THE FATAL
ENVIRONMENT

ALSO BY RICHARD SLOTKIN

The Return of Henry Starr

The Crater

So Dreadfull a Judgment:
Puritan Responses to King Philip's War, 1675–1677
(with James K. Folsom)

Regeneration Through Violence:
The Mythology of the American Frontier, 1600–1860

THE FATAL ENVIRONMENT

The Myth of the Frontier in the Age of Industrialization,

1800-1890

RICHARD SLOTKIN

Wesleyan University Press
Middletown, Connecticut

This book was first published by Atheneum Publishers.

LIBRARY OF CONGRESS CATALOGING-IN-PUBLICATION DATA
Slotkin, Richard, 1942–
    The fatal environment.
    (Wesleyan paperback)
    Bibliography: p.
    Includes index.
    1. Frontier and pioneer life—United States—
Historiography.   2. Little Big Horn, Battle of the,
1876—Historiography.   3. Frontier and pioneer life
in literature.   4. American literature—19th century—
History and criticism.   5. United States—Territorial
expansion—Historiography.   6. Myth.   I. Title.
E179.5.s6   1986   973′.072   86–13184
ISBN 0–8195–6183–5 (pbk. : alk. paper)

All inquiries and permissions requests should be addressed to
the Publisher, Wesleyan University Press, 110 Mt. Vernon
Street, Middletown, Connecticut 06457.

Manufactured in the United States of America

Wesleyan Paperback, 1986

93 92 91 90 89   6 5 4 3 2

FOR IRIS AND JOEL

From far Dakota's cañons,
Lands of the wild ravine, the dusky Sioux, the lonesome
    stretch, the silence,
Haply to-day a mournful wail, haply a trumpet-note
    for heroes.

The battle-bulletin,
The Indian ambuscade, the craft, the fatal environment,
The cavalry companies fighting to the last in sternest
    heroism,
In the midst of their little circle with their
    slaughter'd horses for breastworks,
The fall of Custer and all his horses and men.

... O lesson, opportune, O how I welcome thee!
        WALT WHITMAN, "A Death-Sonnet for Custer,"
        July 10, 1876

General George Armstrong Custer. That beautiful horse cavalry-man . . . But it must have seemed like the wrong career to him when they finished up on that hill near the Little Big Horn, with the ponies making a circle around them in all the dust, and the sagebrush crushed by the hooves of the horses of the other people, and nothing left to him for the rest of his life but that lovely old black powder smell and his own people shooting each other, and themselves, for fear of what the squaws would do to them. And on that hill, to know you'd made one real mistake, finally, and for good, complete with the true handles. Poor horse cavalryman, the end of all his dreams.

        ERNEST HEMINGWAY,
        Across the River and Into the Trees

CONTENTS

INTRODUCTION TO THE WESLEYAN
PAPERBACK EDITION

I envisioned *The Fatal Environment* as the central book of a trilogy that would describe and analyze the historical development of the central myth-ideological trope of American culture: the Myth of the Frontier. I began the project as a graduate student in 1965, at a time when the terms and symbols of that mythology permeated both popular culture and political rhetoric. The 1950s and '60s, in which I grew up, saw the Western movie (and its television spin-offs) become the most prevalent genre of popular-culture narrative. The Western had provided to President Eisenhower his preferred leisure reading. But it provided to President Kennedy a good deal more: it gave him the symbolism of the New Frontier, through which he projected a vision of a revitalized and expansive American liberalism, creating a world in which the strong and powerful (like the chivalric gunfighters of the movies) put their strength and expertise and quick-draw violence at the service of the poor and oppressed. Kennedy's death in Dallas did not diminish the force of the myth he had invoked, but events exceeded his intentions. By 1965 this mythology had begun to reveal its contradictions and incoherences in the most terrible way, as Vietnam became our last and greatest "Indian war," invoking the Frontier Myth's dark side of racism, false pride, and the profligate wastage of lives, cultures, and resources.

The study began with my recognition that the language of values and world-concepts I had learned watching movies, reading comic books, and playing Cowboys and Indians as a child was really the operative language of the political moment—and that belief in its terms was getting most people fooled and some of them killed. The first volume, *Regeneration Through Violence* (Wesleyan University Press, 1973), looked for the bases of the mythology by going back to the earliest emergence of the language of symbols and narrative forms that constituted the Myth of the Frontier. The book began with the Puritans and ended with the American Renaissance of the 1850s; and it showed how a complex literary and ideological language developed out of the efforts of successive generations to describe and narrate their experience of the New World. The book was concerned with the way in which literary culture processes historical events, but its emphasis was on the analysis of texts and documents; and its methods of textual analysis were a mixture of structural anthropology, progressive historiography, archetypalism, and psychoanalysis. The emphasis on textual analysis was necessary and inevitable, since the primary task of the book was to understand the language of the myth. And although my present approach to texts no longer emphasizes either psychoanalysis or archetypalism, those approaches still seem to me to have been appropriate to the kind of material I was working with and the work I had to do.

But *The Fatal Environment* has different concerns, and therefore a different balance of textual and historiographic elements. The problem it addresses is the explanation of how a mythology developed by and for a colonial agrarian society was successfully adapted to the cultural needs of an emerging industrial republic. In the earlier volume the literary texts could be seen as representations (of varying quality) of a place that was in some sense *present* to writer and reader. In the nineteenth century the frontier is increasingly distanced from the center of the culture, in space and finally in time; and the social transformations occurring at the center are far more complex and consequential than those that occurred in the colonies between 1600 and 1800. Hence this book devotes a good deal more attention to describing the social historical matrix into and out of which the mythology played. Because the framework of the study is so different, I thought it necessary to reformulate the theoretical basis laid down in *Regeneration Through Violence,* and to recapitulate and revise the development of the myth from the Puritans through the novels of Cooper (chapters 2–4).

There is also a major difference in the kind of texts discussed. In the period of *Regeneration Through Violence* the dominant forms of printed literature were published pamphlets, books, and small-circulation journals. These forms continued to develop through the nineteenth century, but the context in which they were presented was transformed by the development of mass media—magazines, newspapers, and mass-market books. Although individual works of history and fiction provide special insights into the content of myth and the processes of myth-making, the active center of public myth-making in modern industrial society occurs in mass media. For this reason the central texts of this volume are not novels like Cooper's *Leatherstocking Tales* or Melville's *Moby-Dick,* but case studies from the popular journalism of the period, in which the raw material of history was immediately processed, conflated with ideology and legendry, and transformed into myth.

Taken together the attention given to social and political history, the absence of literary works comparable in stature to those discussed in *Regeneration Through Violence,* and the focus of interpretive energies on journalism may make this work seem (as one reader suggested) less "literary" and more "historical" than *Regeneration Through Violence.* The historical analysis is certainly more detailed and systematic than that in the earlier book, and reflects my increasing engagement with historiographical issues and my response to the "New Social History" of the 1970s. However, the method of *The Fatal Environment* is continuous with that of *Regeneration,* centering the analysis of cultural history in the interpretation of texts whose recurring concerns and formal devices reveal the presence of a continuously evolving system of myth and ideology.

The sheer volume of material to be covered in the study forced me to exclude from *The Fatal Environment* not only some interesting cases, but even some major themes. One reviewer (George Fredrickson) has noted the absence in the book of reference to the way in which the Myth of the Frontier provided a symbolic language for those who resisted the imposition of a corporate ideology on American society.

Since my central theme was the successful adaptation of the Myth of the Frontier to the ideological needs of the new industrial and corporate order, I emphasized those aspects of the myth that served that end. Hence the dominant heroes in the myth are "soldier aristocrats," whose deeds justify a regime in which democratic power is put into the hands of a technological and moral elite. The original draft of the book also included a chapter on "Populist Outlaws" from John Murrell to Jesse James. I omitted it for two reasons. First, it appeared to me that the use *in mass media* of outlaws associated with the frontier as symbols of class or cultural resistance belonged more to the twentieth century than the nineteenth. In folklore, such heroes have always been present. However, my concern is not folk myth, which (as I argue in this book) is different from and often antagonistic to our commercial popular culture; and in popular culture, the populist-outlaw myth acquires weight and force primarily in the late 1880s, and becomes most significant in the movie culture of the 1940s and '50s. To work a discussion of the outlaw myth into *The Fatal Environment* would have increased the already considerable length of the book; and would have cut off that discussion in 1890, just as the outlaw myth was acquiring its greatest significance. I therefore chose to reserve the discussion of the outlaw myth for the last volume of the study, *Gunfighter Nation: The Myth of the Frontier in the Twentieth Century*, which I hope to complete next year.

As I have tried to suggest in this preface, the historical circumstances in which one lives inevitably affect the choice of historical and critical projects and the kinds of concern one brings to them. I finished *Regeneration Through Violence* in 1972, just before a series of economic, political, and cultural events appeared to put a period to America's belief in the Frontier Myth. Defeat in Vietnam between 1973 and 1975 seemed to end our belief in the Indian-fighter mode of international politics; the Arab oil embargo of 1973–74 appeared to inaugurate a regime of resource scarcity, the antithesis of the premise that new sources of limitless wealth are always just across the border; and, as if in response, American film makers virtually eliminated the Western as an active genre of popular culture. It was in this period that I began the present volume, thinking that I could describe not only the birth and growth but also the eventual demise of a central component of the American cultural system. However, before I completed *The Fatal Environment* events showed that the Myth of the Frontier was still quite durable. Although the Western still awaits generic revival, its characteristic forms have been translated into other popular genres; and the rhetoric and ideology of the Reagan administration is not only drenched with frontier imagery, but is, I think, structured and directed in its policies by that mythology. However, that is a subject I will have to reserve for the last volume of the study, *Gunfighter Nation*.

ACKNOWLEDGMENTS

I began work on this book about twelve years ago, and in that time have received so much from friends, colleagues, and students in the way of material help, advice, and useful responses that any list of acknowledgments must be either incomplete or interminable. With apologies to anyone I have omitted:

This work would not have been possible without the grant support provided by the National Endowment for the Humanities (Fellowship for Younger Humanists, Summer Stipend) and the Rockefeller Foundation; and the active support of Wesleyan University, which has provided direct grants-in-aid and four sabbatical leaves during this project. The Wesleyan Center for the Humanities has also provided me with additional time for research, and the stimulus of colleagues from Wesleyan and other academic institutions.

A number of Wesleyan students have served as my research assistants: Jay W. Fliegelman (Stanford) worked on the Custer papers at Yale, and offered insightful comments on the biography; William Holtzman did a thorough job on the Custer, Sheridan, and "Goodenough Horsehoe" files at National Archives; Melissa Totten's undergraduate Honors thesis on Mexican War novels turned up unguessed-at materials and important insights; and Beverly Trefny's work on the Barlow Papers at the Huntington Library provided essential pieces of information. I also want to thank Eleanor M. Gehres and the staff at the Denver Public Library for their help on the Stevens Mine papers; and Duane P. Swanson, for searching out Custer materials in the Northern Pacific Railroad files in Minneapolis.

I particularly want to thank these friends and colleagues for their advice, response to ideas, and willingness to act as readers, hearers, and general sounding boards over the last dozen years: Jeanine Basinger; Sacvan Bercovitch; John G. Cawelti; David Brion Davis; Herbert G. Gutman; David Konstan; Richard Ohmann; Robert O'Meally; Kit and Joe Reed; Michael Rogin; Mark Slobin; Alan Trachtenberg; Clarence Walker; George Ward; Marni and Duffield White.

Thanks to my typists, Linda Costa, Jan Guarino, and Barbara Rivers, for their keen eyes and swift hands.

I am grateful to my editor, Susan Leon, for her patience and care—and toughness—in wielding the scalpel; to my agent, Carl D. Brandt, for his help and advice; and to Iris, for her patience, encouragement, and insight.

PART ONE

Myth Is the Language of Historical Memory

CHAPTER 1

Exposition: The Frontier as Myth and Ideology

Singing my days,
Singing the great achievements of the present,
Singing the strong light works of engineers,
Our modern wonders, (the antique ponderous Seven outvied,)
In the Old World, the east the Suez Canal,
The New by its mighty railroad spann'd,
The seas inlaid with eloquent gentle wires;
Yet first to sound, and ever sound, the cry with thee O soul,
The Past! The Past! The Past!

WALT WHITMAN, "Passage to India"

On July 4, 1876, the American republic celebrated one hundred years of national independence. That century had been characterized by an expansion of territory, population, material wealth and power that appeared almost miraculous. From a colony of England, with a population of four million thinly scattered between the foothills of the Appalachians and the sea, the nation had grown to upwards of forty million, and stretched from the Atlantic to the Pacific. The sites of old trader's posts, mission churches, frontier forts, and Indian battles were now great industrial centers—Pittsburgh, Chicago, Buffalo, St. Louis, San Francisco—generating all of the material wealth, the vast energy, and the inevitable squalor of the modern city. Regions that were known only to Indians and far-ranging trappers when the century began were now beginning to fill up with miners and settlers, and the most distant ends of the continent were linked by those marvels of technology, the telegraph and "the mighty railroad."

The center of the celebration was the Centennial Exposition in Philadelphia, where the republic had been declared a century before; and most of those millions who came to see it arrived by train. As far away as San Francisco American citizens boarded their coach or palace cars, had their tickets duly punched by uniformed conductors, and sped eastward behind a smoking locomotive on a graded road of steel, timber, and pulverized rock that carried them over mountain passes and across chasms, through tunnels shot plumb through hill and mountainside, across vast deserts and prairies of grass where Indians still watched them pass and clouds of buffalo lowered, past green farms and smoking cities to the parks and pavilions on the banks of the Schuylkill. There they found such a Garden of Earthly Delights as might have been jointly designed by Lord Tennyson in a Gothic mood, a pastoral painter of the Hudson River School, and the editors of *Popular Mechanics*. Exhibition halls in the "warehouse Gothic" style were set amid walks and fountains and groves of artificial plantings, threaded by a miniature version of the ubiquitous railroad.

The visitor's first impression was likely to be one of chaotic plenitude, like being dropped suddenly into the midst of one of Walt Whitman's commodious catalogues. There were carpets, perfumes, paints, toys, guns, clocks, a model clothing factory with banks and banks of sewing machines ("too many sewing machines . . . half a mile of sewing machines"), Meissen China, Krupp cannons, McCormack reapers and combines, thousands of silkworms breeding and spinning, ice cream, ice yachts, a section of the Brooklyn Bridge cable, the head of Bartholdi's unfinished statue of "Liberty Enlightening the World," the world's largest cheese, and "a Tuscan column of thirty-eight grindstones, all different, topped by an eagle." There were sideshows with wild children from Borneo, a five-legged horse, and wax figures of famous Indian chiefs. The Wisconsin pavilion featured the eagle mascot of a Civil War regiment, whose cries had sounded amid the carnage of battle—he was a great favorite with tourists, and every day was fed a live chicken. There was a chewing-tobacco machine "run by four Negroes who sang hymns while they worked," and another machine, run by a little girl, that could set 180,000 pins into paper each day. At the center of things, like a principle of order, the great Corliss engine turned all of the machines in Machinery Hall at once.[1]

The Exposition was designed to show that the "American experiment" had produced a society that was not only morally and ethically superior to that of the Old World, but economically more potent as well. Europe and Asia exhibited themselves in Meissen and silk; American was all dynamos and heavy machinery, the Corliss engine a concrete prophecy that the heavy American machines would soon be turning the world. Such colossal size and power in an inhuman mechanism was frightening, despite—perhaps even because of—the productive potential the machine embodied. To one reporter the engine was a "monster which looms up menacing, ready at the touch of a man's finger to show its awful power." To the aging poet of pastoral America, John Greenleaf Whittier, Machinery Hall was "that Ezekiel's vision of machinery": a Valley of Dry Bones made of steel, animated not by the spirit of God or the words of a Prophet but by secular steam and hard currency—an inhuman apocalypse and a resurrection not meant for man. William Dean Howells puzzled through his own ambivalence by metaphorically humanizing the machine into "an athlete of steel," linking it to human magic by calling it the "Afreet"—a djinn from the Arabian Nights. He cast an Arcadian glow over the scene by picturing the engineer reading his newspaper while tending the Afreet "as in a peaceful bower."[2]

The Exposition's proof of American perfection lay in just such a mixture of mechanical symbols of the new age and allusions to an idyllic past. In close proximity to Machinery Hall stood Agricultural Hall—although to be sure the latter exhibited agricultural machinery rather than pastoral bowers. The state pavilions commonly took the form of giant log cabins, evoking memories of a Frontier past. The Pacific Railroad exhibited the tools of its trade, but displayed beside them a tableau of "The Fur Trade in the Rocky Mountains"—thus celebrating that wilderness way of life which it had been the railroad's great task to undo.[3] The hymn-singing Negroes at the tobacco machine, the little girl running the pin-paper machine, the concentrated labor of women seated at half a mile of sewing machines declared further that, in America, industrial progress was not in conflict with humane values and domestic relations, did not lead to class hatred and oppression. American proletarians were docile and efficient, presented in the imagery of Uncle Tom and Little Eva and the housewife seated at her spinning wheel.

The ceremonies on the Fourth of July carried these themes of growth and reconciliation into the realm of civic ritual. The great parade that preceded the afternoon of music, fireworks, and speechifying included a prominent contingent of former soldiers and officers of the Southern Confederacy —a display that was meant to symbolize the binding up of the wounds from the terrible Civil War that had torn the nation apart in four years of battle and twice that many of rancorous and uneasy peace. Union and Confederate veterans, Negro marching societies and lily-white political clubs, exslaves and ex-masters, associations of bankers and manufacturers and organized workingmen marched together through the Exposition grounds to hear the century's achievements praised in oratory and song.[4]

But the imagery was a mask, the oratory hollow. The United States in 1876 was in the midst of the worst economic depression in its history, and of a crisis of cultural morale as well. The reality outside the fairgrounds put the Exposition's triumphant pageantry in a context that was corrosively ironic. The technological marvels enshrined in their pseudo-Gothic temples promised industrial progress; but they also represented new forms of human misery and social danger. If they spoke on the one hand of the growth of Big Business, on the other they implied the bankruptcy and ruin of many small businesses and a new kind of competition that seemed, at times, like a form of warfare. The machines had made possible new forms of production; but they had also created a new and burgeoning class of factory workers, a "proletariat" whose conditions of life and work did not at all conform to the canonical expectations of the American dream—expectations formed long before the war, when small farmers and independent artisans had formed the majority of the "producing classes." This new class had neither independence nor property nor plausible hopes of becoming economically self-sufficient. They were subordinated in their work to the service of the mighty machines and socially subjected to their employers by a wage system that made them dependent. Even in good times, this sort of labor had been plausibly stigmatized as "wage slavery"—a term of powerful import in a society that had so recently fought a bloody war to abolish chattel slavery.

And these times were far from good. The contraction of business after 1873 had thrown large numbers of workingmen and -women out of employment, and onto the scant and incompetent mercy of the community. The problem was compounded by the fact that the new order had fostered the concentration of larger populations in cities and factory towns, an explosive and unplanned urbanization that produced appalling conditions of housing and public health. With so many breadwinners either out of work or absorbing deep wage cutbacks, conditions in the largest cities degenerated (especially in wintertime) toward starvation for many families. Even those workers lucky enough to remain on the job could not evade the imminent threat of a comparable immiseration: capital-starved employers threatened their workers with a choice between dismissal and acceptance of wage rollbacks that the workers regarded as ruinous.[5] In this context organizations of workingmen, and some "philanthropists," had raised anew the cry of "wage slavery," as if the victory of free labor in the Civil War had indeed proved hollow in the end. Within a year violent strikes would flare along the railroad network from coast to coast, raising the specter of revolution and a new kind of civil war, pitting class against class.

The crisis compelled a revaluation of every positive symbol the Exposition deployed. The railroads that bound the nation together and stimulated the forces of industry were also the very institutions that had precipitated the depression. They had managed the business of capitalization, subcontracting, and management in a manner at once so dishonest and so inept that they had "discredited" themselves both literally and figuratively: they fell into bankruptcy as bond buyers lost confidence, and dragged down with them many of the great banks that had plunged so enthusiastically on "the marvel of the age." It was the railroad corporations whose operations had produced the largest urban concentrations of proletarians; and railroads whose importation of labor from Ireland and China had given to the new working class a "foreign" character; and it was in the railroad yards that the fiery labor uprising of 1877 would begin. At the same time, railroad corporations had been undermining public confidence in the moral authority of republican government by the systematic corruption of public officials through bribery, gifts of stock, admission to boards of directors, nepotism, and the like. The scandals that wrecked their financial standing also ruined the reputations of high officials in the Grant administration, and tainted the president himself.

The greatest and most popular military hero since Washington, Ulysses S. Grant had managed in eight years to preside over a veritable circus of corruption and mismanagement, until then unprecedented in American history. Hardly a week passed that did not see some new scandal revealed, implicating cabinet officers, senators, members of the president's family in acts of bribery, influence peddling, and profiteering. Although most observers were willing to accept Grant's personal honesty, they ridiculed his trust and protection of eminently blameworthy and corrupt associates. So low had his standing sunk that he did not appear to address the Exposition in person on the Fourth of July, as it was his "privilege and his duty" to do.

Grant's discomfiture was more than personal. In his person and administration the idealistic motives and reformist ambitions of a generation of Civil War–era liberals were discredited. The program of the postwar Republican Party had been to justify the sacrifices of the war by achieving a thoroughgoing reform of American politics and culture: to establish and protect American industry; to emancipate the slave and uplift the freedman; to open the Great Plains and Far West to homesteading by independent small farmers; to resolve the morally troubling question of the American Indian; to bring moral reform and economic uplift to the denizens of cities as well as to the freeholders of the countryside. Depression in industry, terrorism and political corruption in the Reconstruction South, crime and radicalism in the cities had been the result. Railroads and banks, not farmers, were cashing in on the land opened by the western railroads; and the Indians, betrayed by the reform or "Quaker" Indian policy of Grant, were on the warpath.

Grant was still revered as the victor of Appomattox, but even that great victory had been tarnished and cast in doubt. In the South the issues of the Civil War had recrudesced in a new form. The terrorism of the Ku Klux Klan combined with revelations of corruption in Reconstruction governments to demoralize and displace black and white politicians who still sought genuine reforms. Northern racism, a weariness with southern problems and the "bloody shirt," and disgust with the corruption of Grant's administration deprived southern Reconstructionists of support. When Frederick Douglass attempted to speak at the Exposition on July 4 he was physically blocked from the podium, and responded angrily. A delegation of women's rights activists attempted to speak, and were also denied. But their presence alone was testimony to the fact that the Exposition's imagery of singing darkies and little girls running pin-setters was a mask for the reality of racial inequality, sexual oppression, and child labor.[6]

But it was the West that in fact provided the immediate source of Grant's discomfiture. The outbreak of hostilities with the Sioux and Cheyenne in 1876 was directly attributable to the contradictory forces in Grant's administration, which demanded both "justice for the Indian" and an opportunity to make money by expropriating Indian land or profiteering on reservation supplies. The latest and most damaging of these scandals involved the sale of traderships on western army posts by a syndicate that included Grant's secretary of war, William Belknap, and Grant's brother Orvil. The New York *Herald* had exposed the scandal, apparently with the aid of the famous Indian fighter and Civil War hero George Armstrong Custer, lieutenant colonel of the Seventh Cavalry in Dakota Territory. Stung by Custer's testimony before a congressional committee, Grant had removed him from command of his regiment on the eve of the Sioux War, and reinstated him only after Generals Sherman and Sheridan protested.

Custer had achieved fame during the Civil War as the youngest divisional commander in the Cavalry Corps, a dashing figure who had been dubbed "The Boy General with the Golden Locks." Thirteen years after Appomattox, Custer was still in the rank and command he had reverted to after the war—lieutenant colonel and field commander of the Seventh Cavalry—and the golden locks were thinning. But Custer's wartime fame had been given a new polish by his accomplishments as a leading figure in the military conquest of the Great Plains. After a failed campaign and a damaging court-martial in 1867, Custer had returned from a punitive exile to defeat the Southern Cheyenne at the Washita in 1868; in 1873 he had escorted the Northern Pacific Railroad survey; and in 1874 he had commanded the celebrated military exploration of the Black Hills—an expedition that provided the immediate cause of the Indian war of 1876.

Custer's reports of "gold among the roots of the grass" and of an agricultural "paradise" in the heart of the Sioux territory had stimulated a gold rush, and a movement for seizure of the Black Hills had become irresistible. The expedition had made Custer controversial, and until the Belknap affair broke he was tarred with the brush that soiled Grant, accused of hypocritically "protecting" the Indians out of land and livelihood. But after Custer's open break with Grant, only the most antimilitary of the Friends of the Indian saw Custer as culpable. For most Americans the Boy General of the Civil War, the victorious Indian fighter of the Washita, was now to be seen as a new Daniel Boone or John Charles Frémont, opening up for the American people a new Frontier of fertile land and abundant gold; and doing it at the precise moment when such an acquisition was most needed by an imperiled republic.[7]

Custer and the Seventh Cavalry thus brought together images of all that Americans could take pleasure and pride in remembering: the thunder of Sheridan's cavalry and the flash of their sabers in the Valley of the Shenandoah; the chivalry of soldierly victors to a gallant enemy at Appomattox; the ordered and disciplined blue-and-brass battalions, each company mounted on horses of a single color, paraded on the banks of the Yellowstone behind the flag and their own wind-whipped guidons ready to conquer a new Frontier. To contemplate Custer was to turn from the tragedy of fraternal strife to the classic quest of the republic's heroic ages, the mission to bring light, law, liberty, Christianity, and commerce to the savage places of the earth.

The image of the Boy General riding out to war against the savages of the plains was of the same character as Howell's wishful vision of the Corliss's engineer as the resident of an Arcadian bower. It invoked powerful associations with an America of the past, whose complex realities had been subsumed into the simple and heroic patterns of a myth. The Sioux War was merely the latest in a linked chain of struggles, each of which had pitted white men against Indians, with possession of the land and the power to shape a progressive future as the stakes of battle. Preceding generations of Americans had made of our recurrent Indian wars a historical fable or myth, in which the confrontation of redskin and paleface became the symbolic key to interpreting the meaning of history.

Indeed, even as the Seventh Cavalry marched to battle, Custer's contemporaries began assimilating his adventure to this preexisting body of mythology. They invoked the legendary heroes and triumphs of earlier Frontiers to enlarge and sanctify the adventure. But they were also very much engaged with issues of the present moment—the crisis in the economy, the disorder of politics, the failures of President Grant, and the exigencies of nominating and electing Grant's successor. They made the terms of the Frontier adventure speak to these issues as well: Custer was not only a scourge to Sitting Bull, but a living rebuke to Grant; his triumph over the savages of the plains would not only end the Indian wars, it would point a stern lesson to other forces within the Metropolis—disorderly "tramps," immigrant laborers, recalcitrant blacks—about the will and capacity of the republic to punish its enemies and vindicate its moral and political authority. It might well be that Custer's would be the last of the

Indian wars, and the Great Plains the last of America's liberating Frontiers. Certainly this latest Frontier had not been able to escape the touch and taint of the railroad corporations or of the corrupt bureaucrats in Washington. But the prospective confrontation between Custer and Sitting Bull promised one more grand tournament between representatives of the dying past and the progressive future, between senescence and youth, paganism and Christianity. In that confrontation the pattern of America's hundred-year rise to greatness would be recalled and ritually reenacted, and the golden future made secure.

Walt Whitman caught the mood and turned it to poetry. While preparing the Centennial edition of *Leaves of Grass*, he had been troubled about the state of the nation. Impotence, senility, disease were metaphors for the state of the body politic: "Repondez! Repondez!/ . . . Must we still go on with our affectation and sneaking?" The country's state he identified with his own: a stroke in 1873 had left him half crippled just as the crash of 1873 had left the nation half paralyzed and in despair. The fact of mortality, of impending death, of the closing off of life's golden chances for change and achievement, came home to poet and nation with force. Yet Whitman shared too the wish that the ending of American youth not be a fatal descent into inanition, but a symbolic renewal, a passage to a new stage of life. Therefore his poetry would now link "Death" to the ideas of freedom and democracy he had sung before:

> In former songs Pride have I sung, and Love, and
>   passionate, joyful Life,
> But here I twine the strands of Patriotism
>   and Death.

And it is in speaking of this triumphant and regenerative "Death" that Whitman nearly reaches to prophecy, coining a phrase that would ring loudly before the year was out:

> 'Tis not for nothing, Death,
> I sound out you, and words of you, with daring tone—
>   embodying you,
> In my new Democratic chants—keeping you for a
>   close,
> For my last impregnable retreat—a citadel and
>   tower,
> For my last stand—my pealing, final cry.[8]

On the centennial's "morning after," July 5, the word reached Bismarck, Dakota Territory, and Omaha, and by the next day the *Herald* had it in New York and the War Department in Washington, and Generals Sherman and Sheridan at the Army of the Tennessee reunion in Nashville: "A BLOODY BATTLE / General Custer Killed / . . . General Custer, his two brothers, his nephew and brother-in-law . . . all killed, and not one of his detachment escaped."[9]

"Custer's Last Stand" went against all expectation: even Friends of the Indian had not supposed the redskins could do more than die defiantly under the sabers of the cavalry. More than this—against the proud spectacle of the Philadelphia Exposition—it was as if the perennial scenario of American history had been reversed: red stood and white fell, civilization perished and recoiled and savagery went forward, age triumphed and youth perished, the corrupt escaped unscathed and the righteous fell by the sword. The makers of American myths and ideological formulae— writers, journalists, preachers, and politicians—had another indigestible paradox to add to the ironies of the centennial year. Some saw it as the snatching away of the last promise of an American future shaped by the easy access to wealth that had characterized the period of Frontier expansion. Others saw it as a conclusive rebuke for the corruption and moral failure of American society. For others, Custer's defeat became a kind of atoning sacrifice, almost Christ-like: the representative of American youth, courage, and soldierly virtue violently perishes, but leaves behind a redeeming example that summons his fellow citizens to the purgation of evil, the regeneration of virtue and vigor, and a renewed pursuit of our "ancient struggle" against the forces of darkness.

These were the terms in which Whitman represented Custer's Last Stand in the "Death-Sonnet for Custer," which he published in the New York *Tribune* on July 10. The Boy General becomes a hero of "our race," isolated and surrounded ("the fatal environment") and violently killed by savages; but his death becomes an affirmation of values that are as life giving as "the sun at the center," a redemptive sacrifice that offsets the selfish materialism of the Gilded Age:

> From far Dakota's canons,
> Lands of the wild ravine, the dusky Sioux, the
>   lonesome stretch, the silence,
> Haply to-day a mournful wail, haply a trumpet-
>   note for heroes.
>
> The battle-bulletin,
> The Indian ambuscade, the craft, the fatal
>   environment,
> The cavalry companies fighting to the last in
>   sternest heroism,
> In the midst of their little circle, with their
>   slaughter'd horses for breastworks,
> The fall of Custer and all his officers and men.
>
> Continues yet the old, old legend of our race,
> The loftiest of life upheld by death,
> The ancient banner perfectly maintained,
> O lesson opportune, O how I welcome thee!
>
> As sitting in dark days,
> Lone, sulky, through time's thick murk looking
>   in vain for light, for hope.
> From unsuspected parts a fierce and momentary
>   proof,

(The sun there at the center though conceal'd,
Electric life forever at the center,)
Breaks forth a lightning flash.

Thou of the tawny flowing hair in battle,
I erewhile saw, with erect head, pressing ever
        in front, bearing a bright sword in thy hand,
Now ending well in death the splendid fever of
        thy deeds,
(I bring no dirge for thee, I bring a glad
        triumphal sonnet,)
Desperate and glorious, aye in defeat most
        desperate, most glorious,
After thy many battles in which never yielding up
        a gun or a color,
Leaving behind thee a memory sweet to soldiers,
Thou yieldest up thyself.[10]

"*Fatal environment*": the phrase literally refers to Custer's being surrounded and kill by Indians. But Whitman means it to suggest something more: the idea that Custer's death completes a meaningful myth-historical design, a grand fable of national redemption and Christian self-sacrifice, acted out in the most traditional of American settings. Whitman addresses us as potential believers in a new myth whose form he suggests in the poem. And it is essential to the illusion of this myth that Custer's fate seem somehow implicit in the environment, a moral and ideological lesson which seems to emerge from the very nature of things—as if Nature or God composed the story and assigned its meanings, rather than men. This is the essential illusion fostered by all mythology, even that "primitive" kind whose origins are less easily specified. An environment, a landscape, a historical sequence is infused with meaning in the form of a story, which converts landscape to symbol and temporal sequence into "doom"—a fable of necessary and fated actions.

The Frontier in whose real geography Custer moved and acted was already in his own time a space defined less by maps and surveys than by myths and illusions, projective fantasies, wild anticipations, extravagant expectations. Neither Whitman nor the vast majority of his readers had seen, or would ever see, the real landscape of Dakota. But both could envision and understand it as part of that mythic space called the Frontier —a space so well understood that a few simple clues—"wild ravine," "lonesome reach," "dusky Sioux"—suffice to give it seeming substance. Watching Custer's advance through the medium of popular journalism, they saw a hero at once true to life and infused with a symbolic significance only fictive heroes possess. They knew he had gone to conquer a mythic region whose wildness made it at once a region of darkness and an earthly paradise, a goad to civilization and a barrier to it; whose hidden magic was to be tapped only by self-reliant individualists, capable of enduring the lonesome reach; whose riches were held by a dark and savage enemy with whom white Americans must fight a war to the knife, with the future of civilization itself as the stake. In such a space, whatever the outcome of Custer's battle might have been, his face-to-face meeting with the Enemy would have seemed the fulfillment of a destiny or fate, pregnant with meaning.

The landscape of myth was no less important than battlefield terrain and Indian tactics in creating the "fatal environment" in which Custer was enmeshed. The web of myth that nineteenth-century Americans wove about their Frontier enterprise tangled his feet and obscured his vision as well. And though the bodies of Custer and his dead soldiers went into the ground on a certain hill in what is now the state of Montana, their catastrophe has gone back into the ground of mythology. Custer's Last Stand became part of a renewed and revised Myth of the Frontier, which would be entailed on future generations as the earlier myths had been entailed upon Custer and his contemporaries. It is this industrial and imperial version of the Frontier Myth whose categories still inform our political rhetoric of pioneering progress, world mission, and eternal strife with the forces of darkness and barbarism. It is this myth whose fictive fatalities lurk in the cultural environment we inhabit, whose significance can still be seen behind the silhouettes of skyscrapers, casinos, pipelines, gantries, and freeways.

CHAPTER 2

Myth and Historical Memory

We can easily guess why Custer's Last Stand should have been a six-month wonder to centennial America, and why it was for a generation the metaphor of disaster that came most readily to mind. Victory in the colossal strife of Civil War and in a decade of Indian battles made a defeat such as Custer's as unimaginable as the attack on Pearl Harbor and defeat at Bataan were before 1941. But the significance that Custer's contemporaries saw in his catastrophe has not diminished with the passage of time. If anything, its meanings have multiplied and broadened their range of reference in the last century.

This cultural phenomenon has almost nothing to do with the intrinsic importance of the event itself. Although the Battle of the Little Big Horn was the biggest Indian battle since the War of 1812 in terms of the numbers engaged, it was less decisive than many battles that are hardly remembered now—like Fallen Timbers (1794) or the Battle of the Thames, in which Tecumseh fell (1814). The most that has ever been claimed for it is that it crippled the warmaking power of the hostiles, stirred public support for increases in military spending and troop strength, and made the outcome of the war both speedier and harder on the Indians than it would otherwise have been. But these assertions are questionable, and a more modest conclusion would be that the battle simply delayed by a year the defeat of the Sioux and Cheyenne.[1]

Many other events of the centennial years had far greater impact on the future course of American history. In these years Americans confronted for the first time the explosive potential of industrialization for promoting rapid growth and provoking grave social crises. The railroad networks continued to grow through the cycles of boom and bust, and corporate giants emerged to organize and integrate the hodgepodge of weak and failing lines. In 1877 John D. Rockefeller completed the structure of Standard Oil, the first of the great industrial trusts that would dominate the American economy into the next century. That same year saw a great national railroad strike whose scope and violence appeared to many as a portent of proletarian revolution. In foreign affairs, these years saw the revival of American imperial ambitions in the Caribbean basin, and a more assertive stance in dealings with Europe over a range of economic and political concerns. In 1876 there was a crucial presidential election, whose outcome marked the end of the political struggles of the Civil War and Reconstruction period, and established the balance of partisan power and the terms of conflict for the period of industrialization. It was an election marked by racial violence in the South, and the reemergence of conservative white Democrats as the dominant force in southern politics. It was also an election deadlocked at the polls, and it had to be resolved by the sort of political deal that raised questions about the legitimacy of the democratic process— a deal whose terms included the foreclosure of Reconstruction in the South.

Why then, with all this to choose from, has our culture made of the Last Stand the most *significant* event of the period: that is, the event whose name and character have been longest remembered and have been invested with the heaviest charge of symbolic meaning? Contemporary politicians and journalists of every stripe used the Last Stand as a metaphor, through which they could interpret the election issues of 1876 and the larger crisis of the times. Beleaguered capitalists and besieged bureaucrats were identified (by different parties) as playing "Custer" to the "savage" bloodthirstiness of the dangerous classes in American society—blacks or Klansmen, strikers or policemen, depending on the politics of the speaker.

The metaphor has persisted down to our own time. Military histories and army textbooks alternately offer Custer as the prototype of soldierly heroism or of the evil consequences of failing to be "a team player." Popular literature and art have continually kept the Custer story before the public. Don Russell's exhaustive study of illustrations of the Last Stand has led him to conclude that the Battle of the Little Big Horn is the most frequently depicted moment in all of American history: one thousand different depictions have been reproduced thousands and hundreds of thousands of times in everything from lithographs, calendars, textbooks, to cereal boxes and gum cards, dime novels, comic books. The "Budweiser lithograph" has become an icon of popular illustration, displayed in saloons and delicatessens since 1885; and in 1942 the War Department struck off two thousand copies for distribution to army camps. It might seem that such a depiction of defeat, mutilation, and massacre would have a depressing effect on morale; but the Last Stand motif was an important element in the popular culture in that time of defeat and beleaguerment, and its effect seems to have been that of arousing the grim resolve to fight to the last, neither giving nor expecting quarter. *Life* spoke of MacArthur's defense of Bataan as a "Last Stand," and war movies like *Wake Island* and *Bataan* made the defense of the doomed outpost a movie icon.

Even before Pearl Harbor, Hollywood studios anticipated the coming of war in epic romances about doomed cavalrymen—*They Died with Their Boots On* (1941), one of the best of the Custer movies, was the last of this series. No military figure, and few heroes associated with the West, have been as favored as Custer as a subject for movies. It was the Custer story John Ford used as the basis for *Fort Apache*—the film in which he adapted the language of the Western to the subject matter of the war. During the Vietnam war the Custer story provided moviemakers like Arthur Penn and Sidney Salkow with a fable suitable for addressing the folly and cruelty of an imperial and racial war. In literature and politics, Custer and the Last

Stand have become icons of the language. It is Custer that Hemingway's Robert Jordan thinks about as he listens to the Fascists wiping out El Sordo's guerrillas; and the doomed submariners of *Islands in the Stream* are "fighting Custer's Last Stand in the mangroves." *Custer Died for Your Sins* is the title of Vine Deloria's Indian rights manifesto; "Custeristic" was the adjective applied by nonviolent radicals to proposals for terrorism in the councils of the New Left.[2]

Through long years of cultural usage, the names "Custer" and "Last Stand" have acquired a kind of linguistic resonance. When a writer or moviemaker invokes the name he or she wakes echoes in the memory— bits of lore that we have picked up half-consciously, from sources as various as comic books and history texts and cartoons. But the undertones of this resonance evoke patterns of association that are larger than the specifics of the Custer myth itself. The Custer story has been received as part of a much more comprehensive and complex mythology, "the Myth of the Frontier." This myth provided the terms in which Americans understood the historical catastrophe of 1876; and its terms continue to shape cultural discourse down to the present time.

The Myth of the Frontier is arguably the longest-lived of American myths, with origins in the colonial period and a powerful continuing presence in contemporary culture. Although the Myth of the Frontier is only one of the operative myth/ideological systems that form American culture, it is an extremely important and persistent one. Its ideological underpinnings are those same "laws" of capitalist competition, of supply and demand, of Social Darwinian "survival of the fittest" as a rationale for social order, and of "Manifest Destiny" that have been the building blocks of our dominant historiographical tradition and political ideology.

Like the Custer legend, this larger structure has its roots in historical reality. The Frontier was a material condition of life that shaped the behavior and the ideas of colonists and pioneers. As the colonies and later the nation expanded, the frontiers were pushed farther out from the "Metropolis"; and although more people lived in the West and on the borders than in the early colonial days, the proportion of society actually living in "Frontier conditions" declined as the cities and towns grew. None-theless, the economic and political consequences of frontier expansion continued to be felt throughout the society. Under such conditions it is not surprising that ideas and doctrines would be developed, and stories told, that would explain the meaning of the Frontier to the citizens of the Metropolis, and project policies for dealing with the consequences of growth. It was inevitable too that over time such ideas and stories would take on conventional patterns, become ideologies and myths.

But like the Custer legend, the myth/ideology of the Frontier also outlived the material reality that produced it.

The Myth of the Frontier was developed by and for an America that was a colonial offshoot of Europe, agrarian in economy, localistic in politics, tentative as to nationality, and relatively homogeneous in ethnicity, language, and religion; yet the Myth has been most thoroughly and impressively set forth in the ninety years that followed the closing of the Wild West, in and for an America that is a preeminent world power, urban-

centered and fully industrialized, centralized in government, and heterodox in culture. No historian who lived in the heyday of the real Frontier
saw as much significance in it as the theorists of a post-Frontier historiography, Frederick Jackson Turner and Theodore Roosevelt. The media of
modern mass culture, especially movies and television, have made the
Western at least as significant an element in twentieth-century popular
culture as it was in the days of Fenimore Cooper, "Deadwood Dick," and
Buffalo Bill's Wild West Show.[3]

So if we account for the cultural resonance of Custer's Last Stand by
associating it with a large pattern of persistent myth, all we are doing is
enlarging the terms of the original question. Why has this constellation of
stories, fables, and images been for so long one of the primary organizing
principles of our historical memory?

Myths are stories, drawn from history, that have acquired through
usage over many generations a symbolizing function that is central to the
cultural functioning of the society that produces them. Historical experience is preserved in the form of narrative; and through periodic retellings
those narratives become traditionalized. These formal qualities and structures are increasingly conventionalized and abstracted, until they are reduced to a set of powerfully evocative and resonant "icons"—like the
landing of the Pilgrims, the rally of the Minutemen at Lexington, the
Alamo, the Last Stand, Pearl Harbor, in which history becomes a cliché. At
the same time that their form is being simplified and abstracted, the range
of reference of these stories is being expanded. Each new context in which
the story is told adds meaning to it, because the telling implies a metaphoric connection between the storied past and the present—as, for example, in the frequent invocation of Pearl Harbor in discussions of the need
to prepare for nuclear preemptive strikes; or the invocation of "Munich-style
appeasement" when discussing the possibilities for negotiating with our
adversaries.[4]

In the end myths become part of the language, as a deeply encoded
set of metaphors that may contain all of the "lessons" we have learned
from our history, and all of the essential elements of our world view. Myth
exists for us as a set of keywords which refer us to our traditions, and (as
Martin Green says) transmit "coded message[s] from the culture as a
whole to its individual members."[5] And although these signals are brief,
they are packed with information—for example: the Captain was taking his
company out of Song Be for a Search and Destroy mission against the VC—
one hundred infantrymen in full pack, with rifles, heavy automatics, and a
helicopter gunship flying hover-cover—and he said to the reporter, "Come
on . . . we'll take you out to play Cowboys and Indians."[6]

The war in Vietnam sometimes seemed so alien to American experience
and expectations that it might have been happening on some other planet,
and it had its own special vocabulary whose words and rhythm were native
to its ordered lunacy. But even in that language the reporter knew what
the captain meant, because they'd played that game as children back in
"the World," and they knew how the rules worked. The rules were clear
but flexible, adapting readily to shifts of mood that might be subtle or sud-

den, and might move from a mode in which the deployment of genocidal violence was so indirect or so absurdly motivated that it seemed almost playful, "The Indian idea," one veteran said, "the only good gook is a dead gook." Taking the ears of dead VC was "like scalps, you know like from Indians. Some people were on an Indian trip over there."[7]

General and Ambassador Maxwell Taylor, testifying before Congress in an attempt to explain the difficulties of "pacification" in Vietnam, reached for a metaphor that would at once define the difficulty and suggest the likelihood of final success: "It is very hard," he said, "to plant corn outside the stockade when the Indians are still around. We have to get the Indians farther away . . . to make good progress." Senator Russell Long, rebuking his colleagues for criticizing the war effort, reached for a similar analogy: "If the men who came on the *Mayflower* were frightened to helplessness the first time they had to fight Indians, they would have gone back to England . . . But they fought the Indians and won, meanwhile losing some fine Americans, until this Nation became great." Long's use of the metaphor is vulgarly self-serving, and he stumbles on the ambiguous identification of those "fine Americans" lost in the wars of English settlers and native Indians. But the same language could be deployed with a certain passionate elegance by John F. Kennedy, proclaiming his slogan of the "New Frontier" for a program of renewed economic expansion and forward movement on the borders of the American empire.[8]

Nor was the language of the myth the peculiar property of the "hawkish" factions of our political culture. Its terms were as familiar to left as to right, and were every bit as useful in lending historical resonance and traditional justification to particular political stances and gestures. "Countercultural" radicalism identified strongly with a rather traditional vision of the American Indians as the "Noble Savage" alternative to a civilization gone wrong. The iconography of beads and headbands, the adoption of "tribal" life-styles as a form of communalism untainted by political association with communism, the rationalization of drug use as a form of mystic religiosity, the linkage of political and ecological concerns, the withdrawal to wilderness refuges and the adoption of an outlaw or "renegade" stance toward the larger society—all of these phenomena so special to the sixties were acted out as if they were not innovative at all, but merely repetitions of an older pattern.

The point of repeating the Frontier Myth in that form was to suggest that our history embodied a fatal mistake, which could be corrected by symbolically reenacting the past—only this time, we would live the Frontier Myth as "Indians," not as "Cowboys." The 1960s also saw the appearance of a substantially new genre of "anti-Custer" movies, in which the traditional identification of the audience with the cavalry was inverted, and we were asked to see the bluecoats as murderous "savages" and killers of women and children, and the Indians as defenders of pastoral values, hearths, and homes. Sidney Salkow's *Great Sioux Massacre* (1965) is an early effort in this subgenre, Arthur Penn's *Little Big Man* (1970) the most explicitly Vietnam-oriented.

In *Fire in the Lake* Frances Fitzgerald uses the myth in two ways: she sees it as an ideological cause in American war policy; and she uses it herself as a way of defining a critical position against that policy. According to Fitzgerald, the language of the Frontier Myth "put the Vietnam War into a definite historical and mythological perspective," for Americans; a perspective in which

> The Americans were once again embarked upon a heroic and (for themselves) almost painless conquest of an inferior race. To the American settlers the defeat of the Indians had seemed not just a nationalist victory, but an achievement made in the name of humanity—the triumph of light over darkness, of good over evil, and of civilization over brutish nature. Quite unconsciously, the American officers and officials used a similar language to describe their war against the NLF.

Although the specific application of that language by Fitzgerald reflects ideological disagreement, the language itself represents a kind of consensus— an agreement with Long and Taylor about the largest metaphors of value that will be invoked to interpret the social crisis.[9]

Such metaphors are not merely ornamental. They invoke a tradition of discourse that has historical roots and referents, and carries with it a heavy and persistent ideological charge. All of these public figures and writers speak and think within that tradition of discourse, using a symbolic language acquired by them through the usual processes of acculturation and education. Tradition not only links them with each other as "natives" of the same culture, it associates them backward in time to earlier makers of American culture and ideology. Their association of the struggles against communism with the Indian wars, their belief that racially tinged wars provoke excessive violence, their linkage of such wars with the nation's rise to greatness, their identification with the figure planting corn (or rice) by the stockade would have been as intelligible to Andrew Jackson or Thomas Jefferson or General Custer as it is to us. The readers of Fenimore Cooper in the 1830s or of Helen Hunt Jackson in the 1890s would have been as ready as the audience of *Little Big Man* to see in the Noble Savage an antidote to the discontents of that same triumphant civilization.

The terminology of the Myth of the Frontier has become part of our common language, and we do not require an explanatory program to make it comprehensible. We understand quickly and completely the rules of the Cowboy and Indian game, and what it means to invoke it in a place like Vietnam; we appreciate the mixture of self-irony and self-aggrandizement in Kissinger's identification of himself as the "Lone Ranger" of American foreign policy; we know what the Marines in I Corps meant when they called the territory outside their perimeter "Indian country," and we know what Gerald O'Neill means when he calls his project for "cities in space" *The High Frontier.* That same language can be used to remind us of the evanescence of that past Frontier, and the catastrophe of its closure: Ronald Reagan and his supply-side economists are said to seek a return to "Cowboy economics" and his critics may respond in kind that continued hard times may mean "Supply Side's Last Stand."[10]

These metaphors not only define a situation for us, they prescribe our response to that situation. At the very least, they tell us how we ought to value the situation—whether we are to identify with it or against it, whether our attitude to the "Lone Ranger" and the "Last Stand" is hostile, friendly, or satirical. But they are also ideologically loaded formulations, which aim at affecting not only our perceptions, but our behavior—by "enlisting" us, morally or physically, in the ideological program. Myth is invoked as a means of deriving usable values from history, and of putting those values beyond the reach of critical demystification. Its primary appeal is to ritualized emotions, established beliefs, habitual associations, memory, nostalgia. Its representations are symbolic and metaphoric, depending for their force on an intuitive recognition and acceptance of the symbol by the audience.

Myth does not argue its ideology, it exemplifies it. It projects models of good or heroic behavior that reinforce the values of ideology, and affirm as good the distribution of authority and power that ideology rationalizes. Although its traditional character makes it most useful to conservative ideologies, myth can also be invoked as part of a radically critical ideology. In either case, myth uses the past as an "idealized example," in which "a heroic achievement in the past is linked to another in the future of which the reader is the potential hero." The invocation of the Indian war and Custer's Last Stand as models for the Vietnam war was a mythological way of answering the question, *Why are we in Vietnam?* The answer implicit in the myth is, "We are there because our ancestors were heroes who fought the Indians, and died (rightly or wrongly) as sacrifices for the nation." There is no logic to the connection, only the powerful force of tradition and habits of feeling and thought.

It is this aspect of myth that structuralist critic Roland Barthes has in mind when he speaks of the "buttonholing" character of mythic discourse, its implicit demand that we make of the story a guide to perception and behavior, and its insistence that we acknowledge and affirm the social and political doctrines its terms imply. The moral and political imperatives implicit in the myths are given as if they were the only possible choices for moral and intelligent beings; and, similarly, the set of choices confronted are limited to a few traditional "either/or" decisions. When we play the Cowboy and Indian game only two or three human roles exist—aggressor, victim, avenger—and there are few options for moral choice: A man's got to do what a man's got to do.[11]

If a metaphor like Cowboys and Indians is to work as a device for motivating great masses of people to engage in bloody and protracted war, its terms must do more than suggest that all this has happened before: they must connect what happens to principles that the culture has accepted as valid representations of the nature of reality, of moral and natural law, and of the vector of society's historical destiny. Myth therefore performs its cultural function by generalizing particular and contingent experiences into the bases of universal rules of understanding and conduct; and it does this by transforming secular history into a body of sacred and sanctifying legends.[12]

Myth is history successfully disguised as archetype. In a religious culture, the sacred account of cosmogony and ethnogenesis treats the origins of the world and the nation as if they were shaped by a supernatural and extrahistorical power; and they account for historical events by referring to a sacred paradigm or program set forth in the Word of God. In a more secular culture, similar effects are achieved by associating human actions with natural processes—for example, treating the "Laws of Economics" as if these were as universal and as mechanical as the Law of Gravity. Although scientific method is different from mythology—its assertions are conditional, self-limited, and subject to disproof—"science" as a concept may be used in an ideological and a mythological way, evasive of questions and disproofs. Mythological statements organize thought in a magical or—to use Claude Lévi-Strauss's analogy—a "musical" way. Like a metaphor or a page of a musical score, myth organizes its meanings into a simultaneous expression in which description and meaning are equated and fused—a "bundle of meaning" which is given and must be taken as a whole.[13]

Thus it is myth, as much as any other aspect of reality, that creates the "fatal environment" of expectations and imperatives in which a Custer, or a war correspondent, or a whole political culture, can be entrapped. One of the ways of escaping the fatality of that environment is through the demystifying of specific myths and of the mythmaking process itself. The center of any such effort necessarily involves the rehistoricizing of the mythic subject, and a historical account of its making. "Myth can only have a historical foundation," although its historical sources may be concealed. Even the rules of the Cowboy and Indian game that children play have such origins, although they appear immemorial and changeless. The rules have historical bases, and their character and significance have changed over time in response to ideological cues provided by the adult culture. Tom Sawyer got his sense of the game from Fenimore Cooper; Horatio Alger's heroes got theirs from Ned Buntline; President Eisenhower got his from pulp Westerns and Owen Wister; the generation following got theirs from John Wayne. If appreciated historically, the rules of Cowboys and Indians cease to function as rules and appear as a set of forms generated by a particular set of cultural producers in a peculiar historical moment—and as continually modified from period to period by changing ideological pressures. The present forms in which our myths appear embody not only the solutions to past problems and conflicts; they contain the questions as well, and they reflect the conflicts of thought and feeling and action that were the mythmakers' original concern.[14]

If we can understand where and how in history the rules of the game originated, what real human concerns and social relationships the rules conceal or distort, and what the historical consequences of playing the game have been, we may be able to respond more intelligently the next time an infantry captain or a senator or a president invokes it.

MYTH AND IDEOLOGY

The past two or three decades have seen revolutions in the way historians, anthropologists, and literary scholars think about culture and society. The crucial question in cultural history concerns the relationship between ideas, material conditions, and behavior; and each of the disciplines has its own traditional assumptions about what sorts of factors "determine" the course of events. These traditional explanations were redefined by the work of Lévi-Strauss in developing a structuralist anthropology; by the British labor historian E. P. Thompson, whose work inspired the "new social history"; and by critics like Northrop Frye, who directed attention toward the underlying structures of literary culture. Moreover, the developments in each of these fields have affected all of the others, as scholars have discovered and tried to reach beyond the limitations of their disciplines. The concerns of social history and the methods of structural anthropology meet in the work of "ideological" anthropologists like Clifford Geertz and Marshall Sahlins; of historians of ideology like David Brion Davis, Eric Foner, and David Montgomery; of social historians like Herbert Gutman and Alan Dawley; and of literary critics like Terence Eagleton and Frederic Jameson.[15]

This creative ferment has made the whole vocabulary of cultural analysis a debatable ground. As Raymond Williams says in *Keywords* (1976), "culture" has so many contradictory meanings in present usage that it has ceased to be a single concept; rather, it is a metaphor representing "a complex argument about the relations between general human development and a particular way of life, and between both the works and the practices of art and intelligence."[16] For the purposes of this study it will be useful to think of culture as denoting those works and practices that have to do with the assigning or attribution of meaning and significance to the things, persons, and happenings of the material world. This usage may suggest the existence of a clear distinction between culture and society—a term I generally use to describe the institutional and political-economic organization of human affairs. While such distinctions do describe real differences in the conduct of social life, it is important that we see them as part of a single integrated system, rather than as the "base" and "superstructure" of social reality. Schools of historical and cultural analysis have tended to divide into materialist and idealist camps: in the one, culture is the tail wagged by the dog of History or Economics; in the other it is Myth, or Idea, or Structure that informs and directs the course of behavior. Recent scholarship in social history and anthropology has tended toward a less deterministic view, which (in Raymond Williams's words) sees the historical process as "a continuous interaction between ideology and the material forces of history," in which "a field of mutually if also unevenly determining forces" establishes the tendencies and contradictions of each evolving society.

To say that something is "cultural" is not to say that it is "immaterial" or "occult," as cliometricians sometimes imply. Culture is formed by perceptions, intentions, and acts. It is a form of production or work requiring energy and time, involving human choices and social consequences, engaging materials and labor, and connecting the producer with the network of relationships—social, political, economic—that constitute his society. Although cultural expressions are symbolic, they are not "occult." Those manifold actions that we regard as having or expressing meaning—glances, winks, speeches, credos, deeds—are the active constituents of social reality, and are at least as material as calculations of profit and loss.[17]

In contemporary anthropology and social history the term "ideology" is used to describe the system of belief, values, and relationships that constitute a culture or society. Such an analytical abstraction is a necessary outcome of scholarship, but the actual practice of ideological discourse in the cultures being studied does not always (or even typically) involve the direct presentation of ideological abstractions. The different forms in which ideology is voiced have their own special powers and properties, which affect the substance of the ideological communication and the way in which it will be received. It is particularly important to distinguish what I would call the mode of "ideology proper" from the mode of mythmaking. The vehicles of ideology proper are discursive and argumentative in form, and are typified by the rhetorical structure of the credo, manifesto, polemic, and sermon. The language of myth is indirect, metaphorical, and narrative in structure. It renders ideology in the form of symbol, exemplum, and fable, and poetically evokes fantasy, memory, and sentiment. The logic of myth is the logic of metaphor and narrative. It depends less upon analytical reason than on an instant and intuitive understanding and acceptance of a given meaning. The movement of mythic narrative, like that of any story, implies a theory of cause-and-effect, a theory of history; but these implications are only rarely articulated as objects of criticism, since their operation is masked by the traditional form of the narrative, its conformity to habits of thought, generic conventions, and literary expectations so deeply ingrained that we are unconscious of them.[18]

The roots of myth-making lie in the basic psychological processes of linguistic creativity—specifically in our capacity to make metaphors. Such acts are not simply playful or ornamental, but are essential processes of human learning. Metaphors are primitive hypotheses about the nature of reality, what things mean, how they may be utilized for human purposes. At their most basic, such metaphors involve the association of two varying aspects of material reality, which suggests that some common spirit or power underlies them both—a spirit or power that can be known, appealed to, invoked. For example, the resemblance between the annual cycle of the seasons from spring to winter and the course of human life from childhood to old age suggests a kinship between Man and Nature, perhaps one that can be magically exploited. In the myth of the "Divine King," common to most mythological systems, the life of a single great man represents the Human in Nature; and the continuance of the natural cycles, the seasonal renewal of fertility after winter is linked by sympathetic magic to the life of the king in such a way that the king's health and sexual vigor is felt in the soil itself—and the king's decline toward death may be mirrored in a withering of Nature, an epoch of drought.

Other kinds of metaphor invoke a comparison between remembered experience and immediate perception: these are the metaphoric connections through which the individual deploys memory to make sense of his life, and through which societies utilize their history. By attempting to reconcile "present circumstances and received wisdom" we learn not only the tactical lesson—like the burnt child who shuns fire—but discover also how to use metaphor systematically as a tool for understanding the world. We discover (as Clifford Geertz says) how to go about testing "the states and processes of symbolic models against the states and processes of the world." Memory—any memory, no matter how specific—is only a symbolic model of the experience that generated it, a representation of material reality infused and distorted by feeling, belief, wish, and earlier memory. When we apply memory to the interpretation of immediate experience we attempt to match the symbolic to the material once again; we treat the memory-symbol *as if* it actually reproduced the reality it symbolizes—as if it were reality itself. If the correspondence between symbol and reality is close enough, our belief in the symbol's truth will be confirmed and extended. The process is essentially one of *reification*: of treating ideas about things as if they were the things themselves. When we study cultural history we are examining the processes by which metaphors are generated, projected into a material world, and socially reified.[19]

These processes of learning occur in individuals, but they are also part of the social life in which human beings always participate. On the social plane, the maker of metaphorical hypotheses becomes a human collectivity—tribe, clan, or class—whose projects for historical success are continually matched against a reality that sometimes rewards and sometimes rebuffs the projectors; and from the interacting pressures of projective fantasy, fact, and memory, culture develops.

Myths are stories, and inevitably the central myths of a society will tend to refer to those issues that concern society most deeply, and most persistently over time. Northrop Frye calls these mythological formulations the "myth of concern," which he describes as "a *temenos* or magic circle" drawn around the society, which includes "all its verbal culture." Literature then "develops within a limited orbit of language, reference, allusion, belief, transmitted and shared tradition." The system cannot, of course, be completely closed to new inputs, as Frye's circle metaphor seems to suggest. The original mythology is a kind of net in which new materials will be caught; but when a fish comes along too big for the net to comprehend, the net must either stretch or break, be cast aside or repaired on a new scale. The myths we inherit carry the marks of past reworking, and beneath their smooth surfaces they conceal the scars of the conflicts and ambivalences that attended their making. All of a culture's ideology is contained in myths: the most opposite sides and contradictions of belief are registered in mythic discourse and brought within the frame of its narrative.[20]

Myth is acquired and preserved as part of our language. We observe its operation in the quality of historical (or pseudo-historical) resonance that attaches to terms like "Frontier," "Cowboys and Indians," or "Last Stand." These terms appear to be historical references, but in fact they are metaphors. They implicitly connect the events they emblematize to a system of values and beliefs; and they are usually used in a way that suggests an analogy between the historical past and the present situation. However, even though the referents of myth may be genuinely historical, their resonance and aura of significance derive less from the reality of the past than from the traditions of linguistic or literary usage. It is not western history itself that shapes our sense of these terms, because we have not experienced that history—we know it at second or third hand, through the medium of our literary and historiographical traditions. Rather, our "memory" of the historical significance of these terms derives from the history of the *language* of the Frontier Myth—a history whose events are acts of imagination embodied in prose or pictures and set before the public. Thus when we study a complex ceremonial like the Centennial Exposition, or the journalistic responses to an event like the Last Stand, or the literary fiction of a writer who works in the language of his society's preferred mythology, we engage ourselves with a complex reflecting mechanism, whose complications echo—in a special way—all of the complexities of social life and cultural history.

The language of myth reflects the conditioning of socialized minds to accept as true or valid certain metaphoric renderings of history. But myth has a paradoxical way of dealing with historical experience: although the materials of myth are historical, myth organizes these materials ahistorically. When historical memory is carried by mythological metaphors, it is falsified in the most fundamental way. It is not simply that the making of legends alters or misrepresents the facts of historical cases—it may even be that certain myths are accurate in the representation of important details. What is lost when history is translated into myth is the essential premise of history—the distinction of past and present itself. The past is made metaphorically equivalent to the present; and the present appears simply as a repetition of persistently recurring structures identified with the past. Both past and present are reduced to instances displaying a single "law" or principle of nature, which is seen as timeless in its relevance, and as transcending all historical contingencies.

"Myth is constituted by the loss of the historical quality of things," as Barthes has said. The most important consequence of this is the concealment of human authorship and intention in the creation of ideas and values and the shaping of material conditions. Mythic statements are human statements, and are subject to the various pressures of knowledge, intention, politics, and contingency that shape human discourse. But because they appear merely to be repetitions of ageless and transcendent traditions and principles, myths are things that have lost "the memory that once they were made." They have transformed "history into nature," temporal contingency into divine law. Therefore, those who use mythic speech appear to be vehicles rather than inventors. Their assertions are taken for definitions, their intentions as reflections of natural conditions; their declarations are read "not . . . as a motive, but as a reason." So the complex politics of cultural and social life is concealed beneath a "harmonious display of essences" or embedded in "bundles of meaning" too densely knotted for simple skepticism to unravel.[21]

In the ideal case of successful myth envisioned by the theorists, the "harmonious display of essences" is an exact reflection of the state of the society and culture. Mythic symbolism and ideological meanings harmonize; and this harmony is echoed in the behavior of the people, who live lives that accord with mythic definitions and imperatives. The ideological definitions and categories established by the society's original myth monopolize the culture to such an extent that no event could occur which could not be comprehended in mythic terms. Such a culture would be essentially static, immune to the infection of innovation and progress, free of history. Obviously no such system is possible in human affairs. Myth-ideological systems are affected by crises in material conditions; they are prone to internal contradictions of form and content; and the human intentions that shape cultural politics change, meet with opposition, stumble over difficulties.

It often seems to be the case that in small, relatively simple, preliterate societies myth and ideology are scarcely distinguishable aspects of a homogeneous system of values and behaviors—legends reinforce rituals, rituals reinforce political authority, theology and politics appear to work in accordance with the scheme of cosmic organization. However, the continual agitation and disruption of social forms and systems of value appears to be the characteristic fate of modern and modernizing societies; and in these circumstances, the formal distinction between myth and ideology may become the basis of crucial distinctions. In such societies, the competition of different groups for power in a continually changing society forces the clear articulation of party or class ideology, in a form distinct from the half-spoken understanding of traditional society. As the carrier of "received wisdom," myth is challenged by changes in material conditions or social arrangements. The smooth flow of a narrative in which values appear to be both sacred and self-evident is interrupted by questions arising from substantial changes in the social world. When myths prove inadequate as keys to interpreting and controlling the changing world, systematic ideologies are developed to reestablish the lost coherence between facts and values. As Geertz says, "It is in country unfamiliar emotionally or topographically that one needs poems and road maps." Ideology is the product of "discontent" with a world defined by myth; but the end of ideology is to reintegrate the cultural system, to generate a new narrative or myth that will account for and give value to reality, and so to create the basis for a new cultural consensus. Since even a shattered mythology preserves elements of the cultural past, the new mythology will inevitably find connection with the old; indeed, the readiest way to renew the force of a weakened mythology is to link new ideology to the traditional imagery of existing myth. Thus discontent born of experience creates a cognitive dissonance that disrupts the "harmonious display of essences," degrading sacred myth to secular ideology; and ideology in the hands of a class seeking to establish and justify its hegemony reaches out to coopt myth. This process of mythogenesis, breakdown, cooptation, and mythic renewal informs the history of culture.[22]

We see this operate, over time, in a continuous dialectic between cultural discourse, material conditions, social and political actions. As societies change, developing new technologies or economic systems or moving to new territories, new issues arise which—if they persist—must be interpreted through their "myth of concern." A society of hunters may have mythology centered on the interaction of predator and prey; one of farmers may see gods and men interacting primarily because of their concern with vegetative processes; a modern, industrial, and imperial society may see the basic concern or issue of human history as the struggle for class or racial hegemony in a secular world. Moreover, there is an implied politics in the process of mythmaking. "In every structured society," says Frye, "the ascendent class attempts to take over the myth of concern and make it . . . a rationalization of its ascendency." This activity is necessary because the "myth of concern" has been composed around the culture's central concerns, its interpretation of the central problem of human existence. Thus the ideology of a class striving for ascendancy will seek to appropriate the moral authority of the myth.[23]

In this latter stage of cultural development it becomes possible to identify authorial activity in the production of myth, to specify who the producers are, what their concerns or interests may be, and how they relate to their discipline or art, their materials, their sponsors, their audiences, their fellow producers.

WHOSE MYTH IS IT?

It is essential to my approach to myth to insist that the substance of mythic materials and genres is provided by human "authors": men and women who fabricate or compose the stories, and promulgate them; who bring to the work their needs, intentions, and concerns. However, this premise of human authorship is the very thing that myth is organized to deny. All sacred or religious mythology asserts, for example, that its sources are ultimately divine, whether received through direct speech from the Deity or transmitted through prophets or saints who are privileged to interpret the Lord. Modern literary and anthropological scholarship has not (by and large) accepted a literally transcendent source for mythology. However, important theoreticians in both disciplines have suggested that myths may be produced or generated by structural mechanisms that transcend the capabilities of individual authors.

The theory of mythic archetypes offers one way of accounting for the vagaries of cultural memory, and connecting particular stories to a general theory of cultural expression. The theory developed out of the pioneering anthropological studies of James George Frazer and others in the late nineteenth century, which involved the collection and comparative study of a wide range of mythologies from contemporary "primitive" cultures, classical literature, and folkloric survivals in modern Europe. These studies showed that certain narrative structures, symbolic figures, and motifs recurred in nearly every culture studied whatever their place in historical time or state of social organization. This suggested the existence of an underlying structure of ideas or way of organizing belief common to all men. Those underlying structures were associated with particular mythic genres—the "archetypes" or mythic programs from which the various specific myths of individual cultures were generated. Although the specific formulations of Frazer have been modified and amended by subsequent scholarship, archetypalism persists as a mode of cultural explanation. Jung translated the doctrine into terms appropriate to psychoanalysis; Joseph Campbell and others adapted it to the concerns of students of literature and religion; Northrop Frye and more recently the various schools of structuralists have adapted the conceptual structures of archetypalism to the study of literary forms and genres.[24]

Bruce Rosenberg's *Custer and the Epic of Defeat* (1974) offers a reading of the Custer myth in archetypal terms. The impact and persistence of the myth is said to derive from its evocation of those archetypal myths, whose structures are rooted deep in collective and personal memory, and whose terms engage the most profound and moving concerns of individual psychology and social existence. Rosenberg cites numerous suggestive parallels between several versions of the Custer story and the archetypal hero myths derived from comparative mythography by Lord Raglan, and elaborated by Joseph Campbell in *Hero with a Thousand Faces* (1949). The archetype's roots lie in ancient preclassical myths concerning the vegetative and seasonal cycles, and the necessary and redemptive sacrifice of heroes which magically (or religiously) links the natural process to human and social processes. These ancient myths of sacrifice were integrated with the Western tradition by the Greek and Roman poets, and by the biblical religions whose mythology abounds in sacrificial massacres and "last stands." Finally, the biblical "last stand" mythology was translated into contemporary terms via literature, from the medieval *Chanson de Roland* down to the latest version of the Little Big Horn. The resonance of the Custer story, and its persistence as an American myth, is thus attributed to its resemblance to the classic myths of heroic sacrifice—especially to the Christian myth of expiatory suffering and death, suggested by Vine Deloria's book title, *Custer Died for Your Sins*.[25]

The archetypal qualities of the Custer story are unquestionably significant as factors in its persistence. But as an explanation of the history of the Custer myth, archetypalism mystifies as much as it explains. Archetypes do not exist "in nature." They are abstractions of mythic structures, derived from the study of comparative mythologies by procedures of scholarly analysis. Our current catalogue of archetypes is the end product of a century of scholarship ranging over every extant culture, and many others now known only through archaeology. Archetypes based on that kind of spatial and temporal inclusiveness are abstract to a fault: indeed, it becomes impossible to find any stories whatever that do *not* exhibit one or more of the most important archetypal patterns. Although a key of that kind is useful for highlighting the cognate features of disparate cultural patterns, it becomes nearly useless as a device for distinguishing the important differences of mythic usage and understanding that separate (for example) a culture of farmers from one of hunters, a pre-Columbian Amerindian village from a modern industrial suburb, or Plimoth Plantation from Plymouth, Massachusetts.

The weakness of the archetypal approach is that it must scant the historical particular in the search for the universal structure. Such an approach cannot tell us why the Custer story was chosen for mythic memorialization, when any number of contemporary events—battles, massacres, heroic sacrifices—fit the terms of the archetype as well or better than the Last Stand. Moreover, an archetypal approach cannot tell us why a given version of the archetype has such varying success over time. Although its archetypal qualities remained unchanged throughout its history, the Custer myth has had varying fortunes. It was in the first place never the universal myth-of-choice for all Americans, but rather was preferred by some and rejected or simply ignored by others. Its appeal has varied widely over time, from periods of strong public interest to times of neglect; from phases in which the story is taken in a quasi-religious spirit, to others in which it is reduced to matter for satire, cartoon humor, a spoof on "The Tonight Show." Such changes in the myth's usage, appeal, and appreciation suggest that the operation of social and historical factors is at least as important as archetypal structure in shaping the special history of the myth.

The fundamental flaw in the archetypal approach is its mystification of the processes of mythmaking which it is designed to explain. The making of myths is seen as proceeding from some transcendent suprahuman entity—a "collective mind" or "collective unconscious"—or as something "generated" by the operations of a disembodied and abstract "grammar" of literary tropes and structural rules. In this interpretation the making of myths ceases to appear as human work, in a material world and through historical time, and becomes instead the result of a communion with the Ineffable. In effect, the archetypalist affirms the most important fiction that a myth contains—the implication that its sources are a part of the natural order of things, an expression of some law or rule that shapes a plastic and passive humanity. The memories to which the universal archetypes of Frazer, Campbell, Jung, and Rosenberg appeal are scarcely memories at all, but are primal attributes of a human consciousness conceived of as something prior to (and even outside of) history.[26]

But an archetype couched in historically specific terms is a pattern with demonstrable connections to events, and to the processes of recall. Thus a myth like that of Custer, or the Myth of the Frontier, allows us to test in a more concrete and historical manner our ideas about the way in which mythologies are created.

One of the most appealing aspects of popular culture studies has been the suggestion that the popularity of certain kinds of productions may provide a concrete index to their importance for the culture that produces and purchases them. John Cawelti and Daniel Boorstin provide the clearest discussion of this approach when they posit a process of "natural commercial selection" through which the producers and consumers of cultural productions interact. Their relationship is formed in the marketplace, and is shaped by the same "Invisible Hand" that, in classical economics, shapes all commercial interactions. Producers offer their fables and images, consumers buy or refuse to buy them; producers respond to consumer choices, eliminating those formulas that lack appeal and massively reproducing those that register well by the canons of market research and box office receipts. What emerges at the end is a body of genres or formulas whose

appeal has been commercially validated; and this body of genres and formulas may be taken as the myth/ideology of the mass culture that con-
sumes it, a kind of "folklore of industrial society."[27]

But this metaphoric linkage of human production and natural process
should also alert us to the danger of representing something contingent
and human as something natural and objective. "Natural commercial selection" applies to cultural production the same explanatory and justificatory
models that classic free-market theory applies to economic behavior. The
goals and meanings of production are shaped by an Invisible Hand, which
operates like a natural law or divine fiat; and the end products of the system are seen as the legitimate expressions of the whole society's will and
purpose, rather than as the desiderata of particular interests or classes. To
speak of the end products of popular culture as folklore obscures their
origin and function, and imposes an illusion of consensus on a society that
is, in fact, marked by internal divisions of culture as well as class.

Folklore is the cultural medium of small, homogeneous, premodern
and preindustrial tribal cultures, and of coherent subcultures that have
been partly isolated and impacted within the larger structures of the
nation-state. The culture we call American is distinctly modern and industrial, and is therefore characterized by elaborate fragmentations along
lines of class, status, and ethnic difference. The most basic of these distinctions is built into the modern form of artistic production itself: the alienation of the worker, the consumer, and the means of production. We can
conceive a tribal storyteller as being in important ways a part of his own
audience, a receiver and believer of the myths he transmits. But in an industrial society there is a distinction of function and status between the
proprietors of production/distribution facilities, producers, and consumers;
and, within the category of producers, distinctions between artists, "hacks,"
craftsmen, managers, marketers, and so on. The artist in an industrial society, whether "serious" or "popular," stands at a remove from his final
audience, and must hazard guesses about the ways in which his work will
be understood, the degree to which his statements will be persuasive. He
needs to overcome the distance between himself and his audience; and he
needs a way of tapping into the system of exchange values that will, in-
escapably, mediate his relationship with that audience.

Popular culture and its mass media have developed in time with the
rest of the industrial system; and the systems of popular culture production and distribution have followed the tendency of industries toward
gigantism, corporate rationalization, conglomeration, and oligopoly. The
classic free-market model has therefore tended to become as inappropriate
for interpreting cultural exchange as for understanding economic development. Public choice is really exercised within limits that are set by the
imperatives of particular kinds of media-business; and these in turn are
established by a complex of managerial considerations, only one of which
is a guess—no more than that—about "what the public really wants, likes,
and needs."[28]

We can trace the rudimentary forms of our industrial popular cultural
system back to the late nineteenth century, when a network of political,
business, and cultural institutions developed that was truly national (and

to a degree international) in scope: capable of touching the lives and influencing the behavior of communities in every part of the nation, and relating these disparate lives to a set of central interests or concerns. Between the Civil War and the Great War these institutions existed in "nascent" form, and their power to influence and to organize the behavior or the thinking of a culturally diverse population was limited by the existing technologies of communication and the relatively primitive state of managerial theory and technique. Their power was offset by the tenacity of local institutions and cultural forms, and by the "movement cultures" generated from these subcultures in explicit political opposition to the hegemony of "national" economic and political institutions.

Such areas of subcultural integrity and resistance continue to exist and interact with the commercial popular culture that is produced and marketed for the entire nation. The folklore of persistent and half-assimilated communities, regions, ethnic and religious groups, and movement or work subcultures still exists as an alternative to mass media—sometimes borrowing its terms, sometimes satirically distorting or creatively reconstructing them, sometimes rejecting mass culture outright. But it is now clear that the national culture, the commercial popular culture, contends with these folklores from a position of ubiquitous and overwhelming strength. When we look beyond the family and the neighborhood for a national culture whose symbols we can accept, invoke, or emulate, what we find is commercial popular culture.[29]

If we choose to study national popular culture, we should see it not as a national folklore but as the myth medium of the victorious party in an extended historical struggle. It has come to represent the mythology and ideology of those groups or classes whose political and economic concerns and cultural predilections have by and large dominated and directed the course of American social, economic, and political development—entrepreneurs and corporate directors, salesmen and promoters, entertainers and purveyors of grand ideas.

When year after year the same kinds of stories are produced and marketed by an identifiable community of producers—journalists, writers of historical romances, the movie industry—there is justification for seeing their recurrent themes as myths, which express values and beliefs important to the producers and their society. But do the conventions and tendencies of journalistic practice, historical novels, and Western movies reflect the traditions, values, and preferences of the audience "out there"? Or are they rather the myths of the producers, purveyed to or imposed upon the mass of the body politic?

Before we try to reach conclusions about the "mind" of the audience of myth, we need to be clear about the mythmaking propensities and techniques of those who produce a particular sort of myth. If the themes, symbols, genres, and formulae of popular culture do compose a coherent myth/ideological system—a "folklore" of sorts—then that system should be seen first of all as an expression of the class that produces it. Moreover, by focusing on producers, we also begin to explore the behavior of certain types of audiences as well. The primary audience for any cultural production in modern society consists of those who do the same work, or who participate in its production, reproduction, marketing, or distribution. This is the audience that has the most direct and concrete interest in a work's success or failure, because it must choose for itself whether or not to accept and imitate the work's usage of cultural properties. Its response is also unusually easy to identify and describe, since it consists of direct response (such as reviews) or—more important—in attempts to imitate or reproduce the original. What Cooper's average reader made of Leatherstocking we can only guess; what the man in the street thought of James Gordon Bennett's way of organizing the newspaper version of Custer's Last Stand, or John Ford's way of making a film we do not know for certain. But we do know that literary hacks thought enough of Cooper's work to reproduce innumerable cheap versions of it in dime novels; that moviemakers have elaborated Ford's favorite stories into movie genres and his chosen images into icons.

A producer-centered approach has certain inherent limitations. It will not allow texts to appear as perfect expressions of a "national mind," but will treat them as events in which diverse pressures of personality, ideology, and generic form leave their mark on the product; and in which external phenomena—ideologies, audiences—are not faithfully reflected, but are given to us as distorted by the individual producer's own illusions and predilections. The choices made by the members of such a group, class, or community reflect their own values as individuals and as participants in the life of their trade, and require an interpretation by them of their audience's tastes and needs. Such an interpretation need not reflect reality, but must be a projection—a myth—about who the audience is and what it wants. This myth is then reified in the works of the producer.[30]

Once produced and distributed, their mythology becomes part of a dialectic of cultural and social pressures which it may strongly influence, but which does not consist only of itself. So the significance of such a mythology can be analyzed only when it is seen as part of this dialectic action between audiences and producers, and between competing groups of producers.

The object of this study is to trace the historical development of a single major American myth, and to offer a critical interpretation of its meanings. The object of our study is myth: a set of narrative formulas that acquire through specifiable historical action a significant ideological charge. We will judge the significance of this myth not simply by noting its recurrence and persistence, but by the waxing and waning of its hold on the marketplace in relation to other genres expressive of other myths. We will have to specify *whose* formulation of myth is being examined, and do this by focusing on the producers of myth, and the processes through which works are created, produced, and marketed. And we will have to discuss the elements that make for changes and innovations in mythic formulas: the need to grapple with new historical crises, the inputs of artistic genius, and the special necessities and possibilities that arise from working within specific forms and genres.

The mythmakers in this history are not conveyers of folkloric traditions, but the creators and purveyors of popular literary media. Their productions range from "serious" fiction and history, written by educated men for an educated middle-class or elite audience, to dime novels and the journalism of the penny press which catered to the tastes and the budgetary limitations of the mass of the working and farming classes. During the period covered by the study, these media were all in the process of rapid development and expansion of resources, productivity, and market reach. The development of true *mass* media with a national market begins in the 1830s and 1840s; but it is not complete until the 1890s. Thus throughout the period covered by this study, the nature of the cultural marketplace and the character of the author-medium-audience relationship underwent continual change. Nonetheless, there were certain continuities of theme, form, and authorship that persisted through this period of change. With some exceptions, the authorial "class" in each phase of development, and in each of the different media, can be identified as educated, propertied, and upper-middle or upper class in social identification. Even those writers and editors who assert a role as spokesmen for the working classes identify themselves (or can be unambiguously identified by us) as belonging to a higher class than the average. During this period the primary forms of popular culture myth were literary—that is, dependent upon the printed word—and also *narrative* in form. There were important nonliterary media, such as circuses and traveling "dioramas" or painting shows; and the mass production of printed matter of all kinds fostered a school of popular illustration. However, such media did not have the pervasiveness and presence of literature; and much of their appeal derived from the association of pictures with popular literary texts or histories. Only in the twentieth century, with the advent of movies, did this relationship change; so that now it may be the visual image that cues the production of literature, rather than the other way round.

The dominant themes of the Frontier Myth are those that center on the conception of American history as a heroic-scale Indian war, pitting race against race; and the central concern of the mythmakers is with the problem of reaching the "end of the Frontier." Both of these themes are brought together in the "Last Stand" legend, which is the central fable of the industrial or "revised" Myth of the Frontier. We will see why such a myth was able to speak symbolically to the social and ideological needs of the time; and how it was able to offer a vision—at once placating and reflective of the social crisis—of how the different races and classes that divided American society might restore their "harmony," through a sanctified and regenerative act of violence.

CHAPTER 3

The Frontier Myth as a Theory of Development

The Myth of the Frontier is the American version of the larger myth-ideological system generated by the social conflicts that attended the "modernization" of the Western nations, the emergence of capitalist economies and nation-states. The major cultural tasks of this ideology were to rationalize and justify the departures from tradition that necessarily accompanied these developments. Progress itself was to be asserted as a positive good against the aristocratic and peasant traditions that emphasized stasis and permanence in productive techniques and social relations. The styles, interests, and values of the new classes of entrepreneurs were to be defended against those of old aristocracies and the peasantry. Progress itself was to be interpreted in economic terms—an increase in wealth, of productive capacity, of levels of consumption from year to year and decade to decade. Individualistic assertiveness and achievement were to be justified as values in themselves, and reconciled with the traditional claims of corporate solidarity and deference. Social bonds were to be redefined, with free contract replacing customary fealties, and social standing varying according to achievement as well as birth.

The peculiarities of local circumstances and histories produced significant variations in the kind of bourgeois ideology that developed in each of the Western nations. But the case of the United States has always appeared to be genuinely exceptional. It is the only one of the Western industrial powers to have developed outside the European "cockpit" from purely colonial roots. Its success has been the most spectacular of all, whether measured by its absolute achievement or by the relative rapidity with which it was achieved. Moreover, this success appears to have been achieved without the national and social strife that periodically drenched Europe in blood or filled the streets of European capitals with revolutionary mobs. Its labor history was sufficiently violent to be sure, but America also managed to avoid the sociopolitical impasses that produced the European dichotomies of Jacobin terrorism and Napoleonic reaction, democratic socialism and totalitarian fascism.

The doctrines of American exceptionalism have had an appeal on both sides of the Atlantic that is as much ideological as historiographical. If

American history is indeed exceptional, then Americans are justified in their belief that their society offers a unique example to the world. Revisionist historians in recent years have challenged the central premises of American exceptionalism, and have put a countervailing emphasis on those elements of our national experience that are cognate to or continuous with processes at work in Europe and its other colonies. This movement has of course its own historiographical and ideological biases, some of which resemble those of the "exceptionalists." Both take a Eurocentric approach to the definition of class struggles and ideologies, assuming the European pattern to be a kind of norm and interpreting the American experience in relation to that normative pattern. Each approach produces its own characteristic anomalies. The exceptionalists neglect the real history of class conflict in America, because it does not take the same form as that of European social conflict. The revisionists find all sorts of likenesses, but in the end confront an America in which political culture, ideology, and party structure differ significantly from those of Europe.[1]

The mythologization of American history contains within its structure both a representation of historical reality and an ideological apology or polemic that distorts reality in the service of particular interests. The essence of all that is genuinely exceptional in American history is embodied in those myths that are peculiar to our culture, of which the oldest and most central is the Myth of the Frontier. If we approach this Myth with an awareness of its function as rationalizer of the processes of capitalist development in America, we can begin to see some of the special characteristics of American ideology that link us to—and distinguish us from—the political culture of Europe.

The root of American exceptionalism rests in the fact that American society originated in a set of colonies, abstracted and selected out of the nations of Europe, and established in a "wilderness" far removed from the home countries. These colonies in turn were able to expand into the continent by reproducing themselves in subcolonial settlements, projected at a distance and abstracted from their own bodies politic. The American colonists therefore had a special relationship to the processes of development that were modernizing their European homelands. Although they were engaged in one of the great projects of economic development, they were physically removed from the "Metropolis"—the center of national life and activity. Although they were "modern" people like the citizens of the Metropolis, emigration forced them to accept a temporary regression in conditions of life and work, which were necessarily more primitive in the colonies. Like their European fellows, the colonists experienced the social disruptions and political strife that accompanied the emergence of a new economic and political order, but their isolated position gave these struggles special characteristics. Local factions arose out of economic and political interests peculiar to the colonies' select composition and physical circumstances, and these were often of more importance in the shaping of government policy than the partisan differences of the home country. Moreover, these colonial governments had to contend not only with competing local interest groups, but with two external centers of power: the Metropolitan government and the native tribes.

The myth/ideological systems that developed in the environment took as their central theme the association of all progressive or desirable change —whether of fortune or of moral character—with a physical movement outward from the Metropolis. Emigration was the necessary prelude to any truly American story, since without such a "coming out" there could be no America. This story implied the existence of two geographical poles: the Metropolis, with a predominantly negative character (else why should we leave it?); and the wilderness Frontier, necessarily with a rich endowment of good things to appeal so strongly to us. The achievement of those good things was possible only through a series of ordeals and labors. We had first to separate physically from the homeland and endure isolation; because the land was new and unsettled, we had to undergo regression. The metaphysical energies of these two "places" took a political form in the demands made on the colonist by the resistance of the primitive native, and in the outraged authority of the Metropolitan regime, which wanted to bring the separated colonist back under the wing of authority. The completed American was therefore one who remade his fortune and his character by an emigration, a setting forth for newer and richer lands; by isolation and regression to a more primitive manner of life; and by establishing his political position in opposition to both the Indian and the European, the New World savage and the Old World aristocracy.

The setting of this society in a primitive wilderness held several important economic and political advantages for the upwardly mobile entrepreneur. Because the territory was "virgin land," its resources could be appropriated without the heavy costs of capital and labor required for productive exploitation in the Old World—New World profits were "windfall profits," promising extraordinary returns on investment. And because the New World was unsettled, its political order could be shaped to suit the needs of the moment, out of a dialectic between the colonist and the blend of opportunities and rigors offered by the environment. The enactment of the colonial charter, and its modification by legislative councils on the ground, was therefore a literal acting out of the myth of the social contract. The colonists could leave out or hold at a distance the system of traditions and customary rules that had evolved in Europe during the slow processes of dynastic and class conflict that had produced modern nation-states.

It was the political consequences of life in the New World wilderness that were the center of interest for the first generations of exceptionalist historians in the early nineteenth century. For historians like George Bancroft and Washington Irving, and the ideologists of the early national period, the exceptional phenomenon to be explained was the unique success of the American Revolution and of the federal republic under its written Constitution. The Frontier functioned in this scheme as a very limited phenomenon. It referred primarily to the early colonial phase, when the wilderness was everywhere and the Frontier was a day's ride from the coast; and it served to sum up all of those factors that had allowed the colonial governments to develop in "salutary neglect," in a political dialogue purely between man and Nature, with no interpositions of hoary and outmoded tradition. The triumph of the constitutional regime was the capstone and completion of this development; and to the extent that later

Frontiers tended to reproduce the colonial experience of creating separate and revolutionary colonies apart from the republican Metropolis, they were regarded as threatening or pernicious.[2]

However, the extraordinary phenomenon of the second half of the nineteenth century was not the perfection of republican institutions created by the Founding Fathers. Rather, it was the achievement of unprecedented rates of geographical and economic expansion and industrial development. Even the great political issue of the century—the struggle over slavery—revolved around the imperatives of economic development rather than the niceties of constitutional theory. This shift of emphasis from the political to the economic interpretation of American history began early in the nineteenth century. But it was not fully codified as the dominant American historical explanation until the turn of the century in the work of the Darwinists, the Turnerians, and the Progressives. It was this series of historiographical movements that established as fact the dependence of American democracy and republicanism on an exceptionally fortunate material condition: namely, the existence on the Frontier of a reservoir of cheap, unappropriated, and abundant natural resources, especially in the form of land. These theorists saw the characteristic structure of American economic, political, and cultural life as having emerged from the continuing cycles of development through which the colonies perpetually reproduced themselves in new wildernesses, new Frontiers. This reproduction was not simply a process of duplication, but involved progress from phase to phase. Each new Frontier not only extended the American Metropolis, it made possible a progressive improvement: an increase in wealth, an occasion for technological invention, a new source of productive resources, a new outlet for the productions of the Metropolis itself.[3]

Although the theory (like its predecessor) was essentially a reification of contemporary values and a projection of present tendencies backward into the past, this account of American development had a core of reality. The initial step in American development had involved the emigration of the colonist from his homeland to the wilderness periphery. The availability of cheap and abundant land in America was not a separate and unique phenomenon, but derived from the development of a world market in agricultural products centering in Europe. It was this market that made American land desirable and American agriculture highly profitable, and therefore encouraged a continual expansion of American landholdings and a persistent out-migration from the American Metropolis. This continued experience of emigration, and its persistent association with economic growth and progress in general, suggested the central principle of the myth/ideology of the Frontier—the association of economic development with agrarian expansion on the borders of society.[4]

The development of industrial economies in the nineteenth century ought to have discredited this association, at least in part, since the growth of industry required a shift of population from the countryside and periphery to the Metropolis, where industrial labor was concentrated. European political economists after 1790 understood this, and the enthusiasm for imperial expansion revived only after the industrial basis of Metropolitan society was established. But in America this process was reversed, for even the growth of the Metropolis was connected with emigration: the cities were filled by European immigrants whose journey to America replicated that of the original colonists, while the growth of native population continued to push the borders of productive land out across the continent. Thus the association of economic development with the migration to "new lands" was preserved.

Although the Myth assigns a single name to the "Frontier experience," there were in fact tremendous disparities in the experiences of the early colonists and the later generations of Americans who went pioneering. There were several distinct phases of dramatic Frontier expansion— periods of large-scale land acquisition by American companies and/or governments, followed by substantial and widespread emigrations to the new territories. Each of these waves took off from a different sort of Metropolitan basis. There were different economic and political imperatives at work, which derived from the Metropolis's state of social development; there were different technologies available, different considerations to motivate the emigrants, and different kinds of resistance to be met from the environment, the Indians, rival European powers, Mexicans, and Canadians. Nonetheless, there were enough common features to produce in their literary culture a core group of cognate features and concerns on which a national mythology could be built.[5]

From the early settlement of the eastern seaboard of North America to the thrust of American imperial power into the Pacific and Caribbean there were six or seven major "leaps" forward (and any number of minor "booms"). The first Frontier was the transoceanic, and lasted through the seventeenth century, ending with the firm establishment of colonial settlements along the seaboard. The second phase saw the populations of these colonies swell and extend the rim of settlement from the seaboard to the Alleghenies, in the face of opposition by the French and Indians—a phase that lasted until about 1765. Succeeding phases were shorter, involving accelerated movement and faster, more intensive development—the result of geometrically multiplied population, coupled with advances in the technology of transportation and the development of newer, more efficient modes of economic and political organization. The trans-Allegheny Frontier was opened in twenty years, between 1780 and 1800, to be succeeded by the Mississippi Valley Frontier opened by Jefferson's purchase of Louisiana. Even as population flowed into the valley, Jefferson and his successors were employing army officers to open trails and establish American claims to the Oregon country and the southwestern sector of Louisiana. In the 1820s American settlers in Texas opened the Mexican Frontier; and in the 1840s and early 1850s the population overleaped the Great Plains— for which no economic use had yet been found—to acquire California and Oregon. In the 1850s, with the development of the railroad, came pressure for the settlement of the Great Plains, stimulated by the Kansas competition between the slave and the free states, and by propaganda of railroads interested in disposing of Great Plains land grants for operating capital. Interrupted by the Civil War, the development of this "internal" Frontier—

this area bracketed by the former Frontiers of the Mississippi and California—lasted from 1854 to the 1880s, by which time much of the land was settled or in productive use for mining and grazing.

Each of these Frontiers had a slightly different political and economic makeup, resulting from the tendency of each new movement to build on the economic basis of the one before. The earliest Frontiers of the Atlantic littoral involved the establishment of town-centered communities under close local government; but the Metropolitan base, the source of capital and military force, was overseas. The early trans-Appalachian Frontiers had free land as the basis of their promise of windfall wealth, and they were exploitable by individualistic pioneers and entrepreneurs because of developments in farming, transportation, and weaponry. But these Frontiers also enjoyed the benefit of basing on an American Metropolis, which generated the resources of capital, market demand, and population that made Frontier-going possible and profitable.

Because of the energies generated by Metropolitan growth, the Frontiers of the Great Valley could generate wealth by taking advantage of rising demand for foodstuffs, cotton, and land to grow them on. Small farmers and large landholding companies alike expected to prosper by cashing in on the certain increase of western population as new generations of land seekers entered the territory. Thus western farmers were not merely food growers, but land speculators. The politics of the great wave of Frontier expansion between 1790 and 1820 were shaped by competition between independent farmer/speculators and the large land companies for access to land and authentication of titles; and out of this struggle emerged the ideology and the law of public-land tenure on the Frontier, with its concepts of "squatters' rights," freedom of preemption, and equal access to to public resources. The agitation of these issues in the political arena forced the Metropolis to develop a policy capable of realizing the goals of agrarian democracy, which had hitherto appeared to develop willy-nilly.

This struggle was complicated after 1820 by the emergence of the southern half of the new territories as a sphere for the expansion of African slavery and plantation agriculture. The southern system required large landholdings and large inputs of capital and labor, and both the economic and the ideological imperatives of the plantation system were such as to make the competition between farmer and planter as intense as that between squatter and landlord. Ultimately, that competition made the West the focus of the growing rivalry between North and South that split the Metropolis into warring camps.

Later Frontiers developed out of other kinds of relationships to the Metropolis. The California Frontier offered wealth through the direct exploitation of mineral resources, rather than the laborious process of taking up, developing, and selling land. Its exploitation depended on the development of modern transportation networks and on the prior development of Metropolitan resources capable of creating and sustaining such networks. The Great Plains Frontier was similarly dependent on the development of railroads, and therefore on the industrial and financial basis of the modern corporation. Moreover, successful farming in the region finally would depend on the development of modern dry-land farming technology—requiring considerable capital outlay—and on the development of world markets for American produce that could justify such outlays.[6]

But with all these differences between phases of Frontier development, there remained the recurrent phenomenon of sudden leaps forward of the frontier line, reflecting dramatic new acquisitions of land or the sudden spread of settlement to undeveloped regions. Such leaps were followed by slow phases of apparent stagnation, in which the new territories might "fill up" (relatively speaking). Out of this alternation of leaps forward and slow filling in, this succession of speculative booms and cyclical recessions, the special psychology of Frontier economics emerged, along with a mythology that was its mode of cultural expression. That myth took a folkloric form in local or regional fables, which centered on the adventures of clever Frontier tricksters or *pícaros* who use guile and courage to overcome Indians, moneyed "dudes" from the East, local bigwigs, and their fellow citizens.

But the Frontier Myth also became part of a nascent national ideology and mythology. The economic patterns it rationalized and the individual virtues it celebrated were only exotic and melodramatic versions of the characteristic processes of capitalist development—notably the boom/bust business cycle—and the social types thrown up by an expanding middle class. Thus the story of the Frontier and the materials of local folklore were taken up by the literary and ideological spokesmen of "the nation"—a group that had its own localistic loyalties, but which projected from them an ideology capable of organizing America as a unified nation-state. Their immediate and most intense concern was not given to the Frontier, but to the political economy of the Metropolis, which too was energized by the expectation of extravagant and explosive growth and profit. But the substitution of a Frontier settlement for the Metropolis as the symbolic center of development cast these economic expectations in a special light. As the Frontier community grew from a cabin in a clearing to a functioning agricultural town, it reflected the productive aspects of economic growth: the increase in land values and the rising return on speculative investment provided capital for further investment and expansion. Thus if the Frontier was at once a magic locus of potential wealth, it was also a mirror of its Metropolitan past, and the platform on which future Metropolitan centers would be erected.

Although the economic language of profit-and-loss is appropriate for analyzing the Frontier phenomenon, the language employed by those who "sold" the New World and the Frontier to prospective investors, statesmen, and settlers drew on mythology to support and even to override the facts of colonizing enterprises. In every phase of Frontier development, from the initial transoceanic movements of the Spanish and the English down to the railroad-land salesmen of the 1880s, the prospective colonist or investor was asked to regard the new territory as a Garden of Earthly Delights, "earth's onely paradise" (as Elizabethan poets called it), endowed with fabulous wealth and fertility, gorgeous and exotic to the aesthetic mind, a Garden of Eden to be settled by men forewarned of serpents. Above all, the restorative and regenerative power of the land was emphasized: its ability to redeem the fortunes of those fallen from high estate, improve the lot of the lowly, provide an arena for moral and military heroism. The traditional mythic association of the West with sacred and magic lands— the Hesperides, Valhalla, Avalon from which the once and future king will return—was summoned in evidence of the New World's capacity to fulfill even the most extravagant expectations. The Spaniards went from the paradise islands of the Caribbean to discover the Mexican Empire—a society so exotic and so wealthy as to make the conquistadors feel they had stepped into a dreamworld of strange priest-kings and enchanted castles— and then, as if to confirm the belief in magic, Pizarro repeats the wonder in Peru! Belief in such magic died hard: Coronado searched in vain for El Dorado, and Ponce de Leon died in his pursuit of the Fountain of Youth.

It is easy to patronize Ponce for his folly, but more useful to note the tendency of expectation to leap beyond the matter-of-fact wealth of the New World to some magical source of power and comfort. Although a more scientific age rejected the Fountain of Youth, there was a persistent tendency among promoters of new lands to claim vast restorative powers for their territories. William Bradford in 1620 cited the healthful climate of the New World as a reason for leaving plague-threatened Europe. John Filson's promotional tract on Kentucky, published in 1784, asserted that the region was full of miraculous mineral springs; and similar assertions were made about the Black Hills region, when the American government decided to take them from the Indians in 1874. Such imagery is the extreme form of the more naturalistic—but nonetheless equally compelling—assertion that the Frontier land had the capacity to work grand transformations on the character, fortunes, and institutions of the inhabitants. Each phase of Frontier development carried its own ideas about the kind of transformations the land offered; but all shared a common implication that transformation would be part of the experience.[7]

Definitions of Frontier magic changed as the culture changed. Early notions of the wilderness as a kind of Vale of Avalon, or as a literal English Zion, gave way to more secular kinds of magic: the belief that westward expansion could provide an inexhaustible stimulus to economic growth, and a heritage of property available cheaply to all men and women willing to earn their bread. But by the post–Civil War period, this economic interpretation had been sharpened by the social anxieties attendant on industrialization—the Frontier now became the magic "safety valve" for the discontent of a new industrial proletariat. Each of these images was a wish projection, but behind each lurked a fear: what if the Frontier should somehow be exhausted or closed? In times of expansion and optimism, this question disappeared in the golden haze of expectation. But in times of severe economic contraction and political or social division (such as the 1850s and 1870s) the end of the Frontier was imagined as a permanent expulsion from Eden, to be followed by subordination, poverty, toil, and strife.

These common images of the Frontier as a place of windfall profit, of plenty, of magic, of positive transformation, imply that the Metropolis is the obverse of these things: a place of relative scarcity, in which improvement of conditions can be achieved only by difficult labor within the bounds of custom, where expectation is dimmed by history and self-transformation limited by law and jealousy. This is the "world" of Frederick Jackson Turner's Frontier Thesis, and it has a distinctive bifurcated geography. It is divided between two realms: the "Metropolis," the civilizational center; and the "Wilderness," into which the heroic energies of the Metropolis are projected. The "Frontier" is the ever advancing line that is the interface between these realms. The Metropolis is represented as the highest state of cultural and economic development, but it suffers the defects of its virtues. Its high population density and intensive exploitation of resources threaten it with scarcity, and with a competition for wealth and power that grows fatally virulent as resources wane. In the Metropolis order and organization prevail, society is hierarchically arranged for the wielding of power and distribution of economic rewards. Whatever its productive resources, the Metropolitan economy is essentially one of scarcity: for only the relative scarcity of goods gives them value, and only the promise of valuable rewards induces men to labor and submit to social discipline. But beyond the Frontier exists a world of naturally abundant and unappropriated resources. Since the Frontier lies outside the Metropolis, achievement there is not limited by the competition of a whole society, nor by the rules and hierarchies of the established order: the rules are remade according to the occasion, and after the preferences of the makers; and property is there for the taking.

The Frontier theory posits a one-directional relationship between these realms. The direction of expansion is always progressive, and proceeds from the Metropolis outward. As each new Frontier is met and conquered, it in turn becomes a Metropolis, and as such the base for a new and deeper foray into the Wilderness. The Frontier-goers are motivated by a combination of positive and negative factors; but the crucial determinant is the belief in cheap and abundant resources beyond the Frontier. It is this motive that converts the pioneer from a potential competitor with the striving classes of the Metropolis into an independent agent of Metropolitan civilization as a whole, whose work is to carry the seeds of the Metropolis to newer and more fertile ground.

The Frontier theory holds that the key to economic development is the discovery of abundant and cheap resources *outside* the economic Metropolis. Nature, not labor, gives such resources their value, and hence they are free of the costs and moral claims put forward by the laboring classes in the Metropolis. The most enthusiastic assertion of this doctrine is that advanced by Turner's intellectual heir, Walter Prescott Webb, in *The Great Frontier*. In Webb's book the Turner thesis becomes the key to understanding the development of the entire Western world. Webb asserts that the opening of "free land" frontiers in sparsely inhabited regions of America, Africa, and Australia have provided the material basis for "a boom in Western civilization . . . that lasted as long as the frontier was open, a period of four centuries."[8] This Great Frontier underwrote the expansion of capitalism by providing "windfall" profits, far exceeding what could have been accumulated by labor and self-denial.

Although Webb's language is hyperbolic, there is some validity to his thesis. There is no doubt that the wealth of Europe was increased by the windfall profits of such colonial enterprises as the gold mines of Mexico and Peru, or later the development of "spice islands" in the West Indies. Similarly the discovery of gold in California in 1849 increased America's national wealth by directly infusing precious metals into a cash-poor economy, and by stimulating the trades and industries related to the mining of gold, the support and transportation of miners, and the development of western towns as bases for exploiting the discovered resource. In our own time, we are aware of the important role played by the availability of a vast reserve of cheap American and Middle Eastern oil in underwriting the boom economy of the post–World War II period.

Likewise in our own time, theories of American exceptionalism have died hard. The more recent work of Ray Allen Billington and David Potter offers a critically revised version of this Frontier Thesis of development which takes into account the complexity of economic expansion and the variety of Frontier experiences; and also recognizes the countervailing significance of Metropolitan developments in shaping the course of Frontier history.

Billington is the most systematic student of Turner and his hypothesis, and his revision of the Turner thesis is therefore the most comprehensive. The critics of Turner had pointed out that the Frontier experience was never so unified in form and social or cultural impact as Turner suggested; that Frontier institutions were as often shaped by imperatives carried over from the Metropolis as they were indigenous to the settlements; and that the populations involved in the various phases of Frontier settlement were not typically the simple yeomen or safety-valve-oriented workingmen that Turner spoke of. Billington himself describes a series of "Frontiers," characterized by different Metropolitan bases, by different mixtures of industry and agriculture, and by different "wilderness" environments. Acknowledging the difference between the actualities of Frontier development and the beliefs about the Frontier that motivated both pioneers and Metropolitan policymakers, Billington nevertheless remains committed to the fundamental premises of the Frontier Thesis. Whether the Frontier is seen as agrarian or industrial, whether it is in the fertile forests close to the Metropolis or in deserts flung across a continent, whether it is a real factor in political economy or only a myth in which people believe, the Frontier remains the determinant of the history of development. Even Billington's highly qualified restatement of the Thesis insists that the Frontier generates productivity by providing a reservoir of unappropriated resources that exists outside the bounds of the Metropolis, outside the bounds of property and law, outside the realm in which all things belong to human beings singly and as groups. Billington even affirms that to produce its benign effects, such a Frontier must be circumstanced so as to favor the entrepreneur's pursuit of economic self-improvement.[9]

Recent comparative study suggests that this approach is inadequate to account for the utilization of undeveloped borderlands in other expansive colonial and even Old World societies. Whereas the Frontier Thesis asserts that Metropolitan political economics are transformed by the intervention of an outside force or phenomenon—the discovery of a distant Frontier of superabundant natural wealth—it seems more plausible (and more consonant with economic and social facts) to consider an alternative hypothesis: that the particular forms taken by the developing political economy of the Metropolis—its modes of production, its system for valuing social and economic goods, its peculiar culture and history of social relations, its characteristic political institutions—inform the decision to seek Frontier wealth, and determine the kind of people that will go (or be sent) to the colonies, the kinds of resources they will be interested in, the ways in which they will organize their exploitation and governance of the territory, and so on.

The difference between this and the original Frontier Thesis is one of emphasis and precedence, rather than an either/or distinction. It should not be necessary to deny the truth of the assertion that the discovery of New Worlds and Mother Lodes does indeed reshape Metropolitan expectations and interests, and does materially alter the political economy of both colony and Metropolis. Moreover, the political dialectic between colony and Metropolis is not a marginal phenomenon at all, but a process that affects and alters the political structures of both societies. However, the preponderant voice in that dialectic for the formative years of colonial history is bound to be that of the Metropolis: it is the Mother Country which gives population, language, law, and economic value to the colony, and not the other way round.[10]

No discovery, however rich in potential, can be of any use unless the society whose agents make the discovery possesses already the economic, social, and political resources needed to make that discovery possible and profitable. The New World was discovered by Vikings half a millennium before Columbus sailed, but the discovery was useless to a people whose population, technology, and economic needs were inadequate to sustain a colonial enterprise. The Rocky Mountains and the Great Plains were known to French explorers in the eighteenth century, but the French had neither the need nor the resources for establishing permanent posts and settlements in the region. In the nineteenth century, Americans and Canadians had both the economic motives and the means for exploiting the region's peltry; but only the Americans had the surplus and mobile population, and the transportation network that made settlement of the region feasible and profitable. Even a gold rush diminishes in value if the society that makes the discovery has no need of capital for the support of enterprises.

The disadvantage of acknowledging this process in a theory of American development—and perhaps in bourgeois development as a whole—is that it brings to the fore those patterns of class conflict and oppression that Western democracy is supposed to have abolished. In the American case, attribution of a determining role to Metropolitan events would have the effect of linking national prosperity not with the pioneer farmer, but with the southern slave owner and the northern factory owner. It would note that the special environment of some Frontiers, coupled with developments in the Metropolis, gave business and agricultural enterprises a particularly monopolistic and tyrannical form that was inimical to the "individualism" of entrepreneurs and free workers. The experience of farmers in regions dominated by railroad land companies, of miners and smelter workers in the "hard-rock" mines of Montana and Idaho, and of small ranchers on range coveted by oligarchies like the Wyoming Stock Growers' Association—all in the 1885-99 period—does not bear out the thesis that Frontier conditions in general fostered both individualism and democracy—sometimes conditions favored neither, and sometimes they favored one at the expense of the other. It is an ideological conceit of ours that the two must always go together.

Moreover, since the development of American industry was dependent on expertise developed and capital accumulated in Europe, a Metropolitan-centered account would diminish the American sense of historical exceptionalism. For a society that was, even in Turner's day, still in the process of achieving the nationalization of economic, political, and cultural institutions, such a premise was too painful to be admissible. And for the cold warriors of Billington's day—indeed, in our own—exceptionalism has obvious appeal as an ideological device for sustaining belief in the superiority and unassailability of American institutions.[11]

But the economic developments that generate within a Metropolitan society the demand for discoveries of resources are filled with social and political consequences that are ideologically troubling. The economic expansion of European economies on the eve of Columbus's discovery cannot be described in value-neutral terms as a simple increase in population and productivity. Those quantitative changes were accompanied by necessary shifts in the status and power of different classes, impoverishing and immiserating some while uplifting others, altering traditional arrangements in ways that might be more efficient yet less "just." Similarly, the industrialization of the Metropolis, which was the precondition for later waves of expansion, required the dispossession and uprooting of peasants and farmers, and created the squalor and violence of a new kind of urban culture. Both phases of development provoked social violence within societies and between them, in the form of revolutions and wars. In the industrial period, the working classes were identified as the "dangerous classes" whose development threatened the stability of society. But in the colonial period it was the bourgeoisie itself that was identified as "dangerous." In Europe, the rise of the middle classes and their demand for political power provoked civil wars, wars of religion, and in England the overthrow of monarchy itself.

In the New World, the sort of men who made the Puritan Revolution had an opportunity to have all things their own way, in a world apart from the Metropolis dominated by royalty and feudal aristocracy. Traditional authority was weakly represented in the New World, and for classes whose pursuit of wealth required them to push against or operate outside the boundaries of feudal law and custom the New World offered not only the apparition of windfall wealth; it promised a world in which normal rules and conventions could be evaded or suspended to permit the fullest possible exploitation of a golden opportunity. The magic of the discovery of a New World proved anything was possible; it followed that in exploiting that discovery, everything was permitted. In that case, the moral and political bases of traditional authority were imperiled by the very classes and motives that promised enrichment to the proprietors of American colonies.

This identification of the Frontiersman as a dangerous character persisted beyond the colonial period, and affected Metropolitan responses to all subsequent Frontiers. The "Frontier" was the border between a world of possibilities and one of actualities, a world theoretically unlimited and one defined by its limitations. On one side of the line lay great wealth, and a suspension of normal limitations of law and probability, a dreamworld in which infantile omnipotence became a possibility for the grown man; on the other side lay relative poverty, the necessity of labor and sacrifice, the requirement of sharing. In the Frontier world "the dynamic is furnished, not by the savers, but by the profiteers": in the West personal greed and national good coincide; in the East, moral consequences are social and must be faced. Thus the Frontiersman could embody the negative potential of economic development and the attendant social change, as well as its progressive and positive aspects. The dangerous or dubious form of the bourgeois could be made to disappear into the mystique of the buckskin pioneer. It is for this reason that the Frontiersman became a viable center for a "myth of concern" that sought to explain and justify the processes and exigencies of capitalist development.[12]

The Frontier theory of development offers both a theory of capital development and a theory of social relations. It sees the sources of wealth as lying outside society, in an unappropriated natural wilderness, rather than as the products of social labor; and it sees acquisition of that sort of wealth as an antidote to social conflicts within the Metropolis. This theory in fact masks what it seems to explain. It projects the ideology of capitalism onto the natural world, translating the "law of supply and demand" as the juxtaposition of those two "worlds"—the world of Metropolitan scarcity (demand) and of natural abundance (supply), with the Frontier as the productive interface between them. This projection works especially well in American society because our experience of simultaneous economic and geographical expansion partially justifies it. But the Myth of the Frontier falsifies this core of reality by extending historically limited and contingent phenomena into a "law" of American development. We can rehistoricize the Myth by breaking it down into particular sequences of historical action, and by specifying more accurately the types of economic exchange that are subsumed in the phrase "expanding frontiers."

If we adopt the vocabulary of the Myth, we can speak of three related types of Frontiers, in each of which a realm of scarcity confronts a realm of abundance and stimulates a profitable interchange. Without suggesting a priority, we can begin with the existence of a "resource Frontier," represented by cheap, abundant, arable land and by the existence of reserves of mineral wealth. The resource Frontier provides a stimulus to development by providing a field for the investment of both capital and labor, in which there is a credible promise of great returns for reasonable investment. But the utility of the resource Frontier depends upon the availability of capital and labor to explore it. A "capital Frontier" divides the would-be exploiters of resources from the possessors of surplus capital. Here the abundance/scarcity division between Frontier and Metropolis is reversed, for the city has the capital that the pioneer requires. The development of the American Frontier, and the conflicts that attended that development, cannot be understood without some acknowledgment that the conquest of new territory depended for its sinews on the conquest of the minds and faith of Metropolitan investors—first in Europe, and later in the cities of the East. Finally, without abundant labor there could have been neither the growth of capital nor the growth of population necessary to make Frontier expansion possible. The cheap land Frontier of the West was matched by a "cheap labor" Frontier in the East. That Frontier was located at first in the British Isles and in Africa, from which the colonies drew the labor force that made settlement productive. Slavery provided both positive and negative incentives for Southerners to migrate into new territories before the Civil War. Throughout the nineteenth century, economic development and agrarian expansion were able to coexist because of the continual influx of peoples uprooted and dispossessed by the Industrial Revolution in Europe. Late in the nineteenth century the cheap labor Frontier reached out to the hitherto alien regions of eastern and southern Europe and to the mainland of Asia, from which was drawn the labor for the western end of the transcontinental railroad.[13]

But there were certain features of the American labor Frontier that made it different from that of Europe, and produced different ideological and political results. In Europe, the early stages of industrial development were characterized by an intensified struggle between identifiable social classes, which involved the displacement of peasants from the land, the use of the legal code as an instrument of class power, and the development of ideologies responsive to the needs of the classes engaged in the struggle. Wealth could be accumulated only by drudgery and self-denial, by intensifying labor to increase productivity. In contrast to the squalor and drudgery of the woolens industry or millwork, colonial enterprises offered exotic and adventurous ways of becoming rich. But in Europe's two great waves of imperial expansion, colonial conquests were always distant matters, foreign to the life and politics of the cities and boroughs, separated from the immediate reality of economics and politics by oceanic emptiness. In the United States that distance was annihilated. Within the borders, and within the effective reach of citizens of the Metropolitan East, America possessed a sphere of colonial expansion, a region adapted to an internal imperialism.

To any imperial power, the region of colonization is perceived as a source of great economic advantage, a source of tremendous wealth that can be gotten for relatively minor investment. Colonizable territory is to be mined of its resources, so that the Metropolis may be fed, so that banks may be refreshed with waves of newly mined gold and larders filled with agricultural plenty. For the European such prizes lay at a distance, and were in the possession of native cultures that were substantial in numbers and resources; for the American such prizes lay near at hand, and the natives who "possessed" them were few in number and lacked all semblance of technological advancement or political unity. Thus the processes of industrial development and imperial expansion took different forms on the two American continents, Asia, and Africa.

The idea that imperialism may be an antidote to class antagonisms is a late-nineteenth-century European formulation, but it was almost from the first an essential component of the ideology of American republicanism. Moreover, the "internal" location of the American colonizing enterprise made for a relationship between colony and Metropolis that was closer and more significant for domestic politics than, say, France's possession of Senegal or even Britain's seizure of India. Most important, the American experience differed in its processes of generating the labor pool of industrialization: for while European nations developed by dispossessing their own peasantry, America acquired its work force by means that are associatively linked with the idea of an expanding Frontier: first by exploiting the slave markets of West Africa, acquiring a work force by the means used to gain wilderness land (conquest and purchase); and then by attracting already dispossessed Europeans, who came voluntarily to America as "pioneers" bent on exploiting the rich resources of the "territory" as farmers or as industrial workers in the settled Metropolitan regions.

The confrontations between borrowers and lenders, between laborers and contractors, are therefore as central to the story of Frontier development as the conventional opposition of the white man and the Indian, or the image of Daniel Boone gazing out in wonder on the natural beauty of an untouched wilderness. Yet they are not a part of Turner's Frontier Thesis, nor of the resource-centered theories of development that are its modern successors. Nor were they—except by indirection—a part of the literary mythology or the agrarian ideology that established the tradition in which the Turnerians worked. Frontier Myth and its ideology are founded on the desire to avoid recognition of the perilous consequences of capitalist development in the New World, and they represent a displacement or deflection of social conflict into the world of myth. As we shall see, in that myth the simple fable of the discovery of the new land and the dispossession of the Indians substitutes for the complexities of capital formation, class and interest-group competition, and the subordination of society to the imperatives of capitalist development.

PART TWO

The Language of the
Frontier Myth

CHAPTER 4

Regeneration Through Violence: History as an Indian War, 1675–1820

The language of the Frontier Myth and of its ideological system developed during the colonial and early national periods. These years saw the colonies transformed from coastal enclaves only marginally interested in the hinterland to a nation-state with substantial interest and ambitions in the interior of the continent. The developing language of myth and ideology reflected the shift in intentions toward the undeveloped land and its natives. But the culture itself became more complex as American society expanded and developed, and during the course of this period two related but distinct genres of discourse were developed for reflecting upon the changing character of the Frontier. The development of republican institutions fostered a rich and active political culture whose primary genres were the political speech, pamphlet, or discourse. These genres voiced and re-duced to conventionality Americans' characteristic ways of describing themselves and their purposes. The ideology of Jeffersonian agrarianism codified these ideas in such a way as to make them the core of one of the dominant strains in nineteenth-century American political thought. At the same time, the nascent American book trade and literary culture provided the basis for the emergence of a native school of writers; and these writers drew on the language of colonial myth to create a literary mythology suited to the values and preoccupations of their readers. This literary mythology was systematized by the school of historical romance—writers who took Fenimore Cooper for their model.

Common elements of value and concern mark the agrarian ideology and the literary mythology of the Cooperians as products of the same culture. However, there are crucial differences in the way in which the history of Frontier development is represented in each of these modes of discourse. The literary mythology generally focuses upon the story of In-dian dispossession—that is, on the violent wars of conquest through which the colonists acquired title to the lands they then engaged in developing. Other kinds of social conflict—the tensions between different classes of white land developers, or religious-ethnic differences—are subsumed and reconciled in the conflict of Indians and whites for possession of the land. This literary myth masks the internal social conflicts of the Metropolis by projecting class war outward into racial war on the borders. But the ideology of agrarianism only rarely makes mention of the Indian wars, and then as a distant and unpleasant prelude to the real action of history, which involves the clearing and cultivating of the soil by the diligent democratic husbandman. The ideology of agrarianism thus makes a second order mask for the processes of the development: it substitutes the cultivation of the land, the interaction of man with pure and inanimate nature, for the human conflict of Indian dispossession.

In the mature culture of the nineteenth century, myth and ideology came together to form a whole system of belief that veiled the processes of economic development with considerable success. However, there is an inherent contradiction between the historical view propounded in the myth and that set forth in the ideology. The latter asserts that progress can proceed harmlessly, and that the bases of conflict are essentially immaterial: the abundant resources of land are sufficient to make all conflicts of class and interest unnecessary. On the other hand, the literary mythology represents conflict as the center of the story, and emphasizes the naturalness and inescapability of violence arising where two cultures or races compete for the same territory. These contradictions of course reflect the social reality that the myth/ideology of the Frontier was developed to conceal. By the end of the nineteenth century those social conflicts had proceeded so far that the myth/ideology could no longer rationalize them, and a sharp split developed between the agrarian reading of the past and the "Indian war" reading. These were reflected in the ideologies of populism and progressivism, and were set forth as Frontier hypotheses in the histories of Turner and Theodore Roosevelt. The former offered agrarianism as an antidote to the class antipathies generated by industrialization, while the latter used the Indian war as a model for the rationalization of class subordination at home and imperialism abroad.

THE WARS OF DISPOSSESSION

The myth of the Indian wars is the older part of the system. It acquired its characteristic language of symbols and narrative tropes quite early in colonial history, and it represented a part of the troublesome historical experience that the ideologists of agrarianism wished to explain away. They do that by ignoring the Indian, or by treating the Indian presence as if it were insignificant or marginal. Indian numbers are generally understated, and the threat of substantial Indian opposition to colonization is relegated to another age of history—not all that remote in time, after all, but nonetheless in a different stage of civilization. However, the Indian was an inescapable presence to the colonists throughout their history. As the primitive proprietor of the land and as the human product of the New World, the Indian was taken as a predictor of the long-term consequence of living in America—for good or ill. Relations with the Indians reflected patterns analogous to those between colonists and the natural environment. Sometimes the Indians accepted colonization, at other times they violently resisted; and these shifts of intention paralleled the colonial experience of a land that was by turns inviting and forbidding, hospitable and perilous.

On the one hand, the Indian was seen as embodying the positive qualities of nature in the New World: Edenic innocence, primitive simplicity, generosity, benign magic, the promise of escape and self-transcendence. Early explorers compared them to the fabled folk of the "Golden Age," generous to a fault and "voyd of guile," fit natives of "Earth's onely paradise." On the other hand, the Indian was the antithesis of the European— dark-skinned, pagan in religion, tribal in politics, seminomadic in economy, with a moral system that seemed to sanctify pleasure taking and self-gratification. Moreover, the Indians' presence was a standing threat to colonial order. Indian power and resentment posed a military threat to colonial safety; and the existence of an alternative to the Indian society was a standing temptation to dissentient elements within colonial society to make league with the Indians against their own kind, or to desert civilized order for the relative freedom and seeming license of life among the savages.[1]

The imagistic association of the Indian and the natural world cuts two ways. On the one hand, it humanizes the inanimate world of nature, attributing to it the qualities of generosity, moral innocence, and redemptive power. On the other hand, it dehumanizes the Indians, by treating them simply as an aspect of the inanimate world, a natural obstacle to acquisition—a bear in the path, a stone in the field. Indeed, the objectives of colonial development ensured that the dehumanizing or reifying direction of the metaphor would receive the greater emphasis. In the Spanish colonies (and to some extent in the French) the commodification of the Indian took the form of enslavement or reduction to a state of clientage. But in North America, the Indian population did not exist in a form or a quantity sufficient to employ in plantation farming in those areas. Instead, the English colonies aimed to prosper by displacing the natives, replacing them with white farmers drawn from their own growing population and with black slaves purchased in Africa or bred in the colonies.[2] This fact had important consequences for the development of American ideology and myth. It made feasible the separation of the idea of the wilderness land— the resource base—from the idea of the land's human inhabitants.

This divisibility of the native and the land permitted the formulation of a myth and ideology of expansion in which racial warfare complements the processes of agrarian development. The story of American progress and expansion thus took the form of a fable of race war, pitting the symbolic opposites of savagery and civilization, primitivism and progress, paganism and Christianity against each other. Quite early in the history of white-Indian relations, a conception of Indian warfare developed that tended to represent the struggle as necessarily genocidal. "Savage war" was distinguished from "civilized warfare" in its lack of limitations of the extent of violence, and of "laws" for its application.

The doctrine of "savage war" depended on the belief that certain races are inherently disposed to cruel and atrocious violence. Similar assumptions had often operated in the wars of Christian or Crusading states against the Muslims in Europe and the Holy Land, and massacre had often enough accompanied such wars. But with the Muslims there remained sufficient belief in the possibility of religious conversion to suggest to both sides that evangelism, rather than genocide, was the logical outcome of conflict. It became colonial America's project to convert the idea of racial propensities into a rationale for wars of extermination.[3]

The significance of the Indian wars went deeper than the interface between the two competing cultures. The Indian wars were never isolable from Metropolitan concerns, and during the colonial period the Indian frontier and the colonial cities were nearly side by side. The Indian wars therefore tended to focus the whole range of colonial concerns in a single overwhelming crisis. Relations between governmental authority and the ambitions of individualistic citizens were involved, because the machinations of land-hungry colonists were frequently the cause of friction with the tribes. The administration of Indian affairs and the profits associated with Indian lands and trading posts were points of competition between rival colonial parties, between royal governors and colonists, and between colonial governments and administrators back in England. The Indian wars therefore tended to be seized as occasions for dramatizing the political or moral failings of one party or another. Over time, such stories acquired a certain weight in ideological controversy.

The making of ideological fables out of the experience of Indian warfare was perhaps nowhere as highly charged as in the literature of Bacon's Rebellion of 1676, where the contestants drew on the symbolic languages that had for them the highest moral authority—the idea of the rights and status of English gentlemen. The supporters of Bacon asserted that the governor and his party—alleged to have monopolized the profits of Indian trade—were effectively reducing English gentlemen to the status of vassals or even of servants. The governor, for his part, appealed to the sanctity of secular authority, vested in him by the crown and hence indirectly tied to divine authority. So far their debate conformed to the political vocabulary of their English contemporaries. But for the colonials the issues of rank, privilege, and authority were crossed by a uniquely American category of political opposition: the struggle between whites and Indians for control of the land and its wealth; and the competition between governor's men and private entrepreneurs for access to Indian lands and trade. So Bacon's men accused Governor Berkeley of a sort of treason to his race and nation, in setting Indians to attack his rivals; while the governor's men could respond that the rebels were themselves inclined to a savagery worse than that of the natives. But although the Indian affairs issue was central to the rebellion, and Bacon's men even attacked one unfortunate band, the Indian theme remained marginal in the polemical and narrative literature produced during the Rebellion.[4]

At the same time in the New England colonies, the outbreak of King Philip's War evoked a different ideological response. The Puritans invoked the moral authority of biblical scripture and the religious traditions of evangelical Protestantism to justify their hostilities with the Indians. Although secular concerns of the kind that characterized the literature of Bacon's Rebellion also appeared, they were subsumed in the grander categories derived from biblical mythology. In some respects, this Puritan response was unique. Its intense religiosity, the ideological and religious motives that lay behind its project of colonization, its high rate of literacy, and its concern with disseminating religious doctrine through printing set New England apart from the other colonies. However, the identification of colonization with the Christian enterprise of extending the realm of Protestant control was common to all the English colonies, although New England took the idea more seriously than most. Nonetheless, the importance of New England writings on the Indian wars derives from the region's special experience of warfare. From 1675 until the end of the Revolution, New England was the cockpit of major white-Indian confrontations, first with local tribes and later with the Indians and European soldiers operating out of Canada. Not until the last French and Indian war did the southern and middle colonies experience Indian warfare on a similar scale.

As early as the 1670s, Puritan writings about King Philip's War (1675–76) show the characteristic features of the literary Myth of the Frontier: the use of the Indian war as a metaphor for the entire secular history of the society, and as a link with the sacred mythology of the Bible; the development of a cast of characters representative of the important social and political tensions within the colony. The Puritan colonists in New England had founded their settlements as refuges from religious persecution, and they maintained them as refuges from the taint of heterodoxy even after the triumph of Puritanism in England. Their initial relations with the Indians were friendly, because their numbers were small and their "Errand into the Wilderness" appeared to involve only a temporary or marginal sojourn in Indian country. Yet the persistence of the ideological controversies with the Metropolis was matched by the secular success of the colonies. An attendant increase in population also created continual demand for new lands, which could be gotten only by displacing or restricting the range of the Indians. In such circumstances conflict was perhaps inevitable, and when it came the colonists abandoned their original conception of Indian affairs—that Indians should be Christianized and civilized—for a doctrine of Holy War, which envisioned treating the Indians as the Israelites had treated the Amalekites—exterminating them root and branch.

King Philip's War was the great crisis of the early period of New England history. Although it lasted little more than a year, it pushed the colonies perilously close to the brink of ruin. Half the towns in New England were severely damaged—twelve completely destroyed—and the work of a generation would be required to restore the frontier districts laid waste by the conflict. The war all but wrecked the colonial economy, disrupting the trade in furs and drawing off so much manpower that the fishing fleet and seaborne trade with the West Indies were almost totally inactivated. The colonial treasuries, chronically short of capital in the best of times, spent nearly a hundred thousand pounds on the war, bringing them to the edge of bankruptcy. Beyond the loss in treasure, King Philip's War was (in proportion to population) the costliest in lives of any American war. Out of a total population of some thirty thousand, one in every sixteen men of military age was killed or died as a result of war; and many men, women, and children were killed, were carried to captivity, or died of starvation and exposure as a result of the Indian raids. In a society so relatively small, made up of small towns and hamlets, such extensive losses meant that virtually every community and every family would partake of the common grief. And losses on this scale among the mature male population posed a real threat to the colony's continued prosperity, perhaps even its survival.[5]

The spiritual and psychological immiseration caused by the war, the trauma to the Puritan colonists in their collective spirit, were as deeply felt as the material and personal losses the colonies suffered. For a community that had conceived of itself as the new chosen people of the Lord, as the bearers of Christian light to heathen darkness, the fulfillers of a divinely inspired "Errand into the Wilderness," the catastrophe of the Indian war threatened their most basic assumptions about their own character and their relationship to God and to their new world. Surely the war was a sign of God's anger toward a people that had degenerated from the days of the colonial patriarchs, who had been so wonderfully protected from just such catastrophes.[6] But was the Lord so angered that he would withdraw his sanction from the Puritan enterprise, or was the war merely a warning of the possible consequences of any further degeneration of virtue?

Puritan writers of the 1670s, like Benjamin Tompson, searched the past for answers. His poem on King Philip's War recalled a time when Puritan colonists lived simply and abstemiously, in a harmony of classes and generations that prevented the rich from oppressing and the poor from envying, and kept the son obedient to the father's will:

> The times wherein old *Pompion* was a Saint,
> When men far'd hardly yet without complaint
> On vilest *Cates*; the dainty *Indian Maize*
> Was eat on *Clamp-shells* out of wooden Trayes
> Under thatched *Hutts* without the cry of *Rent*,
> And the best *Sawce* to every Dish, *Content*.
>
> These golden times (too fortunate to hold)
> Were quickly sin'd away for love of gold.[7]

Praise of the past conceals a critique of the present, in which Puritan virtues in dress, deportment, economics, and piety have degenerated, and with them the perfection of social and religious form that supposedly characterized the original colony. (This nostalgia for a past free of commercial conflicts would become an essential element of agrarian ideology.) If, then, the Indian war confirms the end of the Golden Age, it fortunately offers a chance for purgation and renewal.

The Puritans interpreted this struggle by aligning it with the apocalyptic mythology that underlay Protestant Christianity. Histories of the Indian wars, like those written by Increase Mather (and his son Cotton), interpreted history according to the archetypes of sacred typology. Each event of the war would be seen as an act of divine pedagogy, a dramatic "lecture" on the nature of God and his universe and man's place therein. Specific lessons would be drawn and utilized for the reform of the outward behavior of the colonists in manners, economics, and politics. Typological exegesis and historiography are complex techniques, with roots in the

earliest scholarship and theology of the Christian era; it is, however, sufficient for our purposes to note that Mather's typological historiography
interprets temporal history according to an archetype derived from a combination of Old Testament history and prophecy and the myth of Christ in
the New Testament, which is seen as containing a prefigurative model for
the history of mankind's future redemption. Just as the Old Testament
prefigures Christ's coming and martyrdom, the New predicts the pattern
of the Second Coming, Apocalypse, and millennium. The purpose of
Mather's historical writing was to "impose a sacred *telos* on secular events"
by correlating them to prophecies or events in the New Testament (most
particularly in the book of Revelation). Such an "apocalyptic timetable"
(as Sacvan Bercovitch has termed it) gives direction and meaning to the
otherwise incoherent and contradictory flow of events, providences, catastrophes, and triumphs.[8]

Mather's *Brief History* (1676) was composed while the war was still
in progress, not merely to chronicle its course but to account systematically
for the causes of the war, and its moral significance for New England.
The work therefore begins not with a secular history, but with a discussion of a crucial theological disagreement about the interpretation of a
sermon by John Cotton, one of the founding fathers of the Bay Colony.
Cotton's sermon had to do with the symbolism of the Seven Vials in the
book of Revelation, the most important text for typologists seeking the
signs of an imminent Apocalypse. Specifically, Cotton had addressed the
question of whether or not the American Indians were descendants of the
Lost Tribes of Israel, or a unique race of heathens. His aim was to determine the sequence in which their conversion could be expected, since
Jews and heathen were to be converted at different times; and the conversion of each, in proper sequence, was one of the signs by which the Second
Coming could be anticipated. We need not concern ourselves with Mather's
solution to the riddle: the crucial point is that Mather and his audience
saw their relations with the Indians as part of "sacred history" and the
"apocalyptic timetable." Hence their least skirmish was invested with a
tremendous symbolic weight.[9]

Mather's colleague Samuel Nowell was even more explicit in his
suggestion that King Philip's War was preparation for Armageddon. The
Indian war has been a warning. "God in his providence keeps some Nations and people unsubdued, as he did with Israel of old [:] he kept some
people unsubdued on purpose to teach Israel War." The Indians' only
purpose, their only justification within the divine schema, is to provide a
testing ground or a crucible for Puritan martial spirit. Thanks to the
presence of unsubdued Indians, succeeding generations of Puritans—who
would not know the physical and spiritual hardships, the testing of the
Puritan revolution and migration—might maintain the vigor and discipline
of their forefathers. That the Indians might have some claim to the land
does not occur to Nowell. Like Canaan, New England was granted to a
chosen people by God's will.

This hardening and disciplining of the later generations by Indian
warfare is essential if Christianity—represented by New England Puritanism—is to triumph in the larger struggle against paganism, Catholicism,

Islam, and Satan. Armageddon still lies ahead. The unfolding of the events of the war becomes, in Mather's history and Nowell's sermon, a series of "experiments," in which the shifting intentions and dispositions of Jehovah toward his backsliding people are carefully measured.[10]

In these Indian war histories and sermons, the Indians begin to function as a moral benchmark, against which the moral status of all historical actors and events is measured. Mather urges his audience to consider the reasons for God's choice of the Indians as the specific means of chastising his chosen people:

> *Consider how this Judgment is circumstanced,* If we mind where it began and by what Instruments, we may well think that God is greatly offended with the *Heathenisme* of the English People. How many that although they are *Christians* in name, are no better than *Heathens* in heart, and in Conversation? How many Families that live like *profane Indians* without any *Family prayer?* . . . And in most places Instituted Worship (whereby *Christians* are distinguished from *Heathen*) hath been too much neglected.[11]

But the basis of this desertion of the church community is not religious disaffection. Rather, it is greed for land, the motivating principle of emigration to the colonies, and from the colonies to the further frontiers.

> [Whereas] the first Planters that they might keep themselves together were satisfied with one Acre for each person, as his propriety, and after that with twenty Acres for a Family, how have men since coveted after the earth that many hundreds, nay thousands of Acres, have been engrossed by one man, and they that profess themselves Christians have forsaken Churches, and Ordinances, and all for land and elbow-room.[12]

Mather's charge is more general than a critique of frontiersmen and Indian policy. He is also criticizing the worldly spirit of a whole class of Puritans, many of the "rising generation," for whom the New World has become primarily a place in which to achieve wealth and status and for whom the preservation of orthodox purity is less important. Seen in this sense, Mather's sermon is a compelling rebuke to that very spirit of capitalism that later historians have seen as nearly synonymous with the rise of Puritanism.

But although Master rebukes the rich for oppressing the poor, his severest rebukes are reserved for the lower classes. In part, he sees their poverty as a sign of a lack of diligence in their callings, of personal impiety or incontinence, or of divine disfavor. But their chief sin is their ambition to rise, to imitate the style, and hope to acquire the wealth of their social betters. Condemning drunkenness and the delight in "Silk" and "perriwigs," Mather finds these sins directly redressed by the fate of the frontier captives who were mainly of the poorer sort seeking to better their lot in new unprotected settlements. Love of fashion is rebuked when the captive is stripped naked; and the essentially "heathen" character of the victim's sin is revealed when the skin, "exposed to the burning heat of the sun, is burnt and tauned thereby until they become of an hue like unto the Indians."

The minister addressing his congregation becomes, by analogy, a white missionary addressing a mob of unregenerate and recalcitrant heathen who, like the Indians, have refused to show the ministry due respect, who have failed to achieve conversion, and who in effect insult and injure the messenger of Christ's Word. "And what though some [Praying Indians] may be hypocrites," Mather declares, "Are not some *Praying English* as perfidious?" Thus Mather makes a complex association between general sinfulness, the particular sins of the ambitious lower classes (particularly on the frontier), and Indians. This effectively associates the aspirations of the lower classes and frontiersmen with racial degeneration or Indianization. But the force of Mather's jeremiad depends upon a normative belief that the Indian opposition is as fundamental and immutable as that between light and darkness.[13]

Samuel Nowell is more systematic in reducing these observations to doctrine. Nowell stresses the racial antipathy of Englishmen and Indians, by way of emphasizing the permanence and the fundamental character of the conflict (and thereby paralleling it with the Protestant struggle against Rome). He notes that "The Inhabitants of the land will not joyn or mix with us to make one Body," and contrasts this with the biblical efforts of Hamor and Sichem to make peace with Jacob by saying, "*Let us marry together and make one nation.*" This, says Nowell, has always been the French policy, but he notes ironically that though the French "may think thereby to escape some scourge that hangs over them," yet it seems within God's providence that war between Indians and whites (Frenchmen included) is inevitable.

For Nowell, the justification of racial separation and of the racial warfare that accompanies it lies in the divine ordering of nature. He sees the New World as torn between forces representing absolute dark and pure light, embodied in two nations of different blood and religion. Each nation strives to become the master of the world that is yet to be, to control the future of human history and religion. "Two nations [are in] the womb and will be striving." Therefore, "we must either learn to defend ourselves, or resolve to be vassals." No reconciliation between the races can occur, no marriage, for "When God intended the Canaanites to be destroyed, he did forbid Israel to marry with them: they were to be thorns to them, and Israel was to root them out." One or the other must be destroyed or enslaved. This represents a radical shift from the policy of converting the Indians and from the typological interpretation of John Cotton and John Eliot, who had seen the Indians as the Lost Tribes of Israel, rather than as Canaanites (or Amalekites, as Mather would have it).[14]

Moreover, the war polemics of Mather and Nowell were primitive statements of the doctrine of "savage warfare" that later generations conventionalized and codified as part of the Law of Warfare. That doctrine places the moral responsibility for initiating unlimited warfare on the "savages," but there was at least as much projection as observation in the doctrine.

A modern scholar defines the nature of the problem when he cites the fact that in sixteenth-century Mexico an Aztec chieftain was burned to death by the Inquisition—after due judicial procedure—for the crime of engaging in human sacrifice. Such punishments were termed *autos-da-fé*, acts of faith, by their perpetrators, which suggests their own function as ritual sacrifice. What is punished in the Indian is a sin which is shared by the colonial. George T. Hunt's study of *The Wars of the Iroquois* analyzes the tribe that was thought to typify the "Indian" mode of warfare, in its "irrational" devotion to extermination or enslavement of the enemy. Hunt demonstrates quite clearly that before the coming of the white men conflicts between the Iroquois and their neighbors were comparatively bloodless; or, at least, were every bit as discriminate and controlled—or indiscriminate and uncontrolled—as the contemporary warfare of seventeenth-century Europeans. Yet this emphasis on Indians as congenitally prone to exterminating or enslaving other tribes is a normative part of American historical writing, and it is curious, given that it proceeds from a culture that was itself devoted with growing intensity to the extermination or expropriation of the Indians and the kidnapping and enslaving of black Africans.[15]

Moreover, after 1630 the threat of Indians exterminating the colonists was no longer plausible. Indian attacks could wipe out settlements and small military expeditions; but as the eighteenth century progressed it became increasingly obvious that conflict risked the existence of the Indians, not of the whites. Yet the psychology of the early colonial wars, with its sense of total endangerment, was culturally preserved in order to justify the project of dispossessing the Indians.

General Henry Bouquet, a Swiss who served with the British army against Pontiac's Rebellion in 1764, offered a description of Indian warfare that expresses the common sense of the matter shared by eighteenth and nineteenth centuries alike. In a European war, says Bouquet, civilized restraints on the violence that can be offered to prisoners, the wounded, and noncombatants make of war "the exercise of a spirited and adventurous mind." But in an American war, the battle is

> a rigid contest where all is at stake, and mutual destruction the object. . . . In an American campaign everything is terrible; the face of the country, the climate, the enemy . . . victories are not decisive but defeats are ruinous; and simple death is the least misfortune which can happen . . .

Bouquet's account obscures the fact that even in European war, there were occasions when armies were not obliged to give quarter, and when captured towns might be raped by a "licentious soldiery." Nonetheless, folk wisdom from Philip's War to the Little Big Horn—and beyond—held that in a battle against a "savage" enemy you always saved the last bullet for yourself. One side or the other would perish, root and branch, whether by limitless murder and unspeakable torment, or by suicide.[16]

This ideology of savage war has become an essential trope of our mythologization of history, a cliché of political discourse especially in wartime. In the 1890s imperialists like Theodore Roosevelt rationalized draconian military measures against the Filipinos by comparing them to Apaches.

Samuel Eliot Morison, in his multivolume history of naval operations in the Second World War, recounts the posting of this slogan at fleet headquarters in the South Pacific: "KILL JAPS, KILL JAPS, KILL MORE JAPS!" Suspecting that peacetime readers may find the sentiment unacceptably extreme, Morison offers the following rationale:

> This may shock you, reader; but it is exactly how we felt. We were fighting no civilized, knightly war . . . We were back to primitive days of fighting Indians on the American frontier; no holds barred and no quarter. The Japs wanted it that way, thought they could thus terrify an "effete democracy"; and that is what they got, with the additional horrors of war that modern science can produce.[17]

It is possible that the last sentence is an oblique reference to the use of the atomic bomb at the war's end. But aside from that, Morison seems actually to overstate the extraordinary character of the counterviolence against the Japanese (we did, after all, grant quarter) in order to rationalize the strength of his sentiments. Note too the dramatization of the conflict as a vindication of our cultural masculinity against the accusations of "effeteness." The trope of savage war thus enriches the symbolic meaning of specific acts of war, transforming them into episodes of character building, moral vindication, and regeneration. At the same time it provides advance justification for a pressing of the war to the extreme point of extermination, "war without quarter": and it puts the moral responsibility for that outcome on the enemy, which is to say, on its predicted victims.

As we analyze the structure and meaning of this mythology of violence, it is important that we keep in mind the distinction between the myth and the real-world situations and practices to which it refers. Mythology reproduces the world with its significances heightened beyond normal measure, so that the smallest actions are heavy with cosmic significances, and every conflict appears to press toward ultimate fatalities and final solutions. The American mythology of violence continually invokes the prospect of genocidal warfare and apocalyptic, world-destroying massacres; and there is enough violence in the history of the Indian wars, the slave trade, the labor/management strife of industrialization, the crimes and riots of our chaotic urbanization, and our wars against nationalist and Communist insurgencies in Asia and Latin America to justify many critics in the belief that America is an exceptionally violent society.

Because the present study focuses exclusively on the United States, it may be seen as reinforcing that view. But it is worth noting that while the rhetoric we will be studying is brimful of proposals for genocide and wars of extermination, there is in fact nothing exceptional about our history of violence. Just as the history of our economic development can be assimilated to the larger patterns of Western capitalism, the history of American violence can be seen as a significant variation in a more general pattern. Both the Indian wars and the slave trade were part of the general system of European expansion, and have their equivalents in other countries and colonies, ranging from Brazil, Argentina, and South Africa among the colonies to the British conquest of Ireland within the European Metropolis.

The violence of American labor relations likewise is consistent with the general and perhaps universal tendency of industrializing societies. Finally, although American myths have enshrined the "war of extermination" in the cultural imagination in a way that seems to me to be exceptional, we have not in actual fact carried through any of the larger genocidal threats implicit in the myth. Our nearest approaches have been in the episodes of massacre and systematic mistreatment which decimated or destroyed particular tribes or bands of American Indians, and in our sponsorship of the colossal violence within Africa that was essential to the slave trade. But the episodes of anti-Indian genocide predate the full flowering of exterminationist rhetoric, and it might almost be said that the more excessive that rhetoric became, the less murder was actually done. And the violence of the slave trade was the work of many nations and peoples. There are no equivalents in American history of the programs of ethnic genocide carried out by the Turks against the Armenians or the Germans against the Jews; nor of the political genocide practiced by Stalin and Mao against opposition or dissident movements.

What is exceptional in American culture is the *mythology* of violence, the special meanings given to violence of a certain kind, in a certain style. It is symptomatic of that myth's prevalence that (at different times) spokesmen of the right and critics of the left have asserted that America is a preternaturally violent society. Certainly that view has been part of the left critique of America in the atomic era, which focuses on the excessive and irrational violence of the Vietnam war, urban crime and police repression, and our brandishing of the threat of nuclear annihilation. But as this study will show, it was essential to the ideologies of American expansionists, hegemonists, and Progressives in the nineteenth century to claim for our "race" the most extraordinary disposition for battle and the strife of domination.

After 1700 apocalyptic jargon is increasingly overlaid by the vocabulary of secular concerns, which identify the perfection of American life not with that of a Bible commonwealth, but with our possession of republican virtue, democratic idealism, or a perfect economic system. Matherian Puritanism was hostile to this development, and to the spirit of capitalist enterprise that underlay it; and this is reflected in the negative portrayal of the colonial frontiersmen and entrepreneurs in Mather's histories and sermons. Since economic and geographical expansion at the expense of the Indians (and others) was inevitable, Mather's negative myth of the 'Indianization" of the frontiersman would prove too limited a reflection of colonial responses to the New World. What developed after 1700 was a mythology that preserved the racial symbolism while simultaneously introducing a heroic myth in which representatives of colonial culture could engage in struggle with the Indians, become in the process quite close to the Indians, and yet emerge as spiritually regenerate heroes of Christian civilization.[18]

In making this new heroic myth, the Puritans and their successors combined Indian war history with the Christian myth of redemptive blood sarifice. The martyrdoms of Christ and the saints exemplify one sort of sacrifice, in which atonement is made by suffering violence; but the imagery of the Apocalypse offered a second model of redemption, in which the militant crushing of the enemy through divinely inspired violence is the redemptive act. In the literary symbolism of the Myth of the Frontier, these two scenarios are embodied in the stories of the "captive" and the "hunter." These story forms were developed separately during the fifty years after King Philip's War, and they were finally brought together to make a complete literary myth at the end of the eighteenth century.

C A P T I V E   A N D   H U N T E R [19]

The "captivity narrative" is the older literary formula, deriving from Mary Rowlandson's account of her captivity during Philip's War, published in 1682. Mrs. Rowlandson was the wife of a minister and a victim of captivity, not a writer; but she had an extraordinary ability to embody in language her feelings about this catastrophic and overwhelming experience. Because of the power of her writing, and because the values inherent in the captivity narrative were so essential to Puritan ideology, her narrative became the model for a tremendously popular and durable genre, which—in semifictional form—was able to contest the literary marketplace on equal terms with the novels of Cooper and Scott, as late as 1824. The "hunter narrative" is a post-Puritan form, although the first popular work in this mode was by another veteran of Philip's War, Benjamin Church, whose *Entertaining Passages* appeared in 1716.

Both the captivity and the hunter mythologies see the frontier experience as one of regression: civilized men and women leave contemporary society, and enter—willingly or as captives—a primitive, primal world. If they can maintain their racial/cultural integrity in that world, if they can seize the natural, original power that is immanent in that world, and if they can defeat the forces that seek to prevent their return to civilization, then on their return they will be capable of renewing the moral and physical powers of the society they originally left. The pioneer submits to regression in the name of progress; he goes back to the past to purify himself, to acquire new powers, in order to regenerate the present and make the future more glorious. The danger in this experience is that in undergoing regression, in going to the Indian, or to a figurative childhood or infancy, the hero risks the integrity of his or her white soul; he or she may be tempted to remain in the past, become a racial renegade or, on return, may be so altered by the experience of regression that the social responsibilities of adult life in civilization are no longer attractive.

Mrs. Rowlandson saw her captivity as a trial imposed on her by an angry God, rebuking her for her previous religious complacency; and her captivity to the Indians became, for her, the means to an experience of divine grace. Although she speaks of the Indians as devils and her wilderness captivity as hell (she is isolated, made a slave, tormented and mocked, offered sexual temptations and forbidden drugs—tobacco—deprived of her religious practice, deprived of food, shelter, clothing), she also experiences an inward journey, and receives shocking intimations about the true state of her soul and the real power and purpose of that unknowable fanatic, Jehovah. The journey out of civilization becomes a journey into her soul: she recognizes that the Indians are symbolizations of her own sinful inclinations, her own gluttony; she discovers, despite pathetic efforts to resist, that she shares, in some degree, the moral character of the Indians; and it is only when she sees the sinful black Indian in herself, recognizes her sinfulness and distance from God, that divine grace intervenes, exorcises inner-outer demons, and restores her to her broken family.

But her restoration is never fully complete: having experienced the other side of human nature, having passed through Hell and felt the breath of Satan and the hand of God, she is forever altered. People suspect her of having slept with the Indian chief King Philip during her captivity; and for her part, she finds her conversion by captivity has alienated her from her family and the normal world. All temporal objects appear hollow and vain to her: "I can remember a time when I used to sleep quietly of nights, without workings in my thoughts, but now it is other ways with me . . . when others are sleeping, mine eyes are weeping."[20]

Mrs. Rowlandson, and her sister captives, became the colonies' first culture heroes. As captives they had undergone, in dramatically exaggerated form, the essential experience of the American colonist or immigrant: the experience of acculturation, of initiation—in this case, through violence—into the New World. The experience altered perception, in fact changed character; but it also betrayed colonists' fears that they might be mastered by (instead of mastering) their new environment. Not unlogically, then, the captivity narrative eventually made way for an entirely new genre of narrative—those that center on the figure of the white male hunter, who learns from the Indians only in order to destroy them and so make the woods safe for the white woman.[21]

The "hunter myth" represents a very different scenario of relationship between the colonist, the wilderness, and the Indian. The sex of the hunter-hero is always masculine and he enters the wilderness willingly, even enthusiastically, where the captive is dragged kicking and screaming beyond the boundaries of society. He is the heroic agent of an expansive colonial society, rather than the symbol of a colonial culture adrift in an alien landscape and filled with a sense of peril and anxiety. He is an individualist, bent on establishing himself outside the pale of colonial authority, and at times even shares the Indians' antipathy for the colonial authorities—for although the hunter as hero is never a renegade, he speaks for a class of pioneers who were viewed by Metropolitan society as approaching the status of social outcasts, rebels, or renegades.

Like the captivity narratives, the symbolism of the hunter myth derives initially from historical sources, specifically from literary treatment of the lives of a series of real frontiersmen, beginning with Benjamin Church in Philip's War and culminating (but not concluding) with Daniel Boone just after the Revolution. These hunter-heroes—who later came to include Davy Crockett, Kit Carson, and Buffalo Bill—are solitary plebeian adventurers who are the advance guard of civilization—which is to say, of bourgeois democracy in the American mode. Just as the captivity myth embodies contradictory sentiments about colonizing the New World, the hunter myth speaks to the love-hate response of Americans to the processes of social and economic development, to their civilization and its discontents. The hunter speaks for the values of a "natural" and "unfettered" precapitalist Eden. Yet he facilitates the spread of progress and civilization, and himself embodies the go-getter values, the willful and dominant temperament, the pragmatic turn of mind, and the belief in racial superiority that characterized nineteenth-century bourgeois culture.

Within this general structure, we need only look briefly at the two figures who frame the first period of development, Church and Daniel Boone, to understand the essential features of the heroic type, and its historical basis. Both men were "pioneers" who deliberately separated themselves from the jurisdiction of their colonial societies to found communities in territory hitherto occupied only by Indians. Both are represented in historical accounts as strongly individualistic, as expert woodsmen, as adept in Indian warfare, and as men capable of understanding Indians, both diplomatically and sympathetically. Both are represented as having lived as the lone white man among tribes of Indians, and of having formed close relationships with the tribes—Church was said to have had the Squaw Sachem of Sogkonate as his mistress, and Boone was adopted by a Shawnee family during a period of captivity. There is even a parallelism in what is left out of their stories: despite their individualistic styles, both men dealt with the Indians as agents for large land companies—Church, interestingly enough, as agent for a group of investors that included his father-in-law, the Treasurer of Plymouth Colony.[22]

With all of these similarities, there are also significant differences. Although both frontiers did lie outside colonial jurisdiction, Church's frontier was not more than a day's ride from the colonial capital. Indian territory in 1675 lay along the Atlantic coast, and was not topographically distinct from the settled land that lay intermingled with it on every side. Its distance was more symbolic than real, a function of the differences between white and Indian culture and of the limitations of the colonial governments' legal powers. This symbolic distance is nonetheless very real— Church is boastful about his ability to live as the only white man in Indian country, and his frequent conflicts with colonial authorities over their management of Indian affairs suggest a great gulf between the life-styles and knowledge of frontiersmen and Metropolitan leaders. But his real proximity to the Metropolis is revealed at every turn by the ease and speed with which he moves from one world to another, and by the curious use of nautical terms to describe actions in the Indian war—troops "tacking about" rather than changing position in battle and "pilots" rather than scouts or guides leading them into Indian territory. Most important, the primary function of Church is that of Indian fighter. His fame derives exclusively from his role as the conqueror of King Philip, and his disagreements with the colonial authorities concern only their techniques for prosecuting the war. This exclusive focus on combat suggests that the primary business of the mythology at this point is the rationalization of Indian warfare, and the destruction of Indian culture by European settlement.[23]

With Boone the magical qualities of the new land are of equal importance with the drama of racial warfare. Boone's trans-Appalachian

Kentucky is more distant from the Metropolis than Church's Sogkonate, and hence more exotic. At the time when Boone leapt into the American imagination the depression of colonial currency and post-Revolutionary hard times in the East were making emigration especially attractive, particularly to the hundreds of veterans who held land script in lieu of cash payment from the government. Then, too, traditional land hunger, given an edge by the hard times, fed into the enthusiasm generated by the victorious conclusion of the war and into pride in westward expansion and the opening of new territories to republicanism.

Boone himself had been a small farmer on the North Carolina and Virginia frontiers until 1769, when at the age of thirty-six he crossed the border into Kentucky, in search of the trove of game and furs and free fertile land that earlier travelers had reported. Motivated in part by his love of hunting and the untrammeled life of the woods and in part by his speculative bent and ambition, he returned from Kentucky determined to bring his family there, together with sufficient numbers of their neighbors to give them all security from the Indians. He formed a partnership with Colonel Richard Henderson, a colonial land speculator who had illegally obtained a grant of land from the Cherokee; and acting (initially at least) as Henderson's agent, he led settlers across the mountains to found Boonesborough. Not long after, Boone became both an important political leader in Kentucky and a major figure in local folk legends. His character was as fascinating as his adventures were sensational. On the one hand, he was sincere in his abiding love of the hunter's life, which he pursued often in complete solitude; yet he was a devoted and affectionate family man. Simple in his manner, habits, dress, and diet, he nevertheless laid out for himself a baronial tract of forestland in Kentucky—which he subsequently lost through his refusal to "develop" it by converting it from hunting park to plantation. Although he prided himself on his self-sufficiency, he sought government contracts for drayage with the Revolutionary army; and in Kentucky, Virginia, and Spanish Missouri he sought and held public office.

Essential to his character, and later to his legend, is a paradoxical blend of ambition and self-denial, self-indulgence and equanimity in the face of deprivation. Whenever he was disappointed in business or politics, Boone would simply retire to the woods and the chase: rather than contest his landholdings against the lawsuits of newcomers, he deserted Kentucky for Missouri and for the pleasure of the pure freehold, of land won with the rifle, of land unsullied by the mere touch of law. And when the freehold gave way before civilization's advance, rather than abate his enjoyment of the land, he would go west again. Paradoxically he would die absolutely landless, but content, in the midst of a vast progeny and numerous pets, at the age of eighty-eight, after having been an active hunter in the plains and mountains till within two years of his death.[24]

The transformation of Daniel Boone into a mythic hero was begun by John Filson in a little book called *Kentucke* published in 1784. Filson had come west after the Revolution to pursue his career as a schoolmaster and to speculate in land in the new territories. He accompanied Boone on several surveying expeditions, became his friend, and heard from him the story of his adventures. With Boone and several other Kentucky notables, Filson formed a partnership to develop lands along the Ohio, and the pamphlet *Kentucke* was his major contribution to the enterprise. It was an elaborate, poetic, and visionary description of the new lands, intended to promote their sale to prospective emigrants and investors, and to arouse interest in western concerns among the political leadership of the republic.[25]

Filson's literary achievement was his linkage of the heroic fable of Boone's adventures to the mystique of the wilderness land. He framed Boone's adventures in an elaborate description of the territory, which he presents as the quintessence of all those natural and magical powers traditionally associated with the West: a wild and exotic landscape, embellished with weird rock formations, meadows of brilliant flowers, herds of buffalo, medicinal rock springs, and air that restores health and vigor to the refugee from the fumes and dust of the Metropolis. This special valuation of the land is complemented by a new vision of the Indian. Although he is every bit as hostile in Boone's adventures as in Church's, the Indian in *Kentucke* also has the qualities of the Noble Savage—affinity with nature, a religion and moral system based on nature, a patriotic spirit which can be admired even when it leads to opposition to the settlers. In short, the human product of Kentucky bears out the characterization of the land as a wellspring of regenerative natural powers, needing only the work of civilized man to domesticate and perfect it.

Filson sees Boone not merely as an adventurer, but as one who had achieved a remarkable personal philosophy through his career as a hunter. This philosophy, restated in Filson's neoclassic terms as a kind of republican Stoicism, raised Filson's portrayal of Boone in *Kentucke* above the run of frontier narratives, and offered Boone as a model of the republican citizen in a time when the newly independent nation was looking for some self-image appropriate to its status and ideology.

Boone is presented first as the discoverer of this "paradise," but he is not an official explorer. Rather, he follows his own impulses—his love of wilderness hunting and solitary wandering—and these lead him to Kentucky. His first revelation of the power and beauty of the land comes to him as he views the landscape from a "commanding ridge," where he sits in absolute solitude beside the body of a buck he has killed. It is only afterwards that he decides to join himself to others in a social compact for the establishment of communities in Kentucky. This attempt inevitably leads to warfare with the native Indians, and Boone's emergence as a military hero in the manner of Church. With this narrative the hunter-hero story becomes the device that organizes and gives meaning to the conventional tropes of Frontier narrative—specifically the "apocalyptic" fable of Indian warfare that ends with Indian removal or extermination; and the captivity myth, which raises the issue of civilized values imperiled by pioneering.

Like the captivity narrative, the hunter story recounts a conversion or initiation. But here the initiation is triumphant rather than simply traumatic: Boone's adventure involves a course of systematic assimilation to the Indian's world, beginning with his radical solitude and separation from society, and culminating in his captivity and adoption into an Indian tribe. Boone figures as the rescuer of captives, and as a captive who succeeds in circumventing, escaping, and finally defeating the Indians. Thus he emerges at the end as the answer to the problem of the captivity, and as the human agency through which the American errand into the wilderness will be consummated.

THE MYTH AND IDEOLOGY OF AGRARIANISM

The Boone legend was not merely a formulaic development in some autonomous realm of literature, but a development of social mythology that occurred during the period of the Revolution and the consolidation of the federal system. Where Church may be seen as a figure of local celebrity and reputation, Boone is presented from the first as the agent of a national movement to the West, a representative of "American" character and values, and a figure of interest to a "national" reading audience. The first editions of Filson's work were offered directly to political leaders of strongly national identification—Washington and Jefferson; and the propagation of Filson's text, and later of other versions of the Boone legend, made it a staple of popular magazine and cheap-book literature. The popularity of the legend derives from the political relevance of its terms to ideological questions of concern to those classes putting the new republic together.

The hunter/Indian-fighter legend links the development of America with a larger pattern of civilized growth at the expense of primitivism and "savagery," but it also ties that development directly to the activities of men who are notably individualistic. The virtues of the hunter/Indian fighter are primarily those of the entrepreneur, the man on the make. He is self-willed and self-motivated, and—if controlled at all—self-controlled. He stretches the boundaries of society and law by following the dictates of private will and ambition. He is a man of exploit, not of patient labor; a predator before he is a cultivator. He achieves and accumulates wealth not through drudgery and self-denial; but by seeking gratification in adventure, through dramatic discovery and through violent struggle with a great antagonist. Whether seen explicitly as Frontiersman, or as an entrepreneur within the Metropolis, this sort of character is both useful and dangerous. He is continually going beyond bounds of custom and even law; and while he attains results that may be beneficial, it is at the cost of calling custom and law into question. His violent impulses are directed not only outward, against the savage Indian on the western border; they turn also against the restrictive and discriminatory laws and social arrangements of the Metropolis, which seek to limit his freedom. In the context of the Revolution, both of these movements could be seen as acceptable; but once the new government was established, it and its supporters could feel the danger in the Frontiersman's willful determination to keep free of both the wigwam and the Metropolis. Rebellions of frontier farmers stimulated the fear of unchecked democracy which in part underlay the call for the constitutional convention. Popular insurrections on the frontier like the Shays's Rebellion, the Whiskey Rebellions, and the various Regulator troubles and secessionist movements led by former heroes of the frontier wars like George Rogers Clark and Aaron Burr seemed to justify such fears.[26]

This negative side to the Frontier and the Frontiersman had as much to do with the mythologization of the Frontier as the hyperbolic imagery of the West as a new Garden of Eden. It allowed the Frontiersman to serve as a metaphor for the "pure" spirit of individualism, in a republic already committed to entrepreneurship as the characteristic mode of economic expansion. The Frontiersman tests the limits of entrepreneurship as an ideology, and these very drives also make him dangerous to the solidarity of the body politic. Individual enterprise, of course, had energized the colonial economies, individual rights were the center of Revolutionary ideology; but individualism carried too far could be dangerous to the republic: it could atomize the society, dissolving deference, public spirit, and patriotism in a scramble for wealth and position.

The Federalist, or conservative, solution to the problem of frontier insurrection was to increase the coercive power of the state sufficiently to preclude the development of any social, economic, or political tendency capable of threatening the existing order. The ideology of the political opposition, however, articulated by Jefferson and his party offered a more complex and subtle way of dealing with the dual concern for economic freedom and political order. Jefferson's critique of federalism and of the propertied classes it represented noted the tendency of the government to thwart the limited and legitimate ambitions of the lower classes, detach them from the interests of men of property, and cause them to withdraw their consent to be governed. Jeffersonianism thus proposed to resolve the incipient polarization by using the power of government to obtain for the people a reservoir of wealth sufficient to guarantee that all enterprising individuals could obtain property sufficient to make them independent of the coercive power of the existing wealthy classes. With such a wide diffusion of property, the democratic diffusion of the franchise posed no danger to the ideology of property, and no threat to the legal protections enjoyed by existing proprietors. The very energy of individualism that threatened to dissolve the coercive state would become the political cement of the agrarian republic.

The centrality of agriculture in the American economy and its status as a "growth sector" in the 1790s made it logical for Jefferson to identify agrarian enterprise as the characteristic form economic growth would take in the republic. "Agriculture did not figure in his plans as a venerable form of production giving shelter to a traditional way of life; rather, [Jefferson] was responsive to every possible change in cultivation, processing, and marketing that would enhance its profitability."[27]

Thus it is fair to see Jefferson as a representative philosopher of the operative ideology of American capitalism, whose doctrines are not logically inconsistent with the development of industrial entrepreneurship. For Jefferson, however, the agrarian enterprise does have a special character, because of its association with nature and with traditional relations between squires and yeomen. Although opposed in principle to the imposition of deference through a regime confined to the upper classes, he believed in deference as an essential element in preserving social peace, in a society in which perfect distribution of wealth and power could never be achieved. His response to the individual whose definition of enterprise was restricted simply to accumulating capital "for his own account" was uniformly hostile, and he saw this spirit of capitalism as dangerous to civic virtue when carried to its logical extreme.

Behind the ideological rationale of Jeffersonianism, the structures of the Frontier Myth operate as evocative signifiers. The newly acquired lands are a Frontier which promises complete felicity, the satisfaction of all demands and the reconciliation of all contradictions.

In Jefferson's myth language, the "city" is the symbolic place in which class conflicts tend to become irreconcilable, and lead to despotism. The very processes of commerce that bring urban prosperity generate the conditions of collapse, by creating separate and antagonistic classes of the very rich and the very poor. The dependence of poor upon rich, degrading in the best of times, may be converted by hard times into a basis for sans-culottism. To the folk of the city, Jefferson opposes the character and the ideology of the "yeoman farmer"—a free individual, living on his own land, independent of others for the necessaries of life yet depending on his fellow citizens (and society in general) for protection, law, and civilized amenities. Because he possesses a share of property (and therefore of political power) he is a sturdy defender of property as an institution, and of the social system that authorizes and sustains property holding. Because he is not dependent on the rich for his subsistence, he is politically free; but because he acquiesces in the social arrangement, he does not wish to challenge the wealth, standing, or authority of his "betters."[28]

To guarantee a supply of land sufficient to support the property requirements of a growing democracy, Jefferson as president embarked on an ambitious program of expansion, which embroiled the United States in actual and potential conflicts with European colonial powers and with the independent native tribes of the West. But Jefferson did not like to contemplate the wars of dispossession his program would entail. He hoped by an enlightened program of teaching the Indians Christianity and agronomy to avert the necessity of such wars. But although he proposed Indian policies that he hoped would offer an "alternative to extinction," Jefferson's ideology implicitly assumed the inevitability of conflict between true and unredeemed savages and forward-moving agrarian democrats—and the equally inevitable extermination of savagery (if not of savages) by American society. The difference between Jefferson and Filson as makers of myths is one of dramatic subject and emphasis, not ideological intention. Nonetheless, that difference of emphasis is suggestive of a potential contradiction—between a world view that supposes class and racial conflict can be permanently averted, and one that envisions such conflict as history's major and most interesting subject.[29]

These two approaches to making the Myth of the Frontier produce very different kinds of literary fantasy. Filson's "hunter myth" is the progenitor of the grand tradition of literary Frontiersmanship that is first fully voiced by Cooper and culminates in the "Progressive" Frontier Myth of Roosevelt and Wister. The literary fantasy of an agrarian utopia does not have the same distinct novelistic history: it remains a theme rather than a mythic story or narrative formula. Nonetheless, it does project a kind of myth narrative that offers to explain the processes of development and the character of social relations. The best document for illustrating this aspect of agrarianism is Michel Guillaume Jean de Crèvecoeur's *Letters from an American Farmer* (1782)—a classic reflection on American society by an expatriate Frenchman. His book is a mixture of personal philosophy, accurate reportage, and clever pandering to the illusions about America that prevailed among liberal intellects on both sides of the Atlantic.

Crèvecoeur sees America as divided into four metaphorical environments, running north to south through all of the colonies. Each section has its own geography or natural character, which determines the type of economic, social, and political institutions and the sorts of human characters that develop there. The eastern seacoast is described in terms appropriate to our notion of the Metropolis: it faces Europe, engages in trade and exploitation of marine resources; and it is the realm of merchants, adventurous and commercial in character, sharing both the cultural advancement and the "vices" of Europe—greed and ambition for power in particular. At the opposite extreme is the world of the Indian: the wilderness, in which hunting is the mode of subsistence and savagery the form of social organization. The wilderness dweller, too, has particular virtues and vices—he has the "natural" morality and "nobility" of those who live close to nature and far from cities, yet he is also an abysmal barbarian, politically anarchic, violent, capable of great cruelty. Infringing on Indian territory is the third region, the "border" on which adventurous outriders of civilization mingle with the Indians, modifying wilderness in the direction of civilization while themselves acquiring a taste for still wilder freedoms. The borderers are the most dangerous and antisocial characters in the system, for even the Indians have a tribal organizaiton, while the borderer is a solitary individualist, recognizing no law but his own will and appetite.

Between the border and coast, and graded internally according to levels of development, Crèvecoeur locates the realm of the American farmer. It is a utopian district, freed at once of the Indian menace and the corruptions of the city. In this realm of domesticated nature, Crèvecoeur saw the poor of Europe and the east coast acquiring property and status, evolving into model citizens of a model republic. In this realm, nature does not seduce man to savagery, but provides a moral and philosophic tutelage: bees teach the good of labor and organization, the spider teaches patience, the care of soil and kine suggest an economy of enlightened self-interest and mutuality of benefits.[30]

These geopolitical divisions correspond roughly to different stages of civilization. Reading from west to east, we see social organization evolve from savagery to the highest level of social and technological complexity. But this is not the way in which Crèvecoeur would have us read the story embedded in the landscape. The human characters who dot it—most notably Andrew the Hebridean and the "Frontier Man" who flees to the Indians to escape the Revolution—experience the development in reverse order, from east to west. They are regenerated or rescued from the evils of civilization by a physical movement that suggests a social regression toward the primitive—what we may call the "simple regressive" scenario of movement. The contradiction is reconciled in the central region the utopia of the farmers. In this balanced district—the refuge from the alternatives of unchecked regression and progressive decadence—is contained all that man should rationally desire, and the support of the farming district becomes the final end of their endeavors.

Crèvecoeur's system superficially resembles that of Turner's Frontier Thesis, particularly in its depiction of successive stages of development embodied in identifiable regions, its vision of the border as a place for poor men to improve their lot, and its sentimental attachment for the life of the yeoman farmer. But the difference between them is that Turner's system follows a "simple progressive" scenario, appropriate to the values and the historical experience of an age of rapid industrial development. Crèvecoeur wrote at the end of a century of very slow expansion, which had stopped short of the mountain barrier of Appalachia. Moreover, his ideological interest was in providing a new rationale for social stability, not a rationalization of continual social upheaval and change.

But Crèvecoeur's scheme can also be translated as a fable of class relations, which employs a geographical metaphor to describe conflicting tendencies within European and American society. The borderers and merchants represent characteristic traits of the rising or ambitious classes, in two different aspects. The merchant represents a commercially advanced bourgeoisie, capable of putting great pressure on existing governments and of challenging every existing social arrangement affecting all other classes. The borderer represents bourgeois ambition in the "lower orders"—vaguely defined by Crèvecoeur, but suggestively linked with the propertyless classes of the Metropolis, tenant farmers, runaway servants, incipient proletarians who have somehow run wild. The crucial relations for Crèvecoeur are not those between the border and the wilderness, which interested the historian of a society committed to permanent expansion, but rather the internal relations that center on the world of the farmer.

This is the symbolism that underlies Crèvecoeur's famous fable of "Andrew the Hebridean"—the archetypal immigrant boy who makes good in the New World. Andrew's progress is not achieved by any Turnerian adventuring on the border. He is met on the dock by a substantial citizen, himself a prosperous farmer, who guides him through the process of getting work, finding land to rent as a tenant, accommodating to his tame Indian neighbors, and becoming a man of property. All of this action takes place within the boundaries of civilization, in fact on the interface between coast and farms. The only movement beyond the border that Crèvecoeur presents is that of exploration (by the scientist William Bartram) and the extreme case of the "Frontier Man"—who must flee to the Indians only because a corrupt Metropolis has broken out in the madness of revolutionary war. The point of "Andrew the Hebridean" is not only, and not chiefly, the argument that America is a place of opportunity; it is that that opportunity may be seized without excessive individualism, without a disordering of the relations of deference that subordinate poor to rich, with a natural and enlightened self-interest observed by all parties.[31]

But the world created by agrarian expansion sent forward men who were quite different from Filson's Boone or Crèvecoeur's Andrew. The land speculators and ambitious cotton planters and artisan-entrepreneurs who rose to meet the opportunity of the frontier windfall (and a generally expanding commercial economy) did not accept the limitations implied in Jeffersonian ideology. They did not deal deferentially with the established leaders of society, nor adapt manners and morals to the requirements of high culture. Their urge to exploit resources of land and of labor was limited only by self-interest, calculated (by and large) for the short term. They were willing to proceed with the dispossession of the Indians without waiting for the operations of an enlightened Indian policy to justify and ameliorate the process. They were willing to risk the outbreak of class and interest-group conflict in their drive for financial success. Andrew Jackson was, for Jefferson, the type of this rising class, and he regarded Jackson as a sinister figure: a border warrior without Boone's philosophic restraint, who had scrapped his way from low estate to membership in the slave-holding class, but who remained a frontier brawler, duelist, speculator, and demagogue.

In formulating his response to this new class, Jefferson reached for the language of race, and particularly that of Frontier warfare: he called them half-breeds, implying that their character was somehow Indian-like or savage, and their class ambitions akin to the renegadery of white men who desert civilization for the wigwam. Here the self-contradictory character of the myth and its ideology become clear. The white-Indian opposition became sanctified in myth because it appeared to express historical conflict in simple and agreeable terms. Whatever the class, religious, or political differences within colonial or Revolutionary society, the appearance of the Indian challenge evoked instant appreciation of the fundamental common ground.[32]

Jefferson had already rejected the traditional legitimation of class rule by reference to aristocratic birth as inimical to republican principles, to historical experience, and to reason: aristocratic government had produced a regime abusive of privilege in Britain, and so compelled America to rebel. But a class system based purely on wealth did not appeal to Jefferson, whose self-interest might have made him suspicious of the ambition of up-and-coming members of the lower classes. What was wanted was a principle of legitimation based on universally recognized values and the scientific truth of natural law.

The famous exchange of letters between Jefferson and John Adams provided the occasion for defining such a basis for legitimate class subordination. Jefferson and Adams saw themselves as representatives of two crucial oppositions in American life—the cultural opposition of South and North, and the ideological opposition of Democratic-Republican and Federalist—and their adoption of a common viewpoint on the basis of legitimate authority therefore may be taken as representing the consensus of a certain class and generation on these questions. In defining the qualities of a natural aristocracy, Jefferson and Adams reached for the metaphor of race and race conflict, likening the subtle differences of social class to the simple and striking differences that divided whites from Indians or blacks. They asserted their belief that some men were better fitted than others for the exercise of political responsibility because of their possession of a superior moral and intellectual endowment. Thus such men would be safe to entrust with the representative function, not only because their intelligence would enable them to find out the most expedient lines of policy, but because their moral endowment gave them a clear and unselfish sense of devotion to the public good.[33]

Both Adams and Jefferson believed in the essentially biological character of this endowment, and therefore believed that it would typically be found among members of the existing wealthy and educated classes—though provision should be made for finding and promoting those among the lower classes who, by some biological freak, showed the symptoms of aristocratic character. This concept of a biological basis for class differences was not a traditional assumption at the time. The equation of aristocratic status with membership in a particular family lineage was a matter of social definition in European society. The American republicans, seeking to protect a system of social deference while founding a democratic polity, had to base any justifiable difference between men on some operative natural law existing outside the artificial constraints of human laws. Their history taught them that the most profound natural distinctions on the score of moral character and social capability were those that divided all white men from Indians and from blacks. If analogous distinctions in moral or civic capacity existed among whites—between the respectable and the "dangerous" classes, for example, or between men and women—then they could be observed in the resemblance between those classes of whites and the uncivil or savage races.[34]

But this analogy between race and class carried heavy ideological consequences. It implied the relative permanence of "uncivil" traits, and thus suggested that over the course of time republican society must divide into orders of "natural aristocrats" and plebeians, divided according to their greater or lesser capacity to exercise the full power of citizenship, which is the power to rule. Moreover, if the history of Indian relations and of slavery is the model for relations between two such different orders of men, the development of social classes would lead inevitably to "jealousy" and "violence." Jefferson and Adams both note with alarm the tendency of those whom Jefferson calls half-breeds—the newly rich and ambitious classes—to envy and usurp the status, perquisites, and powers of the older families and the educated elite of the Revolution. However, Jefferson's most intensive development of the theme of social jealousy is not occasioned by class politics in Virginia, but by the contemplation of the situation and feelings of his own black slaves. The blacks are certainly jealous of the relative comfort in which their masters live, and of the liberty they enjoy; and such envy is a motive for them to seek both liberty and property. But since they are characterologically unsuited for full civil enfranchisement, these ambitions—laudable in others—become dangerous to civil peace.

Jefferson expresses his sense of the danger in black emancipation by restating the problem of liberty and property in sexual terms. Distinctions of race and class are like differences in the degree of "beauty"—a concept that Jefferson sees as incarnate in the white race. The beauty of whites, like their privileged status, makes them naturally and inevitably the preferred objects of love (or lust) by the lower orders—black preference for whites is "as uniformly [exhibited] as is the preference of the Oranootan for the black woman over those of his own species." By the terms of this analogy, any attempt by the black to act out his preference would produce an outcome as horrific and "unnatural" as the mixture of animal and human orders. This analogy defines the social peril: envying whites, blacks will seek to emulate them by appropriating their attributes and possessions; but because they are closer to the animal than the civil state, their ambitions will assuredly take a brutal form, a violent form. Thus if the blacks were to assert the common right of humanity to revolution for the sake of self-government, the result would be not a repetition of the American Revolution—in which a perfected polity emerged from violent struggle—but a war of mutual and limitless slaughter tending toward anarchy: emancipation would "divide us into parties, and produce convulsions, which will probably never end but in the extermination of the one or the other race."[35]

At the time Jefferson made that prophecy, the chief model for such a war of extermination was the Indian war. Subsequent events provided other models of peculiar relevance to the slavery controversy: the Revolutionary Terror of 1793, in which the Jacobins waged a war of extermination on French aristocrats, and the slave rebellion in Haiti became the model for subsequent visions of black-white race war. But for Jefferson the myth of the Indian or savage war was prior to any conception of a class or servile war tending toward extermination. The fate of the Indian was taken by him as a pattern of the history of all inferior races subjected to free competition with a superior and more energetic one. He had no doubt that should the domesticated sons of African savages be liberated, they would share the destiny of King Philip and Pontiac.

With both Indians and blacks, the "alternative to extinction" was their subjection to a regime established and forcibly maintained by their racial superiors. But if there were classes of whites, even of republican citizens, whose characters were analogous to those of the savages, must such a regime be extended to them? And if it were, would it not vitiate the essential principles and structures of republican government? To a degree, some such vitiation was already accepted in American society as an essential structure of family government: women and children were legally held under the tutelary power of the paterfamilias, and their political dependence was indeed analogous to that of slaves and reservation Indians. There would have to be a deep and severe crisis of social order before committed republicans could envision the extension of such a regime to the governance of substantial numbers of white freemen.

Just such a social crisis arose in Europe in the 1790s, with the triumph and spread of the French Revolution. Those intellectuals in Europe and America who used the American Revolution as a paradigm of enlightened political transformation saw in the French Revolution something far too radical and irrational in its practice and ultimate purposes. Its momentum carried it beyond the reformation of political institutions and the establishment of constitutional checks on royal authority, to become a social war pitting class against class. The antiaristocratic Terror and the descent into

Napoleonic despotism suggested to Jefferson and to French liberal Americanists like Crèvecoeur that the French people were as a whole unprepared for self-government, and perhaps unsuited for it. In this context the race/class analogy acquired a new significance.

Crèvecoeur's handling of it is especially illuminating. In his original *Letters of an American Farmer* he plays with images suggesting that the Americans—living close to nature and even to the Indians—have been able to achieve a unique balance and harmony in their politics. Their proximity to the Indians and their direct experience of the different intermediate stages of development between savagery and metropolitanism have given them a deep knowledge of the fundamental principles of natural law and politics. Hence they can govern themselves without degenerating into an anarchic strife of each against all. There is no need for any principle of order other than this natural and enlightened adherence to natural law and experience, and certainly no suggestion that Americans will require the leadership of a superior man or class to prevent abuses of self-government. America's unique juxtaposition of wilderness and settlement, Indian and pioneer and farmer, is a metaphor of the perfection of social relations in an Enlightenment utopia.

But the experience of revolution caused Crèvecoeur to reinterpret that metaphor. His last American book, the *Journey into Northern Pennsylvania . . .* (1801), is dedicated to Napoleon as the savior of republican principles in France. His concern in the volume is not with the perfection of the world of the yeoman farmer, but with the disorder and degeneration of life on the border. Here the brutalized outcasts of society confront the degenerate remnants of once powerful Indian tribes, and only the moral and military authority of government represented in a few benevolently despotic Indian agents and governors preserves order and peace. In the language of agrarian myth, when social conflict is recognized it is projected outward, to a confrontation on the border between savage and civilized races.[36]

For Jefferson, however, the Frontier conflict did not have this character. Class and race difference within the Metropolis were hard and inescapable, because they arose from the essential processes of economic production. But on the border, the Indian was not essential to production, and so it was not absolutely required that he be integrated into society; nor were his numbers and powers sufficient to threaten the order of society from outside. Jefferson is therefore less harsh in his account of Indians than in his remarks on blacks. Their share of beauty, he says, is greater, and there has been some intermarriage of the "best families" which has improved (or not harmed) them. But it is apparently their racial endowment to grow weaker and to disappear gradually, naturally, before the advance of civilization. In the wild they are doomed to vanish; in society they are so few that their integration presents little problem. Thus for Jefferson the race war on the border was an essentially harmless, productive, redemptive event, while a similar war in the Metropolis was a prelude to social catastrophe.

NATURAL ARISTOCRACY AND
THE CULT OF WASHINGTON

The idea of Indian extinction, the belief that a reservoir of cheap land could buy off class conflict, and the mythologization of figures like Filson's Boone and the "yeoman farmer" are all fantasies of denial, symbols that wishfully negate real and persistent fears and ideological ambivalences. A successful mythology requires heroes who can embody the positive doctrine of the class culture that produces it. To avert the specter of Jacobin anarchy or Napoleonic despotism, more was needed than the assertion that social upheaval was unlikely here. The legitimacy of the "natural aristocracy" needed a positive embodiment to stand against Bonaparte and Robespierre. For the makers of American literary culture—schoolmen, ministers, political leaders—that figure was George Washington. Redeemed from the calumny of partisan politics that dimmed his standing at the end of his life, Washington became the center of a hero cult that transcended party lines. The hagiographic biography by "Parson" Weems established the essential terms of this heroic myth in 1805. Weems presents Washington explicitly as an alternative to Napoleon, and he quotes the French emperor to the effect that he envied Washington his ability to save the American Revolution without having to destroy its liberties.[37]

As developed by Weems, Washington's life unifies in a single heroic career the symbols of disparate social identities. Although he is one of the "wealthy and well-born," he is also represented as in some measure a "self-made man," whose advantages of birth are negated by his father's early death and his own consequent "orphanhood." Early in his career, he abandons the prospect of a career in the Royal Navy to work as a surveyor and soldier for the Virginia government. Weems represents Washington's career as rather Boone-like: a course of solitary exploration, followed by success as a leader of "rangers" under General Braddock, the British commander in chief who suffered ambush and massacre by the French and Indians at Fort Duquesne. Contrary to fact, Weems represents Washington as wielding a tomahawk at Braddock's defeat, dressed in the buckskins of the frontiersman. But this apprenticeship to savage warfare does not make Washington a savage. Rather, it somehow induces in him a sharper sense of the importance of civilized values, and makes of him the Christian gentleman, the unselfish patriot, and the unorthodox general who defeats the British in the Revolution, and leads his country on the path of republicanism.[38]

Although the pattern of the adventure parallels that of the Frontier hero—a birth in civilized farming regions, an immersion in savage warfare, a return to rural domesticity and civic responsibility—Washington is never represented as a plebeian. He is an aristocrat by birth, whose estates are "in reversion," and who has "regressed" to something resembling the status of common man. By rebuilding damaged fortunes, he reacquires (through exhibited merit) authentic title to his original endowment. But he is not a man who starts from scratch; and he ends, not as the most famous man in Boonesborough, but as the wealthiest planter in America and president of the republic. The fable of initiation and success therefore fits exactly the Jefferson-Adams prescription for a "natural aristocrat." The role of the Frontier experience in Washington's development is significant; but it must be emphasized that the frontier is not the primary scene of his heroic accomplishment (as it is for Boone). The natural aristocrat's proper sphere of action is the Metropolis. This is an appropriate symbolization, since the ideological mission of the doctrines of agrarianism and "natural aristocracy" is to provide solutions to the social conflicts of the Metropolis. The former does this by buying off class conflict with a proffer of far-off Frontier land sufficient for all; the latter suggests that for anyone of sufficient natural endowment (and who would willingly denigrate his own natural gifts?) the American system provides a series of initiations through which one may rise to a status comparable to that of barons and earls—and in Washington's case, to saints and demigods.

Weems's proffering of Washington as the "idealized example" toward which Americans must strive is not simply a glorification of the republic's first citizen. It is put forward explicitly as a counter to that threat of social war which has destroyed Rome and the ancien régime and the liberal French republic of Lafayette. As early as 1805 Weems sees in the ideological differences of North and South, Federalist and Democrat, the basis for fratricidal warfare. And the civil war he envisions is one in which "mutual slaughter" will be carried on in the manner of the "war of extermination" associated with the Indian wars. Only by affiliating ourselves with the national ideology symbolized by Washington, and accepting as legitimate the principle of authority Washington represents, can the divergent American factions find a common ground of patriotism. But for Weems, as for Jefferson and Crèvecoeur, the shadow of social warfare is felt as an imminent presence, and a matter of immediate concern for makers of public ideology.[39]

THE DANGEROUS FRONTIERSMAN AND THE GUILT OF DISPOSSESSION

The Washington myth suggested the terms in which the idea of "natural aristocracy" might appeal as the basis for the social and political subordination of one class to another. But practical politicians like Jefferson and Adams knew that universal acknowledgment of merit and ability was not to be expected. Jefferson was materialist enough to believe that political democracy required a material basis in economic equity; and in an agrarian age, such equity must take the form of land. Therefore, he buttressed his own Andrew-the-Hebridean fantasy of the yeoman's realm with an aggressive policy of westward expansion, designed to increase the land available for the "agrarian cupidity" of the poor and the landless and the merely ambitious. This vast reserve of cheap land—which would eventually claim the Louisiana and Oregon territories—was thought to be so extensive that the cupidity of a thousand generations would not be sufficient to exhaust it. Given the spectacularly favorable man/land ratio thus created, Jefferson could reasonably expect that his legacy to America had provided a long-term hedge against the triumph of the Metropolis and its politics of social control over the republic of yeoman farmers.[40]

But he miscalculated—not only the rate of population increase and economic expansion, but the character of the economic and political motives he sought to buy off. During his own lifetime it was already apparent that the arable land available east of the 100th meridian was well on its way to being completely "taken up" and developed, by a burgeoning population of farmers in the North and by spreadeagle plantations in the South. More-over, the prospect of windfall wealth was a stimulant to speculative and entrepreneurial energies, not a soporific. The Jeffersonian expectation that a vast treasury of land would buy off the greed of ambitious Americans was as naive as that of Montezuma, who thought that rich presents of gold delivered to the Spaniards in Vera Cruz would prevent Cortes from march-ing on Tenochtitlan. The Jeffersonian citizen of the Frontier was supposed to have been a buckskin philosopher like Boone or a deferential yeoman like Andrew the Hebridean. But in practice he turned out to be a speculat-ing wastrel like Davy Crockett, or a man like Andrew Jackson, driven by a need for wealth, standing, and power.

In the figure of the dangerous Frontiersman, the ideology of ruthless commercialism is associated with the doctrine of savage warfare derived from the Puritan polemics of Mather and Nowell. Mather had asserted that the greedy land hunger of the frontiersmen had led that class to in-tensify the exploitation and expropriation of the Indians, and so provoked ruinous warfare; and he represented this connection between greed and Indian warfare in the image of the frontiersman as an "Indian at heart." To purify the image of the republican citizen-farmer, it was necessary to dis-connect him from both the sin of excessive greed and self-interestedness. The agrarian ideology found an alternative to this language of slaughter in the metaphorical linkage of the Indian's fate to natural processes like the growth and decay of plants or the rise and fall of contending animal species. Nature, not human choice, is destroying the Indian. Benjamin Franklin caught the spirit of the doctrine in the 1790s, when he wrote:

> Indeed, if it be the design of Providence to extirpate these savages in order to make room for the cultivators of the earth, it seems not improbable that rum may be the appointed means. It has already annihilated all the tribes who formerly inhabited the seacoast.[41]

But of course it was not Providence that made and sold the rum. The moral responsibility for slaughter, though deflected by symbolism, remains.

The fables of the Indian war and the yeoman farmer translate the Metropolitan strife of interest groups and classes into archetypal terms. Instead of interpreting history as a competition for power and resources by classes of fellow citizens, the Myth projects competition outward, and imagines the strife as that between a fully human entity—"civilization"—and an entity that is primarily inhuman. The natural wilderness resists civi-lization with its overgrown plants, strange diseases, and wild beasts; and though the Indians are human, they are so much a part of "nature" as to seem only slightly different from the beasts of the forests. Thus the story of Indian displacement translates a human drama of dispossession into one in which resources are innocently appropriated directly from nature, without human cost.

Nonetheless, the Indians are human, and to dispossess them provokes a sense of guilt that is a recognition of the human character of the conflict. This recognition, and the moral malaise that goes with it, ties the myth of the Indian to the class conflicts of the Metropolis. Here too acts of dispossession occur, ranging from those that detach the peasant from the land and send him to the factory, to the larger dispossession involved in the taking of profit from wages. Thus the story of Indian subjugation can become a metaphor for the Metropolitan struggles that have as their end the subjugation of labor to the disciplines of industrial production. The metaphorical substitution of Indian warfare for class conflict reduces the moral and political complexities of modern life to a terrible simplicity. Racial solidarity against the dark-skinned primitive substitutes for the divisions of class; and by accepting the treatment of the Indian as an aspect of the world of resources—a tree to be cleared off so the field can be farmed—the citizen consents to the commodification of humanity, the reduction of human values—including his own—to the calculus of capitalism.

The rise of industrialism changed the relationship of Frontier and Metropolis in profound ways, the most essential of which was its definitive transfer of the generation of new wealth and economic expansion from the land and the wilderness to the heart of the Metropolis. Especially after the Civil War, the rapid industrialization of the economy made the cities the focus of new emigration—from American farms as well as from Europe. In the "wilderness of cities" the unsubjugated and violent opposition to order was to be found not among redskins, but among Europeans—many of whom were of non-English ethnicity. The representation of the laboring and dangerous classes as "white savages" was more than a simple denigration. It implied, and it rationalized, their dehumanization, their reduction to the status of things or commodities.[42]

But those who act as the agents of dispossession—the Indian fighters in the wilderness, the entrepreneurs in countryside or city—acquire the taint of society's moral malaise and become (in fiction) scapegoats for it. Jefferson imagines such people as "half-breeds," sharing a racial taint, which ties them to the Indians—to the very folk they are most engaged in combating! The association is basic to our literary and political mythology: the Indian fighter is always the man who knows Indians best and has a taint of savagery; the southern planter is seen as sharing the sensuality and indolence attributed to black slaves; the "Lord of the Loom" is represented as sharing the debased and mechanical values attributed to the proletariat. But the most elaborate working out of this fantasy is in the Frontier Myth, in the figure of the hunter-hero. Because of his distance from the controversies and pollutions of the Metropolis, and his engagement with a conflict associated with the historical past, this figure became a safe and appealing vehicle for the expression of these ideological ambivalences. It was James Fenimore Cooper's recognition and exploitation of this figure that made his novels the seminal fictions of American literary history.

CHAPTER 5

Ideology and Fiction: The Role of Cooper

It might be said of James Fenimore Cooper that if he had not existed, it would have been necessary to invent him. Few writers have so deserved the name of literary pioneer, and few have had his influence on the mythological vocabulary and generic structure of their culture's literature. He was not the very first to call for a truly national literature drawing on American materials and values—Charles Brockden Brown preceded him by a quarter century. But no American writer before Cooper made so extensive a use of the materials of American history, none created works that enjoyed equal popularity and respectability, and none sustained so large and thematically coherent a body of work.[1]

Cooper explored his chosen themes both intensively and extensively, and his works divide naturally into series. Some of these, like the sea stories, have a thematic coherence that bonds several disparate fictions together; others, like the Leatherstocking and Littlepage series, are multivolume explorations of a theme, a period, and a constellation of characters and ideas.

His major achievement was the cycle of five historical romances known as the Leatherstocking Tales, a series that takes its name from one of the sobriquets of its central figure—Natty Bumppo, also called Hawkeye, Leatherstocking, Pathfinder, and Deerslayer—and he is an enduring literary character, a central symbol that has continued to exercise an influence on American literary mythology. During the nineteenth century this influence was reflected in the numerous borrowings, imitations, plagiarisms, and parodies of the Leatherstocking formula, which were the stock-in-trade of serious novelists like R. M. Bird and William Gilmore Simms, of the producers of stage melodramas, and of the dime-novel industry that emerged after 1850. Cooper's mythologization of frontier history and his representation of frontier characters also influenced the writing of historians like Bancroft and Parkman, who in effect read Cooper's fiction into the historical record. The classic pairing of white hunter and Indian companion has become an essential structure of American fiction and popular culture, from Melville's *Moby Dick* to Twain's *Huckleberry Finn*, on down to the Lone Ranger and Tonto. The image of the American hero as a man armed and solitary, plebeian but worthy somehow of nobility, fronting a native

wilderness and seeking in action his heart's desire—this figure persists in
Ahab and the Virginian, Robert Jordan and Ike McCaslin, the Great Gatsby
and Ross MacDonald's hard-boiled Lew Archer—who tells a woman in *The
Zebra-Striped Hearse* (1969), "My real name is Natty Bumpo [*sic*] . . . He's
a character in a book. He was a great man and a great tracker . . . I can
shoot a rifle, but as for tracking, I do my best work in cities."[2]

THE CHOICE OF GENRE

Cooper's centrality is not inadvertent. The role of literary pioneer
was one he chose for himself, from motives that were ideological as much
as artistic. Cooper was born in 1789, and grew up during a period of intensifying nationalism in both politics and culture. As the son of a prominent landowner and Federalist judge, he was brought up in the expectation
of his taking a prominent and responsible role in the life of the republic.
When he turned to literary work, after a period of pursuing (with indifferent
success) a career in the Navy and a number of business ventures, he made
literature the field of patriotic action and a forum to address the concerns of
public life. In 1820 he wrote and published his first novel, *Precaution*—an
imitation or parody of Jane Austen which did very badly with American audiences, but paradoxically enjoyed success in England. He later said that he
had attempted to prove that a "typically British novel" could be written by
almost anyone, and that therefore the critical preeminence accorded British
writers was illegitimate. "I take more pains with *The Spy*," he said of his
second novel, "as it is to be an American novel professedly." Its appearance
in 1821 effectively began his career as a professional novelist and as a leading
figure in the developing movement of literary nationalism.[3]

In his early novels, Cooper moved away from the conventions of the
novel of manners and toward the genre known as historical romance, whose
most noted practitioner was Sir Walter Scott. The special character of the
"historical romance" as a literary genre is its simultaneous appeal both to
history and to fiction. Its rise coincided with the rise of European and
American nationalism, and it may be thought of as providing the popular
mythos which both fed and fed upon that cultural and political movement.
The basic convention of the form is its attempted "recovery" of a moment
in the nascent nation's historical past—a moment when tendencies or influences operative in current history can be observed in their embryonic
form. In the resolution of the historical conflict within the novel frame, the
resolution of present tensions is prefigured. The past is mythologized by
being rendered as a symbolic microcosm of persistent tendencies. The
"romance" is to be understood in a double sense: as referring to the fictional
mode, such as the chivalric romance or the artificial epic; and as referring
to the romantic "plot," a love theme in which a sexual/social conflict becomes a metaphor for the historical oppositions of the novel.[4]

To this formula Cooper brought a gift for handling social materials
through projective fantasy rather than through mimetic representation. By
projecting modern social tendencies backward in time and outward in space

he could employ his talent for natural description, and engage also the powerful force of nostalgia for the America of the Founding Fathers. So with Scott rather than Austen as a model, in the years 1821–23 he produced the Revolutionary romances (*The Spy* and *Lionel Lincoln*), the earliest of his sea novels (*The Pilot*), and the first of his Frontier romances: *The Pioneers.*

The choice of the historical romance as his generic form and of literary nationalism as his literary mission made it inevitable that social and political ideology should inform Cooper's fiction. Nonetheless, Cooper's fictional ideology should not be seen as the simple reproduction of the party ideologies of the period. Although ideological distinctions were becoming characteristic of the new parties that emerged in Cooper's time, the bases of political organization were still very closely bound to the particular concerns of locality. Different Democratic factions, and the later Whig-Democratic party split, did not represent ideological constituencies in any systematic way. Conservative and wealthy men, bankers and slaveholding planters, small farmers and artisans, Northerners and Southerners were to be found on both sides—all sides—of party lines, at least until the late 1840s. Cooper himself had all the material attributes, the political education, and even the social values to make him an ideal Whig—yet he was a Jacksonian Democrat, perhaps chiefly because his opponents on immediate local issues were all Whigs.

His political education as the son of Judge William Cooper of Cooperstown served to immerse him in the contradictions of republican ideology. He was reared in a frontier community which was democratic in lifestyle—a widely diffused suffrage, relatively small differentials in conspicuous consumption—but in which political and economic power were vested in men of wealth, education, and standing like his father: the "natural rulers" whose preeminence in politics was presumed by Adams and Jefferson.

Judge Cooper was a perfect embodiment of this class. Beginning with fairly modest means, he had become a man of wealth and political influence who bequeathed an estate valued at nearly $700,000. He took pride in the fact that he had built his fortune in a proper republican manner— not by acquiring bound laborers or slaves for plantation farming, after the manner of the southern planters and the Dutch patroons of New York, but by speculating in and developing frontier lands. He belonged to the class of entrepreneurs whose specialty was the engrossment of large frontier tracts, for sale or rent to pioneer farmers. Although he shared Jefferson's belief that the independent farmer was the basic building block of a stable society, Judge Cooper demanded both social and political deference from his tenants and social inferiors. He was a Federalist hard-case who once told a citizen at the polls, "You cannot know how to vote as well as I can direct you."[5]

Cooper broke with his father's federalism and departed also from the judge's extreme elitism and Anglophilia. But he retained the paternal property interests, and also a belief that resembled his father's in the necessity of social deference in the maintenance of political order. The Revolution, of necessity, had upset and overthrown the existing set of rulers, and it had offered as rationale for its action an ideology that opposed natural rights to traditions of deference. As the son of Judge Cooper and the husband of a De Lancey, Cooper was linked both to the old Tory aristocracy and the new Whig aristocracy that had displaced it. When that American aristocracy was in turn challenged by the economic and political claims of hitherto deferential lower classes, Cooper was equipped with a historical analogy or metaphor that allowed him to interpret it. In some sense, his father's generation could be seen as having initiated the process of its own destruction by undermining the legitimacy of the earlier system of deference; and in his fiction, Cooper began to work out imaginary resolutions for this sin of the fathers, and the social disorder it had entailed on the republic.[6]

His own position, the true position of an American democrat as he saw it, must lie between the extremes of paternal tyranny and filial ingratitude, of political despotism and rebellious anarchy. These gradations of political conditions had historical correlatives, which could be used as the building blocks of historical romance. At the tyrannous extreme is the abusive pre-Revolutionary regime, whose representatives are corrupt or pusillanimous British officers (like Webb in *The Last of the Mohicans* or Warfield in *The Deerslayer*), or unprincipled American Tories. At the anarchic extreme are the Jacobins of the French Revolution, whose radicalism is darkly echoed in the plots of unscrupulous or overambitious Americans, like the Sheriff in *The Pioneers* or the "squatters" in *The Prairie*.

But these political and historical referents posed certain problems for Cooper. On the artistic side, they involved the comparison of disparate historical moments that would seem to resist a coherent novelistic frame. They also posed difficult ideological questions—even the apparently simple opposition of Tory and Patriot, Anglophile and Jacobin, was complicated for Cooper. His own marriage anticipated the conventions of his historic romances, by uniting him with a daughter of the De Lancey family, one of the most notable Tory dynasties left in the country. Setting the family connection aside, a social conservative like Cooper was inevitably attracted by the sober values of Toryism. Similar contradictions affected his response to the radicalism of the French Revolution: he disliked Jacobinism, but disliked as well the reactionary regimes that fought it, and identified with the Francophile party of Jefferson.

The cult of Washington offered a conventionally sanctified device for affecting such broad reconciliations between social and political opposites, and Cooper availed himself of this mythic property in *The Spy*, where Washington functions almost as deus ex machina to clear up the moral and political ambiguities of the struggle. But such a device could not always be used, and Cooper therefore found or created analogues for Washington—characters either historical or fictional in whom the essential qualities of the Washington figure were abstracted and embodied. Thus Cooper translated the terms of the Washington cult into a language of symbols detachable from Washington himself, and hence capable of characterizing a whole class of heroes—professional soldiers or naval captains who are also gentlemen, of middling social origin but natural-aristocratic in moral and intellectual endowment, the acknowledged rulers and moral arbiters of the fictional microcosm. Cooper also abstracted and simplified the ideological complications of his social condition by shifting his source of historical metaphors from the Revolution to the Frontier. On this ground, removed in time and space from the revolutionary divisions of the Metropolis, social and ideological differences could be represented geographically, rather than politically; and the direction of history could be represented not by the dialectic of revolutionary warfare, but by the simple progression of landscapes from wilderness to settlement to town to Metropolis.[7]

The Pioneers, published in 1823, reflects Cooper's formal transition from a novelist of manners to a writer of historical romances. The setting of the novel is Templeton, a fictional version of the Cooperstown of Cooper's youth, and in it Cooper simultaneously explores the material of his personal past and that of American history. The plot of the novel is appropriate to historical romance, in that it pits representatives of historically significant races, classes, and parties against one another in a conflict that symbolizes a major issue in the formation of the nation. But as in the novel of manners, a good deal of time is spent developing in detail a portrait of the social relations of a many-layered community. Thus the novel allows Cooper to utilize his personal past and to develop in some detail a lexicon of social types that would serve him for the rest of his career.

The plot hinges on the question of legitimacy in the exercise of proprietorship and political power. The primitive proprietors of the land have been dispossessed long before—this is a community in the backwash of the frontier, whose Indian population is reduced to the drunken John Mohegan. His chief companion is a white man, the old hunter Natty Bumppo. In the course of the novel, we discover what these two decrepit and down-at-heels men have been in the heroic past—Chingachgook and Hawkeye, the last chief of the ancient Indian race of the Mohicans, and the greatest of the white "scouts" whose heroism had made the wilderness safe for civilization. Power is presently exercised by Judge Temple, a fictional version of William Cooper: the greatest landowner and the primary developer of Templeton. But Temple himself has dispossessed a prior white proprietor, the noble Effingham family, whose English nationality had cost it title to the Templeton lands. The heir of the Effinghams now lives, disguised as a fellow frontiersman, with Natty and Chingachgook, and the romantic plot revolves around the reconciliation of patriot and Tory aristocrats through the marriage of young Effingham with Temple's daughter.

This marriage, and Judge Temple's paternal government, are threatened by the ambitions of another set of would-be proprietors—the up-and-coming class represented by the Sheriff—which uses money and demagogy to attempt an overturn of traditional order. The Sheriff's threat is a direct challenge to Temple's authority; but that authority is vulnerable because its intellectual and moral bases have been undermined by the history of dispossession that established its title. In the long, complex, and subtle Tavern scene, Cooper links these cycles of conflict and dispossession to the catastrophic development of Jacobinism in the French Revolution, which denies (in Cooper's view) the very ideas of legtimacy and property. Indian, white hunter, and aristocrat function as embodiments and voices of primitive and "natural" entitlements to property; and Temple must defend himself against their accusations, as well as against the Sheriff's machinations, to establish his title. In the end, the defense is accomplished not by argument but by action: after a wilderness "rescue," the Judge's daughter marries the son of the aristocrat; and the Indian question removes itself, with the death of the last Indian chief and the willing self-exile of Natty Bumppo.[8]

The writing of *The Pioneers* generated the interests and creative energies that Cooper was to exploit for the rest of his career. In particular, his fascination with the characters of Natty and Chingachgook—the doomed challengers of America's entitlement—engaged him in an intensive exploration of the implications of his story. The fascination held him through the completion of a cycle of Leatherstocking Tales, which reached back into the historical roots of the heroes and forward to Natty's death (*Last of the Mohicans* [1826], *The Prairie* [1827]); and the created myth of Leatherstocking remained so much a part of his artistic memory that he was able to return to it after a lapse of thirteen years to write *The Pathfinder* (1840) and *The Deerslayer* (1841). These tales became a personal myth in much the same way that the "matter of Hannibal" and the Tom and Huck stories are Mark Twain's. But Cooper's reach went beyond the personal and became a fictional codification of ideas about the significance of the Frontier to the ideology of Jeffersonian republicanism.

THE LEATHERSTOCKING MYTH

The antecedents of the Leatherstocking myth as developed during the colonial period and the early republic had centered on a perennial heroic triad—the captive, the hunter, and the savage. Cooper continued and elaborated this scheme by "doubling" and dividing these basic roles, multiplying the varieties of social type they could be made to represent, thus expanding the stories' ideological references. Likewise, he invented elaborate variations on the "plots" of his source narratives, multiplying and varying the scenarios of captivity and rescue. But these variations were not merely arbitrary manipulations of formal entities. Cooper recognized in these source narratives of the captive, hunter, and savage a paradigm of American history and a fable of moral regeneration. Within this general pattern he integrated three distinct, pre-existing plot formulae or scenarios of interaction, defining and valuing the roles of each of the three heroic figures.

The earliest of these to develop was the "conversion" formula, derived from the religious preoccupation of the Puritans, which centered on the female captive's role in the adventure and saw the outcome of the adventure as a spiritual redemption through suffering and humiliation. A chastened but potentially tragic self-knowledge follows, for the victim's suffering breaks her connections to family and home, and her spiritual redemption orients her away from this world and toward death. The other plot forms are secular variants of the conversion. In the "initiation" story, typified by the narrative of Church and the legends of Boone and Washington, the central figure is the hunter, not the captive; but the experience is still one of self-knowledge achieved and of a new relation to the created universe through the wilderness adventure. The initiation differs from the conversion in seeing divinity as resident in nature itself, rather than in pure transcendence of the world; and the acts that allow the hero to achieve self-transformation involve a willed intimacy with the savage and the wilderness, and then a violent attack on and triumph against those elements.

The third variant, the "success" story, is the most secular of all the formulae, and the only one that works as easily for an adventure behind the cutting edge of the frontier as for one in the wilderness proper. Its prototypes exist in pre-1800 literature—in Cotton Mather's biography of William Phipps, in Benjamin Franklin's *Autobiography* (a classic statement of the type), and in the agrarian imagery of Crèvecoeur—but it would be wrong to say that the success story form was as clearly conventionalized as the conversion and initiation fables, and it was certainly not as closely associated with the Frontier before 1820. The hero of this narrative type is out to change his fortunes through his adventure, and in pursuing his private interest he certainly needs to acquire "know-how"—hence his story often involves an initiation into the secular wisdom of nature. It may also happen that in achieving worldly success, this hero grows in grace—this is certainly the way the story is told by Mather, Franklin, and Crèvecoeur. But the success hero's motives have nothing of the self-abnegation of the captive or the hunter's willingness to risk self for the captive's sake. The success hero is a radical individualist, whose know-how is used not only against the savage but to exploit the gullibility of his fellow man. In the popular literature that developed after Cooper's success, this type of hero was exemplified by the "living legend" Davy Crockett and the fictional Simon Suggs. For these heroes, self-transformation takes the primitive form of learning to be "shifty in a new country," and is consummated by the achievement of upward mobility.

Cooper's genius lay in his ability not only to draw on these patterns, but to integrate them into a single narrative line that runs through the entire series of novels. The romantic "plots" of Cooper's fiction are concessions to the sentimental taste of his audience, and their shapes from novel to novel are (with some exceptions) redundant and predictable. But the narrative subtext, in which Cooper carries forward his integrated retelling of the Frontier Myth, develops and grows from book to book, adding meanings rather than merely repeating them.

In the first three Leatherstocking novels—*The Pioneers* (1823), *The Last of the Mohicans* (1826), and *The Prairie* (1827)—Cooper makes his most sustained and intensive effort to comprehend historical movements through the conventions of literary fiction. To do this, he draws heavily on the symbolic language inherited from the writers of popular narratives (especially captivities), on myth-historical accounts like Filson's *Kentucke*, and on the more sophisticated and "analytical" attempts of writers like Crèvecoeur and ideologists like Jefferson to account for America's peculiar history and destiny. In Cooper's hands the fictive "geography" of Crèvecoeur and Jefferson, with its characteristic association of frontier regions with particular social types or classes, is organized and developed as a literary plot and as a historiographical doctrine. But Cooper's concern is to show not only the existence of different phases or stages in American social development, but to exemplify the processes through which one stage impinges upon and finally replaces another. Crèvecoeur's geopolitical map is an allegorical tableau, stable and relatively free of catastrophic change; Cooper's map is active, with lines that break and shift as human actors cross the boundaries in both directions, pursuing a struggle that will end only when one people and one geographical realm has been eliminated from the map.

Such a vision was not readily compatible with the liberal optimism of the intellectual heirs of Jefferson, nor with the philanthropic and evangelical Christianity of the period. It is a vision at odds with the Jeffersonian belief that all human beings share a common moral sense that is the basis and justification of their right to liberty; and at odds with the missionary impulse of romantic and Victorian America, which sought to extend the blessings of Christianity and liberty to all nations and races. Moreover, Cooper's vision of a historical conflict resolvable only by a war of extermination departs radically from the reconciliationist conventions of the historical romance genre established by Sir Walter Scott and his English imitators. If the myth of the "English nation" was proposed in terms of consensus, that of the American nation was proposed in terms of division and exclusion. Yet Cooper's vision is consistent with the tradition of discourse established by Jefferson and Crèvecoeur and Filson. The difference is that where these writers settled for optimistic readings of the signs on the Dark and Bloody Ground, compartmentalized their treatments of Indian wars and republican politics, or offered histories that were inconclusive about final outcomes, Cooper told a complete tale and did not attempt to palliate the presence of darkness or the likelihood of tragedy.[9]

Cooper makes two contributions to the mythologization of American history: he puts the Indian and the matter of racial character at the center of his consideration of moral questions, and he represents the historical process as essentially a violent one. The two conceptions are logically related in Cooper. The racial character of the Indian shows what man is like in his natural, precivilized state; and while some of his propensities are shared with whites (especially primitive or unsocialized whites), his "gifts" are also peculiarly and permanently his own. It is because racial gifts are unique that different peoples respond differently to the same natural environments, the same ethical questions. And given this difference, if two races come together in the same environment, competition between them is inevitable, accommodation unlikely, and the elimination of one or the other logically necessary for there to be social peace. But the case of the Indian is only the most extreme and dramatic expression of this "truth." It is equally applicable to oppositions within society between contending groups whose divisions appear basic and profound: white masters and black slaves, all masters and all servants, the wealthy and the poor, the propertied establishment and the demagogic under-men greedy for wealth.

Indeed, even sexual relations are potentially explicable by the metaphor. For Cooper and his contemporaries race and sex were twinned metaphors of distinctions rooted indubitably in human nature. The impossibility of a black or an Indian becoming fully "white" in character was likened to that of a woman becoming completely and perfectly virile; and the distinction was extended to underscore the differences in mind that divided the savage and dependent classes from their racial and social superiors. In *Last of the Mohicans* this metaphor is literalized in the creation of a series of racially and/or sexually "mixed" characters, whose blended traits test and prove the validity of racialist doctrine. The key figure is Cora, who is of mixed black and Scottish ancestry, and whose personality is a mixture of feminine sensibility and masculine realism and courage. But an analogous set of issues is represented in the characters of Natty Bumppo (Hawkeye, the Leatherstocking) and Magua—the white man raised among Indians, and the Indian who has attempted to affiliate with the whites. The outcome for each of these mixed characters is fatal or tragic.[10]

What is at stake in this symbolism is an essential feature of democratic theory: the belief that all humans are equally capable of exercising moral freedom and are therefore justified in asserting their right of self-government as citizens of the republic. The breadth or narrowness of the scope of republican citizenship depends upon how one interprets and applies Cooper's Indian-war myth—where one draws the line between redskins and palefaces. As an artist, Cooper devoted himself to the intensive exploration of that myth, and *Last of the Mohicans* sets out its tragic logic more completely than anything else he wrote.

The opening pages of the novel elaborately frame the setting in which the drama will unfold. It is 1757, the era of the French and Indian War, we are in the American wilderness near the shores of the Horican or "Holy Lake," called prosaically Lake George by the English. The French are reported advancing with an army "as numerous as the leaves"—a figure that links them to the brooding, threatening, and yet also "Holy" wilderness. The British under General Webb are represented as fearing this advance, evidence of the "imbecility" of British leadership, which has already produced a series of defeats—which will, as any American reader knows, lead in the end to the Revolution. The two daughters of Colonel Munro, Alice and Cora, together with Major Duncan Heyward of the Royal Americans (like Washington, a "Virginian boy"), alone among Webb's garrison have the courage or foolhardiness to go forward in the face of Montcalm's advance, moved by the daughters' desire to reach their father, who commands Fort William Henry on the Holy Lake. They are joined by the psalm singer David Gamut, whose naive faith in his religion and physical incompetence make him a parodic exaggeration of the Christian and sentimental values which the women embody. His presence suggests Cooper's ambivalence about the very values his heroes will be obliged to defend.

Thus, as we cross the border between civilization and wilderness the "normal" order of sexual and social values begins to be inverted—the faint-hearted British soldiers hang back, the women and the minister whom they ought to protect go forward, led by one of the despised Americans. They take with them as guide an Indian named Magua, a savage whose beautiful form and athletic carriage hide a villain's heart. As they prepare to depart, Cora Munro, helplessly fascinated by the movement of Magua's naked limbs, lets fall her veil and we have a glimpse of her:

> . . . in the surprise her veil also was allowed to open its folds, and betrayed an indescribable look of pity, admiration, and horror,

as her dark eye followed the easy motions of the savage. The tresses of this lady were shining and black, like the plumage of the raven. Her complexion was not brown, but it rather appeared charged with the color of the rich blood, that seemed ready to burst its bounds. And yet there was neither coarseness nor want of shadowing in a countenance that was exquisitely regular and dignified, and surpassingly beautiful.[11]

The curiously negative suggestions about Cora's coloring ("not brown") prepare us for the revelation that she inherits through her West Indian Creole mother a fraction of Negro "blood." This racial "taint" is imagistically linked to her superabundant vitality and sexuality, her voluptuousness and her susceptibility to sensuous appeals.[12] She is spontaneously fascinated by Magua and later by Uncas, the son of Chingachgook, and the novel is enlivened by the persistent erotic tension generated between these three: the darkened beauty, a potential rapist, and a potential lover. Her affections are checked by her reason and conscience, and we racialize these two elements of her character, linking her sensuality with her blackness and her reserve with her whiteness. This suggestive association is reinforced by the presence of Alice, whose mother was white and "without a cross" of any other blood—Alice, who is more child than woman, who gazes at Heyward with "infantile dependency," who is lacking in both the passion and the vitality of Cora. Further, it is Cora—never Alice—who excites lust or loving desire in the hearts of Magua and Uncas, as if darkness in the blood called to its fellow.

That the sentiment of love is a litmus test of racial character is "proven" when Heyward approaches Colonel Munro to seek his daughter's hand. Munro assumes Heyward is asking for Cora, and when Heyward denies this, Munro accuses him of a slaveholder's prejudice against Cora for the faint strain of Negro blood. Heyward denies any knowledge of this fact, and denies as well any prejudice against Cora now that he knows; but the fact is that once he had seen Alice, the question of Cora simply never arose for him. Spontaneously, naturally, the whiteness of Alice speaks to the whiteness of Heyward; no call comes to him from Cora. Cooper is here invoking, in rather a subtle way (for Cooper), the nineteenth-century concept of "natural repugnance" between the races, especially marked (it was asserted) on the part of whites toward nonwhites. The doctrine also held that (as Jefferson said) it was "natural" among nonwhites to depart from "natural repugnance," and to prefer the supposedly superior charms of whites—a "natural" tendency of the lower folk to behave "unnaturally." Thus Cora apparently is more strongly drawn to Heyward than he to her; and thus Magua and Uncas are drawn to Cora.[13]

The romantic complications of the plot serve to establish as a central premise the association of sexual and racial identity, and the linkage of sexual and racial qualities to moral character and psychological structure. The linkage uses sexual analogy to establish the immutability of racial character—nonwhite can become white only to the degree that women can become men. So defined, sexual and racial forces appear in the novel as keys to understanding the larger tendencies that work below and shape the surface of the historical events—specifically the siege and massacre of Fort William Henry, and generally the historical triumph of civilization over savagery.

The true characters of the different races and sexes are not clear at the outset. We do not perceive what the difference between Indian and white cultures and characters is unless we see what happens to those who try to cross the border between them. Magua is such a character—a warrior and chief who is drawn to the whites because of his admiration for their apparent superiority in weaponry and wealth. But Magua, as an Indian, cannot abide British discipline; and when Munro has him whipped for drunkenness, his Indian pride is fatally wounded and he becomes the most cruel and implacable of enemies. There are elements of cultural relativism in Cooper's depiction of this conflict—Magua and Munro simply do not understand each other's ways, and the result is tragedy. However, for Cooper the sources of cultural difference are at bottom a matter of blood. Indians are not only unused to discipline and European ideas of manners and restraint, they are inherently incapable of achieving them. Indeed, the best Indians do not even wish to achieve them: just as the white Heyward is not attracted to the gorgeous but un-white Cora, so Chingachgook and his son Uncas do not share Magua's weak predilection for all things white. However, even these Indians—of the pure and unmixed race of the Mohicans, as Cooper tells us—are tempted by friendship and love to gaze (at least) across the border. From these impulses the tension of the novel arises, and is tragically resolved.

The figure who tests these boundaries most significantly is Leather-stocking. He is a white man raised among Indians, but he continually identifies himself as "a man without a cross." The sobriquet is double in meaning, suggesting his non-Christian nurture (and perhaps his Adamic innocence) but referring directly to the purity of his blood line, the fact that he is a white man with no "cross" of Indian blood. In all matters of skill and outward culture, he has adapted to Indian ways, and this allows him to be the most effective of the white warriors; but inside, in all matters of conscience and affection, he is pure white and highly conscious of that fact. Indeed, he represents the irreducible minimum of white racial character —the white man without the extra support of a civilization. Thus it is he who not only scouts the trails, but also scouts the hidden borders between the races and so defines them. He asserts at every opportunity the doctrine that the "pure" and "unmixed" race is best—whether white *or* Indian; and he has scant sympathy with excessively charitable views of Indian character as voiced by Heyward, Munro, or the two girls. Even to Chingachgook he says, "You are a just man, for an Indian."

Character is revealed by its testing in action, and Cooper's way of doing this can be suggested by a brief look at the episode of the combat at Glens Falls (chapters 6–10). Heyward, Alice, Cora, and the psalmist David Gamut now joined by Leatherstocking, Chingachgook, and Uncas, are besieged on a cave-riddled island in the cataract by Magua's Hurons. Cooper uses the natural setting to establish a thematic grounding for the moral drama that follows. The refuge is set amid waters that are at once natural and unnatural. As Natty tells Cora, the river fabricates images and illusions, it leaps about and changes direction "as if, having broke loose from order, it would try its hand at everything." This quality in rivers, as in men, does not appeal to the purist in Leatherstocking.

With their position hopeless, the besieged confront a moral choice: shall they all perish defending the helpless women and the psalmist, or shall some of them try to escape—either to save themselves or to bring rescue when advantage offers? There occurs a moral test which defines clearly the parameters of racial and sexual character. The women and the clergyman do not have to make a choice: their physical weakness is their fate, they must stay and abide the verdict of the action. Chingachgook is willing and eager to go, since it is perfectly sound within the Indian value system (as Cooper defines it) for a valuable warrior to save himself by abandoning the under-valued females. Cooper's Indians are primitive pragmatists, living according to the "natural law" of a wilderness in which fang and claw rule. But natural law is variable, as we have seen. What is natural for an Indian is not "according to the gifts" of a white man. Heyward cannot leave the women to their unmentionable fate, even though that is the practical course. It is, rather, simply inconsistent with his honor as an officer and a white man to go.

Uncas and Leatherstocking experience the moral conflict. As a white man by birth and gifts, Leatherstocking is reluctant to leave the women; but his wilderness pragmatism, learned among Indians, tells on him, out-weighing his white conscience. There is a suggestion that caste as well as race is operative: Natty is no officer and gentleman, and hence is not bound by any code of honor other than Indian pragmatism, which is the antithesis of Christian honor. Still, it is only the prospect that his escape will make possible a later rescue of the women that makes his choice palatable. Uncas ought to feel as his father does; but his attraction to Cora makes him hesitate, and by this we see that his integrity as an Indian has been in some measure breached by love. His behavior, unlike his blood, is no longer unmixed, but like Hawkeye's partakes of both white and Indian elements. While Cooper regards his sympathetic awakening as making him more "advanced" than the rest of his nation, it is also the cause of his downfall.

Among those who are left a further, somewhat more subtle division appears. Although he is a man, Gamut does not "play a man's part" in what follows; and although she is a woman, Cora here shows a capacity for action and courage that is in sharp contrast to Alice's feminine passivity, and suggests her possession of qualities that might almost be called masculine. She urges the Mohicans to leave her, adopting the unsentimental "realism" of Hawkeye. She is indeed a doubly mixed character—a white woman with Negro blood, a female with masculine traits of courage and coolness under stress.

The consequences of these moral choices are evaded in the first part of the novel: the captives are rescued, and make their way to Fort William Henry. There they are besieged, and the incapacity of Webb dooms them to surrender. Montcalm, overawed by Magua, supinely allows the Indians to massacre the refugees from the Fort, and in the melee Magua seizes Alice, Cora, and Gamut and flees into the wilderness.

With this catastrophe, the first volume of the novel ends, and the long pursuit and rescue of the captives begins with a new departure, a new evocation of the deeper and darker wilderness into which the heroes now plunge. This bifurcation of the novel is crucial, for with the massacre we leave the terrain of "history" and enter a world organized by myth. It ceases to matter that the year is 1757, that a certain battle has just been fought. The rescue of the captives, as Cooper well knew, was a motif common to all writing about the frontier from the seventeenth century onward; and the rescue of the daughters of Munro in 1757 is not importantly different in detail or meaning from its probable source—the rescue of Daniel Boone's daughter in 1776, as related by John Filson and others. The narrative finds its cognate structures not in historical accounts, but in the mythic archetype of the captivity narrative, and in a mythological rendering of Indian history based on early anthropological researches. Stepping entirely beyond the border of civilization, we step outside the framework of white history, and into a new framework: the mythologized history of the Indians themselves, played against the white myth of the Indian captivity.[14]

The "historical" framework of Part II is that of "Indian history," as refracted through a pseudo-myth fabricated by Cooper, with borrowings from the writings of Joseph Heckewelder on the Delawares. The pseudo-myth's structure is suggested from the beginning of the novel, when Chingachgook reminds Natty that his people are the "grandfathers" of the Indians, and that he is of the "unmixed" race of chiefs. But the idea is a minor note in the background so long as we are within the frame of white history, worrying about the French and Indian War. Now it comes into the foreground, and is fully revealed when Uncas declares himself to Tamenund, the ancient chief of the Delawares who have captured our heroes. The old chief's role parallels that of Montcalm, and, like him, Tamenund is based upon a historical figure. An Indian of that name was both prophet and chief, and a role as lawgiver was ascribed to him by whites, who took his name (or a variant) for the Tammany Democratic Club of New York politics. Tamenund reveals that Chingachgook and Uncas are the last heirs of the Mohicans, an ancient race of Indians who once dwelt by the "Salt Lake" or ocean. Through the name of Uncas—borne by all members of the family till they gain another by special deeds—Cooper links his Mohicans with the ancient Uncas who befriended the English, and fought with them in the Pequot and King Philip's wars. Their warlike prowess is, by this evidence, linked with a moral superiority that enabled them to appreciate and stay faithful to the English. But war, white men's diseases, and treachery have diminished the Mohicans, until only Uncas and Chingachgook remain—living, like Natty Bumppo, as adopted Delawares.

According to Cooper, the Delawares themselves acknowledge the royalty of the Mohicans; and the tribe had been a worthy vessel for the blood of the Mohicans until the Delawares fell into a kind of degeneracy, and submitted to the "Mingoes" (Iroquois), earning the shameful epithet of "women." It was this episode of subjection in Heckewelder's *History, Manners and Customs of the Indian Nations* that seems to have been the germ of Cooper's conception of the Delaware, and of the myth-history he borrows and invents for his tribe.[15]

Cooper made serious and detailed use of Heckewelder's observations of

Indian customs, manners, and linguistic formulae. But a comparison of *The Last of the Mohicans* with its nominal source reveals that Cooper substantially altered and reinvented Heckewelder's account of Indian history. In Heckewelder it is the Delawares, not the Mohicans, who are the original and "unmixed" race; the Mohicans are described as a late addition to the tribe resulting specifically from intermarriages, and they are represented as possessing (if anything) less courage and grandeur than the Delawares proper. Although sadly diminished, neither Delawares nor Mohicans are on the verge of extinction in Heckewelder's account (written in 1818)—and in fact both tribes survive today. Heckewelder does mention an older, technologically more advanced and physiologically superior tribe, who were the first occupants of the land—the Allegewi (as he calls him), whom we would identify as Mound Builders. But the Delawares were the enemies of these people, not their "grandchildren," and in alliance with the Iroquois they destroyed the Allegewi.

It is clear, then, that Cooper's Indian history is a deliberate and rather elaborate fabrication of "myth" for fictional purposes. Its effect is to unite the fragmentary history of the Indians into a single myth of origin, rise to grandeur, intermarriage, decline and fall—echoing (or, as Cooper would like to suggest prefiguring) the cycle of civilizational rise and fall which was a major concept of contemporary historiography. Cooper's Indian myth is a metaphorical rendering of the pattern of our own civilization, reinforcing the suggestion that in the Indian we see the primitive germ of our own character and fate. In their character as racial "grandfathers" Cooper's Mohicans resemble the various master races cited by historians as the linguistic, cultural, and genetic forebears of the ruling classes or dominant nations of Europe. Like Cooper's Mohicans, these grandfather races—the Aryans, Teutons, the Celts, and so on—were often seen as morally and genetically purer than their technologically more advanced descendants; and like the Mohicans, they were sometimes seen as having been diminished in number or quality by intermarriage or the vicissitudes of war and disease. The idea that their racial career might, like the Mohicans', end in extinction was part of the cyclical theory many racialist historians accepted; and as the nineteenth century went forward, this prophecy of racial mongrelization and extinction became the dominant theme of racialist historiography.

Cooper's projective fantasy of race history requires the representation of the full tragic cycle, and hence the doctrine of extinction is emphasized by him to a degree perhaps greater than that of most prior and contemporary historians. But when Tamenund greets Uncas as a kind of Indian Messiah, we are unmistakably asked to see his role as specifically restorative of the virtues of the Indian "blood" or race; he is not merely to be a new leader and lawgiver, but a genetic renewer, founder and perpetuator of a dynasty that will reverse the course of race-history, drive away the white men and restore the ancient dominion of the red man. The situation is comparable to that in a modern fantasy novel, Tolkien's *Lord of the Rings*, when an heir of the ancient line of the Kings of the Race of Numenor returns to cleanse and restore a darkened world.[16]

This Aryanization of the Mohicans serves to heighten our sense of conflict in the novel. We have left the French and Indian War behind, and at an unfavorable juncture. Now we learn that beneath the surface of that historical combat is a more elemental struggle between savagery and civilization. What is the weak Montcalm against the powerful and subtle Magua? And what would he be as enemy compared to the kingly Uncas? The threat is only implicit, and of course purely novelistic: we know that the English will defeat the French, and that no Indian Messiah will arise to unite the tribes—although our knowledge that Pontiac (1764) and Tecumseh (1809–14) will try lends a degree of credibility to the idea.

If the threat works at all, it is because Cooper has linked the appeal of Uncas-as-Messiah to the erotic appeal of the Uncas-Cora romance. They are the most beautiful and exotic characters in the novel. Uncas is not merely a noble savage, he may be an embryonic god-king, if the prophet Tamenund is to be believed. Cora is regal, brave, clever, evidently possesses all of the queenly virtues to make her a fit mate for a Messianic Uncas. She also combines in her blood the two other racial strains of the New World, black and white. Magua would debase or exterminate these; but in the marriage of Cora and Uncas there would be a fusion, an amalgamation of the warring American races. Thus the union would not be of the lowest types, but of individuals bearing the best of their respective blood lines.

The dynasty of Cora and Uncas becomes part of the Delaware fantasy of what may come from the return of the Last of the Mohicans. Together they may avert the vanishing of the "vanishing American," and make the time of racial history go backward. Both Cora and Uncas are also linked to the fascinating, ubiquitous, and dangerous presence of the "dark" elements in individual psychology. What appeals to Cora from Magua and Uncas, what appeals to Cooper's white reader from Cora—the forbidden, the beautiful-horrible "other"—also appeals to the reader from the pseudo-myth of the Mohican Messiah. It is the appeal of an alternative world and culture, erotically and socially freer than our own, antithetical to and an escape from the civilization that both sustains and discomforts us. Cooper is playing upon *our* "natural attraction to the unnatural," and does this so successfully that he was misread as an advocate of restoring the primitive rights and powers of the subject tribes.

There is a political dimension to the romance as well. The myth wilderness is the antithesis of the disciplined world of white society—a "natural" environment which stimulates and licenses the most "unnatural" human fantasies and actions. In the wilderness of the second half of *Last of the Mohicans* there is no guarantee that boundaries of race, caste, and chastity will be observed; yet this world is one in which things appear "in their harshest and truest colors." The normal order of white society—the order of the historical, French and Indian War world of the first part—is inverted. In Part I, characters are subordinated according to rank and caste, irrespective of "talent and virtue." Munro commands Heyward; Heyward commands Hawkeye; Hawkeye in some sense commands the Mohicans. In Part II the structure is completely reversed. Even before their true character as Indian royalty is revealed, pragmatic considerations make the Mohicans leaders of the hunt, subject only to their deference to the skill of Hawkeye. Heyward follows Hawkeye, and is followed by Munro—whose inexperience and physical and emotional weakness make him the least effective member of the party. As far as the captives are concerned, in the world of civilization Gamut (as man and clergyman) would presumably act as protector or preceptor to the girls, and Alice might enjoy a marginally higher status than Cora. But in the Indian village Cora is treated as a queen, Alice as a nullity, and the foolish Gamut as a holy madman. Inside this looking glass, only Hawkeye—the white man who knows Indians—remains in a comparable position, neither Indian nor white, neither high nor low.[17]

Much can be made of this inversion. Ideologically it appears to confirm the suggestion of Turner's Frontier Thesis that the wilderness was (or was seen as) a place in which virtue and talents could emerge to prominence over inherited wealth or position. Certainly Cooper saw in the wilderness a fantasy refuge from the class ordering and potential strife that marred civilization—a place in which talent could rise above birth *without* the necessity of revolution or even litigation. But one major effect of the inversion in the novel is to place Cora and Uncas at the heads of their respective worlds, especially after his true character is revealed. This reinforces the possibility of a climactic marriage between them, makes it seem appropriate to the reader, and creates a kind of expectation or wish for it.

We know, of course, that there is no Indian Messiah, that the "Last of the Mohicans" is an elegiac phrase. We may even say that Cooper never loves his Indians so much as when he is watching them disappear, and that for him as for General Sheridan—although with different emphasis—the only good Indians were dead. But it is part of the appeal of the romance to make us wish for something that we know is impossible. However, it is also important to Cooper, for ideological reasons, that he suppress whatever in him wishes for the consummation of Cora and Uncas.

Leatherstocking—with occasional assists from Heyward—has tried to teach us the fundamentals of a "realist's" view of the moral universe. They insist on the superiority of "unmixed" races, and they see that the conflict between races of unlike "gifts" is inevitable and inherently unlimited. Men must choose between triumph or extermination in such a war; and their choice is paralleled by the moral problem of the females: an either/or choice between surrendering or defending their virginity, or between losing or preserving the purity of the race. But in his response to Tamenund, as in his love for Cora, Uncas is trapped into tragic ambivalence by a fatal mixture of elements that ought to be kept pure. The friend of Hawkeye and the lover of Cora cannot lead Tamenund's Messianic revolution. Therefore it is not Uncas, but Magua who speaks for the irreconcilability of races, and proposes to lead Tamenund's war of extermination against the whites and their black slaves. But Magua is himself a mixed character, and though he echoes Hawkeye's theme of racial purity his own "mixed" character appears to make him excessively, unappealingly racist. He protests Indian superiority too much, compensating for his own sense of shame and inferiority. Hawkeye also is "mixed" in his nurture, but it is part of his "white gifts" to define racial separation in ways we are meant to find more moderate—and paradoxically more effective—in violently eliminating the Indian. Although we hate Magua for killing Cora and Uncas, hate his way of expressing the doctrine of racial purity, and rejoice when Hawkeye picks him off with his Longue Carabine and sends him plunging like Lucifer headfirst into a chasm, there is yet something in us, in Cooper at least, that consents to the effects if not to the deed of Magua.

Although tempted by the alternative history offered by the pseudo-myth of Uncas, we are not only left with the facts of our past, we *ought* (says Cooper) in good conscience and for the sake of the public peace accept those consequences as good. Even if violence must resolve what marriage cannot be permitted to reconcile—the confrontation of racial/sexual opposites—we must return to the doctrine of purity that Hawkeye continually reiterates. By the novel's end all of the mixed characters are either dead—like Cora, Uncas, and Magua—or settled in a path of sterility (like Gamut, Chingachgook, Hawkeye, and Colonel Munro). Only the pure whites, who have never even yearned for a dark lover, will marry and produce heirs. The future belongs to Heyward and Alice. All the color is dead. And although Cooper mourns that loss, he grapples with the need —equally strong as yearning—to disapprove of it.

In the concluding funeral scene, the Indians mourn Cora and Uncas together:

> They pronounced him noble, manly and generous; all that be-
> came a warrior, and all that a maid might love . . . He was of a
> race that had once been lords on the shores of the salt lake, and
> his wishes had led him back to a people who dwelt about the
> graves of his fathers [i.e., the whites]. Why should not such a
> predilection be encouraged? That she was of a blood purer and
> richer than the rest of her nation, any eye might have seen; that
> she was equal to dangers and daring of a life in the woods, her
> conduct had proved; and now, they added, the "wise one of the
> earth" had transplanted her to a place where she would find con-
> genial spirits and might be forever happy.

They fantasize a union in an Indian heaven beyond the grave—a union too perfect for earth, perhaps, but obviously appropriate in the eyes of the god who had created two such beings.

Munro and Heyward listen uncomprehendingly; but Munro catches the spirit of the prayer, and responds in language that almost seems prophetic of the Fourteenth Amendment: he declares that "the Being we all worship, under different names, will be mindful of their charity; and that the time shall not be distant when we may assemble around his throne without distinction of sex, or rank, or color."

But it is Natty Bumppo—the white man educated as an Indian—who rebukes this extreme statement of religious and social leveling by invoking his version of "natural law." " 'To tell them this,' he said, 'would be to tell them that the snows come not in winter . . .' " The Indians have in fact been saying something quite similar, with Natty listening and shaking his head disapprovingly. He simply refuses to translate their song correctly for Munro. Here, as elsewhere in this novel and others, Bumppo is the strictest and most absolute spokesman for racial and social con-servatism: "I am a man without a cross."[18]

This consciousness of his race is the trait that keeps Leatherstocking true to his own gifts throughout the vicissitudes of his adventures. He is therefore our guide, not only in woodcraft, but in the interpretation of the two "histories." He, who knows both sides of the race war, declares that war to be in its nature irreconcilable. He, who loves Indians, consents to their demise, although he mourns the passing of Uncas and shares the Indians' fate of disappearing without a trace of progeny in the American future. He will mourn throughout his life, sharing the grief of his beloved Chingachgook; yet in the end, they may well end up in segregated heavens, to be rewarded according to their "gifts."

Although Cooper confirms paternalistic and male-dominant values and confirms racial prejudices in his killing off of Cora and Uncas, he also reveals in them possibilities that transcend the conventional limitations assigned to their sex and race, and gives them a greater emotional appeal than his nominal hero and heroine. If he has preached all sorts of moral precepts to us via Leatherstocking, he has also shown us what his limitations are; and in the funeral scene so juxtaposes the elements as to throw Bumppo's prejudices into stark relief by showing them in a less appealing light than the courtesy of Munro. Like most of us, Cooper would like to have had his dilemmas resolved both ways: the races both reconciled and left separate, the wilderness both civilized and preserved in purity, the Indian forever vanishing yet never lost.

The mythology of race, and the linkage of this myth to a larger myth of progressive history, provided Cooper with a resolution to the contradiction between democratic or egalitarian ideals and the perceived need for subordinating one social class (or race) to another. *Last of the Mohicans* extends this mythology by reaching out to link sexuality to race and class, and through a deliberate act of mythogenesis it becomes his first comprehensive rendering of the whole pattern of his myth of American history.

In his next Leatherstocking novel, *The Prairie* (1827), Cooper elaborates the symbolic language of class, sex, and race, and extends it to a new historical phase and a new social problem. The novel was set on the Great Plains or "Great American Desert," in the years just following the Louisiana Purchase. It was to have been the last Leatherstocking novel, and the hero's death in the final chapter was to have signaled the end of the phase of expansion that had begun in the French and Indian War and reached its climax with the removal of the last Indians in the East—an event symbolized in *The Pioneers* by the death of Chingachgook. As in Crèvecoeur, it is nature that determines the social fate of the region. The Great Plains are represented as so arid and intractable to agricultural development that they constitute a permanent barrier to continuation of the frontier.

In this refuge outside the arena of continued historical action, Natty Bumppo has survived his exile from Templeton, and he shares the region with nomadic tribes of horse Indians. Onto this blank screen of desert trundles the caravan of a "squatter" clan, led by Ishmael Bush—a unique combination of the patriarch and the criminal, whose character curiously anticipates the negative stereotypes of John Brown in the late 1850s. Their very presence in this world suggests that they are people whose "gift" it is always to go too far. We learn that they have been driven from the settlements because of their refusal to adapt to the regime of law that must pertain in a postfrontier society—which is what America has become east of the prairie. Thus although they are physically removed beyond the pale of society, the Bush clan brings onto the testing ground of the mythic wilderness the elements within American society that were, in Cooper's view, as threatful to the Metropolis as Indians and Frenchmen had been to the Frontier.[19]

Here Cooper has succeeded in reducing a variety of social and literary types to a compact symbol system. The two types of savage personality complexly developed in Chingachgook/Uncas and Magua are formulaicly rendered in Hard Heart and Mahtoree. Captain Middleton embodies the military-aristocratic principle promulgated in Duncan Heyward and Oliver Effingham—in fact, he is the direct descendant of Heyward and Alice Munro. Leatherstocking himself is realized here as a mythic figure: his first appearance is out of the rays of the noonday sun, which makes him appear to have colossal stature; and at his death he gives up his ghost to the setting sun, surrounded by worshiping Indians. The principle of "female" civilization is represented by Inez, who is so much the incarnation of the qualities of weakness, refinement, and Christianity symbolized by the type that she verges on parody. The social hierarchy developed in *The Pioneers* but missing from *Last of the Mohicans* is represented here by two groups of plebeian frontiersmen. Paul Hover and his beloved Ellen represent the virtues of the yeoman farmer. Although coarser than Middleton, they recognize their proper social relations, and are deferential to Middleton, Inez, and Leatherstocking.

The Bush clan represents the capacity of the common man for evil, and this quality is symbolically expressed by their display of Indian-like qualities. This is shown first of all by their having captured and carried into captivity the aristocratic Inez—the action that is quintessentially "savage" in Cooper's framework. Their disrespect for the woman is related to the contempt they have for the rights of property established in law. Like Indians, they recognize only the rights, the needs, and the code of their clan. Their idea of justice involves the "savage" principle of revenge, and also recalls a kind of Old Testament eye-for-an-eye code. As squatters they would characteristically plant themselves on land legally owned by someone else; develop or simply occupy it, and file a preemption claim hoping to usurp title.[20] Like the pushing and unscrupulous class they represent, the Bushes have a kind of power and grandeur which is primitive and admirable: they achieve things (whether or not by violent means), they are pioneers, they try to make their lives a fable of "success." But like the Indians they are unsuited to civilization, and having broken trail for the progress represented by the yeomen they now find themselves in exile from society.

In their clannishness, their belief in the revenge code, their primitive style of life, and above all in their role as captors, the Bushes are very much like the Indians. In the past, one might have viewed them as precursors of civilization, as Crèvecoeur did. However, in *The Prairie*, the nation seems to have touched the outer limits of arable land. On the rim of the prairie, America confronts the end of the Frontier as it has been known. Neither the

Bushes nor anyone else will be able to plant on the "ocean" of undulating dry prairie that everywhere confronts the eye. Here Leatherstocking finds a last refuge, and the Indians—in diminished numbers and degenerate form—eke out a marginal existence. This is intractable wilderness, pure and simple, from which the actors will recoil once the adventure is done.

Cooper resolves the social/racial tensions of *The Prairie* by the usual means: captivities and rescues, leading ultimately to the union of Middleton and Inez, Paul Hover and Ellen. Leatherstocking dies, honored as a holy man among the remnant of the Indians and mythologized among his own people. The Bushes discover that Abiram, one of their own number, has betrayed the clan for his own self-interest; and the clan slays him, in accordance with its primitive code of justice. But clan justice merely reproduces among whites the vengeance law of savagery. Therefore Cooper must go further to resolve the ideological difficulty posed by the Bush clan. The race tension in *Last of the Mohicans* is resolved by the death of the mediating figures and the "vanishing" of the Indian. *The Prairie*'s class/race tensions are resolved by the vanishing of the Bush clan. The clan returns to the settlements, the older generation broken in spirit and the younger apparently edified by an adventure that has demonstrated the criminal folly of the squatter's code. The triumph of civilization is once again effected by the vanishing of the primitive enemy; although in the case of the squatters, they are only *partly* exterminated, and partly amalgamated. The great promise of the Frontier is that of absolute escape from one's competitors and rivals.[21]

THE COOPERIAN CODE:
RACE, SEX, AND CLASS

Using the terms codified by Cooper, succeeding generations of historical romance writers, historians, and dime novelists elaborated the Myth of the Frontier into a myth-ideological language system, rich in symbols and types that could be deployed as political or literary occasions seemed to require. In its essence, the Cooperian mythology centered on the representation of the history of American development as the confrontation between warring races, Indian and white. In the triumph of the white and the vanishing of the red, the progress of civilization is achieved, in both moral and material terms. From this characteristic historic action of race war, we can gather symbols of value which allow us to interpret conflicts within the white society which succeeds the Frontier. Racial imagery provides a key to interpreting the moral standing of individuals and classes: the Indian represents the primitive natural extreme of human possibilities, and the moral standing of characters can be measured by the extent to which they resemble or "transcend" the qualities of Indians.

Three basic "types" of Indians were evolved, expressing different aspects of American response to the idea of the wilderness and tribal life. Incarnating the evil and hostile force of nature—its resistance to the advance of civilization, its cruelty and cunning coupled with affinity for the environment—is the "great antagonist." Magua in *Last of the Mohicans* is a version of this type, corresponding to King Philip in colonial days, Tecumseh in the early nineteenth century, Pontiac in Robert Rogers's play *Ponteach* (1765) and the *Conspiracy of Pontiac* by Francis Parkman, or Sitting Bull. The antagonist is an Indian chauvinist who sees quite clearly that the advance of the whites means doom for the Indians' power and even their existence. He can be represented with some sympathy, as one who may have suffered at the hands of the whites (Magua, Tecumseh, Black Hawk); his chauvinism may be seen as a primitive patriotism (Rogers's Ponteach, King Philip in Washington Irving's essay "Philip of Pokanoket"), admirable as a quality even if its object is antipathetic.

Like Magua, the antagonist is dangerous because he combines aspects of both white and Indian cultures. He can use the forest like an Indian—being attuned to nature is his racial "gift." Yet he has learned from the whites the arts of political combination (he forms a confederacy or conspiracy); of political corruption (he has renegade whites working for him); and of advanced warfare (he has purchased rifles and other advanced gear for his plotted revolt). This dual affinity links him with the white renegade as a man between the cultures, a kind of half-breed. When this quality takes an extreme form, as with Magua, it is portrayed as his lust for a white woman. But even more sympathetic portraits of antagonist chiefs show them responding—sometimes with a peculiarly intense chivalry—to white women.

Against the antagonist stands the figure of the ally—the trusty Indian scout, loyal to the whites, for whom Chingachgook and Uncas are models. Through the ally, the white hero gains insights into the Indian and the wilderness that would otherwise be closed to him. The ally's brotherhood with the white hunter figure ensures his loyalty: it is a mysterious bond of love, represented as superior to that between man and woman. Through the figure of the ally, we learn that Nature herself—speaking through a good Indian—consents to and cooperates in the overthrow of her Indian children by the whites. The ally's services to the hero do not exempt him or his people from the fate of the vanishing American; but his presence allows the believer in the myth to love his Indian even as he kills him off.

In a curious shadow zone between these two male figures of ally and antagonist is the figure of the red bride: the Indian princess who sexually tempts either the hero or some subordinate white character. Pocahontas is of course the first such figure, and there are others: the Indian "mother" in Daniel Boone's adopted family; the Princess Magawisca in Catherine M. Sedgwick's romance *Hope Leslie*, Cora (in a certain way) in *Last of the Mohicans*. The red bride offers sensual pleasure, and with it the key to an intimate possession of the wilderness-as-wilderness. Her passionate nature awakes forbidden sexual impulses in a form that is at once attractive and repulsive: attractive in that she is a woman outside the taboo structure; repulsive in that the idea of going beyond the taboo brings guilt and certain renegadery. But the sexual issues raised by the red bride made her a troubling figure for nineteenth-century fiction writers; and so she is less frequently met with than the two male types, although when she appears it is with powerful emphasis.[22]

On the white side of the racial spectrum, the myth presents us with an array of figures, ranging from the lowest—the white renegade, given over to Indian-likenesses—to the highest, the military aristocrat. In between these types are the white hunters and yeoman farmers, who in their changing stereotypes register shifting ideas about the place of different classes and social types in American society.

The possession of moral and sentimental attributes of class superiority is attested in Cooper by the character's response to women, especially to white womanhood. Here the racial difference emerges quite clearly: the good Indians recognize the superior moral character of white women, and respond deferentially; whereas the bad Indians want only to kidnap and sexually possess such women, polluting them racially and morally in the name of sensual lust, ambition, or the desire for revenge. Unrepressed lust is therefore expressed as a desire to mate with a woman of superior race; this bespeaks a vile ambition to rise above one's natural place. Moreover, this is the quality that bad Indians share with the "dangerous classes" of whites. Cooper's symbolism thus literalizes Jefferson's metaphoric identification of social climbers as "half-breeds."

The white woman in a Cooper novel plays a role identical with that of the heroine of the Puritan captivity narrative, symbolizing the values of civilization imperiled by savagery. However, she differs in some important respects. First, she is not the protagonist of the tale, but a symbolic property; the male heroes who rescue her are the protagonists, and she is needed largely to evoke their noble qualities. Second, the heroine of the Puritan narratives was generally a mother or wife, often married to a minister or substantial citizen, but equally often simply the wife of a farmer. In Cooper, the captive heroines are typically the daughters of a secular aristocracy, and represent one half of an aristocratic romantic pair. Thus Cooper placed the values of the aristocratic class in the central role previously assigned to the frontier family. Where the "family" of the traditional captivity was an operative economic unit—a married pair plus children engaged in the business of survival and production—the romantic pair is unmarried, and the end of their life's adventure is simply the achievement of marriage. They are not economically engaged during the course of the adventure, and any productive activity they might engage in afterwards is certainly no part of Cooper's story. This absence is, of course, generally shared not only by Cooper's dime-novel imitators, but by writers of romantic fiction in general.

But Cooper's transformation of the captivity myth reveals a social argument that was implicit in the literary convention. The imperiled values symbolized by the traditional captive were very broadly defined as Christian and civilized. Social class referents in these figures were given the slightest emphasis, since the primary argument of the captivity tale was that values common to nearly all classes (in a predominantly bourgeois and agrarian society) had to be defended. By transferring reader identification from the generalized Christian captivity heroine to an aristocratic romantic pair, Cooper substitutes aristocratic (or elitist) values for the more "democratic" and universal values of Christianity. The captivity-myth context provides a kind of cover for this substitution, implying that this new class-specific version of the myth partakes of the sacred and universal character of the original.

On the white side of the racial spectrum, then, Cooper ranks his characters according to their response to racial, class and sexual clues. At the bottom of the moral ladder are those plebeian types—hunters or squatters—who act like Indians in their interaction with white women. The Sheriff, Richard, in *The Pioneers*, is a corrupt engrosser of land and power, who seeks to marry the superior woman, Judge Temple's daughter. The Bush clan in *The Prairie* have actually kidnapped a daughter of the Spanish aristocracy and carried her into Indian territory, acting the role of Indian captors. Their motivation, like that of Magua in *Mohicans*, is revenge. Hurry Harry and Long Tom, in *Deerslayer*, desired marriage to superior white women; and they fight and take scalps like Indians, recognizing none of the restraints appropriate to their racial "gifts." In the Littlepage series of novels, written later in his career, Cooper actually uses the word "Redskins" to describe this class.

The Cooperian status system thus accords quite well with Jeffersonian theory, which held that while one might find some "natural aristoi" among the common people, on the whole the existing aristoi would "breed true": equality in principle reproduces traditional inequalities in fact.

Above the low-level squatters and hunters is the type of the yeoman farmer, represented by several characters in *The Pioneers*, and most notably by Paul Hover, the bee-hunter, in *The Prairie*. These characters are distinctly plebeian, but in their moral character show all the appropriate responses to the racial and sexual tests. Their love objects are women of the appropriate class; and superior women (or men) evoke in them attitudes of deference. They therefore will have a secure place in the settlements, once the Frontier has passed; and will present no danger to the system of moral and social subordination by which society is ruled. They are the perfection of the Jeffersonian yeoman, the farmer of Crèvecoeur who was content with sufficiency and would not contend for wealth. It is worth pointing out that in the Frontier microcosm, the yeoman operates not as farmer, but as hunter. The bee-hunter will become a beekeeper, and the republic of the bees invokes a basic image from *Letters from an American Farmer* of settled industry and hierarchical order. But in the moment of crucial drama, the moment in which the course of history is symbolized, he is *not* a farmer, but an active, wandering, looking-for-new-country hunter.

Ruling the social microcosm of the Cooper novel is a character related to that of Weems's Washington: an American nobleman, typically a soldier-aristocrat. These characters—Oliver Edwards/Effingham in *The Pioneers*, Duncan Heyward in *Last of the Mohicans*, Captain Middleton in *The Prairie*—represent Cooper's attempt to reconcile the democratic imperative of "careers open to talents" with a system of social subordination to the landed gentry from which he himself sprang. Cooper's solution to the problem was to abstract certain traditional features of the aristocrat, detach them from the framework of an actual aristocracy of birth, and thus make the qualities seem available to men of middling circumstances and high natural endowment. The American aristocrat is characterized by innate chivalry: he has a heightened capacity for appreciating the beauties and virtues of the most highly refined female types; and he is therefore an appropriate mate for any of the ladies he rescues (even an aristocrat like Inez in *The Prairie*). Indeed, his manners and breeding are such that he cannot have been raised in a wigwam or frontier cabin, although Cooper often is vague about how many generations intervene between his hero and common, even poor ancestors. Finally, it is the hero's work or profession that distinguishes him: he is not a sentimental tanner or well-spoken blacksmith. For Cooper, the preferred profession is the traditional aristocratic profession of arms, and his aristocrats are gentlemen not by the mere inheritance of a title, but by the achievement of the title of officer and gentleman.[23]

The device is not merely a literary trick. Washington's myth involved a similar combination of aristocratic and military attributes with frontier heroism. The success of Andrew Jackson's personal and political myth follows very much in this military-aristocratic mold. His gentility was achieved (whatever his manners might have been), but its trappings were traditional: the military rank and reputation, earned against both Indians and Europeans, the manorial plantation with its slaves and tenants, the frequent duels and controversies in defense of his own honor and those of the women he admired. To be sure, as a political controversialist, Jackson had opponents who ridiculed each of these attributes; but in a sense, their satire on his manners, battles, and code of honor merely confirmed the importance of these things as values, however they might be misappropriated.[24]

Within the Leatherstocking series the importance of this aristocratic figure seems to be diminished by the dominating presence of Leatherstocking himself: even though the romantic aristocrat is the nominal protagonist who gets the girl and achieves social power at the end of the novel, it is the hunter—most often only a supporting character—who absorbs our interest. It is as if Cooper's novelistic instinct for the interesting character were at war with his social conscience.

Natty Bumppo most completely incarnates the "myth of concern" for Cooper. His character is built purely and entirely out of mythic concerns. Where other characters represent various defined social and racial positions, various solutions to the problem of social order, Natty Bumppo represents the essential problem of social and moral identity. As a white man raised among Indians, he tests the validity of both the racial definition of class and the environmentalist belief in cultural determinism. As a man with duties and affections on both sides of the racial line, his moral decisions implicitly query the basis of loyalty, of social solidarity itself.

In Natty Bumppo all of the good qualities of the Frontier hunter and yeoman are concentrated and all of the bad are left out. Although he has lived with Indians and eaten wild meat, he has, by virtue of his "gift" for racial purism, escaped the curse of Crèvecoeur's renegade hunters: Natty remains true to his race, and faithful in the respect he accords both to white women and—in most circumstances—to the military aristocrat as well. Although his senses of subordination and limitation are like those of the yeoman, he is not a plebeian drudge. As a hunter, adventurer, and warrior he shares the profession and some important attributes of the chivalric hero—an idea Cooper acknowledges in *Deerslayer*, when he invests him with some of the symbolism of Arthurian myth.

If the military aristocrat is the ideological resolution of the contradiction between Jacksonian democracy and social class order, Leatherstocking is the mythic resolution. Here is a white man raised by the Indians, who on all occasions speaks for the immutability and sanctity of racial and class divisions. It is as if Nature herself speaks in validation of the peculiar compromises that characterize American society; and Natty's skill in bringing about the catastrophe of the Indian race reads this notion into the myth-historical record—Nature rejects her own children in favor of the Nature-transcending whites.

Natty Bumppo is a commoner by birth who is lifted beyond the limitations of class by his apprenticeship to the Indians and the wilderness. But unlike the squatters, he never presumes on his special status, or on the peculiar freedom from restraint provided by the wilderness environment. He never attempts to translate his exemption from the class system into higher social standing in a future white community. Sex provides the characterizing metaphor for his social morality: he will not marry an Indian woman, and so compromise his racial integrity; he will not marry a white woman, and so compromise his freedom and assert a social position he does not innately possess. His antipathy for marriage is a metaphor for his antipathy for property and social power. He will never possess his own woman, and thus he symbolically renounces property itself. Hence he will never become a competitor with his social superiors; he will rescue the women of the elite from captivity, but will never romance them. Instead, he delivers them safe to the military aristocrat, and facilitates the resolution of social tensions.

Leatherstocking is a man frozen in stasis between the opposed worlds of savagery and civilization. That stasis is his protection from degeneration toward renegadery on the one hand, and social climbing on the other. He is unique in this attribute, for the Indians, no less than the whites, are obsessed with their right to own and use the land, and assert that right with rage and passion. Leatherstocking's role as mediator between Indian and white is possible because he wants nothing of either world; rather, he responds equally to the claims of each. When the kingly Chingachgook asserts his primitive right to the soil, Leatherstocking sympathizes; and when Chingachgook's bride is captured, Bumppo aids in the rescue. His relation to the Indian aristocracy is identical in many respects to his relation to the white: he is a subordinate knight, Galahad to someone else's Arthur—yet he has his own sanctity, his own value, and remains unique and apart even while he is being serviceable. And like Thoreau at Walden or Boone in *Kentucke*, he is a one-man precapitalist utopia, the wishful denial that society and its contradictions really matter.

The Natty Bumppo character compels our interest because he incarnates the problem, and brings together the contradictory ideological impulses inherent in the Myth of the Frontier. But we should not forget that the resolution of that problem does not lie in Natty's power. He and the constellation of values he represents are doomed to follow the Last of the Mohicans into exile and extinction. It is the military aristocrat and the good yeoman who will survive to beget heirs, and to play the roles of good squire and deferential farmer in the civilized order that follows the Frontier. Only the overwhelming threat of the racial enemy and the conditions peculiar to a wilderness environment compel the aristocrat to take his orders from the plebeian Leatherstocking; for only in such an environment are the specialized skills and peculiar virtues of the hunter morally on a par with those of the aristocrat. Once the special conditions of race war and wilderness have been eliminated, the leader-follower roles are more clearly defined, and the attributes of traditional aristocracy resume their customary status.

As an artist, Cooper preferred to project himself into the Frontier setting, in which social values and status were problematic and in the process of dynamic change. His works played a similar role for American readers, offering them a fictive Frontier that was more permanent than the real thing—a world in which the old issues, the old bases of solidarity, were preserved from change and the destructive contradictions of American ideology. But both the author and his readers were well aware of the impermanence of the Frontier. Cooper always treats the Frontier as belonging to a time and condition of life that have passed or are passing away. His novels are filled with nostalgia—now nobly sad, now bitterly angry—for a heroic age that is no more. The lessons of the Frontier may be applicable to present dilemmas, but the Frontier itself is not likely to remain for long a part of that present reality. The reason for this belief appears clearly in *The Prairie*, which represents the Great Plains region as a vast and intractable desert, in which even so hard a lot as the Bush clan will be unable to make a settlement. This view was held not only by Easterners like Cooper, but by Westerners committed to a general policy of expansion into new territories. Even as devout an expansionist as Thomas Hart Benton doubted whether an America that stretched across the plains to the Pacific could hold together politically.[25]

The Cooperian mythology suggested that such a state of affairs was full of danger for the republic. The moral economy of Cooper's fictive America depended on the maintenance of a balance as exquisite as that in a terrarium or a comedy of manners. On the fictive Frontier, the overwhelming pressure of Indian and wilderness enforce that balance by compelling whites of different classes to unite around common symbols of value. But the post-Frontier world lacks such compulsion, and Cooper represents post-Frontier society as one in which deference is destroyed by the greed and ambition of the lower orders.

The Pioneers gives a closer glimpse of what happens in post-Frontier society: men-on-the-make waste the land, undermine traditional authority and deference, and point society toward the kind of crisis represented by the French Revolution. In Cooper's later works, particularly his dystopian social fantasies (*The Monikins, The Crater*) and the Littlepage or anti-rent novels, this tendency is worked out at length and in detail. In these novels the "redskins" are not the Indians, but the demagogic politicians and anti-rent tenants who use the institutions of republicanism to overturn the authority of the Temples and Effinghams, and to expropriate their property. Cooper thus translates the Frontier Myth into a metaphoric code through which he can interpret the social warfare of a post-Frontier Metropolitan America.

PART THREE
Metropolis vs. Frontier

CHAPTER 6

The Backwash of a Closing Frontier: Industrialization and the Hiatus of Expansion, 1820–1845

The popularity of Cooper's works, and the resonance of his symbolism with the major tendencies in American thought and writing before the Civil War, make it tempting to suggest that Cooper was the inventor of his country's mythology—the fulfillment of the romantic expectations that poets would become the legislators of mankind, forgers of the conscience of their race. It is more accurate to see Cooper as the clarifier, codifier, and popularizer of a language of myth already at work in his society.

As we have seen, his fiction brought together most of the major concerns of post-revolutionary republican ideology, and dealt with them in the imagery of the Myth of the Frontier. His historical fables put at the center of concern the problem of maintaining social equilibrium in a society committed irrevocably to expansion. Moreover, they prophetically extended the Myth to engage in fiction an issue not yet confronted in reality: how to cope with the social consequences of an ultimate closure of the Frontier as a field for expansion. These concerns were developed by a cast of characters representing a broad range of classes, races, and ideological perspectives; and Cooper provided his people with a repertoire of narrative formulas that defined the probable and desirable patterns of historical action.

But neither the ideological problem nor the mythological language was Cooper's exclusive invention. His fictions were parts of a broader cultural response to the changes taking place in American society. Cooper's formulations seemed especially felicitous to his contemporaries because so many of them were already thinking in the terms which he was so adept at using—and which he had had the courage to present as "literature." The problems of the time seemed amenable to just the sort of explanation that the Myth of the Frontier offered. Cooper's novels fixed that explanation in a set of brilliant, appealing, and easily imitated literary structures. At bottom, it was the compatibility of the Cooperian myth code with reality that made the fictions of the Laird of Cooperstown (and his imitators) more than an ephemeral fashion in literary taste. The persistence of Cooper is in part explained by the persistence of the concerns, conditions, and beliefs that Cooper addressed.

Literary fiction and myth represent the dynamic processes of social change by freezing them in narrative formulae. But the processes themselves do not freeze. The Cooperian code had developed out of a dialectical interaction between changing material conditions and the extant structures of a myth-ideological language. Cooper had forwarded that dialectic by adapting the received language to new concerns; and that adapted language in turn became the tradition through which subsequent developments would be interpreted. As material conditions continued to change they exerted pressure on Cooper's successors to adapt and modify the code to preserve its explanatory power, its ability to satisfy our need for historical certainty.

But as the course of development continued, the agrarian Frontier symbolism Cooper had used to interpret the rise and growth of America became less and less adequate to the task of interpreting history. To understand how this process worked, and why it took the direction it did, we need to look first at the changes in American society during the period before the Mexican War, and then at the representation of those changes in literary fiction.

The doctrines of agrarian democracy, as developed by Jefferson and elaborated by Jackson, held that the social cement of the republic must be the self-interest of its citizens. In economic terms, this meant that each citizen must be possessed of sufficient property to guarantee the subsistence of himself and his family, or must at least have a credible prospect of attaining that level of economic independence through his labor. Such a distribution of wealth within the bounds of the existing society would inevitably be limited by the pressure of population growth, the control of existing resources by an already established class of proprietors, and the free competition of individuals for resources presented to them. The reservoir of Frontier land was to provide a guarantee that each citizen would always have a reasonable chance to acquire land, no matter what the distribution of wealth and power in the Metropolis might be. But if social peace in the Metropolis depended on the promise inherent in the Frontier reservoir, then even the threat of a closing of the Frontier must begin to undermine the basis of social peace. In such circumstances the individual's chances for achieving subsistence must be diminished, and the existing classes of established proprietors and successful competitors must become social enemies and the objects of political attacks that would undermine the ideology of property itself. The central themes of Jacksonian politics were therefore sounded in the twin policies of Indian Removal and the "war" against the "monster" Bank of the United States: one cleared the citizen's access to Frontier wealth, the other his access to Metropolitan opportunities.

The long hiatus in American expansion on the verge of the Great American Desert presented the United States with just such a prospect. The forbidding character of those few regions of the Far West that had been explored, the vast distances involved, and the primitive transportation available for the journey suggested that the Great Plains and nearer

Rockies were a permanent barrier to further agrarian expansion. The belief that by 1830 America had reached a "last frontier" was of course premature. When Cooper finished *The Prairie* in 1827, the greatest period of American expansion was still to come; it had barely begun when the last of the Leatherstocking Tales appeared in 1841. But Cooper and his contemporaries had no such hindsight, and from their temporal standpoint it appeared that America might well have reached the natural limits of expansion. Between 1776 and 1784 the United States had defeated England and doubled or tripled its territory, reaching past the Appalachians to the Mississippi. Between 1803 and 1819 this territory was redoubled by the purchases of Louisiana, West Florida, and Florida. But the 1820–45 period was one in which the continued pressure for further expansion was checked by a mixture of natural obstacles (the inadequacy of existing population, capital, and technological resources); and the political disorganization of the Metropolis that arose from sectional and interest-group division on the tariff and slavery issues.

Economic developments in that period were in fact establishing the basis for another great wave of expansion that would last from 1848 to 1890; to continue to exploit the opportunities inherent in an expanding frontier, the United States had to develop at least the rudiments of an industrial system. Government expeditions already in the field were establishing the knowledge base that would facilitate the cross-continental leap. Geographical expansion on such a scale required resources of capital, population, transportation, and production facilities that no agrarian society could muster. The acquisition of Oregon, California, and Texas would require the mobilization of resources for a war with Mexico; the development of that territory would require the building of a vast railroad network (and the industrial plant to sustain it), maintenance of a sizable regular army, new agricultural technology, and stepped-up immigration; all of these things required a reorganization of American labor, of the work life itself, and fundamental changes in social relationships and ideologies.

On the face of it, this would produce a society antithetical to that envisioned in agrarian ideology—a society centering on great urban centers, in which there would be sharply divided classes of capitalists and workers. But as we have seen, the ideology of agrarianism was not as inimical to the values of industrial entrepreneurship as the bucolic imagery of its myth would seem to suggest. The Jeffersonian version of agrarianism treated the farmer as a "contented" entrepreneur in all practical contexts. Jefferson may have fantasized an agrarian social order in which these entrepreneurial farmers would retain the yeoman's habits of deference, but his own presidency made such an order impossible and produced a contradictory set of social imperatives. Social mobility required the entrance of Jefferson's modest farmer into the marketplace and his engagement with cash values; and any such entrance gave him the character, and eventually the function, of a speculator engaged in increasing his capital by all means, including political action. When we consider the indivdual's desire to pass the benefits of an improved standard of living along to his children, the need for a more enterprising yeoman is magnified. The Jeffersonian farmer (in theory) might be content to acquire a small subsistence farm in the Ohio backwoods for himself and his children; the Jacksonian farmer in actual fact would require that farm plus some additional property for surplus production and/or the taking of a speculative profit. The yeoman had emerged as "an expectant capitalist, a hardworking, ambitious person for whom enterprise was a kind of religion, [who] everywhere . . . found conditions that encouraged him to extend himself."[1]

The fantasy of the yeoman as politically passive or deferential was undone by the very ambitions the promise of land was meant to pacify. The basis of the American farmer's hunger for land was, ultimately, as much political as economic. So long as there was a property qualification for voting, the connection was obvious. But even after universal white manhood suffrage was established, the connection between wealth and political power was clear. In the first place, politics was dominated by men of established wealth, the landed aristocracy of the southern and middle states, the commercial aristocracy of New York and New England. In the second, access to wealth and land was determined by federal policies on such matters as sale of public lands in the West, protection of settlers from Indians, assertion of settlers' rights as against those of Indians and/or large land corporations, and sponsorship of improvements in land and water transportation. Thus to be fully "equal" in political terms, the republican citizen had to achieve possession of land—the traditional hallmark of the aristocrat. And to achieve this, he had to get some leverage over policies affecting access to the sources of wealth, initially by agitating for extension of suffrage, and finally by exercising that right so as to elect a member of the dominant class who had expressed himself as favorable to the interests of the common, ambitious man: Jefferson in 1800, Jackson in 1824 and 1828. This political pressure made inevitable a tacit but nonetheless crucial economic decision, which shaped Jacksonian frontier land policy thereafter: that "widespread access to wealth was [to be] preferred over the public capitalization of a great economic asset."[2]

The statement is as much a moral one as it is economic. In Jackson's hands, it became the basis of an attack on the older corporate groups whose legal privileges clogged the routes of access, like the mercantilist regime of the British in the 1770s, or like the holders of toll-way franchises who taxed the marketing farmer. Initially, these policies threw the western and indeed the national economy into a flux of upward and downward mobility. Ultimately, however, they merely facilitated the rise of new privileged groups—the "pet banks," the new limited-liability corporations, and the entrepreneurs of politically franchised transportation (steamboats and railroads). These new groups in turn laid claim to the Jacksonian heritage: as corporate "citizens" they were entitled to both the legal rights and the mythic sanctions accorded any "settler" in new territory. This was to become crucial to the later development of western railroads and the Great Plains phase of frontier expansion.[3]

The hiatus in territorial acquisition from 1819 to 1845 was offset by the expansion of wealth generated by more intensive exploitation of existing resources. Therefore this period saw the establishment of the ideological, social, financial, and technical basis of an industrial economy in the United States. Although the agrarian imagery of a republic of smallholder citizens persisted, it was energized—and implicitly undone—by the ethic of high productivity and profitability that went with belief in democracy-through-mobility. The explosive growth of population, through immigration and an increasing birthrate, provided both a reservoir of labor available for industrial projects and a potential market for increased industrial and agricultural productivity. The development of agricultural regions already acquired effectively expanded the amount of land being brought into cultivation, even though there were no spectacular additions of land beyond the existing borders. The development in the 1820s of manufacturing industries—of large-scale textile manufacturing in New England and of nascent heavy industry in the Pennsylvania–New Jersey–Delaware region—is merely one sign of this process. The industries related to transportation—railroading, shipbuilding, road and canal building—also expanded and stimulated demand for all sorts of manufacturing and maintenance functions, in small towns as well as cities. The growth of transportation and the carrying trade was related to the development of agriculture, and this gave a new gloss to the old symbols of agrarianism. But this was a new kind of agricultural enterprise, more closely and profitably tied to expanding markets than that of the Kentucky pioneers of Boone's day. It was therefore more intensive in its exploitation of land and labor, and it attracted technological developments designed to increase yields and make the farming of larger units feasible. Similarly, in the South the rising demand for cotton fostered an agricultural system that was quasi-industrial in its demand for resources of land, labor, and capital.[4]

These changes altered the economic character and the political stakes of continued westward expansion. The industrialization of the economy in northern factories and southern plantations created a political division in the Metropolis on the issues of slavery protection and extension and the protective tariff. Since these interests were vital to the prosperity of businessmen in the two sections, and hence to politicians, the matter of territorial expansion in the West was increasingly held hostage to resolution of these Metropolitan issues. Northeasterners feared the drain of their labor supply to the new lands; Southerners were concerned that any increase in the number of states would threaten the existing balance of sectional and party power. But the continued growth of the West in population and wealth, and the continued increase in the Westerners' demand for land, made a permanent impasse on the matter of expansion ultimately impossible.

Western growth itself was not simply a matter of farmers' pulling up stakes and lighting out for the territories. Even in recently settled districts, the industrial and urbanizing character of the developing economy induced a pace of urbanization more rapid than that experienced on the older frontiers of the old North- and Southwest between 1795 and 1820. Six years after its seizure, California was the most thoroughly urbanized state west of the Appalachians. There were factors in the California environment that made it to some degree exceptional, notably the presence of gold and the existence of a prior Mexican social base. But these were not entirely unique: parts of Louisiana had enjoyed both prior settlement and access to a lucrative trade with the interior, but had not experienced a similar pattern or pace of development. Rather, the difference derives from the fact that

California was seized during a time when the economic development of the Metropolis had begun to industrialize and accelerate, so that the gold rush opportunity was presented not to a nation of isolated yeomen, but to a society experiencing "the explosion of artisan production and artisan culture into a continental market."[5]

Industrialization and the growth of cities constituted an internal equivalent to the Frontier of expansion at the borders. In the Northeast an industrial base was built by exploiting the resource Frontier of untapped waterpower and local mineral or agricultural resources for raw materials. Technological ingenuity thus found a profitable outlet in industry. Likewise, there was a sufficient pool of labor—initially female, later immigrant—to provide a cheap-labor Frontier which could be profitably exploited. Political spokesmen, particularly those from New England, cited this industrial growth as a tendency which "paralleled and rivalled . . . the frontier" as evidence of American economic and social dynamism. The spread of industrial or artisan production across the continent fostered similar developments in the new cities of the West, where artisans from the East did indeed find the sort of special opportunity that lent credibility to the "safety valve" theory. Indeed, in these new cities, with unformed social hierarchies and cash-poor local economies, artisans who were masters of particular manufacturing processes could and did become industrial entrepreneurs, emerging as part of the business elite in the new territories.

Thus the republican political economy of careers (and resources) "open to talents" was not restricted to the agrarian-yeoman sphere, but included manufacturing as well, and even a certain kind of banking or small-scale moneylending. It followed that the "Jacksonian" ideology, equating democracy with the chance to rise and accumulate property, was not the exclusive program of Jackson and his party. Rather, it was part of a broad consensus, shared by Whigs and Democrats (and later by Republicans and Free Soilers)—a consensus in which there might be different visions of the ultimate economic felicity (the planter on his acres, the farmer in his field, the ironworker in his mill, the merchant or banker at his desk), but in which the form and direction for pursuing happiness were parallel.

And out of this consensus the leading spirit of the northern Whigs, Daniel Webster—as staunch an anti-Jacksonian as there was—could interpret the shape of Americans' political-economic aspirations in terms of these same imperatives of equality of opportunity and of mobility culminating in entrepreneurship. In the debates over the Compromise of 1850, when that consensus was challenged by advocates of a new order based upon slavery, Webster countered with a concise summation of the given principles of that consensus:

> [Who] are the laboring people of the North? They are the North. They are the people who cultivate their own farms with their own hands—freeholders, educated men, independent men. Let me say, sir, that five sixths of the whole property of the North, is in the hands of the laborers of the North; they cultivate their farms, they educate their children, they provide the means of independence;

if they are not freeholders, they earn wages; these wages accumulate, are turned into capital, into new freeholds; and small capitalists are created.[6]

But the new industrial Frontier was subject to the same contradictions that affected the agrarian Frontier. Given the existence of free land, unused water power, and a new manufacturing process, and given also the relative freedom of access to those resources of the "middling sort" as well as the wealthy, there still remained the fact that the seizure and exploitation of such resources demanded capital, usually much more than that required for the taking up of a yeoman's freehold. Moreover, the nature of the new economy determined that once the opportunity was successfully seized—the plantation or factory brought into production—the pretense of classlessness and equality became untenable. Successful entrepreneurs entered a class whose resources of capital and command of labor separated them from the artisan class from which they derived. And as the entrepreneur transformed himself from artisan to employer to full-blown capitalist, the artisans developed into a class characterized by its relative weakness in property endowment and its tendency to evolve into a propertyless proletariat.[7]

These developments paralleled those already apparent in the system of agrarian expansion. The principle of equal access to new territories was championed by Jackson and his party as a principle of democratic egalitarianism. Yet the goal of Jacksonian man was not simply the possession of a subsistence farm, but some grander level of success—represented in Jackson's case by the status of planter-aristocrat, or in the case of the Coopers by the status of squire to a county of tenants and yeomen. Industrial exploitation promised to produce more wealth, and to expand the possibilities for access to high status. Therefore, in the early period of industrialization, artisans or "mechanics" tended to think of themselves as small capitalists—owning their own tools as well as their skills and labor power—and to identify with their employers on issues like tariff protection.

But there were limits on the wealth-generating capacity of industry, just as there were limits on the supply of land—although these were limits imposed by economic and political imbalances rather than geography. Economic historians have disagreed about the precise effects of industrialization on the distribution of wealth in the United States between the Age of Jackson and the Gilded Age, but clearly inequalities increased during this period, reflecting the tendency of wealth to accumulate in a distinct capitalist class, and the corresponding tendency of the laboring classes to become relatively impoverished.[8]

But the assessment of the distribution of capital in the society is not by itself an adequate measure of the impact of industrialization on the political economy of the United States, and on the ideology that sustained that political economy. The character of industrial production required fundamental changes in the social relations between capital and labor. In the agrarian social-economic system envisioned by Cooper and Jefferson it does not matter who is tenant on a given parcel, so long as the rent is paid. But factory work requires a large, disciplined, and relatively stable supply of cheap labor; and for labor to be cheap and amenable to discipline, it would have to be dependent on capital, propertyless itself and tied to the wage system for sustenance. Not surprisingly, then, the first industrial proletariat in the Northeast consisted of women and children, classes traditionally assigned dependent status; and in the South, an analogous productive function was fulfilled by a permanent class of chattel slaves.[9]

In this system, the credible promise that present labor would make possible future "success" constituted an ideological safety valve for class discontent. The agrarian Frontier was one metaphor for this promise, and it had some appeal to the working classes. The working-class National Reform movement led by labor activist and journalist George Henry Evans saw a Homestead Act opening western lands to settlement by small holders as an essential tool of organized labor in establishing a decent wage scale for itself. Like a true Jacksonian, Evans saw the monopolization of resources by the wealthy few as the chief obstacle to the realization of a democratic political economy; and he offered the Homestead plan as an antidote to the "land monopoly" of the large speculative companies, in the same spirit that Jackson had attacked the monopoly of the Bank of United States. Like Jefferson, Evans believed that the creation of a permanent propertyless class—a proletariat—would ultimately prove fatal to republican institutions. The key to preserving the republic lay in making the proletariat (and the tenant farmer) a non-Indian "vanishing American"—a class continually disappearing into the ranks of the propertied classes.

But Evans's identification of the cause of the workingman with agrarian expansion did not stop at advocacy of the Homestead Act. With his colleague George Wilkes—editor of a series of sensation-mongering pro-labor journals, of which *Spirit of the Times* was the most popular—Evans also advocated those expansionist measures most sought by mercantile capitalists and bankers: "Manifest Destiny" in regard to California and the Far West, and the building of a transcontinental railroad. Wilkes and Evans expected that the passage of the Homestead Act and the creation of a government-owned corporation to build the railroad would prevent the new lands from being engrossed by "monster monopolies" and peopled with "degraded labor." This made them (and their cause) a part of the consensus that moved to seize the Far West in 1846 as the essential prior step in creating the new basis of American prosperity; but in the event their expectation of a Homestead Act and a publicly owned railroad was frustrated.[10]

The influence of National Reform or certain of its ideas among liberal intellectuals was considerable. It acquired important advocates in Horace Greeley of the influential New York *Tribune*, and in the popular novelist George Lippard, whose best-selling *Monks of Monk Hall* offered a dystopian vision of an America in which National Reform had *failed*. Its ideas dovetailed at important points with the thinking of Whigs, Free Soilers, and Republicans, and contributed to the general consensus.

However, National Reform had only a limited influence with organized labor proper. Some labor journals did adopt parts of the Reform program, along with other proposals for general social betterment; but few saw any direct interest for organized labor in the public lands policy. Indeed, for most urban workingmen the Frontier was not even a theoretical safety valve, let alone a direct outlet for mobility. They looked to politics, and the control of local and state political institutions, as the means to relief from low wages, bad conditions, and invidious social or economic policies. It would seem, then, that interest in the Myth of the Frontier and its attendant ideology was not universal—that it was not subscribed to with equal enthusiasm by all classes and groups, but only by particular sections of the society: as one historian has noted, "Labor's interest in free public land might actually be rather lukewarm but its sympathizers and opponents both believed that interest to be considerable."[11]

The belief held by Evans and other friends of labor that the interest of the workingmen was deeply engaged by the question of access to public lands was reciprocated by their opponents. The northern manufacturers and their political spokesmen before 1850 often argued that the appeal of western lands drained away their labor surplus, increasing costs of production and —when skilled workmen were enticed—decreasing productivity. But that consensus of opposites speaks to the prevalence of the Frontier Myth as a language for formulating social issues, at least among the educated and nationally oriented elite. Agreement on the terms of the problem facilitated the rapprochement between these groups within the framework of Republican ideology, and allowed former National Reformers, labor spokesmen, and northern manufacturers to support the Homestead Act. This convergence was also aided by the easing of labor shortages because of increased immigration, and the developing interest of northern capitalists in western railroads. Manufacturers did not cease to believe in the myth of a draining away of labor toward the western farms; but they had discovered that the out-migration of workers was less threatening to their interests and their social peace than the class warfare that might result from a closing off of the promise that each workman might become a proprietor. They sought to appropriate for themselves and their party organizations the enthusiasm for property owning implicit in the Homestead component of National Reform, and to dismiss as contradictory that movement's "antiproperty" approach to labor relations.

Here again, the ideological response to the Frontier—as fact and as myth—was being shaped by the immediate concerns of the Metropolis. The language of Frontier symbolism—wilderness, savages, virgin land— was merged with and adapted to the language of an emergent industrialism. Edward Everett—the foremost orator in the country from Jackson's time to Lincoln's, and a spokesman for northern Whig manufacturing interests— gave this new formulation its most characteristic metaphor in the 1830s, when he characterized the western lands as "a safety valve to the great social steam engine." As John Kasson notes in his study *Civilizing the Machine*, the choice of metaphor is industrial, and it implies the specifically industrial character of American society itself.[12]

The Myth of the Frontier was thus in the process of reformulation by a post-Cooperian class of entrepreneurs, journalists, politicians, writers, reformers, and intellectuals, whose aim was to make their traditional Myth responsive to the new political economy. These ideologists were nationalistic in orientation, and their chosen media transcended regional boundaries. The expansion of urban-based commerce and industry into the agricultural hinterland had a cultural correlative in the expansion of urban media into national media. The domestic book-trade—initially localized in the Northeast—became national in its operations. The New York *Herald* and *Tribune* pioneered a tendency of large urban newspapers to become national institutions, with subscribers in every state of the Union and a news-gathering and editorial range that included all of the Americas and Europe. These publications were supplemented by a broad range of periodicals, ranging from cheaply printed sensational, lower-class journals like *Spirit of the Times* and the *Police Gazette*, through middle-brow journals of all sorts (*Harper's Weekly, Frank Leslie's Illustrated*), up to the elite journals—the *Atlantic* and the *North American Review*. Although the reach of these publications was national and even international, their basis was local and therefore urban. The editors of New York papers were intensely involved in city politics, and gave local issues as much and more importance as tariff debates in Congress or revolutions in France. And the elite journals were associated with the intellectual elite of their native regions or cities—the *Atlantic*, for example, was the house organ of New England intellectuals. Consequently they were well adapted to the cultural function of integrating the languages of local and national politics.[13]

In these new national cultural media, the Myth of the Frontier was made to address the general problem of reconciling the conflicting demands for diffusion of wealth and protection of existing privilege. Central to the fantasies of National Reformers, manufacturers, southern expansionists, and Jacksonian politicians is the sense of a conflict between the high expectations of the mass of the population and the apprehension that the resource base will, ultimately, be inadequate to fulfill the justified demands of all comers. Cooper's contemplation of the Great American Desert as an ultimate barrier to agrarian cupidity is merely one metaphor for the larger phenomenon of a contradiction between the imperatives of ideology—for unlimited access to unlimited resources—and the facts of existence. The self-appointed literary spokesmen for our emergent national culture, and spokesmen for the local concerns of western settlers, artisans, manufacturers, and planters, reformulated the language of the Frontier Myth codified by Cooper, transforming both its characters and its plots to make them comfortable to the concerns of this new era.

FACING THE DESERT: THE PROBLEM OF LEADERSHIP IN IRVING'S WEST

As we have seen, implicit in the Cooperian myth is the belief that once the peculiar conditions of the Frontier have disappeared, a social hierarchy based upon birth, breeding, and wealth will "naturally" reassert itself. The military aristocrats of Cooper's novels—Captain Middleton, Duncan Heyward, and their like—are the prototypes of this aristocracy. But Cooper's concern is to show us this acquisition and testing of democratic and civilized values in the special environment of the Frontier, and he seldom made firm and explicit connections between the historical drama of Frontier conquest and the political order of the day. The historical works of George Bancroft and Washington Irving, and of Francis Parkman later in the century while employing a Cooperian vocabulary of social and racial types and paradigm war-dramas, pressed harder for the resolution of the ideological tensions Cooper only played with. This is not only the result of the difference in genre between fiction writing and history. By the time Irving and the others began to address the Frontier issue, Cooper's earliest Leatherstocking works and the agrarian frontier they contemplated were part of the past. Irving's histories of the enterprise of American businessmen and soldiers are set in and around that Great American Desert that Cooper describes in *The Prairie*—a place both real and fictive, which defines a natural limit to the growth of America and the economic resources of the republic.

Washington Irving was already the "dean" of American letters when, in the 1830s, he turned his attention to the subject of western exploration. Like Cooper, he regarded himself as the spokesman of American culture; his fiction tended toward the manufacture of "fake-lore"—stories based on European models, offered as samples of indigenous popular culture. But Irving's most serious contribution (as he saw it) was in the form of multi-volume histories, in which he recounts and values the great figures and movements that (as he saw it) shaped the American republic. In this large scheme, his Frontier writings have a terminal position. They are the closest thing to current-events history in his work, treating as they do events that were only a few years past. They serve as occasions for exhibiting and cele-brating the industry and enterprise of American businessmen, entrepreneurs, traders, and soldiers. However, their view of the future is a problematic one. Cooper in the Leatherstocking Tales could confidently predict that one day the forest scene of Natty's adventures would be populated by prosperous small farms and well-ordered country towns. But Irving's West, like Cooper's in *The Prairie*, is represented as far too arid, wild, savage, and intractable a place for agrarian settlement by yeoman farmers. Rather, the territory exerts its pressure on weaker natures to drive them downward toward savagery. Only those whites of superior endowment, or under the command of a soldier-aristocrat, can maintain themselves in such a region. Thus this West is a final frontier, a permanent wilderness usable only by well-organized entrepreneurial enterprises, a field for Mountain Men but not for the yeoman farmer. Yet even for wealthy and resourceful capitalists, the difficulties are formidable; and in fact the heroes of Irving's frontier histories end their adventures either with outright failure (*Astoria*, 1836) or with only limited and temporary success (*Captain Bonneville*, 1837).[14]

Irving's histories of western enterprise and adventure draw on a vocabu-lary of figures and myths quite close to Cooper's. But as one who combined the roles of novelist, government official, and historian, he tended to be more explicit than Cooper in developing ideas about future western policy from his accounts, casting the plains and mountains of the Great American Desert as the realm of trappers and hunters, and as a last refuge for the savage races. Still, such lands might offer a field for commercial enterprise of a certain kind: a new Frontier, not for the traditional yeoman but for the fur-trade entrepreneur.

Superficially a commercial entrepreneur like John Jacob Astor, hero of Irving's *Astoria*, is an unlikely candidate for a pantheon established on agrarian principles. As the master of large aggregations of capital and political influence, he vitiates both the life-style and the egalitarian ethic of a society which envisions the smallholder as the ideal citizen. He is the master of labor, the commander and director; not himself a toiler. Irving links Astor to the tradition by noting his common origins, his rise from obscurity by hard work and self-sacrifice; and he points to the linkage between this captain of commerce and the commanders of the armies of the republic. Weems democratized the figure of Washington as military aristocrat by giving him a youthful apprenticeship to the life of the Frontier, and by associating his aristocracy of birth with the meritocratic qualities of the soldier. Astor's sanctification is effected by a more distant process of association: while he does not go to the woods or serve as a fighter himself, he makes it possible for others to do so; and he supplies a framework of capital and institutional organization that makes the activities of the hunter and the soldier part of a permanent improvement of America's economic substance. Astor, then, is like the farmer, who uses the hunter's blazed trails to find land which he will cultivate and improve. Of course, in Crèvecoeur's vision, it was the future cultivation of land by the farmer that sanctified the hunter's departure from civilization; but by the time of Cooper, that association of hunter and farmer had served to invest the hunter with the prospective aura of agrarian progress. An enterprise like Astor's could, therefore, partake of the heroic and sanctifying aura of the agrarian Frontier Myth by its linkage with the myth of the hunter. It is interesting that although Irving celebrates Astor, he condescends to those whose impulses are merely commercial. It is the association of the entrepreneur with the hunter and soldier that casts the mantle of glory over the enterprise.[15]

Irving's version of the Frontier Myth appears most characteristically in his history of the adventures of the explorer, soldier, and fur trader Captain Bonneville. Irving met Bonneville in the course of his work on *Astoria*; and this history, unlike *Astoria*, has some of the novelistic coherence that comes from having a central character to provide a strong focus and viewpoint. As Irving portrays him, Bonneville is a type of the military aristocrat. A descendent of a French émigré, and hence a gentleman born, Bonneville is also a gentleman by attainment, having gone to the military academy at West Point. He is not represented as a money-hungry businessman, but as one devoted to the gentlemanly avocations, a reader of good literature, a mathematical scholar, a soldier, officer, and gentleman. In his Rocky Mountain expedition, he "strangely engrafted the trapper and hunter upon the soldier." In this way he combines features of Leatherstocking and of such aristocrats as Captain Middleton, Duncan Heyward, and Oliver Edwards/Effingham. His idea of an exploring and fur-trading venture in the Rockies came not from any motive of private gain, but from a desire to gratify his curiosity and his romantic yearning for western adventure—the motives of Filson's Boone, and of any number of romantic upper-class travelers in the American West. Money was not his object: he was to perform certain tasks for his government, and so combine public utility with private projects.[16]

The wherewithal for the expedition was provided by Alfred Seton, a New York capitalist formerly associated with Astor. Thus Bonneville's work would proceed in a context that bound him quite closely to the Metropolis, however far afield he might roam. He was tied to the army by his career and his orders, and to a commercial enterprise by his link to Seton. Yet whatever the reality of his connection to the Metropolis, the style and structure of his adventure was essentially Frontier: he is physically out of touch with civilization for years, although working for its benefit all that time.[17]

Bonneville's adventure takes the form of a descent into savagery. His companions are a motley mixture of races—Indians and half-breeds, French Creoles and Anglo-American "mountaineers." The latter are superior to the rest in point of pride, vigor, and warlikeness: "A man who bestrides a horse, must be essentially different from a man who cowers in a canoe." However, the wild life of the Mountain Men has separated them forever from their own civilization and made them spiritual half-breeds:

> The wandering whites who mingle for any length of time with the savages, have invariably a proneness to adopt savage habitudes; but none more than the free trappers. It is a matter of vanity and ambition with them to discard everything that may bear the stamp of civilized life, and to adopt the manners, habits, dress, gesture, and even walk of the Indian. You cannot pay a free trapper a greater compliment, than to persuade him you have mistaken him for an Indian brave; and, in truth, the counterfeit is complete . . . it was difficult to persuade oneself that they were white men, and had been brought up in civilized life.[18]

Irving's portrait of the Mountain Men has been discredited as factual description. William Goetzmann has noted they were often as much tied into the success ethic of Jacksonian America as their yeoman counterparts. But like Leatherstocking in Cooper, like the yeoman farmer in Crèvecoeur, the Mountain Man in Irving's book is a fictive alternative to the disruptive commercial ethics of the emerging bourgeois society: a figure standing apart from the success- and mobility-oriented system, content with his "natural" lot.[19]

The Mountain Man, like Leatherstocking and unlike the yeoman, is linked with a dying culture. Irving's Indians of the plains and Rockies are less advanced than those of the woodlands, in effect a degenerate race of Indians (since all Indians are presumed to have descended from a single racial stock). Some of them are little removed from the wild beasts. Bonneville makes some efforts at converting the more susceptible to Christianity, but these efforts are futile. Irving sees the fur-trade frontier—as Cooper saw the eastern woodlands frontier—as "essentially evanescent." With the extinction of furbearing animals, the wild life of the plains and mountains will vanish, to "exist but in frontier story, and seem like the fictions of chivalry or fairy tale." As for the "Great American Desert" itself, he envisions a further degeneration of the form of savage life from its present shape—not a rise to civilization: the barren mountain and desert, he says,

> must ever remain an irreclaimable wilderness, intervening between the abodes of civilization, and affording a last refuge to the Indian. Here, roving tribes of hunters, living in tents or lodges, and following the migrations of the game, may lead a life of savage independence, where there is nothing to tempt the cupidity of the white man. The amalgamation of various tribes, and of white men of every nation, will in time produce hybrid races like the mountain Tartars of the Caucases . . . should they continue their present predatory and warlike habits, they may, in time, become a scourge to the civilized frontiers on either side of the mountains; as they are at present a terror to the traveller and trader.

The utility of Bonneville's adventure, he says, will be to extend the military sway of civilization over that territory, and "put an end to the kind of 'black mail,' levied on all occasions by the savage 'chivalry of the mountains.' "20

This is a very different outcome from that of Boone's adventure fifty years before. Boone returned from his view from the "commanding ridge" of Kentucky determined to bring in families and settle the wilderness. Bonneville's men return scarcely distinguishable from Indians by dress and manners, testimony to the intractability of this last wilderness, its power to render the white man savage before the white man can domesticate it. Bonneville too had his experience of a vision of glorious landscape from a mountain peak; and like Boone, he is said to be overlooking an area sacred to the Indians, like a "Blackfoot warrior" catching his first "view of the land of souls, . . . the happy hunting grounds." Yet the view he sees is more "sublime" and terrible than pastoral: chill winds drive him down, and Irving describes the mountains as "savage, and almost inaccessible."21 Bonneville's heroism lies in his capacity to resist the spell of such wilderness, which turns lesser men into renegades; and to overawe and rule the racially hybrid crowd that accompanies him—prophecy that Bonneville's sort of military man will be able to overawe the future "Tartars," and keep the border safe. But his will be a heroism in defense, not in advance.

FRONTIER PRESIDENTS: TRANSFORMATION OF THE SOLDIER ARISTOCRAT

In the face of such an impenetrable Frontier, the roles assigned to the key characters in the Myth are necessarily revalued. The distinctions of class, ameliorated in Cooperian romance, emerge as real and necessary differences in entitlement to power. Nothing illustrates this process better than the use of the symbolism of the military aristocrat in presidential politics between 1824 and 1850. As their party's standardbearer and the republic's head of state, the presidents (and presidential aspirants) were represented as symbolic repositories of virtues and qualities deemed essential and definitive of national character. Just at the time when Cooper's

fiction elaborated mythic roles for characters like Duncan Heyward and
Captain Middleton, presidential imagery was transformed by the triumph
of Andrew Jackson, who (in many crucial respects) embodies the Cooperian ideal: Jackson was the man of humble birth who had risen—by means
of military deeds against Indians on the frontier, and the British at New
Orleans—to the status of a traditional aristocrat: a plantation owner rich
in land, slaves, and tenants.

The achievement of the promise of American life, if we take Jackson
as its measure, is the achievement of aristocratic status: a social position
so firm that its possession not only entitles one to rule, but also to conceive
of oneself as possessing unique and inherent attributes of virtue and intelligence—attributes that might be inheritable by an heir. Although his politics
and style were anathema to Jefferson—whose roots were in the declining
aristocracy of the pre–cotton gin South—Jackson in fact fulfills the logic
of Jefferson's "natural aristocracy," rising by merit to command, and once
in command is taken for a paragon of the national virtues.

Jackson's power as a figure in popular mythology derived from his
unique combination of aristocratic status with a plebeian or backwoods
style. Like Filson's Boone, he derived the virtues of self-reliance, toughness, vigor, and prowess from his struggle against the Indian and the forest;
unlike Boone, he had so far transcended his origins as to become a nobleman, a chivalric (as opposed to a merely pragmatic) protector of womanhood, an owner of slaves, a duelist, a general. Yet having achieved a
transcendent social status, he did not forget his origins; he remained bluff
and simple in speech and manner, and—most important—he believed sin-
cerely that the power of government should be used to maximize the opportunity of the common man to rise in wealth and status.

To this end Jackson would use the power of the government to set aside
entrenched special privileges and favored classes, to facilitate the wide distribution of cheap public lands and cheap currency for the payment of
debts. In a nation of aspiring capitalists, mortaged both psychologically and
financially to dreams of future prosperity, he represented quintessentially
the promise of abundance inherent in the Frontier. He asserted that the
periodic panics and economic contractions that afflicted the economy were
the work of monopolistic oligarchs, concerned to preserve their special
privileges by preventing the "new men" from rising. Thus in Jacksonian
rhetoric the traits of aristocracy were simultaneously the signs of valid
achievement and the caste marks of illegitimate privilege. What distinguishes the two is the degree of engagement in the project of patriotic
aggrandizement associated with the Frontier. The banker, being exclusively
a man of the Metropolis, has no direct association with the exploits that
win new lands, and his competitors are not Indians but the white citizenry.
Only the soldier and the aggressive statesman can safely possess the marks
of caste and the legitimacy that goes with them, for his aggression is directed outward against the Indians, in the name of the whole public.[22]

This formula was successfully imitated and vulgarized by succeeding
presidents, most notably by William Henry Harrison, who sought to promote his 1840 presidential candidacy as the Whig version of Old Hickory.
Harrison was the scion of wealthy slave owners in Virginia, but he is repre-

sented by his biographers as a log-cabin-born frontiersman, natural gentleman, and Indian fighter in the Jackson mold. James Hall's *Memoir . . . of William Henry Harrison* (1836) represents Harrison as having inherited from his father "little save his noble example," that of a soldier in the Revolution—the one legitimate source of ancestor pride for an American. As a people, says Hall, "it is one of the happiest results of our republican institutions, that no individual can claim respect on account of his parentage," and that Harrison's rise was "dependent on his own exertions."

But for Hall, the crucial transformation of character on the Frontier was not that of poor propertyless Andrew into a freeholding yeoman farmer. Rather, it involved the exchange of agrarian traits for those of the military gentleman. The necessities of Frontier life—that "the savage . . . be expelled; the panther, the wolf and the bear . . . be exterminated; the forest . . . be razed"—transformed "a race of husbandmen . . . into a bold, adventurous, military people." This transformation of racial character involves exchanges of "blood" as well as the influence of Frontier experience. The pioneers became "brave and hardy . . . from their manner of life"; but their higher traits were derived from the infusion of aristocratic blood provided by the numerous settlers from Tidewater Virginia—the native land of Washington and Duncan Heyward. To these Virginians of "education, wealth . . . and talents" are attributed the "hospitality," "polish," and "intelligence" of the Kentucky frontiersmen, and their developing the character of a "chivalrous people." What Hall describes is not the democratization of American character by the Frontier, but the democratic diffusion of characteristics that remain essentially those of an aristocratic ruling class.

Of this new aristo-democracy, William Henry Harrison was (in Hall's view) an appropriate representative. Harrison is seen as a self-made man, particularly after his removal to the West, where Hall represents him as "identified with the people in their domestic hardships, and their arduous labours in founding liberal institutions in the wilderness . . . From these privations and toils none was exempt." Although Harrison was an educated man, as well as a prosperous one (and an official of the government as well), Hall represents him as having received his education "in the field and forest"—after the manner of Boone and Weems's Washington. "It was in this school that Mr. Harrison . . . learned the lessons of political economy . . . [At] the fireside of the farmer, at the camp of the hunter, at the frontier fortress, at the council of the governor, at the festive gatherings of the people . . ." Hall even extends this vision of Harrison as frontiersman down to the present—a major distortion of fact—asserting that "after a long life spent in the public service, he is living upon the fruits of his daily industry—a plain, unassuming man . . ." Harrison was at this point quite well-to-do, a large landowner with white tenants and black servants.[23]

Similar mixtures of imagery were applied to the career of Zachary Taylor, "Old Rough and Ready"—the successful Mexican War general and president from 1848 to his death in 1850. Montgomery's *The Life of Major General Zachary Taylor* (1847) represents Taylor's lineage as aristocratic, "derived from an ancient and distinguished English family," and tied by consanguinity and by marriage to the landed aristocracy of Old Virginia. But Taylor's nurture was said to be all Frontier, after his family's removal to Kentucky when Taylor was six. "His youth was therefore spent, and his character formed, amidst the dangers and difficulties of Indian warfare, and the hardships and privations ever incident to a frontier life." This education developed his manly character, and schooled him to overcome obstacles from which lesser men might shrink. Although the biographer asserts that the Taylor house had to be barricaded against Indians each night and that even the path to school was waylaid by savages, Taylor apparently had no hostile encounters with Indians at all until he began his military service in 1808. His commission, Montgomery admits, was gained by family influence, but Taylor (like Harrison) emerges as self-made through his continual engagement in the "hardships and privations" of frontier life and Indian warfare.[24]

The extent to which the application of myth imagery to the definition of political character could distort reality is attested by *The Rough and Ready*, a newspaper published in Concord, New Hampshire, in 1846, which began plumping quite early for a Taylor presidency. The newspaper's editor was a Democrat, and it was inconceivable to him that any man with a character so like Jackson's—a character to which so much of the sacred imagery of the Frontier and yeoman democracy attached—could be anything other than a Democrat. He thus reports it as an act of "Base Depravity" when a rival journal asserts that Taylor is a Whig-Federalist, "one of the greatest slaveholders in the United States [who] raises babies for the market . . . [and] FURNISHES CREOLE VIRGINS FOR THE 'HELLS' OF NEW ORLEANS . . ." Whatever the truth of the assertion as to Creole Virgins, the vile calumny was of course true: Old Rough and Ready was in fact a Whig, and an extremely wealthy planter and slave owner—in which latter respect he was indeed Jackson's fellow.[25]

The Frontier imagery, therefore, had acquired a considerable power, and it became conventional to attempt to link political candidates with that imagery whenever it was even remotely feasible to do so. Even General Winfield Scott's campaign biographer, in 1852, attempted to link his hero's character with that of Jackson and Taylor, emphasizing his common origins and a Frontier youth, and linking him with Indian fighting—although his services were almost exclusively against European and Mexican regular armies. Perhaps failure of the attempt was inevitable, given Scott's popular sobriquet of "Old Fuss and Feathers"; but that the attempt was made is significant.[26]

These attempts to clothe military aristocrats in Frontier buckskin are motivated by a wish to reconcile the competing ideologies of entrepreneurial democracy, egalitarianism, and paternalism. By adopting the manner and dress of the Frontiersman, the soldier-president-planter affiliates himself with a symbol of the common man: plebeian by birth; educated in the school of experience; energetic and even heroic in his adventurous approach to achievement, productivity, and self-advancement; the unconscious agent of an advancing democracy and an expanding civilization. A democratic style legitimates an aristocratic or elitist politics. But that style is transformed when it is adopted by a Jackson or a Taylor. It ceases to be the final representation of democratic values or natural law, and becomes a stage in the progressive development of Americans toward a "higher" style, a superior form of social organization. Buckskin is a necessary stage through which American heroes pass on their way to presidential broadcloth; and perhaps the things symbolized by the buckskin—egalitarianism, entrepreneurialism without limit, achievement and self-aggrandizement without end—are merely stages of American development, and not the perfected form of republican organization.[27]

TRANSFORMATION OF THE HUNTER: JACKSONIAN OUTLAWS

The absorption of the traits of the Frontier hero by the military aristocrat is one symptom of the ideological shift in American mythology at the start of the period of industrialization. At the same time, there was a reciprocal revaluation of the Frontier hunter-hero himself, which suggested that, in the backwash of a closing Frontier, traits that had been productive and heroic might become antisocial and dangerous.

As Indian fighters, pathfinders, and hunters, the Leatherstockings and Boones of the past had been seen as precursors of the Bonnevilles, the Jacksons, and the Taylors, who represented the triumph of a new, American, republican Metropolis. The hunter could thus be seen as providing the cutting edge for an advancing entrepreneurial civilization, his predatory violence as a prototype of the more productive predation of the "go-getter" ambitious for achievement. Such a figure was projected in Filson's portrayal of Daniel Boone; but there were good reasons for its declining credibility, and for the rise of a dual stereotype of the Frontiersman as an antisocial character—half white-Indian or Leatherstocking, so much the pure wilderness man that he must vanish with the forest; and the outlaw renegade, lingering in the Frontier's aftermath to provide a "dangerous class" in the settlements.

The conditions that gave birth to the Jacksonian Frontiersman-entrepreneur were unique, not to be precisely duplicated again. The territory east of the Mississippi was almost uniformly arable, and its fertility promised bonanza crops. The flow of rivers west and south provided easy access to the new territory, and easy routes of access to foreign markets via New Orleans. In such a territory it was possible for individuals and families to compete on equitable terms with land corporations like the Ohio Company of Associates (1785–90) or the Transylvania Company sponsored by Boone and Henderson (1770–90). The same combination of factors guaranteed that the formation of communities would precede the establishment of official governmental institutions. In the absence of such institutions, temporary institutions acquired the force of established law. Vigilante organizations could suppress those forms of criminality that the community could not live with, such as intramural robbery and murder, while tolerating activities that national law forbade (smuggling, moonshining, filibustering into foreign territory, and even extramural brigandage). Claim clubs, formed by families and by communities of "squatters," could aid individual homemakers to obtain preemption rights against the legally sanctioned chicanery of the land corporations and speculators; more to the point, they could also provide a basis for speculative enterprises by the squatters themselves.

Western communities thus emerged as "competitive units," as economic enterprises in which the homemaker-entrepreneur saw a path to riches in persuading others to join his community, boosting the value of the land. The line dividing the yeoman farmer—the pure homemaker—from the speculator was therefore a vague one at best, since the two roles could be either temporarily merged to take advantage of a local land boom, or permanently altered, if the capital so gained was sufficient to make further speculation possible.[28]

The connection between the two roles becomes clearer when we recognize that behind each wave of settlement was a strongly motivating boom psychology. The opening of a large tract of public land for sale at low prices and with easy terms of credit constituted a kind of windfall to farmers and others hungry for the wealth and political standing that land stood for. The analogy to a gold strike is a close one, since both situations promise a ready way to wealth at less cost in labor and capital outlay than would normally be expected. Given this motivation, the farmer's attitude toward his land might well be an extractive and exploitative one, as opposed to the passion for patient cultivation imagined by Crèvecoeur and Jefferson. That this was indeed the case is suggested by analysis of who went into the new territories: after 1800, at least, there seemed to be a clear tendency for a man who had "gone west" once to be the first to pick up and go again, when opportunity offered, even if his original acquisition was a prosperous one. Indeed, the transcontinental emigrants of the middle 1840s were predominantly of this class. The cost of such a long-distance emigration certainly had something to do with this particular case, but if we look at the society as a whole, it is featured by a kind of universal nomadism, in which westward was only one of many possible directions (for white men at least), but in which no acquisition is anything more than a coign of vantage for surveying future fields.[29]

The West consequently experienced in an acute form the ambivalent association of democratic idealism and unprincipled materialism that characterized the society as a whole. This combination was especially dismaying to those who identified themselves as spokesmen for traditional values—self-restraint, deference, conservative business ethics, religious "otherworldliness." And it was this circumstance that lay behind the emergence of the "Southwestern school" of writers as an important and popular literary tendency in 1835–50.

Usually "Southwestern" stories were concerned with life in the backwash of the frontier, Crèvecoeur's borderland between the realm of the Indian and hunter, and that of the settled and established farming community. Southwestern writers exploited their region and its characters for local color, affecting to stand between the rough characters of the backwash region and their genteel readership in Cincinnati, Philadelphia, or New York. There was a certain amount of realism, an emphasis on the gritty quality of life, crudity of manners, violence, crime, and poverty; a certain amount of sensationalism in the depiction of violence, linked to a folkloric tendency to hyperbole that converted aggression to humor; and a certain amount of condescension to the "types" represented in the stories. The writers of the Southwestern school were mostly Whigs and conservatives, representatives of the professional class, not infrequently politicians. If their stories were intended to popularize and mythologize their region, they were also meant as satires on the primitive side of their section's life-style—satires that pointed, indirectly, toward more respectable values and behavior.[30]

Although the writers themselves were mostly residents of the region and began publishing in local papers, their primary outlets were the nationally oriented urban journals of the Metropolitan North. Magazines like *Police Gazette* and *Spirit of the Times* catered to an urban and lower-class audience, and the preoccupations of that audience shaped their choice of material. Tales of urban criminality tended to make ironic juxtapositions of rich and poor. The law is seen to punish the poor man who becomes an outlaw by robbing the wealthy; but it does not rebuke the wealthy who, by their selfishness, create the conditions of poverty that drive men to crime. One of the conventional plots—which George Lippard treated on an epic scale in *Monks of Monk Hall* (1844)—was that of the poor girl driven to crime or prostitution by an indifferent society and a wealthy seducer. George Wilkes, the pro-labor editor of both *Police Gazette* and *Spirit of the Times*, made a media heroine of sorts out of Helen Jewett—a prostitute murdered by a wealthy man, who was acquitted after a sensational trial.[31]

The context in which the Southwestern stories appeared was therefore entirely Metropolitan; and the juxtaposition of urban and Frontier stories suggested a significant relationship between the two worlds. To some extent the journals preserve the original premise that the Frontier is an alternative to and an escape from the rigors of the Metropolis. These suggestions harmonize with the editorial stance of the papers, which favored the whole range of policies associated with the Frontier Myth—Manifest Destiny, Homestead legislation, and subsidized railroads. But the association of Southwestern with Metropolitan crime stories implies another kind of connection—an identity between the corruptions of Metropolitan society and those of a Frontier approaching closure.

In the Southwest of fiction, the Frontier has passed, and the predatory impulse turned inward produces a society in which economic competition reaches a limit of violent unrestraint that tests the tolerance of social bonding itself. The typical Southwestern heroes are lower-class "confidence men," slick in a horse swap; or men of prodigious capacities for violence. Augustus Baldwin Longstreet's *Georgia Scenes* (1835) offers a typical pantheon of Southwestern types, including two cracker-barrel entrepreneurs who passionately prevaricate, exaggerate, distort, and defraud each other in order to emerge victorious in "The Horse Swap." Pride as well as cash value is at stake: the Frontiersman must overcome his opponent at any cost, competition is a value in itself. In "The Fight," this violence becomes explicitly verbal and physical, and the unrestrained character of a frontier brawl is set before the reader, complete with gouging, kicking, biting off body parts, and foul language. Among themselves, as in their warfare with the Indian, the Frontiersmen have learned to give and take no quarter:

every war is a war of extermination, and every exchange a potential *casus belli*.[32]

The Southwest contains its left-over Leatherstockings as well, and these speak directly of the nature of the change that has overtaken the border. Some old hunters and Indian fighters adjust or even run for Congress like Davy Crockett and Simon Suggs. Others, like the legendary keelboatman Mike Fink, bring to quarrels with fellow whites the same code of violence and revenge that shaped their behavior toward Indians—with the result that they are killed off by the hand of justice or the outcome of blood feud.

Viewed from the perspective of a post-Frontier social order, the Indian fighter of the past becomes a far more ambiguous and threatening figure than Cooper's Leatherstocking. The difference is registered in the critique and revision of Cooper by the western writer James Hall and the southern novelist Robert M. Bird. For Cooper, the Frontier hero had been a mediator between two races representing opposite poles of a spectrum of natural "gifts" or moral propensities. Since Indian and white participate in a common universe of natural and moral law, the Indian's different moral vision has a kind of legitimacy; and through the interpretation of the Leatherstocking figure, Indian morals can even offer a useful critique of civilized values and behavior. To be sure, Cooper's Indians perish and his whites inherit the land; but the mediation of Leatherstocking suggests that this process involves—below the violence—a passing on of legitimate authority from the elder race to the younger. But for Hall and Bird there is no question of Indian legitimacy or moral authority. They criticize Cooper as a sentimentalist for evoking sympathy for Indian values and representing their response to civilization as a moral critique. For Hall and Bird the Indian response is simply the rage of the wild beast against the cage: visceral, unreasoning, an expression of a nature innately incapable of civilization.

By attributing innate depravity to the Indian, Hall and Bird discredit the Frontier hero's role as interpreter and critic of society. Both writers vest the principle of social authority unambiguously in civilized, military-aristocratic characters. Their Frontiersmen are rendered as unstable, dangerous, even schizophrenic by their existence in the void between antitheses of Red and White. The title character of Bird's *Nick of the Woods* (1837) is the most melodramatic version of this sort of hero. Nathan Slaughter had been a fanatical Quaker, who sought license for his hyper-intense religiosity in the isolation of the forest. When his family is massacred by Indians his Christian fanaticism becomes inverted, and he becomes a demonic avenger called by the Indians "Jibbenainosay" and by the whites "Nick of the Woods." The offsetting impulses of gentility and violence (white gifts and Indian nurture) that made Natty Bumppo so capable an interpreter between Indians and whites cannot be balanced in Nathan's world or soul: they split his personality in two. So the principles of savagery and civilization, freedom and order, Frontiersman and citizen are revealed as antithetical.[33]

Hall's portrayal of the type is less sensational in style, and pretends to historical accuracy. But his classic sketch of the "Indian Hater" (1835) points to the same conclusions about the antisocial consequences that follow from a too-devoted enjoyment of the life of the Frontier hero. His brief account of the life of Colonel John Moredock was a well-known and frequently reprinted piece of Frontier history and legend; and after its satirical apotheosis as a parody in Melville's *The Confidence-Man* (1857) it became the work most frequently associated with Hall's name. Hall depicts the Indian hater as a spiritual type common in the Frontier era: a man of solitary and self-willed character who suffers some misfortune at Indian hands—the massacre of family and loved ones—and becomes thereafter a professional Indian killer. The Indian hater's mission is to exterminate red men as a matter of principle, and he will make any sacrifice of health or interest necessary to fulfill this mission. Flint's Boone is represented as an "artist" in his worthy passion of hunting; Hall extends some of this quality to the Indian hater. Yet so closely linked with the animal and the Indian have they become that both the professional hunter and the professional Indian fighter come close to perishing when the things they love to kill have at last been exterminated.

According to Hall, the origin of Indian hating lies in the fact that the people living on the crest of Frontier expansion constitute "a peculiar race," which generation after generation has persisted in keeping ahead of the tide of emigration, "who shunned the restraints, while they despised the luxuries of social life." This race represents a primitive survival of an earlier epoch of our national history, for "America was settled in an age when certain rights, called those of *discovery* and *conquest*, were universally acknowledged; and when the possession of a country was readily conceded to the strongest." Although better notions have entered social life with "the spread of knowledge, and the dissemination of religious truth," such improvements have not touched the consciousness of a pioneer race which persistently flees contact with the more advanced society that follows them. Hall goes so far as to assert that the chief motive of this race is not to kill the Indian or conquer the woods, but simply to escape from civilization: as Melville said, not so much sailing for any haven ahead, as fleeing from all havens astern. Conflict with the Indian rises from his desire to "monopolize" the land, where the pioneer asserts that the hunting grounds must be "free to all."

Hall goes on to give the history of a representative of this pioneer race, Colonel John Moredock, a man of superhuman prowess, whose family was massacred by Indians; and who became, as a result, a passionate hunter and slayer of Indians, who "never in his life failed to embrace an opportunity to kill a savage." Despite this proclivity, he was accounted a good husband and provider, a useful citizen who was considered as a candidate for governor, but declined the honor. In Melville's retelling of the tale, this decline is a sacrifice Moredock makes to his darling passion; but Hall insists on his good qualities as a citizen. The implication in Melville's version is that Moredock's desire for revenge remains a passion, even after the frontier situation which gave birth to it and in a manner justified it has passed; at this point Hall avoids the question or allows it to drop, and ends on a note emphasizing the colonel's eventual socialization. The principle, in both cases, is the same, however: the colonel cannot make one with society unless he lets the obsession for private revenge go and ceases to be "the Indian hater."[34]

Yet the character of Indian fighter or hunter may be, as Hall suggests, as ingrained as a racial trait or a personal identity. Thomas Bangs Thorpe, in his famous short story "The Big Bear of Arkansas," plays with this idea and develops some of its implications. The narrator of the story is the typical "genteel" observer of Southwestern fiction, here journeying down the Mississippi on a steamboat. Into the smoking room bursts Jim Doggett, an "alligator-horse" type of frontiersman, speaking in dialect and calling himself "The Big Bear of Arkansaw." Doggett at first comes on like a Frontier booster as he hyperbolically sings the praises of his home countryside in Arkansas, "the creation State, the finishing-up country—a State where the *sile* runs down to the center of the 'arth, and government gives you a title to every inch of it." However, in his proper character, Jim Doggett is a hunter, a bear hunter—in fact, *the* bear hunter of all the world. As he says of his dog, "I never could tell whether he was made expressly to hunt bear, or whether bear was made expressly for him to hunt." [35]

Jim Doggett's dilemma is that his skill has virtually denuded the country of bears, and those that remain are so demoralized by his skill that they scarcely resist him anymore. The hunter's profession is gone, his competitive prowess no longer evoked by an antagonistic and abundant nature. Life becomes dull and monotonous, until nature responds to Doggett's silent wish and sends him a bear of bears, the "Big Bear of Arkansaw" from which he will take his nickname. The Big Bear is colossal in size, a match for Doggett and his hound in cunning, who also has quasi-magical powers and who, on one occasion, walks right through a fusillade unscathed. Doggett feels that it is not he who hunts bear, but the bear who hunts him. Frustrated and humiliated, he determines to kill the bear, die, or "go to Texas"; and as if in response, the Big Bear comes walking "through his fence," and virtually offers himself to the gun.

The outcome of the hunt is, however, spiritually troubling to Doggett, who is forced to conclude that it was not his skill that gained him the victory, but some mystical choice on the bear's part—that he was "a Creation bear," unhuntable, and died "when his time come." If we are to take Doggett at his word, the killing of the last bear represents the final extinction of the active principle of wildness in the wilderness—an extinction for which man is the instrument, but Nature herself the ordainer. Doggett is left with the name of the thing he killed and of the place whose spirit the animal was—he *is* "The Big Bear of Arkansaw"—but Doggett is also an anachronism, and the last view of him is indeed pathetic: a garrulous, tipsy, backwoodsman booster who vanishes from the steamboat in the night, going back to bear-less Arkansas.

Johnson Jones Hooper's *Some Adventures of Captain Simon Suggs* (1845) presents the quintessential post-Frontier Southwesterner as a rogue and confidence man. In Hooper, the political and social dimensions of the Southwestern version of "the hunter" emerge quite clearly. Captain Suggs is a satire on Andrew Jackson, his border constituency, and his picked successor, Martin Van Buren. Suggs converts the ideology of democracy-in-mobility into a maxim: "It is good to be shifty in a new country." And he makes the most of the ambiguity inherent in the word "shifty," through a career of fraud and chicanery.

The shifty Captain Suggs is a miracle of shrewdness. He possesses, in an eminent degree, the tact which enables a man to detect the *soft spots* in his fellow, and to assimilate himself to whatever company he may fall in with. Besides, he has a quick, ready wit, which has extracted him from many an unpleasant predicament, and which makes him whenever he chooses to be so— and that is always—very companionable. In short, nature . . . sent him into the world a sort of he-Pallas, ready to cope with his kind, from infancy, in all the arts by which men *"get along"* in the world; if she made him, in respect of his moral conformation, a beast of prey, she did not refine the cruelty by denying him the fangs and the claws.[36]

This miracle of predation chooses his victims from within the society, beginning with the cheating and befooling of both his hard-shell Baptist preacher-father and their Negro slave. Neither patriarch nor servant, authority nor subordinate, is safe from exploitation by the shifty Suggs, as he makes his way in the world. His typical victims, however, are not embodiments of traditional authority—noble planters or worthy barristers. Rather, they are representatives of the nouveaux riches the would-be gentlemen of the Frontier, whose pretensions to gentility and status constitute their chief vanity, and the weak spots that Suggs exploits. Thus Suggs overcomes and takes advantage of a Frontier militia muster, where various "worthies" contest his right to the captaincy; of a camp meeting, where a Frontier ranter finds Simon stealing his thunder and his collection; of a puffed-up citizen named General Witherspoon, who is, it transpires, a hog drover by profession.

In Suggs, Hooper finds a voice to satirize Jacksonian man on two levels: through the captain's easy distortion of his victims' pretensions, his showing up of their vanities; and through the captain's own amoral and unrestrained predation. In a true Frontier situation, Suggs's type might have figured as the military aristocrats' sly and ingenious hunter-scout; behind the Frontier, given license to compete for economic and political power, he is something like a menace.

The satiric mode and the presence of resources that are still relatively abundant soften the impact of Suggs's criminality in Hooper's stories. But other Southwestern stories took a darker view, focusing on the careers of the infamous badmen and outlaws who infested the river and forests in the early nineteenth century. James Hall's *The Harpe's Head* is in this vein, and there were any number of paperback potboilers that rendered the careers of Southwestern bandits in the most sensationalistic terms. The Harpes, within this paradigm, represented a survival of two psychopathic primitives into the post-Frontier era. In an earlier time, they would have been renegades like Simon Girty and exhibited their sadism inciting Indians to torture their captives; now they are rapists, robbers and murderers, river pirates and road agents who must be hunted down like wild beasts—yet who can, and do, pass for civilized men in backwoods farming communities.[37]

More troublesome than the throwback Harpes were outlaws of the type of Samuel Rogers and John Murrell—men who carried the striving for success too far, and who turned ferries or taverns or toll stations into bases for the robbery and murder of travelers. Of these, the most notable character was John Murrell, a man who began as a frontier highwayman, but who adjusted his criminal enterprise to suit the new conditions of a post-Frontier society—and so threatened that society profoundly. Murrell's story was told by H. R. Howard in two paperback versions, and also in the *National Police Gazette*. The first of these concentrates on Murrell himself, and was part of a series of books on famous western criminals written by Howard. The second focuses not on Murrell, but on the man who brought Murrell to justice, Virgil A. Stewart.

The Life and Adventures of John A. Murrell, the Great Western Land Pirate (1847) represents the great outlaw as part of that outcast "social refuse" that inhabits Frontier districts and wild tracts. Howard asserts also that the story of Murrell's fall constitutes a significant part of that story of the wilderness's "redemption into civilization" which begins with the Indian wars. However, he sees in Murrell no mere Frontier brigand, but a man of prepossessing intellectual and even moral endowment (phrenologically cast) who converted the motives and energy of the western brigand into "a science . . . confederating all the various elements of the region into a single combination." Murrell is to Frontier outlawry what Astor is to Frontier fur trapping. And like Astor he has "risen" from poverty. That Murrell's parents were poor should not in itself be a motive for a life of crime: but in Murrell's household the mother—who ought to have been the embodiment of all the sacred values—was "course [*sic*] and immodest," taught Murrell to steal, and gave him his "barbarous and vicious nature." Pursuing a career of theft, chicanery, and murder, Murrell eventually arrives in Alabama, where a combination of circumstances give him his great idea. Taking advantage of local panic engendered by rumors of a "servile insurrection," Murrell devises a scheme for a lucrative racket involving seducing slaves to run away from their masters to "freedom" with him. Once in Murrell's confederates' hands, the slave can either be resold, returned for reward, or—if necessity requires it—murdered, gutted, weighted with stones, and dropped in a swamp. Similarly, free northern blacks could be kidnapped and smuggled south. The operation of such a large-scale racket requires a certain amount of conspiracy between Murrell and "respectable" society—law enforcement officers, judges, and of course a class of purchasing planters who would "ask no questions."

Out of the associations created by the runaway-slave racket, Murrell builds a network of political influence and protection which, in Howard's account, amounts to a secret society, a Mafia capable finally of achieving political control of whole districts—and perhaps more. Thus while Murrell follows a course of crime in the Suggsian manner—masquerading as a preacher, a merchant, and so on; a confidence man as much as an armed robber, perhaps more so—he secretly plans his "Mystic Clan" to avenge himself at the expense of a world that had impoverished, scorned, and imprisoned him. The aim of the Mystic Clan is to incite a servile insurrection among blacks in the southwest and Deep South by urging the "malevolent serf[s]" to assert an "equality of hate." In the disorder and terror of the uprising, Murrell's Clan may rise to power, manipulating the ignorant blacks; or if the rebellion looks as if it will fail, they can use it as a cover to loot the plantations, with the cooperation of their black dupes.

Power in the Clan is concentrated in the "Grand Council," with chapters in every community throughout the region. The Council itself meets secretly in a swamp hideout, protected by primitive jungle. Their strategy with the blacks will be to select the most "vicious and daring" of them, then "commence poisoning their minds by telling them how monstrously they are mistreated; that they are entitled to their freedom as much as their masters, and that all of the wealth of the country is the proceeds of black people's labor . . . then sting them with their own degraded condition, by comparing it with the pomp and ease" of their masters. Murrell's agents are told to represent themselves as emissaries from the Free States, and instruct the blacks to "butcher every white man in the slaveholding states." Initiation into this bloody mission requires a bloodcurdling oath sworn on a skeleton, which magically "spoke," and other ceremonies of a Grand Guignol character. Although the plot is appalling, Howard cannot withhold the comparison of his antihero to "Alexander or . . . Napoleon." When Murrell's impulse is thwarted, the rage of the criminal underclass builds. Now Murrell, an Indian-hater/avenger type who has perversely chosen the upper classes of his own race for an object, determines that the basis of the organization will not be profit but "unrelenting massacre. . . . The negroes . . . were promised revenge for past wrongs, possession of the delicate-skinned daughters and wifes of their former masters. . . . Day by day the dark sedition widened."[38]

The downfall of Murrell is recounted in detail in Howard's second book, which features the career of the man hunter Virgil Stewart. Stewart is a diligent small entrepreneur and land speculator who sells merchandise to Indians and settlers and operates a small farm. Asked by a friend to help recover a stolen slave, Stewart comes upon Murrell, and recognizes him; but dissembles, and becomes friendly with the murderous conspirator, learning from him the gory details of Murrell's business. Murrell takes his "friend" to the swamp hideout, for induction into the Mystic Clan. The hideout is described as "the Garden of Eden," a wilderness paradise like the Dark and Bloody Ground of Kentucky—mingling wilderness beauty and fecundity with fearsome shapes of terror and racial war. Stewart, alias "Hues," gains the trust of the conspirators by means of a speech in which he cites the law of the jungle, by which the strongest rule, as justification for their actions: "We consider every thing under the control of our power as our right." Like the "pioneer race" in Hall's account of Moredock, the right of conquest is the only law they recognize. With tongue in cheek, Hues/Stewart compares them to Roman patriots, striking for Liberty.[39]

His situation is not unlike that of the Indian captive—or better, of Daniel Boone among the Indians, feigning acceptance of the ritual of adoption, but yearning for his home and planning escape. Seizing an opportunity, Stewart returns to his community and exposes the plot. Vigilante organizations form (Murrell's Mafia may control the official structure), and the region is swept by a wave of what an unfriendly eye might term witch-hunting. Murrell, himself caught and jailed, turns state's evidence. Suspected blacks and white conspirators are hunted down, lynched or legally executed, or otherwise punished. Yet so powerful is the conspiracy that, years later, Stewart still fears their desire for vengeance will dog him to death.[40]

The fear roused by Murrell's conspiracy was genuine, and well reported in the regional and national press. What Howard and other dime novelists made of Murrell was a national myth, embodiment of destructive forces within a society cut off from expansion at the borders, aggression against passive nature and alien Indians. The story invokes the class/race tensions inherent in the existence of slavery and ties them to poor-white dissatis- factions through the character of Murrell. These in turn are magnified by association with radical abolitionism, "a poisonous swarm" from the "great northern hive of fanatics and incendiaries."[41]

The specter that Murrell's career awakes is the specter of a slave uprising, a war of races that will at the same time be a war of classes, motivated by the resentment of rich and poor. Wars with red savages speak of expansion and progress; those with black savages and white "renegades" speak of social self-destruction. In the backwash of the Frontier, the con- frontation with class differences and conflicts is inescapable; the idea of the *permanence* and necessity of class subordination is inescapable. Yet the Frontier ideology, the Frontier impulse, requires that systems of subordina- tion and limitation be overturned and exploded.

But the same Frontier values that generate the peculiar form of "dan- gerous class" represented by a Murrell offer an antidote to that danger in the figure of the vigilante, a prototype of the private citizen detective. Virgil Stewart is an early version of the type: a common man who is drawn almost inadvertently into the path of adventure; who gains intimacy with the dan- gerous class through a form of disguised captivity; but who ultimately turns the dangerous class's talents for renegadery, conspiracy, and extralegal vio- lence against itself. His adventure parallels that of the Indian fighter, with the difference that for Daniel Boone or Leatherstocking the dangerous class is an unambiguously identified racial "other." Although racial "darkness" taints Murrell and his Clan, it does not entirely define them. Like the Indian fighter, the vigilante is usually represented as a necessary figure in a rela- tively primitive state of society. James Hall delineates the character of the vigilante in the same volume in which he sets forth the character of the Indian hater, and he represents the exponent of "Linch's law" as the representative man of a transitional stage from the world of the Indian hater and pioneer to that of the completed settlement. Like the Indian hater, the vigilante ful- fills a social and civilizing mission by exercising a privilege of violence that goes beyond legal or conventional prohibitions. He thus shares some of the "dangerous" character of the criminals he pursues—just as the Indian hater shares the traits of the savage.[42]

This privilege can safely be exercised only within the primitive frame- work; and if the vigilante pursues his enterprise after the establishment of civilized law, he becomes as antisocial a figure as the Indian hater who persists in secret murder after the time of race war has passed. Hall deals with this dangerous potential anecdotally by informing us that the vigilante abnegates his privilege in deference to the arrival of legitimate and effective law enforcement. The vigilante is more easily assimilated into the political structure of a completed settlement than the Indian hater, for all of his adventure has been within the boundaries of society and defensive of social bonds.

The dubious element in the vigilante figure is not, however, so easily dispelled. We see the persistence of the "dangerous class" identification in Cooper's portrayal of the Bush clan in *The Prairie*. The ending of Virgil Stewart's adventure also represents the vigilante as permanently altered by his adventure, and thus isolated from full participation in his society. Stewart's relation to the society he has rescued is as problematic as that of the returned captive Mary Rowlandson to hers: Stewart is driven into incognito by fear of Murrell's surviving confederates, who have infiltrated legitimate government; and even those whom he has saved doubt the incredible tale he has to tell, and mistrust him for having so readily played the "Clansman," leaving him in a position of moral isolation.

The problem of the dangerous classes behind the frontier, and the vigilante solution to that problem, persisted in both social fact and literary mythology, as we shall see. The vigilante is the prototype of a kind of Frontier hero that would emerge after the Civil War as a substitute for the Indian-fighter/scout type represented by Leatherstocking. His personal characteristics and the special form of his adventure would be fully developed in a new genre, set in the cities rather than the wilderness—the detective story. But the vigilante would also be of persistent importance as a social phenomenon, and not only in Frontier districts. The principle of vigilantism is the assertion of a privilege of extralegal violence in a social setting where some form of law already exists. Consequently it is always a political phenomenon, and may verge on being a revolutionary one. The original vigilantes of California in the 1850s and Montana in the 1860s directed their operations against elected officials and law enforcement officers who were in league with criminal gangs, and used the power of office to protect and mask criminal enterprises. Other movements like the Regulators of eighteenth-century Carolina and the Sons of Liberty employed vigilante-like tactics against officials representing policies that were deemed tyrannous and in violation of "natural rights"—though the officials were not guilty of any common-law crime. Opponents of Radical Reconstruction after the Civil War justified the vigilante terrorism of the Klan in similar terms, representing the Republican state governments as both tyrannous impositions and criminal conspiracies. Similar apologies were made on behalf of the vigilante movement sponsored by the large ranchers of Wyoming in 1888–92; and local and state governments have sometimes encouraged vigilante movements to suppress political movements otherwise protected by law—as happened during the suppression of the IWW in 1917–20.[43]

In all of these cases, vigilantism represents itself as the expression of the will of civilized society as a whole—just as the Indian fighter is taken for the representative of the whole race. But for the vigilante the pretense is thin: in every case, he acts as the agent of only one class or element in his society, asserts his privilege to act and administer violence as if it were mandated by the whole, and even circumvents the will of the majority to achieve his ends. The vigilante identifies his enemy as a tribelike entity

within society, devoted to conspiratorial codes of secret purpose and procedure. Yet the vigilante's own procedures are mirror images of those followed by the tribe or dangerous class he attacks. Since that class probably
represents the interests and views of some part of the community—however
small—there will always be those who will plausibly assert that it is the
vigilante movement that is the conspiracy against the whole, and the supporters of vigilantism, who are the tribe within the settlements, the dangerous class. Virgil Stewart is never free of the taint of linkage to Murrell. The
vigilante as mythic or political response to the dilemma of society's internal
division remains as much an expression of the problem as a vision of its
solution.

CHAPTER 7

Utopia/Dystopia: Plantation, Factory, and City, 1820–1845

The Myth of the Frontier offered one solution to the social divisions arising from economic expansion—the promise of abundant free land and resources for the great mass of the population. When it appeared that the supply of frontier land was approaching a point of exhaustion, the Frontier Myth became a prophecy of disorder, if not of disaster. So long as citizens of the republic were conceived in the terms established by the Myth—as active and ambitious pursuers of wealth and power—the closing of the Frontier would be seen as the clamping down of a safety valve, producing the intolerable internal pressures that are born of the competition of classes for limited resources. The qualities that made a Daniel Boone would be perverted into the predatory commercialism of a Simon Suggs or the outright criminality of a Murrell; and the only counter to a regime of Suggses would be one presided over by authoritative soldier-aristocrats, capable of overawing and disciplining the unruly multitude.

But the literary mythology of the period was not restricted to the vocabulary of the Frontier Myth, and it offered alternative ways of conceiving the character of the citizen and the social consequences of the Metropolitanization of the continent. The Metropolis was not in fact the obsolete survival of Old World decadence that Jefferson invoked in his darker moments. Cities and their immediate hinterlands were the focus of as much and more entrepreneurial energy as the West. Cities were places to which the ambitious artisan or the underemployed farmer's child could go to earn wages and better his or her condition. If Frontier expansion was checked, and the Simon Suggses of the Frontier ran rampant in the backwash, then the city was to be seen as the place in which America's future was being created. Even the South, whose Metropolis was no city but the old-plantation region of the Atlantic littoral, affirmed its version of Metropolitan culture in the exaltation of a "planter aristocracy."

A notable current in literary fiction during this period took a positive view of these developments and developed fictional microcosms that gave shape to fantasies and expectations about the new Metropolitan society. However, these fictions do not exclude the Frontier from their apprehension of reality; indeed, they embody the Myth of the Frontier as a necessary dialectical opposite, and they deploy a similar symbolic language that links class, sex, and race. They even bear out the ideological premise of the Frontier Myth, which sees a regime of class subordination as the necessary consequence of the closing of the Frontier era. The new regime of the Metropolis is regarded as a positive and progressive development; but the literature does this with some awareness that it is abandoning belief in the traditional democratic ethic of aggrandizing and liberating the individual.

These fictions evade the problem of social order bequeathed by the Frontier Myth by obscuring or denying the bases of class conflicts. The Myth of the Frontier achieves a similar belief by imagining that the natural environment is so rich in resources as to render competition harmless, class conflict absurd, and monopoly almost impossible. But the Metropolitan alternative begins with the premise that such a Frontier environment is rapidly disappearing. It therefore bases its faith on a reconception of the character of the citizenry. The fictions of an idealized Metropolis reject the nation of land-hungry and ambitious men-on-the-make conceived in the Myth of the Frontier, and present instead a citizenry whose essential instincts are docile, dependent, and domestic.

In a sense, this fantasy is a restatement of the Jefferson/Cooper ideal of the yeoman farmer; but American society had of course changed since those myths were articulated, and so had the symbolism in which the social character of the citizenry was represented. As the mythical Jacksonian yeoman ceased to be the deferential subordinate of the squire and became the upwardly mobile farmer-speculator-entrepreneur, his abandoned characteristics of dependence, docility, and domesticity were projected onto subordinate races, classes, and sexes—Indians, blacks, women, and children. These were precisely the classes who were the first targets of the aggressive expansionism of the Jacksonian period, and of the industrialization that followed it. The 1828–35 period saw the completion of a massive project of Indian removal from the South; and at the same time, the expansion of plantation agriculture and textile manufacturing brought more black slaves and female or child workers into the nascent industrial system as a primitive proletariat.

In the ideology of social relations arising from these developments we can see the beginnings of a dangerous contradiction in American values. It first appears in the contrast between the active (male) white citizen of the Frontier Myth and the passive (female) nonwhite laborer of the Metropolis. If this is the imagery in which classes and productive roles are conceived, then it is apparent that a white man's acceptance of the status of proletarian (wage worker without property) is equivalent to accepting an unsexing and a racial "degradation." As long as the proletariat was predominantly female and black—with native-born white male workers enjoying the status of independent "mechanics" and artisans—this contradiction could be evaded. But as the mechanization of manufacturing processes proceeded, the class of independent artisans tended to split into entrepreneurial artisans (who made a successful transition to the status of capitalist) and proletarianized artisans (i.e., artisans compelled by necessity to work at wages they could not control, using tools or processes not their own). The demand for unskilled labor in the mechanized factories and the vital sectors of railroad, canal, and house building, coupled with famines and revolutions in Europe, brought in waves of foreign immigrants from Ireland and Germany after 1846; and their employment at once confirmed the degrading character of proletarianization and obscured the symbolic sexual dividing line between "operatives" and "mechanics." The labor of proletarianized workers was now to be seen as "foreign," as well as "black" and "female"; but the foreign workers were as often men as women, and they proved that white masculine labor could indeed become degraded labor.

The literary mythology of the Jacksonian period thus presents a two-tiered representation of America, which juxtaposes "masculine" and "feminine" worlds. In the opposition of the virile Frontier and the effeminate Metropolis, this dualism finds its largest expression. But within the fictional microcosms of Frontier and Metropolis, a similar dualism appears. We have seen how in the Cooperian code the symbolic female acts as a goad to action and moral check on the virility of the Frontier hero. In the Metropolis a similar juxtaposition of masculine and feminine "characteristics" appears in the opposite imperative, masculine entrepreneurship and female resignation; but the resolution is somewhat different. This vision is elaborated in the literary mythology of the "Old South," and in the literature that celebrates the model industrial development of Lowell, Massachusetts. These works present a utopian vision of the social politics of the new order, and the relationship of Metropolis to Frontier. But as we shall see, this utopian vision was inadequate as a means of interpreting and justifying the new order of industrialization. It was challenged from within not only by the resistance of urban workingmen to the role assigned them, but by the refusal of blacks and women to fit the mythic mold established for them; and it was challenged from without by the renewal of Frontier expansion and the persistence of the values embodied in the Frontier Myth.

The central structure of this new ideology was the political arrangement of "paternalism," or (to use a more comprehensive term) "domestication." This involves the projection onto the social and political realms of the values and power relationships characteristic of a "traditional" (read "idealized") bourgeois family. The ruler of this microcosm is a benign but powerful father, whose moral authority and political legitimacy is authenticated by the "natural" sentiments of spousal and filial affection and respect. The father, for his part, mitigates the rigor of his authority by the essentially affectionate and protective attitude he takes toward his dependents; and the dependents, for their part, accept their place in his universe.

This ideology served to mask the changes that were in fact transforming relations between proprietors and dependents both inside and outside the family, as a consequence of economic development. The more problematic such relations became, the more the ideology of paternalism was invoked as a way of containing the resentments of those dependents from breaking out into political dissidence. Recent studies of the development of slavery and the plantation system in the nineteenth century have emphasized the peculiar importance of the paternalistic or domestic ideology as an organizing principle in Southern thought and behavior. Similar ideological formulations emerged at nearly the same time in the North, particularly in relation to the formation of the new mill towns of New England. This suggests that despite the real differences between northern free labor and southern slavery, there were important similarities in the problems of planters and mill owners, and a tendency to resort to similar ideological solutions.[1]

THE PLANTATION AS UTOPIA

The American South was an important "predictor" of what a post-Frontier society might become. Like other Americans in 1784–1820, Southerners had seen the vast territory between the mountains and the Mississippi as a grand field of economic expansion. The southern frontiersman, like his northern counterpart, could expect to gain land for farming and/or speculation by entering Indian territory and establishing his claim. But because his Metropolis was organized around slave labor, the southern pioneer had a different notion of the status to and the means by which he might rise. Slaves, seen by law as capital goods, offered the pioneer the chance to move from subsistence to commercial farming, and eventually to a plantation system that approached the industrial in its scale and organization. But the planter saw himself not as employer/exploiter, but as patriarch, as the baronial ruler of a small tribe enjoying the caste marks of aristocratic superiority.[2]

Southern pioneering was built from the start on the direct and explicit linkage between the cheap-land and the cheap-labor Frontiers—a linkage that was not so apparent in the rest of the nation until after the Civil War. If this situation doubled the kinds of resources available to southern pioneering, it contained a dual liability—the Southerner had to fear the closure of two Frontiers, not just one, and the termination of the African slave trade in 1808 did indeed close off the primitive reserve of black labor. The natural increase of the domestic slave population compensated somewhat for any shortage, but in its expansive phases the southern economy experienced an anxiety about the labor supply that echoed the fears of northern manufacturers.

The economics and agronomics of cotton culture also imposed different pressures on southern perceptions of the Frontier safety valve. Cotton profits encouraged the cultivation of large acreages, but at the same time the crop "mined" the soil. It therefore appeared that the South might be using up its land heritage more rapidly than the North. This situation gave a peculiar shape to the style and direction of southern expansionism. Where Northerners looked to "empty" lands like Oregon for agrarian expansion, Southerners as often looked to the populated regions of Latin America, where a large pool of domestic labor existed alongside undeveloped natural resources. If the yeoman farmer was a pious fiction in the North, in the South the military aristocrat was the Frontier hero—a chevalier, a conquistador, subduing and subordinating the masses of a savage race, the conscious agent not of individual ambition alone, but of corporate will.[3]

Southerners confronted the possibility of closed Frontiers in terms that directed their attention as much to Metropolitan conflicts as to the limitations of nature. It was not merely the intractability of the Great American

Desert or the power of Mexico they envisioned, but an opposing force located within the Metropolitan heart of American society. The boom-bust cycles of the cotton market and the dependence of southern capitalists on northern financial institutions—themselves tied to hostile economic and ideological interest groups among northern manufacturers—fostered a sense of beleaguerment at the borders. Slavery could not expand northward, but free labor might well have a southern Frontier; and to the west, the expansion of slavery faced both the hostility of northern farmers and a climate inhospitable to most southern staples.

In the 1830s southern ideologists, of whom Vice President and later Senator John C. Calhoun was the most important, began transplanting the terms of Jeffersonian agrarianism into a political language appropriate to their new circumstances. They began with the premise that Jefferson's "natural aristocracy" was now a social reality: it was, in fact, the planter class of the older southern states, augmented by the traditional merchant and landowning elites of the North. The transformation of economic production by industrialization and plantation farming, coupled with the natural limits to Frontier expansion, had brought about a premature closure to the period of agrarian expansion prophesied by Jefferson. Whereas an equal access to resources had guaranteed both upward mobility and social peace, the new conditions threatened the peculiar balance of aristocracy and democracy that Jeffersonian policies had achieved. The problem was now one of protecting the power, status, and economic efficiency of the existing "aristocracy" of land, factory, and bank owners from the frustrated rage of masses doomed to eventual disappointment in their quest for upward mobility. How were the lower orders to be placated, without the carrot of expansion held before their eyes as an inducement to submit? How particularly was the southern system to survive, if it excluded poor whites from the laboring masses and the planter aristocracy alike?[4]

The growing financial and political dominance of the North was, as Calhoun saw it, the result of its shift from an expansive to an intensive pattern of development. Yet the commitment of Northerners to democratic ideologies prevented them from perceiving what a southern planter could not avoid knowing: that intensive exploitation depended on labor discipline, and hence was inimical to the infinite subdivision of power. The interest of the capitalist, like that of the planter, is the exploitation of the worker's labor for profit. At some point, the clash of interests will become real: perhaps when the Frontier carrot has been devoured. In the South, this situation was graphically revealed. The continuation of cotton culture required an ever greater reserve of territory. Yet at the same time, climate and soil requirements limited the potential locales of westward extension; and the presence of great numbers of smallholdings forbade its extension to the north. The dependence of the plantation on blacks made more graphic the distance between proprietor and laborer, and made the consequences of worker discontent seem all the more threatening.

Calhoun saw in the growth of northern industries—under that protective tariff which cut against his own section's interests—a threat analogous to Jefferson's fear of the growth of cities, landless urban populations, and unchecked immigration. Where Jefferson had simply correlated the European "city" with the attendant ills of class struggle and mob violence and sought to avoid Metropolitanization, Calhoun acknowledged the necessity of industrialization and concentration of wealth; but he foresaw how the spread of industrialism would inevitably tend to divide society into ever more powerless and impoverished workers, and ever more powerful and greedy capitalists. As the wages of laborers declined before the pressure of monopolized industry, discontent would intensify, and there would be "no want of leaders . . . to excite and direct" the poor toward social revolution.[5]

To forestall such an outcome, northern utopians like the Brook Farmers proposed various socialistic and agrarian nostrums; and the Jacksonian rhetoric about a "nation of small farmers" likewise "dealt" with the problem by proposing to ignore or circumvent the industrial process. What Calhoun (and his followers) proposed was an alliance of northern and southern conservatives. In such an alliance, the South might play two different roles. The first is that of providing a broad and stable base for conservatism. Her peculiar labor system and agricultural economy exempted her from the ills of the North: her lower classes were docile and contented because slavery guaranteed their lifelong nurture; her upper classes were therefore more stable, more firmly in control. The potential rivalry of the poorer whites could be minimized by allowing the slave states to expand to the west, and by reinforcing the doctrines of white supremacy. These measures would guarantee to the ambitious lower-class southern white a continually growing basis of land resources and a permanent class of exploitable slave laborers. It would then appear that there was open access to the future achievement of landed property and the quasi-aristocratic status of "planter," and in the present a politically privileged status that sharply distinguished even the poorest white citizen from the lowest class in society.[6]

In addition, the South offered a model for reform of the northern labor system, an alternative structure of organization. The central paradox of American society—the contradiction of agrarian and industrial values and modes of life and production—was reconciled in the plantation system (and its associated industries): reconciled in a way peculiarly advantageous to the existing holders of wealth. The planters themselves were increasingly conscious of this, and their political rhetoric took on the tones of a critique of northern industrialism from the viewpoint of a society that had achieved the utopian resolution the North sought. Lowell had its women and children, a docile and malleable work force, and yet management was compelled to exploit and repress them, and ultimately to replace them with an alien and sullen labor force. In the South the docility of labor under patriarchal rule was (so the myth said) traditionally established, and its black work force long since domesticated and reconciled to its station by the tutelary labors of the master class. The necessities of political argument required southern spokesmen to distort their claims by contrasting the protected black with the exploited mechanic, the rural plantation with the urban mill. But the direction of their argument was toward a clearer conception of what the whole society might look like after the period of Jacksonian competition closed and the distribution of resources was completed.[7]

Calhoun's ideological forays were supported by the novelists of the "plantation school," many of them Northerners, who saw in the southern plantation a utopian model of industrial relations in a Jeffersonian society. These fictions utilized all sorts of plot forms, from historical romance in the Fenimore Cooper vein to domestic novels-of-manners. What they have in common is a representation of the plantation as a model for civilized social relations. It is a social microcosm presided over by a benign patriarchal figure, whose values are entirely shaped by the need to care for those dependent on him. Women, children, and black slaves make up his large extended family. The particular worship of idealized femininity is the moral center of the microcosm; and the sympathetic and careful administration of the slaves extends the family metaphor into a model of social relations. The active, aggressive, masculine principle is vested in the chivalrous young Southerners who are or will be the inheritors of this microcosm. Their physical and moral lineaments are predicted by Cooper's "Virginians" and military aristocrats. However, the southern novelist is as much or more concerned to show this figure as potential paterfamilias as he is to reveal his capacity for heroic and violent exploits. Southern writers of historical frontier romances like William Alexander Carruthers, Robert M. Bird, and William Gilmore Simms rarely allow their aristocrat heroes to be subordinate to Frontier plebeians—even in the wilderness their superiority is clear. Moreover, there is usually a strong emphasis on the importance of the hero's return to civilization, and to a dominant social role. The hero of Simms's *The Yemassee* (1835) is none other than the royal governor of South Carolina and a British nobleman in disguise; the hero of Bird's *Nick of the Woods* (1837) abandons the Frontier and returns to Virginia as soon as he unmasks the plot that has deprived him of his just inheritance.[8]

But the mainstream of plantation fiction centers on the plantation itself, and paints an idealized portrait of its pastoral pleasures, its familial social relations, its old-fashioned courtesies and deferences. The heroic qualities of the young men are abstracted into a special kind of "virility," which is offered as the special property of southern manhood. One of the conventions of the form is the projection of social and sectional rivalries into sexual politics, and the resolution of conflict in the marriage of a northern girl to the southern man. The sexual identities of the partners suggest that the reconciliation requires the submission of one to the other, with the virile or southern position dominant. The imagery of the plantation novel assimilates to the planter class an abstraction of those heroic traits which had been associated with various figures (and classes) in the Myth of the Frontier.

The language of familial relations masked the essentially exploitive character of the relationship between master and slave. The related concept of "tutelage" masked the real form of labor discipline, which had the character of regimentation. Even Andrew Jackson had invoked the government of the army as a model of the relations that ought to pertain between managers and subordinates in domestic life; and he saw no incompatibility between the aims and manner of military subordination and those of familial paternalism. Even when the setting of a plantation novel is not on or near the frontier, the planter-hero has the character of the Cooperian soldier-aristocrat: breeding, virility, courage, chivalry, a strong sense of race, all the traits needed to identify and defeat the Maguas of the world, and to found dynasties with the Alice Munros.[9]

It is clear that the intention implicit in this imagery is that of representing the plantation as the ideal form of American society, and the final expression of those dynamic and progressive tendencies associated with our history of expansion and conquest. This seems a very optimistic mythology, and when we consider the expansive and prosperous character (despite cyclical depressions) of the cotton business between 1835 and 1860 we might consider it as the mythological expression of the ideology of a rising class.

But the fact is that both the ideology and the mythology of the plantation were anything but optimistic about the future. Most plantation novels are set in times of economic contraction, rather than boom times; and the threat of mortgage foreclosures is as much a part of the plantation scene as Indian raids in a Cooper novel.

Even more threatful was the resistance of blacks to their continued enslavement, and the potential for a division of interest and political commitment between planters and poor whites. The utopian image of the patriarchal plantation was only half of a schizophrenic division in the South's way of imagining its politics: the other half held that the planter was a lonely agent of civilization, living and working in a village of African savages, for whom civilized discipline was hard to learn, painful to suffer, and tempting to throw off. When actual slave revolts occurred (or were rumored to be in preparation), Southerners reverted to the traditional exterminationist presumptions of Jefferson, and to the mythology of Indian warfare which defined the course and objectives of a racial war. The Nat Turner Rebellion of 1831 produced just this sort of response: an identification of the rebels as savages bent on indiscriminate slaughter, even to the extermination of the white race in Virginia; and the evocation in the whites of the reciprocal Indian-hater response, tending toward the extermination of the black savages.[10]

The problem with the plantation myth was that the people who created and gave credence to it were no more capable than northern capitalists of rejecting the central tenet of the Myth of the Frontier—that economies and societies must continue to grow or they will perish in social cataclysm. The plantation microcosm could hold together only in a society in equilibrium, but equilibrium was economically impossible. The depletion of the soil alone was a guarantee that ultimately the plantation would have to grow, transform itself, or die. To improve plantation agronomy or productivity required capitalization, and that created the risk of failure through debt. To provide for the needs of all those ambitious and virile younger sons, let alone the more ambitious and capable of the poor whites, the sphere of plantation agriculture would have to grow. But this would bring the ambitions of planters into conflict with those of entrepreneurs and small farmers. To expand the plantation system, or to improve the productivity of existing land and labor, would require the derangement of the stable "family" of slaves and masters, either through the upgrading of a class of skilled blacks or through the breaking up of slave families via sale for removal to new plantations. Either of these changes threatened the labor peace of the South from within.

In the end, Southern ideology failed to reconcile the contradictions between an ideology of aggressive expansion and an ideology of utopian stability. The proponents of slavery expansion had ultimately to challenge the sectional compromises of 1820 and 1850 by projecting an expansion of slavery into the Caribbean and western territories; while at the same time, they asserted a commonality of interest and technique between themselves and the northern conservatives in creating a politically subservient working class.[11]

THE FACTORY AS PLANTATION

Despite the obvious differences between cotton plantation and textile manufacturing, and between a wage-labor and slave-labor force, the two types of enterprise shared important similarities of structure and iconography. Some important early forms of industrial enterprise had in fact been organized as "plantations," drawing the agricultural and mining activities of a whole district into the organization of the industrial "plant." Joseph E. Walker's 1966 study, *Hopewell Village*, describes such organization in an iron-making community in Pennsylvania. Mining communities in Pennsylvania likewise involved the development of a community of dependent laborers and tenants, engaging in a variety of economic production, centering around and dominated by the management of the mines. The use of "plant" to describe an industrial complex derives in part from "plantation"; and the word plantation itself was in the seventeenth and eighteenth centuries applied to all colonial enterprises.

If the chain of usage suggests anything, it is that the "plant" or "plantation" was to be conceived of as a kind of "colony," planted in a wilderness, in which the wild land and semibarbarous men were to be "developed" and disciplined to productive labor. Both were essentially "industrial" in character, combining large work forces and capital investment and engaging in intensive exploitation of both labor and natural resources, for large-scale commercial production. And both the plantation and the mill town were communities of "dependent laborers" organized around the work place, dominated respectively by the master and owner. The plantation had its infamous slave quarters, Lowell its famous company boardinghouses, where rigid parietal rules enforced industrial discipline outside the factory as well as in. To be sure, the female work force of Lowell was free and used its freedom to attempt to change its conditions; but so, in its own way, did the slave labor force of the South.[12]

The mythology of plantation and factory takes as its wishful premise the realization of a social order characterized by that harmony of classes and interests envisioned in the agrarian myth of Crèvecoeur and Jefferson. Both specifically invoke the myth's iconography. In the plantation and factory, social positions were imagined as stable, divided between a paternalistic aristocratic figure—the Jeffersonian meritocrat in place rather than in potential—and a group of dependent and childlike plebeians, looking to the master for work, protection, and moral guidance. Although the myth lacked a coherent economic program, it did have a clear concept of the form of society most suited to natural law: a society in which the relationships between men are determined not by the cash nexus, but by organic or familial relationships, in which the strong nurture and protect the weak, and the superior rule with the consent of the inferior. In such a society, the absolute dependence of slave on master and worker on capitalist would be tempered and offset by paternalism, and class relations represented by an image of familial bonds (husband-wife, parent-child) rather than by images of conflict (Jacksonian competition, Indian wars). The owner-managerial elite, on plantation or in factory, sought to cloak themselves and their enterprises in the traditional imagery of the landed aristocracy. If the aristocrat was, as Cooper defined him, the patriarchal ruler of a pastoral domain, venerated as a moral superior by both dependents and civic equals, then this was the guise in which the parvenu exploiter of work gangs and assembly lines had to see himself and his operations.[13]

The image of factory and plantation as havens of benevolent and tutelary paternalism set those institutions apart from the rough-and-tumble world of entrepreneurial competition and the commercial exploitation of labor under the rules of laissez-faire. To the extent that rugged individualism was indeed the American ideal, this difference marked planter and mill owner as inimical to the American dream. However, as we have seen, Americans were ambivalent about the consequences and desirability of a regime of pure individualism from the start, and from Puritan times had proposed schemes of social organization making for greater solidarity, unanimity, and discipline.

This tendency persisted in the idealism of reformers before the Civil War, who proposed to confront the evils of commercial individualism by strengthening the family as a model of social relations; and to deal with specific evils by creating institutions set apart from the rough-and-tumble, in which paternalistic tutelage could work to convert the raw material of individual disorder into a set of truly social beings. This was the period of what David Rothman calls "The Discovery of the Asylum," in which models of life- and labor-discipline like those of plantation and factory were applied to (or proposed for) the reform of prisons, workhouses, schools, mental institutions, and Indian reservations—institutions dealing with the "dangerous classes," with fallen women, and with the underclasses, with children, with madmen, with savages. The association of these groups had been suggested in the mythic language of Cooper; but it was now becoming a more explicit and precise way of distinguishing social classes.[14]

In its earliest phase, factory labor was presented as a pathway to achieving the same status of proprietorship and independence that the Jeffersonian yeoman farmer was supposed to be aiming at. The architecture and iconography of Lowell emphasized the analogy and the connection between the idealized rural life of agrarian myth and factory life and labor. If anything, factory work was an intensified and improved form of "cultivation," when compared with farming. Its productivity was higher, by certain measures; its techniques more modern and progressive; its return in wages was supposed to be higher. Even the moral economy of the ideal factory was an improvement on the freehold of Crèvecoeur's American farmer. The latter garnered homey moral truths from observing the bees and manuring his fields; the factory girl, said the Lowell panegyrists, was entering a "manufacturing college," where she could labor along with other young ladies of "good family," in a morally and intellectually "improving" atmosphere. Her labor would be temporary, not a substitute for the maternal role. Moreover, her wages would serve to pay off debts on the family farm, or to send a brother to professional school. Thus her work would exceed that of farm work in its financial and social effects, saving the farm and even providing for upward mobility in the family.[15]

There were, however, elements in the factory situation that undercut the agrarian imagery and Jacksonian pretensions. The labor itself removed workers from the farm, and linked them together in organized groups under the direction of foremen and supervisors. This hierarchical relationship also figured in the extra-factory life of the girls—Lowell was famous for the blue laws and regulations that restricted the socializing of the employed women for the sake of preserving their moral character. Seen in its best light, this relationship was analogous to the "tutelage" extended by the Jeffersonian patrician to his social and racial inferiors—a tutelage described in Crèvecoeur's account of Andrew the Hebridean, for example. The premise of tutelage was its temporariness, its transiency. The test of its validity as a form of American democracy was whether or not it issued in the creation of a new class of independent entrepreneurs. But the economics of the factory system were all against this. Manufacturing required a relatively stable, docile, and large supply of labor: the preference for women and children as workers reflects this need—it constitutes a deliberate selection of the least mobile sector of the population as the basis of industrial labor.

Yet even so there was labor strife at Lowell between management and a work force compelled by condition to set feminine docility aside. Even sympathetic observers noted that the girls were alienated from the healthful life of the open air, were sickened by or experienced psychological harm from their exploitation. The company boardinghouses that were so much a part of the moral-social order of Lowell were always contrasted with the "old country homes" from which the girls had come. As conditions in the mill towns changed, the requirements of industrial labor made the "manufacturing college" idea seem untenable as a vision of the factory. By 1846, on the eve of the great influx of Irish fleeing the potato famine, factory recruiters were combing the farthest reaches of New England for female labor, driving "a long, low, black wagon, termed a 'slaver.'" The "commander" of this vessel was paid by the head, and given premiums to bring girls from a distance, since the farther their home the less likely they would be able to leave the factory.[16]

This folk association of slavery and industrial labor is attested also in the written record. Rebecca Harding Davis's *Margret Howth* (1862) represents the factory as an insidious trap, the place where Davis's title character, daughter of a fallen aristocracy of birth and breeding, comes to suffer her degradation. The power of the factory to degrade and distort is represented for Davis by the figure of a girl dwarf hunchback, who seems also to be a mulatto. The message is clear: the factory takes noble incarnations of all that woman means (Margret) and converts them into physically and morally ugly creatures, whose body and blood is "polluted."[17]

M. W. Tyler's *A Book Without a Title* (1855) carries an even more explicit message. Her heroine, Mira Dana, comes to the factories at Lowell to aid her brother's quest for a professional education. There she faces exploitation and a degrading factory discipline, against which she turns, defying both the mill owners and the male-oriented society that has made her labor merely a function of her brother's ambitions. She leads the mill girls on a strike, which is partly successful. This in turn leads to a brief marriage to a sea captain, who respects her for her independence and spunk. But after his death, she weds a southern planter; and it requires only a brief stay on the plantation to convince her that the life of wife to such a man is very much like the life of a Negro slave; and that life in turn compares at quite a number of points to the factory life she fled. Tyler's book is extraordinary, in that it attacks the Lowell-plantation myth at its root: the myth of female/black dependence. Still, despite its somewhat atypical and advanced ideological stance, it does draw on a similar body of associations—and shows how the same myth that could simultaneously give comfort to the planter and manufacturer could appear to the worker as the realization of nightmare.[18]

This "nightmare" was realized at Lowell with the shift to Irish immigrant labor in the 1840s and 1850s: at this point there was no pretense that Lowell was other than a factory town. If the earlier association of women and blacks had been readily made, that between Irish and blacks was still more dramatic. For one thing, both groups were perceived by native workers as alien in race and spirit; both groups were feared for their potential as reserve armies of the unemployed, acting to depress wages by increasing the labor supply. There was a tendency among upper-class New Englanders to associate the two groups. Hawthorne, for example, responded to both as if they were subhuman, and this was an association that increased with the passage of time. During the Civil War, abolitionists observing the conditions of plantation life at first hand liked to compare the blacks (with whom they were sympathetic) favorably with the Irish; and minstrel-show stereotypes of both groups emphasized similar qualities of shiftiness, stupidity, and brutality. The publication of *Miscegenation* (1864), a Democratic pamphlet designed to scare voters away from Lincoln and the abolition of slavery during the Civil War, drew on this connection in its setting forth of a hoax: a program supposedly being considered by Lincoln to amalgamate the Irish with the blacks, as the two lowest forms of humanity, to produce a large and subordinate work force. Herbert Gutman, in *The Black Family in Slavery and Freedom*, points out that northern and southern elites were alike in depicting the poorer classes of whites—"poor white" and Irish—as being childlike in their need for control and tutelage by the elite classes, as being without self-reliance and ambition, and as like "semi-savages" or mere "animals in search of a richer and fresher pasture."[19]

The portrayal of plantation and factories as utopias of successful and stable paternalism suggests a parallelism in the developing myth/ideologies of industrialism in the North and the South. But the social realities of both sections were such that these fantasies could not provide ideological antidotes for the causes of internal division and instability. The literature reflects not only the paternal values of the planter and the Lowell mill owner, but also the unreconciled elements of resistance from both the laboring classes and from persistent entrepreneurial ambitions in the rising classes. Southern fears of northern abolitionism and the uprising of "contented" slaves on their plantations attests to one form of this fear; and the gingerly substitution of slave for free labor in southern manufacturing enterprises attests to the slaveholders' respect for the resentments and the self-interest of the poor whites. The facts of mill town strikes and the literary insurrections of Margret Howth and M. W. Tyler attest to similar proletarian resistance in the North. Moreover, paternalism in both sections was imperiled by the ambitions of entrepreneurial adventurers, who would risk the stability of class relations and the North-South political balance in order to intensify their exploitation of mill labor, or would increase the supply of workers by importing immigrants or reviving the slave trade, or would seek new lands for plantations in the West or the Caribbean.

The bubble of paternalist utopianism was pricked by the persistence of the commitment to progress through economic expansion in the entrepreneurial mode, and by the persistence of the Jacksonian belief that economic mobility was essential to republican government. As Democratic journalist Frederick Robinson told an audience of workingmen in 1834, "The condition of the people can never remain stationary. When not improving they are sinking deeper and deeper into slavery." Given these values, the great mass of American farmers and artisans could not see the utopias of plantation and mill town in any terms but those of threat. Since they were not by nature dependent types—Negroes or women—they could accept the discipline of Lowell or the plantation only if compelled by force or by poverty at its most extreme. But their hostility to a system of labor that rendered them dependent and enforced their consent to be governed did not take the form of an unambiguous opposition to the degradation of all labor. They perceived the form of labor degradation in racial and sexual terms, and rejected it by affirming their own "innate character" as white males.

In so doing they rejected not only the master of slaves, but the slave as well, perceiving the plantation system as a peculiar marriage of unprincipled men and a race effeminate in its docility. They perceived those sections of the white race which did accept the terms of dependent labor as akin to blacks; or at least, they supposed that the sources of failure and of degradation into the ranks of dependent labor lay in racial, ethnic, or sexual character rather than circumstance. Although this language of class relations made artificial and ultimately destructive distinctions within the working classes, it also gave the cutting edge of racial feeling to the ideological rejection of Lowell and the "Old Plantation."[20]

DYSTOPIA: THE LAST DAYS OF SODOM

This language symbolizing class by race and/or sex was deployed in the most vivid and sensational terms in the literature of urban crime. In its cheapest and most accessible form, this literature was a staple of the magazines edited by working-class politicians like George Wilkes and George Henry Evans, whose *Spirit of the Times*, as we know, was also— and not coincidentally—a primary vehicle for Southwestern fiction. But the most elaborate working out of the genre's premises was achieved by George Lippard, in his monumental and extraordinarily popular *The Quaker City; or, Monks of Monk Hall* (1844).

Lippard was an extraordinary character—a journalist and political figure associated with reform causes, and especially in movements assert- ing the rights of labor; and the author of sensational novels partaking equally of social criticism and Gothic pornography. *Monks of Monk Hall* is a phantasmagoric rendering of the hidden side of the great metropolis of Philadelphia, whose sobriquet of Quaker City—evocative of simplicity, virtue, and nonviolence—becomes bitterly ironic in the face of Lippard's "revelations." Modeling his work to some degree on Eugène Sue's *The Mysteries of Paris* (and other exposés in that vein), Lippard pretended to reveal the true state of affairs in the heart of a great urban center, and to link reportage of the poverty and corruption of city life with grander themes and myths, pointing toward an apocalyptic conclusion. In his Preface, Lippard says that the novel has been written to expose the full horror of the "crime of seduction," a crime akin to homicide; and he makes of the theme of seduction a symbolic key to the social relations that tie the corrupt Quaker City together.[21]

Seduction appears first as a moral crime, in which the unbridled sexual passions of an attractive and clever man lead to his unprincipled suborning of the will and passions of a pure virgin. The consummation of the seducer's lust leaves him puffed up with vanity and a sense of power; while the woman is ruined—morally the very wellsprings of her nature are polluted.

> She knew not that in her own organization, were hidden the sympathies of an animal as well as of an intellectual nature, that the blood in her veins only waited an opportunity to betray her, that in the very atmosphere of the holiest love of woman, crouched a sleeping fiend, who at the first whisperings of her Wronger, would arise with hot breath and blood shot eyes, to wreak eternal ruin on her woman's-honor.
>
> For this is the doctrine we deem it right to hold in regard to woman. Like man she is a combination of an animal, with an intellectual nature. Unlike man, her animal nature is a *passive* thing, . . . But let him play with her animal nature as you would toy with the machinery of a watch . . . and woman becomes like him- self, but a mere animal. Sense rises like a vapor, and utterly darkens soul.[22]

Woman, then, is both purer than man, and less stable in her ability to keep the animal and intellectual natures separate: once arouse her sexually, and the animal defeats all else, and her degradation to the hellish and bestial becomes *total*. This is the pattern of destruction which seduction involves, even where the maiden herself is pure and innocent in her first love—even where, as here in the case of Mary Arlington, she is the victim of a false marriage and of rape.

Seduction is also a type of social crime, and the source of a similarly degrading and pervasive corruption in the body politic. Sex thus provides the metaphor through which class relations are defined. The metaphor of sex suggests the associated metaphor of race. Just as the ruined woman descends to the animal, so degraded man descends in the scale of existence, approaching the animal—and the alien races, the Indian and the Negro. Lippard here plays an American variation on a theme picked up by Sue and others. *London Labour and the London Poor* describes the itinerant laborers and peddlers of England as members of a "nomadic race" like African or Asiatic savages; and Sue's own *The Mysteries of Paris* cites Cooper's Indians as models for the Parisian underclass.[23] For Lippard, the urban savage is embodied in the figure of Devil-Bug, custodian of Monk Hall: a gross and misshapen cripple, deformed in mind as well as body; many times a murderer, a connoisseur of cruelty and injustice who delights at the public execution of innocent victims of injustice, and cooperates in the systematic seductions and rapes that go on in Monk Hall.

Yet even Devil-Bug has had his time of innocence, from which a corrupt world has thrust him. He too once loved a pure woman, only to have her ruined by a seducer. Lost as he is, he still worships the virginity of his long-lost daughter by this woman, and eventually rescues her from *her* seducer. Lippard pictures Devil-Bug standing over her unconscious body, "the Savage reared in the very centre of Quaker City civilization, kneeling at the fair and beautiful woman, wronged and injured by one of the professed Ministers of that civilization!"[24]

His daughter's seducer is none other than her adopted father, the Reverend Algernon Pyne—a wealthy preacher who plays on the anti-Catholic prejudices of the city's poor to provoke riots and distract attention from the manifold oppressions wealth puts upon poverty. The male impulse to arouse woman's animal nature and corrupt her becomes a metaphor for the social processes by which the wealthy and powerful seduce and corrupt the innocent poor, degrading their racial endowment and driving them to crime or self-destruction.[25]

Seduction and rape are Lippard's metaphors for the relationship of classes in the Quaker City; and he establishes the association through the continual reiteration of the seducer/victim theme, in every possible combination, throughout the interminable course of his rambling "plot."

In one such example in the novel, we are introduced to a poor mechanic, "seduced" into depositing his savings in a bank, who loses it all when the bank fails. The mechanic appeals to the banker for his money back, even for a loan, to save himself and his daughter from starvation—and the daughter from the ruin that overtakes females amongst the poor. The banker, protected by bankruptcy laws, still enjoys his carriage and fine house, and declines the loan:

> "God!" [the mechanic] fiercely muttered between his set teeth. "Is there a God? Is he just? Then why have these people fine clothes and warm homes, when *I*, *I*, with honest hands, have no bread to eat, no fire to warm me?"
>
> Your pardon, pious people, your pardon for the blasphemy of this starving wretch! Starvation you know is a grim sceptic, a very Infidel, doubter and a scoffer!

The banker, to be sure, will be blackmailed into suicide by the exposure of his villainies by someone equally as suspect. Our pity is for the mechanic: "Cut his throat because he had no bread to give his child? Can such a thing happen in pious and *Protestant* Philadelphia?"[26]

The class qualities of the seduction metaphor are crystallized in the characters of Gus Lorrimer and Colonel Fitz-Cowles. The latter is a swindler who poses as a southern planter-aristocrat, and who seduces the wife of the merchant Livingstone (her name is Dora) and defrauds the merchant of his money. The business thievery and the theft of the wife's affections go together. Fitz-Cowles is linked with two representatives of alien and degraded races: a dim-witted Negro servant, and a Jewish forger (Van Gelt). The latter is an absolutely unprincipled anti-Semitic stereotype which represents the Jew as at once corrupt in a civilized mode, and primitive in his racial endowment: Van Gelt's features (says Lippard) are those that would have been seen in Palestine thousands of years before, and are still unchanged. This linkage of race and moral status and class character becomes more than implicit when Fitz-Cowles's father arrives, to reveal that he is the bastard son of a Creole slave. Nonetheless, he is the planter's child, and hence a true product of southern aristocracy: corrupt in the love of wealth and power, and corrupt in the forbidden mingling of racial blood. Like the bestialized ruined woman and the degraded Devil-Bug, the evil corruption of the southern planter is figured as a racial degradation.[27]

Gus Lorrimer is the novel's chief seducer: seduction is his profession, just as Indian hating is Moredock's and hunting is Boone's:

> "Know me as I am! Not the mere man-about-town, not the wine-drinking companion, not the fashionable addle-head you think me, but the *Man of Pleasure*! . . . which, in plain English, means— Woman.
>
> "Woman—the means of securing her affection, of compassing her ruin, of enjoying her beauty, has been my book, my study, my science, nay my *profession* from boyhood."

And this profession is likewise a "business," of sorts, albeit one in which speculation and consumption—rather than genuine production—is the aim; and the aim backed by a "capital . . . of one hundred thousand dollars." The function of the earlier linkage of seduction with miscegenation is to allow us to perceive the extremity of "blackness" in the character of a man (and a class) normally seen as white and genteel.[28]

The victims of these two seducers embody the two poles of feminine nature. Mary Arlington, Lorrimer's victim, is pure and innocent, betrayed by her passion and her innocent trust into meeting Lorrimer at Monk Hall, where she is raped and ruined. Dora Livingstone, on the other hand, and to use Lippard's scheme, is a woman whose sensual powers have been aroused prior to her intellectual ones. She is dark where Mary is light, "a perfect incarnation of the Sensual Woman, who combines the beauty of a mere animal, with an intellect strong and resolute in its every purpose." Those purposes speak of her degradation: she has given herself willingly to Fitz-Cowles, and seeks through him to achieve the status of European aristocracy. Though she began life as a "cobbler's daughter" and once prided herself on her rise to be a merchant's wife, she now wishes to take the next step upward in the course of mobility: but in so doing she will not only have to betray democratic principles but also to commit murder. Beautiful as she is, Lippard paints her as possessed by demons. Symptoms of her degradation are her loss of femininity—she puts on man's clothes, symbolizing her loss of the feminine principle of virtue in the male power-drive; and she ultimately places herself in the power of the savage, Devil-Bug.[29]

Monk Hall is the place to which the seducers bring their victims. It is at once a brothel/gambling hell, and the locus of a secret society of "Monks"—evocative of Murrell's Mystic Clan, or of those other secret-society bugaboos that alarmed nineteenth-century political rhetoric—the Masons, Know-Nothings, Illuminati, etc. The hall itself is mysteriously buried in the alleyways of the Quaker City, and sits over a network of catacombs and sewers as elaborate as those of Paris. It was originally the residence of colonial magistrates and governors of wealthy Tories, then a Catholic monastery or cloister—a sinister note. So, linked with the corrupt ruling elites of the past, Monk Hall has become the conclave of a corrupted ruling elite: bribable judges and officers, banker-swindlers, hypocrites who preach the Gospel and support missionary work for the South Sea Islanders, while availing themselves of the corrupt delights of seduction and drink in Monk Hall—and grinding the face of the poor on workdays. Of this haven of elite corruption, the Devil-Bug—incarnating the lowest impulses of the mind and heart, the excesses of the body, the urban "savage"—is the proprietor.[30]

Lippard establishes a situation in which the captivity/seduction of woman is the moral key to interpreting events, and in which the racial guideposts that interpret moral character are used to define a virtuous class (the middle-class producers and their daughters) as against the evil poles of savagery (Devil-Bug) and artificial aristocracy (Lorrimer and Fitz-Cowles). There are even types corresponding to the heroes of Cooperian romance. Luke Harvey, a worthy man born poor who has risen by his merits to be Livingstone's partner, is the Leatherstocking type: he speaks in the vernacular, is the spokesman for a good deal of democratic ideology (it is he who most scathingly attacks Pyne's bigotry), is clever at finding out evil and tracking people to where they have been hidden or are hiding. Like Virgil Stewart, he is a kind of vigilante-detective, like Natty, a "tracker," though his sphere of operations is the city. There are also two semiaristocratic figures, potential romantic heroes of the Heyward/Middleton type: Byrnewood, the brother of the ruined Mary; and Livingstone the merchant, who is (it turns out) descended from true English nobility, where Fitz-Cowles's credentials are forged. In the Cooper model, there would be rescue for the captives prior to their ruin; and in the case of the suspect Dora, a death leaving no innocent parties compromised.

In Lippard's city, such a resolution is impossible. The women are corrupted from the very start: there is no long successful resistance, analogous to Cora's resistance to Magua. Once corrupted, there is no redemption. Even revenge is sterile: Livingstone kills Dora, and commits suicide while the house burns down around them. Lippard likens the scene to the Apocalypse, and to the burning of a church by an anti-Catholic mob. The corrupted sanctuary is destroyed, but nothing takes its place. Similarly, Byrnewood kills Lorrimer; yet Mary, as we learn in the very last line of the novel, remains in love with his ghost, falls in a passionate frenzy before his portrait.

Luke Harvey's capacity to act the rescuer-vigilante is fatally limited by the fact that he himself is in love with the sensual woman (Dora) and the inordinate impulses of ambition and violence she represents. His revelation of Dora's sin to Livingstone has the character of vengeance rather than a restoration of law; and it leads only to the hellish scene of destruction, from which Harvey flees. Harvey at first resists Dora's attempts to seduce him from his loyalty to Livingstone. When he surprises her in the clutches of the deformed savage, Devil-Bug, who is about to rape her, he acts as her rescuer, despite his knowledge of her character. But this action, which most closely parallels the rescue motif in Cooper, is not redemptive at all: it leads, in fact, to Luke's temporary seduction by Dora, and his implicit betrayal of his loyalties.[31]

One further possibility for redemption is offered by the mysterious figure Ravoni—a charismatic philosopher-scientist, who may be a charlatan, and who offers a new religion based on rationalism, perfectionism, and mesmerism. He claims he can raise the dead and cure disease, but only by possessing or dominating the souls of those he saves. Clearly he is not a democratic savior. Yet he may, Lippard suggests, have something genuine to offer—and then he is murdered by Devil-Bug, who suspects him of wanting to seduce his rescued daughter and steal her fortune. So the savage, living by a world view that admits of only sordid motives, strikes down the rationalist messiah.

In all of this, the West is only present by virtue of its absence. It is twice invoked, via pastoral imagery, both times ironically. Lorrimer seduces Mary with his imaginative depiction of the cottage in the mountains, to which they will retire; and it is in just such a sylvan setting that, at the very end, Byrnewood unveils the portrait of Lorrimer: a scene that shows the avenger taking a rather perverse delight in contemplating his victim, and the ruined girl still enthralled by the man who had ruined her.[32]

The climax of the novel—the murder of Lorrimer—occurs on Christmas Eve, ironically juxtaposing vengeance with the birth of the Prince of Peace. The irony is further extended by Lippard's explicit mockery of the hope in redemption through the Frontier. The section begins with the cry of "Land, there to the west—land!" from the masthead of a ship; but instead of white doves from the shore, black ravens rise to greet the sailors. This odd scene, evoking both Columbus and Noah, says in effect that the land itself, like the women, has been permanently corrupted by the sins of Monk Hall. Apocalypse and judgment, not rescue, is the fate of the Quaker City.[33]

This vision of a possible future is realized in the horrific section describing Devil-Bug's dream, "The Last Day of the Quaker City." This is Lippard's modern version of Puritan clergyman Michael Wigglesworth's Day of Doom—the Second Coming brings Judgment for a society steeped in corruption and complacency. In Wigglesworth, this took the form of parents and spouses praising God for casting into Hell their impious children and helpmates. Lippard too has his vision of family relations destroyed in the Apocalypse, and of the casting down of those who, to worldly eyes, are "innocent."

But more than theology is working here. Lippard allows us to perceive the Apocalypse only through the eyes of Devil-Bug, the urban savage; and in his eyes, and the eyes of those like him, pure destruction is sweet. Then too, the sins of which the Quaker City is guilty are distinctly political and social. These are expressed in the differences of class which Devil-Bug initially perceives—"here was the Judge with his visage of solemnity and his pocket-book crammed full with bribes, and here hungry and lean, was the mechanic in his tattered garb, looking to the clear blue sky above, as he asked God's vengeance upon the world that robbed and starved him." Such a figure of destitution informs Devil-Bug that "the lordlings of the Quaker City . . . have turned the sweat and blood of the poor into bricks and mortar, and now as the last act of their crime, they tear down Independence Hall and raise a royal palace on its ruins." The bank directors and others of the corrupt ruling classes—the fellowship of Monk Hall—have now literally made themselves into aristocrats, and mean to replace the republic with a monarchy. This is the final intolerable act which brings the wrath of God on their heads—the republic and Independence Hall embodying, in Lippard's Jeffersonian theology, principles as sacred as Israel and the Holy Temple.[34]

To the juxtaposition of rich and poor a new contrast is added. The dead, past victims of the oppressions of the rich and ancestors dishonored by the treason of the "lordlings," arise and walk about the streets, unseen by all save Devil-Bug. The dead fight out a battle of Armageddon invisibly in the midst of a city that is preparing a festival to honor the coronation of the new monarch. "WOE UNTO SODOM," sing the dead, unheeded, as they pass doom on the Quaker City. The dead here speak for the oppressed poor, whose relationship to the rich parallels their own relation to the living; for so unbearable has life become in the new Quaker City that the poor prefer universal death and destruction to the continuation of life under these circumstances. Better that they and all should perish, than that any should survive under the regime of universal slavery.

This conception of the response of the degraded poor to the destruction of civilization echoes and exaggerates the Jeffersonian analysis of the consequences of class struggles, where one party represents property and other represents its lack. If the poor, like the feudal serfs of France or the slaves of Haiti, should be utterly excluded from the rational hope of property holding, why in their struggles with the rich should they respect the concept of property? And why would they not in their day of revolution overthrow property itself—which Jefferson and his fellows assumed to be the basis of civilization and law—along with the tyrannous ancien régime? Lippard warns that if present tendencies continue—with the rich getting richer and the poor thrust closer to the condition of the propertyless—this calamity may be realized.[35]

The dangerous movement toward the proletarianization of the working class is presented by Lippard in terms apt to the political debates of the 1840s. He visualizes the process as one in which the condition of independent and propertied mechanics—skilled workers who might own their own tools and shops—begins to approach that of southern slaves as the owners of factories appropriate more and more of the wealth and force the independent mechanic into dependence. By "The Last Day of the Quaker City," this process has run its full course:

> Then came the slaves of the city, white and black, marching along one mass of rags and sores and misery huddled together; a goodly tail to the procession of the King. Chains upon each wrist and want upon each brow. Here they were, the slaves of the cotton Lord and the factory Prince; above their heads a loom of iron, rising like a gibbet in the air, and by their sides the grim overseer. Hurrah, hurrah! This is a liberal mob; it encourages manufactures. The monopolist forever, they yelled, his enterprise gives labour to the poor, hurrah, hurrah! The slaves lifted up their eyes at the sound of that tumultuous hurrah, and muttered to each other, of glad green fields, and a farmer's life, and then they clanked their chains together, and gazed at the ruins of Independence Hall.[36]

The lords of the loom and the lords of the lash have become a single class, representing the concentrated power of "Capital and Trade"; and the workers too have become a single class, and slaves. Lippard directs sharply ironic barbs at the "liberal" notion that protectionist trade policies which sponsor manufactures are useful to the laborer—he sees these as fostering monopoly, and the degradation of labor. Nor do other political nostrums attract him: elsewhere he parodies the political slogans of Jackson and his successors, in the dialogue of two ignorant watchmen who blame the world's troubles on either the United States Bank, or the "Seminal Indians."[37] Yet neither the destruction of the "Monster Bank" nor the removal of the Indians resolves the contradictions of Jacksonian democracy.

Lippard offers—in the novel at least—no real solution of his own. His enslaved proletariat continues to dream of green fields and a farmer's life—the old yeoman dream even as the unheeded dead are chanting the preliminaries of their "Redemption." Here as elsewhere, the Frontier Myth appears as a delusion or a snare, rendered so by the corruption of man and society. Perhaps if Lippard's warning were heeded, there might be a return to the "green fields"—Lippard never tells us, though the note of nostalgia is strong. Failing such a restoration, there is only the city, and the entrapment of an environment that is entirely owned, controlled, created, and polluted by society.

Lippard's final metaphor for this new condition is that of the pillar: in a kind of perverse allusion to Devil-Bug's daughter's fate, a pure young maiden stands with her father and her lover on a single pillar in the midst of the final destruction, and Devil-Bug joins them. All around them proceeds the horror of the Last Day, which Lippard terms "the Massacre of Judgment," in which—as in an Indian massacre—all are killed without regard to age or sex. The pillar of clay begins to sway and topple, and the coward lover seizes the maiden, tears her from her clutch on the father's knees, and tries to cast her into the pit, crying "Down . . . There is room for but one upon this isle—down!" The father temporarily rescues the maiden, and falls into the pit himself, locked in a murderous embrace with the false lover; the girl shrieks in despair and horror, and casts herself into the pit. Only Devil-Bug the urban savage survives, to overlook the universal carnage of the Quaker City, capering with glee and delight at the destruction of the rich, the beautiful—and of the innocent as well.[38]

Thus the American dream, moving toward nightmare, shifts from the vision of limitless green fields to the ultimate symbol of crowding and entrapment—a single pillar in the midst of an urban Apocalypse, on which a few survivors struggle for survival and place; and in struggling, they destroy all of the bonds of affection and kinship that make social life possible, ending in mutual murder and despair, leaving behind only the degraded and deformed Devil-Bug to gloat amid the wreckage of civilization.

PART FOUR

Myth of a New Frontier: Renewal and Breakdown, 1845–1850

CHAPTER 8

A Choice of Frontiers: Texas, Mexico, and the Far West, 1835–1850

In 1845 the interrupted course of American expansion was dramatically resumed. The annexation of Texas that year provoked hostilities with Mexico, which in turn brought California and the Southwest into the Union in 1848. At the same time, resolution of the boundary dispute with Britain confirmed American control in the Puget Sound–Columbia River area. The Mexican War marked the return of the federal government as an active and aggressive agent of expansion—a role it had eschewed since forcing the sale of Florida in 1819. The ideological imperatives of a social order based on the promise of economic—and especially agrarian—expansion exerted a pressure sufficient to overcome the doubts and divisions of a quarter century. Those doubts were still embodied in the substantial resistance to the war and the admission of new territories offered by certain factions of the Whig Party; but they did not check the new movement until it had triumphed in battle.

The impetus for expansion was proportional to that of the obstacles it overcame. American expansionists had had the Pacific Coast in view at least since the discovery of the Columbia River by an American trading ship in 1794, and Jefferson had made the establishment of an American claim there part of the mission of Lewis and Clark in 1804–6. But expansion beyond Louisiana was checked by the forbidding character of the "Great American Desert," and the fear that so wide a territory could not be integrated into a single republic. To these technical difficulties were added the politics of the slavery question, which made each new expansion an occasion for putting the political balance of power at risk.

It was the annexation of Texas that tested the strength of these objections—especially the political ones. Until 1836 the American movement into Texas had appeared to follow the classic pattern of company purchase, settlement, and seizure followed earlier in the French-settled regions of the Ohio Valley, and the Franco-Spanish provinces of the Mississippi Valley. The course of the region's economic development and the growth of its population, coupled with the distance of the territory from the political center, gave it a practical autonomy and a strong American cast of features in cultural and political matters despite the presence of a significant

population of Hispanic "Texicans." The Mexican revolution and the ensuing disarray increased Texas's effective independence, while at the same
time throwing up economic and political programs that ran counter to
local interests. The result was a movement toward secession from Mexico;
and since the American element predominated, annexation to the United
States appeared logical and inevitable.

What blocked annexation was the growing importance of the slavery
issue in the Metropolitan United States. Until and unless the impasse over
a distribution of power could be worked out, Texas was inadmissible because it would add to the power of the proslavery parties. Thus the expansive impulses generated by the Metropolitan economy and projected
into Texas were checked by the conflicts of ideology and interest that likewise characterized its new political economy. Yet the appeal of renewed
expansion remained strong, and so the independence of Texas (and its
associated border raids and Indian conflicts) furnished the occasion for a
revival of some of the classic motifs of the Myth of the Frontier. Specifically,
it provided the locale for an important subgenre of dime novels, historical
romances, and "true" captivity narratives. Many of these projected a view
of Mexican-American relations that drew heavily on the old Noble Savage
fantasies of Cooper; and since annexation was the ideological desideratum
of the fantasy, Texican dime novels often featured marriages between
American/Texan "Rangers" and Mexican ladies, following the model of
the Inez/Middleton marriage in *The Prairie*. Others repeated the more
orthodox race-war fantasy of *Mohicans*, with Mexican women or Comanche
princesses as the doomed Cora, rejected from an Americanized Texas.[1]

But the Texas story was also an important matter for popular historical
and journalistic coverage, since the institutional base for national mass
media would be fully in place for the Mexican War. The "living legends" or
celebrity heroes of the Texas wars who populated this growing medium
were more significant cultural properties than any of the dime-novel rangers.
This is testimony to the cultural consequences of the revival of the Frontier—the mythology is not entirely dependent on literature, but draws once
again from history.

HOUSTON, CROCKETT, AND THE
RETURN OF THE FRONTIERSMAN

The two most important figures in the Texas wars in literary and
journalistic culture were Davy Crockett and Sam Houston. Both men had
been prominently associated with the party battles during the Jackson
period, and specifically with the Indian Removal controversy—albeit on
different sides. Both had had spectacularly successful political careers "in
the States" that were suddenly blighted—Houston's by domestic problems
and alcoholism, Crockett's by opposition to Jackson and to Indian Removal.
Both men went to Texas to regenerate their political fortunes and reputations, and in the latter they both succeeded—Crockett via his redemptive
self-sacrifice at the Alamo, and Houston by his emergence as the avenger of

Crockett and the conqueror of General Santa Anna, the "Napoleon of the West," at San Jacinto. Their domination of the mythology of Texican independence therefore links that story with the main themes of Frontier Myth.

In both "legends," the central theme is that of a man seeking self-renewal on the Frontier after experiencing moral or material ruin in the political and social struggles of the Metropolis. Such an explicit and deliberate formulation in turn suggests the centrality of this theme in the myth and ideology of the renewed expansionism of the period, and it is not a connection that is merely suggested or alluded to, as Cooper alludes to "the settlements" in *The Prairie*.

Houston's is the more "Cooperian" career and legend. The major literary vehicles of that legend are not works of fiction, but histories and campaign biographies, most of them written in support of Houston and his policies during the course of his long career. Those from the 1835–50 period mostly concern his desire to obtain the annexation of Texas on favorable terms, and they use his career as an exemplification of the sort of heroic character that Texas will bring into the Union. The later campaign biographies were written in support of his perennial presidential candidacy and offer him as an exemplification of national qualities of virtue and heroism. But whatever the specific polemic, the mythic justification for Houston's heroic status is the same. He is represented as a unique combination of the traits of the hunter and the soldier-aristocrat. Impatient of schooling and discipline—like Boone and Washington before him—he flees to the wilderness, to live as an adopted Cherokee and learn Nature's truths at her breast.

Nonetheless, he retains his natural "gift" for civilized attainment—he reads the *Iliad* between deer hunts, and retains those chivalrous sentiments that characterize the well-born and gently nurtured. When the hero Jackson calls him to fight the Indians, he goes and distinguishes himself as a professional soldier and an Indian fighter. When his hero enters the political fray, to defend the farmers from Monster Banks as he once defended them from savage tomahawks, Houston follows his chieftain, and rises to prominence and high office. It is from this eminence that he suddenly falls, because of a mysterious wound to his honor inflicted by or because of his genteel young wife.

Houston's story to that point had followed the scenario of Cooper's "natural aristocrat," as modeled by Oliver Edwards/Effingham of *The Pioneers* or Duncan Heyward in *Last of the Mohicans*. Beginning as a proto-Leatherstocking and companion of Indians and as a professional soldier, he rises in the scale of social rank and civilization to earn the supreme symbolic accolade of marriage to a white woman of the Elizabeth Temple–Alice Munro type. But the mysterious crisis in the marriage and the estrangement of bride and groom suggests some fundamental incompatibility in the mixture: a bride/civilization too enervated by gentility to accept the rough virtues of the self-made Frontiersman; a hero too much the man of the wilderness to blend his nature with that of civilization's highest type.

This failure reverses the apparent direction of the hero's development. Spiritually desolate, he falls into his old weakness of alcoholism and abandons civilization to return to the Indians—now exiled themselves from his and their native Tennessee, and living a hard life on the buffalo plains of the Indian Territory. A similar reversion and exile to the West inaugurated the terminal phase of Leatherstocking's fictional career at the end of *The Pioneers*. But for Houston it merely begins another repetition of the cycle, as if a certain number of ritual passages were required before the magic of Frontier regeneration would "take." This latest reversion to the primitive has the effect of cleansing and restoring Houston, and giving him back both his honor and his masculine vigor. Dressed as an Indian and vested with the authority of tribal ambassador, he rises from a political grave to return to Washington as defender of the rights of the abused red man.

Houston successfully brought off this "Oliver Effingham" combination of the roles of buckskin hunter, white-man-raised-by-Indians, and soldier-aristocrat. Even the well-substantiated rumors of his "marriage" to a "Cherokee princess" did not discredit him or suggest (except to his opponents) racial renegadery. He impressed the public by living or acting out the full scenario of the fantasy embodied in the Leatherstocking cycle and the larger Myth of the Frontier. Whether that success would have persisted had Houston remained with the Cherokee is another matter; but he did not remain an Indian. The call to go to Texas, says the legend, found him sitting with his Indian brothers, a patriarch presiding over the solemn council in his "wigwam"—actually a tavern on the Cherokee high road. Having gained all he could from immersion in the wilderness, he abandoned the Cherokee and crossed—all alone—into Texas, where his role would be that of a George Washington. The metaphor is appropriate—Washington too was represented as having risen to his military and moral preeminence after a necessary apprenticeship to the life and warfare of the wilderness. If Houston went deeper into the wilderness, stayed longer, and lived its life more fully, that merely reflects the further development and exaggeration of the sanctifying images on which the Washington legend drew.[2]

Crockett's legend is more complex and has proved more durable. This may be because Crockett was already a perfected literary property—as well as a living politician (recently defeated for reelection to Congress)—at the time he went to Texas. His political reputation was based upon a successful projection of the style and values of the fictions of the Southwestern humorist into real politics. Through Crockett a literary persona representing the Mythic Frontier addresses directly the political issues of the age, including both the traditional concerns of the Frontiersman—expansion, Indian policy—and also the Metropolitan concerns of the Whig Party, particularly those relating to tariffs protective of the manufacturing industries.

Crockett's was the most successfully propagated Frontier legend since Daniel Boone's, and the names of the two were linked in historical commentary on the Frontier quite early. The formation by Theodore Roosevelt and others of the Boone and Crockett Club later in the nineteenth century attested to the strength of this long-term association. There are important similarities in the legends of both men, and in the ways by which those legends became part of popular culture. Both were important figures in the frontier communities before being "discovered" by eastern mythmakers.

Boone had his John Filson; Crockett at first promoted himself, and later had several literary-political assistants. Both legends were—in their original media appearance—associated with promotional schemes: Filson's land development projects in Kentucky, and the Whig Party's political program for defeating Jackson. After an initial phase in which the still living hero provided genuine material for the legend to go with the "stretchers," both Boone and Crockett became completely the creatures of fiction makers.[3]

Whereas the Boone myth and its spin-off Leatherstocking myth sanctified the figure of the hunter and Indian fighter by linking these figures to the crucial drama of Indian conquest and to the rescue of the white captive, Crockett's adventures begin in the period of Indian warfare, but they extend into the post-Frontier period portrayed in the Southwestern school's stories. The first Crockett material appeared in the *Narrative of the Life of David Crockett*, published in 1833. This autobiographical account of Congressman Crockett's early career was written primarily by Crockett himself, and it reveals him as a skilled raconteur and a writer adept at both storytelling and the portrayal of character—in this case, his own. It had an instant success, which created a demand for more Crockettiana, and was followed within a year by a second "autobiography," *Sketches and Eccentricities . . .* ghostwritten by James S. French.

Unlike Daniel Boone—whose career and literary fame were precedents—Crockett was truly the author of his own legend. Boone's historical deeds were important enough to speak for themselves and to draw literary attention his way. And since Boone was not literarily inclined, he was content to depend on others to tell his story and create his public persona. Crockett's historical accomplishments in 1833 were nowhere near as significant as Boone's. His reputation and popular fame were essentially by-products of his literary achievement, responses to a literary persona he himself created. It was not the deeds that were important, but the fact that the eccentric Colonel Crockett was the doer.

The success of Crockett's writing, and the ease with which its voice and viewpoint could be reproduced and marketed, raises the question whether Crockett was very shrewd or very lucky in anticipating the demands of the literary marketplace. The answer to this question can tell us something of importance about the relationship of national popular culture and the folklore of communities. One school of Crockett criticism holds that Davy was (at least at the start) a genuinely "folkloric" author, whose materials and way of telling a tale derived from the traditions of small, homogeneous, oral-tradition-bound frontier communities. Certainly much of the literature associated with Crockett has folkloric sources. The various joke books and almanacs attributed to him are filled with tall tales that have a folkloric flavor and structure, and which are (in many instances) traceable to folkloric traditions of the districts in which Crockett lived. This reading suggests that Crockett was originally a folkloric figure, speaking out of a distinctively local and preliterary cultural tradition. His success in the marketplace was initially a matter of luck; and it led to a marketing of a hero that transformed a local legend into a part of national popular culture.[4]

However, most of the folkloric materials associated with Crockett's name were absent from the one literary production that is unquestionably his own—the first autobiography. The tall tales, trickster pranks, and magical triumphs that became staples of Crockettiana first began appearing in French's *Sketches and Eccentricities.* As contemporary reviewers of that book noted, these tales were gleaned from the pages of newspapers and journals from various parts of the country, which had offered them as humorous anecdotes characteristic of western life, manners, or rhetoric. Most of the folkloric stories are of a type so common in American and British culture—and so frequently included in compendia of folklore and fairy tales—that the attribution of the story to the specific traditions of East Tennessee seems unwarranted. Crockett's political and literary success made him a literary commodity, and the obvious way to exploit his appeal was to piece out his historical career with materials drawn from the whole range of myth and legend associated with the Frontier. This process continued, and indeed expanded, even after Crockett's death at the Alamo in 1836. The producers of popular culture did not need Crockett as intermediary between them and folkloric traditions. Their awareness of those traditions was filtered through (and distorted by) the literary mythology with which they worked, and they saw nothing in the folklore they received but what the literary mythology had prepared them to see. They understood and used Crockett as an authenticating device for political and literary ploys whose frame of reference was bounded by the national, commercial, popular culture.

Moreover, Crockett himself may have brought to the original telling of his tale the same kind of literary awareness that characterized the commercial exploiters of his name. Joseph J. Arpad, in his introduction to a modern edition of the *Narrative,* notes that Crockett himself drew heavily on literary sources and on political rhetoric for his own original venture. Arpad notes the influence of congressman Nathaniel H. Claiborne (Virginia) on Crockett's political invective against Jackson; and he further notes that Claiborne's history of the Creek War and the War of 1812 in the South seems to have provided Crockett with both information and a certain kind of symbolism. The "rags-to-riches" theme in the *Narrative* is linked to Franklin's *Autobiography,* a copy of which Crockett is said to have annotated. Finally, the "Major Jack Downing" letters, written by Seba Smith, very much in a Southwestern vein, provided key elements in the Crockett folk-philosopher persona. Arpad's point is to emphasize the self-consciousness with which the Crockett legend was fabricated; he suggests that Crockett fabricated the persona of rude backwoodsman in an almost satirical spirit, revealing himself in direct conversation—like the narrator of the Southwestern story addressing his reader—to be more genteel than the persona, apart from and above his own symbol.[5]

This posturing was deliberate, for Crockett held national political ambitions. His references to his supposed presidential candidacy began as a joke in the *Narrative,* but they became serious; just as Crockett went from being a satire on Jacksonian backwoods values to the embodiment of Whig hopes to "out-Jackson Jackson." This the Whigs eventually achieved, not through Crockett but through William Henry Harrison—a figure of just the same military-aristocratic character as Jackson, for whom a humble past could be fabricated.

Crockett's pose was to attack Jackson in the character of one of that class for whom Jackson was supposed to be the preeminent spokesman: the "hunters of Kentucky," who had helped him win at New Orleans, and for whose benefit Jackson had attacked Spanish Florida, removed the Cherokee Indians, and destroyed the United States Bank. To make this pose effective, Crockett had to distort and alter both the facts of his career and background, and the nature of his opposition to Jackson. Crockett had been elected to represent a squatter constituency in west Tennessee, whose interests were inimical to those of the established planters of east Tennessee—a group that included, most prominently, President Jackson. The issue concerned the disposition of public lands in Tennessee. In exchange for its relinquishment of title to its western lands, North Carolina had stipulated that Congress honor the land warrants issued by the colony and state before 1789. Fraudulent practices and widespread counterfeiting had multiplied these warrants, with the lion's share going to land speculators possessing relatively large capital. This had produced a situation in which even land originally reserved for preemption by squatters had to be put in the pool with land earlier reserved to defray the warrants; and this in turn meant that preemptors, with valid title, could still be put off their land by planters or large speculators holding those early warrants. The rectification of this system was the work of Crockett's congressional life; and it was in fact completed by his son, who succeeded in managing a bill through Congress in 1841.[6]

The attractiveness of Crockett for the national Whig Party lay in the fact that he had been a genuine representative of the resistance of small farmers to the economically and politically privileged, and he could—on the basis of his Tennessee experience—attack Jackson effectively and with complete sincerity as the enemy of the common man. The adoption of Crockett as a spokesman did not, of course, imply that the Whigs would abjure the resistance to Indian Removal or the restrictive policies on public lands and the tariff that were favored by their northeastern leaders and resisted by western farmers. Rather, they expected Crockett to overcome ideological resistance with mythological appeal. Crockett was proof that the true "Hunters of Kentucky" were Whigs; and if those hunters had made Jackson hero of New Orleans and president of the United States, they could do as much for a deserving Whig. But to create the necessary persona of an anti-Jackson Kentucky hunter, details of Crockett's life were altered or invented, converting the living man into a celebrity fiction.

Crockett therefore represents himself as rude and ignorant, until the present moment; as a hunter and farmer who lived chiefly in the backwoods; as one who had office thrust upon him, without his seeking it; and as the hero of a rags-to-riches story, who rose modestly, but by his own efforts. The facts, as Arpad and others point out, are otherwise. Although he had little formal schooling, he was far from being the illiterate that the *Narrative* represents him as being. Where Crockett insists that he remained a private throughout the Creek War, records show him to have held elective office as a sergeant and field officer. He did actively seek office, in both militia and civil posts; and his early service as a magistrate was not the Frontier-vigilante operation he portrays, but something a good deal more regular and legal. He was a good hunter, but a better talker. But his emphasis on his bear-hunting prowess is not simply a distortion of his level of skill and achievement—if he was not the best bear hunter, he was one of the best by all accounts. Rather, the distortion lies in the emphasis given to bear hunting, since at this time bears were becoming quite scarce; wolves, not bears, were the "varmints" most annoying to farmers, and it was against these that most of the hunting went on. By emphasizing bears, Crockett ties himself to a more dangerous and heroic prey, and suggests that his Frontier is a good deal more primitive and backwoodsy than it really was.

Although Crockett did fight in the Creek War, he was not an Indian fighter in the sense that Boone was. For him, the Fort Mimms massacre was something that occurred "out there," and he marched away from home to the wars; Boone fought his on his own doorstep. It is to Crockett's credit that he had a far more humane attitude toward Indians than did Jackson. His sympathy for Indians was practical and consistent, and he authored legislation favorable to them while in Tennessee. His congressional opposition to Jackson's Indian Removal Bill was not simply an opportunistic seizure of an issue likely to gain him Whig supporters in the Northeast. Still, this sympathy is not broadly displayed in the *Narrative*, and his exploits as an Indian fighter are emphasized and exaggerated elsewhere by French and other exploiters of the Crockett mystique. These books and stories linked his persona more closely to that of Boone (and Jackson) than the facts warranted.[7]

The centerpiece of Davy's Indian war experience is not his combat with the savages but his first confrontation with Jackson. Crockett tells a tale about his leading a mutiny among the Tennessee militia against the arbitrary and tyrannical exercise of authority by General Jackson. The point of the scene is to emphasize that Jackson is no more a friend of the "Hunters of Kentucky" than the Indians or the British are. Indeed, Jackson is more like the British martinet of stage melodramas than the border captain of legend. Crockett tells the story in language that makes the connections to contemporary politics inescapable:

> We got ready and moved on until we came near the bridge, where the general's men were all strung along on both sides, just like the office-holders are now, to keep us from getting along to the help of the country and the people. But we . . . had . . . our guns ready primed, that if we were fired on we might fight our way through, or all die together; just as we are now determined to save the country from ready ruin, or to sink down with it. When we came still nearer the bridge we heard the guards cocking their guns . . . But, after all, we marched boldly on, and not a gun was fired, not a life lost; just as I hope it will be again, that we shall not be afraid of the General's Globe, nor his K[itchen] C[abinet], nor

his regulars, nor their trigger snapping; but just march boldly over the executive bridge, and take the deposites [*sic*] back where the law placed them . . .[8]

But the incident described by Crockett is an exercise in historical fiction rather than a bit of genuine reportage. Such an incident did take place, but Crockett played no part in it—he took the details from Claiborne's history of the war. Moreover, the mutiny was squelched by Jackson, who ordered the regulars in his command to fire on the mutineers if they persisted.

The Crockett persona in the *Narrative* tries to assimilate a range of desirable myth-heroic and Frontier qualities. Some of these are self-contradictory, like the assertion that Davy is both vicious Indian killer of the Southwestern flavor and friend of the victims of Removal. Crockett's adventures, and especially his tricksterish flouting of Jackson's authority, link him with the Simon Suggses of the Frontier's backwash, and contribute to the image of Davy as "frontier wastrel" and embodiment of all that was crude, wasteful, and feckless in the pioneer. On the other hand, Crockett tries to represent himself as one who ultimately transcended the Suggsian classes to achieve a position of secure subsistence as a farmer. In fact, both images are falsifications. Davy's career had more of the quality of entrepreneurship and bourgeois ambition about it than it had of the spirit of contented yeomanry. His own father had owned a mill and a tavern in addition to a farm, and after his second marriage (to a woman of some means) Crockett followed suit, building a grain mill, distillery, and gunpowder manufactory. These enterprises all required an input of capital that would have placed him among the wealthier classes in his frontier community. On the other hand, his ascent was not the straight line of progress that flattered both his own ego and the political assumptions of the Whigs. Fire, flood, and financial contractions had ruined Crockett's enterprises, and at the time of his election to Congress he had actually sunk back to the level of tenant farmer.[9]

Nowhere does the Whig effort to extend the applicability of the Crockett version of the Frontier Myth appear more strikingly than in the *Account of Colonel Crockett's Tour to the North and Down East* (1835). This largely ghostwritten account of a speaking tour, undertaken with the hope of promoting both the Whig cause and Crockett's own candidacy, took the "rude backwoodsman" into the heart of the post-Frontier world: the cities and mills of the North. The *Account* does not merely extend the characterization of Crockett by contrasting the naive Westerner and the city slickers—although there are elements of that. Rather, the *Account* attempts to use Crockett's responses to sanctify the new industrial order—and its favorite protective tariff schemes—in the terms of the Frontier Myth. He is represented as approaching the North as a kind of new Frontier, comparing his trepidation before the trip with that experienced before he "braved the lonely forests of the West" or went to fight the Indians in the South; and he compares his fear of sophisticated city audiences with the fear of wild Indians.[10]

With Jefferson, or perhaps even a Daniel Boone, he shares a hostile attitude toward the city as an environment. The city is a place in which people are crammed together, living in squalor and exposed to temptations of all kinds. The racial distinction which elevates the white man over the black is obscured by persistent class divisions: "On my way I saw a white man . . . cursing a white man-servant. I stopped and said to him, 'Hellow, mister! if you talk that way to a white man in my country, he'd give you first-rate hell.'" In the city, it's "Black and white, white and black, all hug-em-snug together." Prominent in the amalgam are the "wild Irish," who form a mob to persecute anti-Jackson speakers. Crockett compares the tendency of city folks to be always "mooving" about with his own domestic stability—a gross misrepresentation in view of the frequent "shifts" recorded in his autobiography. But Crockett is here invoking conventional images of city life, as against the yeoman's life—images that look backward to Crèvecoeur, and forward to Lippard's characterization of the Quaker City.[11]

The city, not the forest, is Jackson's realm, according to Crockett—his natural constituency the wild Irish and the hug-em-snug black/white proletariat rather than the free white hunters of the West. And city people are those whose laziness or viciousness will not allow them to avail themselves of the opportunities offered by the Frontier:

> What a miserable place a city is for poor people; they are half starved, poorly clothed and perished for fire. I sometimes wonder they don't clear out to a new country where every skin hangs by its own tail: but I suppose they think an hour's indulgence in vice is sweet enough for the bitter of the rest.[12]

But the Frontier is not a place where one may rise with little effort. It is a place where the work ethic comes intensively into play; and Crockett asserts that Jackson's policies on the currency, and perhaps on land, offer too much too easily to the land- and money-hungry poor.

> Andrew Jackson . . . can't enact poor men into rich. Hard knocks, and plenty of them, can only build up a fellow's self. Look at my other book, and see how much of the curse of Adam's fall I bore, and tell me if I haven't a right to speak on this poor man subject.

It is the spokesman for the school of "hard knocks," the up-from-poverty frontier hunter, who then points to new Frontiers of opportunity—not only and not chiefly in the West, but in eastern manufacturing cities. He points with pride to the railroads of the Northeast, and notes that there is relatively little speculation in the stock—a remark that is either incredibly partisan or facetious, in view of the reputation of railroad corporations.[13]

But Crockett's highest encomiums are reserved for the mills of Lowell—those factories in which the new working class appear as passive and female, domiciled and disciplined by a paternal corporation—the antithesis of enterprise imagined as a masculine military or predatory adventure. It is the great bear hunter himself who tells us that the worthy capitalists of Lowell use their wealth "in the best possible way—by keeping a great many people busy":

We often wonder how things are made so cheap among the yankees. Come here, and you will see women doing men's work, and happy and cheerful as the day is long: and why not? Is it not much better for themselves and families, instead of sitting up all day busy at nothing? It a'n't hard work, neither. . . .

The girls return from their factory work "as if they were coming from a quilting frolic" in some rural community. He makes the conventional contrast between the fate of working women in Europe and in the United States; and he further notes that since the ultimate consumer of the cheap textiles is the farm wife in the West, the Westerner may consider himself or herself like the "captain on a field muster"—a ruler or aristocrat for whom others labor.[14]

All of this points Crockett toward a "conversion experience" of sorts: he changes from an opponent to a supporter of protective tariffs. An alliance of the western consumer and Eastern manufacturer—basic components of Clay's American System—seems to him now the most natural sort of thing. Among other Whig Party positions he advocates is that of opposition to the Removal of the Cherokee: By doing so just after praising the industriousness of the Yankee character, he aligns himself with those who have seen the Cherokee acquire some of that industrious character, and as having—therefore—acquired the rights of civilized men. In this context Jackson's attack on the Cherokee appears as an attack on the work ethic and on property—which, if left to operate, would convert the urban savage to useful citizenship, as it has already done the Cherokee.[15]

However pleasing and useful Crockett's tour may have been to northeastern Whigs, his own constituents turned him out of office in the next election. Although the Crockett family retained popular support within the state of Tennessee, Davy's national positions were antipathetic to those of his neighbors. They did not share his Whiggish enthusiasm for protective tariffs, nor his antipathy for the personality of Jackson. Nor did they share his apparent concern for the rights of the Cherokee, since they expected (as a group) to profit from the confiscation of Indian lands. It was therefore of no interest to them how the debate on Indian character was resolved: whether, as Jackson claimed, the Cherokee were hunters by their "gifts" of race; or potentially civilized farmers, as Crockett and the Whigs asserted. Expansion of land and resources—not speeches about happy Lowell and the school of hard knocks—were the conjuring themes of the American political economy.

Crockett acknowledged the strength of this imperative personally by his emigration to Texas as a volunteer fighter and prospective political leader. This translation from Metropolitan politico to Frontier warrior finally set the seal of history on Davy Crockett's heroic persona: he fell among the defenders of the Alamo. Crockett's publishers and editorial associates immediately increased the number and circulation of the almanacs that bore Crockett's name, and published a sequel to his earlier autobiographies which purported to be the journal found on his dead body. Newspapers of different political persuasions seized on the event—the Democratic sheets because Crockett died for Texas, the Whigs because

Crockett was a Whig. Some asserted that he had miraculously survived the battle; others "that he died as a United States soldier should die, covered with his slain enemy," battling to free "his adopted land . . . from a savage enemy." In death he took on the lineaments of a Cooperian hero: "To bemoan his fate, is to pay a tribute of grateful respect to Nature—he seemed to be her son."[16]

Within the borders of a closed society the conflicts of class and interest cannot be reconciled, even by an appeal to the authority of a mythic hero. The hero whose career is set in such circumstances becomes problematic, undergoes a kind of degeneration of esteem—Natty Bumppo is put in the stocks in Templeton, and Crockett becomes an ideological comedian. But once projected out beyond the borders again, into warfare against a "savage" foe, the hero regains his lost stature and becomes again a symbol to conjure with.

Even the vexed question of Cherokee Removal confirms this pattern. The arguments for Cherokee Removal were couched in the language of race, and apparently hinged on the question of the mutability of racial gifts—could the Indians adapt to white ways, or were they bound to remain either the violent enemies of civilization or its hapless victims? The underlying economic premises of the controversy had to do with the desire of whites in the Cherokee regions of Georgia, North Carolina, and Tennessee for Cherokee lands; and the argument they made for dispossessing the Indians was a closed Frontier argument—since white American civilization was bound to grow, had to grow to survive, and since resources of land were becoming scarcer, it was "unnatural" and economically unreasonable to permit the Cherokee to maintain their "unproductive" tribal system in that territory. Of course, neither the racial argument nor the economic argument was true—the Cherokees had adapted quite effectively to "civilization," and as farmers were just about as productive as their white neighbors. But facts could not outweigh the ideological belief in the Indians as inherently uncivilizable.[17]

However, once removed to the wilderness of the Great American Desert, the image and mythic function of the Cherokee changed. While Americans could not accept the Cherokee as successful adapters to civilization, the Cooper tradition prepared them to sympathize with the Indians as "vanishing Americans," romantic victims of racial fate and white rapacity. Crockett's plea for the Cherokee was mistimed—such sympathy would not be forthcoming until Removal was completed—and it was also misdirected to a constituency that was directly covetous of those lands.

On the other hand, Houston's use of his Cherokee connection on the eve of the Texas insurrection shows how quickly the mythic role of the Indians could change. In his role as ambassador of the Cherokee, Houston played up his own "Indianization," confirming the romantic image of the Cherokee as savages and suggesting that Jackson had been morally correct in removing them: the Trail of Tears had, in the end, restored them to the feathers and warpaint that belonged with their "racial gifts" better than plows and plug hats. Houston suggested that his kind of Cherokee might be the vanguard of an American movement into the Great Plains region and a source of fighters and supplies for the Texas rebellion, as if the survivors of Removal were willing as a people to play Uncas to Houston's Hawkeye. Indeed, reports had Houston proposing to lead a volunteer force of Cherokee to the aid of the Texicans in 1836, and rumors of a Texas-Cherokee alliance persisted throughout the decade of Texan independence.[18]

The return of old Frontier hunter-heroes like Houston and Crockett to a frontier setting restored the luster of their reputations by connecting them to a renewal of the political economy of the old Frontier. Similarly, the mythic luster of Cherokee character is restored by their regression to the status and circumstances of old-time savages—once again they provide nurture for the solitary hunter-hero, and a force of loyal "scouts" to assist the Frontiersmen against a still-more-savage Mexican foe.

THE CONQUEST OF MEXICO: HUNTERS OR CONQUISTADORES?

Despite its literary appeal, this resurgence of Frontier Myth was not sufficient to provide immediate legitimacy for the move to make Texas the next Frontier. It required a decade of debate and political compromise to make annexation feasible. In the end, the political impasse over Texas was overcome by the development of Oregon as a counterbalancing outlet for Free Soil pioneers; and by the Mexican government's mishandling of the Rio Grande border dispute, which allowed advocates of war with Mexico to present America as the injured party. At first the prospect of conquering Mexican territory was interpreted in the traditional terms of the Frontier Myth. It was assumed that territorial acquisitions would be marginal, restricted to regions that were either uninhabitable wasteland (the Great American Desert) or analogous to the woodland and prairie frontiers of the Mississippi and Ohio valleys. Little account was taken of the settled Mexican populations in the borderlands, let alone of the large Indian populations and their unique political economy. The projection of expectations from old Frontiers to new produced such anomalies as the common use of the Cooperian epithet "Sons of the Forest" to describe the Indians of the Great Plains and Southwest—horse Indians who inhabited a nearly treeless prairie and desert environment.[19]

These allusions and expectations were punctured by the surprising American success in the war itself. General Winfield Scott's spectacular march on Mexico City put the United States in control of the Mexican heartland and raised the possibility of a conquest of an alien Metropolis. At the same time, the military reconnaissance of the borderlands and California revealed that even these "wilderness" regions were not the sort of conquest envisioned in the original Myth of the Frontier. While Oregon could be considered as simply a more distant version of Boone's Kentucky, California was a settled and prosperous agricultural region with a considerable native population; and the Rio Grande Valley included both substantial Mexican settlements and the large, well-organized, and socially advanced Navaho-Pueblo Indian groups, as well as the nomadic Apache and Comanche. These regions were especially suited to southern interests

because of the existence of a relatively large pool of native labor and a tradition of peonage to make the transition to plantation agriculture easy.
California offered a special inducement to northeast mercantile interests, in
the form of port facilities facing Asia and the China trade.

Since so many groups might expect to profit from the Mexican conquest, there was a good deal of support for it at first. But the different patterns of exploitation projected by these diverse interests had already been
productive of intense partisan struggle within the United States. These
differences would finally turn the division of the Mexican spoils into an
occasion for dissolving the consensus and perhaps the Union of the States
as well.

Then as now, North Americans perceived Mexico through a glaze of
preconceptions and expectations born of our own peculiar history and culture. The nation below the Rio Grande could not be seen or understood in
its own terms; it became instead a darkened mirror in which Americans saw
the features of their own culture and society in obscure and exaggerated
forms. The divisions of class and race, the political divisions between entrepreneurs and Jacksonian workingmen and paternalists, were reproduced in
the depiction of Mexico, making that nation an unwilling testing ground for
the definition and resolution of *Yanqui* ideological issues. The land and the
people and the politics of Mexico were interpreted in terms of the current
American vocabulary of myth and ideology. The United States was a nation
that had grown great on the process of agrarian expansion into an Edenic
wilderness. So Mexico, the new field of expansion, is seen as "an earthly
paradise, wild yet beautiful." But modern America was now divided between a dwindling agrarian hinterland and a burgeoning Metropolis. So in
Mexico, the wilderness gives way to poor and crowded towns filled with
"degraded" mestizos; and the lovely buildings set amid tropical gardens,
which appear to be "residences of gentlemen of taste and fortune," are
revealed—"alas for romance!—[as] factories."[20] Even as Americans reached
out for the new paradise as an alternative to Metropolitan limitations, they
confronted in Mexico proof that escape from the issues of a Metropolitan
political economy was impossible.

The most important of these projections concerned the character of
the Mexicans as a race. Since the concept of race encoded for North
Americans all of the most intractable and problematic aspects of class
difference, the resolution of the debate about Mexican racial character
determined the kind of political relationship that might exist between the
two nations. The land of Mexico might be any sort of exotic type of
wilderness; so long as it was undeveloped it could qualify as a field of
pioneering. The presence of towns in such a setting was not more difficult
to reconcile with pioneering than was the existence of New York or St. Louis.
But if the population of wilderness and countryside was not equivalent to
the Anglo-Saxon, then its political status became questionable. Were the
Mexicans to be treated as Indians, fit only for extermination or removal? as
blacks, apt for outright enslavement? or as Irishmen, suited to a proletarian
life, bound to remain poor and unruly and a trouble to the social peace of
the republic?

At the root of the original consensus for conquering Mexico was belief in the concept of history as the story of the strife between advanced and primitive races for control of the resources of nature. This historiographical doctrine had been rendered as literary convention by Cooper, and had been carried over into the writing of history by the romantic historians George Bancroft and William H. Prescott. Bancroft was a Jacksonian Democrat and Prescott a Whig, but they agreed in representing historical change and contingency in the language of natural processes and biological competition. Races and nations, in their history, emerge from the womb of Nature to suffer through their apprenticeship, dependent and weak; then flower into the vigor of expansive youth and enjoy a period of power and contemplation; then, if they have not found the secret of perpetuating racial vigor, they decline into impotent senility.[21]

The United States in 1846 saw itself as "Young America," opposed by a Mexico in which senescent survivals of the Spanish conquest tyrannized over a mestizo population still in the infantile stage of development. President James K. Polk, at forty-nine the youngest man ever elected president, known by his sobriquet "Young Hickory," symbolized the rejuvenescence of the heroic principle embodied in "Old Hickory" Jackson. Prescott, no admirer of either of the Hickories, also represented the war in terms of the opposition of young and old races. His monumental history of the *Conquest of Mexico*, published in 1847, participated in the Romantic enthusiasm for the "Halls of Montezuma" that infected Scott's army, and formulated the rationale of conquest in a more sophisticated way. The Spanish conquered the mighty and numerous Aztec because they represented both an advanced stage of civilization and a race more vigorous than the senescent Indians. But the same historical principles that decreed the sixteenth century triumph of feudalism over barbarism decree in the nineteenth century the triumph of Young America over the remnants of Aztec and conquistador. Anglo-Saxon America embodies in its racial character the traits of pragmatism, realism, liberalism, industriousness, and self-discipline that will shape the industrial and commercial development of the new century. Thus, as Prescott said in a wartime letter, the army of Scott is not only militarily superior to that of Cortes, it is morally superior, and therefore sure of conquering.[22]

The concept of American racial vigor was not exclusively nature-bound. Rather, it deliberately linked natural vigor with the power embodied in industry and in technology. "The Spirit of Young America" is likened in one breath to an eagle that "plumes its young wings for a higher and more glorious flight" and to an engine with "the steam . . . up." Edward D. Mansfield, an army officer whose Mexican War memoir is critical of Polk's provocation of the conflict, regards the struggle itself as an inevitable result of the juxtaposition of two races of different innate endowment; and he describes that endowment in terms that invoke both the natural vigor of agrarian pioneers and the spirit of industrial capitalism:

> The difference of race, religion, and laws, was soon apparent in diversities of sentiment and objects between the old and new inhabitants. The Texan of the United States brought with him, not only greater energy and industry, but a wild and restless ambition —a more intense and speculative pursuit of future objects.

Where differences so deep and original as these exist among different classes of people, they will soon become manifested in external action. The new inhabitants soon seized the direction of all public affairs . . . and looked round for the means of establishing [i.e., by revolution] their own forms of government.

Mansfield's rationale is essentially "scientific"; by his account it becomes the "mission" of the Anglo-Saxon race to conquer the savage and make the New World the home of democracy and economic progress.[23]

The appeal of this doctrine, and its inherent contradictions, can be seen in the coverage of the war by the *Democratic Review*—the premier national organ of the Jackson and Polk Democrats, and the most enthusiastic backer of the Mexican conquest. The magazine makes its case for conquest by asserting first the superiority of the American race, and of American institutions. Its people en masse are a kind of Herrenvolk:

No man with us but has some leisure for thought as well as for toil—none so bowed down by poverty but he stands erect at times in his dignity as a free citizen, and no woman is here unsexed by rude labor and ruder treatment. Democracy is producing the same results with us that it did in ancient Greece. Its influence is seen in the superior classic delicacy of feature and refinement of thought and manner, in universal hightoned courtesy [to] the weaker sex, and in their exquisite gentleness and grace.[24]

But neither superior racial endowment nor the institutions of "democracy alone, even in this enlightened age," are "sufficient to ward off entirely political and social evil." The growth of poor and propertyless classes, especially in the cities, and the related emergence of a privileged class of very wealthy capitalists and merchants threaten Amercia with class warfare. The prospect is aggravated by the rhetoric of abolitionists, who attack the concept of property when they attack slavery, and so pit white against white, class against class. Most of the population is "moral and prudent," but its proportional weight has been diminished by the influx of "pauper" classes as immigrants.

It is plain, that if an increasing population be cramped and confined in too small a space either by artificial or natural restrictions, it will necessarily bring on those evils so prevalent in other countries . . . [If it be so] we must share the fate of older countries; we cannot contravene the laws of nature.[25]

The conquest of Mexico is therefore necessary if both American democracy and the youthful vigor of the American race are to be preserved from revolution and senescence.

This scheme is developed during the war by a mixture of editorials, historical speculations, battle reports, and works of fiction, all of which draw liberally on the language of the Frontier Myth and the associated imagery of racial vigor and technological advancement.

The contrast between Spanish and American modes of conquest is drawn in Prescott's terms:

> While the colonists of other European nations sought, in the wilds of the American continent, only a secure home, in which their industry might meet its reward and their religious scruples be unmolested, the Spanish colonists sought empire by conquest . . . and imposed a regime of oppression and religious bigotry.[26]

There are of course analogies to be made between the ambition of the Spanish and that of the eastern capitalists and abolitionist religious fanatics; but these can be exploited only in other contexts. In speaking of the war, the *Democratic Review* uses its imagery to invoke a consensus and reconcile differences. Editorials availing themselves of the imagery of the Frontier Myth are interspersed with works of fiction, which invoke mythology more directly. During the course of the war itself in 1847–48, the *Democratic Review* ran two serialized "novels." In "The Border Settlement; or, The Tory's Daughter," the Indian conflicts of the Revolution are recalled. The frontier hunter-hero loves the Tory's daughter, but the two are parted by political differences until the consequences of Toryism are made visible in the shape of an Indian attack. Then political partisanship is set aside, and the racial enemy is defeated. War with the Indian on the border, it appears, requires the setting aside of political differences at home. In between the episodes of the novel, an editorial offers the choice "New Territory versus No Territory": the abolitionists who press political issues about slavery will not, it seems, pull together against the Mexican-Indians and so acquire the territory essential to democracy; rather they will take the Indians' part, threatening the United States not merely with the end of expansion (no *new* territory) but perhaps with the loss of the existing domain of republicanism as well.[27]

In 1848, with the debate over whether or not to seize "all Mexico" in full cry, the magazine offered "Chalcahual," a serial novel about the Aztecs and the Spanish conquest. It continued to juxtapose these fictions with its continuing plea for large-scale seizures of Mexican land, but now introduced a third element: minibiographies of noted American entrepreneurs and inventors, embodiments of the progressive spirit of the American race. The first installment of "Chalcahual" opens with a romantic view of Aztec grandeur and invokes the concept of history-as-race-struggle. The Aztec chieftain Chalcahual is pictured surveying the vast ruins of "the Soltees," the nation which preceded the Aztecs, and who by famine, pestilence, and war, had "melted like mist from the land, to give place to the superior race from the north—the Aztecs." We are thus placed in a position to understand that the arrival of Cortes signals yet another chapter in the history of race struggles, superior replacing inferior.[28]

In the case of the "Aztec-Soltee" war, superior strength and cruelty led to the displacement of Indian by Indian. The Spanish arrival pits a culture superior in its mental and spiritual endowment against the mere brawn and prowess of the Aztec. Cortes is not simply a great warrior, he is a man of restraint and forethought. While his companions carelessly enjoy the riches of Mexico, "with Cortes it was different":

> His mind was ill at ease, . . . He saw that his followers were
> rapidly sinking into sloth and a feeling of security, which he knew
> to be the security of those who tread upon a snare . . .

He is like a Jonathan Edwards brooding on the "slippery place" the unregenerate walk in, a Captain Bonneville or Kit Carson holding himself aloof and alert while his Mountain Men comrades debauch themselves: he exercises forethought, self- and social-discipline, and thereby becomes a conqueror and civilizer.[29]

After each of the episodes of Chalcahual, *Democratic Review* offers a biography of an entrepreneur and exponent of advanced technology: Eli Whitney, inventor of the cotton gin; and Henry Miller Shreve, who developed and operated steamboat transportation on the Mississippi. These men represent the "American" spirit now observed to be following in Cortes's footsteps in conquering Mexico. If "Chalcahual" shows the warfare of savages giving way to the feudal conquest of barbarism, the biographies show what the bourgeois-Protestant conquest of feudalism will mean. "A struggle always presents a manly and inspiring spectacle," begins the biography of Whitney—as if a war were to be discussed.[30]

The portrait of Shreve extends this parable between the progress of scientific inquiry and invention and the struggles of warriors and hunters against enemies or against intractable nature. Shreve is explicitly compared to Daniel Boone as a pioneer; and the progress of science and invention is seen as part and parcel of that interaction between expansionism and democratic institutions that produces *American* democracy. The language in which the struggle is represented is drawn from the Frontier Myth. Invention is a "war" pitting intellectual against brute force or the "unwillingness" of nature; and masculine and feminine characters are assigned to the opponents. The triumph of the American race over the Spanish-Mexican-Indian will therefore be the triumph of virile and intellectual qualities over effeminate and brutal ones. As such it is part of a natrual process of historical evolution, in which superior races arise and replace the inferior, and the industrial-technological stage replaces both feudalism and primitive capitalism.[31]

But industrial capitalism is part of the problem to which the conquest of Mexico is supposed to be the solution. The *Democratic Review* appeals to consensus, but it responds to partisan conflict and acknowledges powerful internal divisions in its attacks on Whigs and abolitionists. Moreover, it projects these divisions into the Mexican-American struggle, linking eastern capitalists, who speculate on the labors of the "pioneer army," with the feudal overlords of the Spanish conquest; and associating the religious opposition to slavery with the fanatic bigotry of Spanish Catholic priests. But this projection of the slavery question into the Mexican conflict compromises the *Review*'s assertion that the war is essentially a democratic one, made for the benefit of free labor.[32]

In the early months of the war an effort was made to represent the invasion as a species of liberation for the Mexican poor. This approach affirmed the "gift" of American society for overcoming the class distinction between rich and poor by ignoring American class divisions and projecting the "revolutionary" critique of class outward against an alien society. The passionately expansionist *Democratic Review*—whose editor had coined the phrase "Manifest Destiny"—drew a distinction between the "Spanish" ruling classes of Mexico and the Mexican "nation"—that is, the mass of the people. According to the editorial, the Spanish aristocracy had always treated the Mexican nation as an "inferior race" of Indians, had enslaved them and "exact[ed] from them the proceeds of their labor." As a result, class conflict in Mexico had acquired a racial character, preventing the development of genuine republican institutions capable of obviating the categories of class in that of "citizen." Instead, internal warfare had occurred which had the character of Indian wars like those experienced in the United States, and also like those servile insurrections feared by the southern planters.[33]

These fulminations against Mexican slavery are more than mere propagandistic hypocrisy. They fulfill an ideologically necessary task of scapegoating Mexico for American sins, projecting onto Mexico the unacceptable tendencies of impulses within American society. Earlier generations had done the same thing with Indians, blacks, "squatters," "Tories," and "borderers." But the contradictory character of this ideological approach was obvious from the first. The United States was itself an Indian-killing and slaveholding power, with an ideological commitment to removing all alien races from the path of progress, or subordinating them coercively. It is hard to believe that very many readers could have shared the naive astonishment of the editors of the *Rough and Ready Annual* (1848) at the "singular spectacle" of Mexico as "a people governed by a republican constitution, and claiming republican honors, and yet in fact having its lower classes degraded to the condition of slaves." From its inception the United States had been characterized by just such a mixture. But in Mexico, this condition applies not only to the nonwhites (Indian and African) who are slaves by birth; it is imposed on those Mexicans who have the character of free laborers and operatives. These classes, corresponding to the workmen of American cities, are energetic fellows who try to improve their condition; but in the process they fall into debt, and thence into a form of slavery indistinguishable from that of plantation blacks: "Often the wretched laborer is separated from friends and home, and obliged to toil in helpless misery," like Uncle Tom sold south from Kentucky. But even this portrayal of Mexico draws on familiar American analogies, from the literature of antislavery and from portrayals of urban life like those of Lippard in *Monks of Monk Hall*. The very analogies that make the Mexican tyranny ideologically comprehensible undermine the assertion that American society is a fit and appropriate antidote to that kind of tyranny, for this Mexico is simply Lippard's dystopian vision come true.[34]

The only way in which such an analogy can work in favor of the "liberator" mystique is by denying the identity of racial character between the Mexican *nation* and the American. And in fact the language of class struggle was replaced by the language of racial struggle, in the portrayal of both the Spanish conquest and the American liberation. This is accomplished by first faulting the Spanish for departing from the American model of racial interaction: they have intermarried as well as subjugated, and they have indulged their own national-racial gifts for sensuality and cruelty at the inferior race's expense. The result is that they have blended their own racial character with that of the conquered savages; and although distinctions between Mexican and Spanish savages can still be made, the distinction is analogous to that between the evil Indians of Cooper's fictions and the white renegades who are often more savage than the savages—and never more so than when their ancestry is European and aristocratic.

Thus as the war went forward, the tendency of ideological argument was toward the representation of Mexico as a unitary racial antagonist, rather than as a dark mirror image of the class divisions in republican society. This permitted the portrayal of the Spanish as a renegade class worthy of extermination or expulsion, and the Mexicans proper as a nation fit for racial subservience. The author of the *Rough and Ready Annual's* article on "Slavery in Mexico" represents the Indians as sharing the innately servile temperament attributed by proslavery spokesmen to blacks:

> The Indians of Mexico . . . were made slaves by Cortez, and as such they remain at the present day. They work the mines, execute the public works, and are engaged in the meanest drudgeries. Their children will be slaves after them: servitude is the hereditary legacy of the father; and his sons know not to aspire further. [Their] native atmosphere is slavery, and [they] cannot thrive in any other.[35]

The war itself could now be treated more like an Indian war, and the savage character of the Mexican people emerged as a more serious threat than the cleverness of the Spanish ruling classes. Mexican Indian character, rather than Spanish aristocratic character, was now to be blamed for the "barbarities" supposedly committed against American soldiers and property. G. N. Allen's *Mexican Treacheries and Cruelties . . .* (1847) represents the Mexicans as Indians who butcher the helpless and mutilate the dead—not at the behest of evil rulers, but out of national or racial propensities: "Some of these outrages appear to have opened the eyes of [the naive who imagine the Mexicans to be a wronged and injured people], and induced them to think that this faithless and cowardly nation have been punished no more than they deserve." The Mexican War was now seen in the terms of dimenovel revenge plots: Indian atrocities and captivities must be revenged for the sake of civilization.[36]

"Savagery" is reflected in the association of cruelty and sexuality. Like the Indians, the Mexicans are said to kill the wounded, torture prisoners, and mutilate the dead; and they prefer "concubinage" to civilized marriage, a sure sign of barbarism. The opposition of a savage foe implies that the struggle will by necessity be one of limitless and extraordinary violence for both sides. Since the savage Mexicans recognize no civilized restraints, Americans are in some sense ethically liberated from those restraints as well. The pamphlet does not advocate the massacre or rape of helpless Mexican peasants; but its author does accept such actions by American soldiers as a natural and inevitable response to the savage nature of the war. The precedents for this acceptance are to be found in the traditions of Indian fighting (and Indian hating) and frontier vigilantism. The writer of *Mexican*

Treacheries recounts an incident in which over a hundred Mexican civilians were murdered or lynched, and their women and children saved from a similar fate only by the exertions of American officers. While he deplores "excesses," he affects to understand the outraged feelings of the soldiers, and to a large degree permits us to identify with them.

Once the parties agree to stand on the familiar ground of racial opposition, the Frontier Mythology can work as the basis of a consensus, and the Mexican War can appear as a grand-scale Indian war, with the triumph of civilization and the appropriation of unused resources as the consequence of American victory. But the Mexican "race" is not unambiguously "Indian" in character; it may share either the capacity for freedom of the white race or the capacity for servitude of the black. In either case, the conquest of all Mexico becomes problematical, because it departs from the Frontier model of Indian Removal followed by development: Mexico is already developed, and its people are too numerous and useful to exterminate or to remove as the Indians have been. It therefore remains either to assimilate its "non-white" citizenry, or to treat the Mexicans as a new source of slaves—or else, to decline the conquest and the role of conquistador, and to take only those regions that could accommodate free and independent hunters and pioneers.

In contrast to Mexico, Oregon was "vacant" land—that is, inhabited *only* by Indians—and was well suited to exploitation by small farmers in the traditional Frontier manner. Those interested in continuing expansion in the yeoman-farmer mode had little interest in acquiring territories with large subject populations requiring continued subordination. Alternately, those interested in an industrial type of expansion—plantation owners, capitalists interested in mining, merchants looking for urban bases for Pacific trade—found the idea of seizing populated territory more appealing.

In the prewar period, the "Oregon" partisans tended to oppose engagement with Mexico, in favor of the use of force and diplomacy to guarantee all of Oregon (not just the half eventually gained by compromise). In the South, Oregon held little interest in comparison with the desire to make Texas sure and to extend territory southwestward. The division of opinion was partly sectional, but there were ideological and commercial interests that cut across North/South lines. Southern Democrats were at first almost uniformly enthusiastic about seizing all or most of Mexico, but many southern Whigs were lukewarm on the war, and did not want to attempt the assimilation of large sections of Mexico proper, for fear of provoking a crisis over slavery extension. In the North and West there was a good deal of newspaper agitation for the war and for maximum seizures of territory. But here too opinion divided between those whose motives derived from "agrarian cupidity" and those whose interests were primarily commercial. In every section, including the South, the "middling" classes of white businessmen, artisans, and farmers (the backbone of Jacksonian democracy) resisted the policy of extensive seizures in the most populous regions of Mexico, although they generally supported acquisition of "vacant" or sparsely populated regions.

The strongest and most consistent advocates of seizing "all Mexico" were to be found in the commercial centers of the Northeast (especially in

New York) and in the commercial seaports of the South—that is, in New Orleans and Charleston. It was to these centers of the investment and carrying trades that the acquisition of a large peon population—for plantation and harbor work, as a market of goods—appeared profitable; and they also coveted the Isthmian routes to the Pacific that ran through Mexico. This last group exercised considerable influence over the making of public opinion, through their control of the "penny press" that had developed in the larger cities as a primary means of mass communication. Here were cheaply priced, sensationalistic journals, which catered specifically to the lower middle and poorer classes of the cities and adjacent countryside. Some of these journals developed national circulation, notably the New York *Herald* and the more respectable *Tribune.* These papers represented a variety of political affiliations, ranging from Whiggish or Republican to party-line Democratic, to "independent" like the *Herald* or reformist like the prewar *Tribune.* However, their editors shared a common interest in economic policy, as seen through the filter of New York's commercial banking and investment financing institutions.[37]

Since the success of these papers and the prosperity and political power of their editors depended on mass circulation, proprietors of the penny press became adept at assessing and responding to the mood of their audience—even, at times, of anticipating or shaping that mood. Thus the New York papers—to choose the most important group—were in a unique position of mediating between a vital sector of the ruling elite—the men of commerce and banking—and the newly urbanized and partly proletarianized lower and middle classes of the city. Unlike the agricultural papers of the West, the urban penny press was attuned to the potentially explosive climate of an America in which the safety valve of cheap land and perpetual expansion no longer operated. Their sensitivity to this prospect had been heightened in the forties by economic hard times resulting from financial panics and contraction in 1837, 1839, and 1841. In the West, these had led to disastrous drops in commodity prices, and provoked an escapist enthusiasm for the lush farmland of Oregon. In the East it raised the specter of violent class struggle and revolution by the urban underclasses, increasingly identified with the Catholic immigrant Irish.[38]

Those who proposed the annexation of Mexico and either the enfranchisement or the empeonage of its citizens went against the current of the existing racialist mythology that had been developed from earlier Frontier periods, and in this lay a major cause of their failure. The imperial thrust of the Anglo-Saxon race, according to American mythology, had required movement into unpeopled or sparsely peopled territory—land that could be conquered against the opposition of natural obstacles and the resistance of a small native race, whose resistance would force their final extermination or removal. Through that struggle, the Anglo-Saxon's character would be improved, and at war's end he would be left to master the soil without having had to compromise the purity of his blood—the Roman method of conquer and interbreed was not for the Anglo-Saxon. Part of the justification for the war had also been the assertion that the Mexicans, like the American Indians, made no use (or bad use) of the land given into their hands, declining or failing to "improve" it:

The Mexicans are *Indians*—Aboriginal Indians. Such Indians as Cortez conquered . . . only rendered a little more mischievous by a bastard civilization. The infusion of European blood whatever it is, and that, too, in a highly *illegitimate* way, is not enough . . . to affect the character of the people. They do not possess the elements of an *independent* national existence. The Aborigines of this country have not attempted, and cannot attempt to exist *independently* alongside of us. Providence has ordained it, and it is folly not to recognize the fact. The Mexicans are *Aboriginal Indians*, and they must share the destiny of their race.

It follows as well that the Mexicans are incapable of racial regeneration, and hence can never be acceptable as equal partners in the Union. Mixed races are "inferior to the pure races, and as members of society they are the worst class of citizens." American government is above all "a government of the white race," the "caucasian race—the free white race."[39]

Finally it follows that to restore Mexico its freedom from American power is as antipathetic to the spirit of American civilization as permitting a "reflux of barbarism" in Kentucky and Tennessee. Senator Ambrose H. Sevier (Arkansas), chairman of the Committee on Foreign Relations, carries the logic of the metaphor into advocating seizing "all Mexico." Granted that the Mexican "Indians" are unassimilable as citizens; granted that the American Anglo-Saxon wants land for independent farming, not peons to rule over. He therefore proposes: let the Cherokee policy be applied to Mexico, and the Mexicans removed to distant reservations, like the Indians.[40]

Two points need emphasis here. The first is that the power of the mythologized view of American-history-as-Indian-war was capable of distorting American perceptions of reality to the point where the metaphoric association of Mexicans and Indians could provoke, however briefly, serious proposals for depopulating Mexico by removing the Mexicans to reservations. The second and related point is that the Jacksonian economic ideology carried by the myth, with its emphatic assertion that the universal distribution of cheap land was the guarantee of both progress and democracy, remained the heart of popular political faith, so that even the proponents of seizure of all Mexico had ultimately to resort to it in appealing for support. North or South, there was simply no popular support for the establishment of an American-ruled feudal-industrial state in Mexico; on the other hand, there was great support for any seizures of land which could be made available for exploitation by farmers.

Press responses to the problem of conquest developed according to the pattern already followed by the *Democratic Review*. Initially there was consensus on the reasons for the war, the necessity of Frontier expansion, and the traditional character of that expansion. Gradually, an issue is joined on choice of Frontiers (Mexico vs. Oregon) and of American roles (conquistador vs. pioneer); and these are related to the terms of the political debate over slavery and the place of labor in an industrializing economy.

The New York *Morning News*, in an editorial whose sense was echoed by most of the penny press, distinguished American from European "aggression" in that the Americans' was directed not against civilized fellow nations, but against empty space and natural difficulties. Unlike European powers, "our way lies, not over trampled nations, but through desert wastes, to be brought by our industry and energy within the domain of art and civilization." Not populous Mexico, but the territory north of the Rio Grande is the occasion of enthusiasm: "We are contiguous to a vast portion of the globe, untrodden save by the savage and the beast . . ." Americans, whether competing among themselves or with other states, gain prosperity not by stealing the property of another, but by creating new property or appropriating the unappropriated. This is in the nature of our situation: "Rapacity and spoliation cannot be the features of this magnificent enterprise . . . We take from no man; the reverse rather—we give to man."[41]

In general terms, this doctrine could stand as a device for promoting enthusiasm for the war and encouraging enlistments. A recruiting appeal to North Carolinians, for example, promised that not only would the recruit "get to see the whole Southwest, without the expense incident to travelling," but would "doubtless . . . receive a handsome bounty of the choicest lands" because "Mexico will have to pay the expense of the war," with "California, New Mexico, &c." as "the forfeit of Mexican madness and barbarity." That such promises were effectual is attested to by the protests of New England troops when the army refused to muster them out in the West so they could get a head start on the land grab. Politicians and diplomats likewise accused Britain in Oregon and Spain in California–New Mexico of failing to "improve" the land by cultivation, permitting instead the savage hunter and indolent brave to monopolize the land.[42] The application of the "improvement" standard here is, of course, as indefensible as it is novel: it had never been justified as a basis for assessing the rights of nations. Rather, it was the traditional measure by which whites dispossessed Indians, and rich latecomers displaced white squatters. Were Britain and Mexico in any sense to be seen as "Indians" or "squatters"?

The American challenge to British rights in Oregon was legitimated in the public mind not only by the legalism of prior discovery or by the sanctification of a simple greed for more land; it hinged on the belief that British occupation was equivalent to maintaining the region as the domain of Indian savages, and American conquest meant its development by independent farmers and mechanics. In confronting the issue of incorporating Mexicans, Americans had to resolve the same questions already being asked about excluded groups north of the border: are they capable of "regeneration," of conversion to or spiritual rebirth as a reasonable facsimile of Anglo-Saxon Americans? If they are not, then there is no acceptable basis for incorporating them with the American republic. To attempt to bring them into the Union on any basis would require an immediate choice between two equally unacceptable principles: to grant them citizenship, and also accept the principle of racial equality along with its corollary of full citizenship rights for Blacks and Indians; or, on the other hand, to formally accept the principle that a regime of racial slavery was a permanent and legitimate part of the American future. The final outcome of the negotiations over California and Oregon was not determined by the answers to questions of this kind. There were concrete incentives and assets at stake, and a balance of international relations valuable in itself which had to be maintained by diplomatic circumlocution and compromise. Nonetheless, public concern about the policies worked out by officials and diplomats was articulated in these terms.

Those who favored seizing and ruling all Mexico prophesied ready acquiescence to American rule and speedy conversion of the populace of the level of at least the lowest class of American citizens; those who were leery of territorial cession were pessimistic about the conversion of the Mexicans. An Illinois congressman stated the case in typical terms, citing the "effeminacy" of Mexican character as the basis for an acquiescent attitude to American tutelage:

> Could they be brought under the happy influence of such a Government as our own . . . what might we not hope from them? The Indian population, numbering about four millions, are reputed to be very gentle and quiet in their dispositions, apt to learn, and willing to improve, and, if not possessed of all the manlier virtues, have at least those which ensure their cheerful acquiescence to our control and rapid advancement under it.[43]

The editor of the New York *Sun* wrote that "The [Mexican] race is perfectly accustomed to being conquered, and the only new lesson we shall teach is that our victories will give liberty, safety, and prosperity to the vanquished, if they know enough to profit by the appearance of our stars." The *Herald's* James Gordon Bennett, who veered hot and cold on the "all Mexico" issue (according to his reading of the public mood), went so far as to say that Mexico would be "gorgeously" happy at her annexation and "Like the Sabine virgins, she will soon learn to love her ravisher." Thus what began as rape might end in happy marriage.[44]

The supposed effeminacy of the Mexicans guaranteed not only their conquest, but also promised to facilitate their subjection. But subjection in the context of racial division implied some form of enslavement or peonage, and hence raised again all of those issues the Frontier was supposed to help Americans evade. The editor of the New Orleans *Picayune* illustrates the difficulty perfectly, in his attempt to overcome northern objections by invoking the history of the Puritan-Indian wars as a precedent for the conquest of Mexico, and linking both conquests to the consensus view of Anglo-Saxon racial character:

> We may condemn, we may argue against the tendency of a race of men of higher organization, bolder hearts, more enterprising minds, of superior thews and muscles, and stouter wills, to supplant weak and emasculated tribes—good authority can be evoked to show how wrong all this is—homilies to this day are written against the pilgrim fathers for ejecting the savages from the primeval forests of the North; but until the eloquence of ethics can melt human nature and mould it anew . . . [no] scrap of philosophy, or moral essay, nor political disquisition can countervail the dangerous odor of fields in perennial blossom to an army of Anglo-Saxons.[45]

But the attraction the "Gringos" found in Mexico was not in its agrarian promise of ever blooming fields awaiting the plow. It was the urban character of Mexico that impressed the soldiers, and the masses of people that dominated their portrayal of Mexican abundance. Nonetheless this vision was perceived as threatful by many, including a North Carolina soldier, whose portrait of a crowd in Puebla draws on the imagery of silent sullen masses that Lippard deploys so effectively in *Monks of Monk Hall*— and perhaps also on the imagery of the southern planter surrounded by masses of resentful Africans who want only a leader to set them on the path of blood:

> I thought I had seen large masses of human beings before, but I never saw a shoreless sea of living, moving, animated matter, composed of crowding thousands of men, women and children, ebbing and flowing like the agitated waves of the ocean . . . As I cast my eyes round, I almost shuddered for the fate of our little army. Although I saw no arms or warlike implements of any kind, nor anything like a military organization, yet the immense cloud of hostile citizens that hovered round our little band in dark and portentous gloom, was altogether sufficient to have crushed our whole force into utter annihilation . . . all they wanted was a bold and daring leader who could have given direction and impetus to public feeling, and led the already excited populace in a united and organized body against the heart of the invading foe.[46]

But depictions of Mexico shared the contradictions of images of domestic class relations; and projected solutions for the Mexican involvement evoked the ideological contradictions of a society equally bent on aggrandizing the industrial capitalist and promising equalization in wealth to all white males. An Ohio soldier pondered the simultaneous belief in the moral correctness of egalitarianism and in the inferiority of certain races:

> One thing in particular pleased me much, and that was, *the equality of all ranks before the altar of God.* For here I saw kneeling . . . the haughty Castillian in whose veins flowed the pure blood of the Cortes, the yellow Aztec, the stupid Indian, and the decrepid negro, altogether, side by side; the distinctions of races, of color, of wealth, of rank was disregarded or unknown and they all seemed to regard each other, at least in the Sanctuary, as equal before God. In one instance (and I am satisfied it was of common occurrence) I saw a beautiful, young, fair, Spanish girl, evidently of the highest class, kneeling, and just in front of her, was an old negro beggar in the same attitude, while at the side of the negro was a Castillian gentleman and his little son (about Tom's age) all devoutly offering up their prayers . . . without even a thought of "Negro pews" or "poor seats," and then I wished that it were so in my own, my native land, where we boast that all men are *free and equal.*[47]

Implicit in the accounts of both the Carolinian and the Ohioan is the perception that the actual character of the Mexicans is different from that predicted by the myth of Mexican "effeminacy." From the viewpoint of one committed to their subjection, they appear capable of both resentment and of violent opposition; from the viewpoint of one prepared to sympathize with them, they appear capable of sharing the American's commitment to egalitarianism, and to the achievement of economic and political power that such egalitarianism implies. What is true of the Mexicans is also true of those groups whose supposed racial traits were projected onto the Mexicans. The dispossession of the Indians was rationalized by the myth of their incorrigible savagery; but that myth derived its intensity from the need to resist evidence that Indians were indeed capable of adapting to the new order of things in their own fashion. Likewise the subjection of blacks and women and of the new proletariat of the cities was rationalized by a myth of their innate incapacity for achievement and willingness to be ruled paternally; and this myth also became the focus of ideological fantasy because it was needed to rationalize and explain away the real evidence of economic discontent and political ambitions among those classes of the population.

Thus the war ended by exposing the fallacies of the consensus evoked by the Myth of the Frontier. Within the army of conquest, divisions appeared between those who persisted in seeing the war as a liberation of the Mexican underclass, and those who saw it as the prelude to a national leap into imperialism. Under the ideological divisions, social divisions made themselves felt in intense problems of morale and discipline, and the violence visited upon the Mexicans by occupying troops. Of exceptional interest is the falling away of numbers of Irish and Catholic soldiers from their American loyalty, not simply through desertion but through a transfer of loyalty to Mexico. The famous San Patricio battalion, which distinguished itself at Buena Vista, was formed by Santa Anna from these deserters, whose willingness to fight testified to their motive in deserting. The desertion of the San Patricios has been attributed to the discrimination they had experienced as Catholics and impoverished laborers in American cities; and their affiliation with Mexico has been taken as suggesting an understanding that the Frontier dream of landownership and political or religious freedom was better realized outside the United States.[48]

Together with the slavery issue, the debate over the seizure of "all Mexico" compelled Americans to define more exactly their commitment to democratic equality. In this context, it became difficult to maintain an operative belief in the comfortable paradox which held that society could consist of superior and inferior races, without prejudice to democratic practices or egalitarian faith. Some were moved to a more radical assertion of the need to preserve and extend the regime of Free Labor as against the southern system of degraded labor. Others were compelled to affirm a concept of democracy in which the ideal of equality was no longer sacred.

At the very time that the *Democratic Review* was hailing the army of Taylor as the liberator of the Mexican working class, it was responding to proposals for the abolition of slavery in terms that predicted a very different function for the Gringos. The doctrines of racial equality on which abolitionism is based are not seen as democratic values, but as "the sole instrument by which British aristocracy and feudalism in the Old World, could hope to disturb the march of the great republic." "Feudalism" in Mexico had been, at that stage in the *Review*'s defense of the war, the system of slavery and peonage; yet that same "Feudalism" is here linked with egalitarianism. It is the presence of the racial issue that obliterates any logical address to the problem of establishing a just equilibrium between the classes. For the editor of the *Democratic Review*, abolitionism will create just the form of racially amalgamated and degenerate society here that it attributes to Mexico (and to "ancient Sodom").[49]

Thus the transformation of the Mexican War into an Indian or race war provided only a temporary basis of consensus on the necessity of conquest. Once the analogy was developed it evoked all of the essential disagreements that underlay the ambivalent imagery of "Noble Savages" and "degenerate heathen." The race war analogy totalized the program of conquest into an assault on the entire Mexican nation, and so justified the seizure of all Mexico or any part of it. But analogies apply in two directions, and the application of the race war analogy to Mexico reflected a dangerous split in American ideology. The defenders of slavery projected onto Mexico an antipathy for abolitionism that was potentially as complete as the hatred of Indians; and for their part the enemies of slavery and slavery extension projected onto Mexico their disgust with the southern system of slavery, and their wish to destroy or somehow be rid of it.

The debate over annexing Mexico brought these contradictions to the surface, by compelling ideologists to act upon their fictive premises.

To annex Mexico would require the Americans either to impose an American aristocracy on the sullen and hostile peons—whose hatred of servitude already had provoked revolution against Spanish and Mexican overlords—or to prepare a race strongly tinctured with Indian and Negro blood for full citizenship. The proposal to extend peonage or slavery met with strong objection from all whose interests cut against the aspirations of the South, including both the manufacturing North and the western farmers who hungered for the lands of the Mexican Cession. Even in the South, and generally among the Whigs, there was fear that the strength of the nation was simply insufficient to establish and maintain such rule in Mexico. At the same time, there was widespread agreement, except among committed abolitionist egalitarians, that the colored races were unfit for citizenship; and that to prepare the Mexican for citizenship would require that the Negro and Indian likewise be admitted as equals. James Gordon Bennett, two days after proposing that the rape of Mexico might lead to some permanent union, characterized the "marriage" as "ill-starred and unhappy." The great source of Anglo-Saxon strength, according to most accounts, was its exclusivity, its refusal to mingle its blood with that of lesser races.[50]

In this regard, Bennett found a "strange bedfellow" in the antiwar minister A. A. Livermore, whose *The War with Mexico Reviewed* warned against "introducing into the rights and privileges of American citizens a horde of 'outside barbarians,' the mongrel races of New Mexico and California," which will "cheapen . . . the American birthright." Livermore's response is a complicated one, and revealing of the deep ambivalences that both generated and undermined ideological responses to the Mexican War and slavery issues. As a pacifist, Livermore condemns the military ardor of Americans and their hunger for land—both of which are attributable to the course of frontier expansion and its attendant wars. He also condemns specifically that "pride of race" by which "Anglo-Saxons have been apparently persuaded to think themselves the chosen people, the anointed race of the Lord," with a destiny to Christianize and civilize through conquest—a means which, to Livermore, invalidates the ends.

Yet Livermore also appeals to Anglo-Saxon folk wisdom and to the idea of race superiority in his condemnation of warfare, and in his attribution of large responsibility for the war to the "foreign" element in the population: "hundreds of thousands, with all their old-world ideas, unbaptized into the spirit of liberty except it be as license." Such men, along with criminal elements in the native population, are both excited and armed by warfare for a life of continued violence and rapine—against helpless Mexican citizens now, perhaps against helpless Americans later on. Livermore's warning against incorporating "outside barbarians" has force, because he believes that the nation has already a large share of "inside barbarians," in its frontiersmen and its immigrants. According to Livermore, the school and church have followed the frontiersman too slowly, with the result that the wilderness life has been given time to produce a "rank development of barbaric passions and habits. The tendencies to physical violence, somewhere or upon somebody, it mattered little where or upon whom, have had too little check."[51]

Livermore's response is the traditional one of those groups—often conservative and ministerial—who resisted the rapid development of the frontier ahead of the expansion of religious institutions. The Mathers had condemned the land hunger of the seventeenth-century Puritans in terms not dissimilar to Livermore's; and later writers, for whom racial integrity was more significant than doctrinal purity, had cast the argument in terms of the "mongrelization" of the pioneers, the degeneration into yellow-skinned "lubbers" or white-Indian renegades, the production of "half-breeds." If such considerations could be urged against expansion into sparsely populated Indian country, how much more did they operate in the case of Mexico, whose large population and complex economy and culture offered at once tremendously attractive and seductive temptations (wealth, exoticism), and the threat of a nonwhite population which would be too large to "remove" or "exterminate" as had been done with the Indians.[52]

The agreement of Livermore and Bennett on the inadmissibility of Mexico proper as the sphere of Frontier expansion masks a fundamental contradiction in their use of the consensus-giving Frontier Myth. For Bennett, it is absolutely essential to insist that the consequence of the violence of the war has been the regeneration of both the American economy and the racial vigor of the Anglo-Saxon. Perhaps the course of racial destiny does not yet require that we rule a large subject population; but in the agrarian potential of California and New Mexico there is a field for the exercise of the old pioneer virtues. Racial degeneracy remains the destiny of the Mexicans; and a spiritual taint of that degeneracy is attributed to those whose ideological resistance to the war put them in a position of sympathy with Mexico (and therefore with both Indians and black slaves). For Livermore the terms are inverted. He cites numerous atrocities committed by American troops as evidence that this war has led to a degeneration of the race: Americans have done things "that negroes in a state of insurrection would hardly be guilty of." Some Mexicans are reported to have fled to the Comanches for protection from the Americans —just as Crèvecoeur's "Frontier Man" flees to the Indians to escape the insanity of a war between white men. Livermore echoes Irving's belief that the climate of the new territories will cause the emigrants to degenerate into "ignorance, licentiousness, idleness, intemperance, and every savage and every civilized vice."[53]

So the debate on the Mexican War ends by returning us to the original ground of controversy, the original contradiction in the world represented by the Myth of the Frontier. The categories of class and ideological division within the Metropolis assert their dominance, and the racial symbolism that is meant to invoke consensus becomes the language in which the internal divisions of the Metropolis are expressed.

CHAPTER 9

The Myth That Wasn't: Literary Responses
to the Mexican War, 1847–1850

The ideological premises of the Myth of the Frontier defined
the character of a righteous conquest in terms that forbade the assimilation
of Mexico proper to the United States. Although the Myth permitted racial
warfare as a means of achieving progress, it envisioned such wars as
involving extermination or displacement of small bands of savages by
civilized men, not the conquest and integration of another populous culture
into the American system—whether as fellow citizens or as slaves. The
ideological imperatives that justified a war with Mexico contained contradictory elements that forbade the thoroughgoing treatment of Mexico as an
Indian Frontier. However, those same doctrines were appropriate to the
seizure of territories that were represented as "vacant" or only sparsely
settled, and thus the ideology that failed to assimilate Mexico to its language did indeed assimilate California, Oregon, and the Southwest.

A similar pattern emerges in the literary responses to the Mexican
War. Although there was considerable journalistic excitement about the
Napoleonic battles fought by the armies of Taylor and Scott, in the two
decades after the war itself, very little literary fiction appeared featuring
Mexican War settings—only a few popular books and dime novels, and no
"serious" hardbound fiction of the historical romance type. None of the
published works enjoyed wide popularity or favorable notice, and none
gave birth to series or imitations, as the Frontier romances had done. As
literary territory, the Mexican War barely exists, and certainly occupies less
imaginative ground than the least of the skirmishes with the Iroquois or
(in a later era) the Apache. Some quality in the historical experience itself
appears to have doomed to failure the attempts of writers to assimilate the
experience to the existing language of literary mythology. The chief enduring addition to the vocabulary of American myth made by Mexican War
fiction was the legend of Kit Carson, the conquest of California, and the
gold rush. But the special circumstances of Carson's adventures made it
easy for writers to treat them in the conventional terms of existing myth—
California was simply a marginally Hispanic and somewhat exotic variant
of the "vacant" wilderness frontier, not excessively unlike that of Spanish

Louisiana in Cooper's *The Prairie*; and Carson was simply a modern version of Daniel Boone. But attempts to assimilate the unique and characteristically Mexican aspects of the Mexican War to existing mythology were as unsuccessful as the efforts to assimilate "all Mexico."

DIME NOVELS AND ROMANCES *

Attempts to turn the Mexican War into fictional material began almost as hostilities ceased. Newton M. Curtis and "Harry Halyard" produced six dime novels on the subject in 1847–48; and George Lippard's *Legends of Mexico* and *'Bel of Prairie Eden* appeared in 1847. These three all attempted to utilize the mythic and ideologically charged conventions of the Indian war romance on the Mexican War problem. The problem of Mexican-American relations is posed in the conventional terms of a romantic love crossed by political conflict. According to the formula established by Cooper, the reconcilability of conflicting classes or races is determined by the acceptability of the idea of intermarriage between them. Minor gradations of ethnic character or status are no impediment to marriage between representatives of genuine "natural aristocracies": a noble Effingham may wed a merely well-to-do Temple, a gentlemanly Captain Middleton can wed a Spanish aristocrat (Inez), a Virginian subaltern can marry the daughter of a Scottish colonel and laird. But the more crucial divisions of class and race preclude marriage, and those who attempt to cross such lines transgress laws of man and nature—for which they are punished with death, exile, or the judgment of the law (Magua, Cora, Hurry Harry, the Bushes).

The Mexican War romances divide on precisely this question. Some of them represent Mexicans as a species of savage, or as a people whose only class identity is that of "lower orders." Others present Mexican society as containing a genuinely aristocratic element whose daughters—like Inez in *The Prairie*—are worthy of bearing the children of Anglo-Saxon heroes. The problem is posed in the characterization of Mexican men, particularly in the catchall figure of "the ranchero"; but it is resolved only in the treatment of the women.

The first mention of the ranchero figure is found in newspaper dispatches early in the war. The *Herald* describes *rancheros* as a popular adjunct of the regular Mexican forces—a guerrilla force, akin to scouts or rangers in the American service. Like the rangers, rancheros fight in the manner of Indians. But their half-breed racial character makes them more like the renegades of Frontier mythology—Simon Girty, Magua, Injun Joe. The *Herald* presents them—rather than Mexican officers of Spanish blood—as the most significant and dangerous element of the Mexican opposition:

---

* This discussion is based on material developed by Melissa Totten, "Metaphors of Conquest: The Fiction of the Mexican War, 1846–1848." Honors thesis, Wesleyan University, 1981, done under my supervision.

But, perhaps, the most formidable portion of the Mexican army are the *rancheros*—the Arabs of Mexico. These *rancheros* are a wild, wandering race, half Indian, half Spanish, who live almost entirely in the saddle. . . . They will venture into any danger in pursuit of plunder; but . . . cannot be made effective in a pitched battle, in consequence of the entire absence of discipline that prevails among them.[1]

The *Herald*'s depiction comports with its thesis that Mexico is Indian territory, and liable to the same sort of seizure already visited upon the eastern woodlands. But other writers respond to the civilized character of Mexico by interpreting the ranchero as a social class rather than as a race. The hero of Curtis's *The Hunted Chief* asserts that the rancheros are not at all nomadic savages, but represent a "disreputable" stratum from the "filthy suburbs" of Mexican society. As an oppressed but energetic class they are candidates for liberation by America's democratic army; and in Curtis's account the rancheros show their amenability to American aims by acquiescing in demands for the liberation of their American captives.

Harry Halyard's novels favor the plot convention employed by Cooper in *The Pioneers*, Bird in *Nick of the Woods*, and Simms in *The Yemassee*— the hero is a born aristocrat who has been forced to hide his identity and go into exile, because of a criminal injustice committed against him back in the Metropolis. In *The Heroine of Tampico: or, Wildfire the Wanderer* (1847) the hero is Wallingford, a northern soldier, whose beloved is being forced by her wealthy merchant father to marry a corrupt Mexican nobleman. A military aristocrat of the Middleton-Effingham type, Wallingford is assisted by a Leatherstocking-like Kentucky backwoodsman (Wildfire), who has been by turns a "volunteer of a corps of Kentucky rangers," the adopted father of an Indian girl named Azilca (cf. Telie Doe in *Nick of the Woods*), and a sailor in the navy (another of Cooper's interests). But it transpires that Wildfire is also a displaced member of the natural elite: he began life as member of a wealthy Boston family, "of the higher class of farmers." The villains of the piece are class-proud aristocrat-merchants, one American and one Mexican, and it is from this corrupt alliance that the woman must be rescued.

The *rancheros* of Mexico are no worse impediment to this deeper struggle than are the Indians in the novels of Cooper, Simms, and Bird. It is the heroes' and heroines' adventures among these primitives that lead to the unveiling of their true characters, the undoing of the villains, and the restoration of true lovers and natural leaders to their proper position. A similar plot is used in *The Chieftain of Churubusco*, this time pitting a worthy middle-class American against the machinations of a rich New Yorker and an English aristocrat to keep him from his beloved. Again, in *The Mexican Spy*, the plot involves "another fallen gentleman" who restores his wealth and status through a Mexican captivity-and-rescue.[2]

In all these stories, the Mexican War is merely background to a conflict that pits different elements of American social class and caste against each other. The Frontier Myth operates in a very general sense, since the adventure in Mexico is the occasion through which the right order of society and natural love is restored. However, in none of these stories is it suggested that the successful resolution of the conflict depends on the establishment of a particular and intimate relationship to Mexico. This contrasts with the Indian war romance, in which the rescue of the woman and the consummation of legitimate love is associated with the successful conquest of the wilderness, the integration of Indian territory with civilization, and the "final solution" of the Indian problem. But such an outcome could not be presented without authorial resolution of the problem of what Mexico was, and what America ought to do about "her."

The treatment of captives is the moral litmus test of class and racial character in the Indian war romance, and the test is also applied in fiction of the Mexican War. Curtis's treatments are quite conventional, in that he represents Mexicans as capturing Americans whom they release after their subordination to the will of the American hero. This scenario is perfectly suited to the requirements of wartime propaganda, which naturally preferred to show American invasion not as aggression but as revenge-and-rescue for the abuse and captivity of Americans and American territory. But the propaganda premise was scarcely sustained by the facts, and after 1847 the pretense was dropped altogether: it was America that had captured Mexico, not vice versa; and it was the morality of the American captor that was to be judged by the standard of treatment of captives.

The most extended, serious, and explicit attempt to mythologize the Mexican war in these terms was made by George Lippard. We have seen in *Monks of Monk Hall* that Lippard was moved by a vision of the catastrophe of oppression and class war that awaited the Metropolis in an America deprived of a land Frontier and of the expansive economic conditions such a Frontier created. He greeted the Mexican War with some enthusiasm, in part because it offered just the sort of promise that had been banished from his own fictive "Quaker City." In the year the war began, Lippard had enjoyed a spectacular literary success with a volume called *Legends of the Revolution*, in which he attempted to fabricate something like a "mythology" of the Revolution: a work that would have the moralizing capability of fable, and the authority of history. He attempted to repeat his success by treating the Mexican War in a similar format, alternating chapters of polemic, historical battle-narrative and symbolizing fiction. The work was broken off before the original design was carried to completion, and Lippard wrote instead the short novel *'Bel of Prairie Eden*—a Gothic murdering piece that appears to undercut and undo the optimistic interpretation of the war set forth in *Legends of Mexico*. Together, the books illustrate the failure of existing literary mythology to overcome the ideological contradictions inherent in the Mexican venture.

Lippard begins *Legends* with an apology for the American invasion of Mexico that draws heavily on the mythology of the Indian wars. Our war is a civilizing enterprise, "The Crusade of the Nineteenth Century," undertaken in just revenge for the massacres committed by the Mexicans on "our brothers in Texas." The Mexicans are half-breeds, a "mongrel race moulded of Indian and Spanish blood," as merciless as Indians in battle: "Ask

mercy from the tigress robbed of her cubs, but not from the Mexican
Ranchero!" The Americans are a virile and progressive race, "a new People
created from the pilgrims and wanderers of all nations . . . [whose] lineage
is from God." The American army is an uprising of the common people
"suddenly transformed into a disciplined army." The "hardy mechanic"
joins the "embrowned farmer" and "pale student" to march together in the
ranks, under the command of soldierly aristocrats like Zachary Taylor. The
very classes who figured as hapless victims of bankers and slaveholders in
Monks of Monk Hall form the liberating army—and it is they themselves
who are liberated by this conquest: thus the Mexican War fulfills the promise of the Frontier.[3]

But at another level, Lippard knows better. Hostile himself to slaveholders and slavery, he cannot blink the fact that it is the South which
expects the greatest dividends from Mexico—the South and the Metropolitan bankers, stock villains even in the romances of Curtis and Halyard.
His ambivalence reflects itself in his choice of language. Celebrating the
industrial triumph of "fire and steel" (the artillery) firing on the savage
Mexican hordes, Lippard says that the guns "enchain[] your eye," and he
pictures the infantry in terms he employed for the parade of slaves in
Monks: "an iron mass, composed of muscular forms, muskets and bayonets,
all linked in one." Still more ambiguous is the language he uses to describe
the objects of this industrial militarism: the Mexicans are "slaves," and
that is insulting to their racial character—yet slaves have Lippard's
sympathy in other contexts. Mexicans are like a tigress deprived of her
cubs—but who is it that has entered the lair and taken the cubs?[4]

These issues, concealed under patriotic rhetoric in the historical
chapters, surface with devastating effect in the fictional sections. Lippard's
"legends" all revolve around the single metaphor of seduction and rape—
the metaphor by which he had "unmasked" the cruelty and oppression of
the bankers and merchants of the Quaker City. The "Dead Woman of Palo
Alto" pairs a Cooperian set of lovers, reminiscent of Heyward and the
heroine of *The Prairie*: the hero is a Virginian, the heroine a Mexican lady
named Inez. This Inez has the aristocratic status of Cooper's heroine,
coupled with the dark erotic appeal of Cora in *Last of the Mohicans* and
Judith Hutter in *Deerslayer*. Nonetheless, she is an appropriate mate for the
young Virginian, and their anticipated marriage suggests the unrealized
potential of Mexican-American relations—consummating in a natural alliance, with America as the male partner, instead of mutually destructive
warfare. But the marriage is thwarted by Inez's aristocratic Castilian father,
who imprisons the Virginian and drives Inez to seek refuge among "the
Montezumans"—a fancifully conceived tribe of Mexican Indians. These are
Noble Savages, and they recognize Inez's superiority in their own fashion,
worshipping her as a goddess. She lives in this hidden "garden," idyllically
sheltered from the world. The Virginian meanwhile has escaped, joined
Taylor's army, and slays Inez's father in battle—the latter dies damning
"the accursed race whose destiny is to despoil our land." Wandering in the
wilderness, the hero discovers Inez in her savage garden, and he joins her
as an object of worship. The chief of the Montezumans, gifted with natural

wisdom, perceives the superiority of the pair and the appropriateness of their marriage. He blesses them, hailing the "new race from the North" that will expel the Spaniards.[5]

This "legend" attempts to apply to Mexico the same myth used by Cooper in *Last of the Mohicans,* with this difference: instead of the failure of the Cora-Uncas marriage, and the doom of the nonwhite races, a success-ful cross-cultural marriage is achieved. But it is accomplished only in the isolation of an impossibly utopian Indian village. Outside it, the same wars of extermination are proceeding to their conclusion.

When he deals with the Mexican-American conflict within a real-world setting, Lippard abandons romance for the stronger imagery of rape and seduction. In "Monterrey" his hero (a Pennsylvanian soldier) and heroine meet when the soldier avenges a comrade's shooting by stabbing his attacker, an old man, to death in a doorway. The two crash through the door, into the distracted presence of the old man's two disheveled—and of course voluptuous—young daughters. The American pushes past them pursuing further combat, and this causes yet another tragedy. The brother of the two girls, fearing the American means to rape them, shoots one of the girls and then himself. Simply by pursuing the normal and justifiable course of vengeance—like the larger army revenging the massacres in Texas —and by acting on the violent impulses that are inevitable and laudable in fighting soldiers, the Pennsylvanian has precipitated a domestic catastrophe: he has murdered a father before the eyes of his daughters, threatened the girls with rape, and so precipitated a suicide-murder. But the American is capable of feeling his moral guilt, and at the story's end he has married the surviving daughter and taken her home to Pennsylvania as a "Trophy of War."[6]

As in the first story, marriage resolves the Mexican-American conflict. But here murder and guilt are the bases of that union, and there is an ambiguous quality to the identification of the Mexican bride as a "Trophy of War." Is she merely an object of conquest, and is her marriage therefore merely a sublimated form of rape? James Gordon Bennett's invocation of the rape of the Sabine women as a metaphor for the conquest of Mexico surfaces here in a peculiar form. For Bennett, the rape ends in an imperial marriage and is thereby justified; but for Lippard, as we know, the seduction or rape of virgins is the supreme moral evil, and specifically a metaphor for the evil that is done in the name of capitalism. If the Pennsylvanian's marriage has the taint of rape about it, then it loses its spiritually regenera-tive character and becomes a device for evading guilt.

If the ending of this story is ambiguous on the point, the theme, as developed in *'Bel of Prairie Eden,* leaves no doubt about the guilty con-sequences of the conquest. In this work Lippard abandons the project of combining mythmaking with historical reportage, and composes a pure romance in which the issues of the war are symbolically addressed.

The action of *Prairie Eden,* which spans the period of the Mexican War, is set on an abstracted Frontier—a "prairie Eden"—rather than any histor-ical locale. John and Harry Grywin live there with their father and sister. While they are away with the Texas army their sister is raped and their father hanged by a Mexican, Don Antonio Marin, with the treacherous

help of the Grywins' plantation overseer, Ewen McGregor. Marin is both an
aristocrat and a "ranchero"—he combines the evil features of the corrupt
nobleman and the renegade half-breed, linking the opposite ends of the
social spectrum. The brothers' vengeance is further delayed by their captivity in a Mexican jail; yet this experience does lead to their knowledge of
Marin's own family, which consists also of a father and a sister, Isora. Marin
manages to kill the "girlish" brother, Harry; but John succeeds in murdering
Marin's father, and he begins an extended seduction of Marin's sister. Marin,
fearing retribution, has become a monk, and McGregor has become a "slave"
in the U.S. Navy; but John Grywin manages to entice all of them to an old
Aztec temple on the "Island of Sacrificios." There he induces McGregor to
murder Marin—but only after the latter has been compelled to witness his
sister's deflowering. McGregor is then poisoned.

Thus far the vengeance plot luridly translates the line of American
propaganda on the Mexican War. The invasion and the violence against
Mexico follow the Mexican violation of the prairie Eden, the murder of an
American patriarch and the rape of an American virgin. However, the
vengeance is appalling in its cruelty and sadism; and the Grywins are not
simple husbandmen making a new life in a new world. Old Mr. Grywin is a
Philadelphia merchant, who has fled to his prairie Eden to escape the consequences of his embezzlements and defalcations. McGregor is his former
clerk and accomplice. Moreover, McGregor is described as his "overseer"
—a title that suggests that the ex-merchant of the Quaker City intends to
become a slave driver in Texas: precisely the development Lippard predicted in his indictment of the lords of capital in *Monks of Monk Hall*. This
association is borne out in the description of the guilt-driven McGregor as
a "slave." The transformation of the rapist-murderer Marin into a "monk"
also invokes the Monk Hall connection, as does the linkage of John Grywin's
revenge with rape, murder, and ritual.[7]

What Lippard has done is to extend the symbolic language developed
as a critique of capitalism in *Monks* to the problem of the Mexican War.[8]
It is his way of saying what a polemicist like Theodore Parker would have
stated in analytical terms: that the Mexican War was not at bottom a
simple attempt to rescue and redeem a new prairie Eden, but proceeded
from the greed and ambition of wealthy merchants and slaveholders. In
Legends Lippard uses his symbols to suggest that something genuinely
redemptive may come out of the violence of warfare. That redemption is
figured in the enclosed garden paradise of the "Montezumans," and in the
restored household to which the Pennsylvanian hero brings his Mexican
bride in "Monterrey." But in *Prairie Eden*, the frontier paradise itself has
been shown to rest on a basis of deception and criminality. Moreover, the
form of American vengeance so exactly—and cold-bloodedly—parallels the
original Mexican atrocity that it calls into question the redemptive quality
of revenge.

Lippard then invokes the solution suggested in "Monterrey." The
dishonored Isora has fallen in love with the man who has ruined her; and
John, filled with remorse, marries her and takes her with him back to
Philadelphia. He further protects her innocence by retaining his incognito
—he has been calling himself Juan—and keeping from Isora all knowledge

of what really happened on the Island of Sacrificios. Isora and "Juan" live as aristocrats in the Quaker City, but Grywin is still filled with guilt. The price of his atonement is a marriage based on false pretenses, and the loss of his own American identity—the name change suggests that in imitating the Mexican's deed of blood, he has in some sense become a Mexican. Thus the "marriage" of Mexico and America, which was the traditional historical-romance resolution to the political strife, is not at all redemptive: it is the result of murder and rape, it feeds on hypocrisy and remorse, it debauches the Mexican woman and racially "darkens" the American aggressor. There is, then, no triumph in this outcome, no spiritual regeneration of the kind one would expect from the completion of "the Crusade of the Nineteenth Century." Neither Prairie Eden nor the Halls of Montezuma enable Lippard's heroes to evade the curse of the Quaker City, or the system of exploitation figured in Monk Hall.

FREMONT AND CARSON: HEYWARD AND HAWKEYE IN CALIFORNIA

The only aspect of the Mexican War that had a permanent and positive impact on literary mythology was the seizure of California, and particularly the adventures of Kit Carson—who joined Boone and Crockett in the pantheon of hunter-heroes as a result of his service as a scout for Frémont and General Stephen W. Kearney, the army commander in California. The success and durability of the California/Carson story derived from its compatibility to the traditional requirements of Frontier Myth. Carson himself was treated as a new form of the "Davy Crockett" type of Frontiersman. The relatively "vacant" wilderness of the Rockies and California was out on the far border of Mexico proper. Here the problem of seizing populated territory and ruling a subject race could be scanted in favor of an Indian-war scenario. Moreover, the discovery of gold in 1849, and the huge transcontinental migration that followed obliterated whatever public awareness there had been of California as a settled province of Mexico. It became a new sort of Frontier, a more advanced "Oregon" in which the promise of untapped wealth no longer took the form of land, but was alchemically transmuted directly into the precious metal that is the basis of capital. The California adventure ceased to appear as a struggle between Gringos and Californios, and became an interaction between energetic man and the reluctant virgin of Nature, in a wilderness far from civilization.

Carson first received public notice as the scout who guided the exploring expeditions of John Charles Frémont in the early 1840s, and as Frémont's dispatch rider during the Mexican War—it was Carson who brought to Washington the news of Frémont's seizure of California in 1847. Frémont and Carson figure in journalism and literature as real-life incarnations of the paired heroes of Cooper's novels, the soldier-aristocrat and the hunter-scout. Carson was automatically interpreted as a Rocky

Mountain edition of Natty Bumppo; and Frémont was ideally suited for
the role of the military aristocrat.

Frémont was the illegitimate son of a poor French émigré and the
runaway wife of a Virginia planter, and his youth was marked by poverty
and hard work. From this unpromising beginning, he rose to a captaincy
in the Corps of Topographical Engineers, a technical branch of the army
then being formed to undertake the work of exploring the frontier. His
skill in mathematics, in drawing, and in exact observation were the bases
of this rise; but they served him by bringing him to the notice and patronage of government officers and political figures. His rise was consummated with his clandestine courtship and elopement with the daughter of
Senator Thomas Hart Benton—a leading figure in the Senate and the
most important advocate of expansion to the Pacific. With his own good
record and the support of Senator Benton (now reconciled to his daughter
Jessie's marriage), Frémont obtained command of a series of exploring
expeditions that passed through and mapped vast regions of the Rockies,
the intermountain West, and California.

The Frémont myth developed before the Civil War, in three phases.
The first (1842–47) was dominated by Frémont's own reports of his expeditions, and by newspaper coverage of those reports. It was in this phase
that he received the public sobriquet of Pathfinder—which linked him
explicitly with Cooper's Leatherstocking in the 1840 novel of that name.
The second (1848–50) was dominated by the public prints, as they took
sides in the controversy over Frémont's role in the Bear Flag Revolt in
California, during the Mexican War; and his subsequent court-martial by
General Kearney. The third phase (1856–64) was the period of Frémont's
presidential candidacies, and featured pro- and anti-Frémont campaign
biographies.

Frémont's official reports, prepared during his initial expeditions,
appear to have been composed with an eye toward publication. They were
extremely well written, vivid and even sensational in their accounts of
the beauty of the West and its potential wealth. Like Irving in his histories
of *Astoria* and *Captain Bonneville*, Frémont salted his reports with vignettes
of Indian and Mountain Man life, with tales of love feuds and elopements
and wilderness battles embedded like nuggets in a vein of ore. He seems
to have intended these productions to stimulate interest in the Far West and
in the favored projects of Senator Benton—especially the seizure of California and the intermountain West from Mexico. When the Pathfinder
returned to California in 1846 he came equipped for military action, including secret orders designed by Benton to permit the explorers to turn
filibusters if war broke out with Mexico—as it did.[9]

Frémont's reports were designed to promote their author, as well as
the projects of his father-in-law. Frémont presents himself as the central
and dominant figure in the exploration and conquest of the West. He bears
a strong resemblance to Cooper's soldier-aristocrats and to Irving's Captain
Bonneville: a gentleman, a scholarly observer, a soldier, and a Christian;
but still a man able to take on the manner and skills of the hunter, trapper,
and Indian scout.

His reputation—in truth or by his own manipulation—thus contained all of the essential elements to make him a hero in the Washington/ Heyward-Middleton mode. The circumstances of Frémont's birth—which his enemies used to attack him—were in his early career seen almost exclusively in romantic terms. It was suggested that his father was an exiled and impoverished French aristocrat, a suitable mate for a daughter of Virginia's planter aristocracy. Their elopement was represented as a triumph of romantic love over the tyranny of class, caste, and wealth—an affair at once democratic in its defiance of hierarchy and aristocratic in the character of the principals. The death of his father and the poverty of his youth lent Frémont the aura of self-made man, without contradicting belief in his essentially noble origins—a combination that was also a feature of the Washington myth. Yet Frémont's role in popular literature and mythology was rapidly eclipsed by that of his assistant, Kit Carson; and Frémont's own image underwent a slow but steady degeneration.

The reasons for this lie in Frémont's intense involvement with political controversy, beginning with the Bear Flag Revolt of 1846. As the explorer vanguard of the great "army" of westering pioneers, Frémont was unambiguously a national hero, engaged in expanding the landed heritage of the entire country. But in the seizure of California, Frémont became involved on the wrong side of a dispute over the military government of the new territory, and was court-martialed for disobeying the orders of General Kearney. His trial neither exonerated nor condemned him, but the political infighting that surrounded it linked Frémont with a particularly crass and ignoble level of partisanship. His subsequent explorations were tainted by failure, and by the suggestion that they were undertaken not for the sake of knowledge but for publicity. These negative associations were only intensified by his emergence as senatorial and later presidential candidate of the "abolitionist" Republican Party, which served to encapsulate his legend within strictly partisan bounds.

Moreover, the campaign of 1856 produced numerous anti-Frémont biographies, which read the legend perversely: Frémont's romantic origins become mere bastardy, his knowledge of Indians becomes a lust for Indian maidens, his romantic marriage a cold-blooded alliance of political convenience. The undoing of the legend was completed by Frémont's blundering as a Civil War general, by his attempts to undermine Lincoln in 1861 and 1864, and by his involvement with a postwar railroad-building scheme that ended in failure and scandal. The aura of mythic heroism that invested Frémont as Frontier adventurer simply could not be coined for political use in the Metropolis without losing its magical appeal. The Frontier of myth was a realm in which fantasy was plausible, the Metropolis a realm of inescapable realities, all of which tended to deflate the pretenses of myths and myth heroes. At a distance Frémont could be seen as a man of heroic selflessness and pure motive; on the hustings of the East and in the corridors of power in Washington he could only reveal himself as self-interested, vain, and moved by the same sordid concerns as everyone else in a society based upon ambition and marketplace values.[10]

Kit Carson, on the other hand, was not only more successful than Frémont in his later career; he also had the wisdom or the good fortune to remain in the West, among the scenes that had been part of his legend from the start. He began his career as a runaway apprentice; made his name and the start of a modest business as a Mountain Man, trapper, and trader; became a celebrity as Frémont's scout and Mexican War dispatch bearer; and ended as a successful Civil War general, Indian fighter, and federal administrator in New Mexico.

Frémont's treatment of Carson in his official reports is romantic and even novelistic. As Kent L. Steckmesser points out, Frémont suppressed important details about Carson's character, appearance, and relationship to himself, in the interest apparently of building Carson into a Leather-stocking "foil" for "Captain Frémont." He embroidered tales of Carson's battles and amorous wanderings into fables of revenge and romance. Frémont cleaned up Carson's dialect, so that the hunter spoke respectable English. He also concealed the fact that Carson was often at odds with him, giving Carson instead the deferential manner of a Hawkeye toward a Heyward. His physical description of Carson was sufficiently vague, and his account of his heroic capacities sufficiently grandiose, so that when eastern visitors came west to view the celebrity—much as an earlier generation had sought out Daniel Boone—they were uniformly disappointed to find Carson short, swart, and unprepossessing.[11]

By presenting Kit Carson as a real-life latter-day Leatherstocking, Frémont created the basis for a new "living legend" whose fame would eventually eclipse and outlast that of its "author." The initial effect of Frémont's portrayal of Carson was to enhance Frémont's own mythic stature by annexing to it the properties of Cooperian romance. As Carson's celebrity and appeal developed and were manifested in both journalistic and dime-novel treatments, the functional relationship of the "Frémont" and "Carson" symbols was reversed. Where Frémont's testimony had been necessary to focus public attention on Carson in 1842, by the mid-fifties it was the now legendary Kit Carson whose testimony was sought to validate the pretensions of presidential candidate John Charles Frémont. Frémont's own campaign biographers worked up their hero's linkage with Carson as proof of his democratic manners and amenability to the spirit of frontier democracy. His Democratic opponents appealed to the identical source of authority, and in their pages "Kit Carson" (or a fictive version of him) declares that Frémont was a vain glory grabber, dependent on real frontiersmen for the fame he usurped, capable of getting lost within a half mile of his camp.[12]

Kit Carson's legend followed a course diametrically opposite to Frémont's. Beginning in the Pathfinder's shadow, he soon replaced him as the central figure in the literary mythology of the Rocky Mountain and California frontiers. The fact that Carson remained in the West, and continued to figure as a scout and Indian fighter, undoubtedly helped preserve the currency of his legend. But the original elements of the Carson literary persona were unequivocally those of the Frontiersman—unlike the mixed imagery of scout and aristocrat that invested Frémont.

If we think of Carson in the language of the Frontier romance—Cooper's language—he is associated with the politically and socially impeccable figure of the Leatherstocking. He is so much the "scout," the man of the wilderness, the fighter of Indians and defender of white men of all parties and conditions, that the categories of Metropolitan social and political identity will not adhere to him. He is the agent who resolves in the West an essentially Metropolitan impasse. Thus it is Carson's brand of safe and traditional adventure that renews the idea of finding social salvation in the conquest of the wilderness.

These themes are first developed in Charles E. Averill's *Kit Carson: The Prince of the Gold Hunters* (1848). In it, a young Bostonian of "high" birth (Vernon) is oppressed by a miserly uncle, and is kept drudging as a clerk, surrounded by and associated with the urban poor and exploited apprentices. The hero circuitously learns that his father has not deserted him, but gone to California on a secret mission for the government; and Vernon, pursuing the father, must contact his father's ancient friend and associate, Kit Carson—"the Pride of the Prairie." Pursuit of the father, in company with Carson, brings the oppressed Vernon a restoration of his fortunes and the overthrow of the usurping uncle-tyrant; Kit Carson, Indian fighting, and California gold thus bring about—magically—the redemption of urban poverty and class oppression.

Averill frames his hero's dilemma in terms drawn from the ideology of Jefferson and Cooper. The greedy uncle is clearly one of Jefferson's "half-breeds," who has displaced and degraded a deserving son of the "natural aristocracy." Averill's sympathetic alignment of the displaced "Boston aristocrat" (as he calls Vernon) with the urban poor, against the common enemy—the commercial middle class—matches precisely the agrarian models of Jefferson and Lippard. Boston is a place where the juxtaposition of wealth and poverty tends to produce violent social upheaval. Averill begins his description of the city with an image of wealthy storekeepers and brokers locking their treasures in strong vaults, for fear of the impulses such "lavish display" might arouse in the poor. Even young Vernon is tempted to steal from his employer. But the association of Vernon and the urban poor is fraught with contradiction. He is of a higher *kind*—after all, he does not steal, but seeks restoration of his fortunes in the West. Averill wants the attributes of natural aristocracy to mask the significance of class differences which threaten republicanism; yet he must also insist on the importance of such differences: while Vernon defends some poor 'prentices from a bullying crowd of Harvard boys, he charges that by preventing his going to Harvard, his miserly uncle has deprived him of the education due to his kind.[13]

Salvation from these contradictions, and from the imposition of poverty, is achieved by the adventure in the West. The "strange vagaries [of] fate" that "have mixed up with a man whose home and world is the pathless wilderness" engage Vernon in a ritualistic reenactment of the old pattern of Frontier initiation and achievement. The connection with Carson links him first of all to the traditional Fenimore Cooper frame of reference. Vernon first sees Carson's likeness in a painting called "The Pride of the Prairie," which echoes the title of Cooper's *The Prairie*; and the description that follows is an imitation of the scene of Hawkeye's first appearance to the Bush clan:

Far in the background of the painting, rolled the waving grass of a boundless prairie; amid the silent wilderness of which, towered the noble figure of the hunter-horseman, half Indian, half whiteman in appearance, with rifle, horse and dog for his sole companions . . . while in the clear, gray eye that looked from the thrilling picture forth, there seemed to glance a look of proud indifference to all, and the conscious confidence of ennobling self-reliance![14]

Averill then extends the imagery to connect the Cooperian reference to the more current matter of Mexico and California, and ties him directly to the exploits and the political celebrity of Frémont and "old Rough and Ready" himself. He links him also with "Rogers, who led the Secret Service in the San Juan D'Ulloa," thus assimilating him to the sort of official status Cooper's Hawkeye rarely enjoys. Moreover, he asserts that Carson himself was the discoverer of gold at Sutter's Mill, and hence is the spiritual father of the Gold Rush. All of this suggests that there is more than an ornamental significance to the title "prince of backwoodsmen" which Vernon bestows on Carson. However plebeian his origins, the Frontier hero is clearly tied to the fortunes and partly shares in the status of the "aristocracy" he defends.

The development of the Carson myth sheds light on the tendencies in the development of both the themes of popular mythology, and the forms of popular media. As Steckmesser points out, there were really two myths of Kit Carson: one propagated in dime novels and designed for mass circulation among the lower and middle classes; and another propagated in polite (or politer) fiction and biography, published between hard covers and designed for more "respectable" sectors of the reading public. The genteel biographers tend to bourgeoisify Carson. They clean up his manners and his speech; soft-pedal or deny the existence of his Indian wives and his conversion to Roman Catholicism. Beyond these obfuscations, they fit the Carson story into an elaborate structure, the structure of the success story. Carson is not simply a man of violent exploits and capacities. If Kit carouses with other Mountain Men, he does so only once, then learns his lesson. Each exploit accumulates, like money in a savings account, building a store of moral wisdom and social discipline.

As a result Kit begins to acquire property and standing in New Mexico and the mountains even before Frémont's arrival. He is taken on by the Indian trader St. Vrain as a partner, while still a youth—an event that puts Carson squarely in the pattern that Horatio Alger was later to make standard for the story of youthful progress from rags to riches. If he hunts animals or kills Indians and renegades, his exploits reflect a growing, cumulating awareness of his civilizing function, and make possible his eventual entrance into the life of the settlements as a businessman, Indian agent, soldier, and governor. His progress is marked by a steady movement away from the life of the Indian-like Mountain Man; but he acquires a civilized man's sympathy for Indians, and comes to regard them as victims of white aggression and corruption—an attitude more generally associated with eastern philanthropists than with western adventurers.[15]

These accounts, of course, had a core of fact embedded in the fiction; but it was their contribution to the store of myth rather than to the store of pure information that was significant. In this light, we can see the "genteel" tradition in Carsonian mythology as systematically linking the "myth of the hunter" to the success ethic and the myth of the self-made man and entrepreneur.

The conventions of paperback writing liberated authors from the necessity of dealing with all but the barest and most malleable "facts." The dime-novel Carson is therefore much more obviously a development out of existing myth, rather than a historical personage wrapped in traditional symbol. This Carson is more purely a hero of violent exploits endlessly repeated; and he lives in a world whose moral and racial guideposts do not change, as do those in the biographies which link his career to the development of the West. From the first Carson dime novel in 1848 to those published at the end of the nineteenth century, Carson remains a wild hunter, battling against the eternal types of the Indian and white renegade. The genteel Carson moves from hunter to rescuer of white women to civilized citizen; the dime-novel Carson never escapes from the eternal repetition of the rescue plot, though he does rescue aristocratic males (errant Harvardians or Britishers) as well as females. Carson's character and speech in these accounts does vary between the more contorted levels of dime-novel dialect and polite speech—the caste marks of the commoner and the aristocrat—but his actions remain those of the man of violence, the hunter and avenger. However, these traits of violence are ambiguously linked to images of aristocracy: he is the "prince" or the "king" of guides, one of "nature's noblemen."[16]

Both the genteel and the dime-novel portrayals of Carson's character begin with the hero as an embodiment of the Boone-Leatherstocking myth. Carson is by instinct and inheritance a hunter, drawn to the life of the wilderness. One of the earliest journalistic accounts of his career, reprinted in the *Rough and Ready Annual*, presents him in exactly the terms used by critics and historians to describe Boone and Leatherstocking:

> It is the character of one of those bold and enterprising spirits of the West, whom the peculiar influences of the frontier settlements —between the white man and the red man—are so well calculated to produce. Carson, however, is a master spirit . . . one of the best of those noble and original characters who have sprung up on and beyond our frontier, retreating with it to the West, and drawing from association with uncultivated nature, not the rudeness and sensualism of the savage, but genuine simplicity and truthfulness of disposition, and generosity, bravery, and single-heartedness, to a degree rarely found in society . . . [Living among the mountain men] our hero acquired all their virtues and escaped their vices.

DeWitt Peters's biography presents essentially the same portrait of a man drawn to the wilderness and the Indian, but able to respond to wild nature in the superior fashion of the best of the white race.[17]

But Carson's career is set in an age very different from Boone's. The latter's hunting-trailblazing career takes him from North Carolina to Kentucky, from one farming frontier to another. Carson, on the other hand, begins in half-settled Kentucky, and moves beyond the border of the agrarian Frontier, to make his life among the alien civilization of New Mexico, or among the intractable, inarable, nonagrarian Frontier of the Rocky Mountain/Great Plains fur trade. Although all accounts agree that Carson's adventurous disposition derived from his father—who, too, preferred to move where there was wild game and wild Indians rather than stay in civilization—the fact is that Carson's father apprenticed Kit to a harness maker, and that Kit began his career as a runaway apprentice. This early crisis links the Carson myth directly to the concerns of a developing industrial-commercial society: the boy with the heritage and spirit of a free hunter rejects the discipline of manufacturing labor, to wander among savage and alien races.

To Peters, the hardback biographer, this breach of law must be justified in terms appropriate to the values of bourgeois society. He therefore asserts that Kit was born with capacities for heroic action, for entrepreneurial success, and for political rule, which were ultimately of more value to society than his making of harnesses. He represents Kit as a good and productive worker, who enjoyed "both the confidence and respect of his employer" in the "honorable employment" of saddlery; but the drudgery of the trade could not hold one whose instincts demanded the thrill of the chase and the kill, the exercise of "sinewy muscle" and conquering prowess. Although perhaps guilty of crime in leaving his apprenticeship, Kit redeems his character as workman by working diligently as an employee of various hunting and trading concerns, at the same time that he exercises his military and predatory skills. He imitates and learns from his elders, exhibits good manners even in the heat of battle, shows judgment in leading expeditions against the Indians, and eventually rises to the honorable station of Indian agent—virtually a governor of the territory, as Peters represents it. The whole makes a success story very much in the Benjamin Franklin mode, despite its wilderness setting—and indeed, Peters asserts a physical resemblance between Carson and Franklin in his Preface.[18]

The dime-novel version of this career differs in a number of important respects. Although chivalric enough, Carson is more directly tied to the "old hunter"/Leatherstocking figure, than to the quasi-aristocratic "young hunter" of post-Cooperian dime-novel conventions. The same issues arise in relation to Kit's flight from apprenticeship and from the States, to live among Mexicans and Indians, and mountain half-breeds.[19] But where the "genteel" biographies assimilate Kit to the character of a bourgeois entrepreneur and governor, the dime-novel accounts prefer to leave him as a wild and free hunter, standing out against the encroachments of society forever. For example, the 1872 dime novel biography by Ellis begins by linking Carson's character to that of Boone, then represents his apprenticeship not as an honorable drudgery, but as virtual enslavement, a "captive" in civilization as another man might be a captive among Indians. For Kit, the "captivity" is double: he is held by the law to his drudgery, but his instincts are "captive" to the idea of the hunter's life, "his desire to become the freedman of the wilderness." The language here, in its invocation of captivity and "freedman," directly associates Kit's condition as apprentice with that of the slave.[20]

The genteel historians like to paint the Mexican society to which Kit escaped as combining both Indian-Catholic depravity and an inherited Spanish grace—it is the latter aspect that Kit espouses in his Mexican bride. The dime biography also paints New Mexico as a beautiful land, but with "inhabitants . . . among the most depraved on the American continent, being a race of mixed blood, to a singular degree." Indians and half-breeds are Kit's companions. Conflict and conquest, not patient labor and steady rise in status, are the dream story of success purveyed in the dime novel: it is the underclass's dream of success, not that of the established bourgeois. And where Peters celebrates Carson's appointment as a near partner in a merchant expedition, the Ellis dime biography has Carson preferring to go off and hunt all alone, after the manner of Boone—and not at all after the manner of the Mountain Men, nor of the real-life Carson. Where the genteel biographies pass over Kit's Indian marriages in silence, the Ellis version declares that "the man who alone had vanquished whole parties of bloodthirsty Indians was himself conquered by a single person," who became his "affectionate Indian wife," mother of his "idolized" daughter. The Indian killer is thus tied to the people he has spent his life contesting with; it is the promise of a kind of permanence to his identity as an adventurer among the wild Indians, a "freedman of the wilderness" even in a civilized epoch.[21]

It is worth noting that the dime-novel version of Carson is more grossly racist than the genteel version in its depiction of Indians and half-breeds, and polarizes white-Indian conflicts more sharply. There is certainly a contradiction here, if we interpret the documents as logical ideological statements: how can the same work tell us that Indians are racially despicable, and that the hero will take a wife among them? The difference between the two versions lies in this: the genteel writer takes the view of the Easterner and the man of the government toward the Indian (and, for that matter, toward the white pioneer as well). He sees himself as spokesman for the values of those entrusted with the paternal care of savages and pioneers, and his hero as the agent of Indian policy. Thus he deplores both Indian barbarity and the ambition of unprincipled pioneers which makes hash of Indian policy. The dime novelist feels no responsibility of this kind. Although he wishes to remain within conventional moral boundaries, he intends merely to entertain by pandering to a dream. The dream of escape, of liberation, of the acquisition of great powers over man and nature that is embodied in the Carson figure is spoiled by "responsibility" and even by bourgeois success. Representing the racial enemy as both powerful and colossally evil heightens the thrill of heroic conquest; marriage to the "Indian princess" seals the hero to the dreamworld of that conquest, and allows us to fantasize its continuation.

The dime novels preserve Carson as the Leatherstocking-like central figure of an essentially unchanging fictive Frontier. In that imaginary space Carson is an eternal hunter, "bid[ding] defiance to the encroachments of time . . . as youthful as ever."[22] But the preservation of this Frontier and its resident spirit of undying youth depends on the exclusion of history from the fiction. Once history is readmitted, we are forced to consider Carson from the genteel perspective, as one who will (or will not) make the transition to a post-Frontier society of order, "decency," and repression. The dime-novel Carson is therefore defiant not only of historical time; he also defies the ideology that acceptance of history apparently requires of Americans—the Metropolitan ideology of a tyrannous progress that imposes limitation on freedom and on the chance to rise in the world. This was not the premise of the original Myth of the Frontier, which held that history promised a career of unending youth expressed in interminable conquests of inexhaustible frontiers. Thus by its way of reproducing the Frontier dream, the Carson legend reflects the culture's growing belief that history was undoing the Myth of the Frontier and the democratic ideology based upon it.

PART FIVE

The Railroad Frontier, 1850–1860

CHAPTER 10

Prophecy of the Iron Horse

The ideological function of the Myth of the Frontier had been to substitute the credible prospect of an infinite reservoir of land and economic resources as an alternative to the intense conflict of social classes, economic interest groups, or regional groupings of slave and free states. But in the real-world pursuit of expansion, American political leaders discovered that each new advance of the "territory of Freedom" served to provide new occasions for the acting out of inescapable conflicts. The advance of American settlement in Texas and Oregon did not assuage the anxiety of slave- and free-soil partisans about their respective prospects for growth—it provoked and intensified those anxieties. The projected seizure of "all Mexico" promised a still larger draft of new landed and mineral wealth; but the potential of Mexico as an empire for slavery defeated the project. The rejection of "all Mexico" and the acceptance of a new Frontier more like the old wilderness-agrarian Frontiers of the past—consisting of vast tracts of sparsely inhabited and undeveloped land—ought in theory to have resolved the conflict. But it did not: the promulgation of the 1846 Wilmot Proviso requiring that the new territories be reserved for free-soil settlement transferred to this agrarian Frontier the same issues that had divided the nation in the "all Mexico" debate.

The Wilmot Proviso debates also revealed that the lines of conflict over slavery had both ramified and hardened. To the forces of moral antislavery were added the growing faction of Free Soil Democrats, whose political center was in the former frontier regions of the Old Northwest: a region experiencing rapid growth through a broad range of economic enterprises, from small farming to manufacturing. Moreover, it was from this section (and the border states, where slavery mixed with free farming) that the majority of settlers for the newly conquered territories would come. The idea that physical mobility, movement from Frontier to Frontier, was the classic path to self-improvement, wealth, and social advancement, was a central feature of this region's folklore and ideology.[1]

But the completion of the continental expansion of the United States from sea to sea demonstrated to all that the supply of new lands might very well be finite. With the British confirmed in possession of the Canadian Northwest and "all Mexico" rejected as a Frontier to the south, the lands of the Mexican Cession, Oregon, and the Great Plains could now be seen as the last of the Frontier windfalls. Whatever arrangements were made for settling and organizing these territories would therefore determine, for all the foreseeable future, the degree of access that planters and free farmers would have to the Frontier reservoir.

Another and more systematic compromise between slavery and free-soil interests was therefore required if the impasse over new acquisitions was to be broken. The Compromise of 1850 appeared to answer this need. Its explicit terms provided for the admission of California, the organization of territorial governments in the Mexican Cession, tacit reaffirmation and extension of the Missouri Compromise line dividing potential slave from free territories, abolition of the slave trade in Washington, D.C., and the acceptance by the North of a new and more stringent Fugitive Slave Law. But these provisions were of less importance as legal facts than as symbols of an underlying agreement to avert the public eye from slavery as a question, to keep silent about it and return to business as usual. Michigan Senator Lewis Cass expressed its true meaning when he declared after its passage, "I do not believe any party could now be built up in relation to this question of slavery. I think the question is settled in the public mind. I do not think it worthwhile to make speeches upon it." Cass was an old Warhawk and advocate of expansion since the days of 1812, and the Compromise of 1850 seemed to vindicate the central premise of Manifest Destiny, and the Myth of the Frontier that underlay it: that the promise of wealth inherent in the lands of the West and the gold of California could counterbalance the social and political contradictions of the Metropolis.[2]

But the Compromise lasted only for four uneasy years, and then rapidly fell apart. Moreover, the Frontier wealth which had been the bait of the Compromise provided the occasion for a renewed outbreak of sectional rivalry, of legislative and judicial blow and counterblow, and finally for civil violence between free soil and slavery partisans in the new territory of Kansas. The Compromise of 1850 was undone by a series of political miscalculations, some of which (like the Fugitive Slave Bill) were necessary parts of the package. But the most egregious miscalculation, and the most costly, was Illinois Senator Stephen A. Douglas's Kansas-Nebraska Bill of 1854, which, in effect, undid the Missouri Compromise by permitting territorial legislatures to decide for themselves between slavery and free soil. Ironically, Douglas's primary motive was to acquire for his state and section the means of exploiting the new Frontier: a railroad network tying the Northwest to the Pacific coast.[3]

The crisis it precipitated was perhaps inevitable. The Compromise of 1850 could not contain and reconcile the opposing courses of economic and political development represented by the compromising parties. Its only antidote for division was in denial of these differences, by buying off discontent and rivalry with the "sweetener" of free land. But the new Frontier was not one that could be developed according to the agrarian model of the traditional Frontier Myth. Only in Oregon was there anything like a replication of the conditions of settlement that pertained on the old Frontier. In California and New Mexico the way to wealth lay through mining, merchandising, and transportation, or through the acquisition of huge Spanish or Mexican land grants suitable for tenant farming, peonage—or slavery. The enterprises that produced the most profit and attracted the most settlers were not agrarian at all, but were the industrial and mercantile enterprises associated with railroad building, gold mining, and the ocean-carrying trade to California.

Nor could this new Frontier be settled without a transcontinental railroad to overcome the vast distances separating the Metropolis from the gold of California and the farmlands of Oregon. But such a line could be built only with the active cooperation of the federal government, which would have to explore and survey the prospective routes, protect surveying and working parties from Indians, and use its control of the Treasury and the public lands to attract and secure foreign investment in the project. And—since the railroad would be the essential means to tapping the promised wealth of the Frontier—whichever section the government awarded the eastern terminal of the line would enjoy special advantages of access which might, over time, give that section a position of economic and political superiority both in the territories and in the national government.[4] The promise of Frontier riches was supposed to ensure that such ultimate questions of economic dominance and subordination would never have to be faced. But political and economic realities compelled the parties once again to see the issues in terms of ultimate fates and final consequences.

A complex political compromise like that of 1850 has, in fact, a good deal in common with a cultural mythology. Both are devices for reconciling ambivalent ideologies and conflicting interests, and assimilating them to a common frame of reference, a common fable of historical destiny. The failed Compromise of 1850, like the failed literary mythology fabricated to give meaning to the Mexican War, invoked the Myth of the Frontier as a basis for renewing a vanished consensus. Like Lippard's *Legends of Mexico,* the Compromise represents a willed assertion of a myth/ideology which was no longer capable of explaining, organizing, or justifying the course of historical action to all parties and sections.

But its fatal consequences were not immediately apparent. In the interval between 1850 and the 1854 Kansas-Nebraska fiasco—and even after the outbreak of civil strife in "Bleeding Kansas"—the positive appeal of the new Frontier stirred popular enthusiasm for the West and for all sorts of pioneering projects. Many of these had to do with the prospects for repeating the Gold Rush boom of 1849 in other parts of the West. Mineral strikes throughout the decade sent prospectors rushing to distant regions of California, Nevada, Utah, Idaho, Montana, and Colorado; there were major strikes and gold rushes in western Nevada and around Pikes Peak at the end of the fifties. However, there was also an upswelling of enthusiasm for agrarian pioneering in the distant regions of California and Oregon, and the nearer lands on the eastern rim of the Great Plains. The expectation of connection to Atlantic and Pacific via railroads gave settlement on the eastern plains a special appeal, because it promised both a speculative profit to early settlers and access to markets. The same motives also prompted a renewal of agrarian expansion within the borders of the

Old Northwest. The building of railroads through central Illinois permitted the development of lands that had been unattractive to previous generations of settlers because of their distance from waterborne routes of commerce and river- or lake-port cities. The enthusiasm and rising expectations generated by this limited and partly illusory renewal of the agrarian Frontier gave a special intensity to the sense of crisis that developed when the Kansas-Nebraska struggle appeared to put those expectations at risk.

The central symbol in this false renewal of the agrarian Myth of the Frontier was the railroad. Here was an enterprise that represented "the industrial revolution incarnate," but which at the same time appeared to offer a benign and productive association between the order of industrialism and the ambitions of the yeoman farmer.

Serious and detailed proposals for a transcontinental railroad began to appear in the mid-forties. Their common burden was to express and build confidence in the technical feasibility of throwing a rail line across the prairies and the Rocky Mountains; and their imagery therefore derived from the vocabulary of the "virgin land" myth, which insists on the amenability of nature to the works and projects of mankind. Pastoral imagery coupled with economic appeals was aimed at overcoming agrarian resistance to policies designed to foster railroad projects. But railroad promoters were also divided over the issue of private versus public capitalization and ownership. The Jacksonian experience with the granting of public franchises to private exploiters had created a healthy suspicion of such grants, as the crime literature of the Southwestern school suggests. Jackson's war against the privileged franchise of the "Monster Bank" informed the ideology of such spokesmen of the urban working class as George Wilkes, who declared that private ownership of so vast an enterprise would create "monster monopolies and degraded labor," and by the 1870s it had indeed become clear that this particular method of railroad extension had the effect of making the railroad corporations a serious threat to the economic independence of the small farmer in its capacity to devour "the little man."[5]

But in the 1850s it still appeared that the western farmer had more to fear from the plantation interests than the railroad builders; the consciousness of class struggle on which Wilkes's objections were based were unmanned by the renewal of faith in the capacity of a resource Frontier to render such divisions irrelevant. Although the type of industrial and large-scale capital organization represented by Monster Banks, plantations, and Lowell textile mills was perceived as threatful to the entrepreneurial interests of farmers, artisans, and small businessmen, these were also models of successful achievement; and industry itself was not only a specific mode of production but one of the cardinal virtues. The system of underwriting western railroad construction with grants of public land facilitated their association of railroading with agrarianism. It apparently put the railroads in the role of corporate pioneer, breaking trail and clearing brush for agrarian aftercomers. To be sure, the railroads would take a speculator's profit on the sale or lease of their lands; but that sort of profit taking was just as characteristic of older generations of agrarian pioneers—as much a consideration for the heroic Boones of Kentucky as it was for the gentrified William Cooper or the heavily capitalized Ohio Company.[6]

Agrarian imagery was nowhere in greater evidence than in the aggressive advertising campaigns launched by railroad promoters for the sale of land to farmers recruited from the East and Europe. The Illinois Central Railroad was the first to develop the technique of land-grant promotion. Offices were established in major cities to facilitate immigration, and advertising struck all the mythic chords: Illinois was described as "The Garden State of the West," the land was Edenically unspoiled and incredibly fertile, and the railroad's huge domain was offered as testimony to the grandeur to which enterprises in the region might aspire.[7]

Behind the facade of this agrarian promotion industrial values are clearly at work. The promoters' policy was to favor sales to organized "colonies" over those to individual settlers—which reveals the sensibility of managers imbued with industrial values that admire large-scale, organized, and systematic economic efforts rather than the subsistence achievements of the yeoman farmer. The suggestion that the railroad itself is the model of pioneer enterprise in the region likewise suggests an industrial definition of the scale of "success"—a very different model from that offered by Boone or even Judge Cooper. Moreover, the industrial imagery reveals a contradiction in the railroad promotion that the agrarian imagery masks. Although the men who invested in and promoted railroads like the Illinois Central gained political support for their program of capitalization by associating their enterprise with agrarian values, they themselves were speculative capitalists, who expected to enrich themselves by exploiting the complex opportunities that only an industrial enterprise creates. They were able to take profits on the trading of railroad bonds, on the inflation of land values both inside and outside the land-grant districts, on the sale or lease of railroad lands, and on the subcontracting of construction.[8]

Their activities were in some respects inimical to the policies that had been developed to ensure the agrarian-democratic character of the new regions. The railroad promotions inflated the symbols of agrarianism by their very use of them, and at the same time made those symbols more hollow. The Illinois Central was not unique in its use of an agrarian language to mask an ideology in which industrial values topped the hierarchy of concerns. Cultural historians Leo Marx and John Kasson have shown how American illustrators, advertisers, and spokesmen liked to depict locomotives and factories as parts of a rural landscape of barns and pastures. But these pictures, and the speeches or promotional texts that often accompanied them, were not simply static tableaux. They invoked a fable of history, in which the remnant of wilderness, the plowed fields, and the steaming locomotive represent progressive stages of development. Just as the farm is superior to and replaces the wilderness, so too the railroad represents a further development of civilized power, which always takes the form of establishing human control over nature. The building of railroads allows men to evade the limitations of nature, to construct pathways not carved by rivers or the tracks of beasts and hunters. Daniel Webster, in a speech made at the opening of a New England railroad, begins by contrasting the pastoral pleasures of farm life with the bustle of industry; but while he nostalgically admires the former, he makes it quite clear that it is industrial bustle that represents the appropriate next stage of development. The world of the farm (in his imagery) is like the world of childhood, while the industrial world is that of mature adulthood. We may yearn for the pastoral Eden, but it is our fate to labor productively by the sweat of our brows to increase our bread.

This language involves the same sort of contrast between childish-primitive and adult-advanced cultures and races that lay at the core of the Myth of the Frontier. The difference is that now it is the yeoman farmer who represents the vanishing American, and the railroad man who will be the new lord of the earth.[9]

No one represents this confusion of agrarian and industrial values better than Abraham Lincoln, who became the standard-bearer of the party of "free labor," the Homestead Act, and transcontinental railroading. Lincoln was aware of, and as a lawyer and politician engaged in, the economic and political struggle preliminary to the capitalization and building of the rail-road. He was also deeply engaged in the question of expanding the agrarian frontier as a basis for preserving a government of democratic consensus, and of confronting, theoretically and practically, the problem of the new status of labor in an economy characterized by industrialization in the North and slavery in the South. A speech made by Lincoln at a Wisconsin agricultural fair in 1859 (just after his debates with Douglas) offers a glimpse of the confused thought processes that shaped American responses to the class dilemma presented by industrialization; and it also illustrates how and why the railroad could appeal as an antidote to that dilemma.

Lincoln's speech restates the ideological arguments of Jacksonian or entrepreneurial agrarianism in terms that link farming to industrial enter-prise. He begins with obeisance to the traditional view of the farmer as being "in the nature of things" the mainstay of both economic production and political democracy. But he then moves on to speculate whether or not the universal need for foodstuffs in itself sufficiently guarantees farmers as a class or interest group against a diminution of political or economic power in a changing marketplace. The farmer, he argues, must henceforth look beyond nature to the realm of human industry in order to maintain the solvency of the individual and guarantee the future economic independence —as farmers or something else—of his children.

Lincoln urges his audience to avail itself of mechanical and organiza-tional improvements so as to increase productivity per acre, farming as intensively as possible. Specifically, he recommends the development of a steam plow, because it will make possible *"thorough cultivation*—putting the soil to the top of its capacity—producing the largest crop possible from a given quantity of ground." He cautions against the ambition to acquire broad acreage, since the farming of large plots of land requires excessive "locomotion" in gathering up the crops. Farmers, he says, must balance carefully and in commercial terms their use of soil resources and the expenditure of labor. They must calculate whether machine or animal power is more cost-efficient, in just the way that a mill owner or planter growing a commercial crop must do. In short, Lincoln speaks to the farmers as if to an audience of businessmen, part and parcel of a market economy. And although Wisconsin is still largely virgin land, he recommends small plots and intensive cultivation, the curbing of the urge for land-ownership as such. Cash value, not acreage, is to be the measure, and cost-efficiency in the deployment of capital and labor the test of the farmer's ability to acquire cash. Land *as such* may now be more limited, but an open Frontier of capital acquisition yet remains.[10]

But Lincoln's apparent friendliness toward industrialization is offset by other attitudes that reflect common fears that the new order will degrade both farmer and mechanic. It is the slavery question that focuses Lincoln's uneasiness and gives it ideological form. Following the orthodoxy of Jacksonian democracy, he asserts the priority of labor to capital in both economic and moral (or mythic) terms: the laborer who produces wealth by working with his hands is morally superior to the man who speculates on " 'change." He points with alarm to the development of a new theory of capital/labor relations, the southern or "mud-sill" theory which holds that society rests on its lower classes as a house rests on a permanent earthen sill; and hence, "that whoever is once a *hired* laborer, is fatally fixed in that condition for life; and thence again that his condition is as bad as, or worse than, that of a slave." Lincoln thus associates the factory owner and the planter as capitalists dominating a class of dependent and propertyless laborers—the lords of the loom and the lords of the lash, both of whom degrade and proletarianize the laboring classes.

Lincoln, however, is still addressing an audience in which farmers and small businessmen predominate. So to this doctrine Lincoln opposes the notion that "labor is prior to, and independent of, capital. . . ." Holders of this theory

> do not deny that there is, and probably always will be, *a* relation between labor and capital. The error, as they hold, is in assuming that the *whole* labor of the world exists within that relation. A few men own capital; and that few avoid labor themselves, and with their capital, hire, or buy, another few to labor for them. A large majority belong to neither class—neither work for others, nor have others working for them . . .

He cites as example the farmers in his audience, who work themselves and their families on their own land; and those others who combine their own labor with that of hired men or slaves. And he points to the supposed fact that most farmers in his audience had themselves begun as hired laborers (in agriculture) as refutation of the idea that the mud-sill theory applies to agricultural labor.

Lincoln's premise about his audience may in fact be a questionable one. Statistical studies show that frontier farmers did not in fact begin as hired laborers, but tended to be people who had either owned farms, or who had been children of farming families back east. Lincoln, however, is bent on linking the myth of the yeoman farmer's "success story"—a variant of Crèvecoeur's Andrew the Hebridean—to that of industrial labor, just as he earlier attempted to associate the economic activity of the farmer with that of the industrialist. It is as concise a statement of the free labor ideology as could be made; and it not only defines the world view and social expectations of Lincoln's party, but also states the terms of the new, industrial-era version of the Jacksonian idea of success:

> The prudent, penniless beginner in the world, labors for wages awhile, saves a surplus with which to buy tools or land, for himself; then labors on his own account another while, and at length hires a new beginner to help him. This, say its advocates, is *free* labor— the just and generous, and prosperous system, which opens the way for all—gives hope to all, and energy, and progress, and improvement of condition to all. If any continue through life in the condition of the hired laborer, it is not the fault of the system, but because of either a dependent nature which prefers it, or improvidence, folly, or singular misfortune.[11]

In the nature of things, then, under free labor the normal course of human development will be from rags to riches. No systemic blocks exist: only the grasping for power by the advocates of the mud-sill theory stands in the way of its realization; only defects of human character will prevent the fulfillment of normal development under the system. In Lincoln's historical universe, the individual of prudent character begins in poverty, labors to acquire capital; passes through a phase of independent labor (neither hired nor hiring); and ends as an employer of labor! The stage of independent yeomanry—the stage of Lincoln's audience—is impermanent. Lincoln has implicitly warned them of this in his exhortation to a more efficient use of capital and labor on smaller farms. Reassurance and hope—the Frontier promise and its safety valve—lie in the expectation of becoming an employer of labor or an owner of steam plows (automated labor), whichever is more profitable. The point is a vital one, and very revealing of the ideological imperatives of the changing economy. The independent farmer can become a "vanishing American," not unlike the noble red man. The farmer represents a stage of civilization more advanced than that of the Indian, more advanced than that of the wilderness hunter; but less advanced than that of the employer of labor and machinery, the agricultural/industrial entrepreneur. The vast majority of the poor white or hired labor (let alone the free slaves) in these enterprises leaving the original firm to set up another like it, employing similar numbers who in their turn will go out to establish firms and hire workers—this would seem to require an exponential increase in both landed and productive resources repeated year after year after year. Although the expansive capacity of American industry and agriculture did indeed exceed popular expectations, they did not and could not have been great enough to accommodate that particular kind of growth.

Lincoln was able to see the limitation of the free soil doctrine clearly enough when he looked to the South. The advocates of slavery held that their institution was consistent with democracy, because even the poorest white man could, in theory, become a planter. But to satisfy the planter ambitions of even a significant fraction of the poor white class would have required an extension of territory and an increase in the slave population far beyond anything that was possible without seizing Latin America or reviving the slave trade. Although slavery might be morally condemned as a feudal or barbaric anachronism, the imperatives of the slave economy were precisely those of the entrepreneurial economy idealized by Lincoln— it had to continue to grow explosively, or else confront the possibility of an end to social peace and democratic institutions. That was why the nation could not continue "half slave and half free," but must become "all one thing, or all the other."

Lincoln's theory willfully succeeds in adapting the ethic of success in the Frontier Myth to new conditions; but it contains an absurdity in its projection of a future in which the *normal* expectation of each individual is that he will become an employer of hired labor—of hired labor that will in its turn, for the most part, eventually rise to the employing class. If the supply of cheap land was already deemed insufficient for agrarian cupidity to have its safety valve, how much less sufficient would it be for a more accelerated and intensive industrial cupidity? Industrial production as such would have been inconceivable if, as Lincoln envisioned, the working class was continually "annihilated" by being almost completely absorbed into the owning/employing class. To make such a scheme work one has to envision not only phenomenal population growth (to supply workers for the places vacated by the new class of employers), but also an economy expanding at an inconceivably rapid rate to be able to provide as well for the next genera- tion of new employers as it had for the first. Lincoln spoke in and for an America in which the factory system had not yet become typical of manu- facturing enterprises, and the Northwest was still a region of small farms and artisanal production. It needed an eye educated by the sight of teeming masses in a mill town or the crowded quarters of a plantation to appreciate the impossibility of guaranteeing to every laborer the prospect of becoming an employer of labor.

Lincoln could see the fatal mathematics clearly enough when he looked at the South. He understood that the slavery system had imperatively to grow in order to make good its promise to the poorer whites; and that in the end there could never be enough land or slaves to meet the need. He knew that to include blacks, once freed from slavery, within the terms of that promise would be both socially and economically impossible. But he was able to find credible in the North the same promises he recognized as delusive in the South. He counted upon the unmeasured potential of the new Frontier of the 1850s, and the new technology of railroad building that went with it. By treating the unmeasured as if it were potentially im- measurable, the promises of free labor could be made credible; and perhaps by the faith so engendered (or the magic so invoked) they might even be made good.[12]

The mathematics of this magic was most elaborately developed by the promoters of western railroads, the most eloquent of whom was William Gilpin. They sold their enterprises to the public, to investors, and to political sponsors as devices capable of generating a literally infinite supply of wealth from the finite heritage of Frontier land. Gilpin was a notable booster of and speculator in western land, who had been trained as a soldier, had accompanied one of Frémont's expeditions to the Pacific, and marched with Doniphan's column in its great campaign to Santa Fe during the

Mexican War. He emerged after 1849 as a spokesman for cross-continental migration and for the building of a transcontinental railroad, and he rested his case on a "scientific" analysis of the natural character of the West which appeared to systematize the use of "natural law" as a key to interpreting history and morality. The success of Gilpin's speeches and writings on the West registered in his perennial status as adviser to government and business on western and railroad matters, and his appointment in 1861 as governor of the Colorado Territory.[13] Gilpin's conception of natural law was nonetheless far more mythopoeic than scientific; even his mathematical analyses are more like numerological mysticism than statistics. However, this insistence on scientism was vital to his rhetoric, because his ideological purpose was to substitute the "facts" of natural plenitude for the "senseless" and "illogical" clash of so-called interests and rigid ideologies.[14]

Gilpin insisted that the West contained a reservoir of resources that was unlimited in its capacity to sustain an ever growing population in conditions of universal affluence. This resource reservoir took first of all the form of agricultural land, which was of course finite in extent, but which was capable of sustaining more intensive exploitation by a far larger population than presently existed in the United States. Even so, Gilpin acknowledged that a strictly agrarian Frontier did have outer limits of productivity. But the West also offered a further resource in the form of precious minerals, and Gilpin asserted that his scientific and mathematical analyses proved "that gold *in mass and in position* and infinite in quantity will, within the coming three years, reveal itself to the energy of our pioneers." An infinite supply of gold, coupled with the energies represented by such enterprises as the railroad, would make of the industrial system a substitute for the agrarian Frontier that would offer the same future promise of infinite opportunity for an unlimited population of freemen to fulfill continually rising expectations.[15]

This vision of an industrial Frontier requires a redefinition of the character of pioneering, in which the operative metaphors are not agrarian but military and industrial. Yet Gilpin is aware that such metaphors imply the unacceptable vision of the American pioneer as a military conqueror and as the boss or landlord of a subject people. He "overcomes" the contradiction by a dizzying double-think: the paradox of a "pioneer army" achieving the conquest of Mexico and the dispossession of the Indians "inspired by the universal instincts of peace." Indeed, "Human society is . . . on the brink of a new order of arrangement," and the agency of that transformation is not the simple yeoman cultivating the soil but "a new power, *the People* occupied in the wilderness, engaged at once in extracting from its recesses the omnipotent element of *gold coin*, and disbursing it immediately for the industrial conquest of the world."[16]

Gilpin links this industrial phase of development to the agrarian past by a systematic nature mysticism. As he contemplates the map of the New World, he perceives a tendency for the power and wealth of nature to be gathered into nodes or "centers" of superabundance. The concept is essentially magical, although Gilpin "accounts" for it scientifically. "Center" and "central" are used in an almost incantatory manner, and the structure of his argument becomes at times more like a dithyramb or paean than a scientific discourse. Of all the many nodes or "centers" on Gilpin's map, two particular foci dominate American geography and thus determine the right course of development. The first is the "grand calcareous bowl" of the Mississippi Valley, to which the rivers of the continent concentrically flow. The fertility and shape of this valley determine the agrarian character of America's economic base, and the centralizing tendency of national government and national character. In this concentering structure, the geographical form of America contrasts with that of Europe and Asia, whose central portions are vast ranges of mountains, from which rivers radiate outward.

Thus, while North America opens towards heaven in an expanded bowl to receive and fuse harmoniously whatever enters within its rim; so each of the other continents presenting a bowl reversed, scatters everything from a central apex into radiant distraction. Political empires and societies have in all ages conformed themselves to these emphatic geographical facts. The American Republic is then *predestined* to expand and fit itself to the continent.

This single fact sets at naught the hostilities of squatters and landlords, planters and manufacturers, Northerners and Southerners. Where European nations can amalgamate only by conquest and domination of one over another, by wars predicating mutual "extermination," the "expanded bowl" of America will produce

> a people one and indivisible, identical in manners, language, customs, and impulses: preserving the same civilization, the same religion; imbued with the same opinions, and having the same political liberties. . . . Thus the perpetuity and destiny of our sacred Union find their conclusive proof and illustration in the bosom of nature.[17]

The second node of superabundance is in the Rocky Mountains. The resources of the mountain region are not so broadly abundant as the arable land of the calcareous bowl, but its fecundity is suggested by Gilpin's dubbing the Rockies the "Mother Mountain" of the West, which expresses both fertility and concentrated mineral wealth. Mountain soil is not only fertile enough to sustain "swarms" of "aboriginal cattle," but also holds "all forms of minerals, metals, stones, salts, and earths; in short, every useful shape in which matter is found to arrange itself." The mountains are dotted with "Parcs"—valleys like enclosed gardens, savage Edens in which all of the mineral and vegetable fertility of the Mother Mountain is focused. Gilpin compares these "Parcs" to the fabled oriental Vale of Kashmir; the oriental association suggests that these gardens are the resorts of fabulous leisure, the final reward of a race of heroes who have risen from drudgery to the status of aristocratic consumers or enjoyers of nature's and mankind's "final goods." But the same association also links the denizens of the Parcs backward to the primitive hunter-gatherer, the Indian. The magic of these savage Edens is registered in the Indian's exhibition of religious reverence for them; and Gilpin shares their magical faith in his assertion that the "brilliancy and tonic tone" of the atmosphere are such as to guarantee "health and longevity" to any who settle there.[18]

But even the mountains are not the final stage of development. Beyond them lies the Pacific and the maritime highway to the fabulous markets of the East. It is this that Gilpin sees as the final goal of American aspirations. Despite his enthusiasm for the pioneer army, Gilpin had as little use for "squatters" and "dirt farmers" as Cooper. The final "regeneration" of the American race will be achieved only when we have tapped the wealth and wisdom of the "Celestial democracy" of China. Only in China will we find a market for goods and ideas commensurate with our "infinite" capacity for production. At each stage of our development, new forms of production have arisen in response to population growth and technical capacity, and the final form of America's economy will not be that of a fee-simple utopia, but that of worldwide industrial hegemony.[19]

Gilpin presents his case for this next stage of progress not by citing trade figures, but by invoking the mythology of racial struggle and destiny. Our pioneering past testifies to our race's possession of a mission or destiny to expand the boundaries of civilization, and—more important—to "regenerate" the moral and political character of civilization in the process. The already "transacted destiny" of the American people has been to rise from "nothing" to be "first among the nations existing or in history" in "agriculture, in commerce, in civilization, and in natural strength." The as yet "untransacted destiny" of the American race will be to "subdue the continent—to rush over the vast field to the Pacific Ocean" and by our economic and political example to "animate the many hundred millions" of people, these "herculean masses," and "establish a new order in human affairs." This regenerating mission is not only for the American masses (both present and prospective), but for those "stagnant" peoples of Latin America and Europe, and still further on of Asia, and so "shed blessings round the world."[20]

But violence, despite Gilpin's insistence on the "peaceful" inspiration of the pioneer army, is the necessary means for fulfilling this regenerative mission and "untransacted destiny." Moreover, a corollary of Gilpin's vision of that destiny is not the integration of different stocks into a single American people, but the differentiation of races and classes into virile and passive, young and "superannuated." "War has been to our progressive nation the fruitful season of generating new offspring," Gilpin wrote. If we take the Indian and Mexican War experiences as models of America's interaction with superannuated races, the prospect for peaceful trade with China becomes problematic. Although Gilpin cited the "unity" of Indian races as proof of the unifying tendency of the American continent, he had no brief for preserving Indian title or cultural existence. They were simply obstacles to progress, whose rights were not such as a civilized society must recognize, and were legitimate targets of wars of extermination—those wars that Gilpin asserted were the peculiar geomorphically induced destiny of Europe and Asia.[21]

What will save the American part of the white race from such internecine wars and revolutions will be the projection of "the martial energies and genius of our people" outward into the unpeopled wilderness: "Here is seen an order of progression, the counterpart of what distinguishes the history of European society, but the reverse of it in moral grandeur and

political results." America's exercise of martial energy avoids the consequences of war and tyranny because its projection against nature (rather
than man) is "tempered by a discipline at once voluntary, universal, and
perfect." With our national energies so developed, the national character
so created, the end result will regenerate both the New World and the Old:

> The reclamation of new departments of the wilderness, reflect-
> ing its light through every detail of our industrial populations,
> kindles new fires which become universal to our people, as the area
> for their energies is expanded.[22]

Beneath the enthusiastic confusions of Gilpinian rhetoric we can see
the outlines of the Frontier Thesis that Turner would later systematize.
What gives America its moral-political preeminence among the empires of
the world, what gives American national character its uniqueness, is the
experience of conquering the natural wilderness. Because the martial
temperament of the race is directed against nature alone, its energetic
qualities can be developed without risking the danger that society will
degenerate into militarism, or that economic growth will be based upon
violence and injustice. Gilpin's metaphoric language embodies the doctrine:
he applies military metaphors to the peaceful activity of pioneers and
farmers. But the reverse is also true: he applies the metaphor of peace and
cultivation to the acts of aggression by which territory was expropriated
first from the Indians and then from the Mexicans. Gilpin's langauge is more
revealing than his logical argument. The latter is devoted to the systematic
denial of the facts of American expansion, while the metaphors continually
restate the fact of violence.

To evade that fact, Gilpin (and Turner after him) is forced to omit
from his "universal system" all but the most delicate allusions to the
Indian wars and the Mexican War just concluded. He is likewise compelled
to deny the tendency toward social disorder and civil war in his own
society. He treats slavery and the complex of related issues as the purview
for unscientific malcontents who are too bigoted to take in the large vision
of the American landscape. His approach is perhaps most understandable
in a book written before the Civil War with the intention of substituting
western development for the slavery question; but Gilpin's revised editions,
printed after the war, manage to avoid all but passing allusions to the conflict, and seem to suggest that Gilpin's antebellum prophecy—that the war
was unnecessary and would not take place—had magically been fulfilled.
What we see in Gilpin is an extreme version of an essential tendency of the
whole ideology of the Frontier Myth—the tendency to deny the real bases
for social conflict by substituting "nature" for human antagonists.

Gilpin deals with uncomfortable moral realities by systematic omis-
sions. He omits the blacks from his listing of the races already Americanized
by the experience of conquering the wilderness, just as he omits systematic
treatment of the Indian and Mexican wars from his historical account.
Gilpin's denial of them therefore has the effect of falsifying history, and the
doctrine of development based on his interpretation of nature. But more
than the inadequacy of the theory is at stake. Since this is not just a theory,
but a myth and an ideology, the omission of blacks and Indians is predictive

of their fate in the new order envisioned by Gilpin—they will have no place. And since their presence is real, simple denial will be inadequate as a policy of realizing the "mission of the North American people." Something like a war of extermination or a system of enslavement may be required. Moreover, if it is the case that the "white race" has an ineradicable martial and conquering character, and if the productive pacification of that character has been effected only by the engagement of the Americans in the "peaceful" conquest of the natural wilderness of the "bowl" of America, then why should not the closing of the American Frontier and the projection of American energy into the Eurasian world of "wars of extermination" lead to the eventual undoing of our peculiar democratic system? Only by predicting the discovery of "infinite" resources can Gilpin avoid this theoretical impasse.

Gilpin himself is continually drawn to the language of military conquest and to a racial rationale for subordinating one class or culture to another. This tendency became more marked the more Gilpin grappled with these issues, each strenuous denial of the necessity of social conflict requiring a further elaboration of the myth of conquest. In his early speeches and in his later *The Central Gold Region* (1860), Gilpin is content to vest the right of conquest in a loosely defined "American race," which includes many ethnic subgroups and may even eventually comprehend Orientals and the nobler Indians. But by 1873 this vagueness has been dissipated by a clear-eyed doctrine of racial superiority: in his *The Mission of the North American People* the "American people" become simply "the white race." Likewise the "central railroad" of 1860 metamorphoses into the Cosmopolitan Railroad, which fulfills an imperial destiny beyond the farthest West. But the tendency toward racial explanations of the course of progress inevitably shifts the emphasis from the peaceful and cultivative interaction of man and nature to the struggles of contending races, classes, and cultures for domination.

The recrudescence of the race-war theme in Gilpin's railroad prophecy suggests just how inadequate the railroad-revised version of agrarianism was as a device for buying off the deep social conflicts that the language of the race war represented. The actual politics of transcontinental railroading—the competition for lucrative terminals to conduit trade to the Orient— also revealed that the vision of a railroad-resource Frontier was as inadequate a deterrent to sectional rivalry and the racialization of political rhetoric as Montezuma's gift of gold was to Cortes and his starveling conquistadores. Since the West was the resource base on which future prosperity would be based, it therefore became an important point in the rivalry of the slave-labor and free-labor systems, complicating and delaying the beginning of future American enterprise.

When Senator Douglas attempted to resolve (or manipulate) this competition in a way advantageous to his own political and economic prospects, he found that the railroad issue could not be disentangled from the politics of slavery extension. Once the silence compelled by the Compromise of 1850 was broken, it was impossible to silence the rival demands. What Douglas offered was the traditional antidote of agrarianism: an assertion that "nature" would limit slavery extension and provide lands for free farmers without human political intervention; and a proffer of the venerable Frontier institution of "squatter sovereignty" as a device for settling the issue legally. But neither remedy commanded belief, because the nature of Frontier development had been fundamentally altered. Citizens of an industrial society know that their form of production and labor system can be applied to almost any enterprise, from plantation to small farm, from artisan shop to factory; and can be extended, through technological adaptation, to almost any region or climate. If "degraded" or proletarianized workers could be brought west to build railroads and dig mines, so could black slaves, who were employed in similar enterprises in the South. If peonage worked for the Spanish, why should not a similar organization of farm work be profitable for Americans on the same ground?[23]

The development of an integrated *national* economy and the commitment to both industrialization and expansion made it impossible to continue to evade resolution of the constitutional status of slavery. From the time of the Constitutional Convention to the end of the Mexican War it had been possible to treat slavery as an institution of purely local character, and even as a temporary aberration in the political development of the republic. With this in view, it had been possible even as late as 1850 to resolve crises over slavery by a resort to pragmatic compromises of concrete territorial interest, which tended to preserve and extend slave territory while keeping it segregated from the North. But in an expanding capitalist economy, founded absolutely upon the principle of private property and committed to entrepreneurial mobility and growth, slavery could not remain cloistered and peculiar. Its special and anomalous legal status was safe only in a society in which Southerners made minimal contact with the rest of the nation: never traveled outside on business with slaves, never transported slaves to the territories to form new plantations, never pledged slave property as collateral for loans from northern banks. Indeed, every loan based upon slave collateral was a recognition *in principle* of the right to property in human beings. It was this principle that Chief Justice Roger Taney affirmed in the Dred Scott decision of 1857, declaring that Congress had no power to forbid the transportation of slave property outside the South and invalidating precedents that allowed Negroes the rights of citizens. Thus Taney affirmed the principle later enunciated by Lincoln, that it was literally impossible for the Union to remain a "house divided" between slavery and freedom: that if the law was to maintain its character of consistency it would have to become all one thing, or all the other.

To defend slavery the South had had to seek ever more explicit endorsements in principle; and it had had to buttress these endorsements—never easily won, and subjected to ever increasing dissent from the free states— with an expanding share of political power. The more the North resisted the slavery principle, the more power was required to prevent public sentiment from taking the form of political action. In the end the South would feel that it required not only an equal division of senatorial seats, but a veto power upon the policies and national candidates of the Democratic Party; and in the end, it would believe itself unsafe if it could not ensure the election of a president committed in principle to the perpetuation and extension of slavery.

What the South perceived as defense, the North perceived as aggression. No less than the South, the North was committed to the "safety valve" of democratic politics, seeing in equal access to power the only guarantee of rights, property, and future prospects. The protective measures required by the South in effect gave that section a species of monopoly power within the Democratic Party and potentially in the national government itself. For northern Democrats to consent to such privilege required ever more explicit acts of self-denial and (to such self-assertive men) even of self-abasement. To accept southern vetoes was in effect to accept political subjugation and dependency—the first step toward a species of enslavement.[24]

Thus the defense of free labor in principle became a "vital interest" of the North, to be defended as the South defended slavery, because racial identity and standing were at stake. If the Southerner saw emancipation as lowering white men to the measure of "nigger equality," the Northerner came to see the potential universalization of slavery as lowering him to the status of the black man.

If ideology pressed Americans toward such a division, their mythology enabled them to envision the consequences that would follow. The Frontier Myth provided a model of the war of extermination or subjugation, a war without limits. In the late 1850s this scenario was most frequently invoked as a way of cautioning the sections not to pursue their differences too deeply or too far. In the 1860s, it would provide the rationale for civil war.

C H A P T E R   1 1

The Ideology of Race Conflict, 1848–1858

Gilpin developed his language of geographical determinism as a way of addressing—or denying—the social and political issues that threatened to divide American society. Although these issues were generated by the conflicts of group and class interest arising in the course of industrialization and economic expansion, the peculiar circumstances of American capitalism gave these conflicts a distinctly racial appearance. The initial period of expansion had been characterized by the acquisition of land through warfare against the Indians, and much of it had been developed through the labor of African slaves. The perpetuation and expansion of slavery in the South and old Southwest preserved this association of progress with a labor system dependent on racial subordination.

Although Negro slavery was the most prominent occasion for the racialization of the language of class politics, it was not the only occasion. Other developments throughout industrial society gave the racial metaphor for class an especially poignant relevance, and extended the applicability of the race-war myth to the whole range of American social relations. In the North, the growing influx of immigrants from Ireland and Germany in the 1840s suggested that the new proletariat of the canal and railroad gangs, the mill towns, and the mushrooming cities might well have an alien ethnic character. The latest wars of Mexican conquest, which were meant to effect growth without internal division, repeated the old pattern of achieving progress through the conquest and subjection of a "nonwhite" race. Disagreements about the social and moral consequences of that conquest turned on responses to the racial character of the Mexicans, and back then to the racial character of southern slavery.

These circumstances enhanced the plausibility of a racial explanation of the course of American development. Such explanations were no less illusion-bound than Gilpin's nature mysticism: both doctrines substitute viable myths for unpalatable facts. But where Gilpin's revisionist agrarianism appeals by its evasion of the fact of social conflict, racialism builds upon such conflicts and develops from them a doctrine that justifies the hegemony of the ruling "race" or class. Given the persistence of conflict in the 1850s and the steady movement toward civil war after 1854, the racialist theories are especially telling since they acknowledged and embodied the reality of conflict.

The essential premises of racialist politics and historiography had been part of the Myth of the Frontier at least since the end of the eighteenth century. They underlay the class politics of Jefferson and Adams, the historiography of Bancroft, and the literary mythology of Cooper. But in the 1850s (and thereafter) racialist thinking became far more systematic, and was applied with increasing rhetorical forcefulness to the definition and resolution of social and political issues. During the early fifties, the more assertive spokesmen for racialism were to be found at the political extremes. For the men of the center, like Lincoln, the conflict-charged language of race war was one to be avoided whenever possible; and Douglas resorted to "crying 'Nigger'" only under extreme political stress. But for abolitionists like W. H. Prescott and Theodore Parker and for southern ultras like John C. Calhoun, James Henry Hammond, and George Fitzhugh, the theory of racial division was the basis of political thought and action. With the support of scientific studies that tended to mirror the myth of racial "gifts," these men elaborated and extended the ambiguous racialism of Bancroft and Cooper into a doctrine of social organization.[1]

It is easy to see why spokesmen for an order based on Negro slavery should develop a theory of history and politics that hinges on the rationalization of the hegemony of the white race over all others. It is less easy to see why such doctrines were also appealing to men who identified themselves as advocates of abolition and defenders of liberal principles. Parker was a radical abolitionist who opposed the Mexican War as immoral aggression and as a device for extending slavery. He supported the militancy of abolitionist guerrillas like John Brown, and advocated without compromise the position that all races of men are equal in the eyes of God and in the capacity for moral action, and ought to be equal before the law. Prescott was a conservative Whig, whose revulsion from the slave system eventually turned him to support such radical measures as the violation of the Fugitive Slave Act and the formation of the new Republican Party.

Racialist historiography begins with an extreme form of ethnocentrism, highly charged by ideology. For Prescott and Parker (as for the southern racialists), the starting point of historical analysis was the belief that the American republic represented the fulfillment of the progressive and liberating promises of the Renaissance, the Reformation, and the Enlightenment. This view sees the struggle of Anglo-Americans, French, Spanish, and Indians for hegemony in North America as more than a power rivalry; it is a symbolic contest between groups that "incarnate" particular ideological values. The victory of the English and Americans over the French (or Spanish) and Indians is therefore a victory of "civilization over savagery" and of "progressive/Protestant" values over "feudalistic/Catholic" dogma. Ideological principles tendentiously associated with different cultures and nationalities are read as biological data, expressive of an innate or natural "character." The worldwide triumph of the English over the continental powers argues the racial superiority of the Anglo-Saxon in general; and the victory of the American branch over the English argues the brief for Yankee superiority in particular. The Indian wars provide the paradigm of this model of history and politics, giving the historian the language through which contemporary social and political struggles can be interpreted. Europeans in general are able to conquer savage Indians—this establishes the principle that more advanced races are able to subjugate and destroy more primitive ones. But the French and Indian Wars, the Revolution, and now the Mexican War extend the paradigm, showing that more advanced races of whites are capable of doing to less advanced whites what both together did to the Indians.

For Prescott and Parker, the Mexican War was a precipitant of positive doctrine in both historical theory and political ideology—and this despite the fact that both men opposed the policy of the Polk administration in fomenting conflict and in carrying it out. For both men, the establishment of American hegemony in Mexico was inevitable, given the racial character of the opponents. Prescott detailed its historical antecedents by taking the long way around: in *The Conquest of Mexico* (published in 1847) he posits that the different histories of Latin and North America are the consequence of a fortunate conjunction of races and climes. The greedy, sensuous, fanatical Spaniards landed in a tropical world, populated with Indian civilizations of great size and population—a situation that evoked their racial capacity for proselytizing by the sword, for obtaining and maintaining aristocratic sway over laboring hordes of ignorant Indian peons. The more frugal and self-reliant English landed in a sparsely populated and temperate zone, where their virtues of self-discipline and self-denial could create an agrarian society of independent proprietors, producing wealth by labor rather than by the exploitation of mineral resources and native peons. Prescott defends the American seizure of Mexican territory in 1848 on the ground that "beggarly Mexico" lacks the human energy to make the land productive, while the descendants of the Puritans have proven their capacity to make the wilderness a garden.[2]

Parker, writing some years after Prescott, elaborates the theoretical premises behind these assertions. Although he admits, with Gilpin, that the possession of "God-granted" natural resources is the basis of national prosperity, he emphasizes the absolute necessity that such resources be presented to a people fitted by race for exploiting them. North or South, the Americans are Anglo-Saxon "freemen, possessing some very noble traits of character," including those of industriousness and the love of liberty. These two traits combine into a composite racial gift which is responsible for the tremendous moral and economic progress (the two go together) made by England and her American colonies since the Reformation. That progress is most clearly realized in the conquest of the wilderness and the savages of the New World; and in the triumph here of republican institutions and a competitive industrial economy. But these qualities are not the by-products of the engagement of the Anglo-Saxon with the wilderness. They are innate attributes brought to America along with "the vigorous bodies and sturdy intellect of their race." This "instinct of progress," as Parker calls it,

> exists in different degrees in various nations and races: some are easily content with a small amount thereof, and so advance but slowly; others desire the most of both, and press continually forward.

Of all races, the Caucasian has hitherto shown the most of this instinct of progress, and, though perhaps the youngest of all, has advanced the furthest . . .[3]

In this form, racialism works as the basis of the "egalitarian" ideology associated with Jacksonian democracy. It asserts that *within* the race distinctions of class are of little consequence: all Anglo-Saxons share the core values and capacities of their race, and this is the basis of their solidarity in the face of alien races. Given such a doctrine, it is possible to make the most radical assertions about the necessity of extending the franchise to all white males. But the basis of this sort of radicalism is the exclusion from the democracy of those groups that are neither Anglo-Saxon nor male. So long as the classes of the Metropolis are seen as racially homogeneous— i.e., with Anglo-Saxons as both capitalists and laborers—this approach may even be productive of a stringent critique of class relations in the society. But once it is established (or believed) that the working classes and the owning classes are of different races, the doctrine becomes problematical. The racial distinction then enforces and justifies the distinction of class; or else it compels the ideologist to rethink his racial divisions, and consider whether or not other races may be admitted to the solidarity of Anglo-Saxon equality.[4]

But the concept of race is founded on a historiography that places violence and force at the center of the historical stage. While industriousness and liberality of intellect are not exclusively Anglo-Saxon attributes, racialist historians would argue that what sets the Anglo-Saxons apart from the Greeks of antiquity and other enlightened and imperial races is their extraordinary capacity for violence, both personal and collective. Without this talent for mobilizing violent force, the Anglo-Saxon could not have established his hegemony in the face of opposition from both savage and civilized races. Among more primitive classes of the population (or in primitive conditions), this capacity takes the form of vigilantism or crime; but at its most advanced level, it is the supreme expression of the race's capacity for organizing society and projecting its will upon nature and the lesser races. Complementing this trait is a disposition to avoid amalgamation with other races, to keep the Anglo-Saxon bloodstream "pure." These two traits, coupled with the Anglo-Saxon power of forming combinations, have made them "the most aggressive, invasive, and exclusive people on the earth." Parker speaks with pride as well as moral stricture when he says, "The history of the Anglo-Saxon, for the last hundred years, has been one of continual aggression, invasion, and extermination." It is the Anglo-Saxons' mixture of violence and exclusiveness, rather than their love of the pastoral, that makes them prefer the conquest of virgin lands and savage peoples to that of populous states; rather than rule natives of other races, it is their natural tendency to "exterminate the savages" from whatever territory they conquer.[5]

Although the use Parker makes of this doctrine is determined by the special requirements of his commitment to the moral crusade against slavery, the doctrine itself is drawn from a common historiographical and political mythology. It was stated more crudely by the Mexican War general William Worth—a northern man of southern sympathies and expansionist enthusiasms—who justified the seizure of Mexico with the boast that "our Anglo-Saxon race [have] been land stealers from time immemorial, and why shouldn't they [be]?"[6]

Parker advances the doctrine of the race war a step beyond that taken by Jefferson and Cooper. They asserted that conflict is probable where two races at different levels of social development compete for a common territory; and they believed that such conflicts tend to become wars of extermination because of the prejudices inherent in such a confrontation. Parker asserts that the motive for the war of extermination is inherent in the character of the Anglo-Saxon, as much as or more than in the racial propensities of the savage; and he links that motive directly to the energies that make the Anglo-Saxon both liberal and progressive.

The warfare of whites and Indians fulfills the normative expectations of this doctrine, but the enslavement of Africans violates it. Why have the Anglo-Saxons of the South departed from their racial gifts, cohabited with and multiplied the Africans among themselves rather than exterminating them? Parker's answer lies in the recognition that it is possible for a race to betray its gifts, to degenerate and become corrupt, and he makes the case for degeneration by a consistent application of the racial standard.

Parker begins by establishing the premise that Anglo-Saxons have defeated both Latins and Indians because they are by nature energetic, industrious, interested in combative enterprises, racially exclusive. He then uses the distinction between Spanish and Anglo-Saxon racial traits as a metaphoric device for distinguishing the southern slaveholding Anglo-Saxons from their northern counterparts:

> But America itself is not unitary; there is a Spanish America in the United States . . .
>
> America was settled by two very different classes of men, one animated by moral or religious motives, coming to realize an idea; the other animated by only commercial ideas, pushing forth to make a fortune or to escape from jail. Some men brought religion, others only ambition; the consequence is, two antagonistic ideas, with institutions which correspond, antagonistic institutions.

On the "Spanish" side are the slaveholders and their commercialist allies in the North, both of whom live on the labor of others, both of whom envision the extension of the slave power to rule over Mexican peons and (perhaps) northern laborers as well. The argument is typical of racialist thought, which reasons analogically, defining race in terms of class and class in terms of race as the polemic requires. These "Spanish" Anglo-Saxons have lost the essential attributes of their race. Their "instinct for progress" has atrophied. In opting for the ease and idleness of the master's life, the slaveholder has acquired the character of the unambitious races he rules. The culture of slavery induces degeneracy of habit in Southerners, and these habits continued over decades register finally in the "blood" and biological inheritance: "But what has most affected the ethnological character of the South is the African element. There are three and a half millions of men in the Southern States, of African origin, whereof half a million are (acknowledged) mulattoes, African Caucasians; but those monumental half-breeds are much more numerous than the census dares confess." This biological amalgamation of the races is but the outward sign of a spiritual amalgamation: the Southerner leaves his racial heritage of enterprise and freedom for a life of indolence, sloth, unambitious conservatism, and the enjoyment of the corrupting delights of mastery without labor, government without check. The continuation of slavery, Parker cautions, will only further "Africanize" the white man, rendering him indolent and dependent on the labor of others. He even points to birth statistics and warns that the rising slave population may threaten the dominance of the white. "An Anglo-Saxon with common sense does not like this Africanization of America; he wishes the superior race to multiply rather than the inferior." Thus Parker invokes the threat of an overwhelming black racial tide, which was a cliché of proslavery rhetoric; and he defines the degeneracy of his antagonist by linking him to the standard of racial inferiority—the African and the savage.[7]

This was not a peculiarity of Parker's argument. Northern stereotypes of southern aristocrats emphasized their indolence, sensuality, and tendency toward violence—precisely the traits associated with blacks and Indians, and with backwoodsmen who had wholly or partially "gone Indian." The fear of miscegenation did not exist in the North merely, or even primarily, as fear of black men marrying white northern girls. Rather (as Lippard's work suggests), the image of the domineering white aristocrat exploiting his slaves both sexually and economically, emasculating and "feminizing" the males and sexually "ruining" the females, was a symbolic statement of the white's fear of his own subjection and humiliation. Revulsion with the plantation's sexual scenario was projected from the Northerner's ambivalence about the exploitation of the girls of Lowell and the workmen of New York.[8]

If the regime of slavery is to be ended and the South regenerated, there must be a renascence of Anglo-Saxon *vertu.* It may be that the whites of the South are too far Africanized to redeem themselves. But the processes of racial transformation work both ways, and Parker is radical enough to propose that the South may be regenerated by the infusion of Anglo-Saxon spirit along with Anglo-Saxon blood in the black population. Until the Afro-American acquires "this dreadful Anglo-saxon blood" he cannot stand on terms of equality within the republic; and therefore to regenerate the South the slaves must at least show themselves capable of conceiving the attempt of drowning slavery in "the white man's blood." Thus Parker's rationale for black self-redemption is really an inverse restatement of the central tenets of Anglo-Saxonist racialism, and an application to revolutionary projects of a myth/ideology developed to explain and justify the history of the Indian wars.[9]

At the opposite political extreme from Parker, the southern polemicist and sociologist George Fitzhugh employed similar racial theories to argue not only for the protection of southern slavery, but its universalization as a model of labor relations. Although this position was too extreme for most southern spokesmen before 1858, the premises on which he based his argument were common to the advocates of "slavery as a positive good." Like

Prescott and Parker, Fitzhugh sees history as the story of the struggle of races for dominance, and celebrates Anglo-Saxon triumph in the racial war of extermination. The Negro must be enslaved because he is presently and permanently unfitted for competition with the whites:

> His lot is cast among the Anglo-Saxon race, and what people can stand free competition with that race [?] The Indian is exterminated from Maine to Georgia . . . the Spaniard is hardly heard of in Florida, and Peonage alone can save the Mexican from annihilation. From the days of Hengist and Horsa to those of Houston the same adventurous, rapacious, exterminating spirit has characterized the race. Can the negro live with all his reckless improvidence under the shade of this Upas tree, whose deadly poison spares no other race? Is he fitted to compete with a people whom in the struggle of life, have outstripped and exterminated all other nations with whom they have come in contact? No.

Although in other aspects of his argument Fitzhugh attacks the bourgeois cash-nexus as economic definition of the basis of human relationships, he agrees with Parker and Prescott in seeing economic utility as a determining factor in distinguishing between the value of different races. Anglo-Saxons are the originators of all those arts and sciences that bring technological progress and higher levels of culture. Blacks are worthy of being made exceptions to the universal rule of the extermination of races that fail in competition with the whites because, unlike the Indians, they are useful to the economic program of white culture:

> But there is a peculiar necessity of some measure of this kind, with regard to the blacks, growing out of the antipathies of race. They are threatened with violent extermination. The fate of the Indians shows that they will be exterminated if they continue so useless and so troublesome.

Taking advantage of the docility of the Negro, overcoming his congenital shiftlessness by means of enforcing labor, and providing for his security in a world in which he is otherwise unfit to maintain himself, the white man in the South established an order which has made as much "progress" as that of the North, without at the same time upsetting the proper and traditional ordering of society.

> Men begin to look more closely at what the slaveholders have been doing since our Revolution, and find that they have been exceeded in skill, enterprise and industry, by no people under the sun. They have settled a vast territory from the Alleghany to the La Platte—from the Rio Grande to the Ohio, contending all the while with the blood-thirsty savages and a climate more to be dreaded than even those savages themselves—and are already producing a greater agricultural surplus than any people in the world.[10]

Thus Fitzhugh invokes a set of standards similar to Parker's by which to measure the progressive and industrious character of the South. Where they seem to differ is in their conception of class relations within a productive society. Fitzhugh takes the African slave as the type of the permanent laboring class, and extrapolates from his "inferiority" the necessity of a patriarchal government by a *Herrenvolk* democracy of slave owners. Parker takes the Saxon freeman-farmer or -mechanic of the North as his ideal citizen, and asserts the doctrines of universal competition and entrepreneurship. But Parker also acknowledges the presence in industrial society of classes that appear to lack the energy of the Anglo-Saxon ideal. The indolent slave master is one such type, as is the wealthy Northerner who lives on rent or interest. But a more prevalent type is the new urban proletarian—often but not always of non-Anglo-Saxon heritage—who exhibits the torpidity, indolence, and acquiescence in southern tyranny that are otherwise characteristic of the African.

This class provides the rank and file of the Mexican War army, "idle, drunken, and vicious men out of the low population of our cities," whose distaste for labor would be augmented by the looting of Mexico, and "the idleness, the intemperance, the debauchery of a camp." This same class— especially the Irish—are the slavish adherents of the superstition of "negrophobia," and thus provide political allies for the slaveholders. But more than negrophobia, love of the South, and "Romish superstition" mark this class as inherently antiprogressive. Through their agitation for trade unionism and their recalcitrant response to industrial discipline, they are a drag upon the supreme expression of Anglo-Saxon energy, which is industrialization. Parker envisions Manifest Destiny not as a fee-simple empire, but as "an industrial state," a "great industrial commonwealth from sea to sea."[11]

Parker takes as the hallmark of the "regressive" mentality a desire to "shun all labor" while possessing "all government." Such an attitude is equally characteristic of the aristocrat and the monopolist at one pole of society, and of the savage Indian and the unionizing workman at the other. Parker represents these groups as selfish minorities, whom chance has favored with a privileged position as possessor of wealth, primitive title to the land, or a monopoly of some particular skill. Somewhat paradoxically, given his assertion about the essential laziness of these groups, Parker identifies them as resisting the tendency of modern technology to replace their old ways and undermine their privileged positions. Just as the aristocrat defends feudal privilege and the Indian his primitive land-right, the laborer defends his possession of a job from the encroachment of machinery by a combination of violence (strikes) and abuse of political institutions (demagogy). Thus these workmen too retard the march of progress.[12]

The key historical question for Parker is to determine how much the regressive tendency of any race or class is rooted in "ethnographical misfortune," and how much it is the product of contingent and temporary factors. The expansive energy of the Anglo-Saxon and the savage torpidity of Indians and Hispanics are cases that history has apparently resolved. But for other regressive classes, the issue is still open. This is true for Africans, who have thus far been prevented by slavery from experiencing a full and fair test of their capacities. Hence it is unclear whether "the regressive force . . . belongs to the constitution of the race," or is "an historic accident entailed on them by impression." Parker is inclined to think that torpidity *is* the racial propensity of the African—how else explain the fact that Anglo-Saxons have enslaved blacks, and not vice versa?—but he is willing to postpone final judgment until they have been allowed their chance. But for Parker, the question is also open in respect to white laborers, whose fitness for self-government is likewise being tested. With all his respect for the sanctity of labor, Parker insists that the standard of progress be applied to all judgments; and by this standard, the insistence of striking stevedores that strikebreakers be prevented from working becomes a case of simultaneous monopolism and regression to the primitive. The strikers have declared "that a man who has a head, shall live only by the muscles in his arms, [so] that all merchandise shall be taken out of a ship by an Irishman hanging at the end of a rope." The proper and progressive response presumably would be that of seeking to rise above arm labor to the status of head work.[13]

A similar language for describing class relations in industry characterizes the southern treatments of the labor question. The elder statesman of slavery in the fifties, Edmund Ruffin, echoes Parker's depiction of regressive tendencies in the northern laboring classes: the "disposition to indulge indolence." The image of black and Indian torpidity informs the conception in both sections of the "regressive" element in the working classes, which are seen as indolent by nature, ignorant by inclination, given to licentiousness and insurrection. But Parker's political conclusions do differ from those of Fitzhugh and Ruffin: Parker relies on industrial progress and the spread through education of right values to alter mass conditions for both the blacks and the poor whites, and asserts his faith in democracy; the Southerners are pessimistic, and advocate a paternalistic social order in which the free laborer (white or black) acknowledges his absolute dependence on capital, and resigns to capital the power to govern. Thus competition with the North, in Fitzhugh's eyes, becomes a version of that tendency toward violence and warfare that marks all relationships between free people. The vocabulary of racialism led Fitzhugh and his colleagues to characterize their northern opposites in the same terms otherwise reserved for the regressive or savage races and classes. Northern ideas of free competition are likened to jungle law, harking back to the bestiality of the Indians and Africans whose "freedom is not human freedom, but the wild and vicious license of the fox, the wolf or the hawk." Parker and his fellows responded in kind, and used the language of racialism to distinguish their own Herrenvolk pretensions from those of the planters.[14]

The political and social programs that Parker and Fitzhugh derive from their racialist reading of social class appear to belie the idea of a common vocabulary. But their differences derive more from contingent factors in their immediate economic situations than from any theoretical difference about the significance of race in history. For Parker (as for Abraham Lincoln) a form of Frontier still exists, in western lands and increased industrial productivity; and these Frontiers will allow a prolongation of the period of racial testing, sufficient to reveal which classes and races are of inherently energetic character, and which are inherently torpid or dependent. But what will happen when the inevitable moment arrives when the testing period is finally closed because of the exhaustion of productive resources, or because the competition of the races has produced definitive results?

Northern reformers confronted such situations on the margins of society in their attempts to grapple with the problems posed by the failures and outcasts of industrial society—paupers, criminals and lunatics in the settled regions, seminomadic Indian tribes on the frontier. In every instance, they had adopted institutions that tended to impose on these elements a rigorous but benignly paternal form of government. The inmates of a workhouse, a prison, an asylum, or an Indian reservation had little or no right of self-government, but were coerced into remaining there for the sake of society and to protect them from the violence or cupidity of normal society. Reform consisted in transforming violent coercion into paternal and tutelary forms of government, under which the inmate class had to live until fit for citizenship and self-government. If their defect of character was chronic, incorrigible or innate, that status of subjection had to be permanent.

The southern spokesmen for the idea of slavery as a "positive good" invoked parallels between the reformed prison, asylum, or reservation and the plantation. The difference between the institutions lay in the fact that the northern institutions were marginal, whereas the plantation was the central productive unit of the southern political economy. Yet without the promise of a permanently open-ended and expansive economy, the North would also have to face one day the necessity of imposing order and regularity on the chaos of free competition, and on the indiscipline of the working classes. In such circumstances, it would be justifiable for the people of superior endowment and energy—the aristocrat race, the Anglo-Saxons in their purest form—to assert a benign and paternal, yet forceful, control over society as a whole. This is the role Parker imagines for himself, and plays out in his discussions of slavery—it is he who proposes the "test" that the Africans must pass or fail, he who decides when to give the freed slave a sword and presumably he who must choose when and if that sword shall be taken away.[15]

But beneath the familial imagery that invests plantation and asylum is a concept of social relations that is fundamentally violent. The black man will prove himself to Parker only when he shows himself as capable in violence as the Anglo-Saxon. The southern version of paternalism is more consistently familial in its imagery, but it too reveals a violent core. Fitzhugh contrasts the tendency of slavery to give "full development and full play to the affections" of family feeling, which "Free society chills, stunts and eradicates" through its insistence on competition.

> Is not the head of a large family almost always kind and benevolent? And is not the slaveholder the head of the largest family? Nature compels master and slave to be friends; nature makes employers and free laborers enemies . . . We are better husbands, better fathers, better friends, and better neighbors than our Northern brethren.

Fitzhugh does not restrict this relation solely to blacks and whites, though southern slavery is the highest form of familial government. Vassalage and serfdom, slavery and peonage are alike justified by "the wisdom of the commonlaw" which holds that "guardians, parents, husbands, committees, and officers are but masters by another name. They are all intended to supply in more or less degree, that want of self-control which unfits large classes of the whites for self-government." But when he comes to describe the politics of the family, which ought to be the model of social peace, he reveals that violent antipathies underlie even paternal government:

> A state of independence always begets more or less of jealous rivalry and hostility. A man loves his children because they are weak, helpless and dependent. He loves his wife for similar reasons. When his children grow up and assert their independence, he is apt to transfer his affection to his grand-children. He ceases to love his wife when she becomes masculine or rebellious.

Fitzhugh then reverses the direction of his metaphor: instead of justifying the regime of slavery by associating it with family government, he criticizes family government by holding up slavery as the model of perfect social relations:

> But slaves are always dependent, never the rivals of their master. Hence, though men are often found at variance with wife or children, we never saw one who did not like his slaves.[16]

This suggests that the best form of tutelage, whether for one's own children or for childlike subject races, is one that never eventuates in the subject's achievement of maturity and inheritance of the mantle of adulthood and power. Fitzhugh likens the government of children with that of criminals, and suggests that appropriate equivalents of the slave's or criminal's chain and the lunatic's straitjacket must govern relations with children and wives and free workers:

> Our wiser ancestors made them slaves because as slaves they might be made civilized, useful and christian beings. We subject children till twenty-one years of age to the control of their parents, or appoint guardians for them. We subject wives to the dominion of their husbands—apprentices to their masters. We permit sailors and soldiers to sell their liberties for terms of years. We send criminals to jail . . . and lunatics to hospitals.[17]

The logic of this position requires a step backward not only from democratic forms of political organization—whose real democracy was already limited haphazardly by differentials in wealth—but the adoption of an antidemocratic ideology, the end of the Jacksonian ideology and of the belief in limitless resources for entrepreneurial agrarian mobility. Some southern papers advocating secession in 1860 in fact employed precisely this kind of rhetoric to justify their move, citing fundamental opposition between the "mob law and agrarianism" of the North and the aristocratic organization of the South, and declaring secession to be not merely a move against the northern interest but an assault on the principle of "free society" itself. Secession conventions and the Confederate Congress were organized along largely antidemocratic lines, excluding as they did representation of the poor whites; but this had become traditional in the South. A southern editor could, with impunity, write in 1856:

> Free society! We sicken of the name! What is it but a con-
> glomeration of greasy mechanics, filthy operatives, small-fisted
> farmers, and moon-struck theorists? All the Northern and espe-
> cially the New England States are devoid of society fitted for
> well-bred gentlemen. The prevailing class one meets is that of
> mechanics struggling to be genteel, and small farmers who do their
> own drudgery; and yet are hardly fit for association with a south-
> ern gentleman's body servant. This is your free society. . . .[18]

The racialism of Parker and Prescott on the one hand, and of Fitz-hugh and Ruffin on the other, asserts that certain races by their nature are entitled to dispossess or govern others; and that other races have an equivalent endowment that makes for their defeat in struggle and subordination in the aftermath of defeat. But the Southerners are far more explicit about the sort of regime that the presence of a permanent underclass requires. Parker's doctrine implies that in a contest of genuinely unequal races, or between degenerate and regenerate fractions of a single race, one will lose and the other win. What follows next is uncertain, but the history of the race (as Parker tells it) suggests that the normal and healthy outcome would be extermination of the weaker (or at least dispossession and removal). Enslavement is of course another possible outcome, but Parker regards it as corrupting to the master race more than to the slave. There is no definite answer in Parker's work to the question of what ought to happen if and when the present underclass—black or white—demonstrates by its failure of the "test" of struggle its unfitness for equality with the Anglo-Saxon. This was precisely the impasse that Jefferson and earlier liberal critics of slavery reached, and Jefferson—like Parker—imagined a "war of extermination" as the only possible outcome of the free competition of the Anglo-Saxon and presumably inferior African races. The only thing that stands between Parker and such a vision is his optimism about the future—an optimism based on the belief in an open Frontier, whether in the form of a landed heritage, or of the productive capacity of the new industrialism, or of the moral perfectability inherent in the Anglo-Saxon's racial heritage.

Those more conservative abolitionists who doubted both the Negro's capacity and the prospects for infinite economic expansion saw in the prospect of Negro citizenship "one indiscriminate and irretrievable equality of ruin"—for "history" proved that "the existence of two equal or independent people [of different racial endowment] on the same soil, has always been the cause of exterminating wars." They proposed instead of liberation the creation of a new all-black Frontier on the coast of Africa, where the semicivilized former slaves could regenerate their character and capacities by playing out the myth-drama of "colonizing the wilderness."[19]

For the South's part, Fitzhugh speaks out of a system whose Frontiers were already substantially foreclosed by the intractability of the plains to cotton culture; by southern indebtedness; and by the successful political opposition to the expansion of slavery within the United States. The most favorable field for its expansion lay in the Caribbean, but the South's ability to exploit the Caribbean was sharply limited by the prospect of native resistance, the opposition of northern interests, and the competing interests of European powers. It is not surprising that Fitzhugh sees the planter class as beleaguered and needing to mobilize behind a doctrine informed by the right and necessity of its tutelage over the laboring classes.

But we may wonder where the logic of Parker's racialism would have led him if he had had such grounds for ceasing to believe in the persistence of open Frontiers for the growth of Anglo-Saxon hegemony. In a political economy in which the continuation of industrial progress depended upon the subjugation of one race culture to another, one could only be true to the "instinct of progress" by identifying with the progressive race, declaring the periods of competitive testing to be at an end, and settling down to establish legitimate governance over those races that have been the losers in the competition. This would indeed be the basis of a consensus of northern and southern conservatives after the Civil War, when both sections faced problems of labor discipline in a context of closed or closing Frontiers.

But for the immediate future, the language of racialism was no more able than the language of agrarianism to provide a basis of common understanding between North and South. Instead of uniting on the basis of racial solidarity against some common external foe, each identified the other as a racial enemy, with character traits akin to those of savage Indians or servile blacks.

The logic of this ideological conflict was publicly displayed in the Lincoln-Douglas campaign for the Senate seat from Illinois in 1858. The two men differed radically upon two vital points: Lincoln was convinced that slavery was a moral wrong, and that the logic of American law and political economics dictated that a single system of labor and private property pertain throughout the Union. Douglas denied that the government had any right to address the moral question, and professed indifference to it; and he held that it was possible for different systems, slave and free, to coexist within a union of discrete states. But they also had a very great deal in common. Both were strongly identified with the opening of new territories for small farmers, even at the expense of the Indian tribes; both were strong advocates (within their separate political spheres) of a transcontinental railroad following the "Central Route." They agreed that the American republic was a "white man's government," and that the beneficiaries of territorial expansion must be free white farmers. They even agreed that some classes of men might be of such a "dependent character" as to be unfit for seizing the economic opportunities of American life; and that blacks and Indians in particular were probably unfit for the exercise of political rights. Yet the stress and pressure of their ideological divergence on slavery overrode both their consensus on white superiority and their common material interest. Lincoln exposed the logic of Douglas's position which committed him to acceptance of a universalization of slavery whenever the legal barriers to it should be undermined by a proslavery Democratic Party. Douglas in turn pressed Lincoln to admit that if the black man was entitled to economic liberty, he must in logic be conceded full civil rights as well.[20]

Extending the reasoning of their opponents' arguments, each invoked a part of the Myth of the Frontier in order to project a historical scenario that might follow from the victory of one or the other principle. In Lincoln's scenario, a conspiracy of politicians, planters, and wealthy men could wage a bloodless war of subjugation and enslavement, aimed at making it impossible for democratic action to prevent the establishment and maintenance of slave property in any state or territory. Having nationalized slavery in principle for blacks, slavery or peonage might then be imposed upon vulnerable classes of whites.[21]

Douglas's scenario is more violent and more clearly in the Frontier Myth tradition. Lincoln and the Republicans, by attacking slavery in principle, in effect "make war" upon it wherever it exists, in the South as well as the territories. And the logic of righteous war requires them to "persevere in that war until [slavery] shall be exterminated." In response, the southern states must (by the same logic) make war upon the North, since to defend the moral right of slavery will require them to persevere in their own "war of extermination," which must continue until one side or the other is wiped out or subjugated. Douglas thus follows with fidelity the paradigm of race and cultural conflict articulated in the mythology of the Indian wars: where two unlike and antipathetic races or systems meet, war is inevitable and is fought to the extreme limits of extermination or enslavement.[22] What was for Douglas a polemical device for discrediting Lincoln became by 1860 the South's real-world reading.

In neither scenario is it possible for the natural paradise of western land to offer an alternative to extermination/subjugation. The new land is not the antidote for social strife, but the occasion of it. Its existence and the absolute need of all interests to use it requires each man to follow to the end the premises of his political ideology; and the contradictions of those ideologies, pressed to their limits, evoke the mythological alternative to the "agrarian paradise" version of the Frontier—the myth of the race war.

Lincoln's scenario differs from Douglas's in two crucial respects. Douglas invokes a simplistic model of racial division, which permits an easy identification of the "dark" and "light" parties, the "Indians" and the "settlers" in the prospective race war. Lincoln's depiction of the battle lines is fuzzier, because his attitude toward racial difference is complex and ambivalent. The blacks are the base line of racial reference in these models, and Lincoln has not resolved for himself the question of their humanity and equality—he both affirms and denies it. From this fundamental ambivalence arises his indisposition to declare war upon the issue, and his inclination to translate the conflict into legal and political terms. Even the "attack" which he envisions is visualized not as an armed attack (which is Douglas's trope) but as legislative/judicial conspiracy—which can be met by legitimate electoral countermeasures.

We may also question whether or not Douglas literally expected Lincoln to preside over a war of aggression and extermination. In the context of the political debates engaged in by the two men, Douglas's scenario seems more a polemical ploy or dramatizing device than a literal accusation. But by 1860 Douglas's scenario had indeed been adopted as the literal truth by some of Douglas's most powerful political enemies—the southern

Democrats, who had been driven to the ultimate defense of slavery as a "positive good" and a permanent American institution. For this party, even Douglas's conservative approach to protecting slavery in the South was no longer acceptable because it did not require acceptance of slavery in principle.

The various political initiatives and compromises put forward by Douglas (and other moderates) from 1850 to 1860 depended upon the belief that the mere material abundance of Frontier land could provide an antidote to the agitation of the social question of slavery. But the controversies of the decade shifted the terms of conflict from preoccupation with the distant, golden land to concern with primary matters of right and wrong, justice and injustice, universalized freedom or metastasizing slavery. The issue of slavery in the territories and of access to new lands provided (in Kansas) the most dramatic occasion for acting out the divergent interests of free- and slave-staters. But the land issue by itself was not sufficient reason to start a civil war. Those (like Douglas) who sought to substitute a division of material spoils for resolution of ideological conflict failed, because their belief in the Myth of the Frontier (agrarian version) masked or blurred their perception of the fact that democratic politics itself was the true and persistent safety valve for American discontent. By 1860 both North and South had come to believe that their political safety valve had been shut tight. The southern domination of the Democratic Party, and the attempts of the southern wing to block or destroy the candidacy of the northern Democrats' favorite, Stephen Douglas, convinced northern Democrats that their party could no longer serve as the vehicle of political action or expression. Similarly, the South perceived the legitimate election of Lincoln as evidence that slavery was no longer safe within the Union— because the South had thereby lost the veto upon executive and legislative action that had been its traditional political prerogative.[23]

As the agrarian aspect of the Frontier Myth went into eclipse, it unmasked its active or racialist side—the mythology of the Indian war. Once the "garden of the West" became a battleground between the principles of slavery and free labor, it was no longer possible to see pioneering progress in Gilpin's terms, as the triumph of Man in a struggle with pure, inanimate Nature. Progress now required completion of the struggle between two orders of men, representing fundamentally opposite principles of social and moral organization. The precedent of the Indian wars modeled the sort of battle that would ensue—a "savage" war of extermination or subjugation, with "civilization itself" as the stakes.

CHAPTER 12

The Inversion of the Frontier Hero:
William Walker and John Brown, 1855–1860

By the late 1850s, North and South were radically divided by their common language of myth and ideology. The agrarian benefices that were supposed to buy off political and social discontent became instead the focus of intensified competition. The language of race war, which promulgated a vision of American solidarity in the face of an alien threat, provided instead the imagery that expressed and inflamed internal divisions of ideology and class. The same contradictions that twisted the ideology of Frontier development from its intended function also aborted or inverted the attempts to create literary myths or "living legends" out of the materials of current history. We have already seen how ideological divisions thwarted the creation of a literary myth of the Mexican War. Those war heroes who did achieve something like the "living legend" status of a Boone or a Jackson were either obvious anachronisms like Crockett or Carson, or suffered from their association with the troublesome politics of slavery, like Houston, Frémont, Scott, and Taylor.

The intensification of ideological strife over the transcontinental Frontier thwarted the efforts of entrepreneurs and empire builders to establish and protect trans-Isthmian and cross-continental steamship and rail networks. It also gave a peculiar twist to the representation of those "heroes" who made their reputations by their engagement on these Frontiers. Although both the transcontinental and the trans-Isthmian routes were sought as ways of linking the Metropolis to the California Frontier, the rival interests at stake in each of these routes came to outweigh the existence of a common purpose. The trans-Isthmian sea route became the favored route of southern imperialists and northern merchants—of the latter because it favored the interests of the existing mercantile ports of the East, of the former because it engaged American power in the only region in which the plantation form of production could be propagated. The transcontinental railroad route had its southern partisans, but their enthusiasm was checked by the superior competitive strength of northern railroad interests, by the belief that the territory to be linked was largely unsuited to plantation agriculture, and by the strength of free soil and free labor interests in the North. Northern interests conversely resisted imperial projects in the Caribbean because of their fear of a political and economic hegemony of the slavery interests. Thus the positive interests of each section in a particular route was matched by the negative interest each had in preventing the other from achieving its full purpose.

Each of these developing transcontinental projects produced a representative hero. The filibuster William Walker emerged in 1855 as the hero of the Isthmian and Caribbean Frontier; and in the same year John Brown appeared as the representative of the vigilante-guerrilla fighters of the Kansas Frontier. In the political and literary responses to these two figures we can see what had happened to the Frontier Myth under the pressure of the slavery issue. Myths and heroic types that in the past had represented the solidarity of Americans on their militant march toward progress were now associated with outlawry, piracy, and a perverse tendency to direct violence against the republic itself.

"Filibusters" were private military expeditions, usually invited and organized by Latin American patriots-in-exile or embattled in-country partisans, whose aim was to use American manpower and firepower to achieve victory. In the 1850s the enemies against which expeditions were directed were chiefly the regimes of the surviving Spanish colonies in Cuba and the islands, and the Conservative (also "Servile" or "Legitimist") governments of independent Central America. The American officers and soldiers enlisted for these expeditions were promised land and political offices under the new regime, so that their forays often had the cover of colonization and always the prospect of economic gain. Ostensibly the politics of the filibusters was "liberal": their aim was to liberate Cuba from Spanish colonialism or Mexico from the domination of French influence; to overthrow some local tyranny; or even to attach the colonists' adopted homelands to the United States and its libertarian institutions.

The projected filibuster colonies in Central America had a measure of precedent in the procedures by which Texas had been colonized in 1820–30, and California seized from Mexico in 1846. In both cases, Americans had initially been permitted or even invited to settle on land which Mexico could not immediately develop or defend. Most Americans had come to Texas as members of organized colonial enterprises, whose leaders were given local authority by the Mexican government. After more than a decade they rebelled against Mexican authority and invited "volunteers" from the states to join them. In California Americans had come as individuals, but during the crisis of the Mexican War they were incited and aided to rebel by John C. Frémont, and the "Bear Flag" rebels recruited their forces with volunteers enlisted with the promise of grants of land following victory.

But the context in which the filibustering enterprises of the fifties were formed made it impossible for their projectors to live up to their precedents. The lands they aimed to colonize were in fact already relatively well settled, possessed a large native population and culture; Cuba was a closely governed Spanish colony, while the Central American states had won political independence. In such situations American colonists could not hope to duplicate the Texas/California trick of eventually outnumbering and replacing the native people, or of substituting American for native law and leadership. Whereas the competing European powers were too weak or unwilling to contest American ambitions in Texas and Oregon and California, in Central America the interests of Britain, France, and Spain were heavily engaged. Finally, the new wave of filibuster colonists had to contend with the intensified domestic conflict over the extension of slavery; they could find support only by linking their projects to the ambitions of the most extreme partisans of slavery expansion, who alone possessed a rationale for incorporating a vast nonwhite population on a basis short of full citizenship. Thus even the successful filibusters tripped over the same obstacles that had brought the "All Mexico" movement of 1847–48 to a halt.

Practical filibusterism enjoyed few successes, and those were brief-lived; the political movements that supported the project of a southern empire in the Caribbean moved from blunder to blunder until they were swallowed up in the secession movement. The American-sponsored revolution in Cuba led by Narciso Lopez (1849–50) failed; John A. Quitman's much trumpeted Cuba expedition (1855) never left town; William Walker's brief successes in Sonora and Nicaragua (1854–57) ended in ruin; and the Kinney Colony on the Miskito Coast simply dissolved. The height of official interest in filibustering may have been reached in the issuance of the 1854 Ostend Manifesto by a group of American diplomats in Europe (including James Buchanan, later president, and Pierre Soulé). But this declaration of Manifest Destiny only aroused resentment and resistance among the European nations it was intended to abash; and its association with the ambitions of proslavery men poisoned its appeal to liberal and revolutionary elements in Europe.[1]

Because its projects came to so little in the end, it has been difficult for historians to take filibusterism seriously. But between 1854 and 1857 filibustering and its concomitant of a southern empire in the Caribbean appeared to be serious business. In addition to Quitman's well-publicized Cuba expedition and the Gadsden Purchase (engineered by Jefferson Davis), there were powerful American interests engaged in attempting to purchase or otherwise control trans-Isthmian routes through Tehuantepec in Mexico, through Nicaragua, and through Panama. American businesses and banks had heavy investments in all of these enterprises, and political leaders like President James Buchanan and Ambassador and Senator Pierre Soulé were directly interested in certain of them. Indeed, to some extent the failure of each can be attributed to rivalries with parties interested in one or more of the others. But only in Nicaragua did Americans come close to establishing their own regime in Central America. While he had neither the prestige nor the financial backing of Quitman, William Walker—the Gray-eyed Man of Destiny—proved to have the filibuster's one essential requirement: the ability to act swiftly and decisively, making the maximum use of temporary military advantages to create a political fait accompli.[2]

WILLIAM WALKER: THE
AMERICAN AS CONQUISTADOR

Walker was an unlikely choice for hero of the ultra-partisans of slavery extension. He did not look the hero: small and slight in build, mild-mannered and diffident in public. His most arresting feature was his pale gray eyes, whose mysterious and compelling power became part of Walker's mystique. He was the son of a Calvinist preacher in Nashville—a stern, rigid, unforgiving man who "slew his thousands" in frontier revival meetings —and an invalid mother, who preferred romantic fiction to biblical exegesis. Their son had both the Calvinist sense of personal election and providential mission, and a romantic's egocentric vision of the historical stage and his role thereon. Like Simon Suggs, he felt it good to be "shifty in a new country"—but he preferred the work and status of professional to that of entrepreneur. Seeking his métier, he followed a peripatetic career, first in medicine—actually in mesmerism, which played upon the power of his eyes—then in law and journalism in New Orleans. His political convictions were generally Free Soil, and had to be maintained on the dueling ground as well as the printed page. His romantic spirit expressed itself in his treatment of Ellen Galt Martin—a lovely "deaf-and-dumb" girl whose cure or rescue he undertook. After her death in a yellow-fever epidemic, Walker sought to make a new life in gold rush California, again as lawyer and journalist.

In 1854 he was asked to lead a filibustering expedition to detach Baja California and Sonora from Mexico. The expedition was a fiasco, in part because Walker gave more attention to supplying his men with guns than to the vital matter of food. Since this expedition coincided with the opening debates on the Kansas-Nebraska Bill and with the negotiations for the Gadsden Purchase—arranged by Secretary of State Jefferson Davis to facilitate a southern-based transcontinental railroad—Walker's expedition was seen as part of an all-out offensive by the slavery extensionists. There was in fact no connection between Davis or Gadsden and Walker, and the latter returned from his expedition to participate again as a Free Soiler in politics. It was on the strength of the Baja expedition, and of his reputation as a political liberal, that Walker was invited to bring a corps of soldier colonists to the assistance of the Nicaraguan Liberals, in exchange for the right to plant an American colony in the country.

Although his generalship was suspect and his understanding of Nicaragua shallow, Walker triumphed by a masterstroke of opportunism. In Nicaragua, party ideology was overlaid by the rivalry between the two major cities, León (Liberal) and Granada (Servile or Legitimist). These towns were set inland from the Pacific coast, less than a hundred miles apart, in the midst of the most developed agricultural regions and on the network of interconnected lakes and streams that provided easy routes for transportation. But Granada's position on the great Lake of Nicaragua allowed her to control access from the Liberal northwestern towns to the most important and valuable property of the Nicaraguan republic—the Accessory Transit Corporation's facilities for the Isthmian crossing. These had been developed by the American shipping magnate Cornelius Vanderbilt, under a lease from the Legitimist government that gave the corporation an economic monopoly and effective political authority along its right-of-way. From the start, Walker directed his operations to the capture of the Transit; and when a daring coup de main also gave him possession of Granada almost without a struggle, he had in his hands the means to absolute control of the Transit route and of the conservative pole of Nicaraguan politics.

Walker used his strategic position to impose a political settlement on the warring factions. He himself retained command of the armed forces in the coalition government, and he enforced his government of compromise by appointing an officer of his "American Phalanx" as deputy to each of the Nicaraguan cabinet ministers. Both literally and figuratively there was a heavily armed American or Walker loyalist standing behind each of the Nicaraguan ministers while they ran the country. When the Conservative leader Ponciano Corral attempted to gather Central American support to eliminate Walker, Walker had him shot; and when the Liberal or Leonese party demanded the removal of the capital from Granada (and possession of the Transit route), Walker broke with them as well, and moved (in 1856) to establish an American regime backed by his praetorian guard.

Walker's relatively easy triumph over the Nicaraguan factions reinforced his conviction of heroic destiny, which he generalized into a belief in the racial superiority of North Americans to Central Americans. He had found the Liberals and the Legitimists alike in their incapacity to lead Nicaragua toward self-government. Neither of the parties enjoyed the full support of the Nicaraguan peasantry and Indians. On the contrary, both had earned popular enmity by expropriating lands, taxing and exploiting the farming and laboring population, and—worst of all—conscripting the people into their armies under threat of death and property confiscation for the families of those who refused to serve. By doing away with conscription, disbanding the native armies of both parties, and relying on his own American Phalanx for the heavy combat, Walker earned widespread (though temporary) popular affection and the support of some genuinely popular leaders.[3]

But the success of this policy did not convince Walker of the necessity of establishing his "movement" on the basis of popular consent. On the contrary, it reflected and confirmed his belief that the "native race" was utterly lacking in martial character; and being incapable of self-defense it was therefore incapable and undeserving of self-government. Walker's "revolution" began by proposing the elimination of the traditional Nicaraguan aristocracy, but it did not propose to substitute popular democracy in its place. Instead, Walker moved toward the idea of substituting a North American people for the existing native classes.

To this end he rewrote the laws to encourage massive immigration from the United States and Europe. The government proposed to expropriate from native landowners, and reclaim from the wilderness, great tracts of land, capable of producing a wealth of tropical crops. To provide the large labor force that would be needed to exploit these lands, Walker promulgated a series of laws designed to create a "contract labor" or peonage system; and he (or his agents) began to plan for the reinstitution of slavery and the African slave trade.

Walker's rapid transformation from Free Soiler and Liberator to slavery advocate and military dictator was swift enough to appear opportunistic. Even those who supported Walker out of self-interest or partisanship suspected that his "principles" were lightly held, to be nourished or cast away according to the occasion. Certainly opportunism played a part in Walker's shifts of position. His regime was no sooner established than it was increasingly isolated. By 1857 his enemies included both of the original parties of Nicaragua, as well as the anti-*Yanqui* regimes in neighboring Central America. The British were working on the Miskito Coast to block the American threat to their influence in the Isthmus; and Walker's seizure of the Transit set Vanderbilt against him—a man with the money, will, and ruthlessness to destroy Walker. His native supporters would be loyal to him only as long as he did not require them to fight on his behalf. And their loyalty was bound to be compromised by the influx of American colonists with whom Walker expected to "regenerate" the Nicaraguan economy. It was obviously necessary for him to gain the support of the United States; and since the only faction interested in Caribbean acquisitions was the southern slavery extensionists, it was to that group he appealed. In the event, the appeal was so obviously self-interested and inconsistent with past statements by Walker that even southern extremists viewed it with suspicion. When it was discovered that Walker's proffer of annexation was in fact insincere—he intended to maintain Nicaraguan independence with himself as *caudillo*—Walker was personally discredited with those who had the most interest in his success. Likewise, the annexation ploy destroyed whatever lingering support there may have been for Walker among conservative Nicaraguan nationalists.

But the most devastating error was Walker's promulgation of laws favoring the restoration of the African slave trade and the establishment of a regime of slavery and peonage in Central America. In Nicaraguan terms, this decree put Walker in a position far more reactionary than that of the Spanish regimes that had been overthrown in the 1820s. In the States it allied Walker with a plank in the proslavery platform to which only the most extreme ultras could subscribe—even strong advocates of slavery as a "positive good" feared to agitate revival of the slave trade, which had been execrated and abolished by the civilized world for decades. As an act of Machiavellianism, the decree was "half-smart": if it earned Walker the support of some very vocal Southerners, the Free Soil Democrats who had supported him earlier now saw him as a traitor, exemplifying the perfidy of the proslavery faction of the Democracy.[4]

Walker's development cannot be explained entirely as a maladroit quest for the main chance. Nor was his career so much a repudiation of the antebellum liberalism he had espoused as it was an unintentionally parodic development of its contradictions. The original project for liberating Nicaragua was motivated by both opportunistic cupidity and a sentimental affection for the ideals of political liberation. If there was a contradiction between these two motives, it was one that was denied by the canonical ideologists of American liberalism from Jefferson to Jackson to

Lincoln. The center of the liberal faith was the belief that political democracy must be harnessed to the free expression of individual ambition, as modified by enlightened self-interest; and that the opportunistic seizure of frontier lands was not simply cupidity, but the natural and inevitable means for establishing a resource base sufficient to sustain a democracy of entrepreneurs. Free Soil principles were no deterrent to projects for seizing and colonizing foreign lands—quite the contrary was true, since abundant cheap land was the economic prerequisite of free labor and free soil. If it were not for the "native problem," the liberation of Nicaragua could have been seen as a classic Frontier adventure, a heroic escape from the rigors and limits of Metropolitan conditions, a new garden spot beyond the outer limits of land reached in California—a place to regenerate fortunes and soils, to aggrandize and uplift a new group of pioneers and reclaim new wildernesses for civilization. Even a militant supporter of labor's National Reform like George Wilkes could be temporarily seduced into seeing Nicaragua as a new field for American homesteading.

But the Nicaraguans and their society were there, already in place. To get around the ideological problem they posed, it was necessary to see them as unsuited by their nature for participation in a self-governing republic: to see them either as Indians, fit only for removal or extermination; or as blacks, fit only for enslavement. Here indeed Walker had to choose between Free Soil principles and the interests of his regime. But there were liberal precedents for the choice he made. The Fathers of the republic, in the Constitution of the United States, had accepted the apparent contradiction of slavery in a republic in order to make the new government possible. And the public-spirited Compromisers of 1850 had renewed their commitment to a toleration of slavery, in order to preserve that government and make it safe. If Walker was a hypocrite, then so were the leading men of the last several political generations.

So it was possible for Walker to see and present himself not as a renegade from classic American principles, but as their exemplar, working for republican ends under conditions of extreme difficulty. The grandiosity of Walker's personality, and the loss of contact with reality that went with it, can obscure the ways in which Walker simply exaggerated the general tendencies of style and substance in American romantic nationalism.

For Walker, as for the rest of the "Young America" generation, the principles of democracy were no longer abstract ideas of universal application. They had become identified with "the American nation" and with the Anglo-Saxon race. Walker had begun by identifying the interests of Nicaragua and the United States: both were nations desiring (like all men) independence and democracy, and sharing in addition a common interest in the Isthmian routes that were the key to American development. He had also identified the causes of both countries with himself—an association that is consistent with the premises of romantic fiction and historiography, which identify the hero as the "representative man" of his people and the vindicator of their values. The opportunity for achieving personal power that was offered by the Nicaraguan situation, and the practical measures taken to achieve that power, encouraged Walker to act out and extend the symbolism of his role. Walker the American had conquered Nicaragua: this in itself constituted the victory of liberal principles.[5]

When the Nicaraguans objected to Walker, they rejected the "American movement in Central America" as a whole; and when they rejected America, they imperiled the objective embodiment of democratic principles on the Isthmus, and set themselves against progress and civilization as well. They therefore (as Walker saw it) ceased to be "a people" in the sense of the Declaration of Independence—capable of and eager for self-government—and became instead "them that are not a people" (as the Puritans would have said): savages of the sort permitted by God to test or scourge, but never to replace, his Chosen People.

The Walker regime in 1856–57 presented the absurd spectacle of an isolated army of "Anglo-Saxon" foreigners, besieged by the organized forces of the Nicaraguans and their allies, declaring themselves to be the only legitimate and democratic embodiment of Nicaraguan nationality. Observers at the time, and historians since, viewed this pose as evidence of Walker's cynicism and propagandistic strategy, or as proof of his insanity; and there are elements of both in Walker's career. But the choice of identification, whether cynical or psychotic, tells us something about the system of values in which Walker was reared and to which he believed he could appeal. By a tortuous but coherent logic, Walker had rationalized his substitution of himself and his army for the Nicaraguan people he had come to protect; and that logic was an ironic reflection of the rationale by which English settlers had become "Americans" through the act of dispossessing the Indians and making them alien interlopers in their own country. So to "regenerate" Nicaraguan society was, for Walker, to destroy the society and people he found and substitute another in their place.[6]

The logic of this belief, coupled with the practical exigencies of governing with an alien force of praetorians, impelled Walker to shift the basis of his authority from popular appeal to pure force; and when his material force appeared weak, he supplemented them by creating fear of a "White Terror." This began shortly after his seizure of Granada with the summary executions of two prominent Nicaraguan leaders—one for conspiracy against the regime, and one simply as an example of terror, to cover up a politically embarrassing act of criminal violence by one of Walker's subordinates. To maintain his American army in Granada he had to begin taxing and despoiling the local villages, and the beef-hungry *Yanquis* made heavy inroads into the livestock of the peasantry. The acts of expropriation and the promulgation of the new forced-labor laws that were supposed to encourage foreign immigration made the American regime hateful, and roused both popular and nationalistic opposition—which Walker attempted to cow by terrible deeds on the battlefield, and even by the denial of quarter to surrendering soldiers.[7]

The crowning symbol of Walker's regime was his destruction of his own capital of Granada. Besieged there by an alliance of Central American forces (backed by Vanderbilt), Walker was compelled to leave Granada and fall back on the Transit through which all his own resources were imported. While his troops staved off the assaults of the Allies, other members of the Phalanx deliberately destroyed the city of Granada with hammers, axes, fires, and barrels of gunpowder. As he left, Walker's local commander planted a sign on the ruins, that echoed Scipio's epitaph for Carthage (and Diaz del Castillo's for Tenochtitlán)—"Here stood Granada." Walker justified his action—which was universally condemned as "barbaric"—on the ground that to leave Granada in enemy hands would be to give them political preeminence: as if they had not already achieved that by driving him out of the city. But for Walker, Nicaragua was now synonymous with the American Phalanx, and any action that served to protect that army's position, interest, and reputation for merciless efficiency in war was ipso facto contributive to the ultimate "regeneration" of Nicaragua and Central America. Thus, in the parlance of a later war, Walker had to destroy the city in order to save it; just as he had to propose the destruction of the Nicaraguan population in order to effect its regeneration.[8]

Ultimately Walker's acts of violence could neither save his government nor regenerate Central America. Besieged in Rivas and cut off from the Transit, the heroic charisma of the Gray-eyed Man of Destiny proved insufficient to sustain morale, and his army dissolved around him. He surrendered to an American naval officer in May 1857—abandoning his native collaborators and the mass of his soldiers and colonists to the wrath of the Allies. This abandonment, coupled with his failure, ruined his public reputation as a hero with all but the most devoted "filibusterists."[9]

To overcome the political isolation in which he found himself after 1856, Walker and his supporters had made extensive use of the means of propaganda, producing newspapers, books, and melodramas about the "Gray-eyed Man of Destiny" and the "paradise" of Nicaragua. Their efforts were augmented by those of regular journalists, who were sent by American papers to cover the exciting events on the Isthmus. In the work produced by these men we can see the transformation of mythological and ideological content that paralleled the transformation of Walker's enterprise. Beginning with an emphasis on the similarities between Nicaragua and the traditional agrarian Frontiers of the United States, the Walker mythology moved swiftly toward a reformulation of the Frontier project in terms of racial warfare, with extermination and enslavement as the necessary outcome.

The official newspaper of the regime was *El Nicaraguense*, published in Granada—but in English only, which suggests that its primary audience was in the States and among the American travelers on the Transit route. The first editor of the paper was William V. Wells, Walker's official publicist, and his power as propagandist was not limited by the small circulation of his paper. Walker attempted (with some success) to restrict the flow of uncensored news from Nicaragua, and as a result the stories in American papers tended to be either direct reprintings or paraphrases of stories in *El Nicaraguense*. Thus the basic news stories printed by the New York *Herald* (pro-Walker) and the New York *Tribune* (anti-filibuster) would most often be identical, and positive in tone. But their editorial responses were nonetheless widely divergent, reflecting domestic divisions on slavery extension.[10]

In 1856 Wells returned to the States and published *Walker's Expedi-*

tion to Nicaragua. Based on his newspaper articles, the book was an extended apology for Walker's career which sought to represent the filibustering expedition as the logical extension of Manifest Destiny and the agrarian Frontier. Wells begins by invoking the prospect of a Frontier temporarily closed; but which, thanks to the racial vigor of Anglo-Saxon pioneers will be immediately reopened:

> The term "Manifest Destiny" is no longer a myth for paragraphists and enthusiasts; the tide of American population, stayed on the shores of the Pacific, seeks new channels; and already the advancing step of the blue-eyed race is heard among the plains and valleys of Central America.

The notion of Frontier closure applied to California is patently false: the area had just been conquered, and was scarcely full of population. Indeed, the territory seized from Mexico probably had a man/land ratio smaller than that of any similar frontier district outside of Siberia. But the mythology of the Frontier is clearly operative here, with its suggestion that the achievement of any new Frontier conquest merely postpones the day of final closure and completion.[11]

Wells represents Walker's enterprise not as an act of conquest, but as a "colonizing" expedition: the Americans of the Phalanx are presumably those unable to find land in "crowded" California. The Nicaraguans are represented as "semi-barbarous," a curious mixture of "Indians" and Spanish aristocrats. The opposition party in Nicaragua is termed the "Aristocratic (or Servile) Party"—a phrase that perfectly adumbrates the American linkage of traditional aristocracy with slavery and servility. In this context, Walker appears as liberator and as civilizer in Jacksonian terms, combating at once savage backwardness and aristocratic arrogance. The Nicaraguans, whether rulers or ruled, are alike in their racial inferiority, which Wells defines in the usual terms: effete and decadent descendants of the early Spanish colonists who must eventually give place to the superior Anglo-Saxon activity and intelligence; and a subservient class of Indians and mestizos. But Wells is curiously vague about the exact course which their subordination will take. Will the Americans replace or exterminate only the Spanish ruling class; or will the complete pattern of North American colonization be invoked, and the Indians replaced or enslaved as well? He asserts that Nicaragua is another California for fertility and gold mines—if anything, it is still more lush and well endowed. Like California, it needs "the introduction of an industrious and energetic population" to take advantage of the resources and the "cheap labor" available. This suggests the replacement of Spanish by American *hacendados*; but Wells gives a Jeffersonian flavor to the replacement, by speaking of the prospective colonists as if they were yeoman farmers whose natural labors will "place Nicaragua among the leading nations of the earth." But the advances which Wells envisions are not the increase of the natives, but the colonization of the semibarbarous land by Americans.

Wells portrays Walker as the agent of this great leap forward, playing up the power of Walker's eyes and the sobriquet "Gray-eyed Man of Destiny." The Indians, we are told, regard him as a latter-day Quetzalcoatl, their rescuer and messiah. His acts of warfare have led to his being hailed as "the Liberator and Benefactor of Nicaragua," and he is seen as having "paved the way to regenerate two millions of people, and thrown open to industrious arms one hundred and fifty thousand acres of land." The language of boosterism and of historical romance thus join to aggrandize Walker and his enterprise.[12]

Although at first uncertain about Walker and his projects, the *Herald* became for a time the staunchest supporter of the filibuster regime. Of all the newspapers, James Gordon Bennett's made the most systematic attempt to integrate filibustering with the main principles and symbols of the Frontier Myth in its post–Mexican War, racialist form. The traditional elements of the agrarian myth were not entirely neglected. Bennett's editorials echoed those of *El Nicaraguense* in representing Nicaragua as a paradise of tropical fertility, ripe for the hand of the cultivator. To this he also added the new element of the Gold Rush, predicting that the mines of Chontales would prove more valuable than those of California. This theme develops the premises of Gilpin's work, which associated the natural abundance of fertile soil and mineral deposits as bases of a democratic economy that would be both agrarian and industrial.[13]

But the primary appeal of the Walker regime, as presented by the *Herald*, is its role as agent of Anglo-Saxon Manifest Destiny. A crucial turn in the *Herald's* coverage of Walker occurred in May, 1856, when a British-backed Costa Rican army was advancing on Nicaragua. In one issue, the *Herald's* front-page story on the "Crisis in Nicaragua" is paralleled by a pair of stories on "Indian Battles" in the West and "The Panama Massacre"—a riot in which a number of Americans were killed in the towns along the Panama transit route. On the inside pages, an editorial on "The Slaughter of Americans in Central America" generalizes the Panama riot, and associates it with the Costa Rican attack on Walker as an exhibition of "the savage blood-thirstiness of half-breeds" whose aim is to "exterminate the Anglo-Saxon race in Central America." Walker's appeal now has nothing to do with economic interest, but with the fact that he is "blood of our blood," and is doing battle against the British and the savages in the manner of Andrew Jackson.[14]

From this time until Walker's defeat and expulsion from Nicaragua (May 1857), the *Herald* promoted Walker as a race hero. The "Gray-Eyed Man" legend was given prominent and favorable display in both news stories and editorials, and Walker's victories were compared to the decisive battles of Western civilization—Marathon, Yorktown, and Waterloo. Anglo-Saxon dominion and glory, rather than mere land or gold, would be Walker's primary appeal to Americans; and that glory would be proven through slaughter: "there will be no lack of Anglo-Saxon volunteers for Walker as long as, with a few hundred such men, he can vanquish by thousands his deteriorated mixed Spanish and Indian enemies."[15]

The Filibuster War of 1855–57 coincided with the civil war over slavery in Bleeding Kansas, and the *Herald* offered the Nicaraguan Frontier as a traditional alternative to the strife of sections and parties. Extremists of North and South, said Bennett, were trying to force Americans to choose between "niggerism" and "border ruffianism"—between acceptance of blacks as political and social equals (which Bennett represented as the Republican position); and acceptance of the high-handed and illegitimate manipulation of Kansas politics by slave-state vigilantes. "If niggerism and 'border ruffianism' are to be the paramount . . . elements of our politics, what else but disunion, civil war, anarchy, and a piratical appropriation of public rights and private property, are we to expect. . . ." Bennett pointedly contrasts the disharmony and unpatriotic fanaticism of the Kansas partisans with the glorious celebration of national destiny at a grand demonstration for Walker and Nicaragua held in New York at the end of May 1856. Thereafter, Kansas stories and Nicaragua stories were often juxtaposed, the contrast always tending to show that the tropical frontier was the legitimate extension of the traditional safety valve of the West.[16]

But the promulgation of Walker's slavery decree in October of that year shocked even Bennett, who remarks caustically on the rising value of "nigger stock" in Nicaragua and the South, and links Walker with the "nigger-driving" faction of the Democratic Party. But Bennett rallied quickly, and put the new decree into a broader context. The exposure of Walker's intention to keep Nicaragua independent (rather than seek admission to the Union as a slave state) exonerates Walker of complicity with "border ruffianism." Instead (says Bennett) Walker seeks to establish a Central American Confederacy, based upon slavery and backed by the British and French, which will become in time the "rival" of the United States. We would expect a staunch nationalist like Bennett to share the horror of those former supporters of Walker who now saw the filibuster as a traitor to American interests. But Bennett views the decision under a racial, rather than a national rubric. Walker's Confederacy will substitute an Anglo-Saxon government for the "effete and wretched republics of Central America," and for so doing he will be "ranked among the great benefactors of his race."[17]

Although Bennett was opposed to those slavery partisans who threatened the Union, he did not oppose slavery in principle. On the contrary, he held to the racialist principle that declared that where superior race meets inferior, there must be either a regime of subordination or a war of extermination. Although the *Herald* invokes the mystique of the Indian war to make filibusterism appealing, it never presents Nicaragua as the kind of Frontier for farmers envisioned in the original Myth. This latest incarnation of the "garden of the world," says the *Herald*'s correspondent, is to be enjoyed by southern planters and not individual freeholders. The *Herald* was in fact lukewarm toward the principles embodied in the various Homestead acts, regarding them as a form of unearned and undeserved charity at best, and at worst a mere excuse for enriching speculators. Bennett was particularly sarcastic about the proposals put forward on behalf of labor by the National Reform movement of Evans and Wilkes. On the other hand, Walker's filibustering expedition is presented as the best kind of homesteading: a "redeeming" of land which had been wasted upon a class of demi-savages; an earning of title by the deeds of the sword.[18]

The development of the *Herald*'s portrayal of Walker paralleled the development of Walker's own propaganda, and the political transformations of his regime. Beginning with an invocation of agrarian images and principles, and a vision of the hero as cultivator-colonist, the *Herald* moves toward a definition of the American hero as conquistador—standing above and apart from the race he conquers and the hands that produce wealth and progress in the wilderness "garden."[19] Walker's defeat and surrender suggest that Bennett may have misidentified William Walker as the representative of this new heroic type; but they do not suggest that the principle of heroic government that Walker represented is wrong. If the erstwhile "benefactor of his race" is now seen as deficient in "acumen" and "statesmanship," is is still true that he had "energy, endurance and courage." But these are merely traits he shared with "all Anglo-Saxon Americans"; he was still the representative man of his race, but of its dead average and not of its superior type. Walker's failure proves only that "*private* filibustering on behalf of 'manifest destiny' is used up." The point was not to abandon Walker's project, but to take it up as a nation, and make the "regeneration" of Central America part of a militant and expansionist foreign policy. In this way Bennett acknowledges and applies to international affairs the lesson of industrialization: that the outer limits of individual entrepreneurialism were being reached, and future growth depended upon the systematic, large-scale industrial and national organization of enterprise.[20]

But this conclusion merely returns the *Herald* and its readers to the very impasse which the hero's actions were supposed to transcend. The Frontier hero's achievement is supposed to provide an alternative to social and political conflict in resolving Metropolitan contradictions. In order to provide the kind of leadership required by Bennett in the aftermath of the age of entrepreneurial filibustering, the government would have to resolve the conflict between slavery and freedom. But if it had been capable of resolving that conflict without a social and political breach, it would already have done so. In that case there would have been no critical need for the new Frontier projected by Walker; or if there had been, the individual hero might have received the kind of support given to earlier filibusters (Frémont, Houston) and so achieved success.

The appeal to Myth is made in order to overcome ideological division by invoking symbols of consensus. The development of the Walker legend in the public prints suggests that the ideological division of American society had progressed so far that no such appeal was possible. Rather, all myths had now to be referred to the paramount issue in contention, and interpreted in the light of the slavery/free labor debate. Thus the myths made about Walker by Wells, Bennett, and others appealed only to the already convinced. For the others, Nicaragua (like the Mexican War) was "no myth at all."

The *Tribune's* treatment of filibustering was shaped by its commitment to the cause of abolition, and to a program of related philanthropic reforms which aimed at humanizing the problematic and violent social relations between the decent citizenry and various oppressed or outcast classes—Indians and blacks, the laboring and the dangerous classes, and so on. Its editor, Horace Greeley, rejected Walker's program of invasion and regeneration as a recrudescence of the sort of violence that had unjustly dispossessed and exterminated the eastern Indians, enslaved the blacks, and lately despoiled the Mexicans. Greeley's belief in the importance of the Frontier was literally proverbial—"Go west, young man!"—but the myth of racial violence did not attract him. He saw the Frontier in purely agrarian or more generally economic terms, as a vast reservoir of natural resources ripe for systematic cultivation and exploitation. There was certainly enough of that kind of Frontier already within the boundaries of the nation to make possession of California (in his view) a luxury, and Nicaragua an absolute superfluity— especially since possession of Nicaragua would extend the terrain and resources of slavery.

The *Tribune* therefore dealt with Walker by scarcely dealing with him at all. Where the pro-Walker *Herald* continually held the filibusters up to different lights, to see just how well or badly they fit the Frontier Myth, the *Tribune* treated Walker dismissively as a kind of pirate, and urged its readers to give all their attention to the true Frontier of freedom—in Bleeding Kansas.[21]

The War in Nicaragua (1860) was the work by which Walker sought to recapture his own myth, to vindicate his own heroism, and to turn the domestic political impasse to his advantage. The book developed the Walker legend fully, and linked the Frontier symbolism of the Nicaraguan adventure directly and explicitly to the ideology of the proslavery ultras. The three years between Walker's surrender at Rivas and the publication of his book were the years in which the crisis over the place of slavery in the Union moved with growing momentum toward civil war. The rise of the Republicans as a party capable of exercising national power pushed the South toward a more intensely self-defensive argument for slaveholding as necessary, as morally good, and as an inalienable right of white citizens everywhere in the nation. The Dred Scott decision of 1857 and the "squatter sovereignty" campaign in Kansas asserted the absolute legitimacy of property in slaves, and implicitly invalidated the legislation by which it had been banned in the North and Northwest. Beginning in 1858, the movement to revive the African slave trade intensified, partly as a propaganda device for arguing the legitimacy of slavery, and partly as a "practical" solution to the problem of a scarcity of slave labor: only by reviving the importation of slaves could the southern planters redeem the Jacksonian promise of open access to resources for all classes of whites.

The logic of events and of polemics that pressured southern spokesmen toward these positions had already been lived through by Walker and his regime. Walker blamed the failure of his regime on the South's inability to recognize the prophetic status of the Gray-eyed Man of Destiny and the "American movement in Nicaragua." Nicaragua had been—and in Walker's book would be again—a mirror in which the South could see its own features and destiny made clear; and thus a means to the "regeneration" of the southern will to fight for its rights. One of the primary signs of that regeneration would, of course, be the revival of southern support for Walker's return to Central America, this time with the conscious determination to establish there a slavocratic American colony.

In order to connect his exotic foray into Nicaragua with the main currents of American ideological debate, Walker draws deeply on the primary structures and terms of the Frontier Myth. He appropriates not only the paternalistic rhetoric of Fitzhugh and the proslavery critics of capitalism and free labor, but also the progressive Anglo-Saxonism of

Theodore Parker. Indeed, in many respects Walker is closer to Parker than to Fitzhugh. The charms of slavery in Fitzhugh's argument have to do with the substitution of domestic and nurturing relations for the class conflicts and wars of extermination that characterize the progress of the capitalist order in the North and in Europe. Fitzhugh suggests that the South has passed beyond the period of necessary warfare to a superior kind of social peace. But for Walker, as for Parker, the war of extermination remains the Anglo-Saxon's characteristic approach to expansion and progressive enterprise. Although the end of Walker's project is envisioned in terms of the social peace of slavery described by Fitzhugh, its present and immediate future must be one of purposeful aggression and violence; and it is through this violence that the Anglo-Saxons of Central America will regenerate their personal and racial energies and become a world-conquering race.

The Nicaraguan colony is described by Walker as organized from the first along military lines. He and his fellow invaders are represented as a band of soldierly brothers, held together by a noble "freemasonry" of warriors. They seek to colonize Nicaragua; but their first and chief role is that of professional soldiers or warriors. Walker implicitly invokes the Frontier Myth stereotype of the soldier-aristocrat, who symbolizes the conservative spirit in the wilderness and represents the final arrival of law and order. Employing the third person, Walker portrays his motives for going to Nicaragua as those of a kind of soldier-missionary: "Their views were similar in regard to the state of Central America, and the means necessary for its regeneration." Those means were first an application of American violence—disciplined and directed—to the establishment of order; and from this would flow both economic and cultural progress.[22]

Although he invokes the American Revolution as the model for his nation-building movement, Walker's restatement of Revolutionary principles strips away the democratic premises of the Declaration of Independence. In fact, he is appealing beyond the Revolution to the Indian wars for his justification. The purified government is to be established not as a new social compact among all inhabitants, but by the colonial displacement of one race or people by another. Moreover, Walker openly acknowledges that such a regime would have to be based upon force rather than consent, and upon the premise of slavery rather than that of liberty. The existing native rulers would have to be manipulated like Indian chiefs at first, to win their consent to the original entry of the colonists. But once the "American movement" had established itself, says Walker, it would be its first business to exterminate the native ruling classes. To maintain an American colony large enough to overawe the rest of Central America, it would be necessary to offer colonists huge and unregulated land grants, and supply them with cheap servile labor to work it. Walker therefore advocates the enslavement or empeonage of the Indians, and argues that if the number of Indians proves too small the African slave trade ought to be immediately reopened for Nicaragua's benefit. The new Frontier opened by this military aristocrat was therefore to be a windfall for would-be plantation owners, rather than a Jeffersonian heritage of land for hardworking farmers.[23]

Walker resolves the contradiction between the democratic pretenses of American ideology and the social reality of slavery and subordination by advocating a return to the organic-familial idea of the state. The cult of domesticity that southern paternalists like Fitzhugh proposed as an alternative to capitalism was to be, not a critic's literary abstraction, but a living fact in Walker's Nicaragua. He aims at "the reorganization, not merely of the State, but of the family and of labor . . . Not merely the secondary form of the crystal was to be modified, but the primary form was to be radically changed."[24]

Racial distinction, separation, and subordination thus form the basis of Walker's social theory, and his practice as well. Walker's regime had in fact repealed the decree that had abolished slavery in Latin America; but this had been seen by some as a ploy adopted from necessity rather than principle. Walker now argues forthrightly that slavery in some form is necessary to the continued progress of America and the Anglo-Saxon race. Without the institution of slavery, colonization by Americans would be impossible because there would not be labor enough to work the land. And, says Walker, the Phalanx would then lose its character of pioneering, since the soldiers would not be able to make the transition to cultivators. Instead, they would remain a "praetorian" force, serving hostile native interests— a function for which they are "racially" unsuited.[25]

Slavery then becomes essential to the fulfilling of both Manifest Destiny and the "regenerative" mission of America in the undeveloped countries:

> If we look at Africa in the light of universal history, we see her for more than five thousand years a mere waif on the waters of the world . . . Sunk in the depravities of fetichism, and reeking with the blood of human sacrifices, she seemed a satire on man . . . But America was discovered, and the European found the African a useful auxiliary in subduing the new continent to the uses and purposes of civilization. The white man took the negro from his native wastes, and teaching him the arts of life, bestowed on him the ineffable blessings of a true religion. Then only do the wisdom and excellence of the divine economy in the creation of the black race begin to appear with their full lustre.

Not only does the white man uplift the African and make him useful; but the African, by his slavish dependence, evokes in the white man those conservative qualities essential to the maintenance of order under a regime of liberty:

> A strong, haughty race, bred to liberty in its northern island home, is sent forth with a mission to place America under the rule of free laws; but . . . How are they, when transplanted from their rugged native climate where freedom thrives to retain their precious birthright in the soft, tropical air which woos to luxury and repose? Is it not for this that the African was reserved? And is it not thus that one race secures for itself liberty with order, while it bestows on the other comfort and Christianity?[26]

Slavery, by this account, becomes the true model of an *American* social system. Schemes of libertarian order, like abolitionist doctrines, are European products. "The question involved is whether the civilization of the western world shall be European or American. If free labor prevails . . . the history of American society becomes a faint reflex of European systems and prejudices, without contributing any new ideas, new sentiments, or new institutions to the mental and moral wealth of the world." The political structure of Anglo-America—insofar as it has fostered the creation of a slavery-based "democracy"—has proved progressive. In Spanish America, with the exception of Cuba, slavery was not established, with the result that after independence Central America had "too little slavery to preserve social order." Instead of a society based on racial subordination, evoking obedience and paternalism, Nicaraguan society was "cursed" by the predominance of a "mixed race," for Spain had failed to maintain "the purity of the races." In such a context, the savage system of universal warfare soon comes to prevail.[27]

The American adventure in Nicaragua is therefore a model for both North and South, a test case of "American" principles against the power of savage recalcitrance and the erroneous precepts of European ideology. Walker specifically compares Nicaragua, beleaguered on every side by hostile Central American governments, to the South's beleaguerment by northern interests. His disavowal of a desire for American annexation, seen in this context, is not the cutting of American ties that some writers have taken it to be. On the contrary, Walker asserts a desire to bind the South to his interests. What Walker seems to be suggesting is that the South's true interest, like Nicaragua's, lies outside a federal Union dominated by "free labor." He is not antiannexation—he is prosecession.[28]

But Walker also offers his new order as a model for the North, if it will have it. He criticizes the measures of northern conservatives to order the chaotic economy as devices that—like the reforms of the native Nicaraguans—affect surfaces only, not basic structures:

> The conservativism of slavery is deeper than this; it goes to the vital relations of capital toward labor, and by the firm footing it gives the former it enables the intellect of society to push boldly forward in the pursuit of new forms of civilization. At present it is the struggle of free labor with slave labor that prevents the energies of the former from being directed against the capital of the North through . . . the ballot box and universal suffrage; and it is difficult to conceive how capital can be secured from the attacks of the majority in a pure democracy unless with the aid of a force that gets its strength from slave labor.

Not only plantation capitalism, but capitalism as a whole is to be saved by Walker's military aristocracy standing on its helot base. The analysis is shrewd, in its way: Walker sees in the measures of the "free labor" parties for protective tariffs the program not of labor, but of capital; and he makes the case that ultimately capital will not be able to hoodwink labor, but will confront it in real opposition, and require an appeal to force and the ideology of force. In this prophecy, of course, he was correct; but advocacy of slavery was not, in 1860, the form in which such an argument could be accepted.[29]

To buttress ideological argument, Walker invokes symbolism drawn from the Mythology of the Frontier. He and his men are soldier-aristocrats, in the tradition of Middleton and Heyward, Jackson and Frémont; they are pioneers and colonizers as well, would-be "husbandmen," exponents of republican and agrarian virtues. Their opponents are Indians and half-breeds, a human scum from which Walker gladly lifts his eyes to gaze on the gorgeous pastoral and wilderness landscape. Conflict with such a race is inevitable, just as white-Indian struggles were inevitable in North America:

> That which you ignorantly call "Filibusterism" is not the off-spring of hasty passion or ill-regulated desire; it is the fruit of the sure, unerring instincts which act in accordance with laws as old as creation . . . The history of the world presents no such Utopian vision as that of an inferior race yielding meekly and peacefully to the controlling influence of a superior people. Whenever barbarism and civilization, or two distinct forms of civilization, meet face to face, the result must be war. Therefore, the struggle between the old and the new elements in Nicaraguan society was not passing or accidental, but natural and inevitable.

In such a struggle, the warrior heroes act the part of liberating redeemers, and regenerators—of "rescuers." Walker first plays this role among the Indians of Nicaragua, then in saving American citizens from Nicaraguan attacks on the Isthmian transit. Ultimately he wants us to think of the restoration of the African slave trade as "a commerce for the redemption of African captives" from barbarism to civilization![30]

But the race war requires extermination and removal of those elements of the inferior race which cannot be enslaved. In Nicaragua, says Walker, the "pure Indians" have an attitude toward "the ruling race" which is "more submissive" than that of American Negroes; and with such Indians and pure Africans as auxiliaries, the "white man could become fixed to the soil and they together would destroy the power of the mixed race which is the bane of the country." Neither Indians nor Negroes are fit for the life of a soldier; and hence neither will contest the new military aristocracy's right to rule, but will devote themselves to providing a docile and plentiful labor supply for cultivating tropical products. Walker showed his willingness to fight a war of extermination—or at least a war without restraint—with his "mixed race" opponents when he ordered the city of Granada burned to the ground. This, he said, was punishment for their criminal perfidy in aiding his enemies after all he had done for them. Only those who submit to slavery will avoid extermination: he says of the United States that the triumph of free labor over slavery will lead to the "extermination" of blacks by whites, and only a regime of slavery will make the inevitable conquest of Latin America gentle rather than genocidal.[31]

However, Walker's appeal for a renewal of slavery expansion was delivered in the context of the defeat of slavery's interest in Kansas, and the emergence of a strong Republican Party in the North. In this context, Walker's invocation of the race war has a quality of warning as well as of promise: abandon Nicaragua, and symbolically abandon the principle of universal slavery, and the white race will be undone, the course of American and civilized progress will be reversed, and the united forces of European ideology and savagism will undo all that has been done.[32]

For all its superficial political astuteness, *The War in Nicaragua* is the work of a mind increasingly out of touch with reality, both political and personal. The terrible contradictions and absurdities of Walker's political transformation from Free Soiler to proslavery man are suppressed to create the impression of Walker as a consistent hero of southern principles, scheming from the start to enslave and exterminate the Nicaraguans. But this falsification of his past served only to lock him into a faction that was increasingly isolated by the shift in extremist interest from Caribbean empire to secession from the Union. The more cleverly he maneuvered for support, the narrower his basis of support became. The peculiar third-person perspective and frigid manner of *The War in Nicaragua* also mark a change in Walker's way of voicing his beliefs and representing himself as a public figure. His pre-Nicaraguan journalism is generally vivid, salty, and personal; *The War in Nicaragua* is impersonal, legalistic, unemotional in its recounting of slaughters on the battlefield, snide and sneering in its account of Walker's circumvention of his opponents and betrayal of his Nicaraguan sponsors. There is a real dissociation at work, dividing the man from his experience for the sake of representing him as always knowing, dominant, in control—until the final betrayal by his weak-kneed supporters compels him to retreat. Even the best-made myth has only a limited power to influence a recalcitrant political reality, and Walker's myth was fatally flawed by its own inconsistencies and public knowledge of the reality behind the legend.[33]

His last venture reflected his flight from reality. A British colony on an island off the Honduran coast invited Walker to prevent its return to Honduran rule. Walker put together a small mercenary force, planning to make the island a base for a conquest of Honduras, and Honduras a base for reconquering Nicaragua. He imagined (or professed to believe) that he still had supporters in Nicaragua and among the Liberals of the entire Isthmus, despite his betrayal of their cause in 1856–57. As if this were not fanciful enough, Walker never bothered to warn the Liberal leader, José Trinidad Cabanas, that he was coming—he expected news of his arrival to generate spontaneous native enthusiasm, which would bring Cabanas unsought to join his forces with Walker's. After futile skirmishing and countermarching, Walker's force was besieged in Trujillo; and finally, bereft of support, the Gray-eyed Man surrendered himself to a British naval captain. The officer, anticipating his government's wish to put Walker out of the way, turned him over to the Hondurans—for whom Walker was not only a political enemy, but a drinker of blood, a fire-and-sword man who had laid a neighboring country in ruins. They allowed him shriving time and shot him against a wall in Trujillo. He was thirty-six years old. His tragedy, said *Harper's Weekly*, was that he possessed in excess the American virtue of "self-reliance," which—in the absence of government support—led him to overstep the bounds of prudence in pursuit of America's historic mission.[34]

Although no longer seen by Bennett as a hero capable in practice of fulfilling America's imperial destiny, Walker remained for the *Herald* a viable symbol of Anglo-Saxon virtue imperiled by the strife of "nigger-lovers" and "nigger-drivers." Walker's last expedition coincided with the presidential election of 1860, in which the "Black Republicans" rode to victory on a platform opposing the protection of slavery in the territories. The *Herald* pointedly juxtaposes the quixotic heroism of the filibuster— who was, however incompetently, an agent of Anglo-Saxon racial spirit— with the "niggerism" of the Republicans. "The Last of Walker's Expedition" appears on a front page, strikingly opposed to "The Coming Reign of Terror"—the slave uprisings that will (the *Herald* says) be triggered by a Republican victory. The question of the hour is, "Our Historic Development—Shall It Be Suspended by a War of Races?" The editorial on Walker's death links the Republicans with the forces of British imperialism and Central American savagery—Republican rejoicing over Walker's fall and Lincoln's victory presages "Seward's New Phase of Manifest Destiny," in which white and nonwhite races will be forcibly equalized through amalgamation. Against this, and in memorial to Walker, Bennett asserts the racialist principle:

> It is only by keeping the inferior race subject to the superior mind of the Latin and Teutonic races that civilization and national progress can be maintained. These two [races—i.e., whites and blacks or whites and Indians] cannot mix without degeneracy.

Walker's failure suggests that, in default of a hero to carry the sword of Anglo-Saxonism, the program of "regeneration" through conquest and racial subordination must be accepted by the American people as their own, and made the policy of their government.[35]

Walker's self-mythologization was in some ways a success: he was received by many journalistic media, popular melodramatists, and popular historians in just the romantic terms he preferred. His myth likewise succeeded in linking him with a major ideological tendency, that of the advocates of slavery as a positive good. But these "successes" were the signs of a larger failure. The political polarization of the issue of slavery, and the larger matter of the organization of free labor for industrial production, doomed any myth couched in these terms to political isolation. Moreover, the fate of Walker's myth suggests that the symbolism with which he invested himself had itself been revalued by the crisis over slavery. Walker represented himself clearly as a modern instance of the classic soldier-aristocrat of Frontier romance: pure of race, well-born but not noble in European terms, and in worldly terms a successful self-made man. He is not a trained soldier, but is naturally endowed with martial genius and inclinations; he rises to leadership among men of his own race, and is worshiped by "the Indians," whose racial propensities he well understands. But a hero in these terms, in 1856, has scope for his talents only in Central America, and his triumph there engages the nation in an unacceptable intimacy with the problem of ruling a subject and nonwhite population. Thus the soldier-aristocrat's slaughters of numerous foes cease to figure as heroic rescues, and appear as massacres of helpless victims; and the liberator and re-generator appears as the conqueror and enslaver.

JOHN BROWN: HAWKEYE AS REVOLUTIONARY

Just as the ideology of Parker and Fitzhugh reflected the divergent application of a common racialist doctrine, so the mythologization of John Brown and William Walker reflected a common concept of heroism invoked to rationalize opposing ideologies. The legends of both are directly tied to the problem of the Frontier, and they invoke the mythology that sees extreme and racially oriented violence as a precondition for the regeneration of the individual and the nation. These cognate features were not lost on their contemporaries, even in the opposing camp. Parker and Henry David Thoreau—both strong supporters of John Brown—expressed admiration for the heroic character of Walker, even while they denigrated his principles, because his success proved again the Anglo-Saxon's heroic endowment and his power to impose himself on a whole nation of inferiors. Thoreau describes Brown's Harpers Ferry command as a "northern" or "abolition filibuster army," which is the antislavery party's answer to the "American" or "southern" filibuster army of Walker—as such it proves the equal manliness of the abolitionist. "If Walker may be considered the representative of the South," he wrote, "I wish I could say that Brown was the representative of the North." For their part, the Southerners who condemned Brown's projects professed to admire his "gameness" in the face of wounds, imprisonment, and death, assimilating him perversely to their heroic ideal.[36]

But the ideological uses to which these myths were put forbade the assumption of any common ground. It was no longer possible to compromise divergent models of expansion in the manner of 1845–50, when both Texas and Oregon were annexed and the rival interests of North and South balanced. There was no way in which Nicaragua or Cuba could be accepted as counterweight to a free soil Kansas; instead, political struggle determined that neither program would be carried to completion. If the North blocked a southern empire in the Caribbean, the South could block Kansas's admission as a free state. The code words and symbols that had once evoked common values were translated into the terms of radical disaffection. Walker's acting out of the traditional role of military aristocrat, a Duncan Heyward or a Lord Craven, was rejected by opponents of slavery extension who saw his regime as a perversion of paternalism and his Duncan Heyward manner as a mask for tyranny. The mythology surrounding Walker's anti-type, John Brown, suggested that the Leatherstocking version of the Frontier hero had also ceased to define a cultural consensus. To supporters and enemies alike, John Brown was a radical expression of the values of "agrarianism." But in the South, that word no longer evoked the image of the contented yeoman, or of Natty Bumppo preserving his moral independence by holding aloof from social and trade relations. Rather, it was emblematic of a class bent on obliterating all distinctions of wealth, led by a man who resembled Cooper's Ishmael Bush or Hall's "Indian hater" more than Leatherstocking.

But the basic impulse behind the emigration to Kansas was in fact not different from that which had led to settlement of Kentucky or Iowa. The land hunger of American farmers, the hope for an improved condition, the dream of hitting a speculative jackpot on cheap government lands—these were among the basic forces at work. In 1854–55 this drive was given an impetus by hard times, particularly the drought that affected large sections of Ohio and the Northwest. For those ruined or dispossessed by the drought and the accompanying business contraction new territories offered an opportunity to recoup and rebuild. This northwestern emigration was paralleled by southern emigration from affected areas in the Ohio Valley (Kentucky), from contiguous sections of Missouri—in general from those areas where the pressure of the plantation system squeezed marginal farmers intolerably.[37]

Overlaying this normal pattern of emigration was the ideological issue of "squatter's sovereignty" raised by Stephen Douglas, which again directed national attention on the processes of preemption and heightened the ultimate design of the "Slave Powers" to sinister dimensions. It had always been the case, when new territories were opened, for settlers to preempt as much territory as possible for speculative purposes. Although some of these might eventually settle on the land claimed, they would be likely to spend at least the first few years of their tenure as absentee landholders, making minimal "improvements." The legality of such proceedings was dubious, and it was typical that the first wave of true settlers would "squat" on these lands, make their own improvements, and assert a counterclaim. The raising of the ideological issue by Douglas allowed the Missourian (or proslavery) "claim clubs" to cover their operations with the cloak of ideology, thus purchasing the support of powerful interests in Congress and, given the Democratic presidency, the executive and military branch. Free-state settlers, arriving later, thus had some reason to assert that their struggle to maintain their claim against the original preemptors was both a traditional assertion of "squatter's rights" and an opposition to the "slave interest."[38]

On the other hand, the slavery issue raised by Douglas stimulated abolitionists of means to finance their own emigrant "clubs" and corporations—most notably the New England Emigrant Aid Society. Although operating at a greater distance than the Missouri claim clubs, the Emigrant Aid Society was able to organize, transport, arm, and establish a large community in fairly short order—a measure of the North's greater strides toward large-scale enterprise organization. Planted around Lawrence and Topeka, Kansas, this community was large enough to defend its claims against all comers. Most of them were not themselves abolitionists, but men of small means suffering (like John Brown and his family) from business or agricultural failures. Their hostility toward the plantation system was founded on their fear of competing for limited resources against a large aggregation of capital and labor. They therefore sought to ban not only slavery, but free Negroes as well from the territory, on the grounds that Kansas was to be a field for the independent white yeoman, not the exploitable, cheap-labor black, and not the planter who could exploit him.[39]

The role of the government, then, was more than usually complicated by the mix of ideological and economic factors. As part of the arrangement that opened Kansas, measures were taken to dispossess Indian tribes who had reservations in the area—measures that might have constituted a national scandal had they not been overwhelmed by "Bleeding Kansas." Dispossession was accomplished by a mixture of clever treaty making and outright seizure of Indian lands by squatters. Politicians like Senators Thomas Hart Benton and Douglas, whose commitment to the Pacific railroad required (they believed) the extinction of Indian title to and threats toward the right-of-way, urged the preemptors to "lose no time in commencing [their] pre-emption settlement." The army was reinforced at Fort Leavenworth, nominally to prevent such seizures; but in fact, army officers themselves took up claims of Indian land.[40]

In Kansas the presence of the ideological issue had augmented the normal pressures of partisan politics to make the territorial officials, and particularly the president-appointed civilian agents who served as middlemen for the transfers, ardent proslavery men. Senator David Rice Atchison of Missouri, a leading absentee preemptor and leader of the proslavery forces in Kansas, controlled most federal patronage in the area. When the Lawrence company arrived and sought to set up their claim, they immediately came in conflict with agents J. W. Whitfield and William Clarke, who were to have controlled the disposition of the Ottawa and Peoria Indian lands. Since the government offices of both law enforcement and land distribution were in the hands of their enemies, and since the officers of the army—based in proslavery districts near Forts Leavenworth and Scott—were themselves implicated in the rivalry over land, the Lawrence-Topeka groups had to look beyond Kansas for political support, and beyond the law (what little of it there ever was in unorganized territories) for their own defense. Again, the situation was far from unprecedented: frontier "regulators," vigilantes, armed family clans and claim clubs had always been used to maintain the "rights" of squatters in their rivalry with landlords and corporate speculators. But the slavery issue, inescapable now, gave their actions an ideological coloration, and made inevitable a struggle for control of government itself in Kansas—and beyond this, for control of the national government.[41]

The struggle for land and for the political protection of landed interests in Kansas thus had at its core a similar structure to that which had pertained on earlier frontiers; once again the regenerative potential of western land had been made available to a troubled America, and the fable of our achievement of regeneration would involve a struggle between parties and classes representing ultimate moral and ideological principles—savagery or barbarism or feudalism on one side, civilization, Christianity, and progress on the other. But in Kansas that struggle would not pit whites against Indians or Mexicans, but northern whites against southern—with the blacks (and the Indians) appearing now as helpless victims needing protection and liberation, now as images for the barbaric nature of one's political opposition. In such a struggle, traditional heroic models lose their power to invoke a consensus and become occasions for expressing the extremes of political discontent.

As a figure in contemporary journalistic legendry, John Brown has many of the hunter-hero's distinctive features. But in the new context of civil strife his heroism is a two-edged sword. Like Hawkeye's naturalism, Brown's militant virtue is an implicit critique of his society. But Brown

goes beyond critique to direct action, assuming toward his society a relation more like that of the Indian/rebel Magua or the outlaw Ishmael Bush
than that of the deferential Hawkeye.

In the autobiographical letter he wrote in 1857, Brown links himself
with the frontier, declaring: "When he was Five years old his father moved
to Ohio; then a wilderness filled with wild beasts, & Indians." The phrase
is a formulaic one, which occurs in nearly the same words in biographies
of Daniel Boone, Kit Carson, Zachary Taylor, and William Henry Harrison
—to cite only a few. The phrase is perhaps misleading in its suggestion that
Brown was raised on the cutting edge of the frontier—the hunter-Indian
borderland. However, the course of Brown's life did indeed engage him in
activities and issues central to the life of the "backwash" of the frontier.[42]

In his younger days he too followed in part Simon Suggs's injunction
to be "shifty in a new country," on the agrarian-entrepreneurial level. His
efforts in this line led him in the entrepreneurial direction of Davy Crockett
and of the more advanced types of speculation represented by the "town-
planners." In 1835 he moved to Ohio, invested in land and in the promotion
of a scheme to develop local waterpower and perhaps a canal. The
speculation failed, in part because of the Panic of 1837, and Brown resorted
to a variety of other enterprises: tanning (he was a skilled tanner by
training), horse breeding, raising and trading in cattle and sheep, wool
marketing. None of these efforts prospered, and Brown went bankrupt. In
addition to these business vicissitudes, the hard life of rural poverty had its
effects on the health and character of the Brown family: Brown's first wife
and several of his children died, and his fervent religious temperament was
annealed by the need repeatedly to "submit to the will of the Lord."[43]

In all of this, Brown's responses were in many ways typically those of
a Jacksonian frontiersman-farmer. Despite frequent setbacks, he was convinced of the possibility of success, if only he could persist in industriousness
and in seeking the appropriate place and enterprise for his efforts. To
achieve success—in the form of independence—he was willing to move
anywhere in the country—Connecticut, New York, West Virginia, Ohio,
Kansas—and so were his sons. He saw the cause of his secular misfortunes
in the machinations of powerful interests and combinations—local versions
of the Monster Bank "slain" by Jackson in the 1830s. He was not averse to
using violence to defend his "rights," and once threatened armed resistance
to an effort to dispossess him from land which he tried to preempt. This
was no more, and no less, than the conventional response of the squatter
to rival claimants and hostile law. The principles of vigilante justice embodied in such frontier organizations as "claim clubs" were not unfamiliar
to him.[44]

Brown departs from the western stereotype in his identification of his
own cause with that of the Negro, and in his ultimate "conversion" to the
pursuit of the "Cause" as a substitute for the pursuit of his own interests.
As Brown told the court that condemned him, he did indeed "remember
them that are in bonds, as bound with them." An early article of his called
"Sambo's Mistakes" rebukes blacks for aping white fashions and neglecting
their own interests—which, he says, should be pursued in a disciplined and
militant fashion—and for "tamely submitting" to the aggressions and

humiliations put upon them by the whites. But the article is written in the persona of Sambo: Brown represents himself as a Negro, chides *himself* for the faults of vanity and tame submission and urges *himself* to greater sacrifice and militancy.[45]

True to the implications of this identification, Brown in Kansas resisted the majority, which sought to exclude blacks from the free state. Yet both Brown and his opponents were responding to the same perception of the symbolic meaning of slavery—a perception most dramatically rendered in Lippard's vision of free labor's progressive degradation in political rights and in racial character. Where Brown accepted the identification of slave and workman and sought to save both at once, his free-state opponents sought to avoid the problem by banishing both slavery and the Negro— as if the latter carried the former as a kind of political virus.[46]

Brown also differed from the other Kansas settlers in that his declared purpose in going was not to find land, but to fight against the advance of slavery. His sons went as farmers and became soldiers; from the first, Brown went as a warrior. To the South, this bespoke his personal fanaticism, and "proved" that the movement to Kansas by farmers committed to free labor was an act of deliberate and conspiratorial policy by northern leaders. To Brown's supporters, this was the dimension that raised Brown above the level of those whose chief motives for action were material; and as such, it was an action that brought him closer to the warrior/hunter ideal represented by Hawkeye, Boone and Carson, by Weems's Washington, and even by William Walker; and away from the comfortable yeoman virtues celebrated by Crèvecoeur.

Brown's personal mythology was recognizably Puritan and evangelical in its structure, rather than Jeffersonian or Cooperian. His accounts of himself and his actions were built upon the characteristic narrative structures and metaphoric language of the Puritan conversion narrative and the sermon history. But he was not self-conscious or deliberate in deploying these conventions to make his myth; nor (until his trial) were his words and actions calculated to appear in conformity with a stereotypically heroic role. The shifts of purpose and program that marked his career were seen by him as practical responses to circumstances, modified by the imperatives of religious faith and of a considered revolutionary program. Likewise the language he applied to defining his aims and explaining himself was native to him: he thought and felt in the language of evangelical Protestantism, and read his Bible as a symbolic history filled with lessons for and references to the present and future. His recognition that the struggle against slavery was the form which his own individual "soul warfare" must take is consistent with the concept of the conversion experience passed down from the Puritans. It is perhaps more explicitly political and worldly in its engagements than the conversions of the Puritan Founding Fathers; but it is not different in kind from the connection which a John Winthrop or Roger Williams made between personal conversion and the outward political labors of resistance to impious authority, emigration, and the creation of a new state.[47]

But for most of his career, Brown was not the chief public maker of the "John Brown legend." Only at his trial for the 1859 attack on Harpers

Ferry did his own voice and self-characterization predominate. From the time of his emergence as a guerrilla chief in the Bleeding Kansas struggle of 1855–57 to the Harpers Ferry attack, his deeds were described and rationalized for the most part by other hands—friendly and hostile. When Brown assumed the role of vigilante-avenger in the massacre of slave state men at Pottawatomie, Kansas, in retaliation for the burning of the free-state town of Lawrence, he rationalized the deed according to the canons of religion and the practical exigencies of revolutionary warfare. The Old Testament law of vengeance was the primary source of moral validation for the murders; and for "Captain Brown" the "executions" were necessary and even prudent first steps toward putting the enemies of free Kansas to rout. But journalistic and political partisans who viewed the Kansas struggle from the standpoint of the Metropolis (and took their Bible less literally) found that the readiest way of accounting for Brown was provided by the Frontier Myth.

One of the best and most influential of the contemporary histories of Bleeding Kansas was William Phillips's *The Conquest of Kansas* (1856)—a colorful and highly partisan antislavery account, which originated in a series of articles published in the New York *Tribune*. The paradigm of racial warfare is invoked by Phillips to define the Kansas struggle as one between free-state progressivism and slave-state barbarism. According to Phillips, the Kansas-Nebraska Act was simply a device of the slavocracy for creating a new slave state in Kansas; and the first act of their plot involved them in the illegal and unjust dispossession of the Kansas Indians. But Phillips's critique of the slavocrats' proceedings does not imply pro-Indian sentiments on his part. On the contrary, he asserts that the Indians are by nature incapable of becoming civilized or exercising the privileges of citizenship, and must therefore be either exterminated or removed farther westward to clear the way for civilization. If allowed to remain near white society, they must inevitably degenerate into a dangerous pauper class of "beggars and plagues to society."

According to Phillips, it is the peculiar and characteristic crime of the proslavery party that it rejects the "removal" model of race relations in favor of an "amalgamationist" program. This may seem a strange epithet to apply to a party which asserted its commitment to "a white man's government" as the foundation of its ideology. But Phillips reminds his readers that it is slavery which imports Africans into territories that might otherwise be the exclusive province of the white man, producing a political economy which is racially amalgamated—and which, as a result, reduces free white men to a level like that of the Negro slave.[48]

Phillips develops this racial metaphor in two stages. He first shows how proslavery missionaries and politicians attempted to manipulate the procedures for extinguishing the Indian reservations and bringing the savages in as Democratic Party voters. By so doing they would reap the initial benefit of having a captive constituency; and in the end they would be able to cheat the Indians of their lands, once the protective barrier of the reservation law was breached. Phillips dramatizes the attempts of Democratic politicians to develop and control the "Indian vote," and in the process suggests two things: the racial unfitness of the Indian for the suffrage; and the parallelism between Democratic machine politics in Kansas, and Democratic ward politics in the Irish slums of New York.[49]

This suggestion introduces the second phase of the racial interpretation of Bleeding Kansas, which involves the equation of the proslavery "Border Ruffians" with the barbarous Indians. Phillips repeatedly characterizes the Border Ruffians as "Pukes" and vagabonds, drawing on negative stereotypes of the Frontiersman that go back to the Southwestern-outlaw literature of the 1830s and 1840s, and to Cooper's squatters in *The Prairie*. They are a set of "hard customers," "with yellow complexion, hairy faced, . . . dirty" with a body "of gutta-percha, Johnny-cake, and badly-smoked bacon" and a soul of "Old Bourbon, 'double rectified.' " Like their fellows on Frontiers everywhere they neither know nor respect civil law, and assert their collective power and wisdom in the lynch mob. The portrait of the Ruffians as "yellow-skinned" reinforces the point of the Indian-vote passage, which is that advocates of slavery are racial "amalgamationists," who want to integrate nonwhite (or half-breed) elements into white society, so that they can have a dependent electorate to control and manipulate. To clinch the point, Phillips cites an "atrocious" and "degraded" editorial in a Missouri paper, which asserts that slavery constitutes an essential protection for the chastity of white women by providing lusty white men with black women on whom they can freely copulate. Thus a policy that begins as metaphorically "amalgamationist" is finally revealed to be literally amalgamationist as well.[50]

In contrast to the Ruffians, the Free Staters are an exceptional class of men, not (according to Phillips) the kind found on previous Frontiers. Because they have been sent out by progressive organizations located in those Metropolitan centers of the East, the Kansas pioneers bring with them "more good blood . . . than had ever flowed into any new territory in its youth." These settlers bring not only "intelligence and refinement," but also a new kind of social and economic order, for in Kansas "capital preceded labor." The Kansas Free Staters thus represent the new industrial organization of society, in which the power of organized capital replaces the disorganized labor of uncontrolled individual action.

This new element of organized capital is not simply an economic phenomenon, but signals a change in the nature of social organization. The war in Kansas is to be a class war, with racial overtones. On the free-state side—where "capital precedes labor"—are ranked the organized settlers sent out by eastern emigrant corporations, and a set of western settlers "generally . . . of the better class." Ranged against them are the advocates of slavery, whose people are mustered from "the coon-hunting, soft-soap currency tribe of squatters, who have usually officiated as pioneers."

This class of men have been "good enough . . . in their way," opening new lands in the restless quest for what Boone called "elbow room." But "the Davy Crockett school" of pioneer is now to be "superseded by a class who [have] to keep improvement on the gallop [in Kansas] in order to retain the advantages they had enjoyed in the East. The new class bring with them not only rifles, axes, and livestock but modern plows and equipment for building sawmills and manufactories."[51]

Phillips's book appeared at a time when it seemed that the Border Ruffians had (with the connivance of President Pierce) completed the conquest and subjugation of Kansas. True to his paradigm of racial warfare, Phillips asserts that "the war of conquest may be followed by a war of extermination." If the analogy between Indians and Border Ruffians holds, then such must be the outcome, for races of unlike nature and endowment cannot live together. Since the Free Staters represent the "Anglo-Saxon" component in this situation, the conquest of Kansas by the South represents an inversion of the normal and desirable hierarchy of race (and class) relations. But because the Free Staters represent the white element in the "Indian war," they must in the end gain the victory: "if that war of extermination is begun, it will prove the war of freedom."[52]

The sign that this is so is given by John Brown, and the other free-state guerrillas whose battles are recounted by Phillips. His John Brown is an explosive mixture of the enlightened and progressive new model pioneer, with other elements more obviously derived from Frontier heroes of the past: "a strange, resolute, repulsive, iron-willed, inexorable old man . . . a volcano beneath a covering of snow." He has all the skills of the wilderness fighter, and inspires a "wholesome dread" in his enemies, whom he strikes vigorously and by surprise. Although he acts on the vigilante principles associated with the lynch law of the Ruffians, his motives make the actions justifiable. His attack on the slave-state settlement at Pottawatomie is represented as justifiable vengeance against a set of violent men, who were taken in the act of plotting new acts of persecution and robbery against free-state neighbors. While the civilized man must "shudder" at such deeds, the blame for them lies not with Brown but with the corrupt government that has left Frontier justice in the hands of Pukes and Ruffians. "Lynch-law is terrible always; but Kansas was the seat of guerrilla warfare, and this was its sternest phase." Such warfare is inseparable from Frontier conditions, in which society is challenged by savage Indians and its own uncontrolled white savages. To clinch the point, Phillips asserts that the mutilation of one of the Pottawatomie victims was the work of "Camanches"—a device that places Kansas in the context of old-style wilderness warfare, and at the same time distinguishes the vigilantism of Brown from Indian savagery.[53]

Although Brown acts in the name of free-state principles, his motives for violence are given explicitly in the terms of the Frontier Myth. He acts out of an immediate sense of grievance and persecution, and usually with the aim of protecting his settlement from raiders or rescuing captive members of his family from Ruffian hands. At the "battle" of Black Jack (1856), Brown is "like a wolf robbed of its young," and like a Hawkeye he "stealthily, but resolutely, watched for his foes, which he skirted through the thickets of the Merodesin and Ottawa creeks."

Phillips admires Brown, apologizes for his violence, and denies or obscures his connection with the Pottawatomie massacre. But his portrait nonetheless reveals that the free-state warrior in Kansas must represent a regression of sorts from the values of that progressive class who were to have been the new model pioneers. Phillips acknowledges the necessity of this regression, when he suggests in his conclusion that the Free Staters may have been too "delicate [in] sentiment" to defend themselves effectively when faced with the necessity of war. But the terms of the Frontier Myth suggest a way to absorb this contradiction between progressive ends and regressive means. The central narrative structure of the Frontier Myth requires that the hero-pioneer undergo a regression to the primitive, which in the end will purify and clarify his essentially superior character; and from that regression he derives the basis and the power for a new and higher leap toward the goal of human perfection.[54]

In the later development of the John Brown legend, this mythic structure of regression is presented in the symbolic dress of agrarianism. In going to Kansas—as to any Frontier—the civilized man or farmer undergoes a regression in his manner of living and laboring. Where before he might live by cultivation and trade, he now must live by hunting and fighting, with farming an often marginal activity, frequently interrupted or put off. In so doing, the man sheds the excrescences of civilized life and recovers primitive virtues and skills long buried. In the Brown legend, this "regression" is first seen as bringing out the hidden elements of primitive Puritanism in Brown's character. To abolitionist and journalist James Redpath he is "the last of the Puritans," "the Cromwell of our Border Wars," combining the Puritan and the Frontier warrior. Thoreau compares him to Franklin and Washington, but sees him as an expression of a more original type of patriot: "He was one of that class of whom we hear a great deal, but, for the most part see nothing at all,—the Puritans." He is less the hero of abstract democratic principle than of a primal, racial spirit, expressed in the most elemental of historical struggles. It is said that when he leads his men in battle, he instructs them not to fire until they see the whites of the enemy's eyes—the injunction of Indian fighter Israel Putnam to the militia at Bunker Hill.[55]

Still more immediate models of primitive virtue are found in distinctively western heroes. Thoreau celebrates Brown's western style of dress and speech, rendering him in terms of the Frontier philosopher figure first embodied in Daniel Boone, and carried to its full development in Leatherstocking.

> A Western writer says, to account for his escape from so many perils, that he was concealed under a "rural exterior"; as if, in that prairie land, a hero should, by good rights, wear a citizen's dress only . . . He did not go to the college called Harvard . . . As he phrased it, "I know no more of grammar than one of your calves," but he went to the great university of the West, where he sedulously pursued the study of liberty.

Building on and emphasizing suggestions in biographical accounts of Brown then being prepared by Redpath and others, Thoreau portrays Brown in the character of a surveyor—that role which was closely associated with the careers and characters of Boone, Washington, and Frémont. Thoreau uses the symbol appropriately, to dramatize Brown as an observer of land and manners much in the manner of Boone and Leatherstocking. Redpath, in his portrayal of Brown's last moments, gives to his hero a vision of pastoral landscape that links his sentiments with those of other westward-gazing visionaries, like Filson's Boone or Leatherstocking in *The Prairie*. Redpath quotes Brown as saying that he went to Kansas both for the Cause, and to give his children the benefit of his experience of "pioneer life"—the old hunter or pioneer guiding a new generation back to the origins of American character.[56]

Like Boone and Leatherstocking, Brown is represented as living among, and being succored by, the Indians. Thoreau represents this as a general characteristic of Brown's western experience, and he undoubtedly believed it to be so. Brown himself represented the Indians as befriending him when whites would not. However, Brown himself (and later Thoreau) distorted the reality in the direction of evocative fiction: there was, in fact, a single Indian family that aided Brown. The Indians of Kansas, as a class, were not favorable to the extinction of their title, through which the Free Staters (and others) gained their land. But the image of Brown among the Indians reinforces the image of him as an old-hunter type from the border wars of old. Thoreau invokes the aura of mystery and power that surrounds Leatherstocking in *The Prairie*—and perhaps also the dark power of Jibbenainosay in *Nick of the Woods*—when he speaks of Brown's being regarded by his enemies with a superstitious awe as a supernatural being.

"He was by descent and birth a New England farmer," says Thoreau, but he abandoned that peaceful calling for the life of a warrior, a "ranger" in the manner of the old-time Indian fighters—but with a difference: "Ethan Allen and Stark, with whom he may in some respects be compared, were rangers in a lower and lesser field. They could bravely face their country's foes, but he had the courage to face his country herself when she was in the wrong." Here is the hinge by which the Brown myth takes the Frontier Myth where it was not *meant* to go. Brown abandons the civil life of the farmer for the primitive career of a hunter-warrior *not* in order to kill Indians, but in order to reform his fellow citizens. His violence, even when enacted on the border, is against fellow whites, not Indians; and his move from New York to Kansas is offset by the more significant move from Kansas east to Harpers Ferry. There, in 1859, Brown seized a Federal arsenal as a prelude to a guerrilla war in the South; was trapped by armed citizens, and captured by Federal troops and turned over to Virginia for trial as a traitor.[57]

This reversal of direction for the Frontier hero is justified, in the apologetic literature, by representing the southern invaders of Kansas—the Border Ruffians—as "Indians." Cooper's portrait of the Bush family of squatters provides a prototype for the Border Ruffians. Redpath, in his biography of Brown, makes specific allusion to their "semi-barbaric" character traits. They are seen committing all sorts of atrocities against the helpless and innocent: murdering and torturing free-state men, hacking them to death with hatchets, raping and insulting women, taking scalps. The figure of the white Indian, the renegade *à la* Simon Girty, is taken from the Mythology of the Frontier to define the character of Brown's enemies. Next to these, "pure" Indians and of course blacks show up quite well. Redpath thus proceeds to contrast Pocahontas's saving the first hero of Virginia from her own people, with Virginia's toleration of the lynching

and mutilation of Brown's raiders. The racial association is less compli-
mentary to Indians than shaming to the whites: they are behaving worse
than Indians.[58]

Brown's response to these white Indians is justified in mythic terms.
According to Redpath, the Pottawatomie massacre was not an atrocity, but
a vigilante-style assertion of popular will for law in a place where there
was no law, or a discredited law. According to Redpath, Brown's sons'
daughters and wives had been "insulted" by the Ruffians he murdered,
and the only judge available was himself. The massacre was therefore not a
murder at all, but "one of those stern acts of summary justice with which the
history of the West and of every civil war abounds." Lynch law becomes the
only efficient guarantee of the peaceful citizen from the ruffianism which
distinguishes and curses every new territory. Thoreau concurs in this view,
and carries it a step further: Brown is not merely the exponent of a local
vigilantism against microcosmic evil, but speaks for a cosmic vigilantism
which seeks to confront evil wherever and on whatever scale it is found.[59]

Beyond his vigilantism, Brown is also seen as that essential Frontier
hero, the rescuer of captives. The character is obvious, when applied to
his achievements in combating slavery and in carrying slaves out of Missouri into free territory. As a "redeemer of captives," Brown is seen as
simultaneously Christ-like and Leatherstocking-like—effecting an earthly
rescue which figures a spiritual one. In Redpath's account of the battle of
Black Jack the Border Ruffians are seen first attacking a group of Free
Staters at a church service, then being waylaid and defeated by Brown.
The pattern is a basic formula in Indian war histories and captivity narratives from the time of Increase Mather and King Philip's War on down to
that of Fenimore Cooper and Tecumseh.[60]

After Brown's capture by federal forces following Harpers Ferry, this
captivity imagery is transformed to put Brown in the sanctified role of captive. Thoreau manages to catch the ambiguity of Brown's situation in his
question: "What sort of violence is that which is encouraged, not by soldiers,
but by peaceable citizens, not so much by laymen as by Ministers of the
Gospel, not so much by the fighting sects as by the Quakers, and not so much
by Quaker men as by Quaker women?" The answer is that only violence committed against slavery has the aura of sanctity that attaches to the passive,
"female," and sacred elements in society. But Thoreau's rhetorical device
conflates and so obscures the real practical and theoretical differences between the revolutionary and the nonviolent approaches to antislavery. It
is a powerful evocation of myth, and it is intended to override contradiction
as only myth can—but it cannot in the end conceal the fact of violence and
the necessity for abolitionists to choose between the John Brown and the
"Quaker" model of political action.[61]

It is easy to see that Redpath and Thoreau are attempting to mythologize John Brown's historical career by aligning it with key symbols
drawn from the literary Myth of the Frontier. Thoreau in particular is a
virtuoso in his ability to multiply and vary and invert and recombine the
most diverse symbols from this literature, identifying Brown as Indian and
as pioneer, as avenger and as victim, as rescuer and as captive, as killer and
as Quaker. But the virtuosity of the performance is itself a commentary on

the impossibility of really making John Brown into a hero of the Frontier Myth. Even for Thoreau, he will not stay in character, but changes shape and meaning in response to the pull of contradictory ideological impulses— impulses born of the inescapable politics of the conflict over slavery and Union. With traditional Frontier heroes like Boone and Leatherstocking, the moral center of the character is a fixed point from which we can interpret the changing historical scene; and the attributes that symbolize that moral center—love of wilderness solitude, affinity for Indians, etc.—have a fixed and certain value. In Brown's case the attributes are contradictory and give mixed signals about the content of the hero's moral center. The same attributes that for Thoreau align Brown with Hawkeye and George Washington are the marks of Brown's renegadery for the enemies of abolition.

Public response to Harpers Ferry also invoked the mythic linkage of the hero with the special violence of the Frontier. To be sure, all parties recognized that the primary threat of the Harpers Ferry raid was to begin (or establish a basis for) a social war between slaves and masters, a "war of races." That fear was the special preoccupation of the Metropolis, not of the border (where slaves were few, and slavery excludable). But in seeking metaphors to describe the revolutionary or "unnatural" character of the raid (and southern responses to it), journalists on both sides invoked the Myth of the Frontier.

Southern journals emphasized the project of a "servile war" that must, because of its racial character, become a "savage war" of extermination. Such wars are appropriate to the primitive stage of American history, the Frontier stage; and they engage whites and Indians, not the classes of the Metropolis. Northern journals opposed to the Republicans, like Bennett's New York *Herald*, emphasized the fact that the "lawless violence" tolerated by abolitionists on the "Kansas frontier" had now been projected into the heart of the Metropolis—as if the progress of law and civilization had been made to run backward, with primitive Frontier vigilantism replacing civil law. For their part, the abolitionists cited the recrudescence of "Vigilance Committees" in the South as evidence of that section's regression to barbarism: the lynch law practiced against antislavery advocates and blacks accused of crime is appropriate to the stage of settlement that precedes civilization. When the Wild West gives law to the East, the foundations of society tremble.[62]

After Harpers Ferry, interest in Brown's career became intense, and both his critics and his enemies used the same mythic language to develop the demonic myth of "Old Brown of Osawatomie." The anonymous author of *The Life, Trial, and Execution of Capt. John Brown . . .* (New York, 1859) gives us a biography in the tradition of the "criminal life," like those of John Murrell and the Harpes in the 1830s and 1840s. Although the historical and political significance of Brown's acts is acknowledged, the author evades the central questions raised by the Harpers Ferry attack to dwell on the "romantic" aspects of the story. Brown's Kansas adventures in particular are cited as being "more exciting and romantic than the fabulous history of many a famous hero of romance." That phase of Brown's career can be readily handled in the language of Frontier fiction, but Brown is no Leatherstocking here. Rather, he is a modern version of the classic Indian hater portrayed by James Hall in his sketch of Colonel John Moredock and by Robert Bird in *Nick of the Woods*. Like Nathan Slaughter, the Quaker hero of Bird's romance, Brown begins as a simple and successful husbandman, devoted to farming and family, exceptional only in his perfectionistic insistence on living the Christian life. This fierce devotion is the symptom of "a fierce and relentless nature," which is liberated from the restraints of Christianity and citizenship when the hero suffers insult and outrage.[63]

The Quaker Nathan Slaughter is insulted by Frontier whites for his meekness; and his family is then massacred by Indian savages in contempt for his nonviolence: so Nathan's religious zeal has implicated him in the "slaughter" of his family. These twin outrages make Nathan a solitary, hermitlike figure, still outwardly meek but now—in the persona of "Jibbenainosay"—secretly devoted to expiating his guilt and rage by the hunting and killing and mutilation of any and all Indians within his reach. Like the real-life Indian hater John Moredock, Nathan becomes a "Leatherstocking Nemesis," whose racial "calling" is murder. Brown too is converted from farmer to fanatical man of violence by "the iron of personal wrong, in the form of persecution, oppression and murder"—the killing of one son, the torture and madness of another, the "grossly insulting" treatment of the Brown women by Border Ruffians, the murders of his friends and neighbors. These wrongs were "driven into his soul, and maddened him into the one idea of a life-long, undying war on an institution which he believed to be accursed of God and man." Like Moredock and Nathan/Jibbenainosay, he becomes "the terror of his enemies . . . remorseless and relentless as death itself," praying the more fervently as his blows fall harder. And like Bird's hero, he is implicated in the "desolation" that befalls his own hearth and home (in his case because of his violence, not his piety).[64]

But the objects of Brown's vengeance are not redskins—they are whites, and representatives of legitimate social institutions. The "Indian hater" rationale will not do; this Brown has more of the character of a Murrell or an Ishmael Bush, who share Brown's "perverse" religiosity and antisocial sense of persecution and grievance, defy civil law in the name of their private codes, and engage in acts of vigilantism, murder, kidnapping, and conspiracy. Brown's camp in Kansas closely resembles the Bush clan camp in *The Prairie*—isolated and embattled with both wilderness and society, ruled by an outlawed, law-giving patriarch who holds the power of life and death. Bush, Murrell, and Brown have all taken revenge on society by captivating its dependents—Bush has kidnapped Inez; Murrell steals and smuggles slaves for profit; and Brown expropriates slaves and carries them to the Kansas prairie to liberate them and injure their masters. The difference between Brown and Bush or Murrell is in the degree of fanaticism: Brown is presented as a monomaniac of the Ahab type, whose aims are Promethean and liberating. But Ahab too is simply the "Indian hater" drawn on a cosmic scale, whose object is to slaughter a savage, unjust, and outrageous God. From the perspective of authority, all these heroes are avatars of the Enemy.[65]

Like the Indian hater, Brown represents a fundamental moral and ideological contradiction. The Indian hater fulfills the immediate need of the Frontier society to dispossess and extirpate the Indians; but his excesses suggest a moral queasiness about the legitimacy of dispossession, and a guiltiness over bloodshed. The Brown of *Life, Trial and Execution* addresses the more profound contradiction of a society ideologically committed to both the ideal of freedom and the necessity of maintaining southern slavery. The contradiction is dealt with by acknowledging the authentically Christian and agrarian roots of Brown's sentiments, and even the legitimacy of his personal grievances; then showing how excessive zeal in the pursuit of redress transforms him into a monstrous outlaw, profoundly dangerous to society. His character is rendered paradoxically, reflecting this mix of ideological motives. He is compared to Cromwell, to Peter the Hermit, and to Don Quixote; his enterprise is by turns the disciplined march of a new regiment of Puritan "Ironsides" toward an achievable revolution; an impossible crusade cried up by a fanatic isolated from reality; and a lunatic "mission to rescue all the persecuted damsels in Spain." The shifts of metaphor suggest the author's uncertainty about both the practicability and the justifiability of Brown's enterprise. But these doubts finally infect the moral symbolism by which romance writers resolve their novelistic conflicts—the rescue of damsels is a legitimate reason for taking violent action, but also a Quixotic folly; the assertion of freedom against slavery is a long-standing ideal of Anglo-American society, but also a madman's project.[66]

In the Myth of the Frontier the ineluctable tendency of racial conflict is toward the "war of extermination." So too in the Brown legend the potential for such a war is immanent. Driven by his implacable passion for vengeance, the Brown of *Life, Trial and Execution* characterizes his direct attacks on slavery in the South as attempts to "carry the war into Africa"— a phrase that invokes the same classical allusion deployed by Walker among the ruins of Granada, which recalled Scipio's charge that Carthage must be utterly destroyed. Conversely, the abolitionist accounts of Brown's life in Kansas represent the Free Staters as threatened with a war of extermination by the Border Ruffians. In the case of the Frontier War, exterminating violence is justified as the means to the end of "regeneration"—the renewal of politics, of fortune, of spiritual strength through Indian fighting or vigilantism. There is no more succinct statement of that principle of regeneration through violence than Brown's last public statement from the Charlestown jail: "I John Brown am now quite certain that the crimes of this *guilty land, will* never be purged *away*, but with Blood. I had *as I now think: vainly* flattered myself that without *very much* bloodshed; it might be done."

The idea of blood atonement is common throughout Brown's writings, and it chimes with one of the most basic myths of evangelical Protestantism. However, in the emerging mythology of nineteenth-century America, the myth of blood atonement has a dual and contradictory aspect. On the specifically religious level, it refers to the atonement for man's sins achieved by the sacrifice of Jesus Christ, and renewed in every generation by sacrifice and martyrdom for the sake of religion. But American historiography and mythology used "blood" as the symbol of racial difference—not (as in the evangelical concept) as the universal element binding man to man, and man to God. In the race-war model of human history, atonement through blood sacrifice may take the form of vindicating "blood insult" by an avenging violence. Brown and Theodore Parker both agreed that the moral regeneration of the Negro could be achieved only if the blacks effected their own rescue from captivity and vindication of honor by drowning slavery in "the white man's blood." This disposition to violence was what Parker saw as the secret of the Anglo-Saxon's superiority among the tribes of men—the key to their emergence as the new Chosen People. "The Southerners hold the African in great contempt, though mothers of their children," wrote Parker. "Why? Simply because Africans . . . fail to perform the natural duty of securing freedom by killing their oppressors." According to Thoreau, John Brown is the only northern man whom Governor Wise of Virginia can respect, because only Brown has taken up arms to kill for his principles.[67]

But Brown himself, as he stood in the Charlestown dock, chose to obscure his affiliation with this myth of regeneration through racial violence. He chose to present his action not as a practical beginning to a program of revolutionary guerrilla warfare; but rather as a symbolic act designed only to make visible drama out of impalpable principles. Perhaps his intention arose from practical considerations of legal defense, or the need to protect his supporters; perhaps also from a recognition that, having failed in revolutionary praxis, there was no use to be made of his attempt save as symbolism. But his self-presentation at the trial was carefully and well calculated to present Brown as a Christian martyr and sacrificial atonement, and not as the prophet of regeneration through race war. Perhaps this was the role that came most naturally to him: he had always seen himself as a character in a Bible story; it was Thoreau and Redpath who put him beside the heroes of Frontier romance.[68]

But whatever Brown's intention, his words would inevitably be read in the context of the public legend. Brown's final speech therefore culminates and focuses the significance of his life and myth by unifying in a single expression the two dominant strains of American mythology: the sacred, biblical mythology of evangelical Christianity, with its fables of sin and atonement, salvation and missionary labor and apocalypse; and the secular myth/ideology of the Frontier, with its canonical fables of savage war and rescue, paradise lost and Eden rediscovered. Brown in the Charlestown courtroom has the dual aspect of Frontier hero and biblical martyr, his actions justified by both the unwritten code of western vigilantism and the mystique of religious blood-sacrifice, by the romantic aura of the rescuer and the sacred rhetoric of the preacher. But his distance from the traditional Frontier hero can be measured by comparing Brown in the dock to Leatherstocking in Judge Temple's stocks in *The Pioneers*. The mild and pathetic rebuke which Cooper's hero conveys as the spokesman for the law of "natur'" pales before Brown's prophetic denunciation of the court that condemned him. It is as Old Testament Prophet—a Jeremiah or a Nathan—rebuking the unjust king in the name of God and the nation that Brown was most imposing, most persuasive; and also most terrifying, because that biblical power was assumed by a figure standing outside the laws of the society, a primal recrudescence from the savage Frontier. What was worse, he had turned upon the children of the pioneers those weapons which were sanctified in myth only when used against the racial enemy. As Thoreau wrote, "I know that the mass of my countrymen think that the only righteous use that can be made of Sharps rifles and revolvers is to fight duels with them, when we are insulted by other nations, or to hunt Indians, or to shoot fugitive slaves with them or the like."[69] Although the abolitionist inversion of the traditional color symbolism of Frontier myth made for some splendid ironies and devastating rebukes, the norms founded in the myth retained their force: for most Americans Harpers Ferry was a violation of the myth, a bringing home of the Kansas wars, of the strife that belongs on the borders of an expanding America. Perhaps for that reason, the post-1859 John Brown myth has tended to emphasize the last phase of his life, when his helplessness in jail made him the image of the captive, gentle, wise, atonement-seeking patriarch, bent not upon redress and apocalypse but on the imitation of Christ's crucifixion.

The cases of Brown and Walker have a definite symmetry. Both were engaged in attempts to seize and use the opportunities promised by the new Frontier opened in 1848. Both were trapped in the fallacies and contradictions of that promise; both tried to cover their actions with the gloss of traditional myth and ideology; both in the end were compelled to carry their particular versions of the myth to excess, and so partly to discredit both the myth and the projects it rationalized. Both so believed in their own personal myths that they expected allies would spontaneously rise at the voicing of their names and the news of their presence; both saw their last enterprises fail with that expectation. Like Walker's last expedition to Honduras, Harpers Ferry was a failure that in some part discredited Brown's earlier heroism, by making its motives appear either irrational or profoundly unpatriotic. Both Brown and Walker were executed as criminals, and the large measure of public acceptance of this outcome registers the sense that the course of heroism followed by each had become dangerous to the health of the society whose values the heroes were supposed to aggrandize and affirm. But each had his partisans too, who saw the death of their hero as the martyrdom of some essential American virtue to a legal order that was fundamentally illegitimate.

In Walker's case, this critique of authority rested purely on a racial basis—the contempt for the sovereignty of the Hondurans, and for the racial renegades in the North who prevented Walker's domination of the Isthmus. In Brown's case, the critique of the criminal judgment cut closer to the bone. It required that American law, and the political order it sustained, be found wanting in the scales of Justice; and it followed that if government was created by revolutionary mankind to create justice, then the government itself must now be arraigned, judged, and its behavior enjoined. And if no court of the Metropolis was adequate to the task, then recourse must be had to the primitive Frontier justice of the vigilante.

That the Wild Westerner had reversed direction and pointed his rifles east underlined the fact that the coming test of strength between North and South would determine whether or not the Frontier would be closed to men like the Browns; and that if closure were imminent, the anger of such men would no longer seek redskin, but whiteskin targets. Whatever one thought of Brown's actions, it was clear that what he represented was the Frontier-going impulse frustrated and inverted, gone wrong—or dangerously right—at last.[70]

PART SIX

Toward the Last
Frontier, 1860–1876

CHAPTER 13

Regimentation and Reconstruction: The Emergence of a Managerial Ideology, 1860–1873

The period of the Civil War and Reconstruction is the watershed of American history, a violent rite of passage between one stage of political-economic development and another. As we have seen, both free- and slave-state interests believed in the myth/ideology which held that the Frontier was the economic basis for all future development and prosperity, and the safety valve for the ambitious or envious discontent of the poor and the landless. Each side therefore saw control of access to the land as necessary for the protection of its economic prospects, its present vital interests, and its social and cultural values.

The election of 1860 turned on this issue of slavery in the territories, but it was (as many historians have noted) a disagreement about abstractions and unrealized political-economic prophecies rather than immediate and concrete properties and interests. However, once the election of Lincoln was answered with southern secession, Northerners replaced these abstractions with a concrete and political issue that went right to the heart of the American ideology of self-government—the South's negation of the right of a majority to protect itself through the exercise of the ballot, the true "safety valve" for social discontent in the United States. In the South, northern denial of the right of secession was perceived as a negation of an essential political power vested in a minority for its protection. The alternative to war, in this case, would be the acceptance by either side of a condition of political degradation—a sacrifice of the rights and powers which were the only difference between the status of freedom and the status of slaves, Indians, and women. The war thus unmasked the essentially political character of the disagreements over the territories and the protection of property rights in slave labor. If the issues had been as purely economic as the territorial issue made them seem, it would have been possible to evade conflict through a compromise making fair division of the territorial spoils.

The political struggle over the means of conquering and reconstructing the South produced a similar transposition of political and economic ways of formulating issues—but now overtly political controversies masked a profound social realignment along economic lines. It seems fair to say of Reconstruction that so long as the political status of the ex-Confederacy remained unresolved, the primary political and ideological divisions of American society continued to form around the residual issues of the Civil War—the political rights of the Negro and the division of power between national and state governments. But as these residual matters were pushed toward settlement, as the North first completed its political conquest and then—weary of its southern entanglements—abandoned the enterprise of Reconstruction, the issue of political-economic reorganization arising from industrialization became paramount. This shift of ideological focus in the end produced a major political realignment, involving the foreclosure of Reconstruction and of government sponsorship of liberal reform, and the rejection of the democratic and perfectionistic ideology that underlay those reforms in favor of an ideology protective of the power and status of industrial capitalists and managers.

The material basis for this shift in ideology was laid during the war itself, and the period of hectic speculation and railroad building that followed it. In important ways the project of fighting a modern war acted as midwife to the emergence of the United States as an industrial power. The creation of a huge domestic market for manufactures of all kinds, from shoes and clothing to the heavy gear of armaments, transportation, and machine building, gave a boost to the "demand" side of the equation. Certainly there is little question that the northern economy did expand even while human and financial capital were being wasted on the battlefield, and in the circumstances this was perceived as a revelation of hitherto unguessed capacities for productivity and profitability.

The crucial skills of conceiving and managing large enterprises, of disciplining great masses of men and organizing huge quantities of capital goods, of generating the finance capital necessary to underwrite such enterprises—all of these essential attributes of industrialization were given a powerful boost by the compulsions of the war effort. The triumph of the Republican program added to these general developments the necessary political support, in the form of protective tariffs, and a variety of government measures in support of business. These ranged from supporting employers against striking employees to providing federal resources (land, tax revenues) as collateral for foreign loans. The northern victory also allowed the enactment of the legislative basis for economic development on the Republican/free-labor plan, which involved government underwriting of a transcontinental railroad, a protective tariff to aid industries, and a Homestead Bill to foster agrarian entrepreneurship in the West. It was an essential part of the free labor faith to assume that measures of this kind, coupled with the elimination of the slavery incubus and the southern legislative roadblock, would be sufficient to stimulate a vast range of entrepreneurial activity, which in turn would generate continuous economic expansion.[1]

However, the triumph of the North was not fully perfected until the election of Grant in 1868, following the impeachment of Johnson and the transitional regime of congressional Republicans. Grant used his moral

authority as the preeminent hero of the Civil War to enact a program embodying the reformist ambitions of his party's perfectionistic "philanthropists," while taking a firm hand in suppressing crypto-Confederate
resistance in the South. At the same time Grant put his government firmly
behind the ambitions of northern entrepreneurs, through protective tariffs,
the provision of land grants to railroads as collateral for loans, and a level of
government purchasing and subcontracting unprecedented in peacetime.

With the accession of Grant, the victorious North could contemplate
the most promising set of "Frontiers" ever faced by Americans. In the Far
West the completion of the first transcontinental railroad and the development of the land-grant system appeared to have made possible the productive use of the Great American Desert. Moreover, the gains from this
potential agrarian Frontier would be exceeded by the expected profits from
transcontinental commerce, and from the enterprise of railroad building
itself. The potential for rapid development seemed limitless: the politicians
and investors of 1860 had been able to conceive of only a single transcontinental route, aggrandizing one region at another's expense; the generation of 1865–75 projected a dozen such lines, taking off from every major
city between Duluth and Galveston.

The ruin of the South meant disaster for prewar planters but opportunity for postwar investors, who saw in the South a new kind of Frontier:
equally promising of windfall profits, but unlike the West already largely
developed and possessing a substantial labor supply. The task of making
the South a paying proposition, and of extending productive enterprise to
areas unreachable by the primitive technology and capital-poor economy
of the antebellum South, was one of the most attractive opportunities for
northern and European financiers and managers. At the same time, the
demands of the Civil War armies and the postwar railroads had stimulated
an expansion of mining and manufacturing in the North and Midwest,
whose cities therefore presented an attractive Frontier for investors and for
restless citizens looking for a better job, more money, a chance to accumulate property.[2]

Republican policies supported the exploitation of these various Frontiers by permissive legislation and by direct government subsidy or
sponsorship. In addition, the linkage of economic enterprise with the various
movements for moral and social reform gave to the taking up of opportunities an ideological gloss akin to that of Civil War service. The Myth
of the Frontier had always linked the battlefield triumph of white society
with the secular progress of civilization and an increasing perfection of
moral character and political equity. Thus the expansion of farms and
railroads to the West, of northern capital and management to the South,
and industrialism to the urban North and Midwest, was to be accompanied
in the seventies by programs of education and moral uplift, sponsored by
an alliance of government, missionary sects, and private charity. The least
organized of these was the urban missionary movement, whose objects were
the unorganized, sometimes culturally demoralized members of the new
urban proletariat. But in the South the government sponsored the activities
of the Freedmen's Bureau, which aimed at providing education and Christian nurture for the blacks, along with helpful advice on the management

of secular affairs. In the West a reform Indian policy or "Peace Policy" was adopted, which aimed at a comprehensive peace with the Indians, to be followed by their ingathering to established and guaranteed reservations. There they would be supported by government largesse, and tutored in the arts of agriculture and the doctrines of Christianity by missionary agents, until they were prepared for some form of citizenship.[3]

But the entrepreneurship of the Gilded Age produced two unforeseen effects that threatened the ideological consensus that had sustained the North through the war. Colossal and unprecedented money-making opportunities had made possible great concentrations of wealth and power, and provided both the means and the motives for large-scale attempts by the newly rich to translate their economic power into political privilege. The result was a pervasive corruption of public officials that threatened to discredit the authority of republican government. At the same time, the industrial character of economic expansion was altering the size and social character of American cities. The demand for industrial labor stimulated large in-migrations from the countryside and from overseas, causing the cities to grow beyond the capacities of existing institutional controls. The masses of workers so gathered were ethnically heterogeneous, culturally dislocated by their translation from Europe to America and from farmer/ artisan to industrial-laborer status, and resistant to the impoverishment and economic dependence on capital that went with their new status. The rising crime rates and an increase in strikes in northern cities was a counterpoint to the Klan violence and government corruption associated with the Reconstruction South, and eventually posed a greater and more immediate threat to the culturally elite makers of northern ideology. The wartime alienation or northern and southern conservative leadership was gradually replaced by a sense of shared interest in a common problem, which was that of controlling and directing the potentially destructive energies of a large and racially heterodox "dangerous class." Although this recognition was not sufficient to remove all North/South political differences, it was sufficient to undo the last remnants of Republican reformism in regard to southern freemen and northern proletarians.[4]

The nature and direction of this transformation can be seen in the fate of the various types of Homestead legislation passed during the Civil War and Reconstruction. The Homestead Act of 1862 was the first of these, and it embodied the beliefs and expectations of every generation of liberal ideologists since Jefferson. By its terms the promise of Jefferson's Louisiana Purchase was to be fulfilled, and a reservoir of cheap land provided to ensure the economic self-sufficiency of a thousand generations of yeoman farmers. In the period of congressional Reconstruction this same ideology was applied to the South, in the proposals to break up the former plantations and provide each of the resident freedmen with "forty acres and a mule." This was followed in 1875 by a Southern Homestead Act, which evaded the radical measure of confiscation by opening undeveloped lands for settlement by freedmen and poor whites.

These measures were designed to do more than encourage active settlers to take up and develop new lands. They were part of a large program of social improvement designed finally to purge American society of those nagging disorders that had plagued it. The perennial "Indian question" could now be justly resolved by dividing Indian lands into Homestead-type allotments and having the Indian integrated with civilized society in the sanctified status of yeoman farmer. With the vast reserves of land currently being opened and the ease of transportation created by the new railroads, it would be possible to make the West a true safety valve for discontent and poverty in the urban East; and there were philanthropic programs designed to place the survivors of urban reformatories and orphanages on free land in the West. Even the intractable problem of race relations in the South might be expected to give way in the face of an abundance of landed resources sufficient to satisfy both freedman and poor white.

But in none of these cases was the original intent of the program fulfilled. The economics of farming on the Great Plains did not at all accord with the vision of a "fee-simple empire" embodied in the Homestead Act. Unlike homesteading in the well-watered and forested Middle West, plains farming required considerable investment of capital and a larger scale of operations to make it profitable; and the railroads, whose presence linked the western farmer to his market, used their political and economic leverage to control the best land of the region, and to keep farmers in their debt. Indeed, the greatest beneficiaries of the Homestead legislation were railroad, banking, and landholding corporations; and thirty years after the first Homestead Act, land ownership in the Great Plains states was being steadily consolidated in fewer and fewer hands.

Likewise in the South, the imperatives of the new economy undid the intention of the Homestead legislation. The early rejection of large-scale land reform and the breaking up of plantations revealed that one of the primary concerns of northern Reconstructionists was to restore the profitability of the southern cotton trade. In order to do this it was necessary to keep the plantations together as productive units and to guarantee them a continuous supply of cheap and relatively docile labor. For this purpose the presence of the freedmen was the providential answer—so long as they remained in a state of economic dependence upon the plantation and its owner. Thus instead of the agrarian solution of forty acres and a mule, the reconstruction of the southern labor system involved the reduction of the freedmen to a status akin to that of slaves, via labor contracts, sharecropping, and outright peonage. The Southern Homestead Act of 1875 was written in such a way that it was easy for well-capitalized plantation and lumbering interests to avail themselves of its benefits. Just as the railroads and banks of the Great Plains were able to use their leverage to control the development of Homestead farms in the West, these corporations were able to control development of southern timberlands—actually, to keep them out of production, so as to preserve the market advantages of northern lumber interests.[5]

In the industrial sector similar tendencies were at work. Both western and southern development depended upon the expansion of the railroads. The western transcontinental trunk lines were the most spectacular and capital-attractive of the postwar industrial enterprises; but the rebuilding and expansion of southern systems was of greater initial importance. This new era of railroad building was presented as a multilayered new Frontier, providing new jobs for a growing labor force even while it opened new lands for farmers. But in fact railroad labor was hard and relatively unremunerative. Just as the new owners of southern plantations had to contend with and defeat the land hunger of freedmen to keep them in the fields, so the builders of railroads had to contend with the volatility of their work force—which would move out in order to move up when times were flush, jobs plentiful, or a gold rush in the offing; or would strike for better wages when times were harder. Quite early in the building of the Union Pacific, its builder—General Grenville Dodge—confronted this problem, and dealt with it by using coerced labor: Indians captured during hostilities, Confederate POWs, convicts, and the like. After the Civil War the railroads filled their ranks with workers whose weak or marginal position in American society might be expected to make them relatively more dependent: immigrant Irish in the East, blacks and poor whites in the South, and Chinese "coolies" in the Far West.[6]

Although the Civil War had been fought for the sake of the freedom and economic opportunity of the small farmer and the independent mechanic, the new order the war created was one in which the "producer" and his economic self-sufficiency were no longer the primary political and economic values. The catchwords of agrarianism and free labor remained but the ideology of the party of Lincoln had undergone a profound change. It was essential to Lincoln, as it had been to Jackson, to assert that labor is the source of all wealth, and that therefore the freedom of labor has a moral priority when weighed against the needs of capital. Lincoln himself was inconsistent in the use of this principle, but its moral force in his thinking is unquestionable. Yet the great ideological shift after the war was rooted in a rejection of this premise, in favor of the counter-assertion: that in an industrial state, where the scale of enterprise requires huge drafts of capital and the mustering of masses of labor, it is capital that creates the basis for production, capital that is the generator of national wealth. The ideological shift brought with it a redefinition of the nature of class differences, and the emergence of a new concept of reform—one that aimed not at aggrandizing the individual farmer or laborer with property or political power, but at establishing the tutelary rights of a new managerial elite over the new industrial (and agrarian) proletariat.

In the course of this large ideological and political transformation, the Myth of the Frontier and its attendant ideology of agrarianism also underwent a transformation. The central illusion of the Myth remained the belief that the undeveloped region of the West contained so vast a reserve that it could meet the capital requirements of industrial corporations and still have enough left over to provide each individual with a more-than-sufficient standard of living. However, this vast reservoir would now be tapped by industrial means, rather than by the entrepreneurship of small farmers. The agents of progress would be corporate combinations, chiefly the railroads and the United States Army; and the heroic leaders of these combinations would be of the soldier-aristocrat type—wealthy, culturally elite, professionally expert, charismatically managerial—rather than the democratic Boone-Crockett type. The rituals of war and sacrifice associated with the Frontier conquest would be undertaken not in the name of the family farm but in that of the railroad. All of this implied that within the microcosm of American myth—as within the social microcosm of the work-shop—the subordination of lower- to upper-class figures would become more marked, more like the moral and racial subordination of Indians or blacks to whites.

In these circumstances, the expectation of superabundant wealth which was to be generated by industrial expansion was the symbolic equivalent of the old Frontier. If it could be shown that the new order could guarantee an infinitely expandable and ample provision of resources, sufficient to keep all citizens from poverty and political dependency, then it might be possible to accept industrialization according to the canons of democratic belief promulgated by Jefferson, Jackson, and Lincoln. The most spectacular test case of this new conception of an industrial Frontier was the railroad, particularly the great transcontinental trunk lines, authorized and supported by Congress during or just after the war. The completion of the Union/Central Pacific line in 1869 was expected to inaugurate a new phase of commercial and agricultural growth in the Far and Middle West, and to promote agricultural development of the empty spaces of the Great Plains. But the power and appeal of the railroad as symbol of the new era was not fully attested to until the original line had been joined by half a dozen projected transcontinentals. The plethora of such proposals bespoke the geometrically increasing expectations of wealth and progress that had arisen since the war.

The bellwether of these secondary transcontinentals was Jay Cooke's Northern Pacific Railroad, projected from Duluth to the mouth of the Columbia. Cooke's enterprise not only had the appeal of a colossal economic and technical achievement; it systematically gathered to itself much of the leftover idealism of the Union war effort, and represented its vast landholdings as the new "garden of the West"—that farmer's Eden which Filson had located in Kentucky, Gilpin among the Parcs and valleys of the Rockies, and Walker in Nicaragua. Cooke intended to use the lands of the Northern Pacific as collateral for the loans he needed to get the enterprise started; and he also required the presence of farmers along his developing right-of-way to provide immediately needed revenue and evidence of future profitability. To this end he developed an elaborate propaganda campaign, which borrowed and plagiarized heavily from Gilpin's mystical effusions on the "paradise" of the Far West. Cooke's Gilpinian propaganda was buttressed by fiscal and managerial techniques that had been learned during the Civil War. Cooke had become famous as the financier whose imaginative and aggressive salesmanship had enabled the Union government to float the foreign loans necessary to maintain the war effort; and Cooke attempted to transfer the same mixture of intensive "hype" and political influence peddling to the financing of the NPRR. Similarly, Cooke and his agents applied the techniques of Union army recruiters to the problem of filling their vacant farm lots and manning their work gangs. Information and advertising bureaus were established in major European cities to entice immigrants in the direction of Duluth and to provide them with help in getting there.

But Cooke's enterprise also plumbed the limits of the new order's potential for guaranteeing a golden future to its numerous constituents. No
amount of propaganda could conceal the fact that Cooke's Dakota and
Minnesota lands were hardly the paradise he claimed. Eventually, critics
of the company came to deride the district as "Jay Cooke's Banana Belt."
Cooke's ambitious projections for the taking up of new farms were simply
unrealistic, and the immediate market for the railroad's services fell short
of expectation. What farmers there were in Cooke's territory were as
likely as their fellows farther east to be engaged in political struggles
aimed at regulating freight rates and restricting the railroad's legal privileges. Likewise the labor force, recruited in Europe and the East, was
mobile and demanding in good times, and militantly antimanagement in
hard times. The "magical" expansion of business on which railroad entrepreneurs counted did not—could not—materialize, and Cooke had to
save his existing investment by a resort to chicanery: "cooking" his accounts,
corrupting influential politicians to protect his interests, milking capital
and operating funds to meet debt payments. When European creditors—
alerted by the similar scandals that attended the building of the Union
Pacific—called his notes, the Northern Pacific went bankrupt, and with it
the banking house over which Cooke presided. The failure of Cooke's bank
—one of the largest in the nation, and headed by the most prestigious of
bankers—precipitated a financial panic of unprecedented scale, a "crash"
of the capital market, and a nationwide depression of unparalleled severity.
In that downfall, the projects and expectations of the generation who had
won the Civil War were wrecked or discredited.[7]

The Panic of 1873, and the long and severe depression that followed,
brought the contradictions of the new order to a head. Within four years a
decisive political shift had been accomplished. Reconstruction was definitively foreclosed, and with it a whole range of associated reforms that aimed
at increasing political and economic equality between the races, classes,
and sexes. A new ideological consensus emerged that united southern
"Redeemers" with northern conservatives and a new generation of liberals
or progressives on the fundamental necessity of asserting the authority of
proprietors and managers over the laboring classes. This consensus did not
eliminate divisions of economic or sectional interest, or of party loyalty; it
did instead succeed in disestablishing social justice and reform movements,
exiling them from main-line party politics and so radicalizing them. And
it did produce a political culture that, whatever its other divisions, was
united behind the defense of the privileged status of corporate property
and industrial management.

For the mass of the population, the changes brought by the new order
would be immense, and were already being felt. Before the war, the United
States had been a predominantly agrarian society, in which more than 50
percent of the adult population could be characterized as "self-employed."
Despite the presence of slavery, and of propertyless laborers of all kinds
in all parts of the country, there is some validity to the image of prewar
America as a kind of bourgeois utopia. But by the First World War, almost
40 percent of the work force would be engaged in factory work; in terms
of absolute population, there would be a population shift of eleven million

people from the farms to the cities; and this shift would be augmented by the addition to the population of twenty million immigrants, most of whom settled in cities. While the total labor force would rise by 50 percent in that time, the total number of self-employed individuals would rise only 10 percent, completing the movement from bourgeois utopia to industrial state, complete with industrial proletariat and managerial/proprietary ruling class.[8]

The industrialization of production substantially altered the web of relationships that characterized the social life of preindustrial American communities; and simultaneously it altered the relationship of those communities to each other. The new discipline of the factory required a system that radically differentiated the power and status of employer (and his agents), and employee, which ran counter to the democratic ideology and to the self-esteem which that ideology sustained in the citizen. The distance between manager/owner and worker increased, with the former seeking to rationalize, and the latter to compensate for and overcome, the new arrangement. New technology and new modes of organizing work—notably the assembly line and the various forms of task rationalization later associated with Taylorism—undercut the value of the traditional skills of workmen, or rendered such skills obsolete, with effects that were both economically and psychologically catastrophic for the worker. For those workers who entered the factory from preindustrial economic and social settings—whether from the American countryside or the European or Asiatic peasantry—the transition from preindustrial to industrial culture required a radical, often traumatic reorientation of values and life-styles.

For the workers, these changes were acceptable to the extent that the industrialization of society provided higher wages and a better life-style. But these improvements also fell far short of expectations, and, more important, fell short of providing overall a decent and secure living for the industrial proletariat. American hours of work were longer than those in Europe, and the rate of industrial accidents notoriously worse. Industrial slums might have been an improvement on the worst of European or southern American poverty; but they were still a vile social and hygienic environment. In addition, there could be little job security for the average industrial worker even before the Panic: the economy throughout the period was volatile, waves of prosperity followed by catastrophic depressions, in addition to seasonal unemployment. As the mobility fostered by industrialism undermined the values and resources of the community, the worker was deprived of those support systems he might previously have looked to for sustenance (both physical and moral) in time of adversity; the free soup kitchen and workhouse became regular features of the urban landscape, a charitable enterprise that did little to alleviate suffering—and even that little was condemned as a "coddling" of the idle poor.[9]

These changes did not proceed without resistance, prolonged and violent. Workers in the 1870s could defend themselves by a variety of means. They had labor organizations, some of them of significant historical standing, through which they could organize to bargain with employers. Through these organizations, as well as through political parties, they could use the ballot power which they already possessed to elect officials favorable to labor. So long as the power of national economic organizations did not reach into and dominate local business interests, this power of the ballot could have substantial effects on industrial relations. Indeed in the early phase of industrialization, there was typically a good deal of support for the activities of factory workers among nonproletarian elements in a community—shopkeepers, journalists, and the like, who were tied by economic interest and traditional loyalties to the continued prosperity of the workers in their communities.

The direction of change, however, was against the traditional community and the labor organizations and political refuges it protected. The remainder of the century saw the continuing and culmination of the existing trends toward the industrialization of production, the urbanization and proletarianization of the laboring classes, the concentration of capital in a new wealthy class, and the nationalization (and rationalization) of economic and political institutions. With increasing unemployment and wage cutbacks had come desperate winters in the great cities and mining districts, stories of starvation and an upsurge in crime, and an increase in the number, duration, and violence of labor strikes. Out of the depression came the realization that the United States was no longer a republic of Anglo-Saxon farmers, but a semiurbanized industrializing state, whose cities harbored an alienated and (to a large degree) ethnically alien work force, who were in the process of angrily discovering that the Jacksonian promise of universal property-holding might never be fulfilled for them.[10]

THE MANAGER AS SOLDIER-ARISTOCRAT

The prewar mythology of free labor and the agrarian Frontier had dealt with the problem of class warfare by providing plausible mechanisms of denial and concealment. The imagery of the race war had substituted external conflict with Indians for internal strife between classes; and the belief in an inexhaustible reservoir of land denied that there was any material reason for classes to fight to the finish. The ideology and myth promulgated by the postwar elites do not entirely dispense with these tried and immensely appealing remedies for social acerbity. However, they assert a new spirit of disillusioned "realism" which takes account of the new developments and political imperatives of postwar society. In place of the vague dithyramb to limitless wealth characteristic of prewar Frontier boosterism, they substitute the hardheaded assertion that the new resources are not limitless, and will be difficult and costly to develop and exploit; that their primary value will be industrial, and that therefore the methods of exploitation must follow the industrial path of capitalization, organization, management, and discipline. Instead of refurbishing the Jacksonian mystique of a universalized "producing class," they acknowledge difference and specialization of function, and assign leading roles to the men of capital and organization as against the masses of the laboring classes. Nor do they assert with Lincoln's comprehensiveness the doctrine that each working hand is a potential capitalist: the existence of a permanent proletariat is acknowledged, and regarded as a good and necessary thing.

The vision of such a proletariat had been for Lippard and Lincoln a prophecy of horror: only dependent blacks and racially irreconcilable savages represented fixed and permanent classes; and to speak of or treat white workingmen in these terms was to degrade them, and to court a revolutionary apocalypse. But for the postwar ideology, the vision of the proletarian as contented slave or demented savage became positive doctrine: it justified both the exploitation of the "dependent" worker and the violent military suppression of the rebellious worker; and it put the blame for exploitation and suppression on the natural "gifts" of those classes.

This ideology obviously required a redefinition of the character of laboring classes. As we have seen, the traditional language of myth and ideology divided this class into quasi-entrepreneurial and proletarian subspecies. The ideologies of Jacksonian democracy and free labor saw the former as the dominant and indeed the typical species of American workingman— independent in either his means of production or in his attitude toward his employer, only temporarily dependent on wages for subsistence, upwardly and outwardly mobile through his ambition and his skill, and his equal access to new resources. The condition of permanent proletarian was associated with the status of blacks, women, and chronic paupers—people whose characterological "gifts" supposedly made them inevitably and willingly dependent on the capital, labor, and protective power of their superiors. Yet the prosecution of a great modern war and the management of a great industrial enterprise both required the mustering and the maintenance of just such an essentially proletarian work force—dependent on wages for subsistence, kept in place and in subjection to discipline by more-or-less coercive institutions (as well as by economic pressures).

During the war this transformation of the ideology of class relations could be seen in the measures and rationales adopted on both sides for the mustering of conscript armies and for the management of labor in essential industries. For example, the exigencies of the war required both sides to abandon the volunteer principle of military recruitment with which they had begun, and to adopt legislation designed to coerce or pressure citizens into military service. In both sections these measures were regarded as precedent-breaking departures from traditional definitions of political rights, and as a movement toward the political degradation of the citizenry. This degradation of the individual citizen was justified as necessary to the accomplishment of the larger purpose of preventing the political degradation of the corporate entity of northern (or southern) society. But this apology merely affirmed the idea that corporate rights and powers would now take precedence over those of the citizen. Moreover, the conscription laws were written in such a way as to favor the propertied classes. Conscription could be evaded by the payment of a fee or the purchase of a substitute, the costs of which were beyond the average workingman's or farmer's ability to pay. Thus there was a material basis to the folk wisdom which held the Civil War to be "a rich man's war and a poor man's fight."[11]

The outer boundaries of justifiable proletarianization were tested directly in the North's management of southern plantations during the transition from slavery to emancipation. For economic and political reasons the North was deeply interested in producing and selling cotton on plantations in captured Rebel territory, and to do so northern authorities had to hold on to and utilize the blacks already on the scene. Although some plantations were turned over to former slaves for self-development, the returns were surer and more profitable where a nominally compensated work force was administered by military men or civilian lessees. General Banks, Lincoln's departmental commander in Louisiana from 1862 on, made the army responsible for enforcement of "all the conditions of continuous and faithful service, respectful deportment, correct discipline and perfect subordination"; and he specifically denied the blacks the right to withhold their consent from sharecropping or profit-sharing arrangements desired by the lessees and managers. And although Lincoln himself was firm in his insistence that the abolition of slavery be accepted as a precondition for readmitting southern states to the Union, he was hesitant to propose a full and complete extension of both political and economic rights to blacks and expressed himself as willing to accept projects for emancipation that permitted the retention (temporarily) of the stigmata of political degradation.[12]

The first and only agreed-on meaning of "emancipation" was that it signified the abolition of all "property in persons." But it did not necessarily require that the "laboring, landless, and homeless class" thus created be raised out of its condition of economic dependency and political degradation. The description of the freed blacks could be (and had been) applied as well to existing classes of free white workers—the female proletariat of Lowell, the male proletariat of Lippard's "Quaker City." And these would be the growth class of the Gilded Age: industrial operatives, unskilled laborers whose wandering pursuit of better jobs or flight from unemployment would render them homeless as well as laboring and landless. And surely if it was proper, under the pressure of economic demand and political crisis, to use force to discipline black proletarians in the South, might it not be proper (in similar circumstances) to do the same to the laboring, landless, and homeless proletariat of the North?

The primary ideological barrier to a full identification of the planter/black relationship with that of the employer/wage worker was the clear distinction of race that divided them. For blacks a condition of political degradation and economic dependence had been traditional and customary, and the mythic lore of American culture represented these conditions as appropriate for their racial "gifts." But as we have seen, the "gifts" of white proletarians had always been seen as suspect; and the new circumstances of industrial development intensified these suspicions. The working classes of the eastern coal mines and cities and of the western railroads were increasingly made up of Irish and continental European immigrants, and even "coolies" imported from China as contract laborers. This gave a racialist cast to the perception of class difference that divided the propertied classes of districts like the Pennsylvania coalfields or cities like New York, Philadelphia, and Boston from the laboring classes. Simultaneously, wartime conditions exacerbated class tensions. Real wages declined because of wartime inflation; military power was brought to bear to prevent strikes and enforce systems of contract labor; and the federal policy of emancipation created a "reserve army of the unemployed"—free blacks who could compete with Irish and native workers for jobs, and undercut union activity by working for lower pay.[13]

The result was that racial categories became the readiest symbols for interpreting and acting out class conflicts. The working classes identified the political and economic degradation imposed by federal conscription and labor policies with the condition of Negroes; and in draft riots and political opposition they vented their anger on both blacks and Republicans. The conservative elites who supported the war likewise saw in the opposition of the laboring classes the symptoms of a racially degraded "Celtic character," which was assigned the "savage" and "Negro" attributes of brutality, indiscipline, laziness, and selfish sensuality.

This view of the proletariat was less in harmony with Lincoln's view than it was with the traditional southern ideology of class. There is little to choose between Civil War diarist George Templeton Strong's characterization of Irish draft rioters as a "drove" of "brutes" and the characterization of the northern industrial proletariat as "sons and daughters of Belial" by a southern editor in 1862. The difference between them is that the Southerner believes it possible and desirable to prevent the development of an industrial system in the South: ". . . those who cling with love, which is often the highest form of reason, to the old framework of society, shudder at the thought of a Lowell on the Appomattox or a Manchester in the Piedmont region."[14] For the Northerner (and eventually the Southerner as well) it was clear that Lowells and Manchesters were both inevitable developments and desirable ones. Was it absolutely inevitable, however, that these new cities would be inhabited by the irrepressible and disorderly free proletariat so feared by conservatives? Could not such a proletariat be somehow reduced to a condition of acquiescence like that of the antebellum slave?

During the war northern conservatives attempted to reach some understanding along these lines and to suggest the nature of the ground on which postwar conservatives could unite. Montgomery Blair—a member of Lincoln's cabinet—undertook to reach a rapprochement with conservative Democrats in order to stave off the growing power of Republican Radicals. Speaking for the border state interests whose economic health was tied to the preservation of something like the plantation system even after emancipation, his ideas were also relevant to northeastern manufacturing interests, whose labor-discipline problems were similar. Blair urged the Democrats to accept the restoration of the Union and acceptance of abolition as the basis of peace with the South. But he proposed that conservatives unite to limit emancipation to the simple abolition of property in persons, and prevent the abolition of the conditions of economic and political degradation that held the blacks in service to the plantation master. This would (according to Blair) "reconstruct the parties on the Negro question, as contradistinguished from the slavery question." Such a program would establish anew the Jacksonian consensus between free workers and entrepreneurs in the North and the planters of the South, by identifying democratic politics with the vesting of government in "the white race" as a corporate entity.[15]

If the Jacksonian vision of the American majority as a white "producing class"—free of all internal divisions of class between rich and poor, well-born and common—had itself persisted, such a formulation might have worked. But in a society which was coming to regard its growing proletariat as a separate race, to reconstruct politics along racial lines was to maximize the motives for authoritarian rigidity.

The military experience of the Civil War provided the mystique and the institutional models for the new, managerial social order. Vast resources, both material and human—and fiscal as well—had been generated, mustered, organized, and directed by a central corporate authority, in the name of the highest political and cultural values North and South were capable of articulating. The war made clear just how vast were the resources and the capabilities of American society, once its energies were aroused and systematically directed. Its important corollary was the revelation of how much could be achieved through a coordination of political power with the economic power of private industry and finance. Such a partnership had made possible the creation of the victorious northern war machine; and after the war similar partnerships would make governmental authority the partner and guarantor of western railroad corporations and investor in reconstructed southern plantations. The large scale of postwar enterprises like the transcontinental railroads, the patriotic values associated with their completion, and the direct transfer of methods and personnel from the successful war effort to the tasks of railroad building and Reconstruction suggest that the industrial-financial boom of the Gilded Age was merely the continuation of the war by economic means.

A generation of entrepreneurs, engineers, and managers had learned in the army or through wartime politics the skills of conceiving and managing large-scale enterprises. Jay Cooke and his fellow bankers learned how to capitalize great railroads by helping the government float its war bonds on European exchanges. It was a poor railroad indeed that did not count at least one ex-colonel of volunteers on its Board of Directors, or find for its survey team an impoverished ex-Confederate who had learned to use a theodolite at West Point. The mobilization and maintenance first of a volunteer and then of a conscript army—by both sides—had required the development of skills that would later serve in manning postwar industrial plants and maintaining work discipline. The Union army had first been manned by enthusiastic volunteers, but when the enthusiasm faded and the additional inducement of higher pay (in the form of bounties) failed to yield the requisite manpower, conscription was resorted to; when the draft was resisted, the full coercive power of the military was brought to bear. Similarly, the resistance of workers in wartime factories to the imposition of wage cuts was treated coercively, by the discriminatory use of the draft, the deployment of militia, and the imposition of a ban on strikes and a contract-labor system.

What was emerging was a sense on the part of the officers, managers, and political leaders of society of their distinct identity as a class, of their own power to organize society and to enforce their authority politically. It is important to note that both the suppression of draft dissidence and the restraints put upon labor during the war were policies with a distinct class character. Republican politicians otherwise committed to the doctrine of free labor, and its concomitant of egalitarianism, asserted that the corporate need of society required the granting of privileges to those who had money or who owned factories—the war could not be financed without the bond buying of the one and the productivity of the other. And a nation engaged in an enterprise at once so "grand" and so vital to its national interest must accept as necessary both the fact of privilege and the use of force to protect it. The war, of course, was an extraordinary crisis; but this same rationale was now available for invocation when other kinds of crisis threatened other grand projects and vital interests in the 1870s.

Indeed, as the war became more distant, and as the complexities and conflicts of the new age became more manifest, it was the very *simplicity* of war that was most fondly recalled. Not only had enemies been clearly defined, but one's own society seemed more purposeful and clearly ordered: although the armies had fought, they had also built railroads, run plantations, established governments—and all these amidst the highly charged atmosphere of class and labor strife, of urban riots. The temptation to extrapolate a new government from military order's successes became irresistible, not only to those nostalgic exponents of order, but to progressive liberals like Edward Bellamy and Josiah Royce as well. The image of the society militarized in the name of democratic idealism became, in the decades after the war, a kind of utopian vision.[16]

Central to their thinking, the experience of warfare provided the cultural elites of North and South with the concrete experience of organizing and commanding a colossal human and material enterprise, and for them, the experience of war became a model for optimal social organization. John W. Draper, in his *Thoughts on the Future Civil Policy of America* (1865), interpreted the Civil War as a "school" in which a society inclined to irresponsible individualism "can . . . learn subordination [and] be made to appreciate order. It may be true . . . that men secretly love to obey those whom they feel to be their superiors intellectually. In military life they learn to practice that obedience openly." Draper's interpretation was a common one among members of the northern intellectual elite during and after the war, and it reflected an important shift within that elite from the advocacy of radical individualism and idealistic humanitarianism—as expressed in enthusiasm for Ralph Waldo Emerson, for reform, and for abolition—toward an affirmation of the values of order, loyalty, and discipline.[17]

The ethic of loyalty and service to the state, as George Frederickson's *The Inner Civil War* argues, transformed the concept of the duty of an "aristocrat" and intellectual, pointing toward a rejection of the romantic image of the superior man seeking to make his solitary way through a wilderness: ". . . the gentleman does not become an iconoclast, a wilderness traveler, or an expatriate, but tries to do his 'duty' within the context provided by society."

What was occurring was the transformation of the ideal of the "strenuous life"—which had previously meant retreat into the wilderness—into a social ideal. Rather than following the path of Francis Parkman . . . and seeking adventures outside the confines of civilization, it was now deemed most suitable to do one's duty in a strenuous way within society. . . . The military experience, which had taught the young patrician intellectuals to take pride in a life of service and to emphasize professional skills and professional objectives, had destroyed whatever respect they might have had for anti-institutional thinking, radical individualism, or transcendental hopes of self-fulfillment.[18]

It should be emphasized that the "patrician intellectuals" studied by Frederickson were not the dominant section of the class that was achieving a position of dominance in the postwar economy. The leading financiers, railroad proprietors, and industrial entrepreneurs—the so-called Robber Barons of the Gilded Age—were not usually men of patrician background or intellectual inclination. Nor were they all veterans of the Civil War, since many had taken advantage of wartime conditions and the purchase of draft exemptions to make their fortunes. The new generation of northern intellectuals—the "junior" Charles Francis Adams and Oliver Wendell Holmes, for example—belonged to a class whose power and status was diminished in a nation whose politics were dominated by the economic imperatives and the personalities of big business.

In some respects, the new conservatism of the cultural elite of the North stood in opposition to the principle of "pure materialism" and political corruption represented by the new capitalists, just as their parents had similarly opposed the political power of the Jacksonian "new men." However, the nature of postwar America determined that the major threat to conservative values, expressed in radical democratic ideology, would come not from the nouveaux riches but from the new industrial working classes. Although the cultural elite preserved its sense of difference from, and its right to criticize, the "malefactors of great wealth," the two classes more frequently combined their forces and made common cause. The cultural elite provided a management cadre for corporations that could use their academic knowledge and war-taught professional skills of management and organization, as well as their moral and social credentials. And through the economic and political struggles of the seventies, the two groups moved toward a greater sense of their common interests than of their differences.

This tendency is mythologized in the fiction of the first generation of "realists," most notably that of William Dean Howells. His *Rise of Silas Lapham* (1885) is a mature fable of that tendency, which uses the marriage plot of the old historical romance to represent the integration of patrician values and vigor with the realism, productivity, and disciplined energy of the new commerce. He represents the positive side of this absorption of the younger generation of patrician intellectuals by the tasks of industrialization. He sees it as leading to a democratization of the patrician element through its engagement in the work of the world; while at the same time the patricians' "higher" cultural values are diffused downward for the moral betterment of the "new men." However, this is a symbiotic relationship which does not extend downward to the great mass of the population. The professional and managerial functions made available by postwar industrialism extended into peacetime a distinction of class and function that resembled the officer–enlisted man distinction of wartime. This in turn fostered a reinterpretation of class differences, in which the Anglo-Saxonist racialism of a Parker or a Prescott provided a model for distinctions within the white race, as well as between whites and nonwhites.[19]

This new racialist interpretation of class relations was articulated first as a negation of the perfectionism that provided the rationale for the reform movements and philanthropic enterprises that initially shaped the Reconstruction, Indian, and labor policies of the Grant administration. It involved the derogation of its reformers and philanthropists as "she-males" and sentimentalists, constitutionally unable to meet the stern requirements of the new era. The "sternness" of the times was seen as deriving from the change in the American economy: industrialism might promise a future of prosperity, but for the present it tended to increase the gap between rich and poor, and to require reduction of the working classes to economic dependence and political subordination. The new industrialism—and especially the building of railroads—was the continuation of the Civil War by other means: its objects were "grand" and national in scope, and provided a field in which the virtues of a patrician officer corps could be usefully engaged, as technical experts, as leaders, as imposers of discipline on raw recruits and unruly conscripts.

Nowhere, perhaps, is the process of the patrician class's reeducation more completely and tortuously reflected than in the career of Charles Francis Adams, Jr. He was the grandson of John Quincy Adams and the brother of Henry, and, as the elder brother, heir to the mantle of Adamsian prestige, power, and patriotic *noblesse oblige*. Harvard and his family prepared him for a career as a literary intellectual, perhaps as a professional in law, government, or diplomacy. But the outbreak of the war, and his long and extensive experience in the field, altered his sense of the nature and potentialities of political and economic power in a new age. Early in the war he was engaged directly with the problems of applying political force to the resolution of the political-economic complexities of Reconstruction. During the occupation of the Sea Islands he had to administer contraband camps for confiscated slaves and oversee the management of plantations brought back into production by the military authorities. Later in the war he commanded a black cavalry regiment, which he saw as a microcosm of the "Southern labor problem." These wartime experiences shaped the ideas which he would later apply in his postwar career as a leading spokesman for political reform and reorganization, as a critic and trustee of the Erie Railroad corporation, and as a political leader of New England Republicans.

A conservative abolitionist, Adams was committed to the doctrine that slavery was a primitive institution whose preservation had retarded the development of the South and degraded both the slave and his master. Nonetheless, Adams's closer acquaintance with the South convinced him that "African slavery, as it existed in our slave states, was indeed a patriarchal institution" in which the slaves were protected and happy. This did not make him "like slavery any the better," or diminish his sense that it was "demoralizing" to both races. But it had grown upon him as an "inborn conviction" that the African race had shown a lack of "self-reliance" in its failure to rise against its masters during the war, remaining instead "as supine as logs or animals." He found his cavalry regiment full of "ugly characters," and the race as a whole he saw as "greedy animals" incapable even of fighting for life:

> After all a negro is not the equal of the white man . . . He has not the mental vigor and energy, he cannot stand up against adversity. A sick nigger . . . cannot fight for life like a white man . . . So his animal tendencies are greater than those of the whites.

Adams feared the race would fail in competition with whites if simply turned free after the war; therefore their salvation, Adams speculates, may lie with the militarization of their lives. "The Army . . . is the proper school for the race." Freed of the need for a self-reliance they are racially incapable of exercising, kept to the task by military law, subordinate to the tutelage of men appointed as officers above them, the blacks (says Adams) can learn the necessary skills of each "branch of industry" in which they are capable of productive labor. Adams makes his own regiment sound like a military prototype of Tuskegee: first provide them with manual training and only then permit them the higher elements of education.[20]

After the war Adams extended the principles developed in this analysis to apply more generally to the political problem of combining democracy with industrial enterprise. His involvement with these problems was direct and engaged him as an active politician, a participant in the management of banks and railroads, and as a professional-amateur historian and sociologist. In 1869 he presented a paper on "Protection of the Ballot" to the American Social Science Association, in which he identified the emergence of an urban proletariat as the central political dilemma confronting the enlightened classes in the industrial era. In the "early and relatively undeveloped" stage of American society, it seemed desirable to create a government in which the will of the majority was checked by the fragmentation of authority and by the imposition of barriers to direct election of the executive such as the Electoral College. But as the population grew, simultaneously spreading over a greater area and concentrating in great urban centers, this system tended to "corrupt the ballot" by giving extraordinary weight to votes in urban centers like New York. These are the very places in which a "prole-tariat" has come into existence; and it is the economic and moral character of this new class that makes it inevitably the root of political corruption, through "bossism," bribery, the selling of votes, the cultivation of demagogy. Worst of all, this class is an inevitable by-product of economic development:

> As society develops itself, and wealth, population and igno-rance increase,—as the struggle for existence becomes more and more severe, the inherent difficulties of a broadly extended suffrage will make themselves felt. Starving men and women care very little for abstract questions of general good. Political power becomes one means simply of private subsistence.

The insatiable appetite of industry for "an inexhaustible supply of cheap labor" is fast creating a large and alien-born proletariat. If left un-checked, he warns, our commerce will soon create "a European, and especially Celtic, proletariat on the Atlantic coast; an African proletariat on the shores of the Gulf, and a Chinese proletariat on the Pacific." In such case political democracy and "Universal Suffrage" will simply allow the underclasses to destroy "free institutions" (including private property), because "the proletariat" is simply "the organization of ignorance and vice to obtain political control."[21]

Adams's solution is a sophisticated political variation on his military-government formula for Reconstructing the former slaves. The essential step is a rejection of the ideology of universal suffrage as the fulfillment of democratic ideals, and the reform of governmental institutions so as to eliminate some of the checks on majority rule and make the imposition of national authority simpler. Lastly, the proletariat should be prevented from ever becoming an actual majority of the voting population through the restriction of immigration.

Adams thus redefines the political order, and bases his arguments on assumptions about the social and racial character of the new industrial proletariat. He assumes first of all that proletarian labor is, by its nature, "degraded" labor; but he imputes the degradation to a combination of capitalist greed and the racial disposition of the proletarians. Those races and classes which are inherently degraded (Irishmen, blacks, Orientals) will gravitate naturally to the proletariat; so will those Anglo-Saxons whose "ignorance and vice" are congenital dispositions, or who fall short of the full gift of "successful self-reliance." Adams further assumes that it will be the tendency of this sort of proletariat to increase as civilization moves to a "higher stage." This is paradoxical from the perspective of the liberal perfectionism of prewar reformers. But it is the hallmark of the new tough-minded school of postwar liberals that the necessity of inequality be acknowledged, and accepted as the price of progress. Adams takes it for granted that the lives of the new class will of necessity be miserable and on the border of starvation. Indeed, the social discipline of an industrial society arises from its power continually to confront the citizens with the choice, "to work or to starve." But Adams answers that such immiseration of what is, after all, a minority, appears an inevitable by-product of develop-ments that in general make for the advancement of progress; and his political reforms envision the protection of the privileged from the franchise of the proletariat.

Here is a retreat indeed from the fundamental premise of American liberal thought, which had since 1776 linked political and economic democ-racy as the twin guarantors of social peace. The tendency of American politics during four generations since John Adams's time had been to seek the expansion of both the political franchise and the economic basis of American society. Operating together, political liberty and open access to wealth-producing resources and activities had provided the safety valve for social discontent in this country. When access either to the resource Frontier or to the exercise of representative political rights had been threatened, revolutionary uprisings had occurred—from the time of the Stamp Act resistance of 1765, to Bleeding Kansas in 1855 and the secession crisis of 1860. But for Charles Francis Adams the necessities of the new economic order override the political imperatives of the old. If economic necessity requires that there be a permanent proletariat and a managerial class, then political structures and expectations will have to be modified accordingly. The safety valve of democratic politics has now become a danger to the machine it was invented to protect: its use draws off too much power, diluting and weakening the force of managerial will and talent which drives the machine upon its course. But if the political safety valve is to be closed for the sake of efficiency, then the role of the economic safety valve—of the Frontier, broadly conceived—becomes more absolutely vital than ever before. Unless the new order can generate enough in the way of material benefits to compensate the people for their loss of liberty and the expectation of wealth, then the new managerial class will find itself in the position of the antebellum planter in *Uncle Tom's Cabin*—he will be like a man seated on a steam engine, with the stokers shoveling on the coal and the pressure rising and the relief valve tied down tight, ready at any moment to explode in a fine spray of cogwheels and human blood.

CHAPTER 14

The Reconstruction of Class and Racial Symbolism, 1865–1876

Adams's expectations about the character of the new threefold proletariat—Celtic, African, Chinese—are in sharp contrast to the strain of optimism and self-praise that also figures in American writing of the period—that strain whose leitmotif was the celebration of American workers as the "best paid, best educated, best fed" in the world. Certainly the expansion of American industry in 1865–73 and the inflation of the currency made America attractive to foreign workers on economic as well as political grounds. However, the economic and political developments of the next two decades gave to this optimistic rhetoric a stridently defensive air. Even before the Panic and breakdown of 1873, conditions in the factories and mills and on the railroads were sufficiently bad to produce a rising tide of labor organization, strikes, and sporadic violence. The inadequacy of housing, sanitation, and essential social services in the mushrooming American cities added to the sense and the reality of impoverishment, to the crime rate, and to discontent. When the economic panic produced actual depression, exacerbating these tendencies, the popular journalists and editorialists began to depict the emerging American proletariat in terms of the racial analogy offered by Adams; and they followed Adams's logic in suggesting that a proletariat of this kind must be deprived of its access to political power.

In composing this image of the proletariat, Adams and his journalistic colleagues drew on the traditional American symbolism of class as an aspect of race. That symbolism established the spectrum of class relations on a scale determined by the degree of likeness to the Indian at the lower end of the spectrum, and the Anglo-Saxon natural aristocrat at the other. The Indian is characterized by his savagery, his closeness to nature and to animalism, his lack of a sense of private property and the related inability to recognize and respect Woman; his politics take the form of violence, which is directed to cruel and destructive ends. The Anglo-Saxon is characterized by his amenability to law and civilized order, which in turn is based on respect for property and for Woman; and his violence is both greater than the Indian's and more constructive, because it is controlled by self-discipline and by its functional concentration on civilized goals (i.e., the defense of property and Woman). Before the Civil War two classes of domestic workers had been seen as approaching the "savage" or Indian end of the spectrum: the black slave of the South and the "pauper" class of the northern cities; and these had been treated as wards of the state, entitled to protection but not to political rights. After the war, these three terms—"savage," "slave," and "pauper"—would provide the metaphors through which Americans conceived the development of a proletariat: that is, a class of workers without property, and without the prospect of acquiring property.

As we saw in the writings of Lippard, Americans already had encountered the notion that the proletarianization of the working classes would lead to some kind of social apocalypse. Lippard's "Last Days of the Quaker City" might have seemed an extravagant Gothic fantasy in 1844; but in the 1870s that vague prophecy took on the shape of a real and present threat. The real immiseration of the working class, its "alien" ethnic character, and the rising tide of labor resistance account for a good part of this process; and the Great Strike of 1877 raised legitimate fears of the revolutionary potential of the new proletariat. But the journalism of the years preceding the Great Strike suggests that even before that outbreak, an important part of the American cultural elite were prepared for a sudden, comprehensive, and revolutionary uprising by American workers. Very little in the experience of American labor relations before 1877 justified such expectations. However, there were other experiences on which the observers of the political scene could, and did, draw; and these led them to expect, predict, and perhaps inadvertently foment, the tendency toward revolutionary social violence.

In the editorials of the period, the European experience of revolution is most often cited as the warning of what can happen in an industrializing Metropolitan society. Americans were used to favorable comparisons between their own institutions and those of Europe; and even the excesses of European revolutionaries were excusable on the ground that the moral responsibility for revolutionary cruelty lay in the prior cruelty of European monarchism. But the emergence of revolutionary socialism as a response to European tyranny suggested to American conservatives that the unrestricted importation of European ideas might, in the end, prove dangerous to American capitalism as well as to European monarchism. And with the advent of the Paris Commune of 1871, in which "socialistic" parties proclaimed a revolutionary government and began a "war on property," ideological malaise was converted into political conviction. The "Red Spectre of the Commune" appeared to haunt New York journalists of the seventies whenever any group organized for the support of strikers, the organization of unions, or a protest against starvation and bad housing.

But the "Red Spectre" itself might not have been quite so frightening if Americans had not themselves so recently experienced their own "remorseless revolutionary struggle." The Civil War did not pit class against class or even interest group against interest group in the classic Marxian sense. It had, however, intensified the language of race/class division, and ramified it in unimaginable ways; and at the same time, it showed that the hostilities implied in that system of division could be acted out without restraint, to the full extent of man's capacity for inflicting and suffering violence.

The Civil War had given Americans an extensive education in the capacity of individuals and societies to inflict and to suffer violence—and to justify that violence in terms of sacred mythology. The Protestant myth of blood atonement was perhaps the dominant metaphor through which Americans expressed the conviction that this colossal outburst of murder and destruction must lead to some benign and progressive transformation of society. John Brown's belief that "the crimes of this *guilty land, will* never be purged *away*, but with Blood" is the simplest statement of the belief; but Lincoln also invoked a similar concept, albeit in a more subtle application, in his declaration that:

> . . . if God wills that . . . every drop of blood drawn with the lash shall be paid by another drawn by the sword, as was said three thousand years ago, so still it must be said, "The judgments of the Lord are true and righteous altogether."

The scale of violence, the destruction of property (especially in the South), and the loss of life were on a colossal scale, rivaling in cold fact the apocalyptic fantasies of a Lippard. The economic structure of half the nation was destroyed, and the casualty rate in proportion to population was worse than that experienced in any war that the United States has fought since. Moreover, the political character of the struggle and the possibility of foreign intervention made this a war in which the existence of the nation as such was genuinely at risk.

A struggle so violent and intense, and so far-reaching in its threat of destruction, was bound to add a level of intensity to the language in which American culture framed the bases of social conflict. The racialization of the imagery of class, through association of class antagonists with "savages," became more marked. In the southern press it was common to dwell on the "foreign" character of the northern armies, particularly on the presence of large numbers of Irish and Germans; and the latter were objects of special hostility, described as Huns and barbarians—southern legislators actually debated whether or not to grant surrendering Germans prisoner-of-war status, with hanging being the alternative. Of course, nothing of the kind was done; but something real was reflected in the rhetorical flourish.[1]

Russell Weigley, in *The American Way of War*, has argued that the Civil War established as a norm the expectation that any political struggle eventuating in war must of necessity become a "war of annihilation." The successful strategists of Union victory built their policies on the understanding that the political and social stakes of the war were too fundamental to admit of compromise without military victory, and that battlefield triumph was, in the existing state of military technology and organization, less a matter of decisive battles than of steady commitment to a war of attrition. The strategy recognized the dependence of the military on the political will of the enemy, and the dependence of that will on the maintenance of a productive and secure economic and social structure. Victory therefore demanded not only battles of extermination, in which body counts were seen as more significant than territorial advance; it also required the invention of "total war," in which entire armies could be rationally devoted to the destruction of farms and factories to circumscribe the South's economic capacity to sustain war.[2]

Although Weigley's thesis is a controversial one, which cannot be applied to all American wars after 1865, it is clear that the "total war" concepts developed in 1861–65 as a strategy for civilized conflict did indeed add a significant new element to the ideological vocabulary of American politicians, military men, and public enthusiasts for war. That concept was not invented for civil war. Sherman's march had its roots in colonial- and Revolutionary-era Indian campaigns, and these helped to define the ideological character of Indian wars and to establish expectations about a future "race war" between blacks and whites. What the Civil War added to the ideological mix was the capability for transferring the categories of racial animus and savage war to a struggle of whites against whites, and of one civil society or class against another. This connection was forged during the war, by propagandists, politicians, and the soldiers themselves. And, as we shall see, the Civil War applications of the total war doctrine, in turn, came to rationalize a decade of racial strife in the South and labor strife in the North, and to provide justification for the strategy of "extermination" directed against Indians and the buffalo herds by Sherman and Sheridan in 1866–70. Those Indian campaigns in turn would provide the personnel and the military doctrine that Americans carried into their imperial adventures in Latin America and the Philippines.

The basic terms for interpreting these later struggles were formed in the Civil War. Lincoln's decision to make the war for the Union a war against slavery, for example, evoked the traditional expectations associated with the idea of "race war"—specifically, the belief that such a struggle must become a "war of extermination." Jefferson Davis condemned the Emancipation Proclamation as "a measure by which several millions of human beings of an inferior race, peaceful and contented laborers in their sphere, are doomed to extermination." These were the terms in which Fitzhugh and and Parker had discussed the future of relations between freed blacks and domineering Anglo-Saxons; but they also echoed all the way back to Jefferson's *Notes on Virginia*, which too had envisioned a war of extermination as the only possible outcome of emancipation.

This view was echoed by northern conservatives, ranging all the way from pro-Confederate Democrats like C. L. Vallandigham, through the Unionist Democrat General George B. McClellan, to a hard-war conservative like Sherman. McClellan in 1862 and Sherman in 1864 warned the administration that emancipation or (later) the granting of full citizenship rights to blacks would provoke a rebellion by northern whites, who (in Vallandigham's words) would fear Lincoln meant to free the black and impoverish or enslave the white laborers. Moreover, they asserted that a policy of fostering racial equality would arouse in the South a fierce, last-ditch determination to resist all compromise; this would convert the Civil War into a war of extermination, to be fought by guerrillas even after the destruction of formal military power.[3]

When the North began to use blacks as soldiers, this debate became very serious indeed. Even relatively moderate Southerners were inclined to treat white officers leading black soldiers as fomenters of slave rebellion or as "nigger-stealers," the punishment for which was death; and black war prisoners ran the risk of death or enslavement under the legal code of the South, which did not recognize their status as freemen or soldiers. Only the counterthreat of imprisoning or hanging southern officers, and of forcing Confederate prisoners to labor on fortifications under fire, compelled at least a formal adherence by the South to the laws of war in their treatment of black troops and their officers. After the defeat of the South, the dependence of Reconstruction governments on black troops and voters tended to polarize southern politics along racial lines analogous to those of slavery days—although the power relationships between the parties were very different.

In the North as well the racial metaphor was called into play. Lincoln's conservative Democratic critics linked him to a project for the systematic "miscegenation" of the races. Hostility to immigrants was as potent in the North as in the South, although the Union's need for their political support gave ethnic virulence a patronizing rather than a genocidal form. As the war proceeded and conscription was introduced, the unwillingness of the Irish to fight a Republican war led to an association of ethnic prejudice with anticopperhead sentiment. When Irish resistance to conscription laws that consistently favored the rich burst out in violence in the Draft Riots of 1863, the scenario of "urban savages" tearing down a civilized city was reinvoked—Lippardian imagery, but without Lippard's sympathy for the rebellious despair of the underclass. Southern soldiers were also described in terms suggestive of both Indian "savagery" and the cruelty of the white "squatters" and Southwestern "outlaws." Press reports from the beginning of the war asserted that southern soldiers "are Barbarians and Savages," who "bayonetted our wounded," and found it difficult to advocate being "merciful to such savages," who "have all the craftiness and treachery of the Indian without any of his bravery."[4]

Some of the more significant projects of race/class extermination existed only at the level of polemics—although at the time they were promulgated they might have been thought possible. Early in the war the conservative General McClellan used them as a way of arguing against the Emancipation Proclamation. In his report to the president, McClellan declared that so long as the object of the North excluded emancipation, it was possible to disconnect the southern poor white from the "aristocracy," and make of the Civil War a war against "one class." With emancipation, the war would be against the whole southern branch of the Anglo-Saxon race, and therefore difficult or impossible to win without fighting a war of extermination. Later in the war and during Reconstruction itself, the idea of a war of extermination against the "Barons of the South" became part of the superheated rhetoric of Radicalism. Ties of familial and political kinship across the Mason-Dixon line and the persistence of shared economic interests between southern and northern conservatives of course forbade the implementation of such literally Jacobin proposals. Nonetheless, the projects once conceived and put forward had at least a fictive reality—as such they might even be used as a revolutionary program against those guilty of conceiving them.[5]

THE NEW PATERNALISM

One of the responses to the apocalyptic violence of the Civil War was to revive the wishful antebellum mythology of the "utopia" of dependent labor. Even as the new factory slums were spreading, there was a revival of interest in books and articles about the old days in Lowell, and several books of reminiscences by former "mill girls" appeared and were well received. The most notable writer in this group was Lucy Larcom, whose actual time in the mills had been brief—she was the daughter of a Lowell boardinghouse keeper, one of the groups which both housed and exercised parietal control over the workers. In 1875 she published *An Idyl of Work*, a poetic romance about Lowell which she dedicated "To Working Women . . . By One of Their Sisterhood." The poem gives us an idealized Old Lowell, with clean Yankee girls working their spindles under the supervision of gentlemanly and paternal supervisors. Into this scene comes an English visitor who mistakenly assumes he has happened upon a finishing school of some kind. Larcom's girls find their work morally uplifting, as it enables them to support brothers studying for the ministry or to achieve the skills, maturity, and grace that will make them desirable as wives. One of her heroines marries a fine young gentleman, who takes her to "the far wonderful West," "that great garden-desert [and] prairie paradise." Thus Larcom's "Lowell" is not merely the fictive utopia of an idealized industry, it is also part of a larger fictive universe which still includes an Edenic western Frontier. Yet even Larcom acknowledges that "The conditions and character of mill-labor are no doubt much changed," and that our "morbid desire for wealth, show, and luxury" may be returning us to that primitive "half-civilization" in which labor is indeed degraded.[6]

But even more extraordinary in its denial of history was the revival of the writers and themes of the prewar "plantation school." Northern periodicals and book publishers, even during the heyday of Reconstruction and northern revulsion against the Ku Klux Klan, gave broad play to nostalgic depictions of the "patriarchal institution" in its pristine antebellum form. New articles reporting on life in the successfully Reconstructed parts of the South—some of them by former abolitionists like Harriet Beecher Stowe—suggested that the perfection of Reconstruction involved a partial restoration of antebellum social relations: paternalism and dependence, without the intrusion of actual slavery. Even periodical strongholds of northern liberalism published humorous and nostalgic sketches of darkies and massas "befo' de wah." The American humorist George William Bagby recouped his wartime losses on the lecture circuit with lush depictions of Arcadian plantations and contented workers. For a northern audience confronting the spectacle of the dangerous, and dangerously growing, homeless pauper class known as tramps, Bagby's wistful reminder that in the antebellum South "tramps there were none," was one way of rejecting the new state of things—the rootlessness, the poverty, and the potential radicalism of the new laboring classes—while implicitly registering its impact.[7]

The most successful innovation in popular literary mythology during this period was the series of "urban" dime novels produced by Horatio Alger, which co-opt the tramp figure instead of simply denying him. Alger's books put the reader into the squalor and rough-and-tumble of the mean streets, and his heroes either come from or are compelled to resort to the "dangerous classes" themselves. His most popular hero, "Ragged Dick," is a street boy—one of the rootless class of orphan-tramps who, in other contexts, were seen as the hard core of the criminal classes. But Alger's books simply reproduce the essential ideology of the Lowell/Old South world view, confirming the validity of a patriarchal vision as the model of social relations, but authenticating that vision by a plausible depiction of the "dangerous" contemporary city.

Alger's novels trace the rise of ambitious young boys from the squalor of the gutter to the pride and comfort of "position" and possession of property. Yet his heroes employ no vulgar or dishonest tricks: they rise by serving the interests of benevolent and paternalistic wealthy men with diligence and honesty. They might meet such a man by directing him to his destination in the maze of city streets, or by returning money stolen from him by a criminal, or by rescuing his daughter from ruffians. They would gain his favor by exhibiting frankness, "manliness," and honesty, as well as diligence in doing assigned work. Ultimately their benefactor would raise them to employment or even high position in the business—occasionally a partnership or marriage to the boss's daughter would be the outcome. In short, Alger's heroes face a world in which power is preempted by a benevolent paternal class of rulers, who dispense largesse according to the moral deserts of the individual. The aim of ambition is not to equal or replace the patriarch, but to obtain his good graces and to share (in a small way) his power. If this is not exactly rugged individualism, it is at least a vision of how the dynamism of social mobility could be reconciled with the preservation of order: the ambitious "new man" had simply to limit his demands on society for wealth and power and to conceive of himself as a "boy," a child confronting adults in his political relations with the established classes.

While the Alger hero's success was dependent on his acceptance of subordination, of perpetual childhood, the original mythology of success had called for full adulthood, for the achievement by the common man of near-heroic stature and real political power through his own achievements in a wide-open society. It was of course understood that not every individual would achieve the maximum possibility; but the promise of America had been the promise of a chance to try, without any other restraints than those of skill and "character." But that success story had been played out on a natural frontier, where society's restrictions had not yet arrived, and only natural forces stood between the individual and his achievement. Was there still any alternative to the city of Alger's fables? Even Alger seemed to hope so: as Custer marched against the Sioux in 1876, Alger was on a train, heading west at the behest of his publisher to bring the American "success story" back to its origin in the gold fields of California. Perhaps prophetically, Alger's western stories would have the same structure and plots as his fables of urban paternalism.[8]

The wistful appeal of Alger's fables of success made him perhaps the most popular of the postwar writers. But no fables could alter the realities of urban disorder; neither was nostalgia for Old Lowell and the Old South an antidote for the reality of a society in which "tramps" and "proletarians" were increasing in number and political power in phase with the development of the great industrial corporations. Social scientists, journalists, and fiction writers studied the squalor and tyranny of the industrial towns and depicted their consequences for American life and values. Even the most sympathetic and reform-minded of these observers tended to echo the responses of Adams: these were a different kind of people, whose character was in some sense predisposed to degradation; and though their character and circumstances made them dependent in the near term, in the long run the danger they posed was that of savage violence.[9]

Jonathan B. Harrison was one of the most important spokesmen for urban and industrial reform in the postwar period. His approach to the urban scene combined the training and disposition of a socially engaged Protestant minister with the skills of a journalist and the expertise of a serious amateur social scientist. His major book, *Certain Dangerous Tendencies in American Life* (1880), was a vivid depiction of working-class poverty and a polemic for "realistic" reform measures. (The book made Harrison somewhat famous, and earned him places on a number of official committees to study social problems of the "dependent classes" in cities and on Indian reservations.) Harrison's proposals have a distinctly post-Frontier orientation. Industrialization and its attendant problems of constricted expectations and proletarian discontent are real and permanent phenomena, and will not be disarmed by the existence of cheap western lands. Harrison deplores the living and working conditions of the new working class, the neglect of their moral and physical welfare by the enlightened classes of the country, and regards the industrial town and its population as distinctly alien to the spirit of America, which he equates with the consciousness of his own class:

> It is not safe or wise to allow so large a class to be so far alien and separate from the influences and spirit of our national life. I do not think the mill people are, as a class, inferior in morality . . . to any equally numerous class in this country. On the contrary, I believe they are superior to any class . . . who do not work.
>
> We ought to know more about this sort of people, about their circumstances, their ways of living, their thought, and the tendencies and effects of such a life as theirs upon character and civilization.

In this alienation there is a distinct threat to the continued existence of American society and civilization. Sections of the foreign-born working class are, says Harrison, deeply committed to the revolutionary overthrow of existing institutions. For Harrison their alienation from him and what he represents is expressed in their defensiveness, which reminds him of the behavior of "wild animals."[10]

The remedy, he says, cannot lie in pieties of upward mobility—the "safety valve." There are no Frontiers for such people to take advantage of, even if they had the capability of doing so:

> It does not appear that the earth contains materials for unlimited wealth, or that it will ever be possible for everybody to be rich and live in luxury. The earth does contain materials for sub-sistence for human beings, as long as there are not too many of them. But the overproduction of human beings is a frequently recurring fact in the history of the race.

Here Harrison directly contradicts the confident expectations of Gilpin, and reverts to the humbler ambitions of the "yeoman" myth in the emphasis on nature's provision of the basis for "subsistence." But he also notes that such subsistence is not a guarantee, in the face of overproduction of new births; and he goes on to indicate that "subsistence" in the new mode will explicitly require discipline and subordination to coercive labor control—a mode totally opposite to the independent subsistence envisioned in agrarian myth. He makes these points in the course of stating his opposition to the eight-hour day:

> I think that for most men, including operatives, mechanics, farmers, and clergymen, more than eight hours' labor per day is necessary, in order to keep down and utilize the forces of animal nature and passions. I believe that if improvements in machinery should discharge men from the necessity of laboring more than six hours a day, society would rot in measureless and fatal animalism. . . . It would be well, I think, if we could make it impossible for an idler to live on the face of the earth.[11]

Harrison's comparison of ministerial labors with factory work is (to modern eyes) foolishly self-serving. But Harrison's approach to the proletariat was based on values and assumptions that were basic to the ideology of American liberals, whether conservative or reformist in method. Harrison is invoking the historical myth which sees progress as a rising-above natural or animal limitations and characteristics, and which symbolizes that development in the conflict between "savage" and "civilized" races in America. It is precisely the traits of character traditionally associated with the Indian that are sloughed off as man learns the necessity of productive labor. Instructing the Indian or the African savage in the industrial arts offer him his only chance to rise above his limitations, and survive in the new order of things. Conversely, the social and cultural corruptions of American life which have prevented the new proletariat from learning the essential values of productive labor and social discipline have raised the specter of their degeneration into savagery. Failure to learn will justify a kind of extermination of the class, making their life on earth impossible.

This connection is most strikingly made in the increasing tendency to invoke the Indians as analogues for the proletariat of the city.

PAUPERS, PROLETARIANS, AND INDIANS

Charles Loring Brace, the philanthropist and educator who presided over the Children's Aid Society and the Newsboys' Lodging-House (which Horatio Alger made legendary), had laid down in his book, *The Dangerous Classes of New York* (1872), that America's poor were among the most desperate and dangerous in the world:

> It has been common, since the recent terrible Communistic outbreak in Paris, to assume that France alone is exposed to such horrors; but, in the judgment of one who has been familiar with our "dangerous classes" for twenty years, there are just the same explosive social elements beneath the surface of New York as of Paris.
>
> ... All these great masses of destitute, miserable, and criminal persons believe that for ages the rich have had all the good things of life, while to them have been left the vile things. Capital to them is the tyrant.[12]

Thus they make war against property, which is the basis of civilized life. Brace takes the view that urban society is turning the poor into a species of barbarian, capable of bringing civilization itself down as the earlier barbarians destroyed Rome. Missionary work among the urban poor was of course to be encouraged; but Brace believed that unless the congested communities of the poor could be broken up, the culture of poverty would tend to become hereditary:

> It is well-known to those familiar with the criminal classes, that certain appetites or habits, if indulged abnormally and excessively through two or more generations, come to have an almost irresistible force, and, no doubt, modify the brain so as to constitute an almost insane condition. This is especially true of the appetite for liquor and of the sexual passion, and sometimes of the peculiar weakness, dependence, and laziness which make confirmed paupers.

The "struggle for existence" that produced these present paupers, however, offers a kind of guarantee that hidden within the heredity of the poor are "gemmules" containing the capacity for virtue—since vice, according to Brace, causes the birthrate to decline, the death rate to rise. To bring forth these hidden capacities and overcome the tendency toward degeneration, it is necessary to reengage the poor with the "struggle for existence." To place them in asylums, as the Europeans do, is to monasticize them and reinforce their unproductive character. Brace's alternative is a policy of resettlement, through which the poor and their children would be transported to the West, and engaged in agriculture or adopted by rural families. Here they could begin to realize the American promise of progressive mobility through competitive effort.[13]

The recommendation draws on the ideology of the Homestead Acts and myth of "regeneration through agriculture" which lies at the heart of

Jeffersonian agrarianism. However, it also bears a curious resemblance to the philosophy of Indian Removal, by which the West was made to serve as a safety valve for supposed savages, whose character made them incompatible with the progress of white culture. Brace makes the analogy specific:

> There seemed to be a very considerable class of lads in New York who bore to the busy, wealthy world about them something of the same relation which Indians bear to civilized Western settlers. They had no settled home, and lived on the outskirts of society, their hand against every man's pocket, and every man looking on them as natural enemies; their wits sharpened like those of a savage, and their principles often no better. Christianity reared its temples over them, and Civilization was carrying on its great work, while they—a happy race of little heathens and barbarians—plundered or frolicked, or led their roving life, far beneath.[14]

This comparison tends to maximize both the degradation of the city's pauper-proletarians, and their danger to society. As savages within the gates, they have the potential to do to the city what their redskin analogues do to border settlements. But the analogy is linked to a metaphorical system whose parts are mutually reinforcing. Just as pauper-proletarians are "interpreted" by the Indian analogy, Indians are interpreted by a pauper analogy. Thus Commissioner of Indian Affairs E. P. Smith invokes the connection in his *Annual Report* of 1875, as part of an argument which asserts that the Indians are not entitled to the same rights of property and political representation enjoyed by white men: "The whole spirit of our people and of American institutions revolts against any process that tends to pauperism or taxation for the support of idlers."[15]

This reversible analogy between workers and savages is the most significant new term in the language of American mythology after the war, and it informs the battery of responses that postwar American culture brought to bear on urban problems, southern problems, and on the Indian question. These included the imposition of regimes of tutelary philanthropy, which tended to degrade into political tyrannies; the attempt to apply the Homestead principle as economic and social panacea; and in the end, the rejection of philanthropy as "coddling," and the adoption of a coercive rationale for governing the identified group as an underclass. One of the keys to this is a marked tendency for policymakers and critics who made their reputation in one of these areas to be regarded as "expert" or appointed as policymakers in the others as well. J. B. Harrison's study of the laboring classes drew, as we have seen, on the vocabulary of white-Indian relations. On the basis of this work he was considered to have expertise relevant to dealing with Indians, and in 1880 undertook a tour of inspection of Indian reservations, under government auspices. Oliver Otis Howard, who made a reputation as the head of the Freedmen's Bureau in the South, was later put in charge of western policy. Likewise Vincent Collyer, a businessman and philanthropist associated with early Reconstruction efforts on the Carolina coast during the Civil War, was nominated to serve as a negotiator with the Plains Indians during the formulation of the Peace Policy in 1868–69. It was as if the characteristics of these three problem classes—proletarians, blacks, and Indians—were sufficiently akin so that expertise with one of them was transferable to work with another. Not surprisingly, the policies developed for all three groups shared common features, particularly the insistence that economic advancement—achieved under discipline and tutelage—must *precede* the full recognition of citizenship rights.[16]

The most important intellectual figure among these reform-minded administrators was Francis A. Walker. He was a Civil War veteran, a former staff officer and the official historian of the Army of the Potomac's II Corps; he was also a trained statistician, and a professional social scientist. Although his commitment to bureaucratic reform made him (for a time) an ally of the philanthropic reformers, his scientific reputation gave him credentials for tough-mindedness as a student of human affairs. His work on statistical and economic theory made him a founding father of those newly emergent disciplines. This work, coupled with his studies of the theory of wages in an industrial society, and his sociological analyses of the new working classes and the immigrants, made him perhaps the most respected American political economist in the last three decades of the nineteenth century. His texts replaced those of Francis Wayland as the official curriculum in American colleges and technical schools. In 1866 Walker was appointed a deputy in the U.S. Bureau of Statistics, and in 1869 he became its chief. He reorganized the bureau's work along more scientific lines, and expanded its range of inquiry, beginning a bureaucratic process (culminating in the next century) that would eventually link large-scale government-directed social scientific investigations to a broad range of social, economic, and political concerns. His first great triumph was the Census of 1870, which displayed and justified his new system; and the Grant administration's response to that achievement was to appoint Walker Commissioner of Indian Affairs (1871–72).

Walker's service was unique for his avoidance of those scandals associated with virtually all of Grant's other Commissioners of Indian Affairs; and he was able to make some short-lived reforms in the Indian Bureau's way of doing business. But Walker did not differ from his fellows in his views of the essentials and constants of Indian affairs. He was exceptional in being far more thoughtful and theoretically sophisticated, and in his power for putting the ideology of Indian affairs forward clearly, with a full appreciation of its premises and consequences, and without the slightest imputation of his speaking insincerely or from self-interested motives.

His views were put forward in his annual reports to the Secretary of the Interior (1871–72), and in his book *The Indian Question* (1874). The latter constitutes his major theoretical statement on the relations of savages to industrial civilization.

Although he was nominally committed to the Peace Policy's goal of training the Indian in self-reliance and self-government, Walker supported the Act of 1871, which eliminated the pretense of Indian sovereignty and made the tribes "wards of the nation"—exactly the legal condition of the freed slaves. Walker acknowledged that this action in fact eliminated the vestige of self-government that the Indian had achieved naturally, without white tutelage; and that it unilaterally abrogated all previous treaties, in violation of the revered principle of the inviolability of contracts. It was, he said, an act taken "in the insolence of conscious strength." But the action was justifiable, because it opened up the possibility of an assault on Indian tribal land-title. This assault would be carried on by both speculators and reformers—the latter seeking to make small independent farmers out of the ex-tribal communists, the former seeking to exploit the poverty of the Indian farmer and the cupidity of government allotment officers to acquire more Indian land.[17]

Although he did not underrate the power of the speculative element, Walker thought that the Indians might be protected from the worst of these depredations; and that they would undergo, under the government's power, a transformation into viable citizens, self-reliant, economically independent, participating in republican government as voters. The precondition for this transformation was the absolute sacrifice of all existing "savage" forms of tribal reliance, economic activity (hunting), and political control over their own affairs. Thus independence would be achieved through the acceptance of subordination, and the capacity for self-government developed through acquiescence in the power of the dominant race and its state. Following the pattern of history embodied in the myth of regeneration through violence, Walker summarizes the history of white-Indian relations as a racial struggle in which the superior whites master the techniques of their opponents, ultimately conquering them, and driving them to extinction or subjugation:

> And so the feeble colonies struggled on through those days of gloom and fear, deprecating the anger of the savages as they might, and circumventing their wiles when they could; played off one chieftain against another; made contribution of malice and power to every intestine feud among the natives; bought off tribes, without much scruple as to the ultimate fulfillment of their bargains; postponed the evil day by every expedient, knowing that time was on their side; and when they had, in spite of all, to fight, fought as men who know that they will not themselves be spared— planned ambuscades and massacres; fired Indian camps, and shot the inmates as they leaped from their blazing wigwams; studied and mastered all the arts of forest warfare; and beat the savages with their own weapons, as men of the higher race will always do when forced by circumstances to such a contest.[18]

For Walker the racial character of the Indian is a blend of contradictions, all tending to the image of a chaotic, impulsive being, whose great motives are vanity and desire for physical gratification. In his wild state he is at once "voluptuary and stoic," a greedy, moody, cruel child whose rages are horrific in their consequences. Tamed, he becomes indistinguishable from the commonplace peasant or benighted pauper:

> When broken down by the military power of the whites, thrown out of his familiar relations, his stupendous conceit with its glamour of savage pomp and glory rudely dispelled, his occupa-

tion gone, himself a beggar, the red man becomes the most commonplace person imaginable, of very simple nature, limited aspirations, and enormous appetites.[19]

Such a fate is his inevitable end. "Indian blood . . . has tended decidedly towards extinction."

> Among the greatest figures of the past are those bands and confederacies that have utterly disappeared from the continent, happy that their long, savage independence, and their brief, fierce resistance to the encroachments of the paleface, were not to be succeeded by a dreary period of submission, humiliation and dependence. Other tribes . . . are now represented upon the annuity or feeding-lists in the United States by a few score of diseased wretches, who hang about the settlements, begging and stealing where they can, and quarreling like dogs over the entrails of the beeves that are slaughtered for them.[20]

But Walker's own views of the Indian question look toward a similar conclusion, by different and more gentle means. Although liberal in his advocacy of generous appropriations for Indian subsistence and education, large reservations (to permit restriction of intercourse with whites), and a generous allowance of time for civilizing to go forward, Walker insists on the absolute power of the government first to restrict, then to administer, and finally to discipline its "wards." And although expediency of the moment demands the toleration of Indian vice, crime, idleness, and arrogance, the completion of the railroads and settlements and the destruction of the buffalo will inevitably reduce the Indian to absolute dependence. By stages, the agents will move from feeding and cajoling the Indian chief, to "pointing out the particular row of potatoes his majesty must hoe before his majesty can dine." Finally, the Indian will have to confront the choice which is the last test of civilization: he must be left "to work or starve," like the other citizens of the American Metropolis.[21]

With benevolent intent, the agent cajoles the Indian to acquiesce in his own subjection, to remain peaceful while the sustaining prop of his savage life (the buffalo) is exterminated. To those who would assert that the cajoling of Indians betrays the dignity of the white race, Walker counters, "With wild men, as with wild beasts, the question whether to fight, coax or run, is a question merely of what is easiest or safest. . . . Points of dignity can only arise between those who are, or assume to be, equals." Though equal to whites in the sight of God (as Walker admits), such equality means very little in balance with the reality of their manifest inferiority to whites in the real world of affairs. At best they may acquire some form of equality before the law, but only after they have passed through a tutelary regime of some rigor.

At this point in the argument, Walker shifts from his "wild beast" metaphor to another, somewhat closer to the immediate experience of his audience. In their postsavage, "reservation" state, the Indians are best understood as being in analogous condition to the dangerous classes of the cities—the white "paupers," the unemployed, the criminals, and the insane.

The same principle which underlies the regime of the reservation forms the basis of governing "dangerous classes" wherever these arise, and however they are constituted.[22] In both cases, the alternative to an imposition of order is imagined to be an upwelling of anarchy tending toward social ruination:

> The right of the government to exact . . . all that the good of the general community may require is not to be questioned . . . The condition of eighty thousand paupers and forty thousand criminals . . . affords ample authority and justification for the most extreme measures which may be adjudged necessary to save this race from itself, and the country from the intolerable burden of pauperism, and crime which the race, if left to itself, will certainly inflict upon a score of future states.[23]

Thus Walker, although nominally in favor of a self-governing Indian polity, in fact advocates the establishment of absolute authority in the agent—an authority which is directed to the enforcing of labor on the unwilling tribesman. The analogy to white paupers (and perhaps to blacks in the South) is an important one, as it cuts both ways. If it is proper to enforce labor on the Indian for the sake of public safety, it is proper to do so with half-savage blacks and whites who share the Indian/black traits of idleness and vice. It is the racial character of the underclass which justifies the departure from democratic principles; for the racial nature of their "incapacities" requires tutelage before citizenship can be granted. This implies a limitation on citizenship fundamentally different from the property qualifications for voting which were overturned by Jeffersonian and Jacksonian liberals between 1800 and 1840. It is a limitation rooted in blood and character, requiring almost a biological "conversion" for its removal. When is the racial inferior "ready" for citizenship? Perhaps only when he becomes fully "white," whatever the term may signify.

The underlying theme of this "reform" is the priority given to the breaking up of the "primitive" community structure, the dissolution of its forms of political sovereignty and collective action, and the subordination of the individual to a new political economy in which he cannot exercise his original power of self-government. In the case of the Indian, the undoing of tribal politics involved the direct dismantling of tribal governments, and the indirect task of repealing or discrediting the special legislation of the past which had made the United States government the protector of the tribal rights and lands of the Indians. This latter project required a strong affirmation of the principle that tribal policies by their nature fostered the retrogressive tendencies of the Indians, and had to be removed as obstacles to progress. Because the Indian's "rise" to industrial modernity must begin in the depths of primitive savagery, the Indian's progress (as projected by the reformers) would display the whole scale of human development, and suggest a set of signposts by which the progress of other more-or-less primitive groups could be measured.

Between 1865 and 1880 there were three major groups or classes within the American Metropolis whose case was parallel to that of the Indians: groups that resisted the imposition of an industrial regimen, deployed against it the resources of powerful local political structures, and appealed to the traditional ideologies of Jacksonian democracy and free labor for justification. These were the freedmen of the South, who sought to use their local strength and political leverage to establish themselves as independent small farmers or planters; the "Grangers" and other local organizations of farmers, who sought to use their power in state legislatures to regulate the railroad rates that were driving them into tenancy or out of farming altogether; and the organized working-class, which attempted to use both unionization and the power of local governments to achieve control over their conditions of work and scales of compensation.

From the perspective of a Walker or a Charles Francis Adams, these groups were behaving not unlike a set of Indian tribes, abusing their local autonomy to preserve an outmoded and hence retrogressive set of social and economic relations, retarding the advance of progress. It was therefore necessary to assert against them the sovereignty of the central power, as had been done with the seceding South. But the purpose of that assertion would be not to impose some new form of collectivity, but rather to permit the working out of the logic of economic competition among independent proprietors. Just as the Indian would have to pass from tribesman, to owner of a private allotment, to (perhaps) dispossessed proletarian, the new underclasses—losers of the economic competition—would have to accept their new condition and place in the scheme of things. They would then have to face the radical choice, "to work or starve." If they refused to do so, then they were (by the terms of the analogy) in the position of Indian tribes struggling violently for the power to drive themselves (and everyone else) backward into barbarism. To turn back the political initiatives of these underclass groups and to discredit the ideologies that sustained their popular support, the spokesmen for the new managerial order deployed the "Indian metaphor," which was intended to convince the uncommitted class of "middling" proprietors that collective political action against the new order was a species of tribalism, a throwback to the savage past, a symptom of degeneracy.

THE "PEACE POLICY" IN PRACTICE, 1869–1875

With hindsight it is easy enough to pick out the racialism and the antidemocratic tendencies implicit in policies like those of Reconstruction and the reform of Indian affairs. But it is important to remember that initially both policies were expressions of a genuinely reformist impulse, whose original aims were defined by the same democratic traditions that moved the freedmen, the Grangers, and the friends of labor. The transformation of these programs from instruments of liberation to rationalizers of oppression was therefore a development full of terrible irony, sufficient to shake the bases of belief in American democracy and its institutions.

The chief proponents of Indian policy reform were men and women who been prominent in the abolition struggle, like Wendell Phillips, Lydia Maria Child, Henry Ward Beecher; and like the program of Radical Reconstruction, the reform Indian policy was intended to raise a dark and victimized race of primitives from barbarism (or its near relative, slavery) to the light of Christianity and economic self-reliance. Economic progress and the civilization process would go hand in hand: as the Indian acquired the skills and economic philosophy of the white yeoman, mechanic, or small businessman, his manners would alter, and the religious philosophy of Christianity would come home to him. The emergence of the Indian (and the Negro) as an economically self-reliant Christian would make him unobjectionable as a full and equal citizen in a community of white Christians; and from tolerance, American society would move to an all-embracing commitment to the ideal of a democracy of equal freemen, whose variant racial stocks merely ornamented their common humanity.[24]

The industrial paternalism of the Gilded Age had two different and politically antagonistic tendencies or "moods." Adams speaks for the hardheaded and "masculine" style of paternalism, emphasizing the sternness of necessity in an industrial and urban economy characterized by conflict and scarcity; and emphasizing in consequence a more rigid and authoritarian form of social discipline. The style of the "philanthropic" party or tendency was rather different. It invoked the perfectionist idealism and high expectations characteristic of the prewar reform movements, and tended to take a benign view of human nature and the prospects for economic prosperity. Where hardheaded progressives projected scenarios of social conflict and repression, "philanthropists" saw class relations as involving the gentle tutelage of inferior races/classes by the superior. At bottom, both agreed on the essential doctrine of white male supremacy and the necessity (in the present) for a regime in which the dependent races/classes would be treated as children and denied full civil rights. Both affirmed the need for strong institutions to administer the affairs of the nation's wards. But in southern affairs, philanthropists preferred the tutelary regime of the Freedmen's Bureau while the hardheaded men preferred to see a restoration of political power to the planter elite and its postwar additions. In Indian affairs the hardheads preferred the army as administrator of tribal matters, while the philanthropists marshaled behind the slogans of the "Quaker" or Peace Policy, which aimed at making reservations into schools for civilization. Thus although there were common or convergent tendencies in the ideologies of these two sections of the political elite, there were also sharp divisions on matters of policy.

This situation made for partnerships that might have seemed odd when viewed from a prewar perspective. Northerners like Charles Francis Adams and E. L. Godkin, who had been staunchly against slavery and secession, found themselves making common cause with spokesmen for a renascent southern regime based on the supremacy of the planters. Southern sentimental apologists for slavery could, in the face of the Gilded Age's rampant exploitation of the weak, deploy the prewar slavocrat critique of capitalism on behalf of the oppressed.[25]

Stated in the abstract, there was little to differentiate the ideology of the reformed Indian program from the policies promulgated as far back as the 1820s. As in earlier times, the program was based on the Jeffersonian conception of economic evolution: the barbaric hunting culture, character- ized by nomadism, government-by-custom, and collective ownership, must give way to the agrarian society of settled farmers, living under institu- tionalized law, and holding their property as individuals. Only when private property and its concomitants of individual and religious liberty are estab- lished can higher forms of civilization and social organization be achieved. Nor was the reform insistence on civilian control an innovation; since 1849 the Indian Bureau had been removed from control of the War Department, to the army's lasting chagrin. The difference lay partly in the seriousness with which a major political interest group addressed itself to the problem, and in the dependence of the Republican administration on that group's support. Moreover, the political climate created by emancipation gave a liberal conception of nurturing the Indians toward civilization a broader popular appeal than at any time previously. Underpinning the movement was a sense of optimism generated by the victory of 1865 and the electoral triumph of 1868. This optimism was all the more potent as applied to the Indian question, because the accelerated growth of the western terri- tories had increased the disparity between the embattled races to the point where it appeared—especially from the distance of Boston or Philadelphia— that the hostile Indian was merely the pathetic remnant of a "dying race," more pitiable than fearful.[26]

Thus empowered by public opinion and the favor of Grant, the re- formers put into operation the Peace Policy or "Quaker" Policy. Indian agencies were assigned to Christian missionaries of various sects (a large number of whom were Quakers). The agencies were to provide Indians with instruction in agriculture and manual skills, English and Christianity. To guarantee a constituency for these civilizing missions, a systematic reservation system was adopted. In exchange for an annuity, payable in cash or food, clothing, seeds, and farm implements, Indian tribes promised to cease roaming after the buffalo and to place themselves under the tute- lage of the agent and the paternal care of the government. Their right to the reserved land was guaranteed against white encroachment; but the corollary was that members found off the reservation might be considered as "hostile," and eligible for attack by the military. Reservations had existed before 1869, but there had never been so systematic an effort to turn the reservation into a school for citizens and farmers.

Moreover, the scandal of the old Indian Bureau had involved the cor- ruption of its agents, who used their position to sell off or lease tribal lands to white speculators and to engross profits intended for the benefit of their charges. Measures were enacted to prevent this occurring in the future—but these generally proved inadequate.

Although the Peace Policy apparently prospered for two or three years, its efforts were ultimately nullified by its own weaknesses and the greed of its friends and enemies. The central tenet of the policy was the replacement of the tribal collective by an institutionally democratic polity, based on individual ownership of lands. As Commissioner of Indian Affairs E. P. Smith said, "A fundamental difference between Barbarians and a civilized people is the difference between a herd and an individual." Pursuit

of this goal led to the destruction of existing patterns of tribal government, to the demoralization of the community, reflected in the reduction of tribal nomads to beggary, alcoholism, and anomie, and to the discrediting of those Indians who exercised real power in their tribe. Many of these chiefs had tried to get their fellows to abandon a futile warpath and adapt to agrarian ways—Red Cloud and Spotted Tail in the 1870s, and Sitting Bull in the 1880s are examples of traditional tribalists who left off warring voluntarily and tried to adapt. But for all their accommodations, the great weakness of the old Indian policy remained: Indians occupied lands that were desired by expanding railroads, land-hungry farmers, speculators, and miners; and from these came an unremitting pressure for extinction of their land titles, reduction of reservations, and even extermination of the Indians themselves.[27]

In this climate, all reforms of the methods of Indian landholding and land selling resulted only in the corruption of the agents and the reduction of the Indians' economic base. But a major part of the problem lay in ideology. The commitment to breaking up tribal holdings into individual allotments looked toward the establishment of true private ownership; but this would permit the Indians to sell their land outright, or to be bullied into the sale by any of the techniques used on white or black farmers by speculators and land companies. To protect the Indian by restricting his right of sale would be to betray the ideal of true "self-reliance" which, in nineteenth-century terms, implied the right to ruin yourself and starve. The oscillations of Indian policy on this question indicate that there was no resolution of this problem forthcoming—only a fluid situation in which speculators could profit while Indian leaders could find no clear direction to safety.

Perhaps the final flaw in the policy lay in its assumption of the absolute superiority of all features of white culture to all aspects of Indian culture, and its arrogation of absolute paternal power to bring about its own resolution of the Indian-white disputes. Rather than accepting the tribe as the fundamental social-economic unit and working out a program for tribal development of reserved lands, the policy attacked and ruined tribal structure and the sustaining concepts of moral and personal value that were supported by tribalism. These were replaced with nothing: since Indians could not be trusted to govern themselves, there could be no Indian government; since Indians could not farm, they could not be permitted to hold good land when whites required it, and hence their reserves grew ever smaller and less arable. The culmination of this tendency came in 1871, at the reformers' height of influence, with the passage of the Indian Bill denying the tribes the status of "dependent nations."

Given this sort of conviction on the part of its advocates, the Peace Policy could not be sustained when confronted with a choice between meeting the demands or needs of the Indians and the requirements of "development" of the territory. Both Walker, the reform Indian Bureau chief, and the anti-Indian General Sherman saw the completion of the railroad as the "final solution" to the Indian question, or at least "the beginning of the end"; and among the tasks the Bureau set for itself was that of negotiating Indian acceptance of the completion of the Northern Pacific. Thus the "reformed" Indian Bureau found itself in the same contradictory position as its predecessor, acting simultaneously as the protector of Indian holdings and the disburser of Indians lands to developers. As in the operation of Homestead policy, Reconstruction policy, and labor reform, the liberal program split on the contradiction between industrial imperatives and the moral imperatives of philanthropy and agrarian democracy; and resolved the split by sacrificing the latter to the former. The Indian "underclass" were to be sacrificed—"temporarily"—until a period of labor, tutelage, and subordination rendered them fit for full citizenship in an industrial society.[28]

When the discovery of gold in the Black Hills renewed public interest in the project of taking land away from the tribes of the northern plains, these contradictions surfaced. Walker's successors as Indian commissioner did not share his ideological commitment to eventual Indian self-government; and when economic interests conflicted with existing concepts of Indian rights, the commissioners urged their effective abrogation. In the case of the Black Hills, as we shall see, Commissioner Smith would make the argument that the Indians did not have the same entitlement to property as the white man who sought to develop it, because as savages they were incapable of using it productively and unwilling to tolerate its productive use by others. Yet Smith urged the forced sale of the Hills while being himself fully convinced that this was the only part of the reservation on which the Indians could successfully pursue life as farmers. The decision created a sinister double bind, in which the material basis for Indian farming was destroyed at the same time that the Indian's capacity to learn farming was being touted as the test of the race's ability to become civilized. The policy reflects both the cynicism of the Bureau, and its persistent belief in the immutability of savage racial characteristics.[29]

The policy choices facing officials in Washington in 1868–75 tended to foster the polarization of attitudes on the question. Those who favored the Peace Policy, emphasizing the peaceful settlement of white-Indian disputes and a gradual assimilation of the tribes to modern American life, were pressured by the arguments of the exterminationists into down-playing all evidence of Indian hostility, and giving emphasis instead to the responsibility of white settlers and officials for provoking violence. Indeed, these self-proclaimed "Friends of the Indian" refused to acknowledge that murders committed by Indians could in fact be motivated by a general hostility to the reservation system, and they tended, therefore, to deny the significance of crimes actually committed against settlers and travelers. This tendency ultimately discredited them, first of all with Westerners who had experience of Indian violence (or knew those who had). But the reformers were also wrong about the depth of opposition to the reservation system that existed within the tribes, and that became more potent as the maladministration of Indian affairs and provocative land seizures by whites continued. When these tendencies produced a general war, the Friends found themselves defending the enemy—it was a "copperhead" position whose legal or ethical correctness was no antidote to the hostility of the general public.

Distortions were equally great on the exterminationist side. In their demand for speedy resolution of white-Indian conflicts through Indian subjugation, they made a Peace Policy impossible from the start. Their position demanded the strictest interpretation of the legal definition of Indians as "wards of the nation," and of the racialist characterization of the Indians as permanent inferiors. This precluded any serious recognition of the political and economic rights of Indian communities, in particular the permanent vesting of reservation lands in Indian possession and the right of the tribes to enforce treaty law on Indian land. To accept these Indian rights would have meant delay in obtaining those valuable tracts that were needed by railroads and desired by miners or farmers; it would have delayed or prevented the punishing of Indians actually guilty of crimes against whites, since it was presumed that Indian judges would be as permissive with their guilty brethren as whites were in cases of interracial murder. Yet without permitting some such leeway to Indian self-government, it was impossible that the Indians should regard the reservation as anything other than an open-air prison; and under such a regime, their political expression would inevitably be pressured toward the recrudescence of social violence.

But the exterminationists were in a far better position than the Friends to weather the public storm over the outbreak of an Indian war. Such wars invalidated the predictions of the Friends, but they proved the prophecies of the exterminationists to be valid.

Critiques of both positions were numerous at the time, and the debate has persisted. One of its peculiar features is that the original ideological division has tended to be reproduced in subsequent debates, even among historians. That this is so may be because the issues are not simply of antiquarian interest, but reflect ongoing ideological differences. Some of these arise directly from the persistence of the "Indian question," which, far from "vanishing," is livelier now than it has been since the New Deal. But the ideology of Indian policy also reflects the values and presuppositions we tend to bring to the general problem of dealing with unassimilated racial and ethnic minorities—do we foster their cultural independence and political autonomy, or compel them (gently or firmly) into assimilation? The Indian policy debate recurs in something very like its original form when we confront the problem of crime associated with the underclass that our unassimilated minorities are compelled to inhabit: debates on "crime in the streets" tend to reproduce such mythic figures as the permissive liberal, for whom the responsibility of society outweighs the guilt of the accused; and the hard-liner, for whom the best way with the dangerous classes involves "shoot first" policies and mandatory death sentences.

The great difference between these modern debates on "crime" and the older Indian question is that, because of the Indian's status as a member of a politically autonomous entity (albeit a weak and half-subjugated one), it was deemed logical to categorize all crimes committed by Indians as social acts, that is, as acts of war. It was from this logic that the exterminationist case took off and compelled the Friends to deny the reality of white-Indian violence in the West. In fact, there probably was a good deal of violence perpetrated by Indians—even reservation Indians—against isolated whites. But there were other regions in which the law was similarly lax or lacking, in which other kinds of criminals committed similar deeds. But urban criminals or western bandits like the James gang were not associated with a distinct social entity engaged in political conflict with the government; and therefore it was not proposed that the population of western Missouri be exterminated, or that the army ride through Five Points shooting anyone found on the streets after dark. If the shapers of Indian policy had conceived of Indian violence as mere crime, and had sought justice through means acceptable to the Indians themselves, the self-fulfilling prophecy of inevitable war might have been averted. But this would have required a postponement of the carrying out of economic and political projects which Americans of that time were unwilling to accept; and it would have required the acceptance of Indian tribes as legitimate governments.

The analogy of war with crime deserves further attention. The war/crime distinction is crucial first of all for registering the level of perceived threat associated with a particular group. But it has practical significance as well when applied to the making of policy. The consequences of the difference are suggested by the responses of a popular newspaper like the New York *Herald* to the phenomena of actual KKK violence against blacks and the threat of a new uprising by Plains Indians in 1874. The *Herald* placed the Klan's lynching of blacks under the rubric of "crime": in the first instance, the "crime" was that of a black man against a white man or woman; and in the second, the summary murder of the black accused by a mob was in the nature of a crime of passion or temporary insanity. The *Herald* would not entirely exculpate the lynchers, but would take a liberal view of their motives and offer a general pardon, "telling them to 'go and sin no more.' " At the same time, it urged the doctrine that acts of pillage and murder committed by individual Indians should be punished by attacking the tribe as a whole: "there should be but one policy [in such a case]— Extermination."[30]

The perception of the Indians as both an alien race and a politically self-willed social entity created a context in which crime became an act of social violence or war. So long as groups of white criminals lacked that kind of social and political identification, their actions could be seen as individual aberrations and punished accordingly. But when criminals are perceived as members of a "dangerous class," their actions are set in a context just like that of the Indian, and the society's response to them takes on the character of warfare. During the Civil War, the family clans who later formed the James and Younger gangs served as Confederate guerrillas, and in that capacity they committed robberies and murders as well as participating in conventional military actions against regular troops. The response of the federal authorities in Missouri was to attempt precisely the kinds of measures later employed against the Indians: an order was issued that all law-abiding folk were to come in to towns and forts where the army could keep an eye on them, and those who stayed off the reservation would be considered as hostile. Soldiers enforced the ban by imprisoning civilians, including women and children, and by burning out the farmsteads of the region—an action later paralleled by the extermination of the buffalo to starve the Indians into surrender. The Reconstruction South similarly invoked this pattern to justify a military or terrorist response by both the "Black Reconstruction" regimes and the KKK or Citizens' Leagues: individual crimes were seized as pretexts for general attacks on an entire party, community, or race. Finally, as we will see, this situation was reproduced in the cities, when the rise of labor unionization coupled with the immiseration of the proletariat by the Depression of 1873 caused many Americans to see the working class as a dangerous class, and as an incipient Red Commune like that of Paris in 1871.

The debates on the postwar Indian policy centered on the theme of racial incompatibility, and on the scenarios of genocidal violence "inevitably" arising from unlimited racial competition for land and wealth. But the models of systems capable of imposing rational limits on such competition and reducing the savage to respect for civilized order (if not to participation in it) were derived from the long history of debate on slavery, the question of Negro "character," and the political status of "dependent labor" of all kinds. The coercive and quasi-military system of labor discipline developed to deal with freedmen during the Civil War was not carried over in that same form into the postwar era. But the essential premises about the nature and necessity of disciplining a dependent work force were generalized into a doctrine suited to the needs of both northern industrialists and the new proprietors of southern plantations and mills.

At the heart of this new concept of labor relations was the belief that the new forms of business enterprise required a distinct division of power between owner/manager and worker—a division conceived of as relatively permanent, founded in a difference of natural endowment, and entitling the manager to exercise coercion to maintain the new order. The military government envisioned by Adams reappeared—generalized and expanded upon—in postwar proposals for ordering the life and labor of dependent classes: blacks in the South, the northern proletariat, female and child workers, and western Indians. The policies adopted for dealing with these groups reflected the convergence of ideological themes originally different in emphasis: the prewar mystique of the plantation (and factory) as a paternalist utopia; the mystique of "savage war"; and the analogy between the class identity of lower-class whites and the racial identity of "savages."[31]

In these circumstances, the new Indian policy provided some of the basic concepts and policy options that were, in turn, adopted by those dealing with the labor problem. Harrison's view of the new proletariat, we will recall, drew heavily on the concept of "savage" character and "racial" aliens, and both Harrison and Brace were careful to point out that these savage traits, while not necessarily inbred, could become so after first being induced by industrial poverty. The white man could, under industrialism, degenerate in the direction of the savage; and from this fate he had to be rescued. Labor under a rigorous but fair and equitable regime (rather than a purely exploitive one) was seen as redeeming it from a descent into "animalism."

Walker's work on the labor question applied a similar theory of the necessity for coercive measures. The republic now engaged in making the transition from the agrarian life-style of subsistence farming to the more disciplined and dependent life-style of industrial labor—in which there is no "gathering" from nature's bosom, but rather the confrontation of a choice to work or to starve. Walker anticipated that the Indian's response to this transformation would be violent, and attributed that partly to the Indian's savage nature. White workmen were not savages in the strict sense, but neither were they completely integrated into the new order of civilization. Therefore Walker anticipated similar responses in the two groups—an antipathy for the new order that might very likely express itself in violence of one kind or another. He judged the Indian's response by his knowledge of working-class responses; and he informed his analysis of labor rebellion with the expectations derived from his beliefs about savages.[32]

The crux of the issue between whites and Indians, and between workers and employers, is the issue of property rights. For Walker, civilization depends absolutely upon the system of private property, for it is from the defense of property that equitable laws and liberty are said to arise. The Indian has no "gift" for property holding and cultivation, and unless he can be induced to develop one—through the circumstantial compulsion to "work or starve"—he is doomed to racial inanition or extinction. The white workingman, for his part, has been nurtured from infancy in the ideology of property rights; and with the exception of the 1867–73 interlude of philanthropic "coddling," he has also experienced the "work/starve" discipline. If after all that he chooses to reject his cultural inheritance, and to propose political expropriation—and any form of government support for strikes or control of rents and wages is seen in this light—then he forfeits his racial character and must be treated as a savage. Walker himself does not believe that this terrible logic will hold for the white proletariat; he is uncertain about the Indians, but willing to postpone judgment. However, Walker's contemporaries and successors were not so optimistic. The events of 1873–77 added to their racial and class bias a new element of economic crisis, and with it the infusion of new economic interests and imperatives. These led to a "hardening" of the ideological line against "philanthropy" and the political standing of the underclasses, the termination of Reconstruction, and the end of the Peace Policy in the Indian country.

Among the events that produced this political and ideological change was a series of dramatic developments on the plains centering on the activities of Colonel George Armstrong Custer and the Seventh United States Cavalry. Acting under secret orders, Custer had conducted a grand exploratory reconnaissance of the Black Hills, and the reports he sent back electrified the East with news of "gold among the roots of the grass," and of a garden spot among the prairies filled with sylvan groves and great meadows of wild flowers. It was, the papers said, "The New El Dorado," and it promised to renew at a stroke both the traditional promise of the agrarian Frontier and the more recent promissory notes of the Northern Pacific Railroad, which stood to profit most from the discovery. Custer was the hero of the hour—the "Boy General" of the Civil War now bid fair to become the Frémont of a new Frontier. All it would need was one last, great Indian war.

CHAPTER 15

The New El Dorado, 1874

The Black Hills controversy provides the best case for studying the interaction of western realities and Metropolitan ideologies during this crisis of industrialization. The issues that arose from the Custer expedition and the decision to take the Hills from the Indians restated in the most dramatic terms the underlying contradiction at the heart of liberal ideology: the imperatives of industrial development versus those of social justice or philanthropic reform. Journalists, editorialists, and other makers of public ideology recognized its symbolic importance for the larger problems of the time clearly, and they made the most of its potential meanings. The result was that during the crucial four-year period from the Panic of 1873 to the Great Railroad Strike of 1877, one of the most important organizing metaphors in public ideology was the Black Hills and the Myth of a new—and final—Frontier. For these reasons, it will be worthwhile to look closely at both the facts of the case and representative texts through which they were interpreted.

The Black Hills had attracted the attention of American goldhunters and army reconnaissance parties since the late 1850s, when army expeditions found traces of gold in the streams running out from them. But there was little pressure at that time for exploiting or seizing the Black Hills: the projected lines of trancontinental railroads were far off, and there were far more accessible and promising "strikes" made in Colorado, Montana, Idaho, and Nevada between 1858 and 1868. On the other hand, the Black Hills were essential to both the economic existence and the spiritual life of the most warlike of the Northern Plains tribes, the Sioux or Lakota, the Cheyenne, and the Arapaho. Even today the Hills are a uniquely fertile complex of mountains and valleys, in a region of dry prairie and badlands. The rising heads of the mountains draw rain and lightning from the clouds, creating a relatively lush and uniquely mixed local ecology; it is an area rich in rare plains resources like timber and forage for grazing animals and, consequently, rich in game. Although they came to the Hills late in the eighteenth century, the special qualities of the region affected the religious sense of the Lakota and Cheyenne; and by the mid-nineteenth century, they regarded it as "sacred ground," the hub of ceremonial life and myth as it was the hub of their wanderings through the buffalo range.[1]

At the conclusion of the Bozeman Trail war in 1868, the Lakota and Cheyenne signed a treaty by which they agreed to cease hostilities in exchange for the establishment of a huge "Great Sioux Reservation," comprising the western half of present-day South Dakota, which was to be guaranteed to the Indians in perpetuity. In addition, the treaty recognized Indian claims to a large tract of "Unceded Hunting Land" in North Dakota, Montana, and Wyoming. The duration of Indian title to this district was less clearly defined because it was assumed that the success of the reservation proper would eventually make pursuit of a nomadic buffalo-hunting life unnecessary and undesirable—if the slaughter of the buffalo did not first make it simply impossible.

The Black Hills, which lay on the border between the Unceded Lands and the Great Reservation, constituted at once a promise for the future success of the reservation policy and a threat to its existence. The promise made to the Indians entailed their being prepared for conversion from nomadic hunting to settled farming. But farming on the Dakota plains is a difficult business even with advanced techniques of dry-land cultivation. In the 1870s, most of the land appeared uncultivable, especially by those Indians who were new to farming. The Black Hills represented the largest block of readily arable land on the reservation, the essential reserve fund of land on which a successful program of conversion would ultimately have to draw.

The proposal to make the Lakota into farmers got nowhere until the decade of the eighties. Such a drastic cultural and economic change was resisted by Indian "conservatives"; but its worst enemies were the Indian Bureau and its local agents, who defaulted on promises of tutelage, the provision of tools and seeds, and—worst of all—on the provision of subsistence while the conversion was going on. In this state of affairs, the Hills (and the Unceded Lands beyond them), with their freedom from white intrusion, provided a reservoir of game animals which could be hunted by reservation Indians to supplement the inadequate diet provided by the agencies. But the benefit it provided cut two ways: it may have stayed Indian hunger, but it also undermined the reservation policy whose purpose was to fix the Indians to the agencies and to make them dependent upon the agents for subsistence. The existence of the Black Hills was thus a standing rebuke to the reservation system, a tacit argument that the old ways—still being followed by bands that refused to accept the reservation —were better than the new.[2]

The Treaty of 1868 ensured a measure of peace and safety on the plains and also promised a considerable flow of federal business to towns on the edge of the Indian country. But within two years, rumors of gold in the territory attracted speculators, prospectors, and railroad men to the idea of taking the Black Hills and Unceded Lands away from the Indians. In 1870, the army turned back a foray by the Big Horn–Black Hills Mining and Exploring Association which aimed at establishing a gold mining camp in the Hills. But this evidence of the military's willingness to enforce the Treaty of 1868 did not dampen interest in the Hills; it merely fostered a change of emphasis from mule packing in Dakota to lobbying Congress for government support.[3]

In this endeavor the gold miners had support from other, more powerful interest groups who saw in the prospect of a Black Hills gold rush a larger source of profit than panning for yellow metal could bring. The proprietors of the newly completed Union Pacific needed the increase in its business that a rush to the Black Hills would create. Like all land-grant railroads, the line had been contracted in anticipation of demand, and the sooner that demand could be developed the sooner the line would begin to show a profit. The newly commenced Northern Pacific Railroad likewise hoped for an increase of business on its route; but more than this, it needed to push the Indian reservation's borders farther back from its right-of-way (which ran just north of the Great Reservation) in order to increase the quantity of its disposable land base, to enhance its safety and its appeal to settlers, and so to increase its value as collateral for capitalization. After the collapse of 1873, this last motive became imperative, since without some such increase in its land values, the railroad could not obtain foreign loans for recapitalization. In addition to the railroads themselves, the Black Hills lobby included representatives of local business interests in Cheyenne, Yankton, and Sioux City who hoped that a Black Hills gold or land rush would make their towns prosper as entry points for emigrants, increase their business in the provision and carrying trades, and make them attractive as terminals for railroad branch lines.[4]

The lobbying efforts reached into all levels and areas of government and involved a mixture of advertising hype, ideological appeal, and outright bribery and subornation. The railroads were past masters at this sort of thing, and their corporate character allowed them to offer government officials inducements that were virtually undiscoverable—and if discovered, unpunishable—by existing laws. Juntas of local businessmen could not offer free or discounted stocks and bonds to prospective patrons, but saw in the potential increase in federal business a plethora of profit-making opportunities to take advantage of. Subcontracting for carting provisions to army garrisons, mail contracts, sutlerships at new forts, Indian agencies, post offices—all of these offered multiple opportunities for money-making, first by the corrupt sale of franchises, then by the taking of rake-offs, and latterly by the price fixing made possible by the local monopoly inherent in federally franchised operations.

Some of the projects put forward by local groups were tortuously indirect in the efforts to begin the process of breaking down the Treaty prohibitions against white incursions into the Black Hills. Charles Collins of Sioux City tried (in 1872) to lobby in behalf of a "stumpage corporation" which would pay the Indians a royalty for the cutting of timber in the Black Hills. Under cover of the woodcutting, a survey of the Hills would be made and mineral deposits located and confirmed. The appeal of a gold strike was certain to create the demand for a seizure of the Hills; and through the "stumpage corporation," the "favored friends of the administration" would be able to "secure the choicest tracts" in the Hills.[5]

The railroads had readier access to the seats of power, and they were shamelessly direct in their appeals. In 1870, Jay Cooke wrote General W. S. Hancock, commander of the military district through which the Northern Pacific would pass, ostensibly to ascertain his views on the likelihood of Indian conflict should the line be built near or through the reservation. In fact, the letter was a version of a standard lobbying document which Cooke sent to many officials laying out the arguments for government support of the Northern Pacific. The first argument restates the premises of the agrarian version of the Frontier Myth: the railroad will encourage immigration and colonization of a wasteland by farmers and so promote the spread of civilization. But Cooke went on to assert that completion of the line would enable the army to police the reservations more effectively by increasing mobility and reducing costs. Hancock's reply was frank and favorable, although he did not think that the building of the railroad would lessen the cost of policing the Indians. On the contrary, Hancock was certain that before the railroad could be built the primary surveys and extinction of Indian title would "most probably provoke their hostility . . . and lead to a war ending in their possible destruction. This war in the nature of things will occur before your road is in a condition to carry our supplies . . ." But Hancock hastened to assure Cooke that this practical objection did not in any way reduce the army's enthusiasm for the railroad, which promised inestimable advantages to the whole country; and he assured Cooke that when the Northern Pacific required protection for its surveys, "It will be our duty as well as our pleasure to give all assistance possible."[6]

Cooke's letter to Hancock was a bypassing of official channels, since it sought the kind of policy decision that would normally be made at a higher level—in the White House or the office of army commander Sherman. The personal approach was facilitated in part by the fact that Hancock was a client of Cooke's Philadelphia banking house (as was President Grant), and, hence, a person with a direct interest in Cooke's grand enterprise. Hancock's confidence that the army would support Cooke reflects the considerable autonomy the departmental commander enjoyed in the day-to-day running of his district; moreover, both Hancock and Cooke knew that the Washington bureaucracies most directly involved with the Indian question were already committed to the success of the Northern Pacific and, necessarily, to the diminution of the Great Reservation. Charles Collins claimed that in 1872 he had corresponded with Interior Secretary Columbus Delano—the man entrusted with stewardship for Indian rights—who expressed himself as favorable to the extinction of Indian title to the Black Hills. Jay Cooke was so confident that Indian title to the Hills would be extinguished that his first pamphlet promoting railroad lands (published in 1870) claimed that the government had already made its decision to do just that.[7]

This confidence in the inevitability of a seizure of Indian land derived from the confident expectation of war. Even the 1871–72 reports of Commissioner Walker anticipated some violent outbreak when the progress of the railroad and the further encroachment of civilization compelled the Indians to confront the end of their nomadic way of life. At the same time, Walker had to admit that the Indians had so far accepted the changes necessitated by reservation life, and that only a few malcontents had objected to the railroad surveys on or near their land. Walker's successor, E. P. Smith, likewise reported no evidence of general Indian hostility to the reservation plan or even to the railroad: 'The actual depredations committed by the Sioux have been comparatively few," and none of the reservation Indians had been implicated. Nonetheless, Commissioner Smith advocated the deliberate and unilateral abrogation of the 1868 treaty through the establishment of forts on the reservation—and in the Unceded Lands. Although represented as a response to Indian threats, this action would, in effect, create the conditions for an outbreak which had not materialized as expected, and of which Smith said he had as yet no evidence. The reservation's relative success to date was due in part to the hunting preserves of the Black Hills and Unceded Territory, which remained a supplemental food source and a safety valve for restless tribesmen. To extinguish Indian title to these lands, to drive off the buffalo by building railroads, or to block access by building forts would deprive the reservation of those very elements that compensated for the inefficiency and officiousness of agency administration and the inadequate supplies of food and clothing provided by the government. No wonder that under these circumstances both soldiers and Indian agents expected war—if the Indian's "racial propensities" did not bring it about, the loss of hunting lands certainly would.[8]

The army, too, had its designs on the Hills. Sheridan had long wished to locate a fort there as a central base of operations to control the Great Reservation and the wandering Sioux of the Unceded Lands. Moreover, the long-standing feud between the War and Interior departments for control of the Indian Bureau had recently expressed itself in a second source of rivalry: the contest to control future government exploration and survey expeditions in the West. In the summer of 1873 the War Department and the Department of the Interior had competitive surveying expeditions in the field, the former under Lieutenant George Wheeler and the latter headed by the renowned geologist Ferdinand V. Hayden. The two vied for newspaper headlines, and duplicated efforts by mapping each other's territory. As in the case of the struggle over the Indian Bureau, the competition for control of the surveys had a good deal to do with the indirect benefits accruing to those conducting expeditions. Hayden had made a national reputation akin to that of Frémont on the basis of his reports; and since the content of the surveys was of direct use to mining, railroad, and land interests, those in charge might expect financial benefits as well, either in the form of early investment opportunities, kickbacks, or later employment by the exploiting corporations.[9]

But the army's deepest interest in the Black Hills had less to do with gold and government surveys than with its desire to control the conduct of Indian policy. We must distinguish here between two kinds of motives within the army bureaucracy. The control of Indian affairs, through temporary or permanent militarization of the Indian Bureau, carried perquisites like the right to grant contracts to suppliers, to appoint administrators and agents, to dispose of Indian lands. In that age of political corruption, the Indian Bureau was a rich prize, and control of even a few reservations was lucrative enough for generals, railroad presidents, and government officials to risk discovery in acts of bribery and influence peddling. On the other hand, under the Interior Department, Indian affairs were indeed badly mismanaged—badly enough to create the conditions for war. It was, therefore, the judgment of professional soldiers like Sherman and Sheridan that the army should prepare itself for war by building forts in or near the reservations—despite the violence thereby done to formal treaties.

The crucial determinant of the decision to enter the Black Hills was the belief of Sherman and Sheridan that diminution of the Great Sioux Reservation and an Indian war were inevitable. They shared General Hancock's emotional and ideological commitment to the doctrine of progress and his faith that the railroads were the agency of expanding civilization. They saw the Indian as savage by nature and unchangeable in character, bound despite reason and self-interest to resist the coming of white civilization. Given this premise, they concluded that Custer's expedition must arouse the Indians instantly to war. They therefore prepared him for fighting as well as exploring, providing him with cavalry, infantry, artillery, and Gatling guns—a small army, comparable in size and armament to the Dakota Column of 1876 of which Custer's ill-fated command would be a part. That the expedition would lead to extinction of Indian title and a war of extermination against the Sioux were so much an expectation as to appear, to the generals if not to Grant himself, something like deliberate policy.[10]

The secret history of the Black Hills expedition, with its sordid commercial and bureaucratic maneuverings, was concealed behind an elaborate ideological facade. This facade was erected primarily to persuade public opinion; but it also served to mask the moral status and consequences of their actions from the "insiders" themselves. Collins seems to have been a shameless rascal who delighted (after the fact) in boasting about his cleverness in circumventing the laws, bilking and manipulating public officialdom, and provoking a bloody Indian war for profit. But Cooke, Hancock, Grant, and Walker preferred to see themselves as the agents of a genuine moral and progressive enterprise, compelled by circumstances to get their hands a bit dirty (and of course willing to take a reasonable bit of profit from the exchange), but not fundamentally corrupt.

They masked their actions in the imagery of the Frontier Myth. Cooke's railroad propaganda deployed every bit of Gilpinian nature mysticism and statistical legerdemain that could be assimilated; and it linked railroad agrarianism to the larger theme of the racial struggle between savages and Anglo-Saxons for control of the future. The profit of a bribe from an enterprise of such symbolic appeal must have been all but irresistible: the perfect combination of vile lucre and moral uplift. Collins used the same kind of symbolism in making his appeal for the interests of little Sioux City; but where Cooke worked the bureaucratic side of the street, Collins worked the "populist" side. He presents emigration to the Black Hills as a drama of racial strife and as an occasion for regenerating the Democratic spirit of the Jacksonians. He attacks the reservation system for conferring upon a race lacking in the progressive quality of ambition a privileged "monopoly":

> Right-thinking people with no axes to grind, ask the question, why a country one-third larger than the entire settled portion of the United States, and admitted to be so well adapted to supporting

and supplying the wants of millions of people, should be withheld from those who are now taxed to support the uncivilized hordes who now monopolize it for hunting grounds.

The opening of the Hills will allow a new wave of pioneers to experience for themselves the regeneration of personal and social character undergone by our pioneer forebears, fitting them to rank with the hunter-heroes of legend. The opportunity is priceless—all the more because, Collins says, it may be the last of its kind. Indeed,

> with the settlement and occupancy of the Black Hills, the opportunities for perpetuating careers like those of Daniel Boone and our other historical pioneers, will only be known through story and legend.[11]

Collins carries the logic of this Jacksonian rhetoric to its conclusion by paralleling the Indian "monopoly" with that enjoyed by the great railroad corporations—specifically the Northern Pacific. This was the same kind of linkage that underlay Jackson's simultaneous attacks in the 1830s on the Indian reservations in the South and the Monster Bank in the North. Collins cites one of Jay Cooke's pamphlets to the effect that the government is willing to extinguish Indian title for the sale of the railroad; and by asking why the same should not be done for those citizens without the capital resources and franchised privileges of Jay Cooke, Collins links his cause to the discontent of the Grangers and public disgust with the corrupt bargains between politicians and railroad corporations.[12]

Although Collins's goals were incompatible with the program of philanthropic reform mapped out by the Radical Republicans for Indian affairs, he found ways to disarm their opposition or engage their interest. Between 1866 and 1874 he was active in promoting the establishment of a "military colony" of Irish Fenians in the Black Hills, which aimed at conquering Canada and exchanging it for the freedom of Ireland. The project's mixture of Frontier agrarian expansion and the liberation of an oppressed people attracted an incredible spectrum of supporters: Gilpin endorsed it, and General Custer toasted the project at a Cleveland rally in 1866 called for the purpose of uniting conservatives against the Radical Republicans; but the archradical Ben Butler endorsed it too, along with the most noted of the Friends of the Indian, Wendell Phillips.[13]

Thus on his smaller scale Collins rivals Cooke in his ability to associate ideological opponents in a common project, by appealing to the mythological language which the contending parties share. That unity in turn facilitates agreement on the central matter of extinguishing Indian title, despite the different motives of those who contribute to the movement.

NEWSPAPERS AS MYTHMAKERS

At the bottom of the secret history of the Black Hills affair were the army, which provided the core around which the tangential interests of bureaucrats, politicians, and local businessmen revolved, and the material interests of the railroad. The public history of the event substitutes myth-ideological justifications for the economic motives of profit takers in accounting for the invasion of the Black Hills. But this public history also has its center in the material reality of economic institutions different from—though associated with—the railroad corporations. These were the institutions of mass publicity—newspapers, mass circulation journals, and books—which had been growing in size, complexity, and national circulation ever since the 1840s.

The existence of institutions of mass publicity affected the behavior and policymaking of each of the interest groups involved in the Black Hills. The railroad corporations lived and died by publicity and, therefore, devoted large portions of their dear-bought capital to printing prospectuses, advertising in journals, and suborning editors to their cause. Without such publicity, there would be no emigrants to buy their lands; no capitalists could be "sold" on the high promise of the enterprise; and politicians would feel no constituency pressure to support the railroads as a great national project. With publicity, it was possible to create a public impression of great demand for the Black Hills (or support of the railroad), even where such demand did not exist.

The media involved were journalistic—newspapers, both local and national in circulation; and magazines, ranging in price and pretension from "elite" journals like the *Atlantic* and the *Galaxy*, serious weeklies like *The Nation*, to popular and sensational magazines like *Harper's Weekly* and *Frank Leslie's Illustrated*. Since the Civil War, such enterprises had grown in number, circulation, and influence. Technological improvements had made cheap mass media feasible and speeded up the process of news gathering and dissemination, simultaneously creating a hunger for news and the means of satisfying it. Wire services during the Civil War had given readers far from the battle lines a more immediate sense of the developing crisis than any people had hitherto achieved.

The broad base of the mass media were the newspapers, most of which were still intensely localistic in orientation and circulation. Nonetheless, even local papers drew on wire services and the "national" papers for stories about the great world. Moreover, there were daily newspapers whose editorial concern and subscription lists were national in scope. These were mostly located in New York City and were led by the New York *Herald* (first of the breed) and the *Tribune*. Although these papers and their editor-publishers remained immediately engaged by the affairs of their metropolis—the Tweed Ring, for example—they were also directly engaged with the making of national economic and political policy. And although independent journalism had become an ideal of the industry, in practice most papers were tied directly to some specific interest group. Papers like the *Sun* and the *Independent* were organs of religious interest groups and spoke for them on matters of policy; other papers followed the prewar pattern of serving directly and unabashedly the interest of the particular party or faction that created them. Such a paper was the *World*, started by August Belmont as the vehicle for his own Democratic faction after the war.[14]

But a more potent force in shaping the editorial character of these papers was the fact that their editors and publishers belonged to, or soon became part of, the elite society of New York City. Whatever their nominal party alliances, the Belmonts and Manton Marbles of the *World*, Whitelaw Reid of the liberal-Republican *Tribune*, Henry Raymond of the Republican *Times*, and James Gordon Bennett of the Democratic-leaning *Herald* all inhabited the same world of wealth and position—attended each other's soirées, went to the track or on the hunt together, shared the same essentially conservative attitudes about class and race, the same sense of the crisis of their time. Looking at the personal histories of editors and correspondents in this period, one is struck by the ease with which individuals moved between the worlds of journalism, high finance, and politics. August Belmont was at once publisher of the *World*, head of the banking community, and chairman of the Democratic Party. Henry Raymond of the *Times* was Republican national chairman at the same time. Henry Villard began his career as a correspondent, but parlayed his linguistic skill and acquaintance with men of affairs into a role as international banker, financier, and railroad magnate; and Manton Marble, Whitelaw Reid, and William Eleroy Curtis went from journalism to notable political careers—Reid as nominee for vice president of the United States in 1892.[15]

The editor-publishers and their papers were divided by partisan affiliations which made them intensely antagonistic in their response to electoral choices and to specific partisan issues like the tariff and Reconstruction. Their division was not simply by party but by factions within parties which espoused "hard" or "soft" approaches to civil rights legislation, to philanthropic reforms, and to the questions of currency and loan redemption. Their particularism notwithstanding, the metropolitan editor-publishers found a basis of consensus in the ideological predispositions of their own class, which they identified as a cultural, intellectual, and professional elite. They acknowledged their ties to banking and other "monied interests"— they could not fail to do so—but they saw this as a logical and necessary outcome of their professional attainments and as a necessary means to the fulfillment of their class's special social duty. The core of their ideology was their belief that the Civil War and the industrialization of the economy had transformed the agrarian democracy of the past into a modern corporate state. The scale and complexity of both political and economic enterprise now required the rationalization of different functions and powers for the elite of managers and proprietors and the mass of workers. Like Charles Francis Adams, they envisioned their new relation to the masses as a kind of coercive paternalism—a form of tutelary care and direction, informed by the expectation of resentment.[16]

One of the cultural phenomena of the 1874–77 period is the convergence of these journals and of the factions they represent toward a common program based upon this ideology of corporatism and paternalistic coercion. That convergence never completely eliminated the bases of factional difference or ideological disagreement. Nonetheless, it did permit the operation of a limited consensus on a number of issues of central importance. The first of these was the resolution of the Black Hills affair in favor of the enemies of a reformed Indian policy. This was followed within a year by the final dismantling of Reconstruction and by broad bipartisan agreement on the measures necessary to suppress the labor uprising of 1877 and to prevent its recurrence. We can see the direction (and limits) of convergence in the Republican journals of the period: the *Tribune*'s change of editorship from Horace Greeley to Whitelaw Reid typifies the rejection of an ideology of reform philanthropy for a tough-minded assertion of the privileges of capital. Reid soft-pedaled his paper's commitment to the Peace Policy and Reconstruction, although his commitment to the Republican Party precluded a complete break with the Grant administration. Nonetheless, the *Tribune* was willing to expose the "horrors" of "Negro government" in the South; and it could give its conservative impulses full rein in opposing the activities of labor organizers and "philanthropy" directed at the new proletariat of New York.[17]

The consensual ground toward which papers like the *Times* and *Tribune* moved in this period was already occupied by the newspapers of the conservative "hard money" Democrats, most notably Bennett's *Herald* and the *World*, edited by Manton Marble and owned by August Belmont.

Although its form and institutional character were in a sense typical of the metropolitan daily of the time, the *World* is not a "typical" paper from the political standpoint. It was the organ of the Belmont wing of the Democratic Party—conservative, prosouthern, generally "hard money," wary of immigrants but dependent on their votes, violently racist and anti-black. However, despite its partisan character, the *World* provides a very good index to the ideology of conservatives in both parties on the deeper social issues that underlay partisan politics: divided on the Grant record, they were united in their understanding of the need for returning the South to white rule, for restoring the nation's credit through hard-money policies, for restraint from excessive intervention in the affairs of the poor, and for suppressing the uprising of labor against the discipline of the factory and the depression.[18]

In practice and in the context established by the "philanthropic" reforms of 1865–73, this orientation implied a program of reaction, an undoing of the positive gains made by blacks in the area of civil rights, a limitation on the freedom of workers to organize and strike, a check on the movement of women for political and economic liberties—and, in the West, an undoing of the attempt to preserve intact the tribal polity and landed heritage of the reservation Indians. In the face of the rising militancy of workers, women, blacks, and Indians, this ideology likewise implied advocacy of authoritarian repression by the systematic application of violence: by the military in the case of Indians and strikers, by vigilantes or state authorities in the case of the South. This general ideological orientation provided the framework through which the newsworthy events of 1874 were passed by publisher-editors and their staffs.[19]

Although the publisher-editors of nineteenth-century daily newspapers exercised more direct personal control over style, content, and organization than corresponding figures on modern newspapers, their journals' content depended not only on editorial choice but on the pressure of "real events." The editor could exercise editorial control through his power to assign stories—in some instances even sending out reporters to "create" newsworthy events—and through the power to censor stories by field correspondents on receipt. Together with the composing staff, he could affect the context of stories by setting a given story physically next to another story or group of stories; and by having it headlined in such a way as to emphasize particular elements, tie the particular story to others, and so on. The editor's function can therefore be seen as a nineteenth-century analog of the *auteur*–movie director—providing a shaping intelligence and overall direction to a complex collective enterprise, shaping without absolutely controlling. We can therefore look at the juxtapositions of stories, the borrowings of language from one sort of story to define a response to another, and the relationship of story content to value-assigning headlines and editorials, and see in these the building blocks by which a newspaper, in this case the *World*, presents its mythically valued rendering of current events.

In 1874–76 four story lines figure preeminently in the pages of the *World*. Its interest in restoring the prewar hegemony of conservative Democratic planters in the South disposed the *World* editorialists and reporters to give continuous coverage to the "breakdown of society" under the black Republicans Grant had imposed on Dixie. In covering the "southern story," the *World* worshipfully invokes the traditional literary myth of the antebellum South, and it uses the region as its most explicit case against egalitarianism and philanthropy and for coercive paternalism toward the lower orders. Although accepting the abolition of slavery as a necessary measure of modernization, the *World* finds it unnatural that the administration should continue to refuse a "legitimate part in the restoration of social order" to the "men of ability, trained to deal with great questions of public economy, sound financiers and rational statesmen" in which the South is rich. Where "the better classes" have regained control, the South is now flourishing in "industry, capital, and character." Where philanthropy rules, the natural aristocracy is replaced by a conspiracy of "white demagogues" and "black dupes." The Republican president has "put the criminal and the ignorant above the virtuous and educated. . . . the basest above the best. . . ."[20]

Three other stories were more clearly event-centered and time-limited, and their succession on the *World*'s pages gives narrative direction to the newspaper's portrayal of 1874. The first of these was the Tompkins Square "riot" and the disorders associated with urban unemployment and crime in the depression winter of 1873–74. Like the southern story, the Tompkins Square story poses the issue of class relations in an industrial society; and the *World* resolves the complexities of the issue by treating the event as analogous to the southern Reconstruction and the outbreak of Indian hostilities in the West. The second story was the serial account of Custer's Black Hills Expedition, the results of which the *World* regards as containing the antidote to both the Reconstruction problem and the disorder of the industrial city. Finally, the account of the off-year elections of 1874 draws the culminating political moral of the succession of stories, which is that the American people are ready to repudiate the reformist philanthropy of Grant, together with his Peace Policy and black Reconstruction. What makes the political argument work is the care with which the *World* has made the diverse occurrences of the year appear to be parts of a single coherent narrative line. This is achieved through the systematic assimilation of each story to a common language of mythic metaphor.

The symbol of the savage is the basic value-giving term in this language. In its most obvious application, the symbol identifies a racial group which is seen as more primitive and brutal than the Anglo-Saxon and innately prone to resist civilization and progress. More subtly, the term identifies a set of qualities possessed not only by Indians but by groups within society and partly assimilated to it. Blacks are one such group, but there are also "primitive" groups among the whites. Children are seen as being like savages in some respects until they have been completely socialized; and women are seen as domesticated savages sharing in the dependent status of children. The *World* makes these beliefs mutually reinforcing by systematically associating stories of Reconstruction disorder with Indian outbreaks, Indian outbreaks with urban crime, and each of these with the breakdown of paternal authority under the regime of Radical Reconstruction.

There are generally two devices for effecting the association. The most common—and the least explicit—is by the pairing of news stories through a strong visual juxtaposition: placing them side by side, running them sequentially in a single column, or setting them as "bookends" framing the front page. These visual juxtapositions are usually underscored by a common verbal element or closely related thematic content: for example, both stories might use the words "war" or "savage" or "race" in the main headlines or in a main-and-subhead combination; or they might deploy the thematic association of conflict ("war" and "strife" or "massacre") or racial division ("black" or "Negro" and "redskin" or "reds"). At crucial intervals, the editorial page will take up the issues posed by the news of the day and make a more systematic and explicit relation between the different stories: for example, after some days of Indian conflicts and Reconstruction disorders, an editorial might openly associate the savagery of the Indians with the actions of southern Blacks. The editorial page is the most important part of the newspaper's ideology-making machinery because it translates the "facts" of history into political imperatives. But the editorial page devices work only because the news pages have prepared readers for the association of certain groups of facts. This is also accomplished by a daily linkage of small items no one of which can be considered a major story but which collectively compose a web of associations that support the paper's interpretation of the major stories.

To bring the Indian and Reconstruction analogies home to its New York audience and to extend the range of ideological reference, the *World* associates black/Indian stories with instances of urban crime or "savagery." Since the ideological preference of the editors is for a paternal regime, these crime stories often center on the acts of children (or of blacks displaced into northern cities). Thus an editorial on the "Redemption" of Virginia from its Reconstruction government is paired with an editorial on corporal punishment in the schools titled "Resumption of the Rod." The pairing makes an equation between the government of schoolrooms by adults and the government of a state by its "best classes." Although it was conventional to justify "Redemption" by comparing traditional southern government to a good patriarchal family, in this case, the metaphor runs the other way: the struggle through which the southern elite reestablished its dominion is offered as a model to the urban schoolmaster who (in his present incarnation) may not be up to the task of disciplining the children of free-born Americans: "Principals of the public schools must hereafter be men of nerve and muscle, cautious about entering into a quarrel and once entered into it, resolute unto victory." In short, the problem of the northern elite is that they have followed the Grant/philanthropist model rather than that of the Southerner and the soldier. As a result of this "coddling," the children have run wild: both the literal children of the urban classroom and the figurative child classes who labor in factories and plantations or swarm about the Indian agencies.[21]

The structure of the analogy and the polemic is completed in an editorial called "Maudlin Mercy," which graphically illustrates the horrific results that follow when philanthropic illusions triumph over a realistic appreciation of the character of savages. The editorial concerns "a young werewolf—a creature in the shape of a boy" who had been taken by the Boston police after a series of atrocious child-murders. After luring younger boys to a secluded spot, this fiend had tortured them to death "with a barbarity worthy of an apache."

> People who shrink from the facts of human nature, who refuse to
> believe in the incurable ferocity of certain tribes of savages, con-
> ceived themselves to be doing their duty to society when they sent
> this detestable little monster to a state reform school.

The *World* would rather he had been executed, despite his being a child and insane, because to show any leniency toward the child-savage is to arouse him to more ambitious deeds of destruction.[22] The *World*'s defense of paternal authority begins with the homely imagery of schoolmasters, rods, and spoiled children; but as the metaphor unfolds the child becomes the savage, the rod an application of deadly force, and the schoolmaster a figure torn between kindly philanthropy and the rigor of forcible repression.

This example suggests something of the content and form of the cultural grid through which the *World*'s editorialists interpreted the events of 1874. Although it is possible to abstract and schematize both the partisan character of their credo and its larger ideological dimension—their unabashed anti-Republican and antiphilanthropism; their managerial elitism; their modeling the distinction of social class on the "immutable" symbols of race and sex—to present their ideology in this form would in a sense be to misrepresent it. Popular ideology of this kind was (and is) as much the product of an opportunistic response to real-world events as it was a preconceived system. Indeed, the full articulation of that system was made possible only by the series of historical crises through which American culture passed, which tested, discredited, clarified, and hardened the various ideological tendencies—corporate and entrepreneurial, socialist/philanthropic and laissez-faire—that contended for American allegiance.

To see how this ideology was produced, reproduced, and transformed *in situ*, we need only to observe how its makers responded to the unpredictable course of public events of 1874, from the Tompkins Square "riot" at the start of the year, to the Black Hills expedition in its middle, to the intensifying social and political crisis at its close. And by doing so we shall witness how one newspaper constructed a comprehensive and coherent fable—history with a moral—out of the chaos of events.

THE "RED SPECTRE OF THE COMMUNE"

It was the story of an outbreak of "urban savagery" that provided the *World* with its first major event-centered story sequence of 1874. In January, the workingmen's organizations of New York had called for a large public meeting in Tompkins Square to protest the failure of the city and the business classes to provide for the unemployed during the severe depression winter of 1873–74. Beyond protest, the organizers looked toward some means to relieve the immediate distress of the unemployed and at political measures for reviving trade and employment. The collapse of the economy after the financial panic of September 1873 had found the city's charitable institutions completely unprepared for the unprecedented numbers thrown out of work and home. But the city's financial and political leadership feared that such a meeting would lead to a violent outbreak like the draft riots of 1863 or to unacceptable political demands on the freedom of capital —the use of taxation for relief, for example, or the compulsion of employers to retain workers rather than laying them off. There was in any case a strong ideological objection to the concept of relief itself and a belief that the rigors of unemployment were a necessary and salutary discipline for the working classes. The *World*, like other "popular" papers, at first opposed the meeting and finally called for its suppression by the police as a "communist agitation."[23]

In a sequence of news stories and editorials beginning in September 1873 (before the Panic), the *World* had consistently paired or otherwise linked stories of working-class agitation with stories of impending trouble on Indian reservations. For example, the editorial page of September 4, 1873, juxtaposes an article on a battle between the Sioux and the Pawnee with an account of squabbles between opposing factions in the Socialist International. Beginning in mid-January 1874, this analogy is developed intensively and in detail. The ideological essentials are laid down in an editorial on "Our Indian Policy," published on January 18—and juxtaposed with editorials about the flurry of violent disorders associated with Tompkins Square and with the "Mollie Maguire" agitation in the Pennsylvania coalfields. Since the language of this editorial is also the language later deployed against the workingmen, it is worth quoting key sections, which also offer the *World*'s reading of the history of America's westward movement in clear, racialist terms:

> The sentimental politicians who are fond of reminding us that we are interlopers on this continent and that the whole of it belonged

to the Indians, have never yet attempted to carry their theory to its logical result in action. If the Indians have rights superior to our own, the thing for us to do is to retire from the continent and leave it to the Indians, unless we can acquire it on terms perfectly satisfactory to them . . . In point of fact the country never belonged to the Indians in any other sense than it belonged to the wolves and bears, which white settlers shoot without mercy and in extreme cases even offer a bounty for. We treat the Indians differently, upon the theory that they are accessible to the promptings of interest and fear, and can be made to abstain from depredations without being shot on sight. But the course which has been pursued with them, not according to any legislative or executive device, but according to the necessities of civilization, is the only just one.

This being the case, the Indian has three alternatives: to accept integration into the laboring or farming mass (which goes against his nature); to acquiesce in his removal "to such remote regions as are not needed for the maintenance of civilized man," with the understanding that *when* that land becomes necessary for civilized man the removal will be repeated; or to resist that continued removal, and be punished by death. "The country is not yet so crowded that the Indian must be told to work or die"; a Frontier of unused land still exists into which he can be displaced. But it is now "so crowded that he must be told to behave himself or die," and the day of "work or die" is approaching swiftly.[24]

In the threat that "crowding" will require men to "work or die"—the threat implicit in the idea of the closing of the Frontier—the Indian's situation becomes parallel with that of the urban laborer. For the city *is* nearly that crowded, and the "necessities of civilization" require the maintenance of industrial production. Thus the urban worker faces now the radical choice which will come to the Indian after the Frontier is utterly gone: the choice between working, starving, or dying in futile rebellion. The issue is pointed up in a pair of editorials on January 28 which parallel a discussion of "Starvation Wages" in the city with the actual starvation of the Chippewa on their reservation in Minnesota.[25] The Indian case reveals the folly of intervention by a philanthropically minded government in the natural course of events: the system has ended by corrupting both the savage and the Indian agent (who in this case starved his charges by stealing their food allotments). The editorial avoids evoking sympathy for the Indian victims by treating the whole incident with a lumbering facetiousness. The editorial on the Chippewa eventually arrives at the same conclusion envisioned in "Our Indian Policy," but mixes its comedy with a bit of Social Darwinism:

Mr. GRANT and Secretary DELANO deserve credit for a new, neat, and economical method of solving the Indian problem . . . If the Indians do not eat each other, all will die of famine; if they do take to cannibalism, it is only a question of time, and the survival of the fattest will not be for many moons.[26]

For the urban workers, the starvation theme has a different application. As citizens of the Metropolis, they must directly and seriously choose between work and starvation; and legislative intervention to relieve them will be as unnatural and as productive of crime and anarchy as the Indian policy: "Legislators have interfered to protect American labor . . . The result is what we see."

> A great proportion of the depression and its attendant miseries is due to the human stupidity and arrogance which have undertaken to change the laws of nature by the embodiment of themselves in the legislation . . . Every man is capable to do something which the world wants enough to keep him alive while he is doing it. If he will not do that something he ought to starve.[27]

This is a difficult doctrine for a newspaper and a political party to hold, when its readership and constituency is largely drawn from the lower middle class and the laboring classes themselves. The *World* was thus compelled to register the anger of its constituency, and it did so in a series of articles on the horrible conditions under which workers in the city were living.[28] These muckraking articles established the paper's bona fides as advocate of the working man, and then, in turn, the *World* used that status to give credibility to its resistance to all measures of relief and reform. Recognizing that possession of the ballot as a nominal route to political power constituted the most effective safety valve for underclass discontent, the *World* sought to discredit the use of political power to effect reform by linking such action with the criminality, hypocrisy, and racial disloyalty of the Republican "philanthropists." It did so by exposing the sort of people who provided "Free Soup" and called for suspension of house rent as the same as those who "coddled" and degraded the "redskins" and the "niggers." But it was also necessary to suggest that those people who attended the soup kitchen and demonstrated for suspension of house rent were themselves less like whites than like Indians and blacks—otherwise the readership might identify itself with the dangerous classes rather than the class of property and order. Thus the muckraking portraits of urban poverty were offset by stories and editorials about "The Abuse of Soup-Houses" by lazy workmen, asserting that there was "Plenty of Work But No Workers" and that the clamorous poor were "People Who Are Paupers by Profession." When workingmen organized against the landlords whose malfeasance the *World* had exposed, the newspaper warned them against "adopting a bullying tone towards those who are more fortunate, because, speaking generally, they are better deserving."[29]

The *World* asserted its belief that the new urban-industrial order absolutely required the subordination of the rights of workingmen—especially the right to organized political action "against" property—to the exigencies of capital and the concerns of the owner/manager class. The newspaper couched its opposition to organized labor in the traditional antimonopoly rhetoric of the Jacksonian Democracy; but where the original anathemas were leveled against all combinations in restraint of trade, the *World*'s were now exclusively directed against labor:

Civilized societies are too complex, too close in their interactions, too dependent, man upon man, class upon class, nation upon nation, for any large number of persons to unite in withdrawing their services from the sum of what political economists call exchangeable commodities or things.

Workers may not withdraw the commodity of their labor from the market; yet it remains a fundamental right of capital to dispose of workingmen whenever their inefficiency or the exigencies of trade require it. In this state of affairs, the free modern worker is assigned all of the obligations of servile or dependent labor, without acquiring in exchange any of the slave's moral and legal claim upon the continuing care and benevolence of the master.[30]

In order to defend the new interests of industrial capital against organized labor, conservative journals like the *World* had to contradict the triumphant doctrines of free labor, and undermine the tradition of liberal ideology that produced and sustained those doctrines among the "middle classes"—that large and amorphous group which was neither proletarian nor engaged in the ownership or management of an industrial enterprise. This was a difficult task, if not an impossible one. The liberal program of reform, which the *World* comprehended under the heading of "philanthropy," was rooted deeply in both democratic political theory and in Christian moral idealism. Its traditional appeal as a philosophy was augmented by its prestige as the faith which had provided the moral sinews of the victorious Union.

The only tradition of near equal weight to which it could appeal was the ideology of racialism, which had been for generations the great counterpoise to democratic egalitarianism. By deploying the racialist language of popular mythology against "philanthropism," it was possible to invoke this countertradition without having to mount an explicitly antidemocratic platform. Papers like the *World* therefore attacked liberalism by presenting "philanthropists" in the role of the "renegade" in traditional fables of racial, sexual, and social warfare. They are shown as deluded or fanatical characters, who put the interests and welfare of aliens and savages ahead of the concerns of their own white race and its civilization. At best, their character is like that of Cooper's David Gamut (*Last of the Mohicans*) or Hetty Hutter (*Deerslayer*)—naive to the point of idiocy about the capacities of savages to attain civilization. At worst, they are like the French Jesuit priests in Parkman's histories, like Simon Girty in the Daniel Boone narratives, or the white instigators of Indian uprisings in the romances of Simms and Bird—their missionary work among the savages a mere cover for a profoundly antisocial fanaticism.

Although the "philanthropist" justifies his programs by appealing to the highest values of his nation and race, the *World* argues that the effect of his actions is to reverse or invert the normal and natural order of the social cosmos. Instead of expanding civilization at the expense of savagery, philanthropy protects Indians and retards the growth of railroads. Instead of putting cultivated white minds to the task of reconstructing the ruined South, philanthropy puts ignorant blacks to rule over and abuse deserving southern whites. The *World* defines the depravity of government intervention on behalf of the urban poor by associating proposals for government soup kitchens with the perverse misordering of racial hierarchies in Reconstruction; and then it reverses the metaphor, defining the evils of Reconstruction by comparing the pro-black Republican regimes as "such a spectacle . . . as would be presented if the President interfered to put and keep in power at the City Hall 'Dutch Heinrich' and 'Reddy the Blacksmith.' "[31]

This language of reversible metaphors develops a series of paradoxical images of social and political roles, in which normal identities are continually reversed. Indians are both lazy savages and a leisured class of "aristocrats" or "monopolists" pampered by the government. Workers are "worthy producers," models for the Indian; but they are also Indians themselves, savage in their propensity for violence and evasion of toil, using strikes and mobs to block access to businesses and public squares just as the Indians use violence to block railroad access to the West. Those who stoop to help these dangerous and dark classes sully both garments and character, becoming like those they "pet" and "pamper": philanthropists are seen as having the morals of Italian vendettists or black "Bosjemen"; Samuel Gridley Howe's philanthropies for freedmen and for the blind suggest that Howe's morality is "Blind and Black."

In addition to the inversion of racial order, the key metaphor for demonstrating the perversity of philanthropism is the reversal of sexual roles. The Christian idealism associated with philanthropy had been symbolically vested in "woman" by generations of moralists and romance writers. We can trace this association back to Mrs. Rowlandson and the heroines of Puritan captivity narratives; and forward through the sentimental novels of the eighteenth century to Cooper's Inez (*The Prairie*) and Alice Munro (*Last of the Mohicans*), and the heroines of Harriet Beecher Stowe, Catherine M. Sedgwick, and "Fanny Fern" in the 1850s and 1860s. Moreover, women had played leading roles in the development of reform ideologies and political movements continuously since the 1820s; and in the 1870s a vocal minority of activist women were also putting forward a feminist social and political agenda. From the *World*'s viewpoint, the symbolic association of women and philanthropic ideology was a perfect expression of the liberal fallacy, and a perfect occasion for exposing philanthropic error. The paper accepted as given the necessary affinity between women of high class and character and the values of charity: sympathetic sentiments and the urge to nurture and succor the needy are the peculiar gift and glory of the sex. But the proper sphere for such sentiment and activity is the woman's world of home, church, and neighborhood; in the world of business and politics, the masculine gifts of hardheadedness, analytical rigor, and stern decision must govern. The depravity of philanthropy begins when "effeminate" sentiments take precedence over "manly" strength in the ordering of politics. The efficiency and order of the political economy are impaired, because power is given into weak and effete hands; and both men and women are "unsexed" by the reversal of traditional roles.

This symbolic sexual treason underlies the larger betrayal of race and class interest which philanthropy fosters. Women in their "natural" role are objects of possession and protection by the paternal head of the family; and this familial order provides the model for the subordination of dependent worker to dominant manager in the macrocosm of industrial society. Thus the aggrandizement of women in a philanthropic politics establishes the conditions for a reversal of the economic roles of labor and capital. By linking philanthropic doctrine with feminine values and psychology, the *World* condemns softness and sentimentality. But it also connects the doctrine with more violent and disruptive "female" states of mind: irrationality, hysteria, and madness. Here the female stereotype approaches the racial stereotype of the savage, who is also governed by unreasonable passion, and also opposes the rigor of a white or masculine regime.

The *World* defines the inferiority of blacks, Indians, and women by identifying them with the despised traits of weakness, emotionalism (or proneness to "frenzy"), and dependency; and by linking them as the clients of the illegitimate political favoritism of sentimental philanthropists. Effeminacy is at the heart of these stereotypes, because it is the nonwhites' supposed "weakness" in military and business capacity that renders them dependent on whites, as women are supposed to be dependent on men. Effeminacy is likewise the trait of the liberal philanthropist, whose feminine emotions override the masculine common sense which demands that he exact obedience and order from his dependents. In the new moral order only those who prove themselves according to the standards of Anglo-Saxon virility are entitled to the full privilege of the franchise; the idealism associated with "woman" is to be devalued along with the social position of "the sex."

The political implications of this new standard were especially grim for the recently freed blacks. When the *World* sneered that "the fighting qualities of male negroes are doubtless superior to those of any class of women" it was not being merely facetious. It was suggesting that the black race could never meet the standard of Anglo-Saxon virility that ought to be a prerequisite for full citizenship; and implying as well that the cowardly race would turn its violence against white women, because it feared to confront white men. Moreover, the ideology of race war which was thus invoked justified the severest kind of punishment for those of the subject race who deployed violence against vulnerable whites. The *World*'s December 22 editorial, "A Southern Curse in a Northern Home," cites the rape of a white child by a Negro in Boston as the consequence of the "ghoul-like and emasculating influences" of philanthropic government. Salvation for the North will come only when it follows the pattern of southern white men, and acts upon that intense longing for revenge "which every masculine man . . . must feel." Manhood would be vindicated by a resort to Frontier lynch law—"one hour of Kansas with its hasty ropes"—and from this example might flow an attempt to assert and restore the rightful dignity and privilege of "the ruling race of Europe, of America, and of the world" over "all ignorant and long brutalized races," wherever found.[32]

For the *World*, the essence of social depravity is the attempt to use political power to effect reforms favorable to the subordinate working classes. It sees all of the evils of disorder and economic depression as arising from a "great conspiracy of greed with fanaticism," through which political profiteers manipulate democratic ideology to maintain an unnatural philanthropic government. The dangers of this kind of government have already been manifested in western Indian outrages and in the intransigence of southern blacks. But the true danger (as the *World* sees it) has not been fully manifested until now, in the winter of 1873–74, when urban workingmen and the unemployed lay claim to the ideological mantle of democratic philanthropism to justify a program of "communism." The labor meeting in New York's Tompkins Square in January 1874 brings the issue to a head. Although the demonstrators are ostensibly asking only for relief from starvation through public soup kitchens, and for a suspension of house and room rent, the *World* sees behind them "the red spectre of the commune" which had "frightened Paris from her propriety" in 1871. The demands of the workingmen will probably not be satisfied until labor unions have attained a "monopoly" of the labor commodity, and with it an absolute power of control over the industrial state. The "suffering classes" of America are following the European model, and are becoming "the dangerous classes." And the liberal philanthropist augments this tendency by validating labor's claim to speak with the moral authority of republican ideology.[33]

The real basis of labor radicalism is the resentment of economic underachievers at the disparity between themselves and the newly rich. But this resentment is converted into revolutionary sentiment only because of the involvement of government in protecting privileged corporations. Under the "natural" political economy of free trade and laissez-faire, the "best classes" and the best characters could rise freely to the top of society. This would make it clear to the laboring classes that it is not social privilege but difference of innate character that makes the difference of class. Those who rise are generally better men than those who decline; the unemployed, rather than the employers, are responsible for the misery of the urban poor. But if the parents will not "resume the rod," but instead fall victim to "maudlin mercy," then the child classes will run amok. Order will cease, and with it production and progress. The white striker, the Negro loafer, the Indian "aristocrat" will monopolize the laboring sector. An editorial titled "Charity as a Sin" sums up the *World's* view:

> Charity rages like an epidemic just when all the conditions seem to point towards its proper subsidence. . . . If it is charity to add to the dangerous, diseased element of society . . . if it is charity to encourage idleness and dependence in the lower classes, the city has every reason to congratulate itself. Never has there been greater impetus to worthlessness and vagrancy and so it will continue while begging is more profitable than labor. . . . the disciple of Malthus will think of it as so much squandered in keeping alive a diseased member of the population. . . . Work abounds for all classes. The large class drawn hither by the possibility of living without work should be compelled to return to the country, where their hands are needed, by the stern necessity to work or starve.[34]

The last phrase, echoing as it does the language of "Our Indian Policy," points the moral exactly. In the crowded city, there is no leeway for philanthropy, no time for the savage white man to accustom himself to civilized industry: he must be made to adjust or die.

The choice, however, is a desperate one: the *World* therefore sought a means by which a Frontier situation could be restored to the economy— one in which the opening of new lands or resources created new jobs, new wealth, the stimulus to new investment.

LOOKING FOR PARADISE:
THE FRONTIER AS ESCAPE

Although the labor markets of the cities might be constricting and the Frontier itself rapidly reduced to settlement, the *World* still saw in the West a "safety valve" for the explosive industrial situation. A pair of editorials published on November 11, 1873, juxtaposed accounts of "Useful Charity" for selective relief in New York and an opportunity for "Landless Laborers" from England to make their fortunes in the West. "The Laboring Classes of New York" (January 24, 1874) are filled with Europeans who expected to better their fortunes in a land renowned for high wages and instead find themselves glutting the market and paying higher rents than at home.[35] Only those emigrants who settle in the developing territories of the West and South have attained the promised American prosperity. To be sure, the West was much victimized by the fiscal and political depravities of railroad "monopolies" like that nearly achieved by Cooke; and it also had the accompanying radicalism of the Grangers, who sought to remedy private monopoly by resorting to government action, despite the experience of Reconstruction. Yet it was in the West that the characterological strife of races and classes could be most directly observed and be seen as producing ongoing historical progress from primitivism to civilization; and it was in the latent values of western lands and minerals that the potential for a revival of trade and investment existed.

In the western setting, the heroic role was institutionalized in the army. As the executors of punitive justice against recalcitrant redskins, the army acted the role the *World* imagined for the ruling class as a whole. Unlike the morality of the "philanthropic fanatic," the soldier's morality was a form of chivalry, tempered by practical experience, and committed to a code that was defined legally and institutionally—not according to the "higher law" cited by radical exponents of social reconstruction. There were, in these corrupt times, exceptions to that rule, usually as a result of Grant's favoritism or of the involvement of the army in suppressing white "Redeemers" in the South. Nonetheless, the officers represented the backbone of state power which could be brought to bear on unruly reds, whites or blacks.

Thus in reporting military affairs, the *World* sought to curb the enthusiasm of the southern Democrats for reduction of the army—a device by which they hoped to hasten the removal of occupation troops from

Louisiana, South Carolina, Mississippi, and Florida. The army was never more needed than at this time to police and help open up the last western frontier and to act as counterpoise to the threat of unrest in the cities.[36]

The initial newspaper response to the announcement of the Black Hills expedition reflected the division of national opinion on Indian policy, the army, and westward expansion via the sponsorship of railroads. Papers whose interests were entirely local or regional did not respond to the government's invitation to send reporters and did not give news of the expedition much play until the excitement generated by the bigger papers became infectious. Even in the Northwest, only the states and cities in immediate proximity to the Northern Pacific's line sent correspondents; and the South, intent on the local problem of Reconstruction, was not represented at all. The New York *Tribune* had a traditional interest in the West, and its correspondent had accompanied the Northern Pacific survey in 1873. The Chicago *Inter-Ocean* had a regional interest and was moreover strongly supportive of the administration; it therefore sent its own man, William Eleroy Curtis, anticipating a publicity coup for the Grant regime. Democratic and antiadministration journals in the East did not respond. Even the *Herald*, whose bread and butter was just the kind of sensational story Custer was bound to generate, did not avail itself of the privilege—and was soon to regret it. The New York *World* initially ignored the expedition since anything planned by Grant must by definition be bad news for publisher August Belmont. But at the last minute, the *World* changed its mind and engaged Curtis to serve a second master.[37]

Curtis sent essentially the same sorts of dispatches to both the *Inter-Ocean* and the *World*. A comparison of the context in which the two papers presented those stories therefore throws into relief the effect of editorial ideology in responding to the story as it developed. The *Inter-Ocean* began by being highly interested in the expedition and laudatory of both purposes and personnel. The *World* was first antipathetic, then interested but highly critical. As the story of the gold discovery unfolded, bringing with it the prospect of another outbreak of "savage war" with the progress of civilization as the stake, these roles were reversed. Curtis sent the *Inter-Ocean* longer reports than he sent to the *World*; and, favoring the paper that permanently employed him, he sent them off concurrently with, if not ahead of, his reports to New York. Yet the record shows that the *World* "scooped" the *Inter-Ocean* by two days on the most sensational and newsworthy of all the dispatches—the report of the discovery of the "Floral Valley" and "gold among the roots of the grass." And when the *Inter-Ocean* printed the story, it made as little of it as possible, despite the paper's serving a region directly interested in the discovery of gold; while at the same time, the *World* puffed and expanded upon its reports. If we extend our view to a survey of the other papers reporting on the events, a clear and explanatory pattern emerges: proadministration papers make as little of the events as possible; northern Democratic papers make as much of it as possible. Only in the South, where Reconstruction issues drove out all other concerns, is there any departure from this pattern. The Black Hills expedition, as event and as media event, appeared to serve the interests and the ideology of those who opposed the regime of Grant, of Radical Reconstruction, of "philanthropy." A closer look at the development of the story and its context will reveal why this was so.

Curtis's first dispatches (July 1–31) received very different treatments in the two dailies. At this point, the *Inter-Ocean* was supporting an expedition undertaken by the administration it supported which had in view the opening up of a new region to western enterprise. They therefore gave front-page prominence and editorial support to Curtis's interpretation, which presented the expedition as a fulfillment of the design for development embodied in the ideology of free labor and the Republican platform. For Curtis, it is not the energy of the individual pioneer that will make this new Frontier possible, but the development of industry, and especially the development of federally subsidized transcontinental railroads, that will blaze the trails and smooth the ways:

> The settler can take his family, and leave them in a railroad hotel as comfortably as at the homestead [*sic*] in the East till his claim is established. . . . The days of pioneer hardship are over; prairie schooners are almost obsolete, for the emigrant travels in a Pullman car nowadays. . . . On account of these arrangements, the class of settlers coming to this country is superior, socially, to the general herd. . . . These are the people who develop a country; who carry civilization with them, without waiting for it to come as an aftermath. . . .

Curtis makes a virtue of the fact that the railroad route to the West is more expensive than the old wagon route, suggesting that the pioneer on this new Frontier will be of relatively higher class than the ring-tailed roarers of the antebellum West.[38]

Custer himself is, for Curtis, a perfect hero for this industrial-era Frontier. In a long story published on July 9, he describes Custer at length as a true American aristocrat, at once a man of the people and a paternalistic ruler, the head of a "military family" and a missionary for education and temperance among Wild Westerners and Indians alike:

> At present General Custer is thirty-four years old—a slender, fairheaded, blue-eyed man. His wife [is] a charming lady, who has shared his marches and victories since early in the war . . . and her home is one green spot, if there be no others in the frontier life of the officers of the Seventh. A few evenings since the writer, entering General Custer's library, saw a new phase of this man's character. He sat on a low stool by his desk with a spelling-book in his hand; before him were two little girls, one white and the other colored, the children of his servants, whom he was affording the necessities denied by the lack of schools. Apologizing for my interruption, I was withdrawing, when he cried out in his hearty way, "Come in, come in and see my school." I entered the room, and in a pleasant, familiar way he went on with his teaching, having his scholars spell the words alternately, tell their meaning, and construct sentences. I have found that this has been his custom for several years, and all these little people of his household know of written words is what he has taught them.[39]

This military paterfamilias presides over a regimental community of ethnic and racial "characters" who are represented by Curtis in terms of conventional stereotypes. Among them are a stage Irishman with a thick brogue, and a Negro camp cook (Aunt Sally) who expects that the Black Hills will prove "adapted to the colored race." (Curtis disabuses her—the Hills will be "white man's country.") Other characterizations are drawn in the vocabulary of the Frontier novel: Bloody Knife, Custer's Arikara scout, has more of the "nobility" of Cooper's red man than any of the other Indians Curtis meets. But for the rest of the race, "Shades of Cooper and Natty Bumppo! how the red man has degenerated. . . . [He] prefers peace to war . . . he would rather steal than work" and has a wretched "stench." To make the catalogue of inferior races and classes complete, Curtis brings in the Woman Question: faced with an Indian who has been forced to dress as a woman because of past cowardice, Curtis says: "If Susan B. Anthony wants to vote . . . let her take a scalp."[40]

In all of these attitudes, Curtis's prose is far more compatible to the editorial policy of the *World* than of the *Inter-Ocean*, which was constitutionally bound to pay lip service (at least) to the doctrines of philanthropy on the status of Indians, blacks, women—and above all, on the protection of Indian rights in the land. Indeed, the paper found itself wishfully adopting the belief that the expedition (so dear to local interests) was not a legal violation of the Treaty of 1868, that no threat to the Peace Policy as a whole would necessarily result—a denial of realities which absorbed their ideological energy in rationalization and defense. By contrast, the *World*'s opposition stance and its self-appointed role as maker of national political ideology inclined it to the free and creative development of analogies; and it seems fair to say that it was also assisted in this by the greater degree of consonance between the racialism of Frontier mythology, and the racist attitudes its editors brought to the resolution of the Reconstruction, Indian, and labor problems.[41]

In contrast to the *Inter-Ocean*, the *World*'s initial position on the expedition was an unlikely and unhappy one. It was a project of the Grant administration, and so must be a "job" got up by some faction of the corrupt bureaucracy; so the paper found itself in the uncongenial position of defending the sanctity of an Indian reservation against a military invasion. After delaying coverage until nearly two weeks after the *Inter-Ocean*'s began, the *World* gave a five-column front-page spread to the story, characterizing it as "A Gold-Hunting Expedition to the Sioux' Sacred Retreat" (July 13). The article confidently predicted a successful search for gold and the outbreak of war with the Indians. Editorials characterized Custer as a "pet" of Sherman, Sheridan, and Grant—characterized as Radicals on Reconstruction issues—and condemned the entire project.[42]

Although Curtis's flattering portrait of Custer as the soldier-paterfamilias is entirely omitted, the main line of the story is allowed to stand. It describes the Black Hills in the traditional images of the "wilderness paradise" that go back to Gilpin, to Filson's portrayal of Kentucky, and even to the earliest Virginia promotion narratives. The land is like the Garden of Eden and is compared with sacred groves and valleys from a range of classical and oriental mythologies. It is sacred to the Indian—who is Nature's own child and prophet—and it possesses both material wealth and magical sources of regenerative power. "The Black Hills enclose what may be called the earthly paradise of the Sioux," a "combined deer park and Mecca," the "Sioux Sinai," a circular band of hills enclosing a wilderness garden. On this Holy Ground, the Indians hunt "not for want or wantonness" but as if "the pleasures of the chase" were "a sort of sylvan sacrament." Thus they share the mystique attributed to the hunting of Daniel Boone, for whom predation became a heroic profession of connection with Nature rather than a means to mere survival or profit. Curtis thereby reinforces the implication that in the Black Hills Americans will find a renewal of the opportunity for self-realization and self-transcendence associated with the earlier Frontier of Daniel Boone and Leatherstocking.

The Hills are also a sort of world-navel, focal point of natural and divine energies which are magical, erotic—and dangerous. At its heart are "the springs of immortality." As Curtis recounts it, Indian

> legend has it that a wonderful cave ran through the central hill from side to side. Difficulties and temptations of all sorts surrounded it and made entrance thereto . . . almost to be impossible. Magic deer wooed the hunter to turn aside or back, and he who for a moment was diverted from his path and purpose was torn to pieces instantly by the panthers who guarded the approach. . . . Through this he who passed took a new lease of life till the eagles, whose eyrie was on the summit of the hill, entered another century of their eternal existence.

Curtis then tells the story of a chief who attained immortality but abused the powers achieved thereby and was therefore destroyed by the gods, who closed the immortality spring with rocks. He then proceeds to associate the natural power of the Hills with sexual power: the questing hunter is "wooed" by "magic deer." White men seeking the Hills have had to marry into Indian families, but have been denied admittance or have been literally torn to pieces for their presumption. The Indian defends the Hills "as desperately as any Mussulman could guard his harem." Insanity—that perennial associate of sexual passion—likewise inhabits the Hills, surfacing in the Muslim-like fanaticism of the Indians and in the fear of white officers that troops entering the Hills would become "frenzied with the gold fever" and driven to desertion.[43]

The Indian sources of Curtis's legend are questionable. The geography of Curtis's spring and the panther guardians strongly suggest that Curtis's ideas of Indian myth were shaped by a reading of Charles Brockden Brown's *Edgar Huntly* (1799)—a Gothicized captivity narrative, which also evokes similar archetypes. Curtis universalizes the symbolic reference of his Indian legend by comparing it to Bunyan's *Pilgrim's Progress*, Homer's *Odyssey*, and the *Nibelungenlied*. This reinforces the suggestion that the magic of the Hills is available to white men as well as red, and that in going to the Hills the white man reenacts and recovers the power of the primary myths of his culture.

The snake in Curtis's Garden of the West—the dragon Fafnir to Custer's Siegfried—is the Indian leader Sitting Bull. In the terms of Cooperian mythology, he is more like Magua than Uncas. He is made the incarnation of the characteristic powers and evil propensities of the Indian tribes. He is not merely a wily and unscrupulous warrior but a "charlatan" why cynically manipulates his people's superstitious nature from his position as both war chief and shaman. Curtis, of course, misunderstands and misrepresents Sitting Bull, the Sioux, and the nature of the war chief and shaman institutions among the Indians. But he has chosen his categories carefully to make the Indian reflect evil tendencies that Metropolitan readers are familiar with in their own society. In particular, the identification of Sitting Bull as charlatan and fanatic links him with the religious "fanaticism" of the philanthropists and Radicals—those natural allies of the murderous savage. But Curtis obeys the traditional imperatives of the Frontier Myth, which sees the Indian simultaneously as the source of natural wisdom and insight and the embodiment of savage cruelty. By deploying this paradox, he can emphasize the magical qualities of the new "paradise," while at the same time invoking the scenario that will end with the elimination of the Indians.

The expedition sent to dare the perils of magic, erotic temptation, and frenzy is protected by its purpose and its leadership. It seeks gold, not fantastic immortality; money, not mystery and magic. And its leaders are scientists and soldiers, representing both ordered reason and political authority. Yet the Indians' anger against the invasion will be great enough to put even such forces in peril:

> There is no earthly doubt but that the Sioux will fight and are preparing for conflict. That they should meditate resisting the Long-Haired Chief—so General Custer is known amongst them, his chevelure being as noticeable as it was the day he dashed down the avenue at Washington in the grand review . . . is sufficient proof, particularly after their whipping last year, that their blood is up. A rat will offer a desperate resistance if you pen him in a corner; much more an Indian. Naturally fond of fighting, hating the whites with envenomed hatred, dowered with a pride—or a treacherous ferocity, call it which you will—that no amount of whipping can take out of them; sore from their last year's defeats and the encroachment of the railroad, the Sioux would be certain to fight, even if the expedition did not menace their last refuge and most holy land. Hence there is hardly a man who does not anticipate a very Gravelotte of savage warfare.[44]

The passage invokes an image of Custer remembered from newspaper accounts of an incident during the Grand Review of the Civil War armies in 1865, when Custer inadvertently "charged" down Pennsylvania Avenue with his long hair flowing behind him. Reporters of the *Times* and the *World* then compared him to a "Sioux Chieftain," and the image had stuck with him. Here it serves to remind the reader of Custer's Civil War fame and to recall his likeness to the Indians who are his enemies.[45] This suggests a

Leatherstocking-like aspect of his character, a kinship with his dearest foes that paradoxically enables him to sympathize with them and to be a more effective agent of their destruction. Curtis emphasizes this aspect of him by giving him his Indian sobriquet of Long Hair rather than his more famous Civil War epithet of Boy General with the Golden Locks. Later dispatches develop further the Cooperian aspect of the expedition, and suggest that Custer represents an advance over the traditional Frontier hero. But in general, Curtis wants his readers to see that Cooper's West is no more. The Leatherstockings now serve *under* the Heywards and Middletons, who are their masters in woodcraft as well as in manners; and the Indians have all degenerated. The military aristocrat is, in other words, the mediating figure, the man knowledgeable in two worlds who can deal with the Indian on savage terms in the interests of white civilization.[46]

Curtis is not uncritical of the warmongering character of the expedition, but he refutes the criticism leveled against it from the left by Friend-of-the-Indian Bishop Hare and that from the right by the *World* itself. He denies the accusation—repeated in a *World* editorial printed in that same issue—that the expedition is a "pet affair" gotten up to promote the reputation of President Grant's son Fred (who accompanied Custer) and Custer himself. A bloody and unpopular war is the most likely result of the affair, and that (says Curtis) would not serve the interests of anyone connected with it. Similarly, Curtis dismisses with contempt the moral criticism of Custer leveled by Bishop Hare. He notes that the bishop is "looked upon with horror in army circles," because during the 1868 negotiations he had promised personally to see to it that any white man who violated the treaty would be punished. Curtis acknowledges that this "speech was undubitably founded in justice," but was "of doubtful expediency to be uttered in the presence of such a crowd of treacherous brutes." Given the racial character of the Indians, it is inadvisable to grant self-government and inexpedient even to discuss the question of justice.[47]

Curtis's only objection to the expedition is that it will stir up the Indians, while at the same time depleting the forces assigned to guard the settlements near the reservation. But Custer himself is a hedge against this possibility. "Custer has a reputation among the savages, which in this sort of warfare is worth more than rank," and the threat implied by his presence may check Indian tempers. In any case, as a soldier under orders, Custer cannot be criticized for the decisions of his commander in chief. The reader is therefore invited to admire the expedition's leader as a hero, whatever his criticism of the expedition might be.

This was the position toward which the *World* editorialists now moved. The first symptom of their changing attitude was the reprinting on July 25 of Curtis's portrait of Custer as soldier-paterfamilias, which was followed by a major dispatch on August 1 carrying the theme forward. Here, Curtis contrasts the orderly gardens and shaded streets of Custer's Fort Lincoln with the "gambling-hells, bagnios, rum-mills" of civilian Bismarck—a government of military gentlemen makes a world safe for ladies, while disorderly Frontier democracy peoples the West with roughneck men and sluttish women. This dispatch also develops the portrait of Custer's expected antagonist, Sitting Bull.

> Sitting Bull, the guides believe, will certainly make a stand at the Hills. General Custer affects to disbelieve this . . . [but] I incline to the belief that . . . he would very much like Sitting Bull to attack him. The column is considered about invincible, and Custer "owes Sitting Bull one," in the common phrase, for the fight on the Yellowstone last year. . . .

Custer himself is "as theatrical as ever," and rides just behind the Indian scouts at the head of the column, at once general and pathfinder.[48]

While Custer's expedition marched towards its supposed confrontation with Sitting Bull, across the pages of the *World* its progress was shadowed by other stories related by propinquity on the page and by theme. The most directly related were the stories that dealt with the outbreaks of Indian hostilities elsewhere on the plains—accounts that lent both imagery and credibility to the idea of a war with the Northern Plains Indians breaking out in response to Custer's march. Should that event occur, there would be a total white-Indian confrontation unlike any since Tecumseh's confederacy was broken—war stretching from Canada to Mexico and comprehending Sioux, Cheyenne, Arapahoe, Comanche, Kiowa, Apache, and Ponca. The *World* dubbed this coming struggle "Grant's Indian War," and followed it with an extended summary of white-Indian conflicts, from colonial times to the present—an attempt to set the coming warfare in as large a historical context as possible.[49]

These articles and editorials, and those that followed, were juxtaposed with accounts of Negro disorders in the South, strikes and crime waves in the North, and accounts of the ideological heresies of radicals and philanthropists to create a context in which the approach of Custer to the Hills and the gathering of Indians against him was paralleled by the increase of the assaults of darkness on the citadels of light and virtue. The opposition of the Indians to the railroads is editorially paralleled by *World* correspondents who note an upcoming "Railroad War" between the Granger farmers and the transportation monopolists. The implication is that agrarian radicals who seek to protect their interest through regulatory legislation are spiritual fellows of the Indians who resist the railroad and the civilization it brings: the Indian resists the material form of civilization; the Granger opposes its very spirit, which is "free trade."[50]

The outbreak of Indian attacks is also juxtaposed with instances of urban crime, suggesting both a rationale for the outbreaks (Indians are inherently criminal) and a method for dealing with them (just and severe punishment). Thus on July 14 an editorial on "Grant's Indian Policy" is followed by one on the punishment of a woman who killed her faithless lover ("Maniac or Murderess?"). The leniency of the judge who is inclined to regard the murder as an act of insanity (suggesting some form of care other than prison) is seen in the light of the earlier condemnation of Grant's "policy of palaver" which has permitted the " 'blackmailing' " and " 'redmailing' " of the American people. Contrary to the judgment of the court, the *World* thinks the accused "murderess" should be straitly punished as a lesson against all forms of female intransigence. Similarly, the Grant administration ought to have overawed the Indians, not pampered them to their present pitch of arrogance and hostility. On July 22, a more general discussion of "New Modes of Crime" (and appropriate punishments) is set against with an account of new "outrages" by Indians and the promise that "A More Vigorous Policy" will be "Pursued Towards Them" with "General Sheridan Authorized to Follow the Redskins to Their Reservations." "New Modes of Crime" extends the argument of "Maniac or Murderess?" to further extremes. The editorial notes that the tendency to regard all crime as the result of "morbid impulse" (insanity) has led to an unfortunate relaxation of legal rigor and asserts that whatever the causes of crime, "fear of punishment" is an effective repressive measure. Although the immediate subject of these ruminations is a kidnapper in Philadelphia, the *World* extrapolates its remarks to those groups which it has all along characterized as lazy, parasitical, dependent, and frenzy-prone—women, the white unemployed, blacks, and reservation Indians.[51]

The *World*'s solution for morbid-impulse crime is a blending of regular and "Lynch" law; for the Indian problem, an increase of official vigilance and an unleashing of the official and unofficial forces of the frontier against the redskins. This association of Indian raids and urban crimes, and of military, "popular," and civil retribution, is repeated in succeeding days: on July 23, an account of a "Carnival of Crime" in Philadelphia appears next to an account of "Indian Affairs"; a single item on July 24 combines the lynching of a white miscreant with Indian raids ("Mob Law in Kansas—Indian Outrages in New Mexico"). Similar pairings appeared every day for a week.[52]

The *World* brought its metaphoric argument full circle by reverting to its interpretation of the Black Hills expedition as yet another such action: a criminal invasion or burglary of the Indian reservation committed by Grant and his fellow corruptionists:

> And now suddenly, without a word of warning, the President, who has lured all these nascent communities, all these adventurous pioneers to the westward, turns his back upon his preaching and his proclamations, and with a stealthy bound, like that of the Indian himself, assails the fiercest and most intractable of the tribes for . . . purposes of plunder.[53]

This racial "darkening" of both the white "dangerous classes" and the political opposition serves to reinforce earlier associations of Republicanism with the "retrogressive" forces of primitivism. It also points directly toward a racialist critique of the Republican role in southern Reconstruction. The Reconstruction theme which develops parallel to the Custer story is introduced in a pair of editorials on July 19: "Have We an Indian War On Hand?" is followed by a discussion of "Civil Rights—The White League," an account of the formation of a successor organization to the KKK. Unlike the earlier terrorist organization, which was unfortunately attractive to the lower order of whites, the White League has been formed from the moderate upper classes, many of them former Confederate officers, whose rejection of Negro suffrage was based not on mere bigotry but on "the negroes refusal to co-operate with the whites for any other end than their own supremacy." An editorial on July 23 ("Plain Black and

White") predicts that the Civil Rights Bill "is breeding curses and preparing slaughter throughout regions that but for . . . the Republican party would to-day be orderly and happy sections of a prosperous and law-abiding Union." The alternatives are either a war of races, a "social cataclysm," or an enforced amalgamation:

> A negro demagogue in Vicksburg . . . got up and proclaimed in the public streets . . . not only that he has a right to and could if he would marry any one of a dozen of the better class of white ladies in Vicksburg, but that he would maintain his right to do so against the fathers or brothers of such ladies "revolver in hand." Is there a single town in the North and West outside New England in which a negro could hold such language and advance such pretensions without being promptly thrashed?

Yet such is permitted and protected by the federal authorities in the South.[54]

South and West are peculiarly linked, in that both are underdeveloped areas, attractive to investment capital and useful as safety valves for discontented and impoverished laborers. But in both sections the protection and privilege afforded primitive and antiprogressive races (blacks and Indians) thwarts such development. Indeed, following this very general attempt to place southern affairs in a larger ideological and mythological context, the *World*'s rhetoric escalates. An editorial on 'The Race Issue and Its Origin" (August 2) argues that "the existence of white men and the maintenance of civilization [is] almost impossible where the blacks predominate."

And on August 6, it reports:

> ANARCHY IN LOUISIANA/ A War Between the Races Predicted/Owners of the River Plantations at the Mercy of Their Former Slaves—The State Ruled and Ruined by Knavish Whites and Illiterate Blacks[55]

On August 8, the three left-hand columns of the front pages printed stories on continued riots by southern Negroes, and "The Indian Outbreak" (said to have been caused by "An Indian Prophet Advising His People to Murder All the Whites"). Also published that day was an account of a "Trade-Union Murder in Williamsburg." Printed under the heading "Criminal Record," it picks up the subsidiary theme of labor militancy, presenting it here in the context of criminal activity, and the attempt by racial philanthropists to obstruct progress by favoring the primitive races. This association had appeared earlier in an editorial on "Rattening in Cincinnati" printed on July 23, just following the editorial on amalgamation and race war, "Plain Black and White." In the editorial and the Williamsburg murder article, the *World* characterizes strikers as criminals, intimidators who obstruct free trade in labor by violent means. However, it appeals to elements among the white working class by attempting to associate them with the "intelligent white man" (e.g., upper-class man) of the South, and so to cajole them away from their union allegiance:

Printers are supposed to be among the most intelligent classes of mechanics, if not to constitute quite the most intelligent class. To have such a class insisting that important work shall stop if they are not allowed to do it in their own way and on their own terms is saddening. To find them resorting to actual violence, or to actual threats of violence, in defense of that noble proposition is more saddening still. Surely these men, if anybody, might have been expected to see that the right of a man to sell his labor for whatever it is found in the open market to be worth is a common human right not in any way to be limited by the establishment of trade unions. . . . Ignorant and needy knife-grinders in Sheffield [England] might be pardoned, better than the printers of Cincinnati, who have no excuse for being either ignorant or needy . . . Almost always a strike is idiotic. In this case, it was so wilfully and viciously idiotic as to deprive the strikers of all sympathy whatsoever.

This subtheme of labor-capital conflict would surface more emphatically in the fall, as the onset of winter gave an edge to the miseries of the unemployed and raised once again the specter of large demonstrations and increased crime.[56]

PARADISE DISCOVERED

In the midst of accounts of "The Indian Outbreak," "Negro Outrages in the South," and "An Effort to Introduce the System of [Racially] Mixed Schools" in Washington, there appeared on August 11 a preliminary report on Custer's findings:

ON THE BLACK HILLS / Custer's Expedition Reaches Its Destination / A Region of Gold and Silver Mines and Lovely Valleys Discovered—The Expedition in Good Health and Spirits . . .[57]

Curtis's dispatch thrust the expedition once again into the forefront of the news—this time not as a Grant-corruptionist folly but as a promise of the renewal of the Frontier solution to the problems of American poverty and social tension. The paraphrased summary of the report mentions few deaths, no hostilities, marches "through a valley of transcendent beauty" and the discovery of "indications of surface gold" which grew more plentiful as the command advanced. In Custer Valley

as one of the garden spots has been named, and which the correspondent describes as the most beautiful valley that the eye of man has ever looked on, rich gold and silver mines have been found, both placer and quartz diggings, and the immense section of country bids fair to prove the American El Dorado. The opinion of the geologist with the expedition (Prof. Winchell) fortified as it is by the gold discoveries that have been made already, is that further and elaborate explorations will satisfy the most sanguine expectations.[58]

When the command reaches the heart of the Hills and discovers the famous "Floral Valley," Curtis's prose becomes rapturous—they have found Earth's only paradise. "So beautiful was nature outwardly; so rich was mother earth in the resources of vegetable life, that our miners imagined treasures must be lying under our flower bed." Disappointed at first, the magical expectation proves true, and Curtis reports the camp "aglow with the gold fever."[59]

To this tremendous news, the Republican *Inter-Ocean* had to respond temperately. The effort it made was strenuous:

> We yesterday cautioned the would-be gold seeker against pre-initiate action in the matter and we repeat the warning today. At the same time we cannot but admit that the inducements to emigration are very strong indeed . . . the discoveries of General Custer are of immense importance, and . . . they will and ought to be taken advantage of at once.
>
> There could hardly be a more fortunate event for the country than the confirmation of these reports . . . It would give occupation to thousands who, from the dull condition of business, are now without work, and would stimulate trade and enterprise in every direction . . .

The paper also quotes approvingly the assertion of a miner, Capt. Russell, that "Money is scarce, and the country needs gold":

> The sequence is obvious. There was a crisis in 1848–9; California was opened and helped us out. There was a crisis in 1857; in 1858 Colorado was opened and helped us out. There was a crisis in 1873, from the effects of which we have not yet recovered; the Black Hills will be opened and pull us through.[60]

The Mythology of the Frontier invoked by Curtis and Russell was clearly part of the basic outlook of the *Inter-Ocean*, all of whose stories pointed toward seizing the Black Hills as the inevitable step in the old drama of progress Frontier-style. But the necessity of maintaining a common front with the administration forbade their following the course of the myth to its logical conclusion, and involved them in two years' worth of ideological backing and filling.

The reception of the story in the *World* was quite different. The ideological stances and the invocation of Frontier and racial mythology which was part and parcel of the *World*'s editorial policy throughout the year provided a perfect context for exploiting Custer's discovery. The *World* headline on August 16 depicts the Hills as a second Eden:

> THE BLACK HILLS / General Custer's Official Report / The Reports of Surface Gold Finding Fully Confirmed—A March Amidst Flowers of Exquisite Color and Perfume—The Garden of America Discovered. . . .

Below this unfolded Curtis's account, interspersed with Custer's reports, reprinted in full. In this first extended report, Custer emphasizes the agricultural potential of the Hills equally with, if not more strongly than, the indications of gold. Custer describes them as a vast wilderness park, where Nature seems to have cultivated and formed the landscape after the manner of a Frederick Law Olmsted—the landscape architect whose plan for New York's Central Park was an epitome of mid-nineteenth-century American design. One passage from Custer's report became quite famous in its own right as a visualization of the perfect "Garden of the West." This was his account of the regiment's passage through "Floral Valley," in which the flowers grew so luxuriantly, with such "exquisite colors and perfume," that the soldiers "plucked them without dismounting from the saddle" and decked themselves and their horses in blooms "fit to crown a queen of May."

To this Edenic description Custer added the practical observation that the land must be ideal for human cultivation, if it can yield so abundantly in a wilderness state. And he adds that the virgin wilderness also contains all of the materials necessary to the building of farmsteads, and the supply of heating or cooking fuel (timber and coal). It even has the sort of stone that could provide houses for an urban metropolis. Custer's description thus follows in the tradition of Filson's *Kentucke*, mixing wilderness with pastoral and urban images to suggest that Nature herself— in this perfect place—ordains a plan of progressive development.[61]

But the most sensational find, of course, is the discovery of gold, everywhere and in great abundance. With the discovery of auriferous rock, the Black Hills become the perfect example of a Gilpinian "Parc" in which the natural resources for both agrarian production and the mining of raw capital are superabundant. Custer uses Gilpin's favorite adjective— "inexhaustible"—to characterize the mineral resources. But he goes beyond Gilpin to link raw gold and agrarian promise in a single well-made phrase: "The miners report that they found gold among the roots of the grass." The image was to become the leitmotif of the Black Hills gold rush. This conflation of the agrarian and mineral potential of the Hills in a single phrase-image is not fortuitous, since the next sentences move from gold back into agriculture:

> It has not required an expert to find gold in the Black Hills, as men without such experience in mining have discovered it . . . As an evidence of the rich pasturage to be found in this region, I can state the fact that my beef herd . . . is in better condition than when I started, being now as fat as consistent with marching condition . . . I have never seen as many deer as in the Black Hills. Elk and bear have also been killed. We have had no collision with hostile Indians.[62]

Writers in other New York journals now began to notice that Custer's reports tended to favor the interests of the Northern Pacific Railroad. In the past, the *World* too had been hostile to Cooke and his railroad (because of its association with Grant), and would have been the first to pounce upon the suggestion that a Grant appointee was saving Cooke's interests. But now it was making an ideological investment in Custer, the gold rush, and an Indian war; and by the year's end it would completely reverse its opposition to government relief of the Northern Pacific. Nevertheless, in August, the *World* was less interested in the fate of the Northern Pacific than in the fiscal and political implications of Custer's discovery.[63] The chief consequence of the discovery of a gold and farming country in the Black Hills would be the expansion of the national basis of credit— gold and the value of the public lands—and the development of a Frontier alternative to the confrontation of labor and capital for control of the contracting resources of the depressed East.

PHILANTHROPY, EFFEMINACY, AND CORPORATE PATERNALISM

The Black Hills situation provided the most graphic and uncomplicated proof of the *World's* thesis that Grant's corrupt administration and philanthropic ideology were the primary barriers to a renewal of national prosperity. But its essential political task was to induce its readers to extrapolate from the Black Hills to black Reconstruction, which remained the central ideological and material issue of the political campaign. Editor Marble worked hard at building the analogies between West and South, arguing that in both regions the government's sponsorship of nonwhite "savages" retarded entrepreneurship, investment, and the creation in the region of opportunities for errant laborers and immigrants. The South/West analogy was made more strongly than usual after August 11, paralleling the prospective escalation of the Indian war with the escalating struggle in the South. On August 12, just after the first report of Custer's discovering gold, accounts of Indian outbreaks and "NEGRO LAWLESS- NESS / Disgraceful Conduct of Armed Bands . . . A Fight With the Negroes . . ." appear side by side. An editorial condemns the "riot of savage and infuriated negroes," and portrays the community where it occurred (Austin, Mississippi) as a kind of Frontier outpost of whites "in a region populous with negroes, who have lapsed more nearly towards their ancestral condition of savagery with every year of carpet-bag debauchery . . ." The "outnumbered and besieged whites of Austin will [have to] be rescued or sharply avenged." The front page on the following day reported "THE NEGRO RIOTS / Austin, Miss., Captured by Negroes and Retaken by Whites. . . ." And after the major Custer stories of August 14–16, the front page on the eighteenth reported "Negro War in North Carolina" and the formation of "BLACK LEAGUES / Oath-Bound Organizations of the Louisiana Negroes" to maintain and extend their supposed military-political domination of the whites. Whites were responding by forming "white leagues," and race war threatened.[64]

On August 19, roughly midway between the publication of the Curtis- Custer report published on the sixteenth and the climactic editorial of August 21 on "Custer's Expedition and Grant's Indian Policy," two editorials appeared on "The White Man's Party" and "Negro Reservations." The first was an apology for the formation of white leagues and lily-white Democratic parties in the South, asserting that the artificial divisions between

black and white imposed by Radical Reconstruction were responsible for
an unnatural and unprecedented division of interest. If the Republicans
chose to rule by "monopolizing" the blacks, the Democrats had no choice
but to monopolize whites:

> In that famous partition of the turkey and the crow between
> the Indian and the hunter, it is clear that the Indian would have
> preferred half a turkey with half a crow to the whole crow which
> he got. But as the hunter appropriated the turkey, there was noth-
> ing left for the Indian but the crow.

Only by restoring something like the prewar economic and political dependence of blacks on whites could racial peace and industrial prosperity
be restored.

"Negro Reservations" responds to a proposal by Frederick Douglass
that blacks should emigrate to states in which they can retain a numerical
majority (and hence political control). The *World* asserts that such a plan
would lead to inevitable depression, since "the whites who now inhabit
[such states] will be eager to leave them, and . . . no reasonable man will
put his money into any industrial enterprise of which the returns are so
uncertain as they must be in States given over to the rule of the freedmen."
The editorial then compares Douglass's proposal with the reservation
program of Grant's infamous Indian policy:

> We own surprise at finding so shrewd a person as Mr. Douglass
> giving this advice to his race. It is a confession that negroes and
> whites cannot get on together as equals in communities where the
> blacks are so numerous enough to be troublesome and not numer-
> ous enough to be predominant. It is in effect a suggestion that
> they should be set apart from the whites as the Indians have
> been set apart, on the ground of an incompatibility which forbids
> the two races to live together. But Mr. Douglass ought to know
> that the proposition which virtually he makes, to set off four
> populous and once wealthy States for a negro reservation, will not
> be listened to by anybody for a moment.

The editorial's distortion of Douglass's motivation—the proposal was
motivated by the evidence of white determination as nearly as possible to
reenslave the blacks in those states already "redeemed" by the Democrats
and the Klan—is only part of its interest. The comparison of the black-
dominated Reconstruction state with the Indian reservation points up the
connection between savagery and economic and political regression: Negro
reservations will be like Indian reservations, a domain undeveloped because of the savage indolence of the population. On the other hand, the
editorial defines the limits of comparability. The Indian is economically
dispensable, and hence he may be allowed his reservation in the wastes
until such time as his land is required for civilized men; if he then chooses
not to become civilized, he may be allowed to starve to death or to suffer
violent extermination without substantial loss to white society. The black,
in contrast, belongs to a numerous and useful part of the laboring force.
His participation is too much desired to extend him the privilege of be-

coming a vanishing American—at least, not until sufficient white labor or machinery can be created to replace him.[65]

On the following day, August 20, the *World* printed a scare headline, "THE INDIANS!" which reported an attack on Custer's column by four thousand "Redskins." On August 25, a story on "OUR INDIAN 'POLICY,'" recounting both Quaker corruption and Indian depredations, was followed by a report on "THE PROSTRATE STATE / The Reign of Lawlessness in South Carolina / Riots in All Parts of the State—The Negroes Murdering Each Other . . ." Like the Indians, the blacks have been "maddened with whiskey and inflamed by the most incendiary harangues." The result has been the regression of the community from white civilization to dark barbarism:

> The Indian savage gave place to the civilized White man, who made these beautiful Southern lands blossom like the rose. The whiteman has now been pushed aside, and the negro savage is fast reducing the country to desolation and barbarism. The right of property, the right of the public highway, the right of free speech, indeed all the rights of civilization, were usurped by the mob. . . .

In much the same way, Indians had been represented as insolent in their threats and lacking in respect for the public highways and railroads and the sanctity of white lives and property.[66]

On August 27, the front page again exhibited in adjoining columns "Reported Threats Against General Custer—Four Horns Trying to Organize an Attacking Force" and "NEGRO TROUBLES / Tennessee Negroes Planning the Murder of Whites. . . ." On the twenty-eighth, a pair of editorials titled "Indian Wars and the Indian Bureau" and "The Plots to Incite Negro Riots" directly compared the outbreak of racial hostility in the West and the East. In the West, the idea of a "general war undertaken and carried on in concert" is dismissed as being "quite beyond the intelligence of our scattered bands of savages," divided as they are by barriers of language, custom, and traditional enmity. Since they lack, as a race, the capacity to make a general war or collective policy, the simultaneous outbreaks of Indian hostilities must be the result of failures in prevailing white policies that alternate tardy punishment with "sugar and water" philanthropy.[67]

Like the Indians, the blacks are presumed to lack the intelligence for concerted political and military action. How then explain the widespread outbreak of black discontent, strikes, and riots? To attribute these to a cause like that of the Indian wars would in part imply a widespread incompatibility of interests between blacks and whites throughout the South, and not just in those few Reconstructed sections. The *World* therefore sees the cause of the problem in a Radical conspiracy to foment "negro riots" among the usually docile "wards of the nation" in order to sway northern voters. The August 28 editorial notes the charge that the discontent and militancy of the blacks can come only from demagogic intervention; and that whites and blacks abruptly "subside into amicable relations" when the northern conspirators retire. "Violence between the races [is] generally . . . proved to have originated with the most lawless of both races, while the more worthy element of the population are the sufferers": thus the Republican-Democrat conflict is really another instance of the strife between the producing classes and the dangerous classes.[68]

On August 30, the theme was picked up in both major news stories and editorials. The front page was occupied by accounts, in parallel columns, of "THE INDIAN WAR / Outrages on the Border" and "SOUTHERN WOES / . . . Disgraceful Negro Outrages." The editorial page juxtaposes an account of the government's exposure of helpless Westerners to Indian vengeance with "War of Races—Who is Responsible?" Just as the Indian Bureau has armed the Indians, so the Republicans have armed and incited the Negroes, playing on their desire "to confiscate the whiteman's property" "to ravage, plunder, and murder at will." "Every negro was taught to be an agrarian"—an advocate of land confiscation and redistribution—"and every tenth negro was encouraged to be an incendiary." On September 1, an editorial noted that "the hostility between whites and blacks, which breaks out into open war and bloodshed at times, is the result of a preconcerted arrangement" by Republicans. Front-page articles on September 3 contrast the real outrages of "INDIAN FIGHTING" with the false "'Ku-Klux' Cry" of the Republicans.[69]

On Indian matters, the *World* now found itself in something of a dilemma. It had initially condemned the expedition as evidence of Republican hypocrisy and inconsistency toward the Indian. But having argued that the Black Hills expedition violated the Treaty of 1868, the *World* found itself on shaky ground in advocating the extinguishing of Indian title in the wake of Custer's dispatches. It resolved its difficulties by reminding its readers that it had always opposed any but the most limited reservation system, and had always held that lands which could best be used by whites must never be reserved to Indians. It also distinguished between the public good that could possibly accrue from opening the Hills, and the private profit that had ostensibly motivated Grant's boodlers to order the expedition. Custer himself was now distinguished from the Grant ring: as the discoverer of the Hills and the publicizer of its wealth, he had made the reversal of the Indian policy inevitable and created the conditions for a confrontation between the Indian-loving administration and the pioneer-oriented public.

On August 16 Curtis pointed the direction followed by the *World* by shifting his rhetorical characterization of the Hills as "Indian Holy Land" to one emphasizing the Indians' usual absence from its precincts, their low-level usage of its resources. Their meetings there, initially characterized as sacred and ceremonial, are now presented as conspiratorial and criminal: the Hills serve the savages "as a sort of private backroom," of the kind found in metropolitan saloons with a clientele of thieves. Therefore, if the gold rumors "pan out," Curtis would advocate extinguishing Indian title. Enforced purchase of the Hills must be the government's policy, for "If the Government does not open the way, private enterprise will, backed up by the courage of the Western frontiersman," at a higher cost in blood of both "the red man and his persistent and more hardy opponent."[70]

World editorialists responded to this first dispatch by endorsing the idea of the inevitable opening of the Hills—an event of "very great social and industrial significance"—but characterized the likely takeover as a "usurpation." On the eighteenth, after Custer's full report had been digested, its editorialists look enthusiastically ahead to the prospective increase in national wealth and credit and talk of "usurpation" disappears:

> It would, perhaps, be premature now to predict anything of the future of the Black Hills and their valleys. But a region which combines among its products the flowers of the tropics, the timber of the North, and the grass of Kentucky, and which, in addition to a soil capable of producing the cereals in the greatest abundance, gives every indication of possessing rich mineral deposits, can hardly be long in receiving population and development, and in returning a valuable and yearly increasing contribution to our national wealth.[71]

From the sixteenth to the eighteenth, reports were received and printed indicating that the long-awaited Indian assault on Custer was about to take place. Although affecting to disbelieve the reports, the *World* continued to print them, and to use them as the basis for speculation on the "inevitability" of Indian hostilities that would result from the opening of the Black Hills. The August 21 editorial on "Custer's Expedition and Grant's Indian Policy" offers an interpretation of the Black Hills story in its largest terms, and integrates it with the ideological structure which the *World* has been building since the war. The central premise of the editorial is that the Custer expedition is the first phase of an ineluctable historical process: the expansion of industrial civilization into the undeveloped lands of the West. Although no proposals have yet been put forward for the seizure of the Hills, the *World* already assumes that extinction of Indian title and a war of extermination must follow inevitably in Custer's track. The *World* identifies itself as the voice of that progressive process, and in the name of progress declares that white needs must have priority over Indian rights. The Indians can avoid extermination only by accepting civilization on the same terms offered to the urban working classes: obey the law or die, "work or starve."

The presentation of this choice to the Indians is mere rhetoric. But the editorial presents a more concrete choice to its white urban audience: to identify with philanthropy and savagery, or with military rigor and industrial necessity. It presents the choice in racial and sexual terms, combining the two most important metaphors of social order into a single whole. The editorial begins by noting sarcastically that "From the philanthropic as well as from the financial point of view," it is to be hoped that reports of an attack on Custer are untrue, because any such confrontation must lead to the ultimate extermination of the savages. But the *World* is not "philanthropic," and it suggests that anyone who *is* is either not a full participant in the identity of the ruling race, or—it is nearly the same thing—not completely masculine and adult:

> There are but few grown people, we trust, of the sterner sex in this country, not members of the Society of Friends or immedi-

ately connected with the Department of the Interior, who would
find many tears to shed over the extermination, in whole or in part,
of any of the barbarian tribes which infest our Northwestern
frontiers.[72]

Within this framework, Custer himself now appears as the incarnation
of the heroic, virile, self-restrained, and tough-minded American whose
dominance in government is the *World's* desire. Forgetting its earlier criticism, the paper calls the expedition a "picturesque and instructive military
promenade," and praises Custer for having avoided confrontation and obtained Indian goodwill in a manner to satisfy "the most exacting Quaker."

> That the expedition would be handled as wisely and as skillfully
> as the circumstances in which it was undertaken would permit we
> had no doubt. Nor have we any doubt now that everything
> which could be done to carry the expedition through without com-
> ing to collision with the Indians has been done by General Custer.
> Our confidence as to this reposes not only on the reputation of
> General Custer, both as a man of sense and as a soldier, but also
> on the testimony already furnished to us by our special corre-
> spondent. . . .

The *World* also denies having questioned the expedition's objectives,
now that these have proved so desirable; and in its summary of Custer's
reports of the "remote Arcadia," it added some enthusiastic flourishes of
its own, including "brawling brooks alive with the sly and speckled trout"
(whose presence is specifically denied by the dispatches). "If the expedition has really opened for us a general Indian war, that result must be
attributed to the condition of things created by the headlong and irrational
policy of the Administration, and not to any defect of skill or judgment on
the part of the commanding general." It goes on to announce the doom
of "the already impossible 'Indian policy' of President Grant," and to pro-
claim before

> the Indians of our whole domain, the claim of the United States
> to complete sovereignty over them and over all their lands. . . .
> The life of every settler in the Far West depends henceforth upon
> our doing this. . . . It is our duty to see that they are compelled
> to respect the rights of person and of property of the lowliest
> white settler who ventures in the track of the pioneer beaver . . .
> as completely as they have been compelled to respect the explor-
> ing column of the "Long Haired Chief."[73]

The *World*, then, goes on record in favor of the unilateral extinction
of those pre-1871 treaties which were technically still in force between
Indian "nations" and the United States, and the reduction of all Indians
to the status of subjects or "wards" as envisioned in the 1871 legislation.
To achieve this end, it advocates the placement of Indian affairs in the
hands of the War Department and the army in order to end the policy
of "maudlin philanthropy" that has permitted the "irresponsible marauders"
to avoid realizing "a just understanding of their dependence upon our

authorities and . . . their duties to our people." Custer's success is evidence of their belief that under military control Indian affairs can be handled not by "amateurs" specializing in "gratuitous benevolence" but by "professionals" using "the methods of business." The soldier, in this instance, embodies both the military virtues and the capacities of the businessman, the capitalist; the two groups are identified as the sources of order and efficiency in government, and of industrial prosperity. The only question which remains is, Has the nation the will and resources to "compel [the Indians] to elect between living decent and orderly lives and being driven into the sea"?[74]

Ultimately, the *World's* reversal of attitude toward Custer and his expedition produces a shift even on the vital economic question of refunding the Northern Pacific—hitherto treated as another case of Grant's protecting his corrupt friends. On December 14, the *World* gave an account of the Northern Pacific's petition for congressional relief, emphasizing the railroad's utility in suppressing the "hunting Indians." Custer and other military men were cited as experts endorsing the scheme, and the reporter noted that Custer's "intelligent and successful service . . . in the Northwest . . . gives special weight to his opinion." Reversing its earlier opposition to the railroad as a useless extravagance, the *World* now declared its belief that the NPRR would "realize all its friends and promoters have hoped and dreamed for it," and that it would be a "mighty instrument" for finding a "final and peaceable solution of the Indian question." Moreover, the railroad's recovery (together with the revival of railroad building in general) would help end the depression: "in no other way can the nation, in its organic capacity, so legitimately, so speedily, and so cheaply help itself out of the prevailing business stagnation and depression," and end the unemployment that threatened the cities with a long and brutal winter.[75]

PARADISE POSTPONED

Thus Custer emerged as the hero of the *World's* 1874 edition of the Myth of the Frontier. He became in himself an argument that the government of the "best classes," embodied in a virtuous and professional class of soldierly gentlemen, was America's means to achieving a new chapter of heroic achievement and a renewal of prosperity and social peace. The *World's* account of Custer's slow progress back to Fort Lincoln reads like a kind of Wild West version of the Grand Review of 1865. The paper greeted with pleasure the news that prospectors had already begun gathering around the Hills, and printed travel instructions for the use of interested readers (supplied first by Charles Collins and later by Custer himself). But it evaded the embarrassing necessity of admitting that Grant's decision to send Custer was after all a good one, by declaring that Custer's conduct of the expedition was so expert that it obviated the criminal folly of Grant in having ordered it.[76]

However, Grant's next actions relieved the *World* of any remaining need for ideological hairsplitting. Taken aback by the speed and intensity of public response to the discovery of gold, Grant belatedly recognized what was obvious to everyone else from the first: that the Black Hills expedition was simply incompatible with the successful operation of the Peace Policy. Under pressure from supporters of the Peace Policy, and from army officers unsure of their duties toward Indians and prospectors, Grant issued orders closing the Black Hills to any white incursions.

The news caught the *World*'s gold-rush boosters in full cry. The issue of September 5 reported that the gold hunters were "A Tide That Cannot Be Stopped" and the editorialist mused that even if the reports proved exaggerated, the gold rush itself would benefit more people than it impoverished. Although many would lose their investments, "Disappointed and impoverished gold-hunters . . . make pretty good farmers, and the soil of the Black Hills is said to be rich." But right below the article on this irresistible "Tide" is a bold headline, which arrests the reader's eye: "ALL EXPEDITIONS TO BE STOPPED," datelined Washington.[77] Grant had now "allied" himself with Indians in opposition to the natural forward movement of his own race and culture. But this unnatural alliance was of a piece with the rest of Grant-ism, which had already enlisted white soldiers to protect black Reconstruction in the South. The two policies were interdependent, in the *World*'s view—both practically and ideologically. And both were as foolish and unnatural as King Canute's taking up arms against the tides of the ocean: so much like a force of nature is the drive of white America for progress and dominion.

For the rest of the year the *World* continued to juxtapose glowing accounts of the Hills with stories tracing Grant's mounting opposition to the policy of opening them to settlement. In these stories, Custer figures prominently as typifying the dilemma of the conscientious white officer, bound by obedience to the president's orders and by the imperatives of racial and national destiny. On September 8 the *World* reports miners "mobilizing" to enter the Hills and a mustering of both Indians and soldiers to stop them. Custer declares that he will obey orders to keep the miners out. But on the following day Custer is again quoted giving an enthusiastic account of "The Gold Fever," and detailing the Northern Pacific's facilities for bringing miners out to Dakota cheaply and rapidly. He also informs the reporter that he favors "the extinguishment of the Sioux title . . . for military reasons," and suggests that his views are shared by the army. This was concrete encouragement to the very miners he had sworn to discourage and detain. Chief among these "military reasons" is the "fact" that the Black Hills serve as the nexus of a secret communications network, linking the disaffected tribes as they conspire for a grand race war. He parenthetically expands on the prospects for mining, which are "even better than represented." Although asserting his intention to obey orders and keep the miners out, Custer confesses that it will be difficult to do so; and he urges the miners to wait for the inevitable extinction of Indian title in order to avoid hostilities. Custer then asserts that the Indians have no real need of the Hills, and he borrows Curtis's language of urban crime to characterize the Hills as "a backroom to which they escape after committing depredations." For Custer, then, the Hills are the key to Indian communications, the source of Indian conspiracies which must be disrupted permanently by military occupation.[78]

The headline of the article immediately following this was, taken in context, utterly damning: "THE PARADISE CLOSED / None But the Indians Permitted to Pass Over, Settle Upon, or Reside Therein." An editorial on "The Black Hills and the Gold-Seekers" endorsed Custer's obedience to orders and his hope that Indian title would be speedily extinguished. A September 11 article on the complaints of "Running Antelope" of the Uncapapas about white incursions and his demand for government rifles to repel the miners indicated clearly what the logical outcome of Grant's approach to the matter would be. Even if the Grant administration eschewed the racial treason that arming the hostiles against the miners would engender, its policies effectually supported the Indians' claim that the Hills were held sacred, even against Custer's revelations of their centrality to the Indians' warmaking power. THE BLACK HILLS / Practical Results of the Custer Expedition . . ." argues that the Hills are "An Underground Road Between the Agencies and the Hostile Camps." This suggestively links the Indians (and Quaker agents) with the Underground Railroad of prewar abolitionism—a damning connection for the *World's* readers.[79]

Grant's action forced proadministration newspapers to face up to a contradiction they had hitherto been able to evade. So long as the Black Hills expedition was the project of an administration theoretically committed to Indian rights, it was possible to assert that there was no inconsistency between the projects of protecting the Indians and developing the Black Hills. Now these papers were forced to choose between an open break with the administration and abandonment of the golden prospect of the New El Dorado. Western papers like the *Inter-Ocean* threw their weight behind the project of negotiating a sale of the Hills—a legalistic ploy that was predictably futile given Indian sentiment about the Hills. Other papers like the *Times* and *Tribune* and journals like the *Nation* aligned themselves with the administration and implicitly against Custer (since he continued to advocate opening up the Hills). These papers were not uncritical in their support of Grant and pointed up the inconsistency of his policy; nonetheless, they backed his orders to the army to bar miners and began a subtle denigration of the Black Hills reports, suggesting that with so many parties interested in a gold strike, it was not unlikely that the whole thing was a "job." Thus Custer and his expedition became symbolic integers in a renewed partisan debate which drew on what we may think of as the "countermyth" of the Indian fighter: the view that emphasizes the cruelty and guilt associated with seizing the Frontier, and which seeks to make amends by scapegoating the Frontier hero—painting him as a man of Indian-like violence or as the outlaw agent of antisocial impulses or forces.[80]

But for the *World* and other antiadministration papers, the new phase of the Black Hills story was easily assimilable. What could be more logical, in their story frame, than that the philanthropic coddlers of Indians and blacks should now bar civilized man from access to a new Eden and El Dorado?

The announcement of "Paradise Closed" on September 9 marked the beginning of a new phase of the Black Hills story, in which reprises of Custer's official report, and of those to follow, would be juxtaposed with more, and more strident, accounts of catastrophic events in a safety-valveless Metropolis. On September 11, an account of the Sioux protest against Custer's expedition was printed next to a small item on "Threatened Strike in England." On September 16, "THE RAILROAD WAR" described the continued efforts of the Grangers to obtain government regulation of railroads—another protectionist "folly." On September 19, the front page was divided between accounts of southern disorders in which blacks were said to be engaged (like the Indians) in an "uprising" and in "Drawing Rations" from the government; and opposite these, an account of the "WESTERN WONDERS" discovered by the exploring party of Ferdinand V. Hayden. On September 22, an account of "FIGHTS WITH INDIANS" appeared alongside an account of "A WEAVER'S TROUBLES / Conviction of a Striker in Paterson." An article on "THE INTERNATIONALS" meeting in Brussels reminded readers of the consequences of prolonged labor agitation and economic difficulty as Europe had experienced them; and an editorial on Wendell "Phillips and English Labor" noted the connection between the Friends of the Indian and prolabor radicalism.[81]

Other articles and editorials extended the parallel war of Indians and blacks laid out in the earlier "Negro Reservations." A letter from "An Alabama Lawyer" on "the Negro Problem" appeared on September 26 and painted a bleak picture of the consequences of Radical Reconstruction in the South. These appear very like those forecast for the Black Hills should the Indian title not be speedily extinguished. The *World* had proposed the removal of *all* Indians to waste places where they would subsist until such time as their lands were required, at which time they might either work, starve, or be exterminated. The Alabama Lawyer (citing Adam Smith and Malthus for authority) proposes a similar fate for the freedman, who has surrendered himself

> to all the ills of chronic misgovernment, till such time as the patience of our superior race shall be exhausted, when the process of extermination will be applied, with the same means and the same consequences as to the unfortunate aborigines.
>
> We will then occupy the singular position in history of having exterminated the original proprietors of the soil, of having supplied their places with a captive race, and of having exterminated them also when they were no longer useful to us.

The only alternative to this inevitable race war would be the development of a mixed plantation-farm system in the South which would absorb only those blacks who were capable of independent farming or needed for work on plantations. But what would become of the surplus blacks, forced out of employment by reduced plantations and out of farming by white competition? They might become a drifting proletarian population laboring on middle western farms or in eastern mines and factories—"as long as wages could be had."

> Perhaps the dream of R. J. Walker will be realized, and they will flow over Texas towards Mexico and Central America. At all events, nothing is to be feared from them by any country in which they are not greatly in the majority.

Thus for black labor as for white, the West is a necessary safety valve, without which the pressure cooker of economic competition and racial hostility will produce cataclysm and extermination. Yet the Frontier remains closed, despite Custer's discovery, by Indian depredators and Grant's philanthropists.[82]

The front page on October 14 offers perhaps the most alarming view of the prospects for a continually ramifying series of racial confrontations. Five of the page's six columns concern "THE BLACK LEAGUE / The Secret Society Doings of the Negroes in the South / Semi-Barbarians Led into Horrible Excesses by the Very Scum of Northern Carpetbaggism." In the sixth column, the Yellow Peril rears its head, threatening the crowded cities with "CHINESE EMIGRANTS / The Scum of Asia Floating Over to America / . . . The Coolie Trade Worse Than the African Slave Trade— Disreputable Chinese Women Exported by the Hundreds for Our Western Brothels."

On the inside pages of this issue, and the front page of October 17, this combination of ideas and images is developed and extended by association with Indian battles, and with the archaeological discoveries made by the expedition under Ferdinand V. Hayden in New Mexico. Hayden was a civilian scientist employed by the government to survey unexplored regions of the West with an eye toward their future development; and he promulgated his findings with such flair that he became famous as the "businessman's geologist," as much a promoter of western enterprises as an explorer. Hayden's party had discovered the ruins of ancient pueblos and cliff dwellings, and in his report (reprinted in the *World*) he presented these as relics of an ancient culture's doom and symbols of that tendency to self-destruction, decline, and fall which brings all civilizations low in time. The *World*'s juxtaposition of this sort of speculation with scare stories on race war and the infiltration of white society by black or yellow barbarians points a clear moral: the present social crisis faces America with ultimate ruin.[83]

The crucial political issue is presented in these terms: "*Shall Chinamen Vote?* Asia as Well as Ethiopia Stretching Out Her Hands." As the darker races burgeon among us, they seek a share of power; with numbers and power they will swamp us.

The question of the Chinese gaining the political rights of citizens is important because it restates the problem of black and Indian rights in a context that was especially inflammatory to western organized labor. But all of these various "questions" are part of a single doctrine, which aims at undermining the consensus of belief in the progressive extension of the franchise as the classic means of securing liberty. Just below the article that asks "Shall Chinamen Vote?" are a pair of items that reflect unfavorably on Susan B. Anthony and the suffragist movement. If we deny the vote to white women, they ask, how can we grant it to males of an inferior race? Yet their essential premise is that we must deny the vote to women, to affirm the virile character of the society, and the analogy works against each and all of the disenfranchised.[84]

As for white labor, its prospects worsen as winter approaches with the depression still unabated. The linkage of stories of urban crime with industrial strikes and demonstrations becomes increasingly marked in November, and the beginning of the long strike in the Pennsylvania coal-fields brought into prominence the name of the "Mollie Maguires," a supposed terrorist organization linked to the Irish miners of Pennsylvania. On November 18, for example, the front page carried scare headlines flanking the masthead of "A REIGN OF TERROR / Horrible Murders in the Pennsylvania Coal Regions"—the beginning of the Mollie Maguire scare. Next to this article was an account of the longshoremen's strike; and flanking the masthead on the opposite side, an account of hostilities with "THE RED MAN."

In the face of mounting pressure for seizing the Hills and renewing the Frontier safety valve, the Grant administration launched a counter-attack. Its first aim was to cool the gold fever by issuing denials of Custer's report by on-scene participants Professor Winchell and Fred Grant. The only effect was to provoke Custer's anger at Grant's having effectively called him a liar. Custer, of course, defended himself in spirited interviews, official reports which the papers reprinted, and testimony before government agencies and committees.[85]

His emergence as both the hero of the Black Hills and as an object of harassment by the administration now made him the *World*'s "pet." On November 18, the paper published a long adulatory review of *My Life on the Plains*, Custer's account of his adventures fighting the Southern Cheyenne in 1867–70. The review recalled Custer's fame as a Civil War cavalryman and gave him the chivalric sobriquet of "chevalier *sans peur et sans reproche*." It added that his account of frontier adventure could stir to life even the "tamely" beating pulses of civilized folk, arousing Americans to a sense of the possibility for heroic achievement. It was also an antidote to the "rubbish" of philanthropy in dealing with the Indian question. It notes that Custer has a sense of "the good points of Indian character," but that he is not blinded by a romantic reverence for the Noble Red Man of Cooper or sentiment for the pathetic object of Quaker charity.[86]

From the perspective of the *World* and the other papers opposed to Grant, the celebrity of Custer now took on a new shade of meaning. He had been seen as the Boy General of the Civil War, as the dreaded "Long Hair" of the Indian Frontier—and as a pet of the Grant regime. As a result of his summer's work, his heroic reputation had been renewed: he appeared as the bringer of the glad tidings of gold and a new garden of the West, as the young and terrible enemy of that sinister old savage Sitting Bull; and now he had emerged completely from the shadow of philanthropy and radicalism to appear as the enemy of Indian-coddlers and "she-males," and even as the enemy of the author of all these misguided philanthropies and corrupt bargains—President Grant himself.

And because Custer's standing as a figure in public myth began to matter once again, his real-life relationsip to the world of political affairs acquired a new significance.

PART SEVEN
The Boy General, 1839–1876

CHAPTER 16

West Point, Wall Street, and the Wild West, 1839–1868

The process by which any myth or legend is created is necessarily complex, since each myth reflects in its degree and scale the complexity of the whole "web of culture" on which it draws. Since the symbolic materials that help compose the fable are a given of the cultural vocabulary, there is a sense in which the culture as a whole acts as author. In the creation of the myths of Custer and the Last Stand, the preexisting language of the Myth of the Frontier played a crucial role. It pointed the attention of American writers, journalists, and ideologists toward figures of Custer's type and stories of the kind in which Custer was involved.

A mythological determinist might assert that had Custer not existed, another such figure would have been invented; and the myth would have preserved for us the memory of a different sort of wilderness discovery and a different catastrophic battle. But, in fact, the Custer myth is the product of a special conjunction of historical circumstances and is the handiwork of human authors whose contributions are distinguishable. The journalists who began the process of mythologizing Custer were initially attracted to his story by their recognition that the man and the event were realizations of the myths in which they believed; and they were held to it by the fact that Custer was a principal in several major historical events and in a significant political struggle that affected important government policies. The peculiar ironies of Custer's fate, and the spectacular scale of his 1874 triumph and his 1876 defeat, likewise drew their attention as no other combination of events would have done. Other soldiers won victories like Custer's at the Washita (1868), other army explorers were in the field, other soldiers suffered defeat comparable to Custer's, but none did all of these things in sequence and at a time when western affairs were accorded center stage. Thus the first stage of authorship in the making of the Custer myth was the processing of the story by those who recognized, in the historical events, the acting out of mythic patterns and who then interpreted the events as metaphorically connected to the whole range of current ideological conflicts.

But Custer himself is an author of the story. In a general sense, any responsible historical actor can be said to author his story by the making of choices that express his motives and shape his career. In so doing, he draws, consciously or unconsciously, on the same mythic vocabulary that his contemporary chroniclers will draw on. But Custer is an author of his own myth in a more specific sense. He recognized early in his career the value of reputation, or what we would call image, as a means of affecting the judgment of his social and military superiors. And his experience of public celebrity and rapid promotion as a result (in part) of press coverage of him during the Civil War taught him how he could shape his audience's attitude by playing a role drawn from the lexicon of popular myth. In his maturity Custer became interpreter as well as actor, through a systematic literary exploitation of his public image. We will, therefore, be concerned with Custer's own consciousness of existing mythology and its influences on his actions and his representation of those actions. In this respect, we will be treating him not only as author but as part of the cultural audience for which the myth of his own catastrophe would be made.

If we look at Custer's biography with the eye of a contemporary dime novelist or historical romance writer, with a view toward presenting it as a Frontier fable in the grand tradition of the Leatherstocking Tales and the legend biographies of Boone, Crockett, and Kit Carson, we will be struck by certain structural anomalies. From Benjamin Church down through the Boone legendry of Filson and Flint, the hagiography of Weems's *Life of Washington,* and the up-from-under fables of Crockett and Carson, to the political biographies of Frontier candidates like Jackson and Houston, the story of the Frontier hero follows one general pattern. The protagonist is usually represented as having marginal connections to the Metropolis and its culture. He is a poor and uneducated borderer or an orphan lacking the parental tie to anchor him to the Metropolis and is generally disinclined to learn from book culture when the book of nature is free to read before him. His going to the wilderness breaks or attenuates the Metropolitan tie, but it gives him access to something far more important than anything the Metropolis contains—the wisdom, morality, power, and freedom of Nature in its pure wild form.

The hero's experience of the wilderness is not, however, so much an education as it is a conversion and transformation; and when he returns to civilization, he is seen as a strange and difficult figure. He is either exalted to leadership or treated as a misfit and outlaw because his powers and perceptions are such as to call the normal restraints of social practice into question. Through this figure, in either case, the deep wisdom of the natural wilderness is transmitted to the sluggish life of the Metropolis, informing and energizing it, regenerating its capacity for creative development. The hands which bring this boon to society have been reddened with blood of savage enemies killed; the mind or spirit which transmits the meanings of the wilderness is colored—perhaps even tainted—by the antisocial spirit of the savagery in which it has been tutored. In the case of Washington and the other president-heroes, this tutelage is mastered by an extraordinary endowment of aristocratic self-restraint. For the Frontier hero of literary mythology the case is different. The violent spirit of the warrior hero, and the violent means by which he has gained his wisdom, are inseparable from the regenerative process he initiates. Thus this hero can only function as a social benefactor when he operates on the edge of society, where it confronts the unsocial wilderness. The spectacular violence underscoring his achievement is morally acceptable only when it occurs beyond the borders and when its objects are those primitive and alien races whose existence is antithetical to the triumph of the Metropolis. Violence in the wilderness against the Indian is, as we have seen, the alternative to some form of civil class war which, if allowed to break out within the Metropolis, would bring about a secular *Götterdämmerung*.

Custer's career reverses the order and significance of the roles of Frontier and Metropolis in shaping the hero. Custer was born in New Rumley, Ohio, a distant backwash of the frontier in 1839. In marking out his future, he consistently elected to go east rather than west in search of opportunity. Only after he had graduated from West Point, and made his name as a Civil War hero, did he go west to the wilderness—and then he did so reluctantly and with one eye on the Metropolis. If he was, in the classic Frontier-hero pattern, a poor student, he was nonetheless a persistent student and book learner who came to the book of nature tardily. And although he would figure in myth as a genuine Wild Westerner and a virile rebel against all sorts of old-fogeyism, he was in fact a man who saw his path to fame and fortune as lying within the hierarchical structures of the United States Army and New York's "polite society." He is an early type of organization man, hiding in the costumes of the cavalier trooper and the Frontier buckskin.

The first son of Emmanuel and Lydia Kirkpatrick Custer, "Autie" (as George Armstrong was baby-named) was the pet of their large, disorderly, and affectionate menage. With the family chronically down at heels, and with Mrs. Custer often sickly, the work of childrearing fell to Custer's elder half-sister Lydia Kirkpatrick. In 1849, she married David Reed, a "middling" farmer from Monroe, Michigan, and brought young Autie to live with her. Once installed in her own house, Lydia determined to substitute discipline and respectability for the permissive regime of the Custer household, and her influence on Custer's developing conscience was profound.[1]

Lydia and Emmanuel Custer represent the moral and symbolic poles of his character. Lydia spoke for the bourgeois values of respectability and self-discipline which Custer's society had traditionally vested in "Woman"; and Father Custer represented masculine combativeness, defiance of respectability, and love of display—colorful when measured against Lydian standards, but suspect too. These elements first found symbolic expression in the young boy's search for a personal style. Frequent changes of costume and hair style throughout his life marked his ambivalent play with different roles. His hairstyle was especially symbolic: he alternately grew his hair long and clipped it short, got his head "peeled like an onion" or let his curls swing below his shoulders perfumed with cinnamon oil. The "long-haired" phases suggested his father's flamboyance; yet the style itself made him appear "feminine," and he enjoyed the implications of sensual attractiveness that the adjective implied—and enjoyed also the ambivalent linkage with his half-sister Lydia. Yet "respectable" virtues often required him to shear his locks, Samson-like—it was characteristic of him to clip his mustache and mail it to his wife.[2]

Custer's attraction to a military career was likewise composed of equal parts Lydia and Emmanuel: his father was an enthusiastic celebrant of gaudy militia musters; his sister wanted for him the education and the status of gentleman which the military career would confer. After a stint of schoolteaching, Custer petitioned his congressman, the former Whig and now (in 1856) Republican John Bingham, for a nomination to West Point; and received it on his second try in 1857.[3]

West Point in 1857 had two missions: to provide officers for the army posts that protected the frontier and federal property in the states; and to supply a technical education for topographical, civil, and military engineers. Until 1859 West Point was the only engineering school in the country, and its military-trained engineers provided expertise not only for the building of forts, but for internal improvements, railroad building, harbor and canal work, and mining. Engineering and the closely related discipline of artillery were therefore the centers of the curriculum and attracted the best of the cadets. But Custer's interest in these subjects was minimal. He had come to West Point to "be a soldier," and to acquire the status marks of a gentleman. His concept of soldiering itself seems to have been borrowed from the novels of Charles Lever, which romanticized the adventures of young aristocratic cavaliers in the Napoleonic Wars, and from the southerners who dominated both the social life of the academy and the upper ranks of the army. He maintained friendship with his southern classmates after 1861, and even congratulated them on their personal successes in letters sent through the lines under flag of truce. Custer's prankishness, "gamecock" combativeness, and propensities for gambling nearly cost him a commission; and the demerits he earned for eccentric behavior, hairstyles, and dress lowered his class standing to last.[4]

West Point also offered Custer a grounding in the ideology, values, and moral duties of a would-be member of the republican ruling class. His Ethics class was taught from Francis Wayland's *Elements of Moral Science* (1837), perhaps the most widely used text of the period because of its appealing balance of theological arguments with applied or "Practical Ethics." For Wayland the problem of morality is one of education rather than one of divine grace or predestination. He sees human nature as dual, divided between the body's base animal instincts, and the higher aspirations and affections resident in the mind. By imposing moral discipline in early youth, instilling habits of virtuous obedience, and buttressing these with education in the bases of moral precepts, men can become progressively more moral, more Chirstian as they grow from childhood to adulthood.[5]

At West Point the concept of moral discipline articulated by Wayland was applied allegorically to the relations of command. Although he shares with civilians the general duty of obedience to God and to law, the soldier's responsibility to the institutions of army and government becomes his chief referent for the source of morality. Individual conscience does not exist as an independent faculty; rather, it is equated with habits of feeling and behavior which must be mechanically inculcated, lest the desires of the flesh overwhelm it. Thus in an essay on "Duties and affections which we ought to acquire and possess" Cadet Custer notes three "objections" or obstacles to the achievement of virtue: "The power of directing our thoughts" which may be inadequate to the task of self-discipline; "The recollection that Affections are natural" and therefore subject to distortion by the desires of the flesh; and certain innate propensities of individual character, particularly "Coldness of heart—male violence."[6]

Custer may have recognized in the use of the sexual metaphor to differentiate categories of moral and social behavior a doctrinalization of the roles of Lydia and Emmanuel Custer. This moral theory also conformed to romantic literary convention which assigned to the passive female a moral status higher than that of the male, whose violence is the female's sole and necessary protection. Violence—which was to be his profession—could be exercised with moral impunity to protect or avenge the imperiled "female." Once joined on such an issue, combat was justified and limited only by the efficiency of the fighter, the standards of the profession, and the prohibition against offending the "female" principle. As a male, Custer had to guard against the tendency for his "natural affections" to do violence to the "female," through "coldness of the heart"—that is, a tendency to put personal achievement before the demands of heart and hearth. The fear of proving "wanting in natural affection" was to be a continual theme in his letters home. To rise above his circumstances he had had to leave home, first for Lydia's house in Monroe and later for West Point; the masculine pursuit of fame and success required continual alienation from the sources of affection. Good conscience therefore required that the tie to home be continually affirmed and given homage in the form of letters home, and of grand ethical pronouncements in schoolroom essays.[7]

Like the culture that produced him, Custer was ambivalently drawn to both the "masculine" imperatives of self-assertion and stern command, and the "feminine" morality of subservience and Christian philanthropy. As an adolescent, as an army cadet, as an apprentice citizen of the republic, Custer's role was that of the child seeking to define an adult role for himself, without sacrificing the love or approval of paternal and maternal authorities—parents, God, his commanders, the state. But there was an inherent double bind here, a paradoxical imperative to become a self-reliant man and to remain a child and a subordinate to authority. Custer's response to this psychological impasse was also characteristic of his culture: he split "authority" into masculine and feminine aspects, and played to the preferences of each in a different way. With his feminine authorities— mother, sister, wife—he played the "good bad boy," always getting into scrapes through his high-spirited rebelliousness, but remaining fundamentally good and affectionate at heart—and proving this by turning penitently to his women for forgiveness, approval, and a renewal of love. Thus he simultaneously paid homage to the special moral power of women and Christian ideals, and asserted his manly power to rebel against or exceed them when his personal needs or military necessity required it.

Masculine authority was embodied in the command structure of the army, but Custer needed to personalize this institutional power. He therefore sought to court the sympathies of powerful and favored commanders (or powerful civilians) to turn them into "second fathers": men whose authority and command would direct him in correct paths, but who would temper their sternness with quasi-familial affection for their boyish subordinate. Obedience to such father figures would, in Custer's view, also provide protection from the enmity of jealous peers or rival superiors. The boy soldier could be rebellious against some authorities, so long as he remained filial to his chosen patriarch.[8]

Custer's refashioning of masculine and feminine authority was an adaptive response, which enabled him to do almost as he wished in the world of affairs, so long as he was able to retain the protective loyalty of his military patrons and the affectionate approval of his sister and wife. His role playing with these authorities allowed him to enjoy simultaneously the pleasures of rebellious self-assertion and the good conscience that comes from filial obedience. In the course of his career as Civil War soldier, as Indian fighter, as Gilded Age speculator, as political man, and as self-publicist, Custer inevitably said and did things that were morally questionable. His characteristic way of dealing with such situations was to seek the approval of some figure of authority who was vested, in his eyes, with familial symbolism. In extreme cases he would throw himself upon the mercy of one of his "second fathers," for relief or mitigation of discipline; and always he would write to his sister Lydia and his wife Libbie, protesting his sorrow, remorse, and fundamental innocence. His conscience was, in effect, sequestered in the privileged enclaves of the military fraternity and the bosom of the family.

The combination and familial symbolism with a theory of moral action which stresses obedience to authority tends to produce characters who can comfortably vest their consciences in the persons and doctrines of the society's highest political class. Custer made a very personal application of the teachings of Wayland and West Point, as it was meant he should do. But those teachings were addressed to a larger ideological task than the training of soldiers. They were offered as a general model of republican citizenship, which rooted political authority in the organic and fixed forms of the patriarchal family and the regiment—and not in the changing assertions of the "will of the people," from which the Revolution derived its authority. From the organic or familial model of the state, Wayland was able to deduce and to justify the major institutional characteristics of the capitalist economy as he found it. The system of private property was not a mere appendage of a democratic politics, but as organic to it as sexual roles are to husband and wife, or the Ten Commandments to the nature of Jehovah. It was for his handling of this theme that Wayland achieved his preeminent status as a moral educator.[9]

Wayland's doctrine assimilated Christian idealism to the requirements of a business ethic by presenting the Protestant Reformation's most significant contribution to civilization not in the theology of Luther and Calvin, but as reflected in the concept of privacy in conscience and in the holding of property. Property itself is the basis of all secular progress, and the worst of crimes is the interference of government with the rights of property holders—a secular equivalent of persecution for conscience. This implied acquiescence in the existence of slavery, even though Wayland regarded the institution as morally abominable: the doctrine of property in this crucial case is superior to a purely ethical judgment. As filtered through Custer's West Point instructors, Wayland's precepts became a simpleminded endorsement of the *corporate* values of the nascent capitalist order in America. Indeed in one cadet essay Custer, following Wayland, resorts to some fairly contorted biblical exegesis in order to rationalize the division of society between rich and poor:

> The first Christians had it for a main object of their lives, to exhibit [*sic*] their abhorrence [for] love of money and want of compassion. . . . The Christians made their protest against these vices, by discarding a regard for money. Yet in 1 Tim. vi. 17— Charge them that are rich in this work—*implies that some Christians were rich.*

Coupled with the familial metaphor, his argument suggests that, in society, the men of wealth and command position are "fathers" and the lesser folk "children." As the child grows into the man, so may the propertyless work their way toward its ownership and the status of "fathers." But despite this dynamism, the roles of fathers and sons remain fixed in the social fabric: there are always rich, always poor, just as there are always fathers and children, and one is always subordinate to the other.

For Custer, this vision of class relations had a particular application. His choice of profession was a decision to rise in the world; and the world he had chosen was one in which hierarchy was explicit as a chain of command. Custer therefore looked to his commanders for earthly surrogates of that divine love which Wayland enjoined him to seek; and he expected that with such love would come secular regard and promotion. His letters, even those written after the Civil War, emphasize the paternal affection his commanders have for him and suggest they are like "second fathers." Even as his cadet's essay acknowledged the objection that good deeds without true faith and love "profiteth nothing," he was certain that the chief "considerations by which the above duties are urged upon Christians are that they are the *means of obtaining God's favor.*" It is the promise of reward that motivates the profession of faith.[10]

But the status of the slave posed a problem for this system of belief. If the Christian and familial orders were the models of a social order, why should blacks not be equally entitled to work their way to political freedom and a chance at gaining earthly riches? To accept slavery as good and necessary, Custer had to insist upon the reality of a racial distinction between his own poor white class and the class of the black slaves. This distinction would have to acknowledge that some element in his own class might well correspond to whatever it was that kept blacks in slavery— otherwise, why should the white poor be always with us?—but it would have to permit the possibility that members of the white underclass could indeed transcend their limitations.

The simplest model for such a transition was that of maturation. As the boy grows into the man, he transcends the limitations of the parental household and acquires his freedom. If his capacities are superior to those of his parents, he may rise to a higher status. He may pay for this transcendence with a painful exile from his affectional home, may be visited by nostalgia and by a kind of guilt; but he must recognize the change as inevitable, destined by God and by his own character.

Custer found a perfect vehicle for expressing these sentiments in an essay on "The Red Man," also written in 1858. The traditional view of the Indian as the "child of nature" and the representative of an immature state of society made him serviceable as a metaphor for the childhood state in general; and in portraying Indians as a doomed race, Custer passes sentence on childish things in general. More than this, it suggests a grand historical analogy for the process, linking Custer's personal development to the larger concepts of "progress" and the Myth of the Frontier. He begins with a vision of the Indian as innocent child of nature—conceived of as a doting maternal deity:

> When we first beheld the red man, we beheld him in his home, the home of peace and plenty, the home of nature. Sorrow's furrowed lines were unknown on his dauntless brow . . . His heart did not quake with terror at every gust of wind that sighed through the trees, but on the contrary, they were the favored sons of nature, and she like a doting mother, had bestowed all her gifts on them. They stood in their native strength and beauty, stamped with the proud majesty of free born men, whose souls never knew fear, or whose eyes never quailed beneath the fierce glance of man. But what are they now, these monarchs of the west? They are like withered leaves of their own native forest, scattered in every direction by the fury of the tempest.

There is more than a little suggestion here of a sentimental association between the youthful author and his mythical subject: the "favored son" of *two* "doting mother[s]", now exiled to a cold, distant place:

> The red Man is alone in his misery. The earth is one vast desert to him. Once it had charms to lull his spirit to repose, but now the home of his youth, the familiar forests, under whose grateful shade, he and his ancestors stretched their weary limbs after the excitement of the chase, are swept away by the axe of the woodman.

Yet the end for the Indian is not to achieve manhood by transcending alienation and hardship, but to suffer the doom of his race, perishing even as maternal nature—his protectress—is subjected to the masculine tools of advancing Christian-industrial civilization:

> We behold him now on the verge of extinction, standing on his last foothold, clutching his bloodstained rifle, resolved to die amidst the horrors of slaughter, and soon he will be talked of as a noble race who once existed but have now passed away.[11]

The "Red Man" essay has often been cited as an ironic foreshadowing of Custer's end as the deluded victim of his own illusions. However, its real significance lies in its revelation of the way in which the symbolic vocabulary of the Frontier Myth functioned in the acculturation of one American boy, providing him with a language that simultaneously addressed the public concerns of history and moral philosophy, and the private symbolism of his adolescent psychology.

For the West Point cadet, the catastrophe of civil war was also the path to exceptional personal opportunity. The expansion of the regular army and the creation of a huge force of volunteers and conscripts opened up numerous positions at all ranks, for which trained officers—particularly as those southern-born broke oath and returned south—were few. Men with any sort of military experience or political influence could, with judicious politicking, obtain ranks in a fortnight for which prewar professionals had waited a lifetime. However, Custer's age (twenty-one) and lack of political pull told against him during the early days of the war when demands on patronage were at their highest. He began as a lieutenant in the Fifth U.S. Cavalry, not a very desirable appointment. Advancement in a line regiment would inevitably be slower than in volunteer service because promotions in such regiments had permanent status—as opposed to the temporary or brevet status of the volunteers. But Custer was careful about advancing his career and astute in his analysis of the military bureaucracy: failing to achieve a high rank, he sought out appointments as a staff officer to rising generals of brigade and division, hoping himself to rise through their patronage.[12]

Custer was an able and industrious staff officer who did not shirk the most serious responsibility of his position—giving orders to higher-ranking officers as the agent of his general, sometimes on his own discretion. He was thirsty for distinction and willing to risk his life in seeking it. In the new country of the army he was appropriately shifty at first, moving from general to general, until he finally attracted the attention of the army commander, General McClellan. At that time, McClellan was just past the peak of his fame as the "Young Napoleon," his national reputation tarnished somewhat by his delay in taking the field, but within his own army the object of adoration by nearly all his men. Custer's relationship with McClellan set the pattern for his professional career: he thought of his commander as a patron and a father, giving and demanding absolute loyalty. After McClellan, Generals Alfred Pleasonton and Sheridan played this role. Of Pleasonton he said, "I do not believe a father could love his son more than General Pleasonton loves me. He is as solicitous about me and my safety as a mother about her only child."[13]

McClellan was not only the commander of the nation's principal army but, as the leader of the conservative opposition to the Lincoln government and its policies, a likely candidate to oppose Lincoln at the next election. Throughout his tenure of command, McClellan and his clique of officers corresponded with the leadership of the Democratic Party, speculating on means of overturning Lincoln's policies—which, as soldiers, they were obliged to enforce. Custer is even said to have joined in "staff talk" advocating the military overthrow of Lincoln's government. The McClellan group tended to see the responsibility for secession as lying more with black Republicans and abolitionists than with the actual secessionists; and they hoped and sometimes surreptitiously worked for a rapprochement with their former classmates and colleagues who led the other side. So poisonous did the political atmosphere become that McClellan and his followers often seemed to take satisfaction in Union defeats—even their own defeats—when these seemed to work mischief with Republican plans. "Nigger equality" summed up their notion of the Emancipation Proclamation; and it was McClellan's negative response to that proclamation that, as much as anything else, led to his removal in November 1862. McClellan thus contrived to be one of the most popular generals of the war—and the only major commander about whom rational suspicions of treasonable activities and intentions to make a coup may be maintained.[14]

After his removal, McClellan went to New York City to work with financier and national Democratic Party chairman August Belmont on building a McClellan candidacy. McClellan took one aide with him to help compose his final report, which was also to contain his critique of the administration and a defense of his military career. The aide was Lieutenant Custer. It was at this time that Custer first became acquainted with the financial, political, and journalistic elite of the metropolis; and he was introduced to them under the most favorable auspices, as the loyal aide of their chosen candidate. His letters from this period are happy, if hasty, and not at all concerned that being a McClellan man could hurt him.[15]

This happy phase, however, did not last. Union fortunes prospered without McClellan. Custer could not hang about until 1864 waiting for McClellan to become president. He rejoined the army on the staff of General Pleasonton, one of the McClellan clique who had managed to stay in place. Pleasonton gave him responsible duties and rapidly advanced him to command of the Michigan Cavalry Brigade in June, 1863—promoting him at a single leap from staff captain to brigadier general of Volunteers.

The appointment was especially gratifying to Custer, because he had earlier tried and failed to obtain the colonelcy of one of the brigade's regiments. He had petitioned the Governor of Michigan, and had gone to the extent of asking officers in the regiment to petition on his behalf. While on leave in Monroe he had also courted local Republican leaders, including Judge Daniel Bacon—a notable ex-Whig and perhaps the most respected man in Monroe. Here a complication arose which, in the end, sweetened the triumph of Custer's promotion still further: Custer was introduced to Bacon's daughter Elizabeth, and the two fell in love. The Judge was not unfriendly to Custer's military ambitions, but objected to the idea of a marriage: the Reeds and Custers were not in Bacon's social class; and although Custer was "patriotic" by Republican standards, he did bear the taint of close association with McClellan. However, Libbie was smitten with Custer; and his promotion to brigadier general—coupled with some political assurances—seem to have turned the judge in his favor. He courted his father-in-law assiduously, characterizing himself in formulas that anticipate the language and values of the Alger hero Ragged Dick:

It is true that I have often committed errors of judgment, but as I grew older I learned the necessity of propriety. I am aware of your fears of intemperance, but surely my conduct for the past two years . . . should dispel that fear. . . . I left home when but sixteen, and have been surrounded with temptation, but I have always had a purpose in life.[16]

Custer's marriage to Miss Elizabeth Bacon followed shortly after his promotion to general. Their relationship, though close, affectionate, and persistently romantic, was not the absolute idyll which Elizabeth and her amanuensis Marguerite Merington portrayed in their reminiscences and collections of letters. One unpublished and partly destroyed letter in the Yale collection records a period of near estrangement early in the marriage, possibly over some indiscretion of Custer's; and there were persistent rumors about Custer's flirtations and his alleged keeping of an Indian mistress. However, there seems no reason to question the traditional view of their marriage as generally a happy one. They were childless by choice, were in a sense each other's children, addressing each other as "Boy" and "Little Durl."[17]

Custer and Libbie were frequently separated while he was on campaign, and their extensive correspondence reveals that Libbie was an indispensable audience for him, the mirror in which he could project his desired self-image. He offered her images of himself as sentimentally mourning over the horrors of war and then other images of himself leading charge after charge, crying out "Glorious War!" And although repeating "for your ears only" the praises heaped upon him, he also made effective use of the conventions which permitted a public figure (or his correspondent) to publish private letters or put them in the hands of those capable of doing the sender some good.

Custer's self-dramatizations were vital to him, not merely because they served to advance his cause with his audience—whether Libbie Bacon or her father the judge or some more powerful political or military leader—but because they allowed him to distance himself from realities that were at least unpleasant, and could be morally devastating. The "horrors of war" and its inescapable cruelties come under this head; but Custer was more concerned to keep Libbie ignorant of the political and (later) commercial chicanery through which he had to advance himself. This self-protective style extended to his affective life as well. It is his own statement, confirmed by Libbie, that he was often more passionate in letters than he was face to face, and that, on the whole, he preferred written to direct contact. His courtship of Libbie had been so conducted, partly because of Judge Bacon's early objections—but partly, one suspects, because something about epistolary romance appealed to Custer, and perhaps to Libbie as well.[18]

If Custer was temperamentally inclined toward this manipulative use of correspondence, his experience of wartime politics taught him that such duplicity was essential to the protection let alone the advancement of his career. His reputation as a McClellan man and the son of a proslavery Democrat injured his standing specifically with the powerful Radical Republican senators from Michigan, Zachariah Chandler and Jacob Howard, who controlled army promotions. To justify himself to these men, Custer dissembled his previous political affiliations and the nature of his relationship with McClellan, invoking two prevalent myths to characterize his actions and opinions. The first (and least persuasive) of these was the myth of the apolitical patriotism of the professional soldier—a stereotype discredited by the "treason" of southern officers and the evident political engagement of McClellan and his clique. But Custer was able to associate himself credibly with a more basic mythic structure—the myth of race war, of the war of extermination which is the means to a regeneration of moral and social character.

In his letter to Senator Howard, Custer evades the McClellan connection by advocating the political genocide of the rebels; and he identifies the enemy not by the test of political affiliation but by the invocation of the racial concept of "rebel blood":

> As to "compromise," I know of no compromise with rebels by which we could restore our dignity and self respect as a nation of freemen. If I could decide the question, I would offer no compromise except that which is offered at the point of the bayonet. And rather than that we should accept peace, except on our own terms, I would, and do, favor a war of extermination. I would hang every human being who had a drop of rebel blood in their veins whether they be men, women or children. Then . . . I would settle the whole southern country with a population loyal and patriotic who would not ever forget their obligation to their country and to themselves. . . .

Finding this effort well received, he reiterated his position in a public letter, published in the Detroit *Free Press* in May 1865, and widely reprinted: "Extermination is the only true policy we can adopt toward the political leaders of the rebellion. . . . Then, and not till then, may the avenging angel sheathe his sword, and our country will emerge from this struggle regenerated."[19]

This invocation of a racial metaphor to define political struggle, together with the scenario of regeneration through a war of extermination, reflects Custer's studied response to the ideological pressures of the Civil War. The appeal of such rhetoric to Custer and to Custer's audience suggests how far that kind of thinking was developed by the war; and it shows how the war prepared Americans for the "exterminationist" rhetoric that would later be deployed by Sherman and Sheridan against the Indians, by the Democratic conservatives against the freedmen, and by northern conservatives against "red" agitators and rebellious urban "paupers." However, the wider public stopped far short of acceptance of this rhetoric; even moderate Republican newspapers like the New York *Times* took pains to distance themselves from the kind of language Custer was using, and proposed hanging only for those who were guilty of particular and atrocious war crimes.[20]

Moreover, Custer himself did not believe what he was saying. His friendship with southern officers predated the war and persisted right through it, and his political sympathies and allegiances lay with the conservative Belmont-McClellan wing of the Democracy. As soon as it became feasible, he abandoned this pretense of radicalism.

However, Chandler and Howard were not at all moderate; and even if they discounted Custer's rhetoric by half, they could still feel assured that he wanted to be their man (or their boy, to adopt Custer's own favored epithet). Moreover, the Boy General had credentials which the senators could not ignore, and which made him a valuable potential ally. By the last year of the war Custer had made an enviable military reputation as brigade and division commander; and his flamboyant dress and self-dramatization had captured the imagination of influential sectors of the press. As a general, Custer has had a mixed reputation—the disaster at the Little Big Horn retrospectively discredits his professionalism. The military historian Fletcher Pratt expresses the modern judgment that Custer was "a gallant idiot who could lead a charge supremely well, but do very little else." However, his reputation in 1865 was very different. War correspondents and even some military colleagues compared Custer favorably with Murat, Napoleon's dashing cavalry commander—some even compare him to the young Napoleon himself. Pleasonton, who got Custer his star, asserted that he had the primary requisites of the cavalry general—an eye for terrain, a sense of the proper time for action, and the essentially theatrical qualities necessary to conduct a cavalry attack amid the noise and confusion of battle. However, perhaps the most judicious assessment of Custer's abilities was made just after the war by Whitelaw Reid, who described him as "active, highly energetic, and honorable" although "he gave no evidence of great generalship. As a subordinate, to a leader like Sheridan, he was in his proper sphere. In such a capacity, for quick dashes and vigorous spurts of fighting, he had no superiors, and scarcely an equal."

Under the special circumstances and tasks faced by the Union cavalry late in the war, Custer was in fact able to distinguish himself. Cavalry charges were not at all common during the war, and the superior range of rifles and artillery often rendered futile those that did occur. Custer was fortunate in having, and admirable in seizing, two of the uniquely favorable moments for a saber charge, at Gettysburg and at Cedar Creek. But he also knew how to take advantage of the Union cavalry's superior firepower, as he showed in the closing battles near Petersburg. His talents were particularly suited to the requirements of the cavalry's role in the closing campaigns, which involved rapid pursuit of a beaten enemy deficient in cavalry. The respect accorded him by Sheridan and Grant is testimony to his genuine abilities.[21]

But Custer's Republican judges also had to acknowledge that he had few rivals who could equal his ability to attract the attention of the press and to impress himself vividly on the imagination of its readers. He knew how to court reporters' friendship, and the theatrical qualities that Pleasonton noted in his leadership of cavalry charges served him well in this connection. Before his elevation to general, for example, Custer had apparently been dressed like Huck Finn, Ragged Dick, or Prince Hal at the Boar's Head Tavern—half in ragged clothes captured from the enemy. Such, at least, is the testimony of his unreliable biographer Fred Whittaker, whose 1876 account of Custer's transformation often sounds a good deal like

Mark Twain's *Tom Sawyer*, also published in 1876. In any case, the day after his promotion he appeared rigged out in a suit of black velveteen slathered with gold braid, a bright red scarf that became his trademark, D'Artagnan boots, and a plumed piratical sombrero: in Tom Sawyer's terms, "Respectable Huck Joins the Gang." Reporters loved him: he was good for a story every time he put on, or took off, that hat.

Custer's closest contact in the press corps was E. A. Paul of the New York *Times*, who became his personal friend and promoter. It is interesting that this correspondent, who once rode through Confederate lines to warn Custer of an ambush, and who knew him best, chose to emphasize not the mad gallantry and boyish appearance of the general, but his "coolness," his ability to plan an operation "worthy of a NAPOLEON." Where his career was concerned, Custer wished to associate himself with the imagery of adulthood, paternal authority, the qualities of the masculine and ruling class. However, the greater part of the press preferred to see him as did a New York *World* reporter who, in his account of the victory of Cedar Creek, showed Custer arriving at headquarters in a rush of childish exuberance, lifting Sheridan into the air and carrying him around, and embracing the grizzled General Alfred Torbert so tightly that he cried out, "There, there, old fellow. Don't capture *me!*" In a book published shortly after Appomattox, Colonel Frederic Newhall of Sheridan's staff elaborates on this imagery: Custer's youthful high spirits make him useless in the patient labor of a siege, "but for a sudden dash, Custer against the world." Others associate his youthful energy with a "storm-gale" that sweeps down all before it. When he charges rebel artillery, the guns go off like "firecrackers"—reduced to the playthings of reckless boys.[22]

Custer's wartime image is in fact distinctly dependent on the parallel symbolism of his youthful or adolescent qualities, his ambiguous sexuality, and his resemblance to warriors from a primitive or savage stage of social development. Many correspondents and memoirists emphasized the "almost feminine" qualities of the Boy General—his long fair curls and smooth skin, his high voice that "fairly screeches" calling his troops to charge, his "Merry eye and rosy lip," his vanity and self-display. The imagery has the effect of emphasizing his extreme youth, but this very quality marks him as a source of potential danger and disorder and perhaps as unfitted by temperament to play the role of paternal ruler whose powers lie in reason and coolness. Custer is described as a berserker in battle, "a Viking [in] long yellow locks," a "circus rider gone mad," whose success derives from his ability to channel that mad energy toward the enemy, to make the enemy mad with fear as he is mad with courage. Madness is his element—but that is not the element of a true leader of men. Newhall inadvertently points the ideological lesson when he notes that Northerners habitually refer to their soldiers as "boys" while Southerners call theirs "gentlemen."

Implicit in this association of images is the same mythology of social development we saw operating in the making of Custer's "Red Man" essay and federal Indian policy: that is, the traits of the mature masculine ruler—self-restraint, strength, orderliness, prudence, intellectuality, temperateness —are regarded as the hallmarks of civilization itself. Women, Indians, Negroes, and children are necessarily subject to white masculine rulers because of their lack of these qualities, their indulgence of their passions, the primacy of their physical over their intellectual needs and powers. As civilization ascends from the dark races to the white, so the man-child should grow from boy or boy-savage into adult man.

This pattern of associations came quite early to invest the figure of Custer, as we can see in the description of Custer's showing in the Grand Review of the Army of the Potomac in May 1865. Custer, riding at the head of the cavalry on a captured stallion named Don Juan, suffers an apparent runaway just beneath the reviewing stand—a runaway that allows him to lose his hat and liberate his flowing locks to the breeze, and which affords him a chance to display his mastery of the maddened beast at stage center. Many of his colleagues apparently regarded the event as a carefully planned "accident" intended to throw Custer's personality in sharp relief against the ordered solemnity of the day. But the *Times* wrote up the event as a miniature romantic comedy. The cavalier's "stallion" (surrogate for the man's animal self) becomes unmanageable when a fair damsel throws a bouquet at him:

> [T]he General catches it upon his arm, but the movement so frightens the magnificent stallion which the General rides, that he becomes unmanageable and dashes up the avenue at a frightful speed; but CUSTER is too good a horseman to be so easily unseated; minus hat and saber, holding onto the wreath with one hand, he brings his steed down with the other, and curbing him severely brings him back to his good behavior and in his place at the head of the division, and horse and rider, with superb spirit, have afforded the spectators the finest equestrian exhibition of the day.

Thus brought again under strict discipline by the rider (the intellectual being) the presence of the hero reveals itself.[23]

The New York *World* reporter describes the same scene in terms that later writers would regard as prophetic. Custer and his runaway stallion appear, the General with a "fair and ruddy complexion—a sunrise of golden hair which ripples upon his blue shoulders—on his left arm hangs a wreath of evergreens—scarlet kerchief—white gauntlets . . . in the sunshine his locks, unskeined, stream a foot behind him . . . it is like the charge of the Sioux chieftain." Of course, there is no prophecy involved, but rather the operation in the reporter's mind of an association of images based on conventions that were both historical (dating from Jacksonian sources) and archetypal. The youth of the hero, his vigor and potency, are attested by the ruddy, blood-filled cheeks, emblematically echoed in the flowing scarlet kerchief; images of sunshine associate him with warmth, the source of life; evergreens present the promise of eternal youth; the uncut, unskeined hair speaks of an abundant, as-yet-unchecked flow of animal spirits. That such a figure, evoking a primitive imagery, should also be associated with the Indian, the embodiment for Americans of those animal qualities and the living expression of the "youth" of the human race, is not extraordinary—although "Sioux" is an uncannily lucky hit.[24]

Custer was promoted to Major-General of Volunteers in 1865, perhaps the youngest man to hold that rank since the Marquis de Lafayette during the Revolution. But the imminent demobilization of the volunteer army after Appomattox threatened Custer and his fellow regular officers with the prospect of certain reduction in rank and pay, and possible unemployment. Custer would have reverted to a captaincy in the Regular Army. But the patronage of Sheridan, the favor he had achieved with powerful senators, and his journalistic popularity worked together to spare him that fate. Sheridan was appointed to take an army corps of infantry and cavalry— drawn from volunteer units held unwillingly in service—to occupy and begin the reconstruction of the distant state of Texas. A large force was required, not only because of the proverbial intransigence of Texans and the huge size of the district, but because the government wished to threaten intervention in Mexico, whose people under Juarez were in rebellion against a French army of occupation under the "Emperor" Maximilian.

Custer was made Chief of Cavalry under Sheridan, and allowed to retain his war-time rank and pay. The assignment was a "plum," and indicated that Custer stood very high in the favor of the Radical Republicans who controlled the military and reconstruction committees of the Congress. Taken with his exterminationist letters to the *Free Press* in May 1865, the Texas assignment confirmed the public's image of Custer as a soldier aligned with the Radicals, a "hard-war" man willing to scorch southern earth like Sherman, and take the Jacobins' way with fallen aristocrats.[25] After the conclusion of hostilities put an end to speculations about mass executions of rebel leaders, the test of Radical affiliation became the Reconstruction policy, especially as it regarded the enfranchisement of the ex-slaves. Testifying before the Committee on Reconstruction at the end of 1865, after his return from Texas, Custer expressed himself as favoring the continued disenfranchisement of the ex-Confederates; he praised the work of the Freedmen's Bureau and even went so far as to endorse Negro suffrage.

But Custer's private opinions contradict his testimony and public reputation. Writing in October 1865, Custer had spoken against the employment of Negroes as soldiers, and wished they might be "mustered out rapidly" since "There are white men, veterans, anxious to fill up the Army, to whom preference should be given."

> I am in favor of elevating the negro to the extent of his capacity and intelligence, and of our doing everything in our power to advance the race morally and mentally as well as physically, also socially. But I am opposed to making this advance by correspondingly debasing any portion of the white race. As to trusting the negro of the Southern states with the most sacred and responsible privilege—the right of suffrage—I should as soon think of elevating an Indian chief to the Popedom of Rome.

Apart from the interesting association of Catholics, blacks, and Indians, the passage aligns Custer with Democratic policy in the equation of black suffrage with the "debasing" of white Southerners—since the necessary precondition of Negro suffrage was disenfranchisement of the former Confederates. It also aligns him with that vital sector of Lincoln's free-soil constituency who sought the exclusion of blacks as such from the western territories.

Custer's letter continues, presenting a picture of black workers in Texas that is in direct contradiction to his picture of black diligence given before the committee two months later. It also aligns Custer with those conservatives who put the economic interests of owners and employers above the priorities of democratic reform.

> All advocates of giving suffrage to the southern negro should visit these States and see for themselves. . . . I have travelled over a considerable portion of this State and of Louisiana, and have found no recognized system of labor. Planters are losing extensive and valuable crops because negroes refuse to work.[26]

Custer was therefore in the process of reverting to his prewar politics; and when the break between President Andrew Johnson and the Radicals seemed to offer him a congenial political home among conservatives, he embraced the opportunity with enthusiasm. In the fall of 1866, he helped to organize a pair of political conventions in Philadelphia and Cleveland, designed to build a base of support for a conservative Reconstruction. Such a program would have reversed the recommendations Custer had made before the Committee on Reconstruction, by withholding suffrage from the freedmen and returning a limited form of political power to the southern leadership. The conventions brought together such strange bed-fellows as former Douglas Democrats and Seward Republicans and even an assortment of political opportunists of nominally Radical persuasion— most notably the often disappointed John C. Frémont. The Philadelphia convention rallied on September 17, the anniversary of McClellan's victory at Antietam—a symbolic gesture that was not lost on the Radicals. The Cleveland convention coincided with an apparently unrelated southern convention in Memphis under the aegis of General Nathan Bedford Forrest—the ex-guerrilla and cavalry general who would soon become the first president of the Ku Klux Klan. At the time, Forrest was chiefly noted as the supposed author of the Fort Pillow massacre, in which surrendering black troops were murdered and mutilated, and Memphis was known as the recent scene of an appalling riot directed against the black population. The juxtaposition of the two conventions was underlined by the congratulatory telegrams exchanged by Forrest and a group of the Clevelanders headed by Custer.[27]

Custer's political choices were shaped by career considerations as well as ideological preferences. After his return from Sheridan's Texas expedition, and the consequent demobilization of his division, Custer faced the prospect of reversion to his regular army rank of captain in the Fifth Cavalry at roughly a quarter of his pay as major general. To this prospect was added fact that the estate left by Custer's recently deceased father-in-law had proved disappointingly small. Judge Bacon was apparently "land poor," and most of his assets were committed to supplying an annuity for his second wife. In these circumstances, Custer had to lobby strenuously for promotion and also to consider civilian employment or political office. Rejecting these last possibilities as too risky, he instead sought promotions to military positions that would place him close to the centers of power and to the sources of wealth. He was particularly interested in the position of inspector of cavalry, a major staff position that would give him control over all sorts of perquisites, and present him with money-making opportunities and business contacts in the procurement of supplies. He continued to seek this position (and that of commandant of West Point) even after his appointment as field commander of the Seventh Cavalry.[28]

His design for his future had been crystallized by a return visit to New York City in April 1866. The city had attracted Custer since the time he spent there with McClellan during the composition of the general's report in 1862–63. Since then, his military fame had been most consistently fostered by the New York periodicals and papers—by the *Herald*, which had given him his sobriquet "The Boy General with the Golden Locks"; by his friend the *Times* correspondent who had seen him as a young Napoleon; by *Harper's Weekly*, whose illustrators had flatteringly depicted his great moments. He was therefore something of a lion, as he wrote to Libbie:

> . . . Went with Col. Howe into Wall Street, the financial heart of the country, and was introduced to some prominent capitalists. Then went by invitation to the Brokers' Board . . . a full session, and much excitement. I had scarcely taken my seat when a member unknown to me rose and stated that they had present "one of the bravest and most gallant generals of the War," and proceeded to compliment your boy, by proposing three cheers for Major-General Custer.

During this visit his conservative response to the issues posed by Reconstruction was confirmed, and his allegiance to the Democratic Party (and specifically the Belmont-McClellan wing) was reaffirmed. In turn, his superb war record and pretensions (at least) to the character of a war-to-the-knife man made him a notable catch for the Democrats. Beyond politics, Custer found in the New York financial community a model of success and of the good life toward which he would strive. "Oh these New York people are so kind to me," he wrote to Libbie. "I would like to become wealthy in order to make my permanent home here."[29] Although his immediate opportunities would take him far from Wall Street, this remained the blank of his ambition, and he persistently sought for investment opportunities that would enable him to enter that world. The universe of his aspiration was essentially that of the Horatio Alger hero: a Metropolis in which wealth, power, and position are preempted by a class of kindly and paternal "governors," and in which the hero—an aspiring "boy"— strives to earn the accolade of acceptance to this class, a partnership in the firm.

With this as their goal, neither Libbie nor Custer regarded his assignment to the Seventh Cavalry as particularly desirable. Their Texas experience had taught them that the climate and living conditions would be unpleasant and unsafe. Like most regulars, Custer regarded service against the Indians as a disagreeable chore in which successes were inevitably paltry, but where reputations were easily wrecked in small unit actions against wily savages in impossible terrain. Moreover, the management of a regiment like the Seventh in the postwar army presented difficulties for which Custer was not fully prepared, like how to impose discipline on troops who were not well motivated and were unwilling to endure the hardships and strictures of army life. In Texas in 1865 and later in his Seventh Cavalry days, he tended to resort to punitive measures—including corporal punishment—more frequently and on less provocation than many of his officers (and commanders) thought necessary or prudent. This caused dissension in his command, and on occasion led to official investigations, some of which criticized him. After Custer's success in the Indian wars renewed his reputation, the regiment did attract some troopers eager to serve with the Boy General; but there remained a sharp division among the enlisted men on the quality of Custer's discipline.[30]

More serious difficulties arose in his handling of his fellow officers. During the war, he had had to deal with the jealousy of subordinates whom he had passed in the course of his rapid promotion. But resentments of that kind were limited by the scale of the military operation and the appeal of the national cause. But in the postwar army the stimulus of the cause was lacking. There were so few places available in the higher ranks, that one's initial postwar rank might well be permanent. Moreover, that rank itself was bound to be a reduction in grade from the rank held in the volunteer service. The colonels, majors, and senior captains of the Seventh in 1866 had all been either generals or brigade commanders during the war; and most of the other veteran junior officers had been colonels. In these circumstances, Custer's promotion to lieutenant colonel ahead of many officers who had been senior to him in 1862 was bound to provoke strong resentment.

Custer compounded the problem by excessive use of his privilege of appointing friends and relatives to positions of power in his command. Custer liked the idea of acting as paterfamilias to a large military family; and the resentment of the "Custer Gang" among the other officers added to this the motive of self-protection. By 1876 this gang included his brother, Captain Thomas Custer, snatched out of the ranks of an Ohio infantry regiment in 1864, promoted to colonel, and twice decorated at the instigation of his famous brother; another brother, Boston Custer; his nephew-namesake, Autie Reed; Captain James Calhoun, who married Custer's sister and transferred over from the infantry, and Calhoun's brother-in-law, Captain Myles Moylan; Captain George Yates, a friend of Custer's from Monroe, Michigan; and (until his death at the Washita), Lieutenant Louis McLane Hamilton—an authentic American aristocrat and descendant of Alexander Hamilton—whose father advised Custer on his real estate investments.[31]

In 1867, the army's mission on the southern plains was to protect the builders of the Union Pacific and Kansas Pacific railroads and pacify the hostile Indians who had, since 1864, been raiding settlements and wagon trains. Intermittent warfare had existed on the plains since the Grattan Massacre of 1854, the by-product of increased cross-plains traffic by whites and the consequent shrinkage of the buffalo; the disorder attendant on the Civil War had increased these hostilities. Although substantial power still resided with the peace chiefs of the various tribes, their prestige had been damaged by the fate of Black Kettle, a Cheyenne chief whose people— encamped under an American flag—were horribly butchered by Colorado militia under Colonel Chivington at Sand Creek in 1864. The atrocity of the attack, and of the attendant murders and mutilations of Indians by whites, had much to do with arousing eastern sentiment in favor of the Peace Policy of President Grant, put in place after 1869. But among the Indians, it produced increased intransigence and deep-seated fear of white troops. By 1867, the course of warfare had turned against the Indians, and in anticipation of a move toward a new peace treaty, the Indians of the various warring tribes slackened their raiding efforts. However, there were important groups of whites, in the army and out of it, who saw the security of their investments as lying in successful battle rather than in a negotiation that might leave the Indians their freedom of movement or possession of their choicer territories. The western press generally took this view:

> Nothing is more absurd to the man who has studied the habits of the Indian savage than to talk of making permanent treaty negotiations with these heartless creatures. They are destitute of all the promptings of human nature, having no respect for word or honor. Their only creed is that which gives them an unrestricted license to . . . gratify a heathenish pleasure. To the Indian, destruction is gain. . . . Now and then you will hear a chicken-hearted historian, who knows nothing of the red savage, extolling his noble characteristics and praising his natural knightly endowments. The earnest defenders of this barbarian monster would turn away in disgust could they see him in all of his original desperation. The best and only way to reconcile the blood-washed animal will be to impose upon him a worse schooling than has ever befallen the inferior races.[32]

General Hancock was apparently influenced more by spokesmen for the Kansas Pacific, who mistrusted an Indian peace, than by the Indian Bureau agents who negotiated with the peace chiefs. Writing to the Indian agent charged with bringing in the Cheyenne, Hancock defined his mission in Shermanesque terms: "No insolence will be tolerated from any bands of Indians whom we may encounter . . . We wish to show them that the government is ready and able to punish them if they are hostile, although it may not be disposed to invite war." In April 1867, with foot, horse, and guns, and a spectacularly useless pontoon train, Hancock marched to their first meeting, greeted the chiefs brusquely, and accused them of holding white captives (which seems not to have been the case). The Cheyenne, noting the preparations and manner of Hancock and remembering Sand Creek, refused to negotiate until they had moved their village out of the way of the troops. Hancock responded by ordering Custer to sweep down on the village under cover of darkness and surround it for the purpose of holding the women and children as hostages of the chiefs' good faith. This Custer did, only to find that the Indians—set on edge by Hancock and alerted by the ineptness of the raw troopers—had left their lodges standing and decamped. Hancock thereupon determined that the Cheyenne were ipso facto hostile, burned the village, and ordered Custer in pursuit.[33]

Like most of his fellow officers, Custer was a complete novice where Indian fighting and subsistence on the Great Plains were concerned. But he appears to have learned more rapidly than most in the campaigns of 1866–68. Custer had prepared himself for his first campaign by making reasonably good use of his civilian scouts, and by making frequent hunting expeditions on the plains. This knowledge was extended by his pursuit of the Cheyenne, which taught him to appreciate the Indians' ability to use the terrain and survive its rigors. However, he shared the orthodox army view that the Plains Indians were the degenerate remnants of a vanishing race: his "Red Man" essay had departed from this doctrine only in attributing to the race qualities of nobility in defeat.

Custer was also becoming aware of the West's political significance. Through army channels he was aware of the power struggle then under way between the army and the Indian Bureau for control of the Indian policy. His continuing intimacy with news reporters and his growing contacts with western railroad men and developers (from whom he made purchases of land) gave him a sense of the economic and political stakes of the conflict. Through Libbie, he was aware of the growing sentiment among eastern Republicans for a thoroughgoing philanthropic reform of Indian policy, along missionary lines. Added to these larger matters was Custer's awareness of a significant personal conflict between General Hancock and the commander of the army, Ulysses Grant—the man who would undoubtedly be the Republican candidate for president in 1868. While undertaking his pursuit of the Cheyenne, Custer was cultivating a public persona and a set of attitudes that would align him with the emerging consensus on the Indian question—not an easy task, in view of the contradictory impulses behind current policy decisions. The makers of the Indian policy wanted both to subjugate the Indians—which implied making war—and to establish a regime characterized by peace; they wanted to protect Indian rights, while at the same time extinguishing Indian title to the land to facilitate the building of railroads.

Custer worked out his own approach to the problem in private correspondence, first with Libbie and then in a series of articles for the sporting journal *Turf, Field and Farm* under the pseudonym "Nomad." In both of these he deals with the circumstances surrounding the Indians' flight from Hancock's army. Writing to Libbie on May 2, 1867 (shortly after the event), he exonerates the Indians from the charge that as a group they are hostile to the whites: "I regard the recent outrages as the work of small groups of irresponsible young men, eager for war." The Indians' flight is seen as a response to Hancock's menacing attitude. These positions align Custer with liberal opinion in the East, and they suggest that the responsibility for the war lies with Hancock rather than the Indians—Grant's hostility made Hancock a relatively safe target.

However, Custer had also to take counsel of his own beliefs about Indian character and of the powerful anti-Indian views of western businessmen, of the army in general, and of Sherman and Sheridan in particular. Therefore (he told Libbie), "should a war be waged, none would be more determined than I to make it a war of extermination . . . but I consider we are not yet justified in declaring such a war." His language here is a modulation of that he had used in his wartime letters on the "extermination" of those with "rebel blood": the vocabulary and the scenario of extermination is the same, but he steps back from asserting the present necessity of such a war. Nonetheless, he anticipates the kind of rationale such a war would have by telling Libbie that before they fled, the Indians had raped a little girl and left her covered with blood. This is of course the archetypal raison d'être of the Indian war, and Custer responds appropriately: "Woe to them if I overtake them." This incident figures twice more in Custer's writing about Hancock's War: once in an 1867 *Turf, Field and Farm* article, and again in the extended narrative of *My Life on the Plains* (1874). As we shall see, his version of the incident varied according to his sense of his audience and the politics of the moment.[34]

The pursuit of the Indians was fruitless, and it taxed the material and psychological resources of the Seventh Cavalry to the breaking point. Custer seems to have driven his men and horses beyond their capacities, provoking hostility and desertions. He harassed the hard drinkers among the older officers, and one of these committed suicide—for which Captain Benteen blamed Custer. The discovery of a small party led by Lieutenant Kidder, which had been wiped out by the Indians, unnerved them—the bodies had been burned and mutilated nearly beyond recognition, and it was difficult to tell whether the mutilations had been inflicted on the living or the dead. To cap the failures, the regiment arrived at its post, Fort Wallace, to discover that the army had failed to deliver needed supplies. Custer decided to make a forced march to Fort Riley to expedite these supplies— and this decision led to his court-martial and a year's suspension.

The best research on this incident suggests that Custer's court-martial was designed to make him the scapegoat for Hancock's failed campaign. Hancock was aware of Custer's criticism of his proceedings—and whatever points Custer may have scored with Hancock's enemies were offset by Hancock's power as his immediate commander.

Custer seems to have been within his discretion in going from Wallace to Riley for supplies, although one might question his judgment in not sending a subordinate on the errand. Critics have seen his choice of himself as leader as essentially selfish: he wanted to see his wife, and feared for her safety in the cholera epidemic reportedly raging at Fort Riley. Certainly Custer had the reputation from Civil War days of seizing every chance to leave the front to see her. But his conduct of the march also reflects poorly on his character and capabilities. His ordering the shooting of men who deserted on the march became part of the anti-Custer legend; but the court-martial fudged the question of whether or not these were executions, or represented the shooting of deserters in the act of resisting arrest. The suspect character of the whole proceeding was suggested by the remark of General Grant, that the sentence given Custer was too light if the charges had been proven and unjust if they had not.

As it stood, the court's judgment was a serious stain on Custer's record. To unfriendly eyes it must seem that he had literally gotten away with murder, because of the patronage of former commanders and comrades-in-arms. To others his sentence might seem more a political act than a judicial one; but it still marked him as a man whose political indiscretion would mar his future prospects, and make him a chancy person to befriend. Moreover, in their straitened circumstances Custer's forfeiture of pay during his suspension might impose real hardship on his family. Libbie acknowledged that Custer's jaunt to Fort Riley had been a questionable act, taken for her sake from motives of affection; and amid the despondency of the moment the prospect of making a permanent home for themselves offered a kind of relief: "we are determined not to live apart again, even if he leaves the army otherwise so delightful to us."[35]

Isolated from the army and from the field of action, Custer turned to writing for a new source of income and a possible means of vindicating his reputation. While he was still in Fort Riley awaiting court-martial, Custer's "Nomad" articles began to appear; and he continued to turn out accounts of his adventures after he and Libbie returned to their home in Monroe— now their place of exile. These pieces began to establish Custer as a literary figure as well as a soldier, a man able to speak to cultured people as one of their own—and as a living legend capable of taking charge of the promulgation of his own myth. The first "Nomad" pieces concern a series of competitive buffalo hunts by the regimental officers, recounted in a highly humorous manner. He addresses himself to an audience of gentleman hunters, comparing the hunting of buffalo with sports they will themselves know well, particularly fox hunting. He presents the plains as a hunter's and gourmet's paradise:

> Our table fairly groaned under the load of choice game daily heaped upon it. From a buffalo steak to a broiled quail we indulged *ad libitum*. . . . The flesh of the rattlesnake, when cooked . . . is a dish, which, if called by any other name, would find favor in the opinion of all epicures. I have hunted foxes in Ohio, deer and turkey in Michigan, as well as in Texas, and alligators in the bayous along the Red River. . . .[36]

Custer thus establishes two things: his peculiar expertise and affinity for the life and fare of the plains and his character of gentleman hunter. In this character he addresses the Indian problem and the Hancock campaign. In the first article, he begins by noting the disparity between the comforts of life in New York and the difficulty and inconvenience of the plains, typified by the access to morning papers and to the theater, then featuring the long-running comedy *The Black Crook*, "the predominate feature of which seems to be a display of a universal absence of wardrobe." But, says Custer, "the Plains can offer an equivalent in the spectacle of naked savages and the 'farce' of peace commissioners dealing with them." He titles this plains comedy, "'Lo, the poor Indian' [which is] sometimes particularized by the names of different members of the troupe, such as Sioux, Cheyenne, or Comanches."

The combination is purely, and in every sense of the word, a travelling one, [playing] only to the most *select* audiences. The last point at which we are advertised to appear is at or near Fort Laramie; and in such high estimation are they held by the Government, which, in a legitimate way, desires to encourage and promote histrionic talent wherever found, that Lieutenant General Sherman . . . and an unlimited number of favored ones, have been designated and authorized to proceed to Fort Laramie at the expense of Uncle Sam, and there, by their presence and Uncle Sam's *presents*, give éclat to the opening performance of the season . . . the original play of the Black Crook will be performed; and I might add . . . that this, like most performances of the stage will end with *farce*. The strongest recommendation I can give in favor of this aboriginal troupe is that here we see them in the most primitive style, and in the fullest meaning of the term *au naturel*.[37]

Two features of the passage are noteworthy: the ridicule of Indians through mockery of their rags and nakedness; and the implicit ridicule of those sentimental philanthropists who are taken in by the "histrionics" of Indian claims of victimization. The two themes are united in the play's title, which is an epithet or phrase lifted from Pope's *Essay on Man*:— "Lo, the poor Indian! whose untutor'd mind / Sees God in clouds, or hears him in the wind." It was commonly invoked by papers like the *Herald* and the *World*, who took the hard line against all philanthropies designed to raise nonwhites (Indians and blacks) to the political level of whites. Six years later the expression of such sentiments by Custer would have marked him as an enemy of Grant and the reform Indian policy he sponsored; but in 1867, Grant was more closely associated with hard-liners like Sherman than with the "Friends of the Indian," and Custer's sarcasm cuts against outgoing President Andrew Johnson and outgoing District Commander Hancock.

Custer's most explicit criticisms and ridicule are reserved for Hancock in an article dated October 26, less than two weeks after Custer's sentencing. The "ability and prowess" displayed by Hancock in the war notwithstanding, Custer goes on to claim that "however successful this distinguished officer may have proven himself when combatting a civilized foe," his experience in the past year on the plains has been one of humiliating failure. Custer presents himself as Hancock's antithesis, and he invokes the standard traits of the Cooper-derived Frontier hero and other types familiar from popular fiction and journalism in order to do so. Where Hancock—like Cooper's British generals in *Mohicans*—will not learn till too late to understand and emulate the Indian's skill and the scout's wisdom in wilderness warfare, Custer—like Middleton or Heyward—acknowledges both freely. Where Hancock declines the advice of subordinates, Custer solicits the aid of Delaware Indian scouts (Cooper's favorite tribe) and white plainsmen like Wild Bill Hickok—a scout already celebrated in the eastern press and who had therefore a literary as well as a historical identity. Custer's appreciation of the Indian puts him on the side of the controversial Indian reimbursement claim for the burning of the village by Hancock. And although he responds with horror to the mutilated bodies of some whites at a stage station, he denies Hancock's assertion that his burning of the original Indian village was in retaliation for these murders: Custer points out that the Indians had not yet deserted their village when the station was burned, and the distance between the points is such that "it was not possible that the occupants of the village could have been the perpetrators of the outrages at the station."[38]

Custer thus had begun to establish for himself the public character of sporting gentleman and of enlightened "moderate" on the vexed question of the Indian policy. He aligned himself with the sporting enthusiasms and the racialist attitudes of the class whose patronage he sought—the Belmonts and Astors of New York—yet spoke knowingly and moderately of the Indian, thus evading the appearance of vulgar bigotry. In this seed time of the Peace Policy, this was a useful position to hold; and in future writings intended for a larger audience than the sporting gentry, Custer would further purge his rhetoric of blatant touches of racialism and play up the sympathetic elements. Yet his way was open to advocacy of policies designed to repress the Indian effectively and deprive him of land and power in the interest of the government and its corporate friends.

So however sanguine Libbie may have been about his prospects as a man of letters, Custer had not abandoned his military ambitions. His articles were devices for defending his reputation, criticizing those who had convicted him, and aligning himself with important political interests who might provide sympathy and patronage once he had returned to duty. But the fall and winter of 1867–68 passed, and the summer as well, and other men were commanding his regiment against the Indians, reaping his glories or suffering defeats he might have avoided. If he were to pass from the stage of active western service now, as a convicted man, and just at the beginning of the new cycle of Indian wars, no amount of fine prose would be able to redeem his legend from the back pages of journalism and history. His own brief and inglorious passage of arms with the Cheyenne would be eclipsed by later and greater battles, and his critique of Hancock and of Indian policy would be nothing more than the self-justifying apology of a bitter young man who had missed his chance and failed of his promise.

CHAPTER 17

The Boy General Returns; or, Custer's Revenge, 1868–1876

Custer was saved from premature retirement by a reversal of fortune so melodramatic that it must have convinced him (as it did so many others) that he was the child of destiny, and history a stage designed for the mounting of his legend. On September 24, 1868, he received a telegram from Sheridan summoning him to resume command of the Seventh Cavalry and serve as his old commander's strong right hand in the coming winter campaign.

Hancock's failures in 1867–68 had finally led to his replacement by Sheridan, who bore a commission from Grant and Sherman for an unremitting war against the savages: "The more we can kill this year, the less will have to be killed next year for the more I see of these Indians the more I am convinced that they will all have to be killed or maintained as a species of paupers." What was wanted was the fire-and-sword technique that Sherman had used in Georgia and the Carolinas, and Sheridan in the Shenandoah Valley; and Sheridan remembered Custer as energetic, combative, and a thorough scorcher of enemy earth.[1]

Custer left Monroe almost immediately on receipt of the telegram, and returned to the regiment at Fort Supply, Indian Territory, in the most dramatic fashion—and in circumstances that must have been especially mortifying to the various anti-Custer cliques. He had barely resumed command when Sheridan's scouts discovered an Indian trail leading toward the Washita River. Campaigning in the snow-covered winter prairies was not to the Indians' taste, since forage for their ponies was not to be obtained, buffalo were scarce, and movement difficult. The Washita Valley was a good site for going into winter quarters. If the cavalry under Custer could follow the trail quickly they could catch these Indians fixed in position, and punish them severely. They were (in Sheridan's view) probably one of the bands that had been raiding the territory, and if not themselves raiders, they would certainly lead the soldiers to where large concentrations of hostiles might be found.

In fact, this particular band was not particularly hostile (although it included many braves who had been making war). It was Black Kettle's village—whose people had been massacred at Sand Creek in 1864. Despite this experience, Black Kettle had persisted in efforts to reestablish peace with the whites, and to obtain protection for himself and his people. He had contacted the Indian Bureau agents to propose terms of surrender and a return to the reservation. The agents were Colonel Edward W. Wynkoop, who had been associated with the Cheyenne agency since the Civil War, and Colonel William B. Hazen, once a classmate (not a friend) of Custer's at West Point, now seconded to the Indian Bureau to look after the army's interests. Hazen and Wynkoop opened negotiations and accepted Black Kettle's good faith, but could not conclude peace with the Cheyenne while so many of his tribesmen remained at war and while their own orders required them to treat all off-reservation Indians as full belligerents. They sent Black Kettle back to the winter camp on the Washita without a promise of peace, but in expectation of making one through the chief's efforts. To the same vicinity came other villages of Cheyenne and Arapaho, raiders who still held captured white women and property. Many of these groups also expected that they would soon have to surrender, and planned to use their captives in bargaining for terms.[2]

Custer followed the Indian trail through the snow, and his scouts discovered the village. At dawn on the twenty-seventh of November, Custer divided his command and struck the village from every point of the compass while the regimental band blared away at "Garry Owen." His cavalry rode through the village, shooting men, women, and children indiscriminately in the half light and confusion. A platoon under Major Elliott—who had been associated with the anti-Custer faction—dashed away in pursuit of some fleeing Indians and was cut off and massacred. In the confusion of battle, Custer lost track of Elliott; and when a quick search failed to find him, he was abandoned. For Custer now had other problems: his command was a day's march distant over blizzarded prairie from its supply train, and encumbered with captured Indian women and children and a large pony herd. The soldiers, who had attacked in several parties and were, as usual, confused and maddened by the terror and excitement of the charge, had to be brought back under control. The Indian scouts were also out of hand, and engaged in cutting the breasts off the corpses of Cheyenne women. At this juncture, the pickets noticed a gathering of additional hostiles from the other villages that, unknown to Custer, were located up and down the river. Custer ordered the pony herd slaughtered, marshaled his prisoners, and marched out post-haste for the wagon train and Camp Supply, to which he returned in triumph.[3]

From this battle of the Washita, Custer dated his fame as the premier Indian fighter of the West. From it too derived those suspicions and accusations that made his fame controversial.

Criticism of Custer's battle was of two sorts: there were those who questioned the military skill involved, and those who asserted that the Washita battle was a second Sand Creek. Among the military errors cited were Custer's failure to scout widely enough to discover the other villages that threatened his command after the battle; his division of the command in the face of unknown numbers; his desertion of Elliott to the potential torments of capture, massacre, and mutilation by an enraged enemy; his too precipitous abandonment of the village. Other critics found that the good conduct of the march, and the tactics that conquered the village and extricated the command from its predicament, were more attributable to Chief of Scouts Ben Clark's advice than to Custer himself.

Certainly, Custer went out of his way to avoid mentioning Clark in his several accounts, despite the scout's vital contribution to the success. But if his treatment of Clark marks Custer as a glory grabber, it is no disparagement of his military judgment that he took Clark's advice (if that is what he did). His failure to scout the other villages seems a more serious matter. But strategy favored a quick strike; and this, taken with the depth of the snow, made a thorough reconnaissance difficult. The division of command was likewise a permissible tactic under circumstances where a sizable village, inhabited by whole families instead of warriors alone, was to be assaulted by a contingent of better-armed white troops. Whether the abandonment of Elliott was necessary is a matter impossible to settle; Sheridan apparently had some doubts about it, though not enough to impair his confidence in Custer seriously. But the existence of an unworthy motive in this instance, as in the forced march of the previous year, cast a shadow on the victory.[4]

The chief military fault of the battle was not in its tactics but in the conclusions Custer drew from his success. Failing to appreciate the degree to which his victory was dependent on special circumstances, and perhaps blinded by the magnificence of his own publicity as the winner of the only notable "pitched battle" on the plains since the 1850s, Custer determined that his contempt for the fighting qualities of the Indians was justified, and that the tactics of the Washita could be repeated against any number of Indians under any circumstances.

More serious, in a political sense, were the accusations that the battle of the Washita was merely a repetition of the Sand Creek massacre. Custer was highly sensitive to the charge, concealing in his initial report the fact that the vast majority of the casualties he inflicted were women and children. In his defense he cited the Indians' own abuse of female and child captives (which it was his declared aim to rescue), and the impossibility of distinguishing between men, women, and children in the confusion of battle—particularly since women and children might well be armed for their own defense. He could in any case have known nothing of the arrangement for submission Black Kettle was making with Wynkoop or Hazen.[5]

In a certain sense, Custer's apology is valid. The nature of Indian warfare made it inevitable that the greatest opportunities for white victory would occur when the presence of women and children immobilized the warriors and forced them to defend their ground. The basis of the struggle —the inability of the reservations to support the Indians—likewise made the presence of women and children in the war zone unavoidable. To warn the Indians and challenge battle outside a village would be to lose the chance of corralling them; and in any case, civilian presence had not deterred either army in the various sieges and destructive marches of the Civil War. Ultimate culpability for the "massacre" of the Washita must lie with the makers of the Indian policy—both the bureaucrats who conceived and administered it, the soldiers and civilians who profited from it, and the publicists who exploited the Indians' plight for their own profit.

All this noted, it must also be said that Custer proved himself to be one of the best of the army's Indian fighters in the Washita battle and in the hard campaigning that followed it. His pursuit of the main body of the Cheyenne that spring and his forcing their surrender were enterprises carried through with skill and relatively little loss of life—although to achieve his ends, he was forced (or so he believed) to take hostages under a flag of truce, thus adding one more bit of evidence to the Indian belief in white duplicity. He was, of course, not quite so superlative at his art as he imagined himself to be; but the fame Custer reaped in 1869 had real justifications.

Sheridan himself was pleased that "Custer had struck a hard blow, and wiped out old Black Kettle and his murderers and rapers of helpless women . . ." who had "perpetrated cruelties too fiendish for recital." It is the accusation that the Indians habitually devoted themselves to the capture and rape of white women that Sheridan deploys as his most powerful argument against the supporters of the Peace Policy, and in this polemical context, the cruelties are no longer "too fiendish for recital":

> Still a hue and cry was raised, through the influence of the Indian ring, in which some good and pious ecclesiastics took part, and became the aiders and abettors of savages who murdered without mercy, men, women and children; in all cases ravishing the women sometimes as often as forty and fifty times in succession, and while insensible from brutality and exhaustion, forced sticks up their persons; and, in one instance, the fortieth or fiftieth savage drew his sabre and used it on the person of the woman in the same manner. I do not know exactly how far these humanitarians should be excused on account of their ignorance, but surely it is the only excuse that gives a shadow of justification for aiding and abetting such horrid crimes.[6]

Journalists and writers of popular histories and dime novels tended to echo Sheridan's viewpoint, and to represent Custer as the rescuer and avenger of captive white women, the hero who stands between white civilization and the exterminating fury of the savages. De Benneville Randolph Keim's *Sheridan's Troopers on the Border* (1870) asserts that the triumphant advance of "American Industry" can never be complete until the Indians have been decimated, their buffalo-centered economy eliminated, "villages and ponies [destroyed], all warriors hanged or killed, and women and children imprisoned." A dime novel published in 1869—*General Sheridan's Squaw Spy*—justifies the Washita attack as a response to the discovery of an Indian conspiracy to "exterminate all the white settlers and destroy the railroad to the Pacific." But the dime novel only makes absurdly literal the implicit premises of Sheridan's and Keim's professional analysis of the struggle.[7]

Such accounts were intended to offset the intense propaganda that the supporters of the new Indian policy had mounted about the Sand Creek atrocities. White troops at Sand Creek had mutilated the living and the dead, cut off and displayed as trophies the sexual organs of Indian men, women, and children; shot down Indian women and children without mercy, including pregnant squaws, whose fetuses were cut from them and laid beside their corpses. The tale of atrocities is, in fact, never ending; and even where there was truth to the story, the purposes the facts could be made to serve often had little to do with preventing recurrences. Rather, they were used to justify responses in kind.

For Sheridan and Custer atrocity stories were part of a larger scenario than the simple tale of rape and revenge. The tactical revenge plots with which they filled their reports pointed to a larger strategy of revenge which would justify wars of extermination or subjugation. Similarly, Friends of the Indian availed themselves of this same symbolic language of rape/murder and rescue, but in their scenario, the victims were identified as Indians and the "savages" as soldiers.

The Washita battle news was juxtaposed with reports of the congressional inquiry into the Sand Creek massacre, which was then at its most horrific stage of revelation. The Radical reformers opportunistically linked Custer with Chivington and with those reactionary forces who opposed all philanthropic approaches to dealing with the nation's black and red "wards." The controversy lasted into 1870, when a second massacre was added—that of the Piegans attacked by Colonel E. M. Baker. Wendell Phillips promptly linked Baker, Custer, and Sheridan in a trio of villainy, and thanked God for "a President in the White House whose first word was for the negro, and the second for the Indian." The former abolitionist Lydia Maria Child also attacked the army and linked it to those prewar slaveholders and postwar opponents of Reconstruction who "thought . . . the whip was more efficient than wages to get work out of the black man; and now the approved method of teaching red men not to commit murder is to slaughter their wives and children!" Child's attack on the slaughter of Indian wives is especially telling, given Sheridan's instructions to "bring back all women and children."[8]

One atrocity story that in fact did not reach the press—although it figured prominently in the army rumor mill—concerned the disposition of Custer's captives from the Washita. According to these rumors, Custer turned the Indian women over to the "unbridled lust" (as Sheridan might have called it) of soldiers and officers. It was also said that Custer had taken for himself the daughter of a chief named Little Rock. This girl, Monasetah or Meotzi, later accompanied Custer in the character of an interpreter— although it was noted that she spoke little or no English. At some point, it also began to be said that she considered herself Custer's wife, and that she bore him a child named Yellow Swallow. Custer himself painted an affectionate portrait of the girl in his book *My Life on the Plains*, and some historians have suspected that the book simply suggested a plausible rumor to Custer's many detractors. The argument about the incident has always centered on the question of Yellow Swallow, whose existence was testified to by the notorious Custer-hater Captain Frederick Benteen and by the Cheyenne informants of Thomas Marquis, Charles Brill, and Mari Sandoz, in accounts published between 1915 and 1940. These are hardly disinterested witnesses, and their assertions about the child are cast into doubt by the lack of documentary evidence and by internal inconsistencies about the birth dates of the supposed Custer child (who would have been born in 1869 or 1870) and of an earlier child which Monasetah was carrying at the time of her capture.

But this preoccupation with the question of the child is testimony to the power of myth to distort the nature of the questions historians ask. If the center of our story is the *person* of the hero, then it matters a great deal whether or not Custer himself took an Indian woman as a bed partner, and whether or not the union—affectionate or coerced—produced a child. A more interesting question concerns the general treatment of the Indian women: were they in fact turned over to the officers and soldiers at Camp Supply?

This question reflects on the larger matter of the execution of the Indian policy by the army, and here the testimony is a bit better. The Indian informants of Brill, Sandoz, and Marquis all asserted that the Indian women were indeed sexually coerced, and that Custer himself gave the orders. Brill's informant—an older woman who later accompanied Custer and Monasetah during the latter's service as interpreter—said that after the battle she approached Custer's scout, Romero, with an offer of an Indian girl for a "bride" if he would protect the women from rape. Custer gives a version of this scene in his published account of the battle, but with himself as the primary recipient of the offer. Partial confirmation of these stories is provided by Benteen's correspondence, which independently confirms the tale of Custer's presiding over (or permitting) the distribution of the women—and Benteen's letters to this effect were not published in full until long after the publication of the works of Brill, Sandoz, and Marquis. Sandoz claimed to have seen Medical Corps records—since lost—indicating that Custer and his officers took the treatments prescribed for preventing venereal disease among those who had cohabited with Indian women. This would be persuasive evidence that Custer and his officers had sexual relations with the captive women, although in the Yellow Swallow matter we must reject its use as circumstantial evidence. However, if sexual exploitation, through rape or coercive concubinage, was a part of the scene at Camp Supply in 1869–70, what are we to say of a code that could smirk at the sexual abuse of Indian women while making the Indians' captivity and rape of white women a pretext for massacre?[9]

In fact, the captivity pretext itself is open to serious question. It was public policy, passed down from the president and the army commander and publicly affirmed by Sheridan, that the rescue of captive white women was a primary objective of military operations. The imperative need for speedy rescue was used by Sheridan and Custer to justify actions that might otherwise have seemed precipitate. The rescue objective was a certain way to gain public support for operations against the Indians; and it was particularly important in western communities, which supported operations by providing supplies, quarters, teamsters, and volunteers. Relatives of captive women accompanied field expeditions as aides, scouts, and advisers. So central did this concern appear to be that *General Sheridan's Squaw Spy* describes a fictional "Secret Service" organized among the Indians by Sheridan to locate and rescue captives. But in his private and confidential-official correspondence, Sheridan took a very different stance.

He believed that captive white women would certainly have been raped by their Indian captors, perhaps gang raped or passed from brave to brave and brutalized. Such women, in his view, were no longer worth rescuing, having suffered the "fate worse than death." It would be better for themselves and their families if they were never recovered—although this alternative implied that they would remain alive among the Indians—and best of all if they were somehow to perish: by murder, suicide, or the providentially directed bullet of a would-be rescuer. In the circumstances of the Washita attack, it was as likely that white captives would be killed by charging soldiers as by the Indians—though Custer may have given orders for the troopers to keep an eye open for white skins. Sheridan's views were far from exceptional, as the treatment of many returned captives from this period suggests.[10]

The Peace Policy, like Radical Reconstruction, had indeed triumphed in Grant's first term. Administration of the Indian reservations was given over (in large part) to Christian missionaries of various denominations—with the Quakers or Society of Friends conspicuously over-represented. Their presence, coupled with the pacific objects of the new policy, led to the labeling of Grant's program as the "Quaker Policy"—eventually a term of opprobrium. And the association of "Society of Friends" with the reform group called "Friends of the Indian" gave hostile newspaper editorialists a set of terms that joined all "philanthropists" in a common character of unmilitary soft-mindedness. When the missionary administrators proved to be no less inefficient and corrupt than their predecessors, intimations of religious hypocrisy were added to the "Quaker" image.

But in 1870 the Peace Policy was a new and hopeful beginning in Indian affairs, the "Quakers" were untried but promising, and Custer trimmed his anti-Indian rhetoric to suit the new fashions. There was little immediate call upon his ideas about Indian policy, because the conclusion of the war on the southern plains led to the Seventh Cavalry's reassignment (in 1870) to occupation duty in the South. Custer's headquarters were to be in Elizabethtown, Kentucky, south of Louisville; and contingents of the regiment were scattered as far as Louisiana and South Carolina to combat the anti-Reconstruction and anti-Negro terror of the Ku Klux Klan. Custer had little taste for such duty: his sympathies were more with the opponents of Radical Reconstruction than with the administration, although he was still in Grant's good graces. In any case, occupation duty had a "political" element, which was always dangerous for the career of an officer—the careers of both Hancock and Sheridan had nearly been wrecked by their efforts to enforce administration policy. It was partly for these reasons that Custer sought frequent leaves of absence that enabled him to spend most of 1871 in New York, but there were other reasons as well. Debts further reduced the divided Bacon estate, which had never amounted to more than $40,000, and the Custers' share of it had been small. Custer's army pay was not sufficient to support them in the style they hoped to attain, and his literary income was minimal; and Custer's fondness for gambling and horse racing may have placed additional pressure on their finances. Custer tried to increase their financial security by investing in Kansas real estate. He apparently purchased house lots in the Topeka area, and he took advantage of the favored treatment accorded army officers by the land grant railroads to purchase land from the Kansas Pacific.[11]

But Custer's hopes for wealth were tied most closely to the Stevens silver mine in Georgetown, Colorado. The mine was located on McClellan Mountain, which it shared with another mining company, the Crescent, whose mine had already produced quantities of silver. In the winter of 1870 Custer applied for an extended leave which allowed him to go to New York City to promote sale of the mining stock among the financial leaders who had been so kind to him in 1866. His partner in the enterprise was Jairus W. Hall, an acquaintance from Monroe and ex-colonel of the Fourth Michigan Infantry. At some point in the evolution of the project, General McClellan—now superintendent at the Department of Docks— also joined the combine, although it is not clear in what capacity he participated. McClellan did, however, advise Custer to contact his great friend and political patron August Belmont. Belmont not only invested $15,000, but his fellow financiers, Levi Morton, of Morton, Bliss and Company, and John Jacob Astor, each invested $10,000. These subscriptions brought in W. R. Travers, James H. Barker, and C. J. Osborne, bankers and stockbrokers. Custer himself was listed as subscribing $35,000; neither Hall nor McClellan is listed in the formal prospectus as a subscriber. But there is no record to indicate whether or not any part of Custer's subscription was ever paid by him, and it is therefore unclear whether or not the $35,000 represented an investment by Custer for himself and his partners, or a "broker's share" of the stock for which no money was ever to be paid.[12]

Although the Stevens Mine was a shaft operation, there was nearly enough water in its stock to have operated a sluice. The shares subscribed for by the investors had a face value of $100, but only $50 was actually promised in payment for each share. Of this amount, only half was actually made available for capitalization of the operations of the mine. The prospectus promised a working capital of $100,000 to be raised by this subscription; but when these discounts are taken into account—and when the further possibility is considered that Custer's "subscription" was simply a useful fiction—the capital amounts to far less than that required. Custer and Hall did not attempt to defraud the investors about the quality of the mine—"They have got a mine worth a good deal more than they pay," as Hall said—but Custer and Hall used the "working capital" in ways that were at least unethical if not illegal. Letters written by Hall to Custer in 1874–75 suggested that part of the money that was to have been used to start operations may have gone to pay for a note Custer had given to Frank Dibben, the original owner of the Stevens. The two men apparently milked the mine's capital for personal income. Custer, for his part, needed cash to defray the expenses of his interest in horse breeding and racing, which became serious after he moved to Kentucky in 1872–73; and after August 1874 he was heavily engaged in stock purchases and in some more complicated speculations.

Perhaps to ease the strain on Custer's finances, Hall then devised a "new proposition," which would require the New Yorkers to advance them $48,000 in cash, which when added to the $12,000 received earlier would give them a capital of $60,000. Of this amount, only $10,000 would actually be put into "the hands of the treasurer for a working capital—to build tramways, etc." This would give the partners nearly $50,000 to use as they saw fit; and when the mine began to pay off the subscribers through earnings, Custer and Hall would hold two-thirds of the capital stock. Custer could expect "five or six thousand" immediately, but "to do this we must have charge of management." While this scheme still reflects Hall's belief in the value of the mine, it also offers evidence of Custer's hunger for cash and of his rather flexible business ethics. The Stevens project, however, was not financially successful: Custer continued to importune Hall for cash, to be obtained by selling stock or borrowing against it; and finally, in the winter of 1874–75, he evidently surprised Hall by asking him to sell out his interest entirely.

In 1871, however, Custer's hopes were quite high for "a small fortune" as "the stepping stone to large[r] and more profitable undertakings . . ." He reveled in the New York atmosphere, dining with the wealthy and great—the Belmonts, Bennetts, Astors, and Jeromes—accompanying them to the races at Saratoga, sharing their boxes at the theater. And as one admitted to Belmont's circle, Custer became acquainted with influential figures in journalism and Democratic politics, including a number of congenial ex-Confederates. At a dinner for editors of the New York dailies, Custer dined with Horace Greeley, Bayard Taylor, Whitelaw Reid, Richard Henry Dana, and the poet-journalist Clarence Stedman. Describing it to Libbie, he wrote that

> Mr. Steadman, who sought for an introduction to me, told me that during the war I had been to him, and, he believed, to most people, the beau ideal of the Chevalier Bayard, "knight sans peur et sans reproche" and that I stood unrivaled as the "young American hero." I repeat this *to you alone*, as I know it will please you. Another said no officer holding a commission was so popular with the retired men. . . .

Aside from flatteringly recalling to Custer his boy-general character, the exchange reminded him of his possibilities in politics: popularity with the veterans was crucial for a candidate, particularly a Democratic candidate such as Belmont might sponsor. The Democrats were still the party of the South and of McClellan in the public mind and consequently required war heroes to restore their image. Thus Custer doubly regretted his transfer to the South: "Duty in the South has somewhat of a political aspect, which I always seek to avoid." Such service could, if he were stern, only embarrass him with the Democratic South; and if he were lenient, it might discredit him with the North.

Among the other opportunities offered him was an invitation from the banker Jay Cooke to accompany him on a railroad junket over the line of the newest transcontinental railroad—his own Northern Pacific, slated to stretch from Duluth on the Great Lakes to Puget Sound on the Pacific. Custer was forced by other business to decline, but so began his relationship with Cooke and the Northern Pacific, which was to lead indirectly to his own death five years later.[13]

Custer spent the next two years based in Elizabethtown, where he spent much of his time touring the blue-grass country, purchasing mounts for the cavalry and racehorses for himself—and losing quite a bit of money at the track. In the process, Custer became friends with many of the conservative economic and political leaders of the state, including James Watterson, editor of the Louisville *Courier-Journal* and a potent voice against Radicalism, and General Abraham Buford, formerly of Forrest's cavalry, who would later become Custer's business partner.

Except for some unpleasantness with a unregenerate rebel on a Louisville street, Custer's stay in Kentucky is remarkable for its lack of incident—remarkable because his tenure of command coincided with the height of Ku Klux terror in Kentucky and South Carolina, both of which were patrolled by units of the Seventh Cavalry. Indeed, 1871–72 marks the public reemergence of Custer's traditional southern political affinities, a movement facilitated by the "pull" of friendly southern gentlemen and the "push" of the Fifteenth Amendment, granting suffrage to the despised blacks. Custer was oblivious or indifferent to Klan activities in his district; and he was actively hostile to Major Lewis Merrill of the Seventh Cavalry, who was active in suppressing the Klan in South Carolina.[14]

His financial affairs still in disorder, Custer's public presence was now gaining in potency and value. Beginning in the fall of 1871, Custer began writing up his adventures on the plains for publication by the *Galaxy*—a new literary monthly whose editors intended it to be the New York rival of Boston's prestigious *Atlantic* as an arbiter of intellectual fashion and literary taste. The Church brothers, who owned and edited the magazine, had long been associated with the army as publishers of the *Army and Navy Journal*, which became a semiofficial organ of military opinion.[15]

For this new audience, Custer modified the sportsman's pose and facetious treatment of the Indian that characterized his "Nomad" pieces, and his sarcastic animadversions on Hancock gave way to a more considered critique of "the Indian Policy." The pre-Grant policy which had actually been behind the 1867 war was the nominal focus of these criticisms; but Custer implicitly equates this historical "blunder" with the Peace Policy of Grant, and so his adventures serve as implicit propaganda for the army's present takeover of the Indian Bureau. The articles began appearing in May 1872, and continued until the fall of 1874 when, just as Custer was preparing to leave for the Black Hills, they were issued in book form.

The writing of the book was interrupted by the visit of Grand Duke Alexis of Russia, who wished to make a buffalo hunt on the Great Plains as part of his grand tour. As a noted sportsman and military celebrity, Custer was ordered by Sheridan to join the party. The whole affair was given extensive coverage by the Metropolitan press, especially Bennett's New York *Herald*, whose editor was an avid sportsman as well as an enthusiast for expanding Frontiers. But Custer was upstaged somewhat—at least for Bennett's readers—by the expedition's guide, "Buffalo Bill" Cody, who, as the egregious Ned Buntline's 1869 dime novel hero, was already something of a celebrity himself. The *Herald* gives us his entrance with a flourish:

[Sheridan] has arranged with the genial and daring "Buffalo Bill" to be on hand and act as guide, and this renowned scout was promptly on hand in all his element. He was seated on a spanking charger, and with his long hair and spangled buckskin suit he appeared in his true character of the feared and beloved of all for miles around. White men and the barbarous Indians are alike moved by his presence, and none of them dare do in word or deed contrary to the rules of law and civilization.

The juxtaposition of this Leatherstocking type of Frontier scout with the Russian nobleman and the American gentleman-officer had an appeal that reached back to the literary myth of the Frontier codified by Fenimore Cooper. Both Cody and Custer appreciated the strength of that appeal and made use of it. In 1872, Cody made his own celebrity tour of New York as Bennett's guest, guided Bennett and his friends on a reprise of the 1871 buffalo hunt, and embarked on his own career as showman and dime novelist. Custer himself afterward adopted the "scout" image in dress and manner; and his success in bringing off the role is attested by Curtis's portrayal of him in the Black Hills correspondence of 1874. After the Last Stand, Cody would return the compliment, modifying his own appearance and dramatizing his adventures in a manner designed to emphasize his Custer likeness and his close relation to the Custer story.

But in 1872, Cody was cast as Hawkeye to Custer's Duncan Heyward; and, as was the case with Cooper's heroes, this involved a trade-off: Cody attracted the most interest because of his exotic character as a man of the border, but Custer appeared as the American closest in spirit to the noble prince of Europe, accompanying the Grand Duke in the hunting itself, and in the round of parties and ceremonies that framed it. Moreover, the press also saw in Custer a man of the Frontier, the plebeian scout's match as a wearer of authenticating buckskins, as a tracker and dead shot, and even as a man with special ties with the Indians. The *Herald* reporter echoes the Grand Review description of Custer as resembling an Indian chief in dress and bearing, and as joining with the Grand Duke in offering "gallantries" to the lovely daughter of the Sioux chief Spotted Tail.[16]

Although the expedition was generally treated in a lighthearted manner, the *Herald* did tie it in with the larger political questions that revolved about the Indian policy. Sheridan in particular had been noted for espousing the "extermination" of the buffalo, as a kind of surrogate for extermination of the Indians, since to kill off the buffalo would force the tribes to "settle down" on reservations by depriving them of their food base. The *Herald* editorials whimsically posited an imaginary confrontation between the founder of the ASPCA and Sheridan—a comic version of the battle between "sentimental philanthropy" and tough-mindedness that underlay Indian policy:

> ALEXIS BUFFALOES / It is reported that the meat of three hundred buffaloes, killed by the Grand Duke in his late buffalo hunts, has been sold in the single town of St. Joseph . . . to say nothing to the numbers disposed of in other places. At this rate

a few more such visits of the Grand Duke to the buffalo plains will reduce Red Cloud, Spotted Tail and their Indians to raids upon Sheridan's cavalry for their winter supplies of beef.

This would, of course, produce the Indian war that would settle the Indian question once and for all. What is especially appealing to the *Herald* is the fact that this extermination of the "buffalo tribe" is being carried out not by coarse plebeian hide hunters, but by gentlemen shooting from palace cars. That was a fantasy so appealing that Bennett himself acted it out on a celebrity hunting trip the following autumn.[17]

While Custer was accompanying Alexis and serving in Kentucky, his articles on Hancock's war began appearing in the *Galaxy*. In these articles, Custer took direct charge of the making of his own public persona. Although he quoted General Sherman on the necessity of exterminating the Indians and implicitly concurred in Sherman's belief that they were incapable of civilization, Custer took pains to distance himself from the outright exterminationist position, and he colored the depiction of the Indian's incapacity for civilization with regretful sentiments of the "vanishing American" school.

He establishes his character by playing his own views against the opposed stereotypes of the Noble Savage and Dirty Savage schools. Custer first disparages the philanthropic view of the Indian by linking it with the romantic sentimentality of Cooper's fiction:

> If the character given to the Indian by Cooper and other novelists, as well as by well-meaning but mistaken philanthropists of a later day were the true one; if the Indian were the innocent, simple-minded being he is represented, more the creature of romance than reality, imbued with a veneration for the works of nature, freed from the passions and vices which must accompany a savage nature; if, in other words, he possessed all the virtues which his admirers and works of fiction ascribe to him, and were free from all the vices which those best qualified to judge assign to him, he would be just the character to complete the picture [*i.e.*, of a romantic western adventure, which Custer's book supposedly is not].[18]

Both romance and philanthropic sentiment are associated with a state of immaturity. Grown-up men, who do the work of the world, cannot indulge such fantasies. This metaphor links *My Life on the Plains* to Custer's West Point essay on "The Red Man," which also associated the vanishing Indian with the "childhood" of mankind. In that juvenile essay, Custer identified himself with the Indian—a child separated from the nurturing presence of a maternal spirit (nature for the Indian, Mrs. Custer for Autie), facing a kind of extinction in his absorption by the onrush of mature adulthood (civilization). But now Custer identifies primarily with the aggressor, with adulthood and civilization, acknowledging that as we emerge "from childhood into the years of a maturer age, we are often compelled to cast aside many of our earlier illusions and replace them by beliefs less inviting but

more real, so we, as a people, . . . have been forced . . . to study and comprehend thoroughly the character of the red man." This is a gentler way of
saying what the *World* and *Herald* had been stridently asserting for years:
that no "adult male" member of the white race, other than those "she-males"
unmanned by philanthropy or the profiteers engaged by the Grant administration, could any longer sympathize with "Poor Lo."

But saying that more gently is just Custer's point. As an Indian fighter
of great repute, he had no need to prove himself a hard-liner; and with the
reformers still powerful in government, there was much to be gained by
an appearance of enlightenment and moderation. So Custer says that it "is
to be regretted that the character of the Indian as described in Cooper's
interesting novels is not the true one." Because of the national policy issues
presented by the Indian question, we must "no longer . . . study this problem from works of fiction," but take the testimony of those who have seen
the Indian firsthand. Echoing the sentiments of Mark Twain in *Roughing
It* (1872)—that "up close" Indians forfeit all sympathy—Custer argues that
"stripped of the beautiful romance with which we have been so long willing
to envelope him," and met upon the actual "war-path," the Indian "forfeits his claim to the appellation of 'the *noble* red man' " and "We see him
as he is . . . a *savage* in every sense of the word."[19]

Custer at first postulates a relativist attitude toward the Indian—if
he is a savage, he is "not worse, perhaps, than his white brother would
be, similarly born and bred." But this environmentalist relativism gives
way to something more like the spurious relativism of Cooper: The Indian
is a member of a unique race, "peculiar and undefined . . . incapable of
being judged by the rules or laws applicable to any other known race of
men. . . . He stands in the group of nations solitary and reserved, seeking
alliance with none, mistrusting and opposing the advances of all." And
where "The Red Man" essay had concluded with an image of an embattled
Indian glaring at extinction, this piece concludes regretfully: "Civilization
may and should do much for him, but it can never civilize him."

But the Indian's peculiar racial gifts are of the kind to ensure his
eternal enmity for the white race and its civilization. His "cruel and
ferocious nature" is "so deep-seated and inbred . . . that in the exceptional
instances where the modes and habits of civilization have been reluctantly
adopted, it has been at the sacrifice of power and influence in the tribe,
and the more serious loss of health, vigor and courage as individuals."[20]

> Nature intended him for a savage state; every instinct, every im-
> pulse of his soul inclines him to it. The white race might fall into
> a barbarous state, and afterwards, subjected to the influence of
> civilization, be reclaimed and prosper. Not so for the Indian. He
> cannot be himself and be civilized; he fades away and dies. Culti-
> vation such as the white man would give him deprives him of his
> identity. Education, strange as it may appear, seems to weaken
> rather than strengthen his intellect . . .[21]

That Custer misrepresents Indian character and the course of Indian
responses to civilization should not, at this date, require argument. It
should, however, be noted that Custer here applies to the Indian the

orthodox tests of racialist science and so "proves" that the Indian as a species suffers biological decline under civilization and that he is therefore racially incompatible with whites. Similar arguments had been and were being used to prove the inferiority of blacks. The peculiarity of the Indians, however, is their savagery, their adherence to the violence and freedom of precivilization; whereas the "inferiority" of blacks is rooted in their docility which fits them for at least a marginal association with white civilization.

Part of the heroic persona of the Frontier hero derived from Cooper is the quality of sympathy with the Indians and of yearning for the innocence and freedom of a precivilized wilderness life. Custer identifies himself with this convention in a famous passage, which is often cited as proof of his genuine sympathy with his enemies:

> If I were an Indian, I often think that I would greatly prefer to cast my lot among those of my people who adhered to the free open plains, rather than submit to the confined limits of a reservation, there to be the recipient of the blessed benefits of civilization, with its vices thrown in without stint or measure.

Custer's "sympathy" is expressed here in terms of conventional formulae. The lonely fighter image of the Indian going down to extinction comes straight out of the "Red Man" essay, and the sarcasm about the "vices" of civilization is formulaic rather than personal. "The Indian," the passage continues, "can never be permitted to view the question in this deliberate way. He is neither a luxury nor necessity of life"—that is, he neither adorns nor is useful to the ongoing life of civilization. Custer echoes Parker's vision of the "Saxon race" as a "Juggernaut" which destroys the Indian: "Destiny seems to have so willed it, and the world looks on and nods approval." We can therefore indulge our sentiments in sympathy for the Indian but this need not interfere with the policy of exterminating them; indeed, the inevitability and naturalness of that extermination heightens the intensity and "nobility" of the sentimental response. The free spirit of the wild Indian, with which Custer identifies himself, simply makes this process swifter by bringing about wars in which the vanishing process is accelerated. The Indian's remaining true to his nature thus serves the turn of the Juggernaut's policy.[22]

According to *My Life on the Plains*, Custer is the preeminent hero of this great Indian war because he combines the knowledge, professionalism, and genteel sensibilities of the military aristocrat with the prowess, the affinity for the wilderness and the Indian that characterize the hunter-warrior. His alone is the strategy that leads to the Washita victory and the aftermath of pursuit that ends with the surrender of the Indians in 1869. He avoids any mention of his court-martial and suspension, losing a chance to dramatize his return to action but also avoiding the questions the episode raised about his own actions. He enriches the account with characterizations and dramatic scenes that are suggestive of the influence of historical romances and dime novels. He makes of the scout "California Joe" Milner a true-life version of the trusty, crusty, humorous, dialect-speaking "old hunter" who was a staple of the dime-novel Western formula.

Their relationship in Custer's book is on the order of the Hawkeye/Middleton or the Carson/Frémont pairings; but Custer is Milner's superior as an Indian fighter and pathfinder as well as his social superior.

The Cooper touch is also apparent in the "Indian marriage" scene, in which Custer—amid the burning wreckage of Black Kettle's village—is offered the lovely squaw Monasetah as a bride. In Cooper, the rejection of the possibility of Indian marriage is Leatherstocking's assertion that his racial "gifts" outweigh his acquired affinity for Indian ways. Its thematic purpose is similar here, and Custer deploys the same conventions of description Cooper used to characterize his "dark," sensuous, and racially (or morally) tainted women—Cora in *Mohicans* and Judith in *Deerslayer*:

> [She was] an exceedingly comely squaw possessing a . . . disposition more inclined to be merry than one usually finds among Indians. Add to bright laughing eyes, a set of pearly teeth and a rich complexion . . . [H]er well shaped head was crowned with a luxuriant growth of the most beautiful silken tresses, rivalling in color the blackness of the raven and extending when allowed to fall loosely about her shoulders to below her waist.[23]

Thus, despite his strictures against Cooper as the writer who "more than . . . any other author" has given "people speaking the English language a false and ill-judged estimate of the Indian character," Custer willingly avails himself of the appealing erotic and sentimental elements in Cooperian fantasy. His attack on Cooper is simply one of the devices by which he proves his own hardheadedness, and this lends authenticity to his own essentially romantic fable of his life on the plains. It was, in fact, a technique very similar to Cooper's own methods for authenticating his pretensions to "realism."[24]

While in the midst of publishing the *Galaxy* articles, Custer and the Seventh Cavalry were reassigned to Dakota Territory to provide escort for a surveying party of the Nothern Pacific Railroad. General Alfred Terry would replace Custer's old nemesis, Hancock, as department commander; and Custer would serve immediately under General David S. Stanley. As we have seen, the Army had a special relationship with Jay Cooke and the Northern Pacific. Cooke counted both President Grant and former Department Commander Hancock among his banking clients, and both men had given him personal assurances of government and army support when he assumed control of the railroad in 1869. Hancock's replacement by General Terry did not alter this relationship, and Terry provided military escorts for the surveying parties that the railroad sent into the northern borderlands of the Great Reservation. The army's role in this expedition was somewhat peculiarly defined. It was not merely to provide protection against marauding Indians, but to "subdue and intimidate" them by improving any opportunity for battle, and to survey the area with a view to the establishment of military posts. When a raiding party did attack, Custer not only beat them off but pursued them by night marches for three days. This policy was nominally intended to overawe the Sioux, whose reservation would border on the railroad route; but it also served the purposes of the railroad, which looked toward the eventual liquidation of Sioux title the lands continuous with the railroad's grant and the effective removal of freely roaming Indians from the vicinity.[25]

The bankruptcy of Cooke and the Northern Pacific in September 1873 did not alter this close relationship. The army remained officially committed to the success of the project, and the railroad was as avid as ever in courting good will with the soldiers assigned to protect its interests. Custer was a likely target for such courtship, and the Northern Pacific luckily had on its staff men who had the general's friendship. A. B. Nettleton, the chief of the line's publicity, was a comrade-in-arms of Custer from Sheridan's Shenandoah Valley campaign; and ex-Confederate Tom Rosser, the chief of engineering, was Custer's West Point classmate and his friendly rival from the same Shenandoah campaign. Custer and Rosser were reunited on Stanley's expedition, and Custer immediately received some small favors from the line—a large railroad tent, much more comfortable than government issue, and a lucrative position for Custer's Monroe friend Fred Nims.

For his part, Custer echoed the railroad men's boosterish rhetoric, and, in a letter to Libbie, wondered aloud why Monroe boys did not leave home to make their fortunes as "men" in this new country. But while Custer tried out on Libbie this "Go west, young man" rhetoric, he continued to see his own future prosperity and celebrity in a Metropolitan rather than a wilderness setting. His imagination was no doubt stirred by the Chicago *Post*'s reviving his Civil War sobriquet in praising him as the "Glorious Boy," echoed by both the Republican *Tribune* and the Democratic *World* of New York, who refurbished his wartime laurels in their celebration of the expedition's findings and the victory over the Indians.[26]

It was this resurgence of public acclaim for Custer, coupled with his friendship for Rosser and Nettleton, that made the railroad look to Custer for aid in what suddenly appeared as its darkest hour. The Northern Pacific, thrown into receivership by the panic of 1873, needed more than ever some means of increasing the value of its land grant. At this juncture, too, it was feeling the public backlash against Cooke's overselling of the project and its lands. Among its critics was General Hazen, the same who had clashed with Sheridan and Custer after the battle of Washita. In a letter to the editor of the New York *Tribune*, published February 27, 1874, he attacked the railroad's publicity as "wicked deceptions." Citing a Cooke-inspired article in the December 1873 *Harper's Monthly*—"Poetry and Philosophy of Indian Summer"—as an example of Northern Pacific deceit, Hazen proceeded (as he thought) to demolish Cooke's "poetry" with facts and figures showing the territory to be an arid waste, alternately baked by the sun and frozen by winter winds.[27]

On February 16, 1874, Rosser wrote to Custer asking him to respond to Hazen's attack and suggesting the mode of response:

Dear Custer: Enclosed I send you an effusion of the gallant Col. of the "6th foot," and I think it quite worthy of him. Genl. Hazen has never seen the country he abuses and as you have, I would be glad if you would write, either to me, or to some of our western papers giving your idea of the country you passed over. Of course, we don't claim that *all* the Country we pass over is good, but *all is not as bad as Hazen states.* . . .

A line or two from your pen will render us a great service at this time and I hope you will now come to our aid—You are in better condition to discuss this question than any officer in the Army . . .

Custer agreed, and his letter appeared on April 17, 1874. Custer re-searched his response in the most complete body of literature available on the territory, supplemented with his own experiences. This literature, however, was in large part the product of Northern Pacific surveys as filtered through Northern Pacific publicists. Custer followed their lead, often paraphrasing their words and occasionally reproducing them. He laid careful stress on just those qualities most important to the railroad's land salesmen: the general fertility of the entire region, its aptness for particular crops, the abundance of "representative" harvests, the presence of both wild and cultivated flowers in abundance—a paradisaical touch, and the conventional images by which promoters since Columbus had in-vested their territories with the attributes of the "garden of the world."[28]

But in fact the only aspects of regional fertility to which Custer could have personally attested referred to the availability of grazing and forage for cavalry and pack animals, and when Custer asserted that the region he had passed through was suitable for wheat growing, he exceeded his own agronomic expertise. Moreover, his own earlier report to the army, pub-lished in the *Army and Navy Journal*, described the territory over which he passed as rough, broken, and dry. This was precisely the description given by the *Tribune* correspondent, Samuel Barrows, who had accom-panied the expedition. On balance, however, both Custer and Hazen over-stated their cases. All of the territory was not so bad as Hazen made it; but it was hardly the agricultural paradise Custer portrayed. What is important about the affair is that it marked the beginning of Custer's loyal service as a public advocate of the Northern Pacific's interests; and it established the pattern of his literary treatments of the West, which would follow the model laid down in the Gilpinian propaganda of Jay Cooke.[29]

It was just after the appearance of this letter that Custer was appointed to command the army's exploring expedition into the Black Hills. This appointment marked the high point of his professional career—his first truly independent command, involving a large and important expedition which would require the handling of combined arms, complicated logistics, the supervision of surveying and scientific projects, readiness for combat with the Indians, and the management of public relations. It was a mark of Sheridan's continuing esteem that Custer was appointed; the presence of Grant's son Fred was a sign that Custer and the expedition itself enjoyed the personal support of the president.

Given the circumstances of his appointment, Custer cannot have been in doubt about the role his expedition was to play in the future develop-ment of Indian affairs, nor about the kind of report he was expected to produce. His superiors were on record as anticipating an outbreak of hostilities with the Sioux and Cheyenne over any one of several areas of friction—the encroachment of the Northern Pacific, the invasion of the reservation by prospectors, the corruption and incompetence of the Indian agencies, or the resentment of the off-reservation "hostiles." Since war with the savages was inevitable, the Army wanted to establish fortified posts in the Black Hills; and the high command were willing to do this even though it might very well provide the hostiles with the occasion for starting the war. Nor was the secrecy that surrounded Custer's preparations intended to avoid provoking the Indians, who were bound to react strongly to an "invasion" undertaken without prior warning or approval by the peace chiefs. Rather, it aimed at avoiding the provocation of the philanthropic faction until it was too late to block Custer's departure. The fact that newspapers were invited to send correspondents on the expedition was an indication that the army wanted Custer's procedures and findings to be trumpeted as loudly as possible. And the presence of expert gold miners signaled the army's willingness to have the rumors of Black Hills gold confirmed beyond doubt. Such reports would certainly increase the flow of illegal prospectors to the Hills and the pressure on Washington for extinguishing Indian title, but this appeared not to deter the expedition's military strategists.[30]

Several major newspapers which enjoyed nationwide circulation made arrangements to receive reports from accredited correspondents. Telegraph facilities ensured that field dispatches would be received by the papers almost as soon as army headquarters received them; and the wire services would provide a network for syndicating stories to interested papers across the country. Custer "went the extra mile" for the newspaper people. He wrote to the *Tribune*, which had sent Barrows to accompany the 1873 expedition, to urge them to provide a special correspondent, and he sweetened the note by praising Barrows—despite his anger at being contradicted by him in the controversy with Hazen. He became especially close to William Eleroy Curtis, whose by-line, as we have seen, appeared in both the *Inter-Ocean* and the *World*. Custer may even have made some sort of arrangement with the *World* to provide unsigned correspondence or an advance copy of his preliminary report. In a letter to Libbie which was sent out in mid-expedition with the packet of dispatches entrusted to the scout Charley Reynolds, Custer mentions a "letter to the 'World'" sent out at the same time. Given Custer's acquaintance with Belmont's circle and his practice of making special arrangements with the press, such an arrangement is not out of the question; but no letter over Custer's signature appeared in the *World*, and there is no record of such a letter in the Custer archives.[31]

The most heroic and celebrated episode during the expedition was Charley Reynolds's solitary ride through Indian country to Fort Laramie, where he reported the discovery of gold and gave the world Custer's preliminary report on the "New Paradise," the "New El Dorado." There was no military reason for sending Reynolds at that juncture, and it has always been suspected that the idea was to get word of the discovery to the newspapers in the fastest and most spectacular way possible. It is conceivable that some private arrangement had been made, either with Custer or with Reynolds himself, to get the earliest possible word to particular groups of interested speculators. The tireless Sioux City booster Charles Collins— not the most reliable of sources—claimed he had made such an arrangement with Reynolds for an early warning that would enable him to be ahead of the competition in exploiting the news. In support of his claim, Collins notes that Reynolds did not stop at Laramie but entrained for the east and then rode horseback from Omaha to Sioux City to bring him the word. Why Custer should have acquiesced in Reynolds's deal is not stated; and in any case, Collins had begun preparing for the opening of the Hills before the expedition had been made public. He had already opened an emigration office in Chicago to spread word of the Black Hills' fertility and to route the traffic toward Sioux City. But whether or not Collins made his deal with Reynolds, there is no missing the significance of Custer's sending Reynolds out when and how he did: it was meant to stir excitement about the expedition and its confirmation of the existence of gold, and it did.[32]

But Reynolds's news awaited final confirmation in Custer's own final report, which was not forthcoming until after the expedition returned to Fort Lincoln. As we have seen, by the time Custer returned the enthusiasm stirred by the preliminary reports of Curtis and Reynolds was at fever pitch. With an audience already primed, with the army implicitly behind extinguishing Indian title to the Hills, and with the railroad still needing his help, Custer knew what sort of report was expected of him. And he had a superb example to follow in the works of Ferdinand V. Hayden, the noted explorer and publicist whom historian William Goetzmann has called the businessman's geologist.[33]

In 1873–74, Hayden was at the height of his fame and influence for his expedition into the Rockies. Custer could hardly have been unacquainted with his reputation and character; and since Hayden was the last explorer to visit the Black Hills, it is virtually certain that Custer studied Hayden's reports, his manner of presenting data to an eager popular audience, and his way of combining scientific observation with his skill as a writer to serve the interest of his business patrons, whom he saw as the means through which the Frontier could be conquered and utilized. Hayden had, for example, served Kansas land interests, and especially the Kansas Pacific Railroad, by his scientific argument for the theory that "rain follows the plow." This was designed to convince the "plain and unlearned classes" that the aridity of the railroad's lands would be corrected as soon as farmers had purchased and begun cultivating the soil. When the theory was questioned by other scientists, Hayden's associate "validated" the data by interviewing a select group of railroad presidents with substantial investments in the region—and therefore presumably with great practical as well as firsthand knowledge. It is not surprising that they agreed with Hayden that increased cultivation had induced increases in annual precipitation.[34]

There was also a good deal of firsthand observation in Custer's Black Hills report and justification, too, for his praise of the scenery and its resources. Readers at the time recognized that the style was hyperbolic, but were prepared to accept it as the natural expression of an ebullient young man confronted with a region of real beauty and promise.

But Custer's enthusiastic descriptions were more than exercises in poetic license. They were quite deliberately designed to reproduce and to validate the Northern Pacific's assertions about the value of the land tapped by their railroad. It was because of the railroad's interest that he gave the agricultural potential of the land equal play with the promise of gold, since the railroad's long-term interest depended on the agrarian development of the region. Whatever the evidence before his eyes, in composing his report Custer once again relied upon the texts of railroad promotion brochures in his possession. The clearest example of this is Custer's description of the view from Harney's Peak, which he climbed during the course of the Expedition.

> While in Harney's Peak I could contrast the bright, green verdure of these lovely parks with the sunburned and dried yellow herbage to be seen on the outer plains. Everything indicates an abundance of moisture within the space enclosed by the Black Hills. The soil is that of a rich garden and composed of a dark mold of exceedingly fine grain. We have found the country in many places covered with wild raspberries, both of black and the red varieties. Yesterday and today I have feasted on the latter. It is no unusual sight to see hundreds of soldiers gathering wild berries. Nowhere in the States have I tasted cultivated raspberries of equal flavor to those found growing here, nor have I ever seen them larger or in as great profusion as I have seen hundreds of acres of them here.

The description is extremely well done, and Custer himself is responsible for telling details like the description of the wild berries, and for the rhythm of the piece—spell-casting repetition of words like "abundance" and "profusion." Nonetheless, the description of the green, Edenic verdure is plagiarized in part from a Northern Pacific brochure prepared under Cooke's auspices (that is, before 1873), describing the Red River Valley of Minnesota:

> The eye alone resting upon it can take in the features of this remarkable region. It is a sea of verdure. We ride now through tall rank grass and now through a garden bed. Our horses trample remorselessly on lilies, roses, wild flax, morning-glories and petunias. . . . The Red River and all its tributaries are fringed with timber, and aside from this line of trees there is absolutely nothing for the eye to rest upon except the bright carpet which nature has unrolled upon the floor of this magnificent palace . . . a region which to my mind comes nearer the Garden of Eden than any other portion of the earth . . . gentle swells, parks, groves, lawns, lakes, ponds, pellucid streams—a rare combination of beauty and fertility which will make it in coming years one of the fairest portions of the earth.

Indeed, the Northern Pacific text even anticipates the most striking and unique of Custer's descriptions cited earlier: the cavalry's passage through Floral Valley, and regions that echo the design of Central Park.[35]

Custer, however, had every reason to expect that his report, and the public clamor that followed its appearance, would find favor with the Grant administration. Although there may have been some personal trouble between Custer and Fred Grant about the latter's drinking, Custer had brought the affair off in fine style without the loss of a man and without appearing to provoke an Indian war. He had made exactly the sort of report his superiors expected: one that was calculated to stimulate demand for the immediate establishment of a fortified post in the Black Hills and for the eventual opening up of the region to settlement. If his report served the interests of the Northern Pacific Railroad as well, Sherman and Sheridan had also expressed in writing their enthusiasm for that railroad, and Grant held stock in the corporation received from Jay Cooke himself.

But Grant underwent a sudden change of mind. Whether he had failed somehow to understand what the expedition would mean or whether the "philanthropic" faction of his party now made its strength felt, Grant decided to slam the lid on this Pandora's box of the Black Hills—too late to prevent a host of troubles from flying free, but in time to check Custer in full career. From Custer's viewpoint, Grant's orders to the army to turn back miners heading for the Black Hills were less serious than the statements Fred Grant was induced to make: that he personally had never seen any indications of "gold at the roots of the grass." The expedition's geologist, Prof. N. M. Winchell, concurred.

Custer's response in the *World* (December 13, 1874) was sarcastic, and bad temper made his turn of phrase ambiguous: "Why Professor Winchell saw no gold was simply due to the fact that he neglected to look for it." This left the unfortunate impression that Custer had gone specifically to look for gold and find it whether or not. Winchell and Grant had effectively made Custer look like a liar, and some journals suggested he had been "bought up." Custer considered that he had been betrayed by Grant *père et fils*, insulted and abandoned for the sake of that thrice-accursed Peace Policy.[36]

But there was no immediate break with Grant. Custer expected to lead a second expedition into the Black Hills the next summer to extend his exploration and confirm his findings. Given the start of the gold rush, it was likely that this expedition would also involve action against the off-reservation portion of the Sioux, if not the entire nation. Custer had, therefore, to trim his advocacy of sudden seizure of the "New El Dorado" and conform to the administration line, which required that all miners be expelled from the Hills until negotiations with the Indians settled the issue. However, he would not give his own reports the lie, nor would he disappoint his friends with the Northern Pacific. In an interview with the editor of the Bismarck *Tribune* on September 2, Custer warned that the army would follow presidential orders to keep the miners out. However, he went on record as favoring "the extinguishment of the Indian title at the earliest moment" and the establishment of forts that would "settle the Indian question as far as the Northwest is concerned." Somewhat disingenuously, he invoked his experience with the Stevens Mine as credential for judging deposits, and asserted that his reports of gold "are not exaggerated in the least"; as for agricultural potential, "Nature it would seem exhausted her resources in attempting to beautify and fit for the husbandman these delightful valleys." By May 1875 his relationship with Grant had become more problematic, but the interview he then gave to the New York *Herald* reiterated his main contentions about the Hills while remaining obeisant to the Indian policies of the President.[37]

Custer's report and his well-publicized defense of it had served to identify him with the forces working to open the Black Hills by any means. Thus, even if there had been no public flap over Fred Grant's interview, Grant would have found it difficult to appoint Custer to lead the second Black Hills expedition. But his demonstrated fitness from the strictly military point of view and his familiarity with the region made it hard to refuse Custer the appointment. Grant delayed until April 1875, and then announced that Colonel Richard Irving Dodge would lead the expedition, with Professor Walter Jenney as head of the scientific team. The choice of Dodge suggests that the nature of the government's attitude toward the Hills had not fundamentally changed: Dodge was not widely experienced as a plainsman or a combat officer but was the author of several popular books on the West. He produced exactly the same sort of pen portrait of the Hills as an Eden/El Dorado that Custer had given his superiors—this time at book length. Jenney's findings confirmed Custer's reports in most essentials, although with a caveat for miners to the effect that getting the gold out of the Hills would present substantial technological difficulties not met with in placer mining. Whatever balm such confirmation might bring to Custer, it cannot have compensated for his bitterness at being passed over for the command in favor of someone with similar credentials as publicist and lesser professional standing.[38]

The reports of Custer, Dodge, and Jenney, coupled with the escalation of lobbying and independent "invasions" of the Hills by western prospectors, induced the government to begin the process of extinguishing Indian title to the Black Hills. To avoid the accusation of illegality and impropriety, and to avert Indian hostility, Grant appointed a commission to negotiate the sale with the Indians in June 1875. The proposal caused a deep split in Indian ranks and the outcome of the negotiation was a refusal by the vast majority, under the peace chief Red Cloud, to consider selling the Hills for less than $600,000,000—exactly ten times the price offered by the government. Under the system of private property which the government was teaching the Indians to accept, that ought to have ended the matter. But with such vital interests at stake, the American government could not let the matter drop.

It was at this point that Indian Commissioner Smith abandoned the policy of his agency, which had been to protect Indian title, and urged the application of force to compel the sale of the Hills. He attempted to rest his case on legalistic grounds, declaring that the corporate indebtedness of the Indian tribes to the federal government justified the tribes' being cast in receivership, and the Hills' being appropriated for the creditor. The cynicism of Smith is extraordinary, since the inefficiency and corruption of

Indian Bureau agents was the cause of Indian indebtedness. But the most important element in Smith's *Report* has to do with the Indians' rights of property. The entire program of reform was based on the premise that private property (preferably agrarian) is the basis of civilization, and that the Indians' tutelage in civilization would have to be founded on practical education in the possession and cultivation of property. But now Smith asserts that both theory and circumstance must give way to the necessity of giving the Black Hills to the people who can get the most out of them— that is, to the whites. Moreover, he extends practical exigency into a new ideological argument against the theoretical basis of the whole enterprise of civilizing the Indians and integrating them with American society. In speaking of the Hills, Smith says, "If an Indian can be possessed of rights of country . . . this country [the Black Hills] belongs for occupation by the Sioux." Yet the Bureau's support of the forced sale of the Hills was an explicit acknowledgment that, at least in the present state of their development, the Indians could *not* be said to have any rights at all to the possession of land. This put Smith squarely in the camp of editorialists like those of the *World* and the *Herald*, who had been asserting that doctrine since Custer discovered gold in the summer of 1874.[39]

It was assumed that once the decision had been made to force the sale of the Black Hills, hostilities with the Indians were inevitable. The off-reservation Indians hunting in the Hills and the Unceded Lands were certain to resist as "invaders" any soldiers or civilians they came across; added to their numbers would be partisans of those chiefs who, after rejecting the sale, had been deposed by the government in favor of more cooperative chiefs. On November 3, 1875, Grant met in the White House with Sherman and Sheridan and took a series of decisions that assured hostilities.

The President and his commanders first of all decided to remove army roadblocks from the path of the miners, thus creating the fait accompli of a substantial white settlement. This, in turn, would disarm the administration's opponents by casting the army's role as that of defender of imperiled settlers. It also established a preemptive presence in and claim to the Hills that no amount of Indian resistance or negotiation could undo: despite the Indian war, within a year of Grant's orders the region was in fact thronged with miners, dotted with small camps and boom towns like Deadwood City (where Wild Bill Hickok would be assassinated shortly after Custer's Last Stand). At the same time, any Indians found off the reservations two months following, or after January 1, 1876, were to be considered as at war with the United States and subject to immediate attack. The ultimatum was unprincipled on several counts: it made it an act of hostility for Indians to be found on the Unceded Lands, which were still (in default of successful negotiations) legally Indian territory; moreover, winter conditions made it improbable that off-reservation Indians would receive the announcement, or could travel back to the reservations in time. There was no way in which the Indians could avoid being defined as hostile; and since this was obvious to all concerned, preparations began immediately for a three-pronged pincer campaign against the Indians to begin in the spring by three "columns" of foot, horse, and guns:

the Montana Column under Gibbon from the north; General Crook's Column from the south; and the Dakota Column from the east.

In that campaign, it was inevitable that Custer and the Seventh Cavalry would play a leading role. Despite his public quarrel with Grant over the Black Hills, Custer was still a favorite of Sheridan, who had effective oversight of all operations in the West. Custer's immediate superior, Department Commander Alfred Terry, had no experience as an Indian fighter and no direct knowledge of the terrain, while Custer had achieved notable successes against the Indians and had been over the ground in Dakota Territory more extensively than any other officer of comparable rank. Command arrangements for the march of the Dakota Column were not clearly defined, but Custer seems to have believed that he was intended from the first as its commander. The facts have been obscured by the subsequent political uproar over Custer's role in the impeachment of Secretary of War William Belknap (Custer gave information of the secretary's malfeasance to *Herald* correspondent Ralph Meeker), by his temporary removal from command by Grant, and by his restoration with the stipulation that his command be restricted to the Seventh Cavalry proper. However, there seems to have been ample justification for Custer's belief that he would have effective field command of the Dakota Column, even if Terry should accompany it and assume overall command of the united "pincers." He had had a similar relation to the first colonel of the Seventh, A. J. Smith, ever since the regiment's formation: Smith was the administrative head of the organization and Custer the effective commander in the field.[40]

But for most of 1875, Custer's position was a frustrating and uncertain one. The Stevens Mine investment was reaching its nadir, he had lost his chance to command the second Black Hills expedition, and was at odds with the president. The Dakota Column had not yet been conceived. But disappointment in the West was offset by new literary and financial opportunities in the East. His writings on the West and Indian affairs were much in demand. James Gordon Bennett, Jr., of the *Herald* wanted him to write anonymously on military actions in the West; the *World* offered to send him to Europe as its correspondent—there were wars afoot or brewing in Spain and the Balkans; and James Redpath, John Brown's old publicist, offered to send him on a lecture tour.[41]

And, most fatefully, the acquaintance with New York financial magnates fostered by the Stevens project began to bear fruit. During the spring of 1875, while Custer was on leave in New York, he became involved in the projects of Abraham Buford—the ex-Confederate cavalryman turned Kentucky horse breeder—and Ben Holladay, a former pioneer of transcontinental stagecoach traffic, now a would-be railroad entrepreneur whose Puget Sound holdings gave him control of the Northern Pacific's western terminus.

Buford and Custer met while Custer was on occupation duty in Kentucky in 1871–72; how he had met Holladay is not so certain. Their common interest in the Northern Pacific undoubtedly gave them mutual friends; both were, after a fashion, celebrity Westerners in the big city. And both were drawing heavily on their acquaintances in the banking community to improve their finances and to support failing operations—for Holladay's

Puget Sound rail and steamship franchises were nearly as profitless as the Stevens Mine. Having suffered severely by the Panic of 1873 and having failed to win his suit against the government for losses suffered by his stage lines during the war, Holladay's holdings were then in receivership.

The first evidence we have of a Custer-Buford-Holladay scheme is a hastily composed letter from Buford addressed to "My Dear Custer," written on stationery of the Quartermaster General's Office in Washington, and dated August 22, 1875:

> How long I have waited to be able to write *positively*, but even now I cannot! Ben is still here—of course he expects to leave in two days for Oregon. . . . His financial "buster," Villard, is getting things straight in Europe and doubtless Ben will get the money & *then* the Mare will go!
>
> We want to do a big thing in Black Hills, and we can have half a million money put up to carry it through—We have any amount of Sioux and Valentine Scrip besides—Ben wants to put in Stages and be Sutler to new Posts. He has promise of Interior for Indian Trade . . . Now, what think you! Ben counts much on you—He can put on Stages from Union Pacific also. Now, what should he do to be in the right *place*, right *time*? . . . If I can have control over horse shoes &c, I mean to ask a Board with yourself as President. The Goodenough and Elastic Companies want an Officer to go in Europe. It can be easily managed—if-if-if their shoes are actually the *best*—about which I am doubtful more than half the time. . . .
>
> > Yours truly
> > Buford

Henry Villard, mentioned in the letter, was the agent of Holladay's creditors, and his approval was necessary before Holladay could have his half million released to him. In the spring and summer of 1875, this outcome seemed not unlikely as the two men were on favorable terms. However, Villard was then formulating a plan to take over the Northern Pacific and needed Holladay's holdings for this purpose. An ostensibly friendly stock tip given by Villard to Holladay brought the latter additional financial reverses. By the fall of 1875, Villard had definitively turned down all Holladay's pleas for funds, and the two were enemies.[42]

The Buford letter defines four different but related projects. Buford and Custer were to join Holladay in his reentry to the field of his earliest triumphs, the stagecoach business. A number of lines are suggested between the Black Hills and various points along the line of the Union Pacific, the Northern Pacific, and other railroads. If franchises for carrying the mails could be acquired, these lines could be expected to yield a profit carrying mail and passengers to the forts and mining camps in the Hills. They also hoped to obtain franchises to operate sutlerships on the projected army posts and control of at least one Indian agency—and that a supply depot. These latter enterprises could be highly profitable, especially when dishonestly run—as they most often were. Custer's participation in this part of the scheme is particularly ironic, since he was about to make a huge public splash as the righteous "whistle-blower" on a scandal involving the Indian agencies and the "sale" of post sutlerships by Secretary of War Belknap. Finally, the army was apparently in the market for a new horse-shoe contractor, and Buford hoped Custer could help him sell his product to the army.

The influence of a number of government offices would be required to carry off these schemes. According to Buford, Holladay had an important friend at Interior who could help them obtain their Indian agency, as well as long-standing connections with the post office, from which he would expect to get his mail franchise. Buford's letter is written on stationery of the quartermaster general—an office held in that year by Rufus Ingalls, a confidant of Grant, a man often suspected of corruption but never convicted, and a friend of Custer's.[43]

The offices of Department Commander Sheridan and General of the Army Sherman were also important to the enterprise. The success of the several schemes depended not only on the decision to open the Black Hills, but on early notification of that decision, and of the locations of the projected army posts and mining towns. These decisions were not finalized until the secret meeting in the White House on November 3. As Sheridan's protégé and as the first explorer of the Black Hills, Custer could be expected to provide the early notice that his partners required to "be in right *place*, right *time*." The wording of Buford's letter suggests that both he and Holladay relied heavily on Custer for this part of the scheme, and a similar reliance was placed on him by Buford for the success of the horseshoe promotion.

Custer was to play the roles of technical expert, influence peddler, and respectable "front" for the enterprise—a role similar to that he had played in the Stevens Mine matter. Custer had learned well, and practiced at a high level, the art of lobbying for his friends' promotions and for their business interests—as his favors for Rosser and Nettleton and his letter to Secretary of the Interior Chandler on behalf of a Black Hills promoter reveal. He was not at first expected to provide much in the way of capital; but the withdrawal of Villard's support in September 1875 altered the situation.[44]

The financing of the Black Hills "combination" was highly suspect. It depended in the first instance on the possession of scrip, a highly speculative commodity. Indeed, the Sioux or Half-Breed Scrip which Buford claimed Holladay possessed was not even supposed to be legally transferable. And when Villard's financing definitively fell through, Custer and Holladay turned to a course of intensive speculation in the stock market. The firm of Emil Justh—whose director Custer and Holladay had met through Quartermaster General Ingalls—handled the account. The extent and nature of Custer's transactions came to light in a law suit filed against Holladay by Justh after Custer died and his estate had defaulted on Custer's note to Justh. Testimony revealed that Custer ordered Justh to buy issues of highly speculative railroad stocks without paying anything at all on margin. After the stock was sold, Custer agreed to pay the difference in case of loss, and he would receive the profit in case of a gain. But Custer's transactions were disastrous—he lost all his capital and had to borrow $8,500, for which he signed a note, with Holladay as cosigner. After Custer's death Holladay claimed that the note was invalid because the transactions were in the nature of gambling debts and hence illegal. The ploy recalls that of Indian commissioner Smith who used the indebtedness of the Sioux, caused by the corruption of Indian Bureau officials, as justification for "foreclosing" on the Black Hills.

The interesting thing is that Holladay won his case on appeal. Reviewing the correspondence between Custer and Justh, the court concluded that "It seems to us impossible to read these papers without being impressed with the idea that they refer to an illicit business," and further added that Justh must have been conscious of the gambling character of the transactions, because of the obvious "disparity between the pecuniary ability of Custer and the immense amount of purchases and sales within half a year's time." According to Justh's own testimony and depositions, Custer had represented himself as possessing slightly over $50,000 in assets, chiefly in the Bacon farm in Monroe and in blooded horses; he also said Custer held a draft that he could not present for payment "as there was a lady involved." Justh also claimed that Custer expected to receive $100,000 from Ben Holladay, and this may have been in connection with the Black Hills speculation. But like those of many others, Custer's expectations of financial reward from Holladay were disappointed.[45]

The Buford-Holladay speculation, Custer's dealings in the Stevens Mine matter, his work for the Northern Pacific, and his relationship with Justh and Co. reveal "Custer of Wall Street" as a direct and active participant in the corruption of the Gilded Age. The Northern Pacific matter shows him engaged in an exchange of favors with private businessmen on matters directly affecting public policy. Then in March, 1876, he emerged as one of the chief accusers of Secretary of War Belknap, in a scandal involving bribery in the appointment of post traders at western forts. But the Buford letter shows Custer angling to acquire just such an Indian agency and to purchase just such a post tradership. It was a business capable of corrupting principled men; and the Buford-Holladay matter shows Custer as willing to countenance an attempt to defraud his own branch of the service—by selling it those Goodenough horseshoes which Buford admitted were probably not good enough.[46]

Thus in February of 1876, Custer was in serious financial difficulties. The Black Hills speculation with Buford and Holladay was indefinitely delayed if not aborted; Custer had suffered serious financial losses and was in debt to Justh for $8,500. Justh was apparently dunning him, and Custer had to write a letter pleading for Justh to hold off taking legal action. The "special efforts" he was making to get enough money to settle his account, he said, would be aborted if Justh should sue him in court. It was also at this time that Custer wrote to General Terry requesting an extension of his leave to permit him to resolve these financial matters. If granted, this leave would have allowed him to stay in New York until April 1.[47]

Although Terry had been most accommodating in the past, this time he refused to endorse Custer's application. Such a leave would have kept Custer away from his command during most of the period of preparation for the campaign against the Sioux. If Custer was indeed expected to be the field commander not only of the Seventh Cavalry but of the whole Dakota Column, his absence would have put an inappropriate burden of responsibility on junior officers and would certainly have meant a delay in mounting the expedition. The episode sheds an interesting light on Custer's view of his command responsibility and on the proportional strength of the motives that drew him to the plains and called him back to New York. Even if his role was to have been restricted to command of the Seventh Cavalry, his absence until April would have been a dereliction of his duty to the regiment. But he was willing to scant these duties and jeopardize his chance to command the Dakota Column in order to salvage his fortunes in Wall Street and avoid the financial ruin that faced him and his beloved Libbie. Under Terry's orders, he had perforce to abandon personal matters that touched him very deeply and return to Dakota.[48]

When in March he was suddenly recalled to testify before the congressional committee investigating the Belknap post-traderships sales, Custer tried to avoid giving testimony and cited the necessity of his being with his command during the preparations for the spring campaign. We may suspect Custer's sincerity on this score, since he had been willing to absent himself from the command in order to defend his financial interests. Moreover, he had been working behind the scenes with *Herald* reporter Ralph Meeker to expose Belknap. However, he may have also feared that aspects of his Holladay-Buford dealings might come to light—a classic example of the pot calling the kettle black. But Custer's desire to avoid involvement in the Belknap impeachment was somewhat genuine, since it would further embroil him in Grant's enmity at a time when Grant was still his commander in chief, with power to make or break his military career.[49]

Custer's testimony was characterized as "hearsay," not usable in a court of law; but that is not in itself evidence of impropriety on Custer's part.[50] His appearance before the Clymer committee (investigating Belknap) gave him a chance to accomplish some of the things he had left undone in February, and it also opened up some possibilities. Visiting New York in March, April, and May, he made arrangements with Redpath for a fall lecture tour, after the presumably successful conclusion of the Indian war—and coincident with a presidential election in which Custer was now a factor. He also touched base with his book publishers and with his *Galaxy* editors, who were bringing out his accounts of the 1873 expedition and his "War Memoirs," as well as with newspapers likely to be interested in correspondence from the Dakota Column—he visited the *Herald* offices and spoke with Whitelaw Reid of the *Tribune.*[51]

During this time he also seems to have gotten in touch with Belmont or people close to Belmont about possible political preferment. Anti-Custer writers have asserted that Custer was hopeful of a dark-horse nomination for president at the upcoming Democratic convention in St. Louis and that New York *Herald* owner-editor James Gordon Bennett, Jr., was his chief backer. But there is no hard evidence for this: in fact, Bennett declared in May that no general should ever again be nominated after the experience with Grant. Yet Custer had done the Democratic Party a favor by his testimony against Belknap; and he added to this service by voluntarily testifying against Major Lewis Merrill, an officer of his own regiment who had been active in prosecuting the KKK in South Carolina. Merrill was accused of having accepted a reward for his services and was attacked by Democratic politicians who hoped to discredit further both the Republican administration of Reconstruction and the official propaganda about Klan atrocities. Custer had cherished an enmity for Merrill that went back at least to 1871, when he had attempted to blackmail Merrill into leaving the regiment.[52]

Custer dined in New York with Belmont and on his return to Washington with Senator Thomas Bayard, the son of a prominent prewar senator from Delaware who had presided over the convention of "ultra" southern Democrats in 1860. He was also Belmont's hand-picked candidate for the Democratic nomination against War Democrat Samuel J. Tilden. There were a number of ex-Confederate generals at the dinner as well, which seems to have been arranged to bring together a coalition of military and southern conservatives to back Bayard. While a tie to Senator Bayard would have precluded Custer's own presidential candidacy, it ought certainly to have led to a place in the new administration for the Indian-fighting hero who had stood up to and exposed the corruption of the Republicans. What such a place might have been is anyone's guess: Custer had in the past unsuccessfully applied to be commandant of West Point and inspector of cavalry. Custer's famous remark to his Arikara scouts—that after the expedition of 1876 he would be "their Great Father in Washington"—has suggested to some his presidential ambitions. But the statement also suggests the possibility that Custer might have been appointed head of the Indian Bureau. One of the Democratic platform planks was the return of the Bureau to army control; and as a respected critic of the old Indian policy, Custer would not have been an improbable choice to head up the new.[53]

Custer was, in fact, just then addressing the Indian question and its underlying ideological dilemmas in a series of articles prepared for publication. In a piece prepared for *Turf, Field and Farm* over his old "Nomad" signature (but never completed), Custer abandoned the facetious and denigratory style of those earlier writings. He uses, instead, the moderate and reasonable voice of *My Life on the Plains* and declares himself against the doctrine of "exterminating the Indians." He even states his belief that "no person who at all comprehends the necessities of the Indian question" let alone one who belongs to "a Christian and civilized nation" could "say a word in favor of extermination." Generals Sherman and Sheridan, who had been saying such things for years, might have bridled at this assertion by their protégé; but Custer is not writing for Sheridan here, but rather for that upper-class New York audience who wished to enjoy both the economic fruits of Indian dispossession and the moral satisfaction of sympathizing with "Poor Lo." This was precisely the position of the Belmonts, from whom political preferment might flow: August's son Perry had dined with Sheridan in the spring of 1876 and recorded how appalled he was by Sheridan's restatement of the belief that "the only good Indian is a dead Indian." Custer left off writing just as he was about to offer his own proposals for reform of the Indian policy.[54]

Whatever his specific program might have been, the premises would necessarily have been that the Indian is an obstacle to progress and to progress's most essential work, the railroad. An article published in the July 1876 issue of the *Galaxy* (which appeared while Custer was approaching the Little Big Horn) states this doctrine in just the terms preferred by Custer's sponsors on the Northern Pacific. The article is built around the colorful account of Custer's skirmishes with the Indians in 1873. As in *My Life on the Plains*, Custer himself is the leading figure as fighter, hunter, and scout—this time there is no "California Joe" to contrast with the soldier-hero's social superiority and technical proficiency. There are instead such dime-novel characters as a comical Irishman with a stage brogue— a lower-class type to amuse a condescending writer and audience—and an Indian scout melodramatically called Bloody Knife. But the point of the adventure tale is to provide a validating myth for a systematic restatement of the Northern Pacific's propaganda. Custer reiterates his earlier praises of the railroad's land grant and declares that the railroad's completion is necessary to the fulfillment of the promise implicit in the discovery of the Black Hills: "the opening to settlement of a large tract of valuable country and aiding in the development and successful working of a rich mineral region otherwise inaccessible." But he adds to this assertion that it is the Northern Pacific that will provide the final solution of the Indian question. In the first instance, it will, as Jay Cooke had previously argued, make Indian wars cheaper to fight by providing cheap transportation for troops and material. And in the longer run, it will establish civilization simply by making it impossible for savages to continue to subsist on the Great Plains.

> The experience of the past, particularly that of recent years, has shown too that no one measure so quickly and effectually frees a country from the horrors and devastations of Indian wars and Indian depredations generally as the building and successful operation of a railroad through the region overrun. . . . So earnest is my belief in [its] civilizing and peace-giving influence . . . [A] railroad established and kept in operation [in Indian country] would forever have preserved peace with the vast number of tribes infesting [the Great Plains].[55]

However, Custer is not so forthright as Sheridan in describing the means and processes by which the Indian question is to be settled. The building of the railroads, Sheridan had said, would lead to the extermination of the buffalo herds by meat hunters for the construction gangs, by hide hunters using the railroad as their base, and finally by tourists shooting game from palace-car windows. When the buffalo were gone, the Indian would be faced with the choice of starvation or surrender. However, both Sherman and Sheridan assumed that before that point was reached, the inevitable war of extermination would break out, a scenario they also viewed as desirable; and General Hancock had predicted as much in his letter to Jay Cooke in 1869. In Custer's account, this process is masked by the vaguely statistical assertion that the coming of a railroad "frees" a territory of Indian raids. In fact, the building of the railroad was certain to increase hostilities. As we may recall, Hancock had specifically countered Cooke's claim that the railroad would make Indian wars cheaper and less likely by pointing out that fighting an Indian war was a precondition for building the railroad; and hence, the supposed savings on transportation of Indian fighters could not be realized.

Until the end of April, Custer's eastern sojourn appeared to have gone better than could have been expected. His financial affairs were still in disarray, but he had been able to make some arrangements with Redpath, Justh, and Holladay that might eventually help. His contacts with the Belmont wing of the Democrats were closer than ever, and his testimony had helped him both with the party and with the substantial part of the journalistic community and the voting public who appeared disgusted with the Grant regime. He could now return to the Frontier, take up command of the Dakota Column, and add the laurels of a successful Indian campaign to cap the year's work. He was warned of Grant's anger with him, but he perhaps underrated it. Grant was clearly a tarnished leader and an outgoing one at that. Moreover, the warnings came as friendly advice from two of Grant's closest advisers, Army Commander Sherman and Quartermaster Ingalls; and this suggested that even in the president's circle, Custer had his supporters. At Sherman's suggestion, Custer paid a duty call on Grant before leaving for the West; and when Grant refused to see him, Ingalls went in to urge that he do so. When Grant still refused, Custer left for Dakota. But the duty call was not a mere courtesy; it was required by military regulations. Grant therefore seized Custer's departure as a pretext for putting him under arrest.

Grant's action compounded the political support Custer had earned by his original testimony. To Democratic partisans, Custer's removal was a spiteful attack by a dishonest man who wished to cover the malfeasance of his family and his party by the arbitrary use of military law. Republican papers were divided between those that were embarrassed by Custer's arrest and sought to minimize and downplay the issue; and those that attempted a partisan defense by characterizing Custer as a rash and rude young man, and a witting or unwitting tool of dishonest men and ex-rebels seeking to undo the verdict of Appomattox by undoing its hero. This added an explicit partisan meaning to Custer's role in the ultimate catastrophe, and profoundly affected the myth that was made of it.

But Custer himself was in no position to enjoy the enhanced significance of his yet unwritten legend, nor the possible reward a grateful Democratic Party might bestow. It was not his services that made him valuable but his fame. Nothing he said about politics or railroads or Indian policy was as significant as the fact that it was he who said it: the Boy General, the victor of the Washita, the discoverer of the Black Hills. His arrest left him with a choice of humiliations: he could beg Grant for reinstatement; or he could sit in Chicago while his regiment went out to fight and win the last great Indian war, the war for the region he had discovered and proclaimed to the world. His pride as a soldier and a professional as well as his self-interest required that he beg for reinstatement, and he did so before General Terry, who in turn pleaded Custer's case with Sherman.

Terry wrote to Sherman that he considered Custer's services essential to the success of the campaign—which was indeed the case. Sherman and Sheridan both intervened on Custer's behalf, and Custer himself sent a telegram apologizing for the lapse of protocol and asking Grant to spare him the shame of remaining behind. In the face of this unanimous military advice and public outcry against what was palpably an act of personal spite, Grant relented. But he stipulated that Custer not command the Dakota Column, restricting him to command of the cavalry under Terry— which amounted to command of the Seventh Cavalry alone.[56]

Part of the Custer legend has it that Grant's attack on him drove Custer to desperation and that his subsequent actions reflected a suicidal determination to redeem his honor by victory at any cost, or to die in the attempt. This is the obverse of that anti-Custer "glory hunter" legend which holds that he attacked rashly in order to win a victory that would lead to his nomination for president, and it has as little foundation. Although irked at the reduction of his command, he was elated by his escape from Grant's arrest and by the support of his military superiors and political patrons. His political prospects were bright, his financial affairs had been worse, and his literary career was cresting. He could, if he wished, make the public perceive this campaign in his own terms. Bennett of the *Herald* had hired him secretly to provide unsigned correspondence giving an insider's exclusive on the Indian war.

The army was confident of victory; there was rivalry between the various columns and commands for the honor of being "in at the death." As commander of Terry's cavalry, Custer believed he was in the best position to achieve that object: the plodding infantry and artillery could not catch up with fleeing Indians. He shared with the rest of the high command the belief that this campaign was certain to end once and for all the capacity of the Plains Indians to make war. They expected an arduous campaign because of the difficulty of the terrain and its largely unexplored character. They expected the Indians ranged against them to be unambiguously inclined to fight and more numerous than usual. Official estimates given to the newspapers stated that the army expected to find 15,000 Indians in the field, of whom a third or less would be warriors. However, the army's private assessment was that the actual number of hostiles in the field would be considerably less, and that the Indians' traditional hunting patterns and their timorousness when pursued by the cavalry would make it unlikely that more than 800 warriors would be found in one place. Once the campaign got under way, this estimate was revised upward; and when Custer finally rode out to find the hostiles, he expected to meet perhaps 1,500 warriors. But with its superior firepower and a combat doctrine that regarded attack as desirable even when losses might be severe, the army believed that a regiment like the Seventh Cavalry could handle a number of warriors two or three times its 600 troopers. The primary concern of the column commanders was that the Indians would take advantage of their mobility and scatter before the cavalry could hit them hard enough to make the punishment stick.

What none of the commanders knew was that for once the estimates given to the papers were going to prove accurate. Drawn off the reservation by their need to hunt buffalo and their feelings about the loss of the Black

Hills, the agency Indians did appear in the Unceded Lands in larger numbers than usual. Their receipt of the Indian Bureau's winter ultimatum and an attack on a Cheyenne village by Crook's command in March pressured the wandering bands to join up for counciling and for mutual defense; and when the three columns began their converging pincer movement, they swept most of the remaining wanderers toward a common center. So when Custer, following Terry's orders, traced one such contingent into the valley of the Little Big Horn and determined on an immediate attack, what he would face would be a veritable "Indian city" stretching for miles down the river, whose warrior contingent alone outnumbered his command by between five and ten to one.[57]

His letters to Libbie written just after the start of the expedition were sunny and bumptious and showed a streak of self-congratulation which made Libbie uneasy. Custer boasted that the expedition was utterly dependent on his skills as scout, which exceeded those of Charley Reynolds himself; and he used his superior knowledge to play risky practical jokes on his officers. Libbie warned him against taking unnecessary risks in words most unlike her usual affectionate and personal style: "With your bright future and the knowledge that you are a positive use to your day and generation, do you not see that your life is precious on that account, and not only because an idolizing wife could not live without you?" After-knowledge shadows our sense of her words; she is worried and wants him to be prudent. But the figure she invokes is the one of which he was most proud, the figure he cut in the public prints: a figure still young, still heroic, still linked with the glories of the Civil War and the promise of the New El Dorado.[58]

So the regiment marched out of its base camp on May 17. By some trick of the atmosphere, common in that region, the air above the regiment acted as a mirror so that two regiments—one real in the dust of the riverbank, one mirage in the air above—appeared to be marching westward. The Seventh Cavalry and its commander, both reality and image, were marching to their apotheosis.

The Dakota Column headed west along the survey line of the Northern Pacific Railroad, bucking torrential rains and a freak snowstorm on June 1, then days of heavy heat. The three converging columns of Terry, Gibbon, and Crook were out of touch with each other until Terry and Gibbon joined forces where the Rosebud River enters the Yellowstone. But Crook and Terry maintained contact with army headquarters by using couriers to carry dispatches to advanced telegraph posts whence they were relayed to Sherman and Sheridan in the east. Custer too was in contact with Libbie back at Fort Lincoln, and with his editors at the *Galaxy* and the *Herald*. He sent off the latest installment of his "War Memoirs" to the magazine on June 16. His dispatches to Bennett were short on action, consisting mostly of reprises of Custer's boosterish landscape descriptions of the Northern Pacific's lands, and of his argument with Hazen.

But on June 19 he sent a dispatch criticizing the actions of his second in command, Major Marcus Reno. While commanding a scouting battalion of the Seventh Reno had cut a large Indian trail, followed it up, and then turned aside instead of pushing forward and bringing the Indians to bay. On the 22nd Terry and Gibbon decided to send Custer and the whole of the

Seventh to finish the job, swinging the horsemen across the hills to strike the Little Big Horn valley somewhere upstream, while the slow-moving infantry worked up from the river's mouth. With luck they would catch the Indians between hammer and anvil, but it was more probable that the Seventh would have to hit the Indians before they scattered into the mountains. A victory for Custer was predictable, and adventurous civilians, reporters, and other officers expressed the wish to be "in at the death." As Custer's departing command paraded before Terry and Gibbon, the latter called, "Don't be greedy now, Custer. Leave some for us." His reply was somewhat ambiguous: "I won't."

Three days later Custer's scouts found the Indians, more Indians gathered together than anyone had ever heard of, too many (they said) for the Seventh Cavalry to handle. Custer looked down from the small peak called the Crow's Nest and couldn't read the signs his scouts had seen: shifty shadows that might be heat haze or a vast pony herd, thousands of Indian ponies grazing in the valley. In any case he was committed by character and by training and by the premises of his commanders to the belief that there could not be, in any valley, an Indian force capable of defeating a full regiment of regular cavalry.

When the nearer approach of the soldiers appeared to give the Indians the alarm Custer sent Major Reno with three companies across the Little Big Horn to attack the still-unseen village, without waiting for the scouting detachment of three companies under Captain Benteen to return, or for the pack train to come up with the reserve ammunition. Custer himself took five companies around behind the line of bluffs that paralleled the river to strike the Indians from another direction, just as he had done at the Washita.

Benteen, riding up to join Reno half an hour later, found the Major's command had been routed by overwhelming numbers of Indians, driven in disorder out of the valley and up onto the bluffs with one man in three dead, wounded, or missing. Of Custer there was no word, although heavy firing had been heard from downstream. It took time to rest horses and men after hard riding and fighting in that breathless heat, time to care for Reno's wounded and get his men in hand; time for the pack train to come up; time for Reno and Benteen to sort things out—Reno was in shock after his disaster in the valley, Benteen a junior officer crusty about matters of precedence and seniority, hostile to Reno and Custer. Before anything substantial could be done the Indians came swarming back, besieging the two battalions on the hilltop for a night and a day—they barely held out, there was not much water, and there were more Indians out in the rocks than they could count.

They didn't learn what had happened to Custer until Terry's men relieved them on June 27th, and told them what they had found on the hillside two miles away: Custer and all the men of his five companies, his brothers and his brother-in-law and his nephew and his best friends, all dead, lying as they had for two days in that incredible heat, naked and torn by Indians and animals, fly-blown and swollen with death-gasses. Amid the stench and horror of the scene floated clouds of flies and greenbacks—money which Custer had ordered kept from the men till they had left the sutler's whiskey stores behind. The Indians, having no use for paper currency, left it behind.

PART EIGHT

The Last Stand as
Ideological Object, 1876–1890

CHAPTER 18

To the Last Man: Assembling the Last Stand Myth, 1876

The process of transforming history into myth requires a series of creative acts of transmutation and associative linkage. It begins with an initial selection and dramatic ordering of "breaking" events, which change seemingly intractable bits of factual data into the functioning parts of a fiction. This is as true of the journalistic media who first processed the Custer story as it is of a novelist, who works from invented or remembered events rather than from "breaking" news stories. As the "breaking" events occur they are processed through different sorts of interpretative grids. Some of these have to do with the author's (and audience's) sense of what makes a good—that is, dramatic—tale: so elements that tend to maximize conflict, suspense, irony, and moral resonance may be highlighted at the expense of other no-less-factual elements that do not so palpably serve the tale. Other grids are ideological, and have to do with the attribution of meaning and significance to the events. The meanings to which the story is connected arise from a range of sources: the author's own life, the prevalent ideology of his culture, the language of a current political controversy. There is also the complex grid of historical context: any "breaking" story unfolds in a field which includes many other stories—events most of which will have no logically or materially necessary relation to each other. The process of making a story of the facts, and of attaching significance to the story, also involves the making of connections between the given story and the others in its contextual field. Such connections add drama and meaning by making the story appear to resonate throughout the historical moment in which it occurs, and even to make possible a meaningful interpretation of the whole field of facts and events.

The primary acts of translation that turned the battle of the Little Big Horn into the myth known as Custer's Last Stand were performed by the journalists and editors of the Metropolitan daily newspapers in the summer and fall of 1876. They seem to have had some awareness of the fact that the story they were handling would become a "legend"; and they brought to their telling of it the full range of legendary references and metaphors, from the Trojan War to Horatius at the Bridge, to the Alamo and the Charge of the Light Brigade

Their primary concern was not the making of a legend as such. Theirs was an exercise in applied mythology: they required their legend to address not only the underlying questions of value in their culture, but to speak directly to the issues raised by the platforms of the rival political parties and intraparty factions. A symbolism suited to the grand imaging of the struggle of savagery vs. civilization, or evil vs. good, had to be adapted to the task of representing the dismal intricacies of "hard" vs. "soft" positions on the currency and national debt; the strident and bathetic debate between "tough-minded" and "philanthropic" approaches to social reform in general; and in particular the backbiting and apologetics of the struggle for control of the bureaucracies entrusted with managing the dependent classes. Above all, the symbolism had to represent the central issue of the campaign, the termination or continuation of Reconstruction in the South—an issue of such divisiveness and complexity as to continually distort and disarrange partisan alignments on all the other issues.

Therefore it is no wonder that the Custer legend fabricated by American journalists in 1876 was not a well-wrought fable. The traditional story- and symbol-grids of the Frontier Myth were applied ad hoc and in a rush to meet deadlines, and so were invoked wholesale and haphazardly, without care or consistency in their usage. And these grids in turn were crossed by so many conflicting impulses of partisanship that the making of a single coherent fable was impossible. Nonetheless, these initial accounts performed the essential first task of mythmaking, by establishing Custer and the Last Stand as an important ideological object—a myth whose terms, however variously interpreted, would seem to contain and refer to the conflicts of value that most concerned Americans.

The New York *Herald* played in relation to the Last Stand the same role that the *World* had played in relation to the Black Hills expedition of 1874. It made the first translation of the ongoing historical event into the ideologically charged metaphors of popular mythology, and it used the Custer story as the narrative spine around which the other news stories of the year could be organized. This was a role deliberately undertaken by Bennett, who had approached Custer as early as the spring of 1875 to act as a secret *Herald* correpondent to provide the paper with early information based on an insider's knowledge. Custer's involvement with reporter Meeker in the Belknap affair and his employment as correspondent in 1876 solidified this connection and gave Bennett exactly the kind of information he wanted.

The only surprising aspect of the case is why Bennett delayed so long in connecting with Custer and the Black Hills affair. The *Herald*'s interest in Custer himself was of long standing: James Gordon Bennett, Sr., had been a Custer supporter during the Civil War and had given him the sobriquet "Boy General with the Golden Locks"; and the *Herald* had also given detailed and favorable coverage of his Washita campaign in 1868–69. The *Herald* had been an expansionist paper from the time of its founding in Jackson's second administration and had always taken a hard line in favor of expropriating Indian lands (as well as Mexican and Canadian lands when the mood was right). Yet despite this history of concern with Custer and the West, the *Herald* did not send a correspondent with either the 1873 or the 1874 Custer expedition and allowed itself to be scooped by its rivals, the Republican *Tribune* and the Democratic *World.*

Political priorities probably determined both the lapse of the *Herald's* interest in Custer between 1871 and 1875, and its revival after the Black Hills expedition. Although nominally an independent paper, the *Herald* took a consistently Democratic line in national politics. It had been "soft" on secession and on the readmission of the ex-Confederacy, and "hard" on the treatment of the freedmen and the Indians. In the *Herald's* view, the Black Hills expedition was justifiable primarily as chastisement of the hated Indians; and since the Custer expedition first appeared to be a military incursion, the *Herald* was initially enthusiastic: "Custer Preparing to Take the Warpath," "The Sioux Indians Afraid of General Custer," "Custer is the right man to deal with the Indians, and they dread him. There is nothing like vigor and military promptness to make these people behave themselves." Then, when the "peaceful" and exploratory intentions of the expedition were declared, the *Herald* veered hostile, linking Custer with the despised Grant:

> It is really Custer's expedition, gotten up under his auspices and for his benefit, and that of his brother officers, if it be possible that any good can come of it . . . It is understood by many here that the object of the expedition is to succeed in driving the Indians from the Black Hills . . . so that white adventurers may seize their lands . . . in the wild and crazy search for gold . . . It will also give Custer an opportunity to distinguish himself . . . gratify his restless and rash ambition, and secure his further promotion.[1]

During the course of the expedition, the *Herald* (like the *World*) changed its position, responding to the opportunity it offered to notice the inconsistencies of Grant's Indian policy and to the support for it among its favored army hard-liners, Sherman and Sheridan, whom it quoted as endorsing vengeful retribution against "Our Pampered Outlaws." When Custer's report appeared, the *Herald* hailed it as the discovery of "The New El Dorado" . . . "The Prospective Home of a Thrifty Race of Agriculturists." This lent new credibility to the *Herald's* assertion that instead of holding "communist" rallies, the unemployed ought really to "go West." Custer again became the *Herald's* hero: "The Northern Sioux in Wholesome Dread of Custer," it crowed, and its editorials boostered "THE LAND OF GOLD" in Gilpinish terms—a "central deposit" or mother lode for which the other great gold rush sites were appendages or "outcroppings." While urging the miners to wait patiently for the legal extinction of Indian title, the *Herald* continued to reprint in its editorial columns glowing extracts and paraphrases from Custer's reports by way of making pressure for seizure of the Hills irresistible.[2]

The *Herald's* commercial rivalry with its New York Republican competitors, the *Times* and the *Tribune*, and its division from them on partisan matters led to an editorial rhetoric which maximized the distinctiveness of the *Herald's* positions. However, this superficial partisanship does not conceal the fact that in this 1874–77 period, most of the *Herald's* fundamental principles of economic and political action reflected a consensus position shared with all the largest of the New York dailies; and reflected above all the consensus of that social class which comfortably included bankers, publishers, editors, and sportsmen of both parties. As we have seen, these men shared the "hard-money" gold standard faith, disgust with both the "philanthropy" of Grant and with government corruption, and hostility toward the political movement of working and unemployed men reflected in the Tompkins Square demonstration. Thus the *Herald* employed precisely the same symbolic vocabulary as the *World* in associating developments in "savage" warfare with the struggles over Reconstruction and the resistance of urban labor; and it used that language with the same social ends in view, despite partisan difference as to means.[3]

THE MAKING OF AN IDEOLOGICAL OBJECT: AIMS AND ANTICIPATIONS

The political struggles of 1874–76 imposed a set of difficult ideological problems on the *Herald*, with its long-standing tradition of "sympathy" for the working man and its popularity with the masses; and partly for those reasons, the paper was generally hesitant about committing itself to particular candidates far in advance of the canvass. Bennett's strategy was to use the popular appeal of the *Herald* to stake out a strong conservative ideological position within the anti-Grant consensus; to attract the courtship of candidates eager to appear under *Herald* auspices; and thus to influence the choice of candidates in both parties, and to actually shape the platform of the Democrats. He had in his favor the pervading disillusionment with Grant and with Reconstruction, and the popular enthusiasm for seizing the Black Hills. But there were elements of discord as well. The Black Hills offered a long-term solution to two of the problems that divided the Democrats: the discovery of gold suggested that both hard- and soft-money Democrats could have their way; and the prospect of a major Indian war suggested an attractive way to terminate occupation of the South. But in the short term—with the gold in the Hills and federal troops in the South—there was deep division over the hard-money faction's desire to substitute the gold standard for greenback currency, and over the southern congressional opposition to the army appropriation bill. Moreover, the persistence of the depression had increased the misery and discontent of the unemployed and of urban dwellers generally; and in order to triumph, it was necessary for the Democrats to use that discontent, while at the same time forestalling any political measures favorable to relief or to labor unionization.[4]

Bennett's ideological tasks were therefore to sell the discontented workers and farmers on a conservative fiscal policy and a laissez-faire approach to unemployment and railroad regulation; to reconcile southern suspicion of the army and its hatred of occupation with the West's (and his own) desire for a strong army to deal with the Indians; and to detach northern liberals from any lingering sympathy with the freedmen and the philanthropies of Reconstruction. It was essential to his strategy that each of the *Herald's* ongoing stories—the condition of the unemployed, the "race war" in the South, the Indian war in the West—should reproduce a common world picture and reaffirm a common mythology. The ideological core of that mythology was its justification of the politics of rule by a business elite; and its primary symbolic device was its invocation of racial difference (black vs. white; savage vs. civilized) as an explanatory model of class relations.

Bennett used the "easy" cases of the South and the Frontier to obtain audience sympathy for an ideological position that was in fact inimical to the interests of the *Herald's* main readership: the workingmen and lower middle classes of New York City. Such an audience might be inclined to accept as logical and necessary the subservience of blacks and Indians to white soldiers and officials, but not the application of such a model to themselves. Yet this was exactly what Bennett's program—what the whole project of the new conservatives—envisioned. It was their belief that the requirements of business and industrial society were such that individuals could not expect to enjoy the benefices of liberty and entrepreneurship that had obtained in the heyday of the Jacksonian Frontier. It was not an easy doctrine even for Bennett to adopt, and the appeal of the Black Hills for him was precisely the prospect it held out of further extending the Frontier phase of American history. Nonetheless, he regarded this as probably the last such Frontier, and his editorials urged Americans to scale down their expectations of the "big bonanza" and to accept the discipline of industrial toil.[5]

Bennett's answer to this fundamental ideological dilemma was to cross-link the mythical "savages" of the red, white, or black underclasses with the equally mythical "monopolists" of the Jacksonian demonology. He accomplished this by identifying the "philanthropist" friends of Indians, blacks, and workingmen as a privileged elite, enjoying an exclusive access to political power, and abusing that power to establish and extend a monopolistic control of economic growth. "Protectionism" is the key word here, and it has a double sense. The "philanthropists" were (as orthodox Republicans) exponents of protective tariffs, and of the granting of landed franchises to privileged railroads—economic policies traditionally seen as hostile to the interests of farmers, debtors, and small entrepreneurs. But the true depravity of their doctrine appeared most palpably in their political and economic "protection" of the black and Indian "wards of the nation" against the demands of white men for access to land (in the West) and to the corridors of power (in the South).

Bennett used the developing story of the western Indian war as the mythic fable through which his racialist and elitist ideology could be safely applied to the paramount and immediate social and political questions of the election of 1876. The continuation of labor problems and demonstrations in the North and new outbreaks of violence in the South supplied him with the basis for his allegorical connection of "savage war" to class politics. He employed the same technical devices used by the *World* to establish the connection, beginning with the printing of stories in strong physical relation—either in parallel, in sequence, or as "bookends" of a front page—followed by the borrowing of key terms from one story to define a response to another, and culminating in an editorial explicitly connecting disparate events into a single ideological lesson. Bennett's special relationship with Custer, established far in advance of the Belknap impeachment and the march of the Dakota Column, also gave the *Herald* the luxury of anticipating developments—something the *World* had probably not enjoyed in 1874. Thus Bennett was able to orchestrate the appearance and context of Indian war–related stories with greater preparation and care. There would be no surprises requiring sudden revisions such as had occurred when word of the gold discovery came back in 1874—at least, not until the Last Stand itself.

The first major story of 1876 was the Belknap affair, which broke on February 9 and 10 with the publication of Ralph Meeker's article and an editorial on "Extravagance and Corruption in the War Department." The exposure of Belknap of course cast a general obloquy on the Grant administration, but Bennett also used the case to argue for two of his major planks, the transfer of the Indian Bureau to army control and support of military appropriations for hostilities outside the South. Since Belknap was a swindler, it followed that his budget must be inflated by the cost of his graft; by convicting Belknap and discovering the graft, it would be possible (said Bennett) to effect economies in the army (as the South desired) while actually increasing the amounts being put to real use (as the Westerners desired). Putting army officers in charge of Indian affairs, with an honest administration and adequate financial support, would be "the first real step toward the civilization of these so-called 'wards of the nation'"— a term applied to both Indians and blacks. This measure is linked with the restoration of rule by traditional elites in the South through the suggestive association of Belknap-related stories with accounts of Reconstruction disorders and the progress of a Radical civil rights bill. Both stories are cross-linked to the Indian war by stories in strong visual juxtaposition which tended to show that under the Belknap-Grant regime, the Indians have grown stronger and more spoiled; while the army, divided to occupy the South and weakened by Belknap's wrongdoing, is belatedly girding to fight with inadequate resources.[6]

In keeping with the political aim of associating as many disaffected former "philanthropists" as possible to his own ideology, Bennett also began to evince something very like sympathy for the vanishing American. Editorials printed later in March admit that there may be "something very tragic" in the condition to which the Indian has fallen: "He has been sacrificed by us as fast as sacrifice became necessary to our aggrandizement." The Black Hills gold rush is but a further instance of this tendency, and it will "force us into a war which will cost more, perhaps, than the greatest sum asked by the Indian chiefs last fall."[7]

But Bennett's posturing was totally disingenuous since such statements are made only in editorials about Belknap; in editorials about Indian policy Bennett toes the hard line. He had been, and would be again, an advocate of both the seizure of the Black Hills and the extermination of the Indians. He had opposed accepting the Indians' asking price for the sale of the Hills in the negotiation of 1875, and he would consistently take the line that the value of the Hills outweighed the cost of war in both blood and treasure; he would even go so far as to suggest that it was less expensive to kill Indians than to feed them, as Grant had done.

Sympathy for the Indian in the pages of the *Herald* was a phenomenon to strain the credulity of any reader who had been the least attentive to Bennett's exterminationist diatribes over the last three years. It required a figure of powerful appeal and credibility to obscure the contradiction, and that figure now appeared in the shape of General Custer. A small item on March 28 reported Custer "on His Way to Testify before Clymer's Committee," and on March 31 the burden of his testimony was trumpeted in a large scare-headline: "BELKNAP'S ANACONDA." An editorial under the same heading doubles the metaphor: there are "two monstrous anacondas," both nurtured by Grant, one of which robs the Indians and drives them to war, and the other of which robs the soldiers whom the country must ask to fight the Indians. Bennett thus makes of Belknap the perfect scapegoat, worthy of drawing the wrath of both the Friends of the Indian and the hard-liners who wish the army would go out and make them all "good Indians."[8]

If Belknap was the perfect villain, Custer was the perfect hero and spokesman for Bennett's views. As we have seen, he could, with complete consistency, speak of his sympathy for the Indians, voice his criticism of the administration, and express the desire for peace while preparing to play a leading role in a conflict that appeared inescapable. The *Herald* went to Custer for his estimates of the likelihood of hostilities, the number of Indians the army might face—on this occasion he guessed at 8,000 to 10,000—and for confirmation of its belief that the Indian Bureau should be turned over to the army. Custer told them that if Sherman were to become president, he would settle "the whole business" (i.e., the Indian question) in a single council. The *Herald* thought Custer "a good man to intrust" with preparation for war. And when, in the early spring, there were reports of Indians attacking small settlements and raiding Custer's wagon train, the *Herald* stated its belief that "If anyone can get out of a difficult position in the Indian country it is Custer."[9]

The *Herald* spelled out the ideological premises of the new army-run Indian policy and, at the same time, linked them to a reordering of the policy for dealing with southern blacks, and by implication with the white underclass as well. Philanthropic administration had the effect of making the nation's "wards" into a privileged class, protected from the necessity of work and the discipline of starvation:

> We should deal with Indians as we do with the whites and the blacks. Educate, protect and defend them, compel them to respect the law and earn their bread. . . . An Indian . . . knows when he is hungry, and he should be taught that the way to find bread is to work for it. This is the common sense of the Indian question.[10]

While playing up the Belknap affair, the *Herald* had also been sharpening its comparison of the Indian policy and the failure of Reconstruction. A long article on missionary work includes a letter written by Custer to a missionary with the Santee Sioux in Minnesota, reporting his delight at hearing their singing of Christian hymns. This is the sort of man the army should put in charge of potential Indian converts: a man of Christian sentiments but with a soldier's reputation and the army's force behind him. On the other hand, an editorial on "Fetichism in the South" sounds a favored *Herald* theme: that without the discipline of slavery, blacks were reverting to savagery, that "Freedom seems to have revived [their] instincts for the habits of heathens." The *Herald* notes that the only official objection so far raised to the army takeover of the Indian Bureau has come from General O. O. Howard, who is remembered by Bennett as having "scandalously mismanaged the Freedmen's Bureau." The lesson is clear: with an army run by Grant, Belknap, and Howard, the South has witnessed the subordination of white to black and the degeneration of the blacks into savagery. But a transfer of the army from South to West, and a change of leadership from Howard and Belknap to Sherman and Custer, would realize the hope for "civilizing" the heathen and maintaining a white man's government.[11]

At the same time, another component enters the picture, with the increase in labor disorders and the completion of the Molly Maguire trials in Pennsylvania. An editorial on March 26 referring to the "unenviable notoriety" of the Mollies appears just above an item on General Crook's recent battle (supposedly with Crazy Horse), in which the general asserts that "the hostile redskins were in collusion with those fed, armed and clothed by the government at the agencies. It has always been so with the wards of the nation." In addition to physical propinquity, the stories are associated by the mention that the action occurred "after St. Patrick's Day."

A third strand of the web tying race and class together is taken up on April 3, when Bennett prints a pair of side-by-side editorials titled "The Indian Question" and "The Chinese Question." The Chinese question was closely related to the labor question—that is, to the fact of widespread unemployment and wage rollbacks and to the fear that the growth of population plus immigration from Europe, Asia, and the rural South had created a permanent reserve army of cheap labor to depress wages and weaken unions. The influx of Chinese on the West Coast posed the identical question in a more distant and dramatic way. The anti-Chinese feeling among West Coast labor organizations ran high and ran also to "vigilante" terrorism not unlike that of the Klan in the South.[12] As with the blacks, the *Herald* notes the economic "threat" of the Chinese but emphasizes the "moral" and "racial" aspects of the problem. The Chinese combine the qualities of blacks and Indians: "Their wants are few," and they first drive off American labor by working for a pittance, then take over the trade. "But what is worse, they are disseminating also their debasing practices and immoralities," such as opium smoking and prostitution. "Some way must be found to subject this Chinese question to control, or the leprosy which comes into the country with every ship from China will taint and corrupt not only the body politic but the sanctities of society and the sacredness of religion." The editorial also takes an indirect swipe at other kinds of immigrants: "It is not the intelligence and culture of the Celestial Kingdom which come to America, for these seldom emigrate, and China is no exception to the rule. The lower classes only come here, and they bring with them their base arts and debasing practices, and set them up side by side with our civilization."[13]

The paralleling of this editorial with one on "The Indian Question" serves to underline the racial character of each of the major social conflicts; and it reminds the readership that "monopolists"—the other traditional Jacksonian bugabear—have been a class peculiarly favored by the Republicans. Railroad monopolies, chartered by the government, imported the Chinese. Government "monopolies" of the post traderships and Indian agencies have fattened the president's friends and corrupted good government. And the linkage between the supposed "growing power and numbers" of racially inferior "aliens" in American society is a double one: their growth fosters the greater monopolization of wealth by powerful commercial interests; and at the lower level of the workplace or on the land, it leads to the monopolization of trades by the aliens. So the Chinese have a "monopoly" of cigarmaking in California, and the Indians a "monopoly" of good land in the Black Hills, and the Molly Maguires nearly a monopoly control of labor in the mines. These "monopolies" are seen as being as much a feature of industrial capitalism and as much of a danger to the prosperity and power of the "middle class" as the power of the Robber Barons. While this makes no sense at all economically, it made very good sense politically, drawing as it does simultaneously on class grievances and racial prejudice; and it puts the whole struggle in a context established by the mythology of the race war. Thus, it appropriates and redirects class hostility from Bennett and his colleagues to Grant's monopolistic "philanthropists" and their dark-skinned "pets."[14]

The association of racial and class differences allows Bennett to make important divisions within the working class as well. He assumes (or affects to assume) that the workers who have managed to maintain themselves on the job through the period of contraction—the "successful" workmen—are of a higher caliber than those who have been let go. He makes this explicit in an article and editorial on a bomb plot perpetrated (it is supposed) by strikers against "scabs" and the railroad company that fired them. Like the Indians, the strikers are seen as disaffected with civilized law or disinclined to follow it, as passionately vengeful, and as resentful of "their more intelligent fellows," "the men who would work" when the strikers would not. The *Herald* cites these as "moral elements of destruction" in "our working classes" and compares them to the Molly Maguires and to "the Turks who massacred the other day the Christians in Salonica."[15]

The comparison of the strikers with the Turks invokes another kind of race war in which the savage/civilized dichotomy is supplemented by the Muslim/Christian distinction, and the opposition of monarchial-sultanic tyranny to the democratic rebellion of Balkan nationalists. One of the most important ongoing stories of 1876 was the bloody Turkish repression of the Bulgarian revolt, and the Russian intervention that followed. This temporal juxtaposition of a Balkan race war with an American Indian war was a source of useful associations for Bennett, who used each war in turn to define the horror of the other. On May 20, for example, the editorial page juxtaposes editorials on "The Revolt at Constantinople" and "The Indian

War." The theme of racial hostility, the code words of savagery and revolution, are motifs in each of the editorials, which reinforce the association and give them a common ideological point. The "Indian War" editorial is standard fare for Bennett. The Indians are no longer "tragic" victims, but "are on the warpath, and have massacred our citizens on the Plains, and . . . have gratified their passions by mutilations of the dead." The government's decision to send the army to "punish these savages" is a bit late; if the army were in charge of the Indians, such outbreaks could be prevented. But instead we have "the old, old story [that] will never have an end until the entire Indian policy is revolutionized . . . It is folly to keep up the system of failure for the benefit of speculators, Indian agents and government rings, and for the injury of the whole West and the discouragement of emigration and enterprise."

The "Revolt in Constantinople" story presents a revolution in affairs that is the opposite of what the *Herald* seeks for Indian affairs. Indeed, it is more like the present situation in the Reconstruction South, where Afro-American savages and spoilsmen have massacred and politically suppressed the "better classes." This is, in turn, related to the specter of "Red Revolution" raised by the Paris Commune. In all of these situations, the better classes—the merchants and entrepreneurs, the educated and enlightened Christians—are victimized by savage violence, allied with ideological fanaticism (religious or socialistic). The case of Turkey in the Balkans illustrates how far the consequences of such a regime may go. "European Turkey is . . . a country in which a semi-barbarous minority of Asiatic people hold in subjection many millions of Christians of the first races of the world." These Christians form the commercial and cultural elite of the region and have inevitably tried to redeem their racial dignity by seeking political independence; and their pursuit of this legitimate goal has brought down on them the savagery of Turkish armies and urban mobs:

> In any city in the world it would be a horrible event for the scum of the people to be arrayed against all who are socially their superiors. Paris once had a faint taste of the possibilities of . . . what might happen if all the repressive machinery that commonly preserves order is set aside and the ferocious instincts of the mob are free from every restraint.

Thus, violent strikers are like Turks, Turks are like Communards, Turks are savages—and, therefore, strikers are like savages.[16]

While establishing and elaborating the basic vocabulary of its race-war mythology, the *Herald* continued to focus on its primary real-world concern—the election of 1876. In mid-April and May, the *Herald* covered the Grant administration's counterattack against its critics, which centered on a refutation of the charges made by Custer. The *Herald*, of course, came to Custer's defense and developed a scenario of the controversy that figuratively reduced it to the heroic opposition of Custer and Grant. When Grant followed the former's accusation of perjury by arresting Custer and relieving him of his command, the *Herald's* scenario became literal. Its news coverage was headlined "CUSTER SACRIFICED [to] CAESAR'S SPLEEN"—a metaphor that emphasized the thesis that Grant was a kind of military despot for his handling of Reconstruction and his ambition for a third term; but which also put Custer figuratively in the role of Christian martyr to Roman tyranny.[17]

Since preparations for the Indian war were still going forward, the *Herald* was able to link Grant with those philanthropists and savages who, of course, would rather that the "Long Hair" were kept in Washington than turned loose in Dakota. Grant's decision to relent on Custer's arrest did not cause Bennett to retreat. The decision was represented as showing both weakness and a sense of guilt on Grant's part; thus "it does not wipe out the stain with which he has covered himself" by attempting to humiliate Custer. Since Grant had now withdrawn from the struggle, the *Herald* preserved its dramatic premise by reprinting excerpts from papers around the country commenting on the Custer-Grant affair. Democratic papers, of course, took Custer's part; but the *Herald* also printed excerpts from Republican papers, which naturally supported Grant. These papers represented Custer as a "dime novel hero" and assailed him for everything from perjury to rashness and imprudence in making charges, to being culpably slow in making those charges. The *Herald* thus used these accusations as the basis for entering into an editorial-page dialogue with the political opposition, with Custer as the central figure and the Belknap accusations as the central theme. This not only kept Custer before the public eye as the Indian campaign began; it made the Custer case a symbolic test of political affiliation in the coming electoral canvass.[18]

At about the same time, the *Herald* began its detailed coverage of the opening of the Centennial Exposition in Philadelphia and the patriotic programs and displays associated with the centennial. This coverage would peak during the July 4 ceremonies, and the *Herald* began preparing its symbolism early. It emphasized the Exposition's evidence of the nation's emergence as an industrial power of the first rank, and it associated the future promise of America with technological and industrial development. It also had a political thesis to offer about the reconciliation of North and South on the common ground of patriotic conservatism a decade after the Civil War. The only discordant elements in this picture were the policies of Grant and the Radicals, who were seen as thwarting sectional reconciliation and industrial enterprise. The *Herald* now began applying the adjective "Centennial" to all events of any consequence, by which device it meant to connect these events to the large ideological significance of our "century of progress." Thus, the presidential election became the "Centennial Canvass" and the Indian battles became our "Centennial War"; and there were "Centennial" riots, massacres, strikes, and murders as well.

THE CENTENNIAL WAR

The first news of the Indian war came from General Crook's column, the southern prong of the triple pincers movement. A series of stories printed from May 18 to June 16 recounted Crook's preparations, his expectation of battle with "bloodthirsty" hordes under Sitting Bull, and his animadversions on the Indian Bureau. Editorial treatment of the Indian question ceased to make even the pretense of a fair or sympathetic view of the Indians' situation, and brought Bennett back to his original exterminationist thesis. After asserting his confidence that Crook will "teach these treacherous marauders a salutary lesson," he repeats the work-or-starve, obey-or-be-killed formula which links the language of the Indian question to that of the labor and southern questions. Bennett is working here at a high level of abstraction, presenting ideological premises that pretend to embody generally applicable principles. Thus, his characterization of the Indians applies not only the general epithet of "savage," but the Cooperian convention that associates all Indians with the woodland wilderness:

> For years and years we have been feeding these wild men of the woods in the vain hope that they could be civilized and Christianized, but . . . the savage has gone upon the warpath whenever he has grown tired of eating the bread he has not earned. [The Sioux] . . . must be made to work and required to take his place in the new order of life to which it is necessary that he should conform by force and not merely by moral suasion. If he goes to war the only thing for him and his tribe is extermination. It has long been evident that no other policy would settle this Indian question. . . .[19]

Two editorials on the following day extend this theme. "A Massacre by Sioux Indians" of a group of settlers proves "how relentless is the hatred borne by savages against the whites"; and "The Execution of Lowery" relates the punishment of Indians to that of white criminals (murderers and rapists) whose "lesson of the death penalty must be persistently administered until such villains learn to respect the law and the rights of their fellow men."[20]

On June 19, the first dispatch from Custer appeared anonymously in the *Herald*. Titled "The Indian War" and datelined May 30, the story had little to offer in the way of action, but it served the important function of reestablishing in the forefront of the *Herald*'s readers' attention the mythic paradigm through which the coming events would be interpreted. Much of the article is a lush and romantic landscape description, echoing all of the themes and images associated with Custer's 1874 Black Hills report—the Floral Valley revisited, "a green velvet carpet, interspersed with rare and delicately tinted flowers . . . rich, nutritious grasses" rising to the stirrups of mounted horsemen. The agricultural potential of these Northern Pacific Railroad lands is reasserted, and critics like Hazen debunked again.

The "Garden of the West" theme is augmented by other images invoking the myth of the race war, and the vanishing American. A pair of buttes are identified as "the Maiden's Breasts," and one of them marks the place where "a number of young men, the flower of one tribe, were met and overpowered . . . none escaping to tell the tale." Indians are so scarce that they seem almost "as having belonged to a pre-existent race." We are immersed again in the West of Frontier mythology: a magical place of feminine, virgin beauty and fecundity, seductive and promising; but the promise balanced by the equally mystical threat of annihilation, the flower of a people destroyed, an entire race exterminated or extinct. But beneath the picturesque invocation of vanishing Americans, Custer has some hard things to say about "The Cost of Indian Wars"—and since he is writing anonymously, he can say them without pretense of sympathy for the enemy:

> It has been estimated that the government pays $1,000,000 for every Indian slain in battle, squaws and papooses not counted. This is hardly true of the estimates upon a fair basis, but if the dead Indians cost Uncle Sam so much it would be interesting, and perhaps more to the point, to know how much the self-sacrificing old gentleman is called upon to pay yearly for each live Indian.[21]

Obviously, it is cheaper to kill Indians than to keep them alive.

Articles and editorials in this vein placed the *Herald's* readers in a familiar mythological landscape, and allowed them to see that Custer and his fellows were making progress through that terrain toward the final solution of the Indian question and the possession of the golden West. But this symbolic progress was not matched by the pace of real-world movements. Rain and bad country delayed the Dakota Column, and the *Herald* writers—sitting at the end of the telegraph lines where reports from the separate forces of Terry, Crook, and Gibbon converged—could see that the army pincers might fail to close before the fast-moving Indians had escaped. Dispatches from Custer and the other correspondents in the field told the *Herald* that each column was ignorant of the other's progress; and the editorialists had to warn their readers that it was still possible to be disappointed.

However, on June 21 "The War on the Plains" leaped suddenly into crisis. General Crook's southern column had been attacked on June 17 by a large force of Indians under Sitting Bull, Crazy Horse, and other chiefs— the "Battle of the Rosebud." The dispatch published on the twenty-first was sent before the fight, and reflected Crook's sense that action was imminent, and the correspondent emphasized the mood of crisis by reiterating the army's highest estimate of the force against it, and repeating the by-now-obligatory comparison between Sitting Bull and Napoleon. Then, on the twenty-fourth, the *Herald* carried the story of the battle fought on the seventeenth: "THE INDIAN WAR . . . Almost a Savage Victory." The editorial on "The Battle in the Big Horn Country" reinforced the assertion that it looked "very like a defeat of the soldiers." While suspending judgment of Crook's conduct, the editorial notes correctly that the effect of the battle would be to halt Crook in his tracks, and that therefore it was a strategic victory for "Sitting Bull."[22]

The next day's stories confirmed the worst suspicions. "The News from the Frontiers—a Centennial War" reported that the centennial would not be the festival of peace and reconciliation that the poets and orators had been anticipating. A serious war has begun, and begun badly. While declaring that "we do not wish to criticize an absent commander," the *Herald* was extremely sarcastic about Crook's battle and pointed out that 1,600 regular troops and auxiliaries had been virtually "wiped out" (or at least fought to a standstill) by only 2,500 Indians—when by most military standards, a force of that size should have been able to beat soundly at least double its own numbers. "If the Sioux tribes can meet our regular army with these odds, the Indian question will assume a new and serious aspect."

The *Herald's* anxiety expanded to include the other columns in the field, especially the Dakota Column under Terry and Custer, and it raised the suggestion that Grant's removal of Custer from command had somehow made disaster possible: "Critics of the administration will say that if General Grant had not removed that superb Indian fighter Custer to avenge Belknap, we should not now be mourning ten dead and twenty wounded soldiers." The suggestion is dismissed as "unfair" in the next breath, because there is still insufficient evidence to question Crook's competence. But the suggestion is significant in two respects: first, as an anticipation of what would (thanks to circumstances) become the dominant theme of the *Herald's* campaign to blame the Republicans for Custer's Last Stand; and second, as a reflection of the way in which the *Herald's* position at the center of communications distorted its perception of reality. That position gave the *Herald* writers (and readers) the sense that the events unfolding for each of the three army columns were occurring within the purview of a single interpreting and commanding intelligence. Although the dispatches printed in the *Herald* made it clear that the three columns were out of touch, the idea that Custer might somehow have commanded Crook's column as well as Terry's insistently suggests itself. It did not occur to the *Herald* editors until long after the event that Terry and Custer —encamped so close to Crook's battlefield on the printed map—might know nothing at all of the Battle of the Rosebud, while the citizens of New York were being treated to correspondence, dispatches, and official reports. This illusion complicated the analysis of the newspaper's representation of chronology; but it reinforces the paper's role as mythological rationalizer of disparate and even unrelated events.

If events in the field appeared confused, the ideological progress of the *Herald's* editorial campaign was not. Crook's defeat provided another critical occasion for advancing the paper's case against the reformers' Indian policy. The editorial on June 22 begins in that "sympathetic" voice which the *Herald* had affected earlier in the year to establish its credentials as a "fair-minded" critic of Grant: "Our treatment of the Indians is the blot upon our civilization."

> It is written that we came over the seas; that we found this new land; that we planted empires here—Latin empires, like those in the South; Saxon empires, like those in the North; that in a short time . . . we built upon this open, unknown, savage land, nations that will live with Greece and Rome, England and France. It is written that in doing this we founded a political system which commands the admiration of the elder and the wiser world. But while we may proudly claim all the honors that this implies, it is with shame and sorrow that we think of the Indian and the manner in which we have treated him.

The conceptual framework of Anglo-Saxonist race history invoked here is identical to that deployed by Parker and Prescott in response to the Mexican War and the slavery issue of the 1850s. But the earlier racialism envisioned the possibility that, some day and by some means, the non-Saxon might become Saxonized; and this objective checked the full application of the doctrine to the definition of political statuses. But for Bennett, the question posed by Parker has been negatively answered by the force of violence: the black man and the red man can never be Saxonized. Therefore, Bennett moves from this "sympathetic" or sentimental backward look to the rigorous application of the logic of Anglo-Saxon racialism—which even Parker had seen as entailing the subjection or extermination of any race incapable of somehow becoming Saxonized.

> No one wants to deal hardly with the Indian. We all respect the sentiment which surrounds him. We may not share the poetic conception of Pope or the Romantic ideas of Cooper; . . . we may know the Indian to be a false, cruel, perfidious creature, to whom blood is as much of a passion as it is to the tiger or the shark, who has no possibilities of civilization, and whose fate must be extermination; we may think this, and with justice; but it in no way excuses our treatment of the Indian.

Thus, in the same breath, the *Herald* speaks for both the inevitability and the justice of exterminating the Indians, and condemns the government for going about the procedure in a dishonorable and dishonest way. The *Herald*'s way would be unsentimentally grounded in the realities of the day: "The fact that the whole question is a sentiment is, perhaps, one reason for the way in which we treat it. The Indian, even now, is as much of a romance to us as the caliphs of the 'Arabian Nights.'" The result of our ignorance and wishful thinking has been to neglect the western settlers' need for protection and to allow the Indians to fall into the hands of pious hypocrites, who are really "robbers and adventurers" compelling the Indians to starve so "that the friends of Belknap might live in purple and fine linen." Then the *Herald* proceeds to its final solution of the question, which falls "charitably" short of outright extermination:

> Can we not deal justly with the Indian? . . . of course there will be another battle and a terrible punishment of the Indians. But is this all? Why not end the whole question now? Why not make one job of the Indian business? Why not march against the Indian with force enough to make every one a prisoner? Then why not give them one place to inhabit and keep them within its limits?

To muster such a force would, of course, require removing troops from the South. And where would the Indians be sent? The *Herald* proposes their removal to some distant, desert, and limiting location, and does so by suggesting a parallel between the Indians and the citizens of the Metropolis:

> There are not as many Indians in the whole country as there are inhabitants in the lower wards of New York, and we certainly

could handle them without this constant drain of blood and treasure. We might take Arizona or New Mexico, or we might purchase Lower California and have a territory under military rule where every Indian could live and work out his own salvation.

Thus the Indian, like the white citizen, would finally be overtaken by the Metropolis. But since he is racially "savage," he must be radically segregated through exile to a region whose present emptiness testifies to its barrenness, its incapacity to support life on any large scale; and this segregation must be enforced by the power of a military regime.

But the expulsion of the Indian may paradoxically make possible a postponement of the final closing of the Frontier for Metropolitan whites. The *Herald* now becomes unambiguously enthusiastic about the Black Hills as a new Frontier for miners and farmers, and is therefore able to complete its case for the final solution of the Indian question:

> It is inconsistent with our civilization and with common sense to allow the Indian to roam over a country as fine as that around the Black Hills, preventing its development in order that he may shoot game and scalp his neighbors. That can never be. This region must be taken from the Indian even as we took Pennsylvania and Illinois.[23]

Events of the next few days allowed the paper to develop this doctrine further. Discouraging reports of the fight on the Rosebud continued, and the *Herald* now doubted the wisdom of the converging columns. On June 27, it printed Custer's second unsigned dispatch, dated June 12, "After Sitting Bull / Uncle Sam's Blues Looking for the Hostile Reds" . . . "The Gallant Custer in the Role of a Guide." The use of "Reds" in the headline echoes the terminology used by the *Herald* to discuss the urban and labor crises where "Reds" signified radical agitators and invoked the "Red Spectre of the Commune." The story itself is mainly concerned with focusing our attention on Custer as the chief figure in the expedition. Custer anonymously praises his own work on the march, creating the impression that its forward movement is entirely dependent on himself. It is "the quick eye of Custer" that first discerns figures approaching from an unexpected direction, and Custer who resolves all hesitations about the line of march by a mixture of expert knowledge and natural instinct for the terrain. Although he is an officer and gentleman, he can better the work of all his scouts.[24]

The remainder of the dispatch concerns the plans for the juncture of Terry's and Gibbon's columns and the plans for trapping the hostiles between their columns and Crook's. The correspondent's evident ignorance of the defeat suffered by Crook is disturbing to the *Herald*, and the editorial on "The Hide and Seek After Sitting Bull" emphasizes the peril of the unsuspecting northern columns. For the reader, there is the theatrical *frisson* of seeing the monster lying in wait for the unsuspecting protagonist. Though it was evident that the war was approaching its crisis, the *Herald* did not doubt that the campaign as a whole would probably hurt the Indians more than the army.[25] The important thing was to cultivate the public's present anti-Indian sentiment for the larger project of revolutionizing the Indian policy over the long term.

The *Herald* therefore intensified its rhetoric on "The Indian Question," offering its Metropolitan solution to the Indian reservation problem again and in more detail. The fault with the Indian policy had first of all been to accord the tribes the dignity of "nations" and treaty-making powers— a dignity too recently put to death and then buried too shallowly. The second but related cause is the making of the reservations and the wars themselves a fruitful field for "commercial speculation." The war is not only a commentary on race relations; it is a critique of our business methods, which have relied too heavily on the corrupting tie between government and monopolistic speculators. The selfishness and greed of bureaucrats and business is analogous to the bloody, grasping instincts that motivate the Indian. By rebuking and defeating the Grant regime, this distortion of the business ethic could presumably be corrected. And finally, the *Herald* once again compares the populations of New York and of the Indian country, this time more specifically: the new desert reservations are imagined as places the size of Brooklyn in which the Indians, under the "direct hand of the government," would learn "habits of industry, prosperity and peace"—"if such a thing were possible."

Thus, for the second time in a week, the *Herald* invoked the population and concentration of the poorer wards of New York as a metaphor suggesting the way in which the Indian question could be solved. Stated in its most abstract and simplest terms, said the *Herald*, the problem is simply "How can we arrest and hold three hundred thousand men, women and children?" Its presumption is that the urban slum in fact teaches us how such a thing can be done. However, we have seen that the urban poor were not as yielding to the police power of the government as the *Herald* imagines the Indians will be to the military, and the poor in their active hostility were likened to savages by the *Herald*. The analogy of slum and reservation must therefore be seen as reversible: the lesson of urban concentration teaches us how to deal with Indians; and dealing with Indians may teach us how to deal with uprisings in the urban slums.

An interesting connection occurs in an editorial printed June 29, on "Amnesty for Communists." Praising the government of France for pardoning the last of the Communards, the *Herald*, which had earlier equated them with Turks and savages, then warns those Americans who subscribe to or sympathize with radical movements that they ought to "prove their own fitness for self-government by displaying intelligent moderation." Not all people are capable of living under a regime of self-governing liberty because not all can accept rationally the distinctions of quality and fortune which arise in social existence. Those who advocate self-government for Indian "nations"

> pretend to cure all the evils of humanity by the application of a favorite form of government, but the experience of free peoples in all ages shows conclusively that misery and vice are inseparable from human society, whatever form of government it may adopt. . . .[26]

The period between June 29 and the Fourth of July was largely occupied with intense political speculation—the conventions were making their nominations—and anticipations of the festivities on the Fourth. A brief item on July 3 on "The Indian War" reported General Crook prospecting for gold in the Big Horn mountains, and also rumors of a big fight between part of Terry's column and an Indian village. The *Herald* editorial on "The War with the Sioux" correctly notes that any such fight must be with Custer's detachment from Terry's command, but questions whether news would not have come more swiftly from Terry than from Indian-agency rumor networks.[27] The *Herald* had reason to suppose this, because it had arranged with Custer for a relay of couriers to speed its correspondents' reports from the Yellowstone. Here the odd patterns of news relating, and unequal delays in transmission, produced an interesting confusion: the rumors Crook reported on June 30 that were printed in the *Herald* on July 3, were in fact the first reports of Custer's great battle, which had occurred June 25—two days before Custer's second dispatch (dated June 12) appeared in the *Herald*.[28]

The issues of July 4 and 5 were given over to accounts of the centennial festivities at Philadelphia, and the editorial pages took up the grand historical question appropriate to the hundredth anniversary of Independence. These editorials reiterated, in a more meditative manner, the themes of the previous six months. Consideration of the question "Have We Degenerated Morally?" since 1776 naturally lent itself to aspersions on the honesty of Grant and his cronies as well as to reflections on the criminal propensities of the new dangerous classes. The *Herald* was disposed to exonerate the nation as a whole and to take a favorable view of our moral future; and it cited particularly the soldierly virtues, now on display in the West, as proof that we had not become degenerate. Other stories and editorials put this proof of virtue to the test of action. There were reports of a coming war in the Balkans, which the *Herald* linked metaphorically to Custer's war: Turkey was to be warned, as the *Herald* had warned the Indians, that "the Great Powers . . . cannot idly contemplate the scene while savages from Asia make a desert on the Danube." The "savage" metaphor was also applied close to home in the editorial on "A Brutal Savage" named McCarthy, recently convicted of attempted murder. The *Herald* worried that the soft-hearted philanthropists would return him to society so he could commit "another piece of butchery." This treatment would be the same as that already tried with the Indians, and would have the same results; but if the *Herald's* policy of military rigor was applied, such savagery would be checked: "Such wretches should be permanently exiled from society as unfit to take any share in the blessings of a civilization which they can never appreciate." Thus from the Danube to the slums of the Five Points to the Dakotas, the *Herald* perceives the same essential struggle taking place; and in each of these realms it offers the same solution of rigorous force followed by draconian or military governance.[29]

The *Herald* probably suspected that the crisis of affairs in its metaphorical stage center, the Indian war, would come in close proximity to

the climax of the centennial celebrations. It had received preliminary reports of Crook's battle on the Rosebud River, and it had received word
from Custer that Terry's column was on the Indian trail and preparing a
striking force. Its issue of Thursday, July 6, emphasizes the idea of crisis
and makes it the occasion for a significant development of its position on
the Indian war. Prior to July 6, the *Herald* had professedly declined to
criticize the military operations then under way, although it had not stinted
in its animadversions on the general Indian policy. Now the paper carried
the full report of "The Battle of Rosebud Creek," representing the fight as
a defeat, both tactically and strategically.

The news story (written by someone with the command) absolves
Crook and his gallant troops of blame for the check, but the editorial on
"Details of General Crook's Battle with the Sioux" does not. Crook is blamed
for his faulty conduct of the battle, and compared with General Arthur
St. Clair, whose command had been ambushed and massacred by Indians
in 1792. The editorialist turns the centennial mood of historical reminiscence
to advantage in a passage which recalls Washington's grief at news of St.
Clair's defeat, and the president's justified anger—he had warned St. Clair
to expect a surprise attack and recommended procedures to evade it. But
the chief villain of the piece is President Grant, whose role contrasts with
that of Washington: where the first president had done his best to warn
and protect his soldiers, Grant had done everything to make their work
harder. In particular, his removal of Custer is cited as diminishing the
army's capacity to fight Indians successfully.[30]

The editorial page had evidently been set before the arrival of late
dispatches, for it took no notice of the story appearing opposite: "A
BLOODY BATTLE / An Attack on Sitting Bull on the Little Horn River /
General Custer Killed / The Entire Detachment Under His Command
Slaughtered."

SEIZING THE OCCASION

The dispatch was datelined Salt Lake City, July 5, and it gave
only the briefest account of the battle. Even so, it was apparent that these
early reports anticipated the public outcry and official inquiries that must
inevitably follow, and they have a distinctly exculpatory character which
emphasizes Custer's heroic rashness as the cause of the disaster. With little
time to prepare, the *Herald's* only addition to the dispatch was an obituary
"Sketch of General Custer" which began: "In one of those characteristic
dashes which gave to him the reputation of one of the most reckless cavalry
leaders of the war, General George A. Custer has met his fate." The sketch
described him as having attacked an "entrenched" enemy, superior to him
in numbers, with only "a few hundred men" and without waiting for rein-
forcements. But the sketch also took a critical view of Custer's testimony
before Clymer's committee, which suggests that it was not the product of
Bennett's pen, and probably was not produced at the *Herald*: caught thor-

oughly off guard, Bennett had probably reprinted some western paper's obituary, or a dispatch from a soldier eager to blame Custer and exculpate Terry.[31]

Bennett's own development of the story would take a different ideological tack. However, although he treated Custer as a hero, he also gave a good deal of play to the image of Custer as brave to the point of recklessness, even of madness. At first, this may have been a by-product of interviews with army officers, whose comments often reflected either their long-standing animosity to the Boy General or a desire specifically to exculpate his colleagues in his last fatal campaign. But ultimately Bennett used these criticisms to advantage, building them into the portrait of Custer as a hero whose flaws were the consequences of his virtues, and whose fate is therefore an ennobling American tragedy.

The issues of July 7 and 8 are almost completely dominated by the Custer story, and they allow Bennett and his writers to develop both a mythic dimension of the story and its ideological significance in depth and detail. The first day's stories are simply and starkly headlined, "THE MASSACRE," and the two-page spread begins with an extended account of the battle derived from telegraphic versions of Terry's preliminary report. But the *Herald's* major addition to the tale is an elaborate setting of contexts which has the effect of enlarging the significance of the event beyond the immediacy of military rebuff. The news story includes a summary review of every disaster that ever befell American forces at the hands of Indians, beginning with Crawford's defeat at Sandusky in 1782. Crook's battle on the Rosebud is cast into eclipse, while Custer's Last Stand is added to the roll call of the Indian wars and assigned a place in history.

The critical view of Custer is given in a series of interviews held with Sheridan and his entourage on the occasion of the reunion of the Army of the Cumberland. The longest of these develops the criticism of Custer as reckless in his bravery, hungry for glory, somewhat "mad." Under the subhead "The Inside History" (of the Custer expedition) Sheridan's aide asserts that "the truth about Custer is that he was a pet soldier," favored by Sheridan above others of equal or greater merit. Their relationship is presented as complementary, a useful pairing of opposites: "While Sheridan was always cool, Custer was always aflame. He was like a thermometer." Where Sheridan exemplifies reason and the prose of war, Custer "had a touch of romance about him . . . [he] used to go about dressed like one of Byron's pirates in the Archipelago." While implicitly deriding Custer's vanity and bravado, the officer suggests that these qualities were condescendingly tolerated as the effusions of immaturity and childlikeness—qualities that link Custer to that other childish and dependent class: "You see [said the officer], we all liked Custer and did not mind his little freaks . . . any more that we would have minded temper in a woman."

This analogy recalls the wartime imagery of Custer as the liminal hero, the boy-man whose sexual character is on the border between masculine adulthood and the passionate nature of woman. More important, it avails itself of the central characteristic of the mythic hero: his incarnation of the polar oppositions of a conflict of values or ideological imperatives. Custer is presented as the meeting point of the positive and negative forces in

American culture—masculinity and femininity, adulthood and childhood, civilization and savagery, sanity and madness, order and disorder. As one who balances on a turning point between these orders and qualities, he is able to draw knowledge and power from both; but that very position makes him the embodiment of trouble and conflict, unstable and dangerous as a moral reference point. The very qualities that are his strength as a "Berserker" under Sheridan in 1865 make him a liability in 1876, whose "mad doings on the Yellowstone" will make the Indian problem harder to solve.

But the officer presents a more mundane, and, for Bennett, politically useful basis of criticism when he compares Custer's defeat to the Charge of the Light Brigade—a military blunder precipitated by a quarrel between two officers and the rash anger of the subordinate, suggesting that the Grant-Custer quarrel lies behind Custer's insane rashness.[32] *Herald* editorialists put this material to an ideological purpose that is opposite to that of the interviewee, who obviously means to blame Custer and exculpate Grant. "The Slaughter on the Little Horn—The Death of General Custer" lays the blame squarely on Grant. Bennett borrows the Light Brigade metaphor but emphasizes the Tennyson treatment of the theme: praise for the heroism of the fallen comes before any inquiry into the reasons why, and the accusation that "somebody blundered" is directed toward the president. While Custer may possibly have been "rash . . . we must treat his memory with indulgence," for the gallant Custer had reason to be rash and desperate in his desire for combat. "The brave Custer" was "the best Indian fighter in the army next to Sheridan," and a man who knew at first hand the criminal fallacies of the Indian policy of Grant. Driven by his "keen sense of injustice" and the unmerited dishonor suffered by Grant's degradation, Custer went to battle "with an apparent determination to retrieve his standing by some splendid act of successful daring or die the kind of death which hallows the memory of a soldier." Custer's desperate courage was the response of a brave and honorable man to the deeds of a tyrant; and if culpable at all, he has earned the kind of blame that attaches to a character like Shakespeare's Brutus. Once again, Custer appears as the means of destroying "Caesar" Grant. But to Grant the *Herald* says: "Behold your hands! They are red with the blood of Custer and his brave three hundred."

The next editorial in the column, "Indian Strategy and Personal Government," extends and enlarges this argument. The personal tyranny that is reflected in Grant's Caesarian treatment of Custer has been more generally displayed in his conduct of political affairs, and especially the Indian policy. "Grant's malign influence" appears in the turning over of Indian affairs to his personal favorites, for their personal profit. Thus, "Grant is the author of the present Indian war" and has as much to do with Custer's defeat as Sitting Bull.

Now the *Herald* begins building a mythological context for Custer, comparable to the catalogue of massacres that gave the battle a kind of historical frame: "Never, perhaps, in American history, did a family ever offer up so many lives for the flag in a single engagement. We recall the Curiatii from Roman history and the Maccabees from the Hebrew. Beside them in heroic remembrance must stand the name of Custer." Although characterizing the charge of the regiment as "mad," the *Herald* does not mean the word as criticism, but rather invokes it as divine madness. Like the mythic prototypes cited above, the Custers are defenders of the republic and, in their opposition to Grant, would-be liberators. "They died as grandly as Homer's demigods," yet democratically:

> In the supreme moment of carnage . . . all distinctions of name and rank were blended, but the family that "died at the head of their column" will lead the throng when history recalls their dead. It was mad, it was rash, but, though "some one had blundered," it was
>
>
>
> Theirs not to reason why,
> Theirs but to do or die.
>
>
>
> Success was beyond their grasp so they died—to a man.[33]

On July 8, there was again a huge display given to the Custer stories, including a large map of the territory. The editorials on this day were the most elaborate and extensive yet. The lead editorial on "Custer's Massacre" cites the incredulity of Terry and Sheridan about the Custer disaster as proof that the army underestimated the number and determination of their opponents; and this becomes testimony that exonerates Custer: he attacked believing this false estimate, and "paid the penalty of a mistake [that] was as much their mistake as his." But Bennett is not really interested in blaming Terry and Sheridan. "The deplorable truth is that President Grant is chiefly responsible for the appalling miscarriages which have attended this disastrous campaign against the Sioux. The proper commander of the expedition was General Custer . . . next to Sheridan . . . the ablest Indian fighter in the army," whose "superior fitness" was recognized by the initial decision that he command the column. But:

> Like a man of honor he swore to the truth against Belknap . . . and the soldier who had been selected on grounds of pre-eminent fitness was flung out to gratify a personal pique of the President. Is this kind of personal government to be perpetuated?

An editorial on "Custer's Battle" extends the legend-making aspect of the *Herald*'s case, declaring that "In this recital we see a heroic commander followed to the death by two hundred and forty soldiers of his regiment not less heroic than himself, and all these lives, qualified to make splendid the annals of our race, wasted in a mad battle with from four to five thousand savages not without the virtue of courage." Below this, an editorial on "Our Danger" returns us to the election campaign: if Grant and his ilk continue to rule and expand their corrupt power by "centralization . . . encroachment and usurpation," "the downfall of the Republic would be as certain as the fall of the Roman Empire or the ruin of the Napoleonic dynasty." A news item from Washington notes that even the Commissioner of Indian Affairs has been moved by Custer's fate to say that "a white man's life was worth more than an Indian's," and that "It is not too much to say that the prevailing feeling among the public favors the policy of extermination."[34]

In the days and weeks that followed, the *Herald* developed in greater detail the personal legend of its hero, thus adding to the impact of the catastrophe (and keeping it before the public). Its development was facilitated by a series of startling documents which appeared periodically. A sequence of army reports on the battle published during July and August, for example, added new details to the account of the battle and pictured the pathetic spectacle of the dead lying on the field. They also fueled controversies over the culpability or innocence of Terry and Custer and of Custer's subordinates Reno and Benteen. These controversies intensified the inevitable flood of letters from Custer's former comrades-in-arms, enemies, sympathizers, and detractors. There were also pathetic interviews with Custer's aged parents in Monroe and with Libbie after her return from Dakota.[35]

One of the most spectacular of these occasions was provided on July 11 by the printing of the long-delayed correspondence, sent to the *Herald* by Bismarck *Tribune* correspondent Mark Kellogg and Custer (anonymously) on the eve of the march to the Little Big Horn. Bennett reaped the benefit of his foresight in making arrangements with Custer in a manner neither expected, but one that offered incomparable opportunities for sensationalism. Dramatically headlined "A VOICE FROM THE TOMB," the stories served two purposes: they emphasized and exaggerated Custer's personal heroism on the eve (as it would retrospectively be seen) of martyrdom; and it offered a secondary villain for the drama. A subhead speaks of "Reno's Contempt of Orders," and the story contrasts "Reno Disobeying Positive Orders" with "The Correctness of Custer's Views." The disobedience referred to in this story occurred before the command left Terry, during the course of a scouting foray up the Powder and Tongue rivers: and Custer—anonymously—hints darkly at the likelihood of a court-martial. But this earlier failure of Reno's was now fatally juxtaposed with the accusation that Reno had either failed or refused to obey orders at the Little Big Horn. The conjunction of the two stories in the *Herald's* pages and the public mind—as much as or more than the subsequent investigation—ruined Reno's reputation and made public outcry for a court of inquiry inevitable. "Faint Heart Never Won Fair Lady," writes Custer, in condemning Reno for not going on to attack the Sioux after disobedience to orders had brought him within striking distance. The *Herald* correctly interprets these remarks as showing that Custer, and the rest of the army, believed that the only problem was to find the Indians and that almost any force would whip whatever they discovered. And by condemning Reno's failure, the *Herald* implicitly validates Custer's decision to attack on the twenty-fifth.

Custer describes his own determination to follow up Reno's Indian trail and strike while he can. "Custer takes no wagons . . . but proposes to live and travel like Indians"—the old theme of Leatherstocking's pursuits, indeed of Benjamin Church's hunting of King Philip in the seventeenth century. Mark Kellogg's dispatch then takes up the tale and portrays Custer as both the brains and the "guts" of the expedition. He describes Custer as a dead shot for game, again in the Leatherstocking-Boone-Crockett tradition; gives a rapturous landscape description, out of Cooper by way of Custer and the Northern Pacific brochures; briefly notes that General Terry is "large brained . . . genial, frank and manly," then returns to Custer:

> And now a word for THE MOST PECULIAR GENIUS IN THE ARMY, a man of strong impulses, of great hearted friendships and bitter enmities, of quick, nervous temperament, undaunted courage, will and determination; a man possessing electric mental capacity and of iron frame and constitution; a brave, faithful, gallant soldier, . . . overcoming seeming impossibilities and with an ambition to succeed in all things he undertakes; a man to do right, as he construes right, in every case; . . . Of Lieutenant-Colonel G. A. Custer I am now writing.

The *Herald* itself now began the process of making the Custer story into a hagiographic myth. Under the headline "THE DEAD CAVALRY-MEN" it gave Custer the chivalric epithet of *Le Chevalier Sans Peur et Sans Reproche*. A later editorial presented Custer as the exemplary Christian knight, whose "name will be respected whenever chivalry is applauded and civilization battles against barbarism." Other editorials compare his "hill of death" to Golgotha.[36]

But the death of such a hero did not suggest forgiveness of enemies; rather it implied the need of revenge. The *Herald's* own exterminationist rhetoric now escalated and began to ramify and reach out to include social conflicts other than the Indian war. The metaphorical connections thus developed are complexly interrelated with each other; and all are recurrently associated with the stories that now centered particularly on the personality and heroic fable of Custer himself. In the issue of July 9, all of the important strands of the myth are present, and are presented in a way that reveals their logical (and mythological) relation to each other. The central matter of both the news and editorial pages concerns new revelations about the Custer battle, but its main feature is the reprinting of the pictographic "autobiography" of Sitting Bull which had been copied by a student of Indian culture some years before. This autobiography of Custer's antagonist and presumed slayer completes the cast of characters for the Last Stand tragedy by fleshing out the character of the villain. It also becomes the text for yet another sermon on the character of savages and the best means of governing them. Through the familiar devices of language- and image-borrowing and the physical juxtaposition of articles and editorials, the Custer–Sitting Bull material is related to the grand-scale war of races and religions then materializing in the Balkans; to the continuing problems of "Red" agitation and violence among the "laboring classes and dangerous classes" of the city; to the proposal to build a Custer monument; and to the issues and personalities of the upcoming presidential canvass.

Also on this date, a dramatic event in the South provided a gorgeous opportunity for associating the perpetrators of electoral violence (both blacks and poor whites) with the Indian savages. This event was the "Hamburg Massacre," which a July 9 headline called "A Conflict of Races," and its name alone is sufficient to suggest its aptness for Bennett's purposes. Each of these stories and themes received more or less careful attention from the *Herald* for the rest of the year; and hence, each had its own pattern of development. For the sake of clarity these themes may be explored for discussion separately, but it should be remembered that the *Herald's* artistry was devoted to keeping them continually and inextricably associated.[37]

THE GREAT ANTAGONIST:
SITTING BULL AS METAPHOR

The Sitting Bull story was one of the longest and most elaborately presented stories published by the *Herald* in the whole 1873–76 period. Its only rivals for length are the Black Hills report issues, the Last Stand stories of July 7–8, the Hamburg Massacre, and the presidential election; and none of these stories enjoys the iconographic appeal of the Sitting Bull story, which was illustrated with reproductions of the pictographs done in the chief's own hand. It is also a piece that is central both to the mythology of Custer's Last Stand and to the ideological structure which the *Herald* was engaged in creating. The headline of the autobiography and the subhead of the editorial commentary on it emphasize the exemplary quality of the narrative. It is not simply the autobiography of an Indian, it is "The Life of a Savage," and typical of the species. And since in the *Herald's* view the "savage" character was the key to "antisocial" behavior among the white and black underclasses, the paper's interpretation of this document reflects on its social doctrine generally.

Sitting Bull's pictographs "make up the life of the model savage whom our philanthropists love to feed, the Child of Nature whom the Indian ring is never weary of praising and swindling. There is nothing Arcadian in their savagery." As usual, a romantic view of the Indians (associated with Cooper) is linked with the pious hypocrisy of the Indian missionary agents appointed by Grant. In the case of Sitting Bull, the linkage was particularly unjust, since that chief was distinguished by the fact that he had never submitted to the Treaty of 1868 and had refused to come onto the reservation or to accept support from the whites. However, the *Herald's* aspersions on savages are never disconnected from its attack on those sectors of the political and cultural elite who were principled defenders of the rights of the underclass; for it is this elite, and not the wandering tribesmen or disorganized "dangerous classes" that are contesting with Bennett and his colleagues for mass suffrage and political power.

What discredits the ideology of philanthropic liberalism is the "proof" that the prospective recipient of liberty and political rights is unredeemably "savage" by the rule of his nature. If Sitting Bull is the "model savage," his character therefore becomes the litmus test by which "savagery" is identified in all contexts, and the treatment envisioned for Sitting Bull becomes a generalized response to "savagery" of all kinds. As a portable symbol of savagery, Sitting Bull is even invoked as the measure of the cruelty and regressiveness of the Turkish forces in the Balkans; indeed, a biography of the Turkish Sultan Abdul Aziz is printed side by side with one of the chapters of Sitting Bull's autobiography.[38]

The essence of Indian savagery is that white men are "The Indian's Game," no more in their eyes than beasts to be hunted and killed; yet the *Herald* itself invokes the offering of bounty for the skins of wolves and bears as a model of how civilized men may justly treat the predatory natives of their promised land—whether human or animal. The succession of animal kingdom metaphors here exemplifies the workings of revenge psychology: the predatory motives imputed to the savage arouse an anger which is "savage" in its justification of limitless punishment and cruelty. By attributing the cause of his own "savage" motive to the Indians, Bennett is allowed to indulge freely a level of rage and an advocacy of genocide that would otherwise be unacceptable.[39]

What makes the revenge psychology work is the role of Sitting Bull in the Last Stand myth. Whatever the moral or political responsibility of Grant for the disaster, the fiendish agent of Custer's destruction was taken to be Sitting Bull. There is an attractive symmetry in the opposition of two exemplary protagonists—dark and light, fiend and hero—and the *Herald*, moved by both kinds of appeal, proceeds to make Sitting Bull a dark counterpart of its own hero. This of course exaggerates and distorts the actual role of Sitting Bull in the battle, as well as the political character of the position held by "Old Man Chiefs" and war chiefs among the Lakota and Cheyenne; and it certainly misrepresents the tactics of the Battle of the Little Big Horn and the "command structure" of the tribesmen. Nonetheless, the myth of a great Indian general and antagonist became part of the Last Stand myth.[40]

For Bennett, "it adds a pang to the deaths of Custer and his heroic command that they fell at the hands of such a savage." A representative of the most enlightened and progressive people the world has known has been undone and destroyed by a representative of the most debased and primitive stage of human development. Beyond the horrible irony of that fact lies the question, how could such a reversal of the logic and direction of history have occurred? The *Herald* answers with the assertion that the savage must have been assisted by racial renegades from white civilization. Three groups are identified. According to a rumor reported in the *Herald* (and elsewhere), Sitting Bull had received an education at an Indian school run by French Canadian Jesuits and had been particularly tutored in the study of Napoleon's campaigns. This rumor, to which there was not a shred of truth, became an essential part of Sitting Bull's mystique among the whites—and he acquired the sobriquet of the "Sioux Napoleon." In addition to reinforcing the racial doctrine that savages are relatively harmless unless aided by renegade whites, the Jesuit story has the additional feature of linking anti-Indian attitudes with the nativist and anti-Catholic biases of American Protestantism.[41]

The *Herald* also identifies two classes of American "renegades": a group of white "outlaws" and "squaw men" supposedly residing among the Indians; and, of course, the philanthropists of the Indian Bureau, who

had coddled and armed the savages. The "outlaw" group is treated in such
a way as to link them with the "dangerous classes" of the city; and the
philanthropist group is used as the occasion for linking Grant in particular
and Republicans in general to the guilt of Custer's murder.

Having identified the Indians who killed Custer as the pets of philanthropists, Bennett's next task was to identify the philanthropists as the
dominant force in the Republican Party. The influence of Radicals like
Wendell Phillips was important enough to make the position credible, although friends of the Indian were hardly dominant in the party circles.
Nonetheless, when they took the lead in criticizing the extremism and
cruelty of the *Herald's* exterminationist policy, Bennett was clever enough
in handling their objections to have it both ways. He defended himself
against Wendell Phillips's condemnation of the *Herald's* call for extermination as un-Christian and "savage" by declaring his belief that whether or
not extermination was desirable, it was simply impractical. It was not
simply that the Indians were hard to catch and kill; it was that there were
relatively so few of them that it was not even necessary. The "Brooklyn"
plan of concentrating the Indians under a military regime in a small territory
would accomplish his purpose; and in that desert place they might live or
die, but would in any case cease to matter.[42]

Bennett handled his critics by associating them with Sitting Bull as
murderers of Custer. "The Indian Bureau killed Custer," Bennett repeated
time and again; and he coupled Grant's Republicans with "the false phi-
lanthropical theories of Mr. Phillips and his class," and wished them
swept "into the sea" along with the Sioux. Thus the *Herald* describes the
political activities of New York State Republicans in the following terms:

> Senator [Cornell] and all the braves are up in arms and adorning
> themselves with war-paint and making ready for the warpath.
> Here comes Silver Tongue Curtis . . . Bald Eagle Husted . . . Sit-
> ting Bull Schultz . . . Spotted Tail Fenton . . . all ready for his
> scalp. Cornell, confident in the raid of his chief Red Cloud [Ros-
> coe Conkling] . . . awaits the onset.[43]

The philanthropy of Grant is cited as Sitting Bull's source of power;
and to counter it, the *Herald* begins in this issue a true philanthropy, which
has as its object the building of a Custer monument and provision of a
pension for Mrs. Custer. This was a project that provided the *Herald* with
an unlimited supply of occasions for mourning Custer and berating Grant,
and was particularly useful when the close of active operations for the winter made news from the Indian country scarce. The building of the monument was to be a recognition that Custer and his command represented
civilization and all that was best in America and the white race when they
perished fighting the Indians. To memorialize them did not require agreement on the criticisms of Custer's tactics, nor even on the justice or injustice of the war. Rather, like the European custom of erecting permanent
monuments to its heroes to "hold up the deeds of their brave sons as an
example to all time," it was a point of unification, supposedly enlisting
values that transcended political and sectional differences and class and
racial lines.

But the *Herald*'s apolitical rhetoric was hollow. It turned the Custer monument story to partisan account as it had done with the Last Stand itself. The *Herald* emphasizes that it prefers numerous small contributions from the poor to a few large donations from the wealthy, or from Congress. Custer would thus be compared to the Spartan Leonidas—who held Thermopylae to "the last man" against the Persian barbarians—and appear as the hero of the whole people (as Leonidas's epitaph was addressed to the Spartan people). In support of the fund—which was chaired by August Belmont—the *Herald* printed stories and editorials every day throughout the summer and into the fall. It listed contributors and reprinted the notes that accompanied them—"widow's mites," dimes and nickels from schoolchildren, contributions from "colored waiters" and an English baron, numerous ex-Confederates and veterans of the Michigan brigade, a "cosmopolitan," a "Grecian" immigrant writing broken English, an Errand Boy, a Vassar girl, several "workingmen," a "truck driver," "Former Foeman" . . . and so on. In a time of class strife, Custer was to symbolize the common values shared by rich and poor. The "little people" who devote their hard-earned pennies to the monument show by this gesture their difference from the "dangerous classes." Where the latter squander the wages they dislike laboring for, the contributors are able both to save and to give in charity; where the dangerous classes meditate antisocial revolution, the contributors build a monument to patriotic sacrifice. This contrast is made explicit in the ongoing treatment of "dangerous class" activities that parallels the developing Custer story.[44]

The connection between the dangerous classes and Sitting Bull's warriors had been suggested throughout the year, and the Custer catastrophe now gave that connection an edge. The "Sitting Bull" issue of July 9 marks Bennett's most extensive development of the metaphor. The "Life of a Savage" exemplified by Sitting Bull is characterized by the unwillingness to "earn their bread in the sweat of their brow," which amounts to "rejecting the ways of civilization." The editorial page develops the association in other familiar ways. The legend of Sitting Bull's Jesuit education and his alliance with white criminals links the Last Stand with the threat of the dangerous classes of immigrants and workers. The July 9 editorial on this subject is titled "White Outlaws Lead the Reds"—a formulation that links the Indians and the Communards once again; and identifies as renegades those men (of white race or enlightened class) who aid the race/class enemy.

Another editorial on the same page reiterates the proposal for an Indian reservation "the size of Brooklyn." But this version develops more explicitly the rationale for such an undertaking and, in so doing, emphasizes the connection between savages and dangerous classes. "The Indian Question—Let Us End It Now and Forever" defends the proceeding by arguing that we have come to the end of the Frontier and live in a world in which the conditions of life that pertain in Brooklyn—in the Metropolis—have become universal. So long as we thought we "had plenty of land and could spare it" we could safely tolerate Indian freedom. Under present conditions, only sentimentalists and swindlers will wish to see savages control "more space than the German Empire." Certainly if 300,000 whites live at peace in

Brooklyn, we can expect the Indians to do the same in their little desert place. Of course, Brooklyn—as the *Herald* elsewhere notes—is not entirely pacified itself. But the principle is reversible: force must be used against both whites and reds. But the exile of the Indians to "Brooklyn" is not an immediate threat to the white proletariat, because Indian removal will reopen the vista of Frontier freedom, if only for one more generation: if we "put an end to these Indian immunities . . . these wide rich dominions should be open to civilization."[45]

Bennett was now able to use the "Custer Massacre" as a portable metaphor, through which he could interpret the whole range of election year issues, with all their many twists and turns. He used the metaphor to castigate heartless landlords for raising the rents of the working poor: the landlords, said an editorial, are committing a "massacre" of the poor, while the latter are contributing their pennies to the fund for a Custer monument. He suggests that the authorized strength of the cavalry be increased and that recruiting be energetically carried on among the urban unemployed—thus employing them and making their work of avenging Custer a version of the Frontier safety valve. On the other hand, the Custer Massacre could be used as a symbol for rebuking the "savagery" of certain lower-class elements and the reckless philanthropy of reformers. Bennett speaks of the Sioux government as "communistic" and compares Indian outrages with acts of violence attributed to the Molly Maguire organization in the coalfields, or to the "tramps" and "dangerous classes" of city and countryside. A religious editorial on August 6 makes the parallel between the Mollies and the Indians explicit, and asserts that both are appropriate targets for the power of the authorities and the ministration of the Gospel: "There is growing up in our midst people as ignorant of the Gospel as the savages of Africa . . . and we are doing very little towards enlightening them."[46]

"SIOUX CIVILIZATION" IN SOUTH CAROLINA

The allusion to Africa points us toward the other cockpit of social and racial warfare, the South. The election of 1876 was the first since 1860 in which the Republicans were challenged by a South fully restored to its position in the electoral college, and almost entirely free of the check on Democratic Party power that had been imposed by the Reconstruction governments. Of the three states still under such regimes, South Carolina was the most important because of the dominant role played by the state in the secession movement and because of the gubernatorial election then in progress. The Democratic candidate was Wade Hampton, a representative of the wealthy antebellum planter class and an ex-commander of Confederate cavalry who since the war had been identified with the moderate and "progressive" forces in his state. His party affiliation was Democrat, but his business connections allied him with those conservative northern and nominally Republican businessmen who abhorred the corruption—and still more, the high taxation—imposed by the Reconstruction government.

South Carolina's governors and legislators had become a byword for corruption and for a kind of violence we would associate with gangsterism, involving the misuse of the black militia and various forms of vigilantism. They were, of course, matched and outmatched by the vigilantism of their Klan opponents, and Custer's despised colleague Major Lewis Merrill made —and lost—his reputation suppressing the Carolina Klan. But by 1876, there was a growing tendency to identify the Reconstruction government as the fountainhead of those conditions which made for social violence and corruption. Hampton was therefore put forward as a reform candidate, whose Confederate credentials could appeal to the Democracy and whose conservatism would minimize the resistance of reform-minded Republicans. This view of Hampton was passionately espoused by Democratic journals like the *Herald*; but in doing so, Bennett could draw on a consensus view of Carolina that was shared with Republican conservatives. His favorite nickname for South Carolina was "The Prostrate State," which he borrowed from the title of a series of articles (later a best-selling book) by James Pike, who had gone south in 1872–73 as a reporter for the Republican New York *Tribune*. Pike himself (like editor Whitelaw Reid of the *Tribune*) was an abolitionist converted to an anti-Radical by his abhorrence of blacks as a race and by the spectacle of "Negro Government" imposed on southern whites.[47]

But electoral violence and vigilantism remained a part of the scene. Although Hampton abjured the Klan as a criminal organization, he formed semimilitary units called Rifle Clubs and Red Shirts in emulation of the Italian revolutionaries who followed Garibaldi. Implicitly and explicitly, these units invoked the same threat of violent intimidation that the Klan had attempted to use to defeat black Reconstruction. The Republicans countered by using the black state militia to protect its political meetings. In one of these, at Hamburg, an altercation between black militiamen and an armed mob of whites led to shooting, which left one white man and six militiamen dead. The casualty figures suggested that the white mob, rather than the black agents of Republican Caesarism, were the responsible parties; and the northern Republican papers had a bloody shirt to wave.

The *Herald* had previously expressed itself as hostile to the white perpetrators of such incidents for the stated reason that they provided ammunition to enemies of the South. It urged that such confrontations be especially avoided in this year, since the Democratic prospects looked so promising. In its coverage of Hamburg, the *Herald* therefore sought to disassociate the perpetrators of the massacre from the "aristocratic" party whose triumph—under candidate Wade Hampton—it greatly favored. Pro-Hampton forces feared that riots such as that at Hamburg would discredit the southern Democracy in the North and cost Tilden the presidency, and that they would provoke a renewal of military occupation in South Carolina itself.

The *Herald*'s treatment of the South Carolina election and the Hamburg Massacre went through three major phases. In the first, the paper accused poor white elements of attacking the blacks without provocation and behaving like "savages" in brutalizing the living and mutilating the dead. The editorial page of July 9 speaks of the Hamburg Massacre as "Bloodshed in the South—How to Elect Hayes and Wheeler" (the Republican candidates), and condemns the attack as the work of "Southern white madmen . . . resolved to elect Hayes."[48] In the second phase, the *Herald* sought to shift the focus of blame onto Governor Daniel H. Chamberlain, accusing him of failing to use his own police powers to arrest the Hamburg "savages," preferring to maximize the riot and so obtain federal troops from Grant. In the third phase, the *Herald* accused the Republicans and their black allies of fomenting and provoking riots like Hamburg themselves.

The Indian War and Custer's Last Stand figured both directly and indirectly in this campaign. The fact of the Last Stand was evidence of the need for transferring troops out of the South and into the West, to fight dark-skinned savages rather than "oppressing" progressive southern whites. This was argued through a combination of direct editorial statement and juxtaposition of articles on southern occupation and the inadequacy of western forces. The image of the Last Stand as a battle of a heroic military figure—linked with an idealization of Hampton as a soldier–civil servant— against the dual forces of barbarism and Radicalism also served the *Herald*'s depiction of the ideological struggle in South Carolina. Thus, stories on the Hamburg Massacre and its aftermath often appear in close conjunction with the Last Stand and Custer's monument stories; and language is continually borrowed from the Indian war stories to describe and interpret South Carolina events. Hampton himself figures as a contributor to the Custer myth and monument—in a courtly gesture, Custer's former foe returns to his widow a pair of Custer's field glasses captured during a cavalry fight in 1864.[49]

In the first phase of the developing argument, the poor whites appear as savages. Thus, on July 15, the *Herald* declares that the Hamburg Massacre presages the spread of "Sioux Civilization" to the East, instead of Christian civilization to the savage West:

> SIOUX CIVILIZATION / Sitting Bull is said to be profoundly gratified with the reports of the Hamburg riot. It shows that Sioux civilization and Sioux tactics are spreading. Sitting Bull thinks all the prisoners, and not only four, should have been shot; but still he is not exacting. He knows it requires time to educate a community up to the Sioux standard.

But the role of Radical "philanthropy" in creating the conditions for such "savagery" is not neglected. Below this item appears a note that while Sitting Bull was out of ammunition, he could count on Orvil Grant (the President's brother) to resupply him: the metaphor suggests that Republicans will use Hamburg to foment other provocation.[50]

This was followed by an editorial on July 17 on "How the South Should Regard the Outrages." The editorial points out that classes of ruffians— dangerous classes—now exist in every community; but that in the North, the decent classes vindicate the law against these criminals while their southern peers stand silent or even sympathize. It terms the Hamburg Massacre "A Cruel and brutal outrage . . . worthy of the Sioux," and declares that the governor ought to form up a militia and "shoot down the roughs." Failure to do this will not only cost them the election; it will also embitter the "docile, harmless" Negroes into implacable foes and require at some later time a call from the respectable whites for troops to save them from a Negro uprising. This prospect of racial war is dramatized by the appearance on the same page of a "Warning in Time—Prepare for the Worst," in which the nation is warned of a general uprising of all the western Indians to make "a Golgotha of our frontier settlements." Thus the Indian war makes palpable the implicit threat of race war that looms over the South, and of the class war looming over the North. And in all three instances, "Sitting Bull" and "the Sioux" symbolize the negative or "ruffian" pole of society; Custer and Hampton the positive or soldierly alternative. The apogee of this sort of argument against the "Hamburg ruffians" was reached in an August 3 editorial, which identified their leader, General Matthew C. Butler, as "Sitting Bull Butler."[51]

There were complications to be faced in applying the Indian war as an interpretative grid in this fashion. By identifying Butler as Sitting Bull and the rioters as savages, the *Herald* implicitly cast Governor Chamberlain and his black supporters in the Custer and Seventh Cavalry roles. Obviously it would be necessary to exonerate Hampton from the accusation leveled at his overzealous followers; but more than this, it would be necessary at some point to return to the more orthodox application of mythic symbolism which would identify the blacks as Indians and Chamberlain as the crooked Indian agent. This transition was rather tortuously accomplished when Chamberlain called federal troops to keep order. The *Herald* had reasoned that in the absence of federal troops to "intimidate" southern whites (or prevent their intimidation of the blacks) Hampton would win; but their presence now compelled the *Herald* to revert to type.

First the *Herald* moved to deflate the Indian war metaphor it had used to puff up its attack on the Democratic ruffians. Stories of "A Threatened Race Conflict" to be initiated by the whites were denounced as attempts to reimpose military despotism and as a fraudulent maneuver by Republicans interested in waving the bloody shirt. This bogus, Republican-invented race war in the South was then supplanted by the "real thing": reports and editorials from the West telling us "What Sitting Bull Wants" (the rolling back of the Frontiers, and a race war in the South to draw off the army). In this instance, Sitting Bull is compared to Jefferson Davis— the real race-war enemy, who wants to undo civilization; and the real Civil War advocate, who seeks to set Americans against each other. As the election approached, however, "race war" disorders increased, largely as a result of Democratic efforts to prevent blacks from campaigning, organizing, or voting. But now the *Herald* felt free to put the blame for such encounters on the blacks, accuse them of initiating the hostilities and carrying them out in an especially "savage manner." These stories were often linked or juxtaposed with stories of Indian atrocities and with foreign "race wars" —references to the Haitian rebellion, to the Balkan War, and to Stanley's expedition in Africa: "White Citizens Ambushed and Shot by Colored Militia"; Reign of Terror in the Low Country / Negro Raid on Mount Pleasant."[52]

But if the vicissitudes of the canvass compelled shifts of editorial rhetoric or advocacy, the *Herald* nevertheless constructed a consistent ideological position out of the materials given it by culture and history. The twinned catastrophes of the Custer and the Hamburg massacres worked together to confirm the view that the social crisis could best be interpreted according to the racialist model. Both events tended to see the social order as divided between a civilized ruling class/race and a savage underclass, inimical by its character and nature to the principles of social order. Both tended to legitimate the idea that political authority must be vested in a soldierly ruling class and that the paternalistic regimes of the regiment, plantation, reservation can be extended broadly through the society of the Metropolis. Both saw the subversion of this natural order as leading to a war of extermination in which civilization itself might perish.

This thesis was elaborated with specific reference to the South, but also allowed the *Herald* to extend its "Southern" and "Indian" solutions metaphorically to northern labor as well. The Indian war and Sitting Bull references suggest that wherever two unlike and unequal races contest for a single social space without restraint, wars of extermination result. The "Race Troubles in the South" teach a more complex version of this lesson which Bennett teaches by citing the writings of Jefferson and Calhoun to show that the removal of such restraint by the aristocracy—whether through emancipation of the slaves or the abdication of power in favor of the poor white ruffians—would "tend to produce convulsions" ending in a "war of extermination" by freed blacks against whites, or by unrestrained whites against despised blacks. Although in any such struggle "the negroes would, of course, get the worst of it," the result would be catastrophic for the moral and economic civilization of the South, and indeed of the nation. This is the threat which is raised by carpetbagger government: just when the sure hand and moral authority of the aristocracy would have been of crucial importance to effect the transition to a South without slavery, it was removed by military despotism; and its place usurped by a class of interlopers, crooks, and racial renegades respected by none of the classes concerned.

The significance of the race wars of 1876 is precisely the teaching of this conservative lesson: that the best men of North and South must agree to repudiate the semibarbarous mobs they have demagogically deployed against each other, in favor of a truly conservative redefinition of republican politics. The South must repudiate its Klansmen and White Leaguers; the North its Black and Union Leagues, its bloody shirt, its philanthropic social nostrums. They must find a new unity based first of all on the commonality of race—a concept which must now be understood not only as dividing red, white, and black, but as distinguishing between classes of whites. An editorial on the same page with "Race Troubles" reminds the Southerners who scorn carpetbaggers that "with the exception of Sitting Bull and his people" all Americans are "carpetbaggers." By the terms of this metaphor carpetbaggers and Southern "redeemers" are reconciled on the ground of their whiteness, their "instinct of progress," their proprietary status and interest, and their moral superiority; and they are set against and above unruly lower classes interpreted by the myth as Indians.

Having proposed that the Southerner identify with the carpetbagger, the *Herald* now turns to the northern reader and asks a reciprocal identification: imagine what it would be like if the northern political economy were like that of the South. Northerners tolerated, and even made a positive political mystique out of, rebellions like the Anti Rent War of the 1840s or the recent uprisings of miners in the Pennsylvania coalfields. These riots were small in size and the proletarian element in a minority. "But if fully one half of its people were laborers in the coal mines, with a proportionally numerous body of sympathizers throughout the North, we could not ignore the magnitude of the danger." The lesson of the Hamburg Massacre is not that either the black militia or the white ruffians represent savagery in the South, but that *both* groups share that metaphorical character; and that there are kindred classes in every industrial city and town of the North as well. The connection is explicitly made in editorials on "The Hamburg Massacre and the Mollie Maguires," which compare the labor terrorists first to the White Leagues and then to the black militia— and finally to the Indians, putting "a torch at every man's door and a knife at every man's throat." In an editorial on "The Tramp in a New Character" the *Herald* informed its readers that what had been a "local nuisance" was becoming a national threat, as unemployment sent men wandering across the countryside—the "urban savages" reverting to the nomadic condition of their redskin namesakes.[53]

Thus the final lesson of Hamburg reinforces the lesson of the Last Stand, and it is addressed to the middle classes of the North and Middle West. The disparate struggles of coal corporations with Irish labor-terrorists, of soldiers with Indians, of southern Bourbons with savage blacks and ruffian whites, are really the same struggle of classes and races fitted for governance against those unfit for full self-government.

MYTH, ANTI-MYTH, AND NO-MYTH-AT-ALL

Our discussion has focused on the role of Bennett and the *Herald* in making the Last Stand myth because of all contemporary journalists, Bennett took the story most seriously, and developed its symbolic significance farther than any of his contemporaries. To a considerable degree, his handling of the story and his use of it as ideological metaphor reflect a broader cultural consensus. This consensus exists as the most generalized statement of "concern" for the social, economic, and political crisis of the times—one that involves a new type of class politics and industrialized economy. The consensus also extends to agreement on using the language of race, specifically the Indian war language, to talk about class. And it extends to common acceptance of a set of significant subjects, of which Custer's Last Stand and the Hamburg Massacre are among the most meaningful. Thus the editors of the New York *Daily Graphic*, whose politics differed from Bennett's, depicted the Last Stand and its meanings in rather similar terms. In "Our Indian Impolicy," the editorialist links denigration of the "noble savage" myth to a characterization of the urban underclass as savages; and he justifies the application of stern and forceful measures against both kinds of savages by alluding to the inevitable shrinking of the world of opportunity that comes with industrial progress:

> The Indian is no such creature as he has been represented to our sympathy and imagination. He is a degraded relic of a decayed race, and it is a serious question whether he is worth civilizing, even if he is capable of civilization. . . . Were the money and effort wasted in trying to civilize the Indians wisely expended in reclaiming and educating the savages in our cities the world would be vastly better off in the end. The globe is none too large for the civilized races to occupy, and all others are doomed by a law that is irrevocable and that it is folly to resist.[54]

However, this cultural and linguistic consensus did not produce anything like a political consensus. Traditional differences of sectional and party loyalty, as well as differences arising from the new industrial order, made this symbolic language the instrument for expressing political differences and defining the ground of conflict. The Custer story provided a litmus test of political self-definition, and its treatment by different journals reflects something of the range of conflicts shaping ideological discourse in the 1870s.

Among Democratic papers, the New York *World* still evinced the greatest interest in Custer's adventures. Like the *Herald*, it condemned the removal of Custer as spite work, it predicted that Custer would respond by doing something spectacular, and after July 6, it characterized the Last Stand as "Grant's Indian Policy Come to Fruit." It painted Custer as a perfect hero and martyr, even while acknowledging that Custer might have erred in attacking when and as he did: "we confess with a thrill of pride that it was pardonable in the leader to suppose such soldiers invincible, and pardonable in the soldiers to follow such a leader with heroic faith. They could be killed but not beaten." As with the *Herald*, the *World* called for a kind of moderate or temperate "extermination"—proceeding by stages and directed only against those Indians who would not surrender. "First Exterminate the Agents," one editorial recommended. "After they are eliminated we can more readily dispose of their customers."[55]

On the related issues of labor and the South, the *World* also took the Democratic line. The Hamburg Massacre was an atrocity, but justified in part as the response of whites to their condition of forced subjection to "the most debased and servile elements of her population." A letter on "The Indian War" declared that "an Indian was an Indian" whether "Cherokee . . . Seneca, Sioux . . . [or] Cheyenne," and all should be "lumped together for the same treatment . . ." The *World* then added they "might as well class Fred Douglass and the Hottentots, exactly." Other editorials and paired news stories linked Indians, the Mollie Maguires, and the "criminal classes." An editorial on May 8 described the Mollies as murderous "Thugs," and the crime imagery is extended in another story, "The Union Square Murder," which illustrates the truth that "in New York, as in every other civilized city, there is a class, and not a very small class, of perfectly uncivilized human beings," and blames

> the insufficiency of the class which is created and paid to keep the savage class in check . . . A proper police would have struck such a terror of law into the savage classes as would have made such an assault at such a time a thing not to be thought of by the most reckless and drunken of savages.

A similar item asserting that the "uncivilized classes in Brooklyn are quite as murderous as the savage in Montana" appears right next to the *World*'s second editorial on Custer's Last Stand—"The Custer Disaster."[56]

Other newspapers could not use the event in so straightforward a manner. As we might expect, Republican papers adopted critical attitudes toward Custer and exculpatory ones toward Grant. But they, too, associated the Custer story with the Hamburg story; and this places them within the same mythmaking framework as their Democratic colleagues: although their interpretation of the pattern is different, they perceive the same combination of symbol-events as necessary to the composition of a meaningful picture.

Loyal Republican newspapers in metropolitan centers, like the New York *Times*, of course gave prominent coverage to the great "national" news stories connected with Custer—the Belknap scandal and the Last Stand. But their position as apologists for Grant's policies required them to denigrate or minimize Custer's role and even the significance of these events. The quantity of coverage is less, the tone less strident, the symbolic linkage between Custer's "enemies" and other possible enemies of "good government" or the "white race" are simply not made. Custer himself is represented as rash and imprudent in both the Belknap affair and the Last Stand—the author of his own misfortunes, not the victim of a kind of conspiracy of Grant, Sitting Bull, Wendell Phillips, and Major Reno. The Hamburg Massacre is a better subject for them, and they give it more prominent coverage—and unlike the *Herald* remain quite clear that the whites are the villains in the piece.[57]

The Chicago *Inter-Ocean*, as a western paper tied to local interests, could not so easily follow the administration line on Custer and the Indian question. Although the paper had urged compliance with the administration's original prohibition of prospecting in the Black Hills, and continued to declare its support for the Peace Policy, it had offset these party positions by crying up the gold fever at a time when eastern Republican sheets were trying to talk it down. Thus the paper had been part of the pressure brought to bear in favor of opening the Hills, even at the cost of an Indian war. In 1876, the *Inter-Ocean* reiterated its support for the Peace Policy, both before and after the Last Stand. It published a front-page story refuting the assertion of the Democratic newspapers that the Indian Bureau had supplied the arms the Indians used to kill Custer; but it responded to its constituents' basic prejudices when—without acknowledging any contradiction—it published an editorial asserting that Indian disarmament was essential to peace and that this was the Bureau's responsibility.[58]

This division of sentiment and ideology is apparent also in their treatment of Custer himself. Curtis, the correspondent who had gone on the Black Hills expedition, served as their correspondent again; and the portrait he produced of Custer in an article on "The Custer Tragedy" combined praise and blame in interesting ways. Here personal as well as public considerations also played a role, since Curtis was also a friend of Custer's. He describes Custer as skillful and brave, an "Apostle of Temperance," a gentleman in all senses of the word:

> Custer's strong points as a soldier were his almost unapproachable bravery, his dash, ardor, confidence, and his self-possession and composure that were never shaken in the most desperate resorts. I have seen Custer in circumstances when it was hard for me to believe that he was a man . . .
>
> Yet I have seen tears in his eyes, that were drawn out by the sufferings of a dog . . . He was as dainty as a beau in ladies' society . . . He never swore, nor would he allow an oath to be uttered in his presence. . . . [In] a house on the frontier, where the gentler arts were mingled with the privations and the rudeness of half civilization; with a library, where Ruskin lay beside a revolver . . . where delicate lace curtains were held in place by antlers . . . Custer lived, illustrating in himself the anomaly of a hunter and literateur; an associate of savages and a patron of the arts.

His romance with Libbie, briefly described, fleshes out this romantic portrait of the military aristocrat/Frontiersman.

On the other hand, Curtis notes that Custer was "unpopular with his superior officers" because of his independence of will and judgment. He also claims that the administration's removal of Custer from command was not responsible for the failure of the Indian campaign. In fact, says Curtis, Custer himself said that he preferred commanding the Seventh Cavalry in its active role to commanding the whole expedition from its base in the rear. According to Curtis, this exonerates both Custer and the Grant administration: Custer did not act rashly out of rage and despair at his humiliation, for there was none; and for the same reason, Grant cannot be faulted since he, in effect, gave Custer his wish. The next paragraph, however, suggests that this is a wishful rather than a fair reading: for Curtis notes that before the Belknap matter arose, Custer, in fact, requested command of the expedition and had to defer when Terry chose to command; and Curtis's assertion finally rests on the surmise that command of the Seventh was more suitable to Custer's "disposition." Curtis also resolutely refuses to draw any symbolic significance or major "moral" from the catastrophe. He ends on a most unromantic note, portraying the soldiers who died with Custer as the "driftwood" of society, criminals or indolent refugees from ordinary society, "ambitionless, aimless, indifferent, . . . the foot-balls of fate . . . kicked into an unmarked grave in the wilderness." Considering Curtis's earlier admiration of Custer, this ambivalent portrayal may reflect a sudden disillusionment—or it may reflect Curtis's bending to politically motivated editorial pressure. His fellow editorialists went even further than Curtis. In an editorial on "Custer and His Men" they found Custer guilty of direct and flagrant disobedience of orders and, while acknowledging his courage, convicted him of rashness.[59]

But it is not so much in its echoing of the administration positions on the Custer matter that the *Inter-Ocean* differs from the *Herald,* as in its refusal to make of the event a metaphor for larger struggles. Where the *Herald* continually refers to the Custer matter and relates it to the Hamburg Massacre and other major events, the *Inter-Ocean*—like Curtis—refuses to see the "moral" or make the myth. By isolating the event, rather than symbolically linking it to other events, it minimizes its importance and, hence, its potential "danger" to the administration. Far more coverage is given to the Hamburg Massacre, despite the importance of the western battle for Chicago interests. It is the Hamburg Massacre, and the similar affray at Coushatta (which occurred on August 30), that get the kind of symbolic resonance given elsewhere to the Last Stand. *Inter-Ocean* editorials paralleled the Coushatta Massacre with the Turkish atrocities and the Indian war; and juxtaposed editorials against the cry for Indian extermination with an attack on a "war of races" in the South in which whites proposed to exterminate blacks.[60]

A New York independent Republican paper, the *Tribune,* was critical of Custer from the start—and this despite the fact that editor Reid knew Custer and had been approached by him just before the expedition with an offer of special correspondence. The *Tribune*'s first notice of the battle, "CUSTER'S TERRIBLE DEFEAT," clearly blamed Custer: "The Cause His Fearless Daring." An editorial on "The Montana Slaughter" said, "It is a slaughter, not war," more comparable to Braddock's ignominious defeat than to Balaklava. "A general, skilled in Indian warfare and professedly familiar with every form of savage stratagem, has precipitated himself and his troops into a destruction so unparalleled as to be scarcely credible." It speaks of Custer as reckless and overconfident and says that while his life may have "expiated" his mistake, "the extent of an expiation which costs the country such lives makes the rashness more difficult to forget." It criticizes Democratic praise of Custer as a partisan abuse of the disaster. The only compensation the *Tribune* could see might lie in a new motive for utterly revolutionizing the Indian Bureau along tough-minded lines. In this, the *Tribune* distantly approaches the pattern of mythmaking followed by the *Herald* and the *World.* A later editorial on "Our Incomprehensible Indian Policy" makes a very Bennettian metaphor comparing the feed-them-then-fight-them school of Indian philanthropy to the radical currency policy proposed by the "Greenbackers." It characterizes both as sentimental luxuries left over from our days of abundant resources and open Frontiers and asserts that, in a modern society, the laws of economics can no longer be evaded. The *Tribune* therefore uses the Indians as a stick with which to beat its own version of the *Herald*'s savage-philanthropist axis. For Reid, this includes agrarian reformers of the cheap-money persuasion, Grangers interested in railroad regulation, strikers and unionizers in general, southern poor whites, blacks, and of course Indians. But although it employs a similar pattern of association in support of an ideology of conservatism similar to that of the *Herald,* the *Tribune* does not build this complex around the narrative core of the Custer story in the way that the *Herald* does. For Reid, the story does not signify in quite the same way.[61]

As in the case of the reporting of the Black Hills expedition, political and sectional considerations shaped both the amount and the type of coverage given to the Last Stand by papers nationally. The Yankton *Dakotian* sounded the theme of most far-western papers on July 7 in its headline, "CUSTER AND HIS ENTIRE COMMAND SWEPT OUT OF EXISTENCE BY THE WARDS OF THE NATION AND SPECIAL PETS OF EASTERN ORATORS." The southern press took an anti-Grant position, and generally shared the *Herald's* views. However, southern coverage was nowhere near as extensive as that in the *Herald* and other New York papers. Local issues and preoccupations were overwhelmingly preeminent. In South Carolina, the coming election and the Hamburg Massacre preempted newspaper space in the *News and Courier*. Although some symbolic linkage between Indians and blacks would seem useful from a propagandistic point of view, such linkages were inhibited by persistent hatred for General Sherman and other Union commanders who had ravaged the state during the war. While this antipathy does not lead the journal into actual sympathy with the Indians, it prevents any sort of enthusiasm for the army's struggles.[62]

The Richmond *Enquirer* did use the Custer "massacre" as a device for attacking Grant and for reminding its readers of the primary bonds of racial loyalty. It called for a "war of extermination" on "all the warlike tribes" for the sake of self-preservation. "Either our people must kill the savages or else the savages will destroy our people." Its editorial on "The Indian Policy" noted that whenever a "barbarous and uncivilized race comes into constant contact with a supreme and civilized one, the inferior . . . passes out of existence." While people in the East regard a war of extermination with horror, they must be reminded that "our own welfare and that of our own race and color is nearer to us than that of the 'Red Warriors of the West.'" While the applicability of parts of this rhetoric to the southern race problem is obvious—the same "Easterners" were supposed to be friends of the blacks—the making of large-scale, national myth-ideological structures is beyond the *Enquirer's* scope and concern.[63]

The southern treatments of the story offer a necessary corrective to the impression by the Metropolitan dailies that the Custer battle was an event that had the same kind of significance throughout the whole of American culture. Those media institutions that were engaged in ideologically charged national issues did indeed make the event signify as myth and (in the case of the Republicans) as anti-myth. But for some kinds of cultural media, the Custer story is "non-myth"—it does not signify, or at least does not have the same kind of symbolic resonance as it has in the Metropolitan media. The South is one such case: its media and its culture were still more intensely concerned with the peculiar problems of locale and region than with national matters. A more interesting case is that of the labor journals of the northern cities: papers whose readers inhabited the same physical and cultural space as the readers of the *Herald*, but whose ideological orientation produced rather different kinds of responses to the Last Stand.

A survey of the treatment of the Last Stand and of Frontier issues in general by the labor papers of the 1873–80 period suggests that to the extent that labor spoke as a class "for itself," it did not adopt the myth-ideological framework of the Myth of the Frontier as an interpretive scheme. Moreover, when it did refer to that Myth, it tended to invert its terms and to choose identification with the forces that the Last Stand myth implicitly condemned. During those periods when the front pages of the New York and Chicago daily papers were devoted to displaying the triumphant progress of Custer through the Black Hills, or to mourning the catastrophe on the Little Big Horn, labor papers for the most part ignored these stories. The center of interest for many of them remained very close to home, concerned with affairs in their immediate region or the industry nationally. The *National Labor Tribune*, for example, published in Pittsburgh by the Iron-workers Union, took no notice of the Black Hills expedition in 1874 and mentioned it only in connection with a letter from a former union member who had joined the gold rush—it was a warning not to leave decent jobs for the false promise of sudden wealth, a rather perfunctory refutation of the whole gold-rush mystique on which the Frontier Myth so depended. The same paper briefly noticed the Last Stand but made no comment on it. Even the papers and journals published by organized miners gave little or no play to these stories although a gold rush might be expected to have some appeal for miners. Indeed, it may have been some fear of a loss of members to the gold fields that prompted the turning of a blind eye.[64]

Interest in the Frontier was higher in labor papers published in western cities, where there was a direct regional tie between the market for labor locally and the demand for transportation to the West. *The Work-ingman's Advocate* (published in Chicago, Detroit, and Cincinnati) felt compelled to address the issues presented by the Black Hills gold rush and the Last Stand, but it did so from an ideological perspective that was the direct opposite of the bourgeois dailies, whether Republican or Demo-crat. The issue for March 25, 1876, carried an article with a headline right out of the 1874 New York *World*: "Gold: from the Garden of Eden to the discovery of America." The eye habituated to the association of "gold" and "garden" in the Custer Black Hills dispatches is surprised to discover an analysis of the use of gold currency, the point of which is to analyze and discredit the myth that gold constitutes an absolute or fixed standard of value, and that new discoveries of gold will therefore provide a panacea in the form of money that is both hard and abundant and therefore cheap. An editorial in the same issue exposes "The Black Hills Humbug," by name, warns its readers against the myth of the new "El Dorado" and enjoins them to "*stay away.*" The gold rush is linked to the corrupt practices of stock speculators and government bureaucrats: "The Black Hills excitement will prove as big a fraud as the Emma Mine swindle. A few roving specu-lators and 'outfitters' will no doubt be benefitted . . . but the great masses of the people . . . will find out they have been egregiously fooled."[65]

Reporting on "The Indian Massacre" of Custer on July 10, the paper warned its readers that "It must not be forgotten that in almost every in-stance . . . the American government, through its agents, has been the aggressor." The Indians have been "cheated and wronged by a pack of shameless officials who should protect their interests." In this their condition is not unlike that of the workingmen, likewise driven from property or jobs and bilked of protection by their own government. The paper reiterated its opposition to the Black Hills gold rush in this new context, emphasizing its illegality, but recalling at the same time its admonitions about the relationship of such events to the defrauding of the American worker.[66]

The reactions of the *Irish World* of New York are particularly interesting because the ethnic character of the journal liberated it to some extent from the narrow identification of interest that might characterize ironworkers or coal miners. Moreover, the paper was involved in supporting the movement for Irish colonization of regions in the West and South as a refuge from repression and poverty in the homeland; yet it was ideologically bound to identify itself against the principle of extending Anglo-Saxon rule by dominating other and weaker races or nations. It reversed the language of the *Herald* and the *World* in its treatment of the invasion of Ashantee, equating the British with "Communists" and "barbarians" for their destruction of that African kingdom. Likewise, they condemned the police, not the "red" workers, for the violence that attended the Tompkins Square meeting.[67]

Ideological consistency on behalf of democratic principles outweighed even obvious self-interest in the *Irish World's* treatment of western affairs. Their editorials on the Indian policy published before the Black Hills expedition are essentially the same as those published after: they condemn the belief that "The Indian cannot be civilized" and that we "must have a policy of extermination" and answer that the Indian was eminently suited for civilization, if only treated fairly. Their response to the Last Stand was to print two letters from Wendell Phillips condemning Custer and the opponents of the Peace Policy, and an editorial condemning as "Unmanly Cant" the characterization of the battle as a "massacre." The specific target was the *Herald*, to which it coupled the hated "John Bull" to make a pair of associated villains like the *Herald's* Grant/Sitting Bull combination. They use, of course, the same epithet—"savage"—to characterize the enemy:

> But if SITTING BULL is a savage JOHN BULL is a hundred times a greater savage . . . the New York *Herald* says we should recall his memory with "respect and admiration" . . . "Exterminate them" [i.e., the Indians] Are these men Christianized? Are these journalists civilized? . . . these men are *not* American . . . [but] the descendants by blood or in spirit, of the brutal Tories of a century ago who warred against justice and sought to perpetrate a reign of fraud and wrong over men of all races. . . .

In contrast, Sitting Bull appears heroic and is given laurels for defeating "an accomplished military officer."

> Had SITTING BULL been massacred it would have been a "brilliant victory" and the flaming bulletins of our enterprising papers would flash the joyful news to their civilized readers at next morning's breakfast. SITTING BULL's unpardonable crime was in not letting himself get killed. Had he only granted us that small favor we could forgive him.

SITTING BULL is said to be a savage; and the simple fact that he stood between his people and extermination, by the most approved modern applicances, is to many persons ample proof he is such.[68]

From this, it appears clear that the matter of the West was of little interest and concern to the labor press; and even where western matters cropped up, ideological commitments to progressive principles absolutely determined the response, precluding their development of a racialist myth of the Last Stand. Nonetheless, where there is interest in the Frontier story, we see an infectious use of the term "savage" to identify the enemy. This usage is consistent, across ideological lines, throughout the period. Even Wendell Phillips invoked the metaphor of savage warfare to rebuke those who used the Last Stand as an excuse for exterminating the Indians. The real "Custer massacre," he said, was that committed on the peaceful Cheyenne at the Washita, and not the defeat in battle Custer had suffered at the hands of the Indians—whom Phillips regards as fighters in a cause at bottom more just than Custer's own. But the language of his condemnation is dependent for its force on the ideological language that identifies as "savage" those behaviors that are so unacceptable that they call into question the humanity of those who perform them: bloody indiscriminate violence, a genocidal blood lust extending to the murder of women and children, a morality based on the code of vengeance, a social order that abandons the rational social contract for some terrible bond of blood and fanaticism.

Thus the newspaper coverage of Custer's Last Stand converted that historical event into a myth: an object or symbol whose significations resonated with the full range of social and political conflicts that agitated centennial America. Although the media's varying treatments reflected sharp partisan divisions, they also confirmed the major points of an underlying consensus: an agreement on the appropriateness of the language of racialism to the definition of class difference, on the Indian war as an adequate model of progressive historical change, and on the importance of the Last Stand as a real-world event whose character confirmed the validity of the language and the historiographical model.

CHAPTER 19

The Indian War Comes Home: The Great Strike of 1877

The narrative core of the Last Stand myth centers on the heroic (or anti-heroic) figure of Custer. Every contemporary interpretation of the event, whatever its partisan purpose or ideological mission, necessarily began by offering its own reading of Custer's character and motives, his skill as a commander and degree of culpability for the defeat. The hero myth and the ideological symbol of the Last Stand story refer us to that traditional mythology in which American history is a grand-scale Indian war, and to a progress achieved through regenerative wars of extermination against a primitive racial enemy. But the Last Stand added a genuinely new twist to the ending: that race war might really end in victory for savage darkness.

Although Indian wars continued to occur in the West until 1890, they decreased drastically in scale and significance. The language of the Last Stand myth was consequently applied with more frequency and force to events within the Metropolitan regions of the United States. It was in these regions that the crucial struggles for political power, and for power to shape the relations of labor and management in industry, were being fought out, in struggles that episodically reached an extreme pitch of violence, verging (or appearing to verge) upon revolutionary insurrection. Events like the Great Strike of 1877 drew the concerned attention of myth-makers as a magnet draws iron.

But this shift of emphasis in the content of mythic stories from wilderness to city locales was well prepared by the Metropolitan bias already inherent in the forms, genres, and media of mythological discourse. In the traditional version of the Frontier Myth the nominal subject is an event occurring on the margins of civilization, which poses the most extreme test of the culture's value and its power to shape history. The Indian war symbol was meant to convey the idea that differences of race are the basis of differentials of power, that these distinctions are fixed by nature, and that where two races occupy the same space the weaker must be subjugated or exterminated. But though the symbol explicitly refers to the Frontier, its meanings are intended primarily for citizens within the social Metropolis. They serve as a warning to all classes of the consequences that must follow when a racially defined underclass rejects the tutelage of its natural rulers.

The Last Stand variant of the Frontier Myth has a similar provenance. Although the material consequences of the battle would be most strongly felt in the West, the symbolic force of the Last Stand would be registered most strongly in the Metropolis. Those who promulgated the Last Stand myth addressed it to those sections of the better classes who had been "unmanned" by the soft doctrines of philanthropy and had become reluctant to apply the strong hand of paternal authority. The Indians of the West were only metaphorically a threat to civilization; but their symbolic "race fellows"—the southern blacks, the "unsexed" feminists, the Mollie Maguires and urban tramps—these groups had the numbers, and perhaps in these hard times the motives, to strike a blow at civil order and to deploy their strength in the streets or at the ballot boxes against "the interests of property."

After 1876, the pace of labor strife accelerated, accompanied by larger waves of foreign immigration and further racial violence against blacks in the South and the Chinese on the West Coast. At the same time, the Indian wars ensured the continued employment of the metaphor of savagery as a way of defining the opposition of class and ethnic groups and the diffusion of the metaphor of savage warfare to describe the deepening violence and radicalism of the conflict. The Great Strike of 1877 played a role in organizing the symbolism of this period that is analogous to the role of the Last Stand in interpreting the events of 1873–76. Indeed, the two events drew on the same language and became part of the same myth.

The nature and extent of the labor strife of 1877 has been extensively analyzed elsewhere. Most historians seem to agree that the eruption of strikes along the lines of the major railroads was not a concerted national strike, but the result of the coincidence of widespread dissatisfaction among both organized workers and the disorganized urban poor, in the context of "hard times." The railroad corporations had, as we have noted, been hit extremely hard by the economic contraction that had followed Jay Cooke's bankruptcy in 1873. Railroad owner-managers and their political supporters had played active, perhaps even determining roles in the political struggles of 1874–76; and the settlement of North-South differences by the "Compromise of 1877" (through which Hayes was elected and Reconstruction ended) had been shaped by the pressure of railroad men and railroad interests. A common economic crisis had brought those competitors (or brought many of them) together for a common political end: the redirection of federal concern from southern politics to railroad finances. Federal help of various kinds was expected to help railroads refinance in the long run; and in the short run, the railroad men could also agree on the necessity for reordering their own operations to reduce their cost. The result was a simultaneous, and at least partially concerted, movement by the railroads to roll back the wages of their workers across the board and on every major line in the country.

This nationwide rollback was everywhere met by the counterdemands of workers who, like their employers, were facing hard times with diminished resources (and far fewer sources of outside aid than the railroad proprietors). When strikers resisting the railroads' rollback of wages—and other measures relating to working conditions and labor discipline that were regarded as tyrannical or unjust—actually "turned out" and attempted to obstruct rail traffic in Martinsburg, West Virginia, word of their action (and of the failure of state militia to suppress it) spread along the line of the Baltimore and Ohio Railroad, and onward through the entire national network of lines. Everywhere the similarity of issues and conditions produced similar results: organized railroad workers seizing the yards to combat the rollback, railroad proprietors obtaining militia support from sympathetic state governors. From a small skirmish at Martinsburg on July 16, the strike spread in less than a week to Baltimore and Pittsburgh and thence to every major city from St. Louis to New York. The confrontation between strikers and militia or police attracted crowds of rowdy young men in their teens, the unemployed and disaffected urban poor, and became foci (in some places) of mob action. The heavy-handed and incompetent response of railroad managers and politicians exacerbated class feelings and provoked counterviolence. The most spectacular instance came at Pittsburgh, when the Philadelphia militia—brought in because the local force sympathized with the strike—fired into an unarmed mob, igniting a full-scale riot in which the militia was besieged by strikers and citizens and driven out of the railroad yards, which were then burned. In most cities efforts were made by the organized workers to stave off violent confrontations, and in some cities worker-policemen maintained order; but these efforts were ignored by much of the press. In most places the strike produced a mixture of fear and sympathy. Indeed, one can speak of the nation as radically divided between those who sympathized with the grievances of the strikers and understood, though they might deplore, violence; and those who regarded organized labor by definition as a menace, saw the violence as evidence of "communism," and saw little distinction between the "laboring classes" and the "dangerous classes."[1]

For the large Metropolitan press the equation of the strikers and trade unionists in general with the "dangerous classes" or criminal classes had already become an important device of propaganda. Only by pointing up the differences between "honest workmen" and the "dangerous classes" (who were the Communists' "legitimate prey") could they drive a wedge between the strikers and their middle-class sympathizers. That this class was important is attested not only by the testimony of labor-oriented papers, but by the numerous instances in which militia or police sympathized or joined with strikers, and by the urgency with which the anti-strike press pleaded for a withdrawal of public sympathy from the strikers. The working, managerial, and proprietary classes of the industrial towns still formed a distinct and limited minority of the politically active classes in the United States, and each of them therefore had to bid for the suffrage of a large and ill-defined "middle class"—the class whose primary source of political information would be the newspapers, and the weekly or monthly magazines.

STRIKERS AS SAVAGES

The urban press consequently attempted to turn the middle class against the strikers by applying devices with which we have become familiar: using language from or references to the Indian wars (and other "race wars") to define the character of the dangerous classes and the nature of their threat to society. The New York *Tribune*, the *Graphic*, and the *Herald* ran their strike stories (and editorials) in parallel with their accounts of current Indian wars and the continuing Turkish massacres in the Balkans, just as they had done with Custer's Last Stand, the Hamburg Massacre, and the election in 1876.

However, there were new difficulties in the use of the Indian war metaphor in 1877. For one thing, the major Indian campaign of that year— the so-called Nez Percé War in the Northwest—did not match the Sioux War of 1876 in scale, in the stakes of battle, or in its promise of a clear-cut choice between the forces of civilization and those of savagery. The Nez Percé had been friends of the Americans since first contacted by Lewis and Clark in 1805; had aided the army in earlier Indian campaigns; and their reliance upon the camas root (rather than buffalo) for food made them less dependent on hunting and therefore easier to keep at home than the more nomadic Plains tribes. Moreover, the legislative and administrative acts by which they were deprived of their promised reservation (and their supplies of camas) were so egregiously unjust that even a James Gordon Bennett had to take notice. With the presidential canvass ended, there was no immediate occasion to turn Indian policy into a political football. It may even have been the case that the exterminationist fever of 1876 had burned itself out, leaving a residue of shame from which less threatening tribes than the Sioux might benefit.

But the paramount crisis of the Great Strike was the key factor in the revaluation of the Indian war metaphor in 1877. In 1876 the "war of classes" was merely a threat in the cities of the North; and that threat could be dramatized, and perhaps averted, by invocation of the real blood-and-massacre "war of races" then going on in the West (and perpetually "looming" in the South). In 1877 the polarities of the metaphor (Indian war = class war) were reversed: the reality of the class war far outweighed the reality and the symbolism of the Indian war. Moreover, the working-class "hostiles" were predominantly white, and largely American-born; in some instance, notably in California, they were even rabidly nativist. If the ideological task of the antilabor journalists was to enforce the association between strikers and Indian savages, then the project faced formidable difficulties, and required the making of some powerful new fictions and the revaluation of old ones.[2]

These circumstances forced some uncomfortable twists and turns in the argument of *Harper's Weekly*, which began its coverage of the "Railroad War" by discussing it on the same page with a view of the Nez Percé Indian war then raging in Idaho and Montana. Its editorial on the strike borrowed Indian war language to term the strikers "barbarous" as well as "anarchical" in their attack on "property itself." It spoke of the "massacre of innocent persons"; and it warned strikers of "the hopeless folly of struggling against the unconquerable instinct of the race." But *Harper's* had also to acknowledge that the strikers were members of "the dominant race upon this continent." That suggested the need for a large regular armed force to suppress their insurgency, comparable in quality to the forces used against secession and larger in size than those sent against Indians. However, *Harper's* did not want to face up to the contradictions implied in the "dominant race's principles and moral impulses," and therefore contradicted its call for military force by denying that anything more than "the moral instinct of the people" would be needed to carry the day for "property itself."[3]

The most significant way of tying the strikers to the savages—racially "denigrating" them and characterizing their action as a primitive reversion —was through the mediating symbol of the tramps and criminal classes. In editorials written during the Last Stand summer of 1876, the *Tribune* warned that American immunity from "that fierce and savage cruelty" which has characterized labor struggles in Europe may not be permanent, in view of the increase of lawlessness and other signs of "possible modifications of popular character" in dangerous directions. An editorial on "Molly Maguires and Tramps" warned that the rising tide of terrorism and crime among the laboring and unemployed classes had more than merely "hard times" behind it: "Employment has been scarce and wages low before, yet without developing anything like a dangerous class such as is now to be found in the Western and Middle States, and even in New England." American prosperity and plenty has enabled us to avoid a confrontation with these classes, but the end of an era of expansion may provoke a confrontation, from which the *Tribune* fears "There will be no mercy."[4] When the Great Strike finally erupted, the *Tribune* condemned the strikers as "barbarous" and made no distinction between organized labor and the dangerous classes. Like the Indians, they make war on civilization itself: "Every striker made war upon all civilized society when he countenanced the stopping of trains." But this is a doctrine that can apply more widely to include all those sectors of public opinion that sympathize with the demands of the workingmen.[5] Indeed, it is this group that is the target of the *Tribune*'s persuasive rhetoric.

The Indian analogy partly determined the kind of policy that could be conceived for dealing with the labor problem. The long debate over the Peace Policy had confirmed the long-standing belief that Indians as a race or class of beings were incapable of self-government, and that they could be kept in order or civilized only when put under the tutelage of the white race. Moreover, that tutelage had to be backed by the threat of force, a monopoly of which had to be possessed by the whites, since Indians could not be trusted with enforcing laws made for them. Although reservation authorities were forced to rely on Indian police, that reliance was always uneasy and subject to powerful critiques and interventions by military and other authorities. But the white working class had been—until 1877—presumed to possess the natural right of self-government, and the necessary moral character to use that right wisely. Not only were the legislatures in the hands of the people, but the military force of the state was vested primarily in popular militias, recruited and officered from among "the people." The professionals of the regular army were an almost "alien" force, whose work lay on the borders and beyond the frontiers of the Metropolis; when they had been used as an instrument of internal law enforcement in the Reconstruction South, the results had been problematic to say the least, and disastrous to say the worst. That role was being deliberately terminated by the withdrawal of southern garrisons in 1877.

The outbreak of the Great Strike "against property," and the response of the urban militias to that strike, caused conservative journalists to reassess the distinction between Indians and proletarians. Perhaps the savage-striker metaphor was literally true, and neither tribesman nor workingman was truly capable of self-government. There seemed to be evidence of this in the unwillingness of militiamen to suppress their fellow townsmen, and the marked tendency early in the strike for militia units to fraternize with and even join the strikers.

The solution toward which both the *Herald* and the *Tribune* were drawn—despite their antagonism on so many partisan issues—was the substitution of federal troops for militia in the quelling of internal social disturbances; and the adoption of a policy of "stern repression" and even military government in communities whose people had shown (by striking) an inability to govern themselves. To make the point clear, the *Tribune* parallels the response of militia units in the strike and in the Nez Percé War:

> The better part of valor is conspicuously displayed on each slope of the continent. The Pittsburg[h] home guards fraternized with the mob, and a militia company at Altoona stacked their arms in the depot. At the same time, the volunteers whom Gen. Howard dispatched [against Chief Joseph's Indians] quietly disbanded and retired contemplatively to their homes.[6]

The core of the example is the metaphorical equation of Indians and strikers, who represent a direct and unambiguous threat to society. In neither case are the militia forces drawn from the people capable of playing their assigned and necessary role as enforcers of social discipline. Only through an appeal to the superior, professional elite of the regular army can either struggle be settled.

To persuade the public to accept this policy, it is absolutely necessary for strikers to be perceived as savage and alien, and hence as legitimate subjects for the application of pure and disinterested force. American workers must be looked upon as if they were indeed the "refuse of the Paris Commune," foreign in blood and spiritually alienated from the American belief in property. "What we must come to," said the *Tribune*, is anarchy and communism, for

> so long as we have a large body of ignorant workingmen among us, depending upon daily wages which may at any moment be cut off, easily misled by demagogues, and tempted by the universal timidity of capital and corporations, the danger of mob violence will be a perpetual menace to our society. Many beautiful things

have been spoken and written about the dignity of labor. We shall make a dreadful mistake, however, if we allow ourselves to be deceived as to the real character of a good many of the lower classes in our large cities, in the coal and iron towns, and on the lines of railway. In becoming the refuge for the oppressed of all nations our country accepted a noble mission, but that mission has its perils and difficulties. The oppressed are not always the virtuous. We have taken into our body politic the refuse of the Paris Commune, incendiaries from Berlin and from Tipperary, some hundreds of thousands of European agitators, who are always at war with every form of government thus far known among civilized nations.[7]

The *Herald* initially took a viewpoint less violently antipathetic to the strike and the strikers than the *Tribune's*. However, the difference even at its widest was one of emphasis rather than real content. Both papers agreed on the basic tenets of "free trade" ideology: that labor was a commodity like any other, a species of property to be traded according to laws of supply and demand; that property was the foundation of civilization itself; and that the long-term interests of capital and labor were therefore identical, so that an attack by labor on capital was "insane" or "absurd." Both papers agreed that in this time of economic contraction, both labor and capital had to tighten their belts and "share the suffering"—although the *Herald* gave more weight to the suffering of the workmen than that of the capitalists, while the *Tribune* simply accused the workmen of refusing to bear their fair share. The *Tribune* at one point compares the necessity for workmen to support their families on a dollar a day to the decline in a capitalist's income from $10,000 to $5,000 per year—a shocking comparison, in a time when even army officers of field grade made less than $4,000 a year. The *Herald* takes a more populist tone and castigates the railroad managers sharply for "milking" their enterprises, and for their ostentatious display of ill-gotten wealth in a time of universal hardship.

The *Tribune* editorials addressed themselves primarily to the educated and property-owning classes, although "honest workmen" were also included in the *Tribune's* call. Its opposition to trade unions was an essential ideological principle; and it saw the strike as "Communistic and law-defying, against all law, order, and civilization . . ." The *Herald* conceived of its readership as including more of a working-class constituency; its goal was to convince the "responsible element" among the strikers to "call it off," and to dissuade New York's own laboring classes from participating. But as the "Railroad War" and the "War of Wages" developed and reached into the city, the *Herald's* anxiety increased; and when demonstrations erupted, it became very nearly as antilabor as the *Tribune* (though never quite so nativist).[8]

This change of sympathies was more apparent than real—a device meant to display the *Herald's* "fair mindedness" as prelude to its agreement with the antilabor sentiments of the *Tribune* and other conservative papers. Yet even before the outbreak of the strike in mid-July, it was speaking of dissatisfied Indians as holding "indignation meetings" like white workingmen. As soon as the tendency of the local railroad strikes to become national manifested itself, the *Herald* made the implied association literal. A headline on the front page of the July 23 issue proclaimed, "INSURRECTION! / . . . The Great Railroad Strike Becomes a Savage War." Four days later, an Indian raid on a western settlement is referred to as "The Red Man's Strike."⁹

These literal applications of the metaphor were buttressed by more subtle and indirect, but nonetheless systematic associations, including the borrowing of words with distinctive Indian war connotations for use in strike stories (and vice versa). For example, the *Herald* consistently refers to leading union officials, like the head of the Trainmen's Union, as "Chiefs" —e.g., "Chief Arthur." A story on the pursuit of Chief Joseph's warriors is headlined, "JOSEPH'S BAND / The Murderous Reds Closely Pursued by Federal Troops." Beside this story is an account of the suppression of strikers by government troops. Its headline echoes the Indian war headline in typography and layout, and the content also is parallel: "FIGHTING STRIKERS . . . / Federal Troops Sent." This parallelism is reinforced by the use of "Reds" rather than redskins or some other term in the Chief Joseph headline—the usage is usually reserved to characterize Communards, agitators, and the German Social Democratic Party. Thus the pursuit of "murderous reds" by federal troops becomes a figure that metaphorically unifies the response to both crises.¹⁰

For the *Herald* the events of July 16–22 required a definitive turn toward the task of tying strikers and tramps into a single package. In that period the strikes had burgeoned from sporadic confrontations in backwaters like Martinsburg to large-scale battles for possession of the rail yards of major cities. An editorial (July 24) on "The Situation" warns that the respectable strikers might be losing control of things; and another on "Shifting the Responsibility" asserts that control has already been lost. It does no good, says the *Herald*, to say that strikers did not themselves pillage. By invoking "the spirit of the 'Red Republic' " they liberated the dark forces and dangerous classes ordinarily suppressed in civil life. They are a "dark" and criminal lot, characterized by passions that verge on madness. The "insanity" of the union men has released all the "Unsettled Humors" of society,

> the hard customers, the bummers and tramps, the Mollie Maguires and the Communists, the hoodlums, the pickpockets and many scarcely describable classes of roughs . . . [the strike] was a carnival of disorder, without any other significance so important as that involved in its startling exhibition of the sort of subterranean humanity we are unconsciously producing.

Paradoxically, this upwelling of insane "humors" is not purely irrational: it is directed by a conspiratorial and malign set of intelligences, whose hand is revealed in the simultaneity of the outbreaks, and whose preparations appear in the behavior of the strikers, who go about their destructive work like soldiers drilled for battle. But this is precisely the same kind of paradox exemplified by the Indian war of 1876, in which the unleashing of the violent and insane passions of the red men is given power and direction by the conspiratorial intelligence of the Indian Bureau, and the evil genius of the "Sioux Napoleon" Sitting Bull. It follows that to suppress this kind of uprising, stern measures are required, first involving a complete withdrawal of fellow feeling with the strikers, and ending with a system for forcibly suppressing such outbreaks.[11]

In "A Plan of Operations Needed," the *Herald* declares that the rioters have the advantage of "the public" because they "formed their plan beforehand . . . to starve the public into submission." The only recourse, says the *Herald*, is for the railroads to hire new hands and protect them with armed guards, to break the power of the strike and let the strikers "smell powder." The military flavor of the response is echoed in continual calls for upgrading of the militia and police, or use of the regular army to suppress strikes in the future. The *Tribune* had been enthusiastic about military solutions from the start, and spoke of punishment in the exterminationist terms usually reserved for Indians. "It is a pity that the very first resistance to law was not met by the shooting of every rioter within range of a musket ball . . . Napoleon was right. It is always a blunder as well as a crime to exasperate a mob without exterminating it."[12]

All of the papers took occasion to note that the present regular army could not combine Indian fighting and policing the cities, unless increased: the *Herald* inclined to prefer a well-trained and indoctrinated militia, but the *Tribune* thought "The only safe plan is to have a regular army large enough to be of prompt service in such emergencies." Partisan journals tended to blame "the other political party" for fomenting discontent, and they disagreed on the forms that forceful suppression of strikers should take. However, they agreed that force was required. The New York *Daily Graphic* blamed Democrats for reducing the army appropriation, and at first called for a widespread vigilante movement by the "propertied classes, [which] . . . with their habits of command and cooperation, can easily get the upper hand." This vision of an aristocratic solution by direct action became part of the upper-class myth of the strike; but the *Graphic*, in a more practical mood, sought to embody such principles—order, discipline, command—in a system or institution. It called for a reorganization of the militia, beefing up the regular army for an urban as well as a border mission, and the development of a national police force, to be recruited from the better elements of the working class itself. Here the *Graphic* touches on the underlying linkage of race and class, when it asserts that the government must take the lead in forming such a force, because the railroad capitalists, unlike southern slaveholders, are not "successful in implanting in the breasts of the inferior race sentiments of respect and gratitude," and so fail to gain the "confidence of the laboring classes."[13]

The *Herald* did not go this far, but it too saw military solutions as essential. But it associated military virtue and power not with the disinterested army professionals, but with the managerial class. An editorial on "Arbitration" compares the typical captain of industry to a military commander, in his grasp of affairs and his ability to organize and lead men. This view of the "militaristic" style in labor discipline is paralleled by earlier editorials, in which the turning over of Indian reservations to the War Department is seen as leading to a specifically industrial productivity and discipline—and hence a rise in civilization—among the Indians. "Sitting Bull's Land" declares that "The cheapest and most effective way to civilize savages is to enlist all the able-bodied males as soldiers," and set them to fighting other Indians. This proposal draws on the same philosophy as the *Graphic's* call for a national police drawn from workers. And it recalls too, the managerial ideology behind the proposals of Charles Francis Adams, of using military colonies to civilize the freed blacks by putting them under military discipline and control; such measures, says the *Herald*, will "accustom them to regular habits, cleanliness and settled industry, which can be enforced by military rules and in no other way so well."[14]

The rules themselves are specifically those normally laid down for industrial workers coming to the factory from preindustrial or peasant backgrounds; for the Indian, the specific tasks would be agricultural:

> As a savage he has lived an unsystematic, haphazard life; if he is to be civilized, he must be habituated to regularity, system, order, cleanliness in his person and house; he must be trained to do certain things at certain fixed hours, in certain established ways. Having been brought thus far he ought to be shown the advantage to himself of laboring industriously and productively.

Having begun to produce goods, he can make the transition to participation as small farmer-capitalist in the free market: "If when he has raised a crop he may sell it and pocket the proceeds, he is likely to become habitually industrious." Thus in making the transition to society, the Indian reenacts both the agrarian stage and the industrializing phase through which white America has already passed. But the Indian must do this under military authority, precisely because his rite of passage must be conducted within a post-Frontier society.

It is appropriate that his judge and mentor in this process should be an army officer because (for the *Herald*) this class of men embodies all of the inborn virtues of gentility, hardened and systematized by lifelong training. The West Point officer combines the moral authority of a recognized cultural elite with the authority that resides in the possession of force, and the professional skill to use it. It is not his engineering or technocratic skills that make him a model for the new industrial manager, but his skill in subordinating and controlling the labor of half-civilized white men:

> West Point officers . . . are specifically fitted for this work. Their whole lifelong training has made them rigidly systematic. They are accustomed to exercise authority over rude men . . . they are familiar with the best means ever invented to impress such habits upon persons unaccustomed to them . . . [A] West Point officer of good character is a man thoroughly fitted to take charge of a band of savages and induct them by a slow but entirely effective process into the customs of civilized life. He knows how to exact respect from his inferiors . . . and knows how to drill men after a pattern . . . He knows also how to keep men sufficiently employed, and how necessary it is to do so.[15]

Treating the relationships of employers and employees in terms of the military/reservation-Indian model implies a recognition of the "end of the Frontier"—the end of that time when primitive individualists among the lower orders can be allowed to roam at will and without control in search of fulfillment. In a society made tightly interdependent by the establishment of industrial systems of production, "A strike on the great railway lines," says the *Tribune*, "involves something more" than questions of individual rights and freedoms. "The entire business of the community is disrupted" by a kind of domino effect in which stoppages in one key industry cause shutdowns everywhere.

The burden of the argument is that the complexity of industrial society makes it impossible for America to maintain its full commitment to democratic principles. The organization of workingmen into unions capable of striking, indeed the general use of democratic political power to regulate industry or protect people from the power of corporate wealth, can no longer be permitted or sanctioned by popular political ideology. Like members of hostile Indian tribes, "the innocent" among the workingmen must be made to "suffer with the guilty" because "such is the law of civilized society." The concept is in fact exactly the opposite of what a free-labor ideologist like Lincoln would have called "civilized": what the *Tribune* has done is to equate civilization with the special form of corporate organization adopted by American industrial capitalists.[16]

This position is an extreme reversal of the *Tribune*'s prewar role as spokesman for the more radical programs of democratic reform, abolition, and free labor. And the transformation goes deeper, even to the inversion of the primary commitment to the ideal of a republic of universalized entrepreneurship—a position that, ironically, resembles that of the antebellum southern critics of northern competitive economics and democracy. The *Tribune* even assails the workingmen's desire for self-improvement and better standards of living as the root of the present troubles. It thus rejects the motives for upward mobility which were hitherto seen as the very basis of the worker's stake in American society, the foundation of both our social peace and our economic expansiveness and productivity. "Some Plain Words" condemns workers who have maintained their mobility by continually "throwing away small wages that can be had for the sake of dreamy possibilities of better." And while the *Tribune* does not explicitly endorse the Reverend Henry Ward Beecher's assertion that workers could, in fact, subsist on bread and water if they but had the manly fortitude to try, it does assert that the loss of wages could be made up by "economy and self-denial in . . . indulgences, or in modes of life, rates of living, or places of boarding"—this at a time of increasing food prices and scandalous housing conditions.[17]

But this sort of preachment went hard against the grain of both popular expectations and against the ideological tradition embodied in the Frontier Mythology, both of which tied the continued allegiance of the people to American republicanism to continually expanding land and opportunities. Thus both the *Herald* and the *Tribune* mix their calls for retrenchment and self-limitation with visions of a Frontier safety valve.

Of the two, the *Herald* was the more devoted to the concept, as befitted its Jacksonian traditions and its sponsorship of expansion at the expense of Indians and Mexicans. Its editorial on "The Situation" of July 26, 1877, was devoted to a systematic statement of the doctrine of the Frontier as safety valve, in terms that clearly anticipate the doctrines of Turner and the later Turnerians. Bennett urges the discontented workingmen to look to the prospect of the open land of the West for redress, rather than to labor unions. Although the Frontier is not what it was earlier in the century, "we have still a very great quantity of uncultivated land, which the government offers without charge to actual settlers." This was a rather hyperbolic way to describe the Homestead system as it then existed; but Bennett wants to substitute the appeal of the Frontier Myth for the reality of the wages question, and so he gives his imagination free play in presenting past history and present facts.

According to Bennett, the existence of the Frontier had prevented the rise of socialism and other forms of radicalism because it provided the kinds of opportunity most likely to be seized by the best of the working class: "those who are really strong and influential, and who are discontented with their position and hopes of life in the more densely settled parts of the country"—in short, the natural leaders around whom revolutionary movements would gather in less favored lands. "Hundreds of thousands" of such men, "who would have been dangerous in any European country," have been enabled to make better lives for their families in the West. Thus the existence of the open land of the West has prevented the Communists from enlisting "the brains of the working class"—these have gone west, instead of staying in the Metropolis to "rail at society, or join a trade union, or become strikers."

The material benefit thus conferred by the existence of the Frontier is buttressed by an ideological factor. Because the existence of the Frontier is "so well known and so universally understood among our working people," public opinion has been (or should be) deterred from sympathizing with the strikers. "In Europe," says Bennett, "a striker who claims that he 'must live' has a colorable case; [but] in this country, even in these hard times, it is very well understood by everybody . . . that if a man is dissatisfied with his work or his pay he can . . . go West and settle on public land." If he cannot afford to do so immediately, then he knows that by hard work and frugality he can soon accumulate enough money to do so. "If he declines to do this, and becomes instead a chronic grumbler, he is pretty certain to lose the respect of the community."[18]

Bennett wishfully misrepresents the character of the "opportunity" professed by the Homestead system, the feasibility of workers' saving enough to purchase a homestead, and the community feeling toward labor organizations and strikers. Nonetheless, the appeal of this position was great since it complemented the traditional belief that the prospect of self-improvement was the surest way of holding the lower classes within the existing system of law and property. Even the *Tribune* found the doctrine appealing, suggesting that "A Remedy for Labor Troubles" did indeed lie in the nation's heritage of unused land. In terms reminiscent of

the Bleeding Kansas era, it declared that "The Homestead Law is the im-
perishable barrier which the United States has raised between free labor
and oppression"; and it echoes the assertions made by Lincoln in 1858–59
that a majority of American citizens own property and hire labor or are
looking forward to that position as one surely and speedily within their
reach.

In this context, the Frontier acts as a litmus test dividing the inferior
from the superior types within the working class. Those who resemble Indians in their inability to postpone gratification join unions and strike; those
who are capable of rising to full civilization are abstemious, save money
from their wages, and aim at acquiring a homestead. "The End of It" (the
Great Strike) will come when workingmen in general realize just how
much land is still out there for the taking—the *Tribune*'s August 11 editorial echoes both the sound and the sense of Bennett's on "The Situation."
It ends with a contrast of proletarian and agrarian that might have come
out of the 1840s. The difference in the portrait is that where a Jacksonian
would have emphasized the need of sweeping away monopolistic obstacles
to agrarian cupidity, the *Tribune* places the onus for failure to reach the
Frontier on the character of the worker himself:

> There, next door to all this anarchy and want and vicious idleness,
> are abundance and health, wasting for the industrious man to
> come and take them. Here is the grimy workman with his wife
> stifling in town alleys, and his children imbibing vice at every
> breath, and yonder the farmer, secure among his beeves and
> corn, his family well fed and clothed and in their right minds.
> We only offer these facts as facts. Our readers may make their
> own deductions.[19]

Other papers were more consistent in their rejection of the idea that
the Frontier and the Homestead Law still worked as a practical safety
valve. Some of them noted that the costs of taking up western lands were
hardly as cheap as the *Herald* and the *Tribune* implied (to be had "almost
without money and without price"). But the crux of their rejection of the
idea derived less from an accounting of land prices than from their assessment of the characterological weakness of the new proletariat. The *Graphic*
calls the *Herald*'s "go west" advice "Cheap and Senseless" because "the
ordinary wear and tear of life [in industry] have unfitted them [the
workers] to withstand the diseases and privations inseparable from pioneer
life." Given the human material attracted and produced by industrial society, the Frontier safety valve—even if it can be said to persist—has been
rendered useless. Our policy for dealing with our urban savages therefore
must be based on the same perception of the closing Frontier that underlies
our more rigorous Indian policy.[20]

THE MYTH-IDEOLOGY OF A PROGRESSIVE
RULING CLASS: THE NATION IN 1876-1877

The clearest and most comprehensive and consistent statement of the Indian war approach to the Great Strike and its related issues was that in the *Nation*. Founded by E. L. Godkin, the *Nation* was independent in politics and "liberal" in the classical rather than the modern sense. Godkin had favored the abolition of slavery and certain measures of Reconstruction; but he was essentially elitist in his interpretation of class conflicts and thus opposed the egalitarian and philanthropic aspects of Republican policy. His ideas were highly influential, not only during the period under discussion, but afterwards; and a direct line of descent may be traced from Godkin to the progressivism of Theodore Roosevelt.[21]

Godkin's elitism combined a tacit belief in the inherited superiority of the white race with the belief that existing class differences represented the working out of the logic of characterological superiority. The rich were rich and the powerful powerful because they were more clever, industrious, deserving. "There is hardly a good thing in [the world] that is not the result of successful strife," and the victors in the struggle for property were therefore entitled to their special station by both law and the necessities of natural progress. Philanthropy which seeks to meliorate or undo the necessity of struggle is therefore pernicious to the progress of both the individual and the race. The argument, which was even then a common one, anticipates the codification of such opinions under the banner of Social Darwinism a decade later.[22]

On this ground, the *Nation* condemned the establishment of "Free Soup" kitchens to relieve the distress of the urban poor during the hard winter of 1875–76. Such benevolence served to "degenerate" the moral character of the poor, who would be encouraged to live in idleness rather than seeking work; and deprive them of the chastening experience of suffering and the lesson of the consequences of their faults as workmen—since the *Nation's* presumption was that the fact of unemployment was proof of inadequate ability or diligence on the job. But the worst of "The Educational Influences of Free Soup," the *Nation* declared, were chiefly expressed in the decline of public virtue and respect for the law. The poorest classes of "vagabonds" and "criminals," receiving soup at a police station, would lose that fear of the "baton" which is the only basis of obedience to law and morality among the dangerous classes. At the next level of social order, "the common laborer" will be encouraged by the sight of vagabonds eating free soup to demand of the government a city job—as the Tompkins Square "Communists" had already done. At the next highest level, the "mechanic" will demand laws favorable to his industry and his class—protection as against free trade—and the similarly situated farmer will demand "Granger" laws. Thus, although "we are not to be understood as arguing that free soup alone has actually produced all the harmful theories above indicated," in fact the logic of "Free Soup" does inevitably point to government by philanthropists and radicals, and to the overturn of social order. Therefore, "Free soup must be prohibited, and all classes must learn that soup of any kind, beef or turtle, can be had only by being paid for."[23]

Similar values are applied to the discussion of the Indian and southern labor policies. The *Nation* condemns the corruption of the Indian Bureau which views reservation Indians as a kind of "pauper"—like the vagabond of the cities made so by the provision of an Indian equivalent of free soup. But the Indian's pauper status, while it might be fostered by philanthropy, has its sources in racial character. The theme is echoed in the *Nation*'s review of Richard L. Dugdale's book on *The Jukes*—an early study of the supposed heritability of moral traits and tendencies to criminality. Under the title "Cumberers of the Ground," the reviewer extends Dugdale's study to prove that pauperism is the result of biologically inherited traits— which, in American terms, translate as *racial* traits—rather than being a product of social and economic forces. The review suggests that whole races of paupers and potential paupers exist, some of whom are nonwhite and uncivilized and hence clearly visible. But there are also hidden races of paupers within "white" populations as well, an invisible tribe no more capable of making the latest forward leap of civilization than the Indians have been. These cumberers of the ground, as the epithet implies, are "chaff" and waste matter, and deserve at best exclusion from society—at worst they may merit extermination through judicial punishment or eugenic measures.[24]

The underlying racism of the *Nation*'s views is sharpened in the 1876 discussion of the Hamburg and the Custer massacres. The Hamburg affair found the *Nation* critical of the behavior of the whites towards the blacks. But being politically independent, the *Nation* did not use the occasion, as did the *World* and the *Tribune*, for apologetics either for the Democrats or or the Republicans and Negroes. Rather (like the *Herald*), it condemns the incident as the result of the violent impulses of two classes—white and black—comprising the "lower orders" of southern society. The elites of both parties are to blame for not taking full responsibility for the control of the lower orders that they are supposed to provide. The editorial also distinguishes white from black among the lower orders and expects more from the white than the black. By attacking the Negro militia, the whites have lowered themselves to a Negro level, a savage level comparable to that of the Ashantee—the so-called black Indians of Africa:

> Nothing the Negroes had done or tried to do . . . could make the shooting of the prisoners anything but a piece of atrocious savagery. It is ridiculous for a community in which such things are sanctioned to talk of itself as civilized. There is no use in being white in color if your conduct is that of an Ashantee . . . In resorting to such modes of repressing negro excesses, the Southern men reach the lowest negro level.[25]

However, the wrongs of the white treatment of blacks could be condoned so long as those wrongs pointed toward the ultimate "right" of black subordination and had a favorable effect on economic production:

The devotion of the Southern whites to the past-time of massacring the laboring population of the South since the war has sadly interfered with the development of the old duello. The superior attraction of the new sport cannot be denied, inasmuch as it is much safer, being practised chiefly against unarmed males or women and children . . . and its only drawback—the fear that excessive indulgence in it might lead to a diminution of industry and consequent yield of the arable soil—being entirely removed by the extraordinary fact, proved by experience, that carnage and slaughter of the laboring population has a beneficial effect on the crops, particularly cotton, the yield of which, year by year, shows a steady increase of murder and arson.[26]

The *Nation's* response to Custer's Last Stand focused its use of the race war as a metaphor for the consequences to society of its philanthropically softening the iron laws of supply and demand and of industrial discipline. In an editorial titled "Our Indian Wards," the *Nation* praises the government for doing away with the fiction of Indian self-government and making them wards of the nation like the freedmen. However, it regards the reservation policy as a well-intentioned failure, fatally compromised by its "Free Soup" principles. These have produced a degeneracy in the Indians, but such a philanthropic regimen would "debauch white men of any race; no wonder it debauches savages." In his primitive state, the necessities of hunting for food at least keep the Indian from idleness and indolence. Although we have tried "in a half-hearted way" to translate this predatory energy into agrarian labor, "our main expenditure of funds has been in making him a lazy vagabond, subsisting by alms which he takes for tribute, eating meat he has not worked for, and acquiring the morals of a tramp in lieu of those of a warrior." Echoing Custer in *My Life on the Plains*, Godkin says he prefers "Sitting Bull or any 'wild Indian' " to the "repulsive" though "peaceable" creature seen on the reservation. It is "a disgrace to our civilization" that the Indian eats unearned bread, and is "allowed, in sight of a United States fort, to bring up his children as idle, vicious, ignorant, filthy, and dependent as himself. The whole system is shocking. There is nothing in our religion, or manners, or laws, or traditions, or policy to give it any countenance or support."

This put Godkin for practical purposes in the same camp with Belmont and Bennett, whose projects he otherwise rejected. They were agreed that Indians must be compelled to work or starve, whatever the Treaty of 1868 stipulated; and their title to the land was not to stand in the way of progressive projects requiring that land for their fulfillment. Godkin also accepted the necessity of exterminating the Indians if, as Bennett asserted, they were incapable of consenting to civilization. Our present policies, says Godkin, "degrade the tame Indians into lazy and filthy paupers, preparatory to their extinction through disease, drunkenness and the loss of that vital power which results from total lack of occupation." Thus he concludes— without moral objection—that, "In fact, our philanthropy and our hostility tend to about the same end, and that is the destruction of the Indian race, and there is nothing in our experience to settle which is the more rapid progress." The major grounds of choosing an Indian policy involve an assessment of the relative speed and efficiency of means; they do not affect the end, which is always the same.

But Godkin does not stop at the Indians. He asserts that the Indian policy exemplifies the folly of American philanthropic politics during the last forty years, and more immediately in the Reconstruction of the South. In his peroration, Godkin ties together the philanthropic approach to racial policy (Indians and blacks) with the liberal approach to the laboring and urban population; asserts that in each case these policies have led to degeneration; and poses for each of the problem classes the possibility that failure to integrate with bourgeois society will put them in the way of "extermination." And the justification for all of this is derived from the catastrophe visited upon General Custer and his men—the event that reveals the possible consequences for civilization of taking too lenient a course with savages, white or red. The Custer tragedy has called

> public attention with more than usual earnestness to the treatment of the Indians. There is . . . now a loud demand for their "extermination"—a course for which there is something to be said, if by extermination is meant their rapid slaughter. But if they are to be exterminated, why any longer pauperize them, and then arm them? What would be said if the city of New York, after lodging its thousand tramps in comfortable idleness during the winter, were to arm them on leaving the almshouse in the spring with a good revolver and knife . . . to deliver to them alive the animals they were to eat, and were to allow them to kill them themselves in mock chase with lances? But why should it be worse to do this thing to savage whites than to savage Indians? . . . The agency abomination should come to an end. The tribal organization ought to be broken up, and the people scattered in such a way as to make them easily amenable to the ordinary civilizing influences of our society, and, let us add, to make it easy for the sheriff to get at them. They ought to have no "ponies" which they have bought. Fancy our tramps starting on their spring journey not only armed, but mounted, with saddle-bags for their provisions and flowers in their buttonholes.[27]

The *Nation*, then, adopted as its basic political premises the primacy of the needs of capital (productivity, docility in the under- or working classes) over the moral imperatives of liberal or philanthropic ideology; the relative or proximate coincidence of racial character with class status; and the subordination of the rights of the underclasses—including, perhaps, the right to existence itself (if we take the talk of "extermination" seriously)—to the needs of the capitalist economy and social order. It had adopted these premises unambiguously in relation to Indians, and with some qualifications in regard to blacks—the difference lying in the greater expectation that blacks could be made to accommodate to the productivity requirements of the new order. In regard to white labor, full subscription to these principles was offset by the ideological tradition of informed consent of a majority of "intelligent farmers and mechanics." But insofar as the industrial work force had come to be characterized by immigrant labor, and insofar as it chose unionization over individual bargaining, the *Nation* tended to consider it warily. Indeed, even before the railroad strike of 1877, the *Nation* had published articles condemning the Locomotive Engineers and Trainmen's Unions as "the public enemy." While it recognized the need for some sort of reform in the relations between labor and capital, it held that these should take the form of what later scholars have called "welfare capitalism"—the provision of better housing and certain forms of insurance by the employer to establish a mutual bond of loyalty.[28]

When the Great Strike did break out, the *Nation* ceased to make its earlier qualifications and moved directly into the rhetoric of class war as race war. Its definitive editorial on "The Late Riots" appeared on facing pages with an editorial on responsibility for "The Idaho War"—referring to the Nez Percé troubles. The latter article tended to exonerate the Indians from responsibility for their insurrection: they had been cheated and robbed by an alliance of predatory speculators and Indian Bureau philanthropists. "This desperate rise of a free, warlike, and uncivilized people against insupportable wrong done by its professed guardian has been the natural and necessary result of Congressional neglect . . ." Sympathy for the Indians in this instance contrasts strikingly with the possibility of "extermination" raised in the editorial on Custer's Last Stand. In that instance, the figure of the urban pauper had been invoked, to show how dangerous it was to feed and arm the Indians; here the partially justified rebellion of the Indians is used to point up how *un*justified is the rebellion of the strikers, whose "guardians" have been foolish but not unjust. Further, the Indians' rebellion is seen as their "natural" response because the Indians are "uncivilized" as well as free. When civilized or pseudo-civilized men, living in the heart and not on the border of civilization, assert the same right, they are neither natural nor noble—they imperil the heart of civilization, and must be repressed as sternly as the Indians.[29]

The editorial on "The Late Riots" begins by declaring that the labor insurrection has served to discredit the faith of both American and foreign observers of the American democratic experiment. There had been a "faith" in the idea that outside the exceptional economy of the South, America—aided by a combination of republican institutions and great natural resources (i.e., the Frontier)—had "solved the problem of enabling labor and capital to live together in political harmony, and that this was the one country in which there was no proletariat and no dangerous class." The Great Strike has spoiled not only these hopes, but even "the fondly cherished hopes of many millions about the future of the race"—that is, the general perfectibility of mankind. Unlike other journals, which sought to deny or minimize the importance of the strike and of the strikers and so to preserve the illusion of American exceptionalism, the *Nation* seemingly accepts the strike as the revelation of a new reality: America has a significant proletariat and dangerous class. That class is at war, not with a monarchy or tyranny, but with "society itself" and with the American premise of the perfectibility, good will, and good sense of mankind:

Vast additions have been made to our population . . . to whom
American political and social ideal appeal but faintly, if at all, and
who carry in their very blood traditions which give universal
suffrage an air of menace to many of the things which civilized
men hold most dear.

The equation of the strikers with immigrants has no basis in reality—
the native presence, numerically speaking, was as marked as the foreign,
especially among the organized and skilled workers whom the *Nation* had
declared were the real "public enemies." However, the *Nation* sees the
proletariat as an "alien" presence, a permanently propertyless class of
whites never envisioned in Jeffersonian or Jacksonian ideology; and it
associatively links the alienness of this class with biological/ethnic alienness. The premise is racialist: anti-American ideas are spoken of as an aspect
of "blood," not culture, and hence are as unchangeable as the proverbial
leopard's spots, the Ethiopian's hue, or the Indian's savagery. The consequence of this revelation is the call—implicitly—for a restriction on the
right of "universal suffrage," or at least the posing of a choice between
democratic suffrage and the preservation of civilization.

The theme is taken up and extended in the editorial's conclusion, which
calls for either a change of heart by liberals and philanthropists, or else a
form of self-censorship—since speaking of rights to the new underclass
merely incites them to savage violence and inordinate ambition, in just the
way that treating Indian nations as independent states (rather than wards)
was said to have inflated their sense of both their rights and their wrongs.
The *Nation* demands the

> . . . exercise of greater watchfulness over their tongues by phi-
> lanthropists, in devising schemes of social improvement, and in
> affecting to treat all things as open to discussion, and every ques-
> tion as having two sides, for purposes of legislation as well as for
> purposes of speculation . . . Some of the talk about the laborer
> and his rights that we have listened to . . . such as the South
> Carolina field-hand, to reason upon and even manage the interests
> of a great community, has been enough, considering the sort of
> ears on which it now falls, to reduce our great manufacturing
> districts to the condition of the Pennsylvania mining regions, and
> put our very civilization in peril. Persons of humane tendencies
> ought to remember that we live in a world of stern realities, and
> that the blessings we enjoy have not been showered upon us like
> the rain from heaven.

The passage links the southern Negro field hand with the Pennsylvania
coal miner (here equated with Mollie Maguires), and declares that speaking to such people of their rights threatens the existence of civilization itself. The theme is continued, with parallels being extended to nonwhite
races of Asia and Africa; and the agitation of the labor cause is presented
as something which will reverse the course of both civil and biological
evolution, sending the race back toward savagery and even bestiality:

> Our superiority of the Ashantees or the Kurds is not due to right thinking or right feeling only . . . In trying to carry on the race to better things nobody is wholly right or wise. In all controversies there are wrongs on both sides, but most certainly the presumptions in the labor controversy have always been in favor of the sober, orderly, industrious, and prudent, who work and accumulate and bequeath. It is they who brought mankind out of the woods and caves, and keep them out; and all discussion which places them in a position of either moral or mental inferiority to those who contrive not only to own nothing, but to separate themselves from property-holders in feeling or interest, is mischievous as well as foolish, for it strikes a blow at the features of human character which raise man above the beasts.

Only by placing power in the hands of those classes of the enlightened who have warred on savagery and bestiality, even among their own people, will the progressive trend be preserved and a reversal of direction prevented.

To this end, military force is required, and the principle of force is to be acknowledged as never before in a republican government.

This is because the rebellion of workers took the form of "mob" action, according to the *Nation*; and mob action is essentially irrational, partaking of insanity, "and its conduct has all the fitfulness and incomprehensibleness of that of a wild beast." Appeals to reason when dealing with such beasts or savages are impotent; only a careful indoctrination in *"the habit* of obedience" will answer the problem. But should indoctrination fail, then there must be adequate force to whip the beast back to its den; and the *Nation* sees a larger and better trained regular army as the only solution. The militia is inadequately disciplined and responds to mob provocation either by shooting indiscriminately or by recognizing the striker as a brother and refusing to shoot. On the other hand, the mob knows the regular soldier to be part of a "machine," commanded by one who is a professional, committed unquestioningly to the defense of law and property, an officer and gentleman. The symbolic remedy for the recalcitrant instruments of industry is a force whose very form incarnates the industrial principles of discipline, professionalized or elite central control, obedience by the mass, and high productivity or efficiency. The latter is expressed in terms of the mob's terror of the army, for "when it strikes, [it] strikes like the flail of destiny, without remorse, or pity, or misgiving." In the army, as in industry, man ceases to be man but becomes instrument or machine; and as the highest expression of the industrial ethic, the regular army is the perfect instrument of repression.[30]

The point is reiterated in subsequent editorials. "The Rioters and the Regular Army" asserts that our need of a standing army is even greater than that of England because of the wider spread of "communistic" ideas among the people—the consequence, presumably, of both immigration and native liberalism. A second editorial on "Why the Regular Army Should Be Increased" states the analogy between army and industrial society explicitly, declaring that there will always be a class of "paupers" in society just as every army has its "stragglers and shirks; and we have no reason to expect to see a society without dregs or 'residuum,' until we are able to lay our finger on the very springs of character, and shape a child's destiny in its cradle." The omnipresence of the dangerous class in the cities—"this mass of envious discontent," "the malingerer, the drunkard, the spendthrift, the rogue, the lazy and idle and vicious thousands who every year, from one cause or another, lose their places on the ladder of life"—and the vulnerability of an industrial concentration to sabotage and riot means that "To leave society exposed to such risks, through a sentimental horror of 'bayonets' is to be simply puerile."[31]

To clinch the argument, the editorial compares the cities to the South, where the proletariat is the racially "inferior" black. While noting that the subservient temperament of blacks, the "simplicity" of the southern system's social and economic subordination, and the low level of industrial and urban development have prevented the growth of a "dangerous class" like that in the North, the continued industrial growth of the nation will ultimately bring those problems to the South; and in any case, the effects of rioting on American commerce and credit affect all men of property and enterprise, irrespective of section. Should the liberal or "demagogic" agitation about the rights of labor continue as before, and spread with the growth of industry and the philanthropic mission to the South, the Southerners could face in the blacks a real equivalent of the "dangerous class" of the North—racial inferiors and semisavages, inflamed by having "the most absurd expectations from Government" aroused among them, as these have already been aroused "among poor white men" in the North. "They would, like their Northern confreres, seek out carefully what was widest, most irrational, and mose debased in his [the Negro's] passions and . . . treat us to a species of demagogy . . . the coarseness of which would make even Raoul Rigault smile if he could rise from his grave." (Rigault was a leader of the Paris Commune of 1871.) These sentiments were widely echoed in religious and philanthropic papers as well as in the regular dailies. Suffragist Lucy Stone, writing in the feminist *Woman's Journal*, asserted that it would be worth "a hundred thousand lives and the destruction of every railroad in the country" to suppress the "insurrection"; and the *Independent* approvingly quoted Napoleon's remark "that the way to deal with a mob is to exterminate it."[32]

Thus the race war and Indian war provided a language for interpreting the class struggles attendant on the development of industry and served the ideological function of linking striking workers with racial aliens and primitive savages. The premise, therefore, was that in the struggle of labor and capital, compromise was almost unthinkable. In an Indian battle, one saves the last bullet for oneself because the war is one of extermination and knows no bounds. If victorious in such a war, the "white man"—or his equivalent in the class struggle—acquires the power to shape the richly endowed natural and human world according to his will; if he fails, civilization, as in Tennyson's version of the Arthurian myth, "reels back into the beast." And although the propertied classes were victorious in 1877—and indeed in most struggles thereafter—the possibility of an ultimate defeat, a revolutionary apocalypse, an urban "Last

Stand" remained basic to both the ideological premises of capitalism and the literature that embodied the fantasies of the American and bourgeois social order.

But the Last Stand myth also contains a scenario for avenging the great defeat and restoring the order represented by cavalry. That scenario involves the more rigorous and extensive application of military power, beginning with a war-to-the-knife against the savages and ending with their subjugation to a reservation regime of military character. Translated into Metropolitan terms, this fable suggests (on the literal level) the use of the army against "urban savages." But the regime that will succeed the battle is only figuratively like the military regime of the reservation. It is to have the same clear and well-legitimated lines of command and authority, and the same threat of force to deploy against dissidence; but it is to be ruled by captains of industry rather than captains of horse.

Morgan's Last Stand: Literary Mythology and the Specter of Revolution, 1876–1890

The language of ideology tends inevitably to oversimplify the social and cultural conflicts it represents. This is because it is the language of power, and its function in a crisis is to rationalize and facilitate a particular line of action. Thus it tends to misrepresent the complexity and the ambivalence of perception and intention of the social/cultural entity that produces it. If the newspaper language of the 1870s had been all the culture provided for interpreting the crisis, the definition of opposing sides and the adoption of policy would have been simple. Strikers were Indians, Indians were savages, savages were both primitive and criminal, and the cause of civilization demands that such beings be subjugated or exterminated. But this simple line of argument was offset by the powerful countercurrent of values, which identified virtue with democracy and against elitism, which located central redemptive values in the primitive and the outlawed, and which was as much in love with savagery (mythologically conceived) as it was ideologically opposed to it. This countertendency was given institutional expression by groups like the Greenbackers, labor unionists, Social Gospelers, unreconstructed abolitionists, and feminists.

Literary mythology likewise registers these complexities and ambivalences more sensitively than ideological polemics because its formal and generic structures have been developed for just such a reflective, world-model-making function. Its language is not logical and selective, as ideological polemic must be, but (relatively) cumulative and evocative. The literary mythology is not forced to contort itself to include both Devil Bug and Uncle Tom as images of the proletariat; while Bennett and the *Herald* editors are at once forced into castigating workers as urban savages and to currying their favor by praising them as intelligent mechanics. Literary Indians can be Magua and Chingachgook by turns, because the maker of fictions never has to compose the order of an Indian reservation. What is contradiction to the ideologist is merely the germ of a useful and significant plot conflict to the fiction writer. And therefore it is in fiction that the roles of savage and saint, outlaw and citizen, tyrant and patriarch are most fully and most subtly played out.

In literary fantasy, therefore, the "military" resolution of social and political problems projected by the *Nation* (and others) could be divested of its troubling practical and ideological implications and assimilated to the vocabulary of symbols accepted by the public as the commonplaces of literary mythology. Using the conventional formulae for defining social types in the Frontier romance, it was possible to envision a society very like that which the *Nation* appeared to be calling for, without drawing the ideological ire of libertarians and egalitarians. In such an imagined America, the role and character of the hero would define the ideal traits of a new class of "natural rulers," and the hero story would show those characteristics triumphing over the countervailing powers of an older order. In a Cooper novel, this would have meant contrasting the relative primitivism of Indians or the outmoded Toryism of an ancien régime with the progressive and enlightened sentiments of the "military aristocrat." The white Frontiersman (Leatherstocking) would act as mediator, sympathizing (and fading away) with the primitive, but breaking trail for the progressive. In post–Civil War and post–Great Strike America, the line between progressive and primitive is more significantly drawn within society than on its border with Indian country; yet the structure of the new myth is clearly cognate with the old. The virtues of progress are embodied more definitively in the figure of the military aristocrat, with the Frontiersman clearly his subordinate—a reflection of the deep concern with class discipline in a context of class conflict. The "savage" and "Tory" opponents remain, but are located within Metropolitan society, in the underclasses of the proletariat, and in the representatives of established order and entrenched power—conservative figures resistant alike to savagery and to the challenge of progressive dynamism.

The crisis of 1876–77 was only the beginning of an extended period of social and cultural upheaval which saw both the completion of the project of industrialization and the outbreak of substantial agrarian and working-class radicalism in opposition. During this time, the literary development of the Custer myth registered these changes about the meaning of Frontiers and Frontier heroes in two closely related but formally distinguished streams of development. The first deals with the figure and career of Custer himself and with the pretense, at least, of historical fidelity. These works had the effect of preserving and transmitting the legend and ensuring Custer a place in the pantheon of American myth heroes. They included a range of productions from biographies to dime novels to melodramas to romantic verse narratives and lyric epitaphs. The most seminal of these is the heroic biography of Custer published by Frederick Whittaker in 1876. Although directly addressed to the election year issues, Whittaker's biography has remained a standard source for all popular versions of the Custer story from 1876 down to the era of Western movies. It bears the same relation to the literary mythology of the 1870s and 1880s that Weems's *Washington* or Flint's *Boone* bears to that of the early 1800s. But the development of the larger significances contained in the Custer myth involved the production of works that clearly draw on the Custer story but are not literal repetitions of it.

THE   BOY   HERO: CUSTER,   RAGGED   DICK,
AND   TOM   SAWYER

As ideological object, the Custer/Last Stand myth was constituted by the intersection of a number of different and mutually antipathetic political tendencies. The conservative/Democratic tendency saw
Custer as a martyr to Indian savagery empowered by soft-headed philanthropic liberalism; the radical/Republican tendency saw Custer as the "real
savage" in his representation of the values of racial bigots and aficionados
of violence. In the Custer myth that continued beyond the ideological
context of 1876, these tendencies were assimilated to the traditional symbolism of the Frontier hero myth. That myth had always imagined the
hero as the man at once committed to the defense of racial purity and
spiritually attuned to the mind and heart of the Indian. This ambiguity is
in keeping with the character of myth which seeks to reconcile conflicting
beliefs and tendencies through the telling of a fable. The Frontier hero
before Custer's time had embodied the contradictory attitudes of Americans
toward their own social form: committed to order but yearning for freedom;
committed to equality but thirsting for distinction; ambitious for progress
but lamenting the loss of that world of pure potential and limitless expectation that went with the first approaches to the Frontier. In Custer, those
traditional themes and concerns meet newer ones, born of the special
problems of the Civil War and industrial development: the wish for a
society and an environment indulgent of individual ambitions and desires,
coupled with the recognition that a modern society cannot afford to make
exceptions to its social and economic discipline; the expectation that industrial production will open new vistas of prosperity, coupled with the
fear that America is looking at its last Frontier, its last age of great
expectations.

In the prewar Frontier Myth, the ambivalent tendencies of the Frontier hero were usually seen as linking him more with the Indian wilderness
phase of history than with the Metropolitan phase. Thus the Frontier hero
is seen as passing away along with the Indians with whom he has been
associated in both comradeship and enmity. This tendency was codified in
the literary myth of Leatherstocking and the historical romances of the
1825–40 period. The emphasis on the military aristocrat as hero after
Cooper turned the original hero myth into a more straightforwardly progressive version, in which the hero's development exactly matches that of
society's progress from buckskin to broadcloth. But its major figures are
persistently represented as tied to the lost world of savage warfare. Some,
like the dime-novel Kit Carson, inhabit a fictive Frontier that is independent of history; others, like Davy Crockett, perish in a symbolic last confrontation with the forces against which they had always fought and from
which they had taken the qualities that made them heroes.

Custer's story unifies these different patterns. It gives us the fable of
a boy who first becomes a soldier-aristocrat and a hero in war against a

civilized power; who then goes back to the Frontier and becomes a "buckskin" hero; and who finally perishes in a complex confrontation with the forces of both primitive savagery and Metropolitan corruption. The success of this formula allowed Custer's story to serve as the symbolic meeting ground for his culture's contradictory impulses of ambition and nostalgia, racialism and sympathy for the victims of injustice. In the Custer myth, ideological contradictions become part of a harmonious and significant fable. Phillips's angry assertion that Custer at the Washita proved himself the "real savage," the *World*'s admiring Custer's ride at the Grand Review as "the charge of a Sioux Chieftain," and the *Herald*'s report that Custer intends to "live and travel like the Indians" on his way to battle become the moral tensions that shape a single heroic character. The impulses of youth, its "savage" vigor and "outlaw" impatience of traditional authority, are incarnated in Custer and given a complex interpretation by his fate. On the one hand, these qualities make him a hero and allow him to bring progress by transcending the limits set by tradition and authority; on the other hand, they make him rash and like the savage in the intemperate commitment to personal honor and its redemption in battle— and therefore he perishes surrounded by a small circle of his boys in blue. But this symbolism also makes his fall the death knell of the Indians as well: thus the catastrophe's meanings are doubled, and the doom of cavalry-democracy is ironically mirrored in the doom of noble savagery.

Latent within these complex figures are both a heroic and an antiheroic version of the fable. The latter is the one with which contemporary movies have made us most familiar. This is the view that takes off from an ideological stance close to that of Wendell Phillips, which sees Custer as the embodiment of negative characteristics within American society— characteristics like racism, love of violence and cruelty, moral corruption or dishonesty, the urge to tyrannize over the weak. However, for the nineteenth century it was the heroic version of the Custer story that gained the widest currency and established the base line from which subsequent variants of the myth can be seen to depart.

Frederick Whittaker's *Complete Life of George A. Custer* was the first biography of the Boy General; it was published late in 1876 so hastily as to make it very nearly an "instant biography" of the kind familiar to us in the last decade or so. Whittaker aimed to cash in on the public interest in the recent catastrophe, and he also hoped to make his book a campaign document for use against the Republicans—whose policies, in his view, were responsible for the Indian war and for Custer's defeat. Whittaker was a wartime comrade of Custer's and became in time a friend of the family. He used this status to obtain Libbie's endorsement of his project and access to personal letters in Custer's papers. Mrs. Custer had returned to the East to find her husband's death had stirred up as many detractors as mourners, and she hoped Whittaker would defend her husband in his book and support her efforts to obtain a court of inquiry that would vindicate Custer and condemn the "incompetent" Major Reno.[1]

That Whittaker's biography contains distortions and inaccuracies is easy to show. But what interests us here is the character and meaning of his distortions and the ways in which these serve to link Custer with symbols of value drawn from popular culture mythology. We have seen Custer as both a dashing fighter and as a cautious careerist, seeking to rise through the acquisition of powerful patrons; playing army politics, congressional politics, even presidential politics to serve his needs; filling his regiment with friends and relatives; engaging in dubious business arrangements, exploiting his fame for profit; using his position to aid the Northern Pacific and other business interests while pretending to be objective in reporting on the Black Hills; condemning and secretly seeking to profit from the corruption of the Indian agencies and post traderships.

However, Whittaker's Custer is an amalgamation of a Cooper Frontiersman-aristocrat and an upwardly mobile Horatio Alger boy hero. The Alger element predominates, particularly in the account of Custer's early life, and touches appear that seem to be drawn from that other bestselling "boy" novel of 1876, Mark Twain's *Tom Sawyer*. In the Alger novels, which by 1876 had become formulaic, the young hero begins life in straitened or impoverished circumstances. Richard Hunter, the hero of the Ragged Dick series which were Alger's most successful books, is a street boy, an orphan, whose innate honesty and inborn capacity for hard work and virtuous action earn him the respect of a series of wealthy benefactors. He rises in the world by serving these older men—rescuing them from swindlers and pickpockets, rescuing their daughters in distress—and they in turn give him small amounts of cash and lots of good advice on how to save his money, how and why to obtain an education, how to dress the part of an honest and hardworking young man. As we have seen, Ragged Dick never quite emerges from this tutelage into the status and power of independent adulthood; he remains throughout a boy and, hence, a subject of power. However, some such invisible consummation is clearly promised, for his story is one of continual rise and progress; and from this, his future might be extrapolated—although Alger does not make that extrapolation concrete for his reader.[2]

This formula was so clearly established by 1876 that Twain's *Tom Sawyer* may in part be seen as a parody of Alger's sucess fable and the world view behind it. But the relationship of the Alger to the Twain "boy fable" is a more complex version of the parodically inverted fables of the "Good Little Boy" and the "Bad Little Boy" in Twain's *Sketch Book*, which satirized the kind of morality purveyed in "Sunday school books." Twain's bad little boy flouts all the Sunday school rules and achieves worldly success; the good little boy obeys the rules and is derided, abused, and destroyed. This discredits the moralists' pretension that society and the world are so constituted as to aggrandize good and rebuke evil—the reverse is practically the case. But Twain doubles the satire by his suggestion that the motives of the "good little boy" are just as corrupt in their way as those of the bad—he obeys the Sunday school books not because he is innately moral but because he has been taught to expect that such obedience will earn the reward of praise and worldly goods which the adult "class" has to bestow. This touches the Alger myth close to the quick.

Tom Sawyer works out this satiric concept in a fully realized work of fiction and character creation. Its boy hero is neither priggish nor authority-centered; but like the Alger hero, he mixes "good boy" and "bad boy" qualities. The novel ends with his achievement of success in just the terms the Alger books prefer: he has rescued the daughter of the paternal "governor," Judge Thatcher; he has achieved enough wealth to make him the judge's partner; he has rescued a lower-class friend, Huck Finn, from disreputability (as Ragged Dick does with Mark the Match-Boy); and he's done it all with "pluck and luck." However, Tom's "Way to Wealth" is not based on hard work and respect for authority; it is gained through a long series of rebellions and satires of authority, ending with a treasure hunt that takes a dime novel for its bible.

Between Twain and Alger we can see the common structure of a boy-hero myth. It is essentially a story of success, and its overall thrust is the same whether it is set nostalgically in the backwash of a lost Frontier or in the new slums of a modern Metropolis. Its cast of characters provides a range of responses to authority which include both an identification with it as the source of worldly and moral validation and a rebellion against its illegitimate strictures and pretensions. Twain permits his heroes more leeway in this respect than does Alger; but Alger's choice of heroes from the lower depths is itself a democratic and antiauthoritarian gesture. Both are thus "promising," both fables end with a look toward the future which will be the boys' to shape.[3]

It is against this background that we should read Whittaker's identification of Custer as the model of the "American boy." He links Custer to the conventions of Frontier-hero biography by describing his senses as being "as sharp as those of an Indian even then," and showing him impatient under the tutelage of the schoolroom. However, his impatience of restraint is tempered—indeed, entirely offset—by images of his gentleness and docility in his family and by his ambition to succeed in social terms.

> A strange compound of qualities was this lad in those days, gentle and brave, with an overflowing sense of humor, hating his books, and yet working to the head of his class by fits and starts when he took a notion, obstinate under harsh treatment, opposing the constituted authorities at school with all ingenious evasions, meeting the wily tricks of his pedagogue with tricks still wilier, but ruled by his gentle sister with an absolute sway. He reminds us of one of Thackeray's schoolboys, full of vague poetical yearnings, tempered by the savage freedom of overflowing physical strength and health, a boy all over, a boy of the backbone, with the promise and potency of—who knows what?—of manhood. The ruling traits of his character, as they struck his family, were those of great goodness, of duty performed, of kindness, love and devotion. To this day they seem to think of him, not as the brilliant warrior, but as the exemplary son and brother . . . Inside of all the rough play . . . lay this hidden kernel of gentleness and love, that was to make the foundation of the future knight. And yet he was a plain American boy . . . a thorough American, a Western boy at that.[4]

As a boy, Custer is akin to the savage—full of high spirit, impatient of restraint or discipline. Authority, in its tyrannical form, approaches him as savage to savage, and he matches guile with guile. In its female form,

however, he succumbs to moral authority, like the Cooper frontiersmen and
Indians, whose test of virtue and whiteness is their respect for white
womanhood. Out of this respect will emerge not merely manhood but
knighthood, a species of nobility—but cast in *American* and *Western*
terms. His meeting with Libbie, in a scene recounted in a manner reminiscent of Tom's meeting with Becky in *Tom Sawyer*, points him definitively
in this direction: "spoiled" young Libbie, swinging on her father's gate,
shows off her wit and exercises her "cuteness" by calling out, "Hello! you
Custer boy!" and fleeing into the house.

> A trifle you will say, not worth recording; yet it was the begin-
> ning of Custer's first and last love. The sweet arch face of that little
> girl was the first revelation to the wild young savage, whose whole
> idea of life was that of physical exercise, war, and the chase, of
> something else, of another side of life. It was to him, love at first
> sight, and he then and there recorded an inward vow, that some
> day that little girl should be his wife. He kept the vow through
> many obstacles.[5]

The romance with Libbie becomes the plot around which Whittaker
orders his narrative. Like Cora in *Last of the Mohicans*, like Becky in *Tom
Sawyer*, like Eva in *Uncle Tom*, like Mr. Gregson's daughter in *Ragged Dick*,
Libbie is the redemptive romantic object whose mere glance reveals to the
young "savage" the knowledge of higher things. His attainment of her love
and respect will mark the culmination of Custer's moral development.

The story of that rise, culminating in Custer's wartime marriage and
his achievement of heroic stature in the closing battles of the Civil War,
occupies more than half of the text. Its premises are summarized by Whittaker at the outset:

> This book aims to give to the world the life of a great man, one
> of the few really great men that America has produced. Beginning
> at the foot of the social ladder, with no advantages beyond those,
> physical and mental, given to him by the GOD who made him,
> he rose to the top. His upward career was so rapid and phenom-
> enal in its success as to deceive the world in general as to the
> means by which he rose, and none more completely for a time
> than the present writer of this biography. Much of Custer's success
> has been attributed to good fortune, while it was really the result
> of a wonderful capacity for hard and energetic work, and a ra-
> pidity of intuition which is seldom found apart from military
> genius of the highest order.

Far from being the pet of powerful men, Custer—the American "Bayard"
—reveals his "nobility" by triumphing over tremendous difficulties. He combines in his character and career aspects of the chivalric knight and of
the new man of "that great industrial class from whom so many of our
original men are springing." Like the Boone/Carson type of Frontier hero,
to some degree like Weems's *Washington*, such men are mostly "self-made,"
even though their rise may be cast in an urban or social rather than a
wilderness setting. In Custer's case, the drama of this rise is heightened by

Whittaker's refutation of the view of Custer as McClellan's, Pleasonton's or Sheridan's pet. These commanders merely recognize hard work, brilliance, and virtue when they see it; and Judge Bacon, who first forbids and then assents to Custer's marriage with Libbie, is of this type. But others in the army and out of it see in Custer's youthful promise and high ability a threat to their own positions; and out of fear and jealousy, they thwart and ultimately help to kill him.[6]

This jealousy first surfaces during the war in the response of the old colonels of the Michigan Brigade to the appointment of a "boy general" to command them. Whittaker describes his fanciful uniform, comparing Custer's cavalier "Prince Rupert" hat with the "Praise-God Barebones" regulation model—Custer is a chivalric knight among mean-spirited Puritans. "The boy general looked so pretty and effeminate, so unlike the stern realities of war, that he was certain to be quizzed and ridiculed unmercifully, unless he could compel the whole army to respect him . . . He must do something brilliant to justify the freak." Custer's "effeminacy," his "girl-like" appearance, is used by Whittaker to emphasize his ambisexual *boyishness* and "extreme" youth; and also to emphasize his aristocratic refinement and gentility of character, which coarse-minded Puritans—lacking the chivalric sense of honor—affect to despise.

> Grey-headed Colonels came in to salute him with outward respect, but . . . they were inwardly boiling over with disgust and anger at having this "boy," this "popinjay," this "affected dandy," with his "girl's hair," his "swagger," and "West Point conceit" put "over men, sir, . . . men old enough to be his father, and who knew as much about real fighting, sir, as any epauletted government pensioner . . ."[7]

The opposition here is between youth and age, and also between military professionalism—linked with chivalry—and the prosaic consciousness of the bureaucratic and business worlds. Custer represents youthful merit, which his gray-haired subordinates refuse to admit. But the war offers ample opportunity, and Custer finally makes believers of them. When Custer rides out before his division at Woodstock—in a scene Whittaker embellished if he did not invent—and bows to his enemy Rosser with flourished hat "like the action of a knight in the lists"—his troops cheer and charge with irresistible enthusiasm and show that Northerners are equal in chivalry and prowess to "gallant Southern cavaliers." Like the young nation of which he is (says Whittaker) the embodiment, Custer succeeds against the gloomy prophecies and obstructions of the Old World; his merit and his mobility are both recognized and legitimated by society.[8]

If the story had ended with Custer's triumph and marriage to Libbie, a version of the success-story archetype would have been fulfilled. But the Frontier sequel to the Civil War romance is instead the story of the obstruction or inversion of that promise of romantic fulfillment. Although transferred to the Frontier of America's expanding aspirations, Custer is (according to Whittaker) in fact placed in a post-Frontier context. The contraction of the army after demobilization, the reduction of volunteer to regular ranks, and the straitened prospects for rapid promotion place

the officers of the army in a position not unlike that of the workers in
Lippard's city—fighting and destroying each other for the sake of a place.
The Civil War in the East, not the Indian war in the West, was Custer's
true Frontier:

> Hitherto, Custer had enjoyed a life of constant success. His
> labors had been altogether external and had included no mis-
> fortunes and no serious setbacks. . . . [But] in the present regular
> army of the United States, the great trouble is found in the fact
> that its rewards are so few, its officers so numerous. The conse-
> quence is . . . the most intense jealousy and envy from the major-
> ity towards everyone who possesses any great military merit and
> has attained early distinction.

In this world, seniority rules over merit. Mediocrity prevails, and with it
come both battlefield defeat and political corruption—the symptoms of
incipient degeneracy.[9]

The contrast between the volunteer and the postwar regular army
becomes, in Whittaker's hands, a metaphoric rendering of two models of
industrial society. The professional standing army is one such model. Its
virtues are its discipline and professional efficiency, but as a social model
it is unfortunately antidemocratic, more like slavery than republican freedom. Hence, "the only footing on which standing armies have ever been
tolerated in free republics has been as a police force, to control the criminal classes." In America's past, these classes were chiefly found among the
Indians outside society's Frontiers; but clearly such classes can appear
within the Metropolis, and by their presence justify a standing army. The
alternative model is that of the republican militia, in which voluntarism and
democratic governance are the organizing principles of society and of the
military force that sustains order. As the vessel of popular will, such a
militia republic has the strength and consciousness of virtue that derive
from possession of willing popular support; but the system is weakened and
rendered inefficient by its subjection to shifts of an unstable popular temper, to the multiplicity of demands for satisfaction and shared power, and
to the appeals of demagogues.[10]

During the Civil War (says Whittaker) a perfect synthesis was
achieved. The volunteer spirit brought willing hands to the defense of the
colors; and the rigors of war taught the volunteer army the virtue of command and discipline, unlike "the loose style prevalent at the beginning of
the war when the men elected their officers." The "democratic" principle
gave way to one in which merit, risen by experience from the ranks, was
in command and received from the troops a willing obedience. The army
thus realized the social order dreamed of by Jefferson in which the free
consent of the governed was given to a class in the name of the people.
Even Jeffersonian mobility was preserved:

> The career was open to all, and while the war lasted was excellent.
> This bred between the two classes, i.e., enlisted men and officers,
> a certain mutual respect which was noticeable. The men were
> punctilious in saluting, neat in their dress, and obeyed orders

promptly. The officers were kind in their manner, and only maintained the due distance essential to discipline in public . . . The secret of subordination was that *every man respected the rank he hoped to attain himself.*

This secret of subordination was lost, once the war ended and the contraction of the army ended the promise of mobility upward from the ranks. In addition, the loss of the ideological motive of the war lessened that esprit de corps which contributed to the volunteers' consent to be governed. This, according to Whittaker, lay behind the mutiny of Custer's troops in Texas; and in such a situation, Custer's firm authoritarian handling of the disorder was essential to demonstrate the firmness of American government.[11]

With the Seventh Cavalry, in a purely postwar setting, Custer had to create for himself the kind of soldiers that he needed, in the absence of all those motives and influences—and of the structure of mobility—which had made the volunteer army "ideal." Success in war is compared to success in work, in which "the troops are the tools, the general, the workman." In "normal" circumstances, the making of troops is entrusted to older men, "sergeants, captains and colonels" and the control of battle to young generals whose "adroitness, quickness and magnetic ardor" are more useful in battle than their elders' patience.

During the war, Custer had been content to use troops "made" by others; in the Seventh Cavalry, he would combine the roles of maker and user, "old" trainer and "young" battle leader, "fashioning them out of raw material." In this, Whittaker asserts, Custer was successful; so that in the end, he promised to join the ideal qualities of both age and experience.[12]

Beyond the characterization of Custer's success, Whittaker's imagery links Custer's military enterprise directly and explicitly to the processes of industrialization and to the social problems of subordinating independent and ambitious "volunteers" to the new social discipline required by a post-Frontier and industrial situation. The war period is seen nostalgically as a Frontier in which it was still possible to legitimate subordination by promising the lower classes upward movement through the ranks. However, the first lesson taught by the war is the impossibility of running an efficient army on democratic principles—subordination is absolutely required. Human "volunteers" are transformed into commodities (tools, raw material). Now the voluntaristic mode of subordination must be set aside, and "regular army" discipline enforced rigorously, by heroic authority. This Custer succeeds finally in doing with the Seventh Cavalry. But in the larger society, leaders less chivalric than Custer make a hash of things, being at once too permissive with the "criminal classes" and Indians, and too restrictive and bound by "seniority" to give full scope to the talents of a Custer.

On this "post-frontier" Frontier, age triumphs over youth, mediocrity over merit. Custer's court-martial and his persecution by critics are one symptom of this, but there are others. Whittaker specifically cites the politicization of the army by Congress, the corruption of the Indian Bureau and of Belknap's War Department, the vindictiveness of Grant and his ineptitude as president. In his account of the Black Hills expedition, Whit-

taker contrasts Custer's honest reportage and technically successful management of the expedition with the political and business purposes that
underlay it. Political and business corruptionists and their policies based
on "injustice and cupidity" are responsible for the expedition and the war
that followed.

> It is a sad and humiliating confession to be made, but the irres-
> istible logic of truth compels it, that all the subsequent trouble of
> the Sioux war really sprang from the deliberate violation by the
> United States government of its own freely plighted faith, when
> Custer was ordered to lead his column . . . to the Black Hills. . . .
> Yet we cannot blame Custer. . . . He was a soldier, bound to obey
> orders, and a mere instrument in the hand of power.[13]

It is the treason of the "fathers" that has exposed young Custer to
defeat at the hands of a savage enemy, and not, as his enemies would have
it, that a superior or "different grade of talent [was] required for fighting
Indians," and that it takes "long experience in Indian fighting to produce a
perfect officer." According to Whittaker, Custer was a systematic and scientific Indian fighter, an exemplar of the most moderate and sensible approaches to the Indian problem, a commander who spoke with a voice of
dignity and restraint of the campaigns and battles, an aristocratic foil for the
Leatherstocking-like dialect jokes of California Joe. Whittaker even makes
an incident in which Custer beats up a drunken Indian with his fists into an
occasion for the display of "Indian psychology": Custer turns the occasion
into a lecture to the Indians on the proper respect to be shown to one's commanders—a respect that, says Whittaker, is not enforced in the anarchic
structure of Indian polity. We are clearly in the presence of one of those
Cooperian military aristocrats who are highly competent to deal with the
Frontier, but whose true place and function is to rule within civilized society,
to subordinate and master the forces of social disorder.[14]

All of the Cooperian reference points are here: in the Custer–California Joe pairing, in the stories of Custer's success as a hunter and scout
in the Black Hills. In the Last Stand campaign, Whittaker draws on the
mystique of the trusty Indian scout, in the figures of Bloody Knife and the
"survivor" Curly—whose story of the manner of Custer's death Whittaker
offers as a fact. Whittaker also presents Custer as one well versed in Indian
lore and culture, an expert in sign language, with an ability to think like
an Indian—matching wile for wile, stratagem for stratagem, as he did with
his teachers as a boy. Moreover, his attempts to punish an Indian criminal
named Rain-in-the-Face gain him a particular savage enemy; and the
classic pattern of the vengeance motif, just as with Magua, is played out
when Rain-in-the-Face kills Custer—with a rifle provided by Grant's Indian Bureau. But the Indian, like the boy, has a savage sense of honor and
reverence, and the Indians do not harm Custer's body; whereas the Grant
administration perversely mutilates the hero's reputation after his death.

In Whittaker's version, Custer promises America the kind of heroic
leadership which the new age requires. He carries with him from wartime
experience both an archaic chivalric code—born of West Point and of a
war between equal parties and races, of cavaliers—and the symbolism of

the "volunteer" army, which in turn symbolizes the Jeffersonian utopian social order in which perfect democracy coincides with perfect subordination. As an Indian fighter, he illustrates the application of the highest form of civilized technique and sensibility to the old problem of the vanishing Frontier. He combines the vigor and originality of youth, with the elder's wisdom and capacity for responding authoritatively to challenges from the "criminal classes" and from Indians. But his murder by the Indians and the Republicans thwarts this natural development: senescent seniority outlives youthful vigor, in violation of the natural order of things: the romantic success story ends in a kind of failure—albeit glorious.

For this violation of order, there are certain enemies to blame. Only by punishing the guilty and worshiping the innocent hero can the nation avert impending degeneracy. Only if it is seen as a Christ-like sacrifice will Custer's death serve to regenerate American institutions. This is emphasized by Whittaker in his description of the Last Stand: he cites Curly for authority that Custer had a chance to escape, but chose deliberately to perish with his men. (The only Curly story he rejects is the only demonstrably true one—that Custer fought with carbine and pistols, not a saber):

> When only a few of the officers were left alive, the Indians made a hand to hand charge, in which Custer fought like a tiger with his sabre when his last shot was gone, that he killed or wounded three Indians with the sabre, and that as he ran the last man through, *Rain-in-the-Face kept his oath and shot Custer.*

> . . . So fell Custer, the brave cavalier, the Christian soldier, but dying in harness amid the men he loved.

It is essential for Whittaker that only the officers should have been left for the consummation of the ending; and that of the officers, the highest should be the last to die. Such symmetries have nothing to do with observed fact or probability, but much to do with myth. Custer is the cavalier Christ, the savior-commander: Grant is his Pilate, Reno his Judas, Rain-in-the-Face the soldier who wounds his side and lets out the life.[15]

Although no later biographer of Custer devoted quite so much effort to defining the character and context of Custer's heroism, the Whittaker biography is the model for most of the pro-Custer canon. Between 1876 and 1930, the special features of the hero tended to become conventionalized in the "genteel hero" vein; and these conventions in turn were exaggerated often to the point of caricature. The 1905 novel by Herbert Myrick, *Cache La Poudre: The Romance of a Tenderfoot in the Days of Custer*, sets Custer in the midst of what would have been (in an earlier time) a standard dime-novel plot—now inflated to fill out a standard hard-cover format. Two young eastern stockbrokers—one good, one bad—transfer their competition to the West, where one becomes a renegade and the other a soldier in the Seventh Cavalry. Custer figures as a model of Western heroism and nobility for the young broker-soldier to live up to—a chivalric alternative to the materialist "ethics" of commerce. As Kent Steckmesser notes, Custer's role is similar to that of Kit Carson in the con-

temporary *Kit Carson's Boys* (1904) and the Charles Averill romance *Prince of the Gold Hunters*, published just after the Mexican War. Edward Ellis's hero Deadwood Dick resolves similar conflicts between transplanted Easterners in several dime novels. If there is a difference, it lies in the distinction of class and social function between Carson and Custer: the Mountain Man is a plebeian border scout in the Hawkeye model; the cavalryman is an officer and a gentleman, representative of a managerial and cultural elite.

The aristocratic or cavalier version of Custer reached its apogee in romantic biographies of the kind produced by Frazier Hunt for *Redbook* in 1928. This tendency in the world of literary fiction offset the changing appreciation of Custer among military professionals and historians. The latter had resolved (for the most part) the issue of Custer's responsibility for the disaster at the Little Big Horn. Popular histories of the Indian wars written by military men or "buffs" during this period reflected the judgment of military textbook writers, who blamed Custer as a poor tactician and an egotist incapable of being a good "team player"—an essential trait for the field officer in a complex modern army.

But the most interesting development in Custer fiction by far is the tendency to shift Custer from the role of boy hero to that of governor-patron to some younger boy figure—as if the fictional representation of Custer had somehow "aged" since 1876, like the portrait of Dorian Gray. A similar pattern has already been noted in the development of the Kit Carson legend from its original vision of a hero half-savage and half-Saxon to one embodying genteel values and powers. Custer's literary persona had never been quite so close to the Hawkeye level—boyishness, rather than savagery, had defined his character as a man on the border between worlds of anarchic freedom and order. His gentrification in fiction likewise makes him a more paternal and authoritative figure than Carson had been. Steckmesser lists several Custer-centered dime novels published between 1883 and 1913 in which Custer plays this paternal role. In one of these, *Roving Rifle: Custer's Little Scout* (1883), Custer adopts a waif who serves as a spy among the Indians before the Washita battle—the plot is borrowed from *Sheridan's Squaw Spy* (1869), and owes something to Alger's *Ragged Dick* as well. Custer rewards the youth by sponsoring him at West Point, where he can begin to live the same fable of success that Custer lived before him.[16]

In these fictions, the myth of the "Boy General" as well as the Christian redemptive function Whittaker had asserted for Custer are invoked and applied to surrogates, who survive him to carry forward something of what the "Boy General" has stood for. Although Custer's role in the story is altered, the elements of the story remain consistent through all these changes: the Custer myth tests the ideology of progressive democracy in a fiction whose terms of conflict pit white against Indian, youth against age, and rebellion against authority. Its message is that despite the closing down of old Frontiers, America remains the place in which youthful ambition and the urge for freedom can still successfully play off against authority; and where authority itself assimilates the "liberated" qualities of the boy hero, and paradoxically encourages the freedom it checks.

FROM THE BLACK HILLS TO "BUFFLAND": JOHN HAY'S THE BREADWINNERS

The Custer canon, by its very nature, orbits ceaselessly about the catastrophe of the Little Big Horn, and the questions most closely related to the battle—questions about Custer's character, temperament, and military skill for the most part, with Indian motives and character figuring as a conventional foil for the hero. It requires another kind of work to elaborate the symbolism that is latent in the Custer story—the symbolism that relates the Frontier catastrophe to the conflicts that threaten the Metropolis. John Hay's *The Breadwinners* (1884–85) carries out in a work of literary fiction something very like the scenario of the Great Strike that the *Nation* or *Harper's Weekly* had offered in 1877. Hay was an important political figure: he had been Lincoln's personal secretary during the Civil War, was a leading figure in Republican politics, and would eventually be a powerful Secretary of State under Presidents McKinley and Theodore Roosevelt (1898–1905). A mixture of motives led him to publish the novel anonymously, and to evade for some years the attribution of authorship: the matter was controversial in a Republican Party which still had some affinity for "free labor," and the writing of fiction was perhaps suspect for a man engaged seriously in politics and the evolution of public policy.[17]

The novel was widely praised for its portrayal of the 1877 railroad strike and for its representation of a virile American hero capable of standing up to both the democratic cant of the strikers and their brute physical force. Through his hero, Captain Arthur Farnham, Hay makes an explicit connection between the Indian wars of the Custer era and the new period of labor wars inaugurated in 1877; and he offers a mythological solution to the crisis of authority in which society is reorganized along quasi-military lines, under the guidance of a military aristocrat who is also a big businessman.

Hay's hero is an ex-soldier of aristocratic character and breeding. Although his inherited wealth and position would have allowed him to live a leisured life, he chose instead to serve in the Civil War, and to continue on as a professional soldier fighting Indians on the Great Plains. He anticipates by fifteen years the ideal of the "strenuous life" held out by Theodore Roosevelt, and he foreshadows by two decades Owen Wister's *The Virginian*—likewise a western figure of astonishing virility and sexual presence, great masculine beauty, and unlimited natural capacity. Although *The Virginian* is base-born and Captain Farnham is born well, Hay wants us to think of Farnham as one whose birth is less important than ability and merit: "He seemed, in short, one of those fortunate natures who, however born, are always bred well, and come by prescription to most of the good things the world can give." He is therefore one destined by character to succeed, and deserves success.[18]

Although his birth is eastern, Farnham is distinctly "of the frontier." His frontier service has made a kind of pioneer-in-uniform: his first wife had "die[d] on the Plains from sheer want, though he had more money than he could find transportation for." Yet despite the hardship, he might have remained a soldier had not the responsibility for managing his family's wealth fallen upon him with the death of his grandfather. Although he takes up an urban residence—in "Buffland," a composite of Buffalo, New York, and Cleveland, Ohio—and the onerous chores of a modern life, he thinks longingly of the West he has left—his closed Frontier:

> And even yet, in the midst of a luxury and comfort which antic-ipated every want and gratified every taste, he often looked back longingly on the life he had left. . . . He regretted the desolate prairies, the reaches of barrenness cursed by the Creator, the wild chaos of the mountain cañons, the horror of the Bad Lands, the tingling cold of winter in the Black Hills. But the Republic holds so high the privilege of serving her that, for the officer who once resigns—with a good character—there is no return forever, though he seeks it with half the lobby at his heels.[19]

As a Frontiersman returning to the Metropolis after years in the wilder-ness, Farnham can see his society from the outside. Like Cooper's Leather-stocking, immersion in the realities of nature has given him a standpoint and a standard from which he can critique whatever is false or unnatural in society. But he is of a different social class, and his Frontier has likewise been a different one from Leatherstocking's: he has been a commander, not a free wanderer; and the Frontier to him has meant not liberation from the rigors of hierarchical order, but rather a more perfect commit-ment to hierarchy and against anarchic freedom than the soft society of the Metropolis has had to make. So his critique is not against the strictness of American society and law, but against its laxness and lassitude. There is no Judge Temple in Buffland, no fountainhead of legitimate authority to be questioned by the hero; on the contrary, the wealthy and respectable classes of Buffland have evaded the responsibility for order that is the ob-ligation of the elite. Through Farnham, Hay rebukes his own class for its neglect of politics, its preoccupation with "making money and paying taxes, building fine houses, and bringing their children up to hate politics as they did." The political vacuum left by the *aristoi* is filled by the ignorant masses and their demagogic leaders. While "there was hardly a millionaire . . . who knew where the ward meetings of his party were held," every "Irish laborer in the city . . . knew his way to his ward club as well as to mass."[20]

Cooper had also offered an analogous critique of democratic politics, suggestively in *The Pioneers* and explicitly in *The Redskins*. What is dif-ferent about Hay's critique is its lack of ambivalence or ambiguity about the problem of balancing hierarchy and order with democracy and free-dom: Hay is clearly for hierarchy and order. Moreover, his portrayal of social classes is frank and unapologetic in its avowal of class and ethnic bias. The "rich and intelligent" classes are productive and able beyond the capacities of the lower orders, but lose their grip on politics through culti-vated inertia. The lower classes are divided between the deferential poor, who do their work and know their place; and urban "savages" whose lust for power, wealth—or the women of the upper classes—leads them to challenge the basis of social order.

The negative qualities of the lower classes are embodied in Maud Matchin, Andrew Jackson Offitt, and Sam Sleeny. Maud is a low-born social climber who has been educated beyond the level appropriate to her station and character, and who has thus acquired ideas of upward mobility that will overburden her congenitally weak moral sense. She sets her cap for Arthur Farnham, making illegitimate use of her sexual appeal and her criminal connections to entrap him. Maud is Hay's response to the pretensions of the new would-be middle classes, rising in the world by their wits and wiles and in the process upsetting the right order of things. What would have been in Alger's heyday (or Lincoln's, or Jackson's) proof of the vitality of a democratic political economy—the openness of society to rising men and women—has become a source of social danger.

More dangerous than Maud is Andrew Jackson Offitt, whose greed and power lust take the form of organizing labor against the propertied classes. His name, says Hay, is "in the West, . . . an unconscious brand."

> It generally shows that the person bearing it is the son of illiterate
> parents, with no family pride or affections, but filled with a bitter
> and savage partisanship which found its expression in a servile
> worship of the most injurious personality in American history.

This is a lot to find in a name. Offitt is a socialist, and Hay thus links socialism with a Whiggish interpretation of Jacksonian democracy—reduced here to demagogy, inflation, and hostility to the better classes. But Offitt uses the language of prewar southern Democrats more readily than that of socialism: he tells workmen that labor makes them like "a nigger." His associate, Sam Sleeny, is markedly "alien" in appearance, "dark-skinned, unwholesome looking."[21]

When the great strike comes, the politicians democratically elected by the Irish will not take legal action to protect property. Farnham therefore takes the Frontier-inspired initiative of forming a vigilante force drawn from his own class to protect the homes of the rich from the strikers, and to prepare a nucleus for whatever counterstroke the state will muster. He also finds some allies among the good workmen—a class who differ from the Offitt/Sleeny mob in race as well as character. The representative of this type is Fergus Ferguson, a pure-bred Scot of "shapely build, blond hair and beard, [and] frank blue eyes." But of more use to Farnham are the Civil War veterans, who rally to one they recognize as a Civil War officer. Those who are pure of blood and those who retain the fond memory of military discipline will fight for property and obey Farnham.

This force is able to rout the mob of strikers which the government fears to confront. It does so by virtue of its superior discipline, and by its devotion to principles other than personal gain. The climax of the fight is the rescue of the "white woman"—Farnham's beloved—from Sleeny and Offitt: once again the threat to property is symbolized as a threat to the woman. The rescue is not only effectual in suppressing the strike and saving the girl; it also convinces the fiancé that the virile and even violent qualities that give Farnham his attractiveness and strength are essential ones for a modern man to possess. "I always thought he had such a sweet temper," says his future mother-in-law, "but tonight he seemed to just love to fight." It is that love of battle, as much as anything, that makes Farnham a hero and a model for his class.

Although the origins of Farnham's heroism are rooted in his Frontier past, the form his heroism takes has a distinctly post-Frontier character. Farnham recalls his cavalry days with nostalgia, as a lost heroic age. Unlike the nostalgia of a Leatherstocking, Farnham looks back on his old Frontier from an urban setting, not from some latter-day wilderness; and the past he remembers is not one in which solitary heroes did legendary battle, but one in which a regiment of professionals did a dirty job in loyal servitude to the state and the army. The Frontier skills which Farnham brings to bear on modern problems are not the individualist talents of a Leatherstocking—it is the soldier's skill he calls on, the officer's ability to discipline and command. Frontier individualism, the politics of Crockett and Jackson, is the legacy the Frontier left to Offitt and Sleeny. Frontier militarism, the heroism of the regiment, is its heritage to Farnham.

The original Myth of the Frontier had offered a fictive reconciliation between the conflicting demands of individual ambition and social order, and its panacea had been the offering of external goals for ambition (the virgin land) and external targets for hostility (Indians and renegades). In Hay's world, the terms of the original reconciliation have been dissolved. What remains of individualism is embodied in the charismatic figure of Farnham, and it takes the form of an entitlement to rule. What is left for the mass of men below Farnham is subordination, willing or unwilling.

But the military metaphor was not a monopoly of the right. Perhaps the most popular social and utopian novel of the period was Edward Bellamy's *Looking Backward* (1887). Bellamy saw in the concentration of wealth by the trusts and the increasing immiseration of labor a threat not merely to social peace but to the preservation of republican institutions and ideology. His novel is a thin excuse for projecting a resolution of the conflict and a reorganization of society on a basis both secure and equitable. Bellamy's hero is not an active, virile, soldierly Captain Farnham, but rather a well-meaning, politically passive upper-class Bostonian. His passivity is essential to his role in the novel: he falls into a trance and awakens a hundred years later to find his world has been transformed while he slept. The revolution that has occurred is of a piece with the framing device of the dream. It has been accomplished in nearly bloodless fashion, after a period in which capital and labor finally recognized the fatality of continued strife and the advantages of mutual cooperation, which in turn was effected by means of a scientifically organized social compact. The details of Bellamy's utopia do not concern us here. However, we need to note that the dominant metaphor defining that utopia was military. The members of society have the discipline, sense of collective responsibility, and loyalty to the whole that are characteristics of highly motivated regiments —Civil War volunteer organizations are Bellamy's models. Work is organized on military lines, with "brigades" performing specialized tasks, uniforms to distinguish them, medals for reward, and so on. Although the style of Bellamy's society is military, it is utterly nonviolent. Under the rational reorganization of society, war has become unthinkable.

There is no mention of "the frontier" or "savage warfare" anywhere in the novel, and this accords with its preference for rational, nonviolent, and passive modes of "heroism." The fact tells us something important about the usage of the language of Frontier Myth, specifically its linkage to an ideology which requires us to perceive class and race as linked, which enjoins us to accept racial warfare as inevitable and progressive, and which envisions the outcome of the struggle as one in which a new ruling race (or class) subjugates its opponents. None of those doctrines appeals to Bellamy, and his choice of a most un-Frontier-like hero is therefore appropriate. Nonetheless, even Bellamy is susceptible to the appeal of the "regiment" as a model of social organization; and although his regimental society is commanded by consent and the top ranks are open to all people of ability, the relations between commanders and those they command are those of authority. His utopia is therefore akin to the society envisioned by Hay: a society in which discipline has been established, and in which a natural aristocracy rules with the consent of the governed. The difference between them is that Hay's rulers are selected in the violent struggle of Indian and class warfare, whereas Bellamy's are chosen by the peaceful workings of a merit system.[22]

MYTHOLOGICAL SELF-CRITICISM: MARK TWAIN'S FRONTIER

The most interesting and complex response to these issues and to the language of myth and ideology in which they were understood is that of Mark Twain. His personal experience had carried him through the transformations associated with the Frontier of the Civil War period and the social transformations of the Gilded Age. His understanding of his own experience was enriched by his profound knowledge of the literary culture of his day—a culture whose language he exploited, parodied, and transformed into the tools of creative analysis. His last major novel, *A Connecticut Yankee in King Arthur's Court* (1889), was multilayered satire, which took aim not only at the ideology of Gilded Age industrialism, but also at the ideology of high-minded reformers like Bellamy; and it exposed the fallacies and dangers of American ideology in a language of symbols that drew on the basic sources of popular and high culture, from Cooper to Horatio Alger, from Tennyson and Bellamy to Buffalo Bill.[23]

Twain's relation to the Frontier, and to its myth, was central to his development as man and as writer. He was born in the "backwash" of the frontier, of a family that had been part of the pattern of westward emigration until his father's generation, moving from Virginia to East Tennessee to Missouri. The Frontier of myth, received by way of Fenimore Cooper and the "penny dreadful" newspapers, was basic to his imaginative education. His hometown of Hannibal was a terminal for an abortive transcontinental railroad enterprise, and the deluded optimism of the western railroad business was part of the town's civic life. Faced with the loss of his profession as river pilot and with the danger of conscription as results of the Civil War, Twain followed the traditional path of refuge that led beyond the western borders to the mining regions of Nevada and California.

As he looked back on this experience from the perspective of the successful writer, he adopted toward it an ambivalent attitude of celebration and debunking. This ambivalence is reflected in *Roughing It* (1872), his first extensive treatment of his early life. Twain represents his experience as one of demystification. He presents himself as an "innocent," whose ideas and expectations about the West have been gained entirely from the romances of Cooper and his imitators. He expects to meet noble savages and behold Edenic landscape, to befriend Frontier hunters of the Leatherstocking kind. This literary romance is augmented by the more materialistic elements of the Frontier Myth, specifically the expectation of magical access to incredible wealth—the "gold rush" myth.

By juxtaposing the literary and the economic versions of the Frontier Myth, Twain debunks and demystifies both. On the journey his expectation of gorgeous scenery is disappointed by the monotonous landscape over which the stagecoach journeys like a dust-devouring beetle. His expectation of meeting the Noble Red Man is undone by meeting the "Goshoot" Indians of the Great Basin:

> The disgust which the Goshoots gave me, a disciple of Cooper and a worshipper of the Red Man—even of the scholarly savages in the *Last of the Mohicans* who are fittingly associated with backwoodsmen who divide each sentence into two equal parts: one part . . . refined and choice of language, and the other part just such an attempt to talk like a hunter or a mountaineer, as a Broadway clerk might make after eating a collection of Emerson Bennett's works and studying frontier life at the Bowery Theater a couple of weeks—I say that nausea . . . set me to examining authorities, to see if perchance I had been overestimating the Red Man while viewing him through the mellow moonshine of romance. The revelations that came were disenchanting. It was curious to see how quickly the paint and tinsel fell away from him and left him treacherous, filthy and repulsive—and how quickly the evidences accumulated that whenever one finds an Indian tribe he has only found Goshoots more or less modified by circumstances and surroundings—but Goshoots, after all. They deserve pity, poor creatures; and they can have mine—at this distance.[24]

Twain's disillusionment takes exactly the form suggested by the newspaper and magazine treatments of the Indian question in the 1869–75 period, and he employs the same formulas that Custer borrowed for his anti-Indian essays of 1867–69—particularly the use of Cooper as the archspokesman for the "romantic" and "sentimental" view and the analogy between the sordid comedy of reservation life and that of the Broadway stage. Twain expands on these attitudes in other sketches published in the sixties and seventies. In an essay on his visit to Niagara Falls, he makes the urban savage association: a naive tourist who uses Cooperian terms to address the pseudo-Indians who manufacture souvenirs is beaten up for his pains, and discovers that these noble red men are all Irish immigrants from Limerick.[25]

Such literary "undoing" was essential to the creative task of *Roughing It* in which Twain was not merely retailing his past life but looking for a literary language appropriate to his vision. The language of traditional romance was not merely inaccurate in depicting reality; its highfalutin manner and presumption of moral omniscience were a persuasive falsification of reality which could distort human behavior in the real world. Whereas the Southwest humorists, whose works Twain read and whose techniques he imitated, had seized instead upon the vernacular, they generally did so with the purpose of emphasizing the quaintness and impropriety of Frontier speech. Twain reverses the ideological charge of the contrast, locating truth and virtue in the vernacular. It is the linguistic equivalent of his handling of landscape description: the "realistic" scene is always one that does not glitter, that deliberately invokes a romantic convention in order to undermine or contradict it.

The "gold fever" with its get-rich-quick ideology is another order of romance or illusion. Twain's first attempts to find gold are motivated by the expectation of obtaining a vast fortune for very little expenditure of labor. He learns quite early to suspect the illusory promise of wealth in rocks that are merely gorgeous, and he offers an antiromantic moral: Not only is it true that not all that glitters is gold, but it can be asserted that nothing that glitters is gold. The truth will never be pretty. But this kind of disillusionment does not touch the essential myth of the gold rush, and Twain and his friends persist in thinking they can strike it rich merely by showing up and staking a claim. They stake out a "lumber ranch" on the primeval shores of Tahoe, and through carelessness with fire, burn their forest to ashes. They discover a "blind lead" which will make them millionaires if they will only validate their claim by doing a day's work— and between dreams of future leisure and pursuit of still more glorious illusions of wealth, they somehow fail to do the work. As his adventures proceed, Twain's persona perceives that the essential nature of the illusion offered by the Frontier Myth is its substitution of easy wealth for the necessity of labor. His is a "post-Frontier" sensibility, which insists that "real life" is no longer constituted (if it ever was) to provide farms, ranches, and gold mines to the first comers for no cost. Once Twain discovers his own vocation as reporter and lecturer, he sees the gold rush from a new perspective. It is a "beggar's revel" in which the expectation of wealth produces an economy based entirely on paper values—mining stock whose only value is the expected wealth it symbolizes.

> It was the strangest phase of life one can imagine. It was a beggar's revel. There was nothing doing in the district—no mining— no milling—no productive effort—no income . . . and yet a stranger would have supposed he was walking among bloated millionaires . . . Few people took *work* into their calculations—or outlay of money either; except the work and expenditures of other people. . . . Every one of these wild cat mines—not mines, but

holes in the ground over imaginary mines—was incorporated and had handsomely engraved "stock" and the stock was salable, too. It was bought and sold with a feverish avidity on the boards every day . . .[26]

The Frontier beggar's revel is a crude reflection of the larger economic scene which Twain attacks in his first novel, *The Gilded Age* (1873) written with Charles Dudley Warner. Here the dichotomy between the imperatives of labor and the illusions of an easy way to wealth and status is more elaborately worked out. But his larger theme is that of the corruption of both business and politics by the new profit opportunities offered by Reconstruction and the government sponsorship of railroads. At the heart of the novel is the effort of the ebullient Colonel Sellers to finance his own transcontinental railroad. The passage dealing with the promotion of that enterprise are a deliberate parody of the publicity of Jay Cooke's Northern Pacific and the effusions of Gilpin. The scheme is financed by federal money, obtained through bribery under the cover of a philanthropic project: building a college for Negroes in East Tennessee—an area noted for its lack of black population. Again, the Frontier Myth is exposed as a doctrine which makes its believers liable to fraud and failure. Those characters who build their expectations on the speculative possibilities of Sellers's enterprise are ruined; only those characters who find their work and buckle to it prosper.[27]

But it would be a mistake to reduce Twain's attitude to the ideology of hard work and self-denial he seems to advocate in *Gilded Age*: the pretty illusions of romance and the expectation of a sudden bonanza remained dear to his heart. This ambivalence finds its best reflection in the Tom Sawyer/Huck Finn books which he wrote between 1876 and 1887. Here he reveals his dual allegiance to myth and to realism. Twain's nostalgia for a world in which lost illusions are rediscovered and made good is fully indulged in *Tom Sawyer*. The famous whitewashing episode, and the Bible-ticket "corner" (modeled on Jay Gould's stock market scams) which succeeds it, are celebrations of the boy's cleverness in using the illusions of others—the paper values of his society—for his own real gain. Yet remember that the novel is a parody of Horatio Alger, in which success is achieved precisely by avoiding hard work and good manners, and doing everything just as the bad little boy would do it. Here the contradictions of Twain's viewpoint appear. In *The Gilded Age* he speaks as a respectable adult of the mid–Victorian Age, and he warns the romantic boys that the Frontier is gone, and bread must be earned by the sweat of one's brow. In *Tom Sawyer*, Twain is a boy himself who believes in illusions and prospers nonetheless, who has returned to a world where magic works; where bread is not earned with the sweat of your brow—but rather is loaded with quicksilver (like the processed ore in *Roughing It*), so that it can magically seek you out where you lie hidden across the river. When Tom asserts that robbers are the "most respectable" people in society, the atmosphere of play-fantasy reduces to a mere suggestion one of the bitterest ironies of *The Gilded Age*: that power and prestige were in fact in the hands of Robber Barons and their political lackeys.[28]

The Adventures of Huckleberry Finn brings these contradictions to a head. Huck is faced with a series of crises that compel him to choose between the world of romantic illusion or myth, and reality. He is already disenchanted with Tom Sawyer's robber game when the book begins. When his father forcibly seizes him, imprisons him on the island, and threatens his life, evasion of reality becomes impossible. To survive, Huck has to see through the fictions both of the town (whose religion of legalism and piety is impotent to save Huck) and of Pap—whose claims to the legitimate power of the paternal role are also fictions imposed on reality. Once committed to the real task of escaping from Pap, Huck is required continually to increase his mastery of the borderland between myth and reality: to use the power of lies and fictions effectively against those who would ensnare him, he must himself be quite clear about what is real and what is not. His primary teacher in this process is the slave Jim, who plays Chingachgook to Huck's Leatherstocking—aiding and sustaining Huck, teaching him the lore of the real world, representing the life of authentic feeling which social conventions repress or distort. The mutuality of dependence that unites Huck and Jim in their common quest for escape and survival compels Huck to deal directly with the primary mythology or false religion of his society: the system of chattel slavery, and the ideology of race, social class, and moral authority that sustains the system.

Huck and Jim's adventures on the river provide a series of unavoidable choices that compel Huck to choose between the "illusory" or false values of society—in which, nonetheless, he continues to believe—and the human and material reality of Jim and their friendship. The world of the river is a "magic" and romantic one, described in the romantic terms common to Frontier romances. But in *Huckleberry Finn*, the magic world is a limited one; it cannot spread its power to the world of the shore, in which evil, violence, and greed shape values and behavior. On the contrary, the river itself is invaded, and the raft taken over by the emissaries of the shore.[29]

The contrast of river and shore in *Huckleberry Finn* is an abstraction of the relationship of Frontier to Metropolis. In *Roughing It* this contrast is reflected in the opposition between the "real West" and the illusions of Twain's naive narrator. In *Gilded Age*, the real West is the place of poverty and hard scrabble labor, into which the illusion makers and corrupt speculators of the Metropolis project the false glamour of their mythology and their greed. In *Tom Sawyer*, there is a gentler contrast between the town and the pastoral refuge the boys find on Jackson's Island—described by Twain in the conventional language of Frontier landscape description. But in *Huckleberry Finn*, these variant readings of the symbolic opposition are combined and coordinated into a single symbolism of great complexity and resonance. Huck's successive refuges are Frontiers that fail to live up to the promise, which is to be at once magical in providing happiness and "real"—that is, unprettified, unpretentious, vernacular. Pap's cabin fails as refuge, because Pap is not an alternative to the respectable virtues of the "Metropolis"—merely their perverse inversion. Jackson's Island fails—it is too close to home, and it begins to be assimilated by the Metropolis because slaves and slave catchers can now find the place out. The raft is another kind of refuge, a floating island on which happiness and true speech are possible—but it too is doomed by the flow of river and time which carry it deeper into the slave region. At the Phelps plantation, Tom Sawyer returns and transforms the Underground Railroad (and by analogy, the hope of abolition) into a game whose rules are determined by the conventions of the Metropolis's literary mythology. *Uncle Tom* may have made a war against slavery possible, but as a guide to black liberation it was useless: the vernacular fails, and Jim's liberation becomes a mockery.

Yet at the end, Twain's hero has still not abandoned the hope of finding his way to the mythic Frontier, the place beyond the Metropolis: he is going to "light out for the Territory," for the Indian country. This was a notion which Twain meant to pursue, in a projected sequel whose manuscript version is titled "Tom and Huck Among the Indians." The projected story would have extended the mythology-debunking motif that characterizes much of *Huckleberry Finn*. Tom would approach the Indian territory equipped with ideas out of Fenimore Cooper, like the narrator of *Roughing It*; and he would have found that the savage was far more horrid than even that dime-novel Indian villain Injun Joe. This experience of disillusion is not inconsistent with the logic of *Huckleberry Finn*. Given the rhythmic persistence of the experience of disillusion, of the discovery of Frontiers that fail, it is not difficult to see that Huck's "lighting out for the Territory" will disappoint him. But within the framework of *Huckleberry Finn* that sense derives from evidence that the values of the Metropolis are everywhere and continually encroach on the terrain of freedom. "Among the Indians" has a different basis for hopelessness—it is not the corruption of the Metropolis that spoils the West, but the cruel savagery of the natives.

In the novel, Tom, Huck, and Jim were to join a single-family wagon party, including a beautiful young girl betrothed to a wandering hunter. The family is lulled into a false sense of security, in part because they heed Tom Sawyer's Cooperian "wisdom" about the noble red man more than the warnings of the rough plainsman. In the boys' absence, the wagon party is massacred and the girl taken captive. The boys are met by the hunter, who will guide them and lead the rescue attempt; and he is their man of true speech and vision, who unmasks the myth to show the reality. But "realism" in this case requires an honest treatment of the captivity theme. As the Goshoots passage reveals, Twain's ideas about Indians were those of his "tough-minded" contemporaries. These ideas, reflected in his writings for the *Galaxy* and other New York journals in 1869–74, were reinforced by the research he did for "Among the Indians," which took him back to Custer's account of "Hancock's War" of 1866–69. He was convinced that the necessary and inevitable fate of the young girl in the hands of the Indians would have been gang rape; and his young hunter discovers signs that this has indeed been her fate. At this point, Twain abandoned the project. Perhaps, as some Twain scholars have suggested, it was his squeamishness about the theme of rape and his belief that without at least the invocation of rape as a possibility, he would be betraying his commitment to realism and honesty.[30]

Be that as it may, "Among the Indians" reveals Twain's persistence in employing the vocabulary of the Frontier Myth—or his own version of it— as a way of interpreting the social and moral alternatives available to himself and his fictional surrogates. *Huckleberry Finn* presents the closing of the Frontier from the Frontiersman's perspective, as the loss of freedom to an expanding Metropolis; and it suggests that in primitive character— in the personalities of young women, children, and childlike nonwhite races—lies the only alternative to the dangerous values of the white, adult, male order of society. "Among the Indians" is dialectically opposite to *Huckleberry Finn*—what it challenges is the myth of a primitive nobility, of an alternative in man's wilderness condition. The world then becomes a battleground between the Dukes and Dauphins above and the various kinds of crackers and Comanches below.

Such a reading appears in suppressed passages from his earlier books, most notably in "The French and the Comanches" (1879) which he deleted from *A Tramp Abroad*. The essay begins by invoking "cruelty, savagery, and the spirit of massacre," and asserting that this spirit is not unique to savage races like the Comanches. "It is hard to draw a line here, with any degree of exactness, between the French [and] the Comanches," the only differences being that the Comanches do not massacre one another, and that the French are "more ingenious" in their cruelty. What the Comanche does only to people of alien race and culture, the French do to fellow citizens and Christians. Twain then recounts the massacres perpetrated in the course of French history, between different religious, political, and class entities struggling for power, and cites the torture and legalized rape (*droit de seigneur*) of the ancien régime as evidence of their Comanche-like behavior. On the literal level, Twain appears to find the Comanches on the whole less savage than the French, although the point of the essay is of course to discredit both. Nonetheless, the grounds of the distinction are worth noting. Twain offers it as a norm of racial warfare that the "spirit of massacre" should prevail. Where the French reveal their depravity is in treating competition between classes, parties, or interest groups as if it were racial warfare. What is still more horrible is the persistence of this racialization of class warfare down into the enlightened nineteenth century—a persistence revealed by the massacres of Communards in 1871 directed against the proletariat of Paris.[31]

The symbolic language of Twain's works is the product of reading, experience, introspection, and creative effort, and therefore is a personal and peculiar system. But in its major tropes, symbolism, and structuring principles it is clearly cognate with the myth/ideological system that took shape around the Indian wars and labor struggles of the Last Stand period. The linkage of Indian and class warfare, the expectation of massacre as its result, was basic to both systems. What is different is the greater complexity and ambivalence of Twain's own system—a result of his divided identification, both for and against society, for and against the wilderness.

THE SPIRIT OF MASSACRE AND
THE INSTINCT OF PROGRESS

A Connecticut Yankee in King Arthur's Court is Twain's attempt to work all of this into a coherent fictional scheme. A number of coincident factors shaped his changing intentions about the work and his final treatment of the theme. The warfare of capital and labor was of serious concern to him. He shared Howells's concern about the apparent spread of anarchism among the laboring classes and a spirit of oppression among the masters of capital. Both men read *Looking Backward* and agreed that it might be "a New Bible," pointing the way to resolution of the present difficulties; yet such views were no sooner stated than Twain seems to have begun to doubt them. The "spirit of massacre," he had written, is not a racial trait but "grow[s] naturally out of the social system." The values that Bellamy invoked were, perhaps, unrealistic at best, tyrannous at worst, and in the interim liable to exploitation by cruel and vicious frauds like the scalawags of *The Gilded Age*, Pap or the Duke and Dauphin in *Huckleberry Finn*.

The recently completed cycle of works drawing on the "matter of Hannibal" had sharpened Twain's sense of the ethical consequences of his society's ideology, and had developed to a point of high sophistication his battery of literary tropes—particularly the contrast of "true vernacular" and "false genteel" speech, and the symbolism of race. The cycle had also drawn him back, physically and in memory, to the South and its history: the false "Walter Scott" romanticism of the slave-owning "chivalry," the false promise of Reconstruction, the persistence of racism, greed, and oppression as facts of southern life. His reading provided him with the literary targets for satire which were closely linked with the symbolism in which he perceived these social themes. His rejection of the shallow romanticism of Walter Scott sent him on to read Alfred Lord Tennyson's *Idylls of the King*, whose profounder burden was the struggle between Arthurian order and the disorder of primal savagery. Arthur's continual lament—"All my realm reels back into the Beast"—was a thinly veiled echo of the Victorian fear of the specter of anarchy and social dissolution that awaited a society incapable of resolving peacefully the warfare of labor and capital.

Twain's recent work on "Among the Indians" had also reacquainted him with the language of "savage warfare"—the specifically American version of the conflict between order's "realm" and the anarchy of "the Beast." Among the sources he drew on most heavily was General Custer's *My Life on the Plains*, which gave him a number of natural descriptions and confirmed his ideas about the manner and motive of Indian cruelty. The chapters of that book were being serialized in the *Galaxy* at the same time that Twain's humorous sketches were appearing. The two men may or may not have met each other, but can hardly have missed acquaintance with each other's writing. Twain's continuing interest is also attested by his offering to publish Mrs. Custer's reminiscences of her days with the general on the southern plains. *Tenting on the Plains* appeared in 1887, two years before *Connecticut Yankee*. This Indian war material contributed to the symbolism of class in Twain's story; and the Last Stand may well have been the model for the concluding massacre.[32]

The initial intentions of Twain are reflected in the satiric form of the first half of the novel. Twain apparently meant to contrast the progressive spirit of nineteenth-century American values with the regressive ideologies of traditional aristocracy, political monarchism, and established religion or superstition. The literary voice of the hero narrator, Hank Morgan, would be that of the truth-seeing and -speaking vernacular; and vernacular speech, metaphors, and jokes would continually deflate the pretensions of both the language and the ideology of chivalric romance. The point of the joke is crystallized when the Yankee—who has become Arthur's grand vizier—compels the knights to change their heraldic devices for nineteenth-century billboard advertisements—"USE PETERSON'S PROPHYLACTIC TOOTHBRUSH—IT'S ALL THE GO." As the Yankee himself suggests, the point of the joke—and hence its ideological charge—will be lost on an audience that cannot read and has no notion of either advertising or toothbrushes.

Such satiric ironies, however, are generally buried beneath the strong contrasts Twain offers between Yankee progress and Arthurian "benightedness." The Yankee speaks for science against magic, for egalitarian values against the aristocracy of birth, for a merit system of promotion against one based on connections, for an equitable code of laws against law of might, for a sharing of power against the monopolization of force by a privileged class. He is for religious toleration and against cruel and unusual punishments. He founds a patent office to support technological innovation. He is for free trade in commodities and against monopolies of all kinds. He offers England a chance to avoid its medievalism and to leap into the light of modern Americanism without the pain of intervening stages.

The contrast between medieval and American values is heightened by his invocation of the Indian savage as a metaphor for the mental condition of his Arthurian aristocrats. They have the manners and the morals of "white Indians" or "Comanches." This suggests a kind of innocence in them; and in the case of Arthur, it suggests a degree of truth in the idea of the noble savage. In representing the cruelty and ignorance of his aristocrats, Twain is true to the vision of "The French and the Comanches," which associates the aristocracy and the savage to "the spirit of massacre," violence unchecked by reason or conscience. But in Arthur, he suggests a lingering affinity for the notion of innate nobility as an inherited, racial trait: Arthur's royalty of nature is revealed in his reaction to the smallpox victims, and it is even more admirable than the Yankee's calculated and self-protective response.[33]

The relationship of aristocrats to a semienslaved lower class, coupled with the satire of chivalric myths, suggests the analogy between Arthurian Britain and the South of Mark Twain's past. The analogy is made explicit in the section of the narrative which sees the disguised Yankee and the king taken and sold as slaves—a plot device that was a basic formula of abolitionist fiction in the 1850s. Here the racial analogy with class involves an opposition that complements the white-Indian conflict. If the Arthurian knights are the southern chivalry, then the lower classes are an amalgamation of both the actual slave class—the blacks—and of the poor whites, who were dependent economically on the planters and who gave their suffrage to the system that enslaved the blacks and pauperized themselves. If in the Indian-war analogy the Yankee appears as a civilizer among savages, in the southern analogy he appears as a carpetbag philanthropist who aims at abolishing slavery and substituting in its place the political and economic system of the free North. He is an invader from another culture (or time) who can project a tyrannous reconstruction of society only because he has been able to conquer a position at the top of society.[34]

The slavery-Reconstruction metaphor, buttressed by the "savage" metaphor, suggests a racial model for interpreting the difficulties the Yankee faces. Although his ideology is democratic, he wonders if the population itself is "up to revolution grade." As a nineteenth-century chauvinist, he is convinced that the centuries of experience between Arthur and George Washington have brought the Anglo-Saxon, at least, up to that standard. Yet the terms of the analogy that links Arthurian Britain with nineteenth-century America suggests that we should be doubtful of the Yankee's confidence. If the "hinds" of sixth-century Britain share the consciousness of nineteenth-century crackers, perhaps there is something wrong in the germ plasm of the race—just as there is something right in Arthur's nature. It is a corrosive and corrupting doubt for an exponent of democratic revolution. It weakens Hank Morgan, and it weakened Twain himself.[35]

Hank confronts early on the problem of democratic revolution. He justifies the French Revolution and the Reign of Terror as the only possible response to the longer, crueler Reign of Terror imposed on the peasantry by the aristocracy. He asserts that revolutions must be baptized in blood if they are to succeed, for only by engaging and giving power to the rage of the people does a revolution engage them in the work of making society according to their own will and intention. Revolution imposed from the top may give them the forms of freedom; but only an active seizure of freedom for themselves will make them free in truth. (This had been the John Brown/Theodore Parker thesis about the moral necessity of a slave rebellion.)

But Hank has two reasons for shrinking from fully endorsing Red Revolution. The first is that he does not trust the character of the people in whose name he acts. He persistently finds in them evidence of "slavishness"—they are superstitious, they worship wealth and status instead of merit, they toady to power in hope of preferment, they are vicious to those weaker than themselves. Hank Morgan is an elitist whose sense of worth derives from his triumph in the competitive life of the nineteenth century, and from his easy victory over competing authorities in the sixth. His own pride of place, his enjoyment of power and the position of moral superiority, his preference for his own kind—boys and men whose character is that of nineteenth-century "go-getters" in sixth-century dress—incline him to be protective of the social order he means to replace. By borrowing the authority of the old order, he can begin to construct a conspiracy that will "build the new world amid the ruins of the old." He creates a revolutionary vanguard of sorts in the corps of boys whom he organizes and trains in the secret knowledge of the higher technology—a cadre chosen from among the elite previously selected for his "civilization factories" or colleges. But although his notion of aristocracy has a different basis, the social order he creates is still divided between elite rulers and slavish commoners; and although he calls for democracy, his mistrust of the slavish and savage commons persists.

This mistrust underlies his second reason for refusing to foster revolution: his desire to protect the institutional and economic forms of his "new deal" once he has successfully put it in place under royal sponsorship. Thus his revolution—like that of Reconstruction—does not convert the masses to its cause, nor undermine traditional ideas and authorities. Isolated as much as aggrandized by the privileged position it hopes to protect, Morgan's regime—like that of Reconstruction—is finally and fatally environed by an opposition uniting the old aristocracy with the slavish masses whom they oppress and control.[36]

The ambiguity of Hank's position is fundamental to his character; and as the novel proceeds, the contradictions of his values become more and more crucial. His identification as a "Connecticut Yankee" carries positive connotations of inventiveness, cleverness, a capacity for hard and productive work. Yet it also invokes associations of the carpetbagger—especially in Twain's southern drawl—and of the confidence man. He is "the Boss"—a name that suggests both the owner or manager of a factory and the corrupt patron (and presumed tyrant) of an urban immigrant constituency (à la Boss Tweed). His name links him to the famous pirate Henry Morgan —the real-life plunderer of the Spanish Main. "Morgan" is also the name of the great financier and Robber Baron J. P. Morgan—certainly a "respectable" robber, a real-life version of the thing Tom Sawyer plays at being at the conclusion of his *Adventures*. The new order that Hank Morgan substitutes for that of chivalry is precisely the order of J. P. Morgan. The knights cease to ride on errantry and become, instead, speculators *in* the stock market that has arisen along with Hank's other nineteenth-century improvements—the telegraph, the railroad, and the free press. Hank flatters himself that by following the design of nineteenth-century American progress, he had made possible a society that is both fundamentally stable and yet progressive in just the way that industrial America was progressive: a society in which the holdings and powers of the propertied classes are respected, but which nonetheless is peacefully evolving toward a more perfect democracy.

But Morgan's belief is founded on the literal acceptance of what is only a literary convention. In Twain's earlier books, this type of illusion took the form of belief in literary romance; and it was usually deflated and undone by its parodic confrontation with practical experience and vernacular discourse, of the kind used by Huck Finn. Hank Morgan speaks like Huck Finn, and so we are disposed to accept him as a "realist": yet his romantic illusions also distract him from an attack on the hard realities that still underlie social relations. Hank's illusions take the following form: he believes that since he has parodied and undone the myth of chivalry, altered the basis of privilege from birth to wealth, and changed romantic motives to self-interested ones, he has made impossible the outbreak of disorder that (according to Tennyson) destroyed the Arthurian utopia. Since chivalry is no more, it is impossible that Modred should force a breach between Arthur and Lancelot over Guinevere—romance is less important in these hardheaded days. Hence there will be no war in France, no rebellion by Modred, no last battle, and no reeling of Arthur's realm back into the beast. Such a flattering self-image was very much a part of the Victorian world, which came to believe that the course of progress and economic interdependence had made a world war impossible. But, as Twain shows, the new commercial values merely provide different occasions for strife. Modred and Lancelot fall out over a "killing" made in the stock market, and good nineteenth-century motives destroy Arthur's regime at least as thoroughly as the old chivalric motives in Tennyson.

In its latter portions, Twain's book departs emphatically from the progressive model of Bellamy's *Looking Backward*. Hank has failed as a revolutionary in part because of his Bellamistic faith in rational progress, the organization of society under a managerial elite, and acceptance of the economic tendencies of the trust-building era. The necessity of violence is argued by Hank himself in his meditation on the Reign of Terror, but Hank fails to heed the logic of this meditation. Worse, he fails to understand the nature of the society that has sent him forth. Bellamy's hero fell asleep and awoke to find the revolution accomplished as easily and bloodlessly as in a dream. But Hank Morgan is a "supervisor" at the Colt armaments works, and is thus engaged in expanding society's capacity for administering violence. If Hank is the nineteenth century's man, then Colt's Firearms is the representative of modern industrialism. As a supervisor of work in the plant, Hank is engaged in bossing gangs of workers, dominating them by his wits, but relying in the final analysis on force. It is a blow on the head, suffered in the course of a disagreement with one of his workers "conducted with crowbars," that sends him backward in time. Both the violence that sends him and the direction of travel are antithetical to the ideas of *Looking Backward*: Bellamy dreams his reader past the invisible violence of the present to a future of perfect design; Twain hurls us backward in time, into the primitive past, through a violent confrontation between industrial labor and management.[37]

Instead of applying to the sixth century his own analysis of the violent basis of human society and the necessity of violent revolution, Hank Morgan chooses a mode of violence that belongs to the Myth of the Frontier—as modified by the experience of the Civil War. He first attempts to resolve the problem by eliminating the moral authority of the aristocracy through a symbolic confrontation—a tournament in which he will defeat representatives of the ruling class and so demonstrate the efficacy of his power and values. He arms himself for this battle with just the weapons we might expect him to use against "Indians"—a cowboy's lariat hung from a western saddlehorn, and a pair of Colt's revolvers. This confrontation combines the imagery of the tournament—both the medieval original and its nineteenth-century version—and the Wild West show. Twain had seen Buffalo Bill's Wild West in 1885 and written of it, with a shrewd understanding of the Wild West's implicit myth of American progress.

The final battle invokes images from the same source in a much more complex way. Failing to understand that bourgeois greed can spur violence as surely as romantic illusion, the Yankee has failed to anticipate the outbreak of war between Arthur's party and that of Lancelot and Modred. Failing to educate the masses "up to revolution grade," he has opened his regime to attack by the joint forces of aristocratic reaction and religious superstition. Gathering his elite corps of boys about him, he fortifies an isolated position and prepares to stand off the united forces of the aristocracy and the slavish masses. His position is entrenched, surrounded with dynamite mines and electrified barbed wire and bristling with Gatling guns—a masterpiece of nineteenth-century technology. But against him is arrayed the apparently united mass of "the English nation," peasants and chivalry alike; and his "boys," having learned modern republican patriotism at his hands, balk at making war upon the nation.

Morgan answers their objections ideologically and technologically. He declares that their real strife is not with the nation or "the people" of England, but only with the ruling clerical-chivalric class; and through the magic of modern science (specifically electricity) they will be able to effect the separation of the ruling class from the masses—and exterminate the armored chivalry with the flick of a switch. They will first have to demonstrate to "the nation" the power of Morgan's science, decimating and demoralizing the peasants but not exterminating them. As a preliminary demonstration of power, and to keep their own weapons from being used against them, Morgan orders the blowing up of all the railroads, telegraphs, workshops, and civilization factories—a massive and instantaneous "scorched earth" in which Morgan destroys his civilization in order to save it.[38]

This is followed by the "Battle of the Sand Belt," in which Morgan's dynamite mines, electrified wire, and Gatling guns accomplish the first part of his program. The peasants are thoroughly demoralized, and "the war with the English nation" is ended. But the forces of chivalry are not so easily defeated: it is the source of their power, and of what virtue they have, that they will maintain their right to rule at all costs. Hence the only way to defeat them will be to exterminate them.

The idea of the war of extermination is the central theme of the Myth of the Frontier, and of the myths of class struggle whose origins we have been examining. The notion of an extermination restricted to the ruling class derives from the Civil War variations on this theme. Extermination or removal of the Confederate elite was suggested several times during the war. The Civil War aspect of the metaphor links the battle of the Sand Belt with Twain's southern theme; but the association of both peasants and knights with savages and primitives suggests the Indian war connection as well.

Here the Custer myth is brought into play. The original myth presented the tableaux of his defeat as an image of progressive young soldiers foundering in a sea of rampant savagery, behind which lay the fanaticism and bigotry of false "philanthropists." Falling in with Bellamy's military metaphor, Hank made his military academy, his West Point, the central institution of learning for his new elite. For them, science and military organization go hand in hand—as indeed they had done for Hank, when he exercised his Yankee ingenuity in the Colt Firearms factory. He is the commander of an elite corps of West Pointers and boys—the imagery links him closely to Custer—and with them he is proud to assert that he will challenge the whole of English chivalry to battle, just as Custer dared the entire Sioux nation to oppose him and his single regiment. Hank Morgan's reasons for pride are far more complex than those of Custer, but the kinship is apparent.

The battle that follows ironically combines both the catastrophic reading of the Last Stand and the view of the battle as a redemptive sacrifice. The catastrophic reading of the Last Stand held that it represented the possible destruction of civilization and progress by an uprising of human savagery from below. The optimistic reading emphasized the sacrificial aspect of the battle, showing that Custer's death struggle wounded the Indians and aroused the slumbering spirit of the American nation, leading in the end to revenge on the Indian and the triumph of a chastened and purified people. But the Battle of the Sand Belt combines these readings into a single dark prophecy. The progressive elite deploys its technological might and exterminates its class enemy with appalling thoroughness:

> One thing seemed to be sufficiently demonstrated: our [electric] current was so tremendous that it killed before the victim could cry out . . . I believed the time was come, now, for my climax; I believed that that whole army was in our trap . . . So I touched a button and set fifty electric suns aflame on the top of our precipice.
>
> The sudden glare paralyzed this host . . . I shot the current through all the fences and struck the whole host dead in their tracks. *There* was a groan you could *hear*! It voiced the death pang of eleven thousand men . . . "Stand to your guns, men! Open fire!"
>
> The thirteen gatlings began to vomit death into the fated ten thousand . . . Within ten short minutes after we had opened fire armed resistance was totally annihilated, the campaign was ended, we fifty-four masters of England! Twenty-five thousand men lay dead around us.

But the political failure of Hank Morgan to raise the people as a whole to revolution grade makes it impossible for him to leave his fortress. Although this Custer has massacred all the Indians, his fate is the same: the Yankee falls into a trance caused by Merlin, and his elite corps perish of a pestilence brewed in the piled-up corpses of their slaughtered enemies.[39]

The conclusion is a blow to Bellamiac faith. Violence proves inescapable, and the massive force of the savagery of the lower depths is canceled out by the armed might that reason deploys; but in the end, reason itself sinks into magic, madness, and disease through its surfeit of power and of killing. It is a horrible vision, prophetic in many of its details of the causes and tactics of the Great War, and of the revolutions that grew out of the exhaustion of society's military frenzy. But it is also a brilliant and complex development of the implications of the Custer myth and the ideology of class struggle that it contained—one in which the Last Stand becomes a metaphor for the fate of both savages and cavalrymen, peasants and aristocrats, proletarians and elites; and the "Instinct of Progress" itself willingly calls upon the "Spirit of Massacre."

Twain's work uses the symbolic language of the Frontier Myth tradition, and he shares its traditional preoccupations. But his book is not simply a further elaboration of that tradition; it is a commentary on it, an attempt to turn the language of myth back upon itself. Thus, it does not proffer author or reader the kind of satisfaction mythology has to offer: it does not "naturalize" the social dilemma by assimilating it into a vision of harmonious natural wholeness. _Connecticut Yankee_ presents the Myth of the Frontier in the form of a tragedy. Hank Morgan is a hero because he exemplifies the entrepreneurial skills and egalitarian ambitions of the Jacksonian Frontier hero, and because he has "improved" these basic endowments by adapting them to the task of industrial production and industrial management. He rises to the top of his world not through favor but through merit, particularly of the managerial kind. Yet he discovers that an aristocracy of labor and of merit is still an aristocracy—an order dependent on political and cultural privilege; and in a society divided between privileged and dependent classes (and between rival classes of the privileged), the maintenance of social order is still dependent on force. Indeed, the essence of class privilege, both under chivalry and under Sir Boss's "new deal," is the right to a legitimate monopoly of force. Hank displaces the monopoly of chain mail and battle-ax with a monopoly of barbed wire and Gatling guns; but he cannot himself dispense with his monopoly, even though it kills him. And there is Twain as well: unable, finally, to identify himself and us uncritically with Hank Morgan; but equally unable to reject Morgan, abandon the Gatlings, and merge with the peasantry of the "English nation." To do that would be to abandon Custer for Sitting Bull and civilization for white savagery. Morgan's trap is built into the language of the myth through which he interprets his Last Stand.

CONCLUSION AND PROLOGUE:
THE TURN OF THE CENTURY

Twain's tragic fable of a self-destroying progressivism effectively exhausts the existing vocabulary of the Frontier Myth, developing its ambivalent tendencies to the point at which they reveal their contradictory nature and cancel out. It is in these terms that he poses the dilemma confronting America as it approached the end of the nineteenth century: how to preserve the values and social structures of an entrepreneurial-agrarian democracy in an industrial society. As Twain shows, that way of posing the question suggests that the answer will be an unhappy one because it presupposes the loss or alteration of the very thing we wish to preserve. And if logic alone was insufficient to doom the Frontier Myth to inanition, there was the material fact that the progressive development of the public lands would inevitably, and at no very late date, exhaust that reservoir of "virgin land" which was the economic basis of the Myth.

But culture is tenacious of its values and traditions, even in the face of radical change—perhaps especially so in the face of such change. Faced with the choice of "liquidating" the concept of the Frontier or "renaturalizing" it, Americans chose the latter. By a systematic and highly selective reinterpretation of the language of the Myth, they adapted it to suit the ideological purposes and needs of the new industrial society.

At this point, we can see the completed vocabulary of the language available to them. At the core of the Myth is the belief that economic, moral, and spiritual progress are achieved by the heroic foray of civilized society into the virgin wilderness, and by the conquest and subjugation of wild nature and savage mankind. According to this Myth, the meaning and direction of American history—perhaps of Western history as a whole— is found in the metaphoric representation of history as an extended Indian war. In its original form, this Myth fleshed out the metaphor with the imagery and personalities of agrarian development; it equated the value of the wilderness with land, identified the savage opposition as Indian, and envisioned as heroes men who embodied the virtues and the liabilities of entrepreneurial individualists.

But beneath these agrarian trappings were more general principles which proved to be abstractable from their original settings. Behind the mystique of the "virgin land" lay the principle of the "resource Frontier": the economic doctrine which holds that the Frontier is the discovery and conquest of new lodes of valuable resources—precious metals, industrial ores, supplies of cheap labor, "virgin" markets among the masses of Asia or Europe. Behind the mystique of the Indian war lay a concept of social relations that insisted on the racial basis of class difference, and insisted that in a society so divided, strife was unavoidable until the more savage race was wholly exterminated or subjugated. This was a doctrine applied first of all to social relations in industry and the new cities of postwar America; and it could also apply to the governance of nonwhite populations beyond the seas, when an imperial America went in search of those new lands and virgin markets. Finally, the mystique of the Last Stand connected the system backward in time to the apocalyptic tradition of Puritanism and forward in time to the often prophesied Red Revolution in which "civilization as we know it" would be destroyed—or transfigured. It gave form and shape to the fear of what might come if the world envisioned by the Myth were somehow to repudiate its former sponsorship of progress and civilization in favor of the original savagery; it gave warning of what our fate might be if we ourselves failed to live up to the imperatives enjoined on us by our role in the Myth. And it contained the suggestion of a way to salvation in the notion that Custer's was a re-demptive sacrifice, and that from the ashes of that terminal battle of the last Frontier the shape of a hero for the new age arises: a soldier, a commander of men, a youth vested with the authority of age, a technocrat, a natural aristocrat.

These were the terms available to the makers of myth and ideology as the 1890s began. The decade 1888 to 1898 carried the social conflicts of the Gilded Age to a point of crisis surpassing that of 1876–77; and during this same period, there was a reassessment of the significance of the vanishing American Frontier that was more thoroughgoing, systematic, and self-conscious than anything since Cooper's conception of the Leatherstocking Tales. The opening years of the nineties saw the completion of the "Last Stand" saga with the death of Sitting Bill and the massacre of the Sioux by the Seventh Cavalry at Wounded Knee. The census of 1890 announced the disappearance of a "frontier line" from the population-density map; and this fact provided the basis for the new historiographical theory put forward in 1893 by Frederick Jackson Turner in his address on "The Significance of the Frontier in American History."

At about the same time, Theodore Roosevelt was completing his popular multivolume study of *The Winning of the West*, which converted the history of the Frontier into a myth of origins for the Progressive movement. With an assist from Social Darwinism and new theories of scientific management, this Progressive Frontier Myth provided the language for a triumphant "managerial ideology"—a doctrine capable of rationalizing and justifying the role played by the new class of "Sir Bosses" that directed the civilization factories of an industrial America. And finally, a new popular culture emerged, with tremendously enhanced capacity for reaching audiences en masse, and able to bring to bear a new, more varied, more elaborate battery of media, forms, and genres. The work done in this decade not only salvaged the conventional language of the Frontier Myth for purposes of entertainment, it wove the language of that Myth so deeply into the web of industrial popular culture that it still colors the way we count our wealth and estimate our prospects, the way we deal with nature and with the nations so that the Myth can still tell us what to look for when we look at the stars.

To keep these notes as concise as possible without sacrificing clarity, I have used an abbreviated version of standard footnote form. First entries for books and articles will give author and full title; subsequent entries will give author and short title. Publication dates and places are omitted from the notes, except in the case of primary sources, for which I have indicated the date of first publication in parentheses. Complete entries for all works cited will be found in the Bibliography.

There are a great number of citations from nineteenth-century newspapers, occasionally as many as thirty in a single footnote. For concision I have adopted the following format. The entry will be headed by the name of the newspaper and year of publication, abbreviated in the following manner: New York *Herald,* 1876 = *NYH 76.* This entry will be followed by the title of the article (where necessary), the date it appeared, and the page. However, in the vast majority of instances I have not thought it necessary to give the title of the article in the footnote. In many cases the title is given or the subject clearly described in the body of the text. Wherever I was in doubt about the clarity of the reference I have given the title.

LIST OF ABBREVIATIONS

AHR   *American Historical Review*
AL   *American Literature*
AM   *Atlantic Monthly*
AQ   *American Quarterly*
CBNM   Custer Battlefield National Monument, Museum and Library
CI   *Critical Inquiry*
DR   *Democratic Review*
FA   *Foreign Affairs*
HW   *Harper's Weekly*
HMM   *Harper's Monthly Magazine*
LH   *Labor History*
I-O   Chicago *Inter-Ocean*
JAC   *Journal of American Culture*
JAH   *Journal of American History*
JAS   *Journal of American Studies*
JFC   James Fenimore Cooper
JPC   *Journal of Popular Culture*
JW   *Journal of the West*
LC   Library of Congress
MP   *Marxist Perspectives*
NA   National Archives
NAR   *North American Review*
NLH   *New Literary History*
NYDG   New York *Daily Graphic*
NYH   New York *Herald*
NYSHA   New York State Historical Association
NYT   New York *Times*
NYTRIB   New York *Tribune*
NYW   New York *World*
PMLA   Publication of the Modern Language Association
RHR   *Radical History Review*
SR   *Socialist Review*
WHQ   *Western History Quarterly*

CHAPTER 1

1 Contemporary accounts of the Centennial Exposition and descriptive programs of the fairgrounds and related public celebrations are in *Frank Leslie's Illustrated Historical Register of the United States Centennial Exposition* and James D. McCabe, *The Illustrated History of the Centennial Exposition*. Older secondary sources that give a useful view of the Exposition's impact on Americans of that time are E. Benjamin Andrews, *The History of the Last Quarter-Century in the United States, 1870–1895*, ch. 8; and Ellis Paxson Oberholtzer, *A History of the United States Since the Civil War* 3: ch. 19. Original documents and useful commentaries are in Alan Trachtenberg, ed., *Democratic Vistas, 1860–1880*, chs. 1–5, 12, 17; and Lally Weymouth, ed., *America in 1876: The Way We Were*. Historical and analytical studies of the centennial are Dee Brown, *The Year of the Century: 1876*, esp. ch. 5; William P. Randel, *Centennial: American Life in 1876*, chs. 1, 8; Howard Mumford Jones, *The Age of Energy: Varieties of American Experience, 1865–1915*, ch. 4; and John G. Cawelti, "America on Display: The World's Fairs of 1876, 1893, 1923," in Frederic C. Jaher, ed., *The Age of Industrialism in America: Essays in Social Structure and Cultural Values*, ch. 11. On the overall look of America in 1876, see John Brinckerhoff Jackson, *American Space: The Centennial Years, 1865–1876*.

2 William Dean Howells, "A Sennight at the Centennial," quoted in Trachtenberg, *Democratic Vistas*, p. 85.

3 Randel, *Centennial*, pp. 293–95.

4 On the parades and their significance, see Brown and Randel, above; Andrews, *Last Quarter-Century*, p. 198. New York *Herald, Tribune*, and *Times* for July 5, 1876, have detailed accounts and editorial-page commentaries.

5 Howells, "A Sennight," pp. 85–86, is concerned with the replacement of men by machines as the means to labor's being crushed and dehumanized.

6 These matters are dealt with at much greater length in chapters 15 and 18 below. A *Herald* editorial on July 4 asked, "Have We Degenerated Morally" and offered only a tentative denial. *NYH 76*, July 6, p. 4. For brief centennial-related accounts, see Brown, *Year of the Century*, chs. 4, 6; Weymouth, *America in 1876*, chs. 1–3, esp. ch. 2; Trachtenberg, *Democratic Vistas*, chs. 9, 10, 13, 16; Randel, *Centennial*, ch. 9; Andrews, *Last Quarter-Century*, chs. 4–7; Oberholtzer, *History* 3: ch. 18.

7 See Chapter 18, below. The general shape of the affair is sketched in Andrews, *Last Quarter-Century*, ch. 7; Brown, *Year of the Century*, chs. 4–7; Randel, *Centennial*, ch. 3. The best account is Edgar I. Stewart, *Custer's Luck*, chs. 1–6.

8 Walt Whitman, "*Preface 1876*— Leaves of Grass *and Two Rivulets*," *Leaves of Grass*, ed. by Sculley Bradley and Harold W. Blodgett, pp. 748–49; "In Former Songs," p. 616.

9 *NYH 76*, July 6, p. 5.

10 Whitman, "From Far Dakota's Canons," p. 483.

CHAPTER 2

1 In fact, Congress refused to delay a scheduled cutback in army manpower. On the results of the battle, see Stewart, *Custer's Luck*, pp. 493–95; John S. Gray, *Centennial Campaign: The Sioux War of 1876*, ch. 22; Robert M. Utley, *Frontier Regulars: The United States Army and the Indian, 1866–1891*, ch. 15; Ralph K. Andrist, *The Long Death: The Last Days of the Plains Indians*, pp. 297–98.

2   Brian W. Dippie, *Custer's Last Stand: The Anatomy of an American Myth*, is an excellent survey of the subject. Robert M. Utley, *Custer and the Great Controversy: The Origin and Development of a Legend*, is more narrowly concerned with changing analyses of the battle. Bibliographical compendia are Tal Luther, *Custer High Spots*; and John M. Carroll, *Custer in Periodicals: A Bibliographic Checklist*. On illustrations, see Don M. Russell, *Custer's Last . . .*, on paintings and major illustrations of the battle; and *Custer's List: A Checklist of Pictures Relating to the Little Big Horn*. The Hemingway references are *For Whom the Bell Tolls*, ch. 30; *Islands in the Stream*, p. 459; see also *Across the River and Into the Trees*, pp. 16, 169, 265; and the Last Stand materials in the anthology he edited, *Men at War*, pp. 461–82, and also 221–22, 238–75, 288–301.

3   Richard Drinnon, *Facing West: The Metaphysics of Indian-Hating and Empire Building*, p. 457. On the general prevalence of the Frontier as historiographical theory, ideology, myth, and fact, see, for example, Ray Allen Billington, *America's Frontier Heritage*; Henry Nash Smith, *Virgin Land: The American West as Symbol and Myth*; Richard Slotkin, *Regeneration Through Violence: The Mythology of the American Frontier, 1600–1860*.

4   The definition of myth, and the applicability of the term to ideological materials and the productions of popular culture, are matters of debate among historians, literary critics, and anthropologists. This chapter offers a definition appropriate to the concerns of the book, and an overview of as much of the background theory as is necessary to understand the kind of analysis I will be doing. See also Slotkin, *Regeneration Through Violence*, ch. 1. A good brief definition is Raymond Williams, *Keywords: A Vocabulary of Culture and Society*, pp. 176–78. And compare William H. McNeill, "The Care and Repair of Public Myth," *Foreign Affairs* 61:1 (Fall 1982), 1–13; Thomas A. Bailey, "The Mythmakers of American History," in Nicholas Cords and Patrick Gerster, eds., *Myth and the American Experience* 1:2. This usage is at odds with that evidently preferred by anthropologists and some folklorists, for whom "myth" refers to cosmogonic stories and fables dealing with the gods; while the more human-centered and pseudo-historical matters are dealt with in "legend" and "folktale." See, for example, William Bascom, "The Forms of Folklore: Prose Narratives," *Journal of American Folklore* 78:307 (Jan.–Mar. 1965), 3–20 and esp. 5–6; and Alan Dundes, "Folk Ideas as Units of World View," *Journal of American Folklore* 84:1 (Jan. 1971), 93–103. (I am grateful to Bruce Jackson for bringing these articles to my attention.) My own definition corresponds to the idea of "mythique" suggested in William A. Clebsch, "The American 'Mythique' as Redeemer Nation," *Prospects* 4:79–94; and to certain aspects of the concept of "civic religion" offered by Catherine Albanese, *Sons of the Fathers: The Civil Religion of the American Revolution*, pp. 3–18. But "myth" has been for a generation one of the key terms of cultural analysis in American Studies and comparable fields, and it seems to me more useful to clarify the term—and evoke its connotations of past controversy—than to substitute the narrower "legend," the impressionistic "mythique," or the too specifically political "civic religion." I therefore prefer to use "myth" for describing the fictive and narrative component of cultural discourse, and to couple it with ideology as a "myth/ideological system" when referring to cultural activity as a whole. See also n. 13, below.

5   Martin Green, *Dreams of Adventure and Deeds of Empire*, pp. 54–55.

6   Michael Herr, *Dispatches*, p. 61.

7   Drinnon, *Facing West*, pp. 456–57; Robert Jay Lifton, *Home from the War: Vietnam Veterans, Neither Victims nor Executioners*, pp. 42–43, 48–51, 53–55, esp. ch. 8; Joseph Goldstein, Burke Marshall, and Jack Schwartz, comp., *The My-Lai Massacre and Its Cover-Up: Beyond the Reach of Law*, pp. 99–100, 192–206. S. L. A. Marshall, *Battles in the Monsoon*, notes the frequency with which Indian and Indian-war names were used to encode the names of operations. Slotkin, "Dreams and Genocide: The American Myth of Regeneration Through Violence," *JPC* 5:1 (May 1971), 55–56; Mark Baker, *Nam*, pp. 21–23. The motif is equally strong in such Vietnam-related novels as Philip Caputo, *A Rumor of War*, and James Webb, *Fields of Fire*, pp. 155, 162–63, 401. I'm grateful to my colleague Gerald Burns for his suggestions in this area.

8   Drinnon, *Facing West*, p. 369; Russell Long quoted in Marcus G. Raskin and Bernard B. Fall, eds., *The Viet-Nam Reader*, p. 386.

9   Dippie, *Custer's Last Stand*, is the best source. See also Paul A. Hutton, "From the Little Big Horn to Little Big Man: The Changing Image of a Hero in Popular Culture," *WHQ* 7:1 (Jan. 1976), 19–46; Norman B. Schwartz, "Villainous Cowboys and

Backward Peasants: Popular Culture and Development Concepts," *JPC* 15:4 (Spring 1982), 105–13; Drinnon, *Facing West*, p. 450; Frances Fitzgerald, *Fire in the Lake: The Vietnamese and the Americans in Vietnam*, pp. 484–85, 491–92.

10   This sort of mythological usage is comparable to that described in Karl Marx, *The Eighteenth Brumaire of Louis Napoleon*, p. 97. Vernon Carstensen, "Making Use of the Frontier and the American West," *WHQ* 13:1 (Jan. 1982), 5–16. On Kennedy's New Frontier and the significance of the Frontier ideology in the sixties, see esp. Godfrey Hodgson, *America in Our Time: From World War II to Nixon, What Happened and Why*, pp. 468–73, 493–94. Gerard O'Neill, *The High Frontier: Human Colonies in Space*, esp. ch. 11, "Homesteading the Asteroids," and pp. 321–22, which project a rather Turnerian concept of the old Frontier onto the environment of space. The same catch phrase is used to characterize the Reagan proposal for a buildup of defensive hardware in space: General Daniel Graham, *High Frontier: A Strategy for National Survival* (1983). Robert B. Reich's study of the prospects for an American economic revival is titled *The New American Frontier*. Examples could be multiplied indefinitely.

11   Northrop Frye, *The Critical Path: An Essay on the Social Context of Literary Criticism*, p. 115; Roland Barthès, "Mythology Today," *Mythologies*, p. 124.

12   Bascom, "The Forms of Folklore," distinguishes mythic from legendary stories on the basis of the predominance of sacred, cosmogonic, divinity-oriented content in the former. My point is that whether or not the matter of the story is sacred-timeless or profane-historical, its *composition* can only be the result of human work at some point in real time. See also Stith Thompson, "Myth and Folktales," in Thomas Sebeok, ed., *Myth: A Symposium*, pp. 169–80.

13   Clifford Geertz, *The Interpretation of Cultures*, p. 231; François Jacob, *The Possible and the Actual*; Victor W. Turner, "Process, System, and Symbol: A New Anthropological Synthesis," *Daedalus* (Summer 1977), 1:63–64, 74–75. Marshall Sahlins, *Historical Metaphors and Mythical Realities: Structure in the Early History of the Sandwich Islands Kingdom*, pp. 68, 72; Barthès, *Mythologies*, p. 110. See also George Macklin Wilson, "Time and History in Japan," *AHR* 85:3 (June 1980), 565; Williams, *Keywords*, pp. 176–77; the discussion of Thomas Kuhn's theory of "Paradigm revolutions" in Theodore M. Brown, "Putting Paradigms into History," *MP* 3:1 (Spring 1980), 34–63; and Robert Nisbet, "Genealogy, Growth, and Other Metaphors," *New Literary History* 1:3 (Spring 1970), 350–52.

One of the most useful and interesting books dealing with the role of myth in history, and with the problematic character of historical "demythologizing" is Cords and Gerster, eds., *Myth and the American Experience*, 2 vols., containing essays by historians, critics, and mythographers covering the entire span of American history. James Oliver Robertson, *American Myth, American Reality*, develops a similar line of inquiry. Marx, *The Eighteenth Brumaire*, describes the process of historical mythologization concisely and accurately when he notes the twinned constraints of circumstance and "the tradition of all the dead generations" that limit the creative power of historical actors; and notes the tendency of men in times of social crisis to "anxiously conjure up the spirits of the past to their service and borrow from them names, battle-cries and costumes in order to present the new scene of world history in this time-honoured disguise and this borrowed language" (p. 97). On Marx's own mythopoeic tendencies, see Leonard P. Wessell, Jr., *Karl Marx, Romantic Irony, and the Proletariat: The Mythopoetic Origins of Marxism*, ch. 6.

14   Barthès, *Mythologies*, p. 110; David Glassberg, "Restoring a 'Forgotten Childhood': American Play and the Progressive Era's Elizabethan Past," *AQ* 32:4 (Fall 1980), 366–68.

15   Turner, "Process, System, and Symbol," passim; Gene Wise, "Paradigm Dramas in American Studies: A Cultural and Institutional History of the Movement," *AQ* 31:3 (Bibliography Issue), passim; Frederic Jameson, *The Political Unconscious: Narrative as a Socially Symbolic Act*, esp. chs. 1, 6.

16   Williams, *Keywords*, pp. 76–82.

17   Geertz, *Interpretation of Cultures*, pp. 5, 17. On the historiographical consequences of this approach, see James A. Henretta, "Social History as Lived and Written," *AHR* 84:5 (Dec. 1979), 1303–4. The historian David Brion Davis formulates his definition of ideology and its gestation in terms very close to that of Geertz and his school. Compare David Brion Davis, *The Problem of Slavery in the Age of Revolution, 1770–*

1823, p. 14; and Sahlins, *Historical Metaphors*, pp. 7, 72. The distinction between "immaterial" and "occult" is from E. P. Thompson, *The Making of the English Working Class*, pp. 9–11; see also Alan Dawley, "E. P. Thompson and the Peculiarities of the Americans," *RHR* 19 (Mar. 1979), 35–36; and Eric Foner, *Free Soil, Free Labor, Free Men: The Ideology of the Republican Party Before the Civil War*, pp. 4–10. On the connection between material history, ideology, and literature, see Jameson, *Political Unconscious*, Preface, chs. 1, 6; Raymond Williams, *Marxism and Literature*, esp. pp. 75–89; Terence Eagleton, *Criticism and Ideology*, passim; Thomas E. Lewis, "Notes Towards a Theory of the Referent," *PMLA* 94:3 (May 1979), 459–75; Michael Merrill, "Raymond Williams and the Theory of English Marxism," *RHR* 19 (Mar. 1979), 9–32; Stephen Zelnick, "Melville's 'Bartleby, the Scrivener': A Study in History, Ideology, and Literature," *MP* 2:4 (Winter 1979), 74–92. Louis Chevalier tries to coordinate the "qualitative" documentation of literary fiction with the "statistical information" of quantitative social history, in order to present a total picture of society. See his arguments in *Laboring Classes and Dangerous Classes in Paris During the First Half of the Nineteenth Century*, pp. 1–6, 19, 31, 41–42.

18 Geertz, *Interpretation of Cultures*, pp. 211, 214, and the chapter "Ideology as a Cultural System," which has been widely reprinted; Williams, *Keywords*, pp. 126–30. Geertz's approach is one I find most useful, although the subdivision of ideology into "myth" and "ideology-proper" is not part of his theory. Bill Nichols, *Ideology and Image*, pp. 1–8, offers a very concise statement of the theory, in terms most appropriate to a study of popular culture; as do Michael Omi and Howard Wynant, "By the Rivers of Babylon: Race in the United States," *SR* 13:5 (1983), 40–46. See also Steve Barnett and Martin G. Silberman, *Ideology and Everyday Life: Anthropology, Neo-Marxist Thought, and the Problem of Ideology and the Social Whole*; David E. Apter, ed., *Ideology and Discontent*, esp. chs. 1, 6, 7, 8; Keith L. Nelson and Spencer C. Olin, Jr., *Why War? Ideology, Theory and History*; Peter L. Berger and Thomas Luckmann, *The Social Construction of Reality: A Treatise in the Sociology of Knowledge*.

19 Henretta, "Social History as Lived and Written," 1315, 1318–22; Louis O. Mink, "History and Fiction as Modes of Comprehension," *New Literary History* 1:3 (Spring 1970), 541–48; Nisbet, "Genealogy, Growth and Other Metaphors," ibid., 350–63; Hayden White, *Metahistory: The Historical Imagination in Nineteenth Century Europe*, p. 1–42; Will Wright, *Six-Guns and Society: A Structural Study of the Western*, pp. 10–12, 124–29; Jameson, *Political Unconscious*, ch. 2; and Seymour Chatman, *Story and Discourse: Narrative Structure in Fiction and Film*, esp. ch. 1 and pp. 45–53.

20 On "reification," see Carolyn Porter, *Seeing and Being: The Plight of the Participant Observer in Emerson, Adams and Faulkner*, chs. 1 and 2; Geertz, *Interpretation of Cultures*, pp. 211, 214, 231. The merging of individual mythmaking or reifying processes with the making of social ideology is treated with depth and complexity in Michael Rogin, *Fathers and Children: Andrew Jackson and the Subjugation of the American Indian*, and his more recent *Subversive Genealogy: Politics, Family and Fiction in Herman Melville*. The consequences of reifying propensities for literary culture in a modern society are discussed in Eagleton, *Criticism and Ideology*, esp. pp. 9–19; and Jameson, *Political Unconscious*, ch. 5. One of the consequences most dangerous to scholars is that of reifying their own values, or the ideology of their time and place, by projecting them onto their subjects. This has been a besetting sin of the "myth/symbol school" of American Studies, from which tradition the present work derives. See critiques by Bruce Kuklik, "Myth and Symbol in American Studies," *AQ* 24:4 (Oct. 1972), 435–50; Wise, "Paradigm Dramas," p. 320; Henretta, "Social History as Lived and Written," p. 1297; Guenter H. Lenz, "American Studies—Beyond the Crisis?: Recent Redefinitions and the Meaning of Theory, History, and Practical Criticism," *Prospects* 7 (1983), 53–113. William J. Bouwsma, "The Renaissance and the Drama of Western History," *AHR* 84:1 (Feb. 1979), 1–15 criticizes our "myth of continuity" as a projection of our wish for a historical fable explaining and affirming as good the origins of modernity; but he also says (p. 9) that "a myth is, for the historian, the dynamic equivalent of a model in the social sciences, and we can hardly do without it." A good survey of modern applications of myth study to literature is John B. Vickery, ed., *Myth and Literature: Contemporary Theory and Practice*, esp. pp. 1–136. Frye, *The Critical Path*, pp. 35–36, 107; Sahlins, *Historical Metaphors*, pp. 68, 72; Victor W. Turner, *The Ritual Process: Structure and Antistructure*, pp. 94–97, 102–11, and ch. 5; ———, "Process, System, and Symbol,"

63–64, 72–73; Claude Lévi-Strauss, "The Structural Study of Myth," in Sebeok, *Myth,* pp. 81–106.

21   Barthes, *Mythologies,* pp. 129, 142; Henry Glassie, "Meaningful Things and Appropriate Myths: The Artifact's Place in American Studies," *Prospects* 9 (1979), 1–51; Lévi-Strauss, *Myth and Meaning,* pp. 42–43, 53–54; ———, "How Myths Die," *Structural Anthropology* 2: 256, 268; Alan Jenkins, *The Social Theory of Claude Lévi-Strauss,* pp. 88–155. On the translation of mythic materials into literary and historical narrative, see Frye, *Critical Path,* pp. 38–39, 42–43; and Benjamin Bennett, "Nietzsche's Idea of Myth: The Birth of Tragedy from the Spirit of Eighteenth Century Aesthetics," *PMLA* 94:3 (May 1979), 420–33. On the antihistorical character of myth, and histories employing mythic structures, see David Noble, *Historians Against History: The Frontier Thesis and the National Covenant in American Historical Writing Since 1830,* ch. 1; Henry Nash Smith, *Virgin Land,* ch. 22; Porter, *Seeing and Being,* ch. 1, "American Ahistoricism."

22   Sahlins, *Historical Metaphors,* pp. 8, 64–66, 72, ch. 4: "The dialectics of history . . . are structural throughout. Powered by disconformities between conventional and intentional values, between symbolic sense and symbolic reference, the historical process unfolds as a continuous and reciprocal movement between the practice of the structure and the structure of the practice." Geertz, *Interpretation of Culture,* pp. 218, 220; Wilson, "Time and History," p. 570; Anthony F. C. Wallace, "Revitalization Movements," *American Anthropologist* 58:2 (Apr. 1956), p. 265. On literary forms associated with such renewals of myth, see Frye, *The Secular Scripture: A Study of the Structure of Romance,* ch. 6; Slotkin, *Regeneration Through Violence,* pp. 15–16, 363–64, 370–71; and Philip Wheelwright, "The Semantic Approach to Myth," in Sebeok, *Myth,* pp. 154–68.

23   Frye, *Critical Path,* p. 49, and *Secular Scripture,* ch. 6, which notes the aristocratic bias of romantic genres. See also Wilson, "Time and History," p. 565; Turner, *Ritual Process,* ch. 5; Sahlins, *Historical Metaphors,* ch. 3; Karen I. Blu, *The Lumbee Problem: The Making of an American People,* is a good small-scale case study showing the role that "literary" historical myths can play in a genuine, community-creating folklore. E. P. Thompson, *Making of the English Working Class,* shows the difficulty of tracing a similar interplay of genuinely popular or folkloric culture and class ideology in a modern state. Michael Grant, *Roman Myths,* pp. xiii–xiv, associates the "seizure" of a mythic system by a hegemonic class with classical Roman myth/ideology; in the Roman case even the patent artificiality of a pantheon and mythology imported from Greece did not undermine that system once it was in place. I'm grateful to David Konstan for his ideas on this subject.

24   Joseph Campbell, *The Hero with a Thousand Faces* and *The Masks of God,* 4 vols.; Northrop Frye, *The Anatomy of Criticism*; Carl Gustav Jung, *Psyche and Symbol: A Selection from the Writings of C. G. Jung.* Burton Feldman and Robert D. Richardson, eds., *The Rise of Modern Mythology, 1680–1860* Part 3, reprints original sources (with historical commentary) on the development of myth theory in the late eighteenth–early nineteenth centuries. Robert Jewett and John Shelton Lawrence, *The American Monomyth,* is a good recent example of the strengths and weaknesses of a Campbellian approach.

25   Bruce A. Rosenberg, *Custer and the Epic of Defeat,* pp. 253–86. Although the method has weaknesses from a historical perspective, this is an elegant application of archetypal theory, and it does provide some useful insights into the workings of the legend.

26   Green, *Dreams of Adventure,* p. 53, is the source for "grammar of tropes." A more extended critique of archetypalism is in Slotkin, *Regeneration Through Violence,* pp. 9–14. The critique of the "myth/symbol" approach to American Studies has generated some extremely useful discussion of myth theory and its limitations. See esp. John Cawelti, *Adventure, Mystery and Romance: Formula Stories as Art and Popular Culture,* pp. 1–36; Kuklik, "Myth and Symbol in American Studies," pp. 435–50; Alan Trachtenberg, "Myth, History, and Literature in *Virgin Land,*" *Prospects* 3 (1977), 125–34; Wise, "Paradigm Dramas," pp. 295–96, 319–25; Michael Frisch, "The Memory of History," *RHR* 25 (1980), 9–26; Henretta, "Social History as Lived and Written," 1307, 1316; Lenz, "American Studies—Beyond the Crisis?" esp. 67–92.

27   Cawelti, *Adventure, Mystery and Romance,* pp. 6, 29–30, 32, 35–36; Daniel

Boorstin, "The Rhetoric of Democracy," in Robert Atway, ed., *American Mass Media*, p. 51. The "folklore" association is made specifically by Boorstin; Cawelti describes the system of formulas as performing just the sort of functions I have ascribed to myth and ideology, but he reserves judgment about the social character of the processes of formula production. Compare Sahlins, *Historical Metaphors*, pp. 71–72. Carlos Clarens, *Crime Movies: From Griffith to the Godfather and Beyond*, p. 11, illustrates how this sort of argument works—Clarens seems to be suggesting that the audience somehow creates the formulas that are offered to it; compare Cawelti, p. 231.

28 On popular culture and literary production in the industrial period, see Boorstin, *The Americans: The National Experience*, pp. 325–90; ———, *The Americans: The Democratic Experience* Book 3; Eagleton, *Criticism and Ideology*; Christine Bold, "The Voice of the Fiction Factory in Dime and Pulp Westerns," *JAS* 17:1 (Apr. 1983), 29–46; Eric Breitbart, "From Panorama to Docudrama: Notes on the Visualization of History," *RHR* 25 (1981), 115–26; John P. Diggins, "Barbarism and Capitalism: The Strange Perspective of Thorstein Veblen," *MP* 1:2 (Summer 1978), 138–57, esp. 147–48; Morris Eaves, "Blake and the Artistic Machine: An Essay in Decorum and Technology," *PMLA* 92:5 (Oct. 1977), pp. 903–27; Herbert J. Gans, *Popular Culture and High Culture: An Analysis and Evaluation of Taste*; Garth S. Jowett, "The Emergence of the Mass Society: The Standardization of American Culture, 1830–1920," *Prospects* 7 (1983), 207–28.

The "dime novel" business is the classic case of an "industrial" enterprise producing popular culture in the nineteenth century. See Albert Johannsen, *The House of Beadle and Adams, and Its Dime and Nickel Novels: The Study of a Vanished Literature*, 3 vols., esp. the business history in v. 1: chs. 1–2, 4–6, 11, and the biographies of Beadle authors in v. 2; H. N. Smith, *Virgin Land*, ch. 9.

More recent theoretical studies are Richard A. Peterson, "Five Constraints on the Production of Culture: Law, Technology, Market, Organizational Structure and Occupational Careers," *JPC* 16:2 (Fall 1982), 143–53; Harold L. Wilensky, "Mass Society and Mass Culture: Interdependence or Independence?" *American Sociological Review* 29:2 (Apr. 1964), 173–97; Dorey Schmidt, "Magazines, Technology and American Culture," *JAC* 3:1 (Spring 1980), 3–16; and David Paul Nord, "An Economic Perspective on Formula in Popular Culture," ibid., 17–32. *JPC* 11:2 (Fall 1977) is devoted to "Sociology and Popular Culture," and contains several useful essays.

On the relationship between folklore and popular culture, see Bascom, "Forms of Folklore," pp. 3–20; Alan Dundes, *Interpreting Folklore*, esp. chs. 1 ("Who are the folk?") and 2; ——— and Carl R. Pagter, *Urban Folklore from the Paperwork Empire*, Introduction; Richard M. Dorson, ed., *Handbook of American Folklore*, pp. 1–17, 32–38, 60–85, 326–58; ———, *American Folklore and the Historian*, chs. 1–2, 8–11; ———, *America in Legend: Folklore from the Colonial Period to the Present*, pp. xiii–xv, 1–9; and Joseph J. Arpad, "Between Folklore and Literature: Popular Culture as Anomaly," *JPC* 19:2 (Fall 1975), 403–23 [51–71 alt. numbers].

29 Dorson, *America in Legend*, pp. 253–323; Todd Gitlin, *The Whole World Is Watching: Mass Media in the Making and Unmaking of the New Left*, pp. 2–3, 7; Lawrence Levine, *Black Culture and Black Consciousness: Afro-American Folk Thought from Slavery to Freedom*, pp. ix–xiv, 367–445. On Populist "movement culture," see Lawrence Goodwyn, *Democratic Promise: The Populist Moment in America*, Introduction, chs. 1, 5.

30 Kuklik, "Myth and Symbol," pp. 29–30, suggests a producer focus as antidote to the false generalizations of myth/symbol criticism. The concept of "producing communities" used here has many sources: discussions with Joseph Reed and Jeanine Masinger during the course of a research project on Hollywood movie genres; Boorstin, *The Americans: The Democratic Experience*, pp. 89–166, 537–46; Gitlin, *The Whole World*, pp. 2–18, 249–82. On the institutionalization of myth production, see also Sahlins, *Historical Metaphors*, pp. 71–72; and Turner, "Process, System and Symbol," p. 72. The school of Marxist scholarship deriving from the "hegemony" theories of Antonio Gramsci provides the most insightful work on the connection between such ideology-generating communities and functioning social or political classes. See, for example, Omi and Winant, "By the Rivers . . .," pp. 40–46.

How such communities form, how they develop over time, and how they operate as interpreters of cultural life is best studied in accounts of particular communities.

Those studies that deal with the borderline between folkloric and popular culture institutions are of particular interest: see esp. Mark Slobin, *Tenement Songs: The Popular Music of the Jewish Immigrants*, pp. 1–31. There are numerous studies of movie and television production communities. On history, see, for example, Kevin Brownlow, *The Parade's Gone By*, and *The War, the West and the Wilderness*; I. C. Jarvie, *Movies and Society*, Pt. I; Ted Sennett, *Warner Brothers Presents*; and Tino Balio, ed., *The American Film Industry*, ch. 4. On movie studios' engagement with the problem of audience, see Balio, *American Film Industry*, chs. 8–9 and Pt. III; Jarvie, *Movies and Society*, Pt. II; and Garth Jowett, *Film: The Democratic Art, a Social History of the American Film*, chs. 2, 4, 9, 13, and esp. pp. 179–94. On the dime/pulp "fiction factories," see Bold, "The Voice of the Fiction Factory," pp. 29–46; Johannsen, *The House of Beadle and Adams*, 1: chs. 1–2, 4–6, 11, and 12: pp. 6–8, 24–28, 36–62, 93–100, 155–60, 167–76; and Quentin Reynolds, *The Fiction Factory: From Pulp Row to Quality Street*. On television and journalism, see Gitlin, *The Whole World*; Raymond Williams, *Television: Technology and Cultural Form* and *The Sociology of Culture*; and Peter Braestrup and Burns Roper, *Big Story: How the American Press and Television Reported and Interpreted the Crisis of Tet 1968 in Vietnam and Washington*, 2 vols.

One of the most interesting cases of a "producing community" is the academic establishment, whose dominant ideologies shape the development of literary and historical canons, determine what of history and culture shall be studied, and how they will be interpreted. See Richard M. Ohmann, *English in America: A Radical View of the Profession*; "The Shaping of a Canon: U.S. Fiction, 1960–1975," *CI* 10:1 (Sept. 1983), 199–203; Marx W. Wartofsky, "Art, Artworlds, and Ideology," *Journal of Aesthetics and Art Criticism* 38:8 (Spring 1980), 239–48. Feminist criticism has contributed some of the best recent work on the ideology of academic and literary canons: Ann Douglas, *The Femininization of American Culture*; Annette Kolodny, "Turning the Lens on the 'Panther Captivity': A Feminist Exercise in Practical Criticism," *CI* 8:2 (Winter 1981), 329–45.

CHAPTER 3

1 The critique of American exceptionalism has produced an extensive literature. Of particular interest for this study are Noble, *Historians Against History*, esp. ch. 1; Porter, *Seeing and Being*, ch. 1; Kuklik, "Myth and Symbol," 435–50; Dawley, "E. P. Thompson and the Peculiarities of the Americans," pp. 33–59; Wise, "Paradigm Dramas," pp. 319–37; Walter Hugins, "American History in Comparative Perspective," *JAS* 11:1 (Apr. 1977), 27–44; Laurence Veysey, "The Autonomy of American History Reconsidered," *AQ* 31:4 (Fall 1979), 455–76. Donald K. Pickens, "Westward Expansion and the End of American Exceptionalism," *WHQ* 12:4 (Oct. 1981), 409–18, is a provocative essay with excellent bibliography, marred by a confusing polemic at the end against the new "social myth [of] collectivism" which he sees as underlying the modern critique of Turner's Frontier Thesis. E. J. Hobsbawn, *The Age of Capital, 1848–1875*, is good at summarizing the general tendencies of development in Europe and the U.S.; but the conflations of American and European experiences are sometimes simplistic, for example, pp. 150–53, 157–59. For an overview of the pattern of Western development, see also Richard D. Brown, *Modernization: The Transformation of American Life, 1600–1865*.

2 The Frontier/Metropolis distinction is made by Walter Prescott Webb, *The Great Frontier*, ch. 1, and is reinterpreted in a useful way by William Appleman Williams, *Roots of the Modern American Empire: A Study of the Growth and Shaping of Social Consciousness in a Marketplace Society*, chs. 1–4. See also ———, *The Great Evasion*, pp. 12–13. Catherine L. Albanese, *Sons of the Fathers: The Civil Religion of the American Revolution*, pp. 3–18, 182–225; Lawrence Friedman, *Inventors of the Promised Land*, pp. 3–43; Rogin, *Fathers and Children*, chs. 1, 3; Gordon S. Wood, *The Creation of the American Republic, 1776–1787*, esp. chs. 2, 3, 13.

3 Richard Hofstader, *The Progressive Historians: Turner, Parrington, and Beard*, ch. 4, "The Frontier as an Explanation"; Ray Allen Billington, *Frederick Jackson Turner: Historian, Scholar, Teacher*, esp. chs. 4–5, 8, 18–19.

4 Billington, *Land of Savagery, Land of Promise: The European Image of the American Frontier*, esp. chs. 10, 11, 13; Philip Taylor, *The Distant Magnet: European Emigration to the U.S.A.*, chs. 4, 9–12; David M. Potter, *People of Plenty: Economic Abundance and the American Character*, p. 93.

5 On the sequence and variety of Frontiers see Billington, *America's Frontier Heritage*, and the other works in the series of volumes to which his book is an introduction, esp. Reginald Horsman, *The Frontier in the Formative Years, 1776–1815*; Rodman Wilson Paul, *Mining Frontiers of the Far West, 1848–1890*; and Oscar Osburn Winther, *The Transportation Frontier, 1865–1890*. Margaret Walsh, *The American Frontier Revisited*, is an appreciation of Turner's thesis which nonetheless emphasizes the diversity of Frontier experience Turner slighted. On the patterns of economic development associated with the different epochs of Frontier expansion, see Douglass C. North, *The Economic Growth of the United States, 1790–1860*, and William Greenleaf, ed., *American Economic Development Since 1860*.

6 John D. Barnhart, *The Valley of Democracy: The Frontier versus the Plantation in the Ohio Valley, 1775–1818*, chs. 1, 14; W. A. Williams, *Roots of the Modern American Empire*, pp. ix–xxiv, 132–57; Everett Dick, *The Lure of the Land: A Social History of the Public Lands from the Articles of Confederation to the New Deal*, p. x, chs. 4, 5, 11, 14; Gilbert M. Fite, *The Farmer's Frontier, 1865–1900*, esp. ch. 5; Gene M. Gressley, *West by East: The American West in the Gilded Age*, passim.

7 On the "magic" of the Frontier, see Slotkin, *Regeneration Through Violence*, pp. 31–37, 117–29, 272–73, 280–83; Howard Mumford Jones, *O Strange New World: American Culture, the Formative Years*, esp. pp. 1–34. Joshua C. Taylor, *America as Art*, is a suggestive investigation of visual-art myths and icons, as is Barbara Novak, *Nature and Culture: American Landscape, 1825–1865*. See also Raymond F. Betts, "Immense Dimensions: The Impact of the American West on Late Nineteenth Century European Thought About Expansion," *WHQ* 10:2 (Apr. 1979), 149–66; and Michael McCarthy, "Africa and the American West," *JAS* 11:2 (Aug. 1977), 187–202.

8 Walter Prescott Webb, *The Great Frontier*, p. 43.

9 Potter, *People of Plenty*, chs. 4 and 7; Billington, *America's Frontier Heritage*, pp. 1–22.

10 Thomas C. Cochran, *Frontiers of Change: Early Industrialism in America*, is the most complete discussion of this hypothesis I have seen. See also Cochran, *Business in American Life: A History*, chs. 1–8; ——— and William B. Miller, *The Age of Enterprise: A Social History of Industrial America*, "The Intensive Frontier," ch. 3; Gressley, *West by East*, pp. 18–19, 32–35; Hobsbawm, *Age of Capital*, pp. 28–31, 150–59, 338–39. A collection of comparative Frontier studies is David Harry Miller and Jerome O. Steffen, eds., *The Frontier: Comparative Studies*; see also Walker D. Wyman and Clifton B. Kroeber, eds., *The Frontier in Perspective* and John Francis McDermott, *The Frontier Re-examined*.

11 See for example Melvyn Dubofsky, *We Shall Be All: A History of the Industrial Workers of the World*, pp. 5–87. For specific critiques of Turner's treatment of development, see Everett S. Lee, "The Turner Thesis Re-examined," in Hennig Cohen, ed., *The American Experience: Approaches to the Study of the United States*, pp. 64–71; Potter, *People of Plenty*, ch. 7. Gressley, *West by East*, and Howard Temperley, "Frontierism, Capital, and the American Loyalists in Canada," *JAS* 13:1 (Apr. 1979), 5–28 (esp. 13) criticize Turner's understanding of the relationship between small farmers, entrepreneurs, and capitalists. Jeffrey G. Williamson and Peter Lindert, *American Inequality: A Macroeconomic History*, pp. 10–11, 22, 52, 282, finds inequality of wealth developed with great rapidity on the Frontier. The argument that Metropolitan social and cultural institutions and class divisions tended to be reproduced in western communities is made in: Malcolm J. Rohrbaugh, *The Trans-Appalachian Frontier: Peoples, Societies, and Institutions, 1775–1850*, p. 6, and passim; Don H. Doyle, "Social Theories and New Communities in 19th Century America," *WHQ* 8:2 (Apr. 1977), 151–66; Jackson K. Putnam, "The Turner Thesis and Westward Movement: A Reappraisal," *WHQ* 7:4 (Oct. 1976), 401; R. A. Burchall, "The Character and Function of a Pioneer Elite: Rural California, 1848–1880," *JAS* 15:3 (Dec. 1981), 383; Ronald L. F. Davis, "Community and Conflict in Pioneer St. Louis, Missouri," *WHQ* 10:3 (July 1979), 337–56. Compare Herbert G. Gutman, *Work, Culture and Society in Industrializing America: Essays in American Working Class and Social History*, Pt. 3, which describes a period

of upward mobility in eastern manufacturing cities: mobility was a function of economic expansion, not of location in the West.

12 Webb, *Great Frontier*, pp. 192–93. The centrality of speculators and speculative economics in settling the Great Plains is treated in Dick, *Lure of the Land*, pp. 11–16, 65–68, 133–36, 199–204, 210–13, 360. See also Robert P. Swieringa, "Land Speculation and Its Impact on American Economic Growth and Welfare: A Historiographical Review." *WHQ* 8:3 (July 1977). 283–301.

13 See, for example, the discussion of the relationship of labor supply to development in Carville Earle and Ronald Hoffman, "The Foundation of the Modern Economy: Agriculture and the Costs of Labor in the United States and England, 1800–1860," *AHR* 85:5 (Dec. 1980), 1055–94.

CHAPTER 4

1 This chapter is a summary and revision of ideas and materials presented in detail in Slotkin, *Regeneration Through Violence*.

2 Wilbur R. Jacobs, *Dispossessing the American Indian: Indians and Whites on the Colonial Frontier*, Preface, chs. 1–5.

3 John E. Ferling, *A Wilderness of Miseries: War and Warriors in Early America* argues that the "exterminating" military temperament was imported to the New World by colonists whose military lore derived from the wars of religion in the seventeenth century—wars that had become increasingly merciless and indiscriminate in their violence. However, there were factors in the existing attitudes toward "savages" that created an additional expectation of atrocity. On the peculiar psychology and ideology of Indian-white relations, see Slotkin, *Regeneration Through Violence*, ch. 3; Jacobs, *Dispossessing*, chs. 10–11; Michael P. Rogin, "Liberal Society and the Indian Question," *Political Inquiry* 1:3 (May 1971), 269–312; Robert M. Berkhofer, *The White Man's Indian: Images of the American Indian from Columbus to the Present*. Willcomb L. Washburn, *The Indian in America*, is a good general study. Richard Drinnon, *Facing West*, presents "Indian hating" as the dominant trope in the literature of American expansion; it is a valuable compendium of insights, examples, and documentary references. Don M. Russell, "How Many Indians Were Killed? White Man versus Red Man: The Facts and the Legend," *American West* 10:4 (July 1973), 42–47, 61–63, argues that the exterminationist bark was always worse than the army's real bite; the article is tendentious, and its historical range does not reach back to the periods in which most of the fighting occurred (1740–64, 1774–94, 1809–15). Rogin, *Fathers and Children*, pp. 3–4, n. 6 p. 318, cites other figures and discusses the problems of establishing the data. The concept of "savage war" is discussed in Slotkin, "Massacre," *Berkshire Review: Special Issue on Culture and Violence (1979)*, pp. 112–32, and commentary on pp. 150–59. On the law relating to "savage war," Goldstein, et al., *The My-Lai Massacre and Its Cover-Up*, pp. 198–99; Stuart Creighton Miller, *Benevolent Assimilation: The American Conquest of the Philippines, 1899–1903*, chs. 11–13; ———, "Our My-Lai of 1900: Americans in the Philippine Insurrection," in Marilyn B. Young, ed., *American Expansionism: The Critical Issues*, pp. 110–11; [Moorfield Storey, et al.], *Secretary Root's Record: Marked Severity in Philippine Warfare* (Boston 1902), pp. 21–28, 33, 38, 98. And compare the ideology of lynching as a domestic form in James E. Cutler, *Lynch-Law: An Investigation . . .* (1905).

4 Willcomb L. Washburn, *The Governor and the Rebel: A History of Bacon's Rebellion in Virginia*, is the most complete account.

5 A good general history of the war is Douglas Edward Leach, *Flintlock and Tomahawk: New England in King Philip's War*. Analytical treatments of white-Indian relations are James Axtell, *The European and the Indian: Essays in the Ethnohistory of Colonial America*; and Francis Jennings, *The Invasion of America: Indians, Colonialism, and the Cant of Conquest*. A view that dissents from Jennings's is Alden T. Vaughan, *New England Frontier: Puritans and Indians, 1620–1675*. For a discussion of the cultural impact of King Philip's War, see Slotkin, *Regeneration Through Violence*, chs. 3–6; and Slotkin and James K. Folsom, eds., *So Dreadfull a Judgment: Puritan Responses to King Philip's War, 1675–1677*, Introduction, pp. 3–45.

6   Increase Mather, *Brief History* . . . (1676), in Slotkin and Folsom, *So Dreadfull a Judgment*, pp. 86–87.

7   Benjamin Thompson, *New England's Crisis* (1676), ibid., pp. 215–16.

8   Sacvan Bercovitch, *The Puritan Origins of the American Self*, chs. 2 and 4.

9   Slotkin, "Increase Mather: Puritan Mythologist," in *So Dreadfull a Judgment*, pp. 61–62; Mather, *Brief History*, ibid., pp. 81–85.

10   Slotkin, "Samuel Nowell: Prophet of Preparedness," ibid., pp. 258–70; Samuel Nowell, *Abraham in Arms* (1678), ibid., pp. 283, 286–88.

11   Increase Mather, *An Earnest Exhortation* (1676), ibid., pp. 174–75. See also Slotkin, *Regeneration Through Violence*, pp. 84–86; Ursula Brumm, " 'What Want You Out into the Wilderness to See?': Nonconformity and Wilderness in Cotton Mather's *Magnalia Christi Americana*," *Prospects* 6 (1981), 1–16. Peter N. Carroll, *Puritanism and the Wilderness: The Intellectual Significance of the New England Frontier, 1629–1700*.

12   Mather, *Earnest Exhortation*, pp. 179–80.

13   Ibid., pp. 177, 181, 187; Mather, *Brief History*, p. 90.

14   Nowell, *Abraham in Arms*, pp. 287–88.

15   Marshall Sahlins, "Culture as Protein and Profit," *New York Review of Books* 25:18 (Nov. 23, 1978), 45–53, esp. n. 1; George T. Hunt, *The Wars of the Iroquois: A Study in Inter-Tribal Relations*, pp. 220–27; Richard White, "The Winning of the West: The Expansion of the Western Sioux in the Eighteenth and Nineteenth Centuries," *JAH* 45:2 (Sept. 1978), 319–43. For literary examples, see Roger Wolcott, "Account of the Agency of Governor John Winthrop . . .," *The Poems of Roger Wolcott* (1898), p. 55; Slotkin and Folsom, *So Dreadfull a Judgment*, p. 63. There are numerous collections of true and fictional anecdotes of Indian war incidents and atrocity stories, many of which are repeated from book to book—for example, the accounts of the torture of Colonel Crawford after his defeat by the Indians and Simon Girty at Sandusky in 1782, as given by John Slover and Dr. Knight. Typical of the genre is Archibald Loudon, *A Selection of Some of the Most Interesting Narratives of Outrages Committed by the Indians in Their War on the White People* (1808), 2 vols.

16   [Provost William Smith], *Historical Account of Bouquet's Expedition Against the Ohio Indians, in 1764* (1765), p. 19; Slotkin, *Regeneration Through Violence*, pp. 230–34; Ralph K. Andrist, *The Long Death*, p. 119; Thomas B. Marquis, *Keep the Last Bullet for Yourself: The True Story of Custer's Last Stand*, pp. 172–80.

17   Theodore Roosevelt, "The Strenuous Life" (1899), *Works* 12: 7–8, 19; Samuel Eliot Morison, et al., *The Struggle for Guadalcanal, August 1942–February 1943: History of United States Naval Operations in World War II* 5:187. Racist politicians in the United States during this same period extrapolated the race-war motif to interpret domestic divisions, especially the potential for insurrections by blacks in the South. See the speeches of Hon. John A. Rankin, Feb. 23 and March 10, 1942, *Congressional Record, Appendix*, pp. A768–69, 931. Thanks to Kim Ben-Salahuddin for bringing this to my attention.

18   Ernest Lee Tuveson, *Redeemer Nation: The Idea of America's Millennial Role*; Frederick Merk, *Manifest Destiny and Mission in American History*, pp. 261–64; Perry Miller, *Errand into the Wilderness*, ch. 10, "The End of the World"; Sacvan Bercovitch, "The Typology of America's Mission," *AQ* 30:2 (Summer 1976), 135–55.

19   Slotkin, *Regeneration Through Violence*, chs. 4, 6, 10, deal with the origins of these genres and hero-types. The texts are most easily found in Slotkin and Folsom, *So Dreadfull a Judgment*. See also Roy Harvey Pearce, "The Significances of the Captivity Narrative," *AL* 9:1 (Mar. 1949), 1–20; Hennig Cohen and James Lavernier, *The Indians and Their Captives*; Alden T. Vaughan and Edward W. Clark, eds., *Puritans Among the Indians: Accounts of Captivity and Redemption, 1676–1724*; Robert J. Denn, "Captivity Narratives of the American Revolution," *JAC* 2:4 (Winter 1980), 575–82; Colin G. Calloway, "An Uncertain Destiny: Indian Captivities of the Upper Connecticut River," *JAS* 17:2, 189–210.

20   Mary Rowlandson, *The Soveraignty and Goodness of God* . . . (1682), in Slotkin and Folsom, *So Dreadfull a Judgment*, pp. 312–66, esp. 365; Slotkin, *Regeneration Through Violence*, ch. 3.

21   Ibid., chs. 3, 4; Kolodny, "Turning the Lens," 329–45; J. Norman Heard, *White Into Red: A Study of Assimilation of White Persons Captured by Indians*; Richard

Drinnon, *White Savage: The Case of John Dunn Hunter* is an account of a "returned captive" of the early 19th Century whose career was affected by both captivity and the *myth* of captivity—the latter affecting the response of white society to Hunter. See esp. Pt. I.

22 Slotkin, *Regeneration Through Violence*, pp. 282, 295, 297; "Benjamin Church: King of the Wild Frontier," in *So Dreadfull a Judgment*, pp. 370–76. On the large land companies of colonial and federal times, see Dick, *Lure of the Land*, pp. 1–8, 11, 44, 56, 59, 67.

23 Slotkin, *Regeneration Through Violence*, pp. 169–90.

24 Ibid., ch. 12.

25 Ibid., ch. 9.

26 Ibid., pp. 344–45, 395–98, 414–19; Richard M. Brown, *Strain of Violence: Historical Studies of American Violence and Vigilantism*, pp. 37–89; Dick, *Lure of the Land*, pp. 56, 59–60.

27 On Jefferson and the Jeffersonians, see Dumas Malone, *Jefferson and His Times*, Vol. 4, *Jefferson the President, the First Term, 1801–1805*, chs. 14–19; Merrill D. Peterson, *The Jefferson Image in the American Mind*; ———, *Thomas Jefferson and the New Nation: A Biography*, esp. chs. 9–11. Daniel J. Boorstin, *The Lost World of Thomas Jefferson*; Richard Hofstader, *The American Political Tradition and the Men Who Made It*, ch. 2. On the connection between Jeffersonian agrarianism and commercialism in general, see William H. Goetzmann, *Exploration and Empire: The Explorer and the Scientist in the Winning of the American West*, ch. 1; Horsman, *The Frontier in the Formative Years*, chs. 1–2. The quotation is from Joyce Appleby, "Commercial Farming and the 'Agrarian Myth' in the Early Republic," *JAH* 68:4 (Mar. 1982), 833–49. On Jeffersonian land policies, see Dick, *Lure of the Land*, ch. 2. Despite the differences in their ideology and historical moment, Jefferson's vision of the social function of economic resources in America coincides with Engels's depiction of America as "the last Bourgeois Paradise on earth . . . [where] everyone could become, if not a capitalist, at all events an independent man, producing or trading with his own means, for his own account," Karl Marx and Frederick Engels, *Letters to Americans, 1848–1895: A Selection*, p. 157.

28 Wood, *Creation of the American Republic*, chs. 6, 10, 15; Kenneth A. Lockridge, *Settlement and Unsettlement in Early America: The Crisis of Political Legitimacy Before the Revolution*; Jackson Turner Main, *The Social Structure of Revolutionary America*, chs. 6–7; Stow Persons, *The Decline of American Gentility*. On deference and yeoman/gentry relations, see A. F. C. Wallace, *Rockdale: The Growth of an American Village in the Early Industrial Revolution*, tracing the shift from deference to class conflict; David Spring, "Walter Bagehot and Deference," *AHR* 81:3 (June 1976), 524–31; J. G. A. Pocock, "The Classical Theory of Deference," ibid., 516–23; Richard W. Davis, "Deference and Aristocracy in the Time of the Great Reform Act," ibid., 532–39.

29 On Jeffersonian Indian policy, see Rogin, "Liberal Society and the Indian Question," *Political Inquiry* 1:3 (May 1971), 269–312 and *Fathers and Children*, ch. 1; Bernard W. Sheehen, *Seeds of Extinction: Jeffersonian Philanthropy and the American Indian*; Dippie, *The Vanishing American*, chs. 1–3; Drinnon, *Facing West*, Pt. II.

30 Michel Guillaume Jean de Crèvecoeur, *Letters from an American Farmer* (1782), Letter III. The connection between hunting (as "poaching") and lower-class resistance to the order imposed by the gentry has an explicit historical basis underlying its symbolic appeal. See E. P. Thompson, *Whigs and Hunters: The Origins of the Black Act*. The rituals of "blacking" associated with poacher resistance have cognates in the practices of the Boston Tea Party "Indians" (1773), the South Carolina Regulators, and the Whiskey Rebels of 1794.

31 Crèvecoeur, *Letters*, pp. 203–9, 215, 223.

32 William R. Taylor, *Cavalier and Yankee: The Old South and American National Character*, pp. 2–10, 31; Lester J. Cappon, ed., *The Adams-Jefferson Letters: The Complete Correspondence Between Thomas Jefferson and Abigail and John Adams*, 2:387–91; Hofstader, *American Political Tradition*, pp. 30–31; Billington, *America's Frontier Heritage*, pp. 70–71.

33 Taylor, *Cavalier and Yankee*, pp. 1–5. "Patriarchy" is a peculiar way of describing this sort of aristocratic status. See Jay Fliegelman, *Prodigals and Pilgrims: The*

American Revolution Against Patriarchal Authority, 1750–1800; and Eugene D. Genovese, *The Political Economy of Slavery: Studies in the Economy and Society of the Slave South*, pp. 28–35.

34 Thomas Jefferson, *Notes on Virginia* (1781), pp. 132–39; John P. Diggins, "Slavery, Race and Equality: Jefferson and the Pathos of Enlightenment," *AQ* 28:2 (Summer 1976), 206–28; Alexander Saxton, "Historical Explanations of Racial Inequality," *MP* 2:2 (Summer 1979), 146–48. T. H. Breen and Stephen Innes, *Myne Owne Ground: Race and Freedom on Virginia's Eastern Shore, 1640–1676*, argue that race was not an a priori basis for permanent enslavement or relegation to the underclass during the first period of colonization. On racialist ideas in general, see Winthrop D. Jordan, *White Over Black: American Attitudes Towards the Negro, 1550–1812*, esp. Pt. 5; Thomas F. Gossett, *Race: The History of an Idea in America*, chs. 1–3; George M. Frederickson, *The Black Image in the White Mind: The Debate over Afro-American Character and Destiny, 1817–1914*, chs. 1–5; and Allen Chase, *The Legacy of Malthus: The Social Costs of the New Scientific Racism*, ch. 4, which makes the important connection between the concept of the hereditarian "under-class" and the traditional idea of the "undeserving poor."

35 Jefferson, *Notes on Virginia*, pp. 132–33. Exterminationist expectations acquired renewed force and credibility after slave revolts such as the "New York Conspiracy" of 1741, the Haiti/Santo Domingo Revolution of the 1790s, the Nat Turner rebellion of 1831, and John Brown's Raid of 1859. See, for example, the discussion in Slotkin, "Narratives of Negro Crime in New England, 1675–1800," *AQ* 25:1 (Spring 1973), 12–16, 24–26.

36 Crèvecoeur, *A Journey into Northern Pennsylvania and the State of New-York* (1801), pp. xvi, 10–11, 14, 314–15; Slotkin, *Regeneration Through Violence*, pp. 334–39.

37 Mason Locke Weems, *The Life of George Washington* (1805), p. 1.

38 Weems, *Washington*, pp. 32–33, 43–44, and passim; Taylor, *Cavalier and Yankee*, pp. 77–85, 114–16, 228–33; Friedman, *Inventors of the Promised Land*, pp. 44–78; Marcus Cunliffe, *George Washington: Man and Monument*; Fliegelman, *Prodigals and Pilgrims*, pp. 197–226.

39 Weems, *Washington*, pp. 220–21.

40 Hofstader, *American Political Tradition*, pp. 34–35, 39–40; Billington, *America's Frontier Heritage*, p. 4; Malone, *Jefferson*, 4: chs. 14–19.

41 Benjamin Franklin, *The Autobiography* (1793), p. 133.

42 Mary Young, "The Indian Question Revisited," *MP* 1:1 (Spring 1978), 34–49; Wilbur R. Jacobs, "The Indian and the Frontier in American History—A Need for Revision," *WHQ* 4:1 (Jan. 1973), 34–56.

CHAPTER 5

1 Parts of this chapter were prepared for the Introduction to the Penguin edition of *The Last of the Mohicans*, which I edited.

James Franklin Beard, ed., *The Letters and Journals of James Fenimore Cooper*, is the essential primary biographical source. I have used the biographies by George Dekker, *James Fenimore Cooper: The American Scott*; James Grossman, *James Fenimore Cooper*; Robert Spiller, *Fenimore Cooper: Critic of His Times*; and Stephen Railton, *Fenimore Cooper: A Study of His Life and Imagination*. Railton's is the most recent of these and makes good use of the great body of Cooper scholarship produced since 1950; his approach is psychoanalytic. Dekker and Grossman recapitulate the facts of Cooper's life and production; Spiller emphasizes the importance of politics and political ideas. There are useful essays on special aspects of his life and work in *James Fenimore Cooper: A Reappraisal*, published by the N.Y. State Historical Association in 1954.

For critical responses to Cooper's work during his lifetime, see esp. George Dekker and John P. McWilliams, eds., *Fenimore Cooper: The Critical Heritage*. On Cooper's popularity and influence on popular culture and the book trade, see James D. Hart, *The Popular Book: A History of America's Literary Taste*, esp. ch. 4; and Frank Luther Mott, *Golden Multitudes: The Story of Best-Sellers in the United States*.

Much of the best and most influential writing on Cooper appears in works devoted to larger studies of American literature, politics, and history. His contributions to literary art and language are treated in Louise K. Barnett, *The Ignoble Savage: American Literary Racism, 1790–1890*; Leslie Fiedler, *Love and Death in the American Novel* and *Return of the Vanishing American*; Edwin Fussell, *Frontier: American Literature and the American West*; D. H. Lawrence, *Studies in Classic American Literature*; R. W. B. Lewis, *The American Adam: Innocence, Tragedy and the Tradition in the Nineteenth Century*; Richard Chase, *The American Novel and Its Tradition*; Joel M. Porte, *The Romance in America: Studies in Cooper, Poe, Hawthorne, Melville, and James*, pp. 3–52. Cooper's contributions to American ideology are treated in Drinnon, *Facing West*; H. M. Jones, *O Strange New World*; Vernon L. Parrington, *Main Currents in American Thought; Volume Two, The Romantic Revolution in America*; Rogin, *Fathers and Children* and *Subversive Genealogy*, esp. Prologue; Roy Harvey Pearce, *The Savages of America: A Study of the Indian and the Idea of Civilization*; Arthur K. Moore, *The Frontier Mind: A Cultural Analysis of the Kentucky Frontiersman*; Slotkin, *Regeneration Through Violence*, ch. 13; H. N. Smith, *Virgin Land*, Book II and ch. 21. Cooper's impact on American historiography is discussed in David Levin, *History as Romantic Art: Bancroft, Prescott, Motley and Parkman*, esp. pp. 229–30, 235.

2   Ross MacDonald [Kenneth Millar], *The Zebra-Striped Hearse*, p. 113.

3   Quoted in William Charvat, "Cooper as a Professional Author," in NYSHA *JFC: A Reappraisal*, p. 501. On literary nationalism, see Wayne Franklin, *The New World of James Fenimore Cooper*, ch. 1; Benjamin T. Spencer, *The Quest for Nationality: An American Literary Campaign*.

4   On "romance" as a genre, see Chase, *American Novel and Its Tradition*, ch. 1; Porte, *Romance in America*. Frye, *Secular Scripture*, discusses the medieval and Renaissance bases of the genre and the literary-ideological projects associated with it. Barnett, *Ignoble Savage*, focuses on the Indian war theme in the imitators of Cooper. On Scott, see Donald Davie, *The Heyday of Sir Walter Scott*; George Dekker, "Sir Walter Scott, the Angel of Hadley, and American Historical Fiction," *JAS* 17:2 (Aug. 1983), 211–28; James D. Hart, *Popular Book*, pp. 67–84; Harry E. Shaw, *The Forms of Historical Fiction: Sir Walter Scott and His Successors*.

5   Quoted in Grossman, *James Fenimore Cooper*, p. 11, and see David M. Ellis, "The Coopers and New York State Landholding Systems," NYSHA, *JCF: A Reappraisal*, pp. 412–32; Dekker, *James Fenimore Cooper*, ch. 1.

6   On the "Whig" ideology of Cooper, see John P. McWilliams, *Political Justice in a Republic: James Fenimore Cooper's America*; and Dorothy Waples, *The Whig Myth of James Fenimore Cooper*. On the ideology and sociopolitical basis of American Whiggism, see Wood, *Creation of the American Republic*, esp. Pt. I, "The Ideology of Revolution." The conflict between the republicanism of the Revolutionary "fathers" and that of Cooper's generation is treated in appropriately Oedipal terms by Albanese, *Sons of the Fathers*; and Rogin, *Fathers and Children*, Pt. I, and *Subversive Genealogy*, Prologue and ch. 1. On the social function of gentility and deference see ch. 4, n. 28, above.

7   James Fenimore Cooper, *The Spy: A Tale of the Neutral Ground* (1821); W. R. Taylor, *Cavalier and Yankee*, pp. 78–83.

8   Cooper, *The Pioneers; or The Sources of the Susquehanna* (1823), pp. 156–62; Slotkin, *Regeneration Through Violence*, pp. 485–93.

9   Cooper, *The Last of the Mohicans: A Tale of 1757* (1826), Preface, pp. 3–5, 6.

10   Ann Douglas, *The Feminization of American Culture*, describes a literary marketplace divided along sexual/ideological lines very like those anticipated by Cooper in his Preface—feminine/sentimental on one side and masculine/realistic (or "hard-headed") on the other. According to Douglas, the feminine audience was the stronger market presence, and its tastes are reflected in the predominance of sentimental fiction through much of the middle decades of the nineteenth century. However, Cooper's Preface precedes the exhibition of such market forces, and suggests that the type of "feminine" fiction produced in the period may have been as much a response to pre-existing sex-role stereotypes as to the actual preferences of women; it indicates the sort of role for which nineteenth-century female readers were precast, and for which they were educated.

Lawrence, *Studies in Classic American Literature*, and Fiedler, *Love and Death*, emphasize the miscegenate-erotic and homo-erotic implications of the Cora-Uncas and

Hawkeye-Chingachgook relationships, and suggest that this is the questionable matter Cooper attempted to obfuscate or conceal from his finicky readers. I don't disagree with that judgment. However, Cooper's Preface makes explicit his defiance of female and genteel-masculine readers. And since the tenderness between Hawkeye and Chingachgook is not much in evidence in this book and the interracial romance comes to a typically (and safely) tragic conclusion, I conclude that Cooper intended to defy sentimentality by presenting a world of unmitigated violence, rather than one primarily characterized by uninhibited sexuality—though the two are always linked in Cooper.

11 Cooper, *Mohicans*, p. 24.

12 Compare the description of Cora with Jefferson's discourse on the differences in the "beauty" and sexuality of blacks and whites. The significance of Cora's being able to show a blush, and the hierarchy of sexual passion that draws Magua and Uncas to Cora (but Cora to Heyward), are clearly laid out by Jefferson, *Notes on Virginia*, Query XIV, pp. 132–33. On mixed races, see William J. Scheick, *The Half-Blood: A Cultural Symbol in 19th Century American Fiction*.

13 William Stanton, *The Leopard's Spots: Scientific Attitudes toward Race in America, 1815–1859*, pp. 103–4; Frederickson, *Black Image*, chs. 1, 5.

14 In fact, the pretense of historicity has been thin from the start. Although place names and the names of the leading commanders (including Colonel Monro, translated to "Munro") are historical, and the details of troop movements accurately represented, the motives for crucial historical actions derive from purely fictional causes. For example, the massacre of the Fort's survivors is provoked by Magua to enable him to steal Munro's daughters—a motive without a historical source. See Jacobs, *Dispossessing*, ch. 6.

15 Paul A. W. Wallace, "Cooper's Indians," *JFC: A Reappraisal*, pp. 423–46.

16 On Aryanism and the predecessor theory of Teutonism, see Thomas F. Gossett, *Race: The History of an Idea in America*, chs. 5–6. On the cyclical structure attributed to race history by romantic historians, see Levin, *History as Romantic Art*, chs. 4 and 6. For specific application of the cyclical theory to the Indians, see Dippie, *Vanishing American*, pp. 12–44; and Rogin, *Fathers and Children*, pp. 3–18 and ch. 7. See also Robert Milder, "*The Last of the Mohicans* and the New World Fall," *AL* 52:3 (Nov. 1980), 407–29; and Roy S. Kasson, "The Voyage of Life: Thomas Cole and Romantic Disillusionment," *AQ* 27:1 (Mar. 1975), 42–56.

17 Cooper, *Mohicans*, pp. 204, 223–24, chs. 23, 29–30.

18 Cooper, *Mohicans*, pp. 364–66, 369. The nexus of racial, class, and sexual symbolism in this scene (and Cooper's work in general) is discussed in Slotkin, *Regeneration Through Violence*, ch. 13; Nina Baym, "The Women of Cooper's Leatherstocking Tales," *AQ* 23:5 (Dec. 1971), 696–709; L. Friedman, *Inventors of the Promised Land*, Pt. II; David T. Haberly, "Women and Indians: *The Last of the Mohicans* and the Captivity Tradition," *AQ* 28:4 (Fall 1976), 431–43; and Annette Kolodny, *Lay of the Land: Metaphor as Experience and History in American Life and Letters*, pp. 89–114. On the general character of racial and sexual symbolism in this period and its connection to ideology, see G. J. Barker-Benfield, *Horrors of the Half-Known Life: Male Attitudes Towards Women in Nineteenth Century America*, Pt. I and ch. 10, esp. pp. 8–10 and 37–42, dealing with Cooper; John S. and Robin M. Haller, *The Physician and Sexuality in Victorian America*, pp. ix–xiv; and Barbara Ehrenreich and Deirdre English, *For Her Own Good: 150 Years of the Experts' Advice to Women*, pp. 1–32.

19 Cooper, *The Prairie: A Tale* (1827), ch. 1, and H. N. Smith, "Introduction." See also H. N. Smith, *Virgin Land*, pp. 246–60.

20 Dick, *Lure of the Land*, esp. ch. 5.

21 On Cooper's later years and novels see Ellis, "The Coopers and New York Landholding Systems," *JFC: A Reappraisal*, pp. 412–22; Dekker, *James Fenimore Cooper*, chs. 12–14; and Dekker and McWilliams, *James Fenimore Cooper: The Critical Heritage*, chs. 38–40, 42. Representative of his later works, in which ambitious lower-class whites are equated with "Redskins," are *The Redskins; or, Indian and Injin* (1846); *The Chainbearer, or, The Littlepage Manuscripts* (1845); *Satanstoe; or, The Littlepage Manuscripts, A Tale of the Colony* (1845); and *The Oak Openings; or, the Bee-hunter* (1848). See Alan Leander MacGregor, "Tammany: The Indian as Rhetorical Surrogate," in *AQ* 35:4 (Fall 1983), 391–407.

Cooper's sea fiction offers a different perspective on the political questions addressed in the frontier novels. Although a struggle against an overwhelming natural environment forms a background to these novels as well as to the Leatherstocking series, the white society of the sea is far more orderly and disciplined. The social microcosm of the ship is ruled by a military-aristocratic type, whose legitimacy as arbiter is sustained by the special code of the sea. The conflict of these novels therefore pits one kind of social microcosm (Whig-Republican) against another (piratical or royalist-tyrannical), rather than setting isolated individuals up as lonely types of their race. See Rogin, *Subversive Genealogy*, Prologue, and ch. 9; and Priscilla Allen, "Melville and the Man-of-War Microcosm," *AQ* 25:1 (Mar. 1973), 32–47.

22 Barnett, *Ignoble Savage*, is excellent on the varieties of Indian stereotype in historical romances of this period. See also Slotkin, *Regeneration Through Violence*, pp. 354–68, 426–30, 446–56; and Marilyn J. Anderson, "The Image of the Indian in American Drama During the Jacksonian Era, 1829–1845," *JPC* 1:4 (Winter 1978), 800–10. Representative of the sentimentalization of Indian types are novels like Emerson Bennett, *The Prairie Flower, or Leni Leoti* (1850); George H. Hollister, *Mount Hope; or, Philip, King of the Wampanoags, An Historical Romance* (1851); Lydia Maria Child, *Hobomok; a Tale of Early Times* (1824); and Catherine M. Sedgwick, *Hope Leslie; or, Early Times in the Massachusetts* (1827). "Indian dramas" with a similar orientation were staples of the popular stage: George Washington Parke Custis, "Pocahontas, or the Settlers of Virginia" (1830), in Arthur Hobson Quinn, ed., *Representative American Plays, 1767–1923*, pp. 181–208; John Augustus Stone, "Metamora, or the Last of the Wampanoags" (1829), in Barrett H. Clark, ed., *Favorite American Plays of the Nineteenth Century*, pp. 1–34; Robert M. Bird, "Oralloosa, Son of the Incas: A Tragedy" (ms., 1832); James Eastburn and Robert C. Sands, *Yamoyden: A Tale of the Wars of King Philip* (1820). George Catlin was one of the most energetic and creative promulgators of the romantic view of the Indian, through his ambitious program of painting and public exhibition, his writings on Indian affairs, and his collaboration with Indian affairs administrator Colonel Thomas L. McKenney and the Western author Judge James Hall. The paintings are unique; but the writings are in the Cooper tradition. See George Catlin, *Letters and Notes on the Manners, Customs, and Condition of the North American Indians* . . . (1842); Drinnon, *Facing West*, chs. 13–15; Dippie, *Vanishing American*, ch. 2.

23 Kate Seymour House, *Cooper's Americans*, and Warren S. Walker, *Plots and Characters in the Fiction of James Fenimore Cooper* give a good general "census" of the novels. See also H. N. Smith, *Virgin Land*, Pt. II and ch. 21; Parrington, *Main Currents* 2:222–38; Baym, "The Women of Cooper's Leatherstocking Tales," 696–709; and C. Robert Kemble, *The Image of the Army Officer in America: Background for Current Views*, pp. 17–19.

24 On Jackson, see Rogin, *Fathers and Children*, esp. Pts. I and III; John William Ward, *Andrew Jackson: Symbol for an Age*; Parrington, *Main Currents* 2:145–52; Hofstader, *American Political Tradition*, ch. 3; Edward Pessen, *Jacksonian America: Society, Personality, and Politics*, rev. ed., pp. 1–32. On "aristocratic" character in the U.S., and esp. in the South, see Eugene G. Genovese, *The Political Economy of Slavery: Studies in the Economy and Society of the Slave South*, pp. 28–31; Taylor, *Cavalier and Yankee*, pp. 27–32, chs. 2, 4–5, pp. 301–4; Bertram Wyatt-Brown, *Southern Honor: Ethics and Behavior in the Old South*, Pt. I.

25 H. N. Smith, *Virgin Land*, p. 28.

CHAPTER 6

1 W. A. Williams, *Roots of the Modern American Empire*, chs. 1–3; Hofstader, *American Political Tradition*, ch. 3; Pessen, *Jacksonian America*, ch. 6; Friedman, *Inventors of the Promised Land*, Pts. II–IV.

2 Dick, *Lure of the Land*, pp. 1–2; H. N. Smith, *Virgin Land*, pp. 36–37; Potter, *People of Plenty*, p. 124. The project of equalizing wealth as part of the democratic program was essential to Jacksonian democracy. See, for example, Langdon Byllesby, *Observations on the Sources and Effects of Unequal Wealth* . . . (1826), pp. 81–105; Thomas Skidmore, *The Rights of Man to Property; Being a Proposition to Make It Equal Among Adults of the Present Generation* . . . (1829), ch. 4. Both are excerpted in Joseph

L. Blau, ed., *Social Theories of Jacksonian Democracy: Representative Writings of the Period, 1825–1850*, chs. 24–25. But see Karl Marx's critique of a similar proposition by German-American liberals, *On America and the Civil War*, pp. 3–6.

3 Pessen, *Jacksonian America*, ch. 7; Cochran, *Business in American Life*, ch. 5; ———— and Miller, *Age of Enterprise*, pp. 67–77; Stuart Bruchey, *Roots of American Economic Growth, 1607–1861*, pp. 124–25. Jackson's ideas on monopoly are best expressed in his statements in the controversy with the Bank of the United States, for which see the collection of documents in George Rogers Taylor, ed., *Jackson vs. Biddle: The Struggle Over the Second Bank of the United States*. His "political testament" is reprinted in Joseph L. Blau, ed., *Social Theories of Jacksonian Democracy: Representative Writings of the Period, 1825–1850*, pp. 1–21. Blau also reprints essential texts on monopoly and popular government by Stephen Simpson, John W. Vethake, Gilbert Vale, and Theodore Sedgwick, Jr. (chs. 10, 15–17).

4 T. C. Cochran, *Frontiers of Change*; ————, *Business in American Life*, chs. 4–5, 8; Pessen, *Jacksonian America*, ch. 4; W. A. Williams, *Roots of the Modern American Empire*, chs. 1, 3, 5; North, *Economic Growth*, Pt. II; John N. Ingham, "Rags to Riches Revisited: The Effect of City Size and Related Factors on the Recruitment of Business Leaders, *JAH* LXII:3 (Dec. 1976), 615–37; Gutman, *Work, Culture*, Pt. 3.

5 Alexander Saxton, "George Wilkes: The Transformation of a Radical Ideology," *AQ* 33:4 (Fall 1981), 437–38, 443; David A. Williams, *David C. Broderick: A Political Portrait*, pp. 8–9, 69–70, 180–87.

6 Bruchey, *Roots of American Economic Growth*, pp. xxiii; 74–76; Saxton, "George Wilkes," 437–58; Don H. Doyle, "Social Theories and New Communities," 151–66; Daniel Webster, "Seventh of March Speech," *Congressional Globe*, XXIII, Pt. 1, 1st Session (1849–50), pp. 476–83; Cochran, *Business in America*, chs. 5, 8; Miller, *The Age of Enterprise*, ch. 2; Marvon Fisher, "The Iconology of Industrialism, 1830–1860," in Cohen, *The American Culture: Approaches to the Study of the United States*, pp. 228–56.

7 Saxton, "George Wilkes," pp. 437–38, 456–58; Walter Hugins, *Jacksonian Democracy and the Working Class: A Study of the New York Workingman's Movement, 1829–1837*, chs. 7–10; Wallace, *Rockdale*; James C. Sylvis, ed., *The Life, Speeches, Labors and Essays of William H. Sylvis* (1872), pp. 142–43; Rex Burns, *Success in America: The Yeoman Dream and the Industrial Revolution*, p. 3; Edward Young, *Labor in Europe and America* . . . (1875), p. 5; Rohrbaugh, *Trans-Appalachian Frontier*, p. 6; Burchell, "Pioneer Elite," p. 383; Margo A. Conk, "Social Mobility in Historical Perspective," *MP* 1:3 (Fall 1978), 52–59; Douglas T. Miller, *The Birth of Modern America, 1820–1850*, chs. 3–4.

8 Lee Soltow, *Men and Wealth in the United States, 1850–1870*, esp. p. 183; and Williamson and Lindert, *American Inequality*, esp. Pt. 1, and chs. 10, 13. Soltow notes existing inequalities of wealth, but a tendency for wealth generally to increase in the course of an average male life-span; Williamson and Lindert emphasize the persistence of inequality despite the tendency of wealth to increase with age.

9 The historiography of American slavery would be a book in itself. My analysis of slavery and the ideological responses to it derive from Eugene Berwanger, *The Frontier Against Slavery: Western Anti-Negro Prejudice and the Slavery Extension Controversy*; Breen and Innes, *Myne Owne Ground*; David Brion Davis, *The Problem of Slavery in Western Civilization*; ————, *The Problem of Slavery in the Age of Revolution, 1770–1823*; Foner, *Free Labor*; Robert William Fogel and Stanley Engermann, *Time on the Cross: The Economics of American Negro Slavery*, 2 vols.; and the critique of Fogel and Engermann in Paul A. David, et al., *Reckoning with Slavery: A Critical Study of the Quantitative History of American Negro Slavery*, and Herbert G. Gutman, *Slavery and the Numbers Game: A Critique of "Time on the Cross"*; Eugene D. Genovese, *Political Economy of Slavery*; ————, *Roll, Jordan, Roll: The World the Slaves Made*; ————, *The World the Slaveholders Made: Two Essays in Interpretation*; Gutman, *The Black Family in Slavery and Freedom, 1750–1925*; Edmund S. Morgan, *American Slavery, American Freedom: The Ordeal of Colonial Virginia*; Ulrich B. Phillips, *Plantation and Frontier: The Documentary History of American Industrial Society*, vols. 1–2; Willie Lee Rose, *Documentary History of Negro Slavery in North America*; C. Vann Woodward, *American Counterpoint: Slavery and Racism in the North/South Dialogue*, ch. 1.

I am indebted to my colleague Clarence Walker for his advice and help on this subject.

10   Leo Marx, *The Machine in the Garden: Technology and the Pastoral Ideal in America*, pp. 194–200; Saxton, "George Wilkes," pp. 441–42.

11   Helen S. Zahler, *Eastern Workingmen and National Land Policy, 1829–1862*, pp. 1–49, 74–75; Hugins, *Jacksonian Democracy and the Working Class*, pp. 86–87, 136–60; John R. Commons, *The Labor Movement 1840–1860: Documentary History of American Industrial Society* 7: 287–364; 8: 21–79, on Land Reform. To put the movement in proportion, see Alan Dawley, *Class and Community: The Industrial Revolution in Lynn*, which suggests it had limited impact on eastern manufacturing towns. See also David M. Emmons, *Garden in the Grasslands: Boomer Literature of the Central Great Plains*, pp. 2–3; and Philip S. Foner, *History of the Labor Movement in the United States* 1: 183–88.

12   Edward Everett, *Orations and Speeches . . .* 1: 260 (1860); John F. Kasson, *Civilizing the Machine: Technology and Republican Values in America, 1776–1900*, pp. 44–45; Rogin, *Subversive Genealogy*, pp. 38–39.

13   Frank Luther Mott, *A History of American Magazines* 2: 5, 10, 27–45, 118–21, and ch. 9; Saxton, "George Wilkes," pp. 437–56.

14   William L. Hedges, *Washington Irving: An American Study, 1802–1832*; Lewis Gaston Leary, *Washington Irving*; H. N. Smith, *Virgin Land*, pp. 206–9; Levin, *History as Romantic Art*, pp. 21–25, 142.

15   Washington Irving, *Astoria; or, Enterprise Beyond the Rocky Mountains . . .* (1836), esp. chs. 1–2.

16   Irving, *The Rocky Mountains . . .* (reprinted as *Adventures of Captain Bonneville . . .*) (1837) 1: 3–5; Kemble, *Image of the Army Officer*, chs. 5–7.

17   Goetzmann, *Exploration and Empire*, pp. 147–63, 247–48; ———, "The Mountain Man as Jacksonian Man," in Cohen, *American Culture*, pp. 62–76.

18   Irving, *Rocky Mountains* 1: iii, 26, 33, 92–93, 248.

19   Goetzmann, "The Mountain Man," pp. 62–76; ———, "Mountain Man Stereotypes: A Note," *WHQ* 6:3 (July 1975), 295–302.

20   Irving, *Rocky Mountains* 2: 238; 1: 144, 238–39.

21   Ibid., 1: 244, 247.

22   Rogin, *Fathers and Children*; Hofstader, *American Political Tradition*, pp. 44–46, 50, 109; Miller, *Birth of Modern America*, ch. 5; Ward, *Andrew Jackson*; Pessen, *Jacksonian America*, chs. 2, 5; Parrington, *Main Currents* 2: 145–52.

23   James Hall, *Memoir . . . of William Henry Harrison . . .* (1836), pp. 7, 11–12, 56–57, 323; and ———, *Letters from the West . . .* (1828), pp. 285, 288–90. On Hall, see Slotkin, *Regeneration Through Violence*, pp. 355–56, 405–9; Parrington, *Main Currents* 2: 164–66; Drinnon, *Facing West*, ch. 15.

24   Henry Montgomery, *The Life of Major General Zachary Taylor . . .* (1847), pp. 13–17; *The Rough and Ready Annual* (1847), p. 22, deals with Taylor as rescuer of captives and avenger of victims of the Fort Mimms massacre; see also John Frost, *The Life of . . .* (1849), and Joseph Reese Fry, *A life of . . .* (1848).

25   *Rough and Ready* (Concord, N.H.) 1:1 (Dec. 12, 1846), p. 3.

26   Joel Tyler Headley, *The Lives of Winfield Scott and Andrew Jackson* (1852). See also [   ], *Taylor and His Generals . . .* (1848); and Edward D. Mansfield, *The Life of General Winfield Scott . . .* and *Life and Services of General Winfield Scott* (1852).

27   Rogin, *Fathers and Children*, pp. 256–66; Frederickson, *Black Image*, ch. 4.

28   Boorstin, *The Americans: The National Experience*, pp. 53, 61, 71–76, 122–23; Dick, *Lure of the Land*, pp. 57–62, 132–33, 141–44.

29   Ibid., pp. 10–11; Billington, *America's Frontier Heritage*, pp. 26–27; Boorstin, *The Americans: The National Experience*, p. 95.

30   M. Thomas Inge, ed., *The Frontier Humorists: Critical Views*, is an excellent collection of responses by both contemporary reviewers and later critics.

31   Saxton, "George Wilkes," p. 441; Leslie Fiedler, ed., George Lippard, *Monks of Monk Hall* (1844), Introduction.

32   Augustus Baldwin Longstreet, *Georgia Scenes; Character and Incidents &c.*, pp. 22–64. An excellent collection, with critical introduction, is Hennig Cohen and William B. Dillingham, *Humor of the Old Southwest*, esp. pp. xiii–xxviii, 28–51, 250–66;

F. O. Matthiessen, *American Renaissance: Art and Expression in the Age of Emerson and Whitman*, pp. 635–45; Constance M. Rourke, *American Humor*, chs. 2, 5.

33   Drinnon, *Facing West*, interprets the history of westward expansion in terms of the Indian-hater motif; see esp. Pt. III. Herman Melville, *The Confidence-Man, His Masquerade*, chs. 26–28; Robert Montgomery Bird, *Nick of the Woods* . . . (1837); Slotkin, *Regeneration Through Violence*, pp. 509–15.

34   James Hall, *Sketches of History, Life, and Manners in the West* . . . (1835) 2: 74–76, 87–92; John W. Monette, *The History of the Discovery of the Valley of the Mississippi* . . . (1848) 2: 16–17, 35.

35   Thomas Bangs Thorpe, "The Big Bear of Arkansas," in Cohen and Dillingham, *Humor of the Old Southwest*, pp. 270–71; Slotkin, *Regeneration Through Violence*, pp. 479–84.

36   Johnson Jones Hooper, *Adventures of Captain Simon Suggs* . . . (1848), pp. 9, 12–13.

37   James Hall, *The Harpe's Head* . . . (1833); Parrington, *Main Currents* 2: 164–65. Manly Wade Wellman, *Spawn of Evil*, is a popularly written history of the outlaws of the period.

38   On Murrell, see James Lal Penick, Jr., *The Great Western Land Pirate: John A. Murrell in Legend and History*; H. R. Howard, *The Life and Adventures of John A. Murrell, the Great Western Land Pirate* (1847); and Augustus Q. Walton, *A History of the Detection, Conviction, Life and Designs of John A. Murel [sic]* . . . [n.d.]. The account discussed here is H. R. Howard, *The History of Virgil A. Stewart, and His Adventures* . . . (1836), pp. iii, 5, 22–23, 36, 45–46, 58, 108.

39   Ibid., p. 89.

40   Ibid., pp. 90–93.

41   Ibid., p. 90.

42   Brown, *Strain of Violence*, chs. 1, 4; Hall, *Sketches* 2: 291–92; Cutler, *Lynch-Law*, chs. 2–4; David J. Bodenhammer, "Law and Disorder on the Early Frontier: Marion City, Indiana, 1823–1850," *WHQ* 10:3 (July 1979), 323–36. However, mob violence of a vigilante nature was not restricted to the Frontier; it was as much a part of the Metropolitan as the western scene. See Michael Feldberg, *The Turbulent Era: Riot and Disorder in Jacksonian America*; Leonard L. Richards, *Gentlemen of Property and Standing: Anti-Abolition Mobs in Jacksonian America*; and Jayme A. Sokolow, "The Jerry McHenry Rescue and the Growth of Northern Antislavery Sentiment During the 1850s," *JAS* 16:3 (Dec. 1982), 427–45.

43   Brown, *Strain of Violence*, is a good historical survey.

CHAPTER 7

1   David Montgomery, *Worker's Control in America* . . ., pp. 1–47; David M. Potter, *The Impending Crisis: 1848–1861*, pp. 8–14; David J. Rothman, *The Discovery of the Asylum: Social Order and Disorder in the New Republic*, pp. xiii–xx, 69–70, 154, 179; Pessen, *Jacksonian America*, chs. 3–5; James Oakes, *The Ruling Race: A History of American Slaveholders*, esp. Pt. 3. Michael Stephen Hindus, *Prison and Plantation: Crime, Justice and Authority in Massachusetts and South Carolina, 1767–1878*, points up the common ideological themes of paternal government and social discipline, but contrasts the different institutional policies adopted by each section to enact its beliefs. Taylor, *Cavalier and Yankee*, also finds common ground between northern and southern romance writers on the ideal of patriarchal order (modified by feminine sentiment); see also Barry Hayne, "Yankee in the Patriarchy: T. B. Thorpe's Reply to *Uncle Tom's Cabin*," *AQ* 20:2, 1 (Summer 1968), 180–95. Foner, *Free Soil*, ch. 2, concedes the limited consensus, but emphasizes crucial differences.

On the creation of classes and racialized class lines see Barbara J. Fields, "Ideology and Race in American History," in J. Morgan Kousser and James A. McPherson, eds., *Region, Race and Reconstruction: Essays in Honor of C. Vann Woodward*, pp. 143–77; Edgar T. Thompson, *Plantation Societies, Race Relations and the South: The Regimentation of Populations*, pp. 3–42, 115–17; Gary B. Mills, "Miscegenation and the Free

Negro in Antebellum 'Anglo' Alabama: A Re-Examination of Southern Race Relations," *JAH* 68:1 (June 1981), 16–34; Genovese, *World the Slaveholders Made*, ch. 3.

2   Genovese, *Political Economy*, pp. 19–23, ch. 10.

3   The industrialization of slavery was regarded by Southerners as feasible; and concrete moves were made in that direction in the decade before the Civil War, although these met with resistance on ideological and economic grounds. The history, prospects, and failure of industrial slavery are treated in Robert Starobin, *Industrial Slavery in the Old South*, esp. pp. 9–15, 28–35, 117–25, 148–49, 156–58, 163–64, 167, 178–79, 207, 211; Genovese, *Political Economy*, chs. 7–8; Oakes, *Ruling Race*, ch. 6, "Factories in the Fields"; Ronald L. Lewis, *Coal, Iron and Slaves: Industrial Slavery in Maryland and Virginia*; Fred Bateman and Thomas Weiss, *A Deplorable Scarcity: The Failure of Industrialization in the Slave Economy*; Stanley Elkins and Eric L. McKitrick, "Institutions and the Law of Slavery: The Dynamics of Unopposed Capitalism," *AQ* 9:1 (Spring 1957), 3–21; ———, "Institutions and the Law of Slavery: Slavery in Capitalist and Non-Capitalist Cultures," *AQ* 9:2 (Summer 1957), 157–79; Robert E. Gallman and Ralph V. Anderson, "Slaves as Fixed Capital: Slave Labor and Southern Economic Development," *JAH* 64:1 (Jan. 1977), 24–46; Edward Pessen, "How Different from Each Other Were the Antebellum North and South?" *AHR* 85:5 (Dec. 1980), 1119–66.

3   Taylor, *Cavalier and Yankee*, pp. 182–84, 300–301; H. N. Smith, *Virgin Land*, pp. 174–76; Slotkin, *Regeneration Through Violence*, ch. 12.

4   Genovese, *Political Economy*, ch. 9; Hofstader, *American Political Tradition*, pp. 77–80; George Fitzhugh, *Cannibals All! or, Slaves Without Masters* (1857), pp. 11, 199–200, explicitly ties the closing of the land frontier to the universalization of coercive labor systems (slavery) in the North as well as the South.

5   Ibid., p. 80; Genovese, *Political Economy*, pp. 229–35; Woodward, *American Counterpoint*, ch. 4. Southerners also envisioned revolution in the apocalyptic terms employed by the ministerial successors of the Puritans, and popular writers like Lippard. See Jack P. Maddox, Jr., "Pro-Slavery Millennialism: Social Eschatology in Antebellum Southern Calvinism," *AQ* 31:1 (Spring 1979), 46–62.

6   Hofstader, *American Political Tradition*, pp. 81–83; Genovese, *Political Economy*, ch. 9; Potter, *Impending Crisis*, chs. 2–4; Genovese, *World the Slaveholders Made*, pp. 118–28, 236–37.

7   Genovese, *Political Economy*, p. 121 and ch. 9; Starobin, *Industrial Slavery*, p. 6.

8   Taylor, *Cavalier and Yankee*, pp. 124–25, 300–1; Slotkin, *Regeneration Through Violence*, 460–65, 506–15; Drinnon, *Facing West*, chs. 11–13; William Gillmore Simms, *The Yemassee* (1835).

9   Genovese, *Political Economy*, chs. 7, 10; Rogin, *Fathers and Children*, p. 275; ———, *Subversive Genealogy*, pp. 190–92; Rothman, *Discovery of the Asylum*, ch. 9, on parental roles and institutional equivalents. See also Davis, *Problem of Slavery in the Age of Revolution*, pp. 233–42.

10   On the plantation novel, see Taylor, *Cavalier and Yankee*, chs. 4–5, and p. 133 on the significance of the nostalgic tone; also Lewis P. Simpson, *The Dispossessed Garden: Pastoral and History in Southern Literature*, on the same subject. The work of Mary Eastman is not usually listed with the major productions of this school, but is interesting for her linkage of paternalistic interpretations of the governance of both Indians and blacks. Her most famous work is *Aunt Phillis's Cabin; or, Southern Life as It Is* (1852), a response to Stowe's *Uncle Tom's Cabin*; compare her treatment of Indians in *Dacotah; or, Life and Legends of the Sioux Around Fort Snelling* (1849) and *Romance of Indian Life, with Other Tales* (1853). Eastman's husband was a soldier stationed at Fort Snelling in the 1850s. Her Indian books were reprinted after the Civil War, since their sympathetic paternalism matched the ideology of the "philanthropic" reformers of Indian policy—making for a curious association of former abolitionists with a former advocate of slavery.

Other plantation novels referred to are William Alexander Caruthers, *The Cavaliers of Virginia; or, the Recluse of Jamestown . . .* (1834); ———, *The Knights of the Horseshow; A Traditionary Tale of the Cocked Hat Gentry of the Old Dominion* (1834); John Pendleton Kennedy, *Horse-Shoe Robinson: A Tale of the Tory Ascendancy* (1835); ———, *Swallow Barn; or, A Sojourn in the Old Dominion* (1832); [Thomas Bangs Thorpe], *The Master's House; or, Scenes Descriptive of Southern Life* (1854).

A good source on the Turner Rebellion and its aftershocks is Henry Irving Tragle, ed., *The Southampton Slave Revolt of 1831: A Compilation of Source Material*, pp. 43, 48–53, 69–70, 74, 76, 83, 114–15, 123. It is interesting that abolitionist papers accepted (provisionally) the exterminationist concepts of Southerners: specifically, that blacks would see extermination of whites as the only way to freedom (p. 104) and that whites would respond in kind (p. 63), thus themselves becoming as "savage" as Indians (pp. 103–4). See also Lynn Veach Sadler, "Dr. Stephen Graham's Narration of the 'Duplin Insurrection': Additional Evidence of the Impact of Nat Turner," *JAS* 12:3 (Dec. 1978), 359–68.

11   Rothman, *Discovery of the Asylum*, pp. 69–70, 171–72; Genovese, *Political Economy*, chs. 7, 10; ———, *World the Slaveholders Made*, Pt. II; Potter, *Impending Crisis*, chs. 1, 3, 7–9; Gutman, *Black Family*, chs. 3 and 4, suggests some of the cultural and social consequences of slavery's economic expansion, which were fatal to "patriarchal" values.

12   Joseph E. Walker, *Hopewell Village: The Dynamics of a Nineteenth Century Iron-Making Community*, pp. 11–37, 255–71; Commons, *Labor Movement* 7: 132–45; Peter Temin, *Iron and Steel in Nineteenth Century America: An Economic Inquiry*, p. 85; Thompson, *Plantation Societies*, pp. 43–49, 50–68; Kasson, *Civilizing the Machine*, chs. 1–2; Marvin Fisher, "Iconology of Industrialism," in Cohen, *American Culture*, pp. 228–46; Richard P. Horwitz, "Architecture and Culture: The Meaning of the Lowell Boarding House," *AQ* 25:1 (Mar. 1973), 83–107.

13   Rogin, *Fathers and Children*, ch. 8.

14   Rothman, *Discovery of the Asylum*, chs. 6–7, esp. pp. 107–8, 153–55, 203–4. The treatment of the California Indians in 1850–60 is an extreme example of the application of this model of corrective social relations between races. These Indians were overtly threatened with a war of extermination by whites, then "protected" from white violence (and their own provocative criminal or pauperistic tendencies) by a coercive labor system akin to slavery. See Albert L. Hurtado, " 'Hardly a Farm House—a Kitchen Without Them': Indian and White Households on the California Borderland Frontier in 1860," *WHQ* 13:3 (July 1982), 245–70. Genovese, *Political Economy*, chs. 1, 7, 10; ———, *Roll Jordan, Roll*, ch. 1; Rogin, *Fathers and Children*, p. 275; ———, *Subversive Genealogy*, pp. 190–92; Rothman, *Discovery of the Asylum*, ch. 9; Davis, *Problem of Slavery in the Age of Revolution*, pp. 233–42.

15   Fisher, "Iconology of Industrialism," pp. 237–40. Idealized portrayals of Lowell and its "girls" are William Scoresby, *American Factories and Their Female Operatives . . .* (1845), esp. chs. 4–5, which cites the moral superiority of American working girls and suggests ways of bringing their British sisters up to the Lowell standards; and Henry A. Miles, *Lowell, As It Was, and As It Is* (1845), pp. 9–49, 58–145, which traces the course of progress from Indian times to the flowering of the mills, and celebrates the enlightened government of the women by the "Moral Police" of Lowell.

16   Alice Felt Tyler, *Freedom's Ferment: Phases of American Social History from Colonial Times to the Outbreak of the Civil War*, pp. 212–13; Horwitz, "Lowell Boarding Houses," pp. 83–90. There was a reciprocal use of "Lowell" in the South, as a metaphor for the "negative" effects produced in the character of labor by the rival system. Opponents of southern industrialization feared the "Lowellizing" of the laboring classes (white and black), by which they meant their development of the antipatriarchal tendencies of free workers and politicization of working-place social relations. Although the ideological content of these two metaphors has a different intention, the metaphoric device is the same: the "alien" form of labor infects a peaceful and positive system, altering the racial/sexual character of the participants and fostering a tendency to class struggle and violence. See Genovese, *Political Economy*, pp. 231–34. A crucial difference is that the Northerner who uses "slavery" as a metaphor for industrial labor associates himself with the worker, identifying the employer as the aggressor and perverter of racial/sexual relations; while the Southerner identifies himself with the planter/owner, and identifies the source of aggression and racial perversion in the people and popular movements. Foner, *Free Soil*, ch. 2, esp. pp. 71–72. See also Commons, *Labor Movement*, 7: 81–99, 8: 81–346.

17   Rebecca Harding Davis, *Margret Howth, A Story of Today* (1862), esp. ch. 1.

18   M. W. Tyler, *A Book Without a Title; or, Thrilling Events in the Life of Mira Dana* (1855), pp. iii–iv, 11, 13, 16–17, 22–33. 108–12.

19   Gutman, *Black Family*, pp. 298–99; [David G. Croley and George Wakeman], *Miscegenation: The Theory of the Blending of the Races, Applied to the American White Man and Negro* (1864), pp. 15–16, 18–19, 29–32; Forrest G. Wood, *Black Scare: The Racist Response to Emancipation and Reconstruction*, ch. 4.

20   Friedman, *Inventors of the Promised Land*, Pt. III; Genovese, *Political Economy*, pp. 231–35; Potter, *Impending Crisis*, p. 32; Frederickson, *Black Image*, chs. 4–5; Robinson, quoted in Blau's *Social Theories*, p. 320. The abolitionist critique of slavery became an implicit, and often an explicit, critique of industrial capitalism as well. See Harriet Beecher Stowe, *Uncle Tom's Cabin; or, Life Among the Lowly* (1851), chs. 19, 23; Taylor, *Cavalier and Yankee*, pp. 287–94; Evan Brandstetter, "Uncle Tom and Archy Moore: The Anti-Slavery Novel as Ideological Symbol," *AQ* 26:2 (May 1974), 160–75.

21   Lippard, *The Monks of Monk Hall*, was published as *The Quaker City* in 1844. The modern edition with an informative introduction by Leslie Fiedler is used here. See also George Lippard, *New York: Its Upper Ten and Lower Million* (1853); Eugène Sue, *The Mysteries of Paris* (1845 46). An odd, interesting book in this vein is Cornelius Mathews, *Big Abel and the Little Manhattan* (1845), in which a workingman and his Indian companion wander the "mean streets" and see poverty, labor strikes, luxury; the Cooperian symbolism is used to comment directly on the Metropolis. On the city in American fiction of this time, see Thomas Bender, *Toward an Urban Vision: Ideas and Institutions in Nineteenth Century America*; Adrienne Siegel, *The Image of the American City in Popular Literature 1820–1870*; Janis P. Stout, *Sodoms in Eden: The City in American Fiction Before 1860*. On the literature of crime, see David Brion Davis, *Homicide in American Fiction, 1798–1860*. On working-class life and urban crime, see Bruce Laurie, *Working People of Philadelphia, 1800–1850*; and Eric H. Monkkonen, "A Disorderly People? Urban Order in the Nineteenth and Twentieth Centuries," *JAH* 68:3 (Dec. 1981), 539–59.

22   Lippard, *Monks*, p. 85.

23   Sue, *Mysteries*, p. 3; Chevalier, *Laboring Classes/Dangerous Classes*, pp. 39–40.

24   Lippard, *Monks*, p. 333.

25   Ibid., pp. 206–7, 262–64, 268–69, 295–96, 323–24.

26   Ibid., pp. 405, 441.

27   Ibid., pp. 175, 551.

28   Ibid., pp. 24, 101.

29   Ibid., p. 137.

30   Ibid., pp. 46–47, 55–56.

31   Ibid., p. 362.

32   Ibid., pp. 568–69, 575.

33   Ibid., p. 539.

34   Ibid., pp. 372–74.

35   Ibid., pp. 378–79, 383.

36   Ibid., p. 389.

37   Ibid., p. 401.

38   Ibid., pp. 391–93. There was a corresponding fear among southern poor whites that northern capitalists would eventually enslave them if they stayed within the Union. See James Mills Thornton III, *Politics and Power in a Slave Society: Alabama, 1800–1860*. This attitude carried over into the postbellum period, when it received reinforcement of a material sort from the Reconstruction regime, and the period of agricultural concentration that followed the 1870s. Southern populism has certain of its roots here. It is interesting to note as well the persistence of Lippardian imagery in northern postwar populism; see, for example, Ignatius Donnelly's dystopian novel *Caesar's Column* . . . (1890).

CHAPTER 8

1   William H. Goetzmann, *When the Eagle Screamed: The Romantic Horizon in American Diplomacy, 1800–1860*, esp. chs. 3–4. On Texas historiography in this period, see Stephen Stagner, "Epics, Science, and the Lost Frontier: Texas Historical Writing, 1836–1936," *WHQ* 12:2 (Apr. 1981), 165–82. Early Texas and Texican fiction is a mix-

ture of captivity and Indian-fighting narratives, more or less historical, and works of
fiction that are almost entirely fabricated from existing literary conventions and show
little evidence of an acquaintance with Texas or the Mexican borderlands. See, for example, Timothy Flint, *Francis Berrian, or the Mexican Patriot* (1826); "Anthony Ganilh"
[A. T. Myrthe], *Ambrosio de Letinez; or, the First Texan Novel* (1842). Among the
captivities the most important are collected in Carle Coke Rister, ed., *Comanche Bondage.* . . . On Oregon, see Robert Greenhow, *History of Oregon and California* . . ., esp.
the 1847 edition.

   2 [Charles Edwards Lester], *The Life of Sam Houston: The Hunter, Patriot, and
Statesman of Texas* . . . (1846, 1867); Sam Houston, *The Autobiography of Sam Houston*,
ed. by Donald Day and Harry Herbert Ullom; Marquis James, *The Raven: A Biography
of Sam Houston*; Slotkin, *Regeneration Through Violence*, pp. 429–30.

   3 James Atkins Shackleford, "David Crockett, The Legend and the Symbol," in
Inge, *Frontier Humorists*, pp. 208–18; Catherine L. Albanese, "Savage, Sinner and Saved:
Davy Crockett, Camp Meetings, and the Wild Frontier," *AQ* 33:5 (Winter 1981), 482–
501; M. J. Heale, "The Role of the Frontier in Jacksonian Politics: David Crockett and
the Myth of the Self-Made Man," *WHQ* 4:4 (Oct. 1973), 405–24; Parrington, *Main
Currents* 2:172–79; Slotkin, *Regeneration Through Violence*, pp. 414–17, 553–64; Moore,
Frontier Mind, chs. 4–5, 9–10.

   4 Dorson, *America in Legend*, pp. 65–68, 74.

   5 James J. Arpad, Introduction, to David Crockett, *Narrative of the Life* . . .
(1834), pp. 25–28; James Kirke Paulding, *The Lion of the West* . . . (1831), ed. James N.
Tidwell, puts Davy in an urban setting; see pp. 169–71 below on his visit to Lowell.

   6 Arpad, Introduction, in Crockett, *Narrative of the Life*, pp. 12–13. It is interesting to note the parallel between the Whig/Democratic split in Cooper's district and
that in Crockett's. In both instances the Whigs appeared as the party of smaller farmers
and tenants, while the Jacksonian Democrats were the party of the landlords.

   7 Crockett, *Narrative*, chs. 5–8; Moore, *Frontier Mind*, chs. 9–10.

   8 Crockett, *Narrative*, p. 99.

   9 Ibid., pp. 10–11; Foner, *Free Soil*, pp. 15–18; Calvin Colton, *Labor and Capital,
The Junius Tracts* 7 (1844), is the classic statement of Whig ideas about success and
social mobility.

   10 Crockett, *Account of Colonel Crockett's Tour to the North and Down East* . . .
(1835), pp. 11, 23–25.

   11 Ibid., pp. 45, 48–49.

   12 Ibid., pp. 31, 50.

   13 Ibid., p. 21. Compare Lincoln's use of his own experience of "hard knocks" to
argue the same doctrine in his Wisconsin Agricultural Fair Speech of 1858, cited below.
Foner, *Free Soil*, ch. 1.

   14 Ibid., pp. 62, 91–95.

   15 Ibid., pp. 67–70, 78–79.

   16 Jerry J. Gaddy, ed., *Texas in Revolt: Contemporary Newspaper Accounts*, pp.
52–53.

   17 On Cherokee Removal, see Angie Debo, *And Still the Waters Run*; Grant Fore-
man, *Indian Removal: The Emigration of the Five Civilized Tribes of Indians.* A good
collection of original sources is Louis Filler and Allen Guttman, *The Removal of the
Cherokee Nation: Manifest Destiny or National Dishonor?* See analyses by Rogin,
Fathers and Children, esp. ch. 7; Thompson, *Plantation Societies*, pp. 50–68; Mary
Young, "The Cherokee Nation: Mirror of the Republic," *AQ* 33:5 (Winter 1981), 502–24.

   18 John Dunn Hunter, *Memories of A Captivity* . . . (1824); Drinnon, *White
Savage*, esp. ch. 9; George A. Schultz, *An Indian Canaan: Isaac McCoy and the Vision
of an Indian State.*

   19 Merk, *Mission and Manifest Destiny*, esp. chs. 1–3; George Wilkins Kendall,
The Texan Santa Fe Expedition, pp. 57–60, 75–76, continually refers to Cooper and
Irving, uses "Sons of Forest" quite frequently throughout. Goetzmann, *When the Eagle
Screamed*, ch. 4; Ramón Eduardo Ruiz, ed., *The Mexican War: Was It Manifest Destiny?*;
K. Jack Bauer, *The Mexican War, 1846–1848.*

   20 George Winston Smith and Charles Judah, ed., *Chronicles of the Gringos:
The U.S. Army in the Mexican War, 1846–1848. Accounts of Eyewitnesses and Combattants*, pp. 219, 403–4.

21   Levin, *History as Romantic Art,* pp. 145–57, 163–85; Reginald Horsman, *Race and Manifest Destiny: The Origins of American Racial Anglo-Saxonism,* esp. chs. 7, 11–12.

22   Prescott, *Conquest of Mexico* (1843), pp. 828–30; Smith and Judah, *Gringos,* pp. 406–7.

23   Merk, *Mission and Manifest Destiny,* pp. 53–54; Edward D. Mansfield, *The Mexican War: A History of Its Origin . . .,* pp. 10–11, 321–23; Daniel Webster, *Congressional Globe* 22:1 (1st Session), 31st Congress (1849–50), 476–83.

24   *DR* 23:398. On the ideological commitments of this journal, see Blau, ed., *Social Theories,* pp. 21–37.

25   *DR* 23:30.

26   Ibid., 22: 129.

27   "The Border Settlement, or the Tory's Daughter," *DR* 21: 246–52, 353–60.

28   "Chalcahual," *DR* 22:49.

29   Ibid., 149.

30   Ibid., 69.

31   Ibid., 159–61.

32   Ibid., 401–3.

33   Ibid., 21:93–94.

34   *Rough and Ready Annual* (1848), p. 192.

35   Ibid., pp. 192–93.

36   [G. N. Allen], *Mexican Treacheries and Cruelties . . .* (1847), pp. 1–2.

37   Smith and Judah, *Gringos,* p. 10; Merk, *Mission and Manifest Destiny,* pp. 35–37, 56–57, 139, 144–46. On Bennett and contemporary journalism, see Frank Luther Mott, *American Journalism: A History of Newspapers in the United States Through 250 Years, 1690–1940,* pp. 167–326, esp. 229–38.

38   Merk, *Mission and Manifest Destiny,* pp. 52–53.

39   Quoted ibid., pp. 157–58, 162.

40   Quoted ibid., pp. 157, 165–66.

41   Quoted ibid., p. 25.

42   Smith and Judah, *Gringos,* pp. 14–15.

43   Merk, *Mission and Manifest Destiny,* pp. 160, 164.

44   Ibid., pp. 121–23.

45   Ibid., p. 154.

46   Smith and Judah, *Gringos,* pp. 227–28.

47   Ibid., p. 410.

48   Ibid., pp. 432–33.

49   *DR* 21:92, 524.

50   Merk, *Mission and Manifest Destiny,* pp. 34, 123, 191–92, 162.

51   A. A. Livermore, *The War with Mexico Reviewed . . .* (1849), pp. 6–8, 10–12, 177, 200–1

52   Ibid., p. 11. Compare Irving, *Astoria* 1:232, and above, pp. 121–22.

53   Livermore, *The War with Mexico,* pp. 140–41, 146; Smith and Judah, *Gringos,* pp. 445–47.

CHAPTER 9

1   *NYH 46,* June 1, p. 4; Melissa Totten, "Metaphors of Conquest: The Fiction of the Mexican War, 1846–1848" (honors thesis, Wesleyan University, 1981), p. 90.

2   Harry Halyard, *The Chieftain of Churubusco; or the Spectre of the Cathedral: A Romance of the Mexican War* (1848); ———, *The Heroine of Tampico; or, Wildfire the Wanderer* (1847); ———, *The Mexican Spy; or, The Pride of Buena Vista, A Tale of the Mexican War* (1848); Newton M. Curtis, *The Hunted Chief; or, the Female Ranchero, a Tale of the Mexican War* (1847); ———, *The Prairie Guide; or, the Rose of the Rio Grande, a Tale of the Mexican War* (1847); ———, *The Vidette; or, the Girl of the Robber's Pass, a Tale of the Mexican War* (1848); Ned Buntline [Edgar Z. C. Judson], *The Volunteer; or, the Maid of Monterrey, a Tale of the Mexican War* (1847); J. H. Ingraham, *The Texan Ranger; or, the Maid of Matamoros, a Tale of the Mexican*

War (1847); analysis in Totten, "Metaphors of Conquest," ch. 1; Daryl Jones, *The Dime Novel Western.* See also Charles W. Webber, *Old Hicks the Guide; or, Adventures in the Camanche Country in Search of a Gold Mine* (1848).

3 George Lippard, *Legends of Mexico* (1847), pp. 53–54, 71; Totten, "Metaphors," chs. 2–4.

4 Lippard, *Legends of Mexico*, p. 64.

5 Ibid., p. 47.

6 Ibid., pp. 109–13, 117, 121.

7 George Lippard, *'Bel of Prairie Eden: A Romance of Mexico* (1848), pp. 15–24; Totten, "Metaphors," pp. 103–12. A similar mix of themes and images, tying together Mexican rancheros and Indians, the idea of a prairie Eden, and a romantic fable of abduction (or rape) and vengeance, is in Mayne Reid, *The White Chief: A Legend of North Mexico* (1860); and Webber, *Old Hicks*, pp. 115–16, 219.

8 Totten, "Metaphors," pp. 44–25, and ch. 4.

9 John Charles Frémont, *Report of the Exploring Expedition* . . . (1845), pp. 60–61, is a fair example of his purple prose. See also Stephen Fender, *Plotting the Golden West: American Literature and the Rhetoric of the California Trail.* The best biography is Ferol Egan, *Frémont: Explorer for a Restless Nation.* See also Allan Nevins, *Frémont: Pathmarker of the West*, ch. 15; Goetzmann, *When the Eagle Screamed*, pp. 43–46, 58–59; ———, *Exploration and Empire*, ch. 7; Bernard De Voto, *The Year of Decision 1846*, pp. 39–48, 222–29, 279–83, 365–67, 470–77; William Nisbet Chambers, *Old Bullion Benton: Senator from the New West*, chs. 12, 14; Thomas L. Karnes, *William Gilpin: Western Nationalist*, pp. 85–104; H. N. Smith, *Virgin Land*, 91–94.

10 On Frémont's later career, see Nevins, *Frémont*, chs. 23–36; Ruhl J. Bartlett, *John C. Frémont and the Republican Party*; De Voto, *Year of Decision*, pp. 475–81.

11 Kent Laird Steckmesser, *The Western Hero in History and Legend*, pp. 13, 19, 24, 29–30.

12 John Bigelow, *Memoir of the Life and Public Services of John Charles Frémont* . . . (1856); Samuel M. Smucker, *The Life of Colonel John Charles Frémont, and His Narrative of Explorations* . . . (1856); Charles Wentworth Upham, *Life, Explorations, and Public Services of John Charles Frémont* (1856). These campaign biographies repeat the same materials and themes, presenting Frémont in terms of his "Pathfinder" mystique; tying him to the masses by his humble birth; and linking him to the genteel classes and technological elite through his educational attainments and status as a professional officer.

13 Charles E. Averill, *Kit Carson: The Prince of the Gold Hunters* . . . (1849), pp. 7, 58. This juxtaposition of Frontier heroes and Metropolitan rescue objects is not unique to the Carson canon. J. B. Jones, *Wild Western Scenes* . . . (1856) has Boone giving assistance to similarly placed tenderfeet from the city. Bennett, *The Prairie Flower*, has similar elements, as does Mayne Reid, *The White Chief: A Legend of North Mexico* (1860). This is an exaggeration of the convention established by Cooper, whose female rescue objects are always from the Metropolis—loosely defined as "civilization"; but now the Metropolis is definitively associated with the city.

14 Averill, *Kit Carson*, p. 58.

15 Steckmesser, *Western Hero*, pp. 24–46.

16 As Steckmesser notes (pp. 24–55) the split in the thematic development of the Carson legend corresponds to a split in the form of literary production: the "genteel" Carson is a creature of the clothbound, relatively expensive books of the burgeoning popular book trade; the roughneck Carson remains a denizen of dime novels and the cheaper forms of literature. This differentiation of the literary marketplace is apparent in the 1850s, and increases markedly in each ensuing decade—see, for example, Frank Luther Mott's discussion of the parallel developments in magazines after 1857 in his *History of American Magazines: 1850–1865* 2:5, 27–45. The literary tradition identified by Parrington as "genteel," and by Ann Douglas as "feminized," is associated with the clothbound book and the gentrified Frontier hero; and it is important to note that this was the version of the hero that pretended to historical veracity. The antithetical dime-novel tradition insisted on the Frontier hero as an outlaw of sorts, a man outside society and critical of it, a violent and unmannered man; but made no pretense of being much more than a recombination of favored literary conventions. However, the ideological changes associated with the emergence of progressivism induced a revaluation of these

themes and conventions in the 1890s, with the ironic result that the new "realistic" writers (Garland, Norris, London, Wister) drew on the themes and interests of the "red-blooded" dime-novel tradition, and asserted its authenticity as a vision of western history; while the genteel, feminized, historically pretentious tradition was dismissed as the product of an effeminate sentimentality.

17   *Rough and Ready Annual* (1847), pp. 153–54, 157; DeWitt Clinton Peters, *The Life and Adventures of Kit Carson, the Nestor of the Rocky Mountains . . .* (1858), pp. 15–16; Capt. L. C. Carleton [Edward Sylvester Ellis], *Kit Carson, the Scout; or, the Knight of the Prairie* (1872), p. 9. See also Charles Burdett, *The Life of Kit Carson, the Celebrated Rocky Mountain Trapper and Guide . . .* (1860).

18   Peters, *Life and Adventures of Kit Carson*, pp. vi, 48.

19   John S. C. Abbott, *Christopher Carson, Familiarly Known as Kit Carson . . .* (1873), pp. 30, 37, 42, 46, 64, 165–66, 208, 322. Carson is said to be more of a "merchant" than a "trapper"; and to make his tenderfoot protégés feel as safe as if they were dining on a gourmet supper in the "Astor House on Broadway." Abbott also wrote biographies making similar use of the myths of Daniel Boone and Davy Crockett.

20   Carleton [Ellis], *Kit Carson*, pp. 10–11.

21   Ibid., pp. 11, 20, 36.

22   Ibid., p. 6.

CHAPTER 10

1   Foner, *Free Soil*, pp. 27–29, 256, 311–12; Potter, *Impending Crisis*, ch. 4.

2   Potter, *Impending Crisis*, ch. 5, and p. 115. This discussion of the Compromise of 1850 owes a great deal to Rogin, *Subversive Genealogy*, ch. 4.

3   Potter, *Impending Crisis*, ch. 7.

4   Paul, *Mining Frontiers of the Far West, 1848–1880*, pp. 7–10, 34–35, 48–55; Cochran and Miller, *Age of Enterprise*, pp. 6–8, 30–32, 36–42, 52–56; Winther, *The Transportation Frontier*, esp. chs. 3, 4, 7; Billington, *America's Frontier Heritage*, pp. 31–32; Robert W. Fogel, *Railroads and Economic Growth: Essays in Economic History*, pp. 208–9; Albert Fishlow, *American Railroads and the Transformation of the Antebellum Economy*, pp. 32, 102–5. Fogel makes the strongest case against railroads as a "leading sector" in *Railroads and Economic Growth*, esp. pp. 114, 131–40, 208. A useful case study is John Patterson Davis, *The Union Pacific Railroad: A Case of Premature Enterprise*.

5   Saxton, "George Wilkes," pp. 441–42; Smith, *Virgin Land*, pp. 32–37.

6   Pessen, *Jacksonian America*, ch. 7; Foner, *Free Soil*, pp. 20–23, 31–33.

7   Paul Wallace Gates, *The Illinois Central Railroad and Its Colonization Work*, pp. 160–76, 181, 187–88, 226–27, 232.

8   Ibid., pp. 100–12, 119–20.

9   Marx, *Machine in the Garden*, pp. 194–203, 213; Kasson, *Civilizing the Machine*, ch. 1, and pp. 172–80; Rogin, *Subversive Genealogy*, pp. 37–41.

10   Abraham Lincoln, "Address at the Wisconsin State Agricultural Fair," *The Collected Works* 3: 472–73, 476–77; Foner, *Free Soil*, pp. 32–33, is a succinct critique of this aspect of Republican ideology.

11   Lincoln, "Address," pp. 476–77. Compare the quotation from Webster's 1850 address, above, pp. 114–15, and n. 23, below.

12   Foner, *Free Soil*, pp. 311–12; and the summary view of Republican expansionism, pp. 27–30. See also Kasson, *Civilizing the Machine*, p. 45, which quotes Edward Everett's assertion, "There is no goal; and there can be no pause [in the progress of art and science] . . . Nothing can arrest them which does not plunge the entire order of society into barbarism."

13   The best biography is Karnes, *Gilpin*; see also Smith, *Virgin Land*, ch. 3.

14   William Gilpin, *The Mission of the North American People . . .* (1873), pp. 18–19.

15   Ibid., pp. vi, 234.

16   Ibid.

17   Ibid., pp. 19–20, 117–19.

18   Ibid., pp. 48–49, 70.

19   Ibid., pp. 4, 326; Karnes, *Gilpin*, pp. 126, 227. A similar vision of the reciprocal regeneration of China and America is J. M. Sturtevant, *American Emigration: A Discourse in Behalf of the American Home Missionary Society* . . . (1857), which proposes colonizing China's "vacant lands" with American settlers.

20   Gilpin, *Mission*, p. 124.

21   Ibid., pp. 42, 119, 133.

22   Ibid., pp. 142–43.

23   In the next chapter the proposals for and against indefinite expansion of slavery are discussed at some length. These have to do with the issue of *principle*—the justice or injustice, desirability or undesirability of such extension. The issue here is that of possibility—was it feasible to expand slavery westward, or did the westward environment make that impracticable? In this connection, see Daniel Webster's "Seventh of March Speech" in favor of the Compromise of 1850. Webster argues that demurring on the principle of slavery will not affect the material interests of freedom because California and the other territories are so unsuited for slave agriculture. Note that this assertion depends on a radical underestimation of California's agrarian possibilities. Webster recognizes that peonage is the operative form of labor organization in California and the Southwest; and because peonage is not chattel slavery, he concludes slavery will not work there. From the perspective of the worker or farmer, however, it is clear that a form of dependent labor closer to slavery than freedom did in fact pertain there. Webster's elite perspective allows a reading of the facts which misses the point of his constituents' anxieties. See Webster, "Seventh of March Address," pp. 476–83.

24   Dawley, *Class and Community*, p. 75; Potter, *Impending Crisis*, pp. 151–61, 169, 171–76; Robert Johanssen, ed., *The Lincoln-Douglas Debates*, pp. 14–21, 50–60. This logic was exhibited in the series of crises that followed Kansas-Nebraska: the battles in Bleeding Kansas and the question of approving the proslavery Lecompton constitution for the territory; the Dred Scott decision (1857); the struggle over the nomination of Douglas, which split the only remaining national party and pitted northern Democrats against southern hegemony in their party; and finally, the crisis of secession in 1860. See Potter, *Impending Crisis*, chs. 9–12, 15–16.

CHAPTER 11

1   The historiography of American racism is nearly as extensive as that dealing with slavery. Each generation of scholars has reconceived the problem in terms of current interests and concerns, from the nineteenth-century interest in establishing the reality and social significance of genetic difference, to the twentieth-century concern with the evolution of scientific thought and with redressing past injustices. The work that seems to me to grasp the ideological concerns of antebellum racism most accurately is Horsman, which sees racism as a positive doctrine vaunting the natural "gifts" of Anglo-Americans for conquest and democracy, rather than as a purely negative doctrine for rationalizing the inferiority of blacks and Indians. Horsman sees the Mexican War, rather than the promulgation of new evolutionary or other scientific doctrines by the academic elite, as the precipitant of a fully developed racial Anglo-Saxonism. See also his "Science, Racism and the American Indian in the Mid-Nineteenth Century," *AQ* 27:2 (May 1975), 152–68, which carries the thesis forward to the end of the century; Omi and Winant, "By the Rivers of Babylon . . .," 31–66; and Geoffrey Sutton Smith, "The Navy Before Darwinism: Science, Exploration, and Diplomacy in Antebellum America," *AQ* 28:1 (Spring 1976), 41–55.

A good overview of racialist thought, with an emphasis on its "scientific" basis, is Gossett, *Race: The History of an Idea in America*; and on nineteenth-century race science, see Stanton, *The Leopard's Spots*. On the social and political basis of racialist categories, see Leo Kuper, *Race, Class and Power: Ideology and Change in Plural Societies*; Oliver Cox, *Caste, Class and Race: A Study in Social Dynamics*; and Chase, *Legacy of Malthus*, chs. 4–6.

On racism toward blacks, see Jordan, *White Over Black*; and Frederickson, *Black Image*, esp. ch. 4.

2   On Parker, see Henry Steele Commager, *Theodore Parker: Yankee Crusader*; on Prescott, Levin, *History as Romantic Art*, pp. 3–7, ch. 7 and Clinton Harvey Gardiner, *William Hickling Prescott, A Biography*. Quotations are from William Hickling Prescott, *The Conquest of Mexico and the Conquest of Peru*, pp. civ, cviii, 71. See also Levin, *History as Romantic Art*, chs. 2, 7. For an English view contemporaneous with Parker's and Prescott's, see Robert Knox, *Races of Men . . .*, (1847).

3   Theodore Parker, *The Rights of Man in America*, pp. 100–1, 434, also 213, 446; the sermons cited were delivered between 1850 and 1854. And Prescott, *Conquest of Mexico*, p. xlvi.

4   Pessen, *Jacksonian America*, ch. 5. The classic statement is by Alexis de Tocqueville, *Democracy in America* 1: 343–70.

5   Parker, *Rights of Man*, pp. 198–99, 202. Similar views are attributed to the southern planter and slavery expansionist Alfred St. Clare by Stowe, *Uncle Tom's Cabin*, ch. 23.

6   Quoted in Smith and Judah, *Gringos*, pp. 57–58.

7   Parker, *Rights of Man*, pp. 447–49; and Parker to Frances Jackson, quoted in Louis Ruchames, ed., *John Brown: The Making of a Revolutionary*, p. 262.

8   Ronald G. Walters, "The Erotic South: Civilization and Slavery in American Abolitionism," *AQ* 25:2 (May 1973), 177–201; Charles E. Rosenberg, "Sexuality, Class and Race in Nineteenth Century America," ibid., 131–53. The character Colonel Fitz-Cowles in Lippard, *Monks*, is a version of the type, who turns out to be actually (not just symbolically) of mixed blood.

The view of the southern frontiersman as a semisavage has a long history going back to William Byrd's "Histories of the Dividing Line" (1728) discussed in Slotkin, *Regeneration Through Violence*, pp. 215–22, chs. 10, 12. For a similar view in the antebellum period applied specifically to the slaveholding South, see Robert Lewis, "Frontier and Civilization in the Thought of Frederick Law Olmstead," *AQ* 29:4 (Fall 1977), 385–402.

9   Quoted in Ruchames, ed., *John Brown*, p. 264; Commager, *Theodore Parker*, p. 254.

10   George Fitzhugh, *What Shall be Done with Free Negroes?* (1851), pp. 1–6; on "extermination," see ———, *Sociology for the South; or the Failure of Free Society* (1854), chs. 1, 7. Thomas R. Dew, "Review of the Debate . . .," in Eric L. McKitrick, ed., *Slavery Defended: The Views of the Old South*, pp. 30–31. The best study is Genovese, *World the Slaveholders Made*, Part 2. On the historical background of the "war of extermination" threat in 1830–60, see Sadler, "Dr. Stephen Graham's Narration," pp. 359–68; Steven A. Channing, *Crisis of Fear: Secession in South Carolina*.

11   Parker, *Rights of Man*, pp. 17–18, 35, 93–94, 342; "A Sermon of the Dangerous Classes," *The Collected Works* 7, esp. pp. 80, 111, which likens the pauper class to barbarian "marauders" and "savages" within the city.

12   Parker, *Rights of Man*, pp. 441–42; Commager, *Theodore Parker*, p. 204.

13   Parker, *Rights of Man*, pp. 441–42; compare with Lincoln's version of the "success" myth, and the attribution of failure to "dependent characters," pp. 218–19, above. See also Parker, "Sermon of the Dangerous Classes," which parallels the "perishing classes" of wilderness savages with the "dangerous classes" of the Metropolis, in *Works* 10:137–39; Rogin, *Subversive Genealogy*, pp. 190–91; and Fitzhugh, *Cannibals All!*, p. 137.

14   Edmund Ruffin, "The Political Economy of Slavery" (1853), quoted in McKitrick, *Slavery Defended*, pp. 70–71; Fitzhugh, *Sociology*, pp. 227–29; Fitzhugh, *Cannibals All!*, p. 200.

15   *Ibid.*, ch. 8. On southern paternalism, see Genovese, *Political Economy*, ch. 1. Compare Rothman, *Discovery of the Asylum*; Rogin, *Fathers and Children*, chs. 4, 6, 8, and ———, *Subversive Genealogy*, pp. 190–92; Davis, *Problem of Slavery in the Age of Revolution*, pp. 233–42.

16   Fitzhugh, *Sociology*, pp. 246–48.

17   Fitzhugh, *What Shall Be Done . . .*, pp. 1–2; Fitzhugh, *Cannibals All!*, pp. 151–52, 243–44.

18   Quoted in Hofstader, *American Political Tradition*, p. 118. See also H. N. Smith, *Virgin Land*, pp. 162–65, 174–76. The legislatures that worked actively toward secession in 1860 avoided popular referenda and were themselves dominated by the

planter elite, supplemented by representatives of southern banks, railroads, and merchant houses. See Potter, *Impending Crisis*, chs. 17–18; Bruce Catton, *The Coming Fury*, pp. 32, 104–12, 237, 270; Michael P. Johnson, *Toward a Patriarchal Republic: The Secession of Georgia.*

19 "Amalgamation of Races," *The Colonizationist and Journal of Freedom* (June 1833), 102–6.

20 Lincoln, "Speech of . . .," Springfield, June 16, 1858," pp. 14–21; Lincoln, "Reply," First Joint Debate, Ottawa, Aug. 21, pp. 50–55, 63–67; and compare Stephen A. Douglas, "Speech of . . .," Chicago, July 9, 1858, pp. 27, 33, and "First Joint Debate," pp. 44–46, in Robert W. Johannsen, ed., *The Lincoln-Douglas Debates of 1858*. See also Potter, *Impending Crisis*, ch. 13.

21 Lincoln, in Johannsen, *Debates*, pp. 15–19, 58–64.

22 Douglas, ibid., p. 29.

23 Dawley, *Class and Community*, p. 75; Potter, *Impending Crisis*, chs. 15–16.

CHAPTER 12

1 On the general pattern of filibustering in the 1850s, and its relation to domestic policies, see Robert E. May, *The Southern Dream of a Caribbean Empire, 1854–1861*; Potter, *Impending Crisis*, ch. 8; Goetzmann, *When the Eagle Screamed*, ch. 5; Charles H. Brown, *Agents of Manifest Destiny: The Lives and Times of the Filibusters*, pp. 3–219. Thomas L. Karnes, *The Failure of Union: Central America, 1824–1960*, chs. 1–6, summarizes the political background from the Latin American standpoint. For Frémont as filibuster, see ch. 9 above.

2 The narrative of Walker's career which follows is based on the following sources: Brown, *Agents of Manifest Destiny*, Pt. 3; William O. Scroggs, *Filibusters and Financiers: The Story of William Walker and His Associates*; Albert Z. C. Carr, *The World and William Walker.*

3 Scroggs, *Filibusters*, ch. 7; Brown, *Agents of Manifest Destiny*, pp. 274–76; Carr, *World and William Walker*, chs. 1, 4.

4 Brown, *Agents of Manifest Destiny*, pp. 340–41, 352–55; Scroggs, *Filibusters*, ch. 15.

5 Scroggs, *Filibusters*, p. 145; Rogin, *Subversive Genealogy*, ch. 2; Merle Curti, "Young America," *AHR* 32:1 (Oct. 1926), 34–55.

6 Brown, *Agents*, pp. 338, 349, 352–53. See Isaac Deutscher's discussion of a comparable "substitution" in *The Prophet Armed: Trotsky, 1879–1921*, pp. 89–97, 520–22.

7 Scroggs, *Filibusters*, pp. 118–20, 123, 234–36, 243; Brown, *Agents of Manifest Destiny*, p. 338.

8 Scroggs, *Filibusters*, pp. 261–69; "It became necessary to destroy the town in order to save it," quoted (for example) in Guenter Lewy, *America in Vietnam*, p. 127.

9 Brown, *Agents of Manifest Destiny*, ch. 17.

10 Brown, *Agents of Manifest Destiny*, p. 361; Scroggs, *Filibusters*, pp. 128–29, 254; *NYH* Jan. 30, 1856, p. 1. Brown, *Agents of Manifest Destiny*, has made the widest study of contemporary newspaper and periodical treatments of Walker; his bibliography and analysis of press coverage is more thorough than that of any previous writer on filibusterism, although both Scroggs and Carr have numerous useful quotations from press sources. My own conclusions about press coverage are based on Brown, and on a close study of *NYH* and *NYTrib*, May 1855–October 1857, 1860; *HW*, 1857–60; *Leslie's Weekly*, 1855–57; *U. S. Magazine and Democratic Review*, 1855–57. Taylor, *Cavalier and Yankee*, pp. 194–96, suggests the strong intellectual links between the southern literary mythology of the Indian wars and filibustering.

11 William V. Wells, *Walker's Expedition to Nicaragua* (1856), p. 13. Other sources of a similar nature are *The Destiny of Nicaragua by "An Officer in the Service of Walker"* (1856), and William Frank Stewart, *The Last of the Filibusters . . .* (1857).

12 Wells, *Walker's Expedition*, pp. 13, 17, 43, 57, 118–22, 124.

13 See, for example, *NYH 56* Apr. 9, p. 1; Apr. 17, p. 1; May 2, p. 2; June 2, pp. 1–2; June 3, p. 6.

14   On the "Panama Massacre" and related Nicaraguan stories, see Brown, *Agents of Manifest Destiny*, ch. 15; *NYH 56*, "The Slaughter of Americans . . .," May 2, p. 4; May 1, p. 1; and also Apr. 30, p. 4.

15   *NYH 56*, June 3, p. 6; Nov. 22, p. 4. Similar interpretations of the Nicaraguan war were voiced by a range of newspapers, including both slavery expansionist journals like the New Orleans *Delta* and antiexpansionist journals like the New York *Tribune, Times*, and *Evening Post*. See Brown, *Agents of Manifest Destiny*, pp. 264–65, 309, 349; *NYTrib 55*, May 1, p. 4; *NYT 55*, June 6, p. 4; *NY Evening Post* 1855, July 9, p. 4; and quoted in *National Intelligencer*, Dec. 1, 1855, p. 5; *Putnam's Monthly Magazine* 9:2 (Apr. 1857), 425–35.

16   Issues in which Kansas and Nicaragua are closely associated are *NYH 55*, Dec. 26, p. 4, "No Speaker . . ."; *NYH 56*, Apr. 3, p. 4; May 23, p. 4; May 25, p. 1, "Civil War Begun in Earnest" and "The Nicaragua Mass Meeting"; May 30, p. 4; June 2, pp. 1–2 on Nicaragua, p. 3 on Kansas; June 3, p. 6, editorials on Walker and "Mr. Sumner's Speech"; Oct. 20, p. 4, "Nigger Stock in Nicaragua"; *NYH 57*, May 31, p. 4 editorial on Virginia elections.

17   *NYH 56*, Oct. 20, p. 4; Nov. 21, p. 4; Nov. 22, p. 4. See also June 3, p. 6.

18   On Homestead and Land Reform, see *NYH 55*, May 18, p. 4; and compare Dec. 24, p. 4, "Suspected Filibuster . . .," which describes Walker's sort of homesteading as the best kind. On the governance of inferior races, see *NYH 56*, June 3, p. 6; *NYH 60*, Sept. 21, p. 4, "Seward's New Phase of Manifest Destiny. . . ."

19   The *Herald's* coverage was paralleled by that of other anti-Republican or pro-expansionist journals; Scroggs, *Filibusters*, pp. 147–48, 394–95. Of these, *Harper's Weekly* was (starting in 1857) the most interesting: it presented Walker in the imagery of the chivalric hero, an American King Arthur whose American Phalanx was compared to the "knights of Faerydom." After Walker's fall he became, like Arthur, a Christian martyr, to be compared with Knox and Wesley. See *HW 57* 1: 103, 168, 200, 225–27; *HW 58* 1: 678; and also Anna Ella Carroll, *The Star of the West: National Men and National Measures*, 3d ed., chs. 7–8, on Walker as Protestant hero.

20   *NYH 57*, May 31, p. 4; June 1, p. 4. The expansionist *United States Magazine and Democratic Review* (formerly *DR*) took the same position: "The Nicaragua Question," Feb. 1858, 115–23.

21   Compare *NYTrib 56* coverage of the "Panama Massacre," May 1, pp. 4, 6, with *NYH 56*, May 2, p. 4. Comparisons between the filibuster war and the Indian wars, or the struggle in Kansas, are also made frequently by the *Tribune*, but with an intention opposite to that of the *Herald*: Indian wars are assumed to be the result of white aggression, and the war for Kansas is presented as a more appropriate outlet for the aggressive instincts of civilized men. See *NYTrib 56*, Apr. 2, p. 4; Apr. 3, p. 4; May 2, pp. 4, 5. See also the comparison between filibusters and southern lynch mobs, Apr. 4, p. 4, "Virginia Rampant." Other stories relevant to this comparison are *NYTrib 56*, May 31–June 4 inclusive, stories and editorials on Nicaragua and Kansas; *NYTrib 57*, Oct. 19 and 20, pp. 1, 4; *NYTrib 60*, Sept. 1, p. 20; Oct. 4, p. 13.

There were at least two melodramas about Walker staged during his time in power, both presumably sympathetic to his cause. See for example May, *Southern Dream*, pp. 77–78. A hostile fictional account is [David Deaderick III], "The Experiences of Samuel Absalom, Filibuster," *Atlantic Monthly* 4:26 (Dec. 1859), 653–65; 5:27 (Jan 1860), 38–60. Deaderick represents Walker as a tin-pot Napoleon, whose regime rests on the twin pillars of the pretentions of the southern slave-aristocracy and the greed of northern urban *"sans-culottes"*—two classes which (in Deaderick's view) seek to live at ease by the productive labor of others. The piece is not only an attack on Walker, but a satire on the Nicaraguan version of the Frontier Myth, since the tropics offer only a delusory antidote to the narrator's condition of being "penniless in New York." See esp. 4: 655–56, 658–60, 663; 5: 22–23, 48, 52.

22   William Walker, *The War in Nicaragua* (1860), pp. 53, 23, 27.

23   Ibid., pp. 144–45, 156.

24   Ibid., pp. 251–52.

25   Ibid., pp. 264, 256.

26   Ibid., pp. 271–72.

27   Ibid., pp. 259, 273, 278.

28 Ibid., p. 266.

29 Ibid., pp. 259–60.

30 Ibid., pp. 38, 429–30, 270.

31 Ibid., pp. 260–61, 273, 340–41.

32 Ibid., pp. 428–29. He characterizes the "squatter sovereignty" of Douglas and other proponents of Homestead legislation as an "Indian" doctrine, and associates his English captors with the establishment of "Negro government" in the Caribbean.

33 Scroggs, *Filibusters*, pp. 380–81.

34 *HW 60* 4:645 (Oct. 13), "The Late General Walker."

35 *NYH 60*, Sept. 19, p. 6, "Our Historic . . ."; Sept. 21, p. 4, "Seward's New Phase of Manifest Destiny. . . ." Compare editorials on the "Massachusetts school" of Black Republicans, Aug. 31, p. 4 with "Walker Expedition," Sept. 1, p. 4; and note the strong visual and verbal association of "The Coming Reign of Terror [e.g., insurrectionary Blacks]" with "The Last of Walker's Expedition," Sept. 16, p. 1 (and editorial, p. 4).

36 Henry David Thoreau, "A Plea for Captain John Brown" (1859), *Miscellanies: The Writings . . .* 10: 216. Ruchames, ed., *John Brown*, p. 125, cites the interview in the *NYH* Oct. 21, p. 1, in which the raiders are a "filibuster army"; Richard Owen Boyer, *The Legend of John Brown: A Biography and a History*, p. 532; and see the citations in which Walker's associate Hennigsen and Victor Hugo exchange words over Brown, in American Anti-Slavery Society, *The Anti-Slavery History of the John Brown Year . . .* (1860), p. 162.

37 For biographical narrative I have referred to Stephen B. Oates, *To Purge This Land with Blood: A Biography of John Brown*, passim, and citations from pp. 82, 119; Dick, *Lure of the Land*, p. 110.

38 Ibid., pp. 100–10; Bruce Collins, *The Origins of America's Civil War*, p. 7; Jay Monaghan, *The Civil War on the Western Border, 1854–1865*, p. 122; Paul Wallace Gates, *Fifty-Million Acres: Conflicts Over Kansas Land Policy, 1854–1890*, chs. 1–4, and esp. ch. 4; Potter, *Impending Crisis*, pp. 202–4.

39 Berwanger, *The Frontier Against Slavery*, esp. pp. 3–6, Prologue.

40 Dick, *Lure of the Land*, pp. 114–15; Gates, *Fifty-Million Acres*, pp. 50–55; Oates, *To Purge This Land*, p. 83.

41 Oates, *To Purge This Land*, pp. 104–5; Monaghan, *Civil War/Western Border*, pp. 14, 41; Potter, *Impending Crisis*, pp. 203–8.

42 John Brown, quoted in Ruchames, *John Brown*, p. 44.

43 Oates, *To Purge This Land*, ch. 3; Dick, *Lure of the Land*, pp. 263–71.

44 Oates, *To Purge This Land*, chs. 4, 7.

45 John Brown, "Sambo's Mistakes," in Ruchames, *John Brown*, pp. 69–72.

46 Ibid., p. 119; Berwanger, *Frontier Against Slavery*, is the best discussion of the Negro-exclusion question.

47 This interpretation draws on both Oates's *To Purge This Land*, which adopts the "Brown as Puritan" perspective of Thoreau et al., but interprets the religion psychologically; and W. E. B. Du Bois, *John Brown*, chs. 9–10, 12, which tries to correct the "mad John Brown" legend by considering the rationality and feasibility of his project for guerrilla warfare and revolution.

48 William Phillips, *The Conquest of Kansas . . .* (1856), pp. 18–19.

49 Ibid., pp. 53–58.

50 Ibid., pp. 25, 60–62.

51 Ibid., pp. 24–25, 64–65.

52 Ibid., p. 413.

53 Ibid., pp. 316–17, 332–34.

54 Ibid., and pp. 413–14; see also Thoreau, "Plea," pp. 202–3.

55 James Redpath, *The Public Life of Captain John Brown . . .* (1860), pp. 7, 13, 225; and 41, 49, 153. See also his *Echoes of Harper's Ferry* (1860) for responses by other abolitionist spokesmen.

56 Thoreau, "Plea," pp. 200–5, 209; Redpath, *Public Life*, pp. 81–82.

57 Thoreau, "Plea," pp. 199–201. Orville J. Victor, *History of American Conspiracies . . .*, assimilates Brown's raid to a range of "seditions" in a pattern that suggests the linkage between race wars on the borders and social strife within the Metropolis. There is of course no attempt to systematize that suggestion.

58   Redpath, *Public Life*, pp. 95–96, 115, 118, 141, 143, 254–55; Thoreau, "Plea," p. 204.

59   The organization led by Parker against the slave catchers in Boston (1852–54) was the "Vigilance Committee"; but by 1860, Anti-Slavery Association pamphleteers were citing southern vigilance organizations as proof of southern barbarism, for example, American Anti-Slavery Society, *Anti-Slavery History of the John Brown Year* (1860), pp. 166–91; but see Thoreau, "Plea," pp. 224–25.

60   Redpath, *Public Life*, pp. 36, 126–27; Henry Ward Beecher, quoted in Richard Warch, *John Brown*, pp. 105–7. Compare the account of the attack on Swansea in King Philip's War (1675), Increase Mather, *Brief History*, in Slotkin and Folsom, *So Dreadfull a Judgment*, p. 88.

61   Thoreau, "Plea," pp. 228–29.

62   For southern responses to Harpers Ferry, see Channing, *Crisis of Fear*. *NYH 60*, Oct. 19, p. 6, has Seward and John Brown importing Frontier violence to the East. The *Herald* anticipated Negro insurrection before Harpers Ferry, as a scare tactic to discredit "Black Republicans": see Aug. 31, p. 4; Sept. 16, p. 1, "The Coming Reign of Terror"; Sept. 19, p. 6, "Our Historic Development . . . War of Races"; Sept. 21, p. 4, "Seward's New Phase. . . ." On Harpers Ferry itself, see Oct. 18, pp. 3, 6; Oct. 19, pp. 2, 6; Oct. 21, p. 1; and editorials from October through the completion of the electoral canvass in December.

63   *The Life, Trial and Execution of Capt. John Brown . . .* (1859), pp. 8, 10. For a discussion of the genre of criminal narratives, and of Bird's *Nick of the Woods*, see above, pp. 128–30, 133–7. Compare the description of Brown with that of the Indian hater John Moredock in Hall, *Legends of the West* and *Sketches* 2: 74–82; or Melville, *The Confidence-Man*, chs. 25–28.

64   *Life, Trial*, pp. 10, 11, 14.

65   Ibid., pp. 16–17; and Slotkin, *Regeneration Through Violence*, pp. 547–53; Rogin, *Subversive Genealogy*, pp. 117–18, 123–26.

66   *Life, Trial*, pp. 7–8.

67   Ibid., p. 13; Parker and Brown quotations are in Ruchames, *John Brown*, pp. 69, 167, 255; Redpath, *Public Life*, pp. 60–61; Thoreau, "Plea," p. 221. It is worth noting that Brown does not dwell upon Anglo-Saxon identification of the violence he regards as regenerative.

68   In his second speech on Brown, Thoreau presents the transfiguration of the hero as a movement from Frontier warrior to a vehicle of idealism, whose words are as straight and true as bullets; and finally from wielder of the "Sharps rifle"—both the literal weapon and the figurative rifle of true speech—to wielder of the "sword" of pure Spirit. See Thoreau, "The Last Days of John Brown," *Miscellanies* 10:244–47.

69   Thoreau, "Plea," p. 228.

70   Redpath also invokes the conventional Frontier Myth, in which the promise of rich natural resources functions as the goad to "regeneration," in a promotional book co-authored with Richard J. Hinton, *Hand-book to Kansas Territory and the Rocky Mountains' Gold Region . . .* (1859). However, Redpath and Hinton insist throughout that the American people will not enjoy free access to this new frontier until the Slave Power is suppressed in Kansas, and freedom guaranteed in the new gold districts around Pike's Peak. So political struggle still comes before the enjoyment of Frontier benefits for Redpath and Hinton—an attitude toward the Pike's Peak gold rush very different from Gilpin's, in which the acquisition of the new region substitutes for Metropolitan political strife.

CHAPTER 13

1   The broad pattern of political change that followed the Civil War is discussed in Morton Keller, *Affairs of State: Public Life in Late Nineteenth Century America*, esp. Pt. 1. The studies of Reconstruction I have found most useful are George M. Frederickson, *The Inner Civil War: Northern Intellectuals and the Crisis of the Union*, Pt. 3; Cochran, *Business in American Life*, Pt. 3; Leonard P. Curry, *Blueprint for Modern*

America: Nonmilitary Legislation of the First Civil War Congress, esp. chs. 1, 11; Lawrence Friedman, *The White Savage: Racial Fantasies in the Postbellum South*; Leon F. Litwack, *Been in the Storm So Long: The Aftermath of Slavery*; James M. McPherson, *The Struggle for Equality: Abolitionists and the Negro in the Civil War and Reconstruction*; Edward Magdol, *A Right to the Land: Essays on the Freedmen's Community*; David Montgomery, *Beyond Equality: Labor and the Radical Republicans, 1862–1872*; Michael Perman, *Reunion Without Compromise: The South and Reconstruction, 1865–1868*; Otto H. Olsen, ed., *Reconstruction and Redemption in the South*; Willie Lee Rose, *Rehearsal for Reconstruction: The Port Royal Experiment*; Kenneth M. Stampp, *The Era of Reconstruction, 1865–1877*; ——— and Leon F. Litwack, eds., *Reconstruction: An Anthology of Revisionist Writings*; Allen W. Trelease, *White Terror: The Ku Klux Klan Conspiracy and Southern Reconstruction*; C. Vann Woodward, *Reunion and Reaction: The Compromise of 1877 and the End of Reconstruction*.

2 Cochran, *Business in American Life*, chs. 12–14; ——— and Miller, *Age of Enterprise*, chs. 7–12; Greenleaf, ed., *American Economic Development Since 1860*; Ralph L. Andreano, ed., *The Economic Impact of the American Civil War*; Emerson D. Fite, *Social and Industrial Conditions in the North During the Civil War*, esp. pp. v–vi, chs. 6–7; Robert P. Sharkey, *Money, Class and Party: An Economic Study of the Civil War and Reconstruction*; Howard Mumford Jones, *The Age of Energy: Varieties of American Experience, 1865–1915*, chs. 1–5; H. Wayne Morgan, *The Gilded Age: A Reappraisal*; Winther, *The Transportation Frontier*; Hobsbawm, *The Age of Capital, 1848–1875*, pp. 151–53; Irwin Unger, *The Greenback Era: A Social and Political History of American Finance, 1865–1879*.

3 On the Freedmen's Bureau, see William S. McFeeley, *Yankee Stepfather: General O. O. Howard and the Freedmen*; Litwack, *Been in the Storm*, esp. chs. 7–8; Keller, *Affairs of State*, chs. 3–4. On the Indian Bureau, see Robert Winston Mardock, *The Reformers and the American Indian*, passim, for the inauguration of the Peace Policy, chs. 1–4; and Utley, *Frontier Regulars*, ch. 12.

4 The convergence of northern and southern conservatism is argued in Keller, *Affairs of State*, esp. Pt. 2; Woodward, *Reunion and Reaction*, chs. 2, 4–5, 11; Montgomery, *Beyond Equality*, ch. 9; Cochran, *Business in American Life*, chs. 11–21, esp. 14; William Ghormley Cochrane, *Freedom Without Equality: A Study of Northern Opinion on the Negro Issue, 1861–1870*.

5 On the fate of Homestead legislation, see Dick, *Lure of the Land*, pp. 154–58, 216, and chs. 9–13; Fite, *The Farmers' Frontier, 1865–1900*, pp. 16–24, chs. 2–4. On the Southern Homestead Act, see Woodward, *Reunion and Reaction*, pp. 53–54, and Magdol, *Right to the Land*, pp. 188–91; and on land allotments for freedmen, McFeeley, *Yankee Stepfather*, p. 4. On allotments and Indian Homestead Act, Dippie, *Vanishing American*, chs. 8, 11; Mardock, *Reformers*, pp. 133, 157. See also Paul Wallace Gates, "The Homestead Law in an Incongruous Land System," in Carl N. Degler, ed., *Pivotal Interpretations in American History* 2:1–35; and Robert P. Swieringa, "Land Speculation and Its Impact on American Economic Growth and Welfare: A Historiographical Review," *WHQ* 8:3, 283–301.

6 Woodward, *Reunion and Reaction*, chs. 2, 4, 5, 11, sees the railroad business as central to the convergence of northern and southern conservatism in this period. Winther, *Transportation Frontier*, ch. 8; Fishlow, *American Railroads*, pp. 102, 164, 181, 214; Robert M. Riegel, *The Story of the Western Railroads . . .*, pp. 95, 130–34, 146–47, 229, 233–34, 276–85; Stanley P. Hirshson, *Grenville M. Dodge: Soldier, Politician, Railroad Pioneer*, pp. 159–203; Robert S. Henry, "The Railroad Land Grant Legend in American Historical Texts," in Degler, ed., *Pivotal Interpretations* 2:36–60; Dolores Greenberg, *Financiers and Railroads, 1869–1889: A Study of Morton, Bliss and Company*; Julius Grodinsky, *Transcontinental Railway Strategy, 1869–1893: A Study of Businessmen*, chs. 1–3, 6–8; John Patterson Davis, *The Union Pacific Railway: A Study in Railway Politics, History and Economics*.

7 On Jay Cooke, see Ellis Paxson Oberholtzer, *Jay Cooke: Financier of the Civil War*, 2 vols.; Grodinsky, *Transcontinental Railway Strategy*, chs. 1–2; Matthew Josephson, *The Robber Barons: The Great American Capitalists, 1861–1901*, chs. 2–4. On Northern Pacific propaganda, see Emmons, *Garden in the Grasslands*, ch. 2; Oberholtzer, *Jay Cooke* 2:237–38, 296, 312–14; Josephson, *Robber Barons*, 97–99; Edgar I. Stewart, ed., *Penny-an-Acre Empire in the West*, chs. 1–2, 10–13; John L. Harnsberger, "Land

Speculation, Promotion and Failure: The Northern Pacific Railroad, 1870–1873," *JW*
9:1 (Jan. 1970), 33–45. Examples of NPRR propaganda are Northern Pacific Railroad
Company, *The Northern Pacific Railroad's Land Grant and the Future Business of the
Road* (1870), pp. 4–5, 7–11, 18–20; ———, *The Northern Pacific Railroad: Its Route,
Resources, Progress and Business* (1870); ———, *Guide to the Northern Pacific Railroad
Lands* (1872), pp. 5–6, 9–11, 14–16; George B. Hibbard, *Land Department of the Northern Pacific Railroad Company: Bureau of Immigration for Soldiers and Sailors* (1872), pp.
8–9, 16; "Carleton" [Charles Carleton Coffin], *The Seat of Empire* (1870), esp. pp. 23–
24, 49–50. The cited passages all reflect the "Gilpinian" aspect of the railroad lands:
their gorgeousness, superabundant fertility, and capacity to "regenerate" the health and
fortunes of those who take them up. Gilpin's geophysical analysis, esp. his theory of
the isothermal current, is used without attribution.

On the suborning of politicians and newspaper editors through gifts of stock and
other favors, see Oberholtzer, *Jay Cooke* 2:108, 181, 235–38, 352–54, 389–91, 406–9;
Riegel, *The Story of the Western Railroads*, pp. 122–29; Grodinsky, *Transcontinental
Railway Strategy*, pp. 33–41. A letter typical of Cooke's methods of obtaining the favor
of editors is Jay Cooke to H. C. Bowen, Jay Cooke Papers 3:1870, Baker Library, Harvard University, which spells out the paper's obligation to grant the use of its columns
to the NPRR in exchange for a gift of stock to editor Bowen.

The NPRR also worked to gain the favor of the army by gifts of stock to army,
military division, and district commanders. The railroad also provided special favors and
services to individual officers, as well as to military commands engaged in operations.
See chapter 17, n. 27, below.

8 Melvyn Dubofsky, *Industrialism and the American Worker, 1865–1920*, ch. 1.

9 Seymour Martin Lipset and Reinhard Bendix, *Social Mobility in Industrial Society*, ch. 3; Dubofsky, *Industrialism*, pp. 12–26, reviews the debate on growth of real
wages in this period. See also Gutman, *Work, Culture and Society*, pp. 209–91.

10 Dubofsky, *Industrialism*, is a good overall survey of the period and recent
scholarship on the subject. See also Gutman, *Work, Culture*, esp. pp. 1–78; Montgomery,
Beyond Equality, pp. 3–44; ———, *Workers' Control in America*, chs. 1–2; Daniel T.
Rodgers, *The Work Ethic in Industrial America, 1850–1920*, ch. 1. Contemporary views
of the subject by scholars concerned with informing policymakers are Young, *Labor in
Europe and America . . .* (1875); and Francis Amasa Walker, *The Wages Question: A
Treatise on Wages and the Wages Class* (1876).

11 Dubofsky, *Industrialism*, pp. 40–41, 45, 49; ———, *We Shall Be All*, chs. 1–2;
Montgomery, *Beyond Equality*, ch. 3; Cochran and Miller, *Age of Enterprise*, ch. 5;
Foner, *Labor Movement* 1: ch. 15. Herman Schlüter, *Lincoln, Labor and Slavery: A
Chapter from the Social History of America*, chs. 4, 7; Wayne G. Broehl, *The Molly
Maguires*, pp. 85–95; Bruce Catton, *Never Call Retreat*, 164–65; 205–8. On the effects of
conscription, see Eugene Converse Murdock, *Patriotism Limited, 1862–1865: The Civil
War Draft and Bounty System*.

12 Catton, *Never Call Retreat*, pp. 72, 274–75; Rose, *Rehearsal*, chs. 1, 3, 5.

13 Cochran and Miller, *Age of Enterprise*, ch. 5; E. D. Fite, *Social and Industrial
Conditions*; Montgomery, *Beyond Eqality*, ch. 3; Wayne G. Broehl, *The Molly Maguires*,
pp. 85–95; Catton, *Never Call Retreat*, 205–9.

14 George Templeton Strong, *Diary of the Civil War*, pp. 335–39; Genovese,
Political Economy of Slavery, chs. 8–9; J. D. B. De Bow, *De Bow's Review* (May/Aug.
1862), p. 77.

15 Catton, *Never Call Retreat*, pp. 357–60.

16 Frederickson, *Inner Civil War*, Pt. 3, esp. ch. 14; Daniel Aaron, *The Unwritten War: American Writers and the Civil War*, ch. 10; on the idealization of professional soldiers and militarism in general, see Kemble, *Image of the Army Officer*, Section 4; and Thomas C. Leonard, *Above the Battle: War-Making in America from Appomattox to Versailles*, pp. 1–39.

On the emergence of a managerial elite, see Cochran, *Business in American Life*,
chs. 14–16; Glenn Porter, *The Rise of Big Business, 1860–1910*; Harwood F. Merrill,
ed., *Classics in Management*; Robert Wiebe, *The Search for Order, 1877–1920*, esp. chs.
1–5; Reinhard Bendix, *Work and Authority in Industry: Ideologies of Management in
the Course of Industrialization*, pp. 1–20, 99–116, 198–274; Henry Wood, *Natural Law
in the Business World* (1887), pp. 165, 211.

17 John W. Draper, *Thoughts on the Future Civil Policy of America* . . . (1865), pp. 200–1
18 Frederickson, *Inner Civil War*, pp. 150, 170, 175–76.
19 William Dean Howells, *The Rise of Silas Lapham* (1885); ————, *A Hazard of New Fortunes* (1891); Keller, *Affairs of State*, ch. 12.
20 Charles Francis Adams, Jr., in *A Cycle of Adams Letters, 1861–1865*, ed. by Worthington Chauncey Ford, 1:124–33, 2:194–95, 213–19.
21 C. F. Adams, Jr., "The Protection of the Ballot in National Elections," *Journal of Social Science* 1:1 (June 1869), 91–111, esp. 104–10. Thanks to Herbert Gutman for bringing this article to my attention. See also C. F. Adams, Jr., "The Granger Movement," *NAR* 120 (April 1875), 394–424 and esp. 406–7, in which he argues that political democracy must not apply to economic matters.

CHAPTER 14

1 Catton, *Terrible Swift Sword*, pp. 444–45.
2 Russell F. Weigley, *The American Way of War: A History of the United States Military Strategy and Policy*, ch. 7; William S. McFeely, *Grant: A Biography*, pp. 77–78.
3 Dudley Taylor Cornish, *The Sable Arm: Negro Troops in the Union Army, 1861–1865*, ch. 9, pp. 274–77; Catton, *Terrible Swift Sword*, pp. 327, 444–45; Catton, *Never Call Retreat*, pp. 46, 266, 352–59, 379, 397, 443.
4 Bell Irvin Wiley, *The Life of Billy Yank: The Common Soldier of the Union*, p. 347.
5 Major General George B. McClellan, *The Army of the Potomac: General McClellan's Report* . . . (1864), p. 506; ————, *McClellan's Own Story*, pp. 487–89; Warren W. Hassler, Jr., *George Brinton McClellan: Shield of the Union*, pp. 177–78; Catton, *Terrible Swift Sword*, pp. 442–46.
6 Lucy Larcom, *An Idyl of Work* (1875), pp. 89–90, 191.
7 Rollin G. Osterweis, *The Myth of the Lost Cause, 1865–1900*; Friedman, *White Savage*, chs. 1, 4; Daniel Aaron, *The Unwritten War: American Writers and the Civil War*, chs. 15, 16, 18; George William Bagby, "The Old Virginia Gentleman," in Edwin Anderson Alderman and Joel Chandler Harris, eds., *Library of Southern Literature* . . . 1:151–62.
8 See Horatio Alger, Jr., *Ragged Dick and Mark the Match-Boy* (1867); ————, *Digging for Gold* (1876); ————, *Adrift in New York* (1910). John G. Cawelti, *Apostles of the Self-Made Man: Changing Concepts of Success in America*, chs. 4–5. For general background information on the mystique of boyhood in this period, see Gilman M. Ostrander, *American Civilization in the First Machine Age, 1890–1940*, Pt. 2; Richard Weiss, "Horatio Alger, Jr., and the Response to Industrialism," in Jaher, ed., *Age of Industrialism*, ch. 10. See also Gary Scharnhorst, "Had Their Mothers Only Known: Horatio Alger, Jr., Rewrites Cooper, Melville, and Twain," *JPC* 15:3 (Winter 1981), 175–82; Michael Zuckerman, "The Nursery Tales of Horatio Alger," *AQ* 24:2 (May 1972), 191–209. John Seelye's introduction to *Digging for Gold* contains some important and useful observations.
9 R. H. Davis, *Margret Howth*, p. 16 (for example) offers a sinister image of the new working class of Lowell as "whiskey-bloated and heavy-brained Irish, Dutch, black, with souls half-asleep somewhere and the destiny of a nation in their grasp." An official study of immigration suggested that such concern exaggerated the negative impact of immigration, while at the same time giving reasons for that concern in depth and detail: Edward Young, *Special Report on Immigration* . . . (1872).
10 Jonathan B. Harrison, *Certain Dangerous Tendencies in American Life* (1880), pp. 163–64, 183. See also his *The Latest Studies on Indian Reservations* (1887).
11 Harrison, *Certain Dangerous Tendencies*, pp. 180–81.
12 Charles Loring Brace, *The Dangerous Classes of New York* . . . (1872), p. 29. For a corrective, see Monkkonen, "A Disorderly People?"; ————, *The Dangerous Class: Crime and Poverty in Columbus, Ohio, 1860–1885*. On urban life and its literary representation, see Ira Rosenwaike, *Population History of New York City*, esp. chs. 3–4; Siegel, *The Image of the American City in Popular Literature, 1820–1870*; Stout, *Sodoms*

in Eden; Sam Bass Warner, Jr., *The Urban Wilderness: A History of the American City*, pp. 31–34 and Pt. 2.

13   Brace, *Dangerous Classes*, pp. iii, 26, 43, 45, 76, 111; Victor, *American Conspiracies*, argues that "seditions" tending toward massacre (like the New York draft riots of 1863) tend to arise when social injustice, class division, and racial or ethnic animosity combine. Popular histories of urban riots written in the 1870s suggest that the existence of a "dangerous class" is endemic to urban life; and that it tends to be inhabited by ethnic out-groups like the Irish. See Headley, *Great Riots of New York, 1712–1873* (1873), and ————, *Pen and Pencil Sketches of the Great Riots* . . . (1877). For an analysis of the draft riots, see Adrian Cook, *Armies of the Streets: The New York Draft Riots of 1863*.

14   Brace, *Dangerous Classes*, p. 97.

15   *Annual Report of the Commissioner of Indian Affairs for the Year 1875* (E. P. Smith), p. 6.

16   McFeely, *Yankee Stepfather*, ch. 4; Richard Lowitt, *A Merchant Prince of the Nineteenth Century: William E. Dodge*, ch. 15; Mardock, *Reformers*, pp. 65–70, chs. 3, 5.

17   F. A. Walker, *The Indian Question* (1874), pp. 5, 7, 9–13; and ————, *Wages Question*, chs. 4, 6, 12–24; Parrington, *Main Currents* 3:111–17.

18   Walker, *Indian Question*, p. 7.

19   Ibid., pp. 15–16.

20   Ibid., pp. 14–15, 48.

21   Ibid., pp. 35, 101.

22   Ibid., pp. 35–37, 41. See also Rothman, *Discovery of the Asylum*, esp. ch. 5; Barker-Benfield, *Horrors of the Half-Known Life*, chs. 1, 3, 4, 6, 10; Haller, *The Physician and Sexuality in Victorian America*, ch. 1, pp. 48–68.

23   Walker, *Indian Question*, p. 80.

24   Mardock, *Reformers*, pp. 8–9, 47–48.

25   Charles R. Wilson, "Racial Reservations: Indians and Blacks in American Magazines, 1865–1900," *JPC* 10:1 (Summer 1976), 70–80; Dippie, *Vanishing Americans*, ch. 6. An excellent anthology of postwar racialist theory in England (which influenced American ideas) is Michael D. Biddiss, ed., *Images of Race*. A. D. McCoy, *Thoughts on Labor in the South, Past, Present, and Future*, pp. 19–28, rationalizes the need for a new form of tutelary control of blacks, akin to slavery, because only in such a system can ministers of the Gospel affectively Christianize African heathens, while ensuring they remain economically productive. The rationale is essentially the same as that of the Peace Policy, combining elements of reform with a paternalist politics, and the imperative to bring the "savage" into productive labor quickly—the alternative being something like extermination. For the prewar tradition of this kind of thinking, see, for example, chapter 7, note 10 above, on Mary Eastman. John H. Van Evrie, *White Supremacy and Negro Subordination* . . . (1868), simply reverts to antebellum proslavery arguments to reassert the doctrine that blacks are naturally fitted for slavery.

26   Dippie, *Vanishing American*, Pts. 3–4; Mardock, *Reformers*, pp. 9, 14.

27   *Annual Report of the Commissioner of Indian Affairs for the Year 1873* (E. P. Smith), p. 4.

28   *Annual Report* . . . *Indian Affairs* . . . *1872*, pp. 9, 75–76; *Annual Report* . . . *Indian Affairs* . . . *1871* (F. A. Walker), p. 4.

29   *Annual Report* . . . *Indian Affairs* . . . *1875* (E. P. Smith), pp. 3, 6–9, 184–91. See also Watson Parker, *Gold in the Black Hills*, p. 26.

30   *NYH 74*, Jan. 3, p. 4; Apr. 25, p. 4.

31   The role of northern businessmen and managers in Reconstruction in the South is treated in Stanley Cohen, "North-eastern Business and Radical Reconstruction: A Re-Examination," in Degler, *Pivotal Interpretations* 2:61–87; Richard L. Hume, "Carpetbaggers in the Reconstruction South: A Group Portrait of Outside Whites in the 'Black and Tan' Constitutional Conventions," *JAH* 44:2 (Sept. 1977), 313–30; Rose, *Rehearsal*, chs. 7, 10, 12, esp. pp. 212–29, 298–313. On the tendency to merge class and race as categories, thus associating workers, immigrants, Indians, and blacks, see Reginald Horsman, "Science, Racism and the American Indian in the Mid-Nineteenth Century," *AQ* 27:2 (May 1975), 152–68. Popular imagery linking ethnics, Indians, and blacks became more marked, although it built upon already existing traditions. See Alexander Saxton. "Blackface Minstrelsy and Jacksonian Ideology," *AQ* 27:1 (March 1975), p. 25; Robert C. Toll, *Blacking Up: The Minstrel Show in Nineteenth Century America*, ch. 5.

The theoretical basis of the linkage of racial traits with emergent class characteristics appears (for example) in George Rawlinson, *The Origin of Nations, in Two Parts: On Early Civilizations; On Ethnic Affinities, etc.* (1878).

On the tendency to use southern paternalist models and racialized images of class to justify coercive social orders, see Eric Anderson, *Race and Politics in North Carolina, 1872–1901: The Black Second*; Peter Daniel, "The Metamorphosis of Slavery, 1865–1900," *JAH* 66:1 (June 1979), 88–99; E. Genovese and Elizabeth Fox-Genovese, "Presidential Address: The Slave Economy in Political Perspective," ibid., 7–23; *Prison and Plantation: Crime*; Jay R. Mandle, "The Economic Underdevelopment of the Postbellum South," *MP* 1:4 (Winter 1978), 68–79, esp. 75–76; Donald Spivey, *Schooling for the New Slavery: Black Industrial Education, 1868–1915*; Thomas Wagstaff, "Call Your Old Master—'Master': Southern Political Leaders and Negro Labor During Presidential Reconstruction," *LH* 10:3 (Summer 1969), 324–45; Jonathan M. Wiener, "Class Struggle and Economic Development in the American South, 1865–1955," *AHR* 84:4 (Oct. 1979), 70–106, esp. 979–85.

32 Walker, *Wages Question*, pp. 390–92. See also Bronwen J. Cohen, "Nativism and Western Myth: The Influence of Nativist Ideas on the American Self-Image," *JAS* 8:1 (Apr. 1974), 23–40.

CHAPTER 15

1 Parker, *Gold in the Blacks Hills*, is the most complete history of the gold rush. See also, "The Majors and the Miners: The Role of the U.S. Army in the Black Hills Gold Rush," *JW* 11:1 (Jan. 1972), 99–113; Goetzmann, *Exploration and Empire*, pp. 419–22.

2 Mardock, *Reformers*, chs. 8–9; Dippie, *Vanishing American*, ch. 10; Richard N. Ellis, ed., *The Western American Indian: Case Studies in Tribal History*, pp. 50–89. 97–118.

3 Howard Lamar, *Dakota Territory, 1861–1889: A Study of Frontier Politics*, chs. 1, 4–5.

4 Lamar, *Dakota Territory*, pp. 102–26, traces the complex local shifts on Indian policy; on Black Hills, ch. 5.

5 Charles Collins, *Collins' History and Directory of the Black Hills . . .* (1878), p. 18; Donald Jackson, *Custer's Gold: The United States Cavalry Expedition of 1874*, pp. 3–15; Jane Conard, "Charles Collins: The Sioux City Promotion of the Black Hills," *South Dakota History* 2:2 (Spring 1972), 131–71.

6 Quoted in Oberholzer, *Jay Cooke*, 2:169–70.

7 *The Northern Pacific Railroad's Land Grant* (1870), p. 4; Collins, *History and Directory*, p. 17.

8 *Annual Report . . . Indian Affairs . . . 1871* (F. A. Walker), p. 4; *Annual Report . . . Indian Affairs . . . 1872*, pp. 75–76; *Annual Report . . . Indian Affairs . . . 1873* (E. P. Smith), pp. 5–6, 167, 244.

9 Goetzmann, *Exploration and Empire*, pp. 578–79.

10 Jackson, *Custer's Gold*, pp. 3–7; Utley, *Frontier Regulars*, pp. 243–49.

11 Collins, *History and Directory*, pp. 7, 11–12.

12 Ibid., pp. 15–16.

13 Ibid., pp. 3–4. On O'Neill and the Fenian colony, see ibid., p. 9; William D'Arcy, *The Fenian Movement in the United States, 1858–1886*, pp. 159–61, 303–11, 334–68, 377–82.

14 Mott, *American Journalism*, chs. 24–25; Piers Brendon, *The Life and Death of the Press Barons*, chs. 2, 3, 4.

15 George T. McJimsey, *Genteel Partisan: Manton Marble, 1834–1917*; Royal Cortissoz, *The Life of Whitelaw Reid*, 2 vols.; Irving Katz, *August Belmont: A Political Biography*; David Black, *The King of Fifth Avenue: The Fortunes of August Belmont*; Stephen Birmingham, *Our Crowd: The Great Jewish Families of New York*, chs. 8–9, 17; Anita Leslie, *The Remarkable Mister Jerome*, pp. 58–104, 154–200.

16 Sharkey, *Money, Class and Party*, and Unger, *Greenback Era*, provide the essential background for understanding Belmont's views, and their consonance with those

of his Republican fellow bankers on "hard money." See also Jerome Mushkat, *The Reconstruction of the New York Democracy, 1861–1874*, for analysis of the intraparty divisions.

17 Robert V. Bruce, *1877: The Year of Violence*, pp. 163–64.

18 McJimsey, *Manton Marble*, pp. 93–105, chs. 7–9; Katz, *August Belmont*, pp. 116–24, 186–87, 200–5; Edward L. Gambill, *Conservative Ordeal: Northern Democrats and Reconstruction*, pp. 124–27, 139–42, 148–52.

19 A particularly comprehensive editorial, giving the essentials of the *World's* ideology, is "Human Equality," *NYW 74*, July 4, p. 4; and see "Perpetual President," *NYW 73*, Oct. 5, p. 4.

20 *NYW 73*, "Louisiana and the Law," May 5, p. 4; *NYW 74*, "Friends Indeed," Apr. 14, p. 4; "Texas and the South," Apr. 13, p. 4; "Has the South a Republican Form . . .," Apr., 18, p. 4. A front-page letter from "Ben Zeene, the White Man" (*NYW 73*, May 7, p. 1), links Grant's Indian policy with Reconstruction as twin causes of ruin; and the author's name, which suggests "benzine" used to burn blacks in lynchings, indicates the paper's affinity for racialist violence as a "solution" to the problem.

21 *NYW 73*, "Resumption of the Rod," Nov. 7, p. 4; and compare with coverage of southern news stories *NYW 74*, Feb. 19, p. 2.

22 *NYW 74*, "Maudlin Mercy," Apr. 15, p. 4.

23 On Tompkins Square, see Herbert G. Gutman, "The Tompkins Square 'Riot' in New York City on January 13, 1874: A Re-Examination of Its Causes and Aftermath," *LH* 6:1 (Winter 1965), 44–70; Paul T. Ringenbach, *Tramps and Reformers 1873–1916: The Discovery of Unemployment in New York*, ch. 1; Foner, *Labor Movement* 1:445–48; *NYTrib 74*, Jan. 14, pp. 1, 4, and Jan. 15, pp. 1, 4; and *NYW 74*, below.

24 *NYW 74*, "Our Indian Policy," Jan. 18, p. 4.

25 *NYW 74*, Jan. 28, p. 4; Apr. 14, 18; May 16, p. 4. Note the juxtaposition of editorials concerning blacks and Indians for these dates.

26 *NYW 74*, "Our Indian Policy," Jan. 28, p. 4.

27 Ibid., "Starvation Wages."

28 The series of articles on housing begins *NYW 74*, Jan. 21, p. 1.

29 *NYW 74*, March 29, p. 2; "Unemployed Workingmen," Jan. 10, p. 4.

30 *NYW 74*, June 3, p. 4. The pattern of association exhibited on this page is persistent enough for it to be read as the thematic center of the *World's* metaphors. Its range of reference is continually extended by additional associations, connected to the main theme by similar devices: for example, the pairing of a story on the overthrow of black Reconstruction in Arkansas with an editorial on the treatment of freed blacks by the British in the West Indies. The reference is further extended by a comparison in the editorial between the white proletariat of England and the blacks (the former being felt as a greater threat). *NYW 74*, July 8, p. 4. Editorials on April 26, p. 4, reiterate the West Indies/Arkansas contrast, and couple them with an account of a recent flood in which "reconstructed levees" collapsed. Articles and editorials on strikes in the North are frequently juxtaposed with accounts of "Negro Strikers" or rioters in the South: see, for example, *NYW 73*, Sept. 11, p. 2; *NYW 74*, Jan. 20, p. 1; March 31, pp. 1, 4. The article "Lawlessness in Louisiana," Jan. 19, p. 8, speaks of "Colored Communists [Taking] Their Cue from Northern Reds."

31 *NYW 73*, Oct. 30, p. 4; May 10, p. 4; Sept. 11, p. 2. Other editorials on this subject are Sept. 28, p. 4; *NYW 74*, March 31, p. 4; April 16, p. 4; May 10, p. 4; May 16, p. 4; June 17, p. 4. The free trade argument and linkage of protectionism with "false Philanthropy" are reiterated in nearly every issue; but see, for example, *NYW 73*, Aug. 15, p. 4; Sept. 23, p. 4; *NYW 74*, Apr. 24, p. 4; Sept. 30, p. 4; May 15, p. 4.

32 The quotation about Susan B. Anthony is reprinted in Herbert Krause and Gary D. Olson, *Custer's Prelude to Glory: A Newspaper Accounting of Custer's 1874 Expedition to the Black Hills*, p. 106; this compilation offers the readiest access to newspaper reports of the expedition, but lack the context provided by the original complete issues. The original dispatch which they quote was by William Eleroy Curtis, and appeared in *I-O 74*, July 29, p. 1. Other important editorials linking women (and especially suffragists) with Indians and/or Blacks are *NYH 73*, Oct. 17, p. 4, "Wives for the Wards," which proposes forcibly marrying some noted women suffragists to Indian chiefs to plague two enemies with a single action—in the context of the *Herald's* views of Indian sexuality, this was tantamount to suggesting the women be raped. The quo-

tation about the fighting qualities of male negroes is *NYW 74*, Oct. 5, p. 4, also p. 7; and see also Aug. 1, p. 2 for a reprint of Curtis's dispatch cited above. "A Southern Curse in a Northern Home" is in *NYW 74*, December 22, p. 4.

33 *NYW 74*, Jan. 14, 15, pp. 1, 4; Jan. 10, p. 4; Jan. 28, p. 4; and see note 23 above.

34 *NYW 74*, "Charity as a Sin," March 29, p. 4.

35 *NYW 73*, Nov. 11, p. 4; *NYW 74*, Jan. 24, p. 4.

36 *NYW 73*, May 4, p. 4; Nov. 1, p. 4; *NYW 74*, May 7, p. 4; May 30, p. 4.

37 Krause and Olson, *Custer's Prelude to Glory*, pp. 1–7, 147–48.

38 *I-O 74*, July 1, p. 1; Krause and Olson, *Custer's Prelude to Glory*, p. 99.

39 Ibid., pp. 101–2; *NYW 74*, July 25, p. 5.

40 Krause and Olson, *Custer's Prelude to Glory*, pp. 107–8, 127; *I-O 74*, July 29, p. 1.

41 Krause and Olson, *Custer's Prelude to Glory*, pp. 1, 6–7, 115–17. *I-O 74* on civil rights, May 26, p. 4, and May 30, p. 4; on socialist International, June 16, p. 2; on Indian policy, June 19, p. 4; on Woman Question, July 8, p. 4; on Indian fighting, July 6, p. 2, and June 1, p. 2.

42 *NYW 74*, July 13, pp. 1, 4; the entire dispatch is in Krause and Olson, *Custer's Prelude to Glory*, pp. 149–54.

43 *NYW 74*, July 13, p. 1; and also Aug. 2, p. 1. Compare Filson, *Kentucke*, discussed on pp. 65–8 above; and Slotkin, *Regeneration Through Violence*, pp. 280–85.

44 *NYW 74*, July 13, p. 1.

45 See below, pp. 415–16.

46 *NYW 74*, July 13, p. 1; Krause and Olson, *Custer's Prelude to Glory*, pp. 107, 115–17.

47 *NYW 74*, July 13, p. 1; Krause and Olson, *Custer's Prelude to Glory*, pp. 153–54.

48 *NYW 74*, July 25, p. 5; Aug. 1, p. 1. Krause and Olson, *Custer's Prelude to Glory*, pp. 156–61.

49 *NYW 74*, July 14, p. 4; "Indian Troubles," July 15, p. 1.

50 *NYW 74*, July 13, p. 1; July 14, "Western Grievances," p. 2.

51 *NYW 74*, July 14, p. 4; July 22, p. 4.

52 *NYW 74*, July 23, p. 1; July 24, pp. 4–5. See also July 25, p. 5; July 26, p. 2; July 28, p. 8; July 29, p. 5, for similar arrangements.

53 *NYW 74*, "Indian Affairs," July 23, p. 1.

54 *NYW 74*, July 19, p. 4; July 23, p. 4.

55 *NYW 74*, Aug. 1, p. 4; see also July 29, p. 4, editorials on the South and the West, Indian treaties, and the "Colored Cadet" at West Point; July 28, p. 8; Aug. 1, pp. 1–2; Aug. 4, p. 4; Aug. 6, p. 1; Aug. 7, p. 1—the last of these links British solutions to the Canadian-Indian and West Indian black questions with the failures of Republican philanthropy in the South and the Dakota Territory.

56 *NYW 74*, Aug. 8, pp. 1, 4; see also July 23, p. 4.

57 *NYW 74*, Aug. 11, p. 1. There are a number of interesting questions relating to the content, authorship, and transmission of this dispatch. The assertion that the geologist Professor Winchell confirmed the presence of gold was later denied by Winchell himself; Custer, rising to the controversy, then said he had not discussed the matter with Winchell. Either Winchell reversed himself, was misreported to Custer, or the dispatch misrepresented his testimony.

The dispatch was included with a packet of mail (including Curtis's correspondence) which was carried by Charley Reynolds on his famous ride; but the Custer dispatch was printed five days before Curtis's report, and may have been received earlier. In a letter sent to Libbie at this same time, Custer refers to a "letter to the World," and this suggests that Custer himself may have been in direct contact with the *World* editors—perhaps enjoying the kind of privileged relationship he shared with Bennett and the *Herald* in 1876. See Krause and Olson, *Custer's Prelude to Glory*, p. 171; Marguerite Merington, *The Custer Story: The Life and Intimate Letters of George A. Custer and His Wife Elizabeth*, p. 272; and for additional information on this incident, and the Bennett-Custer relationship, see pp. 415–16, 421, 436–37 below.

58 *NYW 74*, Aug. 11, p. 1.

59   *NYW 74*, Aug. 11, p. 1. Krause and Olson, *Custer's Prelude to Glory*, pp. 120, 126, 128.

60   Ibid., pp. 130–31; *I-O 74*, Aug. 27, p. 1; Sept. 5, p. 1.

61   *NYW 74*, Aug. 16, p. 2; Krause and Olson, *Custer's Prelude to Glory*, pp. 163–78.

62   *NYW 74*, Aug. 16, pp. 1–2.

63   On gold and the resumption of specie payments for greenbacks, see *NYW 73*, Aug. 21, p. 4; *NYW 74*, Sept. 13, p. 4; Dec. 14, p. 5. Nearly every issue in the month of September 1874 has at least one editorial on the subject.

64   *NYW 74*, Aug. 12, p. 4; Aug. 18, pp. 1–2.

65   *NYW 74*, Aug. 19, p. 4. The subject had been treated before in a similar manner: see *NYW 73*, "The Negro in the Future," May 12, p. 4, which represents freedmen as a new kind of "Vanishing American": and compare *NYW 73*, July 6, p. 4, "Wards of the Nation," on Indians, and *NYW 74*, Apr. 8, p. 4, on the Ashantee War (British against the "Black Indians of Africa").

66   *NYW 74*, Aug. 20, p. 1; Aug. 25, pp. 1–2, 8.

67   *NYW 74*, Aug. 27, p. 1; Aug. 28, p. 4.

68   Ibid.

69   *NYW 74*, Aug. 30, pp. 1, 4; Sept. 1, p. 4; see also Sept. 4, p. 4.

70   *NYW 74*, Aug. 16, p. 1.

71   Ibid., p. 4; Aug. 18, p. 4.

72   *NYW 74*, Aug. 21, pp. 1, 4. The editorial is given an impressive context by the long p. 1 story on "Western War Clouds" and the accompanying survey of 200 years of Indian battles with which it concludes.

73   Ibid., p. 4; Oct. 5, p. 4; Oct. 22, p. 4.

74   *NYW 74*, Aug. 21, p. 4; Aug. 28, p. 4.

75   *NYW 74*, Dec. 14, p. 5; also May 12, p. 4.

76   *NYW 74*, Aug. 25, p. 8; Aug. 26, pp. 1, 4; Aug. 28, p. 1; Aug. 29, p. 5; Aug. 31, p. 4; Sept. 1, p. 1.

77   *NYW 74*, Sept. 5, pp. 1, 5.

78   *NYW 74*, Sept. 7, pp. 1, 4; Sept. 8, p. 1.

79   *NYW 74*, Sept. 7, p. 1; Sept. 11, p. 5; Sept. 12, pp. 1–2; Sept. 13, p. 2; Oct. 4, p. 1; Oct. 12, pp. 1, 4.

80   Southern papers: I surveyed the coverage in the Charleston, S. C., *News and Courier*; Louisville, Ky., *Courier-Journal*, and Richmond *Enquirer* for all of 1874. *News and Courier* scarcely covers the story at all, is preoccupied with local and regional politics. The *Courier-Journal* is similarly focused on crucial local political contests to the neglect of western matters. However, the Kentucky paper's lack of interest is worthy of remark, since the state was more directly tied to western railroad and river trade than was South Carolina; and since the paper's editor, Watterson, had been a personal acquaintance of Custer when the latter was stationed in Elizabethtown, Kentucky, in 1871–72 (see Watterson to Custer, correspondence in CBNM). The Richmond *Enquirer* gives the Black Hills story more play, and connects prospects for western expansion with the state's railroad and canal interests. However, the paper's editorial stand was to downplay the appeal of the Hills to forestall emigration, which would complicate the problem of "labor shortages" with which the state was plagued (in part as a consequence of black flight from the South). Its July 16 editorial (p. 2) was titled "A Western Paradise—There's No Place Like Home" (see also Aug. 14, p. 2, and Aug. 28, p. 2); and there were specific appeals to blacks to stay in the South ("Negro Colonization," Aug. 23, p. 2).

Republican papers: The New York *Times* followed the administration line, supporting the project against Democratic critics at the start, soft-pedaling the story when it became politically problematic, veering to opposition to the opening up of the Hills once Grant had made his decision. The editorial on "Custer's Expedition," *NYT 74*, July 4, p. 3, is typical of early coverage; Aug. 18, p. 2 is the high point of the paper's enthusiasm for extinguishing Indian title, with Indians as a "filthy race . . . intolerable to live with," but despite this sentiment, the paper still supported a philanthropic Indian policy, Aug. 27, p. 4. It was at first enthusiastic about Custer's reports (Aug. 24, p. 4) but tried to deflate the public response (Aug. 28, p. 1) and question the existence of gold (Sept. 14, p. 2; Sept. 25, p. 1; Sept. 7, p. 2) when protection of Indian title appeared to become a Republican commitment. By Sept. 1 (p. 1) Custer was being represented as hankering for an Indian war, in accordance with Democratic Party philosophy.

The New York *Tribune* was a Republican journal, but opposed to Grant. Its coverage of the expedition is available in Krause and Olson, *Custer's Prelude to Glory*, pp. 187–232. The *Tribune* took a hard line against preserving Indian title, and for militarizing the Indian Bureau; it opposed Radical Reconstruction and offered its readers devastating critiques of Reconstruction governments and intensely racist portrayals of freed blacks. It was a primary molder of that "tough-minded" ideology which was the antithesis of "philanthropic" reform; but unlike the *Herald* and the *World* it did not see the Democratic Party or the southern "Redeemers" as the men most likely to bring progressive values into public life. It saw in the Hills a chance for the nation to enjoy "the advantages of good currency and the luxury of being honest"—a hard-money approach identical in style and objective to that of the *World* (Aug. 13, p. 4). It praised Custer for his conduct of the expedition, and cited him as the type of soldier who should be given charge of Indian affairs (Aug. 18, p. 4). Important editorials are *NYTrib 74*, Aug. 10, p. 4; Aug. 11, p. 4; Aug. 24, p. 4; Aug. 28, p. 4; Sept. 12, p. 4; Sept. 14, p. 4. However, its reporter Samuel Barrows was frequently cited as contradicting Custer's Northern Pacific–boosterish account of the territory near the railroad.

81   *NYW 74*, Sept. 11, p. 5; Sept. 16, p. 2; Sept. 17, p. 1; Sept. 19, p. 1; Sept. 22, pp. 1, 4.

82   *NYW 74*, Sept. 26, p. 11; also Oct. 12, p. 1; Nov. 9, p. 4. See especially the accounts of the coal strike and the "Black Riots" in South Carolina, in which Radical Republicans attack with "war whoops"—Sept. 27, pp. 1, 3, 4.

83   *NYW 74*, Oct. 13, pp. 1–2.

84   *NYW 74*, Oct. 17, pp. 1, 4.

85   *NYW 74*, Oct. 22, p. 4; Oct. 28, p. 11; Nov. 13, p. 4; Nov. 14, pp. 1, 4; Nov. 18, p. 1; Nov. 21, p. 1; Nov. 23, p. 2. See also Sept. 25, p. 4; and Jackson, *Custer's Gold*, ch. 6.

86   *NYW 74*, Nov. 18, p. 3.

CHAPTER 16

1   Jay Monaghan, *Custer: The Life of General George Armstrong Custer*, pp. 4–8. This is the best biography although it is not definitive—Custer's business engagements, which became as essential to his career as his military activities, are hardly treated at all. The coverage of his education, marriage, and military career is inclined to the most sympathetic interpretations, but is not uncritical and avoids the partisan tone of most Custer biographies. Most other biographies are either intensely pro (Frederick C. Whittaker, *The Complete Life of* . . . [1876]; D. A. Kinsley, *Favor the Bold* . . . 2 vols. [1968]), or violently anti (Frederic F. Van de Water, *Glory Hunter* . . . [1934]; Fred Dustin, *The Custer Tragedy* . . . [1939]). Luther, *Custer High Spots*, is an essential bibliographical source. There are valuable collections of Custer correspondence at Custer Battlefield National Monument (CBNM), and in the Western Americana Collection, Beinecke Library, Yale University. Merington, *Custer Story*, is an indispensable selection of Custer's correspondence, especially with his wife Elizabeth (Bacon) Custer, although Merington's deletions (copies of original letters remain at Yale) occasionally present a too-rosy picture of the marriage. Lawrence Frost, *General Custer's Libbie* is a biography of Mrs. Custer. Utley, *Frontier Regulars*, and ———, *Custer and the Great Controversy*, provide essential backgrounds on military policy, and on the debate in military-historical circles about Custer's Last Stand. Stewart, *Custer's Luck*, is the best study of the battle, and of the events preceding it.

2   Monaghan, *Custer*, pp. 9, 19–20, 33–34; J. H. Kidd, *Personal Recollections of a Cavalryman* . . ., p. 129. An aide to Sheridan, speaking after the Last Stand, said of Custer: "[We] did not mind his little freaks . . . any more than we would have minded temper in a woman," *NYH 76*, July 7, p. 5. Turner, *Ritual Process*, chs. 1, 3, 5, defines these traits as part of the "liminality" that is associated with mythic heroes and ritual agonists as well as adolescents.

3   Monaghan, *Custer*, pp. 6, 10; Bingham quoted in Merington, *Custer Story*, pp. 7–10; Van de Water, *Glory Hunter*, chs. 1–2. The nomination of the son of a notorious Democrat by the highly partisan Republican Bingham has struck later biographers as curious, and led Van de Water to speculate that Custer deserted his father's party to curry favor with Bingham. This presents the paradoxical image of Custer supporting John C. Frémont, whose ideology would have been anathema to Father Custer, but whose heroic myth appealed to the same images that would later invest George A. Custer himself. John A. Bingham represents himself as a disinterested benefactor of an ardent and deserving young patriot; his account has a Horatio Alger flavor to it, reminiscent of the scenes in which Alger's ragged-boy hero receives the favor of a wealthy paternal benefactor. At the time, the favor to Custer may have had less idealized motives: party lines in Michigan in 1856 were not as sharply drawn as they would be later, many Democrats were in fact shifting allegiance toward the new Republican Party; Bingham might have been bidding for just such a conversion in this case.

4   Russell F. Weigley, *History of the United States Army*, p. 147; Raymond H. Merritt, *Engineering in American Society, 1850–1875*, p. 127. Monaghan, *Custer*, chs. 2–3.

5   Francis Wayland, *Elements of Moral Science* (1835) and ———, *Elements of Political Economy* (1837); Jones, *O Strange New World*, ch. 6. Although not used as texts at West Point, Wayland's *Duties of an American Citizen . . .* (1825) and his *Domestic Slavery Considered as a Scriptural Institution . . .* (1845) develop ideas close to those reproduced by Custer.

6   George Armstrong Custer, "Duties and Affections" (1858), CBNM.

7   Monaghan, *Custer*, pp. 29, 32, 35.

8   Custer, "Duties and Affections"; Monaghan, *Custer*, pp. 7, 17, 122–23; Merington, *Custer Story*, pp. 93–95.

9   Custer, "The Duty of Obedience" (1858), CBNM, and see note 5, above.

10   Custer, "Property" (1858), CBNM; Jones, *O Strange New World*, pp. 214–15.

11   Custer, "The Red Man" (1858), CBNM.

12   Monaghan, *Custer*, pp. 35–42, 104; chs. 6, 10; pp. 132–33, 176–77.

13   Merington, *Custer Story*, p. 69.

14   McClellan's military career has been treated sympathetically by Hassler, *Shield of the Union*, and critically by most military historians including Catton (*Terrible Swift Sword, Mister Lincoln's Army*) and Stephen W. Sears, *Landscape Turned Red: The Battle of Antietam*. The political career has never received the same sort of treatment, although the correspondence and political maneuverings of the McClellan men in and out of the army are discussed in Catton, *Terrible Swift Sword*, chs. 5–7; and ———, *Never Call Retreat*, pp. 350–64, 372–76. A firsthand account of the "staff talk" about a coup d'etat is James Harrison Wilson, *Under the Old Flag* 1:126–27. See also Katz, *August Belmont*, pp. 121–48.

15   Custer to Mr. and Mrs. Emmanuel Custer, Mar. 17, 1862, CBNM.

16   Monaghan, *Custer*, p. 123; Merington, *Custer Story*, p. 67; Kidd, *Personal Recollections . . .*, pp. 129–33.

17   Monaghan, *Custer*, chs. 9, 12–13; Merington, *Custer Story*, chs. 4–7, and Frost, *Custer's Libbie*, passim, all present the marriage as a continuous idyll. But see Custer to Elizabeth (Bacon) Custer, July [], 1865, Yale University, which suggests that they too had periods of difficulty and even estrangement.

18   Merington, *Custer Story*, pp. 62–63, 105; this interpretation was suggested by Jay Fliegelman.

19   Hamilton Gay Howard, *Civil War Echoes: Character Sketches and State Secrets*, pp. 306–11; *NYT 65*, May 7, p. 2.

20   *NYT 65*, May 23, p. 4. Sherman's and Sheridan's views on Indian extermination are repeated in nearly every history of the period. See Custer's handling of a classic Sherman quote in *My Life on the Plains; or, Personal Experiences with Indians*, p. 85.

21   Whitelaw Reid, *Ohio in the War . . .* (1868), p. 783; Monaghan, *Custer*, p. 134, ch. 11; David F. Riggs, *East of Gettysburg*, pp. i–ii, 41, 55; Gregory J. W. Urwin, *Custer Victorious: The Civil War Battles of George Armstrong Custer*, ch. 12; Stephen Z. Starr, *The Union Cavalry in the Civil War* 1:420–24, 433–38; 2:294–95. Fletcher Pratt, *Ordeal by Fire: A Short History of the Civil War*, p. 288. Neither Grant nor Sheridan ever trusted Custer with the sort of independent responsibilities they gave to

his chief rival in 1864, James H. Wilson; despite the latter's failure in the spring campaign in Virginia, he was sent to the Army of the Cumberland as chief of cavalry, with Grant's prediction—accurate, as it turned out—that Wilson would make superb use of that arm. Merington, *Custer Story*, pp. 116–7.

22 *NYT 64*, Oct. 27, p. 8; March 20, p. 1; *NYT 65*, Feb. 21, p. 1; Apr. 20, p. 2. Whittaker, *Complete Life*, p. 181; J. Cutler Andrews, *The North Reports the Civil War*, pp. 600, 607; [Frederic C. Newhall], *With Sheridan in Lee's Last Campaign* (1866), pp. 177, 200–1, 211–12.

23 George Alfred Townsend, *Campaigns of a Non-Combattant . . .*, p. 320; Theodore Lyman, *Meade's Headquarters, 1864–1865 . . .*, p. 17; Urwin, *Custer Victorious*, pp. 29, 36, 58. On Custer's romantic escapades, see Monaghan, *Custer*, pp. 112, 155, 157–8, 187–88; Lawrence Frost, *Custer Legends*, pp. 70–73; *NYT 65*, May 24, p. 8.

24 *NYW 65*, May 24, p. 1; Campbell, *Hero with a Thousand Faces*, Pt. 2, ch. 3, esp. pp. 315–34.

25 Monaghan, *Custer*, ch. 19; Merington, *Custer Story*, pp. 169–80.

26 Merington, *Custer Story*, pp. 174–76; U. S. Congress, *Report of the Joint Committee on Reconstruction*, Pt. 4, pp. 73–78; John M. Carroll, *Custer in Texas: An Interrupted Narrative*; Charles William Ramsdell, *Reconstruction in Texas*, ch. 4; James E. Sefton, *The United States Army in Reconstruction, 1865–1867*, p. 62; *NYT 66*, Aug. 22, pp. 4–5; G. A. Custer, "Custer's Reply to the Atrocious Attempts of the Corrupt or Insane Radical Press to Pervert His Testimony," broadside [Cleveland 1866], Beinecke Library, Yale.

27 Dustin, *Custer Tragedy*, p. 19; *NYT 66*, Sept. 4, p. 2; Howard, *Civil War Echoes*, pp. 314–25; Merington, *Custer Story*, p. 186; Mary Rullcotter Dearing, *Veterans in Politics: The Story of the G.A.R.*, pp. 63, 96–97.

28 Merington, *Custer Story*, pp. 178–79, 183.

29 Ibid., p. 181.

30 Robert M. Utley, ed., *Life in Custer's Cavalry: Diaries and Letters of Albert and Jennie Barnitz, 1867–1868*, pp. 46, 49–52; Jackson, *Custer's Gold*, p. 28; Monaghan, *Custer*, ch. 21. Whittaker, *Complete Life*, p. 171, shows the pattern dating back to 1863.

31 Monaghan, *Custer*, p. 336; Stewart, *Custer's Luck*, pp. 168–76; John M. Carroll, ed., *The Benteen-Goldin Letters . . .*, pp. 254–55.

32 Charles J. Brill, *Conquest of the Southern Plains . . .*, pp. 86–87; W[infield] S[cott] Hancock, *Reports of Major-General W. S. Hancock upon Indian Affairs* (1867). Stan Hoig, *The Battle of the Washita . . .*, has a good account of the war; William H. Leckie, *The Military Conquest of the Southern Plains*, chs. 2–5, is the best study of operations. Quote is from the Kearney, Nebr. *Herald*, July 14, 1868, in Mardock, *Reformers*, p. 86.

33 Andrist, *Long Death*, p. 138; Hoig, *Washita*, ch. 1.

34 Custer to Lydia Reed, July 30, 1868, CBNM; Custer to Mrs. Custer, May 2, 1867, CBNM; Merington, *Custer Story*, p. 199. A collection of Indian missionary tracts, reflecting the Bacons' long-standing interest in the subject, is in CBNM. On Hancock's problems with Grant, see W. S. Hancock, *Correspondence Between General W. T. Sherman, U.S. Army, and Major General W. S. Hancock* (1871); and Hancock to Custer, April 5, 1867, CBNM.

35 Lawrence A. Frost, *The Court-Martial of General George Armstrong Custer*, is the definitive work on the subject, although the author is a Custer partisan.

36 "Nomad" [Custer], *Turf, Field and Farm*, Sept. 9, 1867, p. 2; Sept. 21, p. 1; a modern edition of these pieces, edited by Brian Dippie, *Nomad: George Armstrong Custer in Turf, Field and Farm*, reprints these pieces.

37 "Nomad" [Custer], *Turf, Field and Farm*, Sept. 9, p. 1. For another view, see Leonard, *Above the Battle*, p. 44.

38 "Nomad" [Custer], *Turf, Field and Farm*, Oct. 26, p. 1.

CHAPTER 17

1 Monaghan, *Custer*, pp. 305–6; Hoig, *Washita*, ch. 5.

2 Ibid., ch. 6.

3 Ibid., chs. 8–9.

4 Ibid., pp. 147–50; Stewart, *Custer's Luck*, p. 164; Monaghan, *Custer*, pp. 322–23.

5 Hoig, *Washita*, p. 164; for William B. Hazen's critique of Custer's actions, see "Some Corrections of 'Life on the Plains' " [orig. *My Life on the Plains*] in Custer, *My Life*, pp. 383–407.

6 P. H. Sheridan, in *Annual Report of The Secretary of War . . . 1869*, pp. 44–45.

7 De B. Randolph Keim, *Sheridan's Troopers on the Border* (1870), esp. pp. 3, 103, 294–96; [Charles Wesley Alexander], *Sheridan's Squaw Spy . . .* (1869), pp. 19, 27.

8 Mardock, *Reformers*, pp. 41–44, 71–72; Stan Hoig, *The Sand Creek Massacre*; Utley, *Frontier Regulars*, pp. 130–33; Oscar Sherwin, *Prophet of Liberty: The Life and Times of Wendell Phillips*, pp. 568–70.

9 Monaghan, *Custer*, pp. 324–27; Elizabeth B. Custer, *Following the Guidon*, chs. 7–8; Brill, *Conquest of the Southern Plains*, pp. 22, 45–46; Thomas B. Marquis, *She Watched Custer's Last Stand*; Carroll, *Benteen-Goldin Letters*, pp. 258, 271.

10 Hoig, *Washita*, pp. 140, 178–81, 187; Sheridan to Indian Bureau, Nov. 30, 1872, Sheridan Papers, Correspondence, LC; Susan Brownmiller, *Against Our Will: Men, Women, and Rape*, ch. 5, deals with attitudes toward returned captives during this period.

11 Merington, *Custer Story*, p. 231; "Deed to G. A. Custer," Oct. 23, 1869, Kansas Pacific Railroad Company, CBNM.

12 Frost, *Custer's Libbie*, p. 191; Hall misspelled "Hull' by Merington, *Custer Story*, pp. 132, 237; see also pp. 232–37. "The Great Stevens Mine of West Argentine District," Georgetown *Courier*, Jan. 9, 1903, p. 1. Description of the property and Custer's notes on subscriptions from New York bankers including Belmont and Levi Morton are in "The Stevens Lode: Proposition for Sale of the East Half . . . 1871," CBNM. The history of the enterprise can be traced in the letters of Jairus W. Hall to Custer, Nov. 29, 1870; April 20, 24, May 22, June 6, Aug. 8, 13, 19, 21, 1872; Aug. 19, 1874; April 12, June 3, 1875; also Levi Morton to Custer, Feb. 6, 9, 1871; J. Astor to Custer, April 7, 1871; copy of J. W. Hall to William Travis [*sic* Travers], Feb. 23, 1875. A note possibly from McClellan to Custer, on Department of Docks stationery, Feb. 9, 1871, may confirm the McClellan connection. All correspondence is in CBNM.

13 Merington, *Custer Story*, pp. 232–34, 239.

14 Ibid., pp. 281, 183; Trelease, *White Terror*, p. xlvii; Theodore J. Crackel, "Custer's Kentucky, 1871–1873"; *Filson Club Historical Quarterly* 68:2 (Aug. 1974), 147–54; Friedman, *White Savage*, ch. 3; Merington, *Custer Story*, pp. 280–83, 317; Trelease, *White Terror*, ch. 17 on Kentucky, pp. 369–78, on the activities of Major Lewis Merrill, Seventh U.S. Cavalry, in South Carolina, pp. 401–6. For Custer's hostility to Merrill, n. 52, below.

15 Robert J. Scholnick, "*The Galaxy* and American Democratic Culture, 1866–1878," *JAS* 16:1 (Apr. 1982), 69–80; Donald Nevius Bigelow, *William Conant Church and the "Army and Navy Journal*," esp. pp. 233–36.

16 Monaghan, *Custer*, ch. 24; Don M. Russell, *The Lives and Legends of Buffalo Bill*, chs. 12–13; *NYH* 72, Jan. 14, p. 7; Jan. 16, pp. 7, 17; Feb. 5, p. 5; and Jan. 18, p. 3. My thanks to George B. Ward III, whose doctoral dissertation deals with this and other celebrity hunts: "Bloodbrothers in the Wilderness: The Sport Hunters and the Buckskin Hunter in the Preservation of the American Wilderness," doctoral dissertation, University of Texas (Austin), 1980.

17 *NYH* 72, Jan. 6, p. 6; Feb. 4, p. 6; Jan. 23, pp. 6–7.

18 Custer, *My Life*, pp. 13–14.

19 Ibid., and compare Mark Twain, *Roughing It*, ch. 19.

20 Custer, *My Life*, p. 13.

21 Ibid., p. 14.

22 Ibid., pp. 19–22, 201; Leonard, *Above the Battle*, p. 47.

23 Custer, *My Life*, pp. 251–54.

24 Ibid., p. 13.

25 Goetzmann, *Exploration and Empire*, pp. 414–17.

26 Merington, *Custer Story*, pp. 251–52, 257–58, 264. During his tenure of command in Dakota he also had numerous passes for free travel on the line, which enabled him to make frequent trips to the East during the winter. The practice was common, and Generals Sherman, Sheridan, and Terry discussed the need to curtail it. See n. 27, below.

27 Hazen, "Our Barren Lands" (1879), in Stewart, *Penny-an-Acre*, ch. 11, esp. p. 35; ———, "The Great Middle Region of the United States, and Its Limited Space of Arable Land," *NAR* 120 (Jan. 1875), 1–34, esp. 17, 21, 33. On NPRR favors to Custer, see Merington, *Custer Story*, pp. 251, 257, 265, 267. Also H. A. Towne (district supervisor) to General George Stark (vice-president, NPRR), December 27, 1875; Feb. 14, 17, March 11, 14, 16, 1876, Northern Pacific Railway Company Records, Office of the Secretary, Unregistered Correspondence, Box 3-A-6-4F, Minnesota Historical Society (thanks to Duane P. Swanson for locating this file). Army correspondence on the matter appears in General W. T. Sherman to General Alfred H. Terry, Feb. 9, 1871; Sherman Papers, Letter Book, LC; General Philip H. Sheridan to Major George Forsyth, May 2, 1874, Sheridan Papers, Correspondence, LC—an order for officers to return all passes.

NPRR officials contended that Hazen's attack was not only based on misinformation, but was dishonest in its motives. A letter in the NPRR files asserts that Hazen showed a prepublication copy of his article to an NPRR official, and offered to suppress it if the price was right. Chauncey F. Black to George W. Cass, January 29, 1873 [*sic* 1874], NPRR Records, Office of the Secretary, Unregistered Correspondence Box 3-A-5-9B.

28 Hazen, "Our Barren Lands," in Stewart, ed., *Penny-an-Acre*, pp. 79–80, 150–53; Custer, "Custer Letters," ibid., p. 94; Monaghan, *Custer*, chs. 25–26; Jackson, *Custer's Gold*, pp. 20–21; Krause and Olson, *Custer's Prelude to Glory*, pp. 188–89; Thomas Rosser to Custer, Feb. 16, 1874, CBNM.

29 Stewart, ed., *Penny-an-Acre*, pp. 81–82, 86–88, 93–94, 98–101, 104–7. And see above, pp. 287–88, on Jay Cooke's railroad promotional literature.

30 Jackson, *Custer's Gold*, pp. 3–13, 22, 81–91; Utley, *Frontier Regulars*, pp. 243–44.

31 Merington, *Custer Story*, p. 272; and n. 18, ch. 15, above.

32 Collins, *History and Directory*, pp. 19–21. My thanks to Watson Parker for answering a length inquiry on this subject.

33 Goetzmann, *Exploration and Empire*, p. 498.

34 Ibid., pp. 496–501; Emmons, *Garden in the Grasslands*, ch. 6, 131–33.

35 Walter Jenney, *The Mineral Wealth, Climate . . . of the Black Hills* (1875); Jackson, *Custer's Gold*, ch. 6; George B. Grinnell, *The Passing of the Great West: Selected Papers of George Bird Grinnell*, ed. by John F. Reiger, ch. 4, esp. p. 79, on Grinnell's financial interest in the gold strike. The "Harney's Peak" description is *NYW* 74, Aug. 16, p. 2, also in Krause and Olson, *Custer's Prelude to Glory*, p. 174. Compare Oberholzer, *Jay Cooke* 2:127.

36 Jackson, *Custer's Gold*, pp. 109–10; *The Nation* 21:480 (Sept. 10, 1874), 162.

37 Krause and Olson, *Custer's Prelude to Glory*, pp. 231–32; *NYH* 75, May 22, p. 4.

38 Parker, "Majors and the Miners," p. 101; Richard Irving Dodge, *The Black Hills . . .* (1876).

39 *Annual Report . . . Indian Affairs . . . 1875* (E. P. Smith), p. 3, 6–9, 184–91; Parker, *Gold in the Black Hills*, p. 26; Utley, *Frontier Regulars*, pp. 243–47.

40 The plan of campaign for 1876 is described in Stewart, *Custer's Luck*, esp. chs. 4–10, and the issue of Custer's displacement from command is covered in chs. 6, 10.

41 Bennett to Custer, April 14, 1875, CBNM; Montgomery Schuyler to Custer, May 13, 1875, CBNM; Monaghan, *Custer*, pp. 365–69.

42 I have covered this speculative combination more thoroughly in Slotkin, " 'And *then* the Mare will go!': An 1875 Black Hills Scheme by Custer, Holladay and Buford," *JW* 15:3 (July 1976), 60–77. A. Buford to Custer, Aug. 22, 1875, CBNM; Ben Holladay's correspondence of the period is in Oregon State Historical Society, except for letters to/from S. L. M. Barlow (Huntington Library) and Henry Villard (Baker Library, Harvard University). See esp. Holladay to Villard, March 4, April 12, May 25, Aug. 13, 1875, Villard Papers, Box #69, 530. The best biography of Holladay is Ellis Lucia, *Ben Holladay: Giant of the Old West*; see also J. V. Frederick, *Ben Holladay, the Stagecoach King: A Chapter in the Development of Transcontinental Transportation*; and Ben Holladay, *Spoilations Committed by Indians . . .* (1872). For Villard and his technique for seizing control of the NPRR see Henry Villard, *Memoirs of Henry Villard* 2:272–79; Grodinsky, *Transcontinental Railway Strategy*, ch. 2. Biographical information on Abra-

ham Buford is scarce. I am indebted to the staff of the Kentucky State Historical Society for answers to several inquiries, and for the article "General Abraham Buford," Woodford *Sun*, Oct. 9, 1930. There are articles on Buford in the *Dictionary of American Biography* and *The Biographical Encyclopedia of Kentucky* . . ., p. 516. I am grateful to the Filson Club, Woodford County Historical Society, and several citizens of Versailles, Kentucky, for answers to inquiries. Background on Custer's and Buford's common political contacts is in Crackel, "Custer's Kentucky," pp. 147, 149–50, 152–54; and *NYT 66*, Sept. 21.

    43 Monaghan, *Custer*, p. 365; Slotkin, ". . . and *then* the Mare . . .," p. 72, n. 30; Military Division of the Missouri, Headquarters Letters Received, RG 393, Box 20, Items 3003, 3119 in NA.

    44 Slotkin, ". . . and *then* the Mare . . .," pp. 68–74, and n. 29; Monaghan, *Custer*, pp. 176–77; Custer to Zachariah Chandler, Feb. 13, 1876, Chandler Papers, LC; Merington, *Custer Story*, pp. 251, 157, 165, 167.

    45 *Justh* v. *Holladay, Reports of Cases Argued and Adjudged in the Supreme Court of the District of Columbia . . . May 25, 1882 to October 29, 1883*, pp. 348–49, 355–59; *Justh* v. *Holladay, Supreme Court of the District of Columbia, March 6, 1879*, pp. 44–45.

    46 "Abstracts of Reports on the Goodenough Shoe, 1881," *Letters, Reports, and Contracts*, Quartermaster General's Office, NA.

    47 Custer to E. D. Townsend, A. A. G., Jan. 11, 1876, Custer Papers, NA; Maj. Gen. Philip H. Sheridan to Townsend, Feb. 5, 1876, Sheridan Papers, NA; *Justh* v. *Holladay, Supreme Court*, pp. 28–30.

    48 Stewart, *Custer's Luck*, pp. 123–24, 132–33, 137–39.

    49 Ibid., ch. 6. The question of Custer's relationship to Belknap deserves more interest than it usually receives. Custer partisans tend to accept the general's word that he was aware of Belknap's corruption from an early point, treated him coldly when they met, and seized the opportunity offered first by the investigative journalism of Ralph Meeker, and then by Clymer, to expose Belknap. Custer-phobes have tended to see the incident as expressive merely of Custer's hunger for headlines, Democratic loyalties, and personal dislike of Grant and Belknap. It is curious that the only specific statement of Custer's which Belknap chose to refute in public, was the apparently harmless assertion that Custer had given Belknap the "cold shoulder" during a tour of inspection in 1875. Belknap published an exchange of letters between himself and Colonel Forsyth of Sheridan's staff on the subject. Why did both men make so much of so trivial an issue? The visit coincided with the heyday of the Custer-Holladay-Buford speculation; and if Custer had wished to court or purchase support for post-traderships, Belknap was the inevitable source of the favor and the visit a golden opportunity. It is possible that Custer's assertion of "coldness" was an attempt to distance himself from an accusation of complicity; and Belknap's refutation a counterattack and implicit threat against his accuser. See Earl K. Brigham, "Custer's Meeting with Secretary of War Belknap at Fort Abraham Lincoln," *North Dakota History* 9:2 (Aug. 1952), 129–31, which favors the Belknap-Forsyth interpretation of the meeting as "cordial." If Belknap turned down the Custer-Holladay-Buford proposal (for the obvious reason that the combination was starved for capital), Custer would have had additional reasons for disliking Belknap.

    50 Stewart, *Custer's Luck*, p. 121; Monaghan, *Custer*, p. 366. Meeker's letters to Custer suggest that they enjoyed a collegial relationship on the exposé. It was claimed by Belknap's supporters that Custer had received $150 from Bennett for his services; but this appears to have been repayment of money advanced by Custer to Meeker. Custer created a small scandal by attacking and caning one of his accusers in a Washington street. *NYT 76*, Apr. 5, p. 19; May 5, p. 4; Meeker to Custer, Sept. 17, Oct. 5, and Dec. 30, 1875, CBNM.

    51 Monaghan, *Custer*, pp. 365–70; Kinsley, *Favor the Bold: Custer the Indian Fighter* 2:164–65, 183, on Custer's last trip to the East; Cortissoz, *Whitelaw Reid* 1:312; Katz, *August Belmont*, ch. 12.

    52 James Calhoun to Custer, Jan. 2, 1871; Samuel B. Lauffer to Custer, Feb. 6, 1871; Lewis Merrill to Custer, April 26, 1871; Trelease, *White Terror*; George Augustus Armes, *Ups and Downs of an Army Officer* (1900), pp. 322, 343, 407–8. See also the news coverage of Merrill in *NYW 74*, Nov. 3, pp. 1, 4, 5.

53   Merington, *Custer Story*, p. 283; Orin G. Libby, ed., *The Arikara Narrative of the Campaign Against the Hostile Dakotas, June 1876*, pp. 58–63. Stewart, *Custer's Luck*, p. 181, shares the traditional interpretation, which is that (if Custer said these words at all) he was suggesting a run for the presidency, with the support (Mari Sandoz, *Battle of Little Big Horn*, pp. 27–28, 54–55, 181–82) of either Bennett or "Jay Gould" (actually Tom Scott), who had purchased the *World*. But see Bennett's declared opposition to another soldier president (*NYH 76*, May 25, p. 6; June 4, "Great Unknowns," pp. 8, 12).

Among Custer's projects during this period was the writing of his "War Memoirs," which the *Galaxy* began running in the spring of 1876: *Galaxy 76* 21:3 (Mar. 1876), 319–24; 21:4 (Apr. 1876), 448–60; 21:5 (May 1876), 624–32; 21:6 (June 1876), 809–18; 22:3 (Sept. 1876), 293–99; 22:4 (Oct. 1876), 447–55; 22:5 (Nov. 1876), 684–94. Custer's account of the political divisions at West Point on the eve of the Civil War misrepresent his own political enthusiasms for the prosouthern wing of the Democratic Party. But more significant for contemporary politics is his attempt to represent the views of the defecting southern cadets in the best possible light. Among the names he cites as types of southern "honor" are his friend Rosser, and General Young—who sat at Belmont's table with Custer, and was also a member of Belmont's circle. His fascination with southern honor leads him to the absurd assertion that if the federal government had simply refused to accept the resignations of the southern cadets and officers, they would have felt honor-bound to fight for the Union! Such a view was in accordance with the Belmont policy of rehabilitating ex-Confederates as constituents of a new Democratic majority.

54   Custer, "Indian Policy," ms. (1876), CBNM; Randel, *Centennial*, p. 135.

55   Custer, "Battling with the Sioux on the Yellowstone," *Galaxy* 22:1 (July 1876), 91.

56   Stewart, *Custer's Luck*, pp. 132–39.

57   Ibid., pp. 139, 309–12, is the best discussion of this question.

58   Merington, *Custer Story*, p. 304; Stewart, *Custer's Luck*, pp. 210–11.

CHAPTER 18

1   *NYH 74*, May 15, p. 5; June 27, p. 4; July 7, p. 3.

2   *NYH 74*, July 10, p. 5. The editorial on "Hydrophobia," July 12, p. 6, compares Indians to mad dogs, recommends extermination of both. Other Indian policy editorials which echo or vary this line are July 19, p. 6; July 21, p. 6; July 22, p. 6; July 25, p. 6; Aug. 1, p. 4. All of these use Black Hills news as a basis for demanding further reduction of Indian landholdings, tribal autonomy, and population. An editorial on Indian policy, Jan. 3, p. 4, uses Indians as a metaphor for Tompkins Square "rioters" in the same manner as the *World* at the same time; and see also July 6, p. 5. On the prospective use of the Black Hills as a "safety valve" for eastern unemployed and farmers, see Aug. 23, p. 7; Aug. 24, p. 6; Aug. 29, pp. 3, 6, 10; Sept. 19, p. 8.

3   McJimsey, *Manton Marble*, pp. 178–81; Katz, *August Belmont*, p. 218. Editorials that parallel the *World's* hard-money line are *NYH 74*, Jan. 21, p. 8; Jan. 28, p. 9; Mar. 2, p. 10; Mar. 3, p. 4; June 4, p. 6; June 19, p. 6. On southern issues the papers also took similar stands, although the *Herald* was more inclined than the *World* to report (often favorably) the lynching of blacks by whites—perhaps because Belmont was trying to rehabilitate the reputation of southern Democrats by emphasizing their peaceable qualities. As an "independent," Bennett could feel free to exploit the sensationalism of southern violence. For the *Herald*, Reconstruction is simply "Sambo in Excelsis." See *NYH 74*, Jan. 11, p. 11; Jan. 8, p. 3; Jan. 23, p. 4; Feb. 28, pp. 3, 4. On lynching, "Lex Talionis," see Jan. 3, p. 4; Apr. 18, p. 4; Apr. 21, p. 4; Apr. 25, p. 4; Sept. 1, p. 4. For a similar handling of the "Chinese Question," May 4, p. 6.

4   For general ideology, see *NYH 76*, Jan. 17, p. 4; Feb. 1, p. 4; Feb. 12, p. 4; Mar. 1, p. 4; June 21, p. 6. On labor issues, Jan. 17, p. 4; Jan. 19, p. 4. On the army appropriation and proposals for reorganizing, redistributing, and expanding army control of Indian affairs, see Jan. 7, p. 4; Jan. 15, p. 4; Jan. 28, p. 2; Jan. 30, p. 4; Feb. 5, p. 4.

5   *NYH 76*, "False Economy," Mar. 12, p. 3.
6   *NYH 76*, Feb. 10, p. 4; Feb. 28, p. 4; Mar. 28, p. 3; Apr. 5, p. 3. On Mar. 2, p. 5, note visual juxtaposition of stories.
7   *NYH 76*, "The Fall of Secretary Belknap," Mar. 3, p. 6.
8   *NYH 76*, Mar. 28, p. 1; Mar. 31, pp. 1, 4. In the latter, note juxtaposition of Belknap story with Mollie Maguire trials.
9   *NYH 76*, Feb. 17, p. 7; Feb. 18, p. 6; Feb. 19, p. 6; Mar. 8, p. 10; Mar. 9, p. 6.
10 *NYH 76*, Feb. 19, p. 6.
11 *NYH 76*, Mar. 13, p. 4; Mar. 14, p. 6; Mar. 15, p. 5; Mar. 27, p. 4.
12 *NYH 76*, "Mollie Maguires." Mar. 26, pp. 4, 8; Mar. 31, pp. 1, 4; Apr. 3, p. 6.
13 On the Chinese question, see Alexander Saxton, *The Indispensable Enemy: Labor and the Anti-Chinese Movement in California*, chs. 1–5.
14 For articles/editorials on Grangers, see *NYH 74*, Feb. 24, p. 4; *NYH 76*, May 6, p. 6.
15 *NYH 76*, "Explosion in Jersey City," May 8, p. 6.
16 *NYH 76*, May 20, p. 6; May 21, p. 6.
17 *NYH 76*, "Effects of Custer's Exposures," Apr. 18, p. 3; "The President Stands by Belknap," May 4, p. 6; "Grant's Latest Mistake," May 6, p. 6; "CUSTER SACRIFICED," p. 7.
18 *NYH 76*, "Preparing for the Indian War," May 9, p. 7; "The Outrage . . .," May 19, p. 6. The "dime novel" epithet is in *NYH 76*, "Grant and Custer," May 14, p. 4; see also May 11, p. 8; May 12, p. 4; May 13, p. 4; May 14, p. 4.
19 *NYH 76*, "The Hostile Sioux," May 29, p. 6; "The Indian Battle," June 16, p. 6.
20 *NYH 76*, June 17, p. 6.
21 *NYH 76*, June 19, pp. 2, 4. Compare *NYW 74* on the Ashantee War, which estimates costs to British "per nigger killed," ch. 15, n. 65, above.
22 *NYH 76*, June 21, p. 6; June 24, pp. 4, 5.
23 *NYH 76*, June 25, p. 5.
24 *NYH 76*, June 27, p. 7.
25 Ibid., p. 6.
26 *NYH 76*, June 29, p. 6.
27 *NYH 76*, July 3, pp. 4, 5.
28 The chronology of events during this stage of the expedition is established by Stewart, *Custer's Luck*, chs. 10–11. The detachment referred to in this issue is not (as *NYH* supposes) the Custer detachment itself, but the earlier reconnaissance by a battalion of the Seventh Cavalry under Major Marcus A. Reno.
29 *NYH 76*, July 5, p. 4.
30 *NYH 76*, July 6, pp. 3, 4. Note the parallel with "Cross and Crescent" on the fighting between Turks and Christians in the Balkans.
31 *NYH 76*, July 6, p. 5.
32 *NYH 76*, July 7, pp. 3–5.
33 Ibid., p. 6. Note parallel with "Murder of Policeman Scott" by "brutal rowdies" which calls attention to that growing evil, the "dangerous class."
34 *NYH 76*, July 8, p. 6; also pp. 3–5, 7.
35 *NYH 76*, July 9, pp. 3–4; July 10, p. 4.
36 *NYH 76*, July 11, pp. 3–4; July 10, p. 4; Sept. 25, pp. 6, 8.
37 *NYH 76*, "Labor Question in England," and "Negroes and Whites," July 9, pp. 3–4. The latter commences coverage of the "Hamburg Massacre," for which see below.
38 *NYH 76*, July 9, pp. 3–4. For sources of the pictographs, see Stanley Vestal, *Sitting Bull: Champion of the Sioux*, pp. 316–20. On the Turks and Abdul Aziz, see *NYH 76*, July 9, pp. 3–4; July 12, p. 3; July 26, p. 2; Aug. 21, p. 5; Sept. 4, p. 4; Sept. 25, p. 9.
39 *NYH 76*, July 9, p. 4.
40 On Sitting Bull's leadership, see Vestal, *Sitting Bull*, chs. 21–22; Stewart, *Custer's Luck*, pp. 184–87. On the Indian responses to "who killed Custer?" see the pamphlet by Thomas B. Marquis, *Which Indian Killed Custer?*; James H. Howard, *The Warrior Who Killed Custer: The Personal Narrative of Chief Joseph White Bull*; Stewart, *Custer's Luck*, pp. 485–89.
41 *NYH 76*, July 9, pp. 3–4. See also July 15, p. 5; July 17, "A Warning," p. 4; July 18, p. 5; July 20, p. 3; July 21, pp. 4–5; Aug. 19, p. 5; Aug. 21, p. 4. [Robert Dun-

lap Clarke], *The Works of Sitting Bull in the Original French and Latin, with Trans-*
lations Diligently Compared, is devoted to proving he studied Napoleon under the
Jesuits. On Maria Monk and the Canadian-captive tradition, see Slotkin, *Regeneration*
Through Violence, ch. 5, and p. 444.

42 Proposals of this kind were usually accompanied by reiteration of its major
Indian-related platform plans for the '76 elections: transfer of the Indian Bureau to
army control; extinction of Indian title outside small reservations; division of tribal lands
by allotment-in-severalty. See Indian policy editorials *NYH 76*, July 11, p. 6; July 16,
p. 6; July 29, p. 4; July 31, p. 4; Aug. 11, p. 4; Aug. 12, p. 5; Aug. 15, p. 4; Aug. 31, p.
6; Aug. 27, p. 3; Sept. 3, p. 9; Sept. 5, pp. 6, 7; Sept. 6, p. 7; Sept. 8, p. 4; Sept. 20, p.
6; Sept. 24, p. 3; Sept. 27, p. 7; Oct. 1, p. 8; Oct. 2, p. 6; Oct. 5, p. 6; Oct. 24, pp. 5, 6;
Nov. 10, p. 7.

43 *NYH 76*, "Horrors of the Custer Massacre," Sept. 9, p. 4; also July 14, p. 4;
Aug. 6, p. 6; Aug. 14, p. 4.

44 The major Custer monument stories and editorials are *NYH 76*, July 12, p. 6;
July 13, p. 4; July 14, p. 4; July 16, p. 6; July 17, pp. 3, 4; July 18, pp. 3, 4; July 19,
p. 5; July 20, pp. 3, 4; July 21, p. 4 (note also reference to Indian policy platform);
July 22, pp. 4, 6; July 23, p. 4; July 24, pp. 4, 5; July 25, pp. 3, 4 (note contributions
esp. from South and from August Belmont); July 26, p. 4; July 27, pp. 4, 5; July 28, p. 4;
July 29, p. 3; July 30, p. 4; Aug. 8, p. 6. These stories continued to appear for the rest
of 1876, with diminishing length and editorial emphasis. On the congressional reduction
of Mrs. Custer's pension and political moves to raise it, see *NYH 76*, July 30, p. 4;
July 31, p. 4; Aug. 4, p. 4; Aug. 5, p. 4.

45 *NYH 76*, July 9, pp. 3–4.

46 *NYH 76*, July 20, p. 4; Aug. 6, p. 6; Aug. 12, p. 8.

47 James Shepherd Pike, *The Prostrate State: South Carolina Under Negro Gov-*
ernment (1874). On Hampton, see Hampton M. Jarrell, *Wade Hampton and the Negro:*
The Road Not Taken; Albert Brockenbrough Williams, *Wade Hampton and His Red-*
shirts: South Carolina's Deliverance in 1876; Samuel L. Wells, *Hampton and Recon-*
struction; Otis A. Singletary, *Negro Militia and Reconstruction*, esp. ch. 9, and pp. 15,
48, 139–41.

48 *NYH 76*, July 9, pp. 3–4, 7.

49 Pages which reflect these associations with particular force are *NYH 76*, July
13, p. 5; July 24, p. 8; Aug. 7, p. 3. Association of southern and Indian affairs is made
in *NYH 76*, July 18, p. 4; Aug. 17, p. 4; and esp. Aug. 18, p. 5. See Sept. 24, p. 3, for
parallel between "Making Indian Treaties" and "The Strike in the Rice Fields" for a
labor tie-in; and Oct. 17, p. 5; Oct. 27, pp. 5, 6.

50 *NYH 76*, July 15, p. 4.

51 *NYH 76*, July 17, p. 4; Aug. 3, p. 4; see also Oct. 14, p. 4.

52 *NYH 76*, Oct. 20, p. 3; Oct. 23, p. 5; Oct. 17, p. 7; Oct. 18, p. 3 (all on "Cainhoy Massacre"); also Sept. 11, p. 4. Note visual juxtaposition of stories on Oct. 15, p. 9;
Oct. 19, pp. 3, 5. Editorials defining southern policy, vindicating southern leaders, and
excusing southern vigilantism are Aug. 8, p. 4; Aug. 2, p. 4; Aug. 3, p. 4; Aug. 18, p. 5;
Aug. 19, p. 4. An Alabama editorial using "exterminationist" language toward blacks is
cited in *HW 75*, Jan. 9, p. 37; *HW 76*, July 15, p. 66; alliance between KKK and Indian
savages is suggested by Thomas Nast's cover, *HW 76*, July 22, p. 1.

An important group of stories paralleling developments in the South with the progress of white imperialism in Africa began appearing just after the election. The dispatches
of Henry M. Stanley, acting as *Herald* correspondent and explorer, were a major coup
for Bennett's paper; and the publisher sought to reap political gains as well, by contrasting the fruits of "false philanthropy" (symbolized by the "Cainhoy Massacre" and
"Hamburg Massacre") with Stanley's opening of Africa to light and order through the
use of force. These stories are linked in turn to further dispatches on Turkish-Christian
fighting in the Balkans, to link philanthropists with the fanatical "dervishes" on the one
hand, and with benightedness in Africa on the other. *NYH 76*, Nov. 7, pp. 4–5; and also
Oct. 11, pp. 5, 6; Oct. 17, p. 5; Oct. 18, p. 6; Nov. 10, p. 6.

53 *NYH 76*, July 22, p. 4. The paper's final position on the southern question is
detailed Sept. 24, p. 3; Oct. 17, p. 5; Oct. 27, pp. 5–6; Oct. 28, p. 5. For stories linking
Indians, blacks, and workers in this period, see *NYH 76*, Aug. 9, p. 4; Aug. 24, p. 5. July

30, p. 4 is particularly rich in such linkages; and also Aug. 16, p. 4; Aug. 23, p. 5; Sept. 2, p. 3; Sept. 22, p. 7; Sept. 23, p. 7; Dec. 6, pp. 13–14.

54 *NYDG 76*, July 10, p. 59; July 6, p. 10; July 8, p. 46.

55 *NYW 76*, "Justification of Custer," July 11, p. 4; May 2, p. 4; June 27, p. 4; July 7, p. 4; July 6, pp. 1, 4; July 7, p. 4; July 8, p. 4; July 14, p. 4.

56 *NYW 76*, July 15, p. 4; July 17, p. 5; May 10, p. 4; May 8, p. 4; May 9, p. 4; June 29, p. 4; July 7, p. 4. Compare July 9, p. 1, with *NYH 76*, p. 1 of the same date.

57 See the New York *Times* and Boston *Daily Advertiser* for the key dates above, nn. 55–56, esp. for the Belknap affair in March, the Custer dismissal in May, and the Last Stand/Hamburg Massacre coincidence in July and August. *NYDG 76*, July 8, p. 46; July 10, p. 59; July 6, p. 10, mix anti-Indian but pro-Republican views; *HW 76*, July 15, p. 66, July 22 cover, are pro-Indian and -Peace Policy, but regard the Last Stand as a tragedy. Utley, *Custer and the Great Controversy*, pp. 39–47, summarizes variations in press treatment; *NYH 76*, July 9, p. 4, cites many other papers.

58 *I-O 76*, June 26, p. 4; June 27, p. 4; July 6, p. 4; July 10, p. 1; July 27, p. 4.

59 *I-O 76*, July 8, pp. 1, 4.

60 *I-O 76*, July 9, p. 4; "Turks in the United States," June 26, p. 4; June 27, p. 4. Compare *NYH 76*, July 9, pp. 3–4, 7; and n. 49 above on "Sioux Civilization"—the metaphors are similar, the ideological objective different. See *I-O 76* articles supporting blacks against white vigilantism on May 11, p. 4; May 16, p. 5; May 17, p. 4; May 25, p. 4.

61 *NYTrib 76*, July 8, p. 4; July 11, p. 4; July 13, p. 4 (includes Hamburg Massacre). On workers as savages, see "Wages and Murder," Apr. 24, p. 4; on African affairs, analogies between the South and the Ashantee War, "Dahomey," May 11, p. 4.

62 See the Charleston *News and Courier*, Louisville *Courier-Journal*, and Richmond *Enquirer* for the key dates in nn. 55–56 above. Other southern papers are cited passim in sections of reprinted material included in the *Herald*, *Times*, and *Tribune*. See also Utley, *Custer and the Great Controversy*, p. 39.

63 Richmond *Enquirer 76*, July 8, p. 2; July 9, p. 2; July 11, p. 2.

64 *National Labor Tribune 76*, Jan. 1, p. 1.

65 *Workingman's Advocate 76*, Mar. 25, pp. 1–2.

66 Ibid., July 10, p. 2.

67 *Irish World 74*, Mar. 14, p. 7; Apr. 18, p. 4; also Jan. 10, p. 1; Jan. 24, p. 4; Sept. 12, p. 4. The "Colonization" column in each issue is worth careful study.

68 Ibid., "Indians and Agents," Feb. 14, p. 4; Sept. 10, p. 5; *Irish World 76*, July 29, pp. 3, 4; Aug. 19, p. 1. See also Eric Foner, "Class, Ethnicity, and Radicalism in the Gilded Age: The Land League and Irish America," *MP* 1:2 (Summer 1978), 6–55.

CHAPTER 19

1 Dubofsky, *Industrialism*, ch. 2; Gutman, *Work, Culture*, chs. 6–7; Bruce, *1877: The Year of Violence*; Foner, *The Great Labor Uprising of 1877*.

2 *NYTrib 77*, July 20, p. 1; July 24, p. 1; July 30, p. 1, all parallel strike stories with Turkish-Christian battles. For other strike coverage, see below. *NYDG 77*, July 19 parallels the strike ("War in West Virginia") with the starving out of Chief Joseph of the Nez Percé; see also July 20, p. 130; July 27, pp. 178–79. "Gathering of the Strikers" is juxtaposed with a southern story ("War of Races") on July 24, p. 151. *NYH 77*, July 18, p. 4; July 19, p. 5; July 20, p. 4; July 21, p. 5; July 27, p. 3; July 18, p. 4; July 29, p. 9; Aug. 9, p. 4; Aug. 13, p. 4, all have stories or editorials on Indians and strikers printed in close visual juxtaposition, often with some shared term or concept to reinforce the linkage (e.g., "war," "reds," etc.). Other references are to Turkish war. The editorial July 20, p. 4, is more sympathetic to Indians than to strikers.

3 *HW 77*, "Railroad War," Aug. 18, pp. 640–41; "Bright Side," p. 638; "The Strikes," pp. 638–39.

4 *NYTrib 76*, "Wages and Murder," Apr. 27, p. 4; Aug. 14, p. 4.

5 *NYTrib 77*, "Railroad Strike," July 19, p. 4; July 25, p. 4.

6 *NYTrib 77*, July 23, p. 4.

7 *NYTrib* 77, "Great Strike," July 25, p. 4; "First Question," and "What We Must . . .," July 28, p. 4.

8 *NYTrib* 77, "Duty of the Hour," July 23, p. 4; "Workmen and Wages," July 28, p. 4. *NYH* 77, "Right and Wrong," July 20, p. 4; "Some Thoughts . . .," July 24, p. 6; "Belly and the Members," July 25, p. 5. *NYTrib* 77, "Consequences . . .," July 28, p. 4; "Trade-Unions vs. the Government," July 25, p. 4; "Rights and Duties . . .," Aug. 4, p. 4. *NYH* 77, "Great Strike," July 22, p. 8; "Public Meeting," July 24, p. 6; July 25, p. 5; "Communistic Meeting," July 26, p. 6.

9 *NYH* 77, July 23, p. 1; July 27, p. 3; see also Jan. 4, "The Crows."

10 *NYTrib* 77, "Duty of the Hour," July 23, p. 4, links white tramps and nomadic Indians. Compare *NYH* 77, "Home Heathen," Jan. 24, p. 6; Jan. 28, p. 8. Chief Joseph as "vagabond" or "tramp," July 13, p. 6; and "War in Idaho" paralleled with "Tramps in Bands," July 31, p. 4. For strikers as "hostiles," *NYH* 77, July 25, p. 3.

11 *NYH* 77, July 24, p. 6; July 27, p. 5. The image of a well-drilled army of strikers recurs often: for example, July 22, p. 8; July 23, p. 4; July 24, p. 6; Aug. 6, p. 4.

12 *NYH* 77, July 26, p. 6; *NYTrib* 77, July 19, p. 4.

13 *NYDG* 77, July 22, p. 142; "New Vigilance Committees!" July 25, p. 158; July 27, p. 174.

14 *NYDG* 77, July 25, p. 5; July 28, p. 4; "Indian War and Indian Policy," July 14, p. 4; "Sitting Bull," Aug. 4, p. 4.

15 "Indian War and Indian Policy," July 14, p. 4; on acculturation of the working class, Gutman, *Work, Culture,* ch. 1.

16 *NYTrib* 77, July 21, p. 6; "The Commune . . .," July 25, p. 4.

17 *NYTrib* 77, "Some Plain Words," July 26, p. 4.

18 *NYH* 77, July 26, p. 6.

19 *NYTrib* 77, Aug. 7, p. 4; Aug. 11, p. 4.

20 *NYDG* 77, July 26, p. 166.

21 William L. Armstrong, *E. L. Godkin: A Biography,* pp. 104–6, 120–21; Rollo Ogden, ed., *Life and Letters of Edwin Lawrence Godkin . . .,* 2 vols. His conservative views were collected later in E. L. Godkin, *Unforeseen Tendencies of Democracy;* ———, *Problems of Modern Democracy: Political and Economic Essays;* and ———, *Reflections and Comments, 1865–1895.*

22 *Nation* 77, "Universal Suffrage . . ." (Dec. 27), 652:391.

23 *Nation* 76 (Mar. 9), 558–56; (Dec. 28), 600:382.

24 *Nation* 77 (May 1), 619:271; (July 26), 630:60–61.

25 *Nation* 76, "South and the Canvass" (July 27), 578:52.

26 *Nation* 76 (Aug. 17), 581:98.

27 *Nation* 76, "Our Indian Wards" (July 13), 576:21–22. The editorial initiated an exchange of views with Lewis H. Morgan, the pioneer anthropologist, in which Morgan proposed moving the Indians directly into industrial production without passing through the agricultural stage. See *Nation* 76 (July 20), 577:40–1; "Factory System for Indian Reservations" (July 27), 578:58–59; "Indians as Shepherds" (Aug. 10), 580:90.

28 *Nation* 77 (May 3), 618:259; (May 31), 622:318–20.

29 *Nation* 77 (Aug. 2), 631:69–70.

30 Ibid., 68–69.

31 *Nation* 77 (Aug. 9), 632:85–86; (Aug. 30), 635:130–31.

32 *Nation* 77, "Effect on the Negro . . ." (Sept. 6), 636:146–47. On Rigault, see Frank Jellinek, *The Paris Commune of 1871,* pp. 167–68, 231, 252, 292–95. On the role of militias in this period, see Robert Reinders, "Militia and Public Order in Nineteenth Century America," *JAS* 11:1 (Apr. 1977), 81–102. Lucy Stone, quoted in Foner, *The Great Labor Uprising,* p. 192.

CHAPTER 20

1 Monaghan, *Custer,* pp. 295, 399.

2 Alger, *Ragged Dick,* see pp. 306–8, above.

3 Mark Twain [S. L. Clemens], *The Adventures of Tom Sawyer* (1876).

4 Whittaker, *Complete Life,* pp. 8–10; see also ———, *The Dashing Dragoon*

... (1882), p. 1. Compare Whittaker's text of Custer's letter on p. 212, with Merington, *Custer Story*, p. 65. The Horatio Alger elements are stronger in Whittaker, and he has Custer quoting Davy Crockett's motto.

5   Whittaker, *Complete Life*, p. 11.
6   Ibid., pp. 1–2; Lawrence Barrett quoted in Whittaker, p. 629.
7   Ibid., pp. 169–70.
8   Ibid., p. 258.
9   Ibid., p. 406.
10 Ibid., pp. 316, 325.
11 Ibid., pp. 327–38.
12 Ibid., p. 336.
13 Ibid., pp. 501, 512.
14 Ibid., pp. 529, 615, 622.
15 Ibid., pp. 601–2. Custer figures as a Christ figure in (for example) Vine Deloria, *Custer Died for Your Sins* (ironically), and a Leonard Baskin print, commissioned for the Custer Battlefield National Monument brochure but excluded from the final copy. My thanks to Arthur Wensinger for bringing the print to my attention.

16 The best studies of Custer imagery are Rosenberg, *Custer and the Epic of Defeat* and Dippie, *Custer's Last Stand*. Steckmesser, *Western American Hero*, p. 4, covers literary versions.

The core of the Custer canon is Custer, *My Life on the Plains* and the three books by Elizabeth Bacon Custer, *"Boots and Saddles"; or, Life in Dakota with General Custer* (1885); *Following the Guidon* (1890) and *Tenting on the Plains; or, General Custer in Kansas and Texas* (1887). An interesting reprint of *My Life* associates Custer with other western heroes during the heyday of Buffalo Bill's Wild West and of public interest in the Ghost Dance outbreak of 1890: Custer, *Wild Life on the Plains and Horrors of Indian Warfare* (1891).

Dime novel treatments of Custer include [Alexander], *Sheridan's Squaw Spy* discussed above. Some of the most interesting and important dime novel versions were associated with the Ghost Dance outbreak and with Buffalo Bill, and will be discussed in the next volume of this study, *Gunfighter Nation*. Several dime novel treatments appeared in 1876, and in the years immediately following: [Alfred Rochefort Calhoun] "Maj. Ashley Lawrence," *The Custer Avenger; A Story of the Present Sioux War* (1876); William F. Cody, *The Crimson Trail; or, on Custer's Last Warpath. A Romance Founded on the Present Border Warfare* . . . (1876); [Thomas Harbaugh], *Roving Rifle; Custer's Little Scout* . . . (1883); [H. Llewellynn], *Custer's Last Charge; or, The Ravine of Death* (1876); [St. George Henry Rathbone], "Custer's Scout," *Custer's Last Shot; or the Boy Trailer of the Little Big Horn* (1876); [Lu Senarens] "Noname," *Custer's Little Deadshot; or, Custer in the Black Hills* (1876); and Whittaker, *Dashing Dragoon*. The versions by Calhoun, Cody, and Llewellynn and *Sitting Bull*, treat the story as a confrontation between archetypal white and Indian heroes, representing the war as a personal confrontation between Custer and Sitting Bull, or between an "avenger" of Custer and Sitting Bull or some other larger-than-life Indian villain. The other versions treat Custer as a chivalric paternal figure, who engages the loyalty of a boy-hero, acts as a protector in the Horatio Alger manner; however, the boy is unable to fulfill the letter of the Alger scenario, since he cannot save his benefactor in the end.

Novelistic treatments of Custer tend to present him as a paternal figure, acting as a protector to eastern lads out West, or as the mentor and redeemer of young soldiers who have fallen under a moral or romantic cloud: Herbert Myrick, *Cache La Poudre: The Romance of a Tenderfoot in the Days of Custer* (1905); Eldridge S. Brooks, *The Master of the Strong Hearts: A Story of Custer's Last Rally* (1898); Cyrus Townsend Brady, *Britton of the Seventh: A Romance of Custer and the Great North-West* (1914); Edwin L. Sabin, *On the Plains with Custer* (1914); and Frazier Hunt, *Custer, the Last of the Cavaliers* (1928).

For bibliography and analysis of Custer literature see Steckmesser, *Western American Hero*, pp. 213–16; Dippie, *Custer's Last Stand*, pp. 181–201; Russell, Buffalo Bill, pp. 494–503.

17 [John Hay], *The Breadwinners* (1883–84), ed. by Charles Vandersee, Introduction, p. 65.
18 Ibid., p. 65.

19 Ibid., p. 67.

20 Ibid., p. 229.

21 Ibid., p. 123.

22 Frederickson, *Inner Civil War*, ch. 14; Edward Bellamy, *Looking Backward, 2000–1887*; R. Jackson Wilson, "Experience and Utopia: The Making of Edward Bellamy's *Looking Backward*," *JAS* 11:1 (Apr. 1977), 45–60.

23 Henry Nash Smith, *Mark Twain's Fable of Progress: Political and Economic Ideas in* A Connecticut Yankee; Justin Kaplan, *Mr. Clemens and Mark Twain*, ch. 14. John Fraser, *America and the Patterns of Chivalry*, esp. Pt. 1, is the most illuminating study of this theme.

24 Twain, *Roughing It* (1872), p. 146.

25 Twain, "A Visit to Niagara," in *Sketches New and Old* (1875). The association of wild Indians and wild Irish goes back to the seventeenth century: see Slotkin, *Regeneration Through Violence*, pp. 42, 472.

26 Twain, *Roughing It*, pp. 201, 204, 277–78.

27 Mark Twain and Charles Dudley Warner, *The Gilded Age*, 2 vols. (1873), parodies Gilpin's approach to the China trade (chs. 1, 8) and the Gilpin/Cooke school of railroad promotion (1: ch. 17; 2: ch. 28).

28 Twain, *Tom Sawyer*, chs. 2, 4. Compare Judge Thatcher's Sunday school experience in ch. 4 with that of the crooked Senator Dilworthy, *Gilded Age*, 1: ch. 20. The "quicksilver" gold mill is in *Roughing It*, ch. 36.

29 Mark Twain, *Adventures of Huckleberry Finn* (1883).

30 Twain, "Tom and Huck Among the Indians," *Hannibal, Huck and Tom*, ed. by Walter Blair, pp. 84–88 discusses Twain's use of Western sources, esp. Custer, Mrs. Custer, and Colonel R. I. Dodge. For Twain's relations with Mrs. Custer and her books, see Kaplan, *Mr. Clemens*, pp. 339–40; S. L. Clemens to C. L. Webster & Co., July 15, 1888, in Hamlin Hill, ed., *Mark Twain's Letters to His Publishers*, p. 247; Allen Gribben, *Mark Twain's Library: A Reconstruction* 1:169.

31 Mark Twain, "The French and the Comanches," *Letters from the Earth*, pp. 146–49; and on the Commune, see Jellinek, *The Paris Commune*, ch. 11.

32 Smith, *Fable of Progress*; Twain and W. D. Howells, *The Mark Twain–Howells Letters: The Correspondence of Samuel L. Clemens and William D. Howells, 1872–1910*, ed. by Henry Nash Smith and William M. Gibson, 2:579–81, 591–99, 607–15, 621–28, 631; Kaplan, *Mr. Clemens*, pp. 339–40.

33 Mark Twain, *A Connecticut Yankee in King Arthur's Court* (1889), Norton Critical Edition, pp. 19, 73–74, ch. 29.

34 Ibid., pp. 51–52, chs. 34–36, p. 228. The episode uses the conventions of the abolitionist romance, as in *Uncle Tom's Cabin*, *The Octoroon*, etc. See above, pp. 148–50, and Slotkin, *Regeneration Through Violence*, pp. 442–43. To see the Reconstructionist connection compare Albion W. Tourgee, *A Fool's Errand* (1879), for his treatment of the "Chivalry" as barbarians. Tourgee was a not uncritical supporter of Reconstruction who believed that northern capital and know-how could modernize and liberalize the South. His novel shows those liberal hopes defeated by the racialist superstition, and consequent savagery, of white Southerners; and his anti-Yankee party (like that in Twain's novel) is an alliance of "the Chivalry" with the ignorant poor whites. See also Aaron, *Unwritten War*, ch. 13.

35 Twain, *A Connecticut Yankee*, pp. 171–72.

36 Ibid., pp. 65–68, 247.

37 Ibid., pp. 8, 65–68, 101; Bellamy, *Looking Backward*, chs. 1–2.

38 Twain, *A Connecticut Yankee*, pp. 227–29 for "Wild West"; pp. 241–51 for the death of Arthur and Morgan's own Last Stand.

39 Ibid., pp. 254–55. Twain's use of Gatling guns is significant, given the strong association between machine guns and the industrialization of society. See John Ellis, *The Social History of the Machine Gun*, esp. chs. 1–3.

BIBLIOGRAPHY

1. Collections of Manuscripts and Personal Papers

Barlow, Samuel L. M. Papers, Huntington Library, San Marino, California.
Buford, Abraham. File materials, Filson Club, Louisville, Kentucky.
————. File materials, Woodford County Historical Society, Louisville, Kentucky.
Cooke, Jay. Papers, Baker Library, Harvard University, Cambridge, Mass.
Chandler, Zachariah. Papers, Library of Congress.
Custer, George Armstrong. Papers, Custer Battlefield National Monument, Crow Agency, Montana.
————. Papers, National Archives.
————, and Elizabeth (Bacon) Custer. Papers and letters, Western Americana, Beinecke Library, Yale University, New Haven, Conn.
Holladay, Ben. Papers, Oregon State Historical Society, Portland, Oregon.
The Northern Pacific Railway Company Records, Minnesota Historical Society, Minneapolis, Minnesota.
Sheridan, Philip H. Papers, Library of Congress and National Archives.
Sherman, William T. Papers, Library of Congress.
Villard, Henry. Papers, Baker Library, Harvard University, Cambridge, Mass.

2. Official Records and Documents

"Abstract of Reports on the Goodenough Shoe, 1881," *Letters, Reports, and Contracts,* Quartermaster General's Office, National Archives.
"The Chivington Massacre," Appendix to *Annual Report of the Commissioner of Indian Affairs for 1864.* Washington: Government Printing Office, 1865.
"Emil Justh, *Plaintiff* vs. Ben. Holladay, *Defendant,*" *Reports of Cases Argued and Adjudged in the Supreme Court of the District of Columbia. General Term, October, 1883,* pp. 1–28.
————. *Supreme Court of the District of Columbia, March 6, 1879,* pp. 1–56.
Military Division of the Missouri. Headquarters Letters Received, 1869–1876.
Rankin, Hon. John A. "Speech of . . ., February 23 and March 10, 1842." *Congressional Record 1842,* Appendix A 768-9, 931.
Secretary of the Interior, Commissioner of Indian Affairs. *Annual Report of the Commissioner of Indian Affairs for the Year[s] 1868–1876.* Washington: Government Printing Office, 1869–1877.
Secretary of War. *Annual Report of the Secretary of War for the Year[s] 1866–1877.* Washington: Government Printing Office, 1867–1878.
————. *Report of the Sand Creek Massacre.* Senate Executive Documents Number 26, 39th Congress, 2nd Session, 1866–67.
Webster, Daniel. ["Seventh of March Speech"], *Congressional Globe* 22:1, 31st Congress, 1st Session, 1849–50, pp. 476–83.
United States Congress. *Report of the Joint Committee on Reconstruction,* Part 4. 39th Congress, 1st Session. Washington: Government Printing Office, 1866.

United States Congress, Senate. Special Committee Appointed under Joint Resolution of March 3, 1865. *Condition of the Indian Tribes.* Senate Report 156, 34th Congress, 2nd Session.

3. Contemporary Newspapers

Boston *Daily Advertiser*, 1874–1877.
Charleston, S. C., *News and Courier*, 1873–1877.
Chicago *Inter-Ocean*, 1873–1877.
Irish World, 1874–1876.
Louisville, Ky., *Courier-Journal*, 1873–1876.
National Intelligencer, 1855–1857.
National Labor Tribune, 1874–1876.
New York *Daily Graphic*, 1874–1877.
New York *Evening Post*, 1855–1857.
New York *Herald*, 1846–1848; 1855–1857; 1859–60; 1863–1877.
New York *Times*, 1855–1857; 1859–1860; 1863–1866; 1873–1877.
New York *Tribune*, 1855–1857; 1859–1860; 1873–1877.
New York *World*, 1873–1877.
Richmond, Va., *Enquirer*, 1873–1877.
Rough and Ready 1:1, Concord, N. H., December 12, 1846.
Workingmen's Advocate, 1874–1876.

4. Contemporary Magazines and Annuals

Colonizationist and Journal of Freedom, June, 1833.
De Bow's Review, 1855–1857, 1860–1862.
Democratic Review [United States Magazine and Democratic Review], 1844–1850; 1855–1858.
Frank Leslie's Weekly, 1855–1857; 1873–1877.
The Galaxy, 1873–1877.
Harper's Monthly Magazine, 1855–1857; 1859–1860; 1863–1866; 1868–1877.
Harper's Weekly Magazine, 1857–1877.
The Nation, 1873–1877.
Putnam's Monthly Magazine, 1855–1857; 1859–1860; 1873–1877.
The Rough and Ready Annual, 1847–1848.
Turf, Field and Farm, 1867–1874.

5. Books, Articles, Literary Mss., Pamphlets and Theses

Aaron, Daniel. *The Unwritten War: American Writers and the Civil War.* London and New York: Oxford University Press, 1975.
Abbott, John S. C. *Christopher Carson, Familiarly Known as Kit Carson.* New York: Dodd, Mead and Company, 1873.
———. *Daniel Boone, the Pioneer of Kentucky.* New York: Dodd, Mead and Company, 1872.
———. *David Crockett: His Life and Adventures.* New York: Dodd, Mead and Company, 1874.
Adams, Charles Francis, Jr. "The Granger Movement," *North American Review* 120 (April 1875), 394–424.
———. "The Protection of the Ballot in National Elections," *Journal of Social Science* 1:1 (June 1869), 91–111.
———, and Henry Adams. *A Cycle of Adams Letters, 1861–1865.* 2 volumes. Edited by Worthington Chauncey Ford. Boston: Houghton Mifflin, 1920.

Albanese, Catherine L. "Savage, Sinner and Saved: Davy Crockett, Camp Meetings, and the Wild Frontier," *American Quarterly* 33:5 (Winter 1981), 482–501.
———. *Sons of the Fathers: The Civil Religion of the American Revolution.* Philadelphia: Temple University Press, 1976.
Alderman, Edwin Anderson, and Joel Chandler Harris, editors. *The Library of Southern Literature: Compiled Under the Direct Supervision of Southern Men of Letters.* New Orleans and Atlanta: The Martin and Hoyt Company, 1908–13.
[Alexander, Charles Wesley]. *General Sheridan's Squaw Spy and Mrs. Clara Blynn's Captivity Among the Wild Indians of the Prairie; A Thrilling Narrative of Daring Exploits and Hairbreadth Escapes of Viroqua . . .* Philadelphia: Cooperative Publishing House, 1869.
Alger, Horatio, Jr. *Adrift in New York and The World Before Him.* Edited by William Coyle. New York: Odyssey Press, 1966.
———. *Digging for Gold: A Story of California.* Edited by John Seelye. New York: Collier Books, 1968. Reprint of New York, 1892 edition.
———. *Ragged Dick and Mark the Match-Boy.* Edited by Rychard Fink. London: Collier Books, 1962.
[Allen, G. N.]. *Mexican Treacheries and Cruelties; Incidents and Sufferings in the Mexican War . . .* Boston and New York: [n.p.], 1847.
Allen, Priscilla. "Melville and the Man-of-War Microcosm," *American Quarterly* 25:1 (March 1973), 32–47.
American Anti-Slavery Society. *The Anti-Slavery History of the John Brown Year Being the Twenty-seventh Annual Report of the American Anti-Slavery Society.* New York: Negro Universities Press, 1969. Reprint of New York, 1861 edition.
Anderson, Eric. *Race and Politics in North Carolina, 1872–1901: The Black Second.* Baton Rouge: Louisiana State University Press, 1981.
Anderson, Marilyn J. "The Image of the Indian in American Drama During the Jacksonian Era, 1829–1845," *Journal of Popular Culture* 1:4 (Winter 1978), 800–10.
Andreano, Ralph L., editor. *The Economic Impact of the American Civil War.* Cambridge, Mass.: Schenkman, 1962.
Andrews, E. Benjamin. *The History of the Last Quarter-Century in the United States, 1870–1895.* London: K. Paul, Trench, Trübner and Company, Ltd., 1897.
Andrews, J. Cutler. *The North Reports the Civil War.* Pittsburgh: University of Pittsburgh Press, 1955.
Andrist, Ralph K. *The Long Death: The Last Days of the Plains Indians.* New York: Macmillan, 1964.
Appleby, Joyce, "Commercial Farming and the 'Agrarian Myth' in the Early Republic," *Journal of American History* 68:4 (March 1982), 833–49.
Apter, David E., editor. *Ideology and Discontent.* New York: Free Press, 1964.
Armes, George Augustus. *Ups and Downs of an Army Officer.* Washington: [n.p.], 1900.
Armstrong, William L. *E. L. Godkin: A Biography.* Albany: State University of New York Press, 1978.
Arpad, Joseph J. "Between Folklore and Literature: Popular Culture as Anomaly," *Journal of Popular Culture* 9:2 (Fall 1975), 403–23 [51–71].
Atway, Robert, editor. *American Mass Media.* New York: Random House, 1982.
Averill, Charles E. *Kit Carson: The Prince of the Gold Hunters; or, The Adventure of the Sacramento. A Tale of the New Eldorado.* Boston: George H. Williams, 1849.
Axtell, James. *The European and the Indian: Essays in the Ethnohistory of Colonial America.* New York: Oxford University Press, 1981.
Baker, Mark. *Nam: The Vietnam War in the Words of the Men and Women Who Fought There.* New York: Quill, 1982.
Balio, Tino, editor. *The American Film Industry.* Madison: University of Wisconsin Press, 1976.
Barker-Benfield, G. J. *Horrors of the Half-Known Life: Male Attitudes towards Women in Nineteenth Century America.* New York: Harper Colophon Books, 1976.
Barnett, Louise K. *The Ignoble Savage: American Literary Racism, 1790–1890.* Westport, Conn.: Greenwood Press, 1975.
Barnett, Steve, and Martin G. Silberman. *Ideology and Everyday Life: Anthropology, Neo-Marxist Thought, and the Problem of Ideology and the Social Whole.* Ann Arbor: University of Michigan Press, 1981.

Barnhart, John D. *The Valley of Democracy: The Frontier versus the Plantation in the Ohio Valley, 1775–1818.* Lincoln: University of Nebraska Press, Bison Books, 1970.

Barthes, Roland. *Mythologies.* Translated by Annette Lavers. New York: Hill and Wang, 1972.

Bartlett, Ruhl J. *John C. Frémont and the Republican Party.* New York: Da Capo Press, 1970.

Bascom, William. "The Forms of Folklore: Prose Narratives," *Journal of American Folklore* 78:1 (January–March 1965), 3–20.

Bateman, Fred, and Thomas Weiss. *A Deplorable Scarcity: The Failure of Industrialization in the Slave Economy.* Chapel Hill: University of North Carolina Press, 1981.

Bauer, K. Jack. *The Mexican War: 1846–1848.* New York: Macmillan, 1974.

Baym, Nina. "The Women of Cooper's Leatherstocking Tales," *American Quarterly* 23:5 (December 1971), 696–209.

Beard, James Franklin, editor. *The Letters and Journals of James Fenimore Cooper.* Cambridge, Mass.: Belknap Press of Harvard University Press, 1960–1968.

Bellamy, Edward. *Looking Backward, 2000–1887.* Boston: Ticknor and Company, 1888.

Bender, Thomas. *Toward an Urban Vision: Ideas and Institutions in Nineteenth Century America.* Lexington: University Press of Kentucky, 1975.

Bendix, Reinhard. *Work and Authority in Industry: Ideologies of Management in the Course of Industrialization.* Berkeley: University of California Press, 1956.

Bennett, Benjamin. "Nietzsche's Idea of Myth: The Birth of Tragedy from the Spirit of Eighteenth Century Aesthetics," *PMLA* 94:3 (May 1979), 420–33.

Bennett, Emerson. *The Prairie Flower; or, Leni-Leoti.* Cincinnati: U. P. James, 1850.

Bercovitch, Sacvan. *The American Jeremiad.* Madison: University of Wisconsin Press, 1978.

———. *The Puritan Origins of the American Self.* New Haven: Yale University Press, 1975.

———. "The Typology of America's Mission," *American Quarterly* 30:2 (Summer 1976), 135–55.

Berger, Peter L., and Thomas Luckmann. *The Social Construction of Reality: A Treatise in the Sociology of Knowledge.* Garden City, N.Y.: Doubleday, 1966.

Berkhofer, Robert F., Jr. *The White Man's Indian: Images of the American Indian from Columbus to the Present.* New York: Alfred A. Knopf, 1978.

Berwanger, Eugene. *The Frontier Against Slavery: Western Anti-Negro Prejudice and the Slavery Extension Controversy.* Urbana: University of Illinois Press, 1967.

Betts, Raymond F. "Immense Dimensions: The Impact of the American West on Late Nineteenth Century European Thought About Expansion," *Western Historical Quarterly* 10:2 (April 1979), 149–66.

Biddiss, Michael D., editor. *Images of Race: Articles by Alfred Russel Wallace, Francis Galton, John Elliot Cairnes, Charles Mackay, John William Jackson, Frederic William Farrar, Thomas Huxley, Kelburne King, Herbert Spencer, Edward Augustus Freeman and Grant Allen.* New York: Holmes & Meier, 1979.

Bigelow, Donald Nevius. *William Conant Church and the "Army and Navy Journals."* New York: Columbia University Press, 1952.

Bigelow, John. *Memoir of the Life and Public Services of John Charles Frémont.* New York: Derby and Jackson, 1856.

Billington, Ray Allen. *Frederick Jackson Turner: Historian, Scholar, Teacher.* New York: Oxford University Press, 1973.

———. *Land of Savagery, Land of Promise: The European Image of the American Frontier.* New York: W. W. Norton and Company, 1981.

———. *America's Frontier Heritage.* New York: Holt, Rinehart and Winston, 1966.

The Biographical Encyclopedia of Kentucky of the Dead and Living Men of the Nineteenth Century. Chicago: J. M. Gresham Company, 1896.

Bird, Robert Montgomery. *Nick of the Woods; or, The Jibbenainosay: A Tale of Kentucky.* Edited by Curtis Dahl. New Haven: College and University Press, 1967.

———. "Oralloosa, Son of the Incas: A Tragedy." Ms., Library of Congress.

Birmingham, Stephen. *Our Crowd: The Great Jewish Families of New York.* New York: Dell Books, 1967.

Black, David. *The King of Fifth Avenue: The Fortunes of August Belmont.* New York: Dial Press, 1981.

Blau, Joseph L., editor. *Social Theories of Jacksonian Democracy: Representative Writings of the Period, 1825–1850*. New York: Bobbs-Merrill, 1954.

Blu, Karen I. *The Lumbee Problem: The Making of an American Indian People*. Cambridge: Cambridge University Press, 1982.

Bodenhammer, David J. "Law and Disorder on the Early Frontier: Marion City, Indiana, 1823–1850," *Western Historical Quarterly* 10:3 (July 1979), 323–36.

Bold, Christine. "The Voice of the Fiction Factory in Dime and Pulp Westerns," *Journal of American Studies* 17:1 (April 1983), 29–46.

Boorstin, Daniel. *The Americans: The Colonial Experience*. New York: Random House, 1958.

———. *The Americans: The Democratic Experience*. New York: Random House, 1973.

———. *The Americans: The National Experience*. New York: Random House, 1975.

———. *The Lost World of Thomas Jefferson*. Boston: Beacon Press, 1963.

Bouwsma, William J. "The Renaissance and the Drama of Western History," *American Historical Review* 84:1 (February 1979), 1–15.

Boyer, Richard Owen. *The Legend of John Brown: A Biography and a History*. New York: Alfred A. Knopf, 1973.

Brace, Charles Loring. *The Dangerous Classes of New York, and Twenty Years Work Among Them*. New York: Wynkoop and Hallenbeck, 1872. Reprinted by National Association of Social Workers, 1973.

Brady, Cyrus Townsend. *Britton of the Seventh: A Romance of Custer and the Great North-West*. Chicago: A. C. McClurg and Company, 1914.

———. *Indian Fights and Fighters: The Soldier and the Sioux*. New York: McClure, Phillips and Company, 1904.

Braestrup, Peter, and Burns Roper. *Big Story: How the American Press and Television Reported and Interpreted the Crisis of Tet 1968 in Vietnam and Washington*. 2 volumes. Boulder, Colo.: Westview Press, 1976.

Brandstetter, Evan. "Uncle Tom and Archy Moore: The Anti-Slavery Novel as Ideological Symbol," *American Quarterly* 26:2 (May 1974), 160–75.

Breen, T. H., and Stephen Innes. *Myne Owne Ground: Race and Freedom on Virginia's Eastern Shore*. New York: Oxford University Press, 1980.

Breitbart, Eric. "From Panorama to Docudrama: Notes on the Visualization of History," *Radical History Review* 25 (1981), 115–26.

Brigham, Earl K. "Custer's Meeting with Secretary of War Belknap at Fort Abraham Lincoln," *North Dakota History* 9:2 (August 1952), 129–31.

Brill, Charles J. *The Conquest of the Southern Plains; Uncensored Narrative of the Battle of the Washita and Custer's Southern Campaign*. Oklahoma City: Golden Saga Publishers, 1938.

Broehl, Wayne G. *The Mollie Maguires*. [New York]: Vintage Books, 1968.

Brooks, Elbridge Streeter. *The Master of the Strong Hearts: A Story of Custer's Last Rally*. New York: E. P. Dutton, 1910.

Brown, Charles H. *Agents of Manifest Destiny: The Lives and Times of the Filibusters*. Chapel Hill: University of North Carolina Press, 1980.

Brown, Dee. *Bury My Heart at Wounded Knee*. New York: Holt, Rinehart and Winston, 1973.

———. *The Year of the Century: 1876*. New York: Charles Scribner's Sons, 1966.

Brown, Richard D. *Modernization: The Transformation of American Life, 1600–1865*. New York: Hill and Wang, 1976.

Brown, Richard M. *Strain of Violence: Historical Studies of American Violence and Vigilantism*. New York: Oxford University Press, 1975.

Brown, Theodore M. "Putting Paradigms into History," *Marxist Perspectives* 3:1 (Spring 1980), 34–63.

Brownlow, Kevin. *The Parade's Gone By*. New York: Alfred A. Knopf, 1968.

———. *The War, the West and the Wilderness*. New York: Alfred A. Knopf, 1979.

Brownmiller, Susan. *Against Our Will: Men, Women and Rape*. New York: Simon and Schuster, 1975.

Bruce, Robert V. *1877: The Year of Violence*. Indianapolis: Bobbs-Merrill, 1959.

Bruchey, Stuart. *Roots of American Economic Growth, 1607–1861*. New York: Harper Torchbooks, 1965.

Brumm, Ursula. "'What Went You Out in the Wilderness to See?': Nonconformity and

Wilderness in Cotton Mather's *Magnalia Christi Americana*," *Prospects* 6 (1981), 1–16.

"Buntline, Ned" [Edgar Zane Carroll Judson]. *The Volunteer; or, the Maid of Monterrey, a Tale of the Mexican War.* Boston: F. Gleason, Flag of Our Union, 1847.

Burchall, R. A. "The Character and Function of a Pioneer Elite: Rural California, 1848–1880," *Journal of American Studies* 15:3 (December 1981), 377–90.

Burdett, Charles. *The Life of Kit Carson, the Celebrated Rocky Mountain Trapper and Guide; Together with His Hunting Exploits, Thrilling Adventures, and Hairbreadth Escapes Among the Indians . . .* Philadelphia: G. G. Evans, 1860.

Burns, Rex. *Success in America: The Yeoman Dream and the Industrial Revolution.* Amherst: University of Massachusetts Press, 1976.

Byllesby, L[angdon]. *Observations on the Sources and Effects of Unequal Wealth; With Propositions Towards Remedying the Disparity of Profit in Pursuing the Arts of Life, and Establishing Security in Individual Prospects and Resources.* New York: L. J. Nichols, 1826.

[Calhoun, Alfred Rochefort] "Maj. Ashley Lawrence." *The Custer Avenger: A Story of the Present Sioux War. Saturday Night* 14 (September 30–December 23, 1876), 3–15.

Calloway, Colin G. "An Uncertain Destiny: Indian Captivities of the Upper Connecticut River," *Journal of American Studies* 17:2 (August 1983), 189–210.

Campbell, Joseph. *The Hero with a Thousand Faces.* New York: World, Meridian Books, 1949.

Cappon, Lester J., editor. *The Adams-Jefferson Letters: The Complete Correspondence between Thomas Jefferson and Abigail and John Adams.* Chapel Hill: University of North Carolina Press, 1949.

Caputo, Philip. *A Rumor of War.* New York: Holt, Rinehart and Winston, 1977.

Carr, Albert H. Z. *The World and William Walker.* New York: Harper and Row, 1963.

Carroll, Anna Ella. *The Star of the West: National Men and National Measures.* Third edition. New York: Miller, Orton and Company, 1857.

Carroll, John M. *The Benteen-Goldin Letters on Custer and His Last Battle.* New York: Liveright, 1974.

———. *Custer in Periodicals: A Bibliographic Checklist.* Ft. Collins, Colo.: The Old Army Press, 1975.

———. *Custer in Texas: An Interrupted Narrative.* New York: Sol Lewis/Liveright, 1975.

Carroll, Peter N. *Puritanism and the Wilderness: The Intellectual Significance of the New England Frontier, 1629–1700.* New York: Columbia University Press, 1969.

Carstensen, Vernon. "Making Use of the Frontier and the American West," *Western Historical Quarterly* 13:1 (January 1982), 5–16.

Caruthers, William Alexander. *The Cavaliers of Virginia; or, the Recluse of Jamestown. An Historical Romance of the Old Dominion.* New York: Harper and Brothers, 1834–1835.

———. *The Knights of the Horseshoe: A Traditionary Tale of the Cocked Hat Gentry of the Old Dominion.* New York: Harper and Brothers, 1882. Originally published 1834.

Catlin, George. *Letters and Notes on the Manners, Customs and Condition of the North American Indians.* Second edition. New York: Wiley and Putnam, 1842.

Catton, Bruce. *The Coming Fury.* New York: Pocket Books, Inc., 1967.

———. *Never Call Retreat.* New York: Pocket Books, Inc., 1967.

———. *Terrible Swift Sword.* New York: Pocket Books, Inc., 1967.

Cawelti, John G. *Adventure, Mystery and Romance: Formula Stories as Art and Popular Culture.* Chicago: University of Chicago Press, 1976.

———. *Apostles of the Self-Made Man: Changing Concepts of Success in America.* Chicago: University of Chicago Press, 1965.

Chambers, William Nisbet. *Old Bullion Benton: Senator from the New West.* Boston: Little, Brown, 1956.

Channing, Steven A. *Crisis of Fear: Secession in South Carolina.* New York: Simon and Schuster, 1970.

Chase, Allen. *The Legacy of Malthus: The Social Costs of the New Scientific Racism.* New York: Alfred A. Knopf, 1977.

Chase, Richard. *The American Novel and Its Tradition.* Garden City, N.Y.: Doubleday, Anchor Books, 1957.

Chatman, Seymour. *Story and Discourse: Narrative Structure in Fiction and Film.* Ithaca: Cornell University Press, 1978.

Chevalier, Louis. *Laboring Classes and Dangerous Classes in Paris During the First Half of the Nineteenth Century.* Translated by Frank Jellinek. New York: Howard Fortig, 1973.

Child, Lydia Maria. *Hobomok; a Tale of Early Times.* Boston: Cummings, Hilliard and Company, 1824.

Clarens, Carlos. *Crime Movies: From Griffith to* The Godfather *and Beyond.* New York: W. W. Norton and Comapny, 1980.

Clark, Barrett H., editor. *Favorite American Plays of the Nineteenth Century.* Princeton: Princeton University Press, 1943.

[Clarke, Robert Dunlap]. *The Works of Sitting Bull in the Original French and Latin, with Translations Diligently Compared.* Chicago: Knight and Leonard, 1878.

Clebsch, William A. "The American 'Mythique' as Redeemer Nation," *Prospects* 4 (1978), 79–94.

Cochran, Thomas C. *Business in American Life: A History.* New York: McGraw-Hill, 1972.

————. *Frontiers of Change: Early Industrialization in America.* New York: Oxford University Press, 1981.

————, and William B. Miller. *The Age of Enterprise: A Social History of Industrial America.* New York: Harper Torchbooks, 1961.

Cochrane, William Ghormley. *Freedom Without Equality: A Study of Northern Opinion on the Negro Question, 1861–1870.* Minneapolis: University of Minnesota Press, 1957.

[Cody, William F.] "Buffalo Bill." *The Crimson Trail; or, On Custer's Last War Path. A Romance Founded Upon the Present Border Warfare as Witnessed by Hon. William F. Cody, "Buffalo Bill." New York Weekly* 31 (September 25–October 30, 1876), 45–50.

[Coffin, Charles Carleton] "Carleton." *The Seat of Empire.* Boston: Fields, Osgood and Company, 1870.

Cohen, Bronwen J. "Nativism and Western Myth: The Influence of Nativist Ideas on the American Self-Image," *Journal of American Studies* 8:1 (April 1974), 23–40.

Cohen, Hennig, editor. *The American Culture: Approaches to the Study of the United States.* Boston: Houghton Mifflin, 1968.

————. *The American Experience: Approaches to the Study of the United States.* Boston: Houghton Mifflin, 1968.

————, and William B. Dillingham, editors. *Humor of the Old Southwest.* Second edition. Athens: University of Georgia Press, 1975.

————, and James Levernier, editors. *The Indians and Their Captives.* Westport, Conn.: Greenwood Press, 1977.

Collins, Bruce. *The Origins of America's Civil War.* London: E. Arnold, 1981.

Collins, Charles. *Collins' History and Directory of the Black Hills . . .* Central City, Dakota Territory [South Dakota]: By the author, 1878.

Colton, Calvin. *Labor and Capital, the Junius Tracts.* Volume 7. New York: Greeley and McElrath, 1844.

Commager, Henry Steele. *Theodore Parker: Yankee Crusader.* Boston: Beacon Press, 1960.

Commons, John R. *The Labor Movement, 1840–1860. The Documentary History of American Industrial Society.* Volumes 7 and 8. Cleveland: The A. H. Clark Company, 1910–1911.

Conard, Jane. "Charles Collins: The Sioux City Promotion of the Black Hills," *South Dakota History* 2:2 (Spring 1972), 131–71.

Conk, Margo A. "Social Mobility in Historical Perspective," *Marxist Perspectives* 1:3 (Fall 1978), 52–69.

Cook, Adrian. *Armies of the Streets: The New York City Draft Riots of 1863.* Lexington: University of Kentucky Press, 1974.

Cooper, James Fenimore. *The Chainbearer; or, The Littlepage Manuscripts.* New York: Townsend, 1860.

————. *The Deerslayer; or, the First Warpath.* Philadelphia: Lea and Blanchard, 1841.

————. *The Last of the Mohicans; a Tale of 1757*. Edited by William Charvat. Boston: Houghton Mifflin, Riverside Edition, 1958.

————. *The Oak Openings; or, the Bee-hunter*. New York: Townsend, 1860.

————. *The Pathfinder; or, The Inland Sea*. Philadelphia: Lea and Blanchard, 1840.

————. *The Pioneers; or, The Sources of the Susquehanna*. Edited by Leon Howard. New York: Holt, Rinehart and Winston, Rinehart Editions, 1959.

————. *The Prairie; A Tale*. Introduction by Henry Nash Smith. New York: Holt, Rinehart and Winston, Rinehart Editions, 1964.

————. *The Red Rover*. New York: Townsend, 1859.

————. *The Redskins; or, Indian and Injin*. New York: Townsend, 1860.

————. *Satanstoe; or, The Littlepage Manuscripts, A Tale of the Colony*. New York: Townsend, 1860.

————. *The Spy; a Tale of the Neutral Ground*. New York: Townsend, 1860.

Cords, Nicholas, and Patrick Gerster, editors. *Myth and the American Experience*. 2 volumes. Beverly Hills: Glencoe Press, 1973.

Cornish, Dudley Taylor. *The Sable Arm: Negro Troops in the Union Army, 1861–1865*. New York: Longmans, Green and Company, 1956.

Cortissoz, Royal. *The Life of Whitelaw Reid*. 2 volumes. New York: Charles Scribner's Sons, 1921.

Cox, Oliver. *Caste, Class and Race: A Study in Social Dynamics*. New York: Modern Reader Paperbacks, 1948.

Crackel, Theodore J. "Custer's Kentucky, 1871–1873," *Filson Club Historical Quarterly* 68:2 (August 1974), 147–54.

Crèvecoeur, Michel Guillaume St. Jean de. *A Journay to Northern Pennsylvania and the State of New York*. Translated by Clarissa Spencer Bostelmann from the Paris, 1801 edition. Ann Arbor: University of Michigan Press, 1964.

————. "J. Hector St. John" [Michel Guillaume St. Jean]. *Letters from an American Farmer*. Edited by Warren Baston Blake. New York: E. P. Dutton, 1957.

Crockett, David. *Account of Colonel Crockett's Tour to the North and Down East in the Year of Our Lord One Thousand Eight Hundred and Thirty-Four: His Object Being to Examine the Grand Manufacturing Establishments* . . . Philadelphia: E. E. Cavey and A. Hurt, 1835.

————. *Narrative of the Life of David Crockett*. Edited by James J. Arpad. New Haven: College & University Press, 1976.

[Croly, David Goodman, and George Wakeman]. *Miscegenation: The Theory of Blending of the Races, Applied to the American White Man and the Negro*. New York: H. Dexter, Hamilton and Company, 1864.

Cunliffe, Marcus. *George Washington: Man and Monument*. Boston: Little, Brown, 1958.

Curry, Leonard P. *Blueprint for Modern America: Nonmilitary Legislation of the First Civil War Congress*. Nashville: Vanderbilt University Press, 1968.

Curti, Merle. "Young America," *American Historical Review* 32:1 (October 1926), 34–55.

Curtis, Newton M. *The Hunted Chief; or, The Female Ranchero, A Tale of the Mexican War*. New York: Williams Brothers, 1847.

————. *The Prairie Guide; or, The Rose of the Rio Grande, a Tale of the Mexican War*. New York: W. F. Burgess; Cincinnati: Burgess and Wood, 1847.

————. *The Vidette; or, The Girl of the Robber's Pass, A Tale of the Mexican War*. New York: Williams Brothers, 1848.

Custer, Elizabeth Bacon. *"Boots and Saddles"; or, Life in Dakota with General Custer*. New York: Harper and Brothers, 1885.

————. *Following the Guidon*. New York: Harper and Brothers, 1890.

————. *Tenting on the Plains; or, General Custer in Kansas and Texas*. New York: Charles L. Webster and Company, 1887.

Custer, George Armstrong. "Battling with the Sioux on the Yellowstone," *Galaxy* 22:1 (July 1876), 91–102.

————. "Custer's Reply to the Atrocious Attempts of the Corrupt or Insane Radical Press to Pervert his Testimony, &c." [Cleveland, 1866]. Copy in Beinecke Library, Yale University.

————. *My Life on the Plains; or, Personal Experiences with Indians*. Edited by Edgar I. Stewart. Norman: University of Oklahoma Press, 1962. Reprint of New York: Sheldon and Company, 1874.

——— ["Nomad"]. *Nomad: George Armstrong Custer in Turf, Field and Farm.* Edited by Brian W. Dippie. Austin: University of Texas Press, 1980.

———. "War Memoirs," *Galaxy* 21:3 (March 1876), 319–24; 21:4 (April 1876), 448–60; 21:5 (May 1876), 624–32; 21:6 (June 1876), 809–18; 22:3 (September 1876), 293–99; 22:4 (October 1876), 447–55; 22:5 (November 1876), 684–94.

———. *Wild Life on the Plains and Horrors of Indian Warfare . . .* New York: Arno Press, 1969. Reprint of edition published St. Louis: Continental Publishing Company, 1891.

Cutler, James E. *Lynch-Law: An Investigation into the History of Lynching in the United States.* New York: Negro Universities Press, 1969. Reprint of the Boston 1905 edition.

Daniel, Peter. "The Metamorphosis of Slavery, 1865–1900," *Journal of American History* 66:1 (June 1979), 88–99.

D'Arcy, William. *The Fenian Movement in the United States, 1858–1886.* New York: Russell and Russell, 1971.

David, Paul A., Herbert G. Gutman, Richard Sutch, Peter Temin, and Gary Wright. *Reckoning with Slavery: A Critical Study of the Quantitative History of American Negro Slavery.* Introduction by Kenneth M. Stampp. New York: Oxford University Press, 1976.

Davie, Donald. *The Heyday of Sir Walter Scott.* London: Routledge and Kegan Paul, 1961.

Davis, David Brion. *Homicide in American Fiction, 1798–1860: A Study in Social Values.* Ithaca: Cornell University Press, 1957.

———. *The Problem of Slavery in the Age of Revolution, 1770–1823.* Ithaca: Cornell University Press, 1975.

———. *The Problem of Slavery in Western Civilization.* Ithaca: Cornell University Press, 1966.

Davis, John Patterson. *The Union Pacific Railway: A Study in Railway Politics, History and Economics.* Chicago: Griggs, 1894.

Davis, Rebecca Harding. *Margret Howth, A Story of Today.* Boston: Ticknor and Fields, 1862.

Davis, Richard W. "Deference and Aristocracy in the Time of the Great Reform Act," *American Historical Review* 81:3 (June 1976), 532–39.

Davis, Ronald L. F. "Community and Conflict in Pioneer St. Louis, Missouri," *Western Historical Quarterly* 10:3 (July 1979), 337–56.

Dawley, Alan. *Class and Community: The Industrial Revolution in Lynn.* Cambridge, Mass.: Harvard University Press, 1976.

———. "E. P. Thompson and the Peculiarities of the Americans," *Radical History Review* 19 (March 1979), 33–59.

[Deaderick, David, III]. "The Experiences of Samuel Absalom, Filibuster," *Atlantic Monthly* 4:26 (December 1859), 653–65; 5:27 (January 1860), 38–60.

Dearing, Mary Rullcotter. *Veterans in Politics: The Story of the G. A. R.* Baton Rouge: Louisiana State University Press, 1962.

Debo, Angie. *And Still the Waters Run.* New York: Gordian Press, 1952.

De Bow, John D. B. *Industrial Resources, Statistics, &c. of the United States and More Particularly of the Southern and Western States.* New Orleans: De Bow's Review, 1852–53.

Degler, Carl N., editor. *Pivotal Interpretations in American History.* 2 volumes. New York: Harper Torchbooks, 1966.

Dekker, George. *James Fenimore Cooper: The American Scott.* New York: Barnes and Noble, 1967.

———. "Sir Walter Scott, the Angel of Hadley, and American Historical Fiction," *Journal of American Studies* 17:2 (August 1983), 211–28.

———, and John P. McWilliams, editors. *Fenimore Cooper: The Critical Heritage.* London: Routledge and Kegan Paul, 1973.

Deloria, Vine. *Custer Died for Your Sins: An Indian Manifesto.* New York: Macmillan, 1969.

Denn, Robert J. "Captivity Narratives of the American Revolution," *Journal of American Culture* 2:4 (Winter 1980), 572–82.

The Destiny of Nicaragua: Central America as It Is, Was, and May Be . . . by "an Officer in the Service of Walker." Boston: S. A. Bent and Company, 1856.

Deutscher, Isaac. *The Prophet Armed: Trotsky, 1879–1921.* New York: Vintage Books, 1954.

De Voto, Bernard. *The Year of Decision 1846.* Boston: Houghton Mifflin, and Sentry Editions, 1961.

Dick, Everett. *The Lure of the Land: A Social History of the Public Lands from the Articles of Confederation to the New Deal.* Lincoln: University of Nebraska Press, 1970.

Diggins, John P. "Barbarism and Capitalism: The Strange Perspective of Thorstein Veblen," *Marxist Perspectives* 1:2 (Summer 1978), 138–57.

Dippie, Brian W. *Custer's Last Stand: The Anatomy of an American Myth.* Missoula: University of Montana Press, 1976.

———. *The Vanishing American: White Attitudes and U. S. Indian Policy.* Middletown, Conn.: Wesleyan University Press, 1982.

Dodge, Richard Irving. *The Black Hills; A Minute Description . . .* New York: J. Miller, 1876.

———. *Our Wild Indians; Thirty-Three Years Experience Among the Red Men of the Great West . . .* Hartford, Conn.: A. D. Worthington, 1883.

Donnelly, Ignatius. *Caesar's Column: A Story of the Twentieth Century.* Edited by Walter B. Rideout. Cambridge, Mass.: Belknap Press of Harvard University Press, 1960.

Dorson, Richard M. *American Folklore and the Historian.* Chicago: University of Chicago Press, 1971.

———. *America in Legend: Folklore from the Colonial Period to the Present.* New York: Pantheon Books, 1973.

———, editor. *The Handbook of American Folklore.* Bloomington: Indiana University Press, 1983.

Douglas, Ann. *The Feminization of American Culture.* New York: Alfred A. Knopf, 1977.

Doyle, Don H. "Social Theories and New Communities in 19th Century America," *Western Historical Quarterly* 8:2 (April 1977), 151–66.

Draper, John William. *Thoughts on the Future Civil Policy of America.* New York: Harper and Brothers, 1865.

Drinnon, Richard. *Facing West: The Metaphysics of Indian-Hating and Empire Building.* Minneapolis: University of Minnesota Press, 1980.

———. *White Savage: The Case of John Dunn Hunter.* New York: Schocken Books, 1972.

Dubofsky, Melvyn. *Industrialism and the American Worker, 1865–1920.* New York: Thomas Y. Crowell Company, 1975.

———. *We Shall Be All: A History of the Industrial Workers of the World.* Chicago: Quadrangle Books, 1969.

Du Bois, William E. B. *John Brown.* New York: International Publishers, 1962.

Dundes, Alan. "Folk Ideas as Units of World View," *American Folklore* 84:1 (January 1971), 93–103.

———. *Interpreting Folklore.* Bloomington: Indiana University Press, 1980.

———, and Carl R. Pagter. *Urban Folklore from the Paperwork Empire.* Austin, Tex.: American Folklore Society, 1975.

Dustin, Fred. *The Custer Tragedy: Events Leading Up to and Following the Little Big Horn Campaign of 1876.* Ann Arbor, Mich.: Edwards Brothers, Inc. 1939.

Eagleton, Terence. *Criticism and Ideology: A Study in Marxist Literary Theory.* London: NLB, Atlantic Highlands, Humanities Press, 1976.

Earle, Carville, and Ronald Hoffman. "The Foundation of the Modern Economy: Agriculture and the Costs of Labor in the United States and England, 1800–1860," *American Historical Review* 85:5 (December 1980), 1055–94.

Eastburn, James, and Robert C. Sands. *Yamoyden: A Tale of the Wars of King Philip.* New York: James Eastburn, 1820.

Eastman, Mary. *Aunt Phillis's Cabin; or, Southern Life as It Is.* Philadelphia: Lippincott, Grambo and Company, 1852.

———. *Dacotah; or, Life and Legends of the Sioux Around Fort Snelling.* New York: S. Wiley, 1849.

————. *Romance of Indian Life, with Other Tales.* Philadelphia: Lippincott, Grambo and Company, 1853.

Eaves, Morris. "Blake and the Artistic Machine: An Essay in Decorum and Technology," *PMLA* 92:5 (October 1977), 903–27.

Egan, Ferol. *Frémont: Explorer for a Restless Nation.* Garden City, N. Y.: Doubleday, 1977.

Ehrenreich, Barbara, and Deirdre English. *For Her Own Good: 150 Years of the Experts' Advice to Women.* Garden City, N. Y.: Doubleday, Anchor Books, 1979.

Elkins, Stanley, and Eric L. McKitrick. "Institutions and the Law of Slavery: The Dynamics of Unopposed Capitalism," *American Quarterly* 9:1 (Spring 1957), 3–21.

————. "Institutions and the Law of Slavery: Slavery in Capitalist and Non-Capitalist Cultures," *American Quarterly* 9:2 (Summer 1957), 157–79.

Ellis, Edward Sylvester ["Lieut. James H. Randolph"]. *Kit Carson the Guide; or, The Nestor of the Rocky Mountains.* New York: American Novel Publishing Company [1868].

————. ["Capt. L. C. Carleton"]. *Kit Carson the Scout; or, the Knight of the Prairie.* New York: G. Munro, 1872.

————. *Seth Jones.* In Philip Durham, editor. *'Seth Jones' by Edward S. Ellis and 'Deadwood Dick on Deck' by Edward L. Wheeler.* New York: Odyssey Press, 1966.

Ellis, John. *The Social History of the Machine Gun.* New York: Pantheon Books, 1975.

Ellis, Richard N., editor. *The Western American Indian: Case Studies in Tribal History.* Lincoln: University of Nebraska Press, 1972.

Emmons, David M. *Garden in the Grasslands: Boomer Literature of the Central Great Plains.* Lincoln: University of Nebraska Press, 1971.

Everett, Edward. *Orations and Speeches on Various Occasions.* Sixth edition. Boston: Little, Brown, 1860.

Feldberg, Michael. *The Turbulent Era: Riot and Disorder in Jacksonian America.* New York: Oxford University Press, 1980.

Feldman, Burton, and Robert D. Richardson, editors. *The Rise of Modern Mythology, 1680–1860.* Bloomington: Indiana University Press, 1972.

Fender, Stephen. *Plotting the Golden West: American Literature and the Rhetoric of the California Trail.* Cambridge: Cambridge University Press, 1981.

Ferling, John E. *A Wilderness of Miseries: War and Warriors in Early America.* Westport, Conn.: Greenwood Press, 1980.

Fiedler, Leslie A. *Love and Death in the American Novel.* New York: Criterion Books, 1960.

————. *The Return of the Vanishing American.* New York: Stein and Day, 1968.

Filler, Louis, and Allen Guttmann, editors. *The Removal of the Cherokee Nation: Manifest Destiny or National Dishonor?* Lexington, Mass.: D. C. Heath and Company, 1962.

Filson, John. *The Discovery, Settlement, and Present State of Kentucke: and an Essay Towards the Topography, and Natural History of that Important Country: To Which is added, an Appendix, . . .* Wilmington, Del.: James Adams, 1784.

Finerty, John Frederick. *War-Path and Bivouac: The Big Horn and Yellowstone Expedition.* Edited by Milo Milton Quaife. Chicago: R. R. Donnelly, 1955.

Fishlow, Albert. *American Railroads and the Transformation of the Antebellum Economy.* Cambridge, Mass.: Harvard University Press, 1965.

Fite, Emerson D. *Social and Industrial Conditions in the North During The Civil War.* New York: Macmillan, 1910.

Fite, Gilbert M. *The Farmer's Frontier, 1865–1900.* New York: Holt, Rinehart and Winston, 1966.

Fitzgerald, Frances. *Fire in the Lake: The Vietnamese and the Americans in Vietnam.* New York: Vintage Books, 1973.

Fitzhugh, George. *Cannibals All! or, Slaves Without Masters.* Edited by C. Vann Woodward. Cambridge, Mass.: Belknap Press of Harvard University Press, 1960. Originally published Richmond, Va., 1857.

————. *Sociology for the South; or, The Failure of Free Society.* Richmond, Va.: A. Morris [1854].

————. *What Shall Be Done with Free Negroes?* Fredericksburg, Va.: Recorder Job Office, 1851.

Fliegelman, Jay W. *Prodigals and Pilgrims: The American Revolution Against Patriarchal Authority, 1750–1800.* New York: Cambridge University Press, 1982.

Flint, Timothy. *A Biographical Memoir of Daniel Boone: The First Settler of Kentucky; Interspersed with Incidents in the Early Annals of the Country.* Edited by James K. Folsom. New Haven: College and University Press, 1967.

———. *Francis Berrian; or, the Mexican Patriot.* Boston: Cummings, Hilliard and Company, 1826.

Fogel, Robert W. *Railroads and Economic Growth: Essays in Economic History.* Baltimore: Johns Hopkins Press, 1964.

———, and Stanley Engermann. *Time on the Cross: The Economics of American Negro Slavery.* 2 volumes. Boston: Little, Brown, 1974.

Foner, Eric. "Class, Ethnicity, and Radicalism in the Gilded Age: The Land League and Irish America," *Marxist Perspectives* 1:2 (Summer 1978), 6–55.

———. *Free Soil, Free Labor, Free Men: The Ideology of the Republican Party Before the Civil War.* London and New York: Oxford University Press, 1970.

Foner, Philip S. *The Great Labor Uprising of 1877.* New York: Monad Press, 1971.

———. *The History of the Labor Movement in the United States: From the Colonial Period to the Founding of the American Federation of Labor.* Volume 1. New York: International Publishers, New World Paperbacks, 1972.

Foreman, Grant. *Indian Removal: The Emigration of the Five Civilized Tribes of Indians.* Norman: University of Oklahoma Press, 1932.

Frank Leslie's Illustrated Historical Register of the United States Centennial Exposition. New York: Frank Leslie, 1877.

Franklin, Benjamin. *The Autobiography of Benjamin Franklin and Other Writings.* Edited by L. Jesse Lemish. New York: New American Library, 1961.

Franklin, Wayne. *The New World of James Fenimore Cooper.* Chicago: University of Chicago Press, 1982.

Fraser, John. *America and the Patterns of Chivalry.* Cambridge: Cambridge University Press, 1982.

Frederick, James Vincent. *Ben Holladay, the Stagecoach King: A Chapter in the Development of Transcontinental Transportation.* Glendale, Calif.: Arthur H. Clark Company, 1946.

Frederickson, George M. *The Black Image in the White Mind: The Debate over Afro-American Character and Destiny, 1817–1917.* New York: Harper Torchbooks, 1972.

———. *The Inner Civil War: Northern Intellectuals and the Crisis of the Union.* New York: Harper Torchbooks, 1965.

Frémont, John Charles. *Report of the Exploring Expedition of the Rocky Mountains in the Year 1842, and to Oregon and North California in the Years 1843–44.* Washington: Gales and Seaton, 1845.

Friedman, Lawrence I. *Inventors of the Promised Land.* New York: Alfred A. Knopf, 1975.

———. *The White Savage: Racial Fantasies in the Postbellum South.* Englewood Cliffs, N. J.: Prentice-Hall, Inc., Spectrum Books, 1970.

Frisch, Michael. "The Memory of History," *Radical History Review* 25 (1980), 9–26.

Frost, John. *Life of Major General Zachary Taylor; with Notices of the War in New Mexico, California, and in Southern Mexico . . .* New York: D. Appleton and Company, 1874 [1849].

Frost, Lawrence A. *The Court-Martial of General George Armstrong Custer.* Norman: University of Oklahoma Press, 1968.

———. *Custer Legends.* Bowling Green, Ohio: Popular Press, 1983.

———. *General Custer's Libbie.* Seattle: Superior Publishing Company, 1976.

Fry, Joseph Reese. *A Life of Major General Zachary Taylor . . .* Philadelphia: Grigg, Elliot and Company, 1848.

Frye, Northrop. *Anatomy of Criticism: Four Essays.* Princeton: Princeton University Press, 1957.

———. *The Critical Path: An Essay on the Social Context of Literary Criticism.* Bloomington: Indiana University Press, 1973.

———. *The Secular Scripture: A Study of the Structure of Romance.* Cambridge: Harvard University Press, 1976.

Fussell, Edwin. *Frontier: American Literature and the American West.* Princeton: Princeton University Press, 1966.

Gaddy, Jerry J., editor. *Texas in Revolt: Contemporary Newspaper Accounts.* Ft. Collins, Colo.: The Old Army Press, 1973.

Gallman, Robert E., and Ralph V. Anderson. "Slaves as Fixed Capital: Slave Labor and Southern Economic Development," *Journal of American History* 64:1 (January 1977), 24–46.

Gambill, Edward L. *Conservative Ordeal: Northern Democrats and Reconstruction.* Ames: Iowa State University Press, 1981.

"Ganilh, Anthony" [A. T. Myrthe]. *Ambrosio de Letinez; or, the First Texan Novel.* New York: C. Francis and Company [1842].

Gans, Herbert J. *Popular Culture and High Culture: An Analysis and Evaluation of Taste.* New York: Basic Books, 1974.

Gardiner, Clinton Harvey. *William Hickling Prescott: A Biography.* Austin: University of Texas Press, 1969.

Gates, Paul Wallace. *Fifty Million Acres: Conflicts Over Kansas Land Policy, 1854–1890.* New York: Atherton Press, Atheling Books, 1966.

———. *The Illinois Central Railroad and Its Colonization Work.* Cambridge, Mass.: Harvard University Press, 1934.

Geertz, Clifford. *The Interpretation of Cultures: Selected Essays.* New York: Basic Books, 1973.

Genovese, Eugene D. *The Political Economy of Slavery: Studies in the Economy and Society of the Slave South.* New York: Vintage Books, 1967.

———. *Roll Jordan, Roll: The World the Slaves Made.* New York: Pantheon Books, 1974.

———. *The World the Slaveholders Made: Two Essays in Interpretation.* New York: Vintage Books, 1971.

———, and Elizabeth Fox-Genovese. "Presidential Address: the Slave Economy in Political Perspective," *Journal of American History* 66:1 (June 1979), 7–23.

Gilpin, William. *The Central Gold Region: The Grain Pastoral and Gold Regions of North America. With Some New Views of Its Physical Geography; and Observations on the Pacific Railroad.* Philadelphia: Suwer, Barnes and Company, 1860.

———. *The Mission of the North American People: Geographical, Social, and Political.* Edited by Wilson O. Clough. New York: Da Capo Press, 1974. Reprint of Philadelphia, 1874 edition.

Gitlin, Todd. *The Whole World Is Watching: Mass Media in the Making and Unmaking of the New Left.* Berkeley: University of California Press, 1980.

Glassberg, David. "Restoring a Forgotten Childhood: American Play and the Progressive Era's Elizabethan Past," *American Quarterly* 32:4 (Fall 1980), 351–68.

Glassie, Henry. "Meaningful Things and Appropriate Myths: The Artifact's Place in American Studies," *Prospects* 3 (1977), 1–51.

Godkin, E[dwin] L[awrence]. *Problems of Modern Democracy: Political and Economic Essays.* New York: Charles Scribner's Sons, 1898.

———. *Reflections and Comments, 1865–1895.* New York: Charles Scribner's Sons, 1895.

———. *Unforeseen Tendencies of Democracy.* Boston: Houghton, Mifflin, 1898.

Goetzmann, William H. *Exploration and Empire: The Explorer and the Scientist in the Winning of the American West.* New York: Vintage Books, 1966.

———. "Mountain Man Stereotypes: A Note," *Western Historical Quarterly* 6:3 (July 1975), 295–302.

———. *When the Eagle Screamed: The Romantic Horizon in American Diplomacy, 1800–1860.* New York: John Wiley and Sons, 1966.

Goldstein, Joseph, Burke Marshall, and Jack Schwartz, compilers. *The My-Lai Massacre and Its Cover-up: Beyond the Reach of Law?* New York: Free Press, 1976.

Goodwyn, Lawrence. *Democratic Promise: The Populist Moment in America.* New York: Oxford University Press, 1976.

Gossett, Thomas F. *Race: The History of an Idea in America.* New York: Schocken Books, 1965.

Graham, Daniel. *High Frontier: A Strategy for National Survival.* New York: Pinnacle Books, 1981.

Graham, W. A. *The Custer Myth: A Sourcebook of Custeriana.* New York: Bonanza Books, 1963.

Grant, Michael. *Roman Myths.* New York: Charles Scribner's Sons, 1971.

Gray, John S. *Centennial Campaign: The Sioux War of 1876.* Ft. Collins, Colo.: The Old Army Press, 1976.

"The Great Stevens Mine of West Argentine District," Georgetown, Colo. *Courier,* January 9, 1903, p. 1.

Green, Martin. *Dreams of Adventure and Deeds of Empire.* New York: Basic Books, 1979.

Greenberg, Dolores. *Financiers and Railroads, 1869–1889: A Study of Morton, Bliss and Company.* Newark, Del.: University of Delaware Press, 1980.

Greenhow, Robert. *History of Oregon and California and the Other Territories of the Northwest Coast of North America . . .* Fourth edition. Boston: Freeman and Bulles, 1847.

Greenleaf, William, editor. *American Economic Development Since 1860.* New York: Harper Torchbooks, 1968.

Gressley, Gene M. *West By East: The American West in the Gilded Age.* Charles Redd Monographs in Western History, No. 1. Provo: Brigham Young University Press, 1972.

Gribben, Allen. *Mark Twain's Library: A Reconstruction.* 2 volumes. Boston: G. K. Hall, 1980.

Grinnell, George Bird. *The Passing of the Great West: Selected Papers of George Bird Grinnell.* Edited by John F. Reiger. New York: Charles Scribner's Sons, 1972.

Grodinsky, Julius. *Transcontinental Railway Strategy, 1869–1893: A Study of Businessmen.* Philadelphia: University of Pennsylvania Press, 1962.

Grossman, James. *James Fenimore Cooper.* New York: W. Sloane Associates, 1949.

Gutman, Herbert G. *The Black Family in Slavery and Freedom, 1750–1925.* New York: Pantheon Books, 1976.

————. *Slavery and the Numbers Game: A Critique of "Time on the Cross."* Urbana: University of Illinois Press, 1975.

————. "The Tompkins Square 'Riot' in New York City on January 13, 1874: A Re-Examination of Its Causes and Aftermath," *Labor History* 6:1 (Winter 1965), 44–70.

————. *Work, Culture and Society in Industrializing America: Essays in American Working Class and Social History.* New York: Alfred A. Knopf, 1976.

Haberly, David T. "Women and Indians: *The Last of the Mohicans* and the Captivity Tradition," *American Quarterly* 28:4 (Fall 1976), 431–43.

Hall, James. *The Harpe's Head; a Legend of Kentucky.* Philadelphia: Key and Biddle, 1833.

————. *Legends of the West: Sketches Illustrative of the Habits, Occupations, Privations, Adventures, and Spirits of the Pioneers of the West.* Cincinnati: Robert Clarke, 1869.

————. *Letters from the West: Containing Sketches of Scenery, Manners, and Customs; and Anecdotes Connected with the First Settlements of the Western Sections of the United States.* London: Henry Colburn, 1828.

————. *Memoir of the Public Services of William Henry Harrison of Ohio.* Philadelphia: Key and Biddle, 1836.

————. *Sketches of History, Life, and Manners in the West.* 2 volumes. Philadelphia: Harrison Hall [1835].

Haller, John S. and Robin M. *The Physician and Sexuality in Victorian America.* Urbana: University of Illinois Press, 1974.

Halyard, Harry. *The Chieftain of Churubusco; or, The Spectre of the Cathedral: A Romance of the Mexican War.* Boston: F. Gleason, Flag of Our Union, 1848.

————. *The Heroine of Tampico; or, Wildfire the Wanderer.* Boston: F. Gleason, Flag of Our Union, 1847.

————. *The Mexican Spy; or, The Pride of Buena Vista, A Tale of the Mexican War.* Boston: F. Gleason, Flag of Our Union, 1848.

Hancock, W[infield] S[cott]. *Correspondence Between General W. T. Sherman, U. S. Army, and Major General W. S. Hancock.* Minneapolis: [n.p.], 1871.

————. *Reports of Major-General W. S. Hancock upon Indian Affairs.* Washington: [n.p.], [1867].

[Harbaugh, Thomas]. *Roving Rifle, Custer's Little Scout; or, Oath-Bound to Custer.* Beadle's Dime Library, No. 96. New York: Beadle and Adams, 1883.

Harnsberger, John L. "Land Speculation, Promotion and Failure: The Northern Pacific Railroad, 1870–1873," *Journal of the West* 9:1 (January 1970), 33–45.

Harrison, Jonathan B. *Certain Dangerous Tendencies in American Life.* Boston: Houghton, Osgood and Company, 1880.

————. *The Latest Studies on Indian Reservations.* Philadelphia: Indian Rights Association, 1887.

Hart, James D. *The Popular Book: A History of America's Literary Taste.* Berkeley: University of California Press, 1963.

Hassler, Warren W., Jr. *George Brinton McClellan: Shield of the Union.* Baton Rouge: Louisiana State University Press, 1957.

[Hay, John]. *The Breadwinners.* Edited by Charles Vandersee. New Haven: College and University Press, 1973.

Hayne, Barry. "Yankee in the Patriarchy: T. B. Thorpe's Reply to *Uncle Tom's Cabin*," *American Quarterly* 20:2, Pt. 1 (Summer 1968), 180–95.

Hazen, William B. "The Great Middle Region of the United States, and Its Limited Space of Arable Land," *North American Review* 120 (January 1875), 1–34.

Headley, Joel Tyler. *Great Riots of New York, 1712–1873.* New York: E. B. Treat, 1873.

————. *The Lives of Winfield Scott and Andrew Jackson.* New York: Charles Scribner's, 1852.

————. *Pen and Pencil Sketches of the Great Riots: An Illustrated History of the Railroad and Other Great Riots of New York.* New York: E. B. Trent, 1877.

Heale, M. J. "The Role of the Frontier in Jacksonian Politics: David Crockett and the Myth of the Self-Made Man," *Western Historical Quarterly* 4:4 (October 1973), 405–24.

Heard, J. Norman. *White into Red: A Study of Assimilation of White Persons Captured by Indians.* Metuchen, N. J.: Scarecrow Press, 1973.

Hedges, William L. *Washington Irving: An American Study, 1802–1832.* Baltimore: Johns Hopkins Press, 1965.

Hemingway, Ernest. *Across the River and Into the Trees.* New York: Charles Scribner's Sons, 1950.

————. *For Whom the Bell Tolls.* New York: Charles Scribner's Sons, 1940.

————. *Islands in the Stream.* New York: Charles Scribner's Sons, 1920.

————, editor. *Men At War.* New York: Berkeley Publishing Company, 1960.

Henretta, James A. "Social History as Lived and Written," *American Historical Review* 84:5 (December 1979), 1293–1322.

Herr, Michael. *Dispatches.* New York: Alfred A. Knopf, 1977.

Hibbard, George B. *Land Department of the Northern Pacific Railroad Company: Bureau of Immigration for Soldiers and Sailors.* [St. Paul, Minn.]: [Northern Pacific Railroad Company], [1872].

Hindus, Michael Stephen. *Prison and Plantation: Crime, Justice and Authority in Massachusetts and South Carolina, 1767–1878.* Chapel Hill: University of North Carolina Press, 1980.

Hirshson, Stanley P. *Grenville M. Dodge: Soldier, Politician, Railroad Pioneer.* Bloomington: Indiana University Press, 1967.

Hobsbawm, Eric J. *The Age of Capital, 1848–1875.* New York: New American Library, 1975.

Hodgson, Godfrey. *America in Our Time: From World War II to Nixon, What Happened and Why.* New York: Vintage Books, 1978.

Hofstader, Richard. *The American Political Tradition and the Men Who Made It.* New York: Vintage Books, 1974.

————. *The Progressive Historians: Turner, Parrington and Beard.* New York: Alfred A. Knopf, 1968.

Hoig, Stan. *The Battle of the Washita: The Sheridan-Custer Indian Campaign of 1867–1869.* Garden City, N.Y.: Doubleday, 1976.

————. *The Sand Creek Massacre.* Norman: University of Oklahoma Press, 1961.

Holladay, Ben. *Spoilations Committed by Indians . . .* New York: C. Vogt, 1872.

Hollister, George H. *Mount Hope; or, Philip, King of the Wampanoags, An Historical Romance.* New York: Harper and Brothers, 1851.

Hooper, Johnson Jones. *Adventures of Captain Simon Suggs, Late of the Tallapoosa Volunteers; Together with "Taking the Census" and Other Alabama Sketches.* Philadelphia: T. B. Peterson, 1848.

Horsman, Reginald. *The Frontier in the Formative Years, 1776–1815.* New York: Holt, Rinehart and Winston, 1970.

———. *Race and Manifest Destiny: The Origins of American Racial Anglo-Saxonism.* Cambridge, Mass.: Harvard University Press, 1981.

———. "Science, Racism and the American Indian in the Mid-Nineteenth Century," *American Quarterly* 27:2 (May 1975), 152–68.

Horwitz, Richard P. "Architecture and Culture: The Meaning of the Lowell Boarding House," *American Quarterly* 25:1 (March 1973), 83–107.

House, Kate Seymour. *Cooper's Americans.* Columbus: Ohio State University Press, 1966.

Houston, Sam. *The Autobiography of Sam Houston.* Edited by Donald Day and Harry Herbert Ullom. Norman: University of Oklahoma Press, 1954.

Howard, H. R. *The History of Virgil A. Stewart, and His Adventures in Capturing and Exposing the "Great Western Land Pirate" and His Gang, in Connexion with the Evidence* . . . New York: Harper and Brothers, 1836.

———. *The Life and Adventures of John A. Murrell, the Great Western Land Pirate.* New York: H. Long and Brother, 1847.

Howard, Hamilton Gay. *Civil War Echoes: Character Sketches and State Secrets.* Washington: Howard Publishing, 1907.

Howard, James H. *The Warrior Who Killed Custer: The Personal Narrative of Chief Joseph White Bull.* Lincoln: University of Nebraska Press, 1968.

Howells, William Dean. *A Hazard of New Fortunes.* New York: Boni, Liveright, 1889.

———. *The Rise of Silas Lapham.* Norton Critical Edition. Edited by Don Cook. New York: W. W. Norton and Company, 1982.

Hugins, Walter. "American History in Comparative Perspective," *Journal of American Studies* 11:1 (April 1977), 27–44.

———. *Jacksonian Democracy and the Working Class: A Study of the Workingmen's Movement, 1829–1837.* Stanford: Stanford University Press, 1960.

Hume, Richard L. "Carpetbaggers in the Reconstruction South: A Group Portrait of Outside Whites in the 'Black and Tan' Constitutional Conventions," *Journal of American History* 44:2 (September 1977), 313–30.

Hunt, Frazier. *Custer, The Last of the Cavaliers.* New York: Cosmopolitan Book Corp., 1928.

Hunt, George T. *The Wars of the Iroquois: A Study in Inter-Tribal Relations.* Madison: University of Wisconsin Press, 1940.

Hunter, John Dunn. *Memoirs of a Captivity among the Indians of North America, From Childhood to the Age of Nineteen* . . . London: Longman, Hurst, Orme, and Brown, 1823.

Hurtado, Albert L. " 'Hardly a Farm House—a Kitchen Without Them': Indian and White Households on the California Borderland Frontier in 1860," *Western Historical Quarterly* 13:3 (July 1982), 245–70.

Hutton, Paul A. "From the Little Big Horn to Little Big Man: The Changing Image of a Hero in Popular Culture," *Western Historical Quarterly* 7:1 (January 1976), 19–46.

Inge, M. Thomas, editor. *The Frontier Humorists: Critical Views.* Hamden, Conn.: Archon Books, 1975.

Ingham, John N. "Rags to Riches Revisited: The Effect of City Size and Related Factors on the Recruitment of Business Leaders," *Journal of American History* 62:3 (December 1976), 615–37.

Ingraham, J. H. *The Texan Ranger; or, The Maid of Matamoros, A Tale of the Mexican War.* New York: Williams Brothers, 1847.

Irving, Washington. *Astoria; or, Enterprise Beyond the Rocky Mountains.* The Works of Washington Irving, volume 7. New York: G. P. Putnam's Sons, 1868.

———. *The Rocky Mountains; or, Scenes, Incidents, and Adventures in the Far West* . . . 2 volumes. Philadelphia: Carey, Lea and Blanchard, 1837. Retitled *Adventures of Captain Bonneville* in modern editions.

Jackson, Donald. *Custer's Gold: The United States Cavalry Expedition of 1874.* New Haven: Yale University Press, 1966.

Jackson, John Brinckerhoff. *American Space: The Centennial Years, 1865–1876.* New York: W. W. Norton and Company, 1972.

Jacob, François. *The Possible and the Actual.* Seattle: University of Washington Press, 1982.

Jacobs, Wilbur R. *Dispossessing the American Indian: Indians and Whites on the Colonial Frontier.* New York: Charles Scribner's Sons, 1972.

———. "The Indian and the Frontier in American History—A Need for Revision," *Western Historical Quarterly* 4:1 (January 1973), 43–56.

Jaher, Frederic C., editor. *The Age of Industrialism in America: Essays in Social Structure and Cultural Values.* New York: Free Press, 1968.

James Marquis. *The Raven: A Biography of Sam Houston.* Atlanta: Berg, 1970.

Jameson, Frederic. *The Political Unconscious: Narrative as a Socially Symbolic Act.* Ithaca: Cornell University Press, 1981.

Jarrell, Hampton M. *Wade Hampton and the Negro: The Road Not Taken.* Columbia: University of South Carolina Press, 1949.

Jarvie, I. C. *Movies and Society.* New York: Basic Books, 1970.

Jefferson, Thomas. *Notes on Virginia.* New York: Harper Torchbooks, 1964. From the 1801 edition.

Jellinek, Frank. *The Paris Commune of 1871.* New York: Grosset and Dunlap, Universal Library, 1965.

Jenkins, Alan. *The Social Theory of Claude Lévi-Strauss.* New York: St. Martin's Press, 1979.

Jenney, Walter. *The Mineral Wealth, Climate and Rainfall, and Natural Resources of the Black Hills of Dakota.* Washington: Government Printing Office, 1876.

Jennings, Francis. *The Invasion of America: Indians, Colonialism, and the Cant of Conquest.* Chapel Hill: University of North Carolina Press, 1975.

Jewett, Robert, and John Shelton Lawrence. *The American Monomyth.* Garden City, N. Y.: Doubleday, Anchor Books, 1977.

Johannsen, Albert. *The House of Beadle and Adams, and Its Dime and Nickel Novels: The Study of a Vanished Literature.* 3 volumes. Norman: University of Oklahoma Press, 1950–62.

Johannsen, Robert W., editor. *The Lincoln-Douglas Debates of 1858.* New York: Oxford University Press, 1965.

Johnson, Michael P. *Toward a Patriarchal Republic: The Secession of Georgia.* Baton Rouge: Louisiana State University Press, 1977.

Jones, Daryl. *The Dime Novel Western.* Bowling Green, Ohio: Popular Press, 1978.

Jones, Howard Mumford. *The Age of Energy: Varieties of American Experience, 1865–1915.* New York: Viking Press, 1973.

———. *O Strange New World: American Culture, the Formative Years.* New York: Viking Press, 1964.

Jones, J. B. *Wild Western Scenes: A Narrative of Adventures in the Western Wilderness . . .* Philadelphia: J. B. Lippincott, 1869.

Jordan, Winthrop D. *White Over Black: American Attitudes Towards the Negro, 1550–1812.* Baltimore: Penguin Books, 1969.

Josephson, Matthew. *The Robber Barons: The Great American Capitalists, 1861–1901.* New York: Harcourt, Brace and World, Harvest Books, 1962.

Jowett, Garth S. "The Emergence of the Mass Society: The Standardization of American Culture, 1830–1920," *Prospects* 7 (1983), 207–28.

———. *Film, The Democratic Art: A Social History of the American Film.* Boston: Little, Brown, 1976.

Jung, Carl Gustav. *Psyche and Symbol: A Selection from the Writings of C. G. Jung.* Edited by Violet S. de Laszlo. Garden City, N. Y.: Doubleday, Anchor Books, 1958.

Kaplan, Justin. *Mr. Clemens and Mark Twain.* New York: Pocket Books, 1968.

Karnes, Thomas L. *The Failure of Union: Central America, 1824–1960.* Chapel Hill: University of North Carolina Press, 1961.

———. *William Gilpin: Western Nationalist.* Austin: University of Texas Press, 1970.

Kasson, John F. *Civilizing the Machine: Technology and Republican Values in America, 1776–1900.* New York: Grossman, 1976.

Kasson, Joy S. "The Voyage of Life: Thomas Cole and Romantic Disillusionment," *American Quarterly* 27:1 (March 1975), 42–56.

Katz, Irving. *August Belmont: A Political Biography.* New York: Columbia University Press, 1968.

Keim, De Benneville Randolph. *Sheridan's Troopers on the Border: A Winter Campaign on the Plains.* Philadelphia: Claxton, Remsen and Haffelfinger, 1870.

Keller, Morton. *Affairs of State: Public Life in Late Nineteenth Century America.* Cambridge, Mass.: Belknap Press of Harvard University Press, 1977.

Kemble, C. Robert. *The Image of the Army Officer in America: Background for Current Views.* Westport, Conn.: Greenwood Press, 1973.

Kendall, George Wilkins. *Narrative of the Texan Santa Fe Expedition.* Edited by Milo Milton Quaife. Chicago: R. R. Donnelley, 1929.

Kennedy, John Pendleton. *Horse-Shoe Robinson: A Tale of the Tory Ascendancy.* Philadelphia: Carey, Lea, and Blanchard, 1836.

————. *Swallow Barn; or, A Sojourn in the Old Dominion.* New York: G. P. Putnam, 1851.

Kidd, J. H. *Personal Recollections of a Cavalryman.* Grand Rapids, Mich.: The Black Letter Press, 1969. Reprint of 1908 edition.

Kinsley, D[avid] A. *Favor the Bold: Custer in the Civil War.* New York: Holt, Rinehart and Winston, 1968.

————. *Favor the Bold: Custer the Indian Fighter.* New York: Holt, Rinehart and Winston, 1968.

Knox, Robert. *Races of Men; A Fragment.* Philadelphia: Lea and Blanchard, 1850.

Kolodny, Annette. *The Lay of the Land: Metaphor as Experience and History in American Life and Letters.* Chapel Hill: University of North Carolina Press, 1975.

————. "Turning the Lens on the 'Panther Captivity': A Feminist Exercise in Practical Criticism," *Critical Inquiry* 8:2 (Winter 1981), 329–45.

Kousser, J. Morgan, and James H. McPherson, editors. *Region, Race and Reconstruction: Essays in Honor of C. Vann Woodward.* New York: Oxford University Press, 1982.

Krause, Herbert, and Gary D. Olson. *Custer's Prelude to Glory: A Newspaper Accounting of Custer's 1874 Expedition to the Black Hills.* Sioux Falls, S. D.: Brevet Press, 1974.

Kuklik, Bruce. "Myth and Symbol in American Studies," *American Quarterly* 24:4 (October 1972), 435–50.

Kuper, Leo. *Race, Class and Power: Ideology and Change in Plural Societies.* London: Duckworth, 1974.

Lamar, Howard R. *Dakota Territory, 1861–1889: A Study of Frontier Politics.* New Haven: Yale University Press, 1956.

Larcom, Lucy. *An Idyl of Work.* Westport, Conn.: Greenwood Press, 1970. Reprint of 1875 edition.

Laurie, Bruce. *Working People of Philadelphia, 1800–1850.* Philadelphia: Temple University Press, 1980.

Lawrence, D[avid] H[erbert]. *Studies in Classic American Literature.* New York: Viking Press, 1961.

Leach, Douglas Edward. *Flintlock and Tomahawk: New England in King Philip's War.* New York: Macmillan, 1958.

Leary, Lewis Gaston. *Washington Irving.* Minneapolis: University of Minnesota Press, 1963.

Leckie, William H. *The Military Conquest of the Southern Plains.* Norman: University of Oklahoma Press, 1963.

Lenz, Guenter H. "American Studies—Beyond the Crisis?: Recent Redefinitions and the Meaning of Theory, History and Practical Criticism," *Prospects* 7 (1983), 53–113.

Leonard, Thomas C. *Above the Battle: War-Making in America from Appomattox to Versailles.* New York: Oxford University Press, 1977.

Leslie, Anita. *The Remarkable Mister Jerome.* New York: Holt, Rinehart and Winston, 1954.

[Lester, Charles Edwards]. *The Life of Sam Houston, the Hunter, Patriot, and Statesman of Texas; the Only Authentic Memoir of Him Ever Published.* Philadelphia: John E. Potter, 1867.

Levin, David. *History as Romantic Art: Bancroft, Prescott, Motley and Parkman.* New York: Harcourt, Brace and World, Harbinger Books, 1963.

Levine, Lawrence. *Black Culture and Black Consciousness: Afro-American Folk Thought from Slavery to Freedom*. New York: Oxford University Press, 1977.

Lévi-Strauss, Claude. *Myth and Meaning: Five Talks for Radio*. Toronto: University of Toronto Press, 1978.

————. *Structural Anthropology*. 2 volumes. Translated by Claire Jacobson and Brooke Grundfest Schoepf. New York: Basic Books, 1964–76.

Lewis, R. W. B. *The American Adam: Innocence, Tragedy, and Tradition in the Nineteenth Century*. Chicago: University of Chicago Press, 1955.

Lewis, Robert. "Frontier and Civilization in the Thought of Frederick Law Olmsted," *American Quarterly* 29:4 (Fall 1977), 385–402.

Lewis, Ronald L. *Coal, Iron and Slaves: Industrial Slavery in Maryland and Virginia*. Westport, Conn.: Greenwood Press, 1979.

Lewis, Thomas E. "Notes Towards a Theory of the Referent," *PMLA* 94:3 (May 1979), 459–75.

Lewy, Guenter. *America in Vietnam*. New York: Oxford University Press, 1978.

Libby, Orin G., editor. *The Arikara Narrative of the Campaign Against the Hostile Dakotas, June, 1876*. Bismarck, N. D.: [n.p.], 1920.

The Life, Trial and Execution of Captain John Brown: Being a Full Account of the Attempted Insurrection at Harper's Ferry, Va. New York: Robert M. DeWitt, 1859.

Lifton, Robert J. *Home from the War: Vietnam Veterans, Neither Victims nor Executioners*. New York: Simon and Schuster, Touchstone Books, 1973.

Lincoln, Abraham. *The Collected Works*. Volume 3. Edited by Roy P. Basler. New Brunswick, N. J.: Rutgers University Press, 1953–55.

Lippard, George. *'Bel of Prairie Eden; A Romance of Mexico*. Boston: Hotchkiss and Company, 1848.

————. *Legends of Mexico*. Philadelphia: T. B. Peterson, 1847.

————. *The Monks of Monk Hall*. Edited by Leslie Fiedler. New York: Odyssey Press, 1970. Originally published in Philadelphia, 1844, as *The Quaker City*.

————. *New York: Its Upper Ten and Lower Million*. Cincinnati: H. M. Rulison, 1853.

Lipset, Seymour Martin, and Reinhard Bendix. *Social Mobility in Industrial Society*. Berkeley: University of Cailfornia Press, 1959.

Litwack, Leon F. *Been in the Storm So Long: The Aftermath of Slavery*. New York: Alfred A. Knopf, 1979.

Livermore, A[thiel] A[bbot]. *The War with Mexico Reviewed*. Boston: The American Peace Society, 1849.

[Llewellynn, H.]. *Custer's Last Charge; or, The Ravine of Death*. [n.p.]: Champion Novels Number 39, 1876.

Lockridge, Kenneth A. *Settlement and Unsettlement in Early America: The Crisis of Political Legitimacy before the Revolution*. New York: Cambridge University Press, 1981.

[Longstreet, Augustus Baldwin]. *Georgia Scenes; Character and Incidents &c., in the First Half Century of the Republic*. Augusta, Ga.: [n.p.], 1835.

Loudon, Archibald. *A Selection of Some of the Most Interesting Narratives of Outrages Committed by the Indians in Their Wars on the White People*. Carlisle, Pa.: A. Loudon, 1808.

Lowitt, Richard. *A Merchant Prince of the Nineteenth Century: William E. Dodge*. New York: Columbia University Press, 1954.

Lucia, Ellis. *Ben Holladay: Giant of the Old West*. New York: Hastings House [1959].

Luther, Tal. *Custer High Spots: A Guide to Custer Literature*. Ft. Collins, Colo.: The Old Army Press, 1972.

Lyman, Theodore. *Meade's Headquarters, 1863–1865: Letters of Colonel Theodore Lyman from the Wilderness to Appomattox*. Edited by George R. Agassiz. Boston: Massachusetts Historical Society, 1922.

[McCabe, James Dabney]. "Edward Winslow Martin." *The History of the Great Riots . . . Together with a Full History of the Mollie Maguires*. New York: Augustus M. Kelley, 1971. Reprint of New York, 1877 edition.

McCabe, James Dabney. *The Illustrated History of the Centennial Exposition*. Philadelphia: The National Publishing Company, 1876.

McCarthy, Michael. "Africa and the American West," *Journal of American Studies* 11:2 (August 1977), 187–202.

McClellan, George Brinton. *Army of the Potomac: General McClellan's Report of Operations While Under His Command.* . . . New York: [n.p.], 1864.

——. *McClellan's Own Story.* New York: C. L. Webster and Company, 1887.

McCoy, A. D. *Thoughts on Labor in the South, Past, Present, and Future.* New Orleans: Blelock and Company, 1865.

McDermott, John Francis. *The Frontier Re-examined.* Urbana: University of Illinois Press, 1967.

"MacDonald, Ross" [Kenneth Miller]. *The Zebra-Striped Hearse.* New York: Bantam Books, 1964.

McFeely, William S. *Grant: A Biography.* New York: W. W. Norton and Company, 1981.

——. *Yankee Stepfather: General O. O. Howard and the Freedmen.* New Haven: Yale University Press, 1968.

MacGregor, Alan Leander. "Tammany: The Indian as Rhetorical Surrogate," *American Quarterly* 35:4 (Fall 1983), 391–407.

McJimsey, George T. *Genteel Partisan: Manton Marble, 1834–1917.* Ames: Iowa State University Press, 1971.

McKitrick, Eric L., editor. *Slavery Defended: The Views of the Old South.* Englewood Cliffs, N. J.: Prentice-Hall, 1963.

McNeill, William H. "The Care and Repair of Public Myth," *Foreign Affairs* 61:1 (Fall 1982), 1–13.

McPherson, James M. *The Struggle for Equality: Abolitionists and the Negro in the Civil War and Reconstruction.* Princeton: Princeton University Press, 1964.

McWilliams, John P. *Political Justice in a Republic: James Fenimore Cooper's America.* Berkeley: University of California Press, 1972.

Maddox, Jack P. "Pro-Slavery Millennialism: Social Eschatology in Antebellum Southern Calvinism," *American Quarterly* 31:1 (Spring 1979), 46–62.

Magdol, Edward. *A Right to the Land: Essays on the Freedmen's Community.* Westport, Conn.: Greenwood Press, 1977.

Main, Jackson Turner. *The Social Structure of Revolutionary America.* Princeton: Princeton University Press, 1965.

Malone, Dumas. *Jefferson the President, the First Term, 1801–1805.* Jefferson and His Times, Volume 4. Boston: Little, Brown, 1948–81.

Mandle, Jay R. "The Economic Underdevelopment of the Postbellum South," *Marxist Perspectives* 1:4 (Winter 1978), 68–79.

Mansfield, Edward Deering. *The Life of General Winfield Scott.* New York: A. S. Barnes and Company, 1846.

——. *Life and Services of General Winfield Scott* . . . New York: A. S. Barnes and Company, 1852.

——. *The Mexican War: A History of Its Origin and a Detailed Account of the Victories which Terminated in the Surrender of the Capital* . . . New York: A. S. Barnes and Company, 1848.

Mardock, Robert Winston. *The Reformers and the American Indian.* Columbia: University of Missouri Press, 1971.

Marquis, Thomas B. *Keep the Last Bullet for Yourself: The True Story of Custer's Last Stand.* New York: Two Continents/Reference Publications, 1976.

——. *She Watched Custer's Last Stand.* Hardin, Mont.: for the author, 1933.

——. *Which Indian Killed Custer?* Hardin, Mont.: for the author, 1933.

Marshall, S. L. A. *Battles in the Monsoon: Campaigning in the Central Highlands, South Vietnam, Summer 1966.* New York: William Morrow and Company, Apollo Editions, 1967.

——. *Crimsoned Prairie: The Indian Wars on the Great Plains.* New York: Charles Scribner's Sons, 1972.

Marx, Karl. "The Eighteenth Brumaire of Louis Bonaparte," in Karl Marx and Frederick Engels, *Selected Works.* New York: International Publishers, 1968, pp. 95–179.

——, and Frederick Engels. *Letters to Americans, 1848–1895: A Selection.* Translated by Leonard E. Mins. New York: International Publishers, 1953.

——, and ——. *On America and the Civil War.* The Karl Marx Library, volume 2. Edited by Saul K. Padover. New York: McGraw-Hill, 1972.

Marx, Leo. *The Machine in the Garden: Technology and the Pastoral Ideal in America.* New York: Oxford University Press, 1964.

Mathews, Cornelius. *Big Abel and the Little Manhattan*. New York: Wiley and Putnam, 1845.

Mathiessen, F. P. *American Renaissance: Art and Expression in the Age of Emerson and Whitman*. New York: Oxford University Press, 1941.

May, Robert E. *The Southern Dream of a Caribbean Empire, 1854–1861*. Baton Rouge: Louisiana State University Press, 1973.

Melville, Herman. *The Confidence-Man; His Masquerade*. Norton Critical Edition. Edited by Hershel Parker. New York: W. W. Norton and Company, 1971.

Merington, Marguerite. *The Custer Story: The Life and Intimate Letters of George A. Custer and His Wife Elizabeth*. New York: Devin-Adair, 1950.

Merk, Frederick. *Manifest Destiny and Mission in American History: A Reinterpretation*. New York: Vintage Books, 1963.

Merrill, Harwood, F., editor. *Classics in Management*. New York: American Management Association, 1960.

Merrill, Michael. "Raymond Williams and the Theory of English Marxism," *Radical History Review* 19 (1978–79), 9–32.

Merritt, Raymond H. *Engineering in American Society, 1850–1875*. Lexington: University Press of Kentucky, 1969.

Milder, Robert. "*The Last of the Mohicans* and the New World Fall," *American Literature* 52:3 (November 1980), 407–29.

Miles, Henry A. *Lowell, As It Was, and As It Is*. New York: Arno Press, 1972. Reprint of 1845 edition.

Miller, David and Jerome O. Steffen, editors. *The Frontier: Comparative Studies*. Norman: University of Oklahoma Press, 1977.

Miller, Douglas T. *The Birth of Modern America, 1820–1850*. New York: Pegasus Books, 1970.

Miller, Perry. *Errand into the Wilderness*. New York: Harper Torchbooks, 1956.

Miller, Stuart Creighton. *Benevolent Assimilation: The American Conquest of the Philippines, 1899–1903*. New Haven: Yale University Press, 1982.

Mills, Gary B. "Miscegenation and the Free Negro in Antebellum 'Anglo' Alabama: A Re-Examination of Southern Race Relations," *Journal of American History* 68:1 (June 1981), 16–34.

Mink, Louis O. "History and Fiction as Modes of Comprehension," *New Literary History* 1:3 (Spring 1970), 541–58.

Monaghan, Jay. *The Civil War on the Western Border, 1854–1865*. Boston: Little, Brown, 1955.

———. *Custer: The Life of General George Armstrong Custer*. Lincoln: University of Nebraska Press, Bison Books, 1959.

Monette, John W. *History of the Discovery of the Valley of the Mississippi . . .* 2 volumes. New York: Harper and Brothers, 1848.

Monkkonen, Eric H. *The Dangerous Class: Crime and Poverty in Columbus, Ohio, 1860–1885*. Cambridge, Mass.: Harvard University Press, 1975.

———. "A Disorderly People? Urban Order in the Nineteenth and Twentieth Centuries," *Journal of American History* 68:3 (December 1981), 539–59.

Montgomery, David. *Beyond Equality: Labor and the Radical Republicans, 1862–1872*. New York: Vintage Books, 1967.

———. *Worker's Control in America: Studies in the History of Work, Technology and Labor Struggles*. Cambridge: Cambridge University Press, 1980.

Montgomery, Henry. *The Life of Major General Zachary Taylor, Twelfth President of the United States*. Auburn [N. Y.]: Derby, Miller and Company, 1850.

Moore, Arthur K. *The Frontier Mind: A Cultural Analysis of the Kentucky Frontiersman*. Lexington: University Press of Kentucky, 1957.

Morgan, Edmund S. *American Slavery, American Freedom: The Ordeal of Colonial Virginia*. New York: W. W. Norton and Company, 1975.

Morgan, H. Wayne. *The Gilded Age: A Reappraisal*. Syracuse: Syracuse University Press, 1963.

Morison, Samuel Eliot, et al. *The Struggle for Guadalcanal, August 1942–February 1943: History of United States Naval Operations in World War II*. Volume 5. Boston: Litle, Brown, 1949.

Mott, Frank Luther. *American Journalism: A History of Newspapers in the United States Through 250 Years, 1690–1940.* New York: Macmillan, 1941.

————. *Golden Multitudes: The Story of Best-Sellers in the United States.* New York: Macmillan, 1947.

————. *A History of American Magazines.* 5 volumes. Cambridge, Mass.: Harvard University Press, 1930–68.

Murdock, Eugene Converse. *Patriotism Limited, 1862–1865: The Civil War Draft and the Bounty System.* Kent, Ohio: Kent State University Press, 1967.

Mushkat, Jerome. *The Reconstruction of the New York Democracy, 1861–1874.* East Brunswick, N. J.: Fairleigh Dickinson University Press, 1981.

Myrick, Herbert. *Cache La Poudre: The Romance of a Tenderfoot in the Days of Custer.* New York: Orange Judd Company, 1905.

Nelson, Keith L., and Spencer C. Olin, Jr. *Why War? Ideology, Theory and History.* Berkeley: University of California Press, 1979.

Nevins, Allan. *Frémont: Pathmarker of the West.* New York: D. Appleton-Century Company, 1939.

[Newhall, Frederic C.]. *With Sheridan in Lee's Last Campaign.* Philadelphia: J. B. Lippincott, 1866.

New York State Historical Association. *James Fenimore Cooper: A Reappraisal.* Cooperstown: [n.p.], 1954.

Nichols, Bill. *Ideology and Image: Social Representation in the Cinema and Other Media.* Bloomington: Indiana University Press, 1981.

Nisbet, Robert. "Genealogy, Growth, and Other Metaphors," *New Literary History* 1:3 (Spring 1970), 350–63.

Noble, David. *Historians Against History: The Frontier Thesis and the National Covenant in American Historical Writing Since 1830.* Minneapolis: University of Minnesota Press, 1965.

Nord, David Paul. "An Economic Perspective on Formula in Popular Culture," *Journal of American Culture* 3:1 (Spring 1980), 17–32.

North, Douglass C. *The Economic Growth of the United States, 1790–1860.* New York: W. W. Norton and Company, 1966.

Northern Pacific Railroad. *Guide to the Northern Pacific Railroad Lands.* New York: Land Department of the Northern Pacific Railroad Company, 1872.

————. *The Northern Pacific Railroad; Its Route, Resources, Progress and Business.* [Philadelphia]: Jay Cooke and Company, [1871].

————. *The Northern Pacific Railroad's Land Grant and the Future Business of the Road.* [New York]: Jay Cooke and Company, 1870.

Novak, Barbara. *Nature and Culture: American Landscape, 1825–1865.* New York: Oxford University Press, 1980.

Oakes, James. *The Ruling Race: A History of American Slaveholders.* New York: Alfred A. Knopf, 1982.

Oates, Stephen B. *To Purge This Land with Blood: A Biography of John Brown.* New York: Harper and Row, 1970.

Oberholtzer, Ellis Paxson. *A History of the United States Since the Civil War.* Volume 3. New York: Macmillan, 1917–37.

————. *Jay Cooke: Financier of the Civil War.* 2 volumes. Philadelphia: G. W. Jacobs and Company, 1907.

Ogden, Rollo, editor. *Life and Letters of Edwin Lawrence Godkin.* 2 volumes. New York: Macmillan, 1907.

Ohmann, Richard M. *English in America: A Radical View of the Profession.* New York: Oxford University Press, 1976.

————. "The Shaping of a Canon: U. S. Fiction, 1960–1975," *Critical Inquiry* 10:1 (September 1983), 199–223.

Olsen, Otto H., editor. *Reconstruction and Redemption in the South.* Baton Rouge: Louisiana State University Press, 1980.

Olson, James C. *Red Cloud and the Sioux Problem.* Lincoln: University of Nebraska Press, 1965.

Omi, Michael, and Howard Wynant. "By the Rivers of Babylon: Race in the United States," *Socialist Review* 13:5 (1983), 31–66.

O'Neill, Gerard. *The High Frontier: Human Colonies in Space*. Garden City, N. Y.: Doubleday, Anchor Books, 1982.

Osterweis, Rollin G. *The Myth of the Lost Cause, 1865–1900*. [Hamden, Conn.]: Archon Books, 1973.

Ostrander, Gilman M. *American Civilization in the First Machine Age, 1890–1940*. New York: Harper and Row, 1970.

Paine, Bayard H. *Pioneers, Indians, and Buffaloes*. Curtis, Nebr.: The Curtis Enterprise, 1935.

Parker, Theodore. *The Collected Works of Theodore Parker . . . Volume VII: Discourses of Social Science*. Edited by Francis Power Cobbe. London: Trübner & Co., 1864.

———. *The Rights of Man in America*. Edited by Franklin B. Sanborn. New York: Negro Universities Press, 1969: Reprint of 1911 edition.

Parker, Watson. *Gold in the Black Hills*. Norman: University of Oklahoma Press, 1966.

———. "The Majors and the Miners: The Role of the U.S. Army in the Black Hills Gold Rush," *Journal of the West* 11:1 (January 1972), 99–113.

Parrington, Vernon Louis. *Main Currents in American Thought: An Interpretation of American Literature from the Beginnings to 1920*. 3 volumes. New York: Harcourt, Brace & Co., 1927, 1930.

Parrish, Randall. *Bob Hampton of Placer*. Chicago: A. C. McClurg, 1906.

Paul, Rodman Wilson. *Mining Frontiers of the Far West, 1848–1890*. New York: Holt, Rinehart and Winston, 1963.

Paulding, James Kirke. *The Lion of the West; Retitled The Kentuckian, or, A Trip to New York. A Farce in Two Acts*. Edited by James N. Tidwell. Stanford: Stanford University Press, 1954.

Pearce, Roy Harvey. *The Savages of America: A Study of the Indian and the Idea of Civilization*. Baltimore: Johns Hopkins Press, 1953.

———. "The Significances of the Captivity Narrative," *American Literature* 9:1 (March 1949), 1–20.

Penick, James Lal, Jr. *The Great Western Land Pirate: John A. Murrell in Legend and History*. Columbia: University of Missouri Press, 1981.

Perman, Michael. *Reunion without Compromise: The South and Reconstruction, 1865–1868*. Cambridge: Cambridge University Press, 1973.

Persons, Stow. *The Decline of American Gentility*. New York: Columbia University Press, 1973.

Pessen, Edward. "How Different from Each Other Were Antebellum North and South?" *American Historical Review* 85:5 (December 1980), 1119–66.

———. *Jacksonian America: Society, Personality, and Politics*. Revised edition. Homewood, Ill.: The Dorsey Press, 1978.

Peters, DeWitt Clinton. *The Life and Adventures of Kit Carson, the Nestor of the Rocky Mountains, from Facts Narrated by Himself*. New York: W. R. C. Clark and Company, 1858.

Peterson, Merrill D. *The Jefferson Image in the American Mind*. New York: Oxford University Press, 1960.

———. *Thomas Jefferson and the New Nation: A Biography*. New York: Oxford University Press, 1970.

Peterson, Richard A. "Five Constraints on the Production of Culture: Law, Technology, Market, Organizational Structure and Occupational Careers," *Journal of Popular Culture* 16:2 (Fall 1982), 143–53.

Phillips, Ulrich Bonnell. *Plantation and Frontier: The Documentary History of American Industrial Society*. Volumes 1–2. Cleveland: The A. H. Clark Company, 1910–11.

Phillips, William. *The Conquest of Kansas by Missouri and Her Allies . . .* Boston: Phillips, Sampson and Company, 1856.

Pickens, Donald K. "Westward Expansion and the End of American Exceptionalism," *Western Historical Quarterly* 12:4 (October 1981), 409–18.

Pike, James Shepherd. *The Prostrate State: South Carolina Under Negro Government*. New York: Harper and Row, 1968. Reprint of 1874 Edition.

Pocock, J. G. A. "The Classical Theory of Deference," *American Historical Review* 81:3 (June 1976), 516–23.

————. *Politics, Language, and Time: Essays on Political Thought and History.* New York: Atheneum, 1971.

Porte, Joel M. *The Romance in America: Studies in Cooper, Poe, Hawthorne, Melville and James.* Middletown, Conn.: Wesleyan University Press, 1969.

Porter, Carolyn. *Seeing and Being: The Plight of the Participant Observer in Emerson, Adams and Faulkner.* Middletown, Conn.: Wesleyan University Press, 1981.

Porter, Glenn. *The Rise of Big Business, 1860–1910.* Arlington Heights, Ill.: AHM Publishing Corporation, 1973.

Potter, David M. *The Impending Crisis, 1848–1861.* New York: Harper Torchbooks, 1976.

————. *People of Plenty: Economic Abundance and the American Character.* Chicago: University of Chicago Press, 1954.

Pratt, Fletcher. *Ordeal by Fire: A Short History of the Civil War.* New York: Pocket Books, Inc., 1961.

Prescott, William Hickling. *The Conquest of Mexico and the Conquest of Peru.* New York: Modern Library, [1936].

Putnam, Jackson K. "The Turner Thesis and Westward Movement: A Reappraisal," *Western Historical Quarterly* 7:4 (October 1976), 377–404.

Quinn, Arthur Hobson, editor. *Representative American Plays, 1767–1923.* New York: The Century Company, 1917.

Railton, Stephen. *Fenimore Cooper: A Study of His Life and Imagination.* Princeton: Princeton University Press, 1978.

Ramsdell, Charles William. *Reconstruction in Texas.* Austin: University of Texas Press, 1970.

Randel, William Pierce. *Centennial: American Life in 1876.* Philadelphia: Chilton Book Company, 1969.

Raskin, Marcus G., and Bernard B. Fall, editors. *The Viet-Nam Reader.* New York: Vintage Books, 1967.

[Rathbone, St. George Henry] "Custer's Scout." *Custer's Last Shot; or, The Boy Trailer of the Little Horn. Boys of New York,* 51–5 (August 7–September 4, 1876).

Rawlinson, George. *The Origin of Nations, in Two Parts: On Early Civilizations; On Ethnic Affinities, etc.* New York: Scribner, Welford and Armstrong, 1878.

Redpath, James. *Echoes of Harper's Ferry.* Boston: Thayer and Eldridge, 1860.

————. *The Public Life of Capt. John Brown, with an Autobiography of His Childhood and Youth.* Boston: Thayer and Eldridge, 1860.

———— and Richard L. Hinton. *Hand-Book to Kansas Territory and the Rocky Mountains' Gold Region; Accompanied by Reliable Maps and a Preliminary Treatise on the Pre-emption Laws of the United States.* New York: J. H. Colton, 1859.

Reich, Robert B. *The New American Frontier.* New York: Times Books, 1983.

Reid, Mayne. *The Boy Hunters; or, Adventures in Search of a White Buffalo.* Ridgewood, N. J.: The Gregg Press, 1968. Reprint of 1852 edition.

————. *The White Chief; A Legend of North Mexico.* New York: Robert M. DeWitt, 1860.

Reid, Whitelaw. *Ohio in the War; Her Statesmen, Her Generals and Soldiers.* Cincinnati: Wilstack and Baldwin, 1868.

Reinders, Robert. "Militia and Public Order in Nineteenth Century America," *Journal of American Studies* 11:1 (April 1977), 81–102.

Reynolds, Quentin. *The Fiction Factory: From Pulp Row to Quality Street.* New York: Random House, 1965.

Richards, Leonard L. *Gentlemen of Property and Standing: Anti-Abolition Mobs in Jacksonian America.* New York: Oxford University Press, 1970.

Riegel, Robert F. *The Story of the Western Railroads: From 1852 Through the Reign of the Grants.* Lincoln: University of Nebraska Press, 1964.

Riggs, David F. *East of Gettysburg.* Bellevue, Nebr.: The Old Army Press, 1920.

Ringenbach, Paul T. *Tramps and Reformers, 1873–1916: The Discovery of Unemployment in New York.* Westport, Conn.: Greenwood Press, 1973.

Rister, Carl Coke, editor. *Comanche Bondage: Dr. John Charles Beale's Settlement . . .* Glendale, Calif.: Arthur H. Clark Company, 1955.

Robertson, James Oliver. *American Myth, American Reality.* New York: Hill and Wang, 1980.

Rodgers, Daniel T. *The Work Ethic in Industrial America, 1850–1920.* Chicago: University of Chicago Press, 1980.

Rogin, Michael Paul. *Fathers and Children: Andrew Jackson and the Subjugation of the American Indian.* New York: Alfred A. Knopf, 1975.

———. "Liberal Society and the Indian Question," *Political Inquiry* 1:3 (May 1971), 269–312.

———. *Subversive Genealogy: Politics, Family and Fiction in Herman Melville.* New York: Alfred A. Knopf, 1983.

Rohrbaugh, Malcolm J. *The Trans-Appalachian Frontier: Peoples, Societies, and Institutions, 1775–1850.* New York: Oxford University Press, 1978.

Roosevelt, Theodore. "The Strenuous Life," *The Strenuous Life.* The Works of Theodore Roosevelt, volume 12. New York: Charles Scribner's Sons, 1900.

Rose, Willie Lee. *Documentary History of Negro Slavery in North America.* New York: Oxford University Press, 1976.

———. *Rehearsal for Reconstruction: The Port Royal Experiment.* New York: Oxford University Press, 1976.

Rosenberg, Bruce A. *Custer and the Epic of Defeat.* University Park: Pennsylvania State University Press, 1974.

Rosenberg, Charles E. "Sexuality, Class and Race in Nineteenth Century America," *American Quarterly* 25:2 (May 1973), 177–201.

Rosenwaike, Ira. *Population History of New York City.* Syracuse: Syracuse University Press, 1972.

Rothman, David J. *The Discovery of the Asylum: Social Order and Disorder in the New Republic.* Boston: Little, Brown, 1971.

Rourke, Constance M. *American Humor: A Study of the National Character.* New York: Harcourt, Brace and Company, 1931.

Ruchames, Louis, editor. *John Brown: The Making of a Revolutionary.* New York: Grosset and Dunlap, Universal Library, 1969.

Ruiz, Ramón Eduardo, editor. *The Mexican War: Was It Manifest Destiny?* New York: Holt, Rinehart and Winston, 1963.

Russell, Don. *Custer's Last . . .* Fort Worth, Tex.: Amon Carter Museum of Western Art, 1968.

———. *Custer's List: A Checklist of Pictures Relating to the Little Big Horn.* Fort Worth, Tex.: Amon Carter Museum of Western Art, 1969.

———. "How Many Indians Were Killed? White Man versus Red Man: the Facts and the Legend," *American West* 10:4 (July 1973), 42–47, 61–63.

———. *The Lives and Legends of Buffalo Bill.* Norman: University of Oklahoma Press, 1973 [1960].

Sabin, Edwin L. *On the Plains with Custer.* Phildelphia: J. B. Lippincott, 1913.

Sadler, Lynn Veach. "Dr. Stephen Graham's Narration of the 'Duplin Insurrection': Additional Evidence of the Impact of Nat Turner," *Journal of American Studies* 12:3 (December 1978), 359–68.

Sahlins, Marshall. "Culture as Protein and Profit," *New York Review of Books* 25:18 (November 23, 1978), 45–53.

———. *Historical Metaphors and Mythical Realities: Structure in the Early History of the Sandwich Islands Kingdom.* Ann Arbor: University of Michigan Press, 1981.

Sandoz, Mari. *The Battle of the Little Big Horn.* Philadelphia: J. B. Lippincott, 1966.

Saxton, Alexander. "Blackface Minstrelsy and Jacksonian Ideology," *American Quarterly* 27:1 (March 1975), 3–28.

———. "George Wilkes: The Transformation of a Radical Ideology," *American Quarterly* 33:4 (Fall 1981), 437–58.

———. *The Indispensable Enemy: Labor and the Anti-Chinese Movement in California.* Berkeley: University of California Press, 1971.

———. "Historical Explanations of Racial Inequality." *Marxist Perspectives* 2:2 (Summer 1979), 146–68.

Scharnhorst, Gary. "Had Their Mothers Only Known: Horatio Alger, Jr. Rewrites Cooper, Melville and Twain," *Journal of Popular Culture* 15:3 (Winter 1981), 175–82.

Scheick, William J. *The Half-Blood: A Cultural Symbol in Nineteenth Century American Fiction.* Lexington: University Press of Kentucky, 1979.

Schlüter, Herman. *Lincoln, Labor and Slavery: A Chapter from the Social History of America.* New York: Russell and Russell, 1965 [1913].

Schmidt, Dorey. "Magazines, Technology and American Culture," *Journal of American Culture* 3:1 (Spring 1980), 3–16.

Scholnick, Robert J. *"The Galaxy* and American Democratic Culture, 1866–1878," *Journal of American Studies* 16:1 (April 1982), 69–80.

Schultz, George A. *An Indian Canaan: Isaac McCoy and the Vision of an Indian State.* Norman: University of Oklahoma Press, 1972.

Schwartz, Norman B. "Villainous Cowboys and Backward Peasants: Popular Culture and Development Concepts," *Journal of Popular Culture* 15:4 (Spring 1982), 105–13.

Scoresby, William. *American Factories and Their Female Operatives.* New York: Burt Franklin, 1968. Reprint of 1844 edition.

Scroggs, William O. *Filibusters and Financiers: The Story of William Walker and His Associates.* New York: Macmillan, 1916.

Sears, Stephen W. *Landscape Turned Red: The Battle of Antietam.* New Haven: Ticknor and Fields, 1983.

Sebeok, Thomas, editor. *Myth: A Symposium.* Bloomington: Indiana University Press, 1965.

Sedgwick, Catherine M. *Hope Leslie; or, Early Times in the Massachusetts.* 2 volumes. New York: Harper and Brothers, 1842. First published in 1827.

Sefton, James E. *The United States Army in Reconstruction, 1865–1877.* Baton Rouge: Louisiana State University Press, 1967.

[Senarens, Lu] "Noname." *Custer's Little Dead-shot; or, The Boy Scout of the Little Big Horn.* New York: Wide Awake Library, No. 826, 1888.

Sennett, Ted. *Warner Brothers Presents: The Most Exciting Years—from "The Jazz Singer" to "White Heat."* [n.p.]: Castle Books, Inc., 1971.

Sharkey, Robert P. *Money, Class and Party: An Economic Study of the Civil War and Reconstruction.* Baltimore: Johns Hopkins Press, 1959.

Shaw, Harry E. *The Forms of Historical Fiction: Sir Walter Scott and His Successors.* Ithaca: Cornell University Press, 1983.

Sheehen, Bernard W. *Seeds of Extinction: Jeffersonian Philanthropy and the American Indian.* New York: W. W. Norton and Company, Norton Library, 1974.

Sherwin, Oscar. *Prophet of Liberty: The Life and Times of Wendell Phillips.* New York: Bookman Associates, 1958.

Siegel, Adrienne. *The Image of the American City in Popular Literature, 1820–1870.* Port Washington, N.Y.: The Kennikat Press, 1981.

Simms, William Gilmore. *The Yemassee.* Edited by C. Hugh Holman. Boston: Houghton Mifflin, Riverside Editions, 1961.

Simpson, Lewis P. *The Dispossessed Garden: Pastoral and History in Southern Literature.* Athens: University of Georgia Press, 1975.

Singletary, Otis A. *Negro Militia and Reconstruction.* New York: McGraw-Hill, 1963.

Sitting Bull on the War Path; or, Custer in the Black Hills. The Fireside Companion 18 (August 28–December 11, 1876), 461–76.

Skidmore, Thomas. *The Rights of Man to Property; Being a Proposition to Make It Equal Among Adults of the Present Generation; And to Provide for Its Equal Transmission to Every Individual of Each Succeeding Generation . . .* New York: for the author by A. Ming, Jr., 1829.

Slobin, Mark. *Tenement Songs: The Popular Music of the Jewish Immigrants.* Urbana: University of Illinois Press, 1982.

Slotkin, Richard. " 'And *then* the Mare will go!': An 1875 Black Hills Scheme by Custer, Holladay and Buford," *Journal of the West* 15:3 (July 1976), 60–77.

———. "Dreams and Genocide: The American Myth of Regeneration Through Violence," *Journal of Popular Culture* 5:1 (Summer 1971), 38–59.

———. "Massacre," *Berkshire Review: Special Issue on Culture and Violence.* (1979), 112–32; 150–59.

———. "Narratives of Negro Crime in New England, 1675–1800," *American Quarterly* 25:1 (March 1973), 3–31.

———. *Regeneration Through Violence: The Mythology of the American Frontier, 1600–1860.* Middletown, Conn.: Wesleyan University Press, 1973.

————, and James K. Folsom, editors. *So Dreadfull a Judgment: Puritan Responses to King Philip's War, 1675–1677.* Middletown, Conn.: Wesleyan University Press, 1978.

Smith, Geoffrey Sutton. "The Navy Before Darwinism: Science, Exploration, and Diplomacy in Antebellum America," *American Quarter* 28:1 (Spring 1976), 41–55.

Smith, George Winston and Charles Judah, editors. *Chronicles of the Gringos: The U. S. Army in the Mexican War, 1846–1848. Accounts of Eyewitnesses and Combattants.* Albuquerque: University of New Mexico Press, 1968.

Smith, Henry Nash. *Mark Twain's Fable of Progress: Political and Economic Ideas in A Connecticut Yankee.* New Brunswick, N. J.: Rutgers University Press, 1964.

————. *Virgin Land: The American West as Symbol and Myth.* New York: Vintage Books, 1950.

[Smith, "Provost" William]. *Historical Account of Bouquet's Expedition Against the Ohio Indians in 1764.* Edited by Francis Parkman, from the Philadelphia, 1765 edition. Cincinnati: Robert Clarke and Company, 1868.

Smucker, Samuel M. *The Life of Colonel John Charles Frémont, and His Narrative of Explorations and Adventures . . .* New York: Miller, Orton and Mulligan, 1856.

"Sociology and Popular Culture Issue," *Journal of Popular Culture* 11:2 (Fall 1977), passim.

Sokolow, Jayme A. "The Jerry McHenry Rescue and the Growth of Northern Antislavery Sentiment During the 1850s," *Journal of American Studies* 16:3 (December 1982), 427–45.

Soltow, Lee. *Men and Wealth in the United States, 1850–1870.* New Haven: Yale University Press, 1975.

Spencer, Benjamin T. *The Quest for Nationality: An American Literary Campaign.* Syracuse: Syracuse University Press, 1957.

Spiller, Robert E. *Fenimore Cooper: Critic of His Times.* New York: Minton, Balch and Company, 1931.

Spivey, Donald. *Schooling for the New Slavery: Black Industrial Education, 1868–1915.* Westport, Conn.: Greenwood Press, 1978.

Spring, David. "Walter Bagehot and Deference," *American Historical Review* 81:3 (June 1976), 524–31.

Stagner, Stephen. "Epics, Science, and the Lost Frontier: Texas Historical Writing, 1836–1936," *Western Historical Quarterly* 12:2 (April 1981), 165–82.

Stampp, Kenneth M. *The Era of Reconstruction, 1865–1877.* New York: Alfred A. Knopf, 1965.

————, and Leon F. Litwack, editors. *Reconstruction: An Anthology of Revisionist Writings.* Baton Rouge: Louisiana State University Press, 1969.

Stanton, William. *The Leopard's Spots: Scientific Attitudes Towards Race in America, 1815–1859.* Chicago: University of Chicago Press, Phoenix Books, 1960.

Starobin, Robert S. *Industrial Slavery in the Old South.* New York: Oxford University Press, 1970.

Starr, Stephen Z. *The Union Cavalry in the Civil War.* 2 volumes. Baton Rouge: Louisiana State University Press, 1979–82.

Steckmesser, Kent Laird. *The Western Hero in History and Legend.* Norman: University of Oklahoma Press, 1965.

Stewart, Edgar I. *Custer's Luck.* Norman: University of Oklahoma Press, 1955.

————, editor. *Penny-an-Acre Empire in the West.* Norman: University of Oklahoma Press, 1968.

Stewart, William Frank. *The Last of the Filibusters; or, Recollections of the Siege of Rivas.* Sacramento, Calif.: H. Shipley and Company, 1857.

[Storey, Moorfield, et al.]. *Secretary Root's Record: Marked Severities in Philippine Warfare. An Analysis of the Law and Facts Bearing on the Actions and Utterances of President Roosevelt and Secretary Root.* Boston: G. H. Ellis, 1902.

Stout, Janis P. *Sodoms in Eden: The City in American Fiction Before 1860.* Westport, Conn.: Greenwood Press, 1976.

Stowe, Harriet Beecher. *Uncle Tom's Cabin; or, Life Among the Lowly.* New York: New American Library, [1958] 1965.

Streeter, Floyd Benjamin. *Political Parties in Michigan, 1837–1860. An Historical Study of Political Issues and Parties in Michigan from the Admission of the State to the Civil War.* Lansing: Michigan Historical Commission, 1918.

Strong, George Templeton. *Diary of George Templeton Strong.* Edited by Allan Nevins and M. H. Thomas. New York: Macmillan, 1952.

Sturtevant, Julian Monsun. *American Emigration: A Discourse in Behalf of the American Home Missionary Society* . . . New York: American Home Missionary Society, 1857.

Sue, Eugène. *The Mysteries of Paris.* Translated by Charles H. Town. New York: Harper's, 1846.

Swieringa, Robert P. "Land Speculation and Its Impact on American Economic Growth and Welfare: A Historiographical Review," *Western Historical Quarterly* 8:3 (July 1977), 283–301.

Sylvis, James C., editor. *The Life, Speeches, Labors and Essays of William H. Sylvis.* New York: A. M. Kelley, 1968. Reprint of 1872 edition.

Taylor, George Rogers. *Jackson vs. Biddle: The Struggle Over the Second Bank of the United States.* Boston: D. C. Heath, 1949.

Taylor, Joshua C. *America as Art.* New York: Harper and Row, 1976.

Taylor, Philip. *The Distant Magnet: European Emigration to the U. S. A.* New York: Harper Torchbooks, 1971.

Taylor, William R. *Cavalier and Yankee: The Old South and American National Character.* Garden City, N. Y.: Doubleday, Anchor Books, 1963.

Taylor and His Generals: A Biography of Major-General Zachary Taylor; and Sketches of the Lives of Generals Worth, Wool, and Twiggs . . . Hartford: Andrus and Sons, 1848.

Temin, Peter. *Iron and Steel in Nineteenth Century America: An Economic Inquiry.* Cambridge, Mass.: M. I. T. Press, 1964.

Temperley, Howard. "Frontierism, Capital, and the American Loyalists in Canada," *Journal of American Studies* 13:1 (April 1979), 5–28.

Thompson, E. P. *The Making of the English Working Class.* New York: Vintage Books, 1966.

————. *Whigs and Hunters: The Origins of the Black Act.* New York: Pantheon Books, 1975.

Thompson, Edgar T. *Plantation Societies, Race Relations and the South: The Regimentation of Populations.* Durham, N. C.: Duke University Press, 1975.

Thoreau, Henry David. *Miscellanies: The Writings of Henry David Thoreau.* Volume 10. Cambridge, Mass.: Riverside Press, 1894.

Thornton, James Mills, III. *Politics and Power in a Slave Society: Alabama, 1800–1860.* Baton Rouge: Louisiana State University Press, 1978.

[Thorpe, Thomas Bangs]. *The Master's House; or, Scenes Descriptive of Southern Life.* New York: T. L. McElrath and Company, 1854.

Tocqueville, Alexis de. *Democracy in America.* 2 volumes. Translated by Henry Reeve, edited by Francis Bowen, with notes by Phillips Bradley. New York: Vintage Books, 1960.

Toll, Robert C. *Blacking Up: The Minstrel Show in Nineteenth Century America.* New York: Oxford University Press, 1974.

Totten, Melissa. "Metaphors of Conquest: The Fiction of the Mexican War, 1846–1848." Honors thesis, Wesleyan University, 1981.

Tourgee, Albion W. *A Fool's Errand: A Novel of the South During Reconstruction.* Edited by George M. Frederickson. New York: Harper Torchbooks, 1961.

Townsend, George Alfred. *Campaigns of a Non-Combatant; and His Romquat Abroad During the War.* New York: Blelock and Company, 1866.

Trachtenberg, Alan, editor. *Democratic Vistas, 1860–1880.* New York: George Braziller, 1970.

————. "Myth, History, and Literature in *Virgin Land,*" *Prospects* 3 (1977), 125–34.

Tragle, Henry Irving, editor. *The Southampton Slave Revolt of 1831: A Compilation of Source Material.* Amherst: University of Massachusetts Press, 1971.

Travers, J. M. *Custer's Last Shot; or, The Boy Trader of the Little Big Horn.* New York: Frank Tousey, Wide Awake Library, 1894.

Trelease, Allen W. *White Terror: The Ku Klux Klan Conspiracy and Southern Reconstruction.* Westport, Conn.: Greenwood Press, 1979.

Turner, Victor W. "Process, System, and Symbol: A New Anthropological Synthesis," *Daedalus* 3:1 (Summer 1977), 61–80.

―――. *The Ritual Process: Structure and Antistructure.* Chicago: Aldine Publishing Company, 1969.

Tuveson, Ernest Lee. *Redeemer Nation: The Idea of America's Millennial Role.* Chicago: University of Chicago Press, 1971.

"Twain, Mark" [Samuel Langhorne Clemens]. *The Adventures of Huckleberry Finn.* Norton Critical Edition. Edited by Sculley Bradley, Richard Croom Beatty and E. Hudson Long. New York: W. W. Norton and Company, 1962.

―――. *The Adventures of Tom Sawyer.* Hartford: American Publishing Company, 1876.

―――. *A Connecticut Yankee in King Arthur's Court.* Norton Critical Edition. Edited by Allison R. Ensor. New York: W. W. Norton and Company, 1982.

―――. *Hannibal, Huck and Tom.* Edited by Walter Blair. Berkeley: University of California Press, 1969.

―――. *Letters from the Earth.* Edited by Bernard De Voto. New York: Harper and Row, Perennial Library, 1974.

―――. *Mark Twain's Letters to His Publishers.* Edited by Hamlin Hill. Berkeley: University of California Press, 1967.

―――. *Roughing It.* Edited by Franklin R. Rogers and Paul Baender. The Iowa-California Edition. Berkeley: University of California Press, 1972.

―――. *Sketches New and Old.* New York: Harper and Brothers, [n.d.]. Reprint of 1875 edition.

―――, and William Dean Howells. *The Mark Twain–Howells Letters: The Correspondence of Samuel L. Clemens and William D. Howells, 1872–1910.* Edited by Henry Nash Smith and William M. Gibson. 2 volumes. Cambridge: Belknap Press of Harvard University Press, 1960.

―――, and Charles Dudley Warner. *The Gilded Age.* 2 volumes. New York: Harper & Brothers, [n.d.]. Reprint of 1873 edition.

Tyler, Alice Felt. *Freedom's Ferment: Phases of American Social History from Colonial Times to the Outbreak of the Civil War.* New York: Harper Torchbooks, 1961.

Tyler, M. W. *A Book Without a Title; or, Thrilling Events in the Life of Mira Dana.* Boston: for the author, 1855.

Unger, Irwin. *The Greenback Era: A Social and Political History of American Finance, 1865–1879.* Princeton: Princeton University Press, 1964.

Upham, Charles Wentworth. *Life, Explorations, and Public Services of John Charles Frémont.* Boston: Ticknor and Fields, 1856.

Urwin, Gregory J. W. *Custer Victorious: The Civil War Battles of George Armstrong Custer.* East Brunswick, N. J.: Fairleigh Dickinson University Press, 1982.

Utley, Robert M. *Custer and the Great Controversy: The Origin and Development of a Legend.* Los Angeles: Western Lore Press, 1962.

―――. *Frontier Regulars: The United States Army and the Indian, 1866–1891.* New York: Macmillan, 1973.

―――, editor. *Life in Custer's Cavalry: Diaries and Letters of Albert and Jennie Barnitz, 1867–1868.* New Haven: Yale University Press, 1977.

Van de Water, Frederick F. *Glory Hunter: A Life of General Custer.* Indianapolis: Bobbs-Merrill, 1934.

Van Evrie, John H. *White Supremacy and Negro Subordination; or, Negroes a Subordinate Race, and (So-Called) Slavery Its Normal Condition.* New York: Negro Universities Press, 1969. Reprint of 1868 edition.

Vaughan, Alden T. *New England Frontier: Puritans and Indians, 1620–1675.* Boston: Little, Brown, 1965.

―――, and Edward W. Clark, editors. *Puritans Among the Indians: Accounts of Captivity and Redemption, 1676–1724.* Cambridge, Mass.: The Belknap Press of Harvard University Press, 1981.

Vestal, Stanley. *Sitting Bull: Champion of the Sioux.* Norman: University of Oklahoma Press, 1957.

Veysey, Laurence. "The Autonomy of American History Reconsidered," *American Quarterly* 31:4 (Fall 1979), 455–76.

Vickery, John B., editor. *Myth and Literature: Contemporary Theory and Practice.* Lincoln: University of Nebraska Press, 1966.

Victor, Orville J. *History of American Conspiracies; A Record of Treason, Insurrection,*

Rebellion, &c, in the United States of America from 1760–1860. New York: J. D. Torrey [1863].

Villard, Henry. *Memoirs of Henry Villard.* 2 volumes. Boston: Houghton Mifflin, 1904.

Wagstaff, Thomas. "Call Your Old Master—'Master': Southern Political Leaders and Negro Labor During Presidential Reconstruction," *Labor History* 10:3 (Summer 1970), 323–45.

Walker, Francis Amasa. *The Indian Question.* Boston: James R. Osgood and Company, 1874.

————. *The Wages Question: A Treatise on Wages and the Wages Class.* New York: Henry Holt and Company, 1876.

Walker, Joseph E. *Hopewell Village: The Dynamics of a Nineteenth Century Iron-Making Community.* Philadelphia: University of Pennsylvania Press, 1966.

Walker, Warren S. *Plots and Characters in the Fiction of James Fenimore Cooper.* Hamden, Conn.: Archon Books, 1978.

Walker, William. *The War in Nicaragua.* Mobile, Ala.: S. H. Goetzel and Company, 1860.

Wallace, Anthony F. C. "Revitalization Movements: Some Theoretical Considerations for Their Comparative Study," *American Anthropologist* 58:2 (April 1956), 264–79.

————. *Rockdale: The Growth of an American Village in the Early Industrial Revolution.* New York: Alfred A. Knopf, 1978.

Walsh, Margaret. *The American Frontier Revisited.* Atlantic Highlands, N. J.: Humanities Press, 1981.

Walters, Ronald G. "The Erotic South: Civilization and Slavery in American Abolitionism," *American Quarterly* 25:2 (May 1973), 177–201.

Walton, Augustus Q. *A History of the Detection, Conviction, Life and Designs of John A. Murel [sic] Together with His System of Villany [sic] and Plan of Exciting a Negro Rebellion . . .* Cincinnati: [U. P. James], [1836?].

Waples, Dorothy. *The Whig Myth of James Fenimore Cooper.* New Haven: Yale University Press, 1938.

Warch, Richard N., and Jonathan F. Fanton, editors. *John Brown.* Great Lives Observed Series. Englewood Cliffs, N. J.: Prentice-Hall, Inc., 1973.

Ward, George B., III. "Bloodbrothers in the Wilderness: The Sport Hunter and the Buckskin Hunter in the Preservation of the American Wilderness." Doctoral dissertation, University of Texas, 1980.

Ward, John William. *Andrew Jackson: Symbol for an Age.* New York: Oxford University Press, 1955.

Warner, Sam Bass, Jr. *The Urban Wilderness: A History of the American City.* New York: Harper and Row, 1972.

Wartofsky, Marx W. "Art, Artworlds, and Ideology," *Journal of Aesthetics and Art Criticism* 38:8 (Spring 1980), 239–48.

Washburn, Willcomb L. *The Governor and the Rebel: A History of Bacon's Rebellion in Virginia.* Chapel Hill: University of North Carolina Press, 1957.

————. *The Indian in America.* New York: Harper Colophon Books, 1975.

Wayland, Francis. *Domestic Slavery Considered as a Scriptural Institution . . .* New York: L. Colby, 1845.

————. *The Duties of an American Citizen . . .* Boston: James Loring, 1825.

————. *Elements of Moral Science.* [Tenth edition?] Boston: Gould and Lincoln, 1855. First edition, 1835.

————. *Elements of Political Economy.* Fourth edition. New York: Sheldon, Blakeman and Company, 1856. First published 1837.

Webb, James. *Fields of Fire.* New York: Bantam Books, 1979.

Webb, Walter Prescott. *The Great Frontier.* Boston: Houghton Mifflin, 1952.

Webber, Charles W. *Old Hicks, the Guide; or, Adventures in the Camanche Country in Search of a Gold Mine.* New York: Harper and Brothers, 1848.

Weems, Mason Locke. *The Life of Washington.* Edited by Marcus Cunliffe. Cambridge: The Belknap Press of Harvard University Press, 1962.

Weigley, Russell F. *The American Way of War: A History of United States Military Strategy and Policy.* New York: Macmillan, 1973.

————. *History of the United States Army.* New York: Macmillan, 1967.

Wellman, Manly Wade. *Spawn of Evil.* Garden City, N. Y.: Doubleday, 1964.

Wells, Samuel L. *Hampton and Reconstruction*. Columbia, S. C.: The State Company, 1907.
Wells, William V. *Walker's Expedition to Nicaragua*. New York: Stringer and Townsend, 1856.
Wessell, Leonard P. *Karl Marx, Romantic Irony, and the Proletariat: The Mythopoetic Origins of Marxism*. Baton Rouge: Louisiana State University Press, 1979.
Weymouth, Lally, editor. *America in 1876: The Way We Were*. New York: Vintage Books, 1976.
White, Hayden. *Metahistory: The Historical Imagination in Nineteenth Century Europe*. Baltimore: Johns Hopkins University Press, 1973.
White, Richard. "The Winning of the West: The Expansion of the Western Sioux in the Eighteenth and Nineteenth Centuries," *Journal of American History* 65:2 (September 1978), 318–43.
Whitman, Walt. *Leaves of Grass*. Norton Critical Edition. Edited by Sculley Bradley and Harold W. Blodgett. New York: W. W. Norton and Company, 1973.
Whittaker, Frederick C. *A Complete Life of General George A. Custer* . . . New York: Sheldon and Company, 1976.
———. *The Dashing Dragoon: or, The Story of General George A. Custer from West Point to the Big Horn*. New York: Beadle and Adams, 1882.
Wiebe, Robert. *The Search for Order, 1877–1920*. New York: Hill and Wang, 1967.
Wiener, Jonathan M. "Class Struggle and Economic Development in the American South, 1865–1955," *American Historical Review* 84:4 (October 1979), 70–106.
Wilensky, Harold L. "Mass Society and Mass Culture: Interdependence or Independence," *American Sociological Review* 29:2 (April 1964), 173–97.
Wiley, Bell Irvin. *The Life of Billy Yank: The Common Soldier of the Union*. Indianapolis: Bobbs-Merrill, 1952.
Williams, Albert Brockenbrough. *Wade Hampton and His Redshirts: South Carolina's Deliverance in 1876*. Freeport, N. Y.: Books for Libraries Press, 1970. Reprint of 1935 edition.
Williams, David A. *David C. Broderick: A Political Portrait*. San Marino, Calif.: Huntington Library, 1969.
Williams, Raymond. *Keywords: A Vocabulary of Culture and Society*. New York: Oxford University Press, 1976.
———. *Marxism and Literature*. London: Oxford University Press, 1977.
———. *The Sociology of Culture*. New York: Schocken Books, 1982.
———. *Television: Technology and Cultural Form*. New York: Schocken Books, 1975.
Williams, William Appleman. *The Great Evasion: An Essay on the Contemporary Relevance of Karl Marx and on the Wisdom of Admitting the Heretic into the Dialogue on America's Future*. Chicago: Quadrangle Books, 1964.
———. *The Roots of the Modern American Empire: A Study of the Growth and Shaping of Social Consciousness in a Marketplace Society*. New York: Random House, 1969.
Williamson, Jeffrey G., and Peter Lindert. *American Inequality: A Macroeconomic History*. New York: Academic Press, 1980.
Wilson, Charles R. "Racial Reservations: Indians and Blacks in American Magazines, 1865–1900," *Journal of Popular Culture* (Summer 1976), 70–80.
Wilson, George Macklin. "Time and History in Japan," *American Historical Review* 85:3 (June 1980), 557–71.
Wilson, James Harrison. *Under the Old Flag*. 2 volumes. New York: D. Appleton and Company, 1912.
Wilson, R. Jackson. "Experience and Utopia: The Making of Edward Bellamy's *Looking Backward*," *Journal of American Studies* 11:1 (April 1977), 45–60.
Winther, Oscar Osburn. *The Transportation Frontier, 1865–1890*. New York: Holt, Rinehart and Winston, 1964.
Wise, Gene. "Paradigm Dramas in American Studies: A Cultural and Institutional History of the Movement," *American Quarterly* 31:3 (Bibliography Issue), 293–337.
Wolcott, Roger. *The Poems of Roger Wolcott*. Boston: Club of Odd Volumes, 1898.
Wood, Charles R. *The Northern Pacific: Main Street of the Northwest*. Seattle: Superior Publishing Company, 1908.

Wood, Forrest G. *Black Scare: The Racist Response to Emancipation and Reconstruction.* Berkeley: University of California Press, 1970.

Wood, Gordon S. *The Creation of the American Republic, 1776–1787.* New York: W. W. Norton and Company, The Norton Library, 1972.

Wood, Henry. *Natural Law in the Business World.* Boston: Lee and Shepard, 1887.

Woodward, C. Vann. *American Counterpoint: Slavery and Racism in the North-South Dialogue.* Boston: Little, Brown, 1971.

————. *Reunion and Reaction: The Compromise of 1877 and the End of Reconstruction.* Boston: Little, Brown, 1951.

Wright, Will. *Six-Guns and Society: A Structural Study of the Western.* Berkeley: University of California Press, 1975.

Wyatt-Brown, Bertram. *Southern Honor: Ethics and Behavior in the Old South.* New York: Oxford University Press, 1982.

Wyman, Walker Demarquis, and Clifton B. Kroeber, editors. *The Frontier in Perspective.* Madison: University of Wisconsin Press, 1957.

Young, Edward. *Labor in Europe and America; A Special Report on the Rates of Wages, the Cost of Subsistence, and the Condition of the Working Classes, in Great Britain, France, Belgium, Germany, and Other Countries of Europe, also in The United States and British America.* Philadelphia: S. A. George and Company, 1875.

————. *Special Report on Immigration; Accompanying Information for Immigrants . . .* Washington: Government Priting Office, 1872.

Young, Marilyn B. *American Expansionism: The Critical Issues.* Boston: Little, Brown, 1973.

Young, Mary. "The Cherokee Nation: Mirror of the Republic," *American Quarterly* 33:5 (Winter 1981), 502–24.

————. "The Indian Question Revisited," *Marxist Perspectives* 1:1 (Spring 1978), 34–49.

Zahler, Helen S. *Eastern Workingmen and National Land Policy, 1829–1862.* New York: Columbia University Press, 1944.

Zelnick, Stephen. "Melville's 'Bartleby, the Scrivener': A Study in History, Ideology and Literature," *Marxist Perspectives* 2:4 (Winter 1979), 74–92.

Zuckerman, Michael. "The Nursery Tales of Horatio Alger," *American Quarterly* 24:2 (May 1972), 191–209.

INDEX

ABOUT THE AUTHOR

Richard Slotkin is Olin Professor and director of American studies at Wesleyan University, where he has taught since 1966. He was graduated from Brooklyn College (B.A. 1963) and Brown University (Ph.D. 1967). He is the author of *Regeneration Through Violence: The Mythology of the American Frontier, 1600–1860* (Wesleyan, 1973), which won the Beveridge Award from the American Historical Association and a National Book Award nomination; *The Fatal Environment*, which won the Little Big Horn Associates Award in 1985; a novel on the Civil War, *The Crater*, and a Western, *The Return of Henry Starr*, to be published in 1987. His home is in Middletown, Connecticut.